THE ROUGH GUIDE TO

Central
America

There are more than two hundred Rough Guide titles
covering destinations from Alaska to Zimbabwe
and subjects from Acoustic Guitar to Travel Health

Forthcoming travel guides include
The Algarve • The Bahamas • Cambodia • Caribbean Islands
Costa Brava • New York Restaurants • South America • Zanzibar

Forthcoming reference guides include
Children's Books • Online Travel • Videogaming • Weather

Rough Guides Online
www.roughguides.com

ROUGH GUIDE CREDITS

Text editor: Gavin Thomas
Series editor: Mark Ellingham
Editorial: Martin Dunford, Jonathan Buckley, Jo
Mead, Kate Berens, Ann-Marie Shaw, Helena Smith,
Judith Bamber, Orla Duane, Olivia Eccleshall, Ruth
Blackmore, Geoff Howard, Claire Saunders, Alexander
Mark Rogers, Polly Thomas, Joe Staines, Richard Lim,
Duncan Clark, Peter Buckley, Lucy Ratcliffe, Clifton
Wilkinson, Alison Murchie, Matthew Teller, Andrew
Dickson (UK); Andrew Rosenberg, Stephen Timblin,
Yuki Takagaki, Richard Koss (US)
Production: Susanne Hillen, Andy Hilliard, Link Hall,
Helen Prior, Julia Bovis, Michelle Draycott, Katie Pringle,

Mike Hancock, Zoë Nobes, Rachel Holmes, Andy Turner
Cartography: Melissa Baker, Maxine Repath, Ed Wright,
Katie Lloyd-Jones
Picture research: Louise Boulton, Sharon Martins
Online: Kelly Cross, Anja Mutić-Blessing, Jennifer Gold,
Audra Epstein, Suzanne Welles (US)
Finance: John Fisher, Gary Singh, Edward Downey,
Mark Hall, Tim Bill
Marketing & Publicity: Richard Trillo, Niki Smith,
David Wearn, Chloë Roberts, Claire Southern, Demelza
Dallow (UK); Simon Carloss, David Wechsler, Kathleen
Rushforth (US)
Administration: Tania Hummel, Julie Sanderson

PUBLISHING INFORMATION

This second edition published November 2001 by
  Rough Guides Ltd, 62–70 Shorts Gardens,
  London WC2H 9AH.
Distributed by the Penguin Group:
Penguin Books Ltd, 80 Strand, London WC2R ORL
Penguin Putnam, Inc. 375 Hudson Street, NY 10014,
  USA
Penguin Books Australia Ltd, 487 Maroondah Highway,
  PO Box 257, Ringwood, Victoria 3134, Australia
Penguin Books Canada Ltd, 10 Alcorn Avenue, Toronto,
  Ontario, Canada M4V 1E4
Penguin Books (NZ) Ltd, 182–190 Wairau Road,
  Auckland 10, New Zealand
Typeset in Linotron Univers and Century Old Style to an
  original design by Andrew Oliver.
Printed in England by Clays Ltd, St Ives plc.
Illustrations in Part One and Part Three by Edward Briant.

Illustrations on p.1 & p.789 by Henry Iles
© Rough Guides 2001
No part of this book may be reproduced in any form
  without permission from the publisher except for the
  quotation of brief passages in reviews.
848pp – Includes index
A catalogue record for this book is available from the
  British Library
ISBN 1-85828-736-7

The publishers and authors have done their best to
  ensure the accuracy and currency of all the information
  in *The Rough Guide to Central America*; however, they
  can accept no responsibility for any loss, injury, or
  inconvenience sustained by any traveller as a result of
  information or advice contained in the guide.

THE ROUGH GUIDE TO

Central America

written and researched by

Peter Eltringham, Jean McNeil
James Read and Iain Stewart

with additional contributions by

Gary Bowerman and Polly Rodger Brown

ROUGH
GUIDES

TRAVEL GUIDES • PHRASEBOOKS • MUSIC AND REFERENCE GUIDES

 We set out to do something different when the first Rough Guide was published in 1982. Mark Ellingham, just out of university, was travelling in Greece. He brought along the popular guides of the day, but found they were all lacking in some way. They were either strong on ruins and museums but went on for pages without mentioning a beach or taverna. Or they were so conscious of the need to save money that they lost sight of Greece's cultural and historical significance. Also, none of the books told him anything about Greece's contemporary life – its politics, its culture, its people, and how they lived.

So with no job in prospect, Mark decided to write his own guidebook, one which aimed to provide practical information that was second to none, detailing the best beaches and the hottest clubs and restaurants, while also giving hard-hitting accounts of every sight, both famous and obscure, and providing up-to-the-minute information on contemporary culture. It was a guide that encouraged independent travellers to find the best of Greece, and was a great success, getting shortlisted for the Thomas Cook travel guide award, and encouraging Mark, along with three friends, to expand the series.

The Rough Guide list grew rapidly and the letters flooded in, indicating a much broader readership than had been anticipated, but one which uniformly appreciated the Rough Guide mix of practical detail and humour, irreverence and enthusiasm. Things haven't changed. The same four friends who began the series are still the caretakers of the Rough Guide mission today: to provide the most reliable, up-to-date and entertaining information to independent-minded travellers of all ages, on all budgets.

We now publish more than 200 titles and have offices in London and New York. The travel guides are written and researched by a dedicated team of more than 100 authors, based in Britain, Europe, the USA and Australia. We have also created a unique series of phrasebooks to accompany the travel series, along with an acclaimed series of music guides, and a best-selling pocket guide to the Internet and World Wide Web. We also publish comprehensive travel information on our Web site:

www.roughguides.com

HELP US UPDATE

We've gone to a lot of effort to ensure that the second edition of *The Rough Guide to Central America* is accurate and up-to-date. However, things change – places get "discovered", opening hours are notoriously fickle, restaurants and rooms raise prices or lower standards. If you feel we've got it wrong or left something out, we'd like to know, and if you can remember the address, the price, the time, the phone number, so much the better.

We'll credit all contributions, and send a copy of the next edition (or any other Rough Guide if you prefer) for the best letters. Please mark letters: "Rough Guide Central America Update" and send to:
Rough Guides, 62–70 Shorts Gardens, London WC2H 9AH, or Rough Guides, 4th Floor, 375 Hudson St, New York, NY 10014.
Or send email to: mail@roughguides.co.uk
Online updates about this book can be found on Rough Guides' Web site at www.roughguides.com

ACKNOWLEDGEMENTS

The authors would like to thank Gavin Thomas for his patient and expert editing of this guide. Thanks also to Andy Turner for typesetting steadfastly through many chapters; Elaine Pollard for proofreading; Eleanor Hill for pictures; Amy Brown and Narrell Leffman for additional Basics research; Helena Smith for indexing; Melissa Baker and Ed Wright for cartography; and especially to Maxime Burke for keeping a watchful eye on many errant maps. Thanks also to everyone in the London embassies of all the Central American countries who has given so much help and advice, and to Dominique Young, for her contributions to the first edition of this book.

Gary Bowerman: Special thanks to José Antonio Arévalo and Lorena Gomez for their friendship, hospitality and late-night conversations about everything related to El Salvador. Thanks also to Lena Johanessen, Ana Beatriz Rivas, Jaime and the Suchitoto Alcaldía team and Peter Pohlman. A big shout to everyone I met in Nicaragua for their tips, and the surgeon in Rivas who patched up my broken wrist. At Rough Guides, thanks to Gavin Thomas for great editing. Katharine, thanks for all your proofing, support and understanding.

Polly Rodger Brown: Special thanks to all at Costa Rica Expeditions, particularly Richard Edwards, Priscilla Jimenez and Rodolfo Vargas; to Alex Quesada and Europcar; to Jean McNeil for her valuable advice and support; and to all the following for their generous help, hospitality and friendship: George and Susan Atkinson; Byron; Toby and Gloria Cleaver; Rodolfo Cornick; Jack E. Ewing; everyone at La Paloma Lodge; Shawn Larkin; Daryl Loth; Leonel Mata and all his brothers; Paulo Treehouse; Sara and Toine at Montana Linda; and Sofia Stein at Selva Bananito Lodge.

Peter Eltringham: Once again, many thanks to everyone – from archeologists to zoologists – who provided invaluable help and support in Belize. I'll be seeing many of you to thank you personally but I'd also like to add a final word of farewell to my old friend Charles Wright, who knew more about the people and environment of Toledo District then anyone else I'm ever likely to meet.

Jean McNeil: My thanks go first and foremost to Helena Chaverría and Mauricio Hernandez and the support of their outstanding travel agency, Camino Travel. Thanks also to Diego Ferrari, who suffered through long drives in rainstorms and mud; to Polly Rodger Brown, for her wonderful updating; and to all the following for their hospitality: the Arco Iris in Santa Elena; Casa Rigeway in San José; Anita Muktyk in Manuel Antonio; the Mar de Luz in Jacó; and the Sano Banano in Montezuma.

James Read: Thanks to Ivy Vergara of IPAT and Tim Robinson for their help in Panama, and to Emma for sharing all the best bits.

Iain Stewart: In Guatemala: thanks to Lorena Artola; all at Inguat (especially Sandra Monterroso and Migdalia in Guatemala City and Héctor in Antigua); Tom Lingenfelter; Geo Mendoza; José and Lucky for the warmest hospitality; Defensores de la Naturaleza; Phillipa and all at the Rainbow; Ileana; Samuel Martí; and Deedle, Dave, Fiona and Bruce for coming along for the ride.
In Honduras: all at the IHT, but especially Kenia Lima de Zapata; Gracia María Lanza; Howard Rosenzweig and his family in Copán; Andrés at the Posada Arco Iris; Phil and Kaj; the indomitable party girls Claire and Danielle; Alun; Esther; André and all at the Mango Inn and UDC; Mike Wendling; Don Pearly and all the Baymen crew in Guanaja; Sosa Airlines; Ricardo Steiner; Alessandro and Maya Vista in Tela; and all at *Honduras Tips* and *Honduras This Week*.
In the UK: thanks to Gavin Thomas for an efficient, enjoyable and almost pain-free operation; Peter Eltringham for his tireless support and expertise; Kate Berens; all the Rough Guide production team; Dominique Young; Jamie Marshall; Canning House; and all at the Guatemalan and Honduran embassies in London.

THE AUTHORS

Peter Eltringham's first visit to Belize was when he volunteered to do a tour of duty in what was considered a "hardship posting" by the Royal Air Force. After returning briefly to the UK, he set off once again for Central America to co-write the first edition of the *Rough Guide to Guatemala and Belize*. Since then he has researched and co-authored Rough Guides to *Mexico*, *Belize* and *The Maya World*, spending several months each year in the region and contributing articles on Belize to a number of newspapers and magazines.

Jean McNeil is from Nova Scotia, Canada, but has lived in London since 1991. As well as researching and writing the *Rough Guide to Costa Rica* and part of the *Rough Guide to Central America*, she is the author of three books of fiction: *Hunting Down Home*, *Nights in a Foreign Country*, and *Private View*, and the recipient of several awards for fiction writing. She works as a publisher and

researcher at the Latin America Bureau in London.

James Read first went to Latin America in 1991. Expecting to be there for three months, he stayed for three years, working on the reconstruction of pre-Colombian irrigation systems in the high Andes. Since then he has travelled widely in the region, and is currently writing the *Rough Guide to Bolivia*. When not in Latin America, he works as a journalist for the BBC World Service in London.

After two years of travelling the world, **Iain Stewart** ended up in Guatemala and liked it so much that he stayed. Now an author on the *Rough Guides to Guatemala*, *The Maya World*, and *Ibiza and Formentera*, he takes every opportunity to return to Central America. Based in South London, he combines writing Rough Guides with other work as a journalist and restaurant critic.

READERS' LETTERS

Many thanks to all the readers who wrote in with their comments and suggestions (and apologies to anyone whose name we've omitted or misspelt): John Alexander, Karin Amnå, Scott Arneman, Hendrik S. Bakker, K. Behr, Roy and Audrey Bradford, Rachel Bullett, Lorraine Burchell, Chris Callard, Ben L. Campbell, Geoffrey Clover, Francis and Maite Coke, Damon Crowhurst, Alison & Dana Doncaster, Anthony Downing, Linda and Mike Frender, Wolfgang Huber, Andrew van Iterson, Gerard Kohl, Tania Kurland, Bo Lanner, Oliver Marshall, Ted Mau, Kevin McGrath, Martin Mowforth, Toby Northcliffe, Elizabeth Nutter-Valladares, Jaime O'Drisceoil, Emil Olsson, Susan Pot, D.J. Skank, Lucie Zweers van Rosmalen, Peter Schreiner, Ellen Anne Teigen, Jens Vogt, Monika Woltering, Rien van Rosmalen Zweers.

CONTENTS

Introduction xii

PART FOUR   EL SALVADOR   279

PART FIVE   HONDURAS   359

PART SIX   NICARAGUA   461

PART SEVEN COSTA RICA 547

PART EIGHT PANAMÁ 693

PART NINE CONTEXTS 789

LIST OF MAPS

MAP SYMBOLS

Carretera Interamericana	Cave
Other major highways and roads	Museum
Minor highways and roads (paved)	Church (regional maps)
Unpaved highways	Campsite
Pedestrianized street (town maps)	Hotel
Footpath	Restaurant/bar
Railway	Internet access
National boundary	International airport
State boundary	Domestic airport
Chapter division boundary	Bus/taxi stop
Ferry route	Hospital
River	Embassy
General point of interest	Information centre
Border crossing	Public telephone
Bridge	Post office
Mountain range	Fuel station
Mountain peak	Building
Volcano	Cathedral/church (town maps)
Escarpment	Cemetery
Reef	National park
Lighthouse	Biological Reserve
Waterfall	Forest
Marshland	Park
Ruin	Beach
Castle	

INTRODUCTION

H emmed in by the Pacific and Atlantic oceans, the slender land bridge of **Central America** stretches from Mexico to South America – seven piecemeal nations stacked on top of each other in a narrowing isthmus. Its geography is in many ways its destiny: a small but distinctive region which for millennia has been the meeting point of the plants, animals and people of the giant continents to the north and the south. Although Central America has receded in the general public consciousness following the resolution of the conflicts which convulsed it during the 1980s, the region's new-found stability has resulted in something of a tourism renaissance, as thousands of visitors have come to experience its startling natural beauty and biodiversity at first hand, along with a range of man-made attractions ranging from the Maya ruins and traditional highland communities of Guatemala to the modernist skyline of Panamá City.

Central America's position at the volcanic cusp between North and South America, and at the meeting point of tropical and temperate climatic zones, has created a startling, often surreal **landscape**, ranging from the rugged, mountainous cloudforests of Costa Rica and Panamá to the impenetrable swamp-jungles of Mosquitia in eastern Honduras and Nicaragua. Beaches, coves, cayes and island archipelagos hem the coral-laced coasts, while volcanoes – some active – form a backbone of fire that stretches the length of the isthmus. Not surprisingly, given its pivotal geographical and biological position, Central America seems to have been designed for the **ecotourist**, with a complex system of interlocking terrains, from pristine rainforest to rare mangrove, which are home to a fascinating range of birdlife and wildlife, including tropical, temperate and hybrid species. And along with ecotourism go more traditional pleasures: lolling on Costa Rica's palm-draped Caribbean beaches, diving and snorkelling off the coral atolls of Belize, or exploring the sand-fringed islands of Panamá's San Blas archipelago.

Amidst all the hype about the region's natural beauty it's easy to forget that this part of the world was home to one of the Americas' most sophisticated pre-Columbian cultures, the **Maya**, whose splendid civilization flourished in Guatemala – and to a lesser extent in modern-day Belize, Honduras and El Salvador – between 300 and 900 AD. During this period the region was made up of independent and often mutually antagonistic city-states – Tikal in Guatemala, Copán in Honduras and San Andrés in El Salvador being three of the more prominent – which fought each other for prestige and economic dominance while their architects and craftsmen fashioned fabulous cities and stelae and their scientists created the famous Maya calendar, one of the most complex systems of measuring time ever devised.

The high point of Maya civilization had already passed, however, when Central America was "discovered" by the Spanish during **Christopher Columbus's** fourth and last voyage to the Americas in 1502–4. Columbus himself barely set foot in Central America, however, preferring to anchor offshore and write florid letters back home to his sovereign, packed with references to maidens and gold (of which the Spaniards unhappily discovered very little). Nearly ten years later, in 1513, the conquistador **Vasco Nuñez de Balboa** slashed and clambered his way over the scaly mountain spine of Panamá, becoming the first European to set eyes on the American side of the Pacific Ocean.

Within a few years, in 1519, the Spanish had established Panamá City; the city of León, in present-day Nicaragua, followed in 1524; and in 1541, in Guatemala, they established their most important capital, Antigua, from which the region was administered. Still, Central America remained a backwater of the Spanish Empire in the New World:

poor in gold and stuffed with venomous snakes, impenetrable jungles and often hostile natives. In human terms, the ensuing **colonial period** was characterized by the arrival of waves of yeoman farmers from Spain, and the deaths of countless thousands of indigenous people from diseases to which they had no immunity, while many others were taken as slaves to work the mines in Peru.

In the early 1800s, nearly 300 years after Spain's first incursions in the isthmus, the region was caught up in a fervour of **independence**, in part fuelled by the growing anger of the criollos (Spanish people born in the New World), who were barred from advancement and political office by Spain's snobbish insistence on promoting only those born on Spanish soil. By 1823 the collective drive towards autonomy was strong enough for all the Central American states to declare themselves independent, forming a loose federation (with the exception of Panamá, by then part of Colombia, and Belize, which was effectively a British colony). In many of the countries, separate but eerily similar internal conflicts erupted between educated, Europhile liberals demanding egalitarianism and a form of democracy and the monied, land-owning conservatives – a rift between the right and the left which even today remains the most divisive and destructive presence in Central American **politics**.

It was these tensions that sparked the ravaging **wars** of the 1970s and 1980s. Nicaragua's Sandinistas succeeded in shaking off their country's dictator, Anastasio Somoza, though their revolution ultimately failed as a result of the US-sponsored Civil War (1981–1990), while US-fuelled internal conflicts also devastated El Salvador and Guatemala for much of the same decade. Now peace seemingly reigns, although less conspicuous conflicts persist, as in Guatemala, where the state's long-running campaign of repression against its own (mostly indigenous) inhabitants shows signs of continuing, despite the signing of official peace accords.

Nowadays, Central America is keen to shake off its reputation for machine guns and earthquakes, and most of its citizens want to forget about the past and look towards the future. Increasingly, that future is to be found in the overwhelming presence of **North American culture**, whether it be four-wheel drives, shopping malls, fast-food outlets or credit-card spending. American culture has been wholeheartedly embraced by the urban upper middle classes, and trickles down into the poorer echelons in the form of much-prized baseball hats and Nike trainers – any *ropa americana* is better than the homespun equivalent. This relatively new yen for the good life and consumer desirables is one reason why Central American society is described – at least by economists – as "modernizing", and times have changed from when countries like Honduras and Costa Rica were bona fide banana republics, little more than hosts providing land and cheap labour for the huge, US-owned fruit companies. Manufacturing and service industries are increasingly investing in the region, while piecework factories churning out cheap goods for the US market, called *maquiladoras*, still provide many people – particularly women – with employment.

Despite this, there's not much evidence that this new-found investment is trickling down into the pockets of the poorest Central Americans: income differentials here are still among the widest in the world, and much of the population lives in poverty, sometimes abjectly so – you don't need to look further than the faces of begging children on street corners or at border crossings, asking to relieve you of your surplus small change. One product of this widespread deprivation are the high rates of common **crimes** like pickpocketing and burglary, while violent crime against tourists is becoming more common. Certain cities, like Managua and Panamá City, have always had bad reputations, and it has to be said travelling in Central America is hardly risk-free, and visitors should read up on the various dangers before arriving. Fortunately, where dangers are real – mostly in cities – they are well-publicized, and locals will often volunteer warnings and advice.

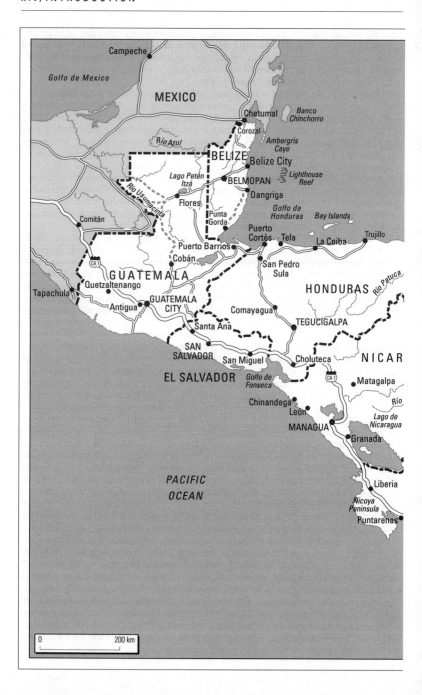

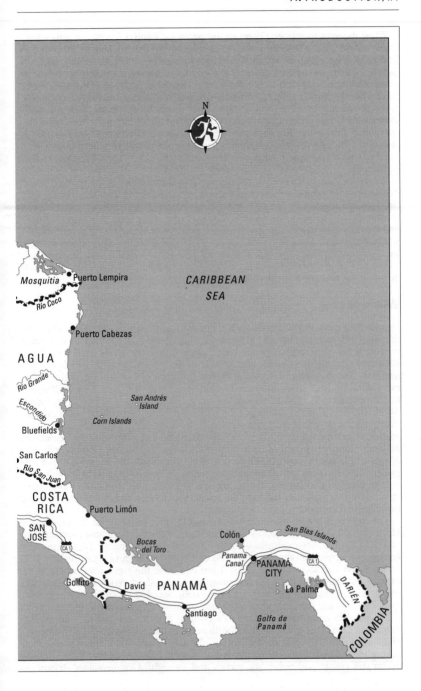

When it comes to relations between the countries, Central America is rather like a family where there's little love lost, but they recognize that sticking together is their best chance for economic survival. Amongst themselves, the nations have oscillated between surprising regional solidarity to outright war, sometimes in the form of incomprehensible conflicts, such as El Salvador and Honduras's infamous "Football War" of 1969, a five-day border conflict ostensibly sparked by a soccer match. National **stereotypes** are bandied back and forth with relish (Costa Ricans think Nicaraguans are intrinsically violent, Nicaraguans think Costa Ricans are placid opportunists, virtually everybody thinks the Hondurans wrote the book on corruption) even while the region's politicians describe neighbour nations as *hermanos* (brothers) and seek to build a Central American trading bloc to neutralize the effect NAFTA has had on their economies.

Wherever you go, it's easy to get around. **Travel networks** in the region are well-developed, with reliable air and road-transport systems. Flying from Guatemala City to San José or Panamá City can save you a lot of time, as what looks like a short hop on the map is often a lengthy road journey thanks to the (often bad) state of the highways and the effects of weather. In the riverine waterways of Mosquitia, boats are the only way to get around, along with light planes. Most of the time, though, you'll be going by **bus** – cheap, frequent, cheerful, and the quintessential Central American experience, where you'll find yourself seated among knitting grandmothers, travelling evangelists, gum-popping teenagers and perhaps the odd chicken.

Where to go

Despite their modest dimensions, each of the seven countries of Central America is distinctively different, and one of the pleasures of a trip through the region is to experience such a diverse range of peoples and culture within a relatively small area. **Costa Rica** draws nature-lovers by the plane-load to its unsurpassed system of national parks and reserves, while English-speaking **Belize**, for much of its history a forgotten fragment of the British Empire, has reinvented itself as a prime diving and snorkelling destination thanks to its offshore national treasury: the second-longest barrier reef in the world. The best place to experience the region's pre-conquest culture is **Guatemala**, which has the strongest indigenous traditions, not to mention a stunning landscape of soaring volcanoes and amethyst lakes, while **Panamá** and **Honduras** are just waking up to the tourist potential of their rainforests, rugged mountain cloudforests, mangroves and beaches. Tourists still tend to avoid Nicaragua and El Salvador – a misguided manoeuvre, as neither is more dangerous for visitors than its neighbours, and despite considerable poverty, the people are welcoming and the basic tourist infrastructure good; plus, they too have the volcanoes, beaches and rainforests that draw travellers to their more popular neighbours.

The archetypal image of Central America is of the grey-white pyramids of the ruined Maya city of **Tikal** rising smokily above the rainforest canopy. Almost everyone who comes to Central America makes tracks for these haunting ruins: Tikal is the best known, but there are other popular sites at Copán in Honduras, San Andrés in El Salvador and Lamanai in Belize. Even if you don't visit the ruins, everywhere in the isthmus you can appreciate the craftsmanship of the Maya peoples, in their technicolour textiles (not just decorative, but a visually encoded social history), exquisite wood carvings and jewellery made from local or imported jade, turquoise and silver.

For **wildlife** enthusiasts, Guatemala's Biotopo del Quetzal and the Monteverde Reserve in Costa Rica will be high on the itinerary. In the pristine forests of Nicaragua's Matagalpa region, the shimmering quetzal, the sacred bird of the Maya, is still abundant; while in Costa Rica's Tortuguero region you can take steamy boat journeys along mirror-still canals, and watch sea turtles nest by night. Commentators struggle to represent this staggering biodiversity in spiralling numbers: 3000 species of moth in Costa Rica's Guanacaste province alone, 850 species of bird (more than in the whole of North America) and literally millions of plants, some as yet uncatalogued.

Life on the **Caribbean coast** of Central America is a shock for those who are used to the formal code of good manners and appearance that are so dear to the highland *ladino* culture. The atmosphere in these slightly rancid coastal towns – Lívingston, Bluefields, Limón and Colón, to name a few – can be raffish; certainly the machete-feuds and drug-running are real. On the Caribbean coast it's Marley, not marimba, you'll hear; English, cricket and herbal teas make an appearance, too. Immigration from Jamaica and Barbados to work on banana plantations and railroads in the late nineteenth and early twentieth century transformed this coast into an area which is more Caribbean than Latin American, dominated by West Indian accents, subsistence agriculture, and a quaint allegiance to the Queen (even if they don't always know which Queen is in at the moment).

For most travellers the **cities** of Central America are not much of a draw in themselves, with their potholed, traffic-choked streets, cheap skyscrapers and gutters full of soapy water and rotting fruits. Yet in each of them, if you can get beyond the initial ugliness you'll find a vibrant, if hectic, urban life with enough cafés, bars, galleries and museums to keep you busy for at least a few days. True city-lovers will want to indulge in spates of salsa dancing, join ice-cream-eating teenagers lolling on the benches of the local park, or improve their Spanish by watching the latest subtitled blockbuster American movie in a theatre filled with sighing matrons and buzzing boys.

When to go

Although located firmly within the tropics, altitude, rather than latitude, governs **climate** in Central America. Covering terrain which ranges between sea level and 3000m the temperature can vary by as much as twenty degrees. The year is divided into just two seasons: a **rainy season**, which lasts roughly from May to October and is often called "winter" (*invierno*), and a **dry season** – or "summer" (*verano*) – from November to April, although the distinction between the two varies wildly, even within small areas. In the highlands of Guatemala or Costa Rica, rainy-season downpours (*aguaceros*) are common in September and October. Meanwhile, on the Caribbean coastline, you'll find it's mostly wet year-round and almost supernaturally humid.

Where there is a rainy season, don't assume it will rain all the time; a common pattern is a fine, sunny dry morning until about noon or 1pm, then a clouding over and an afternoon downpour that sometimes extends into evening showers. It's true that **travelling** in the rainy season can be a little more problematic, due to washed-out roads and swollen creeks on some of the more backroad routes, but the advantages of coming to Central America in the rainy season are many, including lower accommodation prices (especially in heavily touristed areas like Costa Rica), fewer tourists, and the relief of a cooling shower or two.

Yearly average **temperatures** in the region change little, with daytime temperatures in the lowlands the hottest, averaging anywhere from 28 to 32°C. The coastal areas or the low inland plains are where you will feel the heat most uncomfortably. In the mountains the weather can be cooler, fresh, and surprisingly like a fine late spring day in the temperate zone, with temperatures more like 22 to 25°C. For more specific climate details, see the individual country introductions.

AVERAGE TEMPERATURES AND MONTHLY RAINFALL

	Jan	Feb	Mar	Apr	May	Jun	Jul	Aug	Sept	Oct	Nov	Dec
Belize (Belize City)												
Max °C	27	28	29	30	31	31	31	31	31	30	28	27
Min °C	19	21	22	23	24	24	24	24	23	22	20	20
Rainfall (mm)	137	61	38	56	109	196	163	170	244	305	226	185
Guatemala (Guatemala City)												
Max °C	23	25	27	28	29	27	26	26	26	24	23	22
Min °C	12	12	14	14	16	16	16	16	16	16	14	13
Rainfall (mm)	8	3	13	31	152	274	203	198	231	173	23	8
El Salvador (San Salvador)												
Max °C	32	33	34	34	33	31	32	32	31	31	31	32
Min °C	16	16	17	18	19	19	18	19	19	18	17	16
Rainfall (mm)	8	5	10	43	196	328	292	297	307	241	41	10
Honduras (Tegucigalpa)												
Max °C	25	27	29	30	30	28	27	28	28	27	26	25
Min °C	14	14	15	17	18	18	18	17	17	17	16	15
Rainfall (mm)	12	2	1	26	180	177	70	74	151	87	38	14
Nicaragua (Managua)												
Max °C	31	32	34	34	34	31	31	31	31	31	31	31
Min °C	20	21	22	23	23	23	22	22	22	22	21	20
Rainfall (mm)	5	1	5	5	76	296	134	130	182	243	59	5
Costa Rica (San José)												
Max °C	24	24	26	26	27	26	25	26	26	25	25	24
Min °C	14	14	15	17	17	17	17	16	16	16	16	14
Rainfall (mm)	15	5	20	46	229	241	211	241	305	300	145	41
Panamá (Panamá City)												
Max °C	32	33	33	34	31	30	31	31	30	30	30	31
Min °C	23	23	24	24	24	23	23	23	23	22	22	23
Rainfall (mm)	30	10	20	55	200	210	205	200	205	245	250	120

PART ONE

THE

BASICS

GETTING THERE FROM NORTH AMERICA

Getting to Central America from the US and Canada is simplest and usually cheapest by air, and the main US and Central American airlines have daily flights to all Central American capitals from US gateways. The great variety of possible destinations, routes and prices makes any comprehensive listing virtually impossible, but most non-stop flights leave from Miami, Houston, LA, Atlanta and New Orleans; airlines serving these hubs have excellent connections throughout the US and Canada (where gateways are Toronto, Montréal and Vancouver). In addition, several Mexican airlines fly direct from more than twenty cities in the US and Canada to Mexico, with onward connections to Central America – it's particularly easy and cheap to fly to Cancún and continue from there.

You can also travel overland inexpensively and comfortably by bus through Mexico, though this can take between two and four days. From Tapachula and Chetumal, in southern Mexico, buses for Guatemala and Belize take you safely across the border.

SHOPPING FOR AIR TICKETS

In general, the **price** you pay for a ticket to any of the Central American countries depends more on how and when you book your flight and how long you plan to stay than on a particular season. However, prices to most destinations do go up in the **high seasons** of July and August (due mainly to the cost of flights within the US; ironically, this is the rainy season in much of Central

America), and Easter and Christmas, when seat availability can become a problem: it certainly pays to book ahead.

The cheapest of the airlines' published **fares** is usually an **Apex ticket**, generally valid for a maximum stay of three months, which needs to be booked and paid for at least fourteen days before departure. Being a student or under 26 can also help, though you may be subject to eccentric booking conditions.

You can cut costs further by going through a specialist flight agent (see box on p.5–7) – either a **consolidator**, who buys up blocks of tickets from the airlines and sells them at a discount, or a **discount agent**, who in addition to dealing with discounted flights may also offer special student and youth fares and a range of other travel-related services. Bear in mind, though, that penalties for changing your plans can be stiff. Remember too that these companies make their money by dealing in bulk – don't expect them to answer lots of questions. Some agents specialize in **charter flights**, which may be cheaper than scheduled flights, but again departure dates are fixed and withdrawal penalties are high (check the refund policy). **Open-jaw tickets**, where you fly into one city and out of another, are readily available and, depending on which airline you use, often cost little more than a return to one city, particularly if combined with an airpass (for more on which, see p.27).

The companies listed on pp.5–7 are a good place to begin your search, or visit the **eXito Web site** (see p.5).

ROUTES AND FARES

Flights to Central America from the southern US cities of **Miami**, **Houston** and **New Orleans** are always non-stop and usually cost between US$350 and US$550. Flights from **Atlanta**, **Dallas** or **LA** are also non-stop, but tend to cost an extra US$50–100. There are some non-stop flights available from **New York**, **Chicago** and **San Francisco**, though many flights require a change of plane in either the US or Mexico; expect to pay between US$500 and US$700.

From Canada

There are no non-stop flights **from Canada** to Central America – your best bet is to fly to Miami

GETTING THERE FROM THE UK AND IRELAND

There are no non-stop flights from the UK to Central America – as a rule, the journey will involve changing aircraft (and sometimes airline), usually in the US. That said, it's possible to reach most of the Central American

capitals (except Belize City and Tegucigalpa) in one day from London – the best connections are on Continental and American. Obviously you'll have the widest range of options if you fly out of London, though most of the main carriers to the US have two or three regional options available, often at the same fares as you would pay from the capital.

Fares to Central America are almost always higher than those to **Mexico**, so you might want to consider travelling down overland from Mexico City or Cancún (see p.4). Several European airlines fly to Mexico City, although the only direct flights from London are on British Airways, which has three flights a week to Mexico City, plus two weekly departures to Cancún. For a complete list of carriers see the box below. It's also worth checking if your transatlantic carrier has an

SPECIALIST TOUR OPERATORS

Dragoman, Camp Green, Kenton Rd, Debenham, Suffolk IP14 6LA (☎01728/861133, www.dragoman.co.uk). Eight-week overland camping expeditions through Mexico to Panamá for around £1600, plus food kitty. Other trips available.

Exodus, 9 Weir Rd, London SW12 0LT (☎020/8673 0859, www.exodus.co.uk). Fifteen-day escorted tours, staying at hotels, through the Maya region (around £1050) and Costa Rica (£1050). Prices include air fare.

Explore Worldwide, 1 Frederick St, Aldershot GU11 1LQ (☎01252/760000, www.explore.co.uk). Wide range of 2-to-3-week hotel-based tours to Mexico and Central America (except Panamá); some tours run year-round. About £1100 for 15 days in Mexico, Guatemala and Belize; £1400 for a 16-day tour of volcanoes and rainforest in Nicaragua, including air fare.

Global Travel Club, 1 Kiln Shaw, Langdon Hills, Basildon, Essex SS16 6LE (☎01268/541732, info@global-travel.co.uk). Small company specializing in individually arranged tours (including diving trips) to Mexico, Belize and Panamá.

Journey Latin America, 12–13 Heathfield Terrace, London W4 4JE (☎020/8747 3108, fax 8742 1312, www.journeylatinamerica.co.uk). Wide range of high-quality tours and individual itineraries from the acknowledged experts. Around £1700 (fully inclusive) for 11 days' superb wildlife and bird-watching in Costa Rica.

Reef and Rainforest Tours, Prospect House, Jubilee Rd, Totnes, Devon TQ9 5BP (☎01803/866965, fax 865916, reefrain@btinternet.com). Individual itineraries from a very experienced company, focusing on nature reserves, research projects and diving in Belize, Honduras and Costa Rica.

Travelbag Adventures, 15 Turk St, Alton, Hants GU34 1AG (☎01420/541007, fax 541022, www.travelbag-adventures.com). Tours for small groups, staying in hotels, of Yucatán and Central America, including a 16-day trip from Cancún through Guatemala and Belize (around £1299 excluding air fare).

Trips, 9 Byron Place, Clifton, Bristol BS8 1JT (☎0117/311 4400, fax 0117/311 4401, www.tripsworldwide.co.uk). Friendly, experienced company with an inspired range of tailor-made itineraries to all Mexican and Central American destinations.

airpass which links flights in the US and Mexico (usually only Mexico City) – most major US airlines do – for details of the "Visit Central America" pass from Taca, see p.27.

Another option for same-day arrival is to fly on one of the main **European carriers**: KLM (via Amsterdam) has good connections from throughout the UK and Ireland, with flights to Mexico City, Guatemala (arriving early next morning) and Panamá at least three or four times a week. On Iberia (from London via Madrid and Miami) you can reach all the capitals (except Belize City and Tegucigalpa) daily.

SHOPPING FOR TICKETS

Flights to Central America fill up early, **so book as far ahead** as you can. Official **fares**, quoted by the airlines, are generally more expensive than those booked through a travel agent; wherever you book, **peak-season** rates apply in July, August, December and at Easter. If you simply want a plain return ticket, the best deal you'll get is usually an Apex, which means booking at least two weeks ahead and committing yourself to flight dates that you cannot change without paying a hefty penalty. Tickets are usually valid for between three and six months; you'll pay more for one that allows you to stay for up to a year. There's always some deal available for young people or students, though don't expect massive reductions.

For scheduled return flights from London or Manchester to Guatemala City or San José, for example, you should expect to pay around £640–£740 high season, £510–560 at other times. To Mexico City prices are lower but even more variable, ranging from £350 to £500. If you want to travel through several countries in Central America or continue into South America, it's worth considering an **"open-jaw" ticket** (which lets you fly into one city and out of another), or an **airpass** (see p.27).

Web sites in the UK aren't as geared up for Central American destinations as their US counterparts, though a check through *www.cheapflights.co.uk* will give some idea of fares from various UK airports to North America and Mexico, and there are good links to travel agents and other sources of information. The UsitCampus Website (*www.usitcampus.co.uk*) also has a reasonable farefinder.

PACKAGES AND INCLUSIVE TOURS

Many companies offer **package tours** to Central America, which save hassle and can be good value. They're generally relaxed and friendly, usually led by someone from the UK who knows the area well; in many cases there may also be a local guide. Transport can vary from local buses to comfortable minibuses, or from fast launches to light aircraft. The list in the box on p.9 covers the best and most experienced UK operators. Prices quoted are a guide only; some tours also require a local payment for meals. Most operate through the winter only, but several run year-round.

FLIGHTS FROM IRELAND

There are **no direct flights** from Ireland to Central America. The cheapest way to get to

Central America is to take one of the numerous daily flights from Dublin or Belfast to London, and then connect with one of the transatlantic flights detailed on pp.8–9. Alternatively, you can take a direct flight from Ireland to the **US** or **Europe** for easy onward connections to Mexico and Central America. Delta has the widest range of direct flights from Dublin (and several from Shannon) to JFK and Atlanta, with daily connections to Mexico City, Guatemala and Panamá. On Aer Lingus from Dublin (and some from Shannon) you can get same-day connections to Mexico City and San José for example, by flying to New York (JFK); and you can also fly with them from Dublin to Amsterdam and pick up KLM's flights to Mexico and Central America from there. BA also fly from Dublin to meet their connections in London to Mexico City and Cancún. KLM's flights from Belfast connect with their services from Amsterdam to Mexico City and Central America.

Discount fares from Dublin or Belfast to Mexico range from around IR£450 to IR£600 return; the fare from Dublin to Guatemala will cost upwards of IR£570.

USEFUL ADDRESSES IN IRELAND

AIRLINES

Aer Lingus (*www.aerlingus.ie*), Dublin ☎01/705 3333

British Airways (*www.britishairways.com*), Belfast ☎0345/222111; Dublin ☎0141/222 2345

British Midland (*www.britishmidland.co.uk*), Belfast ☎0345/554554, Dublin: ☎01/283 8833

Delta (*www.delta.com*), Belfast ☎028/9048 0526, Dublin ☎1800/414767

Iberia (*www.iberia.com*), Dublin ☎01/677 9846

KLM (*www.klm.com*), Belfast ☎0990/074074, Dublin ☎03458/445588

Ryanair (*www.ryanair.com*), Dublin ☎01/609 7800, Belfast ☎0541/569569

United (*www.unitedairlines.com*), Dublin ☎1800/535300

Virgin (*www.virgin-atlantic.com*), Dublin ☎01/8733388

FLIGHT AND TOUR AGENTS

Maxwell's Travel, D'Olier Chambers, 1 Hawkins St, Dublin 2 (☎01/677 9479, fax 679 3948). Very experienced Latin American operator, and the Irish representative for many of the British specialist tour operators listed in the box on p.9.

Trailfinders, 4–5 Dawson St, Dublin 2 (☎01/677 7888, *www.trailfinders.ie*). Irish

branch of the air fare and independent travel experts.

Usit (*www.usitnow.ie*), 19–21 Aston Quay, O'Connell Bridge, Dublin 2 (☎01/602 1600); Fountain Centre, College St, Belfast BT1 6ET (☎028/9032 4073). All-Ireland student travel agents, with 20 offices (mainly on campuses) in the Republic and the North.

GETTING THERE FROM AUSTRALIA AND NEW ZEALAND

There are no direct flights from Australasia to Central America, but it's easy enough to get there via the US or Mexico. Low-season prices run from mid-January to the end of February and October to the end of November; high season comprises mid-May to the end of August and December to mid-January. Count on paying between A$200 and A$400 more at peak season than the fares quoted below.

The cheapest fares and most direct flights from Australia and New Zealand are with Air New Zealand and Continental/United Airlines, who team up to travel to Central America **via LA** for around A$2100/NZ$2300, depending on your ultimate destination. Qantas also offer a similar deal, though fares are more expensive at A$2300/NZ$2450. Alternatively, you could travel **to Mexico City** via Asia on Japan Airlines (JAL) or Singapore Airlines, and then on to Central America with the relevant national airline; both JAL and Singapore charge around A$1850/NZ$2250 to Mexico City, with add-on return fares costing A$600–700/NZ$720–850. In all cases it's worth checking fares not only with the airlines themselves (see box below) but also with the **discount agents** listed in the box overleaf.

If you're planning to travel a lot around the region you may want to look into an **airpass**, (see p.27) – United Airlines, Taca and Aviateca all offer flight coupons for single flights to Central America. Central America isn't included in any **round-the-world (RTW)** tickets from Australasia – your best bet for getting to Central America on an RTW ticket is to go via LA, though you'll have to pay an extra A$600–700/ NZ$720–850 for the return side-trip to Central America. The best RTW deal from Australia and

---

AIRLINES IN AUSTRALIA AND NEW ZEALAND

Air New Zealand Australia ☎13/2476, New Zealand ☎0800/737 000 or 09/357 3000, *www.airnz.com*. Daily from Sydney, Brisbane, Melbourne and Adelaide to LA, either direct or via Honolulu/Tonga/Fiji/Papeete. Onward connections to all Central American capitals with Continental.

Continental Airlines Australia ☎02/9244 2242, New Zealand ☎09/308 3350, *www.flycontinental .com*. Teams up with Qantas and Air New Zealand to offer a through service to Central America from LA.

Japan Airlines Australia ☎02/9272 1111, New Zealand ☎09/379 9906, *www.japanair.com*. Several flights a week from Sydney, Brisbane, Cairns and Auckland to LA and Mexico City with a stopover in Tokyo or Osaka.

Qantas Australia ☎13/1313, New Zealand ☎09/357 8900 & ☎0800/808 767,

www.qantas.com.au. Daily flights to LA from major Australasian cities with onward connections to all Central American capitals on Continental.

Singapore Airlines Australia ☎13/1011 or 02/9350 0262, New Zealand ☎09/303 2129 or 0800/808 909, *www.singaporeair.com*. Twice weekly to LA from major Australian cities and once weekly from Auckland via Singapore.

Taca & Aviateca Australia Australia ☎03/9329 5211 (no NZ office). Airpasses from LA to Guatemala City and San José.

United Airlines Australia ☎13/1777, New Zealand ☎09/379 3800, *www.ual.com*. Daily direct to LA from Sydney, Melbourne and Auckland with onward connections to all Central American capitals; also sells airpasses.

deal we offer (see box on previous page). A typical travel insurance policy usually provides cover for the loss of baggage, tickets and – up to a certain limit – cash or cheques, as well as cancellation or curtailment of your journey. Most of them exclude so-called dangerous sports unless an extra premium is paid: in Central America this can mean scuba-diving, whitewater rafting and trekking. Many policies can be chopped and changed to exclude coverage you don't need – for example, sickness and accident benefits can often be excluded or included at will. If you do take medical coverage, ascertain whether benefits will be paid as treatment proceeds or only after return home, and whether there is a 24-hour medical emergency number. When securing baggage cover, make sure that the per-article limit – typically under £500 – will cover your most valuable possession. If you need to make a claim, you should keep receipts for medicines and medical treatment, and in the event you have anything stolen, you must obtain a *denuncia* from the police.

RED TAPE AND ENTRY REQUIREMENTS

Information on the entry requirements of the seven Central American countries is liable to sudden change, and it's crucial to contact a consulate before travelling to check **what's required of you. Even when you've checked and armed yourself with the correct paperwork you may find the requests of the immigration officer at variance with the official policy.**

That said, **visas** (with a few notable exceptions) are usually not needed by citizens of EU countries, the US, Canada, Australia and New Zealand to enter Central America as tourists, although you may be required to purchase a **tourist card** on entry. Visitors are usually permitted a stay from thirty to ninety days, depending on the country; again, check with your consulate.

All the Central American countries have consulates in **Mexico City**; there's also a Guatemalan consulate in Comitán; Guatemalan and El Salvadorean consulates in Tapachula; and a Belizean consulate in Chetumal.

VISAS AND TOURIST CARDS

If you need a **visa** it's always best get one in advance; don't bank on picking one up at the border. Apply to the Consular Department of the country you want to visit, preferably before you leave home, though you will usually be able to get one at the relevant consulate in any other country. Visas are valid for at least thirty days, and generally allow you to stay in the country for up to ninety days, depending largely on the mood of the immigration official when you arrive. You may also have to show evidence that you have bought a plane or bus ticket in and out of the country when you apply for a visa. US citizens are strongly advised to check **www.travel.state.gov** for any changes in visa requirements or travel warnings before making travel plans.

Citizens of Australia and New Zealand need a visa to enter **El Salvador**.

Citizens of Canada need a visa for **Nicaragua**.

Citizens of Ireland (Eire) need a visa for **Panamá**.

If you're flying in on a **one-way ticket** (providing the airline lets you board – some countries, Costa Rica for example, refuse travellers with no return tickets) you may have to prove your intention to leave the country; additionally you may have to show "sufficient funds" for your stay, though these conditions are rarely enforced.

Even if you don't officially require a visa or tourist card to enter a particular country, the immigration official may ask you to "buy" one, or pay some form of unspecified "fee" – usually equivalent to a dollar or five (exceptions are Belize and El Salvador, where you'll never be asked for illegal entry or exit fees). How you deal with this depends on how good your Spanish is,

---

CENTRAL AMERICAN EMBASSIES AND CONSULATES

IN NORTH AMERICA

Belize 2535 Massachusetts Ave NW, Washington DC 20008 (☎202/332-9636, www.embassyofbelize.org); Honorary Consul, Suite 3800, South Tower, Royal Bank Plaza, Toronto, ON M5J 2JP (☎416/865-7000, fax 865-7048; in Quebec ☎514/871-4741).

Costa Rica 2114 S St NW, Washington DC 20008 (☎202/234-2945, fax 202/234-2946, www.costarica-embassy.org).

El Salvador 2308 California St NW, Washington DC 20008 (☎202/265-9671, www.elsalvador.org); Consulate, 1724 20th St NW, Washington DC 20009 (☎202/331-4032, fax 331-4036); 209 Kent St, Ottawa, ON K2P 1Z8 (☎613/238-2939).

Guatemala 2220 R St NW, Washington DC 20008 (☎202/745-4952, fax 745-1908, www.guatemala-embassy.org).

Honduras 3007 Tilden St NW, Washington DC 20008 (☎202/966-7702, fax 966-7702, www.hondurasemb.org).

Nicaragua 1627 New Hampshire Ave NW, Washington DC 20009 (☎202/939-6570, Consulate ☎202/939-6531).

Panamá 2862 McGill Terrace NW, Washington DC 20008 (☎202/483-1407, Consulate ☎202/387-6154).

IN THE UK

Belize 22 Harcourt House, 19 Cavendish Square, London W1M 9AD (☎020/7499 9728, fax 7491 4139, bzhc-lon@btconnect.com).

Costa Rica Flat 1, 14 Lancaster Gate, London W2 3LH (☎020/7706 8844, info@embcrlon.demon.co.uk).

El Salvador 3rd Floor, Mayfair House, 39 Great Portland St, London W1N 7JZ (☎020/7436 8282, embasalondres@netscapeonline.co.uk).

Guatemala 13 Fawcett St, London SW10 9HN (☎020/7351 3042, fax 7376 5708).

Honduras 115 Gloucester Place, London W1H 3PJ (☎020/7486 4880, fax 7486 4550, hondurasuk@lineone.net).

Nicaragua Suite 12, Vicarage House, 58-60 Kensington Church St, London W8 4DB (☎020/7938 2373, fax 7937 0952; emb.ofnicaragua@demon.co.uk).

Panamá Panamá House, 40 Hertford St, London W1Y 7TG (☎020/7943 4646 or 7493 4333).

IN AUSTRALASIA

Belize British High Commission, Commonwealth Ave, Yarralumla, ACT (☎06/6270 6666, www.uk.emb.gov.au); British High Commission, 44 Hill St, Wellington (☎04/472 6049, www.brithighcomm.org.nz).

Costa Rica Consulate-General, 30 Clarence St, Sydney (☎02/9261 1177).

El Salvador Honorary Consulate, 3 Donnington St, Carindale, Brisbane (☎07/3398-8658).

Guatemala The nearest representative is in the US.

Honduras Consulate-General, Level 7, 19–31 Pitt St, Sydney (☎02/9350 8118).

Nicaragua The nearest representative is in the US.

Panamá The nearest representative is in Singapore (☎+65/221-8677).

the amount of hassle you're willing to put up with and the attitude of the official. It's certainly annoying to have to pay these **bribes** and, if you know the rules, and stick to the "won't pay" line you'll probably get waved through – eventually. However, in places like Guatemala and Honduras, where there's a semi-institutionalized requirement to pay officials Q10/L20 (around US$1.50), it's usually more bother than it's worth to kick up a fuss. Once you get your stamp (and visa/tourist card if required) you should keep your **passport** with you at all times, or at the very least carry a photocopy, as you may be asked to show it.

Extensions to the permitted period of stay – whether you need a visa/tourist card or not – can be obtained at the immigration department (**migración**) in the country concerned, sometimes only in the capital. The process often takes a full day, so you may prefer to use the services of a *tramitador*, an agency that, for a fee, will deal with the red tape. In many cases it's often easier to leave the country for a few days and re-enter with a new stamp.

COSTS AND MONEY

By European or North American standards **the cost of living in Central America is low. Belize and Costa Rica are the most expensive, while Nicaragua, Guatemala and Honduras are probably the cheapest. There are, of course, exceptions and variations – in El Salvador, for example, one of the cheaper countries overall, accommodation is surprisingly expensive for the region.**

The **US dollar** is the most widely accepted foreign currency in Central America – Panamá's unit of currency, the balboa, *is* the US dollar, and in El Salvador the greenback is now accepted as legal tender alongside local currency for all transactions. Though you can pay for some things by **plastic** – and, more usefully, use it to withdraw currency from ATMs – some countries are less geared up for this than others, and it's always a good idea to have some dollar **travellers' cheques** (though again, these aren't accepted everywhere; see opposite) or **cash dollars**, in case you run short of local currency a long way from the nearest bank. You'll get the best rate for your dollars if you change them for local currency in the country you're in or entering. Most international airports have a bank for **currency exchange**, while at the main land border crossings there might be a bank, or more likely a swarm of moneychangers, who'll give fair rates for cash and occasionally travellers' cheques. At even the most remote border crossing you can usually depend on finding some entrepreneur willing to change dollars, though rates worsen the further you are from a bank.

All prices quoted in the guide are in US dollars.

EXCHANGE RATES

The following exchange rates were correct at time of going to press, though rates will inevitably vary over the course of this edition of the guide in those countries whose currency is not pegged to the dollar.

Belize (Belizean dollar) Bz$2 = US$1

Costa Rica (colón) 306c = US$1

El Salvador (colón) 8.75c = US$1

Guatemala (quetzal) Q7.7 = US$1

Honduras (lempira) L14.9 = US$1

Nicaragua (córdoba) C$13 = US$1

Panamá (dollar/balboa) $1 = US$1

PLASTIC, TRAVELLERS' CHEQUES AND WIRING MONEY

Credit cards are widely used in Central America – though you shouldn't rely on them in Nicaragua or Honduras – and are becoming increasingly accepted even in smaller hotels and restaurants. Visa is the most useful, followed by Mastercard. In most countries there will usually be at least one particular bank which accepts either (sometimes both). You can use your card to get cash (except when crossing land borders, which is where travellers' cheques and cash dollars come in handy) from ATMs, and over the counter at banks. Although most ATMs are in service 24 hours it's wiser to use them when the bank is open: you can see a bank employee if something goes wrong and the machine keeps your card (though this is very rare), and it's also safer. Using your debit card means you don't have to buy and countersign travellers' cheques and, though you pay a handling charge each time you use it, the amount may be less than the commission on cheques and you may also get a better exchange rate.

Travellers' cheques denominated in dollars are a safe way to carry money, as they offer the added security of a refund if they're stolen. To facilitate this, make sure that you have cheques issued by one of the big names, which are also more readily accepted. You should also always carry your proof of purchase when trying to change travellers' cheques, as some places will refuse to deal with you otherwise.

Having money **wired from home** is never convenient or cheap, and should be considered a last resort. Funds can be sent via **Western Union** or **American Express MoneyGram**; both companies' fees depend on the destination and the amount being transferred. The funds should be available for collection at the local Amex or Western Union office within minutes of being sent. It's also possible (for a fee) to have money wired directly from a bank in your home country to a bank in Central America, although this is somewhat less reliable because it involves two separate institutions, and can take between a couple of days and several months. If you go this route, the person wiring the funds to you will need to know the routing number of the bank the funds are being wired to.

COSTS

Life in Central America is generally cheaper than in North America and Europe (though travellers are often surprised by the expense of Belize and Costa Rica, where prices are not that different from in the US). As a general rule, locally produced goods are cheap, and anything imported is overpriced.

To an extent, what you spend will obviously depend on where, when and how you choose to travel. During **peak tourist seasons**, such as Christmas and Easter, hotel prices tend to rise, and certain tourist centres are notably more expensive. **Public transport**, geared to locals, is invariably a bargain – though bear in mind that in some places foreigners are routinely charged more in what's effectively an institutionalized two-tier price system. Travelling by car is expensive, and the cost of renting a car is higher in Central America than it is in the US, as is the cost of fuel – although this is still cheaper than in Europe. **Student cards** may sometimes get you small reductions on standard prices, but unless you need one to get a cheap air fare, it's not worth buying one for the trip.

HEALTH

It's always easier to become ill in a country with a different climate, food and germs, still more so in a poor country with lower standards of sanitation than you might be used to. Most visitors, however, get through Central America without catching anything more serious than a dose of "traveller's diarrhoea", and the most important precaution is to be aware of health risks posed by poor hygiene, untreated water, insect bites, undressed open cuts and unprotected sex.

Above all, it's vital to get the best **health advice** you can before you set off; pay a visit to your doctor or a travel clinic (see box below) as far in advance of travel as possible. Many clinics also sell travel-related accessories, malaria tablets, mosquito nets, water filters and the like. Regardless of how well-prepared you are med-

ically, you will still want the security of medical insurance (see p.13).

VACCINATIONS, INOCULATIONS AND MALARIA PRECAUTIONS

If possible, all **inoculations** should be sorted out at least ten weeks before departure. The only obligatory jab for certain Central American countries is a **yellow fever** vaccination if you're arriving from a "high-risk" area – northern South America and much of central Africa – in which case you need to carry your vaccination certificate. You'll also need a yellow fever jab if travelling in Panamá south of the canal. **Diphtheria** vaccinations are considered essential, and long-term travellers should look at the combined **hepatitis A and B** and the **rabies** vaccines (though see p.21 for a caveat on that one). And all

---

MEDICAL RESOURCES FOR TRAVELLERS

IN NORTH AMERICA

Center for Disease Control, 1600 Clifton Rd, Atlanta, GA 30333 (☎404/639-3311, *www.cdc.gov/travel*). Current information on health risks and precautions, and clear and comprehensive Web pages covering Mexico and Central America.

International Association for Medical Assistance to Travellers (IAMAT), 417 Center St, Lewiston, NY 14092 (☎716/754-4883, *www.iamat.org*); 40 Regal Rd, Guelph, ON, N1K 1B5 (☎519/836-0102). Non-profit organization, supported by donations, which can provide climate charts and leaflets on diseases and inoculations.

Medic Alert, 2323 Colorado Ave, Turlock, CA 95381 (☎1-800/432-5378, *www.medicalert.org*; in Canada ☎1-800/668-1507, *www.medicalert.ca*). Sells bracelets engraved with the traveller's medical requirements in case of emergency.

Travel Medicine, 351 Pleasant St, Northampton, MA 01060 (☎1-800/872-8633, *www.travmed.com*). Sells first-aid kits, mosquito netting, water filters and other health-related travel products.

Travellers Medical Center, 31 Washington Square, New York, NY 10011 (☎212/982-1600). Consultation service on immunizations and treatment.

IN THE UK AND IRELAND

British travellers should pick up a copy of the free booklet *Health Advice for Travellers*, published by the Department of Health; it's available from GPs' surgeries, many chemists, and most of the agencies listed below.

British Airways Travel Clinic, 156 Regent St, London W1R 5TA (Mon–Fri 9am–5.15pm, Sat 10am–4pm; ☎020/7439 9584); other clinics across London (including BA terminal at Victoria station) and over 20 more throughout UK: call ☎01276/685040 or check *www.britishairways.com* to find your nearest branch. Excellent medical advice, vaccinations

and a comprehensive range of travel health items – and you even get air miles. No appointments necessary at the Regent Street branch; call ahead at other clinics.

Hospital for Tropical Diseases Travel Clinic, 2nd Floor, Mortimer Market Centre, Capper St, London WC1E 6AU (Mon–Fri 9am–5pm; ☎020/7388 9600). A recorded health

travellers should check that they are up to date with **polio**, **tetanus**, **typhoid** and **hepatitis A** jabs.

North Americans can get inoculations at any immunization centre or at most local clinics, and will have to pay a fee. Most GPs in the **UK** have a travel surgery where you can get advice and certain vaccines on prescription, though they may not administer some of the less common immunizations. Note too that though some jabs (diphtheria, typhoid) are free, others will incur quite a hefty charge, and it can be worth checking out a travel clinic, where you can receive vaccinations almost immediately, some of them (hepatitis, rabies) at lower prices than at the doctor's. In **Australasia**, vaccination centres are always less expensive than doctors' surgeries.

Malaria is endemic in many parts of Central America, especially in the rural lowlands. The recommended prophylactic west of the Panamá Canal is Chloroquine; Mefloquine to the east of the canal, including the San Blas Islands. However, as Mefloquine (also known as Larium) can have upsetting side effects, it's worth checking with a medical practitioner as to its suitability for you. You need to begin taking the tablets one week before arrival and continue for four weeks after leaving the area. You should still take precautions to avoid getting bitten by insects altogether: sleep in screened rooms or under nets, burn mosquito coils containing permethrin (available everywhere), cover up arms and legs, especially around dawn and dusk when the mosquitoes are most active, and use insect repellent containing over 35 percent Deet. Also prevalent throughout Central America (usually occurring in epidemic outbreaks) is **dengue fever**, a viral infection transmitted by mosquitoes active during the day. There's no vaccine or specific treatment, so you need to pay great attention to avoiding bites.

---

line message on ☎0906/337733 gives hints on hygiene and illness prevention as well as lists of appropriate immunizations.

Malaria Information Line 24-hour recorded message with information about malaria for travellers, provided by the London School of Hygiene and Tropical Medicine (☎0891/600350; calls cost £1 per minute).

MASTA (Medical Advisory Service for Travellers Abroad), London School of Hygiene and Tropical Medicine, Keppel St, London WC1E 7HT. Operates a 24-hour Travellers' Health Line (☎0906/822 4100; calls cost £1 per minute) giving written information tailored to your journey by return of post.

Trailfinders Travel Clinic, 194 Kensington High St, London W8 6BD (☎020/7938 3999); 254–284 Sauchiehall St, Glasgow G2 3EH (☎0141/353

0066). Expert medical advice and a full range of travel vaccines and medical supplies. No appointments necessary in London. Discounts on vaccinations for clients.

Travel Medicine Services, PO Box 254, 16 College St, Belfast 1 (☎028/9031 5220). Operates a travel clinic (Mon 9–11am & Wed 2–4pm) which can give inoculations after referral from a GP, but primarily administers yellow fever vaccine.

Tropical Medical Bureau, Grafton St Medical Centre, 34 Grafton Street, Dublin 2 (☎01/671-9200, *www.iol.ie/-tmb/*).

Yahoo! Health Web Site
(*http://health.yahoo.com*) Gives information about specific diseases and conditions, drugs and herbal remedies, as well as advice from health experts.

IN AUSTRALIA AND NEW ZEALAND
Travellers' Medical and Vaccination Centres:

Adelaide, 27–29 Gilbert Place (☎08/8212 7522)
Auckland, 1/170 Queen St (☎09/373 3531)
Brisbane, 5/247 Adelaide St, Brisbane (☎07/3221 9066)
Christchurch, 147 Armagh St (☎03/379 4000)
Melbourne, 2/393 Little Bourke St (☎03/9602 5788)

Perth, 5 Mill St (☎08/9321 1977), plus branch in Fremantle
Sydney, 7/428 George St (☎02/9221 7133), plus branches in Chatswood and Parramatta
Wellington, Shop 15, Grand Arcade, 14–16 Willis St (☎04/473 0991)

OTHER SIMPLE PRECAUTIONS

What you **eat or drink** while you're travelling is crucial: a poor diet lowers your resistance. Be sure to drink clean water and eat a good balanced diet. Eating plenty of peeled fresh fruit helps keep up your vitamin and mineral intake, but it might be worth taking daily multi-vitamin and mineral tablets with you. It is also important to eat enough and get enough **rest**, as it's easy to become run-down if you're on the move a lot, especially in a hot climate. Don't try anything too exotic in the first few days, before your body has had a chance to adjust to local microbes, and avoid food that has been on display for a while and is not freshly cooked. You should also steer clear of raw shellfish, salads, and don't eat anywhere that is obviously dirty. In addition to the hazards mentioned under "Intestinal Troubles", below, contaminated food and water will also transmit the hepatitis A virus, which can lay a victim low for several months with exhaustion, fever, diarrhoea, and can even cause liver damage. For advice on **water**, see opposite.

More serious are **hepatitis B**, and **HIV** and **AIDS**, all transmitted through blood or sexual contact; you should take all the usual, well-publicized precautions to avoid them. To contemplate casual sex without a condom would be madness; condoms also offer protection from other sexually transmitted diseases.

Two other common causes of problems are **altitude** and the **sun**. The answer in both cases is to take it easy; allow yourself time to acclimatize before you start running up volcanoes, and build up exposure to the sun gradually – only a few minutes on the first day. Use a strong sunscreen and, if you're walking during the day, wear a hat and try to keep in the shade. Avoid dehydration by drinking enough – water or fruit juice rather than beer or coffee. Overheating can cause heatstroke, which is potentially fatal. Lowering body temperature (by taking a tepid shower, for example) is the first step in treatment.

Finally you might want to consider carrying a **travel medical kit**. These range from a box of band-aids to a full compact sterilized kit, complete with syringes and sutures; you can buy them from pharmacies and the specialist suppliers listed in the box on pp.18–19.

INTESTINAL TROUBLES

A bout of **diarrhoea** is the medical problem you're most likely to encounter, and no one, however cautious, seems to avoid it altogether. Its main cause is simply the change of diet: the food in Central America contains a whole new set of bacteria, as well as perhaps rather more of them than you're used to. The best cure is the simplest one: take it easy for a day or two, drink lots of bottled water, and eat only the blandest of foods – papaya is good for soothing the stomach, and is also crammed with vitamins. Only if the symptoms last more than four or five days do you need to worry. **Cholera** is an acute bacterial infection, recognizable by watery diarrhoea and vomiting, and an epidemic has recently swept through Central America, though many victims may have only mild or even no symptoms. However, risk of infection is considered low, particularly if you're following the health advice above, and symptoms are rapidly relieved by prompt medical attention and clean water.

If you're spending any time in rural areas you also run the risk of picking up various **parasitic infections**: protozoa – amoeba and giardia – and intestinal worms. These sound (and can be) hideous, but they're easily treated once detected. If you suspect you have an infestation take a stool sample to a good **pathology lab** and go to a doctor or pharmacist with the test results (see "Getting Medical Help", opposite). More serious is **amoebic dysentery**, which is endemic in many parts of the region. The symptoms are more or less the same as a bad dose of diarrhoea, but include bleeding. On the whole, a course of Flagyl (metronidazole or tinidozole) will cure it; if you plan to visit the far-flung corners of Central America then it's worth carrying these, just in case. If possible get some, and some advice on their usage, from a doctor before you go.

BITES AND STINGS

Taking steps to avoid getting bitten by insects, particularly mosquitoes (see previous page), is always good practice. Sandflies, often present on beaches, are tiny but their bites, usually on feet and ankles, itch like hell and last for days. Head or body lice can be picked up from people or bedding, and are best treated with medicated soap or shampoo; very occasionally, they may spread typhus, characterized by fever, muscle aches,

WHAT ABOUT THE WATER?

Contaminated water is a major cause of sickness in Central America, and even if it looks clean, all drinking water should be regarded with caution. That said, however, it's also essential to increase fluid intake to prevent dehydration. Bottled water is widely available, but stick with known brands and always check that the seal is intact, since refilling empties with tap water for resale is not unknown (carbonated water is generally a safer bet in this respect). Many restaurants use purified water (*agua purificada*), but always check; many hotels have a supply and will often provide bottles in your room. There are various methods of treating water while you are travelling, whether your source is from a tap or a river: boiling for a minimum of five minutes is the most effective method of sterilization, but it is not always practical, and will not remove unpleasant tastes.

   Water filters remove visible impurities and larger pathogenic organisms (most bacteria and parasites). The Swiss-made Katadyn filter is expensive but extremely useful (various sizes are available from outdoor equipment stores). To be really sure your filtered water is also purified however, **chemical sterilization**, using either chlorine or iodine tablets, or a tincture of iodine liquid, is advisable. Both chlorine and iodine leave a nasty aftertaste (though it can be masked with lemon or lime juice), and iodine is more effective in destroying amoebic cysts. Pregnant women or people with thyroid problems should consult their doctor before using iodine sterilizing tablets or iodine-based purifiers. Inexpensive iodine removal filters are recommended if treated water is being used continuously for more than a month or is being given to babies.

   Any good outdoor equipment shop will stock a range of **water treatment products**; their staff will give you the best advice for your particular needs.

headaches and eventually a measles-like rash. If you think you have it, seek treatment.

   Scorpions are common: mostly nocturnal, they hide during the heat of the day under rocks and in crevices. If you're camping, or sleeping in a village cabaña, shake your shoes out before putting them on and try not to wander round barefoot. Their sting is painful (occasionally fatal) and can become infected, so you should seek medical treatment. You're less likely to be bitten by a **spider**, but the advice is the same as for scorpions and venomous insects – seek medical treatment if the pain persists or increases.

   You're unlikely to see a **snake**, and most are harmless in any case. Wearing boots and long trousers will go a long way towards preventing a bite – walk heavily and they will usually slither away. Exceptions are the fer-de-lance (which, thankfully, lives on dense, mountainous territory, and rarely emerges during the day) and the bushmaster (which can be found in places with heavy rainfall, or near streams and rivers), both of which can be aggressive, and whose venom can be fatal. If you do get bitten remember what the snake looked like (kill it if you can), immobilize the bitten limb as far as possible and seek medical help immediately: antivenoms are available in most hospitals.

   Swimming and snorkelling might bring you into contact with potentially dangerous or venomous **sea creatures**. You're extremely unlikely to be a victim of shark attack (though the dubious practice of shark-feeding as a tourist attraction is growing, and could lead to an accidental bite), but jellyfish are common and all corals will sting. Some jellyfish, like the Portuguese man-o'-war, with its distinctive purple, bag-like sail, have very long tentacles with stinging cells, and an encounter will result in raw, red weals. Equally painful is a brush against fire coral: in each case clean the wound with vinegar or iodine and seek medical help if the pain persists or infection develops.

   Rabies does exist in Central America; the best advice is to give dogs a wide berth, and not to play with animals at all, no matter how cuddly they may look. Treat any bite as suspect: wash any wound immediately with soap or detergent and apply alcohol or iodine if possible. Act immediately to get treatment – rabies is fatal once symptoms appear. There is a vaccine, but it is expensive, serves only to shorten the course of treatment you need anyway and is effective for no more than three months.

GETTING MEDICAL HELP

For minor medical problems, head for the **farmacia** – look for a green cross. Pharmacists are knowledgeable and helpful, and many may speak some English. They can also sell drugs over the counter (if necessary) which are only available by prescription at home. Most large cities have **doctors** and **dentists**, many trained in the US, who are experienced in treating visitors and speak good English. Your embassy will always have a list of recommended doctors, and we've included some in our "Listings" for the main towns. Medical insurance (see p.13) is essential, and for anything serious you should to go to the best **private hospital** you can reach; again, these are located mainly in the capital cities. If you suspect something is amiss with your insides, it might be worth heading straight for the local **pathology lab** (*laboratorio médico*), found in all main towns, before seeing a doctor, as the doctor will probably send you there anyway. Many rural communities have a **health centre** (*centro de salud* or *puesto de salud*), where healthcare is free, although there may be only a nurse or health-worker available and you can't rely on finding an English-speaking doctor. Should you need an injection or transfusion, make sure that the equipment is sterile (it might be worth bringing a sterile kit from home) and ensure any blood you receive is screened.

INFORMATION AND MAPS

Information about Central America is available from a number of sources, though much of the promotional puff provided by the official tourist offices is pretty to look at but of little practical use. However, the quality of such information is improving, and if you have specific questions you could try contacting some of the official organizations listed below.

INFORMATION

When digging out information on Central America, don't forget the **specialist tour operators** (see p.6, 9 & 12) and the **embassies** (see p.15). Best of all for practical details, bookmark the recommended **Internet sites**.

CENTRAL AMERICAN TOURIST OFFICES' WEB SITES

Belize *www.belizenet.com*

Costa Rica *www.tourism-costarica.com*, *www.incostarica.net*

El Salvador *www.elsalvadorturismo.gob.sv*, *www.sv*

Guatemala *www.travel-guatemala.org.gt*, *www.guatemala.travel.com.gt*

Honduras *www.hondurasinfo.hn*

Nicaragua *www.intur.gob.ni*

Panamá *www.panamatravel.com*

See also the list of useful Internet sites on p.24.

Amerispan, PO Box 40007, Philadelphia, PA 19106-0007 (☎1-800/879-6640, fax 215/751-1986, *www.amerispan.com*), which has a wide range of resources about learning Spanish and selecting language schools, plus details of volunteer opportunities in Central America.

IN THE UK

In London, **Canning House Library**, 2 Belgrave Square SW1X 8PJ (☎020/7235 2303), has the UK's largest publicly accessible collection of books and periodicals on Latin America (you can visit for free, but you have to be a member to take books out and receive the twice-yearly *Bulletin*, a review of recently published books on Latin America).

Citizens of the UK who are thinking of **working or volunteering** in Central America should take a look at the publications of the Central Bureau for Educational Visits, 10 Spring Gardens, London SW1A 2BN (☎020/7389 4880, *books@centralbureau.org.uk*), particularly *Working Holidays* (updated annually) and *Volunteer Work*, both packed with essential information, including contacts in Mexico and Central America.

For general information on **independent travel** pick up a copy of the excellent *Everything You Need to Know Before You Go* (Abroadsheet Publications, from specialist bookshops); author Mark Ashton has managed to cram an enormous amount of essential advice and tips onto one amazingly well-organized large glossy sheet.

Finally, if you're planning an expedition from the UK, you can (and should) avail yourself of the services of the **Expedition Advisory Centre** (EAC), at the Royal Geographic Society, 1 Kensington Gore, London SW7 2AR (☎020/7591 3080, *www.rgs.org*). As well as expedition planning seminars, the EAC also publishes a range of specialist books.

IN CENTRAL AMERICA

While you're in Central America you'll find **government tourism offices** in each capital city, and sometimes in the main tourist centres. The information they're able to give is variable, but they can usually provide at the very least a city map, a bus timetable and perhaps a list of hotels (and may possibly even call them for you). The addresses (and an idea of how useful a particular office will be) are given throughout the guide. In addition there are some locally run initiatives, often set up by an association of tourism businesses; the tour and travel agents mentioned in the guide are also reliable sources of information.

TOURIST INFORMATION

IN NORTH AMERICA

Belize US ☎212/563-6011 or 1-800/624-0686, *www.travelbelize.org.*

Costa Rica (*www.tourism-costarica.com*) No tourist office in the US or Canada, but calling ☎1-800/343-6332 will connect you to an English speaker at the tourist office in San José at no extra charge.

El Salvador US ☎212/889-3608, Canada ☎613/238-2939.
Guatemala US ☎202/518-4415.
Honduras US ☎1-800/410-9608, *www.letsgohonduras.com.*
Nicaragua US ☎202/939-6571.
Panamá US ☎202/483-1407, *www.panamainfo.com.*

IN THE UK AND IRELAND

Only **Guatemala** has a tourist office in the UK, at the same address as the embassy (see p.15; Mon–Fri 9am–5pm; ☎020/7351 3042). This office and the consular representatives of the other countries (addresses are listed on p.15) will send you information on their respective countries if you send an SAE with a 39p stamp; best give them a call first to check what they have:

Belize	☎020/7499 9728	**Honduras**	☎020/7486 4880
Costa Rica	☎020/7706 8844	**Nicaragua**	☎020/7938 2373
El Salvador	☎020/7436 8282	**Panamá**	☎020/7943 4646

IN AUSTRALASIA

It's difficult to find tourist information about Central America in Australia or New Zealand; your best bet is to have a look at the Web sites listed above or contact the specialist tour operators listed on p.12.

THE INTERNET

The number of pages devoted to Central America on the **Internet** is growing daily. The first place to look is the comprehensive and logically laid-out homepage of the **Latin American Information Center** (LANIC, *www.lanic.utexas.edu*), which has a seemingly never-ending series of superb links for each country. You can reach almost anywhere and anything in Central America connected to the net from here. **Green Arrow**'s pages (*www.greenarrow.com*) while concentrating on Costa Rica, are a good source of travel and environmental information and volunteering opportunities throughout Central America.

The **Latin American Travel Advisor** Web site (*www.amerispan.com/lata*) offers comprehensive information on every Central American country, covering safety, health, politics, culture and the economy. The site also provides general advice on travelling in the region. Another useful site is **Travel Latin America** (*www.travellatinamerica .com*), which offers a selection of news, features and information about travelling in the region, along with a currency converter, consulate details and an impressive selection of Web links for each country. Finally, the ever-helpful members of the newsgroup **rec.travel.latin-america** will answer any query about travel in the region. Most

---

MAP OUTLETS

AUSTRALIA AND NEW ZEALAND

Mapland, 372 Little Bourke St, Melbourne (☎03/9670 4383).

The Map Shop, 6 Peel St, Adelaide (☎08/8231 2033).

Mapworld, 173 Gloucester Street, Christchurch (☎03/374 5399, *www.mapworld.co.nz*).

Perth Map Centre, 1/884 Hay St, Perth (☎08/9322 5733).

Specialty Maps, 46 Albert St, Auckland (☎09/307 2217).

Travel Bookshop, Shop 3, 175 Liverpool St, Sydney (☎02/9261 8200).

Walkers Bookshop, 96 Lake Street, Cairns (☎07/4051 2410).

Worldwide Maps and Guides, 187 George St, Brisbane (☎07/3221 4330).

UK

Daunt Books, 83 Marylebone High St, London W1M 3DE (☎020/7224 2295); 193 Haverstock Hill, London NW3 4QL (☎020/7794 4006).

National Map Centre, 22–24 Caxton St, London SW1H 0QU (☎020/7222 2466, *www.mapsnmc.co.uk*).

Stanfords (*www.stanfords.co.uk*), 12–14 Long Acre, London WC2E 9LP (☎020/7836 1321); c/o British Airways, 156 Regent St, London W1R 5TA

(☎020/7434 4744); 29 Corn St, Bristol BS1 1HT (☎0117/929 9966).

Waterstone's, Deansgate, Manchester M3 2BW (☎0161/837 3000, fax 0161/835 1534, *www.waterstonesbooks.co.uk*).

John Smith and Sons, 26 Colquhoun Ave, Glasgow G52 4PJ (☎0141/221 7472, *www .johnsmith.co.uk*).

US AND CANADA

The Complete Traveler Bookstore, 199 Madison Ave, New York, NY 10016 (☎212/685-9007).

Open Air Books and Maps, 25 Toronto St, Toronto, ON M5R 2C1 (☎416/363-0719).

Rand McNally, 444 N Michigan Ave, Chicago, IL 60611 (☎312/321-1751); 150 E 52nd St, New York, NY 10022 (☎212/758-7488); 595 Market St, San Francisco, CA 94105 (☎415/777-3131); 1201 Connecticut Ave NW, Washington, DC 20003

(☎202/223-6751). For other locations, or for maps by mail order, call ☎1-800/333-0136 ext 2111.

Traveler's Bookstore, 22 W 52nd St, New York, NY 10019 (☎212/664-0995).

Ulysses Travel Bookshop, 4176 St-Denis, Montréal, PQ (☎514/843-9447).

World Wide Books and Maps, 736 Granville St, Vancouver, BC V6Z 1E4 (☎604/687-3320).

have been asked already so there's a huge (and generally accurate) information base to dip into.

MAPS

The best **map of Central America**, covering the region at a scale of 1:800,000, is Kevin Healey's *Travel Map of Central America* produced by International Travel Map Productions (345 West Broadway, Vancouver BC, Canada V5Y 1P8). They also publish **individual maps** of each country at a scale of 1:750,000 (Belize at 1:350,000), but these tend to have a few mistakes. Specialist map shops should sell them and it's wise to try to get what you need before you go, although they are available in many Central American capitals.

ACCOMMODATION

Central American hotels come in all shapes and sizes and it's usually not hard to find somewhere reasonable. Accommodation comes under a bewildering range of names; *hotel*, obviously, but you'll frequently see *pensión*, *casa de huéspedes*, *hospedaje*, *posada*, *alojamiento*, *rancho* and *campamento* – the last two usually refer to some form of camping. The different names don't always mean a great deal: in theory a *casa de huéspedes* is less formal than a *hotel* but in reality the main difference will be the price. You'll soon get used to finding what's on offer in your preferred price range.

Most countries have some form of price (and, in theory, quality) regulation and there's sometimes also a **hotel tax** to pay: always check if this is included in the rate you're quoted. It's a good idea to have a look at the room before you take it; make sure the light and fan work, and if you've been told there's hot water, see just what that means.

BUDGET HOTELS

There's so much variety in standards even among budget hotels that to list every possible permutation of types and furnishings would be impossible. However, a **basic room** in a town will have a light and a fan in addition to the bed, though don't expect a reading light or anywhere to put clothes, and all but the rock-bottom places will also supply a towel, soap and toilet paper. You'll often have the option of a **private bathroom** (ie a toilet and a basic shower), which is usually worth the small extra cost, especially if you're travelling as a couple. If the **price** seems a little high for the type of establishment it's worth asking if there's less expensive room (*¿Tiene un cuarto más barato, por favor?*) – you'll often get the

ACCOMMODATION PRICE CODES

All accommodation reviewed in this guide has been graded according to the following price scales, which represent the cost of a **double room in high season**, excluding any taxes.

① up to US$5	④ US$15–25	⑦ US$60–80
② US$5–10	⑤ US$25–40	⑧ US$80–100
③ US$10–15	⑥ US$40–60	⑨ US$100 and over

same room at a lower price. It's always better to get a room at the back, away from the noise of the street, and upstairs you're more likely to benefit from a breeze. Most small hotels will be family run, and the owners usually take pride in the cleanliness of the rooms. There will usually be a place to hand-wash clothes (a *pila*); ask first before you use it.

In **lowland areas** a fan (*ventilador*) will be more important than hot water (*agua caliente*), but in the mountains you'd probably prefer a hot shower, though there will rarely be any form of heating (*calefacción*); make sure you have enough blankets. The term "hot shower" in Central America can be a bit misleading; the water temperature may just be tepid rather than really hot. And sometimes the "heating element" will be a couple of wires running into a contraption above the shower nozzle – touching this is likely to give you an electric shock.

As a rule budget hotels in the **capital cities** tend to be less attractive than those in smaller towns and tourist areas, though we've listed the exceptions in the relevant chapters. In the bigger cities it's worth paying a little more, or even moving to one grade of hotel higher than you might otherwise, to stay in a more secure place – particularly for your first night. Cheap hotels are often crowded around bus stations and markets; some of these can be very dismal, many of them being used by prostitutes and their clients. However, in every capital there are at least one or two hotels where other travellers congregate (as well as plenty where they don't) to offer company and perhaps security.

Budget hotels in **rural areas** or **coastal locations** which are not touristy are often quite basic; a ramshackle building or perhaps a stick and thatch cabaña. These can be delightful – you'll be less of a guest and more an extra member of the family – but they can also be very uncomfortable, with lumpy mattresses and poor ventilation. This is where serviceable insect proofing can make the difference between misery and a good night's sleep.

Booking ahead for a budget room is not usually necessary (and often not possible, because of the difficulty of paying in advance and the fact that many such establishments don't have a telephone), though it might be worth trying at busy times like Christmas and Easter. Otherwise arriving early at your destination will give you a better selection.

RESORTS AND LODGES

Bigger hotels in cities will have similar facilities to those at home, though often in a more attractive setting and sometimes in a wonderfully restored colonial building. They will almost certainly have air conditioning (*aire acondicionado*); a feature which is also increasingly offered in less expensive places. You'll pay a good deal more for this than you would for a room with a fan and, other things being equal, it may not be worth the extra. Some of the best accommodation in the region, however, is offered by the **resorts** in beach areas and the **jungle-lodges**, often in beautiful, remote locations in or near national parks. Here you'll often have a private thatched cabaña, with a balcony overlooking the forest, lake, beach or other natural attraction. Obviously you'll be paying extra for this, but the experience of a rainforest dawn chorus and the chance of getting close to wildlife makes it worthwhile. These lodges are often used by the adventure and nature tour operators and occupancy varies with the season – if the lodge is open out of season, ask about possible discounts.

YOUTH HOSTELS AND CAMPING

In a region so full of inexpensive hotels you need rarely consider staying in **youth hostels**. In any case, only Costa Rica has a useful hostel network, with many located near national parks. The situation is similar with respect to **camping** and few places outside Costa Rica offer formal campsites. Elsewhere, you'll usually only need a tent if you're hiking really off the beaten track – though you'll probably have a guide who knows where there are shelters to hang a hammock, a tent offers better protection from rain and, more importantly, from insects. Some volcanoes are too high to climb and descend in one day, and if camping at the top you'll need some protection from the cold as well; a good sleeping bag is essential.

GETTING AROUND

Travel within Central America is as varied as the region itself. Since most locals don't own a car, buses are the most common form of public transport, and if you're travelling independently without your own vehicle you'll be spending a lot of time in (and waiting) them.

You're also likely to travel by **boat** – out to and between islands, along rivers, and as the main form of transport in areas like the Mosquito coast of Honduras and Nicaragua. The craft themselves range from precarious-looking dugout canoes and old tubs for ferries, to fast, modern launches, capable of long-distance sea travel.

Each country has at least one domestic **airline**; fares are usually relatively inexpensive, and flying will often save hours of road travel over the region's difficult terrain. If you're covering a lot of territory, **airpasses** can be very good value; see below.

Taxis are readily available in all the main towns; some routes (from airports to city centres for example) have set prices, but meters are a rarity – always fix a price before you set off. Taxis can also be a good substitute for a rental car; you have the advantage of your own transport without the responsibility, and it could even work out cheaper.

Prices vary for **car rental** throughout Central America. The most expensive country is Belize, where companies only offer sport/utility vehicles – the cheapest weekly rate (with Budget) is around US$400. Car rental in Honduras and Guatemala is also quite pricey: expect to pay around US$260 a week for a standard car, or US$320 for 4WD. Other countries are cheaper, ranging from around US$100 in Panamá, US$170 in Costa Rica, and US$200 in El Salvador. If you plan to rent a car make sure you get a good **map** (see p.25) and bear in mind that Central America has some of the highest **accident rates** in the world – and as a foreigner any collision is likely to be construed as your fault, so always take full-cover insurance. If you've succeeded in getting your own car to Central America, any further problems you face are likely to seem fairly minor. If you belong to a **motoring organization** at home, it's

AIRPASSES

If you want to visit the whole region in a fairly short time, the **"Visit Central America Airpass"** can cut costs considerably. For example, the routing Miami–San José–Managua–Guatemala City–LA will cost US$699 low season/US$749 high season – at least one-third less than flying the same route on a normal ticket. The pass links North American gateways with all the capitals and some other cities in Central America, plus some destinations in South America and the Caribbean; the possible routes are mind-boggling. You have to buy the pass – in the form of coupons for each flight – before leaving home, enter the region on one of the participating airlines (Aviateca, Copa, Lacsa, Nica and Taca) and book your route in advance. Free date changes are allowed if space is available (within the 60-day validity of the pass) but a change of route will cost US$50.

The **"Mex-AmeriPass"** combines the extensive networks of Aeroméxico and Mexicana, linking destinations throughout Mexico with several Central and South American cities.

The best way to find out how (or if) an airpass will benefit you is to call JLA in the UK (☎020/8747 3018; *flights@journeylatinamerica.co .uk*); or contact eXito in the US (☎1-800/655-4053 or 510/655-4566, *www.wonderlink.com/exito*).

TRAVEL WARNINGS AND SAFETY INFORMATION

For **British travellers** the **Foreign Office Travel Advice Unit** (Mon–Fri 9.30am–4pm; ☎020/7008 0232, *www.fco.gov.uk*) issues travel advice notices, which give a broadly accurate overview of the dangers facing visitors to Central America. They also produce a worthwhile leaflet for backpackers and independent travellers which gives good advice and explains what a consul can and cannot do for you when you're abroad. The **US equivalent** is the **State Department's Consular Information Service** (*travel.state.gov/travel_warnings.html*), which publishes information sheets about each country, again listing fairly accurately the main dangers to US citizens. If any country is considered particularly dangerous, a travel warning will be issued, though this may in fact simply indicate an isolated incident involving a US visitor. The advice contained in these pages is worth heeding, but don't be put off travelling completely – you could get into more danger in any big city at home than you're likely to encounter travelling wisely in Central America.

expensive jewellery) in a moneybelt under your outer clothes, though this isn't as easy as it sounds, as you'll have to get your passport and money out at border crossings. Trousers with zipped pockets are an idea to deter pickpockets. Border crossings, where you'll often have to change money, surprisingly enough aren't that dangerous; the moneychanger is unlikely to shortchange you (though getting the right exchange rate is another matter), and the presence of armed officials generally discourages thieves in the immediate area of the immigration post. Do the transaction and put your money away out of sight of other people if at all possible. Once away from the post however, you need to be on your guard; beware of people "helping" you find a bus and offering to carry your luggage. In many cases they will genuinely be offering a service in return for a tip, but at times like this you're easily distracted and you should never put your belongings down or let them out of sight unless you're confident they're in a safe place.

You can always register at your **embassy** when (or even before) you arrive – we've listed phone numbers in the Guide. This is advisable if you're spending a long time in or travelling to remote areas of the region, though it's not necessary if you're on an organized tour. Always take photocopies of your passport and insurance documents and try to leave them in a secure place; leave a copy with someone at home too. A second credit card, kept in a very safe location and only to be used in emergencies, will be invaluable if your other cards or funds get stolen.

TRAVEL AND HOTELS

Travelling on **public transport**, particularly by bus, you'll usually be separated from your main bag – it will go either in the luggage compartment underneath or in the rack on top. This is usually safe enough (and you have little option in any case) but keep an eye on it whenever you can. Although the theft of the bag itself is uncommon, opportunist thieves may dip into zippers and outer pockets. You can get small padlocks for backpacks, but for greater security you can put your pack into a coffee or flour sack (*costal*) and put that into a net (*red*). It might look a little outlandish but it's the way the locals transport goods and keeps it clean and dry too – sacks and nets are sold in any market. Once on the bus it's best to keep your small bag on your lap. If you do put it on the inside luggage rack keep it in sight and tie it (or preferably clip it with a carabiner) onto the rack to deter thieves who may try to snatch it and throw it out of the window to an accomplice.

In your **hotel**, make sure the lock on your door works; from the inside as well as out. In many budget hotels the lock will be a small padlock on the outside, and it's a good idea to buy your own (*candado* – readily available on street stalls) so you're the only one with keys. Many hotels will have a safe or secure area for valuables. It's up to you whether you use this; most of the time it will be fine, but make sure whatever you do put in is securely and tightly wrapped; a spare, lockable moneybelt is good for this.

You're less likely to be a victim of a mugging or armed robbery, but when it happens there's little you can do about it, so prevention is essential. Avoid obviously dangerous areas – deserted city centres and bus stations late at night – and wherever possible take taxis after dark. One ploy to watch out for is someone who surreptitiously throws an obnoxious liquid over your pack or clothes – a "passer by" kindly offers to clean it up while another member of the gang snatches your bag. Much worse are the **armed robberies** of tourist minibuses in Guatemala; usually the robbers will go through the passengers collecting money and valuables, but occasionally victims are taken away and assaulted, or even raped. For this reason some tour groups in Guatemala are accompanied by an armed guard.

POLICE

If you have anything stolen, report the incident immediately to the **police** – if there is a tourist police force, try them first – if only to get a copy of the report (*denuncia*) which you'll need for insurance purposes. The police in Central America are poorly paid and you can't expect them to do much more than make out the report – and often you'll have difficulty getting them to

do even this. You may have to dictate it to them (and sometimes they'll demand a fee for their services); unless you're fluent, try to take someone along who speaks better Spanish than you do. And if you can, also report the crime to your **embassy** – it helps the consular staff build up a higher-level case for the better protection of tourists.

Obviously you want to avoid any **trouble** with the police whatsoever. Practically every capital city has foreigners incarcerated for drug offences who'd never do it again if they knew what the punishment was like. Drugs of all kinds are readily available but if you indulge be very discreet: the pusher may have a sideline reporting clients to the police, and catching "international drug smugglers" gives the country concerned brownie points with the DEA. If you are arrested your embassy will probably send someone to visit you, and maybe find an English-speaking lawyer, but they certainly can't get you out of jail.

PART TWO

BELIZE

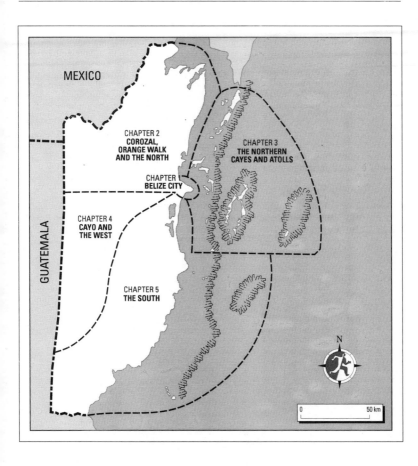

MEXICO

CHAPTER 2
**COROZAL,
ORANGE WALK
AND THE NORTH**

CHAPTER 3
**THE NORTHERN
CAYES AND ATOLLS**

CHAPTER 1
BELIZE CITY

GUATEMALA

CHAPTER 4
**CAYO AND
THE WEST**

CHAPTER 5
THE SOUTH

N

0   50 km

Introduction

Wedged into the northeastern corner of Central America between Mexico's Yucatán peninsula and the Petén forests of Guatemala, **Belize** offers some of the most breathtaking scenery anywhere in the Caribbean. The country actually consists of marginally more sea than land, with the dazzling turquoise shallows and cobalt depths of the longest **barrier reef** in the Americas just offshore. Here, beneath the surface, a brilliant, technicolour world of fish and corals awaits divers and snorkellers. Scattered along the reef, a chain of islands – known as **cayes** – protect the mainland from the ocean swell and offer more than a hint of tropical paradise. Beyond the reef lie the real jewels in Belize's natural crown – three of only four **coral atolls** in the Caribbean.

Belizeans recognize the importance of conservation and their country boasts a higher proportion of protected land (over 40 percent) than any other. This has allowed the **densely forested interior** to remain relatively untouched, boasting abundant natural attractions, including the highest waterfall in Central America and the world's only jaguar reserve. Rich tropical forests support a tremendous range of **wildlife**, including howler and spider monkeys, tapirs and pumas, jabiru storks and scarlet macaws; spend any time inland and you're sure to see the national bird, the very visible keel-billed toucan.

Despite being the only Central American country without a volcano, Belize does have some rugged uplands in the south-central region, where the **Maya Mountains** rise to over 1100m. The country's main rivers rise here, flowing north or east to the Caribbean, forming along the way some of the largest **cave systems** in the Americas, few of which have been fully explored. These caves often bear traces of the **Maya civilization** that dominated the area from around 2000 BC until the arrival of the Spanish. The most obvious remains of this fascinating culture are the ruins of dozens of **ancient cities** rising out of the rainforest.

Officially **English-speaking**, and only gaining full independence from Britain in 1981, Belize is as much a Caribbean nation as a Latin one, but one with plenty of distinctively Central American features, above all a blend of cultures and races that includes Maya, mestizo, African and European. Spanish is at least as widely spoken as English, but the rich, lilting **Creole** is the spoken language understood and used by almost every Belizean, whatever their first tongue. You'll hear this everywhere – and though based on English, it's less comprehensible to outsiders than you might expect.

With far less of a language barrier to overcome than elsewhere in the region, uncrowded Belize is the ideal first stop on a tour of the isthmus. And, although it's the second-smallest country in Central America (slightly larger than El Salvador), the wealth of national parks and reserves, the numerous small hotels and restaurants, together with plenty of reliable public transport make Belize an ideal place to travel independently, giving visitors plenty of scope to explore little-visited Caribbean islands as well as the heartland of the ancient Maya.

■ Where to go

Almost every visitor will have to spend at least some time in **Belize City**, even if only passing through, as it's the hub of the country's transport system. First-time visitors may be shocked by the decaying buildings and the pollution of the Belize River, but it's possible to spend many pleasant hours in this former outpost of the British Empire. In contrast, Belize's capital, **Belmopan**, is primarily an administrative centre with little to offer visitors.

Northern Belize is relatively flat and often swampy, with a large proportion of agricultural land, though as everywhere in Belize there are Maya ruins and nature reserves. **Lamanai**, near Orange Walk, is one of the most impressive Maya sites in the country, and the lagoons here and at **Sarteneja** and **Crooked Tree** offer a superb protected habitat for wildlife. Adjacent to the Guatemalan border is the vast **Rio Bravo Conservation Area.**

The largest of the cayes, **Ambergris Caye**, draws more than half of all tourists to Belize, their main destination being the resort town of **San Pedro**. To the south, **Caye Caulker** is the most popular of the islands amongst independent travellers. Many of the less developed cayes are becoming easier to reach, and organized trips are available to the atolls of **Lighthouse Reef** and **Glover's Reef**.

In the west, the **Cayo District** has everything for the ecotourist: Maya ruins and rainforest, rivers and caves, with excellent accommodation

■ Driving and hitching

Driving in Belize is subject to the same limitations as bus travel. The Northern, Western and Hummingbird highways offer easy motoring and smooth roads, as does much of the Southern Highway, but off these highways roads can be rough. If you want to head off the beaten track you'll need high clearance and 4WD. **Unleaded petrol** is easily available, but expensive at US$3.15 per gallon. **Insurance** (around US$7–10 a day for your own car) is available from an agent just inside either of the land border crossings or in Belize City. Under Belize's **seatbelt law** you'll be fined US$12.50 for not belting up.

All the main **car rental companies** offer cars, Jeeps and 4WDs for between US$75 and US$125 a day, plus up to US$15 per day for insurance. You'll usually have to be over 25 and will need to leave either a credit card, travellers' cheques or a large cash deposit. Many outfits do not offer comprehensive insurance, so the renter is likely to be held liable for any damage to the vehicle, however caused. Note that some companies consider driving a car on minor dirt roads (especially in the south) to be taking the vehicle "off-road", which may invalidate your insurance. Check carefully before signing anything.

In the more remote parts of Belize the bus service will probably only operate once a day, if at all, and unless you have your own transport, **hitching** is the only option. The main drawback is the shortage of traffic, but if cars or, more likely, pick-up trucks, do pass they'll usually offer you a lift, though you may be expected to offer the driver some money.

■ Cycling

Seeing Belize from a **bike** is fairly straightforward and you'll find repair shops in all the towns. Bikes are increasingly available for **rent**, especially in San Ignacio and Placencia. Few Belizean buses have the roof racks that are such a familiar sight in Guatemala; if there's room, the driver *might* let you take your bike onto the bus.

■ Boats

Most **boats** you're likely to use will be fast **skiffs**, usually open boats with two powerful outboard motors (though some are covered, it's advisable to carry a light raincoat just in case). Carrying about 25 passengers, skiffs run from Belize City and mainland destinations out to the **cayes**, and also cover **international routes** from Punta Gorda to Puerto Barrios and Lívingston in Guatemala and from Belize City, Dangriga and Placencia to Puerto Cortés in Honduras – times and destinations are covered in the text. Services are fast, reliable and safe; all registered boats should carry lifejackets and most also carry marine radios. It's worth buying your ticket the day before for early departures from the cayes and on international services if you want to be sure of a place, though there's usually plenty of room.

■ Planes

Maya Island Air (☎02/31140, *www.ambergriscaye .com/islandair*) and Tropic Air (☎02/45671, *www.tropicair.com*) offer a **scheduled service** from Belize international airport and Belize City's municipal airport to all the country's main towns (except Belmopan and San Ignacio) and out to San Pedro and Caye Caulker; there are also several **charter airlines**. A flight from Belize City to San Pedro or Caye Caulker costs around US$27; to Punta Gorda, US$79. The domestic airlines also have several daily flights to **Flores** in Guatemala (for Tikal) and there are daily departures to regional destinations such as **Guatemala City**, **San Salvador**, **San Pedro Sula** and **Roatán** in the Bay Islands, Honduras. Flights to Mexico, however, are plagued by disruptions. Aerocaribe currently fly three times a week to **Cancún**, usually calling at Chetumal.

Costs, money and banks

Belize has a generally well-deserved reputation as being one of the more expensive countries in Central America, and even on a tight budget you'll spend at least forty percent more than in, say, Guatemala. Perhaps as compensation for the general cost of living you can at least travel in the sure knowledge that you'll be paying the same fares as the locals, and you'll never be subjected to mysterious (and sometimes illegal) border crossing charges.

■ Currency, exchange and banks

The national currency is the **Belize dollar**, which is conveniently fixed at two to one with the US dollar (**US$1=Bz$2**); US dollars are also widely accepted (sometimes preferred), either in cash or travellers' cheques. This apparently simple **dual currency system** can be problematic: it's all too easy to assume the price of your hotel room, or trip for example, is in Belize dollars, only to find payment is demanded in the same number of US dollars – a common cause of misunderstanding and aggravation. All Belizean notes (divided into 100 cents) and coins carry the British imperial legacy in the form of a portrait of Queen Elizabeth, while quarters are called "shillings".

You'll find at least one **bank** (generally open Mon–Thurs 8am–2.30pm, Fri 8am–4.30pm) in every town, and also in the main seaside destinations of San Pedro, Caye Caulker and Placencia. Although the exchange rate is fixed, banks in Belize will give slightly less than Bz$2 for US$1 for both cash and travellers' cheques; on the other hand, **moneychangers** at the borders will often give slightly higher rates, especially for larger sums; anywhere else beware of rip-offs. You can usually buy US dollars from the banks and sometimes from hotels or restaurants.

Credit and debit cards are widely used in Belize, with Visa the best option, and are increasingly accepted even in smaller hotels and restaurants, though you might pay an extra 5 or even 7 percent for the privilege – check before you pay. Although banks can give you a Visa/Mastercard **cash advance** over the counter, Barclays is the only bank which doesn't impose an extra charge to use plastic, and also has the only **ATMs** which accept foreign-issued cards.

■ Costs

Even travelling as a couple it's difficult to survive on less than US$18 a day per person – though it can be done – but US$25 a day will cover a decent budget hotel, meals and drinks, bus travel and a short taxi ride, for example. For a **simple room** you can expect to pay at least US$9 single, US$15 double, whereas a night in an upmarket lodge will set you back anything from US$65 to US$150 (though it's always worth asking for a discount out of season). Food and drink are fairly pricey too, with an average breakfast costing around US$4–5, lunch US$5–7, and dinner US$6–8. A small bottle of Belikin **beer**, the only local brew, costs at least US$1.60; imported cans cost twice as much.

Bus travel is much more reasonable, with the longest journey in the country, from Belize City to Punta Gorda, costing US$12. A **taxi** ride within a town costs US$2.50 for one or two people; for more passengers and longer rides agree a price beforehand.

Hotel rooms are subject to a seven percent **tax**, usually added separately (and many of the more expensive places will also impose a **service charge** of around ten percent). There's also an eight percent **sales tax**, which applies to most goods and services (including meals in restaurants, though not to drinks). It doesn't apply to hotel rooms, though some package operators may slap it on anyway; check carefully to see what you're paying.

Leaving Belize you must pay a US$10 **exit tax**, plus the **PACT conservation fee** of US$3.75, at all departure points.

Information

The country's official source of tourist information is the **Belize Tourist Board** (BTB; *www .travelbelize.org*), with offices in Belize City, San Pedro and Punta Gorda, plus an information booth at the airport. The staff are generally quite helpful, and have maps, brochures and local information.

The **Belize Tourist Industry Association** (BTIA) also have numerous offices and representatives around the country and, although they are really an industry organization, staff can help with information and will deal with complaints about hotel standards or service. Perhaps more usefully, most of the **hotels** and all the **travel agents** mentioned in this guide can recommend local guides and attractions.

For the latest information on the growing number of reserves, national parks and associated visitor centres, call or visit the **Belize Audubon Society** in Belize City (see p.56), which administers many of the country's protected areas. For in-depth information on social, cultural, political and economic matters concerning Belize, the place to look is the **SPEAR Web site** (Society for the Promotion of Education and Research) at *www.spearbelize.org*.

Accommodation

Most Belizean **accommodation** is expensive by Central American standards, though fortunately there are budget hotels in all towns except Belmopan and Orange Walk, and the most popular tourist destinations, like Caye Caulker, San

Ignacio and Placencia, have a great deal of choice.

A **simple double** room in Belize usually costs around US$15 (US$9 single) for facilities only a little better than a Guatemalan budget hotel; for the luxury of a private bathroom expect to pay at least US$18. If you've a lot more money to spend you could try one of the delightful, family-run **lodges**, most of which are set in a spectacular natural location, with rooms in the house or in private cabañas. Some of these offer **bed and breakfast**, an increasingly popular style of accommodation.

Finding a room is no problem in Belizean towns: even in Belize City most options are within ten minutes' walk of the main points of arrival. On the whole there's always accommodation available, though during the **peak season**, from December to April (and especially at Christmas and Easter), you may have to look a little longer and prices in resort areas may rise even higher; booking ahead by phone or email is easy.

■ **Camping**

Although there are few proper **campsites** in Belize, it's easy to find somewhere to pitch a tent or sling a hammock in rural areas and coastal villages like Placencia and Hopkins. Camping is not really possible (or recommended) on Caye Caulker or in San Pedro. You can also camp in the area around San Ignacio and in the Mountain Pine Ridge, where several lodges have campsites, some very economical, some surprisingly expensive. Down south a tent will enable you to spend some time wandering inland, around the Maya villages and ancient ruins.

Eating and drinking

Belizean food is a distinctive mix of Latin America and the Caribbean, with Creole "rice and beans" dominating the scene, but with plenty of other important influences. Mexican *empanadas* are as common as pizza, chow mein and hamburgers. In a few places Belizean food is a real treat, with particularly good seafood, but in all too many others it's a neglected art.

■ **Where to eat**

The quality of the food in Belize rarely bears much relation to the appearance of the restaurant it's served in, whether you're eating in a bar, a café or a smart-looking restaurant. Out on the islands and in small seashore villages some restaurants are little more than thatched shelters, with open sides and sand floors, while in other places you'll find upmarket hotels with polished floors, tablecloths and napkins. Most places, however, are somewhere between the two, serving up good food without too much concern for presentation. You'll soon become accustomed to the fact that **lunch hour** (noon–1pm) is observed with almost religious devotion. Abandon any hope of getting anything else done and tuck in with the locals. Only in Belize City, San Pedro and Placencia is there much choice, with fast-food and snack bars sprouting on street corners along with a few surprisingly elegant restaurants.

Travelling, you'll find that food sometimes comes to you, as street traders offer up *tamales*, *empanadas*, hamburgers (literally a slice of canned ham served in a bun) and fruit to waiting bus passengers, although the practice isn't nearly as common as elsewhere in Central America.

■ **What to eat**

The basis of any Creole meal is **rice and beans**, and this features heavily in smaller restaurants. In many cases it means just that, with the rice and beans cooked together in coconut oil and flavoured with *recado* (a mild ground pepper) and often with a chunk of salted pork thrown in for extra taste, but usually it's served with chicken, fish or beef, and backed up by some kind of sauce.

Vegetables are scarce in Creole food but there's often a side dish of potato salad and fried plantains, and sometimes flour tortillas (the maize tortillas so common in Guatemala and some other Central American countries are rarely served here). At its best Creole food is delicious, taking the best from the sea and blending it with coconut and spices. But all too often what you get is a stodgy mass, with little in the way of flavour.

Vegetarians will find the pickings slim. There are no specifically vegetarian restaurants, but in the main tourist resorts there's often a meat-free choice on the menu. Otherwise, you're likely to be offered chicken or ham if you say you don't eat meat. The fruit is good and there are some locally produced vegetables, but they're rarely served in restaurants. Your best bet outside the main tourist areas will be a Chinese restaurant.

Seafood is almost always excellent. **Red snapper** or **grouper** is invariably fantastic, and you might also try a **barracuda** steak, **conch fritters** or a plate of fresh (though usually farmed) **shrimp**. In San Pedro, Caye Caulker and Placencia the food can be exceptional, and the only concern is that you might get bored with **lobster**, which is served in an amazing range of dishes: pasta with lobster sauce, lobster and scrambled eggs, lobster chow mein or even lobster curry. The closed season for lobster is from February to June. **Turtle** is still on the menu in a few places, in theory only during the short open season, but note that this is a threatened species, and by even tasting it – or any other wild animal – you'll be contributing to its extinction.

Chinese food will probably turn out to be an important part of your trip, and when there's little else on offer Belize's many Chinese restaurants are usually a safe bet. Other Belizean ethnic minorities are now starting to break into the restaurant trade: there's a good **Lebanese** restaurant in Belize City and an excellent **Sri Lankan** curry restaurant in San Ignacio.

■ Drinks

The most basic **drinks** to accompany food are water, beer and the usual soft drinks. Belikin, Belize's main **beer**, comes in five varieties: lager-type bottled and draught beer; bottled **stout** (a rich, dark beer); and Lighthouse, Premium and Supreme, more expensive bottled beers and often all you'll be able to get in upmarket hotels and restaurants. The Belikin brewery also produces

bottled **Guinness**. Cashew-nut and berry **wines**, rich and full-bodied, are bottled and sold in some villages, and you can also get hold of imported wine, though it's far from cheap. Local **rum**, in both dark and clear varieties, is the best deal in Belizean alcohol. The locally produced gin, brandy and vodka are poor imitations – cheap and fairly nasty.

Non-alcoholic alternatives include the predictable array of soft drinks. Despite the number of citrus plantations, **fruit juices** are rarely available, though you can sometimes get orange juice. **Tap water**, in the towns at least, is safe but highly chlorinated, and many villages (though not Caye Caulker) now have a potable water system. Pure **rainwater** is usually available in the countryside and on the cayes. Filtered **bottled water** and mineral water are sold everywhere.

Coffee, except in the best establishments, will almost certainly be instant. **Tea**, due to the British influence, is a popular hot drink, as are Milo and Ovaltine (malted milky drinks). One last drink that deserves a mention is **seaweed**, a strange blend of seaweed, milk, cinnamon, sugar and cream. If you see someone selling this on a street corner, give it a try.

Opening hours, holidays and festivals

It's difficult to be specific about **opening hours** in Belize but in general most **shops** are open 8am–noon and 1–8pm. The lunch hour – noon to 1pm – is almost universally observed and it's hopeless trying to get anything done then. Some shops and businesses work a half-day on Saturday, and everything is liable to close early on Friday. **Banks** (generally Mon–Thurs 8am–2.30pm, Fri 8am–4.30pm) and government offices are only open Monday to Friday. Watch out for Sundays, when everybody takes it easy; shops, and sometimes restaurants, are closed, and fewer bus services and internal flights operate. Archeological sites, however, are open every day.

The main **public holidays**, when virtually everything will be closed, are listed overleaf. In Belize it's only in the outlying areas, such as around San Ignacio and Corozal, and in the Maya villages of the south, that you'll find traditional village **fiestas**. Elsewhere, national celebrations are the main excuse for a day-long party, and the

PUBLIC HOLIDAYS

January 1	New Year's Day
March 9	Baron Bliss Day
Good Friday	
Holy Saturday	
Easter Monday	
May 1	Labour Day
May 24	Commonwealth Day
September 10	National Day
September 21	Independence Day
October 12	Columbus Day (Pan America Day)
November 19	Garífuna Settlement Day
December 25 & 26	Christmas

rhythms of the Caribbean dominate the proceedings. But here you'll feel less of an outsider and will be welcome to dance and drink with the locals. **Traditional dance** is still practised by two ethnic groups in Belize: the Maya and the Garífuna. The best time to see Garífuna dances is November 19, Garífuna Settlement Day, in either Dangriga or Hopkins. Maya dances are still performed at fiestas in the south and west, and in many ways resemble their counterparts in Guatemala. Dance is very much a part of Creole culture and all national celebrations are marked by open-air dances.

Mail and telecommunications

Belizean postal services are perhaps the most efficient (and most expensive) in Central America. **Sending letters**, cards and parcels home is straightforward: a normal airmail letter takes around four days to reach the US, under eight days to Europe, and up to two weeks to Australia; **parcels** have to be wrapped in brown paper and tied with string.

Belize has a modern (albeit expensive) phone system with **payphones** found throughout the country. Most of these only accept **phonecards**, which are widely available from BTL (Belize Telecommunications Limited) offices, hotels, shops and gas stations; to use them just scratch off the strip concealing the PIN, dial the access code (printed on the card), the PIN and then the number you're calling. Some rural areas are served by **community telephones** (nowadays often fixed cellular phones), usually located in a

private house; you pay the person who operates the phone. **Calling home collect** is easy using the Home Country Direct service, available at BTL offices, most payphones and larger hotels. Simply dial the access code (printed on some payphones and in the phone book) to connect with an operator in your home country. **Area codes** in Belize range from ☎02 for Belize City to ☎09 for San Ignacio, while numbers prefaced ☎01 or ☎021 through to ☎051 signify a cellular phone, either fixed or mobile; all area codes are included with numbers given in the text. Calling Belize from abroad, the **international country code** is ☎501.

Most hotels and businesses now have **fax** machines and any BTL office will have a public fax you can use. Fax numbers are listed in the pink pages in the telephone directory. Belizean businesses and individuals are also avid users of **email** and the **Internet**, and Internet access is available in all the main towns and for guests at many hotels. Some of the most useful **Web sites** covering Belize are listed on p.24.

The media

Although Belize's English-language media can make a welcome break in a world of Spanish, this doesn't necessarily mean that it's easy to keep in touch with what's happening in the rest of the world. Local news takes pride of place in the **national newspapers** (published weekly on Friday) and international stories receive very little attention. In Belize City, San Pedro and some other main towns you should be able to get hold of **foreign publications**, including *The Miami Herald*, *Time* and *Newsweek*.

There are two national **television** stations, channels 5 and 7, which broadcast mainly imported American shows, with a few local news programmes. Cable TV, however, is the nation's preferred viewing medium, giving saturation coverage of American soaps, CNN and sports. Love FM has the widest coverage of any of the country's **radio stations**, offering easy listening, news and current affairs; sister station Estero Amor broadcasts in Spanish, while More FM plays youth-oriented music. Another major station is KREM FM with the emphasis on talk, reggae and Punta Rock. Each district town also has a local radio station and there's a British forces radio station, BFBS.

Shopping

Compared to its neighbours, Belize has less to offer in terms of traditional **crafts** or neighbourhood **markets**. The latter are purely food markets, but in several places you'll come across some impressive local crafts. **Wood and slate carvers** are often to be found at the Maya sites, and their work, especially the reproductions of glyphs and stelae on slate, is high quality; **ceramics** are less good, but improving. In the Maya villages in southern Belize you'll come across some attractive **embroidery**, though it has to be said that the quality of both the cloth and the work is better in Guatemala. Garífuna and Creole villages produce good basketware and superb **drums**; Dangriga, Hopkins and Gales Point are the places to visit for these.

The excellent **National Handicrafts Center** in Belize City (see p.55) is the best place to buy souvenirs if time is short, with a wide range of genuine Belizean crafts, including paintings, prints and music recordings as well as the items mentioned above. The craftspeople are paid fair prices for their work and no longer have to hawk it on the streets. There are often exhibitions by Belizean artists here too, but the best place for contemporary **Belizean art** is The Image Factory in Belize City (see p.55). For superb **videos** of Belizean wildlife, culture or history, have a look at the series produced by Great Belize Productions, which can be purchased from gift shops. Those with a philatelic bent might appreciate a set of wildly colourful Belize **stamps**; relatively cheap, and certainly easy to post home, they often feature the animals and plants of the country.

For everyday necessities you'll find some kind of shop in every village in Belize, however small, and most of the things you'd find at home are available in Belize, though you may have to hunt around for them. Luxury items, such as electrical goods and cameras, tend to be very expensive, as do other imported goods. **Camera film** is a little more expensive than at home, but easy to get hold of.

One tasty souvenir everyone likes to take home is a bottle (or three) of **Marie Sharp's Pepper Sauce**, made from Belizean *habañeros* in various strengths, ranging from "mild" to "fiery hot". This spicy accompaniment to rice and beans graces every restaurant table in the country – and visits to the factory near Dangriga can be arranged.

Safety and the police

Belize has a bad reputation for **crime**, but while it's true that Belize City has a relatively high crime rate, it certainly doesn't live up to some of the stories you might hear, while crime against tourists in the country as a whole is very low, especially in comparison to other Central American countries. **Violent crime** against tourists is very rare, even in Belize City.

In **Belize City**, theft is now fairly common, the majority of cases involving **break-ins** at hotels: bear this in mind when you're searching for a room. Out and about there's always a slight danger of **pickpockets**, but certainly no greater than in the surrounding countries, and with a bit of common sense you've nothing to fear. The atmosphere on the streets is much less intimidating since the introduction of the **tourism police**, but nevertheless it pays to be aware of the dangers. There's also a chance of something more serious happening, such as a **mugging**. During the daytime there's little to worry about. However, at night you should stick to the main streets and avoid going out alone, especially if you're a

---

SUSPECT SOUVENIRS

Some souvenirs you'll see in Belize are the result of reef and wildlife destruction, so think twice before you buy – they include black coral, often made into jewellery, turtle shells, which look far better on their rightful owners, and indeed marine curios of any kind. Many of the animal and plant souvenirs you may be offered are **illegal** in Belize and may also be listed in Appendix 1 to CITES (the Convention on International Trade in Endangered Species; *www.cites.org*), so you won't be allowed to bring them into the US, Canada or Europe, and will face a fine – or worse – for even trying. Even more illegal are **archeological artefacts** or remains; all such items belong to Belize and theft or trade in them is strictly prohibited; anyone attempting to smuggle such items out of the country could end up in jail in Belize or at home.

woman. If you arrive in Belize City at night, take a taxi to a hotel, as the bus stations are in a fairly derelict part of town – though not bad enough to worry about for daylight arrivals. Having said all this, muggings are really not that common, and your greatest fear is likely to be the mood of intimidation on the streets, which makes Belize City feel far more dangerous than it actually is. If you do need to **report a crime**, your first stop should be the tourism police, where they exist – crime against tourists is taken very seriously in Belize. The **police emergency number** in Belize is ☎90; to contact the **tourism police** in Belize City call ☎02/72222 ext 401.

Verbal abuse is not uncommon, especially in Belize City, where there are always plenty of people hanging out on the streets, commenting on all that passes by. For anyone with a white face, the inevitable "Hey, white boy/white chick – what's happening?" will soon become a familiar sound. At first it can all seem very threatening, but if you take the time to stop and talk, you'll find the vast majority of these people simply want to know where you're from, and where you're heading – and perhaps to try to offer you a deal on boat trips, money exchange, or bum a dollar or two. Once you realize that they mean no harm the whole experience of Belize City will be infinitely more enjoyable. Obviously, the situation is a little more serious for women, and the abuse can be more offensive, but once again it's unlikely that anything will come of it, and it's usually possible to talk your way out of a dodgy situation without anyone losing face.

Homosexuality is still illegal in Belize and some recent prosecutions have resulted in convictions and even a prison sentence. Although no visitors have been prosecuted (or even warned) it's obviously sensible to be very discreet. And given the legal position, it's no surprise to learn that there's no openly gay community and no exclusively gay bars in Belize.

■ Drugs

Belize has long been an important link in the chain of supply between the drugs producers in South and Central America and the users in North America, with minor players often being paid in kind, creating a deluge of illegal drugs. **Marijuana**, **cocaine** and **crack** are all readily available in Belize, and whether you like it or not you'll receive regular offers. *Never* attempt to

buy drugs on the street. All such substances are **illegal**, and despite the fact that dope is smoked openly in the streets, the police do arrest people for possession of marijuana and they particularly enjoy catching tourists. If you're caught you'll probably end up spending a couple of days in jail and paying a fine of several hundred US dollars: expect no sympathy from your embassy.

Work and study

There's virtually no chance of finding paid temporary work in Belize. Work permits are only on offer to those who can prove their ability to support themselves without endangering the job of a Belizean, or to wealthy investors.

There are, however, a growing number of opportunities for **voluntary work** – mainly as a fee-paying member of a conservation expedition or an archeological group. These options generally mean raising at least a thousand dollars and committing yourself to weeks – or months – of hard work, often in difficult conditions. The rewards are personal satisfaction and (sometimes) a genuine contribution to scientific research. Many **conservation expeditions**, aimed at gap-year students, work on rural infrastructure projects such as schools and health centres, or building trails and visitor centres in nature reserves. In addition, at least twenty academic **archeological groups** undertake research in Belize each year, and many of them take paying students (and non-students); check the box opposite for a couple of contacts and have a look at *Archaeology Fieldwork Opportunities Bulletin* (*www.archaeological.org*) or in *Archaeology Magazine* (*www.archaeology.org*).

If you find the initial cost of such programmes a deterrent, you could always **volunteer independently** – many conservation organizations in Belize have volunteer programmes. You'll need to be self-motivated and self-supporting, since no funding will be available, though you'll probably get food and accommodation. Further details are given in the box opposite.

History

Belize is the youngest nation in Central America, gaining full independence from Britain only in 1981, and its history has been markedly different from the Latin republics in the isthmus since at least the mid-seventeenth century. Although all the Central American countries were colonized by European powers from the early sixteenth century, it was the colonial entanglement with Britain that has given Belize its present cultural, social and political structures.

After crossing the **Bering land bridge** the early peoples of the Americas rapidly spread southwards, developing into the so-called **Clovis**

VOLUNTARY WORK AND STUDY CONTACTS

The Web site **www.gapyear.com** has a vast amount of information on volunteering, including organizations dealing with Belize, plus a huge, invaluable database on travel and living abroad. In addition, the comprehensive range of books and information published by *Vacation Work* (*www.vacationwork .co.uk*) is well worth looking at – titles include *Directory of Summer Jobs Abroad, Taking a Gap Year* and *Work Your Way Around the World*; most are updated annually and include work and volunteer opportunities in Central America. The Council on International Educational Exchange (contact Council Travel – see p.5 – for address) also arranges and administers volunteer and study programmes and has information on Belize.

IN BELIZE

Belize Audubon Society, PO Box 1001, Belize City (☎02/35004, *www.belizeaudobon.org*). Volunteer programme in protected areas and in wildlife conservation.

Belize River Archaeological Settlement Survey (*www.lsweb.sscf.ucsb.edu/projects /pilarweb*). Field study programme at El Pilar for paying students.

Green Reef, 100 Coconut Drive, San Pedro, Ambergris Caye (☎026/2838, w*ww.ambergriscaye .com*). Volunteers, including divers, conduct surveys of reef fish and take part in educational programmes.

The Siwa-Ban Foundation (contact Ellen McRae, ☎022/2178, *sbf@btl.net*). Volunteers work on biological surveys of the Caye Caulker Forest and Marine Reserve.

Wildlife Care Center of Belize (contact Robin Brockett, *wildlifecarecenter@yahoo.com*). Opportunities for voluntary work with confiscated and rescued native wildlife.

YWCA Belize (☎02/44971, *ywca@btl.net*). Accepts volunteers to help teach and organize sports and arts activities in the school they run in Belize City (see p.54).

IN THE US

Earthwatch (☎1-800/776-0188, *www.earthwatch .org*); also offices in the UK, Australia and Japan. Earthwatch matches paying volunteers with scientists working on archeological and marine conservation projects in Belize. The cost for a week is around US$1000/£670; longer stints work out less per week.

Ecologic Development Fund (☎617/ 441-6300, *www.ecologic.org*). Internship programmes for volunteers in resource management in partnership with local NGOs.

Peace Corps (☎1-800/424-8580, *www.peacecorps .gov*). Sends American volunteers to Belize to train teachers in rural areas and to work in environmental education and health-related fields.

Western Belize Regional Cave Project (contact Cameron Griffith on ☎812/855-1041 or visit *www.indiana.edu/~belize*). Cave archeology research in Cayo District. Prior field-school or caving experience preferred and students must be in excellent physical condition.

IN THE UK

Trekforce Expeditions, 34 Buckingham Palace Rd, London SW1 0RE (☎020/7828 2275, *www .trekforce.org*). Runs projects in Belize ranging from surveys of remote Maya sites to infrastructure projects in national parks and village communities. Expeditions last two months (£2350) or five months (£3500); the longer programmes also involve learning Spanish in Guatemala and teaching in rural schools.

World Challenge Expeditions, Black Arrow House, 2 Chandros Rd, London NW10 6NE (☎020/8961 1122, *www.world-challenge.co.uk*). Sends 18–25-year-olds to Belize for three- or six-month placements. Tasks could include teaching in a primary school or joining a conservation project. Around £1900, plus £115 per month for food and accommodation.

hunter-gatherer culture by 11,000 BC. Worked stone flakes from this era have been found at Richmond Hill, in northern Belize. Gradually the hunters turned to more intensive use of plants, particularly the newly domesticated **maize** and **beans**, settling into primarily agricultural societies in Belize during the **Archaic** or **Proto-Maya period**, lasting from around 7500 BC until later than 2000 BC. Few visible remains from this period can be seen today, however, and it was only during the subsequent **Preclassic** period (1500 BC–300 AD) that the culture that we recognize as **Maya** emerged distinctly.

City-states emerged, with larger and more elaborate buildings. Temples and palaces were built of stone, using the famous Maya corbelled arch, and characteristic stepped-pyramids rose above enormous plazas. Ceramics found at **Cuello**, near Orange Walk, dating from around 1000 BC, are amongst the earliest in the Maya lowlands. **Cerros**, at the mouth of the New River, and **Lamanai**, on the New River Lagoon, expanded into great trading centres, probably continuing in this role right through the Classic period into the Postclassic era.

■ The Classic and Postclassic periods

Whatever the original construction dates of the Maya sites in Belize, most of what you can see today dates from the **Classic period** (300–900 AD), the greatest phase of Maya achievement. Elaborately carved **stelae** bearing dates and emblem-glyphs tell of actual rulers and of historical events, such as battles, marriages, and the dynastic succession. The best example in the country is at **Nim Li Punit**, north of Punta Gorda.

Developments in the Maya area were powerfully influenced by cultures to the north, above all that of **Teotihuacán**, which dominated central Mexico during the early Classic period until its collapse in the seventh century, an event which sent shockwaves throughout Mesoamerica. However, as the new Maya rulers in Belize gradually established dynasties free of Teotihuacán's military or political control, their cities flourished as never before.

The entire Belize River valley was thickly populated during Classic times, with powerful cities such as **El Pilar** and **Xunantunich** in the west controlling this important trade route. Many Maya centres were much larger than contemporary Western European cities: **Caracol** had an estimated 150,000 people. Exactly how the various cities related to one another is unclear, but it appears that three or four main centres dominated the Maya region through an uncertain process of alliances. **Calakmul**, in Campeche, Mexico, and **Tikal** in Petén, Guatemala, were the nearest of these "**superstates**" to Belize, but in 562 AD Caracol defeated Tikal, as shown by a Caracol ball-court marker. Detailed carvings on wooden lintels and stone monuments at the site depict elaborately costumed lords trampling on bound captives.

The end of the Classic Maya civilization, when it came, was abrupt. By 750 AD political and social changes began to be felt; alliances and trade links broke down, wars increased and stelae were carved less frequently. Most cities rapidly became depopulated and new construction ceased over much of Belize after about 830 AD. By the end of the Classic period there appears to have been strife and disorder throughout Mesoamerica. But not all Maya cities were deserted: those in northern Belize, in particular, survived and indeed prospered, with Lamanai and other cities in the area remaining occupied throughout the **Postclassic** period (900–1540 AD). In the years leading up to the Spanish Conquest, the Yucatán and northern Belize consisted of over a dozen rival provinces, bound up in a cycle of competition and conflict.

■ The Conquest

When the conquistadors arrived in Yucatán from the 1530s onwards, Maya towns and provinces were still vigorously independent, as the Spanish found to their cost on several occasions. Northern Belize was part of the wealthy Maya province of **Chactemal** (the name lives on today as Chetumal, in Quintana Roo, Mexico), with its capital probably at **Santa Rita**, near Corozal. Trade, alliances and wars kept Chetumal in contact with surrounding Maya states up to and beyond the Spanish conquest of Aztec Mexico. Further south was the province known to the Maya of Chetumal as *Dzuluinicob* – "land of foreigners" – whose capital was **Tipu**, located at Negroman, on the Macal River south of San Ignacio. The Maya here controlled the upper Belize River valley and put up strenuous resistance to attempts by the Spanish to subdue and convert them. The struggle was to continue with simmering resentment until 1707, when the population of Tipu was forcibly removed to Lago de Petén Itzá, near Tikal.

The first **Europeans** to set eyes on the mainland of Belize were Spanish sailors in the early 1500s, but they didn't attempt a landing. In 1511 a small group of shipwrecked Spanish sailors managed to reach land on the southern coast of Yucatán: five were immediately sacrificed but the others were taken as slaves. One of them, **Gonzalo Guerrero**, later married the daughter of Nachankan, the chief of Chetumal, and became a crucial military adviser to the Maya in their subsequent resistance to Spanish domination. The archeologist Eric Thompson calls him the first European to make Belize his home.

By 1544 however, **Gaspar Pacheco** had subdued Maya resistance sufficiently to found a town on Lake Bacalar, and a mission was established at Lamanai in 1570. Maya resentment was always present beneath the surface, however, and boiled over into open rebellion in 1638, forcing Spain to abandon the area. The whole region from southern Yucatán to Honduras was never completely pacified by the Spanish, nor were administrative boundaries clearly defined, but it is likely that the Maya of Belize were influenced by the Spanish, even if they were not ruled by them.

■ The arrival of the British

The failure of the Spanish authorities to clearly delineate the southern boundary of Yucatán subsequently allowed **buccaneers** or pirates (primarily British) preying on the Spanish treasure fleets to find refuge along the coast of Belize. When Spain attempted to take action on various occasions to expel the British there was confusion over which Spanish captain-general maintained jurisdiction in the area. Consequently the pirates were able to flee before the Spanish arrived and could return in the absence of any permanent Spanish outposts.

Treasure wasn't always easy to come by and sometimes pirates would plunder piles of **logwood** which had been cut and were awaiting shipment to Europe. Worth £90–110 a ton, the hard and extremely heavy wood was used in the expanding British textile industry to dye woollens black, red and grey. The various treaties signed between Britain and Spain from the late seven-

teenth to mid-eighteenth centuries, initially designed to outlaw the buccaneers, eventually allowed the British to establish logwood camps along the rivers in northern Belize, though they were never intended to permit permanent British settlement of a territory which Spain clearly regarded as falling within its imperial domain. Thus the **British settlements** in Belize and the Bay of Honduras periodically came under attack whenever Spain sought to defend its interests. But the attention of the European powers rarely rested upon the humid, insect-ridden swamps where the logwood cutters, who became known as **Baymen**, worked and lived. The British government, while wishing to profit from the trade in logwood, preferred to avoid the question of whether or not the Baymen were British subjects, and for the most part they were left to their own devices.

Spanish attacks on the settlements in Belize occurred throughout the eighteenth century, with the Baymen being driven out on several occasions. Increasingly, though, Britain began to admit a measure of responsibility for the protection of the settlers and occasionally sent troops to aid the Baymen. Decades of Spanish attacks had fostered in the settlers a spirit of defiance and self-reliance, along with the belief that British rule was preferable to Spanish.

The final showdown between the waning Spanish Empire and the Bay settlers (supported this time by a British warship and troops), the **Battle of St George's Caye**, came as a result of the outbreak of war between Britain and Spain in 1796. The Governor of Yucatán assembled ships and troops, determined to drive out the British settlers and occupy Belize. But this time the Baymen had time to prepare and voted (by a small margin) to stay and fight. **Lieutenant-Colonel Barrow** was despatched to Belize as Superintendent, to command the settlers in the event of hostilities, and the Baymen, now under martial law, prepared for war, albeit grudgingly. A few companies of troops were sent from Jamaica and **slaves** were released from woodcutting to be armed and trained. The sloop **HMS Merlin** was stationed in the bay, local vessels were armed and gun rafts built in preparation for the attack, which was expected at any time.

The **Spanish fleet**, comprising sixteen heavily armed men-of-war and 12,000 troops, arrived just north of St George's Caye in early September

1798, making several attempts to capture the caye and force a passage to Belize. Each time they were beaten back by the Baymen with their small but highly manoeuvrable fleet, with the Baymen's slaves at least as eager to fight the Spanish as their masters were. During the final attack, on the morning of **September 10**, the Spanish fleet, already weakened by desertions and yellow fever, suffered heavy losses before sailing for Yucatán.

■ From settlement to British colony

Though a victory was won, the Battle of St George's Caye was not by itself decisive. Nor did it bring any change to the life of the slaves: even though they had fought valiantly alongside the Baymen, their owners expected them to go back to cutting mahogany – and also enabled them to claim that the slaves were willing to fight on behalf of their masters. Emancipation came no earlier than elsewhere in the British Empire. What the battle did show, however, was that the strength of the Spanish Empire was waning, while British power was expanding. Spain never again attempted to gain control of Belize, and the battle created the conditions for the settlement to become an integral part of the British Empire, with Britain gradually assuming a greater role in its government. Government House, built in Belize Town (later City) in 1814, housed the **Superintendent** (always an army officer) until 1862, when Belize became the colony of **British Honduras**, after which it served as home to the Governor, head of government under British colonial policy.

■ Towards independence

By 1900 Belize had become an integral, though minor, colony of the British Empire. Complacency set in amongst the predominantly white property owners, while the black workers in the forests and on the estates – the descendants of former slaves, known as "creoles" – continued to suffer low wages and restricted freedom of movement. Despite this, Belizeans rushed to defend the "Mother Country" in both **world wars**, but each time the returning soldiers faced humiliation and poverty. In 1919 veterans rioted in Belize City, an event that marked the onset of black consciousness and the beginning of the **independence movement**. Despite this, little changed, and even

after World War II political power still lay with a wealthy elite and with the governor, a Foreign Office appointee, while the devaluation of the British Honduras dollar at the end of 1949 caused additional hardship. The days of the British Empire were numbered, however, and in 1954 elections were held in which all literate adults over the age of 21 could vote. These elections were won with an overwhelming majority by the **Peoples' United Party** (PUP), led by **George Price**.

However, **Guatemala**, as the inheritor of the Spanish colonial territory of that name, had never entirely let go of its claim to the territory of Belize, regarding colonial treaties giving the British settlers rights to cut wood but not to own the land as still applicable in law. These interminable disputes, particularly the 1859 treaty which Britain, despite failing to fulfil the provision to build a road allowing Guatemala access to the Caribbean, regarded as the final settlement of the boundary dispute, rumbled on in the background. The British government never took the Guatemalan claim very seriously and Belize was allowed to proceed down the road to full independence by becoming an **internally self-governing** colony in 1964.

The prospect of what was (notionally at least) the department of "Belice" becoming independent outraged Guatemalan national pride and at least twice, in 1972 and 1977, Guatemala moved troops to the border and threatened to invade, but prompt British reinforcements offered an effective dissuasion. The situation remained tense but international opinion shifted gradually in favour of Belizean independence.

The most important demonstration of the worldwide endorsement of Belize's right to self-determination was the **UN resolution** passed in 1980, which demanded secure independence, with all territory intact, before the next session. Further negotiations with Guatemala began but complete agreement could not be reached: Guatemala still insisted on some territorial concessions. On March 11, 1981, Britain, Guatemala and Belize released the "Heads of Agreement", a document which would, they hoped, eventually result in a peaceful solution of the dispute. Accordingly, on September 21, 1981, Belize became an **independent member of the British Commonwealth**, with Queen Elizabeth II as its head of state.

ETHNIC BELIZE

Belize has a very mixed cultural background, with the two largest ethnic groups, **creoles**, descendants of enslaved Africans and early British settlers, and **mestizos**, descended from Amerindians and Spanish colonial settlers, forming about 75 percent of the population. The **Maya** in Belize are from three separate groups: **Yucatec**, who fled from the Caste Wars in the mid-nineteenth century; **Mopan**, who arrived in southern and western Belize from Petén in the 1880s; and **Kekchí**, who came to Toledo in southern Belize from Alta Verapaz from the late nineteenth century onwards. Together they form around 11 percent of the total population. The **Garífuna**, or **Caribs**, descended from enslaved Africans shipwrecked on St Vincent who mingled with the last Caribs there, settled in Belize in the nineteenth century, and now form around 7 percent of the population.

Since the 1980s, the arrival of an estimated 40,000 **Central American immigrants**, refugees from war and poverty, have boosted Belize's population to around 250,000. These refugees, together with the existing population of predominantly Spanish-speaking mestizos, have dramatically altered the demographic balance, and are now the majority ethnic group in Belize. Though they are treated with tolerance and encouraged to integrate into Belizean society, the recent arrivals are the source of slight racial tension, often referred to as "aliens" and blamed for a disproportionate amount of crime. Some Creoles feel marginalized now that Spanish is the most widely spoken first language, though English, taught in all schools, is certain to remain the official language for the foreseeable future.

The territorial dispute remains a stumbling block in relations between Belize and Guatemala, however, with successive Guatemalan presidents restating the claim to Belize while emphasizing Guatemala's commitment to resolving the dispute though negotiation.

■ Modern Belize

Belize's **democratic credentials** are beyond dispute: at each general election since independence the voters have kicked out the incumbent government and replaced it with the opposition. So far this has meant that the slightly left-of-centre **People's United Party** (PUP) has alternated with the more market-led **United Democratic Party** (UDP). At the last general election, in August 1998, the PUP under the leadership of Prime Minister **Said Musa** captured 25 out of 29 seats in the National Assembly in an unprecedented landslide victory.

Despite a booming **tourist industry** that brings in over US$115 million a year, agriculture remains the mainstay of Belize's **economy**, accounting for over sixty percent of foreign exchange earnings and almost a third of the country's employment. Figures are obviously not available for Belize's income from the lucrative drug transhipment business, but this illicit economy is almost as large as the official one. **Per capita** income is high for Central America, at over US$2500, boosted by the remittances many Belizeans receive from relatives abroad, mainly in the US. This apparent advantage is offset, however, by the fact that many of the brightest and most highly trained citizens leave Belize, fitting in well in English-speaking North America.

Though traditional links with Britain and the Commonwealth countries in the West Indies remain relatively strong, Belize, together with all the other Central American countries, was a signatory to the negotiations held early in 2001 to establish a **Free Trade Area of the Americas**, with December 2005 set as the target date for the agreement to come into force. This step is viewed with alarm by many Belizean workers, who fear that an end to all tariffs will further depress agricultural prices and drive the small manufacturing base into bankruptcy. Even worse, in many people's eyes such proposals might signal an end to the **fixed rate of exchange** with the US dollar, leading to a potentially catastrophic devaluation of the Belize dollar. Regardless of the populist rhetoric of the PUP, however, Belize is already firmly linked to the US-dominated world of international finance, and is likely to face increasing challenges from global competitors in the early years of this century.

CHAPTER 1

BELIZE CITY

he narrow, crowded streets of BELIZE CITY can initially be daunting to anyone who has been prepared by the usual tales of crime-ridden urban decay. Admittedly, at first glance the city is unprepossessing. Its buildings – many of them dilapidated wooden structures – stand right at the edge of the road, and few sidewalks offer refuge to pedestrians from the ever-increasing numbers of vehicles. The hazards of Belize City, however, are often reported by those who have never been here. If you approach the city with an open mind and take some precautions with your belongings, you may well be pleasantly surprised.

The city has a distinguished history, a handful of sights and, particularly during the **September celebrations**, an astonishing energy. The seventy thousand people of Belize City represent every ethnic group in the country, with the **Creole** descendants of former slaves and Baymen forming the dominant element, generating an easy-going Caribbean atmosphere.

Belize City is divided neatly into north and south halves by the **Haulover Creek**, a delta branch of the Belize River. The pivotal point of the city centre is the **Swing Bridge**, always busy with traffic and opened twice a day to allow larger vessels up and down the river. **North** of the Swing Bridge is the slightly more upmarket part of town, home to the most expensive hotels. **South** of the Swing Bridge is the market and commercial zone, the location of all the city's banks and a couple of supermarkets. The city is small enough to make **walking** the easiest way to get around.

Some history

Exactly how Belize came by its name is something of a mystery; it could be a corruption of the name Wallace, a Scotsman and probably a pirate, reputed to have settled here in 1620. Those preferring a more ancient origin believe the name to be derived from *beliz*, a Maya word meaning "muddy", or from the Maya term *belekin*, meaning "towards the east".

What is known is that by the late seventeenth century, buccaneers were cutting **logwood** (used for textile dyes in Europe) in the region, and had settled in a mangrove swamp consolidated with wood chips, loose coral and rum bottles at the mouth of today's Haulover Creek. The settlement became known as **Belize Town**, and by the 1700s it was well established as a centre for logwood cutters, their families and their slaves. The seafront contained the houses of the **Baymen**, as the settlers called themselves; the slaves lived in cabins on the south side of Haulover Creek, with various tribal groups occupying separate areas. After the rains had floated the logs downriver the men returned here to drink and brawl, with riotous Christmas celebrations going on for weeks.

Spain was the dominant colonial power in the region, and mounted several expeditions aimed at demonstrating control over the territory. These raids continued until the **Battle of St George's Caye** in 1798, when the settlers achieved victory with British naval help – a success that reinforced the bond with the British government. The nineteenth century saw the increasing influence of **British expatriates**, with colonial-style wooden housing dominating the shoreline as the "Scots clique" began to clean up the town's image and take control of its administration. Despite fires and epidemics in the nineteenth century the town and settlement grew with immigration from the West Indies and refugees from the Caste Wars in the Yucatán. In 1862 Belize became the colony of **British Honduras**, with Belize City as the administrative centre, and in 1871 Belize was officially declared a Crown Colony, with a resident governor appointed by Britain.

On September 10, 1931, the city was celebrating the anniversary of the Battle of St George's Caye when it was hit by a massive **hurricane** that uprooted houses, flooded the entire city and killed about a thousand people – ten percent of the population. Disaster relief was slow to arrive and many parts of the city were left in a state of squalid poverty. In 1961 the city was again ravaged by a hurricane: 262 people died, and the damage was so serious that plans were made to relocate the capital inland to Belmopan. (Hattieville, on the Western Highway, began life as a refuge for those fleeing the hurricane.) The official attitude was that Belize City would soon become a redundant backwater as Belmopan grew, but in fact few people chose to leave for the sterile "new town" atmosphere of Belmopan, and Belize City remains by far the most populous place in the country. Since independence the rise of foreign investment and tourism has made an impact, and Belize City is now experiencing a major construction boom.

Arrival and information

The main **bus companies** in Belize have their terminals in the same western area of the city, around the Collet Canal and Magazine Road, a fairly derelict part of town known as Mesopotamia. It's only 1km or so from the centre and you can easily walk – or, especially at night, take a taxi – to any of the hotels listed on pp.54–55. **Taxis**, identified by green licence plates, charge US$2.50 for one or two passengers within the city limits. **Boats** returning from the cayes pull in at the Marine Terminal on the north side of the Swing Bridge, or at Courthouse Wharf on the south side, from where it's a short walk or taxi ride to any of the hotels or bus depots. **International flights** land at the **Phillip Goldson International Airport**, 17km northwest of the city; taxis into town cost US$15, or you could walk to the Northern Highway (25min) and try to flag down one of the frequent buses; **domestic flights** come and go from the **municipal airport**, a few kilometres north of town on the edge of the sea; taxis from here to the city centre charge US$2.50.

The **Belize Tourist Board** (BTB; Mon–Fri 8am–noon & 1–5pm; ☎02/77213) is some distance from the centre, at Gabourel Lane in front of the Central Bank building.

HASSLE

Walking in Belize City **in daylight** is perfectly safe if you observe common-sense rules. The introduction of specially trained **tourism police** (☎02/72222 ext 401) in 1995, coupled with the legal requirement for all tour guides to be licensed, has driven away the hustlers and reduced street crime considerably. You'll soon learn to spot dangerous situations, and in the city centre you can always ask the tourism police for advice or directions. They're instantly recognizable by their baseball caps emblazoned with "TOURISM POLICE" and green T-shirts or uniforms – they'll even walk you back to your hotel if it's near their patrol route. That said, it's still sensible to proceed with caution: most people are friendly and chatty, but quite a few may want to sell you drugs or bum a dollar or two. The best advice is to stay cool. Be civil, don't provoke trouble by arguing too forcefully, and never show large sums of money on the street. Women wearing short shorts or skirts will attract verbal abuse from local studs.

The virtual absence of nightlife outside the more expensive hotel bars means there's little reason to walk the streets **after dark**. If you do venture out at night bear in mind that anyone walking alone is in danger of being mugged; it's better to take a taxi.

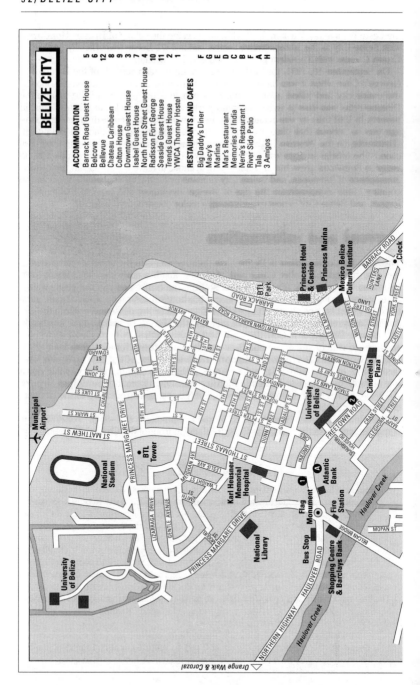

BELIZE CITY

ACCOMMODATION
Barrack Road Guest House	5
Belcove	6
Bellevue	12
Chateau Caribbean	8
Colton House	9
Downtown Guest House	3
Isabel Guest House	7
North Front Street Guest House	4
Radisson Fort George	10
Seaside Guest House	11
Trends Guest House	2
YWCA Thorney Hostel	1

RESTAURANTS AND CAFES
Big Daddy's Diner	F
Macy's	G
Marlins	E
Mar's Restaurant	D
Memories of India	C
Nerie's Restaurant I	B
River Side Patio	F
Tala	A
3 Amigos	H

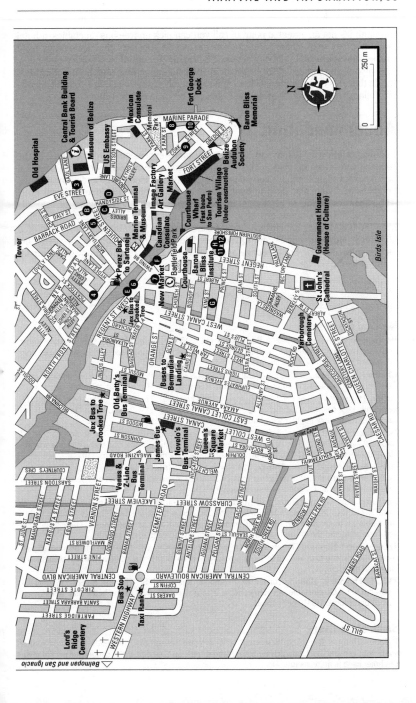

Although it's not an essential point of call you can pick up free bus timetables, a hotel guide and city map, nature reserve brochures and copies of the (sometimes free) **tourist newspapers**. In the city centre the **Marine Terminal** ticket office (see opposite) next to the Swing Bridge has reliable information on **bus and boat schedules**. Inside there's a café, luggage lockers and reasonably clean toilets, and you can change US dollars, Guatemalan quetzales and Mexican pesos in Sunny's shop.

Accommodation

Accommodation in Belize City is generally more expensive than elsewhere in the country, and prices for even budget rooms can come as quite a shock. The selection below covers all price ranges and you can be confident of cleanliness and security in the hotels listed. There's no need to book unless you're eager to stay in a particular hotel – you'll always be able to get something in the price range you're looking for.

Most of the city's hotels are located **north of the river**, and so are a little further from the bus stations but closer to the Marine Terminal, with budget places clustered on or near **North Front St** and **Queen St**. The more upmarket hotels are generally located in the historic **Fort George area**, just north of the river, or along the **seafront** either side of the river mouth, where the houses benefit from sea breezes.

For an explanation of **accommodation price codes**, see p.40.

North of the river

Barrack Road Guest House, 8 Barrack Rd (☎02/36671). Quiet, clean and very secure guesthouse, conveniently located just two blocks from the Marine Terminal. Good value, and run by helpful owners Molly and Leo Castillo. ④.

Chateau Caribbean, 6 Marine Parade (☎02/30800, fax 30900, *www.chateaucaribbean.com*). Comfortable, colonial-style hotel, recently renovated with cable TV, a/c and some sea views. ⑦.

Colton House, 9 Cork St (☎02/44666, *www.coltonhouse.com*). The best guesthouse in Belize, this beautifully kept colonial building has a/c rooms (all non-smoking) with balcony and immaculate private bathrooms; very popular with honeymooners. ⑦.

Downtown Guest House, 5 Eve St, near the end of Queen Street (☎ & fax ☎02/32057, *calista89@hotmail.com*). The best-value budget accommodation in the city, this small and friendly place has secure rooms (some with private bath) plus a kitchen for guests' use. ③.

North Front Street Guest House, 124 North Front St (☎02/77595, *thoth@btl.net*). Two blocks from Marine Terminal, this budget travellers' favourite has small but clean and secure rooms, all with shared bath, and is good for information too. ③.

Radisson Fort George Hotel and Marina, 2 Marine Parade, north side of the harbour mouth (☎02/33333, fax 73820, *www.radissonbelize.com*). Luxurious flagship hotels. The very well-furnished rooms have a huge cable TV, fridge and minibar, and many also have sea views. There's an excellent restaurant and the grounds are an oasis of calm on the edge of the sea. ⑨.

Trends Guest House, 91 Freetown Rd (☎02/36066, *edsan@btl.net*). Five modern, no-smoking a/c rooms with private bath and cable TV in a secure new hotel; the best value in the city at this price. No credit cards. ⑤.

YWCA Thornley Hostel, corner of Freetown Road and St Thomas Street (☎02/44971, ywca@btl.net). Comfortable accommodation in dorm rooms with large beds (not bunks) and shared bathrooms. US$10 per person.

South of the river

Belcove Hotel, 9 Regent St West ☎02/73054, *belcove@hotmail.com*). Recently renovated rooms, some with a/c and most with private bath. Although it's on the edge of the dangerous part of town, the hotel itself is quite secure. ⑤.

Bellevue Hotel, 5 Southern Foreshore (☎02/77051, fax 72353, *fins@btl.net*). The top hotel on the south side of the Swing Bridge, with colonial-style a/c rooms and a relaxing courtyard with palms and a pool. The disco here is a focal point of the city's nightlife, with live music at weekends. ⑦.

Isabel Guest House, across the Swing Bridge, above and behind Central Drug Store (☎02/73139). Small, friendly, mainly Spanish-speaking place, with large rooms and private showers. Good for a group sharing. ⑤.

Seaside Guest House, 3 Prince St, half a block from the southern foreshore (☎02/78339, *friends@btl.net*). Clean, well-run and very secure hotel with hot showers – and you really can see the sea. Good for information, and you get your own key so you can let yourself in and out as you please. Dorm beds US$10 per person, private rooms ④.

The City

Richard Davies, a British traveller in the mid-nineteenth century, wrote of the city: "There is much to be said for Belize, for in its way it was one of the prettiest ports at which we touched, and its cleanliness and order . . . were in great contrast to the ports we visited later as to make them most remarkable."

Most of the features that elicited this praise have now gone, but several of the city's **wooden colonial buildings** have been saved as heritage showpieces, sometimes as museums or galleries, more often by conversion into a hotel or restaurant. Yet even in cases where the decay is too advanced for the balconies and carved railings to be restored, the old wooden structures remain more pleasing than the concrete blocks that have replaced so many of them.

Before the construction of the first wooden bridge in the early 1800s, cattle were winched over the waterway that divides the city – hence the name **Haulover Creek**. The **Swing Bridge**, focal point of the city centre, was made in Liverpool and opened in 1923 – today it's the only manually operated swing bridge left in the Americas. Every day at 5.30am and 5.30pm the endless parade of vehicles and people is halted and the process of turning begins: using long poles inserted into a capstan, four men gradually lever the bridge around until it's pointing in the direction of the harbour mouth.

The north side

Immediately on the **north side** of the Swing Bridge is the **Marine Terminal**, housed inside the beautifully restored former Belize City Fire Station of 1923. The terminal is the departure point for boats to the northern cayes, and is also home to a couple of superbly designed new museums (both Mon–Sat 8am–4.30pm; US$2 for a combined ticket). Downstairs, the **Coastal Zone Museum** contains fascinating displays and explanations of reef ecology, the highlight being a 3-D model of the entire reef system, including the cayes and atolls; upstairs, the **Maritime Museum** exhibits an amazing collection of models and documents relating to Belize's seafaring heritage. Opposite the Marine Terminal is the vast wooden **Paslow Building**, which houses the post office on the ground floor. A block east of the Marine Terminal, at 91 North Front St, **The Image Factory** (Mon–Fri 9am–6pm; free but donations welcome) hosts Belize's hottest contemporary artists. The gallery puts on outstanding, often provocative exhibitions and you often get a chance to chat to the artists themselves.

Continuing east, past the "temporary" market, which often has a greater variety of produce than the official market south of the Swing Bridge, you pass the **National Handicrafts Center** (Mon–Fri 8am–5pm), which sells high-quality Belizean crafts at fair prices. The area beyond here is now undergoing development as a "tourism village", ready to present an ersatz view of Belizean culture to hordes of cruise ship passengers. The tip of the north shore is marked by a small park and the **Bliss**

Lighthouse, a memorial to Baron Bliss (see below). Walking around the shoreline, you pass the *Fort George* hotel and **Memorial Park**, which honours the Belizean dead of World War I. In this area you'll find several well-preserved colonial mansions – many of the finest have now been taken over by embassies and upmarket hotels.

The Fort George area is also home to two of Belize's foremost conservation organizations: the **Belize Audubon Society** (Mon–Fri 8.30am–5pm) at 12 Fort St, which manages several of the country's wildlife reserves, and the **Programme for Belize** (Mon–Fri 8.30am–5pm) at 1 Eyre St, which manages the Rio Bravo Conservation Area (p.67) – both have bookshops selling useful wildlife guides and are worth a visit to pick up news on their latest conservation efforts. A little to the north, at the corner of Hutson Street and Gabourel Lane a block from the sea, is the **US Embassy**, a superb "colonial" building which was actually constructed in New England in the nineteenth century and then shipped to Belize. Just beyond here, in front of the Central Bank building, the former colonial prison is being converted into a **Museum of Belize** and will house colonial and Maya artefacts.

The south side

The **south side** is the older half of Belize City: in the early days the elite lived in the seafront houses while the backstreets were home to slaves and labourers. These days it's the city's commercial centre, containing the ugly new market building just over the Swing Bridge, the main shopping streets, banks and travel agencies. **Albert Street**, running south from the Swing Bridge, is the main commercial thoroughfare. On the parallel **Regent Street** are the former colonial administration and court buildings, collectively known as the **Court House**. These well-preserved examples of colonial architecture, completed in 1926, with columns and fine wrought iron, overlook **Battlefield Park** (named to commemorate the noisy political meetings that took place there before independence), a patch of grass and trees with an ornamental fountain in the centre,

A block behind the Court House, on the waterfront, is the **Bliss Institute**, funded by the legacy of **Baron Bliss**, an eccentric Englishman with a Portuguese title. A keen fisherman, he arrived off the coast of Belize in 1926 after hearing about the tremendous game fishing in local waters. Unfortunately, he became ill and died without ever having been ashore. Despite this he left most of his considerable estate to the colony and, in gratitude, the authorities declared March 9, the date of his death, Baron Bliss Day. The Bliss building is now a **performing arts centre** hosting exhibitions, concerts and plays.

At the end of Albert Street is **St John's Cathedral**, the oldest Anglican cathedral in Central America and one of the oldest buildings in Belize. Looking like a large English parish church, it was begun in 1812, its red bricks being brought over as ballast in British ships. Here, between 1815 and 1845, the kings of the Mosquito Coast were crowned amid great pomp, taking the title to a British Protectorate that extended along the coast of Honduras and Nicaragua.

On the way to the seafront from the cathedral you'll come to the well-preserved, white-painted, green-lawned Government House, now renamed the **House of Culture** (daily 8.30am–4.30pm; free entrance to grounds, US$2.50 to the house). A plush red carpet leads down the hall to a great mahogany staircase, the walls lined with prints and photos of sombre past governors. Much of the collection of this former museum (including silverware, glasses and furniture used during the colonial period) may well have moved to the Museum of Belize (see above) by the time you read this, leaving the House of Culture free to host painting and dance workshops, art exhibitions and musical performances.

Eating, drinking and nightlife

Belize City's selection of **restaurants** is becoming gradually more varied, and there's plenty of seafood and steaks available, though the tasty but monotonous **Creole** fare of rice and beans still predominates. There's a preponderance of **Chinese** restaurants – usually the best bet for **vegetarians** – and some very good **Lebanese** and **Indian** restaurants. The big **hotels** have their own restaurants, which are naturally quite expensive, but with much more varied menus. Be warned that many restaurants are closed on Sunday. In the listings below we have quoted a phone number in places where it is recommended you should **reserve a table** or for those places which offer a **delivery service**.

Restaurants north of the river

Mar's Restaurant, 11 Handyside St. Tasty Belizean food at great prices in a spacious, clean restaurant.

Memories of India, corner of Queen and Handyside streets (☎02/31172). The only Indian restaurant in the city centre and very good, with chicken, lamb and lots of vegetarian curries. Free deliveries.

Nerie's Restaurant, corner of Queen and Daly streets. The best Belizean food north of the river, and fantastically good value. Very busy at lunchtimes, when there's always a daily special.

Tala, 164 Freetown Road (☎02/45841). The best Lebanese food in the country, with delicious tahini, falafel, hummus and kebabs — try the Lebanese plate. Will deliver.

Restaurants and cafés south of the river

3 Amigos, 2b King St (☎02/79936). Small a/c restaurant – plus outside tables on the garden patio – serving what is consistently the best food in the city at great prices. There's a daily special and vegetarian alternatives to the mainly seafood, salad and steak main courses. Closed Sun.

Big Daddy's Diner, upstairs in the new market, south side of the Swing Bridge. Great breakfasts and Belizean dishes, with a daily lunch special, served in clean, bright surroundings. Closed Sun.

Macy's, 18 Bishop St. Long-established, reasonably priced Creole restaurant that's popular with locals and very busy at lunchtimes.

Marlins, 11 Regent St West, next to the *Belcove Hotel*. Good, inexpensive local food in large portions – and you can eat on the veranda overlooking the river.

River Side Patio, at the rear of the market. Try the Mexican-style food, or just relax with a drink as you watch the bridge swing; a small band plays here on Friday and Saturday evenings.

Drinking, nightlife and entertainment

Belize City's more sophisticated, air-conditioned **bars** are found in the most expensive establishments, and there aren't many of those. At the lowest end of the scale are dimly lit dives, effectively men-only, where, though there's the possibility that you'll be offered drugs or be robbed, it's more likely that you'll have a thoroughly enjoyable time amongst easy-going, hard-drinking locals. There are several places between the two extremes, some of them in restaurants and hotels – or try the early-closing *Marlins* restaurant (see above) and *Nu Fenders*, a bar on the corner of Queen and Handyside streets.

Nightlife, though not as wild as it used to be, is becoming more reliable, and the quality of live bands is improving all the time. The *Radisson Fort George* and the *Bellevue* hold regular dances or discos, with **live music** often preceded by a Friday evening **happy hour**. At *Planet Hollywood* (not part of the chain) on the corner of Queen and Handyside streets there's live **punta** and **reggae**, while *Nerie's Restaurant* (see above) hosts local bands upstairs on Friday evenings. A bit further afield the *Lumba Yard Bar*, on the riverbank just out of town on the Northern Highway, hosts the country's top bands on Friday and Saturday evenings.

Listings

Airlines Aerocaribe and Taca, Belize Global Travel, 41 Albert St (☎02/77363); Aerovias, *Mopan Hotel*, 55 Regent St (☎02/75446); American, corner of New Rd and Queen St (☎02/32522); Continental, 80 Regent St (☎02/78309); Maya Island Air, Municipal Airport (☎02/31140 or 026/2345); TACA, at Belize Global Travel, 41 Albert St (☎02/77185, airport ☎025/2163); Tropic Air, Municipal Airport (☎02/45671 or 026/2012).

Banks and exchange The main branches of Atlantic, Barclays, Belize and Scotia banks (all Mon–Thurs 8am–2pm, Fri 8am–4.30pm) are on Albert Street. Barclays does cash advances on Visa with no surcharge (Belize Bank charges US$7.50) and has an ATM which accepts foreign-issued cards. US dollars are usually readily available from the banks, and many shops, hotels and restaurants change travellers' cheques and cash. Guatemalan and Mexican currency is often difficult to obtain, except at the borders, though Sunny's, in the Marine Terminal, usually has quetzales and pesos.

Books Both the Book Center, 2 Church St, opposite the BTL office (☎02/77457), and Angelus Press, 10 Queen St (☎02/35777), have a wide range of Belize-related books and maps.

Car rental The following companies are in Belize City and will arrange vehicle pick-up and drop-off anywhere in the city or at the municipal or international airports at no extra charge: Avis ☎02/34619; Budget ☎02/23435; Crystal (whose cars you're allowed to take over the Guatemalan border) ☎02/31600; IBTM ☎02/32668.

Embassies and consulates Though the official capital is at Belmopan, some embassies remain in Belize City; they're normally open Mon–Fri mornings. Current addresses and phone numbers can be checked under "Diplomatic Listings" in the green pages of the telephone directory. Canada, 83 North Front St (☎02/31060); Costa Rica, Driftwood Bay (☎02/32878); El Salvador (☎02/35162); Guatemala, 8a Street, Kings Park (☎02/33150); Honduras, 91 N Front St (☎02/45889); Mexico, 18 North Park St (☎02/31388); Panamá, Mahogany St (☎02/24551); USA, 29 Gabourel Lane (☎02/77161).

Immigration The Belize Immigration Office (Mon–Fri 8.30am–noon & 1–3.30m; ☎02/24620) is in the Government Complex on Mahogany St, near the junction of Central American Blvd and the Western Highway. Extensions of permitted stay cost US$12.50 and are valid for 30 days only.

Laundry Central America Coin Laundry, 114 Barrack Rd (Mon–Sat 8.30am–9pm, reduced hours on Sun).

Medical care Dr Gamero, Myo-On Clinic, 40 Eve St (☎02/45616); Karl Huesner Memorial Hospital, Princess Margaret Drive, near junction with the Northern Highway (☎02/31548).

Photography For prints, slides and fast passport photos, try Spooners, 89 North Front St.

Police On Queen Street, a block north of the Swing Bridge (☎02/72210). Alternatively, contact the Tourism Police (☎02/72222 ext 401; see p.51).The nationwide emergency number is ☎90.

Post office In the Paslow Building, on the corner of Queen St, immediately north of the Swing Bridge (Mon–Fri 8am–noon & 1–4.30pm).

Supermarkets Brodies and Romacs are opposite each other on Albert St, just beyond the park.

Telecommunications and email There are payphones and cardphones dotted around the city, or visit the main BTL office, 1 Church St (Mon–Sat 8am–6pm), which also has fax facilities and the city's best-value email service.

Travel and tour agents The following travel agents are the best for information and bookings on flights and connections throughout the region; all can arrange tours within Belize: Belize Global Travel, 41 Albert St (☎02/77363, *bzeadventur@btl.net*); Belize Travel Adventures, 168 N Front St (☎02/33064, *www.belize-travel.net*); IBTM, *Princess Hotel*, Newtown Barracks Rd (☎02/32668 or 016/2997, *ibtm@btl.net*).

Moving on from Belize City

Moving on from Belize City by **bus** couldn't be simpler. Most of the bus **companies** are in the same area, along the Collet Canal and Magazine Rd, a short walk from the centre of town. The box opposite lists all the routes from Belize City, including frequencies and duration.

Tours

Most inland **day tours** from Belize City visit two or more of the following: The Belize Zoo, Bermudian Landing Baboon Sanctuary, Crooked Tree Wildlife Sanctuary, Lamanai ruins and Altun Ha ruins. All but the last of these places are very easy to visit independently, though in some cases you'll need to stay overnight. Even when you include the cost of accommodation you're still likely to save money by doing it on your own. If time is short and you'd prefer a guided tour then contact any of the travel agents above or independent naturalist guides David Cunningham (☎02/24400 or 014/9828) or Mary Avila (☎02/31270).

Bus companies and depots

Most of the **bus companies** and bus departure points are in the same area, along the Collet Canal and Magazine Road, a short walk from the centre of town. While the main bus companies have their own depots, there are numerous smaller operators with regular departures but no contact address or telephone number. At the time of writing, **Novelo's**, the largest bus company in Belize (formed by a takeover of Batty's and

BUS SERVICES FROM BELIZE CITY			
DESTINATION	**FREQUENCY**	**COMPANY**	**DURATION**
Belmopan	every 30min 5am–8pm (exp)	NV	1hr 15min
Bermudian Landing	Mon–Sat 2 daily	MF, RU	1hr 15min
Chetumal, Mexico	hourly 5am–7pm (exp)	NV, VE	3hr 30min
Corozal	hourly 5am–7pm (exp)	NV, VE	2hr 30min
Crooked Tree	(NV) Mon–Sat 4 daily, Sun 1 daily (JX) Mon–Sat 3 daily	NV, JX	1hr 30min
Dangriga	12 daily 6am–5pm	JA, ZL	2hr via Coastal Road; 30min via Belmopan
Maskall (for Altun Ha)	Mon–Sat 4 daily	NV	1hr 15min
Melchor/ Guatemala border	every 30min 5am–6pm	NV	3hr 30min
Orange Walk	hourly 5am–7pm	NV, VE	1hr 30min
Placencia	2 daily via Dangriga	ZL	6–7hr via Belmopan
Punta Gorda	10 daily via Dangriga	JA, ZL	8–9hr
San Ignacio	every 30min 5am–9pm	NV	3hr via Belmopan
Sarteneja	3 daily via Orange Walk	PE, VE	3hr 30min

△ *Belmopan & San Ignacio*

Corozal and around

South from the border, the road meets the sea at **COROZAL**, near the mouth of the
New River. The **ancient Maya** prospered here by controlling river and seaborne trade,
and two sites, **Santa Rita** and **Cerros**, are both within easy reach. The present town
was founded here in 1849 by refugees from the massacre in Bacalar, Mexico, who were
hounded south by the Caste Wars. Today's grid-pattern town is a neat mix of Mexican
and Caribbean, its appearance largely due to reconstruction in the wake of Hurricane
Janet in 1955. There's little to do in Corozal, but it's an agreeable place to spend the day
on the way to or from the border, and is hassle-free, even at night. The breezy shoreline park is good for a stroll, while on the tree-shaded main plaza, the **town hall** is
worth a look inside for a vivid depiction of local history in a mural by Manuel Villamar
Reyes. In two corners of the plaza you can see the remains of a small fort, built to ward
off Maya attacks in the late 1800s.

Arrival and information

All **buses** between Belize City and Chetumal pass through Corozal, roughly hourly in
each direction. The Venus bus depot is near the northern edge of town, opposite the

Shell station; Novelo's buses stop on 4th Ave, north of the park. Maya Island Air and Tropic Air operate daily **flights** between Corozal and San Pedro on Ambergris Caye. Jal's travel agency (☎04/22163), at the the southern end of town, beyond Tony's, can organize **international flights**. For reliable tourist **information**, visit the **Corozal Cultural Centre** (Tues–Sat 9am–noon & 1–4.30pm; ☎04/23176, *www.corozal.com*), housed in the restored colonial market building in the waterfront park, just past the new market. The centre also holds a **museum** (US$1.50) with imaginative displays depicting episodes in Corozal's history.

Scotia Bank, on the southeast side of the main plaza, offers the best value for **cash advances**. The **post office** is on the west side of the plaza. For domestic flights and **organized tours** to local nature reserves and archeological sites, contact Henry Menzies at *Caribbean Village Resort* (☎04/22725). Stephan Moerman (☎04/22833), a French biologist, arranges tours to Cerros and Bacalar Chico National Park, at the north end of Ambergris Caye (see p.75).

Accommodation, eating and drinking

Corozal has plenty of **accommodation** in all price ranges, and you shouldn't have any problems finding a suitable room. *Nestor's*, on 5th Ave South, between 4th and 5th streets (☎04/22354, *nestors@btl.net*; ④), is a centrally located budget hotel with private showers and a popular sports bar and restaurant. *Hok'ol K'in Guest House*, facing the sea a block south of the market (☎04/23329, *maya@btl.net*, ⑥), has modern rooms (plus some suites) with large, tiled private bathrooms and hammocks on the balcony. The *Hotel Maya*, on the main road at the south end of town facing the sea (☎04/22082, *stay@hotelmaya.com*; ⑤–⑥), is clean and well-run, with private bathrooms and some new rooms with a/c. Just beyond the *Maya*, the *Caribbean Village Resort* (☎04/22045; ④) offers good-value whitewashed thatched cabins with hot water, set among the palms facing the sea; there's also a trailer park (US$12 per trailer).

Whatever your budget, the best **meals** in Corozal are to be found in the hotels. The popular bar at *Nestor's* serves American and Belizean food, while *Hotel Maya* offers very good Belizean dishes in a quieter environment. *Haley's*, in the *Caribbean Village*, is renowned locally for its fine, inexpensive food. Authentic French pastries can be had at *Le Café Kela*, on the seafront just north of the centre.

Around Corozal: Santa Rita and Cerros

Of the two small Maya sites within reach of Corozal, the closest is **Santa Rita** (daily 8am–4pm; US$2.50), about fifteen minutes' walk northwest of town. To get there, follow the main road in the direction of the border and where it divides take the left-hand fork. Founded around 1500 BC, Santa Rita was in all probability the powerful Maya city known as Chetumal. It was still a thriving settlement in 1531 AD, when the conquistador Alonso Davila entered the town, only to be driven out almost immediately by Na Chan Kan, the Maya chief, and his Spanish adviser Gonzalo Guerrero. The main remaining building is a small pyramid. Excavations here have uncovered the burial sites of an elaborately bejewelled elderly woman and a Classic period warlord.

The remains of the late Preclassic centre of **Cerros** (daily 8am–4pm; US$2.50) are just 5km across the bay from Corozal and best reached by **boat** with a guide from the town. Built in a strategic position at the mouth of the New River, this was one of the earliest places in the Maya world to adopt the rule of kings. Despite initial success, however, Cerros had been abandoned by the Classic period. The site includes three large acropolis structures, ball courts and plazas flanked by pyramids. The largest building is a 22-metre-high temple, whose intricate stucco masks represent the rising and setting sun. In the dry season it's also possible to drive to Cerros via the new chain-winched ferry (daily 6am–9pm; free) which crosses the New River a few kilometres south of Corozal at **Pueblo Nuevo** (the turn-off is signed), allowing access to the site through **Copper Bank** village; in addition, a **bus** (Mon–Sat 11.30am, additional service Mon, Wed & Fri at 4pm; 30min) leaves for Copper Bank from behind the Venus terminal in Corozal. In Copper Bank, *The Last Resort* (✆041/2009, *rickz@btl.net*; ②) offers **budget accommodation** in clean, simple, whitewashed thatched cabins with electricity, mosquito-netted beds and shared showers.

Sarteneja and the Shipstern Reserve

Across Chetumal Bay from Corozal, the largely uninhabited **Sarteneja peninsula** is covered with dense forests and swamps that support an amazing array of wildlife. The only village is **SARTENEJA**, a quiet, Spanish-speaking lobster-fishing centre. A couple of new **hotels** have been built (there's also accommodation at the reserve; see below), and **guides** are available to take you to the lagoons and beyond. The best place is *Fernando's Seaside Guest House* (✆04/32045; ⑤), on the seafront, which has thatched rooms with private bath and a restaurant. The Perez **bus** to Sarteneja from Belize City leaves at noon and 1.30pm; the Venus bus to Sarteneja departs at 12.30pm (both Mon–Sat; 4hr; US$6), stopping at Zeta's store on Main St in Orange Walk ninety minutes later. Buses return from Sarteneja at 5am and 6am.

The **Shipstern Nature Reserve** (daily 8am–5pm; US$5 including guided walk), established in 1981, covers an area of eighty square kilometres. The bulk of the reserve is made up of what's technically known as "tropical moist forest", and includes some wide belts of savanna – covered in coarse grasses, palms and broad-leaved trees – and a section of the shallow Shipstern Lagoon, dotted with mangrove islands. Taking the superb guided walk along the **Chiclero Trail**, you'll encounter more named plant species in an hour than on any other trail in Belize. Shipstern is also a bird-watcher's paradise: the lagoon system supports blue-winged teal, American coot, and huge flocks of lesser scaup, while the forest is home to fly-catchers, keel-billed toucans and at least five species of parrot. Other wildlife in the reserve includes crocodiles, coatis, jaguars, peccaries, and an abundance of wonderful butterflies.

All **buses** to Sarteneja pass the **entrance** to the reserve, 5km before the village. You can **stay** at the headquarters near the visitor centre, where there are two neat four-bed dorms (US$10 per person) with cooking facilities, and a two-roomed house for rent (US$40).

Orange Walk and around

With a population approaching twenty thousand, **ORANGE WALK** is the largest town in the north of Belize and the centre of a busy agricultural region. Like Corozal, less than an hour away along the Northern Highway, it was founded by mestizo refugees fleeing from the Caste Wars in Yucatán in 1849, who chose as their site an area that had long been used for logging camps and was already occupied by the local Icaiché (Chichanha) Maya.

Orange Walk traditionally thrived on the sugar and citrus industries, but a fall in sugar prices has seen it come to depend more heavily on profits from marijuana – though recent pressure from the US government has forced the Belizean authorities to destroy many of the marijuana fields. The town itself boasts few tourist attractions, and Corozal (see p.62) is a preferable place to spend the night. The centre of town is marked by a distinctly Mexican-style formal plaza, and the town hall across the main road is actually called the Palacio Municipal, reinforcing the town's strong historical links to Mexico. The tranquil, slow-moving New River, a few blocks east of the centre, was a busy commercial waterway during the logging days. Now, however, it's a lovely starting point for visiting the ruins of **Lamanai**, and several local operators now offer tours (see pp.66–67).

Practicalities

Hourly **buses** from Belize City and Corozal pull up on the main road in the centre of town, officially Queen Victoria Avenue but always referred to as the Belize–Corozal road. Services to and from Sarteneja stop at Zeta's Store on Main St, two blocks to the east, while local buses to the surrounding villages leave from near the crossroads by the fire station in the centre of town.

The Belize–Corozal road is lined with hotels, restaurants and filling stations, so there's no need to walk far. If you do have **to stay**, then the best option is *St Christopher's Hotel*, 10 Main St (☎ & fax 03/21064; ⑤), which has beautiful rooms (some a/c) with private bath, set in grounds sweeping down to the New River. The best place to **change money** and get cash advances on credit cards is the Scotia Bank, just east of the plaza. The **post office** is at the north end of town on the Belize–Corozal road.

The majority of **restaurants** in Orange Walk are Chinese, though there are a few Belizean-style places serving simple "Mexican" food or rice and beans. *Lover's Restaurant*, tucked away in the far corner of the park at 20 Lover's Lane, offers the best Belizean food, while *Juanita's*, on the side street by the Shell station, has the best Mexican dishes.

Maya sites around Orange Walk

Although the **Maya sites** in northern Belize have been the source of a number of the most important archeological finds in the Maya world, they are not (with the exception of Lamanai) as monumentally spectacular as those in the Yucatán. The area around Orange Walk has some of the most productive arable farmland in Belize, and this was also the case in Maya times – aerial surveys in the late 1970s revealed evidence of raised fields and a network of irrigation canals, showing that the Maya practised skilful intensive agriculture. In the Postclassic era this region controlled the trade in cacao beans (used as currency by the Maya) that were grown in the Hondo and New river

Crooked Tree

Some 38km south of Orange Walk a branch road heads west to **Crooked Tree Wildlife Sanctuary**, a reserve that takes in a vast area of wetlands, covering four separate lagoons. Designated Belize's first **Ramsar site** (to protect wetlands of international importance) the sanctuary provides an ideal resting place for thousands of **migrating and resident birds**, such as snail kites, tiger herons, snowy egrets, ospreys and black-collared hawks. The reserve's most famous visitor is the **jabiru stork**, the largest flying bird in the New World, with a wingspan of 2.5m. Belize has the biggest nesting population of jabiru storks at any one site: they arrive in November, the young hatch in April or May, and they leave just before the rainy season gets under way. The **best months** for bird-watchers to visit are from late February to June, when the lagoons shrink to a string of pools, forcing wildlife to congregate for food and water.

In the middle of the reserve, straggling around the shores of a lagoon, 5km from the main road, is the village of **CROOKED TREE** – effectively an island in the lagoons but linked to the mainland by a **causeway**. At the end of the causeway is the **Sanctuary Visitor Centre**, where you pay the US$4 entrance fee. One of the oldest inland villages in the country, Crooked Tree's existence is based on fishing and farming – some of the mango and cashew trees here are reckoned to be more than a hundred years old – though the main attraction for visitors is simply strolling through the sandy, tree-lined lanes, and along the lakeshore, where you'll see plenty of birds.

Practicalities

There are four **buses** daily to Crooked Tree from Belize City. The Jex service (☎025/7017) leaves once daily from Regent St West (Mon–Sat 10.30am) and twice on weekdays from Pound Yard (Mon–Fri 4.30pm & 5.30pm); there's also one Novelo's service a day (Mon–Fri 4pm, Sat noon & Sun 9am; returning Mon–Sat between 6am and 7am, Sun 4pm). It's always a good idea to check bus times with a village hotel or call the community telephone (☎021/2084)

Most of the **accommodation** at Crooked Tree is in mid-priced resort-type lodges, with meals included, though there are also some inexpensive **bed and breakfast** rooms (③) – ask at the visitor centre. Several of the resorts have **camping** space. Anyone offering accommodation can also arrange boats for **tours**, and should also be able to set you up with one of the village's supremely knowledgeable **guides**. *Bird's Eye View Lodge* (☎02/32040, *birdseye@btl.net*; ⑦ including breakfast), on the lakeshore at the south end of the village, has comfortable private rooms in a two-storey concrete building; there's also a dorm room (US$12.50 per person) and camping (US$5). Though not on the lake, *Sam Tillet's Hotel* (☎021/2026 or 014/7920, *samhotel@btl.net*; ④–⑥) has comfortable rooms (the best value in the village) and camping (US$5), and the garden attracts a variety of birds. *Paradise Inn* (☎025/7044, *www.adventurecamera .com/paradise*; ⑥) has beautiful thatched cabins in a lovely, quiet location, just steps from the lagoon at the north end of the village.

Altun Ha

Fifty-five kilometres north of Belize City and just 9km from the sea is the impressive Maya site of **Altun Ha** (daily 8am–4pm; US$5), which was occupied for around twelve hundred years until abandoned around 900 AD. Its position close to the Caribbean coast suggests that it was sustained as much by trade as by agriculture – a theory upheld by the discovery of trade objects such as obsidian and jade, neither of which occurs naturally in Belize, though both were very important in Maya ceremony. The jade would have come from the Motagua valley in Guatemala and much of it would probably have been shipped onwards to the north.

The core of Altun Ha is clustered around two Classic period plazas, both dotted with palm trees. Entering from the road, you come first to Plaza A. Large temples enclose it on all four sides, and a magnificent tomb has been discovered beneath Temple A-1, the **Temple of the Green Tomb**. Dating from 550 AD, this yielded a total of three hundred pieces, including jade, jewellery, stingray spines, skin, flints and the remains of a Maya book. The adjacent Plaza B is dominated by the site's largest temple, the **Temple of the Masonry Altars**. Several tombs have been uncovered within the main structure, though only two were found intact. In one, archeologists discovered a carved jade head of Kinich Ahau, the Maya sun god. Standing just under 15cm high, it is the largest carved jade to be found anywhere in the Maya world; today it's kept hidden away in the vaults of the Belize Bank.

Outside these two main plazas are several other areas of interest, though little else has yet been restored. A short trail leads south to **Rockstone Pond**, which was dammed in Maya times (and is today home to a large crocodile), at the eastern edge of which stands another mid-sized temple. Built in the second century AD, this contained offerings from the great city of Teotihuacán in the Valley of Mexico.

Practicalities

Altun Ha is fairly difficult to reach independently (though it can be done in a day from Belize City) as the 3km track to the site is located along the **Old Northern Highway** – turn off the Northern Highway at mile 18. There are **buses** (Mon–Sat) from Belize City (call the community phone ☎031/2058 to check times) to the village of **Maskall**, passing the turn-off to the site at the village of **Lucky Strike** (community phone ☎021/2017), 3km from Altun Ha, but you'll probably have to walk in from here. Any travel agent in Belize City will arrange a **tour** (see p.58) and increasing numbers visit as part of a day-trip from San Pedro (see p.76). There's no accommodation at the site, but you can ask the caretaker for permission to camp.

The Community Baboon Sanctuary

West off the Northern Highway, 43km from Belize City, the **Community Baboon Sanctuary** is one of the most interesting conservation projects in Belize. It was established in 1985 by Dr Rob Horwich and a group of local farmers (with help from the World Wide Fund for Nature), who adopted a voluntary code of practice to harmonize their own needs with those of the wildlife. A mixture of farmland and broad-leaved forest along the banks of the Belize River, the sanctuary coordinates eight villages and more than a hundred landowners in a project combining conservation, education and tourism.

The main focus of attention is the **black howler monkey** (locally known as a baboon). They generally live in groups of between four and eight, and spend the day wandering through the leaf canopy feasting on leaves, flowers and fruits. At dawn and dusk they let rip with the famous howl: a deep and rasping roar that carries for miles. The sanctuary is also home to around two hundred bird species, plus iguanas, peccaries and coatis. The **visitor centre** (US$5, includes a short guided walk), at the west end of Bermudian Landing (see overleaf), is home to Belize's first natural history museum, with exhibits and information on the riverside habitats and animals you're likely to see.

Practicalities

The sanctuary comprises eight villages along the Belize River, from Flowers Bank to Big Falls. All of them welcome visitors and you'll find plenty of places where you can rent canoes or horses. Probably the most convenient base is the village of **Bermudian Landing** at the heart of the area, an old logging centre that dates back to the seventeenth century.

At least two **buses** daily (Mon–Sat), leaving early in the morning, run between Belize City and the sanctuary, a journey of an hour and a quarter – see the Belize City chapter, pp.59–60 for departure points and times. You can **camp** at the visitor centre (US$5), while a number of local families offer **bed and breakfast** (④). Behind the visitor centre, *Nature Resort* (☎014/9286, *naturer@btl.net*) has two beautiful cabins (⑤) with private bath, electric lights, fan and coffee maker, and hammocks on the porch; the budget rooms (④) in a nearby wooden house share a separate, clean tiled bathroom. The *Resort* is managed by Alvin Young, who can arrange canoe or horse rental for around US$25 a day; a guide will cost more but the trails are easy to follow on your own. There are a few simple **restaurants and bars** in the village: *Russell's Restaurant*, in the centre on the left-hand side has tables under the thatch overlooking the river.

travel details

BUSES

Addresses and times of services from Belize City are given in the box on pp.59–60.

Belize City to: Bermudian Landing (Mon–Sat 2–3 daily; 1hr 15min); Chetumal (hourly; 3hr–3hr 30min); Corozal (hourly; 2hr 30min); Crooked Tree (4 daily; 1hr 30min); Orange Walk (hourly; 1hr 30min); Sarteneja (3 daily; 3hr 30min).

Bermudian Landing to: Belize City (Mon–Sat 2–3 daily; 1hr 15min).

Chetumal to: Belize City (hourly; 3hr–3hr 30min); Corozal (hourly; 1hr); Orange Walk (hourly; 2hr).

Corozal to: Belize City (hourly; 2hr 30min); Chetumal (hourly; 1hr); Orange Walk (hourly; 1hr).

Crooked Tree to: Belize City (4 daily; 1hr 30min).

Orange Walk to: Belize City (hourly; 1hr 30min); Chetumal (hourly; 2hr) Corozal (hourly; 1hr).

Sarteneja to: Belize City (3 daily; 3hr 30min).

FLIGHTS

Tropic Air (☎026/2012) and Maya Island Air (☎026/2345) each operate three daily flights between **Corozal** and **San Pedro**.

CHAPTER 3

THE NORTHERN CAYES AND ATOLLS

B
elize's spectacular **Barrier Reef**, with its dazzling variety of underwater life and string of exquisite islands – known as cayes – is the main attraction for most first-time visitors to the country. Forming part of the longest barrier reef in the western hemisphere, it runs the entire length of the coastline at a distance of 15 to 40km from the mainland.

Most of the **cayes** (pronounced "keys") lie in shallow water behind the shelter of the reef. A limestone ridge forms larger, low-lying islands to the north, while smaller, less frequently visited outcrops are clustered toward the southern end of the chain – often these are no more than a stand of palms and a strip of sand. Though the 450 cayes themselves form only a tiny proportion of the country's total land area, and only around three dozen have any kind of tourism development, Belize has more territorial water than it does land, and the islands' tourism and lobster fishing accounts for a substantial amount of foreign currency earnings.

The town of **San Pedro** on **Ambergris Caye** has been transformed from a predominantly fishing community to one geared to commercial tourism. There are still some beautiful spots here, however, notably the protected sections of reef at either end of the caye: the **Bacalar Chico National Park** to the north and **Hol Chan Marine Reserve** to the south. South of Ambergris Caye, **Caye Caulker** is less – but increasingly – developed, and remains popular with budget travellers.

Beyond the chain of islands and the coral reef are two of Belize's three **atolls**, the **Turneffe Islands** and **Lighthouse Reef**, regularly visited on day-trips from San Pedro and Caye Caulker. Here the coral reaches the surface, enclosing a shallow lagoon, with some cayes lying right on top of the encircling reef. Lighthouse Reef encompasses two of the most spectacular diving and snorkelling sites in the country – **Half Moon Caye Natural Monument** and the **Great Blue Hole**, an enormous collapsed cave.

A brief history of the cayes

The earliest inhabitants of the cayes were **Maya** peoples or their ancestors. By the Classic period (300–900 AD) the Maya had developed an extensive trade network stretching from the Yucatán to Honduras, with evidence of settlements and trading centres on several of the islands.

Probably the most infamous residents of the cayes were the **buccaneers**, usually British, who lived here in the seventeenth and eighteenth centuries, taking refuge in the shallow waters after plundering Spanish treasure ships. In time the pirates, now calling themselves **Baymen**, settled more or less permanently on some of the northern and central cayes, establishing their first capital on St George's Caye. In 1779 a Spanish

For an explanation of **accommodation price codes**, see p.40.

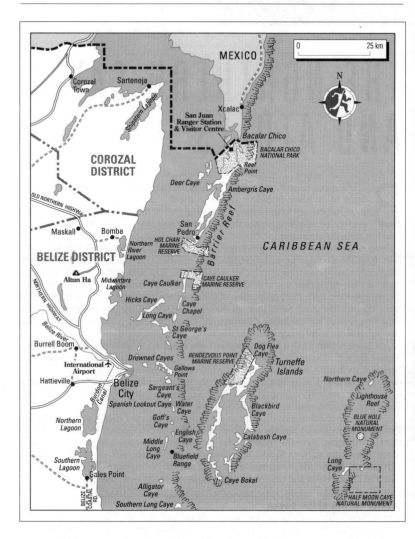

force sacked the caye and imprisoned 140 of the Baymen and 250 of their slaves. The Baymen returned in 1783 and took revenge on the Spanish fleet in 1798, during the celebrated **Battle of St George's Caye**.

Fishermen and turtlers continued to use the cayes as a base for their operations, and refugees fleeing the Caste Wars in the Yucatán towards the end of the nineteenth century also settled on the islands in small numbers. During the twentieth century the island population increased steadily, and the establishment of the **fishing cooperatives** in the 1960s brought improved traps, ice plants, and access to the export market – though there's now the possibility that the lobster-fishing industry will destroy itself by overfishing. At around the same time came another boom, as the cayes of Belize, particularly Caye Caulker, became a hangout on the hippy trail, and then began to attract more lucrative custom. The islanders generally welcomed these visitors and a new-found prosperity began to transform life on the cayes.

Ambergris Caye and San Pedro

The most northerly and by far the largest of the cayes is **Ambergris Caye**, separated from Mexico by the narrow Bacalar Chico channel, dug by the ancient Maya. The island's main attraction is the former fishing village of **SAN PEDRO**, facing the reef just a few kilometres from the caye's southern tip, 58km northeast of Belize City. If you fly into San Pedro the views are breathtaking: the sea appears so clear and shallow as to barely cover the sandy bed, while the pure white line of the reef crest dramatically separates the vivid blue of the open sea from the turquoise water on its leeward side.

San Pedro is not a large town, but its population of two thousand is the biggest of any of the cayes. Although you're never more than a stone's throw from the Caribbean – the town takes up the whole width of the island – in the built-up area most of the palms have died or been cut down, and traffic has increased in recent years, creating deep ruts (which become mud holes after rain) in the sandy streets. But despite development, the town just about manages to retain its feeling of Caribbean charm, with two-storey, clapboard buildings still predominating in the centre. San Pedro is the main destination for most visitors to Belize, and the tourist industry here caters mainly for North Americans – almost all prices are quoted in US dollars. Some of the most exclusive hotels, restaurants and bars in Belize are here; the only budget places are in the original village of San Pedro.

Getting to Ambergris Caye from Belize City is simple. As well as half-hourly **flights**, there are regular **fast boats**, which take around ninety minutes to reach San Pedro; full transport details are given on p.82.

Arrival and information

Arriving boats usually dock at the *Coral Beach* or Texaco piers on the front (reef) side of the island, though the *Thunderbolt* docks at *Cesario's* at the back of the island at the end of Black Coral Street. Arriving at either **dock**, you're pretty much in the centre. If you land at the **airport**, there are golf buggies and taxis to take you to your hotel, though it's only a short walk to anywhere in town. Formerly called Front, Middle and Back streets, the town's three **main streets**, running parallel to the beach, have been given names in keeping with the new upmarket image – Barrier Reef Drive, Pescador Drive and Angel Coral Street – but in any case, it's impossible to get lost.

San Pedro's **tourist office** shares a building with the Ambergris Museum on Barrier Reef Drive (see overleaf) – Ambergris Caye also has one of the best **Web sites** in the country (*www.ambergriscaye.com*), with links to most of the businesses on the island. It's always worth picking up a copy of *The San Pedro Sun* or *Ambergris Today*, the island's **tourist newspapers** (US$0.40), available from most hotels and restaurants, while San Pedro's own **radio station**, Reef Radio, broadcasts good music and news around forthcoming events.

To arrange international flights and trips throughout the country, try Travel and Tour Belize (☎026/2031, *traveltourbelize.com*), on Coconut Drive just north of the airstrip. You needn't worry about **changing money**, as travellers' cheques and US dollars are accepted – even preferred – everywhere; banks on Front Street will give **cash advances**. San Pedro's **post office** (Mon–Fri 8am–4.30pm) is in the Alijua building opposite the Atlantic Bank (best for cash advances). There are two **laundries** on Pescador Drive.

Accommodation

Most of the hotels in San Pedro are just a short walk or taxi ride from the airport. All but a couple are outside the reach of budget travellers, though there are some slightly cheaper options along Front and Middle streets. It's risky turning up at Christmas or Easter unless you've **booked a room**; at other times you should be OK, though if you do book in advance you might get a worthwhile discount.

Caribbean Villas Hotel, just over 1km along the road south from town (☎026/2715, *c-v-hotel@btl.net*). The best-value small hotel in this range, with spacious, very comfortable rooms and suites, all with sea views, and plenty of peace and quiet. ⑧.

Changes in Latitudes, 1km south of town, near the Belize Yacht Club (☎ & fax 026/2986, *latitudes@btl.net*). Very friendly small B&B half a block from the beach, with immaculately clean a/c rooms, and a communal kitchen. The Canadian owner, Lori, is a mine of information. ⑦.

Coconuts, on the beach 1km south of town (☎026/3500, *coconuts@btl.net*). Comfortable modern hotel with clean, well-decorated tiled rooms, all with a/c and balconies. Rates include the free use of bikes and a decent breakfast buffet. ⑧.

Coral Beach Hotel, corner of Barrier Reef Drive and Black Coral Street (☎026/2013, *forman@btl.net*). Nineteen comfortable rooms with private bath, fan or a/c in a rambling wooden building with balconies front and back. Good packages for dive groups. ⑤–⑦.

Hideaway Lodge, 1km south of town, just past the Texaco station (☎026/2141, *hideaway@btl.net*l). Rooms with fan or a/c in a wooden building; especially good value for groups or longer-term stays, and there's a pool and restaurant. ⑥.

Martha's, Pescador Drive, across from *Elvi's Kitchen* (☎026/2053). Clean, comfortable rooms with fan and private bath with hot water. Rooms have better views and increased rates the higher up they are. ⑤.

Ruby's, Barrier Reef Drive, a short walk from the airstrip (☎026/2063, *wamcg@cowichan.com*). Clean, comfortable, family-run hotel on the seafront. Rooms on the higher floors cost more, but all are good value. ④–⑤.

San Pedrano, corner of Barrier Reef Drive and Caribeña Street (☎2054, fax 2093). Quiet, clean hotel in a wooden building set back slightly from the sea, but with good views and breezy verandas. Comfortable rooms with private bath. ⑥.

Exploring the caye and the reef

The **water** is the focus of daytime entertainment on Ambergris Caye, from sunbathing on the docks to windsurfing, sailing, fishing, diving, snorkelling and glass-bottomed boat rides. Many hotels rent equipment, and there are several specialist **dive shops** offering instruction. A word of **warning**: there have been a number of accidents in San Pedro where speeding boats have hit people swimming off the piers. A line of buoys, clearly visible, indicates the "safe area", but speedboat drivers can be a bit macho, so be careful when choosing where to swim.

Before going snorkelling or diving, whet your appetite with a visit to the excellent **Hol Chan Marine Reserve office** (Mon–Sat 8.30am–5pm; ☎026/2247) on Caribeña Street, near the Texaco station on the lagoon side. The staff are happy to answer any questions and there are photographs, maps and other displays on the reserve (see p.76). Equally worthwhile is a visit to the **Ambergris Museum** on Barrier Reef Drive (variable opening hours; US$2.50), whose exhibits – ranging from Maya pottery to weapons and old photographs – illustrate the island's history right up to the 1960s.

Bikes, mopeds and very expensive golf carts can be rented for exploring the caye on the rough tracks that run north and south from town; for bikes, try Joe's Bike Rental, at the south end of Pescador Drive (☎026/4371; US$9 for 24hr, US$39 for a week). Heading **south**, you could ride at least part of the way to **Marco Gonzalez**, a Maya ruin near the southernmost tip of the island, though there's not much to see. **North**, after about ten minutes' walk you'll come up against the **Boca del Rio** channel, crossed by a tiny ferry (US$0.50), on the other side of which are some secluded resorts and beaches. A **fast ferry**, the *Island Express* (US$5 each way), runs several times a day from Fido's dock, in the centre of town, to the resorts in the north of the caye.

You could also take a guided day-trip to some of the **Maya sites** on the northwest coast of the island – Daniel Nuñez (☎026/2314) is one of the best guides. On **San Juan** beach you'll be scrunching over literally thousands of pieces of Maya pottery, but perhaps the most spectacular site is **Chac Balam**, a ceremonial and administrative centre with deep burial chambers. On the way back, you navigate **Bacalar Chico**, the channel separating Belize from Mexico, now a **national park** and marine reserve with a visitor centre and some great snorkelling. At the mouth of the channel the reef is close to the shore; the boat has to cross into the open sea, re-entering the lagoon as you approach San Pedro and so completing a circumnavigation of the island.

Diving

For anyone who has never dived in the tropics before, the **reefs near San Pedro** are fine, but more experienced divers may be disappointed. This is a heavily used area which has long been subject to intensive fishing, and much of the reef has been plundered by souvenir hunters. To experience the best diving in Belize, you need to take a trip out to one of the **atolls**.

Open water certification, which takes novices up to the standard of a qualified sport diver, costs around US$350, while a more basic **resort course** is US$125. For qualified divers a two-tank dive costs around US$50, including tanks, weights, air and boat. One of the best local **operators** is Amigos Del Mar, just north of the centre (☎026/2706). A **live-aboard dive boat**, the *Offshore Express* (☎026/2817), allows you visit the outer atolls, including the Blue Hole and Half Moon Caye (see p.81). A typical two-day trip costs around US$250, including meals and five dives; you can be picked up from Caye Caulker at no extra cost, though you'll usually need to reserve in advance. To book the best dive operators or dive boats contact the Blue Hole Dive Center, on Front Street, near the *Spindrift Hotel* (☎ & fax 026/2982, *bluehole@btl.net*), which has details of all local operators and dive boats. The best dive shops in San Pedro recommend you make a voluntary contribution of US$1 per tank to help fund the town's hyperbaric chamber.

Snorkelling and other trips

Just about every hotel in San Pedro offers **snorkelling** trips, costing around US$20 for three hours, plus about US$5 to rent equipment. **Snorkelling guides** here (who must also be licensed tour guides) have lots of experience and will show you how to use the equipment before you set off. Two of the best local guides are Alfonso Graniel (☎014/5450) and Dino Gonzalez (☎026/2422). Several boats take snorkellers out for a **day-trip to Caye Caulker**, employing a mix of motor and sail and returning to San Pedro around sunset. Boat trips are also available north to the spectacular **Mexico Rocks** or **Rocky Point** or, more commonly, south to the Hol Chan Marine Reserve (see overleaf) and **Shark-Ray Alley**. Day-trips are available on board *Rum Punch II* (☎026/2340; US$45), a ten-metre sailboat, and the 22-metre, motor-powered *Winnie Estelle* (☎026/2982; US$55), with a spacious, shaded deck and an open bar – both supremely relaxing experiences.

At Shark-Ray Alley you can swim in shallow water with three-metre **nurse sharks** and enormous **stingrays** – an extremely popular (but controversial) attraction. Watching these creatures glide effortlessly beneath you is an exhilarating experience and, despite their reputations, swimming here poses almost no danger to snorkellers, as humans are not part of their normal diet. Biologists, however, claim that the practice of feeding the fish to attract them alters their natural behaviour, and at times the area is so crowded that

SAFEGUARDING THE BARRIER REEF

Coral reefs are among the most complex and fragile ecosystems on earth. Colonies have been growing at a rate of less than 5cm a year for thousands of years; once damaged, the coral is far more susceptible to bacteria, which can quickly lead to large-scale irreversible damage. All tour guides in Belize are schooled in reef ecology before being granted a licence (which must be displayed as they guide), and if you go on an organized trip, as most people do, the guide will brief you on the following precautions to avoid damage to the reef.

- Never anchor boats on the reef – use the permanently secured buoys.
- Never touch or stand on corals – protective cells are easily stripped away from the living polyps on their surface, destroying them and thereby allowing algae to enter.
- Don't remove shells, sponges or other creatures from the reef, or buy reef products from souvenir shops.
- Avoid disturbing the seabed around corals – quite apart from spoiling visibility, clouds of sand settle over corals, smothering them.
- If you're either a beginner or an out-of-practice diver, practise away from the reef first.
- Don't use suntan lotion in reef areas – the oils remain on the water's surface. Wear a t-shirt instead to protect your skin from sunburn.
- Check you're not in one of the marine reserves before fishing.
- Don't feed or interfere with fish or marine life; this can harm not only sea creatures and the food chain, but snorkellers too – large fish may attack, trying to get their share!

any hope of communing with nature is completely lost amongst the flailing bodies of other snorkellers. **Night snorkelling**, an amazing experience, is also available.

The best **windsurfing and sailing** rental and instruction on the caye is offered by Sailsports Belize (☎026/4488, *sailsports@btl.net*), on the beach in front of the *Holiday Hotel*. Sailboard rental costs US$20–25 an hour, US$65–75 for a seven-hour day, depending on the style of board; sailboat rental is US$30 an hour, US$115 a day. Seaduced By Belize, run by superb naturalist guide Elito Arceo (☎014/6049, *seabelize@btl.net*), has the best guided **kayak tours** (US$40 per half-day), visiting the lagoons and mangroves to spot birds and other wildlife.

Day-trips from San Pedro to the ruins of **Altun Ha** (see p.68) are increasingly popular. Rounding the southern tip of the island in a fast skiff, you head for the mainland at the mouth of the Northern River, cross the lagoon and travel up the river to the tiny village of Bomba, where a van waits to take you to the site. With a good guide this is an excellent way to spot wildlife, including crocodiles and manatees, and the riverbank trees are often adorned with orchids. The best guide is Daniel Nuñez (☎026/2314).

The Hol Chan Marine Reserve
The **Hol Chan Reserve**, 8km south of San Pedro, at the southern tip of the caye, takes its name from the Maya for "little channel", and it is this break in the reef that forms the focus of the reserve. Its three zones – covering a total of around thirteen square kilometres – preserve a comprehensive cross-section of the marine environment, from coral reef through seagrass beds to mangroves. All three habitats are closely linked: many reef fish feed on the seagrass beds, and the mangroves are a nursery area for juvenile fish. As your boat approaches, you'll be met by a warden who explains the rules and collects the **entry fee** (US$2.50).

A great deal of damage has already been caused by snorkellers standing on the coral or holding onto outcrops for a better look – on all the easily accessible areas of the reef you will clearly see the white, dead patches, especially on the large brain coral heads. **Never touch** the coral – not only does it damage the delicate ecosystem (see box opposite), it can also sting and cause agonizing burns, and even brushing against the razor-sharp ridges on the reef top can cause cuts that are slow to heal.

Eating drinking and nightlife

There are plenty of places to eat in San Pedro, and you'll usually get good service, though **prices** are generally higher than elsewhere in Belize. **Seafood** is prominent at most restaurants, and you can also rely on plenty of steak, shrimp, chicken, pizza and salads. There are several **Chinese** restaurants too, and in the evening several inexpensive **fast-food stands** open for business along the front of Central Park. **Buying your own food** isn't much of a bargain here: there's no market and the supermarkets are stocked with expensive imported canned goods.

Restaurants

Cannibal Café, on the front, just past the *Holiday Hotel*. Tasty, well-priced snacks and light meals on a palm-shaded deck overlooking the sea. Good seafood, and very good fish and chips.

El Patio, towards the southern end of the town, next to the second Rock's supermarket. Fine dining at very reasonable prices in a lovely courtyard.

Elvi's Kitchen, across the road from *Martha's* hotel. The place for seafood, burgers and fries, accompanied by delicious, *licuado*-like fruit drinks. Slick service and upmarket prices.

Jade Garden, Coconut Drive, south of town. The town's best Chinese restaurant – and good value, too.

JamBel, on the park, next to *Big Daddy's Disco*. A friendly, good-value place serving a very tasty blend of Jamaican and Belizean specialities, such as jerk chicken, pork, fish and curry, washed down with Belikin or Red Stripe.

The Reef, near the north end of Pescador. Good Belizean food, including delicious seafood, at great prices.

Ruby's Cafe, Barrier Reef Drive, next to *Ruby's Hotel*. Delicious home-made cakes, pies and sandwiches, and freshly brewed coffee. Opens at 6am, so it's a good place to order a packed lunch if you're going on a trip.

Sweet Basil, 500m north of Boca del Rio (☎026/3869). A gem of a café and deli and well worth making the effort to visit. Great pasta, seafood, salads, Italian specialities and the best selection of cheeses in Belize. Closed Mon.

Woody's Wharf, south of town, behind the *Corona del Mar* hotel. Large portions of good seafood, Tex-Mex and Belizean dishes, and always a great daily special, served in a small *palapa* with a sand floor. A bargain for the island.

Bars and clubs

Some of the hotels have fancy bars, several of which offer **happy hours**, while back from the main street are a couple of small **cantinas** where you can buy a beer or a bottle of rum and drink with the locals. *Sandals Bar*, on the side street between *Martha's Hotel* and the park, is a friendly, long-established bar serving tasty *ceviche* and barbecue in the evenings. For the best beachside happy hour (5–7pm), head for *Crazy Canuk Bar* at the *Exotic Caye Resort*, where the resident band will get you in the party mood.

Big Daddy's **disco**, in and around a beach bar near the main dock, has early evening piano, and a lively reggae band later on; happy hour runs from 5 to 9pm. *Tarzan's Disco and Nite Club*, opposite the park, has the best dance floor, while the new, air conditioned *Barefoot Iguana*, on Coconut Drive just south of the Yacht Club, is home to San Pedro's biggest disco. Beyond here to the right, the tiny *Black and White Reggae Bar* is the focal point for the island's Garífuna community and a good place to enjoy drumming and punta rock.

Caye Caulker

South of Ambergris Caye and 35km northeast of Belize City, **Caye Caulker** is even more relaxed and easy-going than San Pedro, and more accessible for the budget traveller. Until recently, tourism existed almost as a sideline to the island's main source of income, **lobster fishing**, and there are always plenty of lobster for the annual **Lobster Fest**, held in the third weekend of June to celebrate the opening of the season. **Flights** on the San Pedro run stop at Caye Caulker's airstrip, though most visitors still arrive by **boat** from Belize City, from where there are departures every two hours (for full details, see p.82).

Arrival and information

The **airstrip** is about 1km south of the centre, within easy reach of the hotels south of the main dock; alternatively, you can take a golf-cart taxi. If you arrive at either the main "front" dock or the "back" docks, simply follow your nose to the **water-taxi office**, effectively the centre of the village. They can give **information** and will hold your luggage while you look for a place to stay, as will the tour offices listed in "Exploring the caye and the reef" on p.80; if you get a chance, look at the **Web site** *www.gocayecaulker .com* before you arrive. **Leaving for Belize City**, boats depart roughly every two hours from 6.30am to 3pm (5pm on weekends).

There are no street names in Caye Caulker village, but the street running along the shore at the front of the island is effectively "**Front Street**", with just one or two streets running behind it in the centre of the island. The **post office** is on the back street, south of the centre, and the **BTL** office on the corner leading to the main dock. There's **Internet** access at *CyberCafé*, just north of the *Sandbox Restaurant*. The Atlantic Bank, just south of the centre, gives Visa **cash advances** (US$5 fee), and an increasing number of businesses accept plastic. Tina Auxillou, who runs Caye Caulker's **travel agency**, Dolphin Bay Travel (☎ & fax 2214, *dolphinbay@btl.net*), is a fount of local information and can also book domestic and international flights. As yet there is little air conditioning on the island, which is fine most of the time, when a cooling breeze blows in from the sea, but **sandflies and mosquitoes** can cause almost unbearable irritation on calm days. Note that **tap water** on the caye should be regarded as unfit to drink; rainwater and bottled water are widely available.

Accommodation

Most of the year it's easy enough to find an inexpensive room, but to arrive at Christmas or New Year without a **reservation** could leave you stranded. Even the furthest **hotels** are no more than ten minutes' walk from the front dock and places are easy to find.

North from the front dock

Costa Maya Beach Cabañas, towards the Split (☎022/2432, *www.costamaya–belize.com*). New, clean rooms with bedside lights and private bath in hexagonal cabins, run by a friendly family. ⑤.

Mara's Place, towards the Split (☎022/2156). Six simple, comfortable and very good value wooden cabins with private bath, TV and porch. ⑤.

Miramar Hotel, Front Street, past the basketball court (☎022/2357). Good-value budget rooms with shared bath in a wooden building with a large balcony, overlooking the sea. ④.

Sandy Lane Hotel (☎022/2217). Small, clean and inexpensive, with rooms in the original wooden buiding and new ones in a concrete annexe at the back, plus more expensive concrete cabins in the grounds. ③–④.

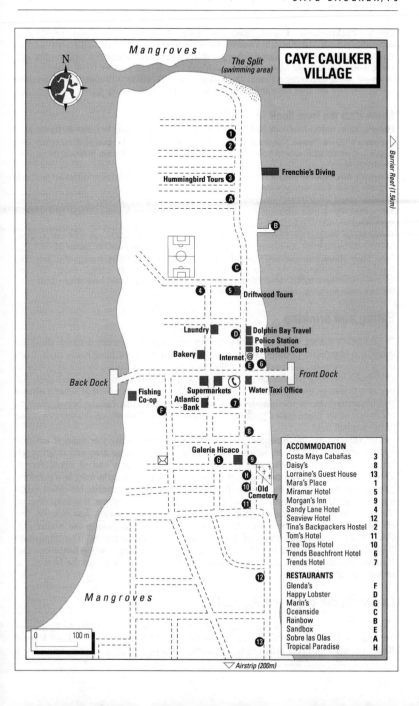

CAYE CAULKER VILLAGE

Mangroves

The Split (swimming area)

N

Barrier Reef (1.5km)

Frenchie's Diving

Hummingbird Tours ❸

Ⓐ

Ⓑ

Ⓒ

❹ ❺ Driftwood Tours

Laundry

Dolphin Bay Travel
Police Station
Basketball Court

Ⓓ

Bakery

Internet @
Ⓔ ❻

Back Dock

Front Dock

Fishing Co-op

Supermarkets

Water Taxi Office

Atlantic Bank

Ⓕ

❼

❽

Galería Hicaco

Ⓖ ❾

Ⓗ

❿ Old Cemetery

⓫

Mangroves

⓬

0   100 m

⓭

ACCOMMODATION

Costa Maya Cabañas	3
Daisy's	8
Lorraine's Guest House	13
Mara's Place	1
Miramar Hotel	5
Morgan's Inn	9
Sandy Lane Hotel	4
Seaview Hotel	12
Tina's Backpackers Hostel	2
Tom's Hotel	11
Tree Tops Hotel	10
Trends Beachfront Hotel	6
Trends Hotel	7

RESTAURANTS

Glenda's	F
Happy Lobster	D
Marin's	G
Oceanside	C
Rainbow	B
Sandbox	E
Sobre las Olas	A
Tropical Paradise	H

▽ Airstrip (200m)

Tina's Backpackers Hostel, 20m past *Costa Maya*, facing the sea (☎022/2214, *dolphinbay@btl.net*). Dorm beds in a wooden house, with communal kitchen; US$10 per person.

Trends Beachfront Hotel, immediately right of the Front Dock (☎022/2094, *trendsbze@btl.net*). Large rooms (⑤) in a new wooden building with comfortable beds and tiled floors. There's another *Trends* round the corner on Front Street (left at the BTL office) with slightly less expensive rooms (④); both are good value and are linked to the *Trends* in Belize City (p.54).

South from the front dock

Daisy's, 250m south of the dock (☎022/2150). Simple budget rooms run by a friendly family. ④.

Lorraine's Guest House, 75m south of the *Seaview* (☎022/2002). A bargain near the beach, with simple but comfortable cabins, run by the friendly Alamilla family; Orlando makes great wooden souvenirs. ④.

Morgan's Inn, opposite Galería Hicaco (☎022/2178, *sbf@btl.net*). Quiet, roomy cabins set just back from the beach. Cold-water showers only. ④–⑤.

Seaview Hotel, (☎022/2205, *seaview@btl.net*). On the beach, south of *Tom's*. Four very comfortable rooms with private bathroom and fridge, plus a one-bedroom wooden cottage for US$225 a week. ⑥.

Tom's Hotel (☎022/2102, *toms@btl.net*). Just beyond *Tree Tops*, with 20 clean, tiled rooms (most with private bathrooms) in a concrete building with all-round balcony, and five cabins. ⑤.

Tree Tops Hotel, just beyond Tropical Paradise restaurant (☎022/2008, treetops@btl.net). The best hotel on the island for the price, just 50m from the water, with very helpful owners. The comfortable rooms have fridge, cable TV and powerful ceiling fans (most also have private bathroom, and one room has a/c); booking advisable. ⑤.

Eating and drinking

Good home cooking, large portions and very reasonable prices are features of all the island's restaurants. **Lobster** (in season) is served in every imaginable dish, from curry to chow mein; **seafood** is generally good value, accompanied by rice or potatoes. Otherwise, evening entertainment mostly consists of relaxing in a restaurant over dinner or a drink, or gazing at the tropical night sky. You can buy food at several **shops** and supermarkets on the island. Many houses also advertise banana bread, coconut cakes and other home-baked goodies, and there's a good **bakery** on the street leading to the football field.

The village's **restaurants** include *Marin's Restaurant*, along the main street one block back from the shore, which has a shady outdoor dining area and is great for breakfasts and seafood. Around the corner, at the southern end of Front Street, *Tropical Paradise* serves good-quality Belizean and American-style food in a comfortable a/c dining room. At the back of the island, *Glenda's* is a favourite breakfast meeting place, serving great cinnamon rolls. The island's best restaurant, the *Sand Box*, by the main dock, serves Italian/American food and is often packed. Just beyond, the *Happy Lobster*, serves good-value local dishes. Walking north along the waterfront, you'll come to a proliferation of **beach bars and restaurants**. The *Oceanside Restaurant* has good food and service and occasional live music, while further on the *Rainbow Restaurant*, on a deck over the water, and *Sobre Las Olas*, are the best of the restaurants this end of the island.

Exploring the caye and the reef

Caye Caulker is a little over 7km long, with the southern, inhabited end curving away west like a hook; the northern tip of the island forms the **Caye Caulker Forest Reserve**, while the reef offshore is a **marine reserve**. At the northern end of Caye

Caulker village you come to "**The Split**", a narrow (but widening) channel cut by Hurricane Hattie in 1961 and a popular place to relax and swim. It's also a glaring example of what happens when mangroves are cut down – the original owner of the beach bar here removed them to build a dock, and the subsequent erosion now threatens to wash the bar away.

The **reef** is certainly an experience not to be missed: swimming along coral canyons accompanied by an astonishing range of fish, with perhaps even the odd shark or two (these will almost certainly be harmless nurse sharks). Here, as everywhere, snorkellers should be aware of the fragility of the reef and be careful not to touch any coral – even sand stirred up by fins can cause damage (see p.76 for reef etiquette).

Trips to the reef by skiff (US$10–20 per person, depending where you go, plus US$3-4 for snorkel equipment rental; around 3hr) are easily arranged; contact Meldie at Driftwood Snorkeling (☎022/2011), on the front north of the centre, or Carlos Ayala (☎014/9986). One of the best day outings is offered by Ras Creek, in his dory *Rice 'n' Beans* (US$12.50), which sails from the main dock in the morning – you're almost certain to encounter nurse sharks and eagle rays. **Kayaks** are available too: try *Daisy's* hotel or ask at the Galería Hicaco (☎022/2178), where you can also rent a **sailboard**. The Galería's owner, marine biologist Ellen McRae, gives really well-informed **wildlife tours** (US$15–25).

Diving trips and scuba instruction are available from Frenchie's, towards the northern end of the village (☎022/2234), who offer enthusiastic, knowledgeable local trips, with some great reef diving and coral gardens, plus day-trips to the Blue Hole (see below). Caye Caulker is a good base for **day-trips** to the **other cayes**, especially Goff's, English and Sergeant's cayes for **dolphin** and **manatee** spotting; ask at Driftwood.

The northern atolls

Although Caye Caulker and San Pedro are the only villages anywhere on the reef, there are a couple of dozen other inhabited islands, some of them supporting fishing camps or upmarket resorts and lodges. Buildings are low-key, wooden and sometimes thatched, and the group you're with will probably be the only people staying there. There are no phones (most are in radio contact with Belize City), electricity comes from a generator, and views of palm trees curving over turquoise water reinforce the sense of isolation. Prices at these resorts are high, but include transport from Belize City or the international airport, accommodation, all meals, and usually diving or fishing.

The virtually uninhabited **Turneffe Islands**, 40km from Belize City, comprise an oval archipelago of low-lying mangrove islands around a shallow lagoon 60km long, enclosed by a beautiful coral reef. You can visit the archipelago as part of a day-trip from Caye Caulker. The construction of resorts on this remote and fragile island has resulted in the controversial destruction of mangroves, while a proposed marine reserve has yet to be established.

About 80km east of Belize City is Belize's outermost atoll, **Lighthouse Reef**, home to the underwater attractions of the Great Blue Hole and Half Moon Caye Natural Monument, while there are also several **shipwrecks** which have formed artificial reefs. The **Blue Hole**, technically a karst-eroded sinkhole, is a shaft over 300m in diameter and 135m deep, which drops through the bottom of the lagoon and opens out into a complex network of caves and crevices; its depth gives it an astonishing deep blue colour. You can visit the atoll either as a day or overnight trip from San Pedro or Caye Caulker.

The **Half Moon Caye Natural Monument**, the first marine conservation area in Belize, was declared a national park in 1982 and became one of Belize's first World

Heritage Sites in 1996. The 180,000-square-metre caye is divided into two distinct ecosystems. In the west, guano from thousands of seabirds fertilizes the soil, allowing the growth of dense vegetation, while the eastern half has mostly coconut palms growing in the sand. A total of 98 bird species has been recorded here, including frigate birds, ospreys, and a resident population of four thousand **red-footed boobies**, one of only two such nesting colonies in the Caribbean. The boobies came by their name because they display no fear of humans, moving only reluctantly when visitors stroll among them – their nesting area is accessible from a platform. The resident reserve wardens will collect the US$5 **visitor fee** and can give permission to **camp** (US$5per person).

travel details

FLIGHTS

Maya Island Air (☎02/31362) and Tropic (☎026/2012 in San Pedro) between them operate flights between Belize City and San Pedro, calling at Caye Caulker on request, every hour from 7am to 5pm (25min).

BOATS

All boats to and from San Pedro stop at Caye Caulker on the way.

Belize City to San Pedro (1hr 25min; US$15): the *Triple J* (☎02/44375) leaves Courthouse Wharf at 9am; *Andrea* (☎026/2578) leaves Courthouse Wharf at 3pm; *Thunderbolt* leaves the Swing Bridge at 1pm. Some services from Marine Terminal to Caye Caulker continue on to San Pedro.

San Pedro to Belize City (1hr 25min; US$15): *Triple J* at 3pm; *Andrea* and *Thunderbolt* at 7am; other boats leave at 8am & 2.30pm.

Belize City to Caye Caulker (45min; US$7.50): from the Marine Terminal approximately every 2hr from 9am to 5pm.

Caye Caulker to Belize City (45min; US$7.50): departures every 2hr between 6.30am and 3.30pm (5pm on weekends). It's best to book a day ahead at the water-taxi office by the main dock (☎022/2992).

CHAPTER 4

CAYO AND THE WEST

H eading west from Belize City towards the Guatemalan border, you travel through a wide range of landscapes, from open grassland to rolling hills and dense tropical forest. A fast, paved road, the **Western Highway**, runs to the border, a route that takes you from the heat and humidity of the coast to the lush foothills of the Maya Mountains. Before reaching Belize's tiny, almost lifeless capital, **Belmopan**, the road passes several places of interest: the **Belize Zoo**, the **Monkey Bay Wildlife Sanctuary** and the **Guanacaste National Park**, at the junction with the Hummingbird Highway to Dangriga.

West of Belmopan, following the Belize River valley, the road skirts the foothills of the **Maya Mountains**, a beautiful area where the air is clear and the land astonishingly fertile. You're now in **Cayo District**, the largest of Belize's six districts and arguably the most beautiful – a sentiment enthusiastically endorsed by the inhabitants when they declare that "the west is the best". South of the road, the **Mountain Pine Ridge** is a pleasantly cool region of hills and pine woods traversed by good dirt roads. **San Ignacio**, on the Macal River, is Cayo's busiest town and the ideal base for exploring the forests, rivers and ruins of western Belize. South of San Ignacio, deep in the jungle of the Vaca plateau, lie the ruins of **Caracol**, the largest Maya site in Belize.

Between San Ignacio and the Guatemalan border, the road climbs past the hilltop ruins of **Cahal Pech** then descends, following the valley of the Mopan River 15km to the frontier bridge. A few kilometres before the border, at the village of **San José Succotz**, an ancient ferry crosses the river, allowing access to the Maya site of **Xunantunich**, from the top of which you can look out over the Guatemalan department of Petén.

Belize City to San Ignacio

Leaving Belize City, the well-paved Western Highway skirts the shoreline, running behind a tangle of mangrove swamps. After 26km the road passes through **Hattieville** (named after the 1961 hurricane), where an unpaved turning north to **Burrell Boom** is used as a short cut to the Northern Highway, bypassing Belize City. If time permits you should allow an hour or two visit the **Belize Zoo**, one of the finest in Latin America. You'd need to stay at least overnight to fully appreciate the **Monkey Bay Wildlife Sanctuary**, but **Guanacaste National Park** is another worthwhile stop right by the roadside. For most people the capital, **Belmopan**, is no more than a break in the bus ride, though if you're heading south for Dangriga or Placencia this is the place to change buses. Beyond Belmopan the landscape becomes a little more hilly and a few unpaved **side roads** head south into the uplands, leading to some of Belize's most spectacular scenery. However, you're better off continuing to the delightful riverside town of **San Ignacio** (see p.87) for a night or two's stay.

For an explanation of **accommodation price codes**, see p.40.

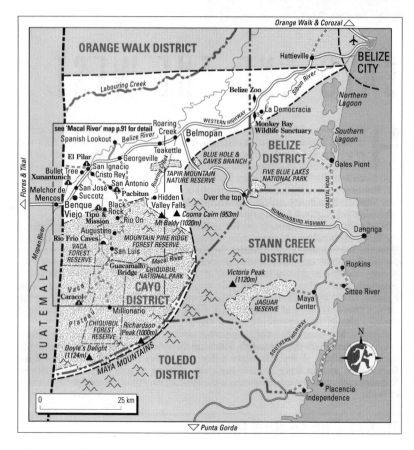

The Belize Zoo

The first point of interest along the highway is the **Belize Zoo**, at Mile 29 (daily 8.30am–5pm; US$7.50; *www.belizezoo.org*), easily visited on a half-day trip from Belize City or as a stop on the way west. Probably the finest zoo in the Americas south of the US, and long recognized as a phenomenal conservation achievement, the zoo originally opened in 1983 after an ambitious wildlife film (*Path of the Raingods*) left Sharon Matola (the film's production assistant, now zoo director), with a collection of semi-tame animals no longer able to fend for themselves in the wild.

The zoo is organized around the theme of "a walk through Belize", and offers the chance to see the country's native animals at close quarters, housed in spacious enclosures which closely resemble their natural habitat – residents include all the Belizean cats, some of which, including the jaguars, have bred successfully here. To **get to the zoo** take any bus between Belize City and Belmopan and ask the driver to drop you at the sign; a 200-metre walk from the entrance and visitor centre.

One kilometre past the zoo, the **Coastal Road** (in good condition, and served by buses) provides an unpaved short cut, marked by a sign and a couple of bars, to Gales Point (see p.100) and Dangriga. A kilometre or so past the junction, on the left, is *Cheers*, a friendly **bar** run by a Canadian family, where you can get good food at reasonable prices, and reliable information.

Monkey Bay Wildlife Sanctuary and Guanacaste Park

Half a kilometre past *Cheers* and 300m off the Western Highway is the **Monkey Bay Wildlife Sanctuary** (☎081/3032, *mbay@btl.net*), a 44-square-kilometre protected area extending to the Sibun River, which offers birding and nature trails through five distinct types of vegetation and habitat. Adjoining the sanctuary is the **Monkey Bay National Park**, enclosing a biological corridor which runs south through karst limestone hills to connect with the Manatee Forest Reserve. Facilities include a field research station for student groups, with an excellent library and small museum. Apart from being a relaxing place **to stay**, either in a bunkhouse (US$7.50) or camping (US$5) on raised platforms under thatched shelters, Monkey Bay is a viable experiment in sustainable living, using solar power, rainwater catchment and biogas fuel for cooking; the food (some of it grown in the station's organic gardens) is plentiful and delicious.

Five hundred metres beyond Monkey Bay along the Western Highway is *JB's Bar* (☎081/3025, *www.jbbelize.com*; ⑤), with comfortable, well-priced **rooms** enjoying views over the forested Sibun valley and a **restaurant** serving Belizean and Tex-Mex food. Just 2km before the turning for Belmopan, a 2.5km track leads off right to the *Banana Bank Lodge* (☎081/2020, *www.bananabank.com*; ⑧ including breakfast) on the north bank of the Belize River, with beautifully furnished wood-and-thatch cabañas and superb horse riding.

At the junction with the Hummingbird Highway, 73km from Belize City, is the **Guanacaste National Park** (US$2.50), where you can wander through a superb area of lush tropical forest at the confluence of Roaring Creek and the Belize River. There's an orchid display at the visitor centre, and several short **trails** which head through the park and along the riverbank The main attraction is a 40-metre **guanacaste** or tubroos tree, which supports some 35 other plant species, including a huge range of bromeliads, orchids, ferns, cacti and strangler figs. As the park is so close to the road, your chances of seeing any four-footed **wildlife** are fairly slim, but howler monkeys use the park as a feeding ground. Birds, however, abound, with over eighty species, among them blue-crowned motmots, parrots and squirrel cuckoos.

Belmopan

From Guanacaste Park the Western Highway pushes on towards San Ignacio and the Guatemalan border, while the **Hummingbird Highway** heads south 2km to the turn-off for **BELMOPAN**, before continuing to Dangriga. Belmopan was founded in 1970 after Hurricane Hattie swept much of Belize City into the sea. The government decided to use the disaster as a chance to move to higher ground and, in a Brasília-style bid to focus development on the interior, chose a site in the geographical heart of the country. The name of the city combines the words "Belize" and "Mopan", the language spoken by the Maya of Cayo. The layout of the main government buildings, designed in the 1960s, is modelled on a Maya city, grouped around a central plaza. In classic new-town terms Belmopan was meant to symbolize the dawn of a new era, with tree-lined avenues, banks, a couple of embassies and telecommunications worthy of a world centre. Today it has all the essential ingredients bar one: people.

Arriving in the market square or bus station, the first thing that strikes you is a sense of space, but unless you've come to visit the government's archeology, archives or immigration departments, there's little reason to stay any longer than it takes your bus to leave.

Practicalities

Buses from Belize City to San Ignacio, Benque Viejo and Dangriga all pass through Belmopan, so there's at least one service every thirty minutes in either direction – the last bus from Belmopan to Belize City leaves at 7pm; to San Ignacio, at 10pm. **Heading south** along the Hummingbird Highway, buses leave roughly every hour from 7am until 6pm. At the moment all buses pull up on the square in front of the small market except Novelo's, which has a terminal and ticket office on the side of the square.

The nearest **restaurant** is the *Caladium*, beside the Novelo's bus terminal, while the nearby *International Café* has vegetarian meals. There are also **banks** close to where the buses stop (including Barclays, for cash advances), a bakery and a small market. **Internet** access is available at *Techno Hub* (Mon–Sat 8am–8.30pm) in the Novelo's terminal. The **immigration** office is in the main government building by the fire station; this building also houses the Land Tax office, where you can buy **topographic maps** of Belize. The **British High Commission** (☎08/22146) is situated on the North Ring Road.

Belmopan to San Ignacio

Beyond Belmopan the scenery becomes more rugged, with thickly forested ridges to the south. The road stays close to the valley of the Belize River, passing through a series of villages. There's been something of an accommodation boom along this route, with a couple of long-established cottage-style lodges now joined by several newer enterprises. One of the best is *Pook's Hill Jungle Lodge* (☎081/2017, *pookshill @btl.net*; ⑨ including breakfast), 9km along a clearly signposted track from Teakettle village, 8km beyond the Belmopan junction. The lodge comprises nine cabañas set in a small clearing above a hillside terraced by the Maya, in a private nature reserve overlooking the thickly forested Roaring River valley, with breathtaking views across the strictly protected **Tapir Mountain Nature Reserve** (no public access) to Mountain Pine Ridge. Superb **horse-riding** across farmland and along forest trails is available.

At Mile 54, about 4km beyond, just across Warrie Head Creek, is the entrance to *Warrie Head Lodge* (☎02/75317, *www.belizenet.com/warrie*; ⑧), formerly a logging camp but now a working farm with comfortable rooms. On Barton Creek, at Mile 60, is *Caesar's Place* (☎09/22341, *blackrock@btl.net*; ⑥), a café and guesthouse with comfortable **rooms**, trailer hookups, space for camping and a fabulous gift shop.

At **Georgeville**, 26km from the Belmopan junction, the Chiquibul Road heads south from the highway to the **Mountain Pine Ridge Forest Reserve** (see p.93), reaching deep into the forest and crossing the Macal River at the Guacamallo Bridge, eventually leading to **Caracol** (see p.95). Twelve kilometres along the road **Green Hills Butterfly Ranch** (daily 8am–5pm; US\$4; ☎091/2017, *www.belizex.com/greenhills.htm*) has Belize's biggest and best collection of butterflies.

The highway continues for 9km to **Santa Elena**, San Ignacio's sister town on the eastern bank of the Macal River, which is crossed by the Hawksworth Bridge, built in 1949 and still the only road suspension bridge in Belize. Traffic from Belize City crosses the river on a low bridge (covered in high water) a little downstream; the suspension bridge is only used by westbound traffic.

San Ignacio and Cayo district

On the west bank of the Macal River, about 35km from Belmopan, **SAN IGNACIO** is a friendly, relaxed town that draws together the best of inland Belize. Surrounded by fast-flowing rivers and forested hills, it's an ideal base from which to explore the region, offering good food, inexpensive hotels and frequent bus connections. The evenings here are usually cool and the days fresh – a welcome break from the sweltering heat of the coast.

San Ignacio town is usually referred to as **Cayo** by locals (this is also the name you'll usually see on buses), the same word that the Spanish use to describe the offshore islands – an apt description of the area, which is set in a peninsula between two converging rivers. The early wave of the Spanish Conquest in 1544 made little impact here, and the area was a centre of rebellion in the following decades. **Tipu**, a Maya city on the Macal River about 9km south of the present-day town, was the capital of the province of Dzuluinicob, where for years the people resisted attempts to convert them to Christianity. **Spanish friars** arrived in 1618, but for years afterwards the population continued to practise idolatry – in 1641, Maya priests conducted a mock Mass to express their defiance towards a group of visiting Spanish clerics, and then threw them out. Tipu retained a measure of independence until 1707, when the population was forcibly removed to Lago de Petén Itzá in Guatemala.

Around this time **British loggers** (Baymen) arrived, seeking mahogany – like many places in modern Belize, San Ignacio probably started life as a logging camp. Spanish influence, never great, was by now in permanent decline, and the British were not interested in converting the remaining Maya – a map of 1787 simply states that the Maya of this general area were "in friendship with the Baymen". In addition to logging, San Ignacio became a centre for the shipment of **chicle**, the sap of the sapodilla tree and the basis of chewing gum. The self-reliant *chicleros*, as the collectors of chicle were called, knew the forest intimately, including the location of most, if not all, Maya ruins. When the demand for **Maya artefacts** sent black-market prices rocketing, some of them turned to looting.

Until the Western Highway was built in the 1930s local transport was by mule or water. It could take ten days of paddling to reach San Ignacio from Belize City, though small steamers later began to make the trip. Nowadays river traffic, which had almost died out, is enjoying something of a revival thanks to the increasing numbers of tourists. Indeed, a good time to visit San Ignacio is at the start of La Ruta Maya **canoe race**, held annually in early March, when teams of paddlers race all the way to Belize City. Anyone can enter, but local guides always win.

Arrival and information

Buses stop in the marketplace, behind Burns Avenue, the town's main street. Novelo's run regular services from Belize City, most of which continue to the Guatemalan border (30min); a shared **taxi** to the border costs only US$2 per person. You can **leave luggage** at Novelo's. too, or at *Mayawalk Bar*, easily visible from the bus stop and also good for information. Although there's no official **tourist office** in San Ignacio, Bob Jones, owner of the long-established *Eva's Bar* on Burns Avenue, is a good source of information. *Eva's* also has **Internet access**, as does *Top Cat* at 8 Hudson St – it's worth visiting the Cayo district's superb Web site at *www.belizex.com/cayo.htm*. Most other facilities can also be found on Burns Avenue, including **banks**, though there's no reliable ATM in town. The **post office** is next to Courts furniture store in the centre of town. **Laundry** can be done at *Martha's* on West Street, behind *Eva's*. For domestic and international **air tickets** go to Exodus Travel, 2 Burns Ave (☎09/24400).

Accommodation

The **hotels** in San Ignacio offer the best-value budget accommodation in the country and you'll almost always find space. For **camping**, try *Cosmos* or *Midas*, both listed opposite.

Central O'tel, 24 Burns Ave (☎09/23734, *easyrider@btl.net*). Simple, clean, good-value budget hotel with shared bathrooms; the balcony with hammocks is a great place from which to watch the street below. ③.

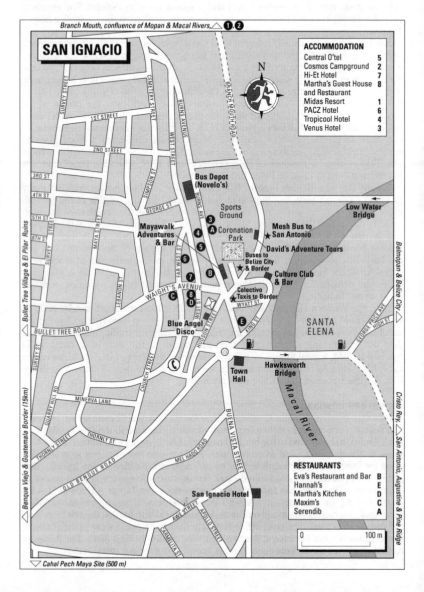

SAN IGNACIO

Branch Mouth, confluence of Mopan & Macal Rivers, △ ❶ ❷

N

ACCOMMODATION	
Central O'tel	5
Cosmos Campground	2
Hi-Et Hotel	7
Martha's Guest House and Restaurant	8
Midas Resort	1
PACZ Hotel	6
Tropicool Hotel	4
Venus Hotel	3

SURVEY STREET
CEMETERY STREET
1ST STREET
2ND STREET
3RD ST
4TH ST
SIMPSON ST
GEORGE ST
5TH ST
6TH ST
SURVEY STREET
MAYA STREET
LEBANON ST
BULLET TREE ROAD
SURVEY ST
QUARRY HILL RD
MINERVA LANE
THORNLY STREET
THORNLY ST
OLD BENQUE ROAD
MEL HADO ROAD
BUENA VISTA STREET
AVE STREET
APOLLO STREET
CARMELITA ST
CHURCH STREET
HUDSON STREET
WEST ST
FAR WEST ST
WAIGHT'S AVENUE
WYATT ST
KING ST
WEST STREET
BURNS AVENUE
BURNS AVE
BRANCH MOUTH ROAD

Bullet Tree Village & El Pilar Ruins ◁
Benque Viejo & Guatemala Border (15km) ◁

Bus Depot (Novelo's)
Sports Ground
Coronation Park
Mayawalk Adventures & Bar
Mesh Bus to ★ San Antonio
David's Adventure Tours
Buses to Belize City ★ & Border
Culture Club & Bar
Colectivo Taxis to Border
Blue Angel Disco
Town Hall
Hawksworth Bridge
Low Water Bridge

Ⓐ Ⓑ Ⓒ Ⓓ Ⓔ
③ ④ ⑤ ⑥ ⑦ ⑧

SANTA ELENA

Macal River

Belmopan & Belize City ◁
GEORGE PRICE AVE
HIGH ST
Cristo Rey, ◁ San Antonio, Augustine & Pine Ridge

San Ignacio Hotel

RESTAURANTS	
Eva's Restaurant and Bar	B
Hannah's	E
Martha's Kitchen	D
Maxim's	C
Serendib	A

0 ——— 100 m

▽ Cahal Pech Maya Site (500 m)

Cosmos Campground, a 15-minute walk from town along the road to Branch Mouth (☎09/22116, *cosmoscamping@btl.net*). Full camping facilities (US$3.50 per person), including showers, flush toilets and a kitchen. There are also clean, simple cabins, some with private bath. ②.

Hi-Et Hotel, West St, behind *Eva's* (☎09/22828). Family-run hotel with four upstairs rooms, each with a tiny balcony, all sharing a bathroom; the least expensive hotel in town, and phenomenally popular. ③.

Martha's Guest House, West St, behind *Eva's* (☎09/23647, *marthas@btl.net*). Very comfortable and good-value rooms, most with private bathroom and balcony, in a homely atmosphere; the restaurant is a favourite meeting place. ④.

Midas Resort, Branch Mouth Rd (☎09/23172, *midas@btl.net*). Very comfortable Maya-style thatched cabañas and newer wooden cabins, all with private bath, set on the riverbank; camping space is also available. ④–⑤.

PACZ Hotel, 4 Far West St, two blocks behind *Eva's* (☎09/22110, fax 22972). Five clean, comfortable rooms at bargain rates, sharing two hot-water showers. ④.

Tropicool Hotel, Burns Ave, 75m past *Eva's* (☎09/23052). Bright, clean budget rooms with shared hot-water bathrooms, a sitting room with TV and a laundry area. ③.

Venus Hotel, 29 Burns Ave (☎23203, *venus@btl.net*). Two-storey hotel, the biggest in town, with good rates and recently renovated rooms, most with tiled bathrooms, a/c and TV. ④–⑤.

Eating, drinking and nightlife

San Ignacio has several good, inexpensive **restaurants**. The Saturday **market** is the best in Belize, with local farmers bringing in freshly harvested produce, and you can pick up good fresh **bread** and and snacks at the Torres Bakery in West Street.

San Ignacio is a popular weekend spot for Belizeans and there's a range of **live music and dancing** on offer. The *Western Bar*, overlooking the market, is a typically Belizean **club**: dark and extremely noisy. Next door, overlooking the river, the *Culture Club* (above *El Cenote* sports bar) is a much better bet, with Latin and Afro-Cuban sounds mixing with Belizean beats. The *Blue Angel* disco, on Hudson Street, has bands at weekends, but has lost its pre-eminent position in the local music scene to the *Cahal Pech Tavern*, on the hilltop next to Cahal Pech Maya site.

Eva's Bar, 22 Burns Ave. Belizean dishes and daily specials, though service is variable. Usually busy in the evenings, when it's a great place to meet travellers and local tour operators.

Hannah's, 5 Burns Ave. Delicious, authentic Indian cuisine, freshly prepared and worth the wait.

Martha's Kitchen, West St, behind *Eva's*. Under the guesthouse of the same name, and just as well-run. Great breakfasts, local coffee, pizza and traditional Creole food. There's usually a vegetarian choice, and always delicious cakes for dessert.

Maxim's, Far West St, behind *Martha's*. One of the best of San Ignacio's numerous Chinese restaurants, with large portions.

Serendib Restaurant, 27 Burns Ave. Excellent Sri Lankan curries and seafood at very reasonable prices, and with good service too.

Around San Ignacio

The people of San Ignacio are justifiably proud of their beautiful river valley and the surrounding countryside, and there's plenty of outdoor action on offer, from relaxing **canoe trips** along the mostly gentle Macal River to tubing or **kayaking** along the faster Mopan River. The nearby farmland and forest is ideal for exploring on **horseback** or **mountain bike** and **caving** is increasingly popular. You can easily use San Ignacio as a base for day-trips with the tour operators listed in the box overleaf, but if you'd like to stay in the countryside, lodges, guesthouses and ranches in the area offer **cottage-style accommodation** and organized trips (see pp.92 & 93).

Cahal Pech

Twenty minutes out of town, clearly signposted along the Benque road, lie the ruins of **Cahal Pech** (daily 8am–5pm; US$5). The name means "place of ticks" in Mopan Maya,

---

INDEPENDENT TOUR OPERATORS IN SAN IGNACIO

Several small-scale, independent local operators offer good-value trips to attractions around San Ignacio and the list below covers a range of adventurous options. As always in Belize, make sure anyone offering you a guided trip is a **licensed tour guide** – they should display their photo-card guide licence. All the guides named below are either based in San Ignacio or will pick you up there. For **bike rental**, check at the *Crystal Paradise* office, across from the marketplace (☎09/22772), or at the *Tropicool Hotel* (☎09/23052).

David's Adventure Tours, office at far side of the marketplace (☎09/23674, *davidstours @hotmail.com*). David Simpson leads half-day canoe tours along an underground river, surrounded by Maya burials, to Barton Creek Cave; around US$25. See also *Guacamallo Jungle Camp*, p.92.

Easy Rider, contact Arts and Crafts on Burns Ave (☎09/23734, *easyrider@btl.net*). Charlie Collins organizes the best-value horse-riding packages in San Ignacio (US$25 for a half day; US$40 for a full day).

Eco Jungle Tours, office across from the post office (☎09/23425, *ecojungletours@hotmail .com*). Orlando Madrid offers canoe floats on the Macal River and jungle trips; around US$25. Also see *Hummingbird Cabañas*, p.92.

Everald's Caracol Shuttle, contact the *Crystal Paradise Resort* (see p.92; ☎09/22772, *cparadise@btl.net*). Everald Tut runs daily trips by minibus to Caracol ruins (US$50).

Mayawalk Adventures, contact the *Mayawalk Bar* (☎09/23070, *www.belizex .com.mayawalk*). Aaron Juan leads amazing trips into the Maya underworld, including the astonishing sacrificial cave of Actun Tunichil Muknal, and overnight caving and rock-climbing expeditions (US$65).

River Rat (☎093/7013, *riverratbelize@btl.net*). Gonzalo Pleitez lives way up the Macal River and arranges excellent whitewater kayak floats and jungle trips (US$45–80).

Toni's River Adventures contact Toni Santiago at *Eva's* or ring ☎09/23292. By far the longest-established and best-value guided canoe trip on the Macal River, costing under US$15 for an expert paddle upriver to the Rainforest Medicine Trail (see below) led by Toni Santiago. Also organizes fantastic overnight camping trips along the river.

---

and is certainly not how the elite families who ruled here in Classic times would have known it. Cahal Pech was the royal acropolis-palace of an elite Maya family during the Classic period, and there's evidence of monumental construction from at least as early as 400 BC, in the Middle Preclassic. There's also a **visitor centre** with a scale model of the site and a small **museum** with good display panels showing pictures of the site in its heyday and some artefacts.

The Macal River

Steep limestone cliffs and forested hills edge the lower **Macal River**, whose main tributaries rise in the Mountain Pine Ridge Forest Reserve and the Chiquibul Forest. In the upper reaches the water is sometimes fast and deep enough for **whitewater kayaking**, though you'll need an expert guide for this (see box above), and there's plenty of accommodation along the river in all price ranges. All the places listed below are also accessible by road, though for a couple of the accommodation options you might also need to cross the river in a canoe.

A canoe trip is by far the best way to visit the **Rainforest Medicine Trail** (daily 8am–noon & 1–4pm; US$5; *www.rainforestremedies.com*), 5km upriver from San Ignacio. The trail is dedicated to Don Eligio Panti, a Maya bush doctor or *curandero* who passed on his skills to Dr Rosita Arvigo at **Ix Chel Tropical Research Station**, where the trail begins. The medical knowledge of the Maya was extensive, and the trail is fascinating: among the plants you'll see the negrito tree, whose bark was once sold in Europe for its weight in gold as a cure for dysentery. The more mundane but equally effective products of the forest range from herbal teas to blood tonic; Traveller's

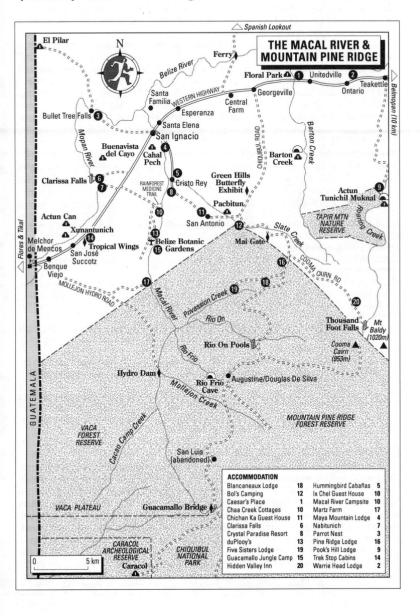

THE MACAL RIVER &
MOUNTAIN PINE RIDGE

ACCOMMODATION

Blancaneaux Lodge	18	Hummingbird Cabañas	5
Bol's Camping	12	Ix Chel Guest House	10
Caesar's Place	1	Macal River Campsite	10
Chaa Creek Cottages	10	Martz Farm	17
Chichan Ka Guest House	11	Maya Mountain Lodge	4
Clarissa Falls	6	Nabitunich	7
Crystal Paradise Resort	8	Parrot Nest	3
duPlooy's	13	Pine Ridge Lodge	16
Five Sisters Lodge	19	Pook's Hill Lodge	9
Guacamallo Jungle Camp	15	Trek Stop Cabins	14
Hidden Valley Inn	20	Warrie Head Lodge	2

Tonic, a preventative for diarrhoea, really works. There's also a comfortable wooden **guesthouse** (☎ 09/23870, *ixchel@btl.net*; ⑤) if you want to stay. A visit to the marvellous **Chaa Creek Natural History Centre**, next to the Medicine Trail (daily 8am–5pm; US$5), is the best introduction to Cayo's history, geography and wildlife, with fascinating displays on the region's flora and fauna, vivid archeological and geological maps, and a scale model of the Macal Valley – if you're spending more than a couple of days in the area try to see this first.

Located at *du Plooy's* resort, a few kilometres upstream from Chaa Creek, the ambitious new **Belize Botanic Gardens** (daily 8am–5pm; US$5) were established in 1997 on fifty acres of former farmland and forest with the aim of conserving many of Belize's native plant species in small areas representative of their natural habitats. The gardens already house four hundred tree species, two ponds with bird hides, several kilometres of interpretive **trails** and a magnificent, specially designed **orchid house**, the only one in Belize, containing 160 species. Expert guide Philip Mai offers **tours** of the gardens.

ACCOMMODATION

Most accommodation on the Macal River is in beautifully located upmarket **cabaña-style resorts**, though there are some budget options (and most places will give discounts to Rough Guide readers, especially out of season between December and Easter). We've listed them in the order you reach them **travelling upriver**; all are also accessible by road.

Hummingbird Cabañas, at the entrance to Cristo Rey village (☎09/23425, *ecojungletours@hotmail .com*). Simple thatched cabins with private bath, plus a good, inexpensive restaurant and canoe rental. For here and *Crystal Paradise* (below) you can get the San Antonio bus to Cristo Rey village; a taxi to the village costs about US$14. ④.

Crystal Paradise Resort, Cristo Rey village, on the east bank of the river (☎ & fax 09/22772, *cparadise@btl.net*). Accommodation is in cabañas (⑧) and rooms (⑥), the majority with private bathrooms, and most rates include two delicious meals a day.

Chaa Creek (☎09/22037, fax 22501, *www.chaacreek.com*). Whitewashed wood and stucco cabañas (⑨) in beautiful grounds high above the Macal River, with a justly deserved reputation for luxury and ambience. Chaa Creek also run the *Macal River Safari Camp* (⑦), just downstream from the resort, where you can camp in comfort, with hot water, clean, tiled bathrooms and big meals.

du Plooy's (☎09/23101, fax 2330, *www.duplooys.com*). Private luxury bungalows (⑨) and jungle lodge rooms, each with a private porch. The "Pink House" has six rooms (⑥) and can be rented by groups. Great for bird-watching.

Guacamallo Jungle Camp (☎09/23674, *davidstours@hotmail.com*). Simple cabins high above the river (which you cross in a canoe) on the edge of a huge Maya site. US$25 per person, including transport, dinner and breakfast.

Martz Farm (☎09/23742, or contact *Eva's* or *Martha's* in San Ignacio). Much further upriver from the other places on the Macal, but well worth the effort, with comfortable thatched cabins perched in trees above a rushing, crystal-clear creek. There's plenty of home-cooked food, plus great horse-riding in the forest which beckons across the river. ④–⑤.

El Pilar Ruins and the Mopan River

Rushing down from the Guatemalan border, the **Mopan River** offers some attractive and not too serious **whitewater rapids**, and it's easy enough to arrange kayak or rafting trips – check at any of the resorts listed below; *Clarissa Falls* or *Trek Stop* (p.96) are best. Five kilometres west of San Ignacio on the river, the village of **Bullet Tree Falls** is the starting point for trips to **El Pilar**, the largest Maya site in the Belize River valley, 15km distant along a rough road over the escarpment. There's no public transport, but archeologists working at the site may give you a lift (ask at *Eva's*); alternatively, a taxi from the village will cost around US$25. Construction at El Pilar's began in the Preclassic era and continued right through to the Terminal Classic, when some of the largest existing temples were completely rebuilt. The site comprises seventy major structures grouped around 33 plazas; one causeway runs west into Guatemala, and the area is now the focus of an international archeological project.

ACCOMMODATION

There's less **accommodation** along the Mopan branch of the Belize River than there is along the Macal, but what's available is more within reach of the budget traveller. The resorts below are listed in order of distance from San Ignacio.

Parrot Nest, in Bullet Tree Falls at the end of the track just before the bridge (☎09/37008, *parrot@btl.net*). Six simple, clean thatched cabins (two sitting very securely up a tree), set in beautiful gardens on the river bank, with shared bathrooms (with hot showers) only. Good, filling meals are available, and there's a free morning and afternoon shuttle for guests from *Eva's* in San Ignacio. ⑤.

Clarissa Falls, along a signed track to the right off the Benque road, just before the Chaa Creek turn-off (☎09/23916, *clarissafalls@btl.net*). Restful place on the river bank with simple, clean, stick-and-thatch cabins with private bathrooms, plus a dorm room (US$8 per person) and camping (US$3.50) with shared hot-water showers. Good home cooking. ⑤.

Nabitunich, off the Benque Road, down a track on the right, just beyond the Chaa Creek turn-off (☎09/32309, *rudijuan@btl.net*). Simple, stone-and-thatch cabins set in beautiful gardens with spectacular views of El Castillo at Xunantunich ruins (see p.96). Great student rate (US$12.50 per person including breakfast; ID needed). ⑥–⑦.

The Mountain Pine Ridge Forest Reserve

South of San Ignacio, running parallel to the border with Guatemala, the **Mountain Pine Ridge Forest Reserve** comprises a spectacular range of rolling hills, jagged peaks and gorges, formed from some of the oldest rocks in Central America. These hills are interspersed by areas of grassland and pine forest growing in nutrient-poor, sandy soil, although in the warmth of the river valleys the vegetation is thicker gallery forest, giving way to rainforest south of the Guacamallo Bridge. The area's rains feed a number of small streams, most of which run off into the Macal and Belize rivers. One of the most scenic is the **Río On**, rushing over cataracts and forming a gorge – a sight of tremendous natural beauty. On the northern side of the ridge are the **Thousand-Foot Falls**, actually over 1600ft (488m) and the highest in Central America. The reserve also includes limestone areas riddled with caves, the most accessible being the **Río Frio Cave** in Augustine/Douglas Silva.

The area is virtually uninhabited but for a few tourist lodges and one small settlement, **Augustine/Douglas Silva**, site of the reserve headquarters. The whole area is perfect for **hiking** and **mountain biking**, but **camping** is allowed only at Augustine/Douglas Silva and at the Mai Gate. For a map of the reserve, see p.91.

Getting to the reserve

There are two **entrance roads** to the Mountain Pine Ridge reserve, one from the village of **Georgeville**, on the Western Highway (see p.86), and the other from Santa Elena, along the **Cristo Rey** road and through the village of **San Antonio**. Tours can be arranged from San Ignacio (see box on p.90) and there are also four Mesh **buses** a day from San Ignacio to San Antonio via Cristo Rey, where there's some budget accommodation (see opposite). A good way to get around is to rent a **mountain bike** in San Ignacio, which you can take on the bus to San Antonio. If you're **driving**, always check road conditions and heed the advice of the forestry officials.

Two kilometres along the Cristo Rey road from Santa Elena you'll pass *Maya Mountain Lodge* (☎09/22164, *www.mayamountain.com*; ⑥–⑦), with comfortable private thatched cabañas and a larger cabin, ideal for groups. There's a good restaurant, a pool, and families are particularly welcome.

San Antonio

The villagers of **SAN ANTONIO** are descendants of Maya refugees who fled the Caste Wars in Yucatán in 1847; many people still speak Yucatec. Their story is told in a fascinating account of the village's oral history, *After 100 Years*, by Alfonso Antonio Tzul, available in some bookshops in Belize and from the Tanah Museum (see below). Nestled in the Macal River valley, surrounded by scattered farms, with the forested Maya Mountains in the background, this is a superb place to learn about traditional Maya ways. The Garcia sisters, who grew up in the village, run the **Tanah Museum** and the simple but comfortable *Chichan Ka Guest House* (☎091/2023, *tanah-info @awrem.com*; ④) at the approach to the village (buses from San Ignacio stop outside). It's a very relaxing place to stay, traditional meals are served and courses are offered in the gathering and use of medicinal plants. The sisters are also renowned for their slate carvings, and their **gift shop** has become a favourite tour-group stop. You can also find out here about guided trips to the brand-new **Elijio Panti National Park**, part of a project to allow the Maya to manage a protected area for conservation and tourism.

The reserve

Not far beyond San Antonio, the roads meet and begin a steady climb to the **reserve**. One kilometre beyond the junction is a **campsite** (US$3.50 per person) run by Fidencio and Petronila Bol, who also operate Bol's Nature Tours; Fidencio can guide you to several nearby caves. About 5km uphill from the campsite is the **Mai Gate**, a forestry checkpoint with information about the reserve as well as toilets and drinking water. Though there are plans to levy an **entrance fee**, for the moment all you have to do is write your name in the visitors' book (to ensure there's no illegal camping).

Once you're in the reserve, the dense, leafy forest is quickly replaced by pine trees. After 3km a branch road heads off to the left, running for 7km to a point which overlooks the **Thousand-Foot Falls** (US$1.50). The setting is spectacular, with rugged, thickly forested slopes across the steep valley – almost a gorge. The waterfall itself is about 1km from the viewpoint, but try to resist the temptation to climb around for a closer look – the slope is a lot steeper than it first appears.

One of the reserve's main attractions is the **Río On Pools** – a gorgeous spot for a swim – where the river forms pools between huge granite boulders before plunging into a gorge. Another 8km from here and you reach the reserve headquarters at **Augustine/Douglas Silva**. If you're heading for Caracol (see opposite), check road conditions with the Forestry Department here. You can **camp** here but you'll probably need to bring all your own supplies as the village store appears to have permanently closed.

The **Río Frio Caves** are a twenty-minute walk from Augustine/Douglas Silva, following the signposted track from the parking area through the forest to the main cave, beneath a small hill. The Río Frio flows right through and out of the other side of the hill here, and if you enter the foliage-framed cave mouth, you can scramble over limestone terraces the entire way under the hill. Sandy beaches and rocky cliffs line the river on both sides.

Accommodation

The **resorts** in Mountain Pine Ridge include some of the most exclusive accommodation in the interior of Belize. These lodges – mostly cabins set amongst the pines and surrounded by the undisturbed natural beauty of the forest reserve, with quiet paths to secluded waterfalls – provide ideal places to stay if you're visiting Caracol.

Three kilometres beyond the Mai Gate, the **Cooma Cairn Road** heads left for 5km to *Hidden Valley Inn* (☎08/23320, fax 23334, *www.hiddenvalleyinn.com*; ⑨ including breakfast and dinner). Rooms are in twelve spacious, well-designed cottages with log fireplaces, set in seventy square kilometres of private reserve – though it's not cheap at US$180 per double per night. Back on the main (Chiquibul) road to Augustine/Douglas Silva, just past the Cooma Cairn junction, *Pine Ridge Lodge* (☎09/23180, *www.pineridgelodge.com*; ⑦ including breakfast), on the banks of Little Vaqueros Creek, has accommodation in thatched or tiled cabins. The grounds and trees are full of orchids and trails lead to pristine waterfalls. A kilometre beyond here, a side road heads right 2km to *Blancaneaux Lodge* (☎09/23878, *www .blancaneauxlodge.com*; ⑨ including breakfast), owned by Francis Ford Coppola, and the most luxurious place to stay in the Mountain Pine Ridge. Sumptuous rooms, cabins and villas decorated with Guatemalan and Mexican textiles are set in lovely gardens overlooking Privassion Creek. At the end of the road past *Blancaneaux*, *Five Sisters Lodge* (☎091/2005, *www.fivesisterslodge.com*; rooms ⑥, cabañas ⑨, including breakfast), has the finest location in Mountain Pine Ridge, with very comfortable palmetto-and-thatch cabañas and lodge rooms set on a forested hillside. The dining-room deck gives tremendous views of the Five Sisters waterfalls cascading over granite rocks, and if you don't fancy the climb down – or back up – you can ride in the only funicular lift in Belize.

The ruins of Caracol

Beyond Augustine/Douglas Silva the ridges of the Maya Mountains rise up to the south, while to the west is the wilderness of Vaca plateau. Here the ruins of **Caracol**, the largest Maya site in Belize, and one of the largest in the Maya world, were lost for several centuries until their rediscovery in 1936. Two years later they were explored by A.H. Anderson, who named the site Caracol – Spanish for "snail" – because of the large numbers of snail shells found there. In 1985 the first detailed, full-scale excavation of the site, the "Caracol Project", began, and research continues today, unearthing artefacts relating to everyday life at all levels of Maya society.

The site is open daily (8am–4pm; US$5) and you'll be guided on your visit by one of the guards or, if excavation is in progress, by an archeology student. The **visitor centre** is the best at any Maya site in Belize and an essential first stop. There's a map of the centre of the site and some excellent display panels, as well as artefacts from the site. Only the core of the city, comprising thirty-two large structures and twelve smaller ones grouped round five main plazas, is open to visitors – though even this is far more than you can effectively see in a day. At its greatest extent, around 700 AD, during the Late Classic period, Caracol covered 88 square kilometres, with a population estimated to be around 150,000. The largest pyramid, **Canaa**, is still one of the tallest buildings in Belize, at 42m high. Over 100 **tombs** have been found, some with painted texts decorating the walls, along with ceremonially buried caches containing items as diverse as a quantity of mercury and amputated human fingers. Hieroglyphic inscriptions here have enabled epigraphers to piece together a virtually complete dynastic record of Caracol's rulers from 599 AD, and glyphs carved on altars tell of war between Caracol and Tikal, when control over a vast area alternated between the two great cities. One altar records a victory of Caracol over Tikal at 562 AD – a triumph that set the seal on the city's rise to power. Caracol is also a haven for **wildlife** (including tapirs, jaguars and ocelots), and birds, among them the orange-breasted falcon and the very rare harpy eagle.

Xunantunich

Back on the Western Highway, around 12km west of San Ignacio on the bank Mopan River, the quiet village of **San José Succotz** is home to the ruins of **Xunantunich** (pronounced Shun-an-tun-ich), "the Stone Maiden", a Classic-period centre. An old chain ferry crosses the river to the site on demand (daily 8am–5pm; free). If you're carrying luggage, you can safely leave it at the *Plaza Restaurant* (also a good source of information), opposite the ferry.

From the riverbank a steep track leads through the forest for a couple of kilometres to the **ruins** (US$5). Your first stop should be the marvellous **visitor centre**, one of the best in Belize, which includes a superb scale model of the city. The site, located on top of an artificially flattened hill, includes five plazas, although the surviving structures are grouped around just three of them. Recent investigations have found evidence of Xunantunich's role in the power politics of the Classic period, during which it probably joined Caracol and the regional superpower Calakmul in an alliance against Tikal. By the Terminal Classic period, Xunantunich was already in decline, though still apparently inhabited until around 1000 AD, after the Classic Maya "collapse" in most other areas.

The track from the entrance brings you out into plaza A-2, with large structures on three sides. Plaza A-1, to the left is dominated by **El Castillo**, at over 40m the city's tallest structure. This is ringed by a decorative stucco frieze, now extensively restored, showing abstract designs, human faces and jaguar heads. The climb up El Castillo can be daunting, but the views from the top are superb, with the forest stretching out all around and the rest of the ancient city mapped out beneath you.

Practicalities

Just before San José Succotz (signed on the left) there's a wonderful budget **place to stay**, *Trek Stop* (☎09/32265, *www.thetrekstop.com*; ④), with eight simple, clean, non-smoking cabins with comfortable beds (US$10 per person) and a **campsite** (US$3.50 per person). The restaurant serves some of the best-value food and largest portions in Cayo, with good vegetarian choices, and there's a self-catering kitchen, while bikes, kayaks and tubes are available for rent at reasonable rates. *Trek Stop* also runs the well-designed **Tropical Wings Butterfly House** (daily 8am–5pm; US$2.50, including guided tour), an enchanting world full of tropical colour.

Benque Viejo and the Guatemalan border

The final town in Belize, 2km before the Guatemalan border, is **BENQUE VIEJO DEL CARMEN**, where Guatemala and Belize combine in almost equal proportions and Spanish is the dominant language. It's a quiet place, but served by a constant stream of buses and shared taxis to and from the border post; some **buses** continue all the way to the market in Melchor. The Belize border is open from 6am to midnight – though you're best advised to cross in daylight – and Guatemalan migración closes at around 8pm.

There's nothing to pay to enter Belize, but **leaving Belize** you pay an exit tax of US$10, plus the PACT Conservation fee of US$3.75; Guatemalan officials routinely charge a Q10 (US$1.25) entry (and exit) tax; if you require a visa (US$10) they can sometimes be issued here, but you might have to go back to the embassy in Belize City, so it's best to equip yourself with one in advance. Buses on to **Flores** (see p.256) call at the migración to pick up passengers, and you'll certainly be approached by drivers of the minibuses which shuttle between the border and **Tikal** (US$10–15) and Flores; ask for Hugo Mayén or Manuel Sandoval.

travel details

The Western Highway **from Belize City to the Guatemalan border** (3hr 30min) is served by half-hourly Novelo's buses from 5am to 9pm, calling at **Belmopan** (1hr 15min) and **San Ignacio** (3hr). Some buses only go as far as **Benque**, from where it's US$1 in a shared taxi to the border. Bus companies and main destinations are covered in the Belize City chapter (see pp.59–60). **Express buses**, stopping only in Belmopan and cutting about 30min off journey times, operate about every three hours. Additionally, Western Transport run daily services **between Belmopan, San Ignacio and Benque**.

From Benque and the border to Belize City buses leave every thirty minutes 4am–5pm; the last bus **from San Ignacio to Belize City** leaves at 6pm; all call at **Belmopan**. To check **bus times** in San Ignacio call ☎09/22058.

Belize City to: Belmopan (every 30min; 1hr 15min); Benque Viejo and the border (every 30min; 3hr 30min); San Ignacio (every 30min; 3hr).

San Ignacio to: San Antonio via Cristo Rey (Mon–Sat 4 daily 10.30am–5pm; 1hr), returning from San Antonio between 6am and 1.30pm.

CHAPTER 5

THE SOUTH

T o the **south of Belmopan**, Belize is at its wildest. Here the central area is dominated by the **Maya Mountains**, which slope down towards the coast through a series of forested ridges and valleys carved by sparkling rivers. As you head further south, the climate becomes more humid, promoting the growth of dense rainforest, rich in wildlife. Population density in this part of Belize is low, with most of the towns and villages located on the coast. **Dangriga**, the largest settlement, is home to the **Garífuna** people, descended from Caribs and shipwrecked Africans. The villages of **Gales Point**, north of Dangriga, and **Hopkins**, on the coast to the south, are worth visiting to experience their tranquil way of life, while offshore, the beautiful cayes of **Glover's Reef** offer budget and luxury accommodation in Belize's largest marine reserve. Further down the coast, **Placencia** is the focus of coastal tourism in southern Belize, and the departure point for yet more idyllic cayes, some of which sit right on the top of the Barrier Reef.

Inland, the Maya Mountains remain unpenetrated by roads, forming a solid barrier to land travel except on foot or horseback. The Belize government, showing supreme foresight, has placed practically all of the thickly forested mountain massif under some form of protection. The most accessible area of rainforest, though still little-visited by tourists, is the **Cockscomb Basin Wildlife Sanctuary**, a reserve designed to protect the area's sizeable jaguar population. The Southern Highway comes to an end in **Punta Gorda**, a final outpost, from where you can head over the sea to Guatemala or inland to visit **Maya villages and ruins** in the southern foothills of the Maya Mountains.

The Hummingbird Highway

Southeast from Belmopan, the well-maintained **Hummingbird Highway** heads towards Dangriga, passing through magnificent scenery as it climbs over the hills and through lush forest. On the right the eastern slopes of the **Maya Mountains** become visible, forming part of a ridge of limestone mountains riddled with underground rivers and **caves**, several of which are accessible.

St Herman's Cave to Five Blues Lake National Park
About 19km out of Belmopan the road crosses the **Caves Branch River**, a tributary of the Sibun River. Just beyond, by the roadside on the right, is **St Herman's Cave** (US$4, includes entrance to the Blue Hole). Follow the marked trail behind the **Visitor Centre** (daily 8am–4pm) for ten minutes to the cave entrance, beneath a dripping rock face; you'll need a flashlight to enter, down steps that were originally cut by the Maya. Inside, you clamber over the rocks and splash through the river for about thirty minutes, admiring the stunning natural formations, before the accessible section of the cave ends.

For an explanation of **accommodation price codes**, see p.40.

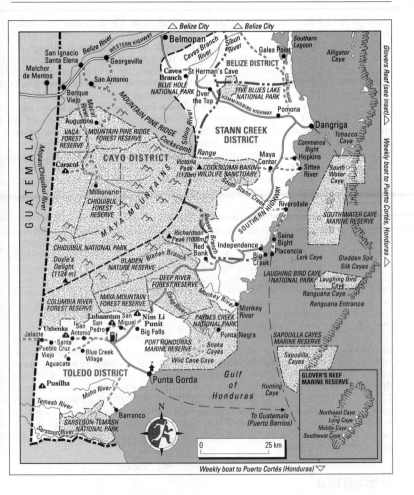

Weekly boat to Puerto Cortés (Honduras) ▽

Two kilometres past the cave, signed from the roadside, is the **Blue Hole National Park**, centred on a beautiful pool whose cool turquoise waters, surrounded by dense forest and overhung with vines, mosses and ferns, are perfect for a refreshing dip – the "Hole" is actually a short but deep stretch of underground river, whose course is revealed by a collapsed karst cavern. Trails lead through the dense surrounding forest and there's a **campsite** 4km from the visitor centre.

Any bus between Belmopan and Dangriga will drop you at the cave or the Blue Hole, but to really appreciate the mysteries of caving in Belize you can **stay** nearby at the *Caves Branch Jungle Lodge* (☎ & fax 08/22800, *caves@pobox.com*; cabañas ⑦, bunkhouse US$15 per person, camping US$5 per person), halfway between St Herman's Cave and the Blue Hole and about 1km from the highway. The **guided cave and rappelling trips** run by the lodge are not cheap (about US$75 per person), but well worth it for the experience. All the caves contain Maya artefacts – ceramics, carvings and the like – furnishing abundant evidence of the Classic-period ceremonies that were held in them.

Beyond the Blue Hole the Hummingbird Highway undulates smoothly through the hilly landscape, eventually crossing a low pass. The downhill slope is appropriately, if unimaginatively, called **Over the Top**. On the way down, the road passes through **St Margaret's Village**, where a women's cooperative arranges B&B **accommodation** in private houses (☎081/2005; ③). *Over the Top Restaurant* stands on a hill at Mile 32, overlooking the junction of the track to **Five Blues Lake National Park**, seventeen square kilometres of luxuriantly forested karst scenery, centred on the lake named for its constantly changing colours. Beyond here is the start of the **Stann Creek valley**, the centre of the Belizean citrus fruit industry, heralded as one of the nation's great success stories – although for the largely Guatemalan labour force, housed in rows of scruffy huts, conditions are little better than on the oppressive coffee fincas at home. The Hummingbird Highway officially comes to an end at **Middlesex**, 18km past Over the Top, and continues as the Stann Creek Valley Road.

Gales Point and the Southern Lagoon

At Melinda, 27km past Middlesex and only 14km from Dangriga, an improved dirt road heads north to the small Creole village of **GALES POINT**. The village straggles along a narrow peninsula jutting into the **Southern Lagoon**, a large body of shallow water which – along with **Northern Lagoon**, to which it's connected by creeks – forms an essential breeding ground for rare wildlife, including jabiru storks, turtles, manatee and crocodiles. The area is bounded on the west by the limestone Peccary Hills, riddled with caves, and the shores of the lagoons are cloaked with mangroves. Gales Point is also a centre of **traditional drum-making**; you can learn to make and play drums at the Maroon Creole Drum School, run by Emmett Young and Randolph (Boombay) Andrewin.

Deborah Callender, who runs the *Orchid Café* (☎014/5621), also publishes the village newsletter, and if you're serious about staying here you should call her for **information** first. There's a range of **accommodation**; several houses offer simple bed and breakfast rooms (④), while *Gentle's Cool Spot* restaurant has a few basic rooms (③) and *Metho's Coconut Camping* (US$3.50 per person) has space in a sandy spot. The most luxurious accommodation is at the *Manatee Lodge* (☎021/2040, *www.manateelodge .com*; ⑦), a two-storey colonial-style building right at the tip of the peninsula; rooms (all non-smoking) are spacious and comfortable and the meals are superb. Gales Point is served by most **buses** on the Belize City–Dangriga route; other traffic passes the junction, 4km from the village.

Dangriga

The last stretch of the Hummingbird Highway is flat and relatively uninteresting; from the junction with the **Southern Highway** to Punta Gorda, it's another 10km further to **DANGRIGA**, the district capital (formerly known as Stann Creek) and the largest town in southern Belize. Though Dangriga is the cultural centre of the **Garífuna**, a people of mixed indigenous Caribbean and African descent, who overall make up about eleven percent of the country's population, it is not the most exciting of places unless you're here during a festival. However, the town is home to some of the country's most popular artists, including painters, drum-makers, the Waribagabaga Dancers and the Turtle Shell Band, and you may catch an exhibition or performance. It's also a useful base for visiting the offshore cayes and the inland jaguar reserve nearby.

Since the early 1980s Garífuna culture has undergone something of a revival, as part of which the town was renamed Dangriga, a Garífuna word meaning "standing waters". The most important day in the Garífuna calendar is November 19, **Garífuna**

Settlement Day, when the arrival from Roatán (see box overleaf) is re-enacted with a landing on the beach in dugout canoes, and expatriate Belizeans return en masse to the town to celebrate wildly with music, drumming, dance and drink.

Arrival and information

Dangriga's airstrip, served by at least eight flights on the run from Belize City to Punta Gorda, is on the shore just north of the *Pelican Beach Hotel*; for both domestic and international **flights** check at *D's Travel Service*, 64 Commerce Street (☎05/22709). Z-Line **buses** from Belize City pull up at their terminal around 1km south of the centre, while James buses stop slightly north of the road bridge over the South Stann Creek which marks the centre of town. From this bridge, the town's main street heads north (as Commerce Street) and south (as St Vincent Street) – almost everything you're likely to need, including hotels, restaurants and banks, is on or near this road. For reliable **tourist information**, call in at the *Riverside Restaurant*, by the bridge on

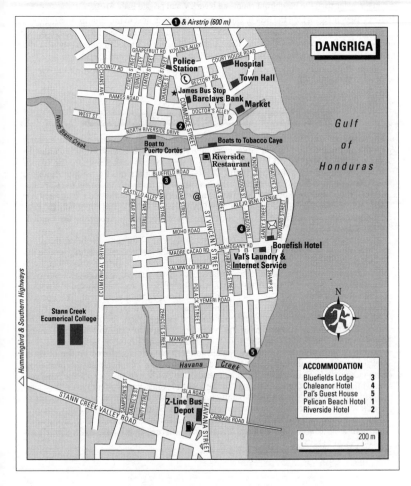

DANGRIGA

Gulf

of

Honduras

ACCOMMODATION

Bluefields Lodge	3
Chaleanor Hotel	4
Pal's Guest House	5
Pelican Beach Hotel	1
Riverside Hotel	2

0   200 m

the south bank of the river; for **bookings and tours** throughout Belize contact Debbie Jones of *Aquamarine Adventures* (☎05/23262, *djones@btl.net*). The **post office** is on Caney Street, in the southern half of town, a block back from the sea.

Accommodation

Dangriga has experienced something of a hotel-building boom in the last few years, resulting in an ample choice of **places to stay**, with some real bargains, so there's no need to stay in a cheap dive – though there are a few of these, too.

Bluefield Lodge, 6 Bluefield Rd (☎05/22742 *bluefield@btl.net*). By far the best budget hotel in town, this secure and well-run establishment has very comfortable and clean rooms, some with private baths. ④.

Chaleanor Hotel, 35 Magoon St (☎05/22587, fax 23038). Clean and spacious rooms, some with private bath, all great value. There's also a rooftop restaurant. ④–⑤.

Pal's Guest House, 868 Magoon St, by the bridge over Havana Creek (☎ & fax 05/22095, *palbelize @btl.net*). Good-value accommodation in two buildings: the budget rooms (some with shared bath) are in the older part; the beachfront rooms all have TV and private bath. ④–⑤.

Pelican Beach Resort, on the beach, 2km north of the town, next to the airstrip (☎05/22024, fax 22570, *www.pelicanbeachbelize.com*). Dangriga's largest and most expensive hotel, though rates do drop out of season – ask for a discount. Rooms at the front are in a wooden colonial-style building; those at the rear are in a two-storey concrete building – most have TV and a/c. ⑧.

Riverside Hotel, right beside the bridge (☎05/22168). Clean rooms with views over the river, and good rates for singles. ③.

A BRIEF HISTORY OF THE GARÍFUNA

The Garífuna trace their history back to the island of **St Vincent**, in the eastern Caribbean, when two Spanish ships, carrying slaves from Nigeria to their colonies in America, were wrecked off the coast in 1635. The survivors took refuge on the island, which was already inhabited by **Caribs**, themselves recent arrivals from South America, who had subdued the original natives, the **Kalipuna**, from whom it is likely the Garífuna derived their own name. At first there was conflict between the Native Americans and the Africans, but the Caribs had been weakened by wars and disease and eventually the predominant race was black with some indigenous blood, becoming known by the English as the **Black Caribs**.

For most of the seventeenth and eighteenth centuries St Vincent was nominally under British control, though in practice it belonged to the Caribs, who successfully fended off British attempts to gain full control of the island until 1796. The British colonial authorities, however, could not allow a free black society to survive amongst slave-owning European settlers, so the Carib population was hunted down and transported to **Roatán**, off the coast of Honduras (see p.453), where the British abandoned them. The Spanish Commandante of Trujillo, on the Honduran mainland, took the 1700 surviving Black Caribs to Trujillo, where they became in demand as free labourers, fishermen and soldiers. Their intimate knowledge of the rivers and coast also made them expert smugglers, evading the Spanish laws that forbade trade with the British in Belize.

In the early **nineteenth century** small numbers of Garífuna moved up the coast to Belize, establishing themselves in the area before the first European settlers arrived in Stann Creek in 1823. The largest single migration to Belize took place in 1832 when thousands fled from Honduras (then part of the Central American Republic) after they supported the wrong side in a failed revolution to overthrow the Republican government. It is this arrival which is today celebrated as **Garífuna Settlement Day**, though it seems likely that many arrived both before and after. An excellent Garífuna Web site – *www .garifuna-world.com* – lists cultural events and current developments in the entire Garífuna community.

MOVING ON FROM DANGRIGA

Returning **to Belize City** (2–3hr), Z-Line buses (☎05/22732) leave every hour or so from 5am to 5pm; most go via **Belmopan**, some travel along the Coastal Road. James Bus Line doesn't have a terminal, but departing buses (currently 4 daily in each direction) pass along the main street. If you're **continuing south**, bear in mind that buses to **Punta Gorda** (4–5hr; eight daily) don't necessarily originate here and delays are possible. All buses to Punta Gorda stop at **Independence** (2hr) – also known as **Mango Creek** – where you can pick up boats to Placencia (see p.107).

There are usually two daily Z-Line services from Dangriga to **Placencia** (2hr–2hr 30min), but departure times are continually changing (they currently leave daily at 11.30pm & 4.30pm) at least one calls at **Hopkins** (40min) and **Sittee River**.

Dangriga is served by **flights** on Tropic Air and Maya Island Air every couple of hours to and from Belize City, continuing south to Placencia and Punta Gorda.

For Puerto Cortés in Honduras (see p.428) a fast **skiff** leaves each Saturday at 9am (US$50; 3hr) from the north bank of the river, two blocks up from the bridge; be there an hour before departure with your passport so that the skipper, Carlos Reyes (☎05/23227), can take care of the formalities.

Eating and drinking

Despite Dangriga's central position in Garífuna culture, there's no restaurant specializing in Garífuna food – you'll find it's generally more readily available in Hopkins (see overleaf). The restaurant at the *Pelican Beach* is the top place in town, with staff skilled in preparing Belizean specialities. The *Riverside Restaurant*, on the south bank of the river just over the bridge, is easily the best place in the town centre, serving tasty Creole food, including great breakfasts and a daily special. *King Burger* (not what you might think) under the *Riverside Hotel* serves good rice, chicken, fish and burgers. Of the several Chinese restaurants on the main street, the *Starlight* is the best value.

Tobacco and South Water Cayes

About 20km offshore from Dangriga is **Columbus Reef**, a superb section of the Barrier Reef with tiny **Tobacco Caye** perched on its southern tip. Ideally situated right in the middle of the reef, Tobacco Caye is easy to reach and has good-value accommodation. **Boats** (40min; US$15) leave daily from near the bridge in Dangriga, though there are no scheduled departures; ask at your hotel or find Captain Buck at the *Riverside Restaurant*. The island is tiny: if you stand in the centre you're only a couple of minutes from the shore in any direction, with the unbroken reef stretching north for miles. Sunsets can be breathtakingly beautiful, outlining the distant Maya Mountains with a purple and orange aura. The island's dive shop, Tobacco Caye Diving (☎014/9907, *www.tobaccocayediving.com*) has a large selection of equipment, including snorkelling gear, and offers PADI courses and trips to the atolls. The best value of caye's **places to stay** is *Gaviota Coral Reef Resort*, which offers cabins on the sand and less expensive rooms in the main building, all with shared bath (☎051/2036; ⑤–⑦ including meals). The owner can arrange discounted boat fares for guests. Alternatively, try *Tobacco Caye Lodge* (☎051/2033, *tclodgebelize@yahoo.com*; ⑦ including meals), which has the largest area of any hotel on the island, stretching from the reef at the front to the lagoon at the back. Accommodation is in three spacious and comfortable two-room houses with deck and hammocks, and there's a good beach bar by the dock.

Eight kilometres south and slightly larger, **South Water Caye** is arguably one of the most beautiful – and exclusive – islands in Belize and the focus of a **marine reserve**.

Like Tobacco Caye it sits right on the reef and offers fantastic snorkelling and diving in crystal-clear waters. With one exception – the very low-key *Bernie's Cabins* (☎014/6553; ⑤), a couple of small, brightly painted wooden cabins with shared bath – the island's **accommodation** is upmarket and expensive and has to be booked in advance, generally as an all-inclusive package. The *Pelican Beach* in Dangriga (see p.102) owns some idyllic wooden houses built on stilts over the white sand and shaded by palms (⑨), plus a two-storey hotel with five rooms (⑨).

The Southern Highway to Placencia

To the **south of Dangriga** the country becomes more mountainous, with development restricted to the coastal lowlands. The only road heading in this direction is the **Southern Highway**, which runs from Dangriga to Punta Gorda. Paving began a few years ago, and at present about two thirds of the road has a good asphalt surface; the remainder is frequently graded and strong bridges have been built. For its entire length the road is set back from the coast, running beneath the peaks of the Maya Mountains, passing through pine forest and vast citrus and banana plantations. Branch roads lead off to settlements, such as **Hopkins**, a Garífuna village on the coast, and the nearby Creole village of **Sittee River**, where you can catch the boat to the idyllic cayes of **Glover's Reef** (see opposite). From the village of **Maya Center**, 36km south of Dangriga, a road leads west into the Cockscomb Basin Wildlife Sanctuary, usually referred to as the **Jaguar Reserve**.

Hopkins

Stretching for more than 3km along a shallow, gently curving bay, the village of **HOPKINS** is home to around a thousand Garífuna people. Garífuna Settlement Day, on November 19, is celebrated enthusiastically here, and at other times it's a pleasant place to spend a few days relaxing, with food and accommodation in all price ranges – you can also rent kayaks, windsurf boards and bicycles. Many hotels can arrange trips to the reef and cayes further out; for **diving**, check with Second Nature Divers (☎ & fax 05/37038, *divers@btl.net*), based in **Sittee River** (see opposite), a few kilometres south of Hopkins.

Arrival and accommodation

The **bus** service to Hopkins is a little unpredictable, but there's at least one daily run to and from the village (currently the 11am Z-Line service from Dangriga to Placencia), though it's vital to check locally for the current situation. Also ask around where the boats tie up by the bridge in Dangriga and see whether anyone from Hopkins is in town who may be willing to give you a lift – this is definitely the best way to arrive. There are no street names in Hopkins; the main point of reference is where the road from the Southern Highway enters the village – dividing Hopkins into north and south – and signs point the way to hotels and restaurants.

Hopkins Inn, 300m south of the centre (☎05/37013, *www.hopkinsinn.com*). Four immaculate white cabins with hot showers and fridge. ⑥ including breakfast.

Sandy Beach Lodge, at the south end of the beach (☎05/37006). Simple, spacious rooms in wood-and-thatch cabins, most with private bath. ③.

Seagull's Nest Guest House, on the beach south of the centre (☎05/37015). Rooms (④) in a wooden house, some with bunk beds (US$10 per person).

Swinging Armadillos on the beach 150m north of the centre (☎05/37016). One private room (④) and some bunk rooms (US$9 per person) perched over the sea alongside a bar and restaurant.

Tania's Guest House, on the right side of the road as you head south (☎05/37058). Bargain rooms, although not directly on the beach, some with private bath. ③.

Tipple Tree Beya, near the south end of the beach (☎051/2006, *tipple@btl.net*). Clean, good-value rooms (one with private bath) in a wooden building, plus a furnished house (US$40 per day) and camping space (US$4.50 per person). ③–④.

Eating and drinking

Although the village now has a number of **restaurants** and **bars**, the choice can be limited out of the tourist season. The *Jabiru Restaurant and Bar*, on the left just before the road from the highway enters the village, is one of the most reliable places to eat, with good Creole and Garífuna dishes served under a thatched roof. Owner Anselma Christiana also runs the *Over the Waves* restaurant, on the beach in the village centre, and is extremely knowledgeable about Garífuna and Hopkins history. The tiny and friendly *Tyson's Diner*, north of the centre, serves good, simple Garífuna and Creole meals, while *Iris's Restaurant*, south of the centre, serves great breakfasts.

If you fancy a **drink** with the locals try the *Tropical Bar* or the *Watering Hole*, north and south of the centre respectively. For **live music** and an early evening **happy hour** check at the *Laru Beya* bar, on the beach where the road from the highway enters the village; nearby the *King Casava* restaurant offers live entertainment at weekends.

Sittee River and Glover's Reef

The 5km sandy road heading south from Hopkins is the "back way" to **SITTEE RIVER** village. Most visitors here are on their way to *Glover's Atoll Resort* (see below), but there are a couple of places to stay, right on the riverbank. The great-value *Toucan Sittee* (☎05/37039; ④) is by far the best option; the bus stops outside. As well as comfortable rooms, there's dorm accommodation (US$8 per person) and **camping space** (US$2 per person). Meals are really good, with lots of fresh fruit and vegetables. Nearby, *Glover's Guest House* (☎051/2016, *glovers@btl.net*; ④), where you check in for the Glover's Reef trip (see below), has dorm beds for US$8 as well as double rooms. There's a restaurant on the riverbank and the boat to the atoll ties up outside. If you need to stock up on supplies for your trip to Glover's Reef the well-stocked Reynold's Store has groceries.

The southernmost of Belize's three coral atolls, **Glover's Reef** lies between 40 and 50km off Sittee River. Named after a British pirate, the reef is roughly oval in shape, about 35km north to south, and its only cayes are in the southeastern section. The whole atoll is a **marine reserve** (US$5 entry fee), with a research station on Middle Caye. What makes Glover's Reef so unusual among the remote atolls is that it offers **accommodation** within the reach of budget travellers at the *Glover's Atoll Resort* (☎014/8351, *www.belizemall.com/gloversatoll*) on **Northeast Caye**. There are twelve simple beach cabins (US$149 per person per week) overlooking the reef, dorm beds in a wooden house (US$99) plus **camping** space (US$80 per week); the weekly rates include transport from Sittee River in the resort's motor-sailboat (leaves Sunday morning, returns following Saturday afternoon; 4hr). Unless you're here on a group package, you'll need to bring most of your own food (some supplies are available) and cook meals on a kerosene stove or campfire. While here you're pretty much left to your own devices and you can choose either to enjoy the simple, desert island experience or take part in activities (paid for separately), including sailing, sea kayaking, fishing, snorkelling and scuba diving, which is spectacular, thanks to a huge underwater cliff and some tremendous wall diving.

Two other cayes at Glover's Reef serve as bases for superb **sea kayaking** expeditions: **Long Caye**, just south of Northeast Caye, is the base camp for Slickrock Adventures from Utah, while **Southwest Caye** serves the same purpose for the Vancouver-based Island Expeditions.

The Cockscomb Basin Wildlife Sanctuary

Back on the mainland the jagged peaks of the **Maya Mountains** rise to the west of the Southern Highway, their lower slopes covered in dense rainforest. The tallest summits are those of the Cockscomb range, which includes Victoria Peak (1120m), the second highest mountain in Belize. Beneath the ridges is a vast bowl of rainforest, over four hundred square kilometres of which is protected by the **Cockscomb Basin Wildlife Sanctuary** – better known as the **Jaguar Reserve**. The basin's luxuriant vegetation is home to a sizeable percentage of Belize's plant and animal species, including tapirs, otters, anteaters, armadillos and, of course, jaguars. Over 290 species of **bird** have also been recorded, including the endangered scarlet macaw, the great curassow and the king vulture, and there's an abundance of amphibians and reptiles, including the red-eyed tree frog and the deadly fer-de-lance.

The sanctuary is reached via a rough ten-kilometre track that branches off the main highway at the village of **Maya Center**, running through towering forest and fording a couple of fresh, clear streams before crossing the Cabbage Hall Gap and entering the Cockscomb Basin. This area was inhabited in Maya times, and the ruins of **Kuchil Balam**, a small Classic-period ceremonial centre, still lie hidden in the forest. Trails have been cut to give visitors a taste of the forest's diversity, leading along the riverbanks, through the forest and even, if you're suitably prepared, on a three-day hike to **Victoria Peak**. The basin could be home to as many as fifty of Belize's 600-strong **jaguar population**, but though you'll almost certainly come across their tracks, your chances of actually seeing one are very slim.

Practicalities

All **buses** heading south from Dangriga pass **MAYA CENTER** (45min). Get off when you see the sign for *Greg's Bar* on the right – owner Greg Sho is one of the most experienced guides in the country. If you're visiting the reserve you'll need to sign in and pay the entrance fee (US$5) at the **craft centre** just past the bar. A small shop just beyond here sells basic supplies and cold drinks and is another good place to find out about guides and transport.

There are a couple of inexpensive and good-value **places to stay** in Maya Center, including the *Mejen Tz'il Lodge* (☎051/2020, *lsaqui@btl.net*), just behind the craft centre, which has a large wooden cabin set in lovely gardens with dorm rooms for US$8 per person. Some 500m up the track to the reserve, the *Nu'uk Che'il Cottages* (☎051/2021, *nuukcheil@btl.net*; ④) offer simple but delightful thatched cabañas with shared bath, plus dorm beds (US$8). Both these places serve good local food, have information about guides to Victoria Peak and can provide transport by truck for the ten-kilometre trip to the **reserve headquarters** (about US$16). At the headquarters there's an excellent **visitor centre** and some simple but comfortable **dorm accommodation** (US$7.50 per person in old, basic cabins; US$15 per person in newer, purpose-built ones) and **camping** space (US$2.50 per person). You'll have to bring your own food, but the cabins do have a kitchen with a gas stove.

The Placencia Peninsula

South of Dangriga, a good dirt road cuts east from the Southern Highway, reaching the sea at Riversdale before heading south down the narrow, sandy **Placencia Peninsula**, through the Garífuna village of **Seine Bight** to the laid-back village of **Placencia**, which sits perched at the tip of the peninsula 75km from Dangriga. Strung out along the peninsula are a dozen or so upmarket **resorts**, most of them owned and operated by expatriate North Americans, where accommodation is usually in cabins with private bathrooms and electricity, with Caribbean beaches a few steps away on one side and the **Placencia Lagoon** close by on the other.

Halfway along the peninsula, on the beautiful stretch of coast called **Maya Beach**, *Barnacle Bill's Beach Bungalows* (☎06/37010, *taylors@btl.net*; ⑨) comprise two large and very well-equipped wooden houses on stilts on a gorgeous sandy beach. A couple of kilometres south, *Maya Playa* (☎06/37010, *mayaplaya@btl.net*; ⑦), has four palmetto-and-thatch A-frame cabañas in a beautiful beachfront location. Friendly owner Chuck Meares has built a very tall *palapa* (thatched hut) on the beach for his kitchen and dining room, and guests are welcome to cook and eat their meals there.

Some 3km further, the small Garífuna village of **SEINE BIGHT** now has several upmarket resorts and one **budget hotel**, *Effie's Guest House* (☎06/24056; ④), with four clean and simple shared-bath rooms upstairs in a wooden house on the beach; friendly owner Effie Hill will prepare delicious meals in her house across the road. The village is worth a visit even if you're not staying: you can hang out and play pool in the *Sunshine Bar*, listen to Garífuna music in the *Wamasa Beyabu Bar*, a distinctive green-and-yellow striped building near the south end of the village, and check out Lola Delgados superb (and affordable) oil and acrylic paintings of village life at *Lola's Art Gallery and Laguñedu Café*, further south behind the soccer field. Lola is also a great cook and serves superb Creole and Garífuna dinners followed by music and drumming – it's a good evening, but call ☎014/2435 to check when she's cooking.

Beyond Seine Bight another series of resorts offers upscale **accommodation**. *Kitty's Place*, just south of Placencia's airstrip (☎06/23227, *www.kittysplace.com*; ⑦–⑧) is one of the best, a convenient 3km north of the village and offering a variety of accommodation, including apartments, beach cabañas and garden rooms. The restaurant serves delicious Belizean and international food.

Placencia village

Shaded by palm trees, cooled by the sea breeze, **Placencia** is one of the few places on mainland Belize with real beaches, and this, together with the abundant and inexpensive accommodation, makes it a great place to relax. The easiest way to get to Placencia is on one of the regular **flights** from Belize City (about 45min). The airstrip is about 3km north of the village; taxis are usually waiting – or it's a five-minute walk to *Kitty's Place*, where you can phone for one. There are usually two direct **buses** a day from Dangriga, which terminate at the beachfront station, right at the end of the peninsula (if you're looking for budget rooms, get off when you see the sign for the *Sea Spray Hotel*, about halfway through the village, then head left for "the sidewalk", a concrete walkway that winds through the palms, and you'll reach a cluster of budget hotels and restaurants). Alternatively you can reach Placencia on the *Hokey Pokey* **ferry** from Independence/Mango Creek, a thirty-minute trip across the lagoon (Independence is on the Dangriga–Punta Gorda bus route; the ferry meets all buses). A **shuttle bus** (US$2.50) runs between Maya Beach and Placencia roughly every two hours from 6am to 7pm. The *Gulf Cruza* leaves Placencia for **Puerto Cortés** in Honduras (US$50; 4hr), every Friday at 9.30am, returning to Placencia on Monday and leaving for Belize City (3hr, US$25) at 2.30pm. For details of onward travel from Independence, see p.110.

The **Placencia Tourism Center** (Mon–Fri 8.30–11.30am & 1–5pm, Sat 8.30–11.30am; ☎06/24045, *www.placencia.com*) is the best place to find out what's going on locally, and you can also call hotels from here and pick up a copy of the *Placencia Breeze*, which has comprehensive local listings. The **post office** is upstairs in the wooden building on the right at the end of The Sidewalk; the **BTL office** is by the sidewalk

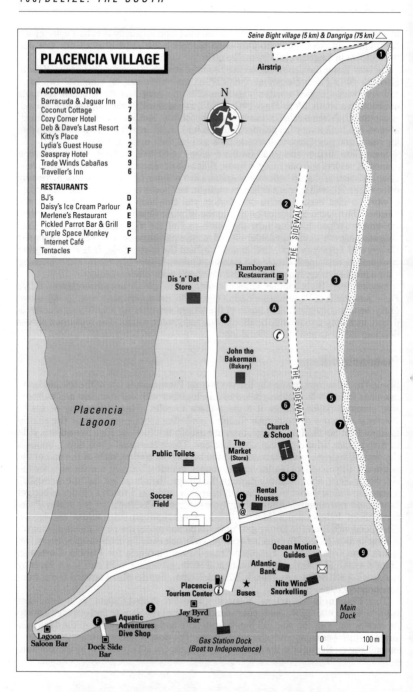

PLACENCIA VILLAGE

Seine Bight village (5 km) & Dangriga (75 km)

ACCOMMODATION

Barracuda & Jaguar Inn	8
Coconut Cottage	7
Cozy Corner Hotel	5
Deb & Dave's Last Resort	4
Kitty's Place	1
Lydia's Guest House	2
Seaspray Hotel	3
Trade Winds Cabañas	9
Traveller's Inn	6

RESTAURANTS

BJ's	D
Daisy's Ice Cream Parlour	A
Merlene's Restaurant	E
Pickled Parrot Bar & Grill	B
Purple Space Monkey Internet Café	C
Tentacles	F

Airstrip

N

Flamboyant Restaurant

Dis 'n' Dat Store

John the Bakerman (Bakery)

Placencia Lagoon

THE SIDEWALK

Church & School

The Market (Store)

Public Toilets

Rental Houses

Soccer Field

Ocean Motion Guides

Atlantic Bank

Nite Wind Snorkelling

Placencia Tourism Center

Buses

Main Dock

Jay Byrd Bar

Aquatic Adventures Dive Shop

Lagoon Saloon Bar

Dock Side Bar

Gas Station Dock (Boat to Independence)

0   100 m

in the centre of the village, and there are several payphones around. The *Purple Space Monkey*, in a large thatched building on the roadside opposite the soccer field, provides excellent **Internet** connections. The Atlantic **bank** (Mon–Thurs 8am–2pm, Fri 8am–4pm), across from the main dock by the filling station, deals swiftly with cash advances.

Accommodation

There's a wide choice of **accommodation** in Placencia and you shouldn't have a problem finding a room except at Christmas, New Year or Easter. Possibilities begin at the sidewalk, and as you wend your way down it seems as though every family is offering **rooms**; you'll also see signs for **houses to rent**.

Barracuda and Jaguar Inn, towards the south end of the village (☎06/23330, *wende@btl.net*). The best value in this price range, with two wooden cabins set in tropical gardens, with fridge and coffee maker and a large deck with lounge chairs and a hammock. There's also a two-bedroom apartment. ⑤–⑥.

Coconut Cottage, on the beach south of the centre (☎ & fax 06/23234, *kwplacencia@yahoo.com*). Two gorgeous, well-decorated and deservedly popular cabins on the beach, with fridge and deck. ⑦.

Cozy Corner Hotel (☎06/23280, *www.cozycornerhotel.com*), on the beach in the centre of the village. Spacious and good-value rooms with tiled floors and private bath, a big wooden deck all round and a good restaurant. ④.

Deb & Dave's Last Resort, on the road, near the centre (☎06/23207, *debanddave:btl.net*). The nicest budget place in the village, offering lovely rooms with shared hot-water bathroom. Bikes and kayaks for rent. ④.

Lydia's Guest House, near the north end of the sidewalk (☎06/23117, *lydias@btl.net*). Clean, secure and very good-value rooms, with tasty meals prepared on request. ④.

Seaspray Hotel, on the beach in the centre of the village (☎06/23148, *seaspray@btl.net*). Popular, well-run hotel offering a range of accommodation, all with private bath and some with fridge and balcony. ④–⑤.

Trade Winds, on the beach at the south point (☎06/23122, *trdewndpla@btl.net*). Brightly painted cabins and rooms with fridge and deck on a spacious and secluded plot facing the sea. ⑥.

Traveller's Inn, on the sidewalk, just south of the centre (☎06/23190). Five basic rooms (③) – the cheapest in the village – with shared bath and a tiny communal porch, plus more comfortable rooms with private bath in a separate building (④).

Eating and drinking

There are plenty of good **restaurants** in Placencia but places change management fast, so it's worth asking locally for the latest recommendations. Most places close early; you'll certainly have a better choice if you're at the table by 8pm. The *Pickled Parrot Bar & Grill*, at the *Barracuda and Jaguar Inn*, is consistently the best restaurant in the village, serving fresh seafood and international dishes. Just beyond here *BJ's Restaurant* serves the best-value Belizean meal in the village. Opposite, the *Purple Space Monkey Internet Café*, which opens early and closes late, offers good coffee, breakfasts and burgers under a huge thatched roof. At the south end of the village (turn right past the gas station), *Merlene's Restaurant* (☎06/23210) is usually the first to open, serving great breakfasts with good coffee; lunch and dinner are equally good, especially for fish, but the place is tiny so you may want to book. A few steps beyond here, built over the water, *Tentacles* has a superb location for enjoying the sunset, though the food – mainly steaks, pasta and seafood – can be variable.

The best-value **food counter** in Placencia, serving fried chicken and rice and beans, doesn't even have a name, but is easy to find: turn left at the end of the road and ask for Pearl. Fresh **bread** is available from John The Bakerman, signed from the sidewalk, and from a number of local women who bake Creole bread and buns. *Daisy's Ice Cream Parlour*, set back from the sidewalk, just south of the *Seaspray Hotel*, has long been deservedly popular for its **ice cream, cakes** and **snacks**, and also serves full meals.

Around Placencia

Trips from Placencia can include anything from an afternoon on or under the water to a week of camping, fishing, snorkelling and sailing. Placencia **lagoon** is ideal for exploring in a canoe or kayak (US$15–30 per day from Dave Vernon, ☎06/23207); you may even spot a manatee. **Diving** at Placencia is excellent, with fringing and patch reefs, but bear in mind that the distance to most dive sites means that trips here are more expensive than elsewhere. Aquatic Adventures (☎06/23182, *glenmar@btl.net*), at the dock in front of the *Paradise Hotel*, offer the best diving instruction, excursions and equipment rental. For **snorkelling** or **manatee-watching** check with Nite Wind Guides (☎06/23487) at the end of the sidewalk. Trips commonly include a visit to uninhabited **Laughing Bird Caye National Park**, beyond which lie the exquisite **Silk Cayes**, where the Barrier Reef begins to break into several smaller reefs and cayes; nearby **Gladden Spit** is now a marine reserve created to protect the seasonal visitation of the enormous yet graceful whale shark.

One of the best day-trips from Placencia takes you by boat 20km southwest to the almost pristine **Monkey River**, which teems with fish, bird life and, naturally enough, howler monkeys. The best tours to the river are run by Monkey River Magic (☎06/23330 or 014/4452; US$45, minimum two people), led by Evaristo Muschamp, a very experienced local guide: a thirty-minute dash through the waves is followed by a leisurely glide up the river and a walk along forest trails. You can get a meal in *Alice's Restaurant* in Monkey River village, and if you want **to stay** there's the *Sunset Inn* (☎061/2028; ③) on a tiny bay at the back of the village, a two-storey wooden hotel with comfortable beds, private bath and fan.

Independence/Mango Creek

Just across the lagoon from Placencia, **Independence** (also called Mango Creek) is a useful travel hub. The *Hokey Pokey* ferry runs from here to Placencia at 8.30am and 2.30pm (30min; US$6), returning from Placencia at 10am and 4pm. Heading north, Z-Line buses leave for **Dangriga** (2hr) at 7am, 10am and 1pm, and south to **Punta Gorda** (2hr 30min) at 1pm, 6pm and 8pm. The James bus from Belize City to Punta Gorda also passes through three or four times daily. With all these transport connections you should be able to avoid getting stuck overnight. If you do, the *Hello Hotel* (☎06/22428; ⑥), mainly used by business people, has some a/c rooms, or you could try the clean and simple *Ursula's Guest House* (③) on Gran Main Street.

The far south

Beyond Independence, the Southern Highway leaves the banana plantations, first twisting through pine forests, and crossing numerous creeks and rivers, then passing through new citrus plantations, their neat ranks of trees marching over the hills. **Red Bank**, on the northern edge of Toledo District, is home to one of the largest concentrations of scarlet macaws in Central America; for details on staying or visiting contact the Programme for Belize in Belize City (☎02/75616) or Geronimo Sho on the Red Bank community telephone (☎06/22233).

About 73km from the Placencia junction, 58km beyond Independence and 1km off the highway is **Nim Li Punit** (daily 8am–4pm; US$2.50), a Late-Classic Maya site, possibly allied to nearby Lubaantun and to Quiriguá in Guatemala (see p.226). The ruins stand on top of a ridge, surrounded by the fields of the nearby Maya village of **Indian Creek**. The **visitor centre** has a good map of the site and explanations of some of the carved texts found there, which include eight stelae, among them **Stela 15**, at over 9m the tallest yet found in Belize. Carvings on this great sandstone slab depict a larger-than-life figure in the act of dropping an offering – perhaps *copal* incense or kernels of corn – into an elaborately carved burning brazier supported on the back of a monster.

Eighteen kilometres further south a road branches off west to **San Antonio** (see p.113), from where you can explore the southern foothills of the Maya Mountains, dotted with ruins and some delightful Maya villages.

Punta Gorda

The Southern Highway comes to an end in **PUNTA GORDA**, the last town in Belize and the heart of the isolated **Toledo District**, an area that has always been hard to reach, though work on paving the highway north from Punta Gorda is well under way. The town is populated by a mixture of Creoles, Garífuna and Maya – who make up more

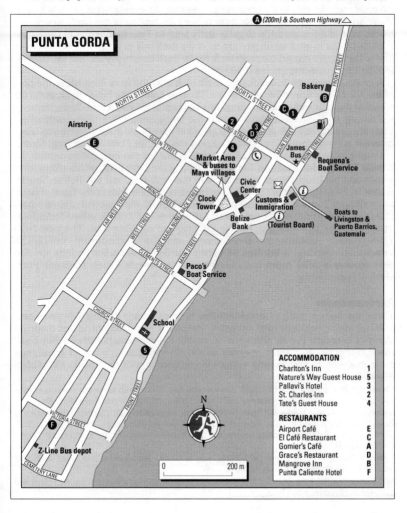

PUNTA GORDA

Ⓐ *(200m) & Southern Highway* △

Bakery Ⓑ
Ⓒ ❶
Airstrip
❷
Ⓔ
❸
Ⓓ
NORTH STREET
NORTH STREET
KING STREET
QUEEN STREET
MIDDLE STREET
MAIN STREET
FRONT STREET
❹
Ⓒ
James Bus
Requena's Boat Service
Market Area & buses to Maya villages
Civic Center
Clock Tower
Customs & Immigration
Belize Bank
ⓘ (Tourist Board)
ⓘ
Boats to Livingston & Puerto Barrios, Guatemala
PRINCE STREET
FAR WEST STREET
WEST STREET
CLEMENTS STREET
JOSE MARIA NUNEZ STREET
BACK STREET
MAIN STREET
Paco's Boat Service
CHURCH STREET
School
❺
VICTORIA STREET
Ⓕ
Z-Line Bus depot
CEMETERY LANE
FRONT STREET
N

ACCOMMODATION	
Charlton's Inn	1
Nature's Way Guest House	5
Pallavi's Hotel	3
St. Charles Inn	2
Tate's Guest House	4

RESTAURANTS	
Airport Café	E
El Café Restaurant	C
Gomier's Café	A
Grace's Restaurant	D
Mangrove Inn	B
Punta Caliente Hotel	F

0   200 m

than half the population of the district – and is the focal point for a large number of villages and farming settlements. The busiest day is Saturday, when people from the surrounding villages come into town to trade. Despite the recent minor building boom, Punta Gorda remains a small, unhurried and hassle-free town. Its position on low cliffs means that cooling sea breezes reduce the worst of the heat, though there's no escaping the rain – this is the wettest part of Belize and the trees here are heavy with mosses and bromeliads.

Arrival and information

Buses from Belize City, via Dangriga, take around eight hours to reach Punta Gorda; Z-Line buses use a depot at the south end of José María Nuñez Street, while James buses stop at an office near the dock. **Skiffs** from Puerto Barrios in **Guatemala** use the main dock, roughly in the centre of the seafront; the **immigration** office is nearby. There are five or six daily **flights** from Belize City, landing at the small airstrip five blocks west of the main dock. Regular skiffs head to **Puerto Barrios** in Guatemala (US$10–12; 1hr in good weather); turn up at the dock half an hour or so before departure so the skipper can get the paperwork ready. You'll have to pay the **exit tax** (US$10) and the PACT conservation fee (US$3.75).

A group of government buildings a block back from the ferry dock house the **post office**, the **BTL office** and a public phone. The only **bank** is the Belize Bank, at the top corner of the main square, across from the Civic Center (Mon–Fri 8am–2pm), but there will usually be a **moneychanger** outside the immigration office when international boats are coming and going; it's best to get rid of your Belize dollars before you leave. **Internet** access is available at *Cyber Café*, just past the *Sea Front Inn* on Front Street.

Despite having relatively few visitors, Punta Gorda has two information centres: the **Toledo Visitors Information Center** (TVIC), by the ferry dock, which offers information and bookings for accommodation in the local area, and the **Belize Tourist Board** on Front Street (☎07/22351) – staff at either office will know the times of buses to the villages. **Tours** of the interior of the Toledo District, the coast and cayes are available from local operators – Green Iguana Adventures (☎07/22475, *wilfred@belizehome .com*) also offer bird-watching, fishing, camping and kayaking trips. The local NGO TIDE (Toledo Institute for Development and the Environment; ☎07/22129, *www.belizeecotours.org*) is involved with many practical conservation projects and also offer **mountain bike tours** and camping trips to **Payne's Creek National Park**, north of Punta Gorda.

Accommodation

There has been a spate of **hotel-building** in town during the last few years and, although visitor numbers have increased, few people spend long here, and there are plenty of bargains. For an alternative to staying in town contact *Nature's Way Guest House* (listed below), which operates an award-winning programme of guesthouse accommodation in surrounding villages in conjunction with the Toledo Ecotourism Association.

Charlton's Inn, 9 Main St (☎07/22197, *charlstin@btl.net*). Rooms with hot-water showers – some also have a/c – in a two-storey concrete building with safe parking. Car rental available. ④.

Nature's Way Guest House, 65 Front St (☎07/22119, *beowulf@btl.net*). The best budget place in Punta Gorda and a good place to meet other travellers and get information. Accommodation is in private rooms or dorms overlooking the sea, and the wholefood restaurant does good meals. Dorms US$9, rooms ④.

Pallavi's Hotel, 19 Main Street (☎07/2414), next to *Grace's Restaurant*. Clean, good-value tiled rooms with private bath in a concrete building. ④.

St Charles Inn, 23 King St (☎07/22149). One of Punta Gorda's smartest options, with clean and quiet carpeted rooms with TV. ⑤.

Tate's Guest House, 34 José María Nuñez St, two blocks west of the town centre (☎07/22196, *teach@btl.net*). Quiet, friendly family-run hotel with some a/c rooms. ④–⑤.

Eating
Restaurants in Punta Gorda tend to be rather basic, though there are a few places where the quality is somewhat higher, and it's certainly easy to get a filling meal for a reasonable price. The *Punta Caliente Hotel* has one of the best restaurants in town, serving Creole and Garífuna dishes and a daily special. In the centre of town *Grace's Restaurant*, opposite the BTL office, serves typical Belizean dishes in very clean surroundings. To the north, along Front Street, the *Mangrove Inn* is a bright place serving seafood, burgers, steaks, Chinese dishes and vegetarian options. A few hundred metres further north *Gomier's Café* (closed weekends) serves delicious organic and soy meals, with a daily special. *El Café*, behind *Charlton's Inn*, does the best coffee in town and opens for breakfast at 6am.

The cayes and the coast

Four hundred square kilometres of the bay and coast north of Punta Gorda are now protected as the **Port Honduras Marine Reserve**, partly to safeguard the many **manatees** living and breeding in this shallow water habitat. The cayes and reefs here mark the southern end of Belize's barrier reef, and the main reef has started to break up, leaving several clusters of islands, each surrounded by a small independent reef. The closest of these islands to Punta Gorda are the **Snake Cayes**, hundreds of tiny islands in the mouth of a large bay whose shoreline is a complex maze of mangrove swamps. Further out in the Gulf of Honduras are the **Sapodilla Cayes**, now a **marine reserve**, of which the largest caye, **Hunting Caye**, is frequented by Guatemalan as well as Belizean day-trippers. Some of these islands already have accommodation, and more resorts are planned, though at present the cayes and reserve receive relatively few foreign visitors and are fascinating to explore.

South of Punta Gorda the coastline is flat and sparsely populated, with rivers meandering across a coastal plain covered in thick tropical rainforest. These include the Temash River, lined with the tallest mangrove forest in the country, and the Sarstoon River, which forms the border with Guatemala. The only village here is **Barranco**, a small, traditional Garífuna settlement of two hundred people which you can visit through the village guesthouse programme arranged by *Nature's Way* (see opposite).

Towards the mountains: Maya villages and ruins

The area inland from Punta Gorda towards the foothills of the Maya Mountains is home to the uniquely Belizean mix of **Mopan Maya** with **Kekchí** speakers from the Verapaz highlands of Guatemala. For the most part each group keeps to its own villages, language and traditions, although both are partially integrated into modern Belizean life and most people speak English. The region's villages are connected to Punta Gorda by road, but while there's a basic bus service from Punta Gorda (check with the information offices for times), getting around isn't that easy: in many places you'll have to rely on hitching – and traffic is sparse – or walking. The easiest village to reach is **San Antonio**, served by regular buses from Punta Gorda.

Blue Creek, San Antonio and Uxbenka
About 4km before San Antonio, at *Roy's Cool Spot* (where you can get a meal and a drink), a branch road heads off west to the village of **BLUE CREEK**, whose main attraction is a beautiful stretch of water that runs through magnificent rainforest.

Whether you're walking or driving you won't miss the river, as the road crosses it just before it enters the village. The best swimming spot is a lovely turquoise pool about ten minutes' walk upriver along the right-hand bank (facing upstream). The source, the **Hokeb Ha** cave, is about another fifteen minutes' walk upriver through the privately owned **Blue Creek Rainforest Reserve**. A guide can take you to Maya altars deep in the cave.

Perched on a small hilltop, the Mopan Maya village of **SAN ANTONIO** has the advantage of *Bol's Hill Top Hotel* (community phone ☎07/22144; ③), which offers simple **rooms** and superb views, and is a good place to get information on local natural history and archeology. The area is rich in wildlife, surrounded by jungle-clad hills and swift-flowing rivers. Further south and west are the villages of the **Kekchí Maya**. The founders of San Antonio were from the village of San Luis, just across the border in Guatemala, and they maintain many age-old traditions, including their patron saint, San Luis Rey, whose church stands opposite *Bol's* hotel. The Maya also adhere to their own pre-Columbian traditions and fiestas – the main one takes place on June 13, and features marimba music, masked dances and much heavy drinking.

Seven kilometres west from San Antonio, towards the village of **Santa Cruz**, are the ruins of **Uxbenka**, a small Maya site, superbly positioned on an exposed hilltop with great views towards the coast. As you climb the hill before the village you'll be able to make out the shape of two tree-covered mounds and a plaza, and there are several badly eroded stelae protected by thatched shelters. Trucks and buses continue 13km further west to **Jalacte**, at the Guatemalan border, used regularly as a crossing point by nationals of both countries, though it's not currently a legal entry or exit point for tourists.

Lubaantun

To visit the ruins of **Lubaantun** (daily 8am–5pm; US$5) from San Antonio, head back along the road to Punta Gorda and after 8km turn left at the track leading to **San Pedro Columbia**, a Kekchí village 4km along the road. Head through the village, cross the Columbia River and just beyond you'll see the track to the ruins, a few hundred metres away on the left. Some of the finds made at the site are displayed in glass cases at the **visitor centre**: astonishing, eccentric flints (symbols of a ruler's power), ceramics and ocarinas – clay whistles in the shape of animal effigies.

Lubaantun ("Place of the Fallen Stones") was a major Maya centre, though it was occupied only briefly, from 700 to 890 AD, very near the end of the Classic period. The city stands on a series of ridges which Maya architects shaped and filled, building retaining walls up to 10m high. There are no stelae or sculpted monuments other than ball-court markers, and the whole site is essentially a single acropolis, with five main plazas, eleven major structures, three ball courts and some impressive pyramids surrounded by forest. A recent restoration has confirmed that the famous Maya corbelled arch was never used here; buildings were instead constructed by laying stone blocks carved with great precision and fitted together, Inca-style, with nothing to bind them. This technique, and the fact that most of the main buildings have rounded corners, give Lubaantun an elegance sometimes missing from larger and more manicured sites.

Perhaps Lubaantun's most enigmatic find came in 1926, when the famous **Crystal Skull** was unearthed here. Carved from pure rock crystal, the skull was apparently found beneath an altar by Anna Mitchell-Hedges (who still has it in her possession), the adopted daughter of the British Museum expedition's leader, F.A. Mitchell-Hedges. The skull was given to the local Maya, who in turn presented it to Anna's father as a token of their gratitude for the help he had given them.

There are several **places to stay** around San Pedro. The best are *Dem Dats Doin* (☎07/22470; ④), a sustainable technology farm with a guest room, 2km from the turn-off on the San Antonio road, and the comfortable wooden cabins of *Fallen Stones Butterfly Ranch* (☎07/22167, *www.fallenstones.co.uk*; ⑨), in a fantastic hilltop location 3km beyond the turn for the ruins.

travel details

BUSES

Journey times south of Dangriga are approximate only.

Dangriga to: Belize City (10 daily; 2–3hr); Hopkins (2 daily; 45min); Independence (8 daily; 2hr); Placencia (2 daily; 2hr–2hr 30min); Punta Gorda (8 daily; 4–5hr).

Placencia to: Dangriga (2 daily; 2hr).

Punta Gorda to: Belize City (8 daily; 8hr); Dangriga (8 daily; 4hr 30min).

FLIGHTS

Maya Island (☎02/31362) and Tropic (☎026/2012) have flights from **Belize City to Dangriga** (35min), most continuing to **Placencia** and **Punta Gorda**. All flights from Punta Gorda to Belize City call at Placencia and Dangriga.

INTERNATIONAL BOATS

Dangriga to: Puerto Cortés, Honduras (1 weekly on Sat; 3hr).

Placencia to: Puerto Cortés, Honduras (1 weekly on Fri; 3hr).

Punta Gorda to: Puerto Barrios, Guatemala (3–4 daily; 1hr).

PART THREE

GUATEMALA

0   100 km

N

MEXICO

BELIZE

CHAPTER 11
PETÉN

CHAPTER 10
COBÁN AND
THE VERAPACES

CHAPTER 7
THE WESTERN
HIGHLANDS

CHAPTER 9
EAST TO THE
CARIBBEAN

HONDURAS

CHAPTER 6
GUATEMALA CITY

CHAPTER 8
THE PACIFIC COAST

EL SALVADOR

Introduction

Spread across a verdant and mountainous chunk of land, **Guatemala** is endowed with simply staggering natural, historical and cultural interest. Though the giant **Maya** temples and rainforest cities have been long abandoned, ancient traditions remain very much alive throughout the Guatemalan highlands. Uniquely in Central America, at least half the country's population is still Native American, and this rural indigenous culture is far stronger than anywhere else in the region. Countering this is a powerful **ladino** society, characteristically urban and commercial in its outlook. All over the country you'll come across remnants of Guatemala's **colonial** past, nowhere more so than in the graceful former capital, Antigua.

It's this outstanding cultural legacy, combined with Guatemala's mesmeric natural beauty, that makes the country so compelling for the traveller. The Maya temples of **Tikal** would be magnificent in any arena but set inside the pristine jungle of the Maya Biosphere Reserve, with attendant toucans and howler monkeys, they are bewitching. Similarly, the genteel cobbled streets and plazas of colonial **Antigua** gain an extra dimension from their proximity to the looming volcanoes that encircle the town. This architectural wealth is scattered to a lesser degree throughout the country – almost every large village or town boasts a giant whitewashed colonial church and a classic Spanish-style plaza. Though most of the really dramatic Maya ruins lie deep in the jungles of **Petén**, interesting sites are scattered throughout the land, along the Pacific coast and in the foothills of the highlands.

The diversity of the Guatemalan **landscape** is astonishing. Perhaps most obviously arresting is the chain of **volcanoes** (some still smoking) that divides the flat, steamy **Pacific coast** from the cool air and pine trees of the largely indigenous western **highlands**, with their green, sweeping valleys, tiny cornfields, gurgling streams and sleepy traditional villages. Further east towards the **Caribbean**, the scenery and the people have more of a tropical feel and at Lívingston, life beside the mangrove and coconut trees swings to reggae rhythms and punta rock.

The **rainforests** of Petén, among the best preserved in Latin America, harbour a tremendous array of **wildlife**, including jaguars, tapirs, spiders, howler monkeys, jabiru storks and scarlet macaws. Further south, you may be lucky and catch a glimpse of the elusive quetzal in the cloudforests close to Cobán or see manatee in the Río Dulce. On the Pacific coast three types of sea turtle nest in the volcanic sand beaches of Monterrico.

All of this exists against the nagging background of Guatemala's turbulent and bloody **history**. Over the years, the huge gulf between the rich and the poor, between indigenous and *ladino* culture and the political left and right has produced bitter conflict. With the signing of the **1996 peace accords** between the government and the ex-guerrillas, the armed confrontation has ceased and things have calmed down considerably, though many of the country's deep-rooted inequalities remain. At the heart of the problem is the red-hot issue of **land reform** – it's estimated that close to seventy percent of the cultivable land is still owned by less than five percent of the population. There is also a chronic lack of faith in the corrupt and inept **justice system**, which has led to a wave of public lynchings of suspected criminals across the country. At the same time the **economy** was destabilized badly by Hurricane Mitch in 1998 and is still chronically weak. Guatemala remains heavily dependent on the export of coffee, sugar and bananas and has very little industry except the foreign-owned *maquila* factories which produce goods for export and typically pay their assembly-line workers under US$5 for a twelve-hour day. Poverty levels are some of the worst in the hemisphere and there's general discontent with the high cost of living.

Despite these structural inequalities, you'll find that most Guatemalans are extraordinarily courteous, and eager to help a lost foreigner catch the right bus or find the local post office. Guatemalans tend to be less extrovert than other Central Americans and are quite formal in social situations. Many will automatically assume you are wealthy, since very few Guatemalans ever get to visit another country. Though you may hear complaints about rising prices, endemic corruption and the lack of decent jobs, this is not to say that Guatemalans are not patriotic and sensitive to criticisms from outsiders.

■ Where to go

Perhaps the most fascinating part of the entire country is the **western highlands**, where not

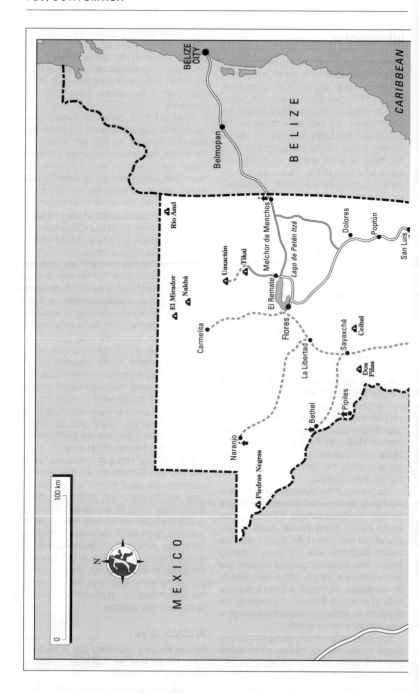

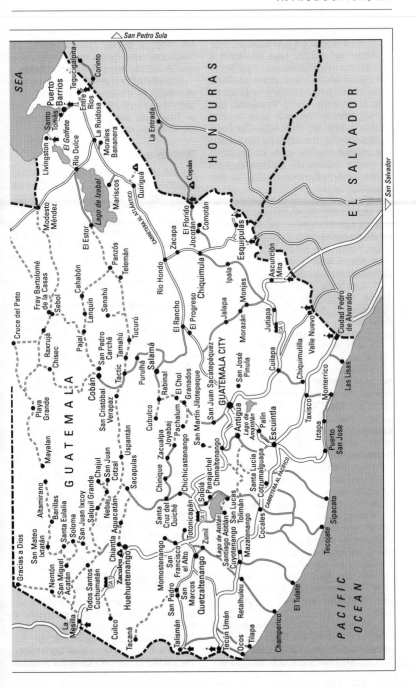

only is the scenery wildly beautiful, but you'll also find the most interesting Maya villages and amazing fiestas and markets. **Lago de Atitlán** is unmissable, a large highland lake, ringed by sentinel-like volcanoes, whose shores are dotted with some of the most traditional indigenous villages in the entire country. **Panajachel** is a booming lakeside town with some excellent restaurants, cafés and shops, while **San Pedro La Laguna** on the other side of the lake has more of a bohemian travellers' scene. For handicrafts, the famous twice-weekly **Chichicastenango market** is unrivalled, with an incredible selection of weavings for sale.

Further scenic excesses lie around the country's second city of **Quetzaltenango (Xela)**, an excellent base for a series of day-trips to nearby hot springs, market towns, pagan shrines and volcanoes. Finally, there are the isolated and traditional villages deep in the mountains of the **Cuchumatanes**: perhaps the two best places to head for are **Nebaj** in the Ixil triangle and **Todos Santos Cuchumatán** to the north of Huehuetenango. Both are intensely rewarding places to visit, with superb scenery, excellent walking and cheap guesthouses.

The *ladino*-dominated **Pacific coast** is generally hot and dull, a strip of black volcanic sand with a smattering of mangrove swamps behind it that blend into the country's most productive farmland. The area is devoted to commercial agriculture and dotted with bustling urban centres; points of interest are thin on the ground. The **beaches** are not as you imagine Pacific beaches to be, except at the wildlife reserve of **Monterrico**, where there is a fine stretch of sand and a maze of mangrove swamps to explore.

If it's real adventure and exploration you seek, nothing can compete with the hidden archeological wonders of **Petén**. This unique lowland area, which makes up about a third of the country, is covered with dense rainforest – only recently threatened by development – that's alive with wildlife and dotted with superb Maya ruins. The only town of any size is **Flores**, from where you can easily reach **Tikal**, the most impressive of all Maya sites. Other dramatic sites like the monumental **El Mirador** require days of tough travel to reach.

In the **east** of the country are the spectacular gorge systems of the **Río Dulce**, the ruins of **Quiriguá** and on the Caribbean coast the funky town of **Lívingston**, home to Guatemala's only black community. Dividing this eastern area from the Petén is another highland region, the **Verapaces**, where there is more stunning alpine scenery and the sleepy coffee centre of **Cobán**.

Guatemala City is of little interest to the traveller except for a couple of museums; it's much better to stay in the colonial capital **Antigua**, just an hour away, where there are great hotels, restaurants and cafés for every budget.

■ When to go

The bulk of Guatemala enjoys one of the most pleasant **climates** on earth, with typically warm or hot days and mild or cool evenings all year round – only in the lowlands does it get really uncomfortably hot and humid.

The immediate climate is largely governed by **altitude**. The Guatemala tourist board calls the country "the land of eternal spring", and since most places of interest are between 1300 and 1600m (including Antigua, Lago de Atitlán and Cobán) there's some justification in this. However, in Quetzaltenango and the Cuchumatanes mountains the climate can be cool and damp and nights distinctly cold. In low-lying Petén it's a different world, with sticky, steamy conditions most of the year. The Pacific and Caribbean coasts are equally hot and humid, but here at least you can usually rely on the welcome relief of sea breezes.

There is also a **rainy season**, roughly from May to October, which Guatemalans call winter, though the rain is usually confined to the late afternoon and the rest of the day is often warm and pleasant. As a rule it's only in remote parts that rain can affect your travel plans. This is especially so in Petén, where the rainy season extends into December and it's advisable to delay any real exploration until February.

The **busiest time** for tourism is between December and March, when many North Americans seek respite from the cold; and again in July and August – this is also the busiest time for the language schools.

Getting around

For most people, travelling in Guatemala means using the anarchic fume-belching **bus system**: a chaotic mix of fun, frustration and discomfort. While it's possible to remove yourself from this chaos to a certain degree by taking **tourist shuttles** and **flights**, you risk missing out on one of

Guatemala's essential experiences. Though in remote areas many buses leave in the dead of night in order to reach the morning markets, we strongly recommend **not travelling after dark** if you can avoid it, due to the greater risk of robbery.

Despite a concerted government campaign to improve things, Guatemala's road network is still alarmingly inadequate and you'll constantly find yourself stuck behind smoking trucks as you climb up the Carretera Interamericana to Lago de Atitlán or drive down to the Caribbean. Fortunately, whatever the pace of your journey, you always have the spectacular Guatemalan countryside to wonder at.

■ Buses

Buses are cheap and convenient, and can be hugely entertaining. There are two types of service. **Second-class** buses – known as *camionetas* to Guatemalans and "chicken buses" to foreigners – are by far the most numerous, and easily distinguished by their trademark clouds of thick black fumes. If they look familiar to North Americans that's because they're old school buses (mainly Bluebirds). Second-class buses will usually stop for every possible passenger, cramming their seats, aisles and occasionally roofs: journeys are certainly never dull. Chickens cluck, merengue assaults your eardrums, snack vendors tout for business and the locals gossip and laugh. Almost all second-class buses operate out of **bus terminals**, often adjacent to the local market. Tickets are bought on board and cost around US$0.75 per hour's travelling, though rip-offs do happen – check out what the locals are paying.

First-class or **pullman** buses, usually old Greyhounds, are faster and more expensive (around $1 an hour) than regular buses and make fewer stops. Each passenger will be sure of a seat to him or herself, and tickets can be bought in advance. They only serve the main routes such as the Carretera al Atlántico and Interamericana, but they will usually stop for you en route if they have space aboard. Pullmans usually leave from the bus company's office rather than the main bus terminal.

■ Taxis

Taxis are available in all the main towns and rates are fairly low. Except in Guatemala City, meters are nonexistent, so it's essential to **fix a price** before you set off. Local taxi drivers will almost always be prepared to negotiate a price for a half-day or day's excursion to nearby villages or sites.

■ Driving and hitching

On the whole, **driving** inside Guatemala is pretty straightforward and it certainly offers unrivalled freedom as traffic is rarely heavy outside the capital. **Parking and security** are the main problems, and in the larger towns you should always get your car shut away in a guarded car park. Most of the main routes are paved but minor roads are often extremely rough. **Fuel** is extremely cheap by European standards, marginally more expensive than in the US. If you plan to head up into the mountains or along any of the smaller roads in Petén, you'll need high clearance and 4WD.

Renting a car takes some of the worries out of driving but is expensive: generally at least US$40 a day (around US$230 a week) by the time you've added the extras. If you do rent, make sure to check the details of the insurance, which often won't cover any damage to your vehicle.

If you plan to visit the more remote parts of the country then it's almost inevitable that you will **hitch** a ride with a pick-up or truck from time to time. You'll usually have to pay for your lift – around the same as the bus fare. Rule number one is **safety**: it's not a good idea for women to hitch alone, and if you don't feel comfortable about getting in someone's vehicle, don't do it.

■ Bikes and motorbikes

Bikes are pretty common in Guatemala and cycling is a popular sport, so you'll be well received and should be able to find a repair shop in most towns. Though cycling is the most exhilarating way to see Guatemala, the country is very mountainous and roads are poor. Most buses will carry bikes on the roof if it all gets a bit too much. You can rent **mountain bikes** in Antigua and Panajachel: see the relevant listings.

Motorbikes can also be an excellent way of getting around and since many locals ride them it's not too hard to locate parts and expertise. There are rental outlets in Guatemala City, Panajachel and Antigua, charging around US$25 a day or US$120 for a week.

■ Boats

Small speedy motorized boats called lanchas have largely replaced ferry routes in Guatemala, though there's still a slow ferry service between Puerto Barrios and Lívingston. The two definitive **boat trips** in Guatemala are through the Río Dulce gorge system, starting in either Lívingston or the town of Río Dulce, and across Lago de Atitlán, usually beginning in Panajachel.

■ Planes

The only internal **flight** most people are likely to take is from Guatemala City to Flores (from US$75 return), with four airlines offering rival services. A domestic airline, **Inter** (part of the Taca group), flies to various other destinations within Guatemala, though they have a poor reputation for overbooking and last-minute flight cancellations. In theory, Inter operates daily return services between Guatemala City and Puerto Barrios, Santa Cruz del Quiché, Quetzaltenango, Retalhuleu, Cobán and Huehuetenango, plus weekend return flights to the Río Dulce. Fares hover around US$40 to US$60 one way.

Costs, money and banks

In May 2001 the **US dollar** became an official currency of Guatemala, alongside the **quetzal**; the exchange rate at the time of writing was Q7.90 to US$1. Both currencies are accepted countrywide, with small change usually being given in quetzales.

Guatemala is an extremely cheap country to travel in. It's certainly possible for **budget travellers** to survive on around US$100 a week in Guatemala by sleeping in simple hospedajes, eating at comedores, travelling by local bus and going easy on the beers. Your wallet will suffer in tourist towns like Antigua and Panajachel, and you'll pay for any indulgences like wine, taxis or shuttle buses. The extremely self-disciplined or fiscally challenged could survive in somewhere like San Pedro La Laguna (see p.197) for as little as US$60 a week. If you can afford to burn a few more quetzales, however, and desire a hotel room with private bath, more varied food and want to take the odd shuttle bus, reckon on US$200 a week. Guatemala has some spectacular hotels at the luxury end of the market – to travel in **real style**, reckon on paying on around US$80 a day, for which you can expect accommodation with period character (plus modern amenities), shuttle buses and the best food in town. Remember that

leaving the country you'll be charged an **airport tax** of US$30, payable in cash (either dollars or quetzales) only.

Travellers' cheques offer one of the safest ways to carry money, with American Express, Thomas Cook, Mastercard, and Citibank cheques being accepted in most banks. It's not a sensible idea to take cheques issued in any currency other than US$ – though Lloyds Bank (branches in Guatemala City, Antigua, Puerto Barrios and Escuintla) will cash sterling travellers' cheques, albeit at poor rates.

Credit cards are widely accepted in upmarket hotels, selected restaurants and most travel agencies. You'll need to pay by cash in most smaller hotels and restaurants. Cards may also be used in the country's network of ATMs; if you've a **Visa** card (by far the most useful) Banco Industrial is the first place to head for. **Mastercard** holders will have much more of a problem finding functioning ATMs, though all branches of Banco G & T Continental should give you an advance. If you have a **debit card**, the **Plus** system (networked with Visa) is by far the most useful, and there's at least one ATM in most towns. **Cirrus** cardholders will really struggle to find functioning ATMs in Guatemala, though there are outlets in the capital (see listings p.156).

Information

The national tourist board, **Inguat**, give out glossy brochures and will try to help you with your trip, but don't expect too much independent travel advice – branches can be found in Guatemala City, Panajachel, Antigua, Flores and Quetzaltenango. In **Petén**, two Flores-based organizations, CINCAP and ProPetén, provide essential support for jungle trekking (see p.258).

Accommodation

Accommodation in Guatemala comes in a multitude of different guises: pensiones, huéspedes, posadas, hospedajes and hotels. The names don't actually mean that much, though most hotels tend to be towards the top end of the price scale and most hospedajes and pensiones towards the bottom. Breakfast is almost never included in the price. As most small towns have a hospedaje or two, staying in peoples' houses is rare, but at fiesta time many families rent out rooms for a little extra cash.

At the **top end** of the scale (above US$80 a night) you'll find magnificent colonial hotels with authentic interiors in most of the main tourist centres, especially Antigua. In the **mid-range** bracket (US$15–80) there are some brilliant deals available: you can still expect character and comfort, and a private bathroom, but perhaps without any extra facilities. Even at the **budget** (under US$10) end of the scale you should be able to find a clean double room in any town in the country (though you may have to look hard in Guatemala City). In some places room prices fall to as low as US$2 a person. Usefully, **prices** are all fixed by Inguat, the tourist board; there should be a price posted behind the door of your room. Despite this, it's well worth trying to **haggle** a little, or asking if there are any cheaper rooms. There are no official youth hostels in Guatemala, but you will find the odd dormitory.

It's only on the Pacific and Caribbean coasts and in Petén that you'll need a **fan** or **air conditioning**; in the highlands you'll sometimes find a logwood fire in the luxury hotels, and heavy-duty blankets in the cheaper places. **Mosquito nets** are very rarely provided, even in the lowland areas, so if you plan to spend some time in Petén or on either coast, it's well worth investing in one, and essential if you plan to so some jungle trekking.

Campsites are extremely thin on the ground in Guatemala. The main cities certainly don't have them and the only places with any decent formal provision for camping are in Panajachel, San Pedro La Laguna, Lanquín, Poptún and Tikal. However, if you decide to set off into the wilds then a **tent** is certainly a good idea, although even here it's by no means essential as most villages have a simple hospedaje – if not, ask for the mayor (*alcalde*), who should allow you to sleep in the town hall (*municipalidad*).

Eating and drinking

Food doesn't come high on the list of reasons to visit Guatemala. In general Guatemalans have fairly unadventurous tastes and seem to survive on a strict diet of eggs, beans and tortillas – in most towns a pizza is considered extremely exotic. However, in the main tourist centres there's much more choice, and in Antigua, Guatemala City and Panajachel you'll be able to feast on numerous different European cuisines, several Asian ones, all-American menus and even Middle Eastern dishes.

Traditionally, Guatemalans eat a **breakfast** of tortillas and eggs, accompanied by the inevitable beans. **Lunch** is the main meal of the day, and this is the best time to fill up as restaurants often offer *comidas corridas*, a set two- or three-course meal that sometimes costs as little as a dollar. It's always filling and occasionally delicious. **Evening meals** are generally more expensive.

■ Where to eat

The first distinction in Guatemala is between the **restaurant** and the **comedor**. Comedores are basic eateries that serve simple food at cheap prices – expect to pay around US$2 for a good feed. In contrast, restaurants are a purely urban phenomenon, and more formal and expensive (US$4 a head and upwards). There are, however, plenty of restaurants with comedor-like menus, and vice versa.

In the larger towns you'll also find **fast-food** joints, modelled on the American originals and often part of the same chains. When you're travelling you'll also come across the local version of fast food: at junctions, buses are besieged by vendors offering a huge selection of drinks, sweets, local specialities and complete meals. Many of these are delicious but you do need to treat this kind of food with a degree of caution and bear in mind the general lack of hygiene.

In most towns there's some kind of pizzeria and a Chinese restaurant: they can make a welcome break from eggs and beans but don't expect anything very authentic. Cakes and pastries are also widely available but tend to be pretty dull and dry.

Vegetarians are hardly catered for specifically, except in the tourist restaurants of Antigua and Panajachel and at a handful of places in Guatemala City. It is, however, fairly easy to get by eating plenty of beans and eggs, which are always on the menu, accompanied by freshly made tortillas. The **markets** also offer plenty of superb fruit and snacks like *tostadas* and *pupusas* (see below).

■ What to eat

Maya cuisine is at the heart of Guatemalan cooking. Maize is an essential – in Maya legend, humankind was originally created from maize – and it appears most commonly as a thin corn pancake, the **tortilla**. The maize is traditionally ground by hand and shaped by clapping it between two hands then toasted on a **comal**, a flat pan of clay or metal placed over the fire. Tortillas are eaten while warm and are usually brought to the table wrapped in cloth. The very best have a slightly burnt, smoky taste and a pliable texture. Mexican-style **tamales** (steamed cornmeal often stuffed with meat, wrapped in a banana leaf) are not that common, but when you can get them are usually delicious.

Beans (*frijoles*) are served as they are in the rest of Central America, either refried (*volteados*) or whole (*parados*) in their own black juice. Almost all truly Guatemalan meals include a portion of beans. In the highlands you'll come across **mosh** (porridge) from time to time. To a lesser extent, **chillies**, usually served in the form of a spicy sauce (*salsa picante*), are the final ingredient in a Maya meal.

Combined with this essentially Maya culinary style, you'll find **ladino-style** food everywhere, often on the same menu. *Bistek* (steak), *pollo frito* (fried chicken) and *hamburguesas* are popular with all Guatemalans. *Chiles rellenos* (stuffed peppers) make a healthy change from other cholesterol saturated dishes and *pepián* (meat stew with vegetables) and *caldos* (meat broths) are usually excellent.

Popular **market snacks** include *pupusas* (thick tortillas topped with crunchy grated salad vegetables) and *tostadas* (corn crisps smeared with avocado, cheese and other toppings).

Finally, on the Caribbean coast there is a distinct **Creole cuisine**, heavily based on fish, seafood, coconuts, plantain and banana.

■ Drinks

To start off the day most Guatemalans drink a cup of weak **coffee**, which is usually loaded with sugar. It's becoming much easier to get a decent cup in tourist-oriented towns, but you're much more likely to be served brown-coloured slops rather than anything resembling the real thing. Through the day locals drink water or *refresco*, a thirst-quenching water-based drink with some fruit flavour added. Coca-Cola, Pepsi, Sprite or Fanta (all called *aguas*) are also common and popular. For a healthy treat, order a *licuado*: a thick, fruit-based drink with either water or milk (milk is safer). **Bottled water** (*agua mineral* or *agua pura*) is available almost everywhere.

Guatemalan **beer** tends to be bland and unexciting and is very rarely available on tap. Woefully, one characterless brew has a near monopoly – the ubiquitous **Gallo** – a medium-strength lager-style beer that comes in 33cl or litre bottles (around US$1 and US$2 respectively in a bar; much less in a supermarket). More interesting but not as widespread is Moza, a dark brew with a slight caramel flavour. The best of the lagers is the premium beer Montecarlo, which is worth the extra quetzal or two when you can get it. You'll also come across Dorada Draft, another dull lager brew, and occasionally Cabro, which has a little more flavour. Imported brands are very rare.

As for **spirits**, rum (*ron*) and *aguardiente*, a clear and lethal sugarcane spirit, are very popular and correspondingly cheap. Ron Botran Añejo is a good rum (around $4 a bottle), while hard drinkers will soon get to know Quezalteca, a local *aguardiente* sold and drunk everywhere, whose power is at the heart of many a fiesta.

Guatemalan **wine** does exist but it bears little resemblance to the real thing. Chilean wines are the best value, with decent bottles available from around US$5 in supermarkets and double that in restaurants.

Opening hours, festivals and holidays

Most offices, shops, post offices and museums are **open** between 8.30am and 5pm, though some take a break for lunch. Bank hours are extremely convenient, with many opening until 7pm (and some as late as 8pm) from Monday to Friday and until 12.30pm or 1pm on Saturdays.

Archeological **sites** are open every day, usually from 8am to 5pm, though **Tikal** is open from 6am to 6pm (until 8pm with permission). The principal public holidays, when almost all businesses

close down, are listed in the box overleaf; in villages, most shops shut during fiestas.

■ Fiestas

Traditional **fiestas** are one of the great excitements of a trip to Guatemala, and every town and village, however small, devotes at least one day a year to celebration.

Guatemalan fiestas can be divided into two basic models: *ladino* and Maya. **Ladino** towns and villages celebrate with daytime processions, beauty contests and perhaps the odd marching band with dance halls by night. In the highlands,

---

GUATEMALAN FESTIVALS

JANUARY
1–5 **Santa María de Jesús**, near Antigua (main days 1st and 2nd)
19–24 **Rabinal**, in the Verapaces (main days 23rd and 24th)
22–26 **San Pablo La Laguna**, Lago de Atitlán (main day 25th)

MARCH
Second Friday in Lent **Chajul**, in the Ixil triangle

APRIL
24 **San Jorge La Laguna**, Lago de Atitlán
25 **San Marcos La Laguna**, Lago de Atitlán

MAY
6–10 **Uspantán** (main day 8th)
8–10 **Santa Cruz La Laguna** (main day 10th)

JUNE
12–14 **San Antonio Palopó**, near Panajachel (main day 13th)
21–25 **Olintepeque**, near Quetzaltenango
22–25 **San Juan Cotzal**, near Nebaj
22–26 **San Juan Atitán** (main day 24th)
27–30 **San Pedro La Laguna** (main day 29th)
28–30 **Almolongo**, near Quetzaltenango (main day 29th)

JULY
21–Aug 4 **Momostenango** (most interesting on July 25 and Aug 1)
23–27 **Santiago Atitlán** (main day 25th)
25 **Antigua**
25 **Cubulco**, in the Verapaces
31–Aug 6 **Cobán**

AUGUST
1–4 **Sacapulas** (main day 4th)
9–15 **Joyabaj**, west of Santa Cruz del Quiché (main day 15th)
12–15 **Nebaj** (main day 15th)
15 **Guatemala City**

SEPTEMBER
12–18 **Quetzaltenango** (main day 15th)
17–21 **Salamá** (main day 17th)
24–30 **Totonicapán** (main day 29th)

OCTOBER
1–6 **San Francisco El Alto** (main day 4th)
2–6 **Panajachel** (main day 4th)
29–Nov 1 **Todos Santos** Cuchumatán

NOVEMBER
1 **All Saints' Day** Celebrations all over, but most dramatic in Todos Santos Cuchumatán and Santiago Sacatepéquez, where massive paper kites are flown
23–26 **Nahualá** (main day 25th)
22–26 **Zunil** (main day 25th)
25 **Santa Catarina Palopó**, Lago de Atitlán
30 **San Andrés Xecul**, near Quetzaltenango
30 **San Andrés Iztapa**, near Antigua

DECEMBER
7 **Bonfires** (the Burning of the Devil) throughout the country
7 **Ciudad Vieja**, near Antigua
13–21 **Chichicastenango** (main day 21st)

however, where the bulk of the population is **Maya**, you'll see a blend of religious and pre-Columbian secular celebration. The very finest ceremonial costumes are usually dusted down and worn, and you can expect to see some hugely symbolic traditional dancing, including the *Baile de la Conquista*, which re-enacts the Spanish victory over the Maya. Whether *ladino* or Maya, festivals tend to be chaotic, drunken affairs with plenty of dancing and fireworks. If you can join in the mood, there's no doubt that fiestas are wonderfully entertaining as well as offering a real insight into both sides of Guatemalan culture.

Many of the **best fiestas** include some specifically local element, such as the giant kites at **Santiago Sacatepéquez**, the religious processions in **Antigua** and the horse race in **Todos Santos Cuchumatán**. At certain times virtually the whole country erupts simultaneously: **Easter week** is perhaps the most important, particularly in **Antigua** and **Santiago Atitlán**, but **All Saints' Day** (November 1), when people gather in cemeteries to honour the dead, and **Christmas** are also marked by celebrations across the land. The festivals listed in the box on the previous page are the pick of the lot.

Mail and telecommunications

Even small towns usually have a branch of **Telgua**, the national phone company, where you can make international phone calls. Most are open daily from 7am to midnight. Telgua tariffs are ridiculously high, however, starting at US$7 for a three-minute call to North America and US$11 to Western Europe. In many places, including Antigua, Flores, Panajachel and Quetzaltenango, you'll be able to find shops, hotels or travel agencies offering much cheaper rates, from as little as US$0.30 per minute to North America and US$0.50 to Western Europe. **Webcall** (phone calls via the Internet) facilities are also beginning to appear in some cybercafés, slashing international call rates to the price of surfing the net, though connections are usually extremely crackle- and delay-prone.

From Guatemala you can only make **collect calls** (reverse charges) to the USA, Canada, Mexico, Italy, Spain, Japan, Switzerland and other Central American countries – not to the UK. Dial ☎171 for the **international operator**. Calling Guatemala from abroad, the **country code** is ☎502. **Local** calls in Guatemala are very cheap, and phone boxes are quite common; it pays to get a **phonecard** if you plan to make a number of calls. **Faxes** can be sent or received from any Telgua branch in the country, or (often more cheaply) through travel agencies, some shops and languages schools. The cheapest method of all for sending a fax is via the **Internet** (see opposite).

Outgoing Guatemalan postal services are fairly efficient by Latin American standards, and you can **send mail** easily from even the smallest of towns – though it's probably safer to send anything of importance through a private firm. The regular mail service is also extremely **cheap** but not very speedy; airmail letters generally take around a week to the US, a couple of weeks or more to Europe. Alternatively, UPS, DHL and Federal Express all operate in Guatemala. **Sending parcels** through the standard mail service is problematic as there are complex regulations about the way in which they should be wrapped. You may want to use a specialized shipping agency instead: see the Antigua and Panajachel listings for recommended companies.

Post coming into Guatemala is less reliable, and the **poste restante** (Lista de Correos) method of holding mail is no longer dependable. Letters and postcards are normally fine, but don't send anything valuable or bulky through the regular mail – use a courier service instead. **American**

Express in Guatemala City at Diagonal 6 10-01, Centro Gerencial Las Margaritas, Zona 10 (Mon–Fri 8.30am–5pm; ☎339 2877) will hold mail for card- or cheque-holders. Alternatively, if you've studied with a language school they'll usually keep your mail for you.

■ Email and the Internet

Guatemala has been quick to embrace the **Internet**, and **cybercafés** are mushrooming throughout the country – you'll find them in numerous towns including all the main (and many minor) tourist centres. In more remote areas Guatemala's antiquated phone system causes frequent connection problems, but in the cities connection speeds are rapid and reliable. Rates vary between US$1.60 and US$6 an hour. Virtually all language schools are online; many offer students discount Internet rates when they enrol for classes.

A vast number of hotels and businesses now have email (and Web sites). Additionally, many towns and regions now boast superb community **Web sites**, replete with information on accommodation, restaurants, culture and entertainment.

The media

After a couple of decades when being a journalist in Guatemala was one of the most dangerous professions on the entire continent, things have cooled down somewhat. The nation's **newspapers** have expanded in both volume and coverage and, in theory, there is little restriction on their freedom, although pressures are still exerted by criminal gangs, the military and those in authority.

Guatemala has a number of daily newspapers with extensive national coverage and a more limited international perspective. Best of the **dailies** are the forthright and outspoken *El Periódico*, which is often tricky to find, and the more widely distributed *Siglo Veintiuno*. The most popular paper is the *Prensa Libre*, a conservative, business-driven institution, though it does have a reasonable sports section. *El Gráfico* is also to the right of centre and broadly supportive of the economic, military and big business elite. Look out for a good **weekly** paper called *El Regional*, published in both Spanish and Maya languages. As for the **periodicals**, *La Crónica* is usually a decent read, concentrating on Guatemalan current political affairs and business news with a smattering of foreign coverage.

Not surprisingly for a country so dependent on tourism, there is a substantial **English-language** press in Guatemala. Both the publications listed below are available in hotels, bookstores and cafés, and are well worth picking up, both for their features and to keep up to date with the current security situation. The free monthly *Revue* magazine, published in Antigua, carries interesting articles about Guatemala and has expanded in recent years to cover Belize, El Salvador and Honduras. It doesn't seek to cover much political stuff but there's often some fascinating cultural or historical coverage, plus comprehensive accommodation, restaurant and shopping listings. Alternatively, the *Guatemala Post* (US$0.40) offers concise, independent coverage of the main Guatemalan news stories.

For really reliable, in-depth reporting, the *Central America Report* excels, with proper journalistic investigation of controversial news stories like the plight of street children in Guatemala City. It's published by Inforpress Centroamericana and available from their offices at 7 Av 2–05, Zona 1, Guatemala City (☎ & fax 232 9034, *www.inforpressca.com*).

As for **foreign publications**, *Newsweek*, *Time* and the *Economist* are all sold in the streets of Guatemala City, particularly on the south side of the main plaza. Some American newspapers are also available: check in the *Camino Real Hotel* bookstore in Guatemala City.

Guatemala has an abundance of **radio stations**, though variety is not their strong point. Most transmit a turgid stream of Latin rock and cheesy merengue, which you're sure to hear plenty of on the buses. There is a host of religious stations, too, broadcasting an onslaught of rabid evangelical lectures, services, "miracles", and so on. If you're visiting Guatemala City, it's worth twiddling your FM dial – there can be some interesting stuff broadcast over the capital's airwaves at weekends.

Television stations are also in plentiful supply. Viewers can choose from five local channels and over a dozen cable stations, all of them dominated by American programmes, either subtitled or dubbed into Spanish. Many upmarket hotels and some bars in tourist areas also have direct satellite links to US stations, which can be handy for catching up with the news on CNN.

Shopping

Guatemalan craft traditions, locally known as **artesanía**, are very much a part of modern Maya culture, stemming from practices that in most cases predate the arrival of the Spanish. Many of these traditions are highly localized, with different regions and even different villages specializing in particular crafts. It's worth visiting as many **markets** as possible, particularly in the highland villages, where the colour and spectacular settings are like nowhere else in Central America

As for **everyday goods**, you'll find that both slide and print film is available in most towns in the country, though monochrome is much less common. Camcorder videotapes are also widely on sale, though digital video tapes are difficult to find.

■ Crafts

The best place to buy Guatemalan **crafts** is in their place of origin, where prices are reasonable and the craftsmen and women get a greater share of the profit. If you haven't the time to travel to remote highland villages, the best places to head for are Chichicastenango on market days (Thurs & Sun) and the shops and street hawkers in Antigua and Panajachel.

The greatest craft in Guatemala has to be **textile weaving**. Each Maya village has its own traditional designs, woven in fantastic patterns and with superbly vivid colours. All the finest weaving is done on the **backstrap loom**, using complex weft float and wrapping techniques. Chemical dyes have been dominant in Guatemala for over a century now and virtually no natural colourings are used.

One of the best places to start looking at textiles is in Antigua's Nim Po't, 5 Av Norte 29 (daily 9am–9pm; ☎ & fax 832 2681), a large store with an excellent collection of styles and designs. Guatemala City's Museo Ixchel (see p.152) is another essential visit.

You should bear in mind that while most Maya are proud that foreigners find their textiles attractive, for them clothing has a spiritual significance – so it's not wise for women travellers to wear men's shirts or men to wear *huipiles*.

Alongside Guatemalan weaving most **other crafts** suffer by comparison. However, if you hunt around you'll also find good ceramics, baskets, mats, silver and jade. Antigua has the most comprehensive collection of shops. For anything woollen, particularly blankets, head for Momostenango Sunday market (see p.209).

■ Markets

For shopping – or simply sightseeing – the **markets** of Guatemala are some of the finest anywhere in the world. The large markets of Chichicastenango, Sololá and San Francisco El Alto are all well worth a visit, but equally fascinating are the tiny weekly gatherings in remote villages like San Juan Atitlán and Chajul, where the atmosphere is hushed and unhurried. In these isolated settlements market day is as much a social event as a commercial affair, providing the chance for villagers to catch up on local news, and perhaps enjoy a tipple or two, as well as selling some vegetables and buying a few provisions. Most towns and villages have at least one weekly event; for a comprehensive list, see p.161.

Safety and the police

Personal safety is a serious problem in Guatemala, partly due to a recent nationwide rise in crime. There is little pattern to these attacks, but some areas can be considered safer than others. It's wise to register with your embassy on arrival, try to keep informed of events by reading newspapers, and avoid travelling at night.

Though relatively few tourists have any trouble, it's essential that you try to minimize the chance of becoming a victim. **Petty theft** and **pickpocketing** are likely to be your biggest worry. Theft is most common in Zona 1 and the bus stations of Guatemala City, but you should also take extra care when visiting markets popular with tourists (like Sololá and Chichicastenango) and during fiestas. Avoid wearing flashy jewellery or waving your money around. When **travelling**, there is actually little danger to your pack when it's on top of a bus; it's the conductor's responsibility alone to go up on the roof and collect luggage.

Muggings and **violent crime** are on the increase in Guatemala City. There's not too much danger in the daylight hours but don't amble around at night, especially if you don't know your way around. Stick to the main streets and use buses and taxis. There have also been a few cases of armed robbery in Antigua and attacks on tourists on the Pacaya volcano.

If you are robbed you'll have to report it to the police, which can be a very long process and may seem like little more than a symbolic gesture; however, most insurance companies will only pay up if you can produce a police statement.

Machismo is very much a part of Latin American culture, and many Guatemalan men consider it their duty to put on a bit of a show to impress the Western *gringas*. It's usually best to ignore any such hassle. *Ladino* towns and *cantinas* are the worst places. Indigenous society is more deferential so you're unlikely to experience any trouble in the western highlands. **Homosexuality** is publicly strongly frowned upon – although not theoretically illegal – so it's sensible to be discreet. There's a small gay community in Guatemala City (see p.155) but few clubs or public meeting places.

■ The police

Guatemala's civilian **police force**, introduced in 1997, was trained by experts from Spain, the USA, France and Chile in an attempt to improve working practices. Despite these efforts, the force still suffers from an appalling reputation for corruption and inefficiency, so don't expect much help if you experience any trouble. Things are a little better in Antigua, where a **tourist police force** (see p.166) has been set up.

If for any reason you do find yourself in **trouble with the law**, be as polite as possible. Remember that bribery is a way of life here, and that corruption is widespread.

■ Drugs

Drugs are increasingly available as Guatemala is becoming a centre for both shipment and production. Marijuana and cocaine are both readily available and cheap heroin is also to be found on the streets.

Remember that **drug offences** are dealt with severely. Even the possession of marijuana could land you in jail – a sobering experience in Guatemala. If you do get into a problem with drugs, it may be worth enquiring with the first policeman if there is a "fine" (*multa*) to pay, to save expensive arbitration later. At the first possible opportunity, get in touch with your embassy and negotiate through them: they will understand the situation better than you. The addresses of embassies and consulates in Guatemala City are listed on p.157. Officially you should

carry your passport (or a photocopy) at all times.

Work and study

Guatemala is one of the best – and most popular – places in the continent to **study Spanish**. The language school industry is big business, with around sixty well-established schools and many more less reliable set-ups. Thousands of foreigners from all over the world study each year in Guatemala – mainly travellers, but also college students, airline crew and business people.

As for **work**, teaching English is the best bet, though there are always opportunities for committed **volunteers**.

■ Studying Spanish

Most schools offer a weekly deal that includes four or five hours one-on-one tuition a day, plus full board with a local family, at an inclusive **cost** of around US$130 a week. It's important to bear in mind that the success of the exercise is dependent both on your personal commitment to study and on the enthusiasm and aptitude of your teacher – if you are not happy with the teacher you've been allocated, ask for another. Insist on knowing the number of other students that will be sharing your family house; some schools pack as many as ten foreigners in with one family. Virtually all schools have a student liaison officer, usually an English-speaking foreigner who acts as a go-between for students and teachers, so if you're a complete beginner there will usually be someone around who you can communicate with.

The first decision to make is to choose where you want to study. By far the most popular choices are the towns of Antigua and Quetzaltenango, though Lago de Atitlán is also starting to become an estabished language centre. Beautiful **Antigua** is undoubtedly an excellent place to study Spanish: though the major drawback is that there are so many students and tourists here that you'll probably end up spending your evenings speaking English. **Quetzaltenango** (Xela) has a very different atmosphere, with a much stronger "Guatemalan" character and far fewer tourists. Despite it being one of the most popular places in the world to study Spanish, it's still possible to really immerse yourself in the language and local culture. Several new language schools have recently been set up in the **Lago de**

RECOMMENDED LANGUAGE SCHOOLS

Many of the schools below have academic accreditation agreements with North American and European universities; some also have US offices – consult the schools' Web sites for more information. The Website www.guatemala365.com is a reliable place to begin the search for a school, with a good list of professional schools and tips about the relative advantages of different study centres.

ANTIGUA

APPE, 6 C Pte 40 (☎832 0720, www.guacalling.com/appe).

Centro America Spanish Academy, inside La Fuente, 4 C Ote 14 (☎ & fax 832 6268, www.quik.guate.com/spanishacademy).

Centro Lingüístico de la Fuente, 1 C Pte 27 (☎ & fax 832 2711, www.delafuenteschool.com).

Centro Lingüístico Maya, 5 C Pte 20 (☎ & fax 832 0656, www.travellog.com/guatemala/antigua/clmaya /school.html).

Christian Spanish Academy, 6 Av Nte 15 (☎ 832 3922, fax 832 3760, www.learncsa.com).

Probigua, 6 Av Nte 41B (☎ & fax 832 0860, http://probigua.conexion.com).

Projecto Lingüístico Francisco Marroquín, 7 C Pte 31 (☎832 2886, www.plfm-antigua.org). Also offers classes in Maya languages.

San José El Viejo, 5 Av Sur 34 (☎832 3028, fax 832 3029, www.guate.net/spanish).

Sevilla, 1 Av Sur 8 (☎ & fax 832 0442, www.sevillantigua.com).

Tecún Umán Linguistic School, 6 C Pte 34 A (☎ & fax 831 2792, www.tecunuman.centramerica .com).

La Unión, 1 Av Sur 21 (☎ & fax 832 7337, www.launion.conexion.com).

QUETZALTENANGO

ALM,15 Av 6–75, Zona 1 (☎761 2877, fax 763 2176, http://travel.to/alm). Also has branches in Antigua and Monterrico.

Casa de Español Xelajú, Callejón 15, Diagonal 13–02, Zona 1 (☎761 5954, fax 761 5953, www.casaxelaju.com).

Centro Bilingüe Amerindia (CBA), 7 Av 9–05, Zona 1, (☎761 1613, www.xelapages.com/cba).

Centro Maya de Idiomas, 21 Av 5–69, Zona 3 (☎767 0352 www.centromaya.org). Also offers classes in six Maya languages.

Educación para Todos, 12 Av 1–78, Zona 3, (☎ & fax 765 0715, www.xelapages.com/paratodos).

English Club International Language School, Diagonal 4 9–71, Zona 9 (☎763 2198). Also offers classes in K'iche' and Mam.

Escuela Juan Sisay, 15 Av 8–38, Zona 1 (☎ & fax 763 1318, www.juansisay.com).

Guatemalensis, 19 Av 2–14, Zona 1 (☎ & fax 765 1384, www.infovia.com.gt/gssxela).

La Paz, 2 C 19–30, Zona 1 (☎761 4243, www.xelapages.com/lapaz).

Atitlán area, in Panajachel and San Pedro La Laguna, with more planned in other lakeside villages. As yet, tuition standards in the Atitlán area are only average, but such is the draw of the lake that the schools have quickly become popular with international travellers. If you already speak some basic Spanish, you could study somewhere where you're unlikely to be able to speak any English at all, such as Huehuetenango, Petén or Cobán.

■ Volunteer and paid work

In Guatemala, the **Project Mosaic Guatemala** 1 Av Sur 21, Antigua (☎813 5758, fax 832 7337, www.pmg.dk), has links to over sixty groups, including projects to help street children and reforestation work. Another good walk-in resource centre in Antigua is **El Arco**, at 5 Av Norte 25B (☎832 0162, fax 832-1540, www .adventravelguatemala.com, elarco@guate.net). The best place to head for in Quetzaltenango is the language school **Casa Xelajú** (see box above), which has excellent contacts with dozens of development projects.

As for **paid work**, teaching English is the best bet: check the English schools in Guatemala City (listed in the phone book). In addition, all Spanish language schools (see box) employ student coordinators to liaise between staff and pupils – but you'll need near-fluent Spanish. In Antigua, there are always a few vacancies for staff in the gringo bars and sales positions in jade showrooms. The English-language press (*The Revue* and the *Guatemala Post*) and noticeboards in the popular bars and restaurants in Antigua and Quetzaltenango

Kie–Balam, Diagonal 12 4–46 (☎761 1636, fax 761 0391, *www.super-highway.net/users/moebius*).
Pop Wuj, 1 C 17–72, Zona 1 (☎761 8286, *www.popwuj.org*).
Proyecto Lingüístico Quetzalteco de Español, 5 C 2–40, Zona 1 (☎761 2620, *www.inforserve.net/hermandad/montana.html*). Also has sister schools on the Pacific coast and in Todos Santos Cuchumatán.
Sakribal, 10C 7–17, Zona 1 (☎ & fax 761 5211, *http://kcyb.com/sakribal*).

LAGO DE ATITLÁN

Escuela Jabel Tinamit, off c/Santander, Panajachel (☎762 0238, *http://members.nbci.com/learnspanish*).
Jardín de América, C 14 de Febrero, Panajachel (☎ & fax 762 2637, *www.atitlan.com/jardin.htm*).
Casa Rosario, south of Santiago Atitlán dock, San Pedro La Laguna (☎767 5795 *www.worldwide.edu/ci/guatemala/schools/34451.html*).
San Pedro Spanish School, between the piers, San Pedro La Laguna (☎703 1100, *www.spanish-schools.com*).

HUEHUETENANGO

Casa Xelajú, contact their Quetzaltenango school (see opposite) for more information.
Fundación XXIII, 6 Av 6–126, Zona 1 (☎764 1478, *www.worldwide.edu/ci/guatemala/schools/10024.html*).

Insituto El Portal, 1 C 1–64, Zona 3 (☎ & fax 764 1987, *www.guatemala365.com/english/schools/schu003.htm*).
Xinabajul, 6 Av 0–69 (☎ & fax 764 1518, *www.spanish-schools.com/huehue/inf/infoe.htm*).

PETÉN

Eco-Escuela, San Andrés, Lago de Petén Itzá (☎928 8106, *www.conservation.org/ecoescuela/about.htm*).
Escuela Bio–Itzá, San José, Lago de Petén Itzá (☎928 8142, *www.conservation.org/ecoescuela/bioitza.htm*).

COBÁN

Active Spanish School, 3 C 6–12, Zona 1 (☎ & fax 952 1432, *www.spanish-schools.com/coban/city/ce.htm*).
Instituto Cobán Internacional (INCO Int), 6 Av 5–39, Zona 3 (☎ & fax 951 2459, *www.worldwide.edu/ci/guatemala/schools/15017.html*).
Muq'b'ilbe, 6 Av 5–39, Zona 3 (☎951 2459 *www.guatemala365.com/english/schools/schu005.htm*). Also offers Q'eqchi' language study.

TODOS SANTOS CUCHUMATÁN

Hispano Maya, (*www.personal.umich.edu/~kakenned*).
Nuevo Amanecer, contact the Centro Maya de Idiomas in Quetzaltenango (see opposite).
Proyecto Lingüístico Mam, contact the Proyecto Lingüístico Quetzalteco de Español (see above).

also occasionally advertise vacancies. To work anywhere in Guatemala you'll need to speak some Spanish.

History

The very first humans to inhabit the area now known as Guatemala were nomadic hunters. By around 1500 BC these nomads had settled into agricultural communities, farming maize, beans, squash and chillies – the staples of today's Central American diet – making pottery and building villages of thatched-roofed houses on the Pacific coast. These early famers are regarded as the first of the **Maya**, and it's thought that most people spoke a proto-Maya language. In the period after 1500 BC, known as the **Preclassic**, the population

began to increase steadily throughout the Maya region (encompassing today's Guatemala and Belize, Mexico's Chiapas, Tabasco and Yucatán peninsula, and western El Salvador and Honduras).

There is little evidence that the early Maya were anything but subsistence farmers until more advanced cultures, the Mexican **Olmec** and **Izapa**, began to filter down the Pacific coast. These Mexican peoples were hugely influential on the Maya region, introducing the Long Count calendar, an early writing system and a polytheistic religion. Evidence of their sculptural skills can be seen at the Pacific coast sites around Santa Lucía Cotzumalguapa and Abaj Takalik, and at the great urban centre of **Kaminaljuyú**, on the outskirts of Guatemala City, where there are substantial Preclassic temple mounds and granite stelae with calendric glyphs.

By the **Middle Preclassic** (1000–300 BC) a unified style of pottery and artefacts – including red and orange jars, dishes and stone *metates* (for grinding corn) – were to be found throughout the Guatemalan Maya lands. It is thought that increased harvests enabled more ambitious constructions to be undertaken, while initial astronomical studies were made. By about 400 BC the settlement of **Nakbé** in Petén had evolved into the most advanced centre in the northern lowlands, with a city boasting over eighty structures, including pyramids and the earliest recorded stelae in the region.

Real advances in architecture came in the **Late Preclassic** (300 BC–300 AD), when large pyramids and temple platforms were built at numerous sites throughout Guatemala in an explosion of Maya culture. The principal centres at this time were the cities of Kaminaljuyú, which dominated the central highlands, and the great early settlements in Petén: El Mirador, Nakbé, Uaxactún and Tikal. Traditionally, the early Maya were imagined as peaceful peasant farmers and traders, led by astronomer-priests, but in fact these new cities were bloodthirsty, warring rivals fighting for hegemony.

Of all the sites dating from this era, it is the colossal triadic structures of **El Mirador** that are the most astounding. Though almost entirely Late Preclassic, the temples are the highest ever built in the Maya world, rising over seventy metres above the forest and connected by a complex system of raised causeways to distant settlements. The scale of El Mirador – covering around sixteen square kilometres – was immense, and the city undoubtedly supported tens of thousands of inhabitants, including engineers, architects, farmers, labourers, and priests. This first great Maya city traded with centres as far away as the Golfo de Mexico, the Pacific and Caribbean coasts and the Guatemalan highlands.

■ The Classic Maya

The development that separates the Late Preclassic from the early **Classic period** (300–900 AD) is the introduction of the Long Count calendar in the Petén lowlands and the development of a recognizable form of writing, which included phonetic glyphs. This appears to have taken place by the fourth century AD and marks the beginning of the greatest phase of Maya achievement.

During the Classic period all the cities we now know as ruined or restored sites were built, almost always over earlier structures. Elaborately carved **stelae**, bearing dates and emblem-glyphs, were erected at regular intervals. These tell of actual rulers and of historical events in their lives – battles, marriages, dynastic succession and so on. As these dates have come to be deciphered they have provided confirmation (or otherwise) of archeological evidence and offered a major insight into the nature of Maya dynastic rule.

Developments in the Maya area were still powerfully influenced by events to the north. The overbearing presence of the Olmecs was replaced by that of **Teotihuacán**, which dominated central Mexico during the Early Classic period. Armed merchants, called *pochteca*, operated at this time, spreading the influence of Teotihuacán as far as Petén and the Yucatán. They brought new styles of ceramics and alternative religious beliefs and perhaps preceded a complete military invasion. Whatever happened around 400 AD, the overwhelming power of Teotihuacán radically altered life in Maya lands. Influence spread south, via the Pacific coast, first to Kaminaljuyú on the site of modern Guatemala City and thence to Petén, where **Tikal's** rise to power must have been helped by close links with Teotihuacán. Both cities prospered greatly: Kaminaljuyú was rebuilt in the style of Teotihuacán, and Tikal has a stela depicting a lord of Tikal on one side and a warrior from Teotihuacán on the other.

Exactly how the various centres related to one another is unclear, but it appears that large cities dominated specific regions though no city held sway throughout the Maya area. Broadly speaking, the culture was made up of a federation of city states, bound together by a coherent religion and culture and supporting a sophisticated trade network. The cities jostled for power and influence, a struggle that occasionally erupted into open warfare.

Intense wars were fought as rival cities sought to dominate one another, with no ruler appearing to gain ascendancy for very long. There were clearly three or four main centres that dominated the region through an uncertain process of alliance. Tikal was certainly a powerful city, but at one time Caracol in Belize defeated Tikal, as shown by a Caracol ball-court marker. Detailed carvings on wooden lintels and stone monuments depict elaborately costumed lords trampling on captives and spilling their own blood at propitious festivals, staged according to the dictates of the intricate and the precise Maya calendar. Copán and Quiriguá were certainly important centres in the southern area, while the cities of the highlands were still in their infancy.

At the height of Maya power, advances were temporarily halted by what is known as the **Middle Classic Hiatus**, a period during which there was little new building at Tikal and after which many smaller centres, once under the control of Tikal, became independent city states. The victory of Caracol over Tikal, some time around 550 AD, may have been a symptom or a cause of this, and certainly the collapse of Teotihuacán in the seventh century caused shock waves through all the civilizations of Mesoamerica. In the Maya cities no stelae commemorating events were erected, and monuments and statues were defaced and damaged. In all likelihood the Maya centres suffered revolts, and warfare raged as rival lords strove to win political power.

However, as the new kings established dynasties, now free of Teotihuacán's military or political control, the Maya cities flourished as never before. Architecture, astronomy and art reached degrees of sophistication unequalled by any other pre-Columbian society. Trade prospered and populations grew: Tikal had an estimated 40,000 people. Many Maya centres were larger than contemporary Western European cities, then in their "Dark Ages".

The prosperity and grandeur of the **Late Classic** (600–800 AD) reached all across the Maya lands: from Bonampak and Palenque in the west, to Labná, Sayil, Calakmul and Uxmal in the north, Altun Ha and Cerros in the east, and Copán and Quiriguá in the south, as well as hundreds of smaller centres. Masterpieces of painted pottery and carved jade (their most precious material) were created, often to be used as funerary offerings. Shell, bone and, rarely, marble were also exquisitely carved; temples were painted in brilliant colours, inside and out. Most of the pigments faded long ago, but vestiges remain, enabling experts to reconstruct vivid images of the appearance of the ancient cities.

■ The Maya in decline

The glory days were not to last very long, however, and by 750 AD political and social changes began to be felt: alliances and trade links broke down, warring increased and stelae were carved less frequently. Cities gradually became depopulated and new construction ceased in present-day Guatemala after about 830 AD. It is uncertain what factors precipitated the downfall of the Maya: an increase in population probably put great strains on food production, perhaps exhausting the fertility of the soil, while climate changes could also have been influential; there may also have been peasant revolts against the ruling elite. By the tenth century, the Maya had abandoned their cities in Petén and those few Maya that remained were reduced to a fairly primitive state.

By the **Postclassic** period (900 AD to the Spanish Conquest) all the city states in Guatemala had collapsed. The decline of Maya civilization in the heartland of Petén brought about a rapid depopulation which prompted an influx of people into the Guatemalan highlands to the south. Along with the Yucatán, this area, formerly a peripheral region of relatively little development, now contained the last vestiges of Maya culture. Small settlements remained scattered throughout the highlands, usually built on open valley floors and supporting large populations with the use of terraced farming and irrigation. Little was to change in this basic village structure for several hundred years.

■ Pre-conquest: the highland tribes

Towards the end of the thirteenth century the central Guatemalan highlands were invaded by a group of **Toltec-Maya**, who had controlled the Yucatán until this time. Their numbers were probably small but their impact was profound, and following their arrival life in the highlands was radically altered.

What once had been a relatively settled, peaceful and religious society became, under the influence of the Toltecs, fundamentally secular, aggressive and militaristic. The well-organized Toltec quickly established themselves as a ruling elite, presiding over a series of competing tribes. The greatest of these were the **K'iche'**, who dominated the central highlands and had their capital, **Utatlán**, to the west of the modern town of Santa Cruz del Quiché. Next in line were the **Kaqchikel**, centred around **Iximché**. On the slopes of the San Pedro volcano on Lago de Atitlán were the **Tz'utujil**, while in the west the **Mam** occupied the area around the modern town of Huehuetenango, with their capital at **Zaculeu**. A number of smaller tribes controlled the high Cuchumatanes mountain region.

To the east, around the modern city of Cobán, were the notoriously fierce **Achi** nation with the **Q'eqchi'** to their north, while around the modern site of Guatemala City the land was controlled by the **Poqomam**. Finally, the **Pipil** occupied the stretch along the Pacific coast. The sheer number of these tribes gives an impression of the extent to which the area was fragmented, and it's these same divisions, now surviving on the basis of language alone, that still shape the highlands today.

The Toltec rulers probably controlled only the dominant tribes – the K'iche', the Tz'utujil, the Mam and the Kaqchikel – initially terrorizing the local highlanders and gradually establishing themselves at the top of a new, rigidly hierarchical society. It was the K'iche' tribe, with strong Toltec influence, that grew to become the dominant power in the highlands, conquering the neighbouring Mam and Kaqchikel tribes under their great ruler, **K'ikab**. After his death in 1475, their empire lost much of its authority and for the next fifty years the tribes were in a state of almost perpetual conflict, fighting for access to the inadequate supplies of farmland. The tribal capitals from this period – Iximché, Zaculeu and Utatlán – are all fortified hilltop sites, surrounded by ravines and man-made ditches.

When the Spanish arrived, the highlands were in crisis. The population had grown so fast that it had outstripped the food supply, leaving a situation that could hardly have been more favourable to the conquistadors.

■ The Spanish Conquest

While the tribes of highland Guatemala were warring amongst themselves to the north, in what is now Mexico, the Spanish conquistadors had captured the Aztec capital at Tenochtitlán. Even amidst the horrors of the Conquest there was one man whose evil stood out: **Pedro de Alvarado**. Ambitious, cunning, intelligent, dashingly handsome and ruthlessly cruel, he could hardly have been better suited to the job of subduing Guatemala.

In 1523, Alvarado arrived in Guatemala via the Pacific coast with a very modest force of a few hundred horsemen, soldiers and Mexican allies. After some minor skirmishes Alvarado confronted the K'iche' army, said to be 30,000-strong, at

Xelajú (present-day Quetzaltenango). Despite the huge disparity in numbers, sling-shot and foot soldiers were no match for cavalry and gunpowder, and the Spanish were able to wade through the Maya ranks. Legend has it that the battle was brought to a close when Alvarado himself slew the K'iche' leader **Tecún Umán** in hand-to-hand combat.

By a series of tactical alliances and brilliant, utterly ruthless military manoeuvres, by 1525 Alvarado's small Spanish force had overpowered all the main highland tribes. First the K'iche' capital, Utatlán, was sacked, then the Tz'utujil were defeated on the shores of Lago de Atitlán with the aid of the Kaqchikel, followed by the Pipil of the Pacific coast. Finally, the last of the major highland tribes, the Mam, were conquered after a siege of their fortified capital, Zaculeu. The support of the Kaqchikel (whose capital, Iximché, they used as a base for their campaigns) during this string of relatively easy gains was probably invaluable.

Dealing with the more remote tribes proved more difficult and it wasn't until the 1530s that Alvarado managed to assert control over the Ixil and Uspantenko. In 1526, the Kaqchikel also revolted and waged a guerrilla war against their former partners, forcing the Spanish from Iximché to a site near the modern town of Antigua (now called Ciudad Vieja). Here, at the base of the Volcán de Agua, they established their first permanent capital on November 22, 1527.

Meanwhile, one thorny problem remained. Despite all his efforts, Alvarado had been unable to conquer the **Achi** and **Q'eqchi'** tribes, who occupied what are now the Verapaz highlands. In the end, Dominican priests under Fray Bartolomé de Las Casas succeeded where gunpowder had failed, and in 1540 the last of the highland tribes were brought under colonial control. Thus did the area earn its name of Verapaz – "true peace".

■ Colonial rule

The early years of colonial rule were marked by a turmoil of uprisings, political wrangling and natural disaster. In 1541, following a massive earthquake, a great wall of mud and water swept down the side of Agua volcano, burying the capital. The surviving colonial authorities moved up the valley to a new site (at present-day Antigua), where a new city was established. The new capital controlled the provinces of the **Audiencia de**

Guatemala (Costa Rica, Nicaragua, El Salvador, Honduras, Guatemala and Chiapas in Mexico) and was the region's centre of political and religious power for two hundred years. By the mid-eighteenth century its population had reached some 80,000 and the city boasted some of the finest buildings in the hemisphere, until another huge earthquake destroyed the city in 1773 and the capital was moved again to its present-day site.

Colonial society was rigidly structured along racial lines, with pure-blood Spaniards at the top, indigenous slaves at the bottom, and a host of carefully defined racial strata in between. There was very little in the way of instant plunder in Central America – certainly none of the gold and silver of Mexico and Peru – and the **economy** was based on agriculture: livestock, cacao, tobacco, cotton and, most valuable of all, indigo were all farmed. At the heart of the colonial economy was the system of *repartamientos*, whereby the ruling classes were granted the right to extract labour from the indigenous population. It was this that established the process whereby the Maya population were transported to the Pacific coast to work the plantations, a pattern (if no longer state-enforced) that continues to this day.

Perhaps the greatest power in colonial times was the **Church**, whose wealth from sugar, wheat and indigo concessions, based on the exploitation of a Maya labour force, fostered the construction of some eighty churches, plus schools, convents, hospitals, hermitages, craft centres and colleges. In the countryside, scattered native communities were merged into new Spanish-style towns and villages, making exploitation that much easier. Though Maya social structures were also profoundly altered, in the distant corners of the highlands priests were few and far between and *cofradía* (brotherhood) groups and *principales* (village elders) developed a religion of Catholic and Maya traditions that has persisted to this day.

Even more brutal than the social changes were the **diseases** that arrived with the conquistadors. Waves of plague, typhoid and smallpox swept through a people lacking any natural resistance to them. It was the devastating impact of these diseases that ensured that the small Spanish invading force was able to maintain control in Guatemala: around ninety percent of the Maya population was wiped out within a few years of the arrival of Alvarado.

Two centuries of colonial rule totally reshaped the structure of Guatemalan society, giving it new cities, a new religion, a transformed economy and a racist hierarchy. Nevertheless, the impact of colonial rule was perhaps less marked than in many other parts of Latin America. Only two sizeable cities were created and many outlying areas received little attention from the colonial authorities. While the indigenous population was ruthlessly exploited and suffered enormous losses at the hands of foreign weapons and imported diseases, its culture was never eradicated. There was little profit for the Spanish in the mountains – no gold, very little silver, and harsh terrain – so the colonists concentrated instead on developing agriculture in more profitable regions like the Pacific coast. In the relative isolation of the highlands, the Maya simply absorbed the symbols and ideas of the new Spanish ideology, fusing Maya and Catholic traditions to create a unique synthesis of old and new world beliefs.

■ Independence

The racist nature of colonial rule had created deep dissatisfaction amongst many groups in Central America. A fundamental issue was Spain's determination to keep wealth and power in the hands of those born in the motherland, a policy that left growing numbers of subjects hungry for power and change. The spark that precipitated independence was Napoleon's invasion of Spain, after which a mood of reform swept through the colonies, including Central America.

Brigadier Don Gabino Gainza, the Captain General of Central America, bowed to liberal demands for independence but still hoped to preserve the colonial power structure when he signed the **Act of Independence** on September 15, 1821. Mexico promptly sent troops to annex Guatemala but by 1823 Guatemala had joined a **Central American federation** with a US-style liberal constitution. Religious orders were abolished, the death penalty and slavery done away with, and trial by jury, a general school system, civil marriage and the Lívingston law code were all instituted.

The liberal era was soon overthrown by a revolt from the mountains. The indigenous population, hit hard by a cholera epidemic and seething with discontent, marched on Guatemala City behind a charismatic leader, the 23-year-old **Rafael Carrera**. Carrera respected no authority other than that of the Church, and upon seizing power he reversed all the liberal reforms with the support of conservative religious and landowning lobbies. Carrera then fought a bitter war against the rest of the Central American federation and Guatemala declared itself a an **independent republic** in 1847. Carrera died in 1865, at the age of 50, leaving the country ravaged by the chaos of his tyranny and inefficiency. He was succeeded by **Vicente Cerna**, another conservative, who was to rule for the next six years.

Meanwhile, the opposition was gathering momentum yet again and 1867 saw the first **liberal uprising**, led by **Serpio Cruz**. His bid for power was unsuccessful but it inspired two young liberals, Justo Rufino Barrios and Francisco Cruz, to follow suit. In the next few years they mounted several other unsuccessful revolts, and in 1870 Serpio Cruz was captured and hanged.

■ Coffee and bananas

A major turning point in Guatemalan politics came in 1871, when Rufino Barrios arrived from Mexico with an army of just 45 men and started a **liberal revolution**.

Rufino Barrios was a charismatic leader with tyrannical tendencies (monuments throughout the country testify to his sense of his own importance), who regarded himself as the great reformer and was intent on making sweeping changes. He was undoubtedly a man of action: he restructured the education system, attacked the power of the Church and modernized the University of San Carlos in Guatemala City. Underneath the new liberal perspective lay a deep arrogance, however. Barrios would tolerate no opposition and developed a network of secret police and an army academy that became an essential part of his political power base.

Alongside all this, Barrios set about reforming agriculture, particularly **coffee farming**. Cultivation had increased fivefold by 1884, creating an economic boom. The railway network was expanded, ports developed and a national bank established. Between 1870 and 1900 the volume of foreign trade increased twenty times. Much of the coffee trade was bound for Germany and many of the plantations were owned by an immigrant German elite – reflecting Barrios's perspective that foreign ideas were superior to indigenous ones; the Maya population were regarded as hopelessly inferior.

Maya society was also deeply affected by the coffee boom as Barrios instituted a system of **forced labour** to safeguard harvests. Up to a quarter of the male population was despatched to work on the fincas, where conditions were appalling and the workforce treated with utter contempt. Many lost not only their freedom but also their **land**. From 1873, the government began confiscating land and selling it to the highest bidder, sparking village revolts throughout the western highlands that continued into the twentieth century. The loss of their most productive land also ensured that the Maya became dependent on seasonal labour.

By the early twentieth century, a new and exceptionally powerful player was becoming involved in Guatemala: the **United Fruit Company**. It first moved into Guatemala in 1901 after previous successes in Costa Rica and initially bought a small tract of land on which to grow **bananas**. Soon after, it was awarded railway contracts and built its own port, Puerto Barrios, giving it a virtual monopoly over transport. Large-scale banana cultivation took off and United Fruit got very rich very quickly. The company's power was by no means restricted to agriculture, and its influence was so pervasive that it earned itself the nickname "El Pulpo" (The Octopus). In 1919, President Carlos Herrera threatened to terminate United Fruit Company contracts. He lasted barely more than a year.

Jorge Ubico became president in 1930 and embarked on a radical programme of reform, including a sweeping drive against corruption and a massive road-building effort which won him great popularity in the provinces. Despite his liberal pretensions, however, Ubico sided firmly with big business when the chips were down, always offering his assistance to the United Fruit Company and other sections of the land-owning elite. Peasants were still compelled to work the fincas by a **vagrancy law** and there were more revolts in the late 1930s and early 1940s.

But while Ubico tightened his grip on every aspect of government through internal security and repression, the rumblings of opposition grew louder. In 1944 discontent erupted in a wave of student violence, and Ubico was finally forced to resign after 14 years of tyrannical rule.

■ Ten years of "spiritual socialism"

The overthrow of Jorge Ubico released a wave of opposition that had been bottled up throughout his rule. Students, professionals and young military officers demanded democracy and freedom. The transformation of Guatemalan politics was so extreme a contrast to previous governments that the handover was dubbed **the 1944 revolution**. A new constitution was drawn up, the vote given to all adults and the president prevented from running for a second term.

Juan José Arévalo, a teacher, won the 1945 presidential elections with 85 percent of the vote. His political doctrine was dubbed **"spiritual socialism"** and he immediately set about effecting much-needed structural reforms. Extensive social welfare programmes were introduced: schools and hospitals were built, an ambitious literary campaign launched, the vagrancy law was abolished, and workers were granted the right to union representation and to strike. Some state-owned fincas were turned into co-operatives, and there were other policies to stimulate industrial and agricultural development, though land reform was not seriously tackled. Unsurprisingly, these sweeping reforms angered conservative interests (the army, Church leaders and large landowners) and there were repeated coup attempts.

The next president, **Jacobo Arbenz**, won the election with ease and immediately set out **land reform** proposals in a direct challenge to the US corporations that dominated the economy. Arbenz enlisted the support of peasants, students and unions to break the foreign dominance and began a series of suits against foreign corporations, seeking unpaid taxes.

In July 1952, the **law of agrarian reform** was passed, stating that idle and state-owned land would be distributed to the landless. The big landowners were outraged. Between 1953 and 1954, around 8840 square kilometres was redistributed to the benefit of some 100,000 peasant families – the first time since the arrival of the Spanish that a government had responded to the needs of the indigenous population. The United Fruit Company lost about half of its property, provoking the US government to accuse the new Guatemalan government of being a communist beach-head in Central America.

In 1954, the CIA (whose director was on the United Fruit Company's board) set up a small **military invasion** of Guatemala to depose Arbenz and install an alternative administration more suited to US tastes. A ragtag invasion army of exiles and mercenaries was put together in Honduras and, under CIA supervision, invaded the country, prompting Arbenz to resign after failing to get the support of the Guatemalan military. The US approved a new "government" and flew it to Guatemala aboard a US Air Force plane. Guatemala's experiment with "spiritual socialism" had ended.

■ Military rule and guerrilla war

Following the overthrow of Arbenz, it was **the army** that rose to fill the power vacuum, with US support; they were to dominate politics for the next thirty years, sending the country into a spiral of violence and economic decline.

Castillo Armas, the new president, immediately swept away all the reforms of the previous ten years: the 1945 constitution was revoked, all illiterates were disenfranchised, left-wing parties were outlawed, and large numbers of unionists and agrarian reformers were simply executed. All the land that had been confiscated was returned to its previous owners. Hardest hit was the indigenous population as the old order of *ladino* rule was firmly reinstated.

In the following years, corruption, incompetence, outrageous patronage, and economic decline caused by a fall in coffee prices brought Guatemala to its knees. Arévalo even threatened to return to Guatemala and contest the 1963 elections. The possibility was too much for the Guatemalan establishment and the US and John F. Kennedy authorized another coup in 1963.

The 1960s saw the start of **guerrilla war** – initially confined to the eastern highlands and ruthlessly fought by the army. Another centre-left government held power until 1970, although it was the army that really controlled affairs. Political assassination became commonplace as **"death squads"** operated with impunity, killing peasant leaders, students, unionists and academics.

In the 1970 elections the power of the military and the far right was confirmed. **Colonel Arana Osorio** was elected president with the support of just four percent of the population (bearing in mind that only a small percentage was enfranchised). Once in power he set about eradicating armed opposition, declaring that "if it is necessary to turn the country into a cemetery in order to pacify it, I will not hesitate to do so". The reign of terror reached unprecedented levels: students, academics, opposition politicians, union leaders and agrarian reformers were particularly targeted.

Some estimate that there were 15,000 political killings in the first three years of Osorio's rule.

Osorio's successor, President Laugerund, was not a great reformer, though he did introduce limited measures to alleviate rural poverty, including opening up parts of the Petén to peasants to farm. However, even these modest concessions were interrupted by a massive **earthquake** on February 4, 1976. The quake left around 23,000 dead, 77,000 injured and a million homeless. The poor suffered the most, whilst on the Caribbean coast, Puerto Barrios was almost totally destroyed and remained cut off from the capital for several months.

In the wake of the earthquake, during the process of reconstruction, many of the victims felt the time had come to take action, and trade unions and a new guerrilla organization, the **EGP**, emerged. The army's response was predictable, with daily disappearances, murders and atrocities. In 1977, US President Carter suspended all military aid to Guatemala because of the country's appalling human rights record. At the same time, Guatemala continued to press its longstanding claim to **Belize**, but failed to gain international support.

In 1978 elections were again dominated by the army, who procured a victory for **Lucas García**, the most murderous of all Guatemala's leaders. All opposition groups met with severe repression. The economy took a battering, while several guerrilla armies started developing strongholds in the highlands. There was a major massacre within a month of García's accession in the village of Panzós, Alta Verapaz, during which a hundred villagers were shot by the army. Political opponents, including rival Christian Democrat politicians, were assassinated by death squads and **Vinicio Cerezo**, the party's leader, was forced into hiding. A peaceful occupation of the Spanish embassy by demonstrators ended with the security forces burning the building to the ground, resulting in the death of 39 people. Spain broke off diplomatic relations for over five years.

Meanwhile, the rural guerrilla war intensified, with Israeli military aid replacing American. The guerrilla groups had an estimated 6000 combatants and some 250,000 unarmed collaborators. Army casualties rose to 250 a month, and the demand for conscripts grew rapidly. Peasants were massacred in their thousands, while in the towns victims included students, journalists, academics, politicians, priests, lawyers, teachers and unionists. Tens of thousands fled to Mexico, and the Catholic Church withdrew all its clergy from Quiché after a number of priests were murdered. It's estimated that around 25,000 Guatemalans were killed during the four years of the García regime.

In 1982 a successful coup was engineered by **Ríos Montt**, who even today remains one of the most powerful political figures in Guatemala. Ríos Montt was a committed evangelical Christian who was, above all, determined to restore law and order, eradicate corruption, and defeat the guerrillas. Repression dropped overnight in the cities, corrupt police and army officers were forced to resign, and trade and tourism began to return.

However, in the highlands the war intensified as Ríos Montt declared that he would defeat the guerrillas by Christmas. By a highly successful (and locally detested) programme, villagers were organized into **Civil Defence Patrols** (PACs), armed with ancient rifles, and told to patrol the countryside. The guerrillas' support infrastructure was immediately undermined and villagers were forced to take sides, caught between the guerrilla's propaganda and the sheer brutality of the armed forces. Significant gains were made against the guerrillas, but as fighting intensified thousands of highland Maya fled into Mexico.

Little progress was made towards democratic reform, however. The Catholic church had become alienated and in 1983 Ríos Montt was overthrown by yet another military coup – this one backed by a US government keen to see Guatemala set on the road to democracy. Although the rural repression, death squads and disappearances continued under the new president, General Mejía Víctores, elections were held for an 88-member Constituent Assembly in July 1984. GAM, a new mutual support group for families of the "disappeared", brought the human rights abuses in Guatemala to international media attention. In November 1985, the first legitimate elections in thirty years were held.

■ Civilian rule

The elections were won by **Vinicio Cerezo**, a Christian Democrat who was not associated with the traditional ruling elite. In the run-up to the election he offered a programme of reform that he claimed would rid the country of repression.

Once in office, however, Cerezo declared that the army still held 75 percent of power and throughout his six-year rule he adopted a non-confrontational approach. Above all he avoided upsetting big business interests, landowners and generals. Political killings did drop but murder was still a daily event in Guatemala in the late 1980s and the guerrilla war continued to rage in remote corners of the highlands.

In many ways the Cerezo administration was a bitter disappointment to the Guatemalan people and by the time the decade drew to a close it was clear that the army was still actively controlling political opposition. The fate of the disappeared remained unsolved, human rights leaders continued to be victims of death squads, land reform had yet to be tackled and 65 percent of the population remained below the poverty line. Acknowledging that his greatest achievement had been to survive, in 1990 Cerezo organized the country's first civilian transfer of power for thirty years.

The 1990 elections were won by **Jorge Serrano**, an engineer and evangelical with a centre-right economic position. His administration once again proved both uninterested and incapable of effecting any real reform or bringing an end to the civil war. The level of human rights abuse remained high, death squad activity continued, the economy remained weak and the army was still a powerful force, using intimidation and murder to stamp out opposition. Economic activity was still controlled by a tiny elite: less than 2 percent of landowners owned more than 65 percent of the land, leaving some 85 percent of the population living in poverty, with little access to health care or education.

Guatemala's dispossessed and poor continued to clamour for change. Maya peasants became increasingly organized and influential, denouncing the continued bombardment of villages and rejecting the presence of the army and the system of civil patrols. Matters were brought into sharp focus in 1992 when **Rigoberta Menchú** was awarded the Nobel Peace Prize for her campaigning work on behalf of Guatemala's indigenous population. In spite of the efforts of the Serrano administration, the country's civil war still rumbled on and three main guerrilla armies, united as the **URNG**, continued to confront the army.

Small groups of refugees began to return from exile in Mexico and start civil communities, though an estimated 45,000 still remained abroad. The territorial dispute with **Belize** was officially resolved when the two countries established full diplomatic relations in 1991, though the decision to recognize Belize as an independent country provoked hostility with ultra-nationalists and the Guatemalan military.

By early 1993 Serrano's reputation had plummeted following a series of corruption **scandals**, including his backing of a casino and race-track development that had suspected links with Colombian drug cartels. Despite his membership of no fewer than four evangelical churches, Serrano had supported a venture dependent on gambling and alcohol consumption that was probably financed by cocaine barons.

In **May 1993** Serrano responded to a wave of popular protests with a **self-coup**, declaring he would rule by decree because the country was endangered by civil disorder and corruption, and that the drug mafia planned to take over Guatemala. Few were convinced, however: the US responded by suspending its annual US$67 million of aid and Serrano was quickly removed from office. Congress finally appointed **Ramiro León de Carpio**, the country's human rights ombudsman, as the new president. One of his first moves was a reshuffle of the senior military command, although he rejected calls for revenge, declaring that stability was the main goal. There was great early optimism at Carpio's appointment, but public frustration quickly grew as the new government failed to address fundamental issues: crime and land ownership, tax and constitutional reform. Some progress was made in peace negotiations with the URNG guerrilla leadership but the question of indigenous rights remained unsolved.

■ Arzú and the peace accords

The **1996 presidential elections** demonstrated the country's increasing lack of faith in the electoral process, which had failed to bring any real change since the return to civilian rule in 1986. Some 63 percent of registered voters stayed at home and it was only a strong showing in Guatemala City, where **Álvaro Arzú** had previously served as mayor, that ensured his election. Arzú represented Guatemala's so-called modernizing right, and his party – **PAN** the National Advancement Party – has strong oligarchic roots and is committed to private-sector-led growth and the free market. Nevertheless, many were surprised as he quickly adopted a relatively progressive stance, shaking up the armed forces in bold early manoeuvres that left seasoned political observers holding their breath in anticipation.

Arzú moved quickly to bring an end to the 36-year civil war, meeting the URNG guerrilla leaders and working towards a final settlement. The **peace accords**, signed on December 29, 1996, concluded almost a decade of talks and terminated a conflict that had claimed 150,000 lives and resulted in the "disappearance" of another 50,000. The core purpose of the peace accords was to investigate previous human rights violations through a Truth Commission overseen by MINUGUA (the UN mission to Guatemala), to recognize the identity of indigenous people, and to eliminate discrimination and promote socio-economic development for all Guatemalans. Though the aims of the peace accords were undeniably ambitious, progress was laboriously slow during the Arzú years. In one of the biggest set-backs, the electorate narrowly turned down a proposal to amend the constitution to allow for greater Maya rights in May 1999. Turnout was woeful – around 18 per cent – with most of the indigenous community failing to vote, a collective rejection that underlined the deep-rooted animosity felt by most Maya towards a political system that had exploited them for centuries.

Though Arzú presided over a token reduction in armed forces numbers, their influence and position as the nation's real power brokers remained unchallenged throughout his term. Blamed for 80 percent of the atrocities of the civil war, army officers implicated in orchestrating massacres successfully avoided prosecution – Arzú simply dared not touch them. Then, in April 1998, two days after publishing a long-awaited investigation into wartime slaughters, **Bishop Juan Geradi** was bludgeoned to death in his own garage in Guatemala City, an event which stunned the nation. Though Guatemalans had long been accustomed to horrific levels of political violence, most thought the days of disappearances and death squads were over – as one newspaper put it, "This wasn't supposed to happen. Not any more."

The acute fragility of the nascent Guatemalan democracy was revealed – most observers immediately recognizing Geradi's assassination as the work of a vengeful military intent on preserving its power base. Despite international and domestic outrage – hundreds of thousands attended a silent protest in the capital days after the killing – the Arzú government seemed paralysed, and incapable of bringing the real perpetrators of the murder to justice. The investigation descended at times to near-farcical levels (including, at one stage, the implication of a priest's dog which had bitten the body), as terrified judges, prosecutors and key witnesses fled abroad following death threats. As Arzú departed the presidential palace in December 1999, Geradi's murderers remained at large and the investigation unsolved.

Despite this horrific killing, levels of political violence fell in the Arzú years, though there was an alarming upsurge in the **crime rate**, with soaring incidences of petty theft, muggings, robberies, drug- and gang-related incidents and murders. In 1997, despite its relatively small population, Guatemala had the fourth-highest incidence of kidnapping in the world, with over 1000 people being abducted. A new police force, the PNC, was retrained by experts from Spain, Chile and the USA, but quickly gained a reputation for corruption and ineffectualness as bad as its predecessor. Not surprisingly, law and order became the key issue of the 1999 election campaign.

■ President Portillo

Former lawyer and professor **Alfonso Portillo** won Guatemala's 1999 presidential elections with a mandate to implement the peace accords and tackle the impunity of both the military and criminal gangs. In the grossest of ironies, Portillo sought to boost his ratings during the presidential campaign by confessing to killing two men during a brawl in Mexico in 1982, declaring, "a man who defends his life will defend the lives of his people". He claimed that he had acted in self defence, then fled the country because he had no chance of a fair trial. The tactic paid off handsomely, as Portillo, leader of the right-wing FRG (Guatemalan Republican Front), won by a landslide after a second round of voting. Portillo campaigned on a populist platform to cut poverty by tackling corruption and tax evasion, though perhaps the decisive factor was the support of his political mentor, the former general **Ríos Montt** and founder of the FRG. Montt himself had been ruled illegible to stand for the presidency because of his role in an earlier coup, but was widely perceived as the real power behind the throne.

Initially, there was a positive groundswell of optimism as Portillo unveiled a diverse cabinet which included academics, indigenous activists and human rights advocates. Nevertheless, many of the key institutions – including the Bank of Guatemala and the Ministries of the Economy, Communications and Interior – were placed under the control of right-wing FRG politicians and pro-business monetarists. In a bold move Portillo broke the military chain of command by appointing a moderate colonel, Juan de Dios Estrada, instead of a general as Minister of Defence, an action which infuriated the army top brass.

Portillo also moved quickly to solve the Geradi murder – another key campaign pledge. Prosecutors arrested three senior military personnel and a priest: in June 2001 they were finally brought to trial and found guilty of plotting Geradi's murder. Despite intense pressure on the prosecution, and a bomb exploding outside the home of one judge on the first day of the trial, justice prevailed, breaking the historically almost complete impunity of the armed forces.

The Geradi case aside, Portillo's brief honeymoon period quickly subsided as he lurched from crisis to crisis as a series of **corruption scandals** were unearthed, crime rates continued to soar and gangsters and corrupt officials continued to enjoy impunity from prosecution. The new president even dispatched his family to Canada in June 2000 after threats from a kidnapping gang, a savage indictment of the security situation. By early 2001, barely a week passed without an armed bank robbery or a public lynching, as rural Guatemalans, frustrated with the country's bankrupt justice system, exacted their own justice, killing suspected criminals. In March 2001, a judge was hacked to death by a crowd in the isolated town of Senahú after he had freed an accused rapist because of a lack of evidence. Confidence in Portillo plummeted to an all-time low in June 2001 following a **mass breakout** from Guatemala's main maximum-security prison. Seventy of the country's most notorious criminals – murderers, rapists, kidnappers and gang leaders – blasted their way out of jail, armed to the teeth with a smuggled arsenal of submachine guns and grenade launchers which they had obviously acquired with internal connivance. Many media figures doubted that Portillo would be permitted to finish his presidential term, as persistent rumours of a military-backed coup swept through the country.

Meanwhile, the **economy** continued to falter, as traditional exports (principally coffee, sugar and bananas) were hit by low commodity prices, and the nation's high interest rates affected investment. The quetzal remained weak against international currencies, prompting the government to introduce **dollarization** in May 2001, with the US dollar becoming an official currency alongside the quetzal, and to sign up for customs union with Honduras, El Salvador and Nicaragua by 2003 in an effort to free up trade and boost the economy.

Away from mainstream politics, the country has witnessed a **Maya cultural revival**, as Guatemala's indigenous people have acquired freedoms denied them for centuries. Important steps to protect indigenous languages have been made, and hundreds of schools founded where Maya children are educated in their own tongue. Increasing numbers of indigenous writers and journalists have emerged, more and more Maya books and magazines are being published and *indígena* radio stations set up. The shifting mood has even influenced youth culture: Maya shamanic courses have become popular and eager young *ladino* university students assert their mixed-race identity by proclaiming a Maya heritage. Yet despite these changes Guatemala is still a divided country. Racism remains endemic and Guatemala's Maya continue to be subject to institutionalized discrimination, while most live in extreme poverty.

In many ways, the years since the peace accords have been a bitter disappointment to many Guatemalans. Though the peace has held, political violence has been replaced by random acts of criminal thuggery, and the unreformed justice system is seemingly moribund. The **economic outlook** remains poor, with low living standards and sub-standard health care and educational opportunities for the vast majority of people. With the issue of land reform still to be tackled and the highest population growth rate in the hemisphere (almost 3 percent per annum), more and more poor Guatemalans have fled to the US as illegal migrants, while those who remain have turned to farming increasingly marginal plots of land, cutting down the country's rapidly diminishing forests and threatening protected reserves and national parks. Though there is ground for optimism in some areas, including a vibrant tourism industry, the key points of the peace accords have not been tackled. Huge obstacles remain, and Guatemala seemingly faces many more difficult years ahead.

CHAPTER 6

GUATEMALA CITY

C haotic, congested and polluted, **GUATEMALA CITY** is in many ways the antithesis of the rest of the country. The capital was moved here in 1776, after the destruction of Antigua, but the site had been of importance long before the arrival of the Spanish. Now the largest city in Central America, its shapeless and swelling mass, ringed by shantytowns, is home to over three million people – about a quarter of Guatemala's population – and the undisputed centre of the country's politics, power and wealth.

Sprawling across a sweeping highland basin, surrounded on three sides by low hills and volcanic cones, the city has an intensity and vibrancy that are both its fascination and its horror, and for many travellers a trip to the capital is an exercise in damage limitation, struggling through a swirling mass of bus fumes and crowds. However, after all these years of neglect and decay, efforts are being made by a small group of conservationists to preserve what's left of the historic centre, **Zona 1**, and a smattering of fashionable new cafés and bars, popular with students, have opened in restored buildings the heart of the city.

Like it or not – and many travellers don't – Guatemala City is the crossroads of the country, and you'll certainly end up here at some time, if only to hurry between bus terminals or negotiate a visa extension. Once you get used to the pace, it can offer a welcome break from life on the road, with cosmopolitan restaurants, cinemas, shopping plazas, a couple of good museums and metropolitan culture. And if you really can't take the pace, it's easy enough to escape: buses leave every few minutes, day and night.

Some history

The pre-conquest Maya city of **Kaminaljuyú**, whose ruins are still scattered amongst Guatemala City's western suburbs, was well established here two thousand years ago. As a result of an alliance with the great northern power of Teotihuacán (near present-day Mexico City) in early Classic times (250–550 AD), Kaminaljuyú came to dominate the highlands and eventually provided the political and commercial backing that fostered the rise of Tikal (see p.263). The city was situated at the crossroads of two trade routes, and at the height of its prosperity was home to a population of some fifty thousand; however, following the decline of Teotihuacán around 600 AD, Kaminaljuyú was surpassed by the great lowland centres that it had helped to establish. Soon after their rise, some time between 600 and 900 AD, the city was abandoned.

Seven centuries later, when Alvarado entered the country, the fractured tribes of the west controlled the highlands and preoccupied the conquistadors. The Spanish ignored the possibility of settling here until the devastating **1773 earthquake** forced them to flee Antigua and establish a new capital. The new city was named Nueva Guatemala de la Asunción by royal decree and was officially inaugurated on January 1, 1776. The splendour of the former capital at Antigua was hard to emulate, however, and the new city's growth was steady but by no means dramatic. An 1863 census listed just 1206 residences and the earliest photographs show the city was still little more than a large vil-

For an explanation of **accommodation price codes**, see p.125.

lage with a theatre, a government palace and a fort. One of the factors retarding the city's growth was the existence of a major rival, Quetzaltenango, though when it too was razed to the ground by a massive earthquake in 1902, many wealthy families moved to the capital, finally establishing it as the country's primary city.

Since 1918, Guatemala City has grown at an incredible rate, mainly due to an influx of rural immigrants. The steady flight from the fields, characteristic of developing countries, was aided and abetted by a chronic shortage of land and, in the 1970s and 1980s, by internal refugees escaping rural violence. Many of these displaced people, for the most part Maya, feel unwanted and unwelcome in the city, and the divisions that cleave Guatemalan society are at their most acute in the capital's crumbling streets. While the wealthy elite sip coffee in air-conditioned shopping malls and plan their next visit to Miami, swathes of the city have been left to disintegrate into a threatening treeless tangle of fume-choked streets, largely devoid of any kind of life after dark. A small army of **street children** live rough, scratching a living from begging, prostitution and petty crime, and there is strong evidence of "social cleansing" by the security forces. Glass skyscrapers rise alongside colonial churches and shoeless widows peddle cigarettes and sweets to designer-clad nightclubbers. Guatemala City has, in many ways, much more in common with Cairo or Bogotá than with the rest of the country.

Arrival and information

Arriving in Guatemala City for the first time, it's easy to feel overwhelmed by its scale, with suburbs sprawling across some 21 **zones**, but you'll find that the central area, which is all that you need to worry about, is really quite small.

Broadly speaking, the city divides into two distinct halves. The northern section, centred on **Zona 1**, is the old part of town, containing the **Parque Central**, most of the budget hotels, shops, restaurants, cinemas, the post office, and many of the bus companies. This part of the city is cramped, congested, polluted and bustling with activity. The two main streets are 5 and 6 avenidas, both thick with street traders, fast-food joints and copious neon.

To the south, acting as a buffer between the two halves of town, is **Zona 4**, home to the Centro Cívico administrative centre, the *migración*, the **tourist office** and the Teatro Nacional. The other great landmark is the Zona 4 **bus terminal**, a crazy world of peripatetic humanity and exhaust fumes.

The southern half of the city, **Zona 9** and **Zona 10**, is the modern, wealthy part of town, split in two by **Avenida la Reforma**. Here you'll find exclusive offices, apartment blocks, hotels and shops and Guatemala's most expensive nightclubs, restaurants and cafés. Many of the embassies and two of the country's finest museums are also here. Continuing south, the neighbouring zonas 13 and 14 are rich leafy suburbs and home to the airport, zoo and more museums and cinemas.

By air

Aurora international airport is on the edge of the city in Zona 13, some way from the centre. The **domestic terminal** is in the same complex, but with a separate entrance on Av Hincapié. There's a Banco del Quetzal (Mon–Fri 6am–8pm, Sat & Sun 6am–6pm) for currency exchange, plus 24-hour cashpoints which accept Visa, Mastercard, Cirrus and Plus cards. There's also a **tourist information office** (daily 6am–9pm; ☎331 4256) on the upper (departures) floor, a Telgua phone office and a post office (both Mon–Sat 7am–9pm).

Much the easiest way to get to and from the airport is by **taxi**: you'll find plenty of them waiting outside the terminal. The fare to or from Zona 1 is around US$10; from Zonas 9 and 10, around US$7. **Buses** also depart from directly outside the terminal, across the

concrete plaza, dropping you in Zona 1, either on 5 Av or 9 Av – the last leaves around 8pm. Virtually all Guatemala City's four- and five-star hotels, and all the guesthouses in Zona 13, offer free pick-ups from the airport if you let them know when you're arriving.

If you're heading to **Antigua**, there are regular shuttle-bus services from the airport (US$10), though they don't run to a fixed schedule and only leave when they have at least three passengers. A taxi from the airport is US$25.

By bus
If you're travelling by **first-class** (Pullman) **bus** you'll arrive at the private terminal of whichever company you're travelling with – there are about a dozen in total, virtually all of them in Zona 1, including all services from the Mexican border and Petén. If you've come by second-class "chicken bus" **from Antigua**, you'll arrive in Zona 1 at the junction of 18 Calle, between 4 and 5 Avenidas. The **Zona 4 terminal** is where second-

---

ADDRESSES IN GUATEMALA CITY

The system of street numbering in the capital may seem a little confusing at first and it is complicated by the fact that the same calles and avenidas can exist in several different zones. Always check the zone first and then the street. For example "4 Av 9–14, Zona 1" is in Zona 1, on 4 Avenida between 9 and 10 calles, house number 14.

class buses to the western highlands, the Pacific coast and some towns in the eastern highlands arrive and depart; the main terminal for San Salvador is very close by on 3 Avenida and 1 Calle.

Information

The Inguat **tourist office** (Mon–Fri 8am–4pm; ☎331 1333, fax 331 8893) is at 7 Av 1–17, Zona 4. At the information desk on the ground floor you can buy a half-decent **map** of the country and city, and there's always someone around who speaks English. For detailed hiking maps, go to the Instituto Geográfico Militar (Mon–Fri 8am–4pm), Av las Américas 5–76, Zona 13.

City transport

As in any big city, getting to grips with the public transport system takes time – even locals can be bamboozled by Guatemala's seemingly anarchic web of **bus routes**. In Zona 1 buses #82 and #83 stop on **10 Av**, while buses to many different parts of the

The main **bus companies**, their addresses and routes are all given at the end of this chapter on pp.158–159.

USEFUL BUS ROUTES

#71 Connects 10 Av, Zona 1, with the Centro Cívico in Zona 4.

#82 Starts in Zona 2 and continues through Zona 1 along 10 Av, then past the Centro Cívico in Zona 4 and on to Av la Reforma before turning left at the Obelisco. The route passes many of the embassies, the American Express office, the Popol Vuh and Ixchel museums and the Los Próceres shopping centre.

#83 To and from the airport from Zona 1 on 10 Av.

Terminal Any bus marked "terminal", and there are plenty of these on 4 Av in Zona 1, will take you to the main bus terminal in Zona 4.

Bolívar/Trébol Any bus marked "Bolívar" or "Trébol" will take you along the western side of the city, down Av Bolívar and to the Trébol junction, for connections to the western highlands.

---

city run along **4 Av**. Destinations are posted on the front of the bus. Buses run from around 6.30am until about 9.30pm. Guatemala City has a ferocious **rush hour** and many roads throughout the city are jammed between 7.30 and 9am and from 4am to 7.30pm.

There are currently both metered and non-metered **taxis**. If you can't face the complexities of the bus system, or it's late at night, the excellent metered taxis are comfortable and cheap; Amarillo (☎332 1515; 24hr) are highly recommended and will pick you up from anywhere in the city; the fare from Zona 1 to Zona 10 is US$4–5. There are plenty of non-metered taxis around too – you'll have to use your bargaining skills with these and fix the price beforehand.

Accommodation

The majority of the city's budget and mid-range hotels are in noisy **Zona 1**, though it's not the safest neighbourhood at night or a great place for wandering around in search of a room. Many travellers are now choosing to stay close to the airport, in **Zona 13**, where there are a number of good new options – all offer free airport pick-ups and drop-offs, though be sure to book ahead. The disadvantage with this quiet, suburban location is that there are very few restaurants and cafés close by, and the bus service is infrequent. Guatemala City's luxury hotels are clustered in a relatively safe part of town, in **Zona 10**, the "Zona Viva", where there's a glut of dining options, bars and nightclubs.

Zona 1

Chalet Suizo, 14 C 6–82 (☎251 3786, fax 232 0429). Friendly, comfortable and, as it's right opposite the police headquarters, very safe. Nicely designed, spotlessly clean and all very Swiss and organized, with left luggage and a new café that's open all day. Private or shared bath. No double beds. ④–⑤.

Hotel Colonial, 7 Av 14–19 (☎232 6722, fax 232 8671, *colonial@infovia.com.gt*). Well-situated colonial-style hotel with dark wood, wrought iron and an attractive tiled lobby. Tasteful and comfortable, but slightly old-fashioned; the rooms come with or without private bathroom. ④.

Hotel Fénix, 7 Av 15–81 (☎251 6625). Safe, friendly and vaguely atmospheric, set in an old, warped, wooden building. There's a quirky café downstairs and some rooms have private bath, though it can be noisy early in the morning. ②–③.

Hotel Hernani, corner 15 C and 6 Av A (☎232 2839). Comfortable old building with good, clean rooms, all with their own shower. One of the better budget deals in town. ②.

Hotel Monteleone, 18 C 4–63 (☎238 2600, fax 238 2509). Rooms are attractively decorated, with quality mattresses and bedside lamps, and some have private bath. Very decent value – clean, safe and right by the Antigua terminal – but not the best area after dark. ②–③.

Hotel PanAmerican, 9 C 5–63 (☎232 6807, fax 251 8749, *www.hotelpanamerican.com*). The city's oldest smart hotel, very formal and civilized, with cable TV, continental breakfast and airport transfer included. Brilliant for Sunday breakfast. ⑥.

Hotel Posada Belén, 13 C A 10–30 (☎253 4530, fax 251 3478, *www.guateweb.com*). Tucked down a side street in a beautiful old building. Supremely quiet, safe and very homely, with its own restaurant. No children under five. ⑥.

Hotel Royal Palace, 6 Av 12–66 (☎ & fax 332 4036). Very comfortable, Best Westin-owned landmark right in the heart of Zona 1, with well appointed, spacious rooms and good service, but be sure to avoid the noisy streetside rooms. Seasonal bargain rates. ⑦.

Hotel San Martín, 16 C 7–65 (☎238 0319). Friendly hotel with very cheap and clean rooms, some with private bath – one of the best deals at the lower end of the scale. ②–③.

Hotel Spring, 8 Av 12–65 (☎232 2858, fax 232 0107). An excellent deal and a safe location, though it's often full of Peace Corps volunteers. The fairly spacious rooms, with or without private bath, are set around a pretty colonial courtyard; there's also a new block where all rooms have cable TV. Breakfast available, plus free mineral water. ②–③.

Pensión Meza, 10 C 10–17 (☎232 3177 or 253 4576). Infamous budget travellers' hangout; cheap and laid-back, with plenty of 1960s-style decadence. Fidel Castro and Che Guevara stayed here – the latter in room 21. Pretty dilapidated dorms (US$2.50 per person) and doubles, some with private shower. There's a useful noticeboard, ping-pong, all-day music, and the helpful owner, Mario, speaks good English. ①.

Zona 13

Dos Lunas, 21 C 10–92 (☎ & fax 334 5264, *www.xelapages.com/doslunas*). Clean, secure and friendly guesthouse set in quiet suburban surrounds a short drive from the airport. Free pick-up, drop-off and breakfast, plus excellent travel information and tips from the dynamic young Guatemalan owner. Very popular, so it's essential to book well ahead. ④.

Economy Dorms, 8 Av 17–74, Col Aurora I (☎331 8029). Basic dormitory accommodation with free continental breakfast and airport transfers. US$10 per person.

El Aeropuerto Guest House, 15 C A 7–32 (☎332 3086, fax 362 1264, *hotairpt@guate.net*). A pleasant, convenient and comfortable place five minutes' walk from the international airport (call for a free pick-up or walk across the grass outside and follow the road to the left). Rooms have cable TV, private showers and fluffy towels. Continental breakfast is included and there are email and fax facilities for guests. ⑤.

Hotel Hincapié, Av Hincapié 18–77 (☎332 7771, fax 337 4469, *aruedap@infovia.com.gt*). Under the same management as the *El Aeropuerto* and conveniently located for the domestic terminal. Rates include local calls, continental breakfast and transport to and from the airport. ④.

Patricia's Bed and Breakfast, 19 C 10–65, Col Aurora II (☎331 0470, *www.geocites.com /xelaju2001*). Small, family-run guesthouse a short distance from the airport with pleasant rooms and a friendly atmosphere. ④.

Zona 10

Camino Real, Av la Reforma and 14 C, Zona 10 (☎333 4633, fax 337 4313, *www.quetzalnet. com/caminoreal*). Landmark hotel, now run by the Best Westin group, long favoured by visiting heads of state and anyone on expenses, though the chintz-heavy decor is beginning to look rather dated. Excellent location in the heart of the Zona Viva, plus bars, shops and sports facilities – including two pools. Rooms from US$167. ⑨.

Holiday Inn, 1 Av 13–22, Zona 10 (☎332 2555, fax 332 2584, *www.guatered.com/holidayinn*). First-class hotel within walking distance of the city's best upmarket shops, bars and restaurants. Commodious rooms and suites, plus a fully equipped business centre and an in-house Internet café. Rooms from US$140. ⑨.

Hotel Casa Santa Clara, 12 C 4–51, Zona 10 (☎339 1811, fax 332 0775, *www.hotelcasasantaclara .com*). Small, beautifully appointed hotel in the Zona Viva, with tastefully decorated modern rooms and a quality in-house Mediterranean restaurant. ⑦.

Hotel Inter-Continental 14 C 2–51, Zona 10 (☎379 4444, fax 379 4447, *www.interconti.com*). This spectacular new Zona Viva hotel is now the city's most stylish five-star address. Among its many charms are a monumental lobby featuring fine art, modern sculpture and a modish bar, sumptuous bedrooms, a fine French restaurant and a wonderful outdoor pool. Rooms from US$145. ⑨.

The City

Though few people come to Guatemala City for the sights, there are some places which are well worth visiting while you're here. The Ixchel, Popol Vuh and Archeological **museums** are particularly good; there's the odd impressive building in **Zona 1** and, dotted across the southern half of the city, some more outlandish modern structures.

Zona 1: the old city

The hub of the old city is **Zona 1**: a squalid world of low-slung, crumbling nineteenth-century town houses and faceless concrete blocks, broken pavements, parking lots and plenty of noise and dirt. Having been left by the city authorities to rot for decades, tentative signs of regeneration are now beginning to emerge, as a committed group of planners and architects attempt to preserve the capital's heritage, and clusters of new bars and cafés open in historic buildings. It's a process that will take decades to complete, however, and the area remains plagued by pollution and noise from fume-belching buses and beset by social problems. Despite all this, the Zona's streets do possess a certain brutal fascination and are undeniably the most exciting part of the capital.

The heart of the city, and the country's political and religious centre, is the windswept **Parque Central**, from where all distances in Guatemala are measured. Despite its importance, the Parque is a soulless place, patronized by bored taxi drivers, *lustradores* (shoeshiners) and pigeons, which only really comes alive on Sundays (when there's a good *huipil* market) and public holidays, when a tide of Guatemalans come to stroll, gossip and snack. The new spirit of Guatemala is detectable here, as soldiers chat with Maya girls, and you may even hear politics being discussed – something unthinkable a decade or so ago. Next to the giant Guatemalan flag is a small box containing an **eternal flame** dedicated to "the anonymous heroes for peace". For many Guatemalans this is a place of pilgrimage.

The Parque's most striking building is the **Palacio Nacional**, a grandiose stone-faced structure started in 1939 under President Ubico. For decades it housed the executive branch of the government, and from time to time its steps have been fought over by assorted coupsters. The palace is currently being converted into a **museum** of the history of Guatemala. If you can get inside, it's worth a look at its most imposing features – two Moorish-style interior courtyards and the stained-glass windows of the former **Salas de Recepción** on the second floor.

On the east side of the plaza is the blue-domed **Cathedral** (daily 8am–1pm & 3–7pm), completed in 1868. Its solid, squat design was intended to resist the force of earthquakes and has, for the most part, succeeded. Inside there are three main aisles, all lined with arching pillars, austere colonial paintings and intricate altars housing an array of saints. The cathedral's most poignant aspect is outside, however: etched into the twelve pillars that support the entrance railings are the names of thousands of the dead and "disappeared", victims of the civil war, including an astonishing number from the department of Quiché.

Around the back of the cathedral is the **Mercado Central**, housed in three sickly blue-and-yellow layers of sunken concrete; a structure which the architect apparently modelled on a nuclear bunker, sacrificing any aesthetic concerns to the need for strength. Inside, the top floor sells textiles, leatherware and jewellery, the middle floor has flowers, fruit and vegetables, and the bottom has **handicrafts** – mainly basketry and típica clothing.

Heading south from the Parque Central are **6 and 7 avenidas**, thick with clothes shops, fast-food joints and neon signs. On the corner of 6 Av and 13 C is the **Iglesia de San Francisco**, dating from 1780 and famous for its carving of the Sacred Heart. It's said that cane syrup, egg whites and cow's milk were mixed with the mortar to enhance its resistance to earthquakes. Another block to the south is the **police headquarters**, an outlandish-looking mock castle with imitation medieval battlements.

Just 300m east of the police headquarters along 14 Calle, at the corner with 8 Avenida, **Casa Mima** (Mon–Sat 9am–12.30pm & 2–5pm; US$2) is an immaculately restored late nineteenth-century town house with original furnishings from various periods, including Moderne, Art Deco and French neo-Rococo, offering a fascinating glimpse into a wealthy middle-class household of the late nineteenth and early twentieth centuries. There are excellent explanatory leaflets, and usually an English-speaking guide on hand, plus a delightful little **café** on the rear patio, with good coffee and cookies.

As you head south from Casa Mima, along 8 Avenida, things go into a slow but steady decline, until you finally emerge in the madness of **18 Calle**, a distinctly sleazy part of town which is probably best avoided day or night. An assorted collection of grimy nightclubs and "streap-tease" joints, this is the street that most of the city's petty thieves, prostitutes and low-life seem to call home. At the junction of 18 Calle and 9 Avenida is the wooden shell of the former **train station**, badly damaged by a fire in 1996, from which regular passenger services used to leave for Tecún Umán and Puerto Barrios.

At the southern end of the old city, separating it from the newer parts of town, the distinctively 1960s architecture of the **Centro Cívico** area marks the boundary between Zonas 1 and 4. Looming over 7 Avenida is the **Banco de Guatemala** building, bedecked with bold modern murals and stylized glyphs designed by Dagoberto Vásquez – the images recount the history of Guatemala and the conflict between Spanish and Maya. Just to the south you'll find the main office of **Inguat** (see p.147) and opposite is the lofty landmark **Teatro Nacional**, also referred to as the Miguel Asturias cultural centre, one of the city's most prominent and unusual structures, completed in 1978. Designed along the lines of an ocean liner, painted blue and white with portholes as windows, it has superb views across the city and hosts regular cultural events in its auditorium and the adjoining open-air space. There's also a little-visited **museum** dedicated to the Guatemalan military, though it's really only of interest to would-be *comandantes*.

The new city

The more spacious southern half of the city, with its broader streets, is, roughly speaking, divided into two by 7 Avenida. To the south of the Centro Cívico, at the junction of 7 Av and 2 C, in Zona 4, is the landmark **Torre del Reformador**, Guatemala's answer to the Eiffel Tower. The steel structure was built in honour of President Barrios, whose liberal reforms transformed the country between 1871 and 1885. Unfortunately you can't go up it. Just to the north on the junction with Ruta 6 is the **Yurrita Church**, built in an outlandish neo-Gothic style more reminiscent of a horror movie set than the streets of Guatemala City.

A block east from the Torre is **Avenida la Reforma**, the new city's main transport artery, which divides zonas 9 and 10. Many of the city's important sites and buildings are to be found on or just off this tree-lined boulevard, including the **Jardín Botanico** (Mon–Fri 8am–3.30pm; US$1.20) of the San Carlos University, whose entrance is on 0 C. Inside you'll find a beautiful little garden with quite a selection of species, all neatly labelled in Spanish and Latin. There's also a small and not terribly exciting **natural history museum**, with a collection of stuffed birds, including a quetzal and an ostrich, along with geological samples, wood types, live snakes and some horrific pickled rodents.

Far more worthwhile are the two privately owned **museums** in the campus of the University Francisco Marroquín, reached by following 6 C Final off Av la Reforma to the east. The **Museo Ixchel** (Mon–Fri 8am–5.50pm, Sat 9am–12.50pm; US$2.50) is strikingly housed in its own purpose-built cultural centre. Probably the capital's best museum, the Ixchel is dedicated to Maya culture, with particular emphasis on traditional weaving. There's a stunning collection of hand-woven fabrics, including some very impressive examples of ceremonial costumes, with explanations in English, plus information about the techniques, dyes, fibres and weaving tools used and the way in which costumes have changed over the years. Don't miss the miniature *huipil* collection in the basement.

Right next door, on the third floor of the *auditorio* building, is the city's other private museum, the excellent **Museo Popol Vuh** (Mon–Fri 9am–5pm, Sat 9am–1pm; US$2.50), home to an outstanding collection of artefacts from sites all over the country. The small museum is divided into Preclassic, Classic, Postclassic and Colonial rooms, and all the exhibits are top quality. In the Preclassic room are some stunning ceramics, stone masks and *hongo zoomorfo* (mushroom heads). The Classic room has an altar from Naranjo, some lovely incense burners, and a model of Tikal; the Postclassic contains a replica of the Dresden code. The colonial era is represented with some ecclesiastical relics and processional crosses.

Back on Av la Reforma and heading south brings you to the smart part of town, a collection of leafy streets filled with boutiques, travel agents, banks, office blocks and sleek hotels. A little to the east, around 10 C and 3 Av, is the so-called **Zona Viva**, some ten small city blocks housing a bunch of upmarket hotels, restaurants, nightclubs and, at the bottom of La Reforma, the upmarket Los Próceres shopping mall. To get to Av la Reforma from Zona 1, take bus #82, which runs along 10 Av in Zona 1, past the Yurrita Church and all the way along Av la Reforma.

West of 7 Avenida

West of 7 Avenida it's quite another story, and while there are still small enclaves of upmarket housing, and several expensive shopping areas, things are really dominated by commerce and transport, including the infamous **Zona 4 bus terminal**, at 1 C and 4 Av. This area is probably the country's most impenetrable and intimidating jungle, a brutish swirl of petty thieves, hardware stores, bus fumes and sleeping vagrants. Around the terminal the largest **market** in the city spreads across several blocks. To get to the bus terminal from Zona 1, take any of the buses marked "terminal" from 4 Av or 9 Av, all of which pass within a block or two.

Some 2km further to the south in Zona 13, reachable by bus #63 from 4 Avenida or #83 from 10 Avenida, **Parque Aurora** houses the city's remodelled **zoo** (Tues–Sun 9am–5pm; US$1.20), home to African lions, Bengal tigers, crocodiles, giraffes, Indian elephants, hippos, monkeys and all the Central and South American big cats, including some well-fed jaguars. Most of the larger animals have a reasonable amount of space; many smaller animals do not.

On the other side of Parque Aurora is a collection of three state-run **museums** (all Tues–Fri 9am–4pm, Sat & Sun 9am–noon & 1.30–4pm). The best of these is the **Museo Nacional de Arqueología y Etnología** (US$5), which has a world-class selection of Maya artefacts, though the design and displays are somewhat antiquated. The collection includes sections on prehistoric archeology and ethnology and features some wonderful stelae and panels from Machaquila and Dos Pilas, spectacular jade masks from Abaj Takalik and a stunning wooden temple-top lintel from Tikal. However, it's the exhibits collected from Piedras Negras, one of the remotest sites in Petén, that are most impressive. Stela 12, dating from 672 AD, brilliantly depicts a cowering captive king begging for mercy, and there's a monumental carved stone throne from the same site, richly engraved with superb glyphs and decorated with a twin-faced head.

Right opposite the archeological museum, the city's **Museo Nacional de Arte Moderno** (US$1.70) also suffers from poor presentation and layout but can boast some imaginative geometric paintings by Dagoberto Vásquez, vibrant semi-abstract work by the indigenous artist Rolando Ixquiac Xicará and a collection of startling exhibits by Efraín Recinos, including a colossal sculpture made from the unlikely combination of a marimba (signifying Maya culture) and a tank (signifying the military). There's also a permanent collection of bold Cubist art and massive murals by Carlos Mérida, Guatemala's most celebrated artist, which draw strongly on ancient Maya tradition. The most neglected of the three museums, the **Museo Nacional de Historia Natural** (US$1.70), features a range of mouldy-looking stuffed animals from Guatemala and elsewhere and a few mineral samples. Close by on 11 Avenida is a touristy **handicraft market**, while to the south is Aurora airport.

Kaminaljuyú

Way out west on the edge of the city is the long thin arm of Zona 7, which wraps around the ruins of **Kaminaljuyú** (daily 9am–4pm; US$4). Archeological digs on this side of the city have revealed a Maya city that once housed around fifty thousand people. More than three hundred mounds and thirteen ball courts have been discovered, though unlike the massive temples of the lowlands, these structures were built of adobe, and most of them have been lost to centuries of erosion and a few decades of urban sprawl. Today, the archeological site, incorporating only a tiny fraction of the original city, is little more than a series of earth-covered mounds, and though it's now a favourite spot for football and romance, it's virtually impossible to get any impression of Kaminaljuyú's former scale and splendour.

To get to the ruins, take **bus #35** from 4 Av in Zona 1. Alternatively, any bus from the Parque Central that has a small "Kaminaljuyú" sign in the windscreen passes within a block or two.

Eating, drinking and entertainment

Despite its role as the country's economic centre, Guatemala City isn't a great place for indulging in hedonistic pleasures. Most of the population hurry home after dark and it's only the very rich who eat, drink and dance until the small hours. There are, however, **restaurants** everywhere in the city, invariably reflecting the type of neighbourhood they're in. Movie-watching is also popular and there is a good selection of **cinemas**. **Nightclubs** and **bars** are concentrated in Zona 10.

Restaurants and cafés

When it comes to eating cheaply in Guatemala City, stick to **Zona 1**, where there are some good comedores and dozens of fast-food chains. In the smarter parts of town, particularly **Zonas 9** and **10**, the emphasis is more on upmarket cafés and glitzy dining, and there's also more choice, including Mexican, Middle Eastern, Chinese and Japanese options.

Zona 1

Altuna, 5 Av 12–31. Spanish/Basque food in a wonderfully civilized old colonial mansion. Very strong on fish and seafood, but also pasta and Castilian treats like Manchego cheese and *jamón serrano*. Not cheap, but worth a splurge for the elegant ambience.

Cafebreria, 5 Av 13–32. Part bookshop, part Internet café, serving coffee, snacks and more substantial dishes on a quiet covered patio. The owner also plans to open a budget hotel upstairs.

Café de Centro Histórico 6 Av 9–50. Stylish café on the upper floor of a beautifully restored 1930s building replete with original tiles, wood panelling and evocative monochrome photographs. Simple menu of inexpensive Guatemalan dishes, pies and salads, plus great coffee.

El Gran Pavo, 13 C 4–41. Massive portions of genuinely Mexican food, moderately priced. It's riotous on the weekend when mariachi bands prowl the tables. Other branches at 6 C 3–09, Zona 9; 15 Av 16–72, Zona 10; 13 C and 6 Av, Zona 10

Europa Bar, 11 C 5–16. The most popular expat hangout in Zona 1, set inauspiciously beneath a multi-storey car park. Primarily a bar, with CNN and sports on screen, but there are also cheapish eats. Owner Judy is a mine of local information. You can trade US dollars here and make local calls. Closed Sun.

Fu Lu Sho, 6 Av and 12 C. Popular, inexpensive Chinese restaurant with an Art Deco interior, opening onto the bustle of 6 Avenida.

Long Wah, 6 C 3–75, west of the Palacio Nacional. One of the best of the many Chinese restaurants in this neighbourhood, with a good inexpensive menu.

Rey Sol, south side of Parque Centenario. "Aerobic" breakfasts (sic), *licuados* and very good selection of vegetarian dishes. The shop sells wholemeal bread, granola and veggie snacks.

Tao Restaurant, 5 C 9–70. The city's best-value three-course veggie lunch. There's no menu; you just eat the meal of the day at tiny tables around a plant-filled courtyard.

Zone 4

Cafe Restaurant Pereira, inside the Gran Centro Comercial mall, 6 Av and 24 C. Just a couple of blocks west of Inguat, this is a very popular comedor with excellent set meals of typical Guatemalan food. There's another branch at Av la Reforma 14–43, Zona 9.

Zonas 9 and 10

Jake's, 17 C 10–40, Zona 10. Lunch and dinner from an international menu, very strong on fish and with terrific desserts. Pleasant, candle-lit atmosphere, excellent service and correspondingly high prices. Closed Sun & Mon.

La Lancha, 13 C 7–98, Zona 10. French-owned restaurant, with a superb menu of very reasonably priced traditional Gallic dishes, plus a daily special and a tremendous wine list. Open for lunch Mon–Fri, dinner Thurs & Fri only.

Los Alpes, 10 C 1–09, Zona 10. A haven of peace, this garden café has superb pastries, pies and crêpes and a relatively inexpensive breakfast menu considering the smart location. Closed Mon.

Los Antojitos, Av la Reforma 15–02, Zona 9. Good, moderately priced Central American food – try the *chiles rellenos* or guacamole.

Luigi's Pizza, 4 Av 14–20, Zona 10. Very popular, moderately priced Italian restaurant serving delicious pizza, pasta and baked potatoes.

Olivadda, 12 C 4–51, Zona 10. Very smart restaurant with a stylish interior and a leafy terrace garden, majoring in authentic, moderately priced Mediterranean fare.

Palace, 10 C 4–40, Zona 10. Pasta and snacks, cakes and pastries in a cafeteria atmosphere.

Piccadilly, Plaza España, 7 Av 12–00, Zona 9. One of the most popular European restaurants with tourists and Guatemalans alike. Decent range of pastas and pizzas, served along with huge jugs of beer. Moderate prices. There's another branch in Zona 1 on 6 Av and 11 C.

Puerto Barrios, 7 Av 10–65, Zona 9. Excellent but pricey seafood restaurant in a slightly comical boat-like building.

Tamarindos 11 C 2–19A, Zona 10. Uber-chic bar-restaurant with modish Italian furniture, sensitive lighting, European chill-out music and a very hip, moneyed clientele. The pan-Asian menu matches the site, with delicious, beautifully presented Thai, Malay and Chinese influenced dishes at far from outrageous prices – expect to pay around $15 a head.

Nightlife and entertainment

Despite appearances, Guatemala City quietens down very quickly in the evenings, and **nightlife** is certainly not one of its strengths. The best bet for a night out in Zona 1 is to start at somewhere like *El Tiempo* (see overleaf) and then check out what's on at *La Bodeguita del Centro*. If you crave low life, then stroll on down 18 C, to the junction with 9 Av, and you're in the heart of the **red-light district**, where the bars and clubs are truly sleazy.

The **Zona Viva** in Zona 10 is where the wealthy go to have fun, though it's anything but an egalitarian experience. House music is now firmly established in Guatemala, though you'll be lucky to get anything other than the standard, commercial "handbag" strain. Most city DJs spin a mix of pan-Latin sounds and pop-rave hits, with the merengue of the Caribbean often being spiced up with raggamuffin vocals. There are also specialist clubs for **salsa** fanatics. The city's premier **reggae bar** is *La Gran Comal* on Via 4 between 6 Av and Ruta 6, Zona 4. Radiating rhythm, it's relaxed, but not as worn-out as the clubs of Zona 1, and a favourite haunt of black Guatemalans from Livingston and the Caribbean coast – well worth a visit.

Guatemala City's **gay nightlife** is mostly underground and concentrated around two (almost entirely male) clubs: *Pandora's Box*, Via 3 and Ruta 3, Zona 4, and *Eclipso* at 12 C 6–61, Zona 1. There are no specifically lesbian clubs or bars in the city.

Bars and clubs

Altos del Cairo, first floor, 9 C 6–10, Zona 1. Raucous drinking den with simple bench seating, draught beer, and rock, pop and salsa nights.

El Establo, 14 C 5–08, Zona 10. Large, stylish European-owned bar with polished wood interior, good food and a soundtrack of decent jazz and Western music.

El Tiempo, Pasaje Aycinema, 9 C between 6 and 7 Av, Zona 1. Very lively bar in the heart of the historic centre that's a magnet for the city's bohemian youth, hedonists and thinkers, with sporadic musical jams, protest poetry readings and the like.

Kahlua, 15 C and 1 Av, Zona 10. Currently one of the most happening clubs in town with two dance floors and a chill-out room. Attracts a young crowd with a reasonable mix of dance and Latin pop.

La Bodeguita del Centro, 12 C 3–55, Zona 1. Large, left-field venue with live music, comedy, poetry and all manner of arty events. Free entry in the week; around US$4 at weekends. Definitely worth a visit for the Che Guevara memorabilia alone.

Las Cien Puertes, Pasaje Aycinena, 9 C between 6 and 7 Av, Zone 1. Funky, artistic bar in a beautiful run-down colonial arcade. Good Latin sounds, very moderate prices and some imaginative Guatemalan cooking. Recommended.

Sesto Senso 2 Av 12–81, Zona 10. Hip, lively bar-restaurant venue with superb menu of global food, plus great coffee and snacks, and often some live music in the evening.

Shakespeare's Pub, 13 C 1–51, Zona 10. Small basement bar with friendly staff, mainly catering to middle-aged expat North Americans.

Xtreme, 3 Av and 13 C, Zona 10. Industrial decor, with a dark interior full of steel and aluminium, plus a tooth-loosening sound system make this club one of the coolest places in town. The Latin dance, house and chart pop attracts a rich, young crowd.

Cinemas

Most movies are shown in English with Spanish subtitles. There are four **cinemas on 6 Av** between the Parque Central and the Police HQ. Elsewhere, the very best for sound quality is the Magic Place on Av las Américas, Zona 13. Also recommended are Cine las Américas, Av las Américas between C 8 and 9, Zona 13, and Cine Tikal Futura, Tikal Futura, Calzada Roosevelt, Zona 11. Programmes are listed in the two main newspapers, *El Gráfico* and *Prensa Libre*.

Listings

Airlines Airline offices are scattered throughout the city, with many along Avenida la Reforma. It's fairly straightforward to phone them and there will almost always be someone in the office who speaks English. Aerocaribe (see Mexicana, below); Aerovías, Av Hincapié 18 C, Zona 13 (☎332 5686); Air Canada, 12 C 1–25, Zona 10 (☎335 3341); American Airlines, *Hotel El Dorado*, Av la Reforma 15–45, Zona 9 (☎334 7379); Aviateca (see Taca, below); British Airways, 1 Av 10–81, Zona 10, 6th floor of Edificio Inexa (☎332 7402); Continental, 12 C 1–25, Zona 10, Edificio Géminis 10, 12th floor, Torre Norte (☎331 3341); Copa, 1 Av 10–1, Zona 10 (☎361 1567); Delta, 15 C 3–20, Zona 10, Centro Ejecutivo building (☎337 0642); Iberia, Av la Reforma 8–60, Zona 9 (☎334 3816); Inter (see Taca, below); Jungle Flying, Av Hincapié & 18 C, domestic terminal, Hangar 21, Zona 13 (☎360 4917); Lacsa (see Taca, below); Mexicana, 13 C 8–44, Zona 10, Edificio Edyma (☎333 6048); Nica (see Taca, below); Taca Group (Aviateca, Inter, Lacsa, Nica), Av Hincapié 12–22, Zona 13 (☎334 7722); Tikal Jets, La Aurora airport, international terminal (☎334 5631); United Airlines, Av la Reforma 1–50, Zona 9, Edificio el Reformador (☎332 2995).

American Express Diagonal 6 10–01, Centro Gerencial, Las Margaritas, Zona 10 (Mon–Fri 8.30am–5pm; ☎339 2877, fax 339 2882).

Banks and exchange At the airport, Banco del Quetzal (Mon–Fri 6am–8pm, Sat & Sun 6am–6pm) gives a good rate, takes most European currencies, and has a 24hr Mastercard and Cirrus cashpoint; Visa and Plus cardholders should head for the nearby 24hr Bancared cashpoint. In Zona 1, Credomatic, on the corner of 5 Av and 11 C, gives Visa and Mastercard cash advances (Mon–Fri 8.30am–7pm, Sat 9am–1pm) and will cash travellers' cheques. In Zona 10, head for the Centro Gerencial Las Margaritas, at Diagonal 6 10–01, where there are numerous banks where you can cash travellers' cheques, three 24hr cashpoints for Visa and Plus cards and another, inside the Banco de Central América (Mon–Fri 9am–5pm, Sat 9am–1pm), that accepts Mastercard and Cirrus cards.

Books The pleasantest bookshop in town is Sopho's, Av la Reforma 13–89, Zona 10, where there's a decent selection of English-language fiction and literature – you can also get good coffee here. Over the road in Zona 9 the Librería del Pensativo, 7 Av and 13 C, Edificio La Cúpula, is worth a browse, while in Zona 1 try Arnel, in the basement of the Edificio El Centro on 9 C, corner of 7 Av. Finally Géminis, 3 Av 17–05, Zona 14, is also worth a visit if you're in the south of the city.

Car rental Renting a car in Guatemala is quite expensive and you should always keep a sharp eye on the terms, as there are usually large deductible penalties if you damage the vehicle. Jeeps can be rented for a little under US$55 a day and cars start from US$35. Car rental agents include: Adaesa Renta Autos, 4 C A 16–57, Zona 1 (☎220 2180, *masifre@hotmail.com*); Americar, 6 Av 3–95, Zona 10 (☎361 8641, *www.america.com*); Autorrentas (Budget agent), Av Hincapié 11–01, Zona 13 (☎332 2024, *budget@infovia.com*); Avis, 6 Av 11–24, Zona 9 (☎334 1057, *avis@guate.net*); Hertz, 7 Av 14–76, Zona 9 (☎334 2540, *rentauto@guate.net*); Rental (also the only company to rent motorbikes), 12 C 2–62, Zona 10 (☎361 0672, fax 334 2739); Tabarini, 2 C A 7–30, Zona 10 (☎332 2161, fax 334 1925); Thrifty, Av la Reforma 8–33, Zona 10 (☎332 1220, *thrifty@guate.net*).

City Tours Excellent walking tours of the historic centre of the city are organized by Antañona, 11 Av 5–59, Zona 1 (☎238 1751, *walkingtour@hotmail.com*); tours leave from their offices Mon–Fri at 9.30am and cost US$10 per person. Plenty of agencies offer guided city tours that usually include the main museums and sites and transport, including Clark Tours (see "Travel agents", below).

Embassies Most of the embassies are in the southeastern quarter of the city, along Avenida la Reforma and Avenida las Américas, and they tend to open weekday mornings only unless otherwise indicated. Belize, Av la Reforma 1–50, 8th Floor, Suite 803, Edificio el Reformador, Zona 9 (Mon–Fri 9am–1pm & 2–5pm; ☎334 5531 or 331 1137); Canada, 13 C 8–44, 8th Floor Edificio Edyma Plaza, Zona 10 (Mon–Thurs 8am–4.30pm, Fri 8am–1.30pm; ☎333 6102); Colombia, 12 C 1–25, Zona 10 (☎335 3602); Costa Rica, Av la Reforma 8–60, 3rd floor, Torre 1, Edificio Galerías Reforma, Zona 9 (☎ & fax 332 0531); El Salvador, 4 Av 13–60, Zona 10 (☎366 2240); Honduras, 12 C 1–25, 12th floor, Edificio Géminis, Zona 10 (☎338 2068); Mexico, 15 C 3–20, Zona 10 (Mon–Fri 9am–1pm & 3–5pm; ☎333 7254 or 333 7255); Nicaragua, 10 Av 14–72, Zona 10 (☎368 0785); Panamá, 5 Av 15–45, Torre II, Edificio Centro Empresarial, Zona 10 (☎333 7176); United Kingdom, 16 C 0–55, 11th floor, Torre Internacional, Zona 10 (Mon–Fri 9am–noon & 2–4pm; ☎367 5425); United States, Av la Reforma, 7–01, Zona 10 (Mon–Fri 8am–5pm; ☎331 1541).

Immigration The main immigration office (*migración*) is conveniently located on the second floor of the Inguat HQ at 7 Av 1–17, Zona 4 (Mon–Fri 9am–3pm; ☎634 8476).

Internet Guatemala City is under-endowed with Internet cafés compared to Antigua, and rates are much higher, typically around US$5 an hour. In Zona 1, Cafebreria at 5 Av 13–32 is well set up, while in Zona 10 head for the Próceres shopping mall at 16 C and 2 Av where you can surf at Café Virtual at ground level or Wizards on the third floor.

Laundry Lavandería Obelisco, Av la Reforma 16–30, next to the Samaritana supermarket (Mon–Fri 8am–6.45pm, Sat 8am–5.30pm), charges around US$3 for a self-service wash and dry, and there's also a self-service laundry at 4 Av 13–89, Zona 1.

Libraries The best library for English books is in the IGA (Guatemalan American Institute) at Ruta 1 and Vía 4, Zona 4. There's also the National Library on the west side of Parque del Centenario, and specialist collections at the Ixchel and Popol Vuh museums.

Medical care Your embassy should have a list of bilingual doctors, but for emergency medical assistance dial ☎125 for the Red Cross, or head for the Centro Médico, a private hospital with 24hr cover, at 6 Av 3–47, Zona 10 (☎332 3555). Central Dentist de Especialistas, 20 C 11–17, Zona 10 (☎337 1773), is the best dental clinic in the country, and superb in emergencies.

Pharmacies Farmacia Osco, 16 C and 4 Av, Zona 10.

Photography Colour transparency and both colour and monochrome print film is easy to buy, though expensive. There are several camera shops on 6 Avenida in Zona 1. Foto Sittler, 12 C 6–20, Zona 1, and La Perla, 9 C and 6 Av, Zona 1, repair cameras and offer a three-month guarantee on their work.

Police The main police station is in a bizarre castle-like structure on the corner of 6 Av and 14 C, Zona 1. In an emergency dial ☎120.

Post office The main post office, 7 Av and 12 C (Mon–Fri 8.30am–6.30pm, Sat 8.30am–4.30pm), has a Lista de Correos and will hold mail for you.

Telephone You can make long-distance phone calls and send faxes from Telgua, one block east of the post office (daily 7am–midnight).

Travel agents There are plenty of travel agents in the centre and along Avenida la Reforma in Zonas 9 and 10; flights to Petén can be booked through all of them. Clark Tours, Diagonal 6, 10–01, 7th floor, Torre II, Las Margaritas, Zona 10 (☎339 2888, fax 339 2909, *www.clarktours.com*), organizes trips to many parts of the country; Ecotourism & Adventure Specialists, 4 Av A 7–95, Zona

14, (☎337 0009, *www.ecotourism-adventure.com*), offers well co-ordinated trips to Petén and many remote parts of the country; Maya Expeditions, 15 C 1–91, Zona 10 (☎363 4955, fax 363 4164, *www.mayaexpeditions.com*), specializes in ecotourism adventure and rafting trips. Viajes Tivoli, 6 Av 8–41, Zona 9 (☎339 2260, *viajes@tivoli.com.gt*), and 12 C 4–55, Zona 1 (☎238 4771), is a good all-round agent with competitive rates for international flights.

Work Hard to come by. The best bet is teaching at one of the English schools, most of which are grouped on calles 10 and 18 in Zona 1. Check the classified sections of the *Guatemala Post* and *Revue*.

Moving on from Guatemala City

There are frequent **international** flights from Guatemala City's Aurora airport to Mexico, Central America and North America, and eight daily flights to Flores in Petén, the only other international airport in the country – most of these leave early in the morning, between 6.30 and 9am, enabling day-trippers to visit Tikal and get back to the capital. Tickets for the fifty-minute flight can be bought from virtually any travel agent in the capital, and cost around US$75 return in a small plane or US$110 in the larger Tikal Jets aircraft. To get to the international terminal of Aurora airport from Zona 1, either take bus #83 from 10 Av (30min) or a taxi (around US$10); from Zona 10, a taxi costs around US$7. There's a US$30 departure tax on all international flights, payable in either quetzales or dollars.

A new **domestic** airline, Inter (☎334 7722), operated by the Taca group, in theory operates daily return services between Guatemala City and Puerto Barrios (US$60 each way; 1hr), Santa Cruz del Quiché (US$55; 25min), Quetzaltenango (US$40; 30min), Retalhuleu (US$40; 35min), Coatepeque (US$55; 1hr), Cobán (US$45; 30min) and Huehuetenango (US$55; 50min), plus return flights to the Río Dulce at weekends (US$50; 1hr). Note, however, that their schedules are subject to change and cancellation. Note that all Taca and Tikal Jets internal flights leave from the international terminal. For the **domestic terminal**, in the same complex as the international terminal but only accessible from Av Hicapié, you'll need to take a taxi; the domestic departure tax is US$0.80.

If you're leaving by **first-class bus**, departures are all from the offices of the relevant bus company (see opposite). The **Zona 1 terminal**, spread out around the streets surrounding the old train station at 18 C and 9 Av, is the most important transit point, with departures to Puerto Barrios, Cobán, the Pacific highway, the Mexican border and Petén. Moving on by **second-class bus** the main centre is the chaotic **Zona 4 terminal**, where services run to all parts of the country. To get there take any city bus marked "terminal"; you'll find these heading south along 4 Av in Zona 1.

BUSES FROM GUATEMALA CITY

The abbreviations we've used for the bus companies are as follows:

KQ	King Quality	**TA**	Transportes Alamo
L	Lituega	**TB**	Ticabus
LA	Líneas Américas	**TD**	Transportes Dulce María
LD	Línea Dorada	**TE**	Transportes Escobar y Monja Blanca
LH	Los Halcones		
MI	Melva Internacional	**TG**	Transportes Galgos
P	Pulmantur	**TM**	Transportes Marquensita
RO	Rutas Orientales	**TR**	Transportes Rebuli
RZ	Rápidos Zacaleu	**TV**	Transportes Velásquez
SJ	San Juanera		

TO	COMPANY	BUS STOP	FREQUENCY	JOURNEY TIME
Antigua	various (2nd)	18 C & 4 Av, Zona 1	15min	1hr
Chichicastenango	various (2nd)	Zona 4 terminal	30min	3hr 30min
Chiquimula	RO (1st)	19 C & 9 Av, Zona 1	15 daily	3hr 30min
Cobán	TE (1st)	8 Av 15–16, Zona 1	14 daily	4hr 30min
Cubulco	TD (2nd)	19 C & 9 Av, Zona 1	10 daily	5hr
Escuintla	various (2nd)	Zona 4 terminal	30min	1hr 15min
Esquipulas	RO (1st)	19 C & 9 Av, Zona 1	15 daily	4hr
Flores	various (1st/2nd)	17 C & 8 Av, Zona 1	16 daily	9hr
	LD (1st)	16 C 10–55, Zona 1	3 daily	9hr
Huehuetenango	LH (1st)	7 Av 15–27, Zona 1	3 daily	5hr 30min
	TV (1st)	20 C 1–37, Zona 1	9 daily	5hr 30min
	RZ(1st)	9C 11–42, Zona 1	3 daily	5hr 30min
La Mesilla	TV (1st)	20 C 1–37, Zona 1	9 daily	7hr
Monterrico	various (2nd)	Zona 4 terminal	5 daily	4hr
Panajachel	TR (2nd)	21 C 1–54, Zona 1	11 daily	3hr
Puerto Barrios	L (1st)	15 C 10–40, Zona 1	18 daily	5hr 30min
Quetzaltenango	LA (1st)	2 Av 18–74, Zona 1	6 daily	4hr
	TA (1st)	21 C 1–14, Zona 1	5 daily	4hr
	TM (1st)	1 Av 21–31, Zona 1	8 daily	4hr
	TG (1st)	7 Av 19–44, Zona 1	6 daily	4hr
	SJ (2nd)	Zona 4 terminal	10 daily	4hr 30min
Rabinal	TD (2nd)	19 C & 9 Av, Zona 1	10 daily	4hr 30min
Salamá	TD (2nd)	19 C & 9 Av, Zona 1	10 daily	3hr 30min
San Salvador	MI (1st)	3 Av 1–38, Zona 9	11 daily	5hr
	TB (1st)	11 C 2–72, Zona 9	1 daily	5hr
	KQ (1st)	Col Vista Hermosa II, Zona 15	2 daily	5hr
	P(1st)	Hotel Raddison Suites, 1Av 12–43, Zona 10	2 daily	5hr
Santa Cruz del Quiché	various (2nd)	Zona 4 terminal	30min	4hr
Tecún Umán	various (1st)	19 Av & 8 C, Zona 1	30min	5hr
Talismán	various (1st)	19 Av & 8 C, Zona 1	30min	5hr 30min
Tapacula	LD (1st)	16 C 10–55, Zona 1	2 daily	7hr
	TG (1st)	7 Av 19–44, Zona 1	2 daily	7hr
Zacapa	RO (1st)	19 C & 9 Av, Zona 1	15 daily	3hr

CHAPTER 7

THE WESTERN HIGHLANDS

G uatemala's **western highlands**, stretching from Guatemala City to the Mexican border, are perhaps the most captivating and beautiful part of the entire country. The area is defined by two main features: the chain of awesome volcanoes that lines its southern side, and the high mountain ranges that dominate its northern boundaries, the greatest being the **Cuchumatanes**, whose granite peaks rise to over 3800m. Between the two is a bewitching pattern of twisting, pine-forested ridges, lakes, gushing streams and deep valleys.

It's an astounding landscape, blessed with tremendous fertility but cursed by instability. The hills are regularly shaken by earthquakes and occasionally showered by volcanic eruptions. Of the thirteen cones that loom over the western highlands, three volcanoes are still active: **Pacaya**, **Fuego** and **Santiaguito**. Two major **fault lines** also cut through the area, making earthquakes a regular occurrence. The most recent major quake, in 1976, centred on **Chimaltenango** and left 25,000 dead and around a million homeless. But despite its sporadic ferocity, the countryside is outstandingly beautiful and the atmosphere calm and welcoming, with irrigated valleys and terraced hillsides carefully crafted to yield the maximum potential farmland.

The highland landscape is shaped by many factors, all of which affect its appearance. Perhaps the most important is **altitude**. At lower elevations the vegetation is almost tropical, supporting dense forests and plantations of coffee, cotton, bananas and cacao, while higher up the hills are often wrapped in cloud and the ground is sometimes hard with frost. Here trees are stunted by the cold, and maize and potatoes are grown alongside grazing land for herds of sheep and goats. The **seasons** also play their part. In the rainy season, from May to October, the land is superbly green, with young crops and lush forests of pine, cedar and oak, while during the dry winter months the hillsides gradually turn to a dusty yellow.

Some history

The western highlands are home to one of the American continent's largest groups of indigenous people, the **Maya**, who have lived in this land continuously for over two thousand years. Despite the catastrophe of the Spanish Conquest, their society, languages and traditions remain largely intact, and they continue to form the vast majority of the population in the western highlands.

The highlands are still divided up along traditional tribal lines. The **K'iche'** language is spoken by the largest number of people, centred on the town of Santa Cruz del Quiché and reaching west into the Quetzaltenango valley. The highlands around Huehuetenango are **Mam**-speaking, while the **Tz'utujil** occupy the southern shores of

For an explanation of **accommodation price codes**, see p.125.

Lago de Atitlán, and the **Kaqchikel** the east. **Smaller tribal groups**, with distinct languages and costumes, such as the Ixil and the Awakateko, also occupy clearly defined areas in the Cuchumatán mountains.

Though pre-conquest life was certainly hard, the **arrival of the Spanish** in 1523 was a total disaster for the Maya population. In the early stages, **Alvarado** and his army met with a force of K'iche' warriors in the Quetzaltenango basin and defeated them in open warfare. Legend has it that Alvarado himself slew the great K'iche' warrior, **Tecún Umán**, in hand-to-hand combat. The Spanish made their first permanent base at **Iximché**, the capital of their Kaqchikel Maya allies, but this uneasy alliance was to last only a few years. Alvarado then moved to a site near the modern town of Antigua, from where the Spanish gradually brought the rest of the highlands under a degree of control. The damage done by Spanish swords, however, was nothing when compared to that of the **diseases** they introduced. Waves of smallpox, typhus, plague and measles swept through the indigenous population, reducing their numbers by as much as ninety percent in the worst-hit areas.

In the long term, the **Spanish administration** of the western highlands was no gentler than the Conquest, as indigenous labour became the backbone of the Spanish Empire. Guatemala offered little of the gold and silver that was available in Peru or Mexico, but there was still money to be made from **cacao** and **indigo**. As well as being at the heart of Spanish Guatemala, **Antigua** also served as the administrative centre for the whole of Central America and Chiapas (now in Mexico). In 1773, however, the city was destroyed by a massive earthquake and the capital was subsequently moved to its modern site.

The departure of the Spanish in 1821 and subsequent **independence** brought little change at village level. *Ladino* authority replaced that of the Spanish, but Maya were still required to work the coastal plantations and, when labour supplies dropped off, they were simply press-ganged and forced to work, often in horrific conditions. It's a state of affairs that has changed little even today, and remains a major burden on the *indígena* population.

In the late 1970s, **guerrilla movements** began to develop in opposition to military rule, seeking support from the indigenous population and establishing themselves in the western highlands. The Maya became the victims in this process, caught between the guerrillas and the army. A total of 440 villages were destroyed; around 200,000 people died and thousands more fled the country, seeking refuge in Mexico. Indigenous society has also been besieged in recent years by a tidal wave of American **evangelical churches**, whose influence undermines local hierarchies, dividing communities and threatening to destroy Maya culture.

MARKET DAYS

Make an effort to catch as many market days as possible – they're second only to local fiestas in offering a glimpse of the traditional Guatemalan way of life.

Monday: Antigua; San Juan Atitán; Zunil.
Tuesday: Chajul; Patzún; San Lucas Tolimán; San Marcos; Totonicapán.
Wednesday: Cotzal; Huehuetenango; Momostenango.
Thursday: Aguacatán; Antigua; Chichicastenango; Jacaltenango; Nebaj; Panajachel; Sacapulas; San Pedro Sacatepéquez; Santa Cruz del Quiché; Soloma; Totonicapán; Uspantán.
Friday: Chajul; San Francisco El Alto; Santiago Atitlán; Sololá.
Saturday: Antigua; Cotzal; Santa Clara La Laguna; Santa Cruz del Quiché; Todos Santos Cuchumatán; Totonicapán.
Sunday: Aguacatán; Chichicastenango; Huehuetenango; Jacaltenango; Joyabaj; Momostenango; Nebaj; Nahualá; Panajachel; Sacapulas; San Juan Comalapa; San Pedro Sacatepéquez; Santa Cruz del Quiché; Santa Eulalia; Soloma; Uspantán.

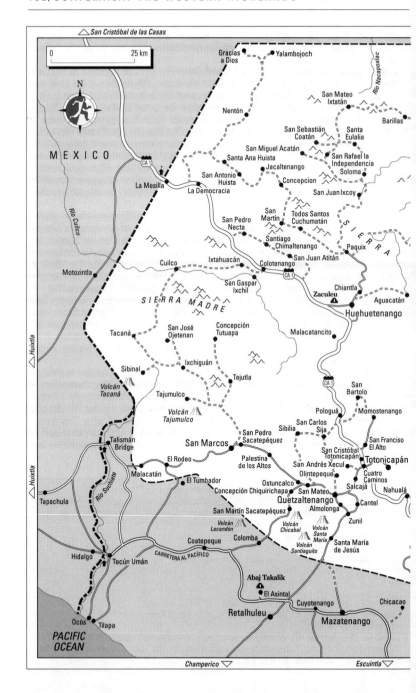

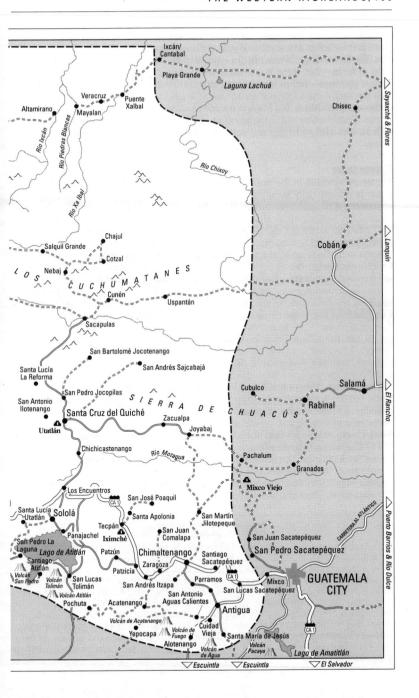

Today, following the signing of the 1996 **peace accords**, tensions have lifted and there is evidence of a new spirit of self-confidence amongst the highland Maya population. Fundamental problems remain – poverty, racism and the still unsettled issue of **land reform** – but there is a reawakened sense of pride in Maya identity. Despite intense pressure – and an increasing migration of young Maya men north to the US to look for work – the traditional structures of society are still largely in place. Rejecting *ladino* commercialism, the Maya see trade as a social function as much as an economic one. Conservative and inward-looking, they live in a world centred on the village, with its own civil and religious hierarchy, and the subsistence farming of maize and beans.

Where to go

Almost everywhere in the western highlands is of interest to the traveller. The landscape is exceptionally beautiful, dotted with highland villages of adobe houses and whitewashed colonial churches. **Antigua**, the former capital, is unmissable: a beautiful colonial city nestling in the shadow of giant volcanoes, it also has the most cosmopolitan restaurant scene in Central America. **Lago de Atitlán** is another jewel – a lake of astounding natural beauty, ringed by volcanoes and some of the most traditional Maya villages in all Guatemala. Home to perhaps the most famous market in the country, **Chichicastenango** is a sleepy highland town steeped in Maya/Catholic ritual. There are tremendous markets, too, at **Sololá** and **San Francisco El Alto**.

For real adventure, spectacular scenery and myriad hiking possibilities, the **Ixil triangle** in northern Quiché and the mountainous countryside around **Todos Santos Cuchumatán** are unmatched. Both are remote, intensely traditional areas that lie at the end of tortuous bus journeys; both suffered terribly in the civil war. Much easier to get to are the villages around **Quetzaltenango** (Xela), Guatemala's second city. Though Xela itself is a fairly unexciting provincial centre, close by you'll find the villages of Zunil, San Francisco El Alto, the stunning hot springs of Fuentes Georginas and the near-perfect cone of Volcán Santa María.

The scenery, villages and living Maya culture are the main attractions in the highlands, but there are also interesting **Maya ruins**, including the pre-conquest cities of **Iximché**, **Utatlán** and **Zaculeu**, and assorted smaller sites, many still actively used for Maya religious ritual and ceremony. These ancient cities don't bear comparison to Tikal, Copán and the lowland sites, but they're fascinating nevertheless.

The **Carretera Interamericana** runs through the middle of the western highlands, served by a constant flow of buses, some branching off along minor roads to more remote areas. Travelling in these areas can sometimes be a gruelling experience, particularly in northern Huehuetenango and Quiché, but the scenery makes it well worth the discomfort. The most practical plan of action is to base yourself in one of the larg-

---

TOURIST CRIME

While there is no need to be paranoid, visitors to the heavily touristed areas around Antigua and Lago de Atitlán should be aware that **crime against tourists** – including robbery and rape – is a problem. Pay close attention to security reports from your embassy and follow the usual precautions with extra care. In particular, avoid walking alone, especially at night or to isolated spots during the day. If you want to visit viewing spots like the *cruce* overlooking Antigua, inform the Tourist Police and they will accompany you or even give you a ride there on one of their Jeeps or motorbikes. Though there have been very few attacks on hikers in the Lago de Atitlán area recently, it's still safer to walk in a group. Similarly, don't amble around Panajachel alone late at night. In the more remote highlands, where foreigners are a much rarer sight, attacks are extremely uncommon.

er places and then make a series of day-trips to markets and fiestas, although even the smallest of villages will usually offer some kind of accommodation.

Antigua

Superbly sited in a sweeping highland valley between the cones of Agua, Acatenango and Fuego volcanoes is one of Central America's most enchanting colonial cities: **ANTIGUA**. In its day, Antigua was one of the great cities of the Spanish Empire, ranking alongside Lima and Mexico City and serving as the administrative centre for all of Central America and Mexican Chiapas, and the magnificent colonial churches, monasteries and mansions built during this era have ensured the city's continuing prosperity as one of Guatemala's premier tourist attractions.

Antigua was actually the third capital of Guatemala. The Spanish settled first at the site of Iximché (see p.178) in July 1524, and then at a site a few kilometres from Antigua, now called Ciudad Vieja, but when this was devasted by a massive mudslide from Volcán Agua in 1541, the capital was moved to Antigua. Antigua grew slowly but steadily as religious orders established themselves one by one, competing in the construction of schools, churches, monasteries and hospitals, all largely built by the sweat and blood of conscripted Maya labourers.

The city reached its peak in the middle of the eighteenth century, after the 1717 earthquake prompted an unprecedented building boom, and the population rose to around fifty thousand. By this stage Antigua was a genuinely impressive place, with a university, a printing press and a newspaper. But, as is so often the case in Guatemala, **earthquakes** brought all of this to an abrupt end. For the best part of a year the city was shaken by tremors, with the final blows delivered by two severe shocks on September 7 and December 13, 1773. The damage was so bad that the decision was made to abandon the city in favour of the modern capital. Fortunately, despite endless official decrees, many refused to leave and Antigua was never completely deserted.

Since then, the city has been gradually repopulated, particularly in the last hundred years or so, and as Guatemala City has become increasingly congested, many of the conservative middle classes have moved to Antigua. They've been joined by a large number of resident and visiting foreigners, attracted by the relaxed and sophisticated atmosphere, lively cultural life, the benign climate and largely traffic-free cobbled streets.

Efforts have been made to preserve Antigua's grand architectural legacy, especially after it was listed as a UNESCO World Heritage site in 1979 – local conservation laws protect the streets from overhanging signs, and house extensions are severely restricted. Though many colonial buildings lie in splendidly atmospheric ruin or else are steadily decaying, many more have been impeccably restored and sympathetically converted into hotels or restaurants.

Thanks to its relaxed atmosphere, Antigua is a favoured hangout for jaded travellers to refuel and recharge. The bar scene is always lively and there's an extraordinarily cosmopolitan choice of restaurants. If you can make it here for **Semana Santa** (Easter week) you'll witness the most extravagant and impressive processions in all Latin America. Another attraction are the city's **language schools**, some of the best and cheapest in all Latin America, drawing students from around the globe. Expats from Europe, North and South America and even Asia contribute to the town's cosmopolitan air, mingling with the Guatemalans who come here at weekends to eat, drink and enjoy themselves. The downside of this settled, comfortable affluence is perhaps a loss of vitality – this civilized, isolated world can seem almost a little too smug and comfortable. After a few days of sipping cappuccinos and munching cake, it's easy to forget that you're in Central America at all.

SEMANA SANTA IN ANTIGUA

Antigua's **Semana Santa (Holy Week) celebrations** are perhaps the most extravagant and impressive in all Latin America. The celebrations start with a procession on Palm Sunday, representing Christ's entry into Jerusalem, and continue through to the really big processions and pageants on Good Friday. On Thursday night the streets are carpeted with meticulously drawn patterns of coloured sawdust, and on Friday morning a series of processions re-enacts the progress of Christ to the Cross, accompanied by sombre music from local brass bands. Setting out from La Merced, Escuela de Cristo and the village of San Felipe, teams of penitents wearing peaked hoods and accompanied by solemn dirges and clouds of incense carry images of Christ and the Cross on massive platforms. The pageants set off at around at 8am, with the penitents dressed in either white or purple. After 3pm, the hour of the Crucifixion, they change into black.

It is a great honour to be involved in the procession, but no easy task as the great cedar block carried from La Merced weighs some 3.5 tonnes, and needs eighty men to lift it. Some of the images displayed date from the seventeenth century and the procession itself is thought to have been introduced by Alvarado in the early years of the Conquest, imported directly from Spain.

Check the exact details of events with the tourist office, who should be able to provide you with a map detailing the routes of the processions. During Holy Week hotels in Antigua are often full, and the entire town is always packed on Good Friday. But even if you have to make the trip from Guatemala City or Panajachel, it's well worth coming for, especially on the Friday.

Arrival and information

Antigua is laid out on the traditional grid system, with avenidas running north–south, and calles east–west. Each street is numbered and has two halves, either a north (*norte/nte*) and south (*sur*) or an east (*oriente/ote*) and west (*poniente/pte*), with a plaza, the **Parque Central**, at the centre. Despite this apparent simplicity, poor street lighting and the lack of street signs combine to ensure that most people get lost here at some stage. If you get confused, remember that Volcán Agua, the one that looms most immediately over the town, is to the south.

Arriving by bus, you'll end up in the main **bus terminal**, a large open space beside the market. The street opposite (4 C Pte) leads directly to the plaza. The city is easy to get around on foot, but should you need a **taxi** you'll find one on the east side of the plaza close to the cathedral; alternatively you can call one on ☎832 0479. Mountain bikes and cars can also be rented – see p.175.

The **tourist office** (daily 8am–6pm; ☎ & fax 832 0763) on the south side of the plaza dispenses reasonable if occasionally overcautious information. The **tourist police** (☎832 7290) are just off the Parque Central on 4 Avenida Norte; officers escort visitors twice daily up to the Cerro de la Cruz, from where there's a panoramic view of Antigua and the surrounding volcanoes. **Noticeboards** in various tourist venues advertise everything from private language tuition to apartments, flights home and shared rides – probably the most read are those at *Doña Luisa's* restaurant, 4 C Ote 12, and the *Rainbow Reading Room*, 7 Av Sur 8. For **tours** of the city, contact Geovany at Monarcas, 7 Av Nte 15a (☎832 4779, *www.angelfire.com/mt/monarcastravel*), who looks at Maya influence on Antiguan architecture and also at the flora around the city, or Elizabeth Bell's Antigua Tours, at 3 C Ote 28 (☎832 0140 ext 341, *www.antiguatours.com*), for excellent historical walking tours of the town.

Antigua is also one of the most popular places in Latin America to **study Spanish**. For a full list of recommended schools, see pp.132–3.

Accommodation

Hotels in Antigua are in plentiful supply, although like everything else they can be a bit hard to find due to the absence of overhanging signs. Be warned that rooms get scarce (and prices increase) around Semana Santa.

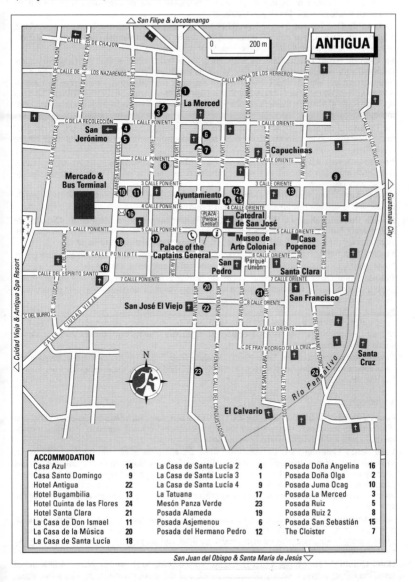

ACCOMMODATION					
Casa Azul	14	La Casa de Santa Lucía 2	4	Posada Doña Angelina	16
Casa Santo Domingo	9	La Casa de Santa Lucía 3	1	Posada Doña Olga	2
Hotel Antigua	22	La Casa de Santa Lucía 4	9	Posada Juma Ocag	10
Hotel Bugambilia	13	La Tatuana	17	Posada La Merced	3
Hotel Quinta de las Flores	24	Mesón Panza Verde	23	Posada Ruiz	5
Hotel Santa Clara	21	Posada Alameda	19	Posada Ruiz 2	8
La Casa de Don Ismael	11	Posada Asjemenou	6	Posada San Sebastián	15
La Casa de la Música	20	Posada del Hermano Pedro	12	The Cloister	7
La Casa de Santa Lucía	18				

BUDGET TO MODERATE

Hotel Bugambilia, 3 C Ote 19 (☎832 5780, *www.theantiguajournal.com*). Clean, safe place in a quiet location with parking, but rooms are a little plain. The owners are very helpful and hospitable. Snacks available. ③.

Hotel Santa Clara, 2 Av Sur 20 (☎ & fax 832 0342). Tranquil location on the east side of town and very spacious, comfortable rooms, most with two double beds and all with private bath, set around a pleasant little courtyard. Parking available. ③.

La Casa de Don Ismael, 3 C Pte 6 (☎832 1939). Attractive rooms with towels and soap provided, a lovely little garden, free mineral water and free tea or coffee in the morning. Communal bathrooms are brightly painted and kept spotless. Very fair prices. ②.

La Casa de Santa Lucía, Alameda Santa Lucía Sur 5 (☎832 6133). Recently refurbished, good-value and very popular hotel with secure, spacious rooms and private hot-water baths. There are three further and almost identical offshoots of the same original elsewhere in town: *La Casa de Santa Lucía 2*, Alameda Santa Lucía Nte 21; *La Casa de Santa Lucía 3*, 6 Av Nte 43 A; and *La Casa de Santa Lucía 4*, Alameda Santa Lucía Nte 5 (no phones) – all similarly well equipped and value for money. ②.

La Tatuana, 7 Av Sur 3 (☎832 1223, *latatuana@micro.com.gt*). Small hotel with bright, imaginatively decorated rooms, all with private bath, and comfortable beds. Extremely good value for the price. ④.

Posada Alameda Alameda Santa Lucía Sur 18 (☎832 7349, *alameda@intelnet.net.gt*). Good new hotel close to the bus terminal, with six comfortable rooms, all with cable TV, plus baggage storage and security boxes. ③.

Posada Asjemenou, 5 Av Nte 31 (☎832 2670, *cangeletti@hotmail.com*). Comfortable, colonial-style rooms with or without private bath, set around a courtyard. ④–⑤.

Posada Doña Angelina, 4 C Pte 33 (☎832 5173). Popular budget option. Many of the 42 rooms are a bit gloomy, but there's usually space here, and there's a secure store room where you can leave your baggage. Close to the bus terminal, so not the most tranquil place in town. ②–③.

Posada Doña Olga, Callejón Campo Seco 3A (☎832 0623). Exceptionally good value new guesthouse, with very clean rooms, all with private bath, and a rooftop sun terrace. ②.

Posada Juma Ocag, Alameda Santa Lucía Nte 13 (☎832 3109). Superb, very well managed new place. The nine cheery, comfortable rooms are excellent value: all have wardrobes and private bath, and are draped with local fabrics. ③.

Posada La Merced, 7 Av Nte 43a (☎832 3197, *posadalamerced@hotmail.com*). Large refurbished hotel with a good choice of attractive rooms (some set around a pretty garden patio at the rear), all with spotless private bathrooms and nice decorative touches. The very helpful Kiwi owner is a good source of local information. ④.

Posada Ruiz, Alameda Santa Lucía Nte 17; **Posada Ruiz 2**, 2 C Pte 25 (no phones). Pretty grim, small rooms with no frills, but rates are extremely cheap and both are a short stumble from the bus terminal. ①.

EXPENSIVE

Casa Azul, 4 Av Nte 5 (☎832 0961, fax 832 0944, *www.infoguate.com/casazul*). Choice location, just off the plaza, with huge, very stylish rooms in a converted colonial mansion. Facilities include sauna, Jacuzzi and a delightful small rooftop pool. ⑧.

Casa Santo Domingo, 3 C Ote 28 (☎832 0140, fax 832 0102, *www.casasantodomingo.com.gt*). Probably the most atmospheric hotel in Guatemala, set in a spectacular colonial convent which has been sympathetically converted into a hotel and restaurant at a cost of several million dollars. Rooms and corridors are bedecked in ecclesiastical art and paraphernalia and there's no lack of luxury. High-season rates start at US$132, but there are substantial discounts at quiet times of the year. ⑨.

Hotel Antigua, 8 C Pte 1 (☎832 0288, fax 832 0807, *www.hotelantigua.com.gt*). Venerable establishment, popular with Guatemala's elite families, and decorated with tasteful colonial-style furniture. There's a large swimming pool set in expansive gardens, and the pleasant rooms have open fires to ward off the winter chill. ⑨.

Hotel Quinta de las Flores, C del Hermano Pedro 6 (☎832 3721, fax 832 3726). A little out of town, but the attractive, tastefully decorated rooms and the spectacular garden, with a swimming pool and many rare plants, shrubs and trees, make it a wonderful place to relax. ⑦.

La Casa de la Música, 7 C Pte 3 (☎832 0335, *www.lacasadelamusica.centroamerica.com*). Sumptuous guesthouse with a selection of very attractive bedrooms and characterful suites, all with fireplaces and antique furniture. There's a large garden, with plenty of space for children to play, a guests' lounge with an extensive library and plenty of family games. Very friendly and efficient service, breakfast is included and additional meals are also available. ⑥–⑦.

Mesón Panza Verde, 5 Av Sur 19 (☎ & fax 832 2925, *mpv@infovia.com.gt*). Small, immaculately furnished hotel spread across two colonial-style buildings that are also home to one of Antigua's premier restaurants. Supremely comfortable suites (⑧), some with four-poster beds, plus good-value doubles (⑥). There's also small swimming pool, faultless service and a healthy breakfast is included in the price.

Posada del Hermano Pedro, 3 C Ote 3 (☎832 2089, fax 832 2090). Comfortable hotel in a huge, tastefully converted colonial mansion just behind the main square. The pleasant rooms all have cable TV. ⑥.

Posada San Sebastián, 3 Av Nte 4 (☎ & fax 832 2621). Very quiet, charming establishment. Each room is individually decorated with antiques, there's a gorgeous little bar and the location is very convenient. Excellent value. ⑥.

The Cloister, 5 Av Nte 23 (☎ & fax 832 0712, *www.thecloister.com*). Small, elegant hotel, set almost under Antigua's famous arch, with beautifully furnished rooms around a flowering courtyard. There's a real air of tranquillity here, plus a well-stocked private library and reading room. ⑧–⑨.

The City

Antigua has an incredible number of ruined and restored **colonial buildings**, and although these constitute only a fraction of the city's original splendour, they do give an idea of its former extravagance. If the prospect of visiting all the sights listed below is too overwhelming, make La Merced, Las Capuchinas, Casa Popenoe and San Francisco your targets.

The Parque Central

The focus of the colonial city was its central plaza, the **Parque Central**. For centuries the Parque served as the hub of the city, bustling with constant activity, while a huge market spilled out across it, being cleared only for bullfights, military parades, floggings and public hangings. The calm of today's shady plaza, with its risqué fountain, is relatively recent.

The most imposing of the surrounding structures is the **Catedral de San José**, on the eastern side. The city's first cathedral was begun in 1545 but an earthquake brought down much of the roof and, in 1670, it was decided to start on a new cathedral worthy of the town's role as a capital city. The scale was astounding – a vast dome, five aisles, eighteen chapels and an altar inlaid with mother-of-pearl, ivory and silver – but in 1773, the new cathedral was destroyed by an earthquake. Today, two of the chapels have been restored, and there's a figure of Christ by the colonial sculptor Quirio Cataño inside. Behind the church, entered from 5 C Oriente, are the **ruins** (entrance fee US$0.40) of the rest of the original structure – a mass of fallen masonry and some rotting beams, broken arches and hefty pillars. Buried beneath the floor are some of the great names of the Conquest, including Alvarado, his wife Beatriz de la Cueva, Bishop Marroquín and the historian Bernal Díaz del Castillo. At the very rear of the original nave, steps lead down to a burial vault that's regularly used for Maya religious ceremonies – an example of the coexistence of pagan and Catholic beliefs that's so characteristic of Guatemala.

Along the entire south side of the square runs the squat two-storey facade of the **Palace of the Captains General**, originally constructed in 1558, but rebuilt after earthquake damage. The palace was home to the colonial rulers and also housed the barracks of the dragoons, the stables, the royal mint, law courts, tax offices, great ballrooms, a large bureaucracy, and a lot more besides. Today it contains the local government offices, the headquarters of the Sacatepéquez police department and the tourist office. Directly opposite is the **Ayuntamiento** (City Hall), which dates from 1740 and survived undamaged until the 1976 earthquake. It now holds a couple of minor museums: the **Museo de Santiago** (daily 9am–6pm; US$1.30), housed in the old city jail and containing a collection of colonial artefacts, and the **Museo del Libro Antiguo** (same hours; US$1.30), in the rooms that held the first printing press in Central America. A replica of the press is on display, alongside some copies of the works produced on it. From the upper floor of the Ayuntamiento there's a wonderful **view** of the three volcanoes that ring the city, especially fine at sunset.

Southeast of the Parque Central

Across the street from the ruined cathedral is the **Museo de Arte Colonial** (Tues–Fri 9am–4pm, Sat & Sun 9am–noon & 2–4pm; US$3.20), located on the site of a former university, whose deep-set windows and beautifully ornate cloisters make it one of the finest architectural survivors in Antigua. The museum contains a good collection of dark and brooding religious art, sculpture, furniture and murals depicting life on the colonial campus.

Further down 5 Calle Oriente, at the corner with 1 Avenida Sur, is the **Casa Popenoe** (Mon–Sat 2–4pm; US$0.90), a superbly restored colonial mansion, which offers an interesting insight into domestic life in colonial times. Originally owned by a Spanish judge, it was abandoned for some time until its painstaking restoration by Dr Wilson Popenoe, a United Fruit Company scientist. Among the paintings are portraits of Bishop Marroquín and the menacing-looking Alvarado himself. The kitchen and servants' quarters have also been carefully renovated: you can see the original bread ovens, the herb garden and the pigeon loft, which would have provided the mansion's occupants with their mail service. Go up to the roof for great views over the city and Volcán Agua.

A little further down 1 Avenida Sur is the imposing church of **San Francisco** (daily 8am–6pm). One of the oldest churches in Antigua, dating from 1579, it grew into a vast religious and cultural centre that included a school, a hospital, music rooms, a printing press and a monastery. All of it was lost, though, in the 1773 earthquake. Inside the church are buried the remains of **Hermano Pedro de Betancourt**, a Franciscan from the Canary Islands who founded the Hospital of Belén in Antigua. Pilgrims come here from all over Central America to ask for the benefit of his powers of miraculous intervention. The **ruins** of the monastery are among the most impressive in Antigua, with pleasant grassy verges and good picnic potential.

One block west and one block north of San Francisco is **Parque Unión**, a pretty palm-tree-lined plaza which doubles as an open-air típica textile street market – women travel here from as far away as Lago de Atitlán and the Ixil triangle to sell their wares. Two churches face each other at opposite ends of the Parque: at the western end is **San Pedro Church**, dating from 1680; at the eastern end is **Santa Clara**, a former convent which in colonial times was a popular place for aristocratic ladies to take the veil – the hardships were not too extreme, and the nuns gained a reputation for their fine cooking. The convent was twice destroyed in the earthquakes of 1717 and 1773, but the current building with its ornate facade survived the 1976 tremors intact. In front of Santa Clara is a large washhouse where village women gather to scrub, rinse and gossip.

North and west of the Parque Central

At the junction of 2 C Ote and 2 Av Nte are the remains of **Las Capuchinas** (Tues–Sun 9am–5pm; US$1.30), dating from 1726, the largest and most impressive of the city's convents, whose ruins are some of the best preserved but least understood in Antigua. The

---

VOLCANO TOURS FROM ANTIGUA

A number of outfits in Antigua run guided tours to climb **Volcán Pacaya** near Guatemala City, a spectacular and very active volcano which regularly erupts towering plumes of smoke and brilliant orange sludge. These trips cost around US$7 per person, and virtually all the daily tours (no matter who you book with) leave Antigua around 1.30pm and return by around 10.30pm, enabling you to see the volcano by night without having to camp out. Though in the past a number of cowboy operators set up robberies of their own tourists, things have settled down considerably, and in the last few years and there have been only very isolated reports of trouble. To be safe, check the latest situation with your embassy (see p.15) or Antigua's tourist office (see p.166) before booking a trip. One of the most reputable operators in Antigua is Gran Jaguar Tours, 4 C Poniente 30 (☎832 2712, *www.granjaguar.com*).

Capuchin nuns who lived here were not allowed any visual contact with the outside world: food was passed to them by means of a turntable and they could only speak to visitors through a grille. The ruins are the most beautiful in Antigua, with fountains, courtyards, massive earthquake-proof pillars, and a unique tower, or "retreat", with eighteen tiny cells set into the walls on the top floor and a cellar supported by a massive pillar, that probably functioned as a meat storage room. The exterior of the tower is also interesting, ringed with small stone recesses representing the Stations of the Cross.

A couple of blocks to the west, spanning 5 Avenida Norte, the arch of **Santa Catalina** is all that remains of the original convent founded here in 1609. The arch was built so that the nuns could walk between the two halves of the establishment without being exposed to the pollution of the outside world. Somehow it has managed to defy the constant onslaught of earthquakes and is now a favoured, if clichéd, spot for photographers, as the view to the Volcán Agua is unobstructed from here.

Walking under the arch and to the end of the street brings you to the church of **La Merced**, which boasts one of the most intricate facades in the entire city. Look closely and you'll see the outline of a corn cob, a motif not normally used by the Catholic Church and probably added by the original Maya labourers. The church is still in use, but the cloisters and gardens (entrance US$0.25), including a monumental triple-tiered fountain, lie in ruins exposed to the sky.

Continue west down 1 Calle Poniente to the junction of the tree-lined Alameda Santa Lucía, and you reach the spectacular remains of **San Jerónimo** (daily 9am–5.30pm; US$1.30), a school built in 1739. Well-kept gardens are woven between the huge blocks of fallen masonry and crumbling walls, and the site is regularly used as a spectacular venue for classical music concerts.

Eating and drinking

The choice of **food** in Antigua is even more cosmopolitan than the population. You can munch your way around the world in a number of reasonably authentic restaurants for a few dollars a time, or dine in real style for around US$10 a head. The only thing that seems hard to come by is authentic Guatemalan comedor food – which will be quite a relief if you've been subsisting on eggs and beans in the mountains.

Cafés

Condesa, west side of Parque Central – go through the Casa del Conde bookshop. Extremely civilized, though pricey, place to enjoy an excellent breakfast, coffee and cake or full lunch. The gurgling fountain and period charm create a nice tone for the long, lazy Sunday brunches favoured by Antiguan society. Alternatively, grab a *latte* from the adjoining take-away window.

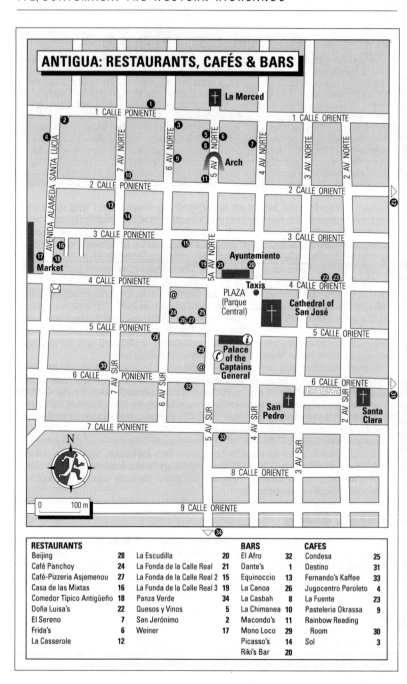

ANTIGUA: RESTAURANTS, CAFÉS & BARS

RESTAURANTS

Beijing	28	La Escudilla	20
Café Panchoy	24	La Fonda de la Calle Real	21
Café-Pizzeria Asjemenou	27	La Fonda de la Calle Real 2	15
Casa de las Mixtas	16	La Fonda de la Calle Real 3	19
Comedor Típico Antigüeño	18	Panza Verde	34
Doña Luisa's	22	Quesos y Vinos	5
El Sereno	7	San Jerónimo	2
Frida's	6	Weiner	17
La Casserole	12		

BARS

El Afro	32
Dante's	1
Equinoccio	13
La Canoa	26
La Casbah	8
La Chimanea	10
Macondo's	11
Mono Loco	29
Picasso's	14
Riki's Bar	20

CAFES

Condesa	25
Destino	31
Fernando's Kaffee	33
Jugocentro Peroleto	4
La Fuente	23
Pasteleria Okrassa	9
Rainbow Reading Room	30
Sol	3

Destino, 1 Av Sur 8. Diminutive café pit-stop, popular with language students, that's ideal for a caffeine hit or a slab of home-made cake, though the convivial American owner will rustle up a bacon sandwich for those in need.

Fernando's Kaffee, 7 C Pte 11. Simple premises but unquestionably the finest coffee in town – ground, roasted and served by a perfectionist – plus delicious home-made pastries.

Jugocentre Peroleto, Alameda Santa Lucía Nte 36. Excellent budget hole-in-the-wall cabin with cheap, healthy breakfasts, fruit juices and yummy cakes.

La Fuente, 4 C Ote 14. Vegetarian restaurant/café where you can eat stuffed aubergine and falafel or sip good coffee in one of the most attractive restored courtyards in town. On Saturdays village women set up a *huipil* market around the fountain.

Pasteleria Okrassa, 6 Av Nte 29. Great for croissants, cinnamon rolls and healthy drinks – try the raspberry juice.

Rainbow Reading Room, 7 Av Sur 8. Relaxed bohemian atmosphere in this favourite travellers' hangout. Great vegetarian menu of imaginative salads and pasta dishes, epic smoothies and decent cappuccinos, plus friendly, prompt service. Also home to one of Antigua's best travel agents, a good secondhand bookshop, and regular musical jams.

Sol, 1 C Pte 9. Simple courtyard café serving home-baked bread, healthy snacks and tasty sandwiches and cakes, plus Internet, fax and phone facilities.

Restaurants

Beijing, 6 Av Sur and 5 C Pte. Antigua's best Chinese and East Asian food, with good noodle dishes, soups and Vietnamese spring rolls prepared with a few imaginative twists. Fairly expensive.

Café Panchoy, 6 Av Norte 1B. Good-value cooking with a real Guatemalan flavour, served around an open kitchen. Dishes include top steaks and some traditional favourites like *chiles rellenos*. Excellent margaritas too. Closed Tues.

Café-Pizzeria Asjemenou, 5 C Pte 4. A favourite for its legendary breakfasts, and also very strong on pizza and calzone, though the service can be erratic.

Casa de las Mixtas, 1 Callejón, off 3 C Poniente. A basic comedor, but nicely set up with attractive decor and cooking that's executed with more flair than most. Open early until 7.30pm.

Comedor Típico Antigüeño, Alameda Santa Lucía Sur 5. Excellent canteen-like comedor opposite the bus terminal and market, with bargain set lunches and meals, all including a soup starter.

Doña Luisa's, 4 C Ote 12. One of the most popular places in town. The setting is relaxed but the menu could do with a revamp – the basic line-up of chilli con carne, baked potatoes, salads and hamburgers is a little uninspired. An adjoining shop sells bread and pastries baked on the premises.

El Sereno, 4 Av Nte 16. Superb colonial setting with beautiful dining rooms and a lovely roof terrace with some of the finest views in Antigua. The extensive and expensive menu features many seasonal specialities, plus a decent wine list.

Frida's, 5 Av Nte 29. Lively atmosphere and the best Mexican food in town, including tasty enchiladas and fajitas, served up amidst 1950s Americana.

La Casserole, Callejón de la Concepción 7. This elegant, expensive restaurant, in a pretty patio location, serves the finest French cooking in Antigua. Leave some room for the epic desserts. Closed Mon.

La Escudilla, 4 Av Nte 4. Tremendous courtyard restaurant, in the same premises as *Riki's Bar*, which is usually extremely busy thanks to its excellent-value, good-quality food. Dishes include good pasta, delicious salads and plenty of tasty vegetarian choices, while the US$3 all-day, all-night set meal is exceptional value. You may have a wait, though, when it's busy.

La Fonda de la Calle Real, one branch upstairs at 5 Av Nte 5, another over the road at 5 Av Nte 12, and a third (the nicest location) at 3 C Pte 7. Probably the most famous restaurant in Antigua, and patronized by Bill Clinton during his 2000 visit. Try the excellent Guatemalan specialities including *pepián* (spicy meat stew) and *caldo real* (chicken soup) or the sizzling grilled meats. Prices are moderate to expensive. Closed Wed.

Panza Verde, 5 Av Sur 19. One of Antigua's most exclusive restaurants, featuring exemplary European cuisine, professional service and a nice setting, with well-spaced tables grouped around a courtyard garden. Try the trout or sea bass meunière.

Quesos y Vinos, 5 Av Norte 32. Very stylish Italian-owned restaurant with a reliable reputation for good home-made pasta and pizza, and wines from Europe and South America. Moderate.

San Jerónimo, Alameda Santa Lucía Nte and 1 C Pte. This pleasant, simple patio-based comedor is a good bet for an early breakfast (it opens at 7am) and also does tasty and very inexpensive lunches and snacks.

Weiner, Alameda Santa Lucía Sur 8. Especially good for well-priced, filling breakfasts, as well as lunchtime specials (US$2.50), good coffee and herbal teas, and a fair selection of bottled beers.

Nightlife and entertainment

Evening activity is officially curtailed in Antigua by a "dry law" which forbids the sale of alcohol after 1am. The places listed below on 5 and 7 avenidas norte are particularly popular with the gringo crowd and all open at around 7pm. Antigua's dance scene is burgeoning, drawing a big crowd from Guatemala City. The venues tend to be very quiet Monday to Wednesday, busy Thursday and heaving at weekends.

There are a number of small video **cinemas** that show a range of Western films on a daily basis – *Trainspotting*, *Salvador* and *Buena Vista Social Club* are on almost permanently. Fliers with weekly listings are posted on noticeboards all over town. The main cinemas are Cinema Bistro (5 Av Sur 14), Cinemaya (6 C Pte 7), and Maya Moon (6 Av Nte 1A), while the Proyecto Cultural El Sitio (5 C Pte 15) also shows a good choice of Latin American and art-house movies.

Bars and clubs

El Afro, 6 C Pte 9. Funky, sociable bar, usually crammed at weekends with a salsa-stepping crowd, though space is tight for really serious dancing.

La Canoa, 5 C Pte between 4 and 5 avenidas. A small, unpretentious club where people come to dance to mainly Latin sounds. Merengue is the main ingredient, spiked with a dash of salsa and reggae; they also play a few tracks of Western and Latin pop/rock. Good mix of locals and foreigners and reasonable drink prices, though perennial licensing problems means it shuts down from time to time. US$2 entrance at weekends, free in the week.

La Casbah, 5 Av Nte 30. Spectacular venue in the ruins of an ancient church, attracting a well-heeled crowd from Antigua and Guatemala City. The music can occasionally match the site, with deep bassline-driven dance mixes, though drinks are expensive. Gay night on Thurs. Mon–Wed free, Thurs, Fri & Sat around US$3.50.

La Chimanea, 7 Av Nte 7. One of the more popular bars, though the music selection is disturbingly eclectic – expect everything from Rod Stewart to Black Sabbath.

Dante's 7 C Pte 6B. Arguably the hippest place in town, this large, stylish bar hosts live bands and regular Cuban and house music club nights.

Equinoccio 7 Av Nte and 2 C Pte. Bar-cum-club that's *the* place to groove to Latin music – predominantly merengue and salsa, but occasionally a little Cuban hip-hop – with a dark bar zone and a large dancefloor. Moderate drink prices.

Macondo's, 5 Av Nte and 2 C Pte. Probably the closest thing Antigua has to a pub, though the themed nights (Wed is ladies night) and constant visual barrage of music videos spoil things somewhat.

Mono Loco 2 Av Nte 6B. Popular gringo bar, with full US and some European sports coverage, though the music selection can be banal.

Picasso's, 7 Av Nrte 16. No-nonsense drinking-hole that can get quite lively in high season. Usually closed Sun.

Riki's Bar, 4 Av Nte 4. Unquestionably the most happening place in town due to its excellent site inside *La Escudilla*, to the eclectic funk, nu jazz and downbeat music policy, and to the unrivalled happy hour (7–9pm), which means this place is packed most nights.

Listings

Adventure sports Maya Mountain Bike Tours, 3 C Pte and 7 Av Nte (☎832 3743, *www.mayanbike* .com), have an excellent range of trips, plus bike rental and whitewater rafting; Old Town Outfitters,

Guatemala City buses, Guatemala

Looking south over Glover's Reef, Belize

Garífuna women, Lívingston, Guatemala

Keel-billed toucan, Belize

Tikal, Guatemala

Sololá man, Guatemala

Hidden Valley Falls, Cayo, Belize

Lago de Atitlán, Guatemala

Terminal Oriente, San Salvador, El Salvador   Cathedral, San Salvador, El Salvador

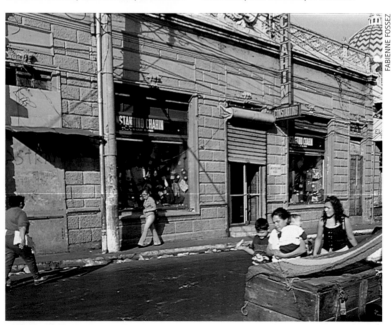

El Centro, San Salvador, El Salvador

6 C Pte 7 (☎832 4243, *www.bikeguatemala.com*), run mountain-bike excursions and rock-climbing trips for all levels, and offer tent, sleeping bag, pack and bike rental.

Banks and exchange Banco Industrial, 5 Av Sur 4, just south of the plaza, has a 24hr ATM for Visa and Plus cardholders; Lloyds, in the northeast corner of the plaza, changes sterling travellers' cheques. Note that the Banco del Quetzal Mastercard/Cirrus cashpoint on the north side of the plaza routinely accepts cards but fails to dispense money.

Bike rental Aviatur, 5 Av Norte 35 (☎ & fax 832 2642), and Maya Mountain Bike Tours and Old Town Outfitters (see "Adventure sports" opposite) rent mountain bikes for around US$8 a day, US$25 weekly.

Bookstores Casa Andinista, 4 C Ote 5A; Casa del Conde, on the west side of the plaza; Un Poco de Todo, also on the west side of the plaza. The Rainbow Reading Room, 7 Av Sur 8, has by far the largest selection of secondhand books.

Car and motorbike rental Avis, 5 Av Nte 22 (☎ & fax 832 2692), and Tabarini, 2 C Pte 19A (☎ & fax 832 3091, *www.centroamerica.com/tabarini*), both have cars from around US$45 a day and Jeeps from US$60, including unlimited mileage and insurance. La Ceiba, 6 C Pte 15 (☎832 0077), rent out motorbikes from US$25 a day.

Horse riding Ravenscroft Stables, 2 Av Sur 3, in the village of San Juan del Obispo, on the road up to Santa María de Jesús (☎832 6229).

Internet There are over twenty places where you can send and receive email; rates are set at around US$1.50 an hour, though there are discounts for heavy users. The best set-up places include La Ventana, 5 Av Sur 24 (daily 8am–9pm), and Enlaces, 6 Av Nte 1 (daily 9am–9.30pm). Conexión, in the La Fuente cultural centre at 4 C Ote 14 (daily 8am–8pm), is probably the best place to head for real computer queries.

Laundry Rainbow Laundry, 6 Av Sur 15 (Mon–Sat 7am–7pm). A wash typically costs around US$2.

Libraries and cultural institutes El Sitio, 5 C Pte 15 (☎832 3037), has an active theatre, library and art gallery, and regularly hosts exhibitions and concerts; see the *Revue* or *Guatemala Post* for listings.

Medical care There's a 24hr emergency service at the Santa Lucía Hospital, Calzada Santa Lucía Sur 7 (☎832 3122). Dr Aceituno, who speaks good English, has a surgery at 2 C Pte 7 (☎832 0512).

Pharmacies Farmacia Santa María, west side of the plaza (daily 8am–10pm).

Police The police HQ is on the south side of the plaza, next to the tourist office (☎ & fax 832 0572). The tourist police are just off the plaza on 4 Avenida Norte (☎832 7290).

Post office Alameda de Santa Lucía, opposite the bus terminal (Mon–Fri 8am–4.30pm). DHL are at 6 Av Sur 16 (☎832 3718, fax 832 3732, *ecastill@gtl-co.gt.dhl.com*), and Quick Shipping is at 3 Av Nte 26 (☎832 2595).

Supermarket La Bodegona at 4 C Pte and Alameda Santa Lucía.

Telephones The Telgua office is just south of the plaza on 5 Avenida Sur (7am–10pm), but rates are higher here than anywhere else and you'll have to queue. Several places now offer Internet-linked phone facilities, including La Ventana (see "Internet", above), enabling you to call North America for US$1.50 an hour, or Europe and the rest of the world for a little more, though lines can be very fuzzy. The cheapest conventional phone connections are at Kall Shop, 6 Av Sur 12A (daily 8am–8pm), where you can call North America for US$0.25 a minute, Western Europe for US$0.45, and Australia and New Zealand for US$0.64 a minute.

Travel agents There are dozens of travel agents in Antigua; the following are the most professional and reliable: The Rainbow Travel Center, 7 Av Sur 8 (daily 9am–6pm; ☎832 4202, fax 832 4206, *rainbowtravel@gua.gbm.net*), is fully computerized and has some of the best deals in town, as well as friendly and efficient staff. Viajes Tivoli, at 4 C Ote 10, on the west side of the plaza (Mon–Sat 9am–6pm; ☎832 4274, fax 832 5690, *antigua@tivoli.com.gt*), is another recommended all-rounder. Monarcas, 7 Av Nte 15A (☎ & fax 832 4779, *www.angelfire.com/mt/monarcastravel*), is a highly recommended specialist agency with some fascinating Maya culture and ecology tours and daily connections to Copán in Honduras. Adventure Travel Center Viareal, 5 Av Nte 25B (☎ & fax 832 0162, *viareal@guate.net*), is particularly good for adventure and sailing trips and shuttle bus services. Perfect for backpackers, Quetzalventures, 1 C Pte 12 A (☎832 5827, *www.quetzalventures.com*), offers a number of good, inexpensive trips to Petén and the Verapaz highlands; all profits aid Guatemalan street children. Vision Travel, 3 Av Nte 3 (☎832 3293, fax 832 1955, *www.guatemalainfo.com*), has very high standards of service and is consistently recommended.

Around Antigua

The countryside around Antigua is superbly fertile and breathtakingly beautiful. The valley is dotted with small villages, ranging from the *ladino* coffee centre of Alotenango to the traditional *indígena* village of Santa María de Jesús. None of them is more than an hour or two away and all make interesting day-trips. For the more adventurous, the volcanic peaks of Agua, Acatenango and Fuego offer strenuous but superb hiking, best done through a specialist agency.

Santa María de Jesús and Volcán Agua

Up above Antigua, a smooth new sealed road snakes through the coffee bushes and past the village of San Juan del Obispo before arriving in **SANTA MARÍA DE JESÚS**, starting point for the ascent of Volcán Agua. Perched high on the shoulder of the volcano, the village is some 500m above Antigua, with magnificent views over the Panchoy valley and east towards the smoking cone of Pacaya. The village was founded at the end of the sixteenth century and is of little interest, though the women wear beautiful purple *huipiles*. There's also a good little hospedaje here, *El Oasis* (☎832 0130; ①), just below the plaza, if you want to make an early start. **Buses** run from Antigua to Santa María every hour or so from 6am to 5pm, and the trip takes thirty minutes.

Volcán Agua is the easiest and by far the most popular of Guatemala's big cones to climb – on some Saturday nights hundreds of people spend the night at the top. The trail starts in Santa María de Jesús: head straight across the plaza, between the two ageing pillars, and up the street opposite the church doors. Take a right turn just before the end, and then continue past the cemetery and out of the village. From here it's a fairly simple climb on a clear path, cutting across the road that goes some of the way up. The climb can take anything from four to six hours, and the peak, at 3766m, is always cold at night. There is shelter (though not always room) in a small chapel at the summit, however, and the views certainly make it worth the struggle.

Jocotenango and San Andrés Itzapa

Just 2km north of Antigua, the unappealing suburb of **JOCOTENANGO**, "place of bitter fruit", set around a huge, dusty plaza and long notorious for its sleazy bars, now boasts a couple of interesting new attractions. **Casa K'ojom** (daily 9am–5pm; US$2.50 including tour; *www.kojom.com*) is a purpose-built museum dedicated to Maya culture, especially music. The history of indigenous musical traditions is clearly presented from its pre-Columbian origins, through sixteenth-century Spanish and African influences – which brought the marimba, bugles and drums – to the present day, with audio-visual documentaries of fiestas and ceremonies. Other rooms are dedicated to the village weavings of the Sacatepéquez department and the cult of Maximón (see below). Next door, the **Museo de Café** (daily 9am–5pm; US$2.50), based in the Finca La Azotea, a 34-hectare plantation dating from 1883, offers the chance to look around a working organic coffee farm. All the technicalities of husking, sieving and roasting are clearly explained, and you're served a cup of the aromatic home-grown brew after your tour. Buses from the Antigua terminal pass Jocotenango every thirty minutes on their way to Chimaltenango; the museums are 500m west of the plaza, down a dirt road.

The road from Antigua to Chimaltenango continues beyond Jocotenango, ascending the Panchoy valley, past dusty farming villages, before a dirt track branches off to **SAN ANDRÉS ITZAPA**, one of the many villages badly hit by the 1976 earthquake. San Andrés is home to the cult of **San Simón** (or Maximón), the "evil saint" – a kind of womanizing and rapacious combination of Judas Iscariot and the conquistador Pedro de Alvarado – who is housed in his own pagan chapel. Despite San Andrés being just 18km from Antigua, few tourists visit this shrine, and you may feel less intrusive and more welcome here than at his other places of abode, which include Zunil (see p.208) and Santiago Atitlán (p.195). Uniquely in Guatemala, this San Simón attracts a largely *ladino* congregation and is particularly popular with prostitutes. To reach the saint's "house" ("Casa de San Simón") head for the central plaza from the dirt road into the village, turn right when you reach the church, walk two blocks, then up a little hill and you should spot street vendors selling charms, incense and candles. If you get lost, just about any village kid will take you there for a quetzal tip. You can only visit the saint between sunrise and sunset, as the Maya believe he sleeps at other times. Local stores stock candles and incense and there are also books on witchcraft for sale.

Once you've tracked down the dimly lit shrine, you'll find that Maximón lives in a fairly strange world, his image surrounded by drunken men, cigar-smoking women and hundreds of burning candles, each symbolizing a request: red for love, white for health, and so on. The walls are adorned with hundreds of plaques from all over Guatemala and Central America, thanking San Simón for his help. You may be offered a *limpia*, or soul cleansing, which, for a small fee, involves being beaten by one of the resident women workers with a bushel of herbs. A bottle of the firewater *aguadiente* is also demolished: some is offered to San Simón, some of it you'll have to drink yourself and the rest is consumed by the attendant, who sprays you with alcohol (from her mouth) for your sins – all in all, quite an experience.

To get to **San Andrés Itzapa** from Antigua, take any bus heading to Chimaltenango from the terminal (every 20min, 5.30am–7pm) and get the driver to drop you off where the dirt road leaves the highway. From there you can hitch, or else it's a thirty-minute walk.

The Carretera Interamericana

Leaving Guatemala City to the west, the serpentine **Carretera Interamericana** cuts right through the central highlands as far as the border with Mexico. In its entirety, this road stretches from Alaska to Chile (with a short break in southern Panamá), and here in Guatemala it forms the backbone of transport in the highlands. As you travel around, the highway and its junctions will inevitably become all too familiar since, wherever you're going, it's invariably easiest to catch the first local bus to the Carretera Interamericana and then flag down one of the buses heading along the highway.

Heading west from the capital, you climb steadily up a three-lane highway to **San Lucas Sacatepéquez**, from where a well-maintained side road descends to Antigua. There are other major junctions on the Interamericana which you'll soon get to know well. The first of these is **Chimaltenango**, an important town and capital of its own department. From its ugly sprawl along the highway you can also make connections to or from Antigua. Continuing west, **Los Encuentros** is the next main junction, where one road heads off to the north for Chichicastenango and Santa Cruz del Quiché and another branches south to Panajachel and Lago de Atitlán. Beyond this, the highway climbs high over a mountainous ridge before dropping to **Cuatro Caminos**, from where side roads lead to Quetzaltenango, Totonicapán and San Francisco El Alto. The Interamericana continues on to Huehuetenango before reaching the Mexican border at La Mesilla. Virtually every bus travelling along the highway will stop at all of these junctions and you'll be able to buy fruit, drink and fast food from a resident army of vendors, some of whom will storm the bus looking for business, while others are content to dangle their wares outside your window.

Leaving Guatemala City, the first place of interest is **SANTIAGO SACATEPÉQUEZ**, 1km or so to the north of the highway. The road branches off from San Lucas Sacatepéquez and buses shuttle back and forth along the branch road. The best time to visit Santiago is on November 1, for a local fiesta to honour the **Day of the Dead**. Massive kites made from paper and tobacco are flown in the cemetery to release the souls of the dead from their agony. The festival is immensely popular, and hundreds of Guatemalans and tourists come every year to watch the spectacle. Teams of young men struggle to get the kites aloft while the crowd looks on with bated breath, rushing for cover if a kite comes crashing to the ground. There's also a **market** in Santiago on Tuesday and Sunday.

Chimaltenango

Founded by Pedro de Portocarrero in 1526, on the site of the Kaqchikel centre of Bokoh, **CHIMALTENANGO** was later considered as a possible location for the new capital. It has the misfortune, however, of being positioned on the continental divide and suffered terribly from the earthquake in 1976 which flattened much of the surrounding area. Today's town (its centre is just to the north of the main road) is still suffering from that disaster, with dirt streets, breeze-block buildings and an air of weary desperation. The town extracts what little business it can from the stream of traffic on the Interamericana, and the roadside is crowded with cheap comedores, mechanics' workshops, and sleazy bars that become brothels by night. **Buses** passing through Chimaltenango run to all points along the Carretera Interamericana. For Antigua they leave every twenty minutes between 5am and 7pm from the market in town – or you can wait at the turn-off on the highway.

Tecpán and Iximché

Further west along a fast section of the Carretera Interamericana is the small town of **TECPÁN**, ninety minutes or so from Guatemala City. Tecpán may well have been the site chosen by Alvarado as the first Spanish capital, to which the Spanish forces retreated in August 1524, after they'd been driven out of Iximché. Today it's a place of no great interest, though it has a substantial number of restaurants and guesthouses catering to a mainly Guatemalan clientele.

About 5km south of Tecpán on a beautiful exposed hillside are the ruins of **Iximché** (daily 8am–5pm; US$3.50), the pre-conquest capital of the Kaqchikel, protected on three sides by steep slopes and surrounded by pine forests. The Kaqchikel allied themselves with the conquistadors from the early days of the Conquest, so the structures here suffered less than most at the hands of the Spanish. Since then, however, time and weather have taken their toll, and the majority of the buildings that once housed a population of ten thousand have disappeared, leaving only a few stone-built pyramids, plazas and a couple of ball courts. Nevertheless, the site is strongly atmospheric and its grassy plazas, ringed with pine trees, are marvellously peaceful, especially during the week, when you may well have the place to yourself. The ruins are still actively used as a focus for Maya worship: sacrifices and offerings take place down a small trail through the pine trees behind the final plaza.

To get there, take any bus travelling along the Carretera Interamericana between Chimaltenango and Los Encuentros and ask to be dropped at Tecpán. To get to the ruins, simply walk through Tecpán and out the other side of the plaza, passing the Centro de Salud, and follow the road through the fields for about 5km – an hour or so on foot. With any luck you'll be able to hitch some of the way, particularly at weekends when the road can be fairly busy. There's **camping** at the site, but bring your own food as the small shop sells little more than drinks. Iximché's shady location is perfect for a picnic or barbecue. If you're not planning to camp, be back on the Carretera Interamericana before 6pm to be sure of a bus.

Chichicastenango

The road for Chichicastenango and the **department of El Quiché** leaves the Carretera Interamericana at the **Los Encuentros** junction, thirty kilometres past the Iximché turnoff. Heading north from Los Encuentros, the highway drops down through dense, aromatic pine forests, plunging into a deep ravine before bottoming out by a tributary of the Río Motagua.

Continuing upwards around endless switchbacks, the road eventually reaches **CHICHICASTENANGO**, Guatemala's "mecca del turismo". If it's market day, you may get embroiled in one of the country's very few traffic jams – a rare event outside the capital – as traders, tourists and locals all struggle to reach the town centre. In this compact and traditional town of cobbled streets, adobe houses and red-tiled roofs, the calm of day-to-day life is shattered on a twice-weekly basis by the **Sunday and Thursday markets** – Sunday is the busiest. The market attracts myriad tourists and commercial traders, as well as Maya weavers from throughout the central highlands.

The market is by no means all that sets Chichicastenango apart, however. For the local Maya population it's an important centre of culture and religion. The area was inhabited by the Kaqchikel long before the arrival of the Spanish, and over the years Maya culture and folk Catholicism have been treated with a rare degree of respect – although inevitably this blessing has been mixed with waves of arbitrary persecution and exploitation. Today, the town has an incredible collection of Maya artefacts, parallel *indígena* and *ladino* governments, and a church that makes no effort to disguise its acceptance of unconventional pagan worship. Traditional weaving is also adhered to here and the women wear superb, heavily embroidered *huipiles*. The men's costume of short trousers and jackets of black wool embroidered with silk is highly distinguished, although it's very expensive to make and these days most men opt for Western dress. However, for the town's fiesta (December 14–21) and on Sundays, a handful of *cofradres* (elders of the religious hierarchy) still wear traditional clothing and carry spectacular silver processional crosses and incense burners.

Arrival and information

There's no bus station in Chichi, but the corner of 5 C and 5 Av operates loosely as a terminal. **Buses** heading between Guatemala City and Santa Cruz del Quiché pass through Chichicastenango every thirty minutes, stopping in town for a few minutes to load up with passengers. In Guatemala City, buses leave from the terminal in Zona 4, from 4am to about 5pm. Coming from Antigua, you can pick up a bus easily in Chimaltenango. From Panajachel, you can take any bus up to Los Encuentros and change there; on market days there are also several direct buses, supplemented by a steady flow of special tourist shuttles run by various companies. There are also special shuttle services from Antigua on market days.

There's a small Inguat **tourist information** office (daily 8am–noon & 2–6pm; ☎756 1015) beside Santo Tomás church on 8 Calle; they usually have a good stock of leaflets about the department. If you're bitten by market fever and need to **change money**, there's no problem in Chichi, even on a Sunday: try Banco Ejército on 6 Calle (Tues–Sun 9am–5pm) or, almost opposite, Banco Industrial (Mon 10am–2pm, Wed–Sun 10am–5pm) for Visa card holders. The **post office** (Mon–Fri 9am–5.30pm) is behind the church on 7 Avenida, and **Telgua** office (Mon–Fri 8am–6pm, Sat 9am–1pm) is on 6 Avenida. for **Internet** access try Acses at 6 C 4–52 (US$4 per hour).

CHICHICASTENANGO

△ Santa Cruz del Quiché (19km)

Buses to Santa Cruz
Buses to Interamericana & Guatemala City

Banco Industrial

Centro Comercial

El Calvario   Plaza

Museo Rossbach   Santo Tomás
Former Monastery

Mask Shop

Pascual Abaj

0   200 m

ACCOMMODATION
Colonial El Centro   7
Hospedaje El Salvador   8
Hospedaje Girón   3
Hotel Chalet House   2
Hotel Chugüilá   4
Hotel Posada Belen   9
Hotel Santo Tomás   5
Maya Inn   6
Posada El Arco   1

RESTAURANTS AND CAFÉS
Buenadventura   C
Casa San Juan   E
Comedor Gumarcaj   B
La Fonda del Tzijolaj   D
La Villa de Los Cofrades   A

▽ Los Encuentros & Guatemala City

Accommodation

Hotels can be in short supply on Saturday nights before the Sunday market, but you shouldn't have a problem on other days. Prices can also rise on market days, though at other times you can usually negotiate a good deal.

Colonial El Centro, 8 C and 6 Av (☎756 1249). Friendly, family-owned guesthouse, very close to the plaza, with clean, inexpensive rooms, some with private bath. ②–③.

Hospedaje El Salvador, 5 Av 10–09 (☎756 1329). Decent budget hotel, with a vast warren of bare but cleanish rooms, a bizarre external colour scheme and cheap prices. Insist that the owners turn on the hot water. ②.

Hospedaje Girón, 6 C 4–52 (☎756 1156, fax 756 1226). Pretty, well-priced pine-trimmed rooms, with or without private bath, plus parking. Good value for single travellers. ③–④.

Hotel Chalet House, 3C C 7–44 (☎756 1360, *multiple@concyt.gob.gt*). Excellent new hotel in a quiet street on the north side of town. The ten rooms are all very clean and have nice touches like high-land wool blankets and textiles, plus comfortable beds and private bathrooms. There's also a tiny dining room where you can get breakfast, and a rooftop terrace. ④.

Hotel Chugüilá, 5 Av 5–24 (☎756 1134, fax 756 1279). Attractive if rather old-fashioned rooms, all on different levels and some with fireplaces, with lovely greenery and pot plants everywhere. Secure parking. ⑤.

Hotel Posada Belen, 12 C 5–55 (☎ & fax 756 1244). Not the most attractive rooms, though half have private bath and many have good views. Cable TV available for a little extra. ②–③.

Hotel Santo Tomás, 7 Av 5–32 (☎756 1061, fax 756 1306). Very comfortable, well-appointed rooms set around two colonial-style courtyards. Rooms 29–37 are the ones to book if you can – they have great mountain views. Restaurant, swimming pool, sauna and Jacuzzi. ⑦.

Maya Inn, 8 C and 3 Av (☎756 1176, fax 756 1212). Chichi's longest established tourist hotel offers very comfortable rooms with old-fashioned period furnishings and fireplaces. Though its character is undeniable, prices are a bit steep, and you pity the staff decked out in mock-traditional dress. ⑧.

Posada El Arco, 4 C 4–36 (☎756 1255). Superb new guesthouse, run by friendly English-speaking brothers, with seven huge, attractive rooms with good wooden beds, reading lights and appealing decor, including local Maya fabrics. Rooms 6 and 7 have access to a pleasant terrace, and there's also a beautiful garden and stunning countryside views. ④.

The Town

Though most visitors come here for the market, Chichicastenango also offers an unusual insight into traditional religious practices in the highlands. At the main **Iglesia de Santo Tomás**, in the southeast corner of the plaza, the K'iche' Maya have been left to adopt their own style of worship, blending pre-Columbian and Catholic rituals. The church was built in 1540 on the site of a Maya altar, and rebuilt in the eighteenth century. It's said that indigenous locals became interested in worshipping here after Francisco Ximénez, the priest from 1701 to 1703, started reading their holy book, the Popul Vuh.

Before entering the church, it's customary to make offerings in a fire at the base of the steps or to burn incense in perforated cans, a practice that leaves a cloud of thin, sweet smoke hanging over the entrance. Inside is an astonishing scene of avid worship. A soft hum of constant murmuring fills the air as the faithful kneel to place candles on low-level stone platforms for their ancestors and the saints. For these people, the entire building is alive with the souls of the dead, each located in a specific part of the church. Don't enter the building by the front door, which is reserved for *cofrades* and senior church officials; use the side door instead and be warned that taking photographs inside the building is considered **deeply offensive** – don't even contemplate it.

Beside the church is a former monastery, now used by the parish administration. It was here that the Spanish priest Francisco Ximénez became the first outsider to be shown the Popol Vuh. His copy of the manuscript is now housed in the Newberry Library in Chicago: the original was lost some time later in the eighteenth century. The text itself was written just to the north of here, in Utatlán, shortly after the arrival of the Spanish, and is a brilliant poem of over nine thousand lines that details the cosmology, mythology and traditional history of the K'iche'.

On the south side of the plaza, often hidden by stalls on market day, the newly renovated **Rossbach Museum** (Tues, Wed, Fri & Sat 8am–noon & 2–4pm, Thurs & Sun 8am–1pm & 2–4pm; US$0.15) houses a wide-ranging collection of pre-Columbian artefacts, mostly small pieces of ceramics (including some demonic-looking incense burners), jade jewellery and stone carvings, some as old as two thousand years, that had been kept by local people in their homes. A second room, due to open in 2002, will be dedicated to local artesanías, including weavings, masks and carvings.

Facing Santo Tomás across on the west side of the plaza, the whitewashed **El Calvario** chapel is like a miniature version of Chichi's main church. Inside, the atmosphere is equally reverential as prayers are recited around the smoke-blackened wooden altar, and women offer flowers and stoop to kiss a supine image of Christ, entombed inside a glass cabinet.

THE CEMETERY AND SHRINE OF PASCUAL ABAJ

The town **cemetery**, down the hill behind El Calvario, offers further evidence of the strange mix of religions that characterizes Chichicastenango. The graves are marked by anything from a grand tomb to a small earth mound, and in the centre is a Maya shrine where offerings of incense and alcohol are made.

The church and cemetery are certainly not the only scenes of Maya religious activity: the hills that surround the town, like so many throughout the country, are topped with shrines. The closest of these, **Pascual Abaj**, is less than a kilometre from the plaza and regularly visited by tourists, but it's important to remember that any ceremonies you may witness are deeply serious – you should keep your distance and be sensitive about taking photographs. The shrine is laid out in a typical pattern with several small altars facing a stern pre-Columbian sculpture. Offerings are usually overseen by a *brujo*, a type of shaman, and range from flowers to sacrificed chickens, always incorporating plenty of incense, alcohol and incantations.

To get to Pascual Abaj, walk down the hill beside Santo Tomás, take the first right, 9 Calle, and follow this as it winds its way out of town. You'll soon cross a stream and then a well-signposted route takes you through the courtyard of a workshop that churns out wooden masks. If you look up, you may see a thin plume of smoke if there's a ceremony in progress. The path continues uphill for ten minutes through a dense pine forest.

Eating

If you've come from Panajachel or Antigua, the dining scene here may come as a bit of a shock to the system. You won't find sushi or Thai curries in Chichi, just simple, good-value Guatemalan comedor food. The plaza on **market day** is the place to come for authentic highland eating: try one of the makeshift food stalls, where you'll find cauldrons of stew, rice and beans.

Buenadventura, upper floor, inside the Centro Comercial. Bird's-eye view of the vegetable market and simple, no-nonsense food – the breakfasts are the cheapest in town.

Café-Restaurant La Villa de Los Cofrades, 6 C and 5 Av, first floor. Good set meals – soup, a main dish and salad, fries and bread – for under US$4, plus superb breakfasts and real coffee.

Casa San Juan, west side of the plaza, beside the El Calvario. Stylish bar-restaurant with a brightly painted interior and plenty of artwork, with good, imaginative Guatemelan cooking, including a US$2.50 set meal. Live music some nights.

Comedor Gumarcaj, opposite the *Hotel Santo Tomás*. Simple, scruffy but cheap and friendly comedor that serves up a mean chicken and chips and lush *licuados*.

La Fonda del Tzijolaj, upper floor of the Centro Comercial. Yes, the name's unpronounceable, but the food is probably the best in town and the balcony views of the church of Santo Tomás and the market are excellent. Try the delicious *chiles rellenos*.

Santa Cruz del Quiché and around

The capital of the Department of El Quiché, **SANTA CRUZ DEL QUICHÉ** lies half an hour north of Chichicastenango. A good paved road connects the two towns, running through pine forests and ravines, and past the **Laguna Lemoa**, a lake which, according to local legend, was originally filled with tears wept by the wives of K'iche' kings after their husbands had been slaughtered by the Spanish.

The Catholic church suffered terribly in El Quiché in the late 1970s and early 1980s, when priests were singled out and murdered for their connections with the co-operative movement. The situation was so serious that Bishop Juan Geradi withdrew all his priests from the department in 1981. They have since returned to their posts, but the bishop himself was later assassinated in April 1998.

On the central **plaza**, there's a large colonial **church**, built by the Dominicans with stone from the ruins of Utatlán. Beside the church, the large clock tower is also said to have been built with Utatlán stone stripped from the temple of Tohil, and in the middle of the plaza, a defiant **statue** of the K'iche' hero, Tecún Umán, stands prepared for battle. His position is undermined somewhat by an ugly urban tangle of hardware stores, bakeries and trash that surrounds this corner of the square and the looming, spectacularly ugly **market** building.

Arrival and information

The **bus terminal**, a large, open affair, is about four blocks south and a couple east of the central plaza. Connections are generally excellent from Quiché. There's a constant stream of second-class **buses** to Guatemala City, going every thirty minutes between 3.30am and 5pm (3hr 30min); all pass through Chichicastenango (30min) and Los Encuentros (1hr). There are also regular services to Nebaj between 8.30am and 4pm (5 daily; 3hr 30min), to Uspantán four times daily between 9am and 2pm (5hr), and to Quetzaltenango (7 daily; 3hr). Inter airlines also serve Quiché with daily **flights** from Guatemala City (25min; US$55 one way). The airstrip is 4km south of the town centre.

The street directly north of the terminal is **1 Avenida**, which takes you up into the heart of the town. Two **banks** will change your travellers' cheques: Banco G&T Continental, 6 A 3–00 (Mon–Fri 9am–7pm, Sat 9am–1pm), and Banco Industrial, at the northwest corner of the plaza (Mon–Fri 8.30am–5.30pm, Sat 8.30am–12.30pm), which also advances cash on Visa. If you're heading into the Ixil triangle (see p.185), you may need to stock up on film: try the Kodak or Fuji shops, both one block northeast of the central church.

Accommodation

There's a limited range of **hotels** in Quiché and nothing luxurious. The cheapest are some extremely basic dives right beside the bus terminal. Most of the others are between the terminal and the plaza.

Hospedaje Tropical, 1 Av and 9 C. Extremely basic place: no hot water but dirt cheap. ①.

Hotel Maya Quiché, 3 Av 4–19, Zona 1 (☎755 1464). Friendly place with big clean rooms, some with bathroom. ②–③.

Hotel Rey K'iche, 8 C 0–39, Zona 5 (☎755 0824). Two blocks north, one east from the terminal. Well-run, extremely clean and welcoming place with 26 rooms, most with cable TV and private bath, plus a good comedor. ②–③.

Hotel San Pascual, 7 C 0–43, Zona 1(☎755 1107). Walk up 1 Avenida, and turn left into 7 Calle. Large, clean rooms and equally well-kept communal bathrooms. ②–③.

Posada Calle Real, 2 Av 7–36, two blocks from the terminal. Good-value budget deal: rooms are smallish but clean and the bathrooms (with reliable hot water) are well scrubbed. ②.

Eating and drinking

There's very little to get excited about in Quiché. Most restaurants and cafés are grouped around the plaza. *El Torito Steakhouse*, 7 C 1–73, just southwest of the plaza, is the smartest place in town, with kitsch cowboy decor and a menu that's a real carnivore's delight – try the sausages or fried chicken. On the west side of the plaza, *La Pizza de Ciro* dispenses reasonable pizzas that taste fine if you've come from remote Nebaj and pretty poor if you've arrived from cosmopolitan Antigua. Close by are several uninspiring bakeries with dry pastries and cakes, and also *Café La Torré*, a friendly place for a coffee, snack or a delicious piece of cheesecake. For no-nonsense comedor meals, try *Restaurante Las Rosas*, 1 Av 1–28.

Utatlán (K'umarkaaj)

Early in the fifteenth century, riding on a wave of successful conquests, the K'iche' king Gucumatz (Feathered Serpent) founded a new capital, K'umarkaaj. A hundred years later, the Spanish arrived, renamed the city **Utatlán**, and then destroyed it. Today you can visit the ruins, about 4km to the west of Santa Cruz del Quiché.

According to the Popol Vuh, Gucumatz was a lord of great genius, assisted by powerful spirits, and there's no doubt that his capital was once a great city, with several separate citadels spread across neighbouring hilltops. It housed the nine dynasties of the tribal elite, including the four main K'iche' lords, and contained a total of 23 palaces. The splendour of the city embodied the strength of the K'iche' Empire, which at its height boasted a population of around a million.

By the time of the Conquest, however, the K'iche' had been severely weakened and their empire fractured. They first made contact with the Spanish on the Pacific Coast, suffering a heavy defeat at the hands of Alvarado's forces near Quetzaltenango, with the loss of their hero, Tecún Umán. The K'iche' then invited the Spanish to their capital, but the suspicious Alvarado captured the K'iche' leaders, burnt them alive and then destroyed the city.

The site (8am–5pm; US$2) is not as dramatic as some of the ruins in Guatemala, but impressive nonetheless, surrounded by deep ravines and pine forests, a setting which makes up for the lack of huge pyramids and stellae. There has been little restoration since the Spanish destroyed the city and only a few of the main structures are still recognizable, most buried beneath grassy mounds and shaded by pine trees. The small **museum** has a scale model of what the original city may once have looked like.

The central plaza is almost certainly where Alvarado burned alive the two K'iche' leaders in 1524. Nowadays, it's where you'll find the surviving three **temple buildings** of Tohil, Auilix and Hacauaitz, all of which were simple pyramids topped by thatched shelters. In the middle of the plaza there used to be a circular **tower**, the Temple of the Sovereign Plumed Serpent, and its foundations can still be made out. The only other feature that is still vaguely recognizable is the **ball court**, which lies beneath grassy banks to the south of the plaza.

Beneath the plaza is a long **tunnel** that runs underground for about 100m. Inside are nine **shrines**, perhaps signifying the nine levels of the Maya underworld, Xibalbá. Each is the subject of prayer and devotion, but it is the ninth, housed inside a chamber, that is the most actively used for sacrifice and offerings of incense and alcohol. Why the tunnel was constructed remains uncertain, but some local legends have it that it was dug by the K'iche' to hide their women and children from the advancing Spanish, whom they planned to ambush at Utatlán.

Perhaps the most interesting thing about the site today is that *brujos*, traditional Maya priests, still come here to perform **religious rituals**, practices that predate the arrival of the Spanish by thousands of years. The entire area is covered in small burnt circles – the ashes of incense – and chickens are regularly sacrificed in and around the plaza. If there is a ceremony taking place you'll hear the mumbling of prayers and smell incense smoke as you enter the tunnel, in which case it's wise not to disturb the proceedings by approaching too closely.

A **taxi** from Santa Cruz del Quiché with an hour at the ruins costs around US$7. To **walk**, head south from the plaza along 2 Av, and then turn right down 10 C, which will take you all the way out to the site – it's a pleasant forty-minute hike. You're welcome to **camp** close to the ruins, but there there are no facilities or food.

To the Cuchumatanes: Sacapulas and Uspantán

The land to the north of Santa Cruz del Quiché is sparsely inhabited and dauntingly hilly. About 10km out of town, the paved road passes through San Pedro Jocopilas, and from there presses on through parched mountains, eventually dropping to the isolated town of **SACAPULAS**, ninety minutes from Quiché. In a spectacular position on the Río Negro, beneath the foothills of the Cuchumatanes, Sacapulas has a small colonial church, and a good market every Thursday and Sunday beneath a huge ceiba tree in the plaza.

With its strategic position, Sacapulas should be a transport hub but, alas, it's not. Getting to Sacapulas isn't too difficult – catch any bus from Santa Cruz del Quiché to Uspantán or Nebaj – but leaving is far more difficult: the four daily buses for Quiché leave between 2am and 6am so you may have to **hitch**. Wait by the bridge as traffic heading for Quiché can turn left or right after crossing the river. There's a daily Transportes Rivas bus to Huehuetenango at 5am (4hr) and four buses to Uspantán (2hr 30min) between 1pm and 5pm, but all services in this remote region are erratic and subject to delays and cancellations. Hitchhike by truck or pick-up whenever possible and expect to pay the same rate as you would on the bus. At least if you get stuck there's a half decent place to **stay**, the *Restaurant Río Negro*, which offers basic but clean rooms (①). The cook, Manuela, serves good **meals** and excellent banana, pineapple and papaya milkshakes.

East of Sacapulas, a dirt road rises steeply, clinging to the mountainside and quickly leaving the Río Negro far below. As it climbs, the views are superb, with tiny Sacapulas dwarfed by the sheer enormity of the landscape. Eventually the road reaches a high valley and arrives in **USPANTÁN**, a small town lodged in a chilly gap in the mountains and often soaked in steady drizzle. Rigoberta Menchú, the K'iche' Maya woman who won the 1992 Nobel Peace Prize, is from Chimel, a tiny village in this region. But probably the only reason you'll end up here is in order to get somewhere else. With the **buses for Cobán** and San Pedro Carchá leaving at around 3am, the best thing to do is go to bed. There are three friendly pensiones, all basic but clean and very cheap: *Casa del Viajero* (①) just southeast of the plaza, *Galindo* (①) on 5 Calle, and *La Uspanteka* (①) on 4 Calle. **Buses** for Uspantán, via Sacapulas, leave Quiché at 9am, 11am, noon and 2pm, returning at 11.30pm, 1am, 2am and 3am – a five-hour trip.

The Ixil triangle

High up on the spine of the Cuchumatanes, in a landscape of steep hills, bowl-shaped valleys and gushing rivers, is the **Ixil triangle**. Here the three small towns of Nebaj, Chajul and Cotzal, remote and extremely traditional, share a language spoken nowhere else in the country. This triangle of towns forms the hub of the **Ixil-speaking region**, a massive highland area which drops away towards the Mexican border and contains at least 100,000 inhabitants. These lush and rain-drenched hills are hard to reach and notoriously difficult to control, and today's relaxed atmosphere and highland charm conceal a bitter history of protracted conflict. It's an area that embodies some of the very best and the very worst characteristics of the Guatemalan highlands.

Before the arrival of the Spanish, the town of Nebaj was a sizeable centre, producing large quantities of jade, and possibly allied in some way to Zaculeu (see p.212). The Conquest was particularly brutal in these parts, however. After many setbacks, the Spanish managed to take Nebaj in 1530, and by then they were so enraged that not only was the town burnt to the ground but the survivors were condemned to slavery as punishment for their resistance. Things didn't improve with the coming of independence, when the Ixil people were regarded as a source of cheap labour and forced to work on the coastal plantations. Many never returned. Even today large numbers of local people are forced to migrate in search of work and conditions on many of the plantations remain appalling. In the late 1970s and early 1980s, the area was hit by waves of horrific violence as it became the main theatre of operation for the **EGP** (the Guerrilla Army of the Poor). Caught up in the conflict, the people have suffered enormous losses, with the majority of the smaller villages destroyed by the army and their inhabitants herded into "protected" settlements. With the peace accords, a degree of normality has returned to the area and new villages are being rebuilt on the old sites.

Despite this terrible legacy, the fresh green hills are some of the most beautiful in the country and the three towns are friendly and accommodating, with a relaxed and distinctive atmosphere.

Nebaj

NEBAJ is the centre of Ixil country, a beautiful old town, by far the largest of the three, with white adobe walls and cobbled streets. The weaving done here is unusual and intricate, the finest examples being the women's *huipiles*, which are an artistic tangle of complex geometrical designs in superb greens, yellows, reds and oranges, worn with brilliant red *cortes* (skirts). On their heads, the women wear superb headcloths decorated with pompom tassles that they pile up above their heads; most men no longer wear traditional dress. You'll find an excellent shop, selling goods produced by the Ixil weaving co-operative, on the main square.

The small **market**, a block east of the church, is worth investigating. On Thursday and Sunday the numbers swell as traders visit from out of town with secondhand clothing from the USA, stereos from Taiwan and Korea and chickens, eggs, fruit and vegetables from the highlands. The town church is also worth a look, although it's fairly bare inside. If you're here for the second week in August, you'll witness the **Nebaj fiesta**, which includes processions, dances, drinking, fireworks and marathon marimba-playing.

Arrival and information

The **plaza** is the focal point for the community with the major shops, municipal buildings and police station around the square. The market and **bus terminal** are on 7 C nearby. The Bancafe **bank**, 2 Av 46, near the market (Mon–Fri 8.30am–4pm, Sat 9am–1pm), exchanges both cash and travellers' cheques; there's a new **Internet café** next door, with modern terminals, cheap rates and discounted international call facilities.

Getting to Nebaj is straightforward with **buses** from Santa Cruz del Quiché every ninety minutes between 8.30am and 4pm (4hr), plus a daily service from Huehuetenango every morning (6hr); alternatively, take a bus to Sacapulas and change there. **Leaving Nebaj** is more problematic with the schedules being subject to frequent changes: departures for Quiché are usually in the early hours, and the Huehuetenango bus generally leaves at 5am. Check at the terminal for the latest information and arrive early to grab a seat. **Pick-ups and trucks** supplement the buses; the best place to hitch south is on the road out of town, a little further past the *Hotel Ixil*.

Accommodation

You'll find little in the way of luxury in Nebaj, although what there is does have an inimitable charm and prices here are some of the lowest in the country. There are few street signs, so you'll probably have to rely on the gang of children who act as guides – none of the hotels in town is more than a few minutes' walk from the terminal.

Hospedaje Esperanza, northwest of the plaza. Friendly, simple but very basic for the price – and you'll have to pay extra for a hot shower. Not the best deal in town but a good place to stay if you're interested in learning to weave – ask the owner's daughter for lessons. ②.

Hospedaje Ilebal Tenam, three minutes from the plaza on the road to Chajul/Cotzal. Tremendous hospedaje with simple but very clean rooms, exhilaratingly hot showers and safe parking. ①.

Hospedaje Las Tres Hermanas, a block northwest of the plaza. Despite its damp rooms, ancient mattresses and shabby apperance, this is one of the most famous hotels in Guatemala. During the troubles of the 1970s and 1980s this place put up a virtual *Who's Who* of international and Guatemalan journalists, including Victor Perera, George Lovell and Ronald Wright. It is still run by two of the original three sisters, who must have some stories to tell. ①.

Hotel Ixil, on the main road south out of town. The large, bare rooms are a little on the damp side, though the setting is pleasant, around a courtyard in a nice old colonial house, and there's a warmish shower. Better quality rooms, with private bath and hot showers, are available in a nearby house if you ask the friendly staff. ①–②.

Hotel Posada de Don Pablo, one block west of the plaza, opposite *Irene's* comedor. Attractive hotel, with smallish but spotless, pine-trimmed rooms, comfortable beds, private bathrooms and safe parking. ③.

Nuevo Hotel Ixal, three blocks south of the plaza. Good, secure little hotel with a charming courtyard. The pleasing rooms have private baths, and those on the upper floor enjoy mountain views. ②.

Posada Maya Ixil, four minutes northwest of the plaza, just off the road to Chajul/Cotzal. Excellent new hotel, easily the smartest in town, with real character. The large, comfortable rooms come with private bath and are decorated with vibrant local textiles and rustic furniture and pottery. ③.

Eating

The best **comedor** in town is *Irene's*, just off the main square, with several others in the plaza itself. The *Maya-Inca* on 5 C is owned by a friendly Peruvian/Guatemalan couple and serves delicious Peruvian and local dishes, though the portions are small, while there are reasonable pizzas at *Cesar's* on 2 Av opposite Bancafe. In addition, there's always something to eat at the market. For entertainment, most of the raving in town is courtesy of Nebaj's burgeoning neo-Pentecostal church, with four-hour services involving much wailing and gnashing of teeth.

Walks around Nebaj

There are several beautiful **walks** in the hills surrounding Nebaj, with one of the most interesting taking you to the village of **ACUL**, two hours away. Starting from the church in Nebaj, cross the plaza and turn to the left, taking the road that goes downhill between a shop and a comedor. At the bottom of the dip it divides: take the right-hand fork and head out of town along a dirt track. The track switchbacks up a steep hillside, and heads over a narrow pass into the next valley, where it drops down into Acul.

The village was one of the original so-called "model villages" into which people were herded after their homes had been destroyed by the army. If you walk on through the village and out the other side, you arrive at the Finca San Antonio, run by an Italian family who have lived here for more than fifty years, making some of the country's best cheese, which they sell at pretty reasonable prices.

A second, shorter walk takes you to a beautiful little **waterfall**, La Cascada de Plata, about an hour from Nebaj. Take the road to Chajul and turn left just before it crosses the bridge, a kilometre or two outside Nebaj. Don't be fooled by the smaller version you'll come to shortly before the main set of falls.

San Juan Cotzal and Chajul

To visit the other two towns in the Ixil triangle, it's best to time your visit to coincide with **market days**, when there's more traffic around: Cotzal is on Wednesday and Saturday; Chajul on Tuesday and Friday; and Nebaj on Sunday. **Buses** run to an irregular schedule, but on Sunday transport returns to both Cotzal and Chajul from Nebaj after 10am. Pick-ups supplement the buses. Look out too for aid-agency and MINUGUA (United Nations) 4WDs. It's certainly possible to visit both towns in one day from Nebaj if you get an early start.

SAN JUAN COTZAL is closer to Nebaj, up to an hour and a half away, depending on the state of the road. The town is set in a gentle dip in the valley, sheltered somewhat beneath the Cuchumatanes and often wrapped in a damp blanket of mist. Cotzal attracts very few Western travellers, so you may find that many people assume you're an aid worker or attached to an evangelical church.

Intricate turquoise *huipiles* are worn by the Maya women in Cotzal, who also weave bags and rope from the fibres of the maguey plant. There's little to do in the town itself but there is some great hill-walking close by. If you want to **stay**, there's a small and very basic unmarked pensión called *Don Polo* (②) two blocks from the church, or you may find the *farmacia* in the corner of the plaza will rent you a room. For **eating**, the *La Maguey* restaurant, housed in someone's front room a block behind the church, serves up reasonable, if bland, food. **Buses** should return to Nebaj daily at 6am and 1am; at other times you'll have to hitch.

Last but by no means least of the Ixil settlements is **CHAJUL**. Made up almost entirely of old adobe houses, with wooden beams and red-tiled roofs blackened by the smoke of cooking fires, it is also the most determinedly traditional and least bilingual of the Ixil towns. The women of Chajul wear earrings made of old coins strung up on lengths of wool and dress entirely in red, filling the streets with colour – you'll see them washing their scarlet *cortes* and *huipiles* at the stream that cuts through the middle of the village. Here boys still use blowpipes to hunt small birds, a skill that dates from the earliest of times but is now little used elsewhere.

The colonial church, a massive structure with huge wooden beams and gold leaf decoration, is home to the **Christ of Golgotha** and the target of a large pilgrimage on the second Friday of Lent, a particularly good time to be here. If you want somewhere to **stay** for the night, the *Hospedaje Cristina* (①) initially looks a pretty depressing option, though the upstairs rooms are OK; alternatively, there's the basic but clean *Hospedaje Esperanza* (①), close to the church. Some local families also rent out beds in their houses to the steady trickle of travellers now coming to Chajul; you won't have to look for them, they will find you; alternatively, ask at the post office, where one of the workers rents out rooms.

A number of unscheduled trucks bump along the two-hour route between Nebaj and Chajul, and on **market** days (Tues & Fri) there are regular morning **buses** from 4am. Return buses leave at 11.30am and 12.30pm, and there's usually a **truck** at 3.30pm (you'll share the covered trailer with firewood and vegetables – not recommended for anyone who is claustrophobic.) You can also **walk** here from San Juan Cotzal, two to three hours away through the spectacular Ixil countryside. Follow the unpaved road that branches off to the main Nebaj–Cotzal road just before you enter Cotzal. The final uphill part of the walk is quite tough, especially if the sun is shining.

Lago de Atitlán

Lake Como, it seems to me, touches the limit of the permissibly picturesque; but Atitlán is Como with the additional embellishments of several immense volcanoes. It is really too much of a good thing. After a few days of this impossible landscape one finds oneself thinking nostalgically of the English Home Counties.

Aldous Huxley, *Beyond the Mexique Bay* (1934).

Whether or not you share Huxley's refined sensibilities, there's no doubt that **Lago de Atitlán** is astonishingly beautiful. Most people find themselves captivated by its scenic excesses – indeed, the effect is so overwhelming that a handful of gringo devotees have been rooted to its shores since the 1960s. The lake itself is an irregular shape, with three main inlets. It measures 18km by 12km at its widest point, and shifts through an astonishing range of blues, steely greys and greens as the sun moves across the sky. Hemmed in on all sides by steep hills and massive volcanoes, it's some 320m (nearly 1000 feet) deep.

Another astonishing aspect of Atitlán is the strength of Maya culture evident in its lakeside settlements, still some of the most intensely traditional villages in Guatemala,

San José
Chacayá

Sololá

Santa Lucía
Utatlán

Santa Cruz
La Laguna

San Jorge
La Laguna

San Andrés
Semetabaj

Jaibalito
Tzununá

Paxanax

Panajachel

San Marcos
La Laguna

San Pablo La Laguna

Santa Catarina
Palopó

Godínez

San Antonio
Palopó

Santa María
Visitacion

Lago de Atitlán

San Pedro
La Laguna

San Juan
La Laguna

*Volcán
San Pedro
3020 m*

CERRO DE ORO

Agua Escondida

Santiago
Atitlán

San Lucas
Tolimán

*Volcán Tolimán
3158 m*

*Volcán Atitlán
3537 m*

Pochuta

LAGO DE ATITLÁN

0   5 km

Cocales (25 km) & Carretera al Pacífico

despite the thousands of tourists that pour in here from Europe and North America every year. **San Antonio Palopó**, **Santiago Atitlán** and, above the lake, **Sololá** are some of the very few villages in the entire country where Maya men still wear traditional costume, and two languages, **Tz'utujil** and **Kaqchikel**, are spoken on the lake's shores.

There are thirteen villages on the shores of the lake, with many more in the hills behind, ranging from the cosmopolitan resort-style **Panajachel** to tiny, isolated **Tzununá**. The villages are mostly subsistence farming communities and it's easy to hike and boat around the lake staying in a different one each night. The area has only recently attracted large numbers of tourists and for the moment things are still fairly undisturbed, but some of the new pressures are decidedly threatening. The increase in population has also had a damaging impact on the shores of the lake, as the desperate need to cultivate more land leads to deforestation and accompanying soil erosion.

You'll probably reach the lake through Panajachel, which makes a good base for exploring the surrounding area. "Pana" has an abundance of cheap hotels and restaurants and is well served by buses. To get a real sense of a more typical Atitlán village,

---

TRANSPORT ON THE LAKE

All lakeside villages are served by small fast boats called **lanchas**. Lanchas do not run to a fixed schedule but depart when the owner has enough passengers to cover fuel costs, so you may have to wait around a while, sometimes up to an hour at quiet times of the year.

There are two **piers** in Panajachel. The pier at the end of Calle Rancho Grande is for Santa Catarina, San Antonio, San Lucas, Santiago Atitlán and lake tours. The second pier at the end of Calle del Embarcadero is for all villages on the northern side of the lake: Santa Cruz, Jaibalito, Tzununá and San Marcos; some services continue on to San Pablo, San Juan and San Pedro. There are also direct lanchas to San Pedro which cut straight across the lake in a white-knuckle twenty-minute ride. The last boats on all these routes leave around 6.30pm.

Unfortunately, **rip-offs** are the rule for tourists: you'll be asked for two or three times what locals normally pay, so unless you can convince the boat owners that you're a resident, expect to pay around US$1.30 per trip. Another scam is charging more for the last boat of the day. **Tours of the lake** (US$8–10), visting San Pedro, Santiago Atitlán and San Antonio Palopó, can be booked in virtually any travel agent (see p.195); all leave around 9am and return by 4pm.

---

however, travel by boat to Santiago Atitlán or San Antonió Palopó. **San Pedro La Laguna** is now the village with the most established travellers' "scene", and a surplus of extremely cheap hotels. **Santa Cruz** and **San Marcos** are the places to head for if you're seeking real peace and quiet, and there are good hikes on this side of the lake.

All things Atitlán seem to be covered by the excellent **Web site** *www.atitlan.com*, including good accommodation options, and plenty of historical and cultural information.

Sololá

Perched on a natural balcony overlooking the lake, **SOLOLÁ** is a fascinating place, ignored by the majority of travellers. In common with only a few other towns, it has parallel *indígena* and *ladino* governments and is probably the largest Maya town in the country, with the vast majority of the people still wearing traditional costume.

The town itself isn't much to look at: a wide central plaza with a recently restored clock tower on one side and a modern church on the other. However, its **Friday market** is one of Central America's finest – a mesmeric display of colour and commerce. From as early as 5am the plaza is packed, drawing traders from all over the highlands, as well as thousands of local Sololá Maya, the women covered in striped red cloth and the men in their outlandish "space cowboy" shirts, woollen aprons and wildly embroidered trousers. There's another smaller market on Tuesday. Another interesting time to visit Sololá is on Sunday, when the *cofradres*, the elders of the Maya religious hierarchy, parade through the streets in ceremonial costume to attend the 10am Mass.

Panajachel

Ten kilometres beyond Sololá, from which it's separated by a precipitous descent, is **PANAJACHEL**. Over the years, what was once a small Maya village has become something of a resort, with a sizeable population of long-term foreign residents whose numbers are swollen in the winter by an influx of North American seasonal migrants and a flood of tourists. Panajachel was a premier hippie hangout back in the 1960s and 1970s and developed a bad reputation amongst some sections of Guatemalan society as a haven for drug-taking gringo drop-outs. Today "Pana" is much more integrated into the tourism mainstream and is as popular with Guatemalans and other Central Americans as Westerners. The lotus-eaters and crystal-gazers have not all deserted Panajachel, however. Many have re-invented themselves as (vaguely) conscientious capitalists who own restaurants and export *típica* clothing. In many ways, it's this **gringo** crowd that gives the town its modern character and identity.

Not so long ago (although it seems an entirely different age) Panajachel was a quiet little village of **Kaqchikel** Maya, whose ancestors were settled here after the Spanish crushed a force of Tz'utujil warriors on the site. Today the old village has been enveloped by the new building boom, but it still retains a traditional feel, and most of the Maya continue to farm in the river delta behind the town. The Sunday market, bustling with people from all around the lake, remains oblivious to the tourist invasion.

For travellers, Panajachel is one of those inevitable destinations. It's a comfortable base for exploring the lake and central highlands, and, although no one ever owns up to actually liking it, everyone seems to stay for a while. The old village is still attractive and, although most of the new building is fairly nondescript, its lakeside setting is superb. The main **daytime activity** is either shopping – weaving from all over Guatemala is sold with daunting persistence in the streets here, but you'll need to bargain hard as prices can be high – or simply hanging out. There's an amazing selection of places to eat and drink or surf the net, plus reasonable swimming and sunbathing at the **public beach**, where you can also rent a kayak for a few hours (mornings are usually much calmer) or scuba-dive with ATI Divers (see p.201). Alternatively, if you're seduced by the bohemiam ambience and easy-going pace of lakeside life, Panajachel now boasts a number of new language schools where you can **study Spanish** (see p.133).

Arrival, information and accommodation

The bus drops you beside the Banco Inmobiliario, very close to the main drag, C Santander, which runs down to the lakeshore. Straight ahead, up C Principal, is the old village. The **tourist office** (Mon–Sat 9am–5pm; ☎762 1392) is on the lakeshore, with English-speaking staff, basic hotel information, and boat and bus schedules. There are a dozen or so **Internet** cafés in Pana and rates are very cheap, at around US\$1.40 an hour. Amongst the best are the *Green Earth,* midway along Calle Santander, and *Café Pulcinella* at C Principal 0–72.

The streets of Panajachel overflow with cheap **hotels**, and there are plenty of "**rooms**". If you have a tent, first choice is the *Campaña* **campsite** (☎762 2479; US\$2 per person), on the corner of the road to Santa Catarina and C del Cementerio, over the river bridge. Here, happy campers will find kitchen and storage facilities and there are also sleeping bags and tents for rent. Don't bother camping at the public beach: your stuff will be ripped off.

BUDGET

Casa Linda, down an alley off the top of Calle Santander. Popular backpackers' retreat: the central garden is undeniably beautiful, but the rooms, some with private bath, are a shade pricey for a hospedaje. ②–③.

Hospedaje Eli, Callejón del Pozo, off Calle de los Árboles (☎762 0148). Ten clean, cheap rooms overlooking a pretty little garden in a quiet location. ①.

Hospedaje Montufar, down an alley off the top of Calle Santander (☎762 0406). Quiet location and the rooms are cleaned with true evangelical zeal by a very accommodating family. Triples also available. ②.

Hospedaje Santander, Calle Santander (☎762 1304, *www.atitlan.com/roomssantander.htm*). Leafy courtyard, friendly owners and clean, cheap rooms, some with private bath, though hot showers cost a little extra. ①–②.

Hospedaje Villa Lupita, Callejón El Tino (☎762 1201). Impressive new family-run hotel on a quiet alley close to the church. Fourteen excellent-value rooms, all with bedside lights, rugs and mirrors, some with private bath. There's also a sun terrace and free purified water. ②–③.

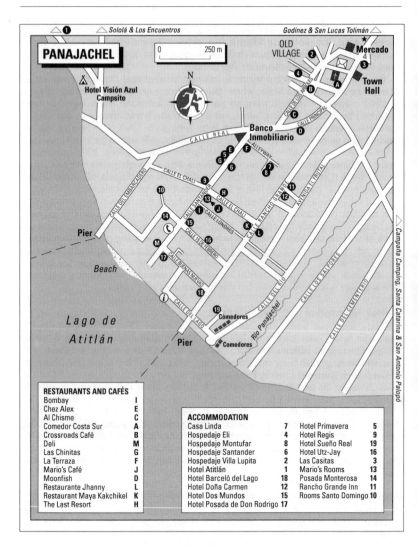

RESTAURANTS AND CAFÉS

Bombay	I
Chez Alex	E
Al Chisme	C
Comedor Costa Sur	A
Crossroads Café	B
Deli	M
Las Chinitas	G
La Terraza	F
Mario's Café	J
Moonfish	D
Restaurante Jhanny	L
Restaurant Maya Kakchikel	K
The Last Resort	H

ACCOMMODATION

Casa Linda	7	Hotel Primavera	5
Hospedaje Eli	4	Hotel Regis	9
Hospedaje Montufar	8	Hotel Sueño Real	19
Hospedaje Santander	6	Hotel Utz-Jay	16
Hospedaje Villa Lupita	2	Las Casitas	3
Hotel Atitlán	1	Mario's Rooms	13
Hotel Barceló del Lago	18	Posada Monterosa	14
Hotel Doña Carmen	12	Rancho Grande Inn	11
Hotel Dos Mundos	15	Rooms Santo Domingo	10
Hotel Posada de Don Rodrigo	17		

Hotel Doña Carmen, just off Calle Rancho Grande (☎762 2035, *losgarcia10@hotmail.com*). Nicely situated in a quiet corner of town, this pleasant family-run place offers simple, clean budget rooms, some with private bath, set off a huge shady garden. ②.

Hotel Sueño Real, Calle Ramós (☎762 0608, fax 762 1097). Excellent new hotel, very close to the lakeshore in a quiet location and owned by a friendly, helpful family. The seven attractive, secure rooms – all with private bath – are superb value for money. ③.

Las Casitas, Calle Principal, near the market (☎ & fax 762 1224, *hotelcasitas@yahoo.com*). Very clean, friendly and safe, with tastefully decorated rooms sporting good-quality beds and reading lamps; most also have private bath. There's also free email access for guests, and an upstairs dormitory is planned. ③.

Mario's Rooms, Calle Santander (☎762 1313). Good choice of pleasant, very clean rooms, some airy and light with private bath, others are more basic. Hot water is available on request for a few quetzales. ②–③.

Posada Monterosa, Calle Monterrey (☎762 0055). Attractive little hotel with ten spotless rooms, all with pine furnishings and private bath, and safe car parking. ③.

Rooms Santo Domingo, down a path off Calle Monterrey (☎762 0236). One of the cheapest places in town, set well away from the hustle. Very simple wooden rooms (①) all face a charming little garden, with more expensive options (③) with private bath upstairs.

MODERATE TO EXPENSIVE

Hotel Atitlán, on the lakeside, 1km west of the centre (☎ & fax 762 1441 or 762 1416, *www.atitlan .com/hotelatitlan.htm*). The swankiest hotel in the Panajachel area with a stunning lakeside location, lovely gardens and a swimming pool. Rooms are very comfortable and tastefully decorated. ⑨.

Hotel Barceló del Lago, right on the lakeshore (☎762 1555, fax 762 1562, *www.atitlan.com/barcelo .htm*). Opulent, all-inclusive colossus complete with pool, Jacuzzi and gym. Very corporate, "international" flavour – only the great volcano views remind you you're in Guatemala. Doubles US$110 low season, US$162 high season. ⑨.

Hotel Dos Mundos, Calle Santander (☎762 2078, fax 762 0127, *www.atitlan.com/dos_mundos.htm*). Italian-owned hotel, just off the main drag, offering comfortable rooms set to one side of a private garden, where there's also a small swimming pool; breakfast is included. The attached *Lanterna* restaurant has authentic Italian cuisine at moderate prices. ⑥.

Hotel Posada de Don Rodrigo, Calle Santander, facing the lake (☎ & fax 762 2322 or 762 2329, *www.centramerica.com/posadadedonrodrigo*). Colonial-style hotel by the lakeside, with a large outdoor pool, sauna and squash court. Most of the accommodation in the main block is on the small side, so try to book a room in the superb new wing (rooms 301–311) – they're supremely spacious and boast bathtubs and stunning volcano views. ⑧.

Hotel Primavera, C Santander (☎762 2052, fax 762 0171, *www.atitlan.com/primavera.htm*). Stylistically, the design of this minimalist hotel is almost revolutionary for Guatemala: all blond wood, magnolia walls and a notable absence of típica textiles or rustic clichés. Elegant rooms, a tiny Zen-like garden zone and a classy restaurant, *Chez Alex*, downstairs, is very good value too. ⑤.

Hotel Regis, Calle Santander 3–47 (☎762 1149, fax 762 1152, *www.atitlan.com/regis.htm*). Age-old colonial-style establishment with attractive individual bungalows and rooms, all with cable TV, though the real attraction is the wonderful natural hot spring. ⑥.

Hotel Utz-Jay, Calle 15 de Febrero (☎762 0217, fax 762 1358, *www.atitlan.com/utz-jay.htm*). Oustanding new hotel set in a large, tranquil garden, with five very stylish adobe-and-stone houses (all sleep up to four and have private bath), decorated with nice homely touches. In-house *tuj* herbal sauna, plus a selection of excellent tours available. Book ahead, though there may be more rooms shortly as the owners are busy constructing accommodation next door. ④.

Rancho Grande Inn, Calle Rancho Grande (☎762 2255, fax 762 2247, *www.atitlan.com /ranchogrande.htm*). A long-standing Panajachel institution with very attractive, nicely appointed bungalows, superbly kept gardens and helpful staff. Breakfast included. ⑥.

Eating, drinking and entertainment

Panajachel has an abundance of **restaurants**, all catering to the cosmopolitan tastes of its floating population. You'll have no trouble finding tasty Chinese, Italian, Mexican and Mediterranean dishes. For really cheap and authentically Guatemalan food there are plenty of comedores on and just off the new beach promenade and close to the market.

CAFÉS AND RESTAURANTS

Al Chisme, Calle de los Árboles. A smart, European-style restaurant and bar adorned with black-and-white photographs of former customers. The food – including bagels, sandwiches, crêpes and pasta – is delicious but a little pricey. Closed Wed.

Bombay, halfway down Calle Santander. Eclectic vegetarian food which, despite the name, has little Indian about it, instead featuring offerings such as Indonesian *gado-gado,* epic pitta-bread sandwiches (try the falafel), and organic coffee, plus a US$3 daily set menu.

Chez Alex, halfway along Calle Santander. Unquestionably the flashest place in town, with an over-designed peach interior and gilt-tinted plates and cutlery. Heavyweight menu, majoring in European classics – the food's good, though not outstanding. Expensive.

Comedor Costa Sur, near the church in the old town. Clean and attractive comedor, loudly bedecked with Mexican blankets and serving great breakfasts, lunchtime dishes and *licuados*.

Crossroads Café, Calle del Campanario 0–27. Easily the finest coffee in town: selected, blended and roasted by perfectionists, and with a multitude of combinations and flavourings, including lattes and mochas, plus real hot chocolate and fresh pastries. Closed Mon and for siesta 1–2pm.

Deli, southern end of Calle Santander. Excellent range of healthy meals, snacks and drinks, including salads, sandwiches, pastries, bagels, cakes, wine and tea, in a pretty garden setting. Service is friendly, but often lethargic.

Las Chinitas, towards the northern end of Calle Santander. Excellent pan-Asian cuisine in a pretty patio setting. Nonyan (Malay-Chinese) cooking is the main draw, with Thai and Japanese dishes at moderate prices. Closed Mon.

La Terraza, northern end of Calle Santander. One of the finest restaurants on the lake, though quite formal and expensive, with a classy European menu plus a few Asian-influenced dishes.

Mario's Café, halfway down Calle Santander. A limited range of budget food: huge salads, delicious yoghurt and pancakes.

Moonfish upper floor, C Principal 0–72. Scruffy-chic bohemian dive popular with travelling scenesters, with a fine line-up of inexpensive *tempe* burritos and sandwiches, plus yoghurt *licuados*. Eclectic sounds – drum 'n' bass, reggae, rock – plus live music some nights.

Restaurante Jhanny, halfway down Calle Rancho Grande. Ignore the fairylights and head inside for a superb Guatemalan-style *menú del día* (US$2.50); tables are nicely arranged around a little garden.

Restaurant Maya Kakchikel, C el Chali 2–25. Bright little comedor, great for Guatemalan food, excellent filling breakfasts and crêpes.

The Last Resort, Calle el Chali. Looks vaguely like an English pub, but does the best American buffet breakfasts in town, along with pasta, steaks and vegetarian dishes, all served in huge portions.

NIGHTLIFE

Panajachel has a gregarious party spirit at weekends and during the main holiday season, when many young Guatemalans head to the lake to drink and flirt, though things are less lively at other times. The town's prime bar and dance scene is centred around the southern end of Calle de los Árboles, where there's a cluster of busy places including the long-running *Circus Bar, Porque No* and *El Aleph* for **live music**, plus the *Chapiteau* **nightclub**. For a less frenetic environment head for *Moonfish* or *The Last Resort* (see "Cafés and Restaurants", above), or *Ubu's Cosmic Cantina*, on Calle de los Árboles, where there's a big screen for sports fans, movie buffs and news addicts. Finally, there are occasional **poetry** recitals at *Delante's Bookshop* off Calle Buenas Nuevas, video **movies** at Carrot Chic and Turquoise Buffalo cinemas on Calle de los Árboles, and a **pool hall** in the old village, near the post office.

Listings

Banks and exchange Banco Inmobiliario, at C Santander and C Principal (Mon–Fri 9am–7pm, Sat 9am–12.30pm), or Banco Industrial, on Calle Santander, which has a 24hr ATM for Visa card holders. Try the AT travel agency or *Hotel Regis*, both on Calle Santander, for Mastercard transactions.

Bicycle rental Moto Servicio Queche, C de los Árboles and C Principal, rents mountain bikes for US$1 an hour, US$5 a day.

Bookstores Delante, down an alley off Calle Buenas Vistas, has a friendly atmosphere and a very comprehensive selection of secondhand books. The Gallery, on Calle de los Árboles, stocks a reasonable choice of secondhand titles and a few interesting new books in English.

Laundry Lavandería Automatico, C de los Árboles 0–15 (Mon–Sat 7.30am–6pm), US$3.50 for a full load washed, dried and folded.

Medical care Dr Edgar Barreno speaks good English; his surgery is down the first street that branches to the right off Calle de los Árboles (☎762 1008).

Motorbike rental Moto Servicio Queche, C de los Árboles and C Principal (☎762 2089), rents 185cc bikes for US$6 an hour, US$25 for 24 hours, US$100 for the week.

Pharmacy Farmacia La Unión, Calle Santander.

Police On the plaza in the old village (☎762 1120).

Post office In the old village, down a side street beside the church (Mon–Fri 8am–4.30pm), or try Get Guated Out on Calle de los Árboles (☎762 0595, *gguated@c.net.gt*) for bigger shipments.

Telephone To make a phone call or send a fax, check first with businesses in Calle Santander for the best rates; many advertise discounted calls. Otherwise, Telgua (daily 7am–midnight) is near the junction of C Santander and C 15 de Febrero.

Travel Agents Rainbow Travel, C Principal near the junction with C Santander (☎762 1302), is a good all-rounder, with competitive international flight prices; Sevicios Turisticos Atitlán, C Santander, near C 14 de Febrero (☎762 2075, fax 762 2246, *www.atitlan.com*), is another recomended agent.

Panajachel to San Antonio Palopó

On the eastern shore of the lake, backed up against the slopes, are a couple of villages, the first of which, **SANTA CATARINA PALOPÓ**, is just 4km from Panajachel. The people of Santa Catarina used to live almost entirely by fishing and trapping crabs, but the introduction of black bass into the lake to create a sport-fishing industry has put an end to all that, as the bass eat the smaller fish. They've now turned to farming and migratory work, with many of the women travelling to Panajachel and Antigua to peddle their weaving. The women wear stunning *huipiles*, in vibrant turquoise and purple zigzags.

Much of the shoreline as you leave Santa Catarina has been bought and developed, and great villas, ringed by impenetrable walls and razor wire, have come to dominate the lakeside. Here you'll find the landmark *Hotel Villa Santa Catarina* (☎762 1291, fax 762 2013, *villasdeguatemala.com*; ⑦), which enjoys a prime lakeside plot, with 31 very comfortable rooms, two banqueting halls, a pool and restaurant. Beyond here, the road winds around the shore for another 3km until you reach the upmarket *San Tomas Bella Vista Retreat* (☎762 1566, *www.santomasatitlanlodge.guate.com*; ⑦), with fourteen attractive bungalows, all boasting great views, plus a pool and restaurant.

Another 5km brings you to **SAN ANTONIO PALOPÓ**, a larger and more traditional village, squeezed in beneath a steep hillside. Because it is on the tour-group itinerary, the villagers have become a bit pushy in selling their weavings. But, despite this, the village is quite interesting and certainly very traditional. The hillsides above San Antonio are well irrigated and terraced, reminiscent of rice paddies, and most men wear the village *traje* of red shirts with vertical stripes and short woollen kilts. Women wear almost identical shirts, made of the same fabric with subtle variations to the collar design. The whitewashed central church is also worth a look; just to the left of the entrance are two ancient bells.

Regular **pick-ups** run between Panajachel and San Antonio, passing through Santa Catarina and leaving approximately every thirty minutes (the last one returns to Panajachel from San Antonio at 5pm) – and of course there are **boats** (see p.190).

If you decide **to stay** in San Antonio there are two options: the fairly upmarket *Hotel Terrazas del Lago* (☎7621288; ⑤), down by the water, with beautiful views, or the very simple but clean pensión (①) owned by Juan López Sánchez near the entrance to the village. Try the comedor below the church for a cheap **meal**.

Santiago Atitlán

On the opposite side of the lake from Panajachel, **SANTIAGO ATITLÁN** is set to one side of a sheltered horseshoe inlet, overshadowed by the cones of the San Pedro, Atitlán and Tolimán volcanoes. It's the largest and most important of the lakeside villages, and also one of the most traditional, being the main centre of the Tz'utujil-speaking Maya. At the time of the Conquest, the Tz'utujil had their fortified capital, **Chuitinamit-Atitlán**, on the slopes of San Pedro, while the bulk of the population lived spread out around the site of today's village. Alvarado and his crew, needless to say, destroyed the capital and massacred its inhabitants, assisted this time by a force of Kaqchikel Maya, who arrived at the scene in some three hundred canoes.

Today, Santiago is an industrious but relaxed sort of place. During the day the town becomes fairly commercial, its **main street**, which runs from the dock to the plaza, lined with weaving shops. There's nothing like the Panajachel overkill here, but the persistence of underage gangs trying to sell weavings and artesanía can still be a bit much. By mid-afternoon, once the ferries have left, things revert to normal and the whole village becomes a lot more friendly. There's not a lot to do in Santiago other than stroll around soaking up the atmosphere, or enjoying the market – Friday is the main day, though there's a smaller event on Sundays.

The old colonial Catholic **church** is well worth a look, however. The huge altarpiece which was carved when the church was under *cofradía* control culminates in the shape of a mountain peak and a cross. The cross symbolizes the Maya world tree, which supports the source of all life, including people, animals and the corn ears that you can see on the cross. In the middle of the floor is a small hole which Atitecos believe to be the centre of the world. The church is also home to a stone memorial commemorating Father Stanley Rother, an American priest who served in the parish from 1968 to 1981. Father Rother was a committed defender of his parishioners in an era when, in his own words, "shaking hands with an Indian has become a political act". Branded a Communist by President García, he was assassinated by a paramilitary death squad like hundreds of his parishioners before and after him. His body was returned to his native Oklahoma for burial but his heart was removed and buried in the church.

As is the case in many other parts of the Guatemalan highlands, the Catholic Church in Santiago is locked in bitter rivalry with several evangelical sects, who are building churches here at an astonishing rate. Their latest construction, right beside the lake, is the largest structure in town. Folk Catholicism also plays an important role in the life of Santiago and the town is well known as one of the few places where Maya still pay homage to **Maximón**, the drinking and smoking saint. Any child will take you to see him; just ask for the "Casa de Maximón".

The traditional **costume** of Santiago, still worn a fair amount, is both striking and unusual. The men wear long shorts which, like the women's *huipiles*, are striped white and purple and intricately embroidered with birds and flowers. The women also wear a *xk'ap*, a band of red cloth approximately 10m long, wrapped around their heads, which has the honour of being depicted on the 25 centavo coin. Sadly this headcloth is going out of use and on the whole you'll probably only see it at fiestas and on market days, and then worn mainly by older women.

Practicalities

Boats to Santiago leave from the beach in Panajachel at 5.45am, 9.30am, 11.30am and 3pm – the trip takes about an hour – but there are also unscheduled lancha services at other times. The village is also astonishingly well connected by **bus** with almost everywhere except Panajachel (see opposite).

As for **accommodation**, a backpackers' favourite is the *Hotel Chi-Nim-Ya* (☎721 7131; ①–②), where some rooms have private bath; it's on the left as you enter the village from the lake. The good-value *Hotel Tzutuhil*, in the centre of town (☎721 7174; ②), is a five-storey concrete building with spectacular views from the top floor and a restaurant. For something special, there are a number of good options, all can be reached by road or water-taxi from the dock. The *Posada de Santiago*, on the lakeshore 1km south of the town (☎ & fax 721 7167, *www.atitlan.com/posada.htm*; ⑥), is a luxury American-owned bed and breakfast, with rooms in stone cabins, each with its own log fire, a few budget rooms and a fine restaurant. A kilometre north of the dock, the *Bird House* (☎716 7440, *thebirdhousetk@hotmail.com*; ③–④) is another good choice, with attractive rooms and apartments, nice lakeside gardens, a library and great home-made food. About 500m further north, *Hotel Bambú* (☎416 2122; ⑤) has beautiful thatch-roofed stone bungalows and rooms, plus an excellent restaurant with Spanish specialities. Next door, there's quite a scene developing at *Las Milpas* (☎416 3395, *las_milpas @hotmail.com*; ③), a great new bohemiam retreat-cum-hotel run by an ex-Grateful Dead roadie, with four comfortable cabañas, camping (US$4 per person), a hot tub and sauna, tasty vegetarian food, plenty of live music and full-moon cruises.

There are three **restaurants** at the entrance to the village, just up from the dock, all fairly similar. In the centre of the village you can eat at the *Hotel Tzutuhil* or, if you really want to dine in style, head out to one of hotel restaurants above.

Leaving Santiago, buses depart from the central plaza and head via Cocales to Guatemala City (6 daily between 2.30am and 2pm). For Panajachel there are four daily boats (plus supplementary lanchas); there are nine daily boats for San Pedro La Laguna between 6am and 3pm (40min).

San Pedro La Laguna

Around the other side of Volcán San Pedro is the village of **SAN PEDRO LA LAGUNA**, which has now usurped Panajachel as the pivotal centre of Guatemala's travelling "scene". It isn't Goa, but it does have a distinctively bohemian feel about it. Things certainly seem very mellow here but it hasn't always been so. Crack cocaine arrived in San Pedro in the early 1990s and the locals got so fed up with wasted gringos that they wrote to a national newspaper demanding that the freaks get out of town. Today things seem to have settled down again and, despite the obvious culture clash between locals (most of whom are evangelical) and travellers, everyone seems to get on reasonably well. San Pedro has also started to establish itself as a **language school** centre in recent years, the beautiful location drawing increasing numbers of students, though the quality of tutition is pretty variable at present (see p.133).

Again, the setting is spectacular, with Volcán San Pedro rising to the east and a ridge of steep hills running behind the village. To the left of the main beach, as you look towards the lake, a line of huge white boulders juts out into the water – an ideal spot for an afternoon of swimming and sunbathing. Two sets of **thermal pools**, adjacent to each other halfway between the two docks, offer further opportunities to relax. The best of these, Thermal Waters (☎206 9658; open late afternoon only; US$2.50 per person), also offers fine organic vegetarian food and camping.

There are two docks in San Pedro. All **boats** from Panajachel and villages on the north side of the lake, including Santa Cruz and San Marcos, arrive and depart from the Panajachel dock on the north side of town, while boats from Santiago Atitlán use a separate dock to the southeast, a ten-minute walk away. It's also easy to travel by **bus** to San Pedro from the Guatemala City's Zona 4 terminal: there are three daily buses between noon and 4pm; buses return from San Pedro plaza at 3am, 4am and 7am; the journey time is 3hr 15min.

Most of the village is based around the Catholic church in the centre of town, where you'll find the marketplace (busiest on Thurs and Sun), post office and, a block to the south, Banrural **bank** (Mon–Fri 9am–5.30pm, Sat 9am–12.30pm), which will change travellers' cheques. There are very few phone lines in town, and consequently just one place, Solar Pools, between the docks, currently offering international call and **email** facilities – most visitors head into Panajachel, where there are much speedier and cheaper connections.

Volcán San Pedro, which towers above the village to a height of some 3020m, is largely coated with tropical forest and can be climbed in four to five hours. Most of the village guides are reliable – including Samuel Cumatz Batzin (☎762 2487) who can often be found at *Casa Elena* (see below) – and it's well worth using their services, as the foliage is dense and the route can be tricky to find. Get an early start in order to see the views at their best and avoid the worst of the heat. If you'd rather do something a little more relaxing, Excursion Big Foot (☎204 6267), just left of the Panajachel dock, rents out **horses** for US$2.50 an hour, **bicycles** for US$10 a day and **canoes** for US$2 for two hours.

Accommodation

San Pedro has some of the cheapest **accommodation** in all Latin America, with a number of basic, clean guest houses that almost all charge less than US$2 a person per night. There's nothing in the way of luxury. If you plan to stay around for a while then you might want to consider **renting a house**, which works out incredibly cheap.

Casa Elena, left after *Nick's Place*. Owned by a friendly Maya family, with nine tidy rooms with twin beds, some right on the lakeshore. ①.

Hotel Bella Vista, by the docks (turn left after *Nick's Place*). Decent budget hotel with really cheap rates and clean, bare rooms. The mattresses are foam slabs, though. ①.

Hotelito El Amanecer Sakcari, between the docks (☎812 1113). Friendly, family-run place with ten attractive tiled rooms, all with private bath, and most with wonderful lake views too. ②.

Hotel Mansión del Lago, right above the Panajachel dock (☎811 8172). Bulky, somewhat obtrusive new place, with spotless, excellent-value rooms that are unquestionably the smartest in town: all have nice pine beds, private bath and balcony areas with lake views. ②–③.

Hotel Ti'Kaaj, near the Santiago dock. Very basic rooms, but the lovely shady garden, replete with orange trees and hammocks, certainly helps compensate. ①.

Hotel Valle Azul, turn right at the Panajachel dock (☎207 7292). Hulking concrete monster of a hotel, but the views are excellent and the good-value rooms, some with private bath, are reasonable enough. ①–②.

Hotel Villa Sol, beside the Santiago Atitlán dock (☎334 0327, fax 360 0994). Plenty of space here, but the 42 clean, perfunctory rooms are set in somewhat souless twin-deck blocks. Bizarrely – despite the location – none enjoy lake views. ①–②.

Eating and drinking

The steady flow of gringo travellers has given San Pedro's **cafés** and **restaurants** a decidedly international flavour, and most places are also excellent value for money. Vegetarians are well catered for, though there are also a few typical Guatemalan comedores in the centre of the village and by the Santiago dock. The San Pedro **drinking** scene is centred around the English-owned *D'Noz* bar, above *Nick's Place*, where you'll find an eclectic musical selection, plus free video movies (nightly at 7pm) and tasty food. Between the docks there are more drinking holes, including the Dutch-run *Tony's Sports Bar* and *Torj's Bar* over the pathway. The guys at *D'Noz* also organize DJ-driven **full moon parties** on the lakeside close to San Pedro most months of the year, though events are sometimes cancelled in the rainy season.

Café Luna Azul, 400m west of the Panajachel dock. Wonderful lakeside location, with a good dock for swimming and sunning, plus great breakfasts, lunches and treats – try the chocolate fudge cake. Open daily 9am–4pm.

Comedor Francés, between the docks. Reasonably priced Gallic fare including coq-au-vin at less than US$2 and yummy crêpes.

Matahari, turn right from the Santiago dock. The best comedor in San Pedro, with a tasty line-up of Guatemalan dishes and amazingly good fries.

Nick's Place, by the Panajachel dock. Great-value grub (chicken and chips at US$2) and a lakefront location make this the most popular place in town. There's another branch serving Italian food beside the Santiago dock.

Pinocchio, between the two docks. Consistently good Italian, where you can feast on bruschetta and pasta in a pretty garden setting.

Restaurant Rosalinda, a short walk uphill from Santiago dock. Excellent comedor, with fresh lake fish, grilled meats and a warm welcome.

Restaurant Ti'Kaaj, opposite the hotel of the same name. Stunning views of the lake and volcanoes from the upper floor, and a lovely garden out front. Famous for its burgers, though it also does great breakfasts and pasta.

Tintin, between the docks. Pleasant patio setting and a delicious menu of pitta bread sandwiches, Thai and Indonesian dishes.

San Juan La Laguna

The northern side of Atitlán harbours a string of isolated villages, many inaccessible to cars. From San Pedro, a rough dirt road runs as far as Tzununá and from there a spectacular path continues all the way to Sololá via Santa Cruz. Most of the boats between San Pedro and Panajachel call at all the villages en route but the best way to see this string of isolated settlements is **on foot**: it makes a fantastic day's walk. A narrow strip of level land is wedged between the water and the steep hills most of the way, but where this disappears the path is cut into the slope, providing dizzying views of the lake below. To walk from San Pedro to Santa Cruz takes between five and six hours and if you want some real peace and quiet this is the section of the lake to head for. There are also some excellent **places to stay** in San Marcos, Jaibalito and Santa Cruz.

From San Pedro you follow a dirt road to **SAN JUAN LA LAGUNA**, just 2km or so away at the back of a sweeping bay surrounded by shallow beaches. The village specializes in the weaving of *petates*, mats made from lake reeds, and there's a large weaving co-op, Las Artesanías de San Juan, where they welcome visitors and have plenty of goods for sale – it's signposted on the left as you walk from the dock. On the other side of the street is the simple *Hospedaje Estrella del Lago* (①) with eleven secure rooms, none with private bath, while uphill, in the centre of the village, you'll find a quiet comedor, *Restaurant Chi'nimaya*, and a very under-used branch of *Nick's Place* which does American-style sandwiches and meals. Behind the church and basketball court, there's a shrine to **Maximón** (see p.176), the evil saint, dressed in local garb, though this shrine attracts fewer visitors here than those elsewhere, so you may want to bring him some liquor or a cigar. Leaving San Juan, you'll pass below the Tz'utujil settlement of **San Pablo La Laguna**, perched high above the lake a fifteen-minute walk away, and connected to the Pan-American highway by a torturous road. After this, the villages start shrinking considerably.

San Marcos La Laguna

Guatemala's premier New Age centre, the tiny village of **SAN MARCOS LA LAGUNA**, is about a two-hour walk from San Pedro, or a twenty-minute ride in one of the regular pick-ups that bump along the road between the villages. The land close to the lakeshore, densely wooded with banana, mango, jocote and avocado trees, is where San Marcos' bohemian hotels and guest houses have been senstively established, while the Maya village is centred on higher ground away from the shore – relationships between the two communities remain reasonably good. Apart from a huge new stone **church**, built to replace a colonial original destroyed in the 1976 earthquake, there are no sights in the Maya village.

San Marcos has a decidedly tranquil appeal – there's little in the way of partying and no bar scene at all. The main draw is the *Las Pirámides* yoga and meditation retreat (see "Accommodation", overleaf), with a surplus of auxiliary practioners and masseurs, plus the requisite organic bakery and healing centre. There's excellent swimming from a number of wooden jetties by the lakeshore, and a mesmering view of Atitlán's three volcanoes, including a perspective of the double-coned summit of Tolimán, plus glimpses of the grey 3975m peak of Acatenango, over 50km to the east.

Accommodation

To **get to** any of the places listed below, get off at at the westernmost of San Marcos' two docks where *Posada Schumann* and *Las Pirámides* have jetties (look out for the mini pyramid): all accommodation is signposted from there.

El Paco Real (☎801 2297). Attractive French-owned place, with pleasant, well-constructed stone bungalows, some sleeping up to four, set in a garden dotted with chairs. No private bathrooms, but the communual facilities are kept spotless, and there's a terrific in-house restaurant too. ③.

Hotel Quetzal (☎306 5039). Good-value private rooms and a small dormitory in a sturdy-looking two-storey house. ②.

Hotel San Marcos. Six cheap but clean rooms in a concrete block, none with private bath. ②.

Las Pirámides (☎205 7151, *www.laspiramides.com.gt*). Meditation retreat centre set in leafy grounds, where monthly courses beginning the day after full moon (though you can also enrol on a daily or weekly basis) include hatha yoga, healing and meditation techniques, plus days of fasting and silence and plenty of esoteric pursuits. All accommodation is in comfortable pyramid cabañas, and there's delicious vegetarian food. US$10–12 per person per day including all courses but not food.

Posada Schumann (☎202 2216). Stylish, solar-powered hotel with a wonderful lakeside plot and accommodation in rooms or stone bungalows (sleeping between two and six); numbers 8 and 10 have stupendous volcano views. There's also a decent restaurant, a private wooden jetty for sunbathing and swimming, and a tiny, smoky, Maya-style sauna. ④–⑤.

Unicornio. Quirky English-Guatemalan-owned set-up with small A-frame huts in a nice garden, with a kitchen and sauna. Massages available. ②.

Eating

There's a limited choice of places to eat in San Marcos. Inexpensive Guatemalan food is available at the *Comedor Marquensita* and *Sonoma* close to the church, and you can get pretty decent pizza and pasta at *Rudy's Place* at the back of the village, though it's best to order in advance. Otherwise, any of the hotels closer to the lakeshore have restaurants attached, with superb but pricey French food at *El Paco Real*. There's also excellent healthy eating (including delicious sandwiches and salads) at *Las Pirámides*, while *Posada Schumann* also has a good menu.

Tzununá to Paxanax

Continuing east from San Marcos, it's a thirty-minute walk along a dirt road to the next lakeside village, **TZUNUNÁ**, where the women often run from oncoming strangers, sheltering behind the nearest tree in giggling groups. Here the road indisputably ends, giving way to a narrow path cut out of the steep hillside, which can be a little hard to follow as it descends to cross small streams and then climbs up again around the rocky outcrops. The next, slightly ragged-looking place is **JAIBALITO**, an isolated lakeside settlement nestling between soaring *milpa*-clad slopes. Though the village remains resolutely Kaqchikel – very little Spanish is spoken, and few women have ever journeyed much beyond Lago de Atitlán – the opening of two new hotels means that outside influence is growing. Almost lost amongst the coffee bushes, 70m north of the main pathway, the Norwegian-owned *Vulcano Lodge* (☎410 2237, *www.atitlan.com/vulcano.htm*) is tranquil and beautifully maintained, its well-tended garden bursting with bouganvillea and flowering shrubs and scattered with sun loungers and hammocks. There's a bright little restaurant decorated with antique *huipiles*, and a choice of spotless, comfortable double rooms (④) and very stylish two-bedroomed suites (⑥) with balconies, ideal for families.

Heading west, it's a steep five-minute walk up along the cliff path to the spectacularly sited *La Casa del Mundo* (☎204 5558, fax 762 2333, *www.atitlan.com/casamundo .htm*; rooms ④, suite ⑨). It's a simply magnificent place, the culmination of twelve years' work by the warm American host family, with a range of atmospheric accommodation including a budget room, doubles (rooms 1 and 3 have the best views), detached stone cabins, and a glorious suite with private Jacuzzi, kitchen and balcony. Guests can rent kayaks – the hotel boasts its own dock – and use the lakeside hot tub.

From Jaibalito it's around an hour to Santa Cruz along a glorious, easy-to-follow path gripping the steep hillside. Set well back from the lake on a shelf 100m or so above the water, **SANTA CRUZ LA LAGUNA** is the largest in this line of villages with a population of around 4000. If you arrive here by boat it may appear to be just a collection of **hotels**, as the village is higher up above the lake. There isn't much to see in Santa Cruz, apart from a fine sixteenth-century church, and most people spend their time here walking, swimming or just chilling out with a book. Alternatively, there's some excellent **hiking**, including a walk to a waterfall above the village football pitch, and another to Sololá along a spectacular path that takes around three hours.

On the shore, opposite a line of wooden jetties, you'll find the *Iguana Perdida* (*www.atitlan.com/iguana.htm*; ②–③), owned by an English-American couple, with undoubtedly the most convivial atmosphere in Lago de Atitlán. The rooms are fairly basic, ranging from dorms (US$2.50) to twin-bedded doubles, but it's the gorgeous, peaceful site overlooking the lake and volcanoes that really makes this place. Dinner (US$4.50) is a wholesome three-course communal affair. The *Iguana* is also home to Lago de Atitlán's only **dive school**, ATI Divers (in Panajachel ☎762 2646, *www.atitlan .com*), a professional PADI outfit that can train all levels up to assistant instructor. Next door is another good place, the slightly more expensive and comfortable *Hotel Arca de Noé* (☎306 4352, *www.atitlan.com/arcadenoe.htm*; small rooms ③, larger rooms ⑤), with a selection of attractive rooms, most with private bath, and uninterrupted views of the lake from the spacious terraced gardens. There's good home cooking here as well, with large breakfasts for US$4 and dinner for US$7. On the other side of the main dock, the *Posada Abaj* (*www.atitlan.com/abaj*; ④), offers beautiful, peaceful gardens, decent, though unexceptional, rooms and a restaurant. However, service standards are not always the highest, and perhaps consequently the hotel is less popular than others nearby.

Beyond Santa Cruz a lakeside path wriggles past luxury villas for a kilometre to the small bay of **Paxanax**, ringed by about twenty holiday homes, where a magnificent and superb-value luxury guest house, *Villa Sumaya* (☎762 0488; *www.villasumaya.com*; ⑤–⑥) enjoys stupendous lake views. All the seven rooms and one suite have sumptuous beds, stylish decor and balconies with hammocks, and there's a fine Mediterranean restaurant and a hot tub and sauna. Beyond Paxanax a path runs directly to Panajachel, though it's very hard to follow, and distraught walkers have been known to spend as long as seven hours scrambling through the undergrowth. Lanchas will call in at Paxanax if they see you waving from the pier beside *Villa Sumaya*, but as there's very little traffic from here it's often best to go back to Santa Cruz and pick up a boat from there.

Quetzaltenango and around

To the west of Lago de Atitlán, the highlands rise to form a steep-sided ridge topped by a string of forested peaks. On the far side of this is the **Quetzaltenango basin**, a sweeping expanse of level ground that forms the natural hub of the western highlands. It was here that the conquistador Pedro de Alvarado first struggled up into the highlands and came upon the abandoned city of Xelajú (near Quetzaltenango), entering it without any resistance. Six days later he and his troops fought the K'iche' in a decisive battle on the nearby plain, massacring the Maya warriors. Legend has it that Alvarado himself killed the K'iche' king, Tecún Umán, in hand-to-hand combat.

Totally unlike the capital and only a fraction of its size, Guatemala's second city, **QUETZALTENANGO** (**Xela**, pronounced "Shay-La"), has the subdued provincial atmosphere that you might expect in the capital of the highlands, its edges gently giving way to corn and maize fields. Bizarre though it may seem, Xela's character and appearance is vaguely reminiscent of an industrial town in northern England – grey, cool, slightly dour and culturally conservative. Ringed by high mountains and bitterly cold in the early mornings, the city wakes slowly, only getting going once the warmth of the sun has made its mark.

Some history

Under colonial rule, Quetzaltenango flourished as a commercial centre, benefiting from the fertility of the surrounding farmland and good connections to the port at Champerico. When the prospect of independence eventually arose, the city was set on deciding its own destiny and Quetzaltenango declared itself the capital of the independent state of **Los Altos**. The separatist movement was unsuccessful, however, and the city has had to accept provincial status ever since, although during the coffee boom at the end of the last century Quetzaltenango's wealth and population grew so rapidly that it began to rival the capital in status.

All this, however, came to an abrupt end when the city was almost totally destroyed by the massive **1902 earthquake**. Rebuilding took place in a mood of high optimism: all the grand Neoclassical architecture dates from this period. A new rail line was built to connect the city with the coast, but after this was washed out in 1932–33 the town never regained its former glory, gradually falling further and further behind the capital.

Today Quetzaltenango has all the trappings of wealth and self-importance: the grand imperial architecture, the great banks, and a list of famous sons. But it is completely devoid of the rampant energy that binds Guatemala City to the all-American twentieth century. The city has a calm and dignified air and Quetzaltecos have a reputation for formality and politeness – an ideal antidote to the chaos of Guatemala City.

Arrival and information

Unhelpfully for the traveller, virtually all buses arrive and depart Quetzaltenango from nowhere near the centre of town. If you arrive by **second-class bus** you'll almost certainly end up in the chaotic **Minerva Bus Terminal** on the city's northwestern edge. Walk through the covered market place to 4 C and catch a local bus marked "Parque" to get to the plaza from there. An extremely useful transport hub is a roundabout called the **rotunda** at the far end of Calzada Independencia, east of the city centre, where virtually all **long-distance buses** stop on their way to and from the city. Three main companies operate **first-class buses** to and from the capital, each with their own private terminal: the Líneas Américas terminal is just off Calzada Independencia at 7 Av 3–33, Zona 2, (☎761 2063), Alamo is at 4C 14-04, Zona 3 (☎767 7117), and Galgos is at C Rodolfo Robles 17–43, Zona 1 (☎761 2248). There are also **daily flights** to and from the capital with Inter airlines (30min; US$55 one way); the airstrip is 5km east of the town centre.

The helpful **tourist office**, on the main plaza (Mon–Fri 8am–1pm & 2–5pm, Sat 8am–noon; ☎761 4931), has maps and local information. Xela is an excellent place to **study Spanish**, with dozens of schools, many of a high standard. For a list of recommended language schools, see pp.132–3.

Quetzaltenango is laid out on a standard grid pattern, somewhat complicated by a number of steep hills. The oldest part of the city, focused around the plaza, is made up of narrow streets, while in the newer part, reaching out towards the Minerva terminal, the blocks are larger. The city is also divided up into **zones**, although for the most part you'll only be interested in zonas 1 and 3, which contain the plaza area and the Minerva Bus Terminal respectively. When it comes to **getting around**, most places are within easy walking distance (except the terminal). To get to the Minerva terminal you can take any bus that runs along 13 Av between 8 C and 4 C in Zona 1. To head for the eastern half of town, along 7 Av, catch one of the buses that stops in front of the Casa de la Cultura, at the bottom end of the plaza.

Accommodation

Most accommodation in Quetzaltenango tends to be a little dour, but several bright new places have opened in recent years. Once you've made it to the plaza, all the places listed below are within ten minutes' walk.

Casa Argentina, 12 Diagonal 8–37 (☎761 2470, *casaargentina@trafficman.com*). The most popular budget place in town with 25 very comfortable single rooms, two dorms (US$2.50 a bed), a kitchen and very friendly owners who are an excellent source of information. It's also the home of Quetzaltrekkers (see p.207). ②.

Casa Kaehler, 13 Av 3–33 (☎761 2091). Attractive place with spotless rooms set around a patio, some with private bath. Decent value, secure and very central, but be sure to book ahead as it's always popular. ②.

Casa Mañen, 9 Av 4–11 (☎765 0786, fax 765 0678, *www.comeseeit.com*). Luxury boutique hotel, very stylish and exceptional value for money. Beautiful rooms, some with fireplaces, all with *ikat* fabrics and rugs and cable TV, plus two huge split-level suites with sofas and fridges and a wonderful rooftop terrace with Jacuzzi. Breakfast included. ⑥–⑦.

Hotel Casa Florencia, 12 Av 3–61 (☎761 2811, *www.xelapages.com/florencia/index.htm*). The lobby isn't going to win any design awards, but the nine large rooms with wood-panelled walls and fitted carpets are comfortable enough, and all come with private bath. ④.

Hotel Modelo, 14 Av A 2–31 (☎761 2529, fax 763 1376, *www.xelapages.com/modelo/index.htm.*). Civilized and quiet, but a bit gloomy for the price and decidedly old-fashioned. The nicest rooms face a small garden courtyard, or try the separate annexe which is better value. ④–⑤.

Hotel Occidental, 7 C 12–23 (☎765 4069). In a good location just off the plaza, with large plain rooms and good beds, some with private bath. ②–③.

Hotel Río Azul, 2 C 12–15 (☎ & fax 763 0654, *rioazul@c.net.gt*). Very reminiscent of an English boarding house, but spotless and welcoming. All rooms have private bath. ③.

Pensión Altense, 9 C 8–48 (☎761 2811). Just above the budget range, this place has plenty of clean spacious rooms, all with private bath, plus safe parking. ③.

Pensión Andina, 8 Av 6–07 (☎761 4012). Very cheap and centrally located; the rooms are pretty plain but fairly clean – some have private bath (hot water 6–9am only). ①.

Pensión Bonifaz, northeast corner of the plaza (☎761 2182, fax 761 2850). The hotel, founded in 1935, has character and comfort, a reasonable (though overpriced) restaurant and a quirky bar. Very much the backbone of Quetzaltenango society, with an air of faded upper-class pomposity, but still one of the best places in town. ⑥.

The City

There aren't many things to do or see in Quetzaltenango, but if you have an hour or two to spare then it's worth wandering through the streets, soaking up the atmosphere and taking in the museum in the Casa de la Cultura. The hub of the place is the central plaza, officially known as the **Parque Centro América**, whose mass of mock-Greek columns and imposing banks exude an atmosphere of dignified calm – there's none of the buzz of business that you'd expect, except on the first Sunday of the month when the plaza hosts a good artesanías market with blankets, basketry and piles of típica weavings for sale. The northern end of the plaza is dominated by the grand old **Banco del Occidente**, complete with sculptured flaming torches. On the west side is Bancafé and the impressive but crumbling **Pasaje Enríquez**, planned as a sparkling arcade of upmarket shops but left derelict for many years, though it has now been partially revived. Inside you'll find the *Salón Tecún Bar* (see p.206), the hippest place in town, and a good place for meeting other travellers.

At the bottom end of the plaza, next to the tourist office, is the **Casa de la Cultura** (Mon–Fri 8am–noon & 2–6pm, Sat 9am–1pm; US$1), the city's most blatant impersonation of a Greek temple, with a bold grey frontage. The main part of the building is given over to an odd mixture of local exhibits. On the ground floor, to the left-hand side, you'll find a display of assorted documents, photographs and pistols from the liberal revolution and the State of Los Altos (see p.202), along with sports trophies and a room dedicated to the marimba. Upstairs there are some modest Maya artefacts, historic photographs and a bizarre natural history room. Amongst the dusty displays of stuffed bats, pickled snakes and animal skins are the macabre remains of assorted freaks of nature, including a sheep born with eight legs and a four-horned goat.

Along the other side of the plaza is the **Cathedral**, with the new cement version set behind the spectacular crumbling front of the original. There's another piece of classical grandeur, the **Municipalidad** (Town Hall), a little further up. Take a look inside at the courtyard, which has a neat little garden set out around a single palm tree. Back in the centre of the plaza are rows and circles of redundant columns, a few flowerbeds, and a monument to Rufino Barrios, president of Guatemala from 1873 to 1885.

CENTRAL QUETZALTENANGO

Minerva Bus Terminal △   Mercado La Democracia △

N

Teatro Roma
Teatro Municipal
Cine Paraíso

19 AVENIDA
14 AVENIDA A
14 AVENIDA
15 AVENIDA

1 CALLE
2A CALLE
2 CALLE
3A CALLE
3 CALLE

CALZADA SINFOROSO AGUILAR

4 CALLE
5 CALLE
6 CALLE
7 CALLE

DIAGONAL 12
DIAGONAL 11

Plaza
Municipalidad
Cathedral
Casa de la Cultura

11 AVENIDA
10 AVENIDA
9 AVENIDA
8 AVENIDA

DIAGONAL 13

8 CALLE
9 CALLE
10 CALLE
11 CALLE

Buses to Zunil
Buses to Rotunda

Minerva

0   100 m

RESTAURANTS & CAFÉS

Blue Angel Video Café	K
Café Baviera	F
Café Colonial	L
Café El Mana	G
Cardinali's	C
Deli Crêpe	B
El Rincón de los Antojitos	D
La Luna	J
La Polonesa	E
La Salida	N
La Taquería	I
Royal Paris	A
Sagrado Corazón	M
Salón Tecún	H

ACCOMMODATION

Casa Argentina	8
Casa Kaehler	3
Casa Mañen	6
Hotel Casa Florencia	4
Hotel Modelo	1
Hotel Occidental	7
Hotel Río Azul	2
Pensión Altense	10
Pensión Andina	9
Pensión Bonifaz	5

Away from the plaza, the city spreads out, a mixture of the old and new. The commercial heart is 14 Avenida, complete with pizza restaurants and neon signs. At the top of 14 Avenida, at the junction with 1 Calle, stands the restored **Teatro Municipal**, another spectacular Neoclassical edifice. Further afield, the city's role as a regional centre of trade is more in evidence. Out in Zona 3 is the **Mercado La Democracia**, a vast covered complex with stalls spilling out onto the streets. There's another Greek-style structure right out on the edge of town, the **Minerva Temple**, built to honour President Barrios's enthusiasm for education and making no pretence at serving any practical purpose. Beside the temple is the fairly miserable **zoo** (Tues–Sun 9am–5pm; free) and a children's playground. Below the temple are the sprawling **market** and **Minerva Bus Terminal**, and it's here that you can really sense the city's role as the centre of the western highlands, with *indígena* traders from all over the area doing business.

Eating, drinking and entertainment

There are more than enough **restaurants** to choose from in Quetzaltenango, with a strip of reasonable pizza places on 14 Avenida and a number of new cafés spread across the city. Note that almost nowhere opens before 8am in the morning, so forget early

breakfasts. After dark, things are generally quiet in the week, but there are a number of lively **bars** that fill up at the weekend, plus a small **club** scene, with a couple of venues in the centre of town, and other alternatives in the suburbs.

Cafés and restaurants

Blue Angel Video Café, 7 C 15–22, Zona 1. Intimate, friendly and popular gringo hangout with a daily video programme and great vegetarian food.

Café Baviera, 5 C 12–50, Zona 1, a block from the plaza. Spacious pine-panelled coffee house, dripping with photographic nostalgia and serving quality cakes and decent coffee, though the set breakfasts are a little pricey.

Café Colonial, 13 Av and 7 C, Zona 1. Large café-cum-restaurant with tasty barbecued meats, decent sandwiches and rich *licuados*.

Café El Mana 13 Av and 5 C, Zona 1. Tiny, very friendly family-run café with an excellent selection of inexpensive breakfasts – including *mosh* (highland porridge) pancakes and granola – lunches and real coffee. Closed Sun.

Cardinali's, 14 Av 3–41, Zona 1. Without doubt the best Italian food outside the capital, at reasonable prices. Make sure you are starving when you eat here because the portions are huge. For a pizza delivery call ☎761 0924.

Deli Crêpe, 14 Av & 3 C, Zona 1. Looks a bit gloomy from the outside, but wait till you try the *licuados*, pancakes and delicious sandwiches.

El Rincón de los Antojitos, 15 Av and 5 C, Zona 1. Despite being run by a French–Guatemalan couple, this friendly little restaurant has a purely Guatemalan menu, with specialities such as *pepián* (spicy chicken stew) and *hilachas* (beef in tomato sauce).

La Luna, 8 Av 4–11, Zona 1. Stylish new place, ideal for a relaxing cup of coffee and a yummy cake. They also do very fine chocolates.

La Polonesa, 14 Av 4–55, Zona 1. Great little place with an unbeatable selection of set lunches (with daily specials), all under US$2, and served at nice solid wooden tables.

La Salida, 9 Av and 10 Av Zona 1. Diminutive vegetarian café, with delicious food including tempe and tofu, Oriental treats like *pad thai*, wholesome soups, and lassis. No alcohol. Closed Wed.

La Taquería, 8 Av 5 C, Zona 1. Best Mexican food in town, moderately priced and served in a pleasant courtyard patio setting – try the enchiladas or the *caldo Tlalpeño* soup, washed down with cheap litres of beer.

Pan y Pasteles, 18 Av and 1 C, Zona 1. The best bakery in town, run by Mennonites whose fresh pastries and breads are used by all the finest restaurants. Tues & Fri only, 9am–6pm.

Pensión Bonifaz, in the hotel of the same name, corner of the plaza, Zona 1. Always a sedate and civilized spot for a cup of tea, a cake and the chance to rub shoulders with the town's elite, though the restaurant is expensive and overrated.

Royal Paris, 14 Av A 3–06, Zona 1. Superb, moderately priced French-owned restaurant with a winsome menu of really flavoursome dishes including cassoulet and onion soup, plus snacks like croque monsieur. Special weekday lunches are a steal at US$2.

Sagrado Corazón, 9 C 9-00, Zona 1. Excellent little comedor, with great-value breakfasts, filling meals and very friendly service.

Drinking and nightlife

Considering the size of Quetzaltenango, there's not that much going on in the evenings and the streets are generally quiet by about 9pm. There are a few **bars** worth visiting. however. At the popular *Salón Tecún*, on the west side of the plaza, you can down *cuba libres*, enjoy draught beer and great bar food, and listen to the latest sounds imported by the gringo bar staff. The more sedate but classy *Don Rodrigo*, 1 C and 14 Av, has leather-topped bar stools, more draught beer and good, but pricey sandwiches. Close to the Teatro Municipal is a cluster of hip new places including the bar *El Zaguan*, at 14 Av A and 1 C, Zona 1, and the club *Bukana's*, almost next door, for salsa and merengue. Of the **clubs** on the outskirts of town, the *Music Center* attracts a loyal young local clientele, while *Loro's* appeals to an older crowd.

Quetzaltenango is a good place to catch movies, with a number of **cinemas**, though you shouldn't have to stray further than the excellent Cine Paraíso on 14 Avenida A, near the Teatro Municipal, which shows a very varied selection of independent movies from all over the world, plus the odd quality Hollywood production. For **theatre** head for the refurbished Teatro Roma, also on 14 Avenida A, which often stages interesting productions. The *Casa Verde* (also known as the *Green House*), at 12 Av 1–40 (☎763 0271), has a lively **cultural programme** including theatre, dance and poetry readings, plus salsa nights at weekends. To find **what's on** in Xela, pick up a copy of the free listings magazine, *Fin de Semana*, available in many of the popular bars and cafés.

Listings

Banks and exchange Banco Inmobiliario, Banco del Occidente and Bancafé (with the longest opening hours: Mon–Fri 8.30am–8pm, Sat 10am–1.30pm) are all in the vicinity of the plaza and will change travellers' cheques. Banco Industrial, also in the plaza, has an ATM that takes Visa.

Bike and car rental Guatemala Unlimited, 12 Av and 1 C, Zona 1 (☎761 6043), has mountain bikes for around US$6 a day; alternatively, try the Vrisa bookstore (see below).

Bookstore Vrisa, 15 Av 3–64, opposite Telgua and the post office, has over 4000 used titles, plus a newsroom with *Newsweek* and *The Economist*, a message board, espresso coffee and bike rental.

Consulates Mexican Consulate, 9 Av 6–19, Zona 1 (Mon–Fri 8–11am & 2.30–3.30pm). A Mexican tourist card costs US$1. Hand in your paperwork in the morning and collect in the afternoon.

Email and Internet access There are at least a dozen places in Xela where you can surf the Net, including Maya Communications, above Salón Tecún in the Plaza Central; Casa Verde, 12 Av 1–40, Zona 1; and Alternativas at 16 Av 3–35, Zona 3 (all open until 9pm or later; around US$1.40/hr).

Laundry MiniMax, 4 Av and 1 C, Zona 1 (Mon–Sat 7am–7pm); US$2 for a full-load wash and dry.

Medical care Dr de León at the Hospital San Rafael 9 C 10–41 (☎761 4414) speaks English.

Photography For camera repairs try Fotocolor, 15 Av 3–25, or one of the several shops on 14 Av.

Post office At the junction of 15 Av and 4 C.

Telephone office The best rates in town are at Kall Shop, 8 Av 4–24 Zona 1, where calls to the USA and Canada are US$0.25 and Europe US$0.45 per minute. Maya Communications (see "Email and Internet access" above) is also competitive. You'll pay much more at the main Telgua office, 15 Av and 4 C.

Tours and travel agencies Adrenalina Tours, inside Pasaje Enríquez, Plaza Central (☎761 0924, *http://adrenalinatours.xelaenlinca.com*), offers city tours, daily transport to Fuentes Georginas and volcano climbing. Casa Iximulew, 15 Av and 5 C, Zona 1 (☎765 1308, *iximulew@trafficman.com*), runs organized trips to most of the volcanoes and sights around Xela. The Guatemalan Birding Resource Center, 7 Av 19–18, Zona 1 (☎767 7339), offers excellent guided tours to the surrounding countryside. Guatemala Unlimited, 12 Av and C 35, Zona 1 (☎ & fax 761 6043), is a good all-rounder with tours all over the country. Quetzaltrekkers, inside *Casa Argentina* (see "Accommodation", p.203), offers hiking trips to volcanoes and to Lago de Atitlán, with all profits going to a charity for street children.

Weaving For weaving classes contact the Ixchel school at 8 Av 4–24, Zona 1 (☎765 3790).

Around Quetzaltenango

It's easy to spend a week or two exploring this part of the country – making day-trips to the markets and fiestas, basking in hot springs, or hiking in the mountains – and Quetzaltenango is the obvious place to base yourself, with bus connections to all parts of the western highlands. The valley is heavily populated and there are numerous smaller towns and villages in the surrounding hills, mostly indigenous agricultural communities and weaving centres. The area also offers excellent **hiking**. The most obvious climb is the **Volcán Santa María**, towering above Quetzaltenango itself. To the south, straddling the coast road, is **Zunil** and the hot springs of **Fuentes Georginas**, overshadowed by breathtaking volcanic peaks. To the north are **Totonicapán**, capital of the department of the same name, and **San Francisco El Alto**, a small town perched on an outcrop overlooking the valley. Beyond that lies **Momostenango**, the country's principal wool-producing centre and a centre of Maya culture. For organized **tours** to all these places, contact the travel agents in Quetzaltenango listed on the previous page.

Volcán Santa María

Due south of Quetzaltenango, the perfect cone of **Volcán Santa María** rises to a height of 3772m. From the town only the peak is visible, but seen from the rest of the valley the entire cone seems to tower over everything around. The view from the top is, as you might expect, spectacular, and if you're prepared to sweat out the climb you certainly won't regret it. It's possible to climb the volcano as a day-trip, but to really see it at its best you need to be on top at dawn, either sleeping on the freezing peak, or camping at the site below and climbing the final section in the dark by torchlight. Either way you need to bring enough food and water for the entire trip; and make sure you're acclimatized to the altitude before attempting the climb.

Zunil and Fuentes Georginas

Ten kilometres south of Quetzaltenango is the traditional village of **ZUNIL**, a vegetable-growing market town surrounded by steep hills and a sleeping volcano. The plaza is dominated by a beautiful white colonial church with a richly decorated façade; inside an intricate silver altar is protected behind bars. The women of Zunil wear vivid purple *huipiles* and carry bright shawls – the plaza is awash with colour during the Monday market. Just below the plaza is a **textile co-operative**, where hundreds of women market their beautiful weavings. Zunil is also one of the few remaining places where **Maximón** (or San Simón), the evil saint, is still worshipped. In the face of disapproval from the Catholic Church, the Maya are reluctant to display their Judas, who also goes by the name Alvarado, but his image is usually paraded through the streets during Holy Week, dressed in Western clothes and smoking a cigar. Virtually any child in town will take you to his abode for a quetzal.

In the hills above Zunil are the **Fuentes Georginas**, a spectacular set of luxuriant hot springs. A turning to the left off the main road, just beyond the entrance to the village, leads up into the hills to the baths, 8km away. You can walk it in a couple of hours, or rent a pick-up truck from the plaza in Zunil. Prices are officially set at US$5 for the trip, no matter how many passengers hitch a ride – it's an exhilarating journey up a smooth paved road which switchbacks through magnificent volcanic scenery. If you're not staying the night you'll have to arrange the return trip (another US$5) a few hours later with the driver. The baths (US$1.30) are surrounded by fresh green ferns, thick moss and lush forest, and to top it all there's a restaurant and a well-stocked bar (with decent wine) beside the main pool. It's easy to spend an afternoon or more here soaking up the scene, though you can also rent one of the very pleasant rustic stone **bungalows** for the night (no phone; ③) complete with bathtub, two double beds, fireplace and barbecue.

Buses to Zunil run from Quetzaltenango's Minerva Bus Terminal every half-hour or so, though you can also catch a ride from a bus stop closer to the centre of town, beside the Shell gas station at 10 C and 9 Av in Zona 1. The last bus back from Zunil leaves at around 6.30pm.

San Francisco El Alto

The small market town of **SAN FRANCISCO EL ALTO** overlooks the Quetzaltenango valley from a magnificent hillside setting, and it's worth a visit for the view alone, with the great plateau stretching out below and the cone of Volcán Santa María on the horizon. Another good reason for visiting the village is the **Friday market**, possibly the biggest in Central America and attended by traders from every corner of Guatemala –

many arrive the night before, and some start selling by candlelight as early as 4am. Throughout the morning a steady stream of buses and trucks fill the town to bursting; by noon the market is at its height, buzzing with activity.

The town is set into the hillside, with steep cobbled streets connecting the different levels. Two areas in particular are monopolized by specific trades. At the very top is an open field used as an **animal market**, where everything from pigs to parrots changes hands. The teeth and tongues of animals are inspected by the buyers, and at times the scene degenerates into a chaotic wrestling match, with pigs and men rolling in the dirt. Below this is the town's plaza, dominated by textiles. On the lower level, the streets are filled with vegetables, fruit, pottery, furniture, cheap comedores, and plenty more. These days most of the stalls deal in imported denim, but under the arches and in the covered area opposite the church you'll find a superb selection of traditional cloth. For a really good **photographic** angle and for views of the market and the surrounding countryside, pay the church caretaker a quetzal and climb up to the **church roof**. By early afternoon the numbers start to thin out, and by sunset it's all over – until the following Friday.

There are plenty of **buses** from Quetzaltenango to San Francisco, 16km away, leaving every twenty minutes or so from the rotunda; the first is at 6am, and the last bus back leaves at about 5pm (45min).

Momostenango

A further 22km from San Francisco, down a paved road that continues over a ridge behind the town then drops down through lush pine forests, is **MOMOSTENANGO**, a small, isolated town and the centre of wool production in the highlands. Momostecos travel throughout the country peddling their blankets, scarves and rugs – years of experience have made them experts in the hard sell and given them a sharp eye for tourists. The wool is also used in a range of traditional costumes, including the short skirts worn by the men of Nahualá, San Antonio Palopó and the jackets of Sololá. The ideal place to buy Momostenango blankets is in the **Sunday market**, which fills the town's two plazas.

A visit at this time will also give you a glimpse of Momostenango's other feature: its rigid adherence to tradition. Opposite the entrance to the church, people make offerings of incense and alcohol on a small fire, muttering their appeals to the gods. The town is famous for this unconventional folk-Catholicism, and it has been claimed that there are as many as three hundred Maya **shamans** working here. Momostenango's religious calendar, like that of only one or two other villages, is still based on the 260-day *Tzolkin* year – made up of thirteen twenty-day months – that has been in use since ancient times.

As a visitor it's best to visit Momostenango for the market, unless you can coincide your visit with the start of the Maya new year or the fiesta on August 1. If you decide to stay for a day or two then you can take a walk to the *riscos*, a set of bizarre sandstone pillars, or beyond to the **hot springs** of Pala Chiquito, about 3km away to the north.

The best place **to stay** in Momostenango is the *Hotel Estiver*, 1 C 4–15, Zona 1 (☎736 5036; ②), which has clean rooms, some with private bathrooms, great views from the roof and safe parking. For **eating**, there are plenty of small comedores on the main plaza or try the one inside the *Hospedaje Paglóm*. There's a Bancafé **bank** at 1 C and 1 Av (Mon–Fri 9am–4pm) which accepts Visa, cash and travellers' cheques.

Buses run here from Quetzaltenango, passing through Cuatro Caminos and San Francisco El Alto on the way. They leave the Minerva terminal in Quetzaltenango every hour or so from 9am to 4pm (1hr 15min) and from Momostenango between 6am and 3pm. On Sunday, special early-morning buses leave Quetzaltenango from 6am: you can catch them at the rotunda.

Totonicapán

Capital of one of the smaller departments, **TOTONICAPÁN** is reached down a road leading east from Cuatro Caminos. Surrounded by rolling hills and pine forests, the town stands at the heart of a heavily populated and intensely farmed little region. There is only one point of access and the valley has always held out against outside influence, shut off in a world of its own, and it's still a quiet place, ruffled only by the Tuesday and Saturday **markets**, which fill the two plazas to bursting. Until fairly recently a highly ornate traditional costume was worn here, but this has now disappeared and the town has instead become one of the chief centres of commercial weaving. To take a closer look at the work of local artisans, head for the town's visitor centre, the **Casa de la Cultura**, on 8 Av 2–17 (Mon–Sat 9.30am–5pm; *http://larutamayaonline.com/aventura .html*), which organizes pricey tours of the town (US$6–14) and classes in weaving and wood carving (US$21–49 per person, depending on class size); the funds raised help benefit the community. The only other sight is located in the northern of the two plazas: a grand though somewhat faded Neoclassical **theatre**, echoing the one in Quetzaltenango – it's currently undergoing restoration.

There are good connections between Totonicapán and Quetzaltenango, with **buses** shuttling back and forth every half-hour or so. Totonicapán is very quiet after dark, but if you want to stay, the best **hotel** is the *Hospedaje San Miguel*, a block from the plaza at 8 Av and 3 C (☎766 1452; ②–③): it's pretty comfortable and some rooms have bathrooms, but beware price rises before market days. The *Pensión Blanquita* (①) is a friendly and basic alternative opposite the filling station at 13 Av and 4 C.

Huehuetenango

In the corner of a small agricultural plain, 5km from the Carretera Interamericana at the foot of the mighty Cuchumatanes mountain range, lies **HUEHUETENANGO**, capital of the department of the same name. Though Huehue is the focus of trade and transport for a vast area, its atmosphere is provincial and relaxed. Before the arrival of the Spanish, it was the site of one of the residential suburbs that surrounded the Mam capital of Zaculeu (see p.212), and under colonial rule it became a small regional centre with little to offer other than a steady trickle of silver and a stretch or two of grazing land. The supply of silver dried up long ago, but other minerals are still mined, and coffee and sugar have been added to the area's produce.

Today's Huehuetenango has two quite distinct functions – and two contrasting halves – each serving a separate section of the population. The large majority of the people are *ladino*, and for them Huehuetenango is an unimportant regional centre far from the hub of things. Here the mood is summed up in the unhurried atmosphere of the attractive **plaza** at the heart of the *ladino* half of town, where shaded walkways are surrounded by administrative offices. Overlooking it, perched above the pavements, are a shell-shaped bandstand, a clock tower and a grandiose Neoclassical church, a solid whitewashed structure with a facade that's crammed with Doric pillars and Grecian urns.

A few blocks to the east, the town's atmosphere could hardly be more different. Around the **market**, the hub of the Maya part of town, the streets are crowded with traders, drunks and travellers from Mexico and all over Central America. This part of Huehuetenango, centred on 1 Avenida, is always alive with activity, its streets packed with people from every corner of the department and littered with rotten vegetables.

Arrival, information and accommodation

Huehue is fairly small so you shouldn't have any problems finding your way around, particularly once you've located the plaza. You'll arrive at the purpose-built **bus terminal** halfway between the Carretera Interamericana and town. Minibuses make constant trips between the town centre and the bus terminal. Daily **flights** from Guatemala City land at the airstrip 3km south of the centre of town (50min; US$60 one way).

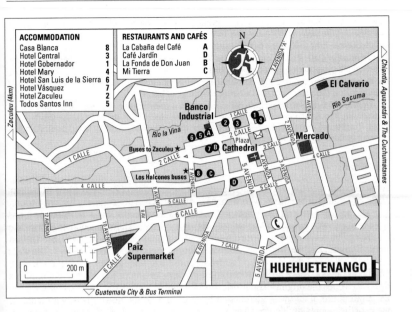

ACCOMMODATION
Casa Blanca	8
Hotel Central	3
Hotel Gobernador	1
Hotel Mary	4
Hotel San Luis de la Sierra	6
Hotel Vásquez	7
Hotel Zaculeu	2
Todos Santos Inn	5

RESTAURANTS AND CAFÉS
La Cabaña del Café	A
Café Jardín	D
La Fonda de Don Juan	B
Mi Tierra	C

There's a **post office** at 2 C 3–54 (Mon–Fri 8am–4.30pm), a **Telgua** office at 4 Av 6–54 (7am–10pm) and two **Internet cafés**: *Génesis* at 2 C 6–37 and *Mi Tierra* at 4 C 6–46 – both charge around US$3.80 an hour. Huehue also boasts a couple of decent **language schools** (see p.133).

Casa Blanca, 7 Av 3–41 (☎ & fax 769 0777). Modern upmarket hotel, built in colonial style; all rooms have private bath and cable TV. The fine restaurant and spacious garden terrace are well worth a visit too. ⑤.

Hotel Central, 5 Av 1–33 (☎764 1202) Classic budget hotel, with large, scruffy rooms in a creaking old wooden building, plus a fantastic comedor. No singles or private baths. ①.

Hotel Gobernador, 4 Av 1–45 (☎ & fax 764 1197). Excellent budget hotel run by a very friendly family, with attractive rooms, some with bath, and reliable hot showers. ②.

Hotel Mary, 2 C 3–52 (☎764 1618, fax 764 7412). Centrally located with small but pleasant rooms, most with private shower, and loads of steaming hot water. ②–③.

Hotel San Luis de la Sierra, 2 C 7–00 (☎ & fax 764 1103). Spotless modern hotel with small but very attractive rooms, all with good showers and cable TV; some have wonderful views of the mountains. ④.

Hotel Vásquez, 2 C 6–67 (☎764 1338). Cell-sized rooms around a bare courtyard, but clean and safe, with secure parking. ②.

Hotel Zaculeu, 5 Av 1–14 (☎764 1086, fax 764 1575). Large, comfortable hotel, something of an institution. Some of the older rooms surrounding a leafy courtyard are a bit musty and gloomy, while those in the more expensive new section are larger and more spacious. All come with cable TV and private bath. There's also parking and a reasonable restaurant. ④–⑤.

Todos Santos Inn, 2 C 6–74 (☎7641241). Good, secure budget hotel, though the rooms do vary in quality – some are bright and cheery with bedside lights, others are less attractive. An excellent deal for single travellers. ②–③.

Eating, drinking and entertainment

Most of the better **restaurants** are in the central area around the plaza. **Films** are shown at the cinema on 3 Calle, half a block west of the plaza.

Café Jardín, 4 C and 6 Av. Friendly place serving inexpensive but excellent breakfasts, milkshakes, pancakes and the usual chicken and beef dishes.

Hotel Central, 5 Av 1–33. Very tasty, inexpensive set meals, and a particularly good breakfast.

La Cabaña del Café, 2 Calle, opposite *Hotel Vásquez*. Logwood café with an excellent range of coffees (including cappuccino), great cakes and a few snacks.

La Fonda de Don Juan, 2 C 5–35. Attractive place with gingham tablecloths, serving good, if slightly pricey, pizza and pasta, and a reasonable range of beers.

Mi Tierra, 4 C 6–46. Attractive little restaurant set in a covered patio with nice decor and a good atmosphere. The flavoursome menu is more imaginative than most – great for house salads, *churrascos* (barbecued meat) and cheesecake – plus very cheap and healthy breakfasts. Also has Internet facilities and a good noticeboard.

Zaculeu

A few kilometres to the west of Huehuetenango are the ruins of **Zaculeu** (daily 8am–6pm; US$3.20), capital of the **Mam**, who were one of the principal pre-conquest highland tribes. The site includes several large temples, plazas and a ball court, but unfortunately it has been restored with an astounding lack of subtlety (or accuracy). Its appearance – more like an ageing film set than an ancient ruin – is owed to a latter-day colonial power, the **United Fruit Company**, under whose auspices the ruins were reconstructed in 1946–7. The walls and surfaces have been levelled off with a layer of thick white plaster, leaving them stark and undecorated. There are no roof-combs, carvings or stucco mouldings, and only in a few places does the original stonework show through. Even so, the site does have a peculiar atmosphere of its own. Surrounded by trees and neatly mown grass, with fantastic views of the mountains, it's also an excellent spot for a picnic. There's a small **museum** on site (daily 8am–noon & 1–6pm) with examples of some of the unusual burial techniques used and some interesting ceramics found during excavation.

The site is thought to have been a religious and administrative centre housing the elite, while the bulk of the population lived in small surrounding settlements or else scattered in the hills. Zaculeu was the hub of a large area of Mam-speakers, its boundaries reaching into the mountains as far as Todos Santos Cuchumatán. However, to put together a history of the site means relying on the records of the K'iche', a more powerful neighbouring tribe. According to their mythology, the K'iche' conquered most of the other highland tribes, including the Mam, some time between 1400 and 1475. Following the death of the K'iche' leader, Quicab, in 1475, the Mam managed to reassert their independence, but no sooner had they escaped the clutches of one expansionist empire than the Spanish arrived with a yet more brutal alternative.

Pedro de Alvarado despatched an army under the command of his brother, Gonzalo, which was met by about five thousand Mam warriors. The Mam leader, Caibal Balam, quickly saw that his troops were no match for the Spanish and withdrew them to the safety of Zaculeu, where they were protected on three sides by deep ravines and on the other by a series of walls and ditches. The Spanish army settled outside the city and besieged the citadel for six weeks until starvation forced Caibal Balam to surrender.

To get to Zaculeu from Huehuetenango, take one of the **pick-ups** or **buses** that leave close to the school from 7 Av between 2 and 3 calles – make sure it's a Ruta 3 heading for Ruinas Zaculeu (not Zaculeu Central).

The Cuchumatanes

The largest non-volcanic peaks in Central America, the **Sierra de los Cuchumatanes** rise from a limestone plateau close to the Mexican border and reach their full height of over 3800m above Huehuetenango. This is magnificent mountain scenery, ranging from wild, exposed craggy outcrops to lush, tranquil river valleys. While the upper parts of the slopes are almost barren, scattered with boulders and shrivelled cypress trees, the lower levels, by contrast, are richly fertile and cultivated with corn, coffee and sugar. Between the peaks, in the deep-cut valleys, are hundreds of tiny villages, isolated by the enormity of the landscape.

Despite the initial devastation, the arrival of the Spanish had surprisingly little impact in these highlands and the communities here include some of the most traditional in Guatemala. A visit to the mountain villages, either for a market or fiesta (and there are plenty of both), offers one of the best opportunities to see Maya life at close quarters. In the late 1970s and early 1980s this was the scene of bitter fighting between the army and the guerrillas, a wave of violence and terror that sent thousands fleeing across the border to Mexico. Nowadays, though, with the fighting over, things are much calmer.

The most accessible of the villages in the vicinity, and the only one yet to receive a steady trickle of tourists, is **Todos Santos Cuchumatán**, whose horse-race fiesta on November 1 is one of the most interesting and outrageous in Guatemala. To the east a road struggles through the mountains past the interesting village of **Aguacatán** on its way to Cobán in Alta Verapaz (see p.244).

Todos Santos Cuchumatán

Spectacularly sited in its own remote deep-cut river valley, **TODOS SANTOS CUCHU-MATÁN** is many travellers' favourite place in Guatemala. Though the sheer beauty of the alpine surroundings is one attraction, it's the unique culture that is really astounding. The *traje* worn here is startling: the men wear red-and-white candy-striped trousers, black woollen breeches and pinstripe shirts, decorated with dayglo pink collars, while the women wear dark blue *cortes* and superbly intricate purple *huipiles*. It's the tradition and isolation that have made the village so attractive to visitors, photographers in particular, though such attention has not always been welcome. In 2000, an angry mob attacked and killed a Japanese tourist and his Guatemalan guide, believing that the former, who was taking pictures of local children, was a Satanist baby stealer. Though the perpetrators have been jailed, and the community as a whole was stunned and deeply remorseful, the depth of misunderstanding serves to highlight the cultural chasm between this remote, highly superstitious mountain community and the developed world. There have been no incidents since, but it's obviously very important to respect local sensitivities and be very judicious about taking photographs, particularly of children.

The Todosanteros are perhaps the proudest of all Guatemala's Maya people – there is a distinctive swagger in the step of the men – and the **fiesta** (on November 1) is one of the most famous in the country, during which the village is taken over by unrestrained drinking, dancing and marimba music. The three-day event opens with an all-day horse race, and there is a massive stampede as the inebriated riders tear up the course, thrashing their horses with live chickens, their capes flowing out behind them. On the second day, "The Day of the Dead", the action moves to the cemetery, with marimba bands and drink stalls set up amongst the graves – a day of intense ritual that combines grief and celebration. By the final day of the fiesta, the streets are littered with bodies and the jail packed with brawlers. The Saturday **market**, although nothing like as riotous, also fills the village.

The village itself is pretty – a modest main street with a few shops, a plaza and a church – but is totally overshadowed by the looming presence of the Cuchumatanes mountains. Above the village – follow the track that goes up behind the *Comedor Katy* – is the small Maya site of **Tojcunanchén**, where you'll find a couple of mounds sprouting pine trees. The site is occasionally used by *brujos* for the ritual sacrifice of animals.

Todos Santos is home to two interesting **language schools** (see p.133) where you can study Spanish or Mam; a percentage of the profits from both schools goes to local development projects.

Practicalities

Buses leave Huehuetenango for Todos Santos from the main bus terminal four times a day: at 5.45am, 10am, 1pm and 2pm – get there early to mark your seat and buy a ticket. Some carry on through the village, heading further down the valley to Jacaltenango and pass through Todos Santos on the way back to Huehuetenango; ask around for the latest schedule.

The best places **to stay** are *Hospedaje Casa Familiar* (②), 30m above the main road past *Comedor Katy*, where views from the terrace café are breathtaking, and *Hospedaje Las Ruinas* (①), further up the track on the right, which has four large rooms in a large twin-storey concrete structure. Turning left just before you reach the *Casa Familiar* (①) brings you to the orange *Hotel Mam*, another good option with hot showers, while the new *Hotelito Todos Santos* (②), just east of the plaza, is a fairly decent choice with cleanish rooms. There are two other very cheap "hotels" in Todos Santos, *Hospedaje La Paz* (①) and *Las Olguitas* (①), but both are extremely rough.

The best place **to eat** is the delightful *Comedor Katy*, with tasty and cheap meals; there's also good food at the *Casa Familiar* and the gringo-geared restaurant/cafés *Cuchumatán* or *Tzolkin* nearby. There's a **post office**, while the Banrural **bank** (Mon–Fri 8.30am-5pm & Sat 9am–1pm) on the plaza will change travellers' cheques.

Though most of the fun of Todos Santos is in simply hanging out, it would be a shame not to indulge in a traditional **smoke sauna** (*chuc*) while you're here. Most of the guesthouses will prepare one for you. If you want to take a shirt, pair of trousers or *huipil* home with you, you'll find an excellent co-op selling quality weavings next to the *Casa Familiar*.

Walks around Todos Santos

The village of **SAN JUAN ATITÁN** is around five hours from Todos Santos across a beautiful isolated valley. Follow the path that bears up behind the *Comedor Katy*, past the ruins and high above the village through endless muddy switchbacks until you get to the ridge overlooking the valley where, if the skies are clear, you'll be rewarded by an awesome view of the Tajumulco and Tacaná volcanoes. Take the easy-to-follow central track downhill from here past some ancient cloudforest to San Juan Atitán. There are two hospedajes (both ①) if you want to stay, and morning **pick-ups** return to Huehue from 6am (1hr). Market days are Mondays and Thursdays.

Alternatively, you can walk down the valley along the road from Todos Santos to **San Martín** and on to **Jacaltenango**, a route which also offers superb views. There's a basic hospedaje (①) in Jacaltenango, so you could stay the night and then catch a bus back to Huehuetenango in the morning. Some buses from Huehue also continue down this route.

Aguacatán

To the east of Huehuetenango, a dirt road turns off at Chiantla, weaving through dusty foothills along the base of the Cuchumatanes to **AGUACATÁN**, a small agricultural town strung out along two main streets, shaped entirely by the dip in which it's built. During the colonial period, gold and silver were mined in the nearby hills – the Maya are said to have made bricks of solid gold for the king of Spain in an attempt to persuade him to let them keep their lands – though today the locals survive by growing vegetables, including huge quantities of garlic, much of it for export. The area is also the only place in the country where the Akateko language is spoken.

Aguacatán's huge Sunday **market** gets under way on Saturday afternoon, when traders arrive early to claim the best sites. On Sunday morning, a steady stream of people pour down the main street, cramming into the market and plaza, and soon spilling out into the surrounding area. Around noon the tide turns as the crowds start to drift back to their villages, with donkeys leading their drunken drivers. Despite the scale of the market, its atmosphere is subdued and the pace unhurried: for many it's as much a social event as a commercial one.

The traditional costume worn by the women of Aguacatán is unusually simple: their skirts are made of dark blue cotton and the *huipiles*, which hang loose, are decorated with bands of coloured ribbon on a plain white background. This plainness, though, is set off by the local speciality – the **cinta**, or headdress, in which they wrap their hair, an intricately embroidered piece of cloth combining blues, reds, yellows and greens.

Aguacatán's other attraction is the **source of the Río San Juan**, which emerges fresh and cool from beneath a nearby hill, making a good place for a chilly dip. To get there, walk east along the main street out of the village for about a kilometre, until you see the sign. From the village it takes about twenty minutes.

Eight daily **buses** run from Huehuetenango to Aguacatán between 6am and about 2.45pm (1hr). There are two small and very simple places to stay: the *Nuevo Amanecer* (②) and the *Hospedaje Aguateco* (①). **Beyond Aguacatán** the road runs out along a ridge, with fantastic views stretching out below, eventually dropping down to the riverside town of **Sacapulas**.

West to the Mexican border

From Huehuetenango the Carretera Interamericana runs for 79km to the Mexican border at **La Mesilla**. There are hourly buses between 5am and 6pm (2hr). If you get stuck at the border there's **accommodation** at the *Hotel Maricruz* (②–③), a clean place with private bathrooms and a restaurant, or the cheaper *Hospedaje Marisol* (②). The two sets of customs and *migración* are 3km apart. There are taxis, and on the Mexican side you can pick up buses running through the border settlement of **Ciudad Cuauhtemoc** to **Comitán**, or even direct to **San Cristóbal de las Casas**. Heading into Guatemala, the last bus leaves La Mesilla for Huehuetenango at around 5pm.

travel details

BUSES

Antigua to: Chimaltenango (every 20min 5am–7pm; 40min); Guatemala City (every 15min Mon–Sat 4am–7.30pm, Sun 6am–8pm; 1hr); Panajachel (1 daily; 2hr 30min); Santa María de Jesús (every 30min; 30min).

Chichicastenango to: Guatemala City (every 30min 5am–4.30pm; 3hr); Quetzaltenango (7 daily; 2hr 30min); Santa Cruz del Quiché (every 30min; 30min).

Huehuetenango to: Aguacatán (8 daily; 1hr); Guatemala City (14 daily; 6hr); La Mesilla (10 daily; 2hr); Quetzaltenango (14 daily; 2hr); Todos Santos Cuchumatán (4 daily; 2hr 30min).

Panajachel to: Antigua (1 daily at 11am; 3hr); Chichicastenango (5 daily Thurs & Sun, 1–2 daily at other times; 1hr 30min); Cocales (9 daily; 2hr 30min); Guatemala City (8 daily; 3hr 30min); Quetzaltenango (6 daily; 2hr 30min); Sololá (every 20 min; 30 min). There are also three daily tourist

shuttles to Antigua and on to Guatemala City, and five daily to Chichicastenango on market days.

Quetzaltenango to: Chichicastenango (6 daily; 2hr 30min); Guatemala City (19 daily; 4hr); Huehuetenango (14 daily; 2hr); Momostenango (hourly; 1hr 15min); Panajachel (6 daily; 2hr 30min); San Francisco El Alto (every 30min; 45min); Totonicapán (every 30min; 1hr); Santa Cruz del Quiché (7 daily; 3hr); Zunil (every 30min; 25min).

Santa Cruz del Quiché to: Guatemala City (every 30min; 3hr 30min); Nebaj (5 daily; 3hr 30min); Quetzaltenango (7 daily; 3hr); Sacapulas (9 daily; 1hr 45min); Uspantán (4 daily; 5hr).

FLIGHTS

Huehuetenango to: Guatemala City (daily; 50min).

Quetzaltenango to: Guatemala City (daily; 35min).

Santa Cruz del Quiché to: Guatemala City (1 daily; 25min).

CHAPTER 8

THE PACIFIC COAST

Beneath the chain of volcanoes that bounds the southern side of the highlands is a strip of sweltering, low-lying land some 300km long and 50km wide, known by Guatemalans simply as **La Costa Sur**. This featureless yet supremely fertile coastal plain – once a wilderness of swamp, forest and savanna – is today a land of vast fincas, scattered with uninteresting commercial towns and small seaside resorts.

The **Pacific coast** was once as rich in wildlife as the jungles of Petén, but while Petén has lain relatively undisturbed, the Pacific coast has been ravaged by development. Its large-scale agriculture – sugar cane, palm oil, cotton and rubber plantations – accounts for a substantial proportion of the country's exports. Only in some isolated sections, where mangrove swamps have been spared the plough, can you still get a sense of the maze of tropical vegetation which once covered it. The **Monterrico Reserve** is the most accessible protected area, a swampy refuge for sea turtles, iguanas, crocodiles and an abundance of bird life.

As for the archeological sites, they too have largely disappeared, though you can glimpse the extraordinary art of the **Pipil** (see p.220) around the town of **Santa Lucía Cotzumalguapa**. Here, a few small ceremonial centres, almost lost in fields of sugar cane, reveal a wealth of carvings, some of them still regularly used for religious rituals. The one site that ranks with those elsewhere in the country is **Abaj Takalik**, whose

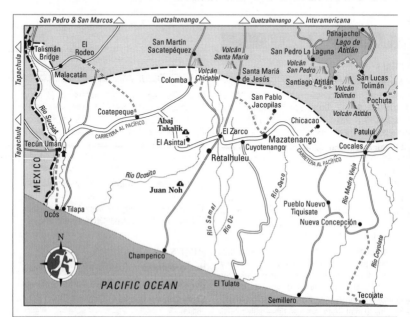

For an explanation of **accommodation price codes**, see p.125.

ruins are well worth a detour on your way to or from Mexico, or as a day-trip from Quetzaltenango or nearby Retalhuleu.

The main attraction should be the **beach**, but as nature has cursed the coast with mosquitoes and unpredictable sea currents, and man has added filthy palm huts, pig pens and garbage, it's not. The hotels are also some of the country's worst, so if you're desperate for a dip and a fresh shrimp feast, it's best to visit as a day-trip from the capital or Quetzaltenango. The one glorious exception to this rule is the nature reserve of **Monterrico**, which harbours an attractive village and what may be the country's finest beach, with a superb stretch of clean sand.

The main route through the region is the **Carretera al Pacífico**, which runs from the border with Mexico at Tecún Umán into El Salvador at Ciudad Pedro de Alvarado. It's the country's swiftest highway and you'll never have to wait long for a bus. Venture off the Carretera al Pacífico, however, and things slow down considerably, with irregular bus services and poorly maintained roads.

Some history

Before the arrival of the **Ocós** and **Iztapa** tribes from the north, little is known of the history of the Pacific coast. By 1500 BC, however, these Mesoamerican tribes had developed village-based societies with considerable skills in the working of stone and pottery. Between 400 and 900 AD, the whole coastal plain was again overrun by Mesoamericans; this time it was the **Pipil**, who brought sophisticated architectural and artistic skills which they used in building ceremonial centres.

The first Spaniards to set foot in Guatemala did so on the Pacific coast, arriving overland from the north. Alvarado's first confrontation with the Maya happened here, in the

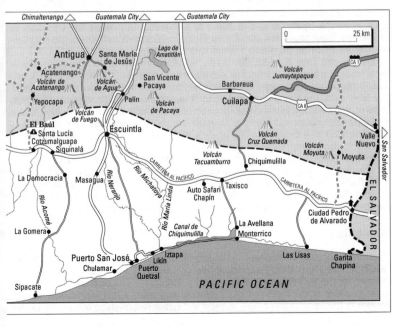

heat of the lowlands, before the Spanish moved north to Quetzaltenango. Once established there, they despatched a handful of Franciscans to convert the Pipil coastal population. In **colonial times**, the land was used for the production of indigo and cacao and for cattle ranching, never becoming anything more than a miserable, disease-ridden backwater. It was only after **independence** that commercial agriculture began to dominate this part of the country.

Today this coastline is the country's most intensely farmed region, with coffee grown on the volcanic slopes and entire villages effectively owned by vast cotton- and sugar-cane-growing fincas. Much of the nation's income is generated here, and the main towns are alive with commercial activity and dominated by the assertive machismo of *ladino* culture. In the past, the highland Maya were forcibly recruited to work the plantations here; even today many thousands come to the coast for seasonal work and continue to be exploited by the fincas.

From the Mexican border to Cocales

The coastal border with Mexico is the busiest of Guatemala's frontiers, with two crossing points, both open 24 hours. The northernmost of the two posts is the **Talismán Bridge**, also referred to as **El Carmen**, where there's little more than a few huts, a couple of basic pensiones (both ①) and a round-the-clock flow of buses to Guatemala City. If you're heading towards Quetzaltenango or the western highlands, take the first bus to Malacatán and change there. On the Mexican side, over the bridge, a constant stream of minibuses leave for Tapachula.

The **Tecún Umán** crossing is favoured by most Guatemalans and all commercial traffic. It has an authentic frontier flavour, with all-night bars frequented by lost souls, dealers in contraband and moneychangers. There are some cheap hotels: the *Hotel Vanessa 2* (②) and the *Hotel Don José, 2 C 3–42* (☎776 8164; ②) are two of the best, but it's probably a much better idea to get straight out of town – everyone else does. Once again, there's a steady stream of buses to Guatemala City along the Carretera al Pacífico via Coatepeque and Retalhuleu. If you're Mexico-bound, there are very frequent bus services to Tapachula (30min) over the border.

Heading east from the Mexican border, **COATEPEQUE** is the first place of any importance you come to, a town that's in many ways typical of the coastal strip. A furiously busy, purely commercial centre, this is where most of the coffee produced locally is processed. The action is centred on the **bus terminal**, an intimidating maelstrom of sweat, mud and energetic chaos. Buses run every thirty minutes from here to the two border crossings, and hourly to Quetzaltenango and Guatemala City. The town is also connected with Guatemala City by daily **flights** (1hr; US$55 one way), arriving at the airstrip about 3km southwest of the centre.

The best place to **stay** in Coatepeque is the *Hotel Villa Real*, 6 C 6–57 (☎775 1308, fax 775 1939; ④), a modern hotel with clean rooms and secure parking. A bit cheaper is the family-run *Hotel Baechli*, 6 C 6–35 (☎775 1483; ④), which has plain rooms with fan and TV, plus secure parking. There are two **banks** on the plaza that will change travellers' cheques and a **Telgua** office (daily 7am–10pm) at 5 Av and 7 C.

Retalhuleu

About 40km beyond Coatepeque is the largest town in the region, **RETALHULEU**, usually referred to as **Reu**, pronounced "Ray-oo". Set away from the highway and surrounded by the walled homes of the wealthy, Retalhuleu has managed to avoid the worst excesses of the coast and has a relaxed, easy-going air. It was founded by the Spanish in the early years of the Conquest and remains something of an oasis of civilization, with a plaza of towering Greek columns and an attractive colonial church. If you have time to kill, pop into the local **Museo de Arqueología y Etnología** in the plaza (Tues–Sun 8am–1pm & 2–5pm; US$0.20), home to an amazing collection of anthropomorphic figurines, mostly heads, and some photographs of the town dating back to the 1880s.

Budget **accommodation** is in short supply in Retalhuleu. The best is at the *Hotel Hillman* (②), 7 Av 7–99, where most rooms have a private bath. Elsewhere, rates go up steeply: the *Hotel Modelo* (☎771 0256; ③), 5 C 4–53, has decent basic but clean rooms with private bath, while over the road the good-value *Hotel Astor*, 5 C 4–60 (☎771 0475, *hotelastor@infovia.com.gt*; ④), has rooms with fan, TV and bath, set around a pleasant courtyard. If you want a bit more luxury, try the modern *Hotel Posada de Don José*, 5 C 3–67 (☎771 0180, *www.don-jose.com*; ④), which has good a/c rooms, a reasonable restaurant and a pool.

The **plaza** is the hub of the town's activity. Here you'll find the **post office** (Mon–Fri 8am–4.30pm) and three **banks**, including the Banco del Agro and, close by, the Banco Industrial with a 24-hour Visa ATM; the **Telgua** office (daily 7am–10pm) is just around the corner. The best **restaurants** are also on the plaza: try the *Cafetería la Luna* or, for cakes and pastries, *El Volován*.

Buses running along the coastal highway almost always pull in at the Retalhuleu terminal on 7 Av and 10 C, a ten-minute walk from the plaza. There's an hourly service to and from Guatemala City, the Mexican border and Quetzaltenango, plus regular buses to Champerico and El Tulate. Inter airlines **fly** daily to and from the capital (35min; US$40 one way), using the airstrip about 10km southwest of the town centre on the Champerico road to the coast. Retalhuleu has the only **Mexican consulate** on the Pacific coast, at 5 C and 3 Av (Mon–Fri 4–6pm).

Abaj Takalik

Currently undergoing excavation, the site of **Abaj Takalik** (daily 9am–4pm; US$3.20) has already provided firm evidence of an **Olmec** influence reaching this area in the first century AD. Excavations have so far unearthed some enormous stelae, several of them very well preserved, dating the earliest monuments to around 126 AD. The remains of two large **temple platforms** have also been cleared, and what makes a visit to this obscure site really worthwhile are the carved sculptures and stelae found around their base, including rare and unusual representations of frogs and toads (monument 68) and an alligator (monument 66). Amongst the finest carvings is stela 5, which features two standing figures separated by a hieroglyphic panel which has been dated to 126 AD. Look out for a giant Olmec head, too, showing a man of obvious wealth with great hamster cheeks. A small building acts as the site **musuem**, containing a model of Abaj Takalik and assorted carvings and ceramics. You should be able to get a warm *agua* near the entrance, but there's no food available.

To **get to Abaj Takalik**, take a local bus from Reu 15km east to the village of El Asintal, from where it's a 4km walk through coffee and cacao plantations. If you're using your own transport, take the highway towards Mexico and turn right at the sign.

Champerico, Mazatenango and Cocales

Some 42km south of Retalhuleu, a paved road runs to the beach at **CHAMPERICO**, which, though it certainly doesn't feel like it, is the country's third port. The town enjoyed a brief period of prosperity when it was connected to Quetzaltenango by rail, but there's little left now apart from a rusting pier. The **beach** is much the same as any-where else, although its sheer scale is impressive (watch out for the dangerous under-tow). Delicious fried shrimp and fish **meals** are widely available: try the *Restaurant*

Monte Limar or the *Alcatraz* for fried shrimp and fish, or, for a treat, feast on paella at the *Hotel Miramar* (☎773 7231) at 2 C and Av Coatepeque, which also has a fantastic wooden bar and dark, windowless rooms (②). **Buses** run between Champerico and Quetzaltenango every hour or so passing through Retalhuleu. The last bus for Retalhuleu leaves Champerico at 6pm.

Back on the highway, heading east, the next place of any size is the unremarkable town of **Cuyotenango**, where a side road heads off to the sweeping and almost undeveloped beach of **EL TULATE**. The surf is less dangerous here, and there's a handful of very simple fried fish 'n' shrimp cookshacks, but no hotels. Infrequent buses struggle down to El Tulate from Cuyotenango at weekends from Reu and Mazatenango.

The next stop on the highway is **MAZATENANGO**, another seething commercial town which also has a quieter, calmer side centred on the plaza. *Maxim's*, at 6 Av 9–23, serves excellent Chinese food and barbecued meats, or try *Croissants Pastelería* on the plaza for coffee and cakes. There are also a couple of cinemas, plenty of **banks**, a few run-down pensiones and, on the main highway, the decent, clean *Hotel Alba* (☎872 0264; ④), which has secure parking.

About 30km beyond Mazatenango is **COCALES**, a crossroads from where a road runs north to Santiago Atitlán, San Lucas Tolimán and Lago de Atitlán. If you're heading this way you can wait for a connection at the junction, but don't expect to make it all the way to Panajachel unless you get here by midday. The best bet is to take the first pick-up or bus for Santiago and catch a boat from there to other points on the lake. The last transport to Santiago Atitlán leaves Cocales at around 5pm.

Santa Lucía Cotzumalguapa and around

Another 23km brings you to **SANTA LUCÍA COTZUMALGUAPA**, another uninspiring Pacific town a short distance north of the highway. The main reason to visit is to explore the **archeological sites** that are scattered around the surrounding cane fields. You should bear in mind, though, that getting to them isn't easy unless you have your own transport or hire a taxi.

As usual, the **plaza** is the main centre of interest. Santa Lucía's shady square is disgraced by one of the ugliest buildings in the country (although there's plenty of competition), a memorably horrific green and white concrete municipal structure. Just off the plaza you'll find several cheap and scruffy **hotels**, the *Pensión Reforma* (①), 4 Av 4–71, and the *Hospedaje el Carmen* (①), around the corner on 5 C. The nearest upmarket place is the *Caminotel Santiaguito* (☎882 5435, fax 882 2285; ④), a slick motel on the highway at km 90.5, which has a swimming pool and restaurant.

Back in town at least three **banks** will change your travellers' cheques – try Banco Corpativo in the plaza, which accepts most varieties. For **food**, the *Comedor Lau* on 3 Av does reasonable Chinese meals, or there's a huge *Pollo Campero* on the north side of the square; there's a *Sarita* ice-cream parlour on 3 Av. For a drink, *Cevichería La Española* on 4 Av, south of the plaza, is the best bet.

Pullman **buses** passing along the highway will drop you at the entrance road to town, ten minutes' walk from the centre, while second-class buses from Guatemala City go straight into the terminal, a few blocks from the plaza. Buses to the capital leave the terminal hourly until 4pm, or you can catch a pullman from the highway.

Pipil sites around Santa Lucía Cotzumalguapa

A tour of the three **Pipil sites** around Santa Lucía can be an exhausting and frustrating process, taking you through a sweltering maze of cane fields. Doing the whole thing on foot is certainly the cheapest way – you can find children in the plaza or by asking in your pensión who'll act as guides – but it's far easier to hire a taxi in the plaza; reckon on US$10 to visit all three sites. If you want to see just one of them, choose Bilbao, just 1km or so from the centre of town, which features some of the best carving. If you get lost at any stage, ask for "*las piedras*", as they tend to be known locally.

In 1880, more than thirty Late Classic stone monuments were removed from the Pipil site of **Bilbao**, and nine of the very best were shipped to Germany. Four sets of stones are still visible in situ, however, and two of them perfectly illustrate the magnificent precision of the carving, beautifully preserved in slabs of black volcanic rock. To **get to** the site, walk uphill from the plaza, along 4 Av, and bear right at the end, where a dirt track takes you past a small red-brick house and along the side of a cane field. About 200m further on is a fairly wide path leading left into the cane for about 20m. This brings you to two large stones carved with bird-like patterns, with strange circular glyphs arranged in groups of three: the majority of the glyphs are recognizable as the names for days once used by the people of southern Mexico. In the same cane field, further along the same path, is another badly eroded stone, and a final set with a superbly preserved set of figures and interwoven motifs.

The second site is about 5km further afield in the grounds of the **Finca El Baúl**, reached by following 3 Av, the only tarmacked road that heads north out of town. The hilltop site has two stones, one flat and carved in low relief, the other a massive half-buried stone head, with wrinkled brow and patterned headdress, possibly that of Huhuetéotl, the fire god of the Mexicans, who supported the sun. The site itself is still actively used for pagan ceremonies, particularly by women hoping for children or safe childbirth. In front of the stones is a set of small altars on which local people make animal sacrifices, burn incense and leave offerings of flowers.

The next stones of interest are at the **finca** itself, a few kilometres further away from town, where the carvings include some superb heads, a stone skull, a massive jaguar and an extremely well-preserved stela of a ball-court player (monument 27) dating from the Late Classic period. Alongside all this antiquity is the finca's old steam engine, a miniature machine that used to haul the cane along a system of private tracks. As the finca has its own **bus service** you may be able to get a ride: buses leave from the Tienda El Baúl, a few blocks uphill from the plaza, four or five times a day, the first at around 7am and the last either way at about 6pm.

On the other side of town is the third site, at **Finca Las Ilusiones**, where there's another private collection of artefacts and some stone carvings. Perhaps the most striking figure here is a pot-bellied statue (monument 58), probably from the middle Preclassic era. There are several other original carvings, including some fantastic stelae, plus some copies, and a small museum crammed with literally thousands of small stone carvings and pottery fragments. To **get there**, walk east along the highway for about 1km, and turn left by the second Esso station.

La Democracia

The next town along the highway is Siquinalá, a run-down sort of place from where another branch road heads to the coast. Nine kilometres south along this road is **LA DEMOCRACIA**, home to a collection of archeological relics taken from the site of **Monte Alto** to the east of town and now displayed around the town plaza under a vast ceiba tree. These so-called "fat boys" are massive stone heads with simple, almost child-like faces, carved in Olmec style and thought to date from the mid-Preclassic period, possibly from as far back as 500 BC. Some are attached to smaller rounded bodies and rolled over on their backs clutching their swollen stomachs like stricken Teletubbies. Also on the plaza, the town **museum** (Tues–Sun 8am–noon & 2–5pm) houses carvings, a wondeful jade mask, yokes worn by ball-game players, pottery, grinding stones and a few more carved heads.

Escuintla and south to the coast

Located at the junction of the two principal coastal roads from the capital, **ESCUINT-LA** is the largest and most important of the Pacific towns. There's nothing to do here, but you do get a good sense of life on the coast, its pace and energy, and the frenetic commercial activity that drives it. Escuintla lies at the heart of the country's most productive region, both industrially and agriculturally, and the department's resources include cattle, sugar, cotton, light industry and even a small Texaco oil refinery.

Below the plaza a huge, chaotic **market** sprawls across several blocks, spilling out into 4 Av, the main commercial thoroughfare, which is also notable for a lurid blue mock-castle that functions as the town's police station.

There are plenty of cheap **hotels** near 4 Av, most of them sharing in the general air of dilapidation. The *Hospedaje Oriente*, 4 Av 11–30 (①), is cheap and pretty clean; for a/c and secure parking, head for *Hotel Costa Sur*, 4 Av and 12 C (☎888 1819; ③). As for **banks**, there's a Banco Industrial at 4 Av and 6 C, and a Lloyds at 7 C 3–07. Among the **places to eat**, the best deal is at *Pizzería al Macarone*, 4 Av 6–103, which has lunch specials for US$1.50. There are also two **consulates** in town, Honduras, at 6 Av 8–24, and El Salvador at 16 C 3–20.

Buses to Escuintla leave from the Treból junction in Guatemala City frequently until 7pm, returning from 8 C and 2 Av in Escuintla. For other destinations, there are two terminals: for places en route to the Mexican border, buses run through the north of town and stop by the Esso station opposite the Banco Uno (take a local bus up 3 Av); buses for the coast road and inland route to El Salvador are best caught at the main terminal on the south side of town, at the bottom of 4 Av (local bus down 4 Av). Buses leave every thirty minutes for Puerto San José, hourly for the eastern border, and six times daily for Antigua via El Rodeo.

Puerto San José

South from Escuintla an excellent, smooth highway heads through acres of cattle pasture to **PUERTO SAN JOSÉ**, which, in its prime, was Guatemala's main shipping terminal, funnelling goods to and from the capital. It has now been made virtually redundant by Puerto Quetzal, a container port a few kilometres to the east. Today both town and port are somewhat sleazy and the main business is local tourism: what used to be rough sailors' bars pander to the needs of the day-trippers from the capital who fill the beaches at weekends.

The shoreline is separated from the mainland by the **Canal de Chiquimulilla**, which starts near Sipacate, west of San José, and runs as far as the border with El Salvador, cutting off all the beaches in between. Here in San José, the main resort area is on the other side of the canal, directly behind the beach. This is where all the bars and restaurants are, most of them crowded at weekends with big *ladino* groups feasting on seafood. The **hotels** are some of the worst value in the country, and cater to a largely drunken clientele – you could try *Casa San José Hotel*, Av del Comercio (☎776 5587; ③), which has a pool and restaurant, or, for a really cheap option, *Hospedaje Viñas de Mar* (②), which is basic but right by the beach.

Buses between San José and Guatemala City run every thirty minutes or so all day. From Guatemala City they leave from the terminal in Zona 4, and in San José from the plaza.

Monterrico

The setting of **MONTERRICO**, further east along the coast, is one of the finest on the Pacific coast, with the scenery reduced to its basic elements: a strip of dead straight sand, a line of powerful surf, a huge empty ocean and an enormous curving horizon. The village is friendly and relaxed, separated from the mainland by the waters of the Chiquimulilla canal, which weaves through a fantastic network of **mangrove swamps**. Mosquitoes can be a problem during the wet season, but that said, Monterrico is certainly the best place on the coast to spend time by the sea, though take care in the waves as there's a vicious undertow – lifeguards are on duty at weekends.

Beach apart, Monterrico's chief attraction is the **Biotopo Monterrico-Hawaii nature reserve**, which embraces the village, the beach – an important **turtle** nesting ground – and a large slice of the mangrove swamps behind, covering a total area of some 28 square kilometres (sadly, however, the reserve's protected status does not stop the dumping of domestic rubbish and the widespread theft of turtle eggs). The reserve encloses four distinct types of mangrove, with dark, nutrient-rich waters flowing between a dense mat of branches, interspersed with narrow canals, open lagoons, bulrushes and water lilies. The tangle of roots acts as a kind of marine nursery, offering small fish protection from their natural predators, while above the surface the dense vegetation and ready food supply provide an ideal home for hundreds of species of bird and a handful of mammals, including racoons, opossums, ant-eaters and armadillos, plus iguanas, caimans and alligators. The best way to travel is in a small *cayuco* (kayak); ask around at the dock for a boatman or organize a trip through *Iguana Tours* (☎238 4690), on the main street close to the football field. The reserve's **visitor centre** (daily 8.30am–noon & 2–5pm), just off the beach between *Hotel Mangle* and the *Pez d'Oro*, has plenty of information about the environment (Spanish only) and an important turtle hatchery; caimans and iguanas are also bred at the centre for release into the wild.

Monterrico, like most places on the Pacific coast, is very quiet during the week but fills up at **weekends** with Guatemalans from the capital and increasing numbers of language-school students from Antigua. Though the beach is far too expansive to get packed, the atmosphere tends to be raucous, with some of the more frenzied visitors ripping up and down the sands on their motorbikes.

Getting to Monterrico

The best way to **get to Monterrico** is via the coastal highway at **Taxisco**. From here, trucks and buses run along the 17km of paved road to **LA AVELLANA**, a couple of kilometres from Monterrico on the opposite side of the mangrove swamp, where boats shuttle passengers and cars back and forth. There's a steady flow of traffic between Taxisco and La Avellana, the last bus leaving Taxisco at 6pm and La Avellana at 4.30pm – you'll find the latest schedules posted in several hotels, including the *Baule Beach*. Several direct **buses** run between La Avellana and the Zona 4 bus terminal in Guatemala City, taking around three and a half hours; alternatively, get on any bus heading for Taxisco and change there. An altogther easier, though pricey (US$25 return), option if you're staying in Antigua is to use one of the **shuttle-bus** services, which leave every Friday afternoon and return on Sundays around 3pm.

Hourly buses also continue from Taxisco along the Carretera al Pacífico to the border with El Salvador at Ciudad Pedro de Alvarado, just over an hour away. The border is a fairly quiet one, as most traffic uses the Valle Nuevo post to the north, but there are a couple of basic hospedajes (①–②) and some comedores if you get stuck.

Accommodation

Most of Monterrico's **accommodation** is concentrated in the mid-range, with few good budget rooms available. Everything is centred right on or just off the beach. As there are **no phones** it isn't that easy to book in advance, though many places have reservation numbers in Guatemala City and others use cellular phones. As elsewhere on the coast, prices can increase by up to fifty percent at weekends, when it's also best to book ahead.

Eco Beach Place, turn left at the beach, walk for 250m (cell phone ☎309 2505, Guatemala City ☎369 1116 or 365 7217). Very attractive new guesthouse, set away from the others, run by a friendly Italian-Guatemalan with large comfortable doubles – all but one have private bath. There's good grub, a nice lounge and bar area and stunning Pacific vistas from the veranda. ④.

Hotel Baule Beach, next door to the *Kaiman* (Guatemala City ☎478 3088, *baulebeach @hotmail.com*). For many years this was a very popular place, but a recent change in management has seen service levels plummet and a general air of decay set in. All rooms have private bath and mosquito net and there's a tiny pool. Avoid the food. ③.

Hotel El Mangle, beside the *Baule Beach* (Guatemala City ☎369 8958 or 514 6517, fax 369 7631). Friendly place with thirteen very pleasant but small budget rooms – all have private shower, fan, nice wooden furniture and little terrace with hammocks – and there's a small pool. ④.

Hotel La Sirena, turn right at the beach, walk for 100m. Huge, unattractive concrete hotel which nonetheless offers a decent choice of digs: from tiny twin-bed rooms to larger apartments. There's also a pool and a reasonable restaurant. ②–④.

Johnny's Place, turn left when you reach the ocean and it's the first place you'll come to (cell phone ☎206 4702, *www.backpackamericas.com/johnnys.htm*). Selection of reasonable, though not wildly attractive, self-catering bungalows sleeping between two and four, each with little bathing pools, plus four gloomy but cheap rooms. The new management team promises substantial renovation. ③/⑤.

Kaiman Inn, turn left at beach and walk for 200m. The large rooms have mosquito nets and fans but are a little run-down, and it can be noisy here. There's a pool and a variable, overpriced Italian restaurant. ④.

Pez de Oro, the last place as you head east down the beach (cell phone ☎204 5249, Guatemala City ☎368 3684, *laelegancia@guate.net*). The nicest cottages in Monterrico – well-spaced, comfortable and tastefully decorated. Most are detached and all have ceiling fans and balconies with hammocks. The pretty swimming pool is shaded by coconut palms and there's a good Italian restaurant with excellent pasta and wine by the glass. ⑤.

Eating and drinking

When it comes to **eating** in Monterrico, you can either dine at one of the hotels on the beach – though the food is pricey – or at one of the comedores in the village, the best being the *Divino Maestro*, where they do a superb shark steak with rosemary. For a relaxing **drink,** head for the *Caracol* bar, which boasts a lethal cocktail list and good tunes.

travel details

BUSES

Coatepeque to: Guatemala City (hourly; 4hr); Retalhuleu (every 30min; 50min); Quetzaltenango (hourly; 2hr); Talismán and Tecún Umán (12 daily; 40min).

Cocales to: Escuintla (14 daily; 30min).

Escuintla to: Antigua (6 daily; 1hr 30min); Ciudad Pedro de Alvarado, El Salvador (hourly; 2hr 30min); Guatemala City (18 daily; 1hr 15min).

Guatemala City to: La Avellana (4 daily; 3hr 30min); Puerto San José (every 30 min; 1hr 30min); Taxisco (hourly; 3hr); Tecún Umán and Talismán via all towns on the Carretera del Pacífico (19 daily; 5hr); Tapachula, Mexico (3 daily; 6hr).

La Avellana to: Guatemala City (4 daily; 3hr 30min).

Retalhuleu to: Champerico (8 daily; 1hr); Cocales (14 daily; 50min); Guatemala City (10 daily; 4hr); Mazatenango (12 daily; 30min); Quetzaltenango (10 daily; 1hr 15min).

Talismán to: Guatemala City (10 daily; 5hr).

Tecún Umán to: Guatemala City (14 daily; 5hr); Quetzaltenango (10 daily; 2hr 30min).

FLIGHTS

Coatepeque to: Guatemala City (daily; 1hr).

Retalhuleu to: Guatemala City (daily; 45min).

CHAPTER 9

EAST TO THE CARIBBEAN

T he land to the **east of Guatemala City** is some of the most varied in the entire country, ranging from the cacti-spiked near-desert around the El Rancho junction to the permanently lush Caribbean coast. Although the coastal area was fairly densely populated in Maya times, it was largely abandoned until the end of the nineteenth century. Its revival was due to the arrival of the United Fruit Company, who cleared the land for the banana plantations that still dominate the area. Fruit-laden trucks thunder along the road to the coast, following the **Motagua valley**, a broad river corridor dividing two high mountain ranges. A couple of hours before you reach the coast, the route passes the ruins of **Quiriguá**, a small site with some of the finest stelae and carvings in the entire Maya world. At the end of the road is the faded, slightly

For an explanation of **accommodation price codes**, see p.125.

seedy port of **Puerto Barrios**, a steamy, largely *ladino* town, from where it's possible to cross the border into Honduras.

To the north of the Motagua valley is **Lago de Izabal**, a vast expanse of fresh water ringed by lonely villages and swamps, its largely unpopulated shores home to a tremendous variety of **wildlife** (most of it threatened), including alligators, iguanas, turtles, toucans and manatee. The best base for exploring this region is sleepy, one-street **El Estor**, from where you can easily venture into the **Bocas del Polochic** nature reserve. Sailing towards the Caribbean from Lago de Izabal you pass through El Golfete lake and the towering, jungle-covered gorge systems of the **Río Dulce**. At the end of the river is **Lívingston**, a very funky coconut-and-ganja town, home to Guatemala's black Garífuna people.

Also included in this chapter are the **eastern highlands** – dry *ladino* territory, intermittently scarred by ancient, eroded volcanoes and hot, dusty towns. Though the scenery is superb, there is little for the traveller here, save the beautifully isolated **Volcán de Ipala**, with its stunning crater lake, and the curious holy town of **Esquipulas**, whose huge basilica – containing an image of the black Jesus – is the focus for Central America's largest annual pilgrimage.

The Motagua valley

Leaving the capital, the Caribbean highway passes through the hilly, infertile terrain of the upper **Río Motagua**. As you head further down the valley, the land rapidly becomes bleak, dry and distinctly inhospitable, until you come to the first place of any note: the **Río Hondo junction**. Here you'll find a waiting army of food sellers swarming around every bus that stops, and a line of blue and red Pepsi-sponsored comedores. If you need refreshment, there are usually fresh coconuts for sale, too. The road divides here, with one arm heading south to Esquipulas and the three-way **border** with Honduras and El Salvador, and the main branch continuing on to the coast. There are a number of motels scattered around Río Hondo which, bizarre as it may seem, is viewed by middle-class Guatemalans as something of a weekend retreat, due to the presence of the large *Valle Dorado* waterworld park-motel (☎941 2542, fax 941 2543; ⑥), close by at Km 146.

On down the valley the landscape starts to undergo a radical transformation: the flood plain opens out and the cacti and scrub are gradually overwhelmed by a profusion of tropical growth. It was this supremely rich flood plain that attracted both the Maya and the United Fruit Company, to the great benefit of both.

Quiriguá

Set splendidly in an isolated pocket of rainforest, surrounded by an ocean of banana trees, the ruins of **Quiriguá** (daily 7.30am–5pm; US$4) may not be able to match the enormity of Tikal, but they do have some of the finest Maya carving anywhere. Only neighbouring Copán (see p.406) offers any competition to the magnificent stelae, altars and so-called "zoomorphs", covered in well-preserved and superbly intricate glyphs and portraits.

The **early history** of Quiriguá is still fairly vague, but during the Late Preclassic period (250 BC–300 AD) migrants from the north, possibly Putun Maya from the Yucatán peninsula, established themselves as rulers here. Later, in the Early Classic period (250–600 AD), the centre was dominated by Copán, just 50km away, and doubtless valued for its position on the banks of the Río Motagua, an important trade route, and as a source of jade, which is found throughout the valley.

It was the during the rule of the great leader **Cauac Sky** that Quiriguá challenged Copán, captured its leader 18 Rabbit in 737, and was able to assert its independence and embark on an unprecedented building boom: the bulk of the great stelae date from this period. For a century Quiriguá dominated the lower Motagua valley and its highly prized resources. Under **Jade Sky**, who took the throne in 790, Quiriguá reached its peak, with fifty years of extensive building work, including a radical reconstruction of the acropolis. From the end of Jade Sky's rule, in the middle of the ninth century, the historical record fades out, as does the period of prosperity and power.

Entering the site beneath the ever-dripping ceiba, jocote, palm and fig trees, you emerge at the northern end of the **Great Plaza**. To the left-hand side of the path from the ticket office and new site **museum** (due to open in 2002) is a badly ruined pyramid and, dominating the site at the southern end of the plaza, the untidy bulk of the **acropolis**. Liberally scattered amidst the luxuriant grass of the plaza are the finely carved **stelae** for which Quiriguá is justly famous. The nine stelae in the plaza are the tallest in the Maya world (the largest; stela E, rises to a height of 8m and weighs 65 tons), while their sides are all similarly covered with glyphs and portraits of the city's rulers, with Cauac Sky depicted on no fewer than seven (A, C, D, E, F, H and J). Two unusual features are particularly clear: the vast headdresses, which dwarf the faces, and the beards.

As you head down the path towards the acropolis you can just make out the remains of a **ball court** on your right, before you reach the other features that have earned Quiriguá its fame. Squatting at the base of the ruined acropolis are the **zoomorphs**: six bizarre, globular-shaped blocks of stone carved with interlacing animal and human figures – look out for the turtle, frog and jaguar. The best of the lot is zoomorph P, which shows a figure seated in Buddha-like pose, interwoven with a maze of other detail.

Practicalities

The **ruins** are situated some 70km beyond the junction at Río Hondo, and 4km down a side-turning from the main road. All **buses** running between Puerto Barrios (2hr) and Guatemala City (4hr) pass by. There's a fairly regular bus service from the highway to the site itself, plus assorted motorbikes and pick-ups. You shouldn't have to wait too long to get a ride back to the highway, or you can walk it in around forty-five minutes.

There are a couple of simple places to **stay** in the village of **QUIRIGUÁ**, just off the main highway 5km from the ruins; the village can be reached either by following the old railtrack (which is halfway between the ruins and the highway) west for 3km or heading back to the highway itself and getting a ride from there. The best option is the pleasant *Hotel y Restaurante Royal* (☎947 3639; ②–③), alongside the former hospital for tropical diseases, with large old rooms downstairs and modern rooms on the upper floor; the *Hotel el Eden* (☎947 3281; ②), just off the tracks next to the old station, is another reasonable budget option, and also serves **meals**.

Puerto Barrios

Founded in the 1880s by President Rufino Barrios, the port of **PUERTO BARRIOS** soon fell into the hands of the United Fruit Company, who used their control of the railways to ensure that the bulk of trade passed this way. Puerto Barrios was Guatemala's main port for most of this century, and the Fruit Company were exempt from almost all tax.

These days the boom is over and the town distinctly forlorn, with a smattering of strip clubs, all-night bars and brothels. The streets are wide, but they're poorly lit and badly potholed, and the handful of fine old Caribbean houses is now outnumbered by grimy hotels and hard-drinking bars. The reason most travellers come here is to get somewhere else: to Honduras via the new border crossing at Corinto (see p.229), to Livingston, or to Punta Gorda in Belize (see p.111) by boat.

Arrival and information

There's no purpose-built bus station in Puerto Barrios. Litegua **buses**, which serve all destinations along the Caribbean Highway, have their own terminal in the centre of town on 6 Av, between 9 and 10 C. All second-class buses, including ten daily services to Chiquimula and four daily to Esquipulas, arrive and depart close by from several bays grouped around the central market opposite. **Taxis** seem to be everywhere in Barrios; drivers toot for custom as they drive through the streets. A daily Taca **flight** from Guatemala City lands at the airstrip about 3km northeast of the town centre (call Taca on ☎334 7722 for details).

There's no Inguat tourist office in town: check at the Litegua terminal for bus schedules and at the **dock** at the end of 12 C for boat departures to Lívingston and to Punta Gorda in Belize. You have to clear **migración** (daily 7am–noon & 2–5pm; ☎334 7722) before you can buy a ticket, which is best done the day before departure: the *migración* is at the end of 9 C, two blocks north of the dock. The **Telgua** office (daily 7am–midnight) is at the junction of 8 Av and 10 C, though you'll find the best international call rates at **Comunitel**, 7 C and 5 Av (daily 8am–10pm); the best **Internet** café is *Cafenet* at 13 C and 6 Av (daily 9am–9pm). There are a number of **banks** in Puerto Barrios: you'll find Lloyds on the corner of 7 Av and 15 C (Mon–Fri 9am–4pm, Sat 9am–1pm), Banco G & T Continental (for Mastercard) at 7 C and 6 Av (Mon–Fri 9am–7pm, Sat 9am–1pm), and Banco Industrial (with a 24hr Visa-friendly ATM) at 7 Av and 7 C. The **post office** is at 6 C and 6 Av (Mon–Fri 8am–4.30pm).

Accommodation

Cheap **hotels** are plentiful in Puerto Barrios and there is a slice of Caribbean charm in amongst the squalor. This is a very hot and sticky town, so you'll definitely want a fan, if not air conditioning.

Hotel Caribeña, 4 Av between 10 and 11 calles (☎948 0384). Large and friendly place with very good-value rooms, including doubles, triples and quadruples. The management is friendly and there's a quality seafood restaurant attached which also does cheap breakfasts. ②.

Hotel Cayos del Diablo, across the bay, reached by a regular free boat service from the jetty (in Guatemala City ☎333 4633). Lovely Best Western-owned hideaway hotel, discreetly set above a secluded beach, with beautiful thatched cabañas, a swimming pool, good restaurant, tennis courts and kayaks available for rent. The definitive luxury option on this stretch of coastline, with special packages available. ⑧.

Hotel del Norte, 7 C and 1 Av (☎ & fax 948 0087). Built entirely from wood, this is an absolute gem of a hotel, and a magnificent colonial time-warp. The clapboard rooms aren't especially comfortable or very private, but there's a nice swimming pool, and the location, overlooking the Caribbean, is magnificent. Best of all is the incredibly classy, mahogany-panelled restaurant and bar – though the food doesn't quite match the decor. ④–⑤ with bath, ③ without.

Hotel Europa 2, 3 Av and 12 C (☎948 1292). Clean, safe and friendly place, ideally located for the ferry to Lívingston. All rooms have fan and private shower and there are good rates for single travellers. The almost identical *Hotel Europa 1* is at 8 Av and 8 C (☎948 0127). Both ③.

Hotel Internacional, 7 Av and 16 C (☎948 0367). Very well priced motel-style set-up, with a small, heat-busting swimming pool. All rooms have private shower and TV, and come with the choice of either a/c or fan. ④ with a/c, ③ without.

Hotel Xelajú, 9 C, between 6 and 7 avenidas (☎948 0482). Though it looks a little rough from the outside, this reasonable budget place is safe, has clean rooms, and doesn't allow visiting señoritas. ②–③.

Eating, drinking and nightlife

There's an abundance of cheap **comedores** around the market, such as *Cafesama* and *El Punto*, although the *Restaurant Fogón Porteño*, close by on 6 Av and 9 C, has a nicer setting. One of the best places in town is the *Rincón Uruguayo* (closed Mon), which does meat cooked South-American style on a giant *parrilla* (grill), plus vegetarian dishes like barbecued spring onions and *papas asados* – it's a ten-minute walk south of the centre at 7 Av and 16 C. For **fish and seafood** there's plenty of choice: try *Safari*, ten minutes north of the centre on the seafront at 5 Avenida, which is good, if a little pricey, and serves huge portions; *Mar Azul*, also right on the seafront, at the end of 6 Calle, which is a little cheaper; or *La Caribeña*, 4 Av between 10 and 11 calles, which does a superb *caldo de mariscos* (seafood soup). Finally, there's the unique period charm of the *Hotel del Norte* restaurant (see opposite).

Puerto Barrios also has more than its fair share of **bars** and **nightclubs**, offering the full range of late-night sleaze. None of these is hard to find – a lot of the action is centred around 6 and 7 avenidas and 6 and 7 calles. Reggae and punta rock are the sounds on the street in Puerto Barrios, and you'll catch a fair selection at weekends in the *Bric a Brac Disco* on 7 C and 7 Av.

Overland to Honduras

Getting to Honduras from Puerto Barrios is now straightforward, thanks to the opening of the new Arizona bridge over the Río Motagua. Minibuses depart from the marketplace in Puerto Barrios (every 30min; 6.30am–4.30pm) and head via the small town of Entre Ríos to the Arizona bridge (1hr), where there's a new Guatemalan *migración* – you may be asked for an unofficial "exit tax" (US$1). You then have to catch a pick-up to the village of **Corinto**, just inside Honduras a further 8km away, where you'll find the Honduran *migración* and plenty of moneychangers offering fairly reasonable rates. (Note that these details might change, as there are plans to open a bi-national border post close to Arizona in 2002 or 2003 as part of a Central American trade initative.) Buses depart from Corinto to Puerto Cortés (every 90min; at least 3hr) via the pretty village of Omoa (see p.428). If you set out early from Puerto Barrios, you should get to San Pedro Sula (see p.421) the same day, and it's certainly possible to make an afternoon flight out to one of the Bay Islands. San Pedro Sula is extremely well connected with Puerto Cortés by Citul and other buses (every 30min 5am–7.30pm; 1hr 15min); the Citul terminal is located just across the plaza from the *migración*.

Lívingston, the Río Dulce and Lago de Izabal

At the mouth of the Río Dulce, and only accessible by boat, **LÍVINGSTON** is a very funky town that not only enjoys a superb setting but also offers a unique fusion of Guatemalan and Caribbean culture in which marimba mixes with Marley. Along with several other villages in Central America, Lívingston provides the focus for the displaced **Garífuna**, or black Carib people, who are now strung out along the Caribbean coast between southern Belize and northern Nicaragua (for a brief history of the Garífuna, see p.448). To a lesser extent, Lívingston also acts as a focal point for the Q'eqchi' Maya, many of whom moved into the area to escape the fighting during the guerrilla war.

Lívingston is undoubtedly one of the most fascinating places in Guatemala, and many visitors find the languid rhythm of life here hypnotic. The town is as popular with weekending Guatemalans as it is with international travellers, and offers a welcome break from mainstream Guatemalan culture. Garífuna **food** is generally excellent and more varied than the usual comedor dishes, and Garífuna punta rock and reggae make a pleasant change from the standard merengue. While certainly not unaffected by the pressures of daily life in Central America (crack cocaine use is growing), the general atmosphere is very chilled.

Lívingston is a small place, and you can see most of what there is to see in an hour or so. While there's not really that much to do in town itself other than relaxing in local style, a few places nearby are worth a visit. The local **beaches**, though safe for swimming, are not of the Caribbean dream variety, with the exception of the wonderful white-sand **Playa Blanca**, though this can be visited only on a tour (see overleaf).

Women should note that it is not safe to walk alone along the local beaches, as a number of rapes have been reported in recent years.

The most popular trip out of town is to **Las Siete Altares**, a group of waterfalls some 5km to the northwest. Unfortunately, there have been sporadic **attacks on tourists** walking to the falls. Though incidents have diminished in recent years, you should ask about the current situation before setting out; if you do decide to go, don't take anything of value. The safest option is to hire a local guide or visit as part of a tour (see below). If you decide to go it alone, continue down the street past the *Ubafu* bar and turn right by the *African Place* hotel to the beach, then follow the sand away from town. After a couple of kilometres, wade across a small river and, just before the beach eventually peters out, take a path to the left. Follow this inland and you'll soon reach the first of the falls; to reach the others, scramble up, and follow the water. All of the falls are idyllic places to swim, but the highest one is the best of all.

Arrival and information

The only way to get to Lívingston is **by boat**, either from Puerto Barrios, the Río Dulce, Belize, or, occasionally, from Omoa in Honduras (see p.428 for more details). Boats arrive at the main dock on the south side of town; straight ahead, up the hill, is the main drag with most of the restaurants, bars and shops. The **migración** (daily 7am–9pm) is on the left as you walk up the hill, a block or so before the *Hotel Río Dulce*. For **changing money**, try the Banco de Comercio, down the road to the left as you walk up the hill from the docks, or Bancafé, on the main drag; on Sundays, when the banks are closed, try the Almacen Koo Wong in the centre of town. The **Telgua** office (daily 7am–midnight) is on the right, up the main street from the docks, next door to the **post office**. There are several places with **Internet** access, try @ or Happy Fish on the main drag, or Explorer Travel, just west of the dock – rates are around US$6 an hour.

Exotic Travel (☎947 0049, *kjchew@hotmail.com*), in the same building as the *Bahía Azul* restaurant, and Happy Fish (☎902 7143), just down the road, are the best **travel agents** in town. The helpful owners can arrange a variety of trips around the area: up the Río Dulce (US$9); along the coast to the lovely white-sand beach of Playa Blanca (US$10); to the Sapodilla Cayes off Belize (see p.113) for **snorkelling** (US$30); and to the Punta Manabique reserve for **sports-fishing** (US$14). All these trips only depart if there are sufficient people; sign up early and be prepared to wait a day or two. Several companies, including Exotic Travel and Happy Fish, run morning boat trips up the Río Dulce (US$9 per person) – Explorer Travel's are a little more leisurely than most, with greater opportunities to soak up the scenery.

Scheduled **boats** leave for Puerto Barrios daily at 5am and 2pm (1hr 30min), supplemented by **speedboats**, which leave when full (roughly every 30min; 6.30am–5.30pm; 25min). Boats also run to Punta Gorda in **Belize** on Tuesdays and Fridays at 8am (1hr) and to Omoa in **Honduras** when there are sufficient numbers (US$35 per person, minimum 6 people; 2hr 30min).

Accommodation

There is a pretty decent selection of **hotels** in town and though rooms fill up at weekends and during holidays, you should always be able to find a bed.

Hotel California, turn left just before the *Bahía Azul* restaurant. Clean hotel, painted a vivid green and offering reasonable rooms, all with private bath. ②.

Hotel Caribe, along the shore to the left of the dock as you face the town (☎948 0053). Basic, budget hotel with bare rooms, some with private shower and fan. ①–②.

Hotel Casa Rosada, about 300m left of the dock (☎ & fax 947 0303, fax 947 0304, *info@hotelcasarosada .com*). Relaxing and charming American-owned establishment, with a harbourfront plot and lush, spacious grounds. The small but cheery wooden cabins (④) have nice hand-painted touches but are a little overpriced (and lack private bath); alternatively, some very smart duplex bungalows (⑥) with private bath are currently being built. Excellent vegetarian meals.

Hotel Doña Alida, turn right immediately after the *Tucán Dugú*, then walk north 250m (☎ & fax 947 0027, *hotelalida@hotmail.com*). Very welcoming owners and a selection of spacious modern rooms, some with excellent sea views, in a quiet cliffside location with a little beach below. ④.

Hotel El Viajero, turn left after the dock, past the *Hotel Caribe*. A good budget choice, with safe and clean – if slightly shabby – rooms, all with fan and some with private bath. There's a shoreside snack bar, too. ②.

Hotel Garífuna, turn left off the main street towards the *Ubafu* bar, then first right (☎948 1091, fax 948 0184). Squeaky-clean, locally owned guesthouse with good-value, secure and spotless rooms, all with fan and private shower. ②.

Hotel Vista al Mar, about 350m left of the dock (☎947 0131, fax 947 0134). Secure, simple wooden huts, three with private bath, set close to the sea and run by amiable locals. ②–③.

Tucán Dugú, first on the right, uphill from the jetty (☎947 0072, fax 947 0614, *www.tukanis.com.gt*). Lívingston's only luxury hotel, with attractive modern rooms set above the bay, a pleasant bar, swimming pool and gardens. ⑦–⑧.

Eating and drinking

There are plenty of places to **eat** in Lívingston, two of the best for local food being *Tiburón Gato* and *Margot* (where Mama Helén serves up a mean *tapado*). For a memorable **vegetarian** meal, check out the *Hotel Casa Rosada* (see above), though it's not priced for budget travellers. The *Bahía Azul*, on the main street, is probably the most popular place in town, with an excellent terrace for watching Lívingston streetlife. There are also plenty of cheap, small comedores on the main street, all selling decent **fried fish**: try *Comedor Coni* or the *Lívingston*.

For evening **entertainment** there are lots of groovy bars (*Ubafu* is usually the most lively), movies at the *Black Sheep* next to the *Bahía Azul*, and a disco on the beach where you'll hear Jamaican reggae and pure Garífuna punta rock.

The Río Dulce

Another very good reason for coming to Lívingston is to venture up the **Río Dulce**, a truly spectacular trip that leads eventually to the town of the same name about 30km upriver. The total journey takes some two to three hours and can be organized through any of the travel agents in Lívingston (see opposite).

From Lívingston the river heads into a system of **gorges** between sheer rock faces 100m or so in height. Clinging to the sides is a wall of tropical vegetation and cascading vines, and here and there you might see some white herons or flocks of squawking parakeets. Six kilometres from Lívingston there's a delightful river tributary, the **Río Tatín**, which some boatmen will venture up if you ask them, where there's a good guesthouse, the *Finca Tatín* (☎902 0831, *www.geocities.com/fincatatin/index.htm*; ②), set in dense shoreside jungle and only reachable by boat. Run by hospitable Italians, the four wooden huts are very basic, but the remote, peaceful location is the real draw, and there's excellent healthy food, kayaks for hire, walking trails and Spanish classes available.

Continuing up the Río Dulce for another kilometre or so, you'll pass an excellent place for a swim, where warm sulphurous waters emerge from the base of the cliff. Past here, the river opens up into the **Golfete** lake, surrounded by swampy lowlands, the north shore of which has been designated the **Biotopo de Chocón Machacas** (daily 7am–4pm; US$5), designed to protect the **manatee** – though the huge mammals are extremely timid and you'll be very lucky to see one. The reserve also protects the forest that still covers much of the lake's shore, and there are some specially cut trails where you might catch sight of a bird or two, or, if you've plenty of time and patience, even a tapir or jaguar. Heading on upstream, the river closes in again and passes the marina and

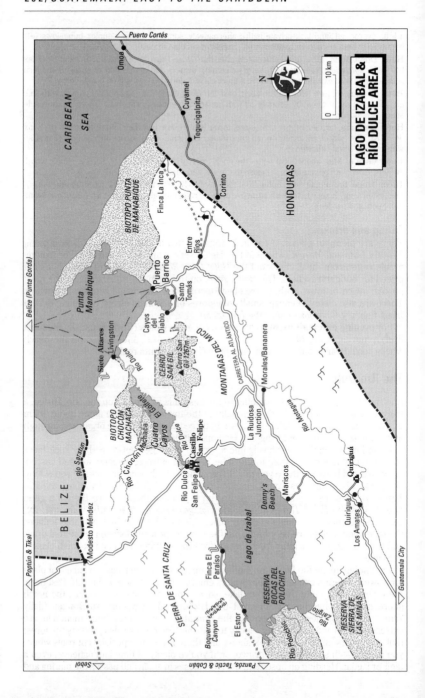

LAGO DE IZABAL &
RÍO DULCE AREA

bridge at the squalid town of **Río Dulce** (also known as Fronteras). This part of the Río Dulce is a favourite playground for wealthy Guatemalans, with boats and hotels that would put parts of California to shame. The area is also popular with European and North American yachties on account of its sheltered waters, stores and repair workshops. The road for Petén crosses the river here and the boat trip comes to an end.

Río Dulce town

The town of **RÍO DULCE** itself is little more than a truck stop, where traffic for Petén pauses before the long stretch to Flores. The town is actually formed out of older settlements, Fronteras to the north and El Rellano to the south, connected by a monstrous concrete road bridge. The road between them is lined with cheap comedores and stores, and you can pick up buses here in either direction.

A good, inexpensive **place to stay** is the *Hotel Backpackers* (☎208 1779, fax 331 9408, *casaguatemala@guate.net*), a budget set-up underneath the south side of the bridge, with dorm beds, hammock space and private doubles (③). The hotel is owned by the nearby Casa Guatemala children's home, and many of the young staff are former residents. It's also a good place to pick up information, and there's a noticeboard with information about yacht-crewing opportunities and sailing courses; they also rent canoes. The comfortable *Hotel Río Dulce*, on the north side of the bridge (☎930 3179; ③), has spotless doubles with fans and showers. Very close by, under the bridge, *Bruno's* (☎930 5174, *rio@guate.net*) has modern and comfortable but overpriced rooms (⑥) with terraces, along with some less attractive but cheaper accommodation (④); there's also a swimming pool and bar-restaurant. *Hacienda Tijax* (☎902 0858, *www.tijax.com*), two minutes by water-taxi from the bus stop on the north side of the bridge, is a working teak and rubber farm with a pleasant lakeside plot and tasty, slightly pricey food, hiking trails and horse riding. Accommodation is either in rooms (③), cabins (④) or bungalows (⑥), and you can also **camp** here (US$2 per person).

As for **restaurants**, *Río Bravo*, on the north side of the bridge, is the best place to meet other travellers (and yachties), eat pizza or pasta and drink the night away – you can also make radio contact with most places around the river and lake from here. *Bruno's* serves up international food and offers the chance to catch up with the latest news and North American sports events – it's very popular with the sailing fraternity – they have **Internet** facilities here too. For cheap grub, there's a strip of pretty undistinguished comedores on the main road close to the bus stop. There are three **banks** in Río Dulce that will change travellers' cheques.

Moving on from Río Dulce, there are buses every thirty minutes or so to Guatemala City, and to Flores via Poptún until around 6pm. If you're heading towards Puerto Barrios, take the first bus or minibus to La Ruidosa junction (every 30min) and pick up a connection there. Heading to El Estor, there are buses around the lakeshore every two hours (1hr 45min) between 6am and 4pm; they all pass the hot springs and Boquerón canyon en route, and some continue on up the Polochic valley towards Cobán and the Verapaces. If you're heading for Lívingston via the Río Dulce gorge, the lancha **boat** captains will ambush you as soon as you step off a bus; services do not run to fixed schedules, but there are several daily (US$10), mostly in the afternoon. There are also **flights** connecting Río Dulce with Guatemala City on Fridays, Saturdays and Sundays. Telephone Taca (☎334 7722) for details, but be warned that cancellations are frequent. Río Dulce is also the base for *That*, a remarkable nineteen-metre (62ft) trimaran operated by ATI Divers (☎ & fax 762 2646, *atidivers@yahoo.com*) of Santa Cruz, Lago de Atitlán (see p.201). Wonderful seven-day sailing trips through the Río Dulce gorge to the Belize cayes cost US$390 for snorkellers and US$490 for divers, including all equipment rental, tanks and meals.

There's a useful **Web site** covering the Río Dulce region, *www.mayaparadise.com*, with good links and listings.

Castillo de San Felipe

Looking like a miniature medieval castle, the **Castillo de San Felipe**, 1km upstream from the bridge at Río Dulce, was damaged by a large earthquake in July 1997 and closed to visitors at the time of writing, but should open again soon (entrance will be US$1.30). Marking the entrance to Lago de Izabal, the *castillo* is a tribute to the audacity of British pirates, who used to sail up the Río Dulce to raid supplies and harass mule trains. The Spanish were so infuriated by this that they built the fortress to seal off the entrance to the lake, and a chain was strung across the river. Inside there's a maze of tiny rooms and staircases, plenty of cannons and panoramic views of the lake.

A kilometre from the castle, close to the waterside village of **SAN FELIPE**, is the *Rancho Escondido* (☎ & fax 369 2681; ②–③), a friendly American-Guatemalan guesthouse, with hammock space and a restaurant. If you call or radio from the *Río Bravo* or *Bruno's* (see p.233), they'll come and pick you up.

Lago de Izabal

Beyond the *castillo*, the broad expanse of **Lago de Izabal** opens up before you, with great views of the highlands beyond the distant shores. Hotels in Río Dulce town, including the *Hacienda Tijax* and *Hotel Backpackers*, can arrange a tour around the lake with a local boatman, or you can easily explore the north shore along the new road to El Estor. The **hot spring waterfall** (daily 8am–6pm; US$0.65), 25km from Río Dulce and 300m north of the road, is one of Guatemala's most remarkable natural phenomena. Bathtub-temperature spring water cascades into pools cooled by a secondary flow of chilly fresh river water, creating a steamy, spa-like environment where it's easy to soak and bathe away an afternoon. Above the waterfall are a series of **caves**, their interiors crowded with extraordinary shapes and colours – made even more memorable by the fact that you have to swim by torchlight to see them (bring your own flashlight).

Two kilometres south of the hot waterfall on the lakeshore, the *Finca El Paraíso* (☎949 7122; ⑤–⑥) has two rows of large, comfortable, but rarely occupied cabañas and a reasonable, if overpriced restaurant. The hotel enjoys a delightfully peaceful location and there's good swimming from the black-sand beach. **Buses** and pick-ups between Río Dulce and El Estor pass the hot springs and hotel hourly in both directions.

Continuing west along the lakeshore it's a further 7km to the **Boquerón canyon**, just 500m from the road but completely hidden. Near-vertical cliffs soar to over 250m above the Río Sauce, which flows through the bottom of the jungle-clad gorge, the river bed dotted with colossal boulders. To see Boquerón, you'll have to find Hugo, a campesino-cum-boatman who lives at the base of the canyon at the end of a signposted track from the main road; he will paddle you upstream in his logwood canoe for a small fee. The return trip takes around thirty minutes, though it's possible to continue exploring Boquerón – which extends for a further 5km – on foot if you have sturdy footwear and don't mind a scramble.

El Estor

Heading west beyond Boquerón, it's just 6km to the sleepy lakeside town of **EL ESTOR**. Allegedly named by English pirates who came up the Río Dulce to buy supplies at "The Store" of Lago de Izabal, it's an easy-going, friendly place which was briefly energized in the 1970s when a vast nickel plant flourished just to the west, but quickly settled back into provincial stupor when the commodity price plummeted. Though El Estor remains off the tourist trail, the completion of the paved road to Río Dulce has helped revive local optimism that the town can now capitalize on the vast ecotourism potential of the surrounding area.

There's not a lot to do in El Estor, although it does have a friendly and relaxed atmosphere, particularly in the warm evenings when the streets are full of activity. Don't miss the pool in the plaza, which harbours fish, turtles and small alligators. You could spend a delightful few days exploring the surrounding area, much of which remains untouched – you can rent **bikes** at 6 Av 4–26. For **tours**, try Hugo at *Hugo's Restaurant*, or Oscar Paz, who runs the *Hotel Vista del Lago* and is an enthusiastic promoter of the area – he can arrange boats and guides to explore the surrounding countryside, plus fishing trips on the lake or visits to the hot springs at *Finca El Paraíso*.

Considering the size of the place, there's an excellent choice of quality budget and mid-range **accommodation**. The most atmospheric hotel is undoubtedly *Hotel Vista del Lago* (☎949 7205; ③), a beautiful, colonial-style wooden building by the dock, claimed by the owners to be the original store that gave the town its name; it offers clean rooms with private bath, with those on the second-floor boasting superb views of the lake. A block up, the *Hotel Villela* at 6 Av 2–06 (②) is a reasonable budget deal, with rooms, some with private shower, surrounding a pretty garden. On the east side of the plaza, the *Posada de Don Juan* (②) has large rooms with well-maintained bathrooms set around a grassy courtyard, while just north of the plaza, *Hotel Central* (☎949 7244; ②) has pleasant, clean, modern rooms, all with private bath and fan. For a really cheap deal, the *Hospedaje Santa Clara* at 5 Av 2–11 (☎948 7244; ①–②) has basic, clean rooms, some with their own shower. Finally, a kilometre east of the centre, in a prime, tranquil lakeside plot, the bungalows at the *Hotel Ecológico Cabañas del Lago* (☎ & fax 949 7245; ④) are comfortable, spacious and attractive – Hugo, the owner, will take you there if you drop in at his restaurant in the plaza.

For good inexpensive **breakfasts** and snacks try the clean and friendly *Cafetería Santa Clave*, three blocks west of the plaza at 3 C 7–75. For something a little more substantial head for *Hugo's Restaurant*, on the main plaza, for steaks and burgers, or the lakeside *Restaurant Chaabil*, though you'll pay extra for the location.

Reserva Bocas del Polochic

Encompassing a substantial slice of lowland jungle on the west side of the lake, the **Reserva Bocas del Polochic** is one of the richest wetland habitats in Guatemala. The green maze of swamp, marsh and forest harbours at least 224 different species of bird, among them golden-fronted woodpeckers, Aztec parakeets and keel-billed toucans. It's also rich in mammals, including howler monkeys, which you're virtually guaranteed to see (and hear), plus rarely encountered manatees and tapirs.

You can **stay** next to the tiny Q'eqchi' village of **SELEMPÍM** in the heart of the reserve – accommodation is in a large, screened wooden house with bunk beds (US$12 per person per day, including three substantial meals) which is managed by the reserve and provides villagers with employment. Locals also lead walking tours up into the foothills of the Sierra de las Minas and kayak tours of the river delta. The drawback is that there's no road to the reserve and you'll have to rent a lancha to get there – due to fuel costs this can amount to US$35 for a day-trip, or as much as US$80 to get to Selempím and back, though obviously it's much cheaper if you can get a group together. To **get to** the reserve contact Defensores de la Naturaleza at 5 Av and 2 C, El Estor (☎949 7237, *rbocas@defensores.org.gt*), which organizes excellent **tours** into the heart of the refuge. To visit the zone nearest to El Estor, contact Hugo or Oscar in El Estor (see above), both of whom run good day-trip excursions.

The eastern highlands

The **eastern highlands** southwest of the capital have to rank as the least-visited part of Guatemala. The population is almost entirely Latinized, speaking Spanish and wearing Western clothes, although many are by blood pure Maya. The *ladinos* of the east have a reputation for behaving like cowboys and supporting right-wing politics, and violent demonstrations of macho pride are not uncommon. Not surprisingly, the military recruits much of its personnel here.

The landscape lacks the immediate appeal of the western highlands: the peaks are lower and the volcanoes less symmetrical. The region's towns are almost all pretty featureless and perennially hot and dusty, so you're unlikely to want to hang around for long. **Esquipulas** is certainly worth a visit, though, for its colossal church, the most important pilgrimage site in Central America. It's also positioned very close to the border with Honduras and El Salvador, though if you're heading into Honduras, you're most likely to end up spending the night in **Chiquimula**, a dull town that's the gateway to the ruins of Copán just over the border. Finally there's the spectacular crater lake of on top of the **Volcán de Ipala**, an idyllic spot whose isolation adds to its appeal.

Chiquimula

Set to one side of the broad San José river valley is the town of **CHIQUIMULA**, an unattractive, bustling *ladino* stronghold – if you've just arrived from Honduras, things only get better from here. Most travellers who come here are on their way to or from the Maya ruins of Copán, just over the border in Honduras (see p.406), and though the town has long been an important transport terminal, there's little else of note save a massive ruined colonial church on the edge of town beside the highway.

Everything you're likely to need in Chiquimula is east of the plaza, and close to the bus terminal on 3 Calle, which leads towards the main highway. Of the town's **hotels**, *Pensión Hernández* at 3 C 7–41 (☎ & fax 942 0708, *hotelh@guate.net*; ②–③) is the first place to try, with plenty of very clean, simple rooms, all with fan and some with television and private shower. It also has safe parking, a small pool and the owner speaks good English. A little further down the road, at 3 C 8–30, *Hotel Central* (☎942 6352; ③) has five pleasant rooms all with private bath and cable TV, while *Pensión España*, also on 3 Calle at 3 C 7–81 (①), is very cheap and basic. A couple of blocks south from here, *Hotel Posada Don Adán* at 8 Av 4–30 (☎942 0549; ③) is comfortable, if old-fashioned; most of its eighteen large rooms have a/c and cable TV, and there's parking too.

When it comes to **eating**, there are plenty of good, inexpensive comedores in and around the **market**, which is centred on 3 C and 8 Av, as well as *Magic Burger* and *Cafe Paíz*, both on 3 Calle, for predictable fast food and good fruit juices. For something a little more ambitious, try *Bella Roma*, 7 Av 5–31, which specializes in pizza and pasta. *Las Vegas*, on 7 Avenida off the plaza, with fairly high prices and garish decor, is where the town's upwardly mobile gather – you can forget the cocktails here, but the food's reasonable. Otherwise the only evening entertainment in Chiquimula is at the Cine Liv on the plaza.

For **changing money** there's a branch of the Banco G & T Continental at 7 Av 4–75 (Mon–Fri 9am–7pm, Sat 10am–2pm) and a Bancafé on the north side of the plaza with a cashpoint that accepts Visa cards. There's **Internet** access at Email Center at 6 Av 4–51 (daily 9am–9pm); the Telgua office (daily 7am–midnight) is on the corner of the plaza.

The **bus terminal** is at 1A C, between 10 and 11 avenidas, midway between the plaza and the highway. There are frequent **buses** from here to Guatemala City (every 30min 3.30am–6pm; 3hr 30min), Esquipulas (every 15min 5am–7pm; 1hr), Jalapa via Ipala (hourly 6am–4pm, 3hr) and Puerto Barrios (hourly; 3hr). For Copán, there are hourly buses to the border at El Florido (1hr 30min).

The Volcán de Ipala

Reached down a side road off the main highway between Chiquimula and Esquipulas, the **Volcán de Ipala** (1650m) may at first seem a little disappointing – it looks more like a rounded hill than the near-perfect conical peaks of the western highlands.

However, it's well worth heading for if you yearn for some real solitude: extremely few visitors make it out this way and the chances are that if you visit on a weekday you'll have the place to yourself. The cone, inactive for hundreds of years, is now filled by a beautiful little **crater lake** ringed by dense tropical forest – you can walk round the entire lake in a couple of hours. It's beautifully peaceful up here and the lake makes a wonderful place to **camp**, though you'll have to bring all your own supplies as there are no shops or other facilities. It's possible to climb the volcano from the village of Ipala itself, a distance of around 10km, but the easiest ascent (2hr) is from the south, setting out from close to the village of Agua Blanca (see below). If you have your own transport, head for the tiny settlement of Sauce, at Km 26.5 on the Ipala–Agua Blanca road, park close to the small store and follow the dirt track up to the summit.

AGUA BLANCA is a *ladino* moustache-and-cowboy-hat kind of place, with a good little hospedaje, the *Maylin* (①), and a couple of comedores, the best of which is the *El Viajero*. It's a pretty straightforward route to the lake; ask the way to the Finca El Paxte and continue to the top from there. The village of **IPALA**, 20km to the north of Agua Blanca, down a fast sealed road, is connected by bus with Jutiapa to the south, Jalapa in the west, Chiquimula to the north and Esquipulas to the east. The village itself is a pretty forlorn place with a few shops and three **hotels**, the best of which is the basic *Hotel Ipala Real* (☎923 7107; ②), where rooms have en-suite showers and toilets, plus cable TV if you want it.

Esquipulas

Southeast from Chiquimula a beautiful road heads through the hills, running beneath craggy outcrops and forested peaks before emerging suddenly at the lip of a huge, bowl-shaped valley, with the town of **ESQUIPULAS** below. The final town on the eastern highway, Esquipulas is the most important Catholic shrine in Central America, and is entirely dominated by the four perfectly white domes of its **church**, which are brilliantly floodlit at night. The rest of the town is a messy sprawl of cheap hotels, souvenir stalls and restaurants which have sprung up to serve the pilgrims who flock to the town year-round from all over Central America, creating a booming resort where people come to worship, eat, drink and relax, in a bizarre combination of holy devotion and indulgence. The principal day of **pilgrimage** is January 15, when even the smallest villages save enough money to send a representative or two, filling the town to bursting point. Esquipulas's other claim to fame is as the place where the first **peace accord** initiatives to end the civil wars in El Salvador, Nicaragua and Guatemala were signed in 1987.

As a religious shrine, Esquipulas probably predates the Conquest. When the Spanish arrived, the Maya chief surrendered rather than risk bloodshed; the grateful Spaniards named the town in his honour and commissioned the famed colonial sculptor Quirio Cataño to carve an image of Christ for the church. Perhaps in order to make it more appealing to the local Maya, he chose to carve it from balsam, a dark wood. Things really took off in 1737 when the bishop of Guatemala, Pardo de Figueroa, was cured of a chronic ailment on a trip to Esquipulas. The bishop ordered the construction of a new church, which was completed in 1758, and his body was buried beneath the altar.

Inside the church today there's a constant scurry of hushed devotion amid clouds of smoke and incense. In the nave, pilgrims approach the image on their knees, while others light candles, mouth supplications or simply stand in silent groups. The image itself is approached by a side entrance: join the queue to shuffle past beneath it and pause briefly in front before being shoved on by the crowds behind. Back outside you'll find yourself among swarms of souvenir and relic hawkers, and pilgrims who, duty done, are ready to head off to eat and drink away the rest of their stay.

Practicalities

When it comes to staying in Esquipulas, you'll find yourself amongst hundreds of visitors whatever the time of year. **Hotels** probably outnumber private homes but bargains are in short supply – the bulk of the budget places are grubby and bare. Prices are rarely quoted in writing and are always negotiable, depending on the flow of pilgrims. Avoid Saturday nights, when rooms cost double.

Many of the **budget** options are clustered together in the streets off the main road, 11 C. The family-run *Hotel Villa Edelmira* (②–③) is one of the best, or look for a room at *La Favorita* on 10 C and 2 Av (②). For a touch more luxury, head for 2 Avenida, beside the church, where you'll find the *Hotel Los Ángeles* (☎943 1254; ③), whose rooms have private bath and cable TV, and the *Hotel Esquipulao* (☎943 1143, fax 943 1371; ④), a cheaper annexe of the *Hotel Payaquí* (same numbers; ⑤), which has rooms with TV and fan, and a pool.

There are also dozens of **restaurants** and **bars**, most of them overpriced by Guatemalan standards. Breakfast is a bargain, however, and you shouldn't have to pay more than US$1.50 for a good feed. There's a decent range of lunch specials later on, though dinner can be expensive. The *Hacienda Steak House*, a block from the plaza at 2 Av and 10 C, is one of the smartest places in town, while many of the cheaper places are on 11 Calle and the surrounding streets. Banco Industrial has a branch with a 24-hour ATM at 9 C and 3 Av, and there's also a Banco G & T Continental (Mon–Fri 9am–7pm, Sat 10am–2pm) almost opposite.

Rutas Orientales runs a superb hourly **bus** service between Guatemala City and Esquipulas; its office is on the main street at 11 C and 1 Av. There are also buses across the highlands to Ipala and regular minibuses to the borders with **El Salvador** (every 30min; 6am–4pm; 1hr) and **Honduras** at Aguacaliente (every 30min 6am–5.30pm; 30min). If you want to get to the ruins of Copán, you'll need to catch a bus to Chiquimula and change there for the El Florido border post (see p.413). There's a **Honduran consulate** (Mon–Fri 8am–1pm & 3–6pm) in the *Hotel Payaquí*, beside the church.

travel details

BUSES

Agua Blanca to: Guatemala City (3 daily; 5hr).

Chiquimula to: El Florido for Copán (hourly; 1hr 15min); Esquipulas (every 15min; 1hr); Guatemala City (14 daily; 3hr 30min); Ipala (8 daily; 1hr); Puerto Barrios (10 daily; 3hr).

El Estor to: Cobán (10 daily, 8hr); Guatemala City (3 daily, 6hr); Río Dulce (12 daily, 1hr 15 min).

Esquipulas to: Aguacaliente for Honduras (every 30min; 30min) and El Salvador (1hr); Chiquimula (minibuses every 15min; 1hr); Guatemala City (hourly 2am–6pm; 4hr); Puerto Barrios (4 daily, 4hr).

Puerto Barrios to: Chiquimula (10 daily; 3hr); Esquipulas (4 daily; 4hr); Entre Ríos for Honduras border (15 daily; 1hr); Guatemala City (19 daily; 5hr), passing Quiriguá (1hr 30min).

BOATS

Lívingston to: Río Dulce (3–4 daily; 3hr); Puerto Barrios (2 ferries daily at 5am & 2pm; 1hr 30min; 6–10 speedboats daily; 30min); Omoa, Honduras (chartered trips only, minimum 6 people; 2hr 30min); Punta Gorda, Belize (Tues & Fri 8am, minimum 4 people; 1hr).

Puerto Barrios to: Lívingston (2 ferries daily at 10am & 5pm; 1hr 30min; 6–10 speedboats daily; 30min); Punta Gorda, Belize (daily at 10am & 2pm; 1hr 30min).

FLIGHTS

Puerto Barrios to: Guatemala City (1 daily; 1hr).

Río Dulce to: Guatemala City (1 daily Fri, Sat & Sun; 1hr 20min).

CHAPTER 10

COBÁN AND THE VERAPACES

The twin departments of the **Verapaces** harbour some of the most spectacular mountain scenery in the country, yet attract only a trickle of tourists, perhaps because there's less obvious evidence of Maya tradition and costume than in other parts of the country. If you've time to spare, however, you'll find the highlands of **Alta Verapaz** astonishingly beautiful, with their fertile limestone landscapes and mist-soaked hills. The mountains here are the wettest and greenest in Guatemala – locals say it rains for thirteen months a year. To the south, the department of **Baja Verapaz** could hardly be more different: a low-lying and sparsely populated area of cactus country which gets very little rainfall.

The hub of the area and the capital of Alta Verapaz is **Cobán**, an attractive mountain town with some good accommodation and restaurants. Though a little subdued once the rain really settles in, it's still the best base for exploring the area, particularly in August when it hosts the National Folklore Festival. In Baja Verapaz, the towns of **Salamá**, **Rabinal** and **Cubulco** also have famous fiestas, where incredible costumes are worn and traditional dances performed. Northeast of Cobán are the exquisite natural bathing pools of **Semuc Champey**, surrounded by lush tropical forest and fed by the azure waters of the Río Cahabón.

The main **road** into the Verapaces climbs up from the El Rancho junction on the Carretera al Atlántico past the turn-off at La Cumbre, and skirts the Quetzal Sanctuary before arriving at Cobán – a journey very well served by frequent pullman buses. Virtually all other roads in the region are unsealed and covered only by a limited service of second-class buses and pick-ups, so the going can be slow.

Some history

The history of the Verapaces is quite distinct from the rest of Guatemala. Long before the Conquest the local **Achi Maya** had earned themselves a unique reputation as the most bloodthirsty of all the region's tribes, and were said to sacrifice every prisoner that they took. Their greatest enemies were the **K'iche'**, with whom they were at war for a century. So ferocious were the Achi that not even the Spanish could contain them by force. Alvarado's army was unable to make any headway against them, and eventually he gave up trying to control the area, naming it *tierra de guerra*, the "land of war".

The church, however, couldn't allow so many heathen souls to go to waste, and under the leadership of **Fray Bartolomé de Las Casas**, they made a deal with the conquistadors. If Alvarado would agree to keep all armed men out of the area for five years, the priests would bring it under control. In 1537 Las Casas and three Dominican friars set out into the highlands, befriended the Achi chiefs, learnt the local dialects and

For an explanation of **accommodation price codes**, see p.125.

translated devotional hymns. By 1538 they had made considerable progress and had converted large numbers of Maya. At the end of the five years, the famous and invincible Achi were transformed into Spanish subjects, and the king of Spain renamed the province Verapaz (True Peace).

Since the colonial era the Verapaces have remained isolated and, in many ways, independent. All their trade bypassed the capital by taking a direct route to the Caribbean, along the Río Polochic and out through Lago de Izabal. The area really started to develop with the **coffee boom** at the turn of the century, when German immigrants flooded into the country to buy and run fincas, particularly in Alta Verapaz, around Cobán. The Germans quickly prospered and exported huge quantities of coffee back to Europe, only to be expelled during World War II, when the USA insisted that Guatemala remove the enemy presence. Today, the Verapaces are still dominated by the huge coffee fincas and the wealthy families that own them, and there are also hints of Germanic influence here and there. Taken as a whole, however, the Verapaces remain very much *indígena* country: Baja Verapaz has a small **Achi** outpost around Rabinal, and in Alta Verapaz the Maya population is largely **Poqomchi'** and **Q'eqchi'**. The production of coffee and, more recently, cardamom for the Middle Eastern market has cut deep into their land and their way of life, with many people being driven off prime territory and onto

---

MARKET DAYS IN THE VERPACES

Monday: Senahú, Tucurú.
Tuesday: Chisec, El Chol, Cubulco, Lanquín, Purulhá, Rabinal, San Cristóbal Verapaz, San Jerónimo.
Saturday: Senahú.
Sunday: Chisec, Cubulco, Lanquín, Purulhá, Rabinal, Salamá, San Jerónimo, Santa Cruz, Tactic.

---

marginal plots. Traditional costume is also worn less here than in the western highlands. The northern, flat section of Alta Verapaz includes a slice of Petén rainforest, and in recent years Q'eqchi' Maya and landless mestizos from the south have expanded into this region, carving out sections of the forest and attempting to farm, a process which offers little security for the migrants and also threatens the future of the rainforest.

Baja Verapaz

The main approach to both departments is from the Carretera al Atlántico, where the road to the Verapaz highlands branches off at the **El Rancho** junction. Beyond El Rancho this road climbs steadily into the hills, the dusty browns and dry yellows of the Motagua valley giving way to an explosion of greens as dense pine forests and alpine meadows begin to cover the mountains. Some 48km beyond the junction is **La Cumbre de Santa Elena**, where the road for the main towns of Baja Verapaz turns off to the west, descending into the **Salamá valley**, surrounded by steep hillsides and seemingly cut off from the outside world.

Salamá

At the western end of the valley is **SALAMÁ**, capital of the department of Baja Verapaz. The town has a relaxed and prosperous air and, like many of the places out this way, its population is largely *ladino*. There's not much to do other than browse in the Sunday market, though the crumbling colonial bridge on the edge of town and the old church, with its huge, gilded altars, darkened by age, are worth a look. The **fiesta** in Salamá runs from September 17 to 21.

If you decide **to stay**, the pick of the hotels is the modern *Hotel Real Legendario* at 8 Av 3–57 (☎940 0187; ③), with very clean rooms, all with private bath, good beds and cable TV, or you could try the *Hotel Tezulutlán* just south of the plaza (☎940 1643; ③), though the rooms, set round a courtyard, are less attractive. For something cheaper, *Pensión Juárez* (☎940 0055; ②) is a good budget hotel at the end of 5 Calle past the police station. For **eating**, there are several places around the plaza: *El Ganadero* is the best restaurant and *Deli-Donus* scores for coffee and snacks. The Bancafé opposite the church will cash travellers' cheques; the post office (Mon–Fri 8am–4.30pm) is almost next door.

Hourly **buses** run from Guatemala City to Salamá (6am–4pm; 3hr 30min). There's also a steady shuttle of minibuses to and from La Cumbre, for connections with pullman buses between Cobán and Guatemala City.

Rabinal

An hour or so from Salamá, **RABINAL** is another isolated farming town that's also dominated by a large colonial Baroque church. Here the proportion of *indígena* inhabitants is considerably higher, making both the Sunday market and the fiesta well worth a visit. Founded in 1537 by Bartolomé de Las Casas himself, Rabinal was the first of the settlements to be included in his peaceful conquest of the Achi nation. Sights are few in Rabinal itself, though the town's small **museum** (Mon–Fri 9am–4pm; free) beside the church is worth a visit, with exhibits on traditional medicinal practices, local arts and crafts and the impact of the civil war in the region – there were four massacres in 1982 alone in the Río Negro region north of the town. The hills around Rabinal are scattered with Maya ruins, including the remains of **Cahyup**, 3km northwest of the plaza, a thirty-minute hike away.

Rabinal's **fiesta** (Jan 19–24) is noted for its dances. The most famous of these, an extended dance drama known as the "Rabinal Achi", re-enacts a battle between the Achi and the K'iche' tribes and is unique to the town, being performed annually on January 23. Other dances include the *patzca*, a ceremony to call for good harvests, using masks that portray a swelling below the jaw, and wooden sticks engraved with serpents, birds and human heads. If you can't make it for the fiesta, the **Sunday market** is a good second-best – Rabinal has a reputation for producing high-quality artesanía, including carvings made from the *árbol del morro* (calabash tree) and traditional pottery.

Of the several fairly basic **hotels** in Rabinal, the best is the *Posada San Pablo* at 3 Av 1–50 (①–②), a decent budget hotel with immaculate rooms, some with private bath; if it's full, try the *Hospedaje Caballeros*, 1 C 4–02 (①). For somewhere really comfortable, see if the new three-storey *Gran Hotel Rabinal Achi* (due to open in late 2001) is operational; if it is, you'll find 36 comfortable rooms, a pool and a café. For an inexpensive **meal** try *Cafetería Mishell del Rosario* on 1 Calle behind the church. Hourly **buses** run between Salamá and Rabinal (1hr) between 6am and 5pm.

Cubulco

Another hour of rough road brings you down into the next valley to the isolated *ladino* town of **CUBULCO**, surrounded on all sides by steep, forested mountains. Cubulco is again best visited for its **fiesta**, this being one of the few places where you can still see the **Palo Volador**, a pre-Conquest ritual in which men throw themselves from a thirty-metre pole with a rope tied around their legs, spinning down towards the ground as the rope unravels, and hopefully landing on their feet. It's as dangerous as it looks: most of the dancers are blind drunk and deaths are not uncommon. The fiesta still goes on, though, as riotous as ever, with the main action taking place on July 25. The best place to stay is the *Hospedaje Pías* (①) next to the large *farmacia* in the centre of town, where some rooms have private bath. There are several good **comedores** in the market, but the best place to eat is *La Fonda del Viajero*, which serves up big portions of Guatemalan food at reasonable prices.

Hourly **buses** run between Salamá and Cubulco via Rabinal. If you'd rather not **leave** the valley the same way that you arrived, a bus leaves Cubulco daily at around 9am, heads back to Rabinal and then, instead of heading for La Cumbre and the main road, turns to the south, crossing the spine of the Sierra de Chuacús and dropping directly down towards Guatemala City. The trip takes you over rough roads for at least eight hours, but the mountain views and the sense of leaving the beaten track help to take the pain out of it all.

The Biotopo de Quetzal

Back on the main highway towards Alta Verapaz and Cobán, the road sweeps around endless tight curves below forested hillsides. Just before the village of Purulhá (Km 161) is the **Biotopo del Quetzal** (daily 7am–4pm; US$3.85), an 11.5-square-kilometre nature reserve designed to protect the habitat of the endangered bird. The forest is also

THE RESPLENDENT QUETZAL

The **quetzal**, Guatemala's national symbol, has a distinguished past but an uncertain future. The feathers of the quetzal were sacred from the earliest of times, and in the strange cult of Quetzalcoatl, whose influence spread throughout Mesoamerica, the quetzal was incorporated into the plumed serpent, a supremely powerful deity. To the Maya the quetzal was so sacred that killing one was a capital offence, and the bird is also thought to have been the *nahual*, or spiritual protector, of the Maya chiefs. When Tecún Umán faced Alvarado in hand-to-hand combat his headdress sprouted the long green feathers of the quetzal; when the conquistadors founded a city adjacent to the battleground they named it **Quetzaltenango**, the Place of the Quetzals.

In modern Guatemala the quetzal's image permeates the entire country, appearing in every imaginable context, as well as lending its name to the nation's currency. Citizens honoured by the president are awarded the Order of the Quetzal, and the bird is also considered a symbol of freedom, since caged quetzals die from the rigours of confinement. Despite all this, the sweeping tide of deforestation threatens the existence of the bird, and the sanctuary is about the only concrete step that has been taken to save it.

The more resplendent of the birds, and the source of the famed feathers, is the male. The heads of males are crowned with a plume of brilliant green, the chest and lower belly is a rich crimson, and trailing behind are the unmistakeable oversized, golden-green tail feathers, though these are only really evident in the mating season. The females, on the other hand, are an unremarkable brownish colour. The birds nest in holes drilled into dead trees, laying one or two eggs at the start of the rainy season, usually in April or May. Quetzals also can be quite easily identified by their strangely jerky, undulating flight.

known as the Mario Dary Reserve in honour of one of the founders of Guatemala's environmental movement, Mario Dary, a lecturer from San Carlos University in Guatemala City, who pioneered the establishment of nature reserves in Guatemala and campaigned for years for a cloudforest sanctuary to protect the quetzal – he was murdered in 1981, possibly as a result of his upsetting powerful timber interests. The reserve he instituted comprises steep and dense rain- and cloudforest, pierced by waterfalls, natural pools and the Río Colorado, which cascades through the reserve towards the valley floor.

Paths through the undergrowth from the road complete a circuit that takes you up into the woods and around above the reserve headquarters (from where you can get maps). There are reasonable numbers of quetzals hidden in the forest but they're extremely elusive. The **best time** to visit is at sunrise, just before or just after nesting season (March–June). A favoured feeding tree is the broad-leaved *aguacatillo*, which produces a small avocado-like fruit. Whether or not you see a quetzal, the forest itself, usually damp with a perpetual mist the locals call *chipi-chipi*, is well worth a visit: a profusion of lichens, ferns, mosses, bromeliads and orchids, spread out beneath a towering canopy of cypress, oak, walnut and pepper trees.

Less than a kilometre or so past the entrance to the reserve is the rustic *Hospedaje Ranchito del Quetzal* (☎953 9235; ②–③), where you can **stay** in clean basic rooms with or without private bath; there's also a simple comedor, though the menu is usually limited to eggs and beans. Quetzals are often seen in the patch of forest around the hotel; staff sometimes insist on charging an entrance fee even if you just want to come in and look around for birds. For something more luxurious try the *Hotel Posada Montaña del Quetzal* at Km 156.5 (☎331 0929, *www.medianet.com.gt/quetzal*; ⑤–⑥), which has very attractive stone and timber bungalows containing pleasant rooms with fireplaces, warm private showers and great forest views – there's also a restaurant, bar and swimming pool.

Buses from Cobán pass the entrance every thirty minutes, but make sure they know you want to be dropped at the reserve, as it's easy to miss.

Alta Verapaz

Beyond the quetzal sanctuary, the main road crosses into the department of Alta Verapaz, and another 13km takes you beyond the forests and into a luxuriant alpine valley of cattle pastures, hemmed in by steep, perpetually green hillsides. The first place of any size is **TACTIC** – a small, mainly Poqomchi'-speaking town adjacent to the main road, which most buses pass straight through. The colonial **church** in the centre of the village, boasting a Baroque facade decorated with mermaids and jaguars, is worth a look, as is the Chi-ixim chapel high above the town. If you fancy a cool swim, head for the Balneario Cham-che, a crystal-clear spring-fed **pool**, on the other side of the main road, opposite the centre of town. The simple *Pensión Central* (①), on the main street north of the plaza, is a reasonable budget bet, or for a little more comfort try *Hotel Villa Linda* (☎953 9216; ③) close by, where the rooms have private baths.

About 10km past Tactic is the turn-off for **San Cristóbal Verapaz**, a pretty town almost engulfed by fields of coffee and sugar cane, set on the banks of the Lago de Cristóbal. From here a rough road continues to **Uspantán** in the western highlands (see p.185), from where there are connections on to Santa Cruz del Quiché, Nebaj and Huehuetenango. To get from San Cristóbal Verapaz to Uspantán you can either hitch or catch one of the **buses** that leaves San Pedro Carchá (see p.248) at 10am and noon, passing through San Cristóbal about forty minutes later.

Cobán and around

The heart of this misty alpine land and the capital of the department is **COBÁN**, where the paved highway comes to an end. Cobán is not a large place: suburbs fuse gently with nearby meadows and pine forests, giving the town the air of an overgrown mountain village. When the rain settles in, Cobán can have something of a subdued atmosphere, and in the evenings the air is usually damp and cool. That said, the sun does put in an appearance most days and the town makes a useful base to recharge, eat well and sleep soundly – and also has some genteel cafés in which to sample some of the finest coffee in the world. In addition, Cobán is a hub for all kinds of **ecotourism** possibilities in the spectacular mountains and rivers nearby.

Arrival, information and tours

Transportes Escobar Monja Blanca, one of Guatemala's best **bus** services (their *especiales* have onboard TV and video), operate half–hourly departures between Guatemala City and Cobán, a journey of four to five hours; their office is on the corner of 2 C and 4 Av, Zona 4. Buses to **local destinations** such as Senahú, El Estor, Lanquín and Cahabón leave from the terminal, down the hill behind the town hall. There are also some long-distance and local departures from **San Pedro Carchá** (see p.248), a few kilometres away. It's also possible to **fly** between Guatemala City and Cobán: Inter run a daily service (30min) to and from the capital from the small airstrip a few kilometres southeast of the town centre.

Inexcusably, Inguat currently choose not to grace Cobán with a tourist office, but luckily a couple of hotels more than adequately fill the **information** gap. The first place to try is the *Hostal d'Acuña* (see p.246), who have helpful staff, a good folder with maps and bus times and a useful noticeboard; the *Hostal Doña Victoria* also provides useful information. Another source of information is Access, in the same complex as *Café Tirol*, with bilingual owners and **Internet access**, though you'll find the best Internet rates and connections at Cybercoban, 3 Av 1–11, Zona 4. **Telgua** has its main office in the plaza (daily 7am–midnight); the **post office** is at 2 C and 2 Av (Mon–Fri 8am–4.30pm). To change **travellers' cheques** and get Visa cash advances, try Banco

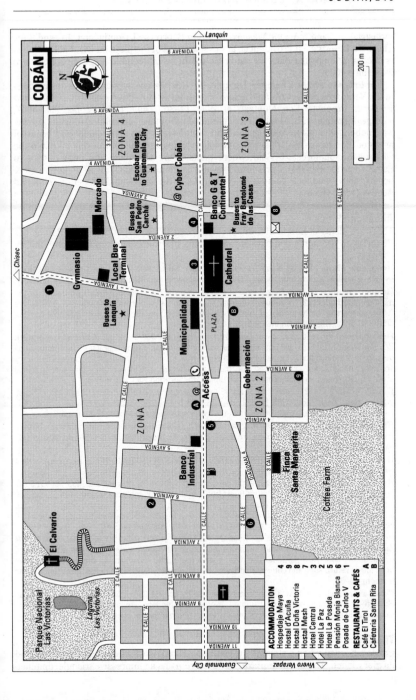

COBÁN

△ Lanquín

△ Chisec

N

200 m

ZONA 4

ZONA 3

ZONA 1

ZONA 2

Parque Nacional
Las Victorias

Laguna
Las Victorias

El Calvario

Gymnasio

Mercado

Local Bus
Terminal

Municipalidad

PLAZA

Cathedral

Gobernación

Banco G & T
Continental

Banco
Industrial

Access

Finca
Santa Margarita

Coffee Farm

@ Cyber Cobán

Escobar Buses
to Guatemala City ★

Buses to San Pedro
Carchá ★

Buses to Lanquín ★

Buses to
Fray Bartolomé
de las Casas ★

△ Guatemala City

▽ Vivero Verapaz

6 AVENIDA
5 AVENIDA
4 AVENIDA
3 AVENIDA
2 AVENIDA
1 AVENIDA
5 AVENIDA
6 AVENIDA
7 AVENIDA
8 AVENIDA
10 AVENIDA
11 AVENIDA
2 AVENIDA
3 AVENIDA

1 CALLE
2 CALLE
3 CALLE
4 CALLE
5 CALLE
6 CALLE
DIAGONAL 4
2 CALLE A

❶ ❷ ❸ ❹ ❺ ❻ ❼ ❽ ❾
Ⓐ Ⓑ
@

ACCOMMODATION
Hospedaje Maya   4
Hostal d'Acuña   9
Hostal Doña Victoria   8
Hostal Mesh   7
Hotel Central   3
Hotel La Paz   2
Hotel La Posada   5
Pensión Monja Blanca   1
Posada de Carlos V   6

RESTAURANTS & CAFÉS
Café El Tirol   A
Cafetería Santa Rita   B

Industrial, 1 C and 2 Av; for Mastercard, go to Banco G&T Continental, 1 C and 2 Av. There's a **laundry**, La Providencia, at the sharp end of the plaza on Diagonal 4. Cobán is becoming a popular place to **study Spanish**; recommended language schools are listed on p.133.

For **tours** to Semuc Champey, Lanquín, the Rey Marco caves and other destinations in the Verapaces contact *Hostal d'Acuña* or Aventuras Turísticas inside the *Hostal Doña Victoria*. Proyecto Eco Quetzal, at 2 C 14–36, Zona 1 (☎ & fax 952 1047, *bidaspeq@guate.net*), is a highly recommended adventure and cultural tourism special-ist, enabling visitors to really get off the beaten track and visit remote and beautiful areas of the Verapaces. Trips, all using local guides, include a three-day hike into the Chicacnab cloudforest (US$55), where quetzals are abundant, and two-day trips to Laguna Lachuá (US$34). **Car rental** is available from Tabarini, 7 Av 2–27, Zona 2 (☎ & fax 952 1504), and local company Geo Rentals, in the same building as *Café Tirol* and Access (☎952 1650).

Accommodation

There are plenty of **hotels** in town, plus **camping** (US$2.50 per person) at Parque Las Victorias on the northwest side of town, which has toilets and running water, but no showers.

Hospedaje Maya, 1 C 2–33, Zona 4, opposite the Cine Norte (☎952 2380). Large, basic hotel used by local travellers and traders. Bargain rates, warm showers and friendly staff, but smelly toilets. ①.

Hostal d'Acuña, 4 C 3–17, Zona 2 (☎951 0482, fax 952 1547, *uisa@amigo.net.gt*). Undoubtedly the most popular budget choice in town, offering spotless rooms with comfortable bunks, plus dorms (US$5 per person) in the garden of a colonial house. Guests can also enjoy excellent home cooking on the veranda. Highly recommended. ②.

Hostal Doña Victoria, 3 C 2–38, Zona 3 (☎951 4213, fax 952 2213, *aventour@intelnet.com.gt*). Beautiful refurbished colonial house dripping with antiques and oozing character. The commodious bedrooms are individually furnished and all come with private bath, though the streetside rooms are rather noisy. There's also a good café/bar and restaurant. The owners also run a second hostal at 1 Av 5–34, Zona 1 – equally comfortable, though the location isn't as good. ⑤.

Hostal Mesh, 3 C 4–27, Zona 3 (☎ & fax 952 1605, *hostalmesh@hotmail.com*). Small hostel boast-ing two clean dormitories with bunk beds (US$4.50 per person) and safety boxes. Breakfast is included, there's a café/bar at the rear and the owners also organize tours of the region. ②.

Hotel Central, 1 C 1–79, Zona 4 (☎ & fax 952 1442). Germanic decor and friendly staff, but the rooms, set round a nice little garden, are a little gloomy for the price – though they do have private baths with reliable hot water. ③.

Hotel La Paz, 6 Av 2–19, Zona 1 (☎952 1358). Safe, pleasant budget hotel run by a very vigilant *señora*. Some rooms have private bath. ②.

Hotel La Posada, 1 C 4–12, Zona 2, at the western end of the plaza (☎ & fax 952 1495, fax 951 0646, *laposada@c.net.gt*). Probably the city's finest hotel, in an elegant colonial building with a beautiful, antique-furnished interior. The rooms, many with wooden Moorish-style screens (and some with four-poster beds), are set around two leafy courtyards and offer all the usual luxuries, though traf-fic noise can be a problem. There's also an excellent restaurant and café. ⑥.

Pensión Monja Blanca, 2 C 6–30, Zona 2 (☎951 1900 or 952 0531, fax 951 1899, *www.sitio.de /hotelmonjablanca*). A wonderfully old-fashioned atmosphere and a variety of rooms, all set around two stunning courtyard gardens. The older rooms are a little run-down but the newer ones have been nicely refurbished and come with private bath; all are very quiet. Don't miss the Victorian-style tearoom. ②–③.

Posada de Carlos V, 1 Av 3–44, Zona 1 (☎952 3502, fax 951 3501). Mountain chalet-style hotel close to the market, with pine-trimmed rooms and modern amenities including cable TV. Comfortable if not memorable. Check out the lobby photographs of old Cobán. ④.

The Town

Cobán's heyday, when it stood at the centre of its own isolated world, is long gone, and its glory faded. The elevated **plaza**, however, remains an impressive triangle, dominated by the cathedral, from which the town drops away on all sides. Check inside to see the remains of a massive, ancient, cracked church bell. A block behind, the **market** bustles with trade during the day and is surrounded by food stalls at night. Life in Cobán revolves around **coffee**: the sedate restaurants, tearooms, trendy nightclubs and overflowing supermarket cater to the town's affluent elite, while the crowds that sleep in the market and plaza, assembling in the bus terminal to search for work, are migrant labourers heading for the plantations. For a closer look at Cobán's principal crop, take the guided tour offered by the **Finca Santa Margarita** (Mon–Fri 8am–12.30pm & 1.30–5pm, Sat 8am–noon; US$2), a coffee plantation just south of the centre of town at 3 C 4–12, Zona 2. The interesting tour (an English-speaking guide is usually available) covers the history of the finca, examining all the stages of cultivation and production, and takes you on a walk through the grounds. You also get a chance to sample the crop and, of course, purchase some beans.

One of Cobán's most attractive sights is the church of **El Calvario**, a short stroll from the town centre. Head west out of town on 1 Avenida and turn right up 7 Avenida until you reach a steep cobbled path. You'll pass a number of tiny **Maya shrines** on the way up – crosses blackened by candle smoke and decorated with scattered offerings. There's a commanding view over the town from the whitewashed church, which has a distinctly pagan feeling – Christian and Maya crosses hang from the roof inside hundreds of corn cobs (sacred in indigenous religion). Another place worth a look is the **Vivero Verapaz** (Mon–Sat 9am–noon & 2–5pm; US$0.75), a former coffee finca just outside town now dedicated to the growing of orchids, which flourish in these sodden mountains. The plants are carefully grown in a shaded environment, and a farmworker will show you around and point out the most spectacular blooms, which are at their best between November and January. The farm is on the old road to Guatemala City, which you reach by leaving the plaza on Diagonal 4, the road that runs past the *Pensión Familiar*, turn left at the bottom of the hill, go across the bridge and follow the road for 3km. Any taxi driver will be able to take you.

Eating, drinking and entertainment

Eating in Cobán comes down to a choice between fancy European-style restaurants and very basic, cheap comedores. For really cheap food, your best bet, as always, is the **market**, but remember that it's closed by dusk, after which street stalls set up in the plaza selling barbecued meat and warm tortillas.

Bistro Acuña, 4 C 3–17, Zona 2. The most relaxed place to eat in town, and a good place to meet other travellers, with a stunning period setting, uplifting classical music and attentive service. A full-scale blow-out will cost around US$8 a head but there are many cheaper options, including great cannelloni. Make sure you leave room to sample something from the cake cabinet.

Café and Restaurant La Posada, 1 C 4–12, Zona 2, at the west end of the plaza inside *Hotel la Posada*. The smartest restaurant in town, with traditional Guatemalan specialities as well as international cuisine. The café on the veranda outside serves superb breakfasts, bagels and muffins.

Café El Tirol, 1 Calle, on the north side of the plaza. Relatively upmarket by Guatemalan standards, though cheaper than the *La Posada* (see above). Serves 52 different types of coffee, pretty good breakfasts, hot chocolate, pancakes and sandwiches, though service can be hit and miss. Closed Mon.

Cafetería Santa Rita, 2 Calle, on the plaza close to the cathedral. Good comedor with friendly service and decent nosh. Very Guatemalan, in the unlikely event you're sick of all those European-style cafés.

Kam Mun, 1 C and 9 Av, Zona 2. Excellent, hyper-hygienic Chinese restaurant, with a good line-up of economical Oriental choices.

NIGHTLIFE

Generally speaking Cobán is a pretty quiet place, particularly in the evenings. In addition to the usual cantinas, however, there are some half-decent **bars**: *Tofuba*, at 2 C and

6 Av, is one of the hippest places, with a cosmopolitian atmosphere, modern Latin sounds and good snacks, while *Tacobán* at 1 Av and 4 C can get lively at weekends with a sociable crowd and house music. The best **club** in town is *Keops*, 5 Av and 3 C, where the merengue and Latin dance draw a funky bunch of groovers. There are two **cinemas:** the CineTuria on the plaza, and the Cine Norte, on 1 Calle.

San Pedro Carchá

A few kilometres from Cobán, **SAN PEDRO CARCHÁ** is a smaller version of Cobán, with silver instead of coffee firing the economy and a stronger Maya character. These days the two towns are merging into a single urban sprawl, and many of the buses that go on towards Petén, or even over to Uspantán, leave from Carchá. Local buses between Cobán and Carchá leave from the terminal in Cobán and from the plaza in Carchá.

If you've an hour to spare, the **regional museum** (Mon–Fri 9am–noon & 2–5pm; US$0.75), in a street beside the church, is worth a look. Alongside a collection of Maya artefacts are dolls dressed in local costumes and a mouldy collection of stuffed birds and animals, including the inevitable moulting quetzal. A little further afield, the **Balneario Las Islas** is a stretch of cool water that's popular for swimming; you can also **camp** there. It's a couple of kilometres from the town centre: walk along the main street beside the church and take the third turning on the right, then follow the street for about 1km and take the right-hand fork at the end.

If you're planning a speedy departure then you might prefer **to stay** in Carchá – the *Hotel la Reforma*, 4 C 8–45 (☎952 1448; ②), is a good option. For **changing money** there's a branch of the Banco del Ejército on the plaza. **Buses** to local destinations such as Senahú, El Estor, Lanquín and Cahabón leave from the plaza. Two buses a day (10am & noon) leave from beside the *bomberos* **to Uspantán** in the western highlands, for connections to Sacapulas, Nebaj and Quiché.

San Juan Chamelco

A few kilometres southeast of Cobán, easily reached by regular local buses from the terminal, **SAN JUAN CHAMELCO** is the most important Q'eqchi' settlement in the area. Most of your fellow bus passengers are likely to be women dressed in traditional costume, wearing beautiful cascades of old coins for earrings, and speaking Q'eqchi' rather than Spanish. Chamelco's focal point is a large colonial **church**, whose facade is rather unexpectedly decorated with twin Mayanized versions of the Hapsburg double eagle – undoubtedly a result of the historic German presence in the region. Inside the belfry is hidden the village's most significant treasure, a church bell that was given to the Maya leader Juan Matalbatz by the Holy Roman Emperor Charles V. The best time to visit the village is for its annual **fiesta**, on June 16. Participants in the wild processions dress up in a variety of outfits, including pre-Conquest Maya costumes and representations of local wildlife, in celebration of the local Q'eqchi' culture and environment.

Just outside Chamelco are the **Grutas de Rey Marcos** (daily 9am–5pm; US$3 including the services of a guide, plus hard hat and boot rental), a kilometre-long series of caves, though the tour only takes you a little way into the complex – you have to wade across an underground river at one stage to see some of the best stalactites and stalagmites, including one that's a dead ringer for the leaning tower of Pisa. The caves are a pleasant five-kilometre walk from Chamelco down a signposted road 150m west of the plaza; alternatively you can catch a pick-up from 0 C and 0 Av heading for the village of Chamíl. Just 500m from the caves is a great place **to stay**, *Don Jerónimo's* (☎308 2255, *www.dearbrutus.com/donjeronimo*; ④ for full board), a vegetarian guesthouse/retreat in sublime countryside, run by a friendly American who has been living off the land here for a good twenty years.

Lanquín and Semuc Champey

Northeast of Cobán, a rough, badly maintained road heads off northeast into the hills, connecting a string of coffee fincas. The road soon drops down into rich land as the valleys open out – their precipitous sides are patched with cornfields, but the level central land is saved for the all-important coffee bushes. As the bus lurches along, clinging to the sides of the ridges, there are fantastic views of the valleys below.

The road divides after 43km at the **Pajal** junction, three hours from Cobán, where one branch turns north to Sebol and Fray Bartolomé de Las Casas and the other cuts down deep into the valley to **LANQUÍN**, 12km away, a very sleepy, modest Q'eqchi' village superbly sheltered beneath towering green hills. Don't count on practising your Spanish here – the language has yet to gain much influence. Of the village's several **pensiones**, the good, cheap hospedaje-cum-store-cum-comedor *Divina Providencia* (①) is the best, offering good grub, steaming hot showers and the only cold beers in town. The clapboard rooms are comfortable enough, though you'll probably get to know all about your neighbours' nocturnal habits. More luxurious is the *Hotel El Recreo* (☎952 2160, fax 952 2333; ④) on the entrance-road to the village, with a choice of rooms in wooden huts, a restaurant and a pool. There is electricity only between 6pm and 9pm, though, and prices rise at weekends. Perhaps the best place to stay, however, is *El Retiro* (*elretirolodge@hotmail*.com; ②), a ten-minute walk from the village along the road to Cahabón. This wonderful English/Q'eqchi'-owned lodge has palm leaf-thatched cabañas with mosquito screens and hammocks by the Lanquín river, plus **camping**. There's a camp fire and music most nights, and the owners run tours to sights in the region.

A couple of kilometres from the village on the road back to Cobán are the **Lanquín caves** (US$1.30), a maze of dripping, bat-infested chambers, stretching for at least 3km underground. An illuminated walkway complete with ladders and chains cuts through the first few hundred metres, but it's very slippery so take care. It's also well worth dropping by at dusk when thousands of bats emerge from the mouth of the cave and flutter off into the night. A small car park near the entrance to the caves has a covered shelter where you're welcome to camp or sling a hammock.

Semuc Champey

The other attraction around Lanquín are the extraordinary pools of **Semuc Champey** (US$2.50, parking US$0.75), which are a great deal more spectacular than the caves. The problem can be **getting there**, however. If you're very lucky and there are enough tourists in town you can catch a pick-up at about 8am, returning around noon. Another option is to hire Rigoberto Fernández's pick-up for US$10 return trip, including two hours at the pools – you can find him in the unnamed, vivid green shop beneath the central park. Alternatively, tours run from Cobán (around US$30 per person), and the *Hostal d'Acuña* runs a shuttle bus on Wednesday and Saturday (same price) when there's sufficient demand.

The hard way to get to the pools is to walk, which takes nearly three hours and can be extremely tough going if the sun is shining – take plenty of water. Leave the village along the gravel road that climbs the hill to the south, then drops into another valley. From here the track wanders through thick tropical vegetation where bananas, coffee and the spear-leafed cardamom plants grow beside scruffy thatched huts. After crossing a suspension bridge the road climbs uphill again to the car park, where you may be asked for the entry fee. Finally, follow the muddy track that brings you, at long last, to the pools.

The effort of getting here is rewarded by a natural staircase of turquoise waters suspended on a limestone bridge, with a series of idyllic **pools** in which you can swim. The bulk of the Río Cahabón runs underground beneath this natural bridge, and by walking a few hundred metres upstream over a slippery obstacle course of rocks and roots you can see the aquatic frenzy for yourself. The river water plunges furiously into a cavern, cutting under the pools to emerge downstream. If you have a tent or a hammock it makes sense to stay the night. There's a thatched shelter here and the altitude is sufficiently low to keep the air warm in the evenings. Be warned, though, it's not safe to leave your belongings unattended.

Beyond Lanquín

Beyond Lanquín the road continues 24km to **Cahabón**, which has two basic pensiones, the best being *Hospedaje Carolina* (①). From here, a very rough road heads south towards Panzós (see opposite), cutting high over the mountains through superb scenery. **Buses** to and from Cahabón via Lanquín leave Cobán five times daily, except Sundays when there are only three services. Moving on from Cahabón, two daily buses (4am & 12.30pm) leave for the three-hour trip to El Estor (see p.234), while pick-ups ply the same route more frequently.

Heading north, buses pass the Pajal junction for **Fray Bartolomé de Las Casas** (from where you can head northeast to Poptún) and **Raxrujá** (see opposite) twice each morning at around 6.30am & 8.30am.

The Polochic valley

If you're planning to head out towards the Caribbean from Cobán, or are simply interested in taking a short trip along Guatemala's back roads, then the **Polochic valley** is an ideal place to spend a day being bounced around inside one of the hourly buses which travel the length of the valley's dirt road from Cobán to El Estor. To begin with the scenery is pure Alta Verapaz, with V-shaped valleys where coffee commands the best land and fields of maize cling to the upper slopes wherever they can. The villages along the road are untidy-looking places where the Q'eqchi' and Poqomchi' Maya are largely Latinized and seldom wear their traditional brilliant red *huipiles*. Later on the scenary undergoes an immense transformation as the road drops down through the coffee-coated mountains to emerge in the lush, tropical lowlands.

The first two villages in the upper end of the valley are **Tamahú** and **Tucurú**. High above Tucurú in the mountains to the north is the **Chelemá Reserve**, a large protected area of pristine cloudforest which contains one of the highest concentrations of quetzals anywhere in the world, not to mention an array of other birds and beasts including some very vocal howler monkeys. The forest is extremely difficult to reach; contact Proyecto Eco Quetzal in Cobán (see p.246), who can arrange accommodation with local families in the village of Chicacnab.

Beyond Tucurú the road plunges abruptly and cattle pastures start to take the place of the coffee bushes, while both the villages and the people begin to take on a more tropical look. Next comes **La Tinta** and then **Telemán**, from where a side road branches off north to **SENAHÚ**, climbing high into the lush hills past row upon row of neatly ranked coffee bushes. Set back behind the first ridge of hills, Senahú is a small coffee centre set in a verdant, steep-sided bowl, and is an ideal starting point for a short wander in the Alta Verapaz hills. Three **buses** a day run from Cobán to Senahú, the first returning at 4pm (check with the drivers for the latest times); or you could easily hitch a ride on a truck from Telemán. There are a couple of simple **pensiones** here, plus the *Hotel El Recreo Senahú* (☎952 2160; ③) in the centre of the village, with twelve pleasant rooms. From here, you can trek to some nearby caves, the **Cuevas de Seamay**, used by Maya shamen for ceremonies, and on to Semuc Champey and Lanquín in a couple of days – ask for a guide at the *Hotel El Recreo Senahú*. Another stunning hike is to Cahabón, a trip which you can also do in a 4WD, weather permitting.

Panzós

Heading on down the Polochic valley you reach **PANZÓS**, the largest of the valley villages. Its name means "place of the green waters", a reference to the swamps that surround the river, swarming with alligators and bird life. In 1978, Panzós made the international headlines when a group of campesinos attending a meeting to settle land disputes were gunned down by the army and local police, in one of the earliest and most brutal massacres of General Lucas García's military regime. García had a personal interest in the matter, since he owned over 300 square kilometres of land around Panzós. The event is generally regarded as a landmark in the history of political violence in Guatemala, after which the situation deteriorated rapidly. Over 100,000 people attended a protest rally in Guatemala City after news of the massacre broke.

Getting to Panzós is straightforward: ten daily buses from Cobán pass through the town en route to El Estor, while two daily buses and sporadic pick-ups leave Panzós for the uphill struggle to Cahabón, from where it's easy to continue to Lanquín and Semuc Champey. Beyond Panzós the road pushes on towards Lago de Izabal, passing a huge, deserted nickel plant, yet another monument to disastrous foreign investment, just before you come to El Estor (see p.234).

North towards Petén

In the far northern section of Alta Verapaz, the lush hills drop away steeply onto the limestone plain that marks the frontier with the department of Petén. At present, two rough roads head north: the first from Cobán **via Chisec** and the second from San Pedro Carchá **via Pajal**. From the Pajal junction it's a very slow, very beautiful journey north through typical Verapaz scenery – a verdant green landscape of impossibly green mountains, tiny adobe-built hamlets, pasture and pine forests. After three hours or more of twists and turns you'll reach **Sebol**, a beautiful spot on the Río Pasión where tributary waterfalls cascade into the main channel and a road heads off for Fray Bartolomé de Las Casas and Poptún. The next stop is the small settlement of **Raxrujá**, where the buses from Cobán finish; currently only pick-ups and trucks head north for **Cruce del Pato** and onwards, either up to Sayaxché and Petén or west into the Ixcán.

Just 8km from Sebol is **FRAY BARTOLOMÉ DE LAS CASAS**, where there are several **hotels** – the best are the clean *Hotel Diamelas* (②) and the basic *Pensión Ralíos* (①) – and a couple of banks. Buses leave Las Casas to Cobán (7hr) six times daily, and also head northeast to Poptún (see p.256) daily at 3am (5hr 30min).

Raxrujá and the Candelaria caves

RAXRUJÁ is the best place to get a pick-up, a truck or, if you're very lucky, a bus north to Sayaxché and Flores or west to Playa Grande and the Ixcán. Little more than a few streets and an army base straggling round the bridge over the Río Escondido, a tributary of the Pasión, Raxrujá has the only **accommodation** for miles around and you may end up staying here. *Hotel Raxruhá* (①), next to the Texaco garage, is the best on offer, and there are plenty of quite reasonable places to **eat** in town, including *Comedor Vidalia*. The Banrural (Mon–Fri 8am–5pm, Sat 9am–1pm) next to *Hotel Raxruhá* will cash travellers' cheques. Buses leave for Cobán at 4am, 9am and 1pm; heading north, it's pick-ups only.

The limestone mountains to the west of Raxrujá are full of caves. Some of the best are the **Candelaria caves**, 10km west, whose series of caverns stretches for around 18km and includes some truly monumental chambers such as the 200-metre-long "Tzul Tacca". The caves are located on private property a short walk from the road, and are jealously guarded by Daniel Dreux, who has set up the **Complejo Cultural de Candelaria** conservation area. Entrance to the complex, including a two-hour tour and a guide to the first cave system, costs US$4 per person, while a two-day tour by lancha

---

THE "DISCOVERY" OF CANCUÉN

In September 2000 newspapers across the world trumpeted the re-discovery of the ancient Maya city of **Cancuén**, lost for 1300 years, by an American-Guatemalan team of archeologists on the banks of the river Pasión. While the reality was very different – Cancuén had been discovered in 1907 and was even plotted on tourist board maps of the country – the sheer size of the ruins had certainly been underestimated, while new investigations revealed the site to be enigmatic in other ways. Uniquely, Cancuén seems to have lacked the usual religious and defensive structures characteristic of Maya cities and appears to have existed as an essentially secular, trading city. For most of the twentieth century, the absence of soaring temple-pyramids led archeologists to assume that Cancuén was a very minor one, and it was ignored for decades. However, the vast amounts of jade, pyrite, obsidian and fine ceramics found recently indicate that this was actually one of the greatest trading centres of the Maya world, with a paved plaza (which may have been a marketplace) covering two square kilometres. Cancuén is thought to have flourished because of its strategic position between the great cities of the lowlands, like Tikal and Calakmul, and the mineral-rich highlands of southern Guatemala. The vast, almost ostentatious **palace** complex, with 170 rooms and 11 courtyards, is Cancuén's most arresting feature and it's hoped that ongoing investigations here by Guatemala's Institute of Anthropology and the National Geographic Society will help uncover much about Classic period life.

---

costs US$35 per person. Alternatively, contact one of the Cobán travel agents (see p.246) or the official agents, PTP, 15 C 3–20, Zona 10 in Guatemala City (☎363 4404, *www.ptpmayas.com*), to organize a trip. The complex's wonderfully atmospheric **accommodation** (US$50 per person per day including two meals) is often block-booked by French tour groups, but you can **camp** (US$2.50 per person) close to the entrance at the *Rancho Ríos Escondidos*.

The area beyond Raxrujá, where the rolling foothills of the highlands give way to the flat expanse of southern Petén, is known as the **Northern Transversal Strip**, dubbed the "Generals' Strip", as huge parcels of land, complete with their valuable mineral resources, were dispensed to military top brass instead of needy campesinos. In the heart of this region, 11km north of Raxrujá, is the large Maya site of **Cancuén** (see box) where a huge Classic period palace has been unearthed. At the moment the only way to visit the site is with the specialist tour operator Maya Expeditions (see p.158); don't be tempted to hike to the site, as you'll have to dodge past fields of grazing water buffalo through land owned by the ex-military dictator Lucas García.

Playa Grande

Continuing west from Raxrujá, trucks make the 90km journey over rough roads to **PLAYA GRANDE** (at least 6hr), the bridging point of the Río Negro. The town is an authentic frontier settlement with cheap hotels, rough bars and brothels. If you need to **stay**, the best options are the basic but clean *Hospedaje Torre Visión* or *Reyna* (both ①).

One point of interest in this area is the **Parque Nacional Laguna Lachuá**, a beautiful little lake, 4km off the main road east of Playa Grande. One of the least visited national parks in Central America, this is a beautiful, tranquil spot, with a clear, almost circular lake completely surrounded by dense tropical forest. Though it smells slightly sulphurous, the water is good for swimming, with curious horseshoe-shaped limestone formations by the edge that make perfect individual bathing pools. You'll see otters and an abundance of birdlife, but watch out for mosquitoes. There's a large thatched *rancho* (shelter) by the shore, ideal for camping or slinging a hammock (available for rent). There are also canoes for rent and fireplaces and wood are provided, though you'll need to bring food and drinking water.

You can get to Playa Grande **from Cobán** on one of a stream of trucks and pick-ups which leave from the corner of the bus terminal in the early morning – a journey of around six hours. Heading south **from Sayaxché** you need to catch a bus or pick-up to Playitas via Cruce del Pato and take another pick-up or truck from there. There are also regular **flights** from the airstrip in Cobán.

Into the Ixcán

The Río Negro marks the boundary between the departments of Alta Verapaz and Quiché. The land to the west, known as the **Ixcán**, comprises a huge, swampy forest, some of which was settled in the 1960s and 1970s by peasants migrating from the highlands, and which became the scene of bloody fighting in the 1980s. The Ixcán has recently become a focus for *repatriado* settlement as refugees who fled to Mexico in the 1980s are resettled in a string of "temporary" camps west of the river.

The journey further west across the Ixcán and into northern Huehuetenango, though no longer hazardous, is still very arduous – it can take up to two or three days to get from Playa Grande to Barillas. **Veracruz**, 20km (1hr 30min) from Playa Grande, is the first place of note, a settlement at the crossroads beyond the Río Xalbal. Some buses continue to Mayalan, 12km away, across the presently unbridged Río Piedras Blancas. Here the road ends and you'll have to walk 15km (4–5hr) to **Altamira** on the far bank of the Río Ixcán, past several tiny villages; the path is easy to follow. At the last village, **Rancho Palmeras**, ask for directions to the crossing point on the Ixcán, where boys will pole you across the flowing river. Once across, Altamira is still a few kilometres away, up the hill. From here a regular flow of trucks make the 30km (4hr) journey to Barillas, over some of the worst roads in the country. It's a spectacular journey, though, especially as you watch the growing bulk of the Cuchumatanes rising ever higher on the horizon. You can also get trucks over the border in **Mexico**, taking you to Chajul on the Río Lacantún in Chiapas, but you'll need a Guatemalan exit stamp first, probably best obtained in Cobán or Flores.

travel details

BUSES

Cobán to: Cahabón (3–5 daily; 4hr); Chisec (5 daily; 4hr); El Estor (10 daily; 8hr); Guatemala City (30 daily; 4–5hr); Lanquín (4 daily; 3hr); San Cristóbal Verapaz (hourly; 45min); San Pedro Carchá (every 15min; 20min); Senahú (3 daily; 7hr); Tactic (hourly; 45min).

Cubulco to: Guatemala City via El Chol (1 daily; 9hr); Guatemala City via La Cumbre (5 daily; 5hr 30min); Rabinal (hourly; 30min); Salamá (hourly; 1hr 30min).

Rabinal to: Cubulco (hourly; 30min); Guatemala City via El Chol (1 daily; 8hr) and via La Cumbre (hourly; 4hr 30 min); Salamá (hourly; 1hr).

Raxrujá to: Cruce del Pato (pick-up to Canleche, 1hr, then pick-up to Cruce del Pato; 20min).

Salamá to: Cubulco (hourly; 1hr 30min); Guatemala City (hourly; 3hr 30min); Rabinal (hourly; 1hr).

San Pedro Carchá to: Cobán (every 15min; 20min); Fray Bartolomé de las Casas (5 daily; 6hr 30min); Raxrujá via Sebol (2 daily; 7hr); Uspantán via Cobán (2 daily; 5hr).

FLIGHTS

Cobán to: Guatemala City (daily; 30min); irregular flights to Playa Grande.

CHAPTER 11

PETÉN

T he vast northern department of **Petén** occupies about a third of Guatemala but contains less than three percent of its population. This huge expanse of swamps, dry savannas and tropical rainforest forms part of an untamed wilderness that stretches into the Lacandón forest of southern Mexico and across the Maya Mountains to Belize. Totally unlike any other part of the country, much of it is all-but-untouched, with ancient ceiba and mahogany trees that tower 50m above the forest floor. Undisturbed for so long, the area is also extraordinarily rich in **wildlife**. Some 285 species of bird have been sighted at Tikal alone, including a great range of humming-birds, toucans, blue and white herons, hawks, buzzards, wild turkeys, motmot (a bird of paradise) and even the elusive quetzal, revered since Maya times. Beneath the forest canopy are many other species that are far harder to locate. Among the mammals

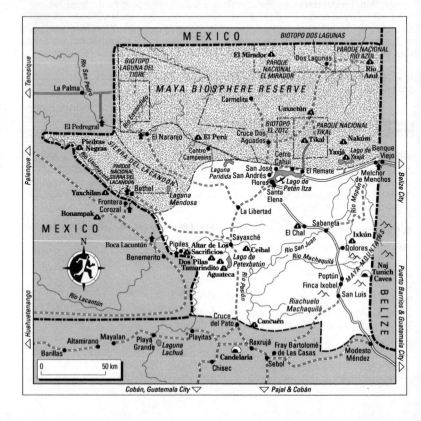

For an explanation of **accommodation price codes**, see p.125.

are the massive tapir or mountain cow, ocelots, deer, coatis, jaguars, monkeys, plus crocodiles and thousands of species of plants, snakes, insects and butterflies.

Recently, however, this position of privileged isolation has been threatened by moves to colonize the country's final frontier. Waves of **settlers**, originally lured by offers of free land, have cleared enormous tracts of jungle, while oil exploration and commercial logging have cut new roads deep into the forest. The population of Petén, just 15,000 in 1950, is today estimated at over 400,000, a number which puts enormous pressure on the remaining forest. Various attempts have been made to halt the tide of destruction, and in 1990 the government declared that forty percent of Petén would be protected by the **Maya Biosphere Reserve**, although little is done to enforce this.

The new interest in the region is in fact something of a reawakening, as Petén was once the heartland of the **Maya civilization**, which reached here from the highlands some 2500 years ago. Maya culture reached the height of its architectural, scientific and artistic achievement during the Classic period (roughly 300–900 AD), when great cities rose out of the forest, and the ruins at Tikal and El Mirador, among the most spectacular of all **Maya sites**, represent only a fraction of what was once here. At the close of the tenth century the cities were mysteriously abandoned, and many of the people moved north to the Yucatán, where Maya civilization continued to flourish until the twelfth century.

By the time the Spanish arrived, the area had been partially recolonized by the **Itzá**, a group of Toltec-Maya who inhabited the land around Lago de Petén Itzá. The forest proved so impenetrable however that it wasn't brought under Spanish control until 1697, more than 150 years after they had conquered the rest of the country. The Spanish had little enthusiasm for Petén, though, and under their rule it remained a backwater. Independence saw no great change, and it wasn't until 1970 that Petén became genuinely accessible by car. Even today the network of roads is skeletal, and many routes are impassable in the wet season.

The twin lakeside towns of **Flores** and **Santa Elena** form the hub of the department. You'll probably arrive here, if only to head straight out to the ruins of **Tikal**, Petén's prime attraction, though the town is also the starting-point for adventures to more distant ruins – **El Mirador, El Zotz** and **Río Azul**. Halfway between Flores and Tikal is the tranquil alternative base of **El Remate**. The caves and scenery around **Poptún**, on the main highway south, justify exploration, while down the other road south, **Sayaxché** is surrounded by yet more Maya sites. From Sayaxché you can set off **into Mexico** and the ruins of **Yaxchilán** either via the road to Bethel, or along the Río Pasión.

Getting to the Petén

Many visitors arrive in Petén by bus or plane directly from **Guatemala City. By air** it's a short fifty-minute hop to Flores. A number of internal airlines fly the route daily and **tickets** can be bought from virtually any travel agent in the country; prices range between US$70 and US$120 depending on the airline. Demand is heavy and overbooking is common. **By bus** it can take anywhere between eight and ten hours. Numerous companies provide around twenty services a day from Guatemala City to Flores. If you don't want to do the 554-kilometre trip in one go, it's easy enough to do it in stages – the best places to break the journey are at **Quiriguá** (see p.226), **Río Dulce** (see p.231) and **Poptún** (see overleaf).

Coming from the Guatemalan highlands you can reach Petén along the backroads **from Cobán** in Alta Verapaz, a long and adventurous route (see p.244). **From Belize or Mexico**, you can enter the country through Petén. The most obvious route is from Belize through the border at Melchor de Mencos, but there are also two river routes that bring you through from Palenque or Tenosique in Mexico. All of these are covered on pp.274–277.

Poptún and around

Heading north from the Río Dulce, the smooth paved highway to Flores cuts through a degraded landscape of small *milpa* farms and cattle ranches that was jungle a decade or two ago. Some 95km from Río Dulce, at an altitude of 500m, the first settlement of any interest is the small town of **POPTÚN**. For many travellers this dusty frontier settlement is the embodiment of rustic bliss and organic food – thanks to the proximity of the *Finca Ixobel* (see below). There's no particular reason to stay in the town itself, but you may well stop by to use the Telgua office or banks. If you do get stuck here, you can **stay** at the friendly *Hotel Posada de los Castellanos* (☎927 7222; ②), where you get hot water and a bathroom. The best food in town is at the *Fonda Ixobel 2*, which bakes good bread and cakes.

For a more rural setting, head 4km north of Poptún to *Cocay Camping* (☎927 7024; ①), set in peaceful isolation on the banks of the river just past the village of Machaquilá. This isolated site has camping space, very simple huts, and vegetarian and European food. Over the bridge to the right, nicely located in a patch of forest, are the splendid cabañas of the *Villa de los Castellanos* (☎927 7541, fax 927 7307, *www.ecovilla.com*; ⑨ – check also for special backpacker rates), offering a comfortable base for adventurous visitors to explore the forests, rivers and caves of central Petén. Carlos, the owner, is an excellent source of information – botanical, historical and logistical.

Finca Ixobel

A couple of kilometres' walk north of Poptún, surrounded by aromatic pine forests in the cool foothills of the Maya Mountains, is the *Finca Ixobel* (☎927 7363, *www.fincaixobel .conexion.com*), a working farm that provides **accommodation** to passing tourists. The farm was originally run by Americans Mike and Carole DeVine, but on June 8, 1990, Mike was murdered by the army. This prompted the American government to suspend military aid to Guatemala, and after a drawn-out investigation which cast little light on their motives, five soldiers were convicted of the murder in September 1992. Others involved have managed to evade capture and their commanding officer, Captain Hugo Contreras, escaped from jail shortly after his arrest. Carole fought the case for years and remains at the finca.

Finca Ixobel is a supremely beautiful and relaxing place, where you can swim in the pond, walk in the forest, dodge the resident "attack" parrots and stuff yourself stupid with delicious home-grown food. There are **hikes** into the jungle, horse-riding trips, rafting, 4WD jungle jaunts, and short excursions to nearby caves. Accommodation is in attractive bungalows with private bathroom (④), regular rooms (②–③) or dorms (US$3.50 per bed), and there's also camping and hammock space (US$3) and tree houses (②). You run up a tab for accommodation, food and drink, paying when you leave – which can be a rude awakening. To get to the finca ask the bus driver to drop you at the gate (marked by a large sign), from where it's a fifteen-minute walk through the pine trees; after dark, it's probably safest to head for the *Fonda Ixobel 2* restaurant (see above) in Poptún and they'll call a taxi (US$1) to drop you off.

Flores and around

FLORES, the capital of Petén, has an easy pace and a sedate, old-world atmosphere diametrically opposed to the commerce and hustle that typify most of Petén's towns. Its genteel cobbled streets, ageing houses and twin-domed church are set on a small island in Lago de Petén Itzá, connected to the mainland by a short causeway. The frontier mentality lies just across the water in **SANTA ELENA**, a chaotic, featureless town which is dusty in the dry season and mud-bound during the rains.

The **lake** was a natural choice for settlement, and its shores were heavily populated in Maya times, with the capital of the Itzá, **Tayasal**, occupying the island that was to become modern Flores. Cortes passed through here in 1525, on his way south to

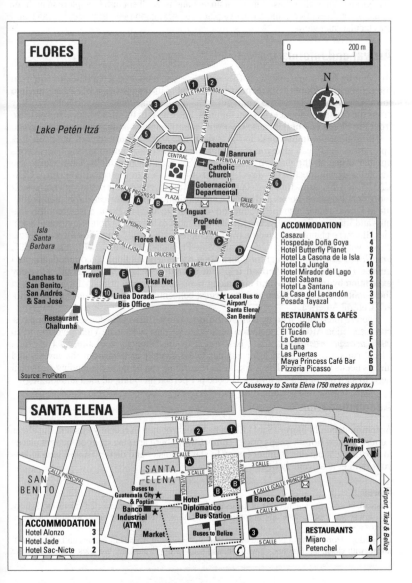

FLORES

Lake Petén Itzá

Isla Santa Barbara

Lanchas to San Benito, San Andrés & San José

Restaurant Chaltunhá

Source: ProPetén

CALLE FRATERNIDED
AV. LA LIBERTAD
CALLE LA UNIÓN
CALLEJÓN EL REDONDO
PASAJE PROGRESO
CALLEJÓN PEDRITO
CALLE 30 DE JUNIO
CALLEJÓN
EL CRUCERO
AV REFORMA
AV BARRIOS
AVENIDA FLORES
CALLE EL ROSARIO
CALLE 15 DE SEPTIEMBRE
CALLE EL ROSARIO
CALLE ANA
AVENIDA SANTA ANA
CALLE CENTRAL
CALLE CENTRO AMÉRICA

CENTRAL
PLAZA

Cincap ⓘ
Theatre
Banrural
Catholic Church
Gobernación Departmental
Inguat
ProPetén
Flores Net @
Martsam Travel
Tikal Net
Linea Dorada Bus Office
★ Local Bus to Airport/ Santa Elena/ San Benito

0   200 m
N

ACCOMMODATION

Casazul	1
Hospedaje Doña Goya	4
Hotel Butterfly Planet	8
Hotel La Casona de la Isla	7
Hotel La Jungla	10
Hotel Mirador del Lago	6
Hotel Sabana	2
Hotel La Santana	9
La Casa del Lacandón	3
Posada Tayazal	5

RESTAURANTS & CAFÉS

Crocodile Club	E
El Tucán	G
La Canoa	F
La Luna	A
Las Puertas	C
Maya Princess Café Bar	B
Pizzeria Picasso	D

▽ *Causeway to Santa Elena (750 metres approx.)*

SANTA ELENA

SAN BENITO

SANTA ELENA

1 CALLE
1 CALLE A
2 CALLE
2 CALLE
3 CALLE A
3 CALLE
4 CALLE (CALLE PRINCIPAL)
4 CALLE A
5 CALLE
CALLE PRINCIPAL
5 AVENIDA
4 AVENIDA
3 AVENIDA
2 AVENIDA

Avinsa Travel

Buses to Guatemala City ★ & Poptún
Banco Industrial (ATM)
Market
Hotel Diplomatico Bus Station
Buses to Belize
Banco Continental

▷ *Airport, Tikal & Belize*

ACCOMMODATION

Hotel Alonzo	3
Hotel Jade	1
Hotel Sac-Nicte	2

RESTAURANTS

Mijaro	B
Petenchel	A

Honduras, and left behind a sick horse which he promised to send for later. A horse-worshipping cult started as a result, and later visitors were sacrificed to the equine deity. Tayasal was eventually destroyed by Martín de Ursúa and an army of 235 in 1697. For the entire colonial period (and indeed up to the 1960s) Flores languished in virtual isolation, having more contact with neighbouring Belize than with the capital.

Today, despite the steady flow of tourists passing through en route to Tikal, the town retains an urbane air. It has little to detain you and is small enough to explore in an hour or so, but it does offer some attractive places to stay, good restaurants, cybercafés and spectacular lake views.

Arrival and information

Arriving by **bus** from Guatemala City or Belize, you'll be dropped a block or two from the causeway to Flores. The **airport** is 3km east of the causeway, a US$2 taxi-ride into town. **Local buses** cover the route but entail a time-consuming change halfway. They cross the causeway about every ten minutes. Returning to the airport, local buses leave from the Flores end of the causeway every twenty minutes or so.

The staff at the Inguat desk in the arrivals hall at the airport (daily 7am–noon & 3-6pm; ☎926 0533), can give you reasonable maps and **information** in English. There's another office on the plaza in Flores (Mon–Sat 8am–4.30pm; ☎926 0669), where the helpful staff will most likely direct you across the plaza to the resource centre, **CIN-CAP** (Mon–Fri 9am–1pm & 2–6pm; ☎926 0718), a very useful resource centre with more detailed maps, books and leaflets, and exhibitions on historical and contemporary life in Petén. This is also the production office of *Destination Petén*, a free monthly listings and **information magazine**, available at most of the town's hotels and travel agencies. If you're planning to go on a trip to remote parts of the Maya Biosphere Reserve, check with **ProPetén** on C Central (Mon–Fri 8am–5pm; ☎926 1370, fax 926 0495, *propeten@guate.net*) for current information on route conditions, accommodation and guides. They also run **organized trips**, including the "Scarlet Macaw Trail", a five-day expedition by truck, horse and boat along rivers and through primary forest, taking in the remote ruins of **El Perú** and the largest concentration of scarlet macaws in northern Central America.

If you're interested in doing some **voluntary work**, the wildlife conservation and rescue association **ARCAS** (Asociación de Rescate y Conservación de Vida Silvestre; ☎926 0946, *arcaspeten@intelnet.net.gt*), based next to the Petencito zoo, 4km east of Santa Elena, runs a rescue service for animals taken illegally as pets from the forests and always needs volunteers. The work, while rewarding, can be quite demanding and you'll need to sign up for at least a week (US$80 per person including all food and lodging).

Accommodation

Accommodation in Flores/Santa Elena has mushroomed in recent years and the sheer number of new **hotels** keeps prices competitive. There are several good budget places in Flores itself, making it unnecessary to stay in noisier and dirtier Santa Elena unless your budget is extremely tight.

Flores
Casazul, close to the northern tip of the island (☎926 1138). Stylishly converted colonial-style mansion house with light, tastefully decorated rooms, all with two double beds, wooden furniture, fridges and a/c. ⑨.

Hospedaje Doña Goya, north end of the island (☎926 3538). Excellent family-run budget guesthouse, with clean, light rooms, all with fan, and some with private bath; the ones at the front have balconies. Also offers a book exchange, roof-top terrace with hammocks and trips to nearby caves. Good rates for single travellers. ②.

Hotel Butterfly Planet, near the Linea Dorada office (☎926 0357, *martsam@guate.net*). Clean, inexpensive rooms with shared cold-water bath. Run by Benedicto Grijalva of Martsam Travel, so very good for information and tours. ②.

Hotel la Casona de la Isla, Calle 30 de Junio (☎ & fax 926 0593, *www.corpetur.com*). The arresting citrus and powder-blue paint job conceals attractive modern rooms with private bath and a/c, plus a swimming pool and spectacular sunset views from the terrace bar-restaurant. ⑤.

Hotel La Jungla, southwest corner of the island (☎926 0634). Decent value in this price range, with gleaming tiled floors and private baths with hot water, plus rooftop views over the town and lake and a good restaurant. ③.

Hotel Mirador del Lago, Calle 15 de Septiembre (☎926 3276). Easily the best just-above-budget hotel in Flores, with well-furnished rooms with private bath and fan. Friendly owner Mimi Salguero (who speaks a little English) keeps the lobby fridge stocked with beer and soft drinks, and has tables on a lakeshore terrace at which to enjoy them. Great sunset views from the roof. ③.

Hotel Sabana, at the northern tip of the island (☎ & fax 926 1248, *www.sabanahotel.com*). Large, modern and good-value place with a small pool and nice lake views, especially from the restaurant. All 28 rooms have a/c and cable TV. ⑤.

Hotel Santana, southwest corner of Flores (☎926 0492, fax 926 0662). Recently modernized three-storey building with a small pool and patio overlooking the lake. Very comfortable, spotless rooms with fan and private bath; first-floor rooms have private lakeside terraces and a/c. ⑤.

La Casa del Lacandón, on the lakeshore, Calle Fraternidad (☎926 3592). Good new hotel with a range of rooms, all with private bath. Those downstairs are clean and reasonable value, but the upstairs rooms are larger and more attractive, especially rooms 101 and 105, which have stunning lake views. ③.

Posada Tayazal, Calle la Unión near the *Doña Goya* (☎ & fax 926 0568). Well-run budget hotel with decent, basic rooms (either with private or shared bath) plus roof terrace, information service and tours to Tikal. ②.

Santa Elena

Hotel Alonzo, 6 Av 4–99 (☎926 0105). Reasonable budget rooms, some with balconies and a few with private hot- or cold-water bath (the shared bathroom is grubby). There's also a restaurant and a public telephone. ②–③.

Hotel Jade, 6 Avenida. A backpackers' stronghold. Shambolic, but the cheapest place in town. ①.

Hotel Sac-Nicte, 1 C 4–45 (☎ & fax 926 0092). Clean rooms with fan and private shower; second-floor rooms have views of the lake. ②.

Eating and drinking

Flores unquestionably offers the most cosmopolitan dining in Petén and there are a number of good restaurants, many with delightful lakeside views, though prices are a little higher than elsewhere in Guatemala. **Santa Elena** has a very limited selection of comedores, so even if you're staying there you may want to cross the causeway for an evening out. Many restaurants here also serve **wild game**, often listed on menus as *comida silvestre*. Virtually all this has been taken illegally from reserves and you should avoid ordering items such as *tepescuintle* (paca, a large relation of the guinea-pig), *venado* (deer), or *coche de monte* (peccary, or wild pig).

Flores

Crocodile Club, Calle Centro América, near Martsam Travel and under the same ownership. Really good, filling meals (some vegetarian) and bar snacks in a friendly atmosphere, plus music, movies, book exchange and information.

El Tucán, a few metres east of the causeway, on the waterfront but reached from Calle Centro América. Good fish, enormous chef's salads, great Mexican food and the best waterside terrace in Flores, but prices are higher than they used to be and there's wild game on the menu.

La Canoa, Calle Centro América. Popular, good-value place serving pasta, great soups, and some vegetarian and Guatemalan food, as well as excellent breakfasts.

La Luna, at the far end of Calle 30 de Junio. The best restaurant in town, though not that expensive, set in a wonderfully atmospheric old building. Meat, fish and pasta, plus home-made soup and a few vegetarian dishes – and it doesn't serve wild game. Also great for an espresso.

Las Puertas, signposted from Calle Santa Ana. Paint-splattered walls and live music as well as very good pasta and healthy breakfasts. Worth it for the atmosphere.

Maya Princess Café Bar, Avenida Reforma. Moderate prices and an interesting creative international menu – teriyaki chicken, salad with basil leaves – and a sociable vibe make this a deservedly popular place. Free movies shown at 4pm and 9pm daily.

Pizzeria Picasso, across the street from the *Tucán* and run by the same family (☎926-0637). Great pizza served under cooling breezes from the ceiling fans; they also deliver.

Santa Elena

Mijaro, two branches. one on the road from the causeway, the other round the corner on Calle Principal. The best Guatemalan restaurants in Santa Elena, with good food at local prices and a daily special. You can also usually leave luggage here while you look for a room.

Restaurant Petenchel, 2 Calle, past the park. Simple, good food. The nicest place to eat within two blocks of the main street and you can leave your luggage here.

Listings

Banks and currency exchange For Visa cash advances try Banco Industrial (which has a 24hr ATM); for Mastercard transactions try Banco G&T Continental. You can also cash travellers' cheques at one of the recommended travel agents listed below.

Bike rental Cahuí, 30 de Junio, Flores, for US$1 per hour (daily 7am–7pm; ☎ & fax 926 0494).

Car rental Several firms, including Budget, Hertz and Koka, have offices at the airport. All offer cars, minibuses and Jeeps, with prices from around US$65 a day for a Jeep.

Doctor Centro Medico Maya, 4 Avenida near 3 Calle in Santa Elena, down the street by the *Hotel Diplomatico* (☎926 0180), is helpful and professional, though no English is spoken.

Language schools San Andrés and San José, two very attractive villages on the north shore of the lake, both have good Spanish schools and, since few of the villagers speak English, are excellent places to learn and practise the language. The Eco-Escuela in San Andrés (☎928 8106, *www .conservation.org/ecoescuela/about.htm*) is larger and has been established longer than the Escuela Bio-Itzá in San José (☎928 8142, *www.conservation.org/ecoescuela/bioitza.htm*), but the instruction in the latter is just as good and San José is arguably the prettier village. Official rates (around US$170 a week for lessons, food and lodging) may seem more expensive than schools in Antigua or Quetzaltenango, but you may get a discount if you contact the school directly or ask one of the recommended travel agents (below) to call for you – they won't charge you extra for this. Lanchas for the villages leave regularly from Flores, and there are buses from Santa Elena.

Laundry Lavandería Amelia, behind CINCAP in Flores; Lavandería Emanuel on 6 Avenida in Santa Elena.

Post office Two doors away from the Inguat office in Flores; at 2 C and 7 Av, two blocks east of the *Hotel San Juan*, in Santa Elena (both offices Mon–Fri 8am–4.30pm).

Telephones and email The Telgua office is in Santa Elena on 5 C, but you're better off using Tikal Net, at 4 C and 6 Av, for all phone, fax and Internet services; they also have another branch in Flores at Calle Centro America (both offices daily 8.30–10.30pm).

Travel agents and tour operators Every hotel in Flores – and a good many in Santa Elena – seems to be offering tours, but most actually only sell minibus trips to Tikal or bus and plane tickets. The best travel agent in Flores is Martsam Travel (☎ & fax 926 3225, *martsam@guate.net*), at the western end of Calle Centro America; the owners speak English, run a daily trip to Yaxhá (p.260) and know Belize well. Avinsa (☎929 0808, *www.tikaltravel.com*), a few blocks east along Calle Principal in Santa Elena, arranges first-class tours throughout Guatemala and the entire Maya region, and is the only agent able to issue international airline tickets beyond Mexico or Belize; staff speak English and German. Evolution Adventures (☎926 0633, *evolution@internetdetelgua.com.gt*), off Calle Centro America, opposite Tikal Net, offers overnight backpacking trips to the more remote ruins of the Maya Biosphere Reserve, such as El Perú, Río Azul and El Mirador, formerly very difficult to reach on your own; it's owned by a Canadian, David Jackaman. EcoMaya, at Calle 30 de Junio in Flores (☎926 1363, *www.ecomaya.com*), is also recommended for trips to remote ruins including El Zotz and Mirador and the Scarlet Macaw trail inside the Laguna del Tigre reserve. The *Hotel San Juan* travel agency in Santa Elena is not recommended.

Around Flores: Lago de Petén Itzá

If you have a few hours to spare, the most obvious excursion is a **trip on the lake**. Boatmen can take you around a circuit that takes in a *mirador* and small ruin on the peninsula opposite and the **Petencito zoo**, 3km east of Flores (daily 8am–5pm), with its small collection of sluggish local wildlife, pausing for a swim along the way (beware the concrete waterslide by the zoo – it's caused at least one death). Boatmen loiter with intent below the *Hotel Santana* in Flores, or around the start of the causeway. If you'd rather paddle around under your own steam you can rent a canoe for around US$2 an hour.

Of the numerous **caves** in the hills behind Santa Elena, the most accessible is **Aktun Kan** (daily 8am–5pm; US$1.20) – simply follow the Flores causeway through Santa Elena, turn left when it forks in front of a small hill, and then take the first right. Otherwise known as *La Cueva de la Serpiente*, the cave is the legendary home of a huge snake; the guard may explain some of the bizarre names given to the various shapes inside.

San Andrés and San José

Though accessible by bus and boat, the traditional villages of **San Andrés** and **San José**, across the lake from Flores, have until recently received few visitors. Sloping steeply up from the shore, the streets are lined with one-storey buildings, some fashioned out of palmetto sticks and thatch, some coated with plaster, and others made from brightly painted concrete. Pigs and chickens wander freely.

Getting to the villages is best achieved by using the lanchas (US$0.50 to San Andrés, 25 min; US$0.75 to San José, 30 min) which leave regularly from the beach next to the *Hotel Santana* in Flores and from **San Benito**, a suburb of Santa Elena. A chartered *expreso* from Flores or San Benito will cost around US$9. Regular morning **buses** leave from the market in Santa Elena for San Andrés (some continue on to San José; if not, it's an easy 2km walk downhill from Santa Elena). Lanchas and buses return when full throughout the day at regular intervals until 5pm.

Most outsiders in **SAN ANDRÉS** are students at the village's **language school**, the Eco-Escuela. Since nobody in the village speaks English, a course here is an excellent opportunity to immerse yourself in Spanish without distractions, though it may be daunting for absolute beginners (see opposite for more details).

There are currently no hospedajes in the village, but 3km to the west you'll find the luxurious *Hotel Nitún* (☎928 8132, fax 928 8113, *www.nitun.com;* ⑥ including transport from Flores), which offers accommodation in thatched stone cabañas with hardwood floors and private bathrooms; the restaurant serves superb food. The hotel is also the base for Monkey Eco Tours (same contact details), who organize well-equipped expeditions to remote archeological sites.

Perched above a lovely bay, 2km east along the shore from San Andrés, **SAN JOSÉ** is even more relaxed than its neighbour, and also has a language school, the Escuela Bio-Itzá (see opposite for more details). The village is undergoing something of a cultural revival: Itza, the pre-conquest Maya tongue, is being taught in the school, and you'll see signs in that language dotted all around. Over the hill beyond the village is a secluded rocky beach where there's a shelter to sling a hammock and a couple of cabins to rent.

Beyond San José a signed track on the left leads 4km to the Classic period **ruins of Motúl**. The site is fairly spread out and little visited (though there should be a caretaker about), with four plazas, stelae and pyramids. It's a secluded spot, ideal for bird-watching, and probably best visited by **bicycle** – borrow one from either of the villages or rent one in Flores.

El Remate

On the eastern shore of Lago de Petén Itzá, 30km from Santa Elena on the road to Tikal, the quiet and friendly village of **EL REMATE** offers a pleasant alternative to staying in Flores and makes a convenient base for visits to Tikal. **Getting to El Remate** is easy: all minibuses to Tikal pass through the village, or catch any bus heading for the Belize border and get off at the village of **Puente Ixlú** (also called El Cruce), from where it's a two-kilometre walk down the Tikal road. **Returning to Flores**, three local buses pass through El Remate between 5.30am and 8am and a swarm of minibuses from Tikal also ply the route – there are more from midday onwards.

On the north shore of the lake, 3km along the road from the centre of El Remate, the **Biotopo Cerro Cahuí** (daily 6am–4pm; US$5) is a 6.5-square-kilometre wildlife conservation area comprising lakeshore, ponds and some of the best examples of undisturbed tropical forest in Petén. The smallest and most accessible of Petén's reserves, it contains a rich diversity of plants and animals, and is especially recommended for birdwatchers. There are hiking trails, a couple of small ruins and two thatched *miradores* on the hill above the lake; pick up maps and information at the gate where you sign in, close to the *El Gringo Perdido* hotel. Unfortunately there have been attacks on visitors inside the Biotopo, so check the current security situation before setting out.

There's lots to explore in the rich tropical environment around El Remate, including boat tours of the eastern end of the lakeshore operated by the *Casa de Don David*. Plenty of places also rent out canoes for a dollar an hour.

Accommodation and eating

Most of the places listed here have a distinctive charm. There a few simple comedores offering inexpensive Guatemalan food, and most of the hotels also provide meals. Accommodation options are listed in the order you reach them from Puente Ixlú.

Camping Sal Itzá, 100m down a signed track opposite the lakeshore right at the beginning of the village. Simple stick-and-thatch cabins and camping on a steep hillside with lake views. Run by a very friendly family, headed by Juan and Rita, who cook tasty local food on request. ②.

El Mirador del Duende, high above the lake, reached by a stairway cut into the cliff (*miraduende@hotmail.*com). An incredible collection of globular whitewashed stucco cabañas decorated with Maya glyphs, plus space for hammocks and tents. There's also a wonderful terrace overlooking the lake and a restaurant serving cheap vegetarian food. ②.

La Mansión del Pajaro Serpiente, just below *El Mirador del Duende* (✆ & fax 926 4246, *nature@ietravel.com*). The most comfortable accommodation on the road to Tikal, with thatched, two-storey stone cabañas in a tropical garden and smaller rooms, all with superb lake views. Good food is also available, and there's a small swimming pool. The owners vary their prices according to demand, so it can be a bargain at quiet times of the year. ④–⑤.

Hotel Ixchel, just off the Tikal road close to the junction. Simple but fairly comfortable wood cabins, run by a very friendly local family. ②.

Casa de Bruno's Place, just past the *Ixchel*, at the junction. Four basic, functional rooms with shared bath, behind the village store. ②.

La Casa de Don David, 300m beyond *La Mansión*, right on the junction (✆306-2190, *www .lacasadedondavid.com*). Comfortable, spacious and secure wooden bungalows and rooms with private hot-water baths, set in grassy grounds just back from the lakeshore. Owners David and Rosa Kuhn offer great hospitality and home cooking. David is a mine of information about Petén, and can change money, arrange trips, and sell bus tickets for Belize and Guatemala City; the staff know the times of local buses. There are usually a couple of bikes for guests to borrow. ④.

Casa Mobego, 500m down the road to Cerro Cahuí on the right. Good budget deal right by the lake. Simple, well-constructed stick-and-thatch cabañas, plus camping, canoe rental, a good, inexpensive restaurant and swimming. ②.

Casa de Doña Tonita, 800m down the road to Cerro Cahuí on the right. Four basic clapboard rooms, built high above the lake, with great views. The owner also runs a pleasant thatched-roofed restaurant next door with vegetarian food and snacks. ②.

El Gringo Perdido, on the north shore, 3km from *Don David's* (☎ & fax 334 2305, *ecoadventure @mail2.guate.net*). Long-established place in a supremely tranquil setting offering rooms with bath, a mosquito-netted bunk, good-value basic cabañas and camping (US$3 per person). The restaurant is less impressive. Guided canoe tours available. ③–⑤.

Tikal

Towering above the rainforest, **Tikal** is possibly the most magnificent of all Maya ruins. The site is dominated by five enormous temples, steep-sided granite pyramids that rise up to 60m from the forest floor, while around them are literally thousands of other structures, many half-strangled by giant roots and still hidden beneath mounds of earth.

The site itself is deep in the jungle of the **Parque Nacional Tikal**, a protected area of some 370 square kilometres, on the edge of the even larger Maya Biosphere Reserve. The trees around the ruins are home to hundreds of species including howler and spider monkeys, toucans and parakeets. The sheer scale of the place is overwhelming, and its atmosphere spellbinding. Whether you can spare as little as an hour or as long as a week, it's always worth the trip.

Plane schedules are designed to make it easy to visit the ruins as a day-trip from Flores or Guatemala City, but if you can spare the time it's well worth **staying overnight**, partly because you'll need the extra time to do justice to the ruins themselves but, more importantly, to spend dawn and dusk at the site, when the forest canopy bursts into a frenzy of sound and activity. The air fills with the screech of toucans and the roar of howler monkeys, while flocks of parakeets wheel around the temples, and bats launch themselves into the night. With a bit of luck you might even see a grey fox sneak across one of the plazas.

Arrival and information

The best way to reach the ruins is in one of the **tourist minibuses** which meet flights from the capital and are operated by just about every hotel in Flores and Santa Elena, starting at 4am to catch the sunrise. In addition a **local bus** (Pinita) leaves the market at 1pm, arriving at Tikal about two hours later, then continuing to Uaxactún (see p.270), before returning to Santa Elena at 5am. If you're travelling from Belize to Tikal, there is no need to go all the way to Flores; get off instead at **Puente Ixlú** – the three-way junction at the eastern end of Lago de Petén Itzá – to change buses. The local bus from Santa Elena to Tikal and Uaxactún comes through at about 2pm, and there are passing minibuses all day long, at their most frequent in the mornings.

Admission to the national park costs US$6.40 a day (payable every day you stay at the site; if you arrive after 3pm you'll be given a ticket for the next day). The ruins are **open** daily from 6am to 6pm; extensions to 8pm can be obtained from the *inspectoría* (7am–noon & 2–5pm), a small white hut to the left of the entrance to the ruins. A **licensed guide** (US$40 for a 4hr tour) is an extremely worthwhile investment if you can afford it. Many, including Eulogio López García and José Luis Morales Monzón, speak excellent English, and they all know the site really well. You'll find them waiting for business by the visitor centre and the *inspectoría* gate.

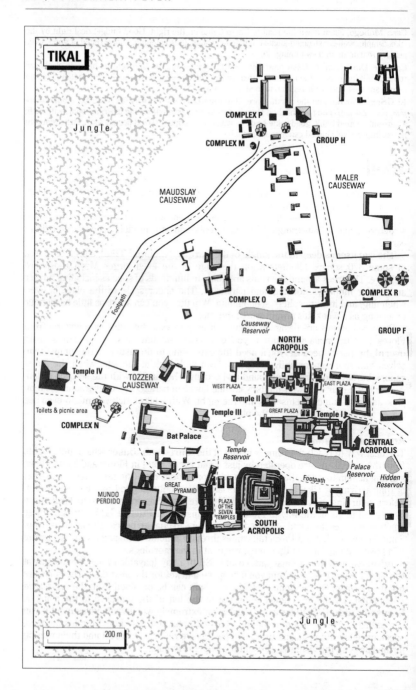

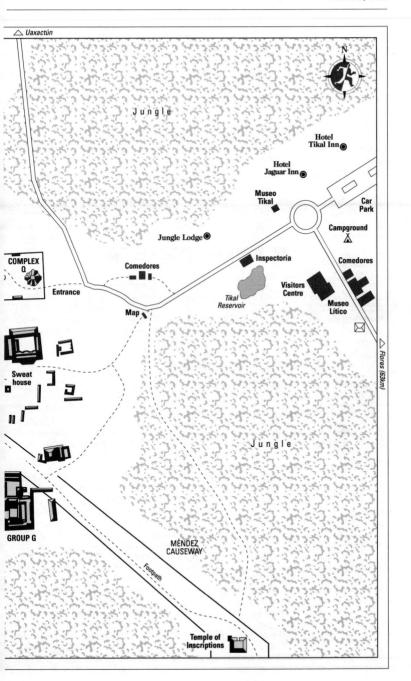

Uaxactún

Jungle

N

Hotel
Tikal Inn

Hotel
Jaguar Inn

Museo
Tikal

Car
Park

Jungle Lodge

Campground

COMPLEX
Q

Comedores

Inspectoría

Comedores

Entrance

Visitors
Centre

Tikal
Reservoir

Map

Museo
Lítico

Sweat
house

Flores (63km)

Jungle

GROUP G

MÉNDEZ
CAUSEWAY

Footpath

Temple of
Inscriptions

The site also has a **post office**, shops and **visitor centre**, where you'll find an over-priced café-restaurant, souvenir stalls and the **Museo Lítico** (Mon–Fri 9am–5pm, Sat & Sun 9am–4pm; free), which houses nineteen stelae, though they're very poorly labelled and there is no supplementary information in English. Two **books** of note are usually available: Michael Coe's *Tikal: A Handbook to the Ancient Maya Ruins* is the best guide to the site, while *The Birds of Tikal*, although by no means comprehensive, is useful for identifying some of the hundreds of species you might come across as you wander round.

At the entrance, between the *Jungle Lodge* and *Jaguar Inn* hotels (see opposite), the one-room **Museo Tikal** (Mon–Fri 9am–5pm, Sat & Sun 9am–4pm; US$1.30) houses some of the artefacts found in the ruins, including jewellery, ceramics, obsidian eccentric flints, the jade jewellery found in tumba 116 and the magnificent Stela 31, which shows the Tikal ruler Smoking Frog bearing a jaguar-head belt and a jade necklace. There's also a spectacular **reconstruction of Hasaw Chan K'awil's tomb**, one of the richest ever found in the Maya world, containing 180 worked jade items in the form of

THE RISE AND FALL OF TIKAL

According to archeological evidence, the first occupants of Tikal arrived around 900 BC, probably attracted by its position above the surrounding seasonal swamps and by the availability of **flint** for making tools and weapons. The first definite evidence of buildings dates from 500 BC, and by about 200 BC the first ceremonial structures had emerged, including the first version of the **North Acropolis**. Two hundred years later, at around the time of Christ, the **Great Plaza** had begun to take shape and Tikal was already established as a major site with a large permanent population. Despite development and sophisticated architecture, Tikal remained very much a secondary centre, dominated, along with the rest of the area, by **El Mirador**, a massive city about 65km to the north (see p.271).

The closing years of the **Preclassic** (250–300 AD) era were marked by the eruption of the Ilopango volcano in El Salvador, which smothered huge areas of Guatemala in a thick layer of volcanic ash. Trade routes were disrupted and the ensuing years saw the decline and abandonment of El Mirador, creating a power vacuum with bitter disputes between the cities of Tikal and Uaxactún. Tikal eventually won under the inspired leadership of Toh Chac Ich'ak (Great Jaguar Paw), probably with the aid of the powerful highland centre of **Kaminaljuyú** – on the site of modern Guatemala City – which was itself allied with **Teotihuacán**, the ancient metropolis that dominated what is now central Mexico.

The victory over Uaxactún enabled Tikal's rulers to control central Petén for the next three centuries, developing into one of the most elaborate and magnificent of all Maya city states. This extended period of prosperity saw temples rebuilt, while the city's population grew to somewhere between 50,000 and 100,000, and its influence reached as far as Copán in Honduras.

In the middle of the sixth century, however, Tikal suffered a major setback. Already weakened by upheavals in central Mexico, where Teotihuacán was in decline, the city now faced major challenges from the east, where the city of **Caracol** (see p.95) was emerging as a regional force, and from the north, where **Calakmul** was becoming a major power. In an apparent attempt to subdue a potential rival, **Double Bird**, the ruler of Tikal, launched an attack (known as an "axe war") on Caracol and its ambitious leader, Yahaw-te, **Lord Water**, in 556 AD. Despite capturing and sacrificing a noble from Caracol, Double Bird's strategy was only temporarily successful; in 562 AD Lord Water hit back in a devastating "star war", which crushed Tikal and almost certainly resulted in the capture and sacrifice of Double Bird. The victors stamped their authority over the humiliated nobles of Tikal, smashing stelae, desecrating tombs and destroying written records, ushering in a 130-year hiatus during which no inscribed monuments were erect-

bracelets, anklets, necklaces and earplugs, and delicately incised bones, including the famous carving depicting deities paddling canoes bearing the dead to the underworld.

Accommodation, eating and drinking

There are three **hotels** at the ruins, all of them fairly expensive and not especially good value, though they offer discounts out of season. The largest and most luxurious is the *Jungle Lodge* (☎476 8775, fax 476 0294, *www.junglelodge.com*; ④/⑥), which offers good bungalow accommodation with two double beds per bungalow, and some fairly comfortable "budget" rooms, though they lack private baths and are often booked up; there's also a restaurant and a pool. Next door is the overpriced *Jaguar Inn* (☎926 0002, fax 926 2413, *www.jaguartikal.com*; ⑥), with nine bungalows with little verandas and camping (US$3.20 per person), but no pool. Close by, the *Tikal Inn* (☎926 0065, fax 594 6944, *tikalinn@internetdetelgua.com.gt*; ⑤) is a better bet, with nice thatched bungalows, pleasant rooms and a glorious swimming pool. Alternatively, for US$4.80 you can **camp** or sling a **hammock** under one of the thatched shelters in a cleared space used

ed and Tikal was overshadowed by Caracol, supported by its powerful ally, Calakmul. Another effect of Caracol's assault was to free many smaller centres throughout Petén from Tikal's influence, creating fresh and disruptive rivalry.

Towards the end of the seventh century, however, Caracol's stranglehold had begun to weaken and Tikal gradually started to recover its lost power. Under the formidable leadership of Hasaw Chan K'awil, **Heavenly Standard Bearer**, who reigned from 682–723 AD, the main ceremonial areas were reclaimed from the desecration suffered at the hands of Caracol. By 695 AD, Tikal was powerful enough to launch an attack against Calakmul, capturing and executing its king, Yich'ak K'ak or **Fiery Claw/Jaguar Paw**, and severely weakening the alliance against Tikal.

The following year, Hasaw Chan K'awil repeated his astonishing coup by capturing **Split Earth**, the new king of Calakmul, and Tikal regained its position among the most important of Petén cities. Hasaw Chan K'awil's leadership gave birth to a revitalized and powerful ruling dynasty: in the hundred years following his death Tikal's five main temples were built and his son, Yik'in Chan K'awil, or **Divine Sunset Lord** (who ascended to the throne in 734 AD), had his father's body entombed in the magnificent **Temple I**. Temples and monuments were still under construction until at least 869 AD, when Tikal's last recorded date is inscribed on Stela 24.

The cause of Tikal's final **downfall** remains a mystery, but what is certain is that around 900 AD almost the whole of lowland Maya civilization collapsed. Possible causes range from an earthquake to a popular uprising, but the evidence points in no particular direction. We do know that Tikal was abandoned by the end of the tenth century.

Little more is known of Tikal until 1848, when it was **rediscovered** by a government expedition led by Modesto Méndez. Later in the nineteenth century a Swiss scientist visited the site and removed the beautifully carved wooden lintels from the tops of Temples 1 and 4 – they are currently in a museum in Basel – and in 1881 the English archeologist Maudslay took the first photographs of the ruins. The site could only be reached on horseback and the ruins remained mostly uncleared until 1951, when the Guatemalan army built an airstrip, paving the way for a cultural invasion of archeologists and tourists. The gargantuan project to excavate and restore the site started in 1956, and involved teams from the University of Pennsylvania and Guatemala's Institute of Anthropology. Most of the major work was completed by 1984, but thousands of minor buildings remain buried in roots, shoots and rubble. There's little doubt that an incredible amount is still buried around the site – as recently as 1996 a workman unearthed a stela (Stela 40, dating from 468 AD) while mowing the grass on the Great Plaza. A ten-year project to restore Temple 5 (at 58m the second highest structure at Tikal) is currently being co-ordinated with help from the Spanish government, and should be completed by 2007.

as a campsite. Hammocks and mosquito nets (essential in the wet season) can be rented either on the spot or from the *Comedor Imperio Maya* opposite the visitor centre. There's a shower block at the entrance to the campsite, but water is sporadic. It's illegal to camp or sleep out among the ruins.

The three simple **comedores** at the entrance to the ruins, and a couple more inside, offer a limited menu of traditional Guatemalan specialities – eggs, beans, grilled meat and chicken. For more extensive and expensive menus, there's an adequate restaurant in the *Jaguar Inn*. It's essential to buy some water before setting out, though cold drinks are sold at a number of spots around the ruins.

The ruins

The sheer scale of the ruins at Tikal can at first seem daunting. The **central area**, with its five main temples, forms by far the most impressive section; if you start to explore beyond this you can wander seemingly forever in the maze of smaller, **unrestored structures** and complexes. Compared to the scale and magnificence of the main area, they're not that impressive, but armed with a good map (the best is in Coe's guide to the ruins), it can be exciting to explore some of the rarely visited outlying sections. Whatever you do, Tikal is certain to exhaust you before you exhaust it.

From the entrance to the Great Plaza

From the entrance, a path leads past **Complexes Q and R**, twin pyramids built by **Chitam**, Tikal's last known ruler, to mark the passing of a *katum* (twenty 360-day years). Set to one side is a copy of the superbly carved Stela 22 (the original is now in the Museo Lítico). Bearing to the left after Complex R, you approach the **East Plaza**; in its southeast corner stands an imposing temple, beneath which were found the remains of several severed heads, the victims of human sacrifice. Behind the plaza is the **sweat house**, which may have been similar to those used by highland Maya today. It's thought that Maya priests would take a sweat bath in order to cleanse themselves before conducting religious rituals.

From here a few short steps bring you to the **Great Plaza**, the heart of the ancient city. Surrounded by four massive structures, this was the focus of ceremonial and religious activity at Tikal for around a thousand years. Beneath the grass lie four layers of paving, the oldest of which dates from about 150 BC and the most recent from 700 AD. **Temple 1**, towering 44m above the plaza, is the hallmark of Tikal – it's also known as the Jaguar Temple because of the jaguar carved on its door lintel (now in a museum in Basel). This temple was built to contain the magnificent tomb of **Hasaw Chan K'awil** (682–721 AD) by his son and successor Yik'in Chan K'awil. The skeleton was found in the tomb at the temple's core, facing north and surrounded by an assortment of jade, pearls, seashells and stingray spines, the last a symbol of human sacrifice. There's a reconstruction of the tomb (tumba 116) in the Museo Tikal. Standing opposite, like a squat version of Temple 1, is **Temple 2**, known as the Temple of the Masks for the two grotesque masks, now heavily eroded, that flank the central stairway. As yet no tomb has been found beneath this temple, which now stands 38m high, although with its roof comb intact it would have equalled Temple 1. It's an easy climb up the staircase to the top.

The **North Acropolis**, which fills the whole north side of the Great Plaza, is one of the most complex structures in the entire Maya world. In true Maya style it was built and rebuilt on top of itself, and beneath the twelve temples that can be seen today are the remains of about a hundred other structures. As early as 100 BC the Maya had constructed elaborate platforms here supporting temples and tombs. Archeologists have removed some of the surface to reveal these earlier structures, including two four-metre-high **masks**. One facing the plaza, protected by a thatched roof, is clearly visible; the other can be reached by following the dark passageway to the side – you'll need a torch. In front of the North Acropolis are two lines of **stelae** with circular altars at their bases, all of which were originally painted a brilliant red.

The Central Acropolis and Temple 5

On the other side of the plaza is the **Central Acropolis**, a maze of tiny interconnecting rooms and stairways built around six smallish courtyards. The buildings here are usually referred to as palaces rather than temples, although their precise use remains a mystery. Possibilities include law courts, temporary retreats, administrative centres, and homes for Tikal's elite. Behind the acropolis is the palace reservoir, which was fed with rainwater by a series of channels from all over the city. Further behind the Central Acropolis is the 58-metre-high **Temple 5**, which supports a single tiny room at the top thought to be a mortuary shrine to an unknown ruler. The temple is currently the subject of a huge restoration project, due to be completed by around 2007, when the view from the top will be superb, with a great profile of Temple 1 and a side view of the central plaza.

From the West Plaza to Temple 4

Behind Temple 2 is the **West Plaza**, dominated by a large Late Classic temple on the north side, and scattered with various altars and stelae. From here the Tozzer Causeway – one of the raised routes that connected the main parts of the city – leads west to **Temple 3** (55m), covered in jungle vegetation. A fragment of Stela 24, found at the base of the temple, dates it at 810 AD. Around the back of the temple is a huge palace complex, of which only the **Bat Palace** has been restored. At the end of the Tozzer Causeway is **Temple 4**, at 64m the tallest of all the Tikal structures. Built in 741 AD, it is thought by some archeologists to be the resting place of the ruler **Yik'in Chan K'awil**, whose image was depicted on wooden lintels built into the top of the temple. Twin ladders, one for the ascent, the other for the descent, are attached to the sides of the temple. Exhausting as the climb is, one of the finest views of the whole site awaits, with the forest canopy stretching out to the horizon all around you, interrupted only by the great roof-combs of the other temples.

The Mundo Perdido, Plaza of the Seven Temples and Temple of the Inscriptions

To the south of the Central Acropolis, reached by a trail from Temple 3, you'll find the **Plaza of the Seven Temples**, which forms part of a complex dating back to before Christ. There's an unusual triple ball court on the north side of the plaza, and to the east is the unexcavated South Acropolis. To the west, the **Mundo Perdido**, or Lost World, is another magical and very distinct section of the site with its own atmosphere and architecture. Little is known about the ruins here, but archeologists hope that further research in this area will help to explain the early history of Tikal. The main feature is the **great pyramid**, a 32-metre-high structure whose surface hides four earlier versions, the first dating from 500 BC. The top of the pyramid offers awesome views towards Temple 4 and the Great Plaza and makes an excellent place from which to admire the visual dramatics of sunrise or sunset.

Finally, there's the **Temple of the Inscriptions**, reached along the Méndez Causeway from the East Plaza behind Temple 1. The temple (only discovered in 1951) is about 1km from the plaza. It's famous for its twelve-metre roof comb, at the back of which is a huge but rather faint hieroglyphic text.

The far north

Away to the north of Tikal, lost in a sea of jungle, are several other substantial **ruins** – unrestored and for the most part uncleared, but with their own unique atmosphere. Twenty-four kilometres north of Tikal, strung out by the side of a disused airstrip, are the village and ruins of **UAXACTÚN** (pronounced "Wash-ak-toon"). With a couple of places to stay, several comedores and a daily bus to Santa Elena, the village is an ideal jumping-off point for the more remote sites of **El Zotz**, **Río Azul** and **El Mirador**, the bulk of whose temples are coated in an anarchic tangle of roots and shoots, with only the tallest roof combs visible. Dirt tracks go as far as Río Azul and El Zotz, offering the perfect destinations if you're in search of adventure and want to see virtually untouched Maya sites.

Uaxactún

Substantially smaller than Tikal, the ruins at **Uaxactún** are thought to date from the same era. During the Preclassic period Uaxactún and Tikal coexisted in relative harmony, both being dominated by El Mirador, but by the first century AD, with El Mirador in decline, a fierce rivalry developed between Tikal and Uaxactún. The two finally clashed in 378 AD, when Tikal's warriors conquered Uaxactún, forcing it to accept subordinate status.

The overall impact of Uaxactún may be a little disappointing after the grandeur of Tikal, but for a sense of the forest this is an excellent spot to make for, and you'll probably have the site to yourself. The most interesting buildings are in **Group E**, east of the airstrip, where three reconstructed temples, built side by side, are arranged to function as an observatory. Viewed from the top of a fourth temple, the sun rises behind the north temple on the longest day of the year and behind the southern one on the shortest day. Beneath one of these temples the famous **E-VII** was unearthed, the oldest building ever found in Petén, once thought to date back to 2000 BC, though a much later date is now accepted. The original pyramid had a simple staircase up the front, flanked by two stucco masks, and post holes in the top suggest that it may have been covered by a thatched shelter. Over on the other side of the airstrip is **Group A**, a series of larger temples and residential compounds, some of them reconstructed, and some impressive stelae.

PRACTICALITIES

A **bus** from Flores passes through Tikal en route for Uaxactún at around 3.30pm; alternatively, you could take one of the **tours** run by a number of companies in Flores. **Staying overnight** you have two options: the *EcoCampamento* (☎926 0077) has rooms (②), tents and hammocks (US$3 per person), protected by mosquito nets, under a thatched shelter; the welcoming *Campamento Ecológico El Chiclero* (☎926 1033, fax 926 1095; ②) offers clean rooms without bath, or you can camp or sling up a hammock for US$2.50 a head. Owner Antonio Baldizón also organizes 4WD trips to Río Azul, and his wife Neria prepares excellent food.

Uaxactún's guide association has a small **information office** at the end of the airstrip and will organize **camping trips** to any of the remote northern sites, into the jungle or east to Nakúm and Yaxhá. Equipment is carried on horseback and the price (US$30 per person per day for a group of three or more) includes a guide, horses, camping gear and food. Check at CINCAP or ProPetén in Flores for advice and help with putting together excursions, or contact Evolution Adventures (see p.260).

El Zotz

Thirty kilometres west of Uaxactún, along a rough track not always passable by Jeeps, is **El Zotz**, a large Maya site set in its own nature reserve. To **get there** you can rent vehicles in Uaxactún, or hire a pack horse, guide, food and camping equipment from

Uaxactún's guide association. After about four hours – almost halfway – you come to **SANTA CRUZ**, where you can camp if necessary. At the site itself you'll be welcomed by the guards who look after the reserve headquarters. You can camp here and, with permission, use their kitchen and drinking water; remember to bring some food to share with the guides.

Totally unrestored and smothered by vegetation, El Zotz has been systematically looted, although there are guards on duty all year. Zotz means "bat" in Maya and each evening at dusk you'll see tens, perhaps hundreds of thousands of **bats** of several species emerge from a cave near the campsite. It's especially impressive in the moonlight, the beating wings sounding like a river flowing over rapids – one of the most remarkable natural sights in Petén.

Continuing beyond El Zotz, it takes about four and a half hours to walk to **CRUCE DOS AGUADAS**, a crossroads village on a bus route to Santa Elena (bus leaves at 7am), where you'll find shops and the *Comedor Patojas*, where you can sling a hammock or camp. Northwards, the road goes to Carmelita for El Mirador and west towards El Perú (not passable in the rainy season).

Río Azul

The remote site of **Río Azul**, almost on the border where Guatemala, Belize and Mexico meet, was discovered in 1962. The city and its suburbs had a population of around five thousand and probably reached a peak in the Preclassic era. Although totally unrestored, the core of the site is similar to a small-scale Tikal, with the tallest temple (AIII) standing some 47m above the forest floor, surfacing above the treetops and giving magnificent views across the jungle.

Several incredible **tombs** have been unearthed here. Tomb 19 is thought to have contained the remains of one of the sons of Stormy Sky, Tikal's great expansionist ruler. Nearby tombs contained the bodies of warriors, dressed in clothing typical of Teotihuacán in central Mexico – further supporting evidence of links between Tikal and that mighty city. Extensive **looting** occurred after the site's discovery, with a gang of up to eighty men plundering the tombs and removing some of the finest murals in the Maya world once the archeological teams had retreated to Flores in the rainy season. Mercifully, despite its chamber being looted in 1981, Tomb 1's walls remain almost intact, and today there are two resident guards.

It's 95km north by **road** from Uaxactún to Río Azul, though it's only passable in the dry season, when it can be covered by 4WDs in as little as four hours, depending on conditions. **Walking** or on **horseback** it's four days each way – three at a push. Trips can be arranged through *El Chiclero* in Uaxactún or through ProPetén and CINCAP (see p.258) or a number of agents in Flores. Once you arrive at Río Azul you'll be welcome to **stay** at the guard's camp (bring some supplies).

El Mirador

El Mirador is perhaps the most exotic and mysterious of all Petén's Maya sites. Still buried in the forest, this massive city matches Tikal's scale, and may even surpass it. Rediscovered in 1926, it dates from an earlier period than Tikal, having flourished between 150 BC and 150 AD, and was almost certainly the first great city in the Maya world. It was unquestionably the dominant city in Petén, occupying a commanding position above the rainforest, at an altitude of 250m, and was home to tens of thousands of Maya. Little archeological work has been done here but it's clear that the site represents the peak of Preclassic Maya culture, which was perhaps far more sophisticated than was once believed.

The core of the site covers some sixteen square kilometres, stretching between two massive pyramids that face each other across the forest. The site's western side is marked by the massive **Tigre Complex**, made up of a huge single pyramid flanked by two smaller structures, a triadic design that's characteristic of El Mirador's architecture. The base of this complex alone would cover around three football fields, while the height of the 2000-year-old main pyramid touches 70m, equivalent to an eighteen-storey building and the tallest structure anywhere in the Maya world. In front of the Tigre Complex is El Mirador's sacred hub: a long narrow plaza, the **Central Acropolis**, and a row of smaller buildings. Burial chambers unearthed in this central section contained the bodies of priests and noblemen, surrounded by the obsidian lancets and stingray spines which were used to pierce the penis, ears and tongue in ritual bloodletting ceremonies. The spilling of blood was seen by the Maya as a method of summoning and sustaining the gods, and was clearly common at all the great ceremonial centres.

To the south of the Tigre Complex is the **Monos Complex**, another triadic structure and plaza, named after the resident howler monkeys. To the north the **León pyramid** and the **Casabel Complex** mark the edge of the site. Heading away to the east, the Puleston Causeway runs to the smaller East Group, the largest of which (about 2km from the Tigre Complex) is the **Danta Complex**. This is another triadic structure, rising in three stages to a height just below that of the Tigre pyramid, but with an even better view since it was built on higher land.

The area **around El Mirador** is riddled with smaller Maya sites, and as you look out across the forest from the top of either of the main temples you can see others rising above the forest canopy on all sides – including the giant Calakmul in Mexico. Among the most accessible are **Nakbé**, 10km south, where a huge Maya mask (5m by 8m), was found in September 1992, and **El Tintal**, around 21km southwest, which you'll pass on your way in from Carmelita.

Getting to El Mirador is a substantial undertaking, involving a rough 60km bus or pick-up journey from Santa Elena to the chicle- and *xate*-gathering centre of **Carmelita**, followed by two days of hard jungle hiking – you'll need a horse to carry your food and equipment. The journey is impossibly muddy in the rainy season, and is best attempted from mid-January to August; February to April is the driest period. The trip offers an exceptional chance to see virtually untouched forest, and perhaps some of the creatures that inhabit it. ProPetén (see p.258) and EcoMaya (see p.261) offer five-day **tours** (around US$200 for two people) from Flores, including guide, packhorse and digs in Carmelita, or you can travel **independently**, arranging a guide in Carmelita (about US$30 a day), who will then organize packhorse, food, water and camping gear for you – ask for Luís Morales, president of the Tourist Committee, who can sort out guides for the trip. You should definitely bring some supplies for the guards, who spend forty days at a time in the forest, subsisting on beans and tortillas. Whether you take a tour or go independently, you're advised to examine the information and maps at ProPetén and CINCAP see p.258 first.

There's a daily **bus** at 1pm from Santa Elena to Carmelita via San Andrés (see p.261) and Cruce Dos Aguadas (see p.271). There's basic but clean **accommodation** in Carmelita at the *Campamento Nakbé* (②), 1.5km before the village, where the large thatched shelters have mosquito nets and hammocks, or, if you have your own tent, you can **camp** (US$2 per person). For a good feed, visit the *Comedor Pepe Toño* in the centre of the village, run by Brenda Zapata, who is a mine of information about the area and can introduce you to the local guides.

Sayaxché and around

Southwest of Flores, on a bend in the Río Pasión, the easy-going frontier town of **SAYAXCHÉ** makes an ideal base for exploring the surrounding forest and its huge collection of archeological remains. The town is the supply centre for a vast surrounding area that is being steadily cleared and colonized. The complex network of rivers and swamps that cuts through the forested wilderness here has been an important trade route since Maya times, and there are several interesting ruins in the area. Upstream is **Ceibal**, a small but beautiful site in a wonderful jungle setting; to the south is **Lago de Petexbatún**, on the shores of which are the small ruins of **Dos Pilas** and **Aguateca**. Both sites offer great opportunities to wander in the forest and watch the wildlife.

Sayaxché practicalities

Getting to Sayaxché from Flores is very straightforward, with several Pinita **buses** (5.30am, 8am, 10am, 1pm & 4pm; 2hr) and one Del Rosio service (5am) plying the fairly smooth 62-kilometre dirt road. At other times hitching a ride in a **pick-up** is not too difficult. A ferry takes you over the Río Pasión, directly opposite Sayaxché.

Hotels in Sayaxché are on the basic side. The *Guayacán* (☎926 6111; ③), right beside the river, is the first you come to, with plain functional rooms, some with private bath, and lovely sunset views from the terrace. For a cheaper room, head right from the dock to the friendly *Hotel Posada Segura* (②), which has decent, clean rooms, some with private bath; alternatively, head left down the street above the *Guayacán* to the basic but cheap *Hospedaje Mayapan* (①), where you may be able to rent a **bike** for visiting Ceibal.

There are plenty of reasonable places to **eat**, the best being the *Restaurant Yaxkin* (closes 8pm), which is a little pricey, though the portions are huge. There's also decent food at *Guayacán* and *La Montaña*, 100m south on the same street, a restaurant owned by the knowledgeable and helpful Julián Mariona, who can arrange **trips** to the nearby ruins (around US$40 a day). You'll find plenty of **boatmen** eager to take you up- or downriver, though they tend to see all tourists as walking cash-dispensers and quote prices in dollars. Try Pedro Méndez Requena of Viajes Don Pedro (☎ & fax 928 6109) who offers **tours** of the area from his office on the riverfront. You can change **travellers' cheques** at Banora, a block up from the *Guayacán*.

Ceibal

The most accessible and impressive of the sites near Sayaxché is **Ceibal**, which you can reach either by land or river. It's easy enough to make it there and back in an afternoon **by boat**; haggle with the boatmen at the waterfront and you can expect to pay around US$40 (for up to six people). The boat trip is followed by a short walk through towering rainforest. **By road**, Ceibal is just 17km from Sayaxché. Any transport heading south out of town passes the entrance track to the site, from where it's an 8km walk through the jungle to the ruins.

Surrounded by forest and shaded by huge ceiba trees, **the ruins** of Ceibal are a mixture of cleared open plazas and untamed jungle. Though many of the largest temples lie buried under mounds, Ceibal does have some outstanding and well-preserved carving: the two main plazas are dotted with lovely **stelae**, centred around two low platforms. During the Classic period Ceibal was a relatively minor site, but it grew rapidly between 830 and 930 AD, apparently after falling under the control of colonists from what is now Mexico. Outside influence is clearly visible in the carving here: speech scrolls, straight noses, waist-length hair and serpent motifs are all decidedly non-Maya. The monkey-faced Stela 2 is particularly striking, beyond which is Stela 14, another impressive sculpture straight ahead down the path. If you turn right here and walk for ten minutes you'll reach the only other restored part of the site, set superbly in a clearing in the forest – an unmissable massive circular stone platform which was either an altar or observation deck for astronomy.

Lago de Petexbatún: Aguateca and Dos Pilas

A similar distance to the south of Sayaxché is **Lago de Petexbatún**, a spectacular expanse of water ringed by dense forest and containing plentiful supplies of snook, bass, alligator and freshwater turtle. The shores of the lake abound with wildlife and Maya remains and, though the ruins themselves are small and unrestored, their sheer number suggests that the lake was an important Maya centre. **Aguateca**, perched on a high outcrop at the southern tip of the lake, is the furthest away from Sayaxché but the most accessible site, as a boat can get you to within twenty minutes' walk of the ruins. The atmosphere is magical, surrounded by dense tropical forest and with superb views of the lake, and you can clearly make out the temples and plazas, dotted with well-preserved stelae. Lamentably, in 2000 a gang of armed looters destroyed some of the superbly executed carvings, but there's still plenty to see, including images of rulers, captives, hummingbirds, pineapples and pelicans. The resident guards may give you a well-informed tour of the site. You can reach Aguateca on a boat trip from the *Posada El Caribe* (see below), and it may also be possible to reach the site by mule or truck during the dry months.

A slightly closer (and therefore cheaper) option is **Dos Pilas**, another unrestored site, buried in the jungle a little way west of the lake. Dos Pilas was the centre of a formidable empire in the early part of the eighth century, with a population of around ten thousand. The ruins are quite unusual, as the major structures are grouped in an east–west linear pattern. Around the central plaza are some tremendous stelae, altars and four **hieroglyphic stairways** decorated with glyphs and figures. To get to **Dos Pilas** you have trek 12km on foot from the *Posada El Caribe*, passing the small site of **Arroyo de Piedra**, where you'll find a plaza and two fairly well-preserved stelae. As with Aguateca, it may also be possible to get to the site by mule or truck during the dry season.

It's a 45-minute speedboat trip from Sayaxché to the northern tip of Lago de Petexbatún, where you'll find the *Posada El Caribe* (☎928 6114, fax 928 6168; ⑦ full board), with clean, screened cabins, good food and boat trips to Aguateca. Three kilometres south of here on the western shore of the lake, the *Chiminos Island Lodge* (☎335 3506, fax 335 2647, *www.chiminosisland.com*, US$85 per person including all meals) is a stunning alternative base, with five beautiful bungalows set in thick jungle next to some minor ruins.

Routes to Mexico and Belize

There are a number of possible routes **into Mexico** from Petén, all of which offer a sense of adventure, a glimpse of the rainforest and involve shuttling between buses, boats and immigration posts. Travellers should bear in mind, however, that at the time of writing, Mexican border officials were only issuing **two-week visas** to travellers entering the state of Chiapas from Guatemala, due to the armed conflict in the region. Getting to **Belize** is much more straightforward, with numerous daily buses connecting Flores with the border at Melchor de Mencos and good bus services onward on the Belizean side.

From Sayaxché to Benemérito

Downriver from Sayaxché the **Río Pasión** snakes its way through an area of forest, swamp and small settlements to **Pipiles,** which marks the point where the rivers Salinas and Pasión merge to form the Usumacinta. All boats stop here at the migración, where you can get your exit stamp. Not far from Pipiles is the small Maya site of **Altar de los Sacrificios**, commanding an important river junction. This is one of the oldest sites in Petén, but these days there's not much to see beyond a solitary stela. Following the Usumacinta downstream you arrive at **BENEMÉRITO** in Mexico, a sprawling frontier town at the end of a dirt road from Palenque. The eight-hour trip costs around US$8–10, though some cargo boats can take a couple of days to get this far. There are basic hotels and restaurants in Benemérito and you can head on to Yaxchilán from here directly by boat or, much cheaper, by bus to Frontera Corozal (where there are basic beds and camping) and then by boat. **Buses** leave Benemérito for Palenque (9hr) at least six times a day; make sure you stop at the **Mexican migración** for your tourist card.

From Sayaxché via Bethel to Frontera Corozal
The cheapest and most straightforward route to Mexico from Sayaxché is along the rough road to **BETHEL** on the Río Usumacinta, where there's a Guatemalan **migración** post. Three buses a day leave Flores for Bethel (5am, 8am & 1pm; 4-5hr depending on season), passing the El Subín junction north of Sayaxché a couple of hours later. At Bethel it's relatively easy to find a lancha heading downstream (US$7, 30min) to Frontera Corozal. Alternatively, it's usually possible to get off the bus, obtain your exit stamp in Bethel and continue on the same bus for a further 12km to the tiny settlement of **Técnica**, where you can cross the Usumacinta (US$0.7) to Corozal on the opposite bank. At the time of writing there are no accommodation or other facilities in Técnica.

If you need to stay, Bethel itself is a pleasant village; you can **camp** above the river-bank and there are several **comedores** and shops. The **Bethel ruins**, 1.5km from the village, are today little more than tree-covered mounds, but there's an excellent **eco-campamento** here, the *Posada Maya* (☎926 0525, *centromaya@guatenet*) with comfortable rooms (④), tents (including mattresses and clean sheets) under thatched shelters (②) or hammocks (①) on top of a wooded cliff high above the river. Frontera Corozal, over the border, has a **migración**, plus comedores and very basic hotels. Fairly regular **buses** and shared minibuses leave Frontera Corozal for Palenque until 3pm (4hr).

For further adventure, the spectacular ruins of **Yaxchilán** are 15km from Bethel, set around a great loop in the Usumacinta just over the border in Mexico; **hiring a boat** for the beautiful trip will cost around US$60 return. Even further downstream from Yaxchilán are **Piedras Negras**, some of the most remote ruins in the Maya world, accessible only by boat. Several tour operators run trips down the Usumacinta to Piedras Negras, including two-day trips run by the *Posada Maya* in Bethel (see above), which cost US$450, including a boat for up ten people and all meals. The best-organized operator is undoubtedly Maya Expeditions (see p.158), a specialist whitewater rafting operation based in Guatemala City who also run numerous pricey but excellent trips to sites all over Guatemala with prominent archeologists as guides.

El Naranjo to La Palma
A less popular and more expensive route **from Flores to Mexico** runs along a part-ly paved road to **EL NARANJO** (several buses daily until 2.30pm; 4hr). El Naranjo is a rough spot, consisting of little more than an army base, a **migración**, where you'll be asked for a "leaving tax" of a US dollar or two, stores (offering poor exchange rates), comedores and basic hotels. The best place **to stay** is the friendly, family-run *Posada San Pedro* across the river (☎926 1276 in Flores; ③). The other places in town are pretty filthy.

From El Naranjo, you head by boat down the Río San Pedro; there's usually a **boat** (US$20 per person; 4hr to La Palma) for Mexico at around 1pm. Your first port of call should be the Mexican **migración**, about an hour away from El Naranjo, beyond which is the small riverside village of **LA PALMA** in Mexico. La Palma is a good transport hub, with basic rooms and bus connections to Tenosique (last bus 5pm). Some agencies in Flores (see p.260) now offer tickets direct to Palenque using this route (US$30 per person), though it's a bit cheaper to do it independently.

From Flores to Belize

The hundred kilometres from Flores to the Belizean border at Melchor de Mencos (2hr 30min) takes you through another sparsely inhabited section of Petén. Hourly **buses** leave from the market place in Santa Elena. Alternatively, Linea Dorada/Mundo Maya operate a 5am **express service** to Belize City (5hr; US$20) and on to Chetumal (8hr; US$30), leaving from their offices on C Principal in Santa Elena. Though more than twice as expensive as the public bus, this service is quicker and connects with services in Chetumal to Cancún.

Lago de Yaxhá

About halfway between Puente Ixlú and the border is **Lago de Yaxhá**, a shallow limestone depression ringed by dense rainforest and home to two isolated Maya sites: Yaxhá and Topoxté. The turn-off to the lake is clearly signposted and the bus driver will stop if you ask. If you haven't travelled as part of a tour (see p.260); you'll probably be faced with a sweltering two-hour walk to get there, though there is some traffic to and from the village of La Máquina, 2km before the lakes of Yaxhá and Sacnab, which is just to the east. Just before you reach the lakes you pass a **control post** where you may be asked to sign in. From here it's 3km to the site: head along the road between the lakes then turn left (signed) for Yaxhá.

    Yaxhá (daily 8am–5pm; free), covering several square kilometres of a ridge overlooking the lake, is primarily a Classic-period city. The early history of the site is unclear, though the sheer scale of the ruins (in Guatemala only Tikal and El Mirador are larger) confirm it was undoubtedly a major player in the central Maya region. Although some restoration has been completed, don't expect the manicured splendour of Tikal. What you can count on, though, is real atmosphere as you explore the many parts of the city still half hidden by the forest. The ruins are spread out over nine plazas and around five hundred structures have been mapped so far, including several huge pyramids and large acropolis complexes. The tallest and most impressive pyramid, **Structure 216**, 250m northeast of the entrance, rises in tiers to a height of over 30m; the recent restoration enables you to climb to the top for spectacular views over the forest and lake. If you're not on a guided trip one of the guards will show you around for a small tip.

    Topoxté, a much smaller site on an island close to the west shore of the Lago de Yaxhá, is best reached by boat from *El Sombrero* (see below). There's a four-kilometre trail to a spot opposite the island but you still have to get over to it – and large crocodiles inhabit the lake. The structures you see are not on the scale of those at Yaxhá, and date mainly from the Late Postclassic, though the site has been occupied since Preclassic times. Work is in progress to restore some structures.

    If you want to **stay** nearby, the wonderful, solar-powered *Campamento El Sombrero* (☎926 5229, fax 926 5198, *sombrero@guate.net*; ④), 200m from the road on the south side of the lake, has thatched rooms in wooden jungle lodges and space for **camping**; the Italian owner can arrange boat trips on the lake and horseback riding; she'll pick you up from the bus stop if you've called in advance. There's another *campamento*, run by locals on behalf of Inguat, on the far side of the lake, below Yaxhá, where you can **pitch a tent** or sling a hammock beneath a thatched shelter for free.

    The unrestored **ruins of Nakúm**, another larger site, are about 20km north of Lago de Yaxhá, though the road is rarely passable so you'll probably have to walk. The most impressive structure is the residential-style palace, which has forty rooms and is similar to the North Acropolis at Tikal. There are two guards here who will show you where you can camp or put up a hammock. It's also possible to **walk to Tikal** in a day from Nakúm (around 25km), though you'll need to persuade a guard to act as a **guide**, or bring one with you – speak to Inguat or see CINCAP in Flores (see p.258).

The border: Melchor de Mencos

Despite the differences between Guatemala and Belize, border formalities are fairly straightforward; you have to pay a small departure tax on leaving Guatemala. **Money-changers** will pester you on either side of the border and give a fair rate. There's also a **bank** (Mon–Fri 8.30am–2pm) just beyond the **migración**, next to the *Hotel Frontera Palace* (☎ & fax 9265196; ④), which has rooms in pleasant thatched cabins, hot water and a restaurant.

Buses leave **for Belize City** every hour or so (3hr) right from the border. Indeed, most actually begin their journey from the market in Melchor; for other destinations you may have to take a shared taxi to Benque Viejo or to San Ignacio (US$2 per person; 20min).

t r a v e l   d e t a i l s

BUSES

Flores to: Belize City (2 daily; 5hr); Bethel (3 daily; 4–5hr) ; Chetumal (2 daily; 9hr); Cruce del Pato (2 daily; 4hr); El Naranjo (8 daily; 4–5hr); Guatemala City (around 30 daily; 8–10hr); Melchor de Mencos (10 daily; 2hr 30min); Río Dulce (around 30 daily; 4hr); Sayaxché (6 daily; 2hr); Tikal (1 daily at 1pm; 2hr; plus innumerable private minibuses; 1hr); Uaxactún (1 daily; 3hr).

Poptún to: Flores (around 30 daily; 2hr); Río Dulce (around 30 daily; 2hr).

Sayaxché to: Cruce de Pato (2 daily; 2 hr); Flores (6 daily; 2hr).

Tikal to: Flores (1 daily, 2hr; plus minibuses, 1hr). Uaxactún (1 daily; 3hr).

BOATS

From **Flores/San Benito** to San Andrés, boats leave when full, in daylight hours only (25min).

From **El Naranjo** to La Palma in Mexico there's a daily boat at 1pm.

From **Sayaxché** to Benemérito, Mexico, a trading boat leaves most days (at least 12hr); rented speedboats take 2hr 30min–3hr.

FLIGHTS

From **Flores** there are 10 flights a day to Guatemala City (50min), plus international services to Belize City (4 daily), Cancún (1 daily) and Palenque and Chetumal (both 3 a week).

You can also charter flights to Uaxactún, Dos Lagunas, El Naranjo, Sayaxché, Poptún, Río Dulce, Lívingston and to the Honduras border.

PART FOUR

EL SALVADOR

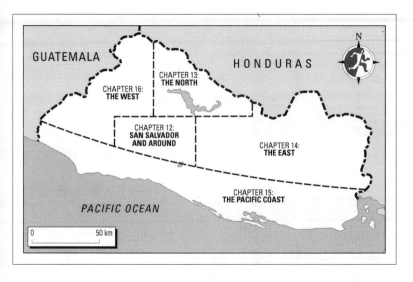

Introduction

The smallest and most densely populated country in Central America, El Salvador is chiefly remembered for the vicious **civil war** of the 1980s, when streams of harrowing news stories brought this tiny country to the attention of the world. For a decade, atrocity followed atrocity in a seemingly unstoppable sequence. Then in 1992, with both sides having fought each other to a standstill, **Peace Accords** were signed, and the attention of the world's press moved elsewhere, leaving behind a brutalized country faced with the immense task of rebuilding itself.

Tourism in El Salvador has lagged behind that of its Central American neighbours. Despite its compactness and considerable natural beauty, many would-be visitors are deterred by the half-remembered headlines and the country's reputation for violence, danger and difficulty. Its geographical position doesn't help, either: tucked into the Pacific underbelly of the isthmus, El Salvador is easily bypassed. Those that do make it here, however, are well rewarded by the sheer physical beauty of the place, with lush Pacific lowlands sweeping up through fertile hills and coffee plantations to rugged mountain chains. Almost every journey in El Salvador yields photogenic vistas of the majestic cones of towering **volcanoes**, while some of the secluded pacific **beaches** are as fine as any in Central America.

As in Nicaragua, another country pulled apart by a decade of civil war, travelling in El Salvador brings you into contact with some of the most engaging and interesting **people** in the region. With a well-deserved reputation for hard work and business acumen, the Salvadoreños (or *gua-nacos*, as they're often affectionately described) – predominantly mestizo – live life with a vigour that's hard to match. That said, however, as the people here slowly find ways to come to terms with their brutal past and uncertain future, some residual hostility to foreigners – particularly Americans – remains, and initial reactions to tourists can be, on occasion, cool. If you persist, however, in the face of what may seem like outright hostility, and make an effort to speak Spanish, you will find that people begin to unbend and bring you into their lives. They may or may not be willing to talk about the civil war. Many aren't. What is important now is the future, and this Salvadoreans approach with sardonic humour, designed to lessen the travails of daily life, the corruption of politics and everything else that seems insurmountable.

Perhaps unsurprisingly, **tourist infrastructure** is at times sorely lacking. This is not the country for those who like everything on tap, and there's little luxury outside the cities, but for those with a spirit of adventure, El Salvador has plenty to offer. One feature particular to the country is its network of government-run tourist centres, or **turi-centros**. Aimed more at locals than tourists, these provide bathing, eating and recreation facilities in areas of natural beauty. Some, like Los Chorros, just outside San Salvador, offer a convenient way to take advantage of natural facilities safely and comfortably.

Travelling around El Salvador is a lesson in humility. Contrasting with the vibrant colour and sweep of the landscape, the overwhelming evidence of the endemic **poverty** and social divisions that sparked the Civil War in the first place hits you right between the eyes. As El Salvador enters its second decade of peace it remains a

---

THE 2001 EARTHQUAKES

In January and February 2001, a series of powerful **earthquakes** (the strongest measuring 7.6 on the Richter scale) ripped through El Salvador, killing over 1000 people and causing widespread destruction. The earthquakes produced over 600 landslides and destroyed more 145,000 homes, along with schools and hospitals across the country. Few towns remained unaffected, while main arterial roads and infrastructure were also badly damaged. The cost of repairing the devastation is estimated at US$2.8billion, and rebuilding will take years to complete.

The hardest hit areas were the **central departments** of San Vicente and Cuscatlán and the **coastal regions** of Sonsonate, La Paz and Usulután. As a result of the devastation caused by the earthquakes, some of the information in this guide may no longer be accurate, especially in the most badly affected towns, such as San Vicente, La Libertad, Zacatecoluca, Sonsonate and Ahuachapán. Although some parts of the capital, San Salvador, were damaged, the city was not badly affected, while the popular northern town of Suchitoto escaped totally unscathed.

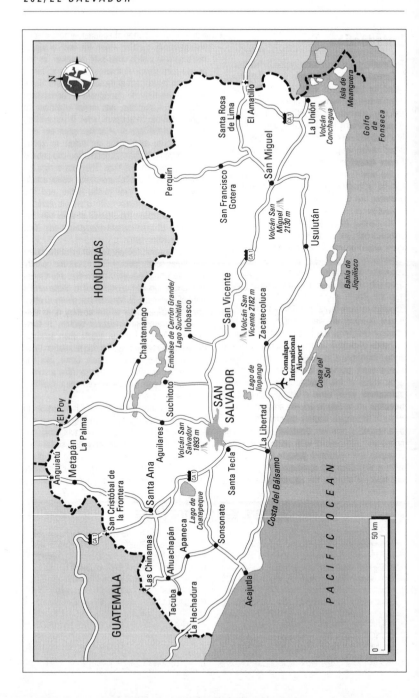

country painfully divided between haves and have-nots, and the full benefits of redevelopment projects and an improving economy have yet to trickle down to the majority of the population. From the muddy shanty towns of San Salvador to the broken-down shacks in the countryside, many people live in squalor, eking out a living selling fruit, sweets, household goods and sundry odds and ends on the street. In addition, the ever-growing population – at 6.2 million, the densest in Central America – is placing unprecedented pressure on the country's **natural resources**, with rampant deforestation a particular problem. And while political violence is now a thing of the past, **civil violence** has grown to alarming proportions. Guns are common, and people use them, while recent years have seen an increased number of kidnappings of prominent businessmen. The casual visitor is unlikely to be directly affected by this, but you can't ignore the underlying sense of tension.

■ Where to go

San Salvador is a frenetic and polluted city whose sometimes tangible sense of menace often creates extremely negative first impressions among visitors. Things are improving, however: the city authorities are making a determined effort to clean up the Centro Histórico, while all the central parks and plazas have received a makeover and extra police have been deployed on the streets. San Salvador also offers a thriving nightlife, along with facilities unavailable elsewhere in the country. For beaches, swimming and sun you don't have to stray too far from the capital, to the crater lake of **Ilopango** or, an hour's journey away, the small Pacific coast resort of **La Libertad**. Also within easy reach are the small Maya ruins of **San Andrés** and **Joya de Cerén** which, although they pale visually in comparison to sites in Guatemala – El Salvador was at the furthest fringe of Maya culture – are nonetheless important. The World Heritage Site of Joya de Cerén, in particular, gives the most complete picture yet of what daily village life was like in Maya times.

Western El Salvador is the most relaxing and perhaps most scenic part of the country, with the lovely old colonial city of **Ahuachapán** making a convenient entry point from Guatemala, and the laid-back city of **Santa Ana** making a good alternative to San Salvador as a place to stay a few nights. In addition to the Maya ruins of **Tazumal** there is the exquisite cloudforest of **Montecristo**, bursting with exotic plants and wildlife.

For something slightly more energetic, the nearby volcanic peaks of **Izalco**, **Volcán Santa Ana** and **Cerro Verde** provide good and varied hiking, while nestling at their base is the magnificent crater lake of **Coatepeque**, whose deep blue waters are perfect for snorkelling, diving and swimming.

The **north** and **east** of El Salvador, though rough and wild, and less accommodating to travellers, hold a number of attractions. North of the capital is **Suchitoto**, considered the finest colonial town in the country. **La Palma** and **Ilobasco** are famous for their artesanías, producing wooden handicrafts, pottery and hammocks, while the small city of **San Vicente** is an enjoyable base for trips to the volcano of **Chichontepec** and the lagunas of **Apastepeque**. The larger city of **San Miguel** hosts one of the largest carnivals in Central America each November, drawing visitors from all over the country and beyond. The **Ruta de la Paz** winds up through the poor but beautiful mountainous department of Morazán towards the thought-provoking civil war museum at **Perquín**, unmissable for anyone interested in learning about El Salvador's recent history.

Up and down the glorious sweep of the **Pacific coast** lie long, palm-fringed stretches of beach, the most beautiful of which are **Barra de Santiago** in the west and **El Espino, El Tamarindo** and **El Cuco** to the east. Close to the capital are the famous surf beaches around **La Libertad**, while further east are the mangrove swamps of the **Bahía de Jiquilisco** and, still further down the coast near the border with Honduras, the idyllic islands of Meanguera and Conchagüita in the **Golfo de Fonseca**.

■ When to go

The best time to visit El Salvador is during the **dry season** from November to February. Though temperatures reach a high of around 30°C – and in the coastal lowlands, it feels much hotter because of the humidity – it's easiest to get around at this time and even the back roads are accessible. Towards the end of the dry season, in March and April, temperatures increase to around 34°C and, in the lowlands, can feel unbearable. During the **wet season** – May to October – the heat and humidity are temporarily relieved by daily downpours, though these rarely last for more than a couple of hours, and there are spectacular lightning storms in the mountains around San Salvador. Travel is difficult, as mud roads in the back country become impassable. Sometimes, between September to November, El Salvador is affected by the tail end of **hurricanes** out in the Pacific; when this happens, as occurred during Hurricane Mitch in 1998, the rain can last for days, and cities begin to flood. Whatever the season, the climate is coolest in the **mountains**, where temperatures are moderated by altitude, being far fresher by day and cool at night.

Getting around

The best way to get around El Salvador is **by bus**. Short distances (the longest journey you're likely to take in one stretch, from San Salvador to La Palma for example, is around four hours), and relatively good main highways mean that the few **internal flights** that do exist (on private or military flights) are far more trouble than they're worth.

■ Buses

Hundreds of companies operate **buses** to everywhere from everywhere every few minutes during daylight hours, although very few buses depart after dark. Buses are brightly painted, and all have their route number and the name of their final destination emblazoned across the front. On the back roads you do have to plan ahead a little to avoid getting stuck in the middle of nowhere for hours (or even overnight). Though ideally you

should confirm what time buses leave as soon as you get to a place, printed **timetables** – if they exist at all – are only adhered to if the weather is good. If roads are bad because of rain, everything gets delayed. Except for routes to the cities in the east there is only one **class** of bus – and everyone travels on it. It's much easier to cope if you have small bags; larger luggage gets thrown in a heap at the back or, occasionally, on the roof. Buses can be **hailed** at the side of the road and you can get off at virtually any point. Tickets are bought on board (retain your ticket as it may be checked during the journey); at bus stations, simply turn up a few minutes before it's due to leave, earlier if you want to guarantee a seat. Buses are extremely **cheap**: from San Salvador to Santa Ana (2hr 30min), costs just US$0.80, while San Salvador to Santa Rosa de Lima by fast bus (around 3hr 30min) will cost around US$2.20.

Virtually every town has departures to San Salvador; if you're trying to reach somewhere small *from* the capital, however, it's usually quicker to go to the nearest major town and change. Heading **east** to San Miguel, Santa Rosa de Lima and La Unión the direct ("*directo*") buses are marginally more comfortable and make fewer stops, knocking about an hour off the standard journey.

■ Taxis

Taxis in El Salvador are yellow, painted with black numbers and a "taxi" sign. They can be hailed anywhere on the street – in fact, they usually see you and honk before you see them – and also tend to congregate in the main square and around bus stations in towns and cities. **Fares** should be agreed before you set off (be prepared

FINDING YOUR WAY AROUND EL SALVADOR'S CITIES

Orientation in Salvadorean cities is initially confusing but logical. Streets running north–south are **avenidas**; those running east–west are **calles**. The main avenida and calle will have individual names (along with a few of the others) and the heart of any city are at their intersection. North or south of this intersection avenidas are Norte or Sur, while east or west calles are Oriente or Poniente. Avenidas lying to the east of the main avenida are numbered evenly, rising the further out you go; west of the main avenida, the numbers are odd.

Similarly, calles have even numbers south of the main calle and odd numbers to the north. Named avenidas/calles sometimes (though not always) change name either side of the intersection.

Addresses can be given either as the street name/number, followed by the building number, or as the intersection of two streets. So: "12 C Pte #2330, Col Flor Blanca" is number 2330, 12 Calle Poniente in the district (*colonia*) of Flor Blanca, while "10 Av Sur y 3 C Pte" is the intersection of 10 Avenida Sur and 3 Calle Poniente.

to bargain). Expect to pay US$2–5 for most city trips, and anything upwards of US$30 for a half-day driving around the countryside (a good way to see some of the remoter spots if you're in a hurry). **Tipping** is not usual unless you've rented the taxi for the day.

■ Driving and hitching

Driving in El Salvador is relatively straightforward on the major roads and a perfect way to reach some of the more inaccessible beaches along the Pacific coast. There are **filling stations** in every town and at most major highway junctions, and no road is so long that you should have to worry about running out of fuel. Finding parts for US and Japanese models is not usually a problem if you have your own car. However, some back roads become impassable at times during the rainy season, even to 4WD; ask locally about conditions before you set off. More worrying is the recent increase in armed **hold-ups** of private cars on quieter roads, especially in the northern departments of Chalatenango – it will be automatically assumed that foreigners have something of value to steal. Keep an eye on the latest news and, if in doubt, seek police advice. In cities, thefts – particularly of newer-model cars – are common, and it's wise to leave your car in a guarded or locked car park. **Car rental** prices are on a par with those in the West: from US$40 a day for a small car to US$90 and upwards for a jeep. See p.312 for a list of **rental companies** in San Salvador. Take great care if driving on Sunday afternoons or public holidays as drink-driving-related road accidents tend to increase at these times.

Hitching is common in remote areas and around La Libertad, where the lack of regular bus services means that any passing vehicle is fair game. Having said that, hitching carries obvious risks, and we do not recommend it. If you *do* hitch, it's polite to offer payment – about the same as the bus fare – for the journey.

■ Cycling

Cycling is an extremely common way of getting around, and even the smallest of places usually has a repair shop. Mountain bikes, in particular, can take you to places that even the buses don't reach. The main highways, however, can be more than slightly nerve-racking for those on two

wheels; you might want to consider putting them on top of a bus for sections of your journey. Unfortunately there are no formal places to **rent bicycles** from; your only option is to do a private deal with someone local.

Costs, money and banks

Since January 1, 2001, El Salvador has operated a dual-currency economy, with both the local currency, the **colón** (often called the peso), and the **US dollar** recognized as legal tender for all transactions. The colón, however, is slowly being withdrawn from circulation, and the dollar will become the sole unit of currency from 2003.

The colón is divided into 100 centavos. There are coins of 5c, 10c, 25c and 1 colón, and banknotes of 1, 5, 10, 25, 50, 100 and 200 colones. All US dollar notes and coins are now in free circulation.

■ Exchange and banks

There is a fixed exchange rate of US$1=8.75 colones (see box below for a full series of conversions), and banks do not charge a commission for changing either currency into the other. All goods and services can legally be paid for in either dollars or colones, though in practice some vendors still prefer one or other. Outside the top-end hotels and restaurants, the best way to pay is in **cash**. **Travellers' cheques** are becoming more

CONVERTING DOLLARS AND COLONES

The following shows conversion rates between colones and dollars based on the fixed exchange rate of US$1=8.75 colones

US$	Colones
1	8.75
2	17.50
5	43.75
10	87.50
20	175.00
50	437.50
100	875.00
1000	8,750.00
Quarter ($0.25)	2.19
Dime ($0.10)	0.88
Nickel ($.05)	0.44
Penny ($0.01)	0.09

widely recognized, but at present can only be changed in banks (you'll need have your proof of purchase in order to change them). A few **ATMs** (*cajeros electrónicos*, mainly operated by Banco Agrícola, Banco Salvadoreño, Banco de Comercio and Banco Cuscatlán) accept foreign-issued Visa and Mastercards (Visa is more widely accepted) and dispense US dollars. Opening hours for banks are 8.30 or 9am until 4 or 5pm, and some of them close for an hour at lunch. Some banks in the larger cities also open between 9am and midday on Saturday. There are **casas de cambio** in San Salvador, Santa Ana and San Miguel (generally open daily 9am–5pm). **Moneychangers** can be found at borders, and along Alameda Juan Pablo II in San Salvador, but exercise caution.

■ Costs

Day-to-day living is, for foreigners at least, very cheap in El Salvador. A cup of coffee will cost US$0.25–60, while a soft drink will be US$0.50 and fresh juice US$1. Cigarettes are around US$1.40 a packet, while a meal in an ordinary café will set you back around US$2–3. Also very good value are **bus fares** (see p.284).

In expensive hotels and restaurants, service charges and **taxes** are added to the bill automatically; room taxes are 13 percent while service charges are 7–10 percent. If you're spending less than around US$30 a night for a room however, the tax is usually not charged. There's no entry tax if you arrive by bus or plane (though you'll have to purchase a US$5 entry card); travellers entering by car have to pay a fee – there have been stories about people bringing cars into the country being overcharged, so it's best to check with a Salvadorean embassy for the correct schedule of prices before you arrive. The airport **departure tax** is currently US$28, which must be paid in cash.

Information

The helpful government organization Corporación Salvadoreña de Turismo, or **Corsatur**, at Blvd del Hipodrome #508, Col San Benito, San Salvador (Mon–Fri 8am–noon & 1.30–5pm; ☎243 0427, fax 243 0427, *corsatur@salnet.sv*), has a useful bilingual guide, *Destination El Salvador*, which gives an overview of what there is to see in the country. They can also provide information (Spanish only) on national parks and archeological sites in El

Salvador, and details of local specialist tour operators.

The Instituto Salvadoreño de Turismo, or **ISTU**, C Ruben Darío, 9a–11a Av Sur, San Salvador (Mon–Fri 8am–4pm, Sat 8am–noon; ☎222 8000) is responsible for some of the national parks and the network of *turicentros*. Staff are extremely unhelpful, however, and will, more than likely, refer you to Corsatur.

Although El Salvador is gradually waking up to its own tourism potential there are, as yet, no tourist offices **outside the capital**, and the concept of independent tourism is still in its infancy. If you have any questions, head for the largest and most expensive hotel, or strike up a conversation with a taxi driver. Alternatively, it might be possible to obtain information from municipal cultural centres (*casas de la cultura*), offices of the government-run culture development agency *Concultura*, or the city hall (*alcaldía*).

Useful **Web sites** include *www .elsalvadorturismo.gob.sv* and the comprehensive *www.sv*, the Web site of the Republic of El Salvador.

Accommodation

The widest choice of **accommodation** is, inevitably, in San Salvador. Elsewhere, choices are fewer, and occasionally you'll find nothing between extreme luxury and total squalor – though in most places new hotels are beginning to open, offering travellers a greater range of options. Hotels on the coast and near the country's lakes are usually empty during the week but busy at weekends, and many hotels are busy around **Easter Week** and **Christmas** and/or at the time of a large festival; at these times it's worth reserving in advance. Always ask to see more than one room and, if you're staying for a few days, ask if there's the chance of a discount. Many hotels also have multi-bed rooms, which can cut costs a lot if you're travelling in a group.

In **San Salvador** you'll need to pay at least US$10, probably more, for somewhere clean and secure, since the city's cheapest rooms are located in the worst and most dangerous part of town. By contrast, the city's top-end establishments – the *Camino Real*, the *Princess*, the *Alameda* and others – have everything you would expect of an international-standard hotel, with soft lighting, room service, cocktail bars and piped music swirling along carpeted corridors.

Outside the capital, top-of-the-range hotels are relatively few and far between, although there are a good number of comfortable places to stay. In general, expect to pay at least US$8 for an acceptable double room, rising to around US$10–12 with private bath.

Camping (and hammock-slinging) is possible on many beaches, but the only formal provision elsewhere is in the parks of Cerro Verde and Montecristo. Hiking in the mountains may also throw up some possibilities, but ask for local advice on safety in the area before you go, and get permission from the landowner. Note, too that sudden downpours are common and, in the winter, can last for hours.

Eating and drinking

Refined cooking is not one of El Salvador's strong points, although there are a few exceptions, with gourmet cuisine available in San Salvador and smart restaurants serving excellently prepared local dishes in the provincial cities. Most local people, however, eat in **comedores**, the ubiquitous café, where you can get a nutritious and substantial meal for around US$2–3. The cleanliness of these places varies, as does the quality of the food; if in doubt, choose one that's busy.

The main meal of the day is lunch – look out for **comida a la vista**, basically a cheap and cheerful set lunch served up at comedores across the country. Generally, unless it's a fiesta, people don't eat out a lot and places close relatively early; around 9pm. Only in the cities, and mostly at weekends, will restaurants be full and stay open late.

■ What to eat

The mainstay of Salvadorean food is the *pupusería*, serving **pupusas**, the cheap and filling national snack. These small tortillas are served piping hot and filled with cheese (*queso*), beans (*frijoles*), pork (*chicharrón*) or all three (*revuelta*), and cooked on a hot plate. *Pupusas* are normally made from cornmeal (although the crispier rice-meal version is worth trying), and are served with optional hot sauce and/or *curtida*, a jar of pickled cabbage, beetroot and carrots. *Pupuserías* range from humble street-corner grills to huge, barn-like places filled with families at the weekends – most of them, however, only start serving from the late afternoon onwards.

Other Salvadorean **specialities** include *mariscada* (seafood in a creamy sauce), *tamales* (meat or chicken wrapped in maize dough and boiled in a leaf), *ceviche* (raw, marinated fish), and *sopa de frijoles* (black or red bean soup – often a meal in itself). *Panes con pavo* are bread-rolls filled with turkey and served with salad – many restaurants specialize in these alone – and *bocas* are small appetizers, often meat and/or pickles and vegetables, served with drinks or before a meal.

There are US-style **fast-food** and **pizza** chains throughout the country. **Chinese** and **Tex-Mex** restaurants are reasonably common too, as are **Italian** places in the larger cities, though their authenticity varies.

So far, El Salvador has not been struck by a cholera epidemic. If freshly cooked in front of you, **street food** is generally safe to eat, although there's a lot of dust and dirt in the air and hygiene standards are not always what they should be.

■ Drinking

Locally produced **coffee** is very good, usually drunk black and strong at breakfast and with an afternoon snack of *tamales*. In small villages it will be served *lista*, boiled up with sugar cane and surprisingly tasty. El Salvador's abundance of tropical fruits go to make delicious **juices** in the form of *jugos*, *licuados* and *frescos*. *Jugos* are pure juices mixed with ice, most commonly made of orange, papaya, pineapple and melon. *Licuados* (sometimes called *batidos*), blend the fruit juice with sugar, ice and sometimes milk, while *frescos* are a fruit-based, sweet drink, made up in bulk and served with lunch or dinner. Unless you ask otherwise, sugar will be added to *jugos* and *licuados*. **Horchata**, another favourite, is a rather heavy milk drink with a base of rice, sweetened with sugar and cinnamon.

The usual international-brand **soft drinks** are available, as well as local equivalents, such as *Kolashanpan*. **Water** is safe to drink in San Salvador only; elsewhere check that the water and ice used in drinks is purified. Bottled mineral water is available almost everywhere, as are bags of pure spring water, while most hotels provide drinking water. El Salvador produces three excellent **beers**, the most popular of which is *Pilsener*, followed by *Regia* and *Suprema*. **Aguardiente** is a sugarcane-based liquor, produced under government control and sold through licensed outlets called *expendios*.

Opening hours, holidays and festivals

Opening hours throughout the country tend to vary. The big cities and major towns generally get going quite early in the morning, with government offices working from 8am to 4pm and most businesses from 8.30/9am to 5/5.30pm. Some close for an hour at lunch, some don't; **archeological sites** are usually closed on Monday. Generally, **banks** are open from 8.30 or 9am until 4/5pm;

PUBLIC HOLIDAYS	
Jan 1	New Year's Day
Mar–Apr	Easter (3 days)
May 1	Labor Day
Aug 3–6	El Salvador del Mundo
Sept 15	Independence Day
Oct 12	Columbus Day
Nov 1	Day of the Dead
Nov 2	All Saints' Day
Dec 25	Christmas Day

some close for an hour at lunch. On **national holidays**, everything will be shut, with some businesses also closing on the day of local fiestas.

All towns and villages have their own **fiestas patronales** commemorating the local saint. The scope of these varies wildly, with some lasting only a day and some, like those at San Miguel (see p.329) and Sonsonate (see p.340) lasting weeks and encompassing a programme of arts and other events. Most commonly, the fiesta is a time for relaxation and holiday-making; large amounts of alcohol are consumed and towards the late evening things can get rather wild. Generally the last day will be the main event.

Mail and telecommunications

Letters from San Salvador generally take about one week to the US and nine or so days to Europe. The **main post office** in San Salvador (see p.313) is open Mon–Fri 8am–5pm and Sat 8am–noon; it

LOCAL FIESTAS	
Jan 8–15 Cristo Negro, Juayúa	**Aug 1–6** Fiesta al Divino Salvador del Mundo, San Salvador
Jan 12–21 San Sebastián, Cojutepeque	**Sept 12–14** Santa Cruz de Roma, Panchimalco
Jan 25 to Feb 2 Virgen de la Candelaría, Sonsonate	**Sept 15** Independence Day, San Salvador
1st week of Feb Dulce Nombre de Jesús, Ahuachapán	**Nov 14–30** Virgen de la Paz, San Miguel
3rd week in Feb Dulce Nombre de María, La Palma	**Nov 26** Nuestra Señora de los Pobres, Zacatecoluca
2nd Sun in May Las Palmas, Panchimalco	**Dec 12** Virgen de Guadalupe, San Salvador
July 1–26 Nuestra Señora de Santa Ana, Santa Ana	**Dec 12–31** San Vicente Abad y Mártir, San Vicente

offers a parcel service, but if you're sending anything of value it's better to use one of the **courier services**. The safest place to **receive letters** is at the *lista de correos* (window 14) of the main post office; alternatively, there's the American Express office (see p.312), while some embassies (see p.312) hold mail addressed to their citizens. Post offices in smaller cities and towns keep the same hours as in the capital but aren't recommended as places to receive mail, while letters posted here take longer to arrive at their destinations.

Telecom, the recently privatized phone company, has newly renovated offices (all open daily 7am–10pm) in every town from where you can make local, long-distance and international calls. Offices in the larger towns also offer **Internet** services. Reverse charge (collect) calls can be made to the US and Canada, but not to the UK. A three-minute minimum call to Europe costs about US$8, and direct-dial services are available to the US (AT&T, MCI, Sprint). The **telephone code** for the whole of El Salvador is ☎503.

Most public phones in El Salvador are now **cardphones**: either the yellow **Telecom** booths (with instructions in both Spanish and English) or the lime-green **Telefónica** booths (instructions in Spanish only). Both require prepaid cards which can be purchased at many stores, gas stations and the *Mister Donut* restaurant chain; the Telefónica card uses a unique number code which must be keyed in before use (don't insert the phonecard). You can make international calls from both types of cardphone, but it's cheaper to go to a Telecom office. There are also a limited number of red **coin-operated phones**, but they don't always work and you can't make international calls from them. Rates for local calls are the same at Telecom offices; a minimum call costs 1 colón.

Faxes can be sent from Telecom offices, but don't expect great service, and all hotels with a fax machine will usually send one for you, though at a considerable premium. Most towns now have places with **Internet** access, particularly around universities and in shopping malls. Connections are generally very good and prices range from US$2 to US$4 per hour.

The media

There are two main daily **national newspapers** in El Salvador: *La Prensa Gráfica* (*www .laprensa.com.sv*) and *El Diario de Hoy* (*www.elsalvador.com/noticias*). Both have full coverage of regional and international affairs – albeit from a very conservative standpoint – and the Friday and Saturday editions are good for arts and cultural events. *El Mundo* and *Diario Latino* are smaller afternoon papers with a moderate stance, while *Marca* is a more sensationalist, tabloid-style affair. *Tendencias* is a liberal monthly magazine with in-depth analysis of political and social affairs. Daily papers are sold everywhere on the streets. The bigger hotels stock US newspapers and magazines, and the embassies have copies of papers from their respective countries.

There are seven national **television stations** and numerous cable channels showing programmes from South America, CNN and CNN en Español, and films. Over seventy **radio stations**, including Radio Venceremos (owned by the FMLN), transmit pop, rock, Latin sounds and religious programming. The BBC World Service can be picked up in El Salvador on 15220, 12095 and 9915 kHz (shortwave).

Shopping

El Salvador produces a number of instantly recognizable **artesanías**, such as the brightly painted, naif-style wood and ceramics from La Palma, hammocks from Concepción Quezaltepeque, and interesting ceramics at Ilobasco. These are far cheaper in their place of manufacture, but the **Mercado Cuartel** and the **Mercado de Artesanías** in San Salvador both have an extensive selection of goods from across the country at reasonable prices; a number of more expensive shops around town also carry smaller selections. Hammocks can usually be found for sale in the parque central in San Salvador.

The outlets in the **malls** of San Salvador and San Miguel sell US clothing at US prices. For something a little more down to earth, local **markets** (open daily in most towns) sell clothing, fresh fruit, vegetables and much more besides. Most towns also have at least one **supermarket**.

Safety and the police

Sadly, given the beauty of the country and the character of the people, El Salvador can be a dangerous place to travel in. Since the signing of the Peace Accords in 1992 **street crime** and delinquency have risen, and levels of **civil violence** continue to spiral upwards. Carrying weapons is commonplace, and holidays and festivals in particular can act as flashpoints. While the chances of being caught up in a violent incident are low, basic rules should be followed.

In **San Salvador**, very few people stay on the streets after dark, particularly in the centre, and the streets themselves are generally poorly lit. Outside the centre, the intimidation and threat is usually more potential than actual, but do not walk around alone (this especially applies to women), and always take taxis after dark, even if you are only travelling a short distance. Outside the capital things are more relaxed, but when walking around cities stick to the main roads and take taxis at night. On the street don't flash large amounts of money or obviously expensive cameras, watches or jewellery. Try not to look too obviously lost and walk with confidence; if you think you've inadvertently strayed into the wrong part of town simply retrace your steps. The **civil police** are plentiful in San Salvador and other city centres, and a pilot **tourist police force** has recently been set up in the Zona Rosa and richer parts of the capital.

Bus hold-ups occasionally occur and there is nothing much you can do about it; keep a close eye on the latest news about various areas before you decide where to travel. Generally hold-ups are still comparatively rare and affect the local population far more than tourists; whatever happens, your life is far more important than anything you might be carrying. **Police checks** occur on some buses entering the capital. Don't be alarmed if you are asked to get off the bus to have your bag and body searched. Be polite and patient and have a copy of your passport ready for presentation.

Work and study

Unlike Guatemala and Costa Rica, El Salvador is not well equipped with **language schools**, although there are vague plans to set up schools in the more touristed areas like Apaneca and Panchimalco, with profits going to local communities – contact Corsatur (see p.286) to see how far things have progressed. The Academia Europea, 99a Av Nte #639, Col Escalón, San Salvador (☎263 4355 or 264 0237, *www.euroacad.edu.sv*) has schools in all the country's major cities with private classes for US$12 per hour and group classes starting at US$50 for a thirty-hour course; classes are aimed at business residents and accommodation isn't arranged. If you're looking to **teach English**, contact the Academia Europea directly, or check the listings for *Academias de Idiomas* in the yellow pages.

Of more lasting benefit may be **voluntary work**, particularly if you have specific skills. **CIRES** (Comité de Integración and Reconstrucción para El Salvador), 2a C Pte #2137 at 41a Av Sur, San Salvador (☎298 9410) is a non-governmental agency with a remit to set up development programmes in the wake of the Peace Accords. It works in fifty areas around the country, with national and international funding, on credit loans, agricultural cooperatives, housing, potable water schemes and primary health-care schemes, particularly for women and children; they are always interested to hear from foreigners with relevant medical, technical and administration skills.

History

The first settled peoples of El Salvador were the **Maya**, who had arrived in the territory from Guatemala by 1200 BC or earlier. By 500 BC they had developed several large settlements in the west and the centre, the most important of which was Chalchuapa – close to present-day Santa Ana – trading in ceramics and obsidian across Mesoamerica. A catastrophic eruption of Volcán Ilopango around 250 AD spread ash over ten thousand square kilometres and all but wiped out many of these settlements, forcing their inhabitants to flee north. Over the next two hundred years, during the early Classic Period (300–900 AD), the land began to be repopulated, with important cities developing at San Andrés, Tazumal, Cara Sucia and, in the east, Quelepa. West of the Río Lempa the **Maya-Quiché** predominated, with the Chortís (Chortí being a dialect of Quiché) settling around Santa Tomas and Tejutla in what is today the department of

Chalatenango. To the east of the river the **Lenca** – a mix of the early nomadic tribes and groups of Maya-Quiché, with linguistic links to the South American Chibchan group – established themselves and developed in overall isolation from their neighbours.

Around 900 AD, when – for reasons still unclear – the Classic Maya culture began to crumble, these cities were abandoned. During the early Postclassic period (900–1200 AD), waves of Nahuat-speaking groups began to migrate south from Mexico, seeking land and power. These settlers, who established themselves in west and central El Salvador and in the northwest around Metapán, came to be known as the **Pipils**. New seats of power were built at Cihuatán, Tehuacán and Cuscatlán; unusually, the deserted Maya city of Tazumal was also reoccupied. The new settlers planted maize, beans, cocoa and tobacco, lived in highly stratified societies under a hereditary system of military rule, had highly developed arts and sciences and worshipped the sun and the idols of Quetzalcoatl (man), Itzqueye (woman), Tlaloc (rain) and Mictlanteuctli (god of the underworld). Trade links with the west and north were strong, based on the exchange of cocoa, which was extensively cultivated.

Final waves of Nahuat speakers arrived in the thirteenth and fourteenth centuries, threatening and occasionally displacing the already established communities and disrupting the network of trade, possibly contributing to the abandonment of Cihuatán and Tehuacán. Chief among the new immigrants were the **Nonualcos**, who settled around what is now the city of Zacatecoluca, and the **Pok'omans** who moved in around Chalchuapa.

■ The Conquest of El Salvador

The first **conquistador** to set foot on El Salvador was Andrés Niño who, exploring the Pacific coast of the isthmus, landed on the island of Meanguera in the Golfo de Fonseca on May 31, 1522. The Spanish returned in June 1524 when **Pedro de Alvarado**, commanding a force of around 250 Spanish troops and 5000 indigenous people, entered what is now the department of Ahuachapán from Guatemala. The region was fertile and densely populated, with two rival city-states, Cuscatlán, more or less where the city of San Salvador now stands, and Tecpa Izalco,

around the Sonsonate area. The Spanish called all this new territory **Cuscatlán**, a name which is still used today in presidential speeches, stirring newspapers and the like to evoke national pride.

Defeating the Pipils at Acajutla and then at Tacuxcalco, Alvarado advanced up the Zapotitán valley to the city of Cuscatlán, only to find it deserted, its army having fled to the mountains. Wounded and forced to return to Guatemala, Alvarado reported that the region would take time and effort to conquer. No doubt he exaggerated, but it is thought that the Pipil forces were up to twice as numerous as those of the Spanish, with the population of the territory as a whole put variously at between 130,000 and one million. Not until April 1528 did a third Spanish force under **Diego de Alvarado** succeed in subduing the Pipils and establishing the foothold of Villa San Salvador near present-day Suchitoto.

Once established, the Spanish almost immediately began to think about advancing east, motivated both by the persistent belief that the undiscovered territories would yield riches and by the need to remain dominant to the rival group of conquistadors advancing up the isthmus from Panamá under Pedrarias Davila. In 1530 Alvarado dispatched Luis de Moscoso from Guatemala to finalize the conquest of the east. Ten years later, despite a number of indigenous uprisings, the Spanish hold upon the territory was secure.

■ Colonial rule

Though the new territory never yielded the fabled riches of the mythical El Dorado, the fertile lands provided sufficient wealth for those Spanish who chose to take advantage. The **encomienda** system was established and haciendas developed, producing balsam and cocoa for export (this latter proved to be a particular source of wealth, with an ever-increasing demand for the delicacy from Europe). Cattle were also introduced and flourished – the indigenous farming method of slash and burn had created fertile pastures for grazing – providing a firm source of food and income.

As across Latin America, the impact of the Spanish arrival was catastrophic for the indigenous inhabitants. Susceptible to European diseases, cut off from food sources as lands were enclosed by the *encomenderos*, forced into a different system of beliefs, the indigenous population of El Salvador went into freefall. By the end of the sixteenth century at least half had perished. The Lencas and other groups living east of the Río Lenca – considered by the Spanish to be more primitive and less malleable than the Pipils in the west – were particularly badly affected.

The decline in the indigenous population left the Spanish *encomenderos* with insufficient labour to work the land. In the early years of the seventeenth century **black slaves** were imported, though this came to a halt in 1625 when two thousand slaves gathered in the centre of San Salvador during Semana Santa, apparently to foment rebellion. The plans came to nothing, but the slaves were henceforth considered too dangerous to use. Thereafter, the *encomienda* system was gradually abandoned, largely replaced by the end of the seventeenth century with a system of **peonage**. Work on the haciendas was rewarded by payment in vouchers, redeemable only in the hacienda shop, whose prices were set significantly higher than in the open market. Money for daily expenses, however, was advanced by the landowner, creating over time a debt that the worker, or "peon", was unable to repay and which, moreover, devolved upon his family and heirs.

Haciendas became enclosed, self-sufficient worlds; the workers found all their needs provided for, but in return became reliant upon the landowner for everything and unable to leave. Workers could get ahead by serving their patron in all areas, legal or illegal, while he in turn boosted his power by commanding such resources. Such patterns were to continue in El Salvadorean society in later years – not least in the private armies, raised by landowners, that developed into the death squads of the 1970s and 1980s.

From the early eighteenth century, landowners switched from the production of cocoa to that of *añil* (**indigo**). Although long cultivated, it was not until protection measures in the European markets were removed that it became viable to produce the crop on a large scale. Growing demand for the superior dye produced in Latin America ensured that by the mid-1700s indigo had become the primary export crop. The principal beneficiaries of this were – despite the efforts of the Spanish Crown to ensure small-scale production – the hacienda owners and *comerciantes*, the middle-men handling the sale and shipping of the crop.

By the end of the eighteenth century El Salvador was a rigidly stratified society, whose European elite consisted of the small number of Spanish-born Crown functionaries and priests and a few hundred Creole (Latin American-born) hacienda owners and *comerciantes*; these last two groups were allocated some responsibility in the management of local affairs on behalf of the Crown. Of available agricultural land, around half was held in private haciendas. The vast majority of the population, mestizo and indigenous, existed at subsistence level, cultivating maize.

■ Independence

Following the deposition of Mexican leader Augustín Iturbide in 1822, which brought an end to the hopes of a Mexican Empire, the Salvadorean Manuel José Arce was elected first president of the **Federal Republic of Central America** in April 1825. Beset by the deep divisions between Conservatives and Liberals, Arce attempted to unite the rival groups by force. Though himself a Liberal, he allied with the Conservatives of Guatemala and almost immediately plunged the federation into civil war, the first of a series of many to plague the five states during the short-lived union (it dissolved in 1839) and on into full independence. Between 1825 and 1876 El Salvador was in an almost perpetual state of turmoil as rival Liberals and Conservatives battled for power, aided more often than not by similar groupings in the surrounding states. Not until the presidency of **Rafael Zaldívar** – in power between 1876 and 1885 – did the country achieve any measure of stability.

■ A coffee oligarchy: 1860–1931

Commercial production of **coffee** became widespread from 1860 onwards, fuelled by the collapse in demand for indigo following the development of synthetic dyes – and the growing popularity of coffee in Europe and North America. Other exports – sugar cane, beef – also expanded, but it was coffee which came to dominate and be seen as the best hope for the Salvadorean economy. Unusually, compared to El Salvador's neighbours, finance for the boom was provided and controlled domestically. Government encouragement for and promotion of coffee created a **"coffee elite"**. The most significant piece of government policy was the privatization, in 1882,

ANASTASIO AQUINO AND THE INDIGENOUS REBELLION

The most serious challenge to the nascent government of El Salvador came in 1833 with the indigenous uprising led by **Anastasio Aquino**. Ostensibly a protest against the practice of forced conscription among hacienda workers, the month-long rebellion was also a response to the instabilities in society generated by the new state of independence. In particular it focused resistance against a new decree stating that all land not in use should be converted into private property. The hacienda owners expanded their estates, while the indigenous and other groups living on subsistence agriculture found that much of the land needed for slash and burn cultivation had been transferred into private hands.

A worker on an indigo plantation near Santiago Nonualco, Aquino rebelled following the arrest and detention – and presumed conscription – of his brother by the hacienda owner. He and his followers, the so-called **"Army of Liberation"**, attacked army posts, releasing and arming the forced conscripts and sacked haciendas; according to legend the spoils from these were distributed among the poor. The well-disciplined forces of the rebellion were successful in early confrontations with government troops and at one stage looked capable of advancing on, and taking, San Salvador. Instead, Aquino chose to march on the nearby cities of Zacatecoluca and San Vicente, giving the government time to marshall its forces. On February 16 Aquino arrived in San Vicente and had himself crowned **"Emperor of the Nonualcos"** with a crown taken from the statue of San José in the Iglesia Nuestra Señora del Pilar.

He then returned to Santiago Nonualco where, on February 28, he was defeated by the resurgent government forces. Finally captured on April 23, Aquino was **executed** in San Vicente in July. His head was put on public display, a primitive act in accordance with the status of "primitive rebel" which the government accorded him.

of lands worked under the *ejido* system, that is communally. Growing numbers of small-scale farmers and families dependent upon subsistence agriculture were displaced, with no access to land. Over time, as small-scale producers found themselves unable to compete profitably in the world market, land became concentrated into fewer and fewer hands, creating a tiny but powerful **oligarchy**. This trend became particularly apparent from the early twentieth century onwards, with three-quarters of all land eventually held by less than two percent of the population.

Descended mainly from the original colonial European elite, the oligarchy monopolized coffee production and trade, extending its interests into other agricultural sectors, industry and finance. As the interests became more firmly entrenched, so did the oligarchy's willingness to take action to defend them. The first example of this came in 1885, when President Zaldívar was forced from office. Over the next decades, until a military coup in 1898, private interests were the motivating force behind all changes in government.

■ The early twentieth century

On the back of the profits from the coffee boom, the first decades of the twentieth century were a period of relative **economic stability** and development for El Salvador. Transport links, including railways, and a communications system were put into place, education expanded and a functioning civil judicial system established. It was, however, also a period of deepening **social polarization**. The elite dominated business and the state machine, working alongside a small, mainly urban, middle class. The vast majority, however, lived in the most basic of conditions, marginalized both in the countryside and, increasingly, in the urban centres. Despite regular elections, democracy existed in name only, with the bulk of the population denied access to both the political process and the coffee profits. Despair and anger at conditions was reflected in growing civil and criminal **violence**, in turn dealt with by increasing repression – of which the Guardia Nacional (National Guard), formed in 1912, soon became a highly feared instrument.

The surprise election of Liberal president **Pío Romero Bosque** in 1927 was, for the majority, a sign that things could change for the better. Vowing to make El Salvador a truly democratic society, Romero took steps to restrain the worst excesses of the police and Guardia Nacional and – to the alarm of the oligarchy – ensure that civil rights were observed for all. Romero's successor Arturo Arujo, winning what was possibly the first truly democratic election in 1931, also vowed to continue on the same course.

■ 1932 and "La Matanza"

Despite some initial success, Romero's and Arujo's plans for democratic consolidation were brought to an abrupt end by international events. The **Wall Street Crash** in November 1929 and the Great Depression that followed were catastrophic for El Salvador. Virtually all – 95 percent – of her exports were coffee. As the market for this collapsed after 1929, so did the country's economy. All were affected, in particular the landless poor, for whom living conditions deteriorated appallingly. Unrest both amongst the destitute masses and the elite grew, and in December 1931 Arujo's brief period in office was ended by a **military coup**, engineered by the vice-president General Maximiliano Hernández Martínez.

Social unrest over the deteriorating conditions suffered by campesinos and the urban poor grew, exacerbated by growing repression meted out by the new government. On the night of January 22, 1932, thousands of campesinos – the majority indigenous – led by the Communist Party, **rebelled**. Armed mainly with machetes they attacked military installations and haciendas in the west of the country, assassinating hundreds of civilians including government functionaries and merchants. Mainly because plans to rebel had been widely known in the days before the event, the rebellion itself was rapidly quashed by superior government forces. The ringleaders were arrested and later executed.

The scale of **government repression** in the wake of the failed rebellion was unprecedented in the history of the country. The army, the police, the Guardia Nacional and the private forces of the hacienda owners engaged in a week-long orgy of killing. During **"La Matanza"** ("the massacre"), as it became known, anyone suspected of connections to the rebellion, anyone wearing indigenous dress or anyone simply perceived to be guilty was shot out of hand. In some cases, whole villages disappeared. Exact figures have never been known, but the death toll is estimated at up to 30,000 people, although the government itself insisted that only 2000 were killed. For El Salvador's indigenous population, the effects of the massacre went far beyond the immediate death toll. As it became increasingly

dangerous to be identified as *indio* (indian), traditional dress, language and customs largely disappeared.

■ Military government 1932–80

The rebellion and its bloody aftermath ushered in a era of **military rule** as the oligarchy, desperate to defend its interests, handed political power to the army while retaining economic control. For the next fifty years the two groups worked together in a symbiotic relationship. Successive groups of **tandas** – cliques of military officers – assumed power, felled by coups and counter-coups as factions within the military itself fought for supremacy. The economic business of state was handled by the oligarchy, who relied on the army to protect its interests. Depending on the faction in power, occasional limited **social reforms** were made, although leaving the fundamental structures unchanged. A number of political parties were allowed to operate, but elections were widely perceived as a sham.

After World War II, economic interests diversified into production of sugar, cotton and beef for export. During the 1960s and 1970s, some limited industrialization also occurred. Needless to say, the profits and benefits deriving from this expansion remained firmly in the hands of the oligarchy, with social inequalities unchanged. The vast majority of the population had no access to land and – at best – only tenuous means of survival. The census of 1971 recorded that 64 percent of agricultural land was held by 4 percent of landowners, while two-thirds of rural families had either no land or worked plots that were insufficient to provide daily needs.

A downturn in export markets in the 1970s again led to a steep deterioration in conditions, with a subsequent increase in militant pressure for change. The elections of 1972, won by the Christian Democratic Party (PDC) led by **José Napoleón Duarte**, should have signalled a mandate for democratic change. The PDC advocated a peaceful road to reform, but following the election the army installed its own candidate, **Colonel Arturo Molina**, as president. Duarte and other opposition leaders were exiled, the National University closed down and trade union and reform activists persecuted and killed.

The cycle of repression continued throughout the 1970s as Molina's successor, **Carlos**

Humberto Romero, took power in elections, again rigged, in 1977. Shortly after Romero took office, news programmes around the world showed footage of the army firing upon unarmed civilians during a protest in front of the cathedral in central San Salvador on February 28 – as many as three hundred people died. In 1979 the ineffectual Romero was himself deposed in a coup, replaced initially by a civilian military junta and then by a group of hard-line army officers in January 1980. The army accepted an offer from Duarte to form a provisional government on condition that certain reforms be introduced, yet repression continued, culminating in the **assassination of Archbishop Oscar Romero** on March 24, 1980 – a murder planned by serving army officer Roberto D'Aubuisson. Though preliminary reforms were implemented and agreement secured for a transfer of power from military to civilian hands, these were insufficient to halt a deepening cycle of extra-judicial violence.

The developments of the 1970s and continuing military domination had convinced many that change could only come through violence. Far-right paramilitary death squads waged campaigns of terror in the countryside and against those advocating reform. At the opposite end of the spectrum, left-wing guerrilla groups were mobilizing and advocating radical change. Archbishop Romero's assassination signalled the point from where descent into civil war became inevitable.

■ The 1980s

In October 1980 the formal integration of all left-wing guerrilla organizations led to the foundation of the Frente Faribundo Martí de Liberación Nacional, or **FMLN**. Three months later, in January 1981, the FMLN launched its first general offensive, gaining territory in the eastern and northern departments of the country and forcing the government into defensive action.

Events within El Salvador were watched closely abroad, particularly in the White House. The newly installed Reagan administration, paranoid about communist insurgency in the region, began to pump aid to the government to expand and equip fighting forces. Between 1980 and 1992 this aid totalled over US$1 billion, while aid channelled through covert sources is estimated to be at least a further US$500 million. The

money flowed despite concerns over the army's *modus operandi* and close connections between government security forces and the death squads. The **El Mazote massacre** in December 1981 – when US-trained troops systematically murdered more than a thousand people – was first denied then ignored by both Salvadorean and US authorities and only fully investigated in the early 1990s. Despite US support, the army remained hampered by insufficient organization, leadership and endemic corruption, unable to confront with success the guerrillas' organized ambush tactics and targeted attacks against strategic infrastructure and economic installations. Army response, tending towards the blanket attack of large areas of "free fire" zones, rebounded most heavily upon the civilian population. During the course of the war eighty thousand people were killed and more than 500,000 fled the country as refugees.

Against a background of continued fighting, the promised transfer of power from military to civilian hands was completed, with **parliamentary elections** in 1982 and a new constitution introduced in 1983. In 1984 presidential elections brought Duarte to power on a mandate for continuing reform, although the FMLN remained outside the political process, disrupting ballots in this and subsequent local and national elections. Sporadic attempts at peace talks foundered upon the seemingly irresolvable demands for fundamental changes in the role and structure of the army and for incorporation of the FDR (the political wing of the FMLN) into political life.

Widely perceived as incompetent and corrupt, Duarte was succeeded in 1989 by **Alfredo Cristiani**, candidate of the right-wing **ARENA** (Alianza Republicana Nacionalista) party founded by Roberto D'Aubuisson. Regarded internationally as a moderate leader, Cristiani began to unpiece economic reforms achieved over the previous decade. The response of the FMLN was to renew offensives against the government, most spectacularly during its **"final offensive"** of November 1989, when areas of major cities, including San Salvador, were occupied. In turn, the death squads and the military intensified their activities. Suspected FMLN sympathizers, trade unionists and Church activists were intimidated and assassinated. Thousands died when San Salvador and other cities were indiscriminately bombed by the air force and – in an incident that caused international outrage – six Jesuit priests, their housekeeper and her daughter were massacred in their rooms on the campus of the Universidad de Centroamérica on November 16, 1989.

■ Steps towards peace

At the close of 1989, an end to the fighting seemed a remote dream. Yet in April 1990, representatives of both the FMLN and the government, under the chairmanship of the UN, met in Geneva for the first of a series of **negotiations** that would lead to peace. This was achieved largely due to global changes: the end of the Cold War had reduced Central America's strategic importance, and both the US and USSR switched policy to an active encouragement of conflict resolution. Increasingly isolated and drawn into a military stalemate, both the government and the FMLN bowed to US and UN pressure to seek a negotiated solution.

A protracted negotiating process resulted in a UN-brokered agreement, the **Chapultepec Accords**, signed on January 16, 1992, followed on February 1 by a formal ceasefire. The FMLN agreed to disengagement and demobilization of its forces; the government to a purge of the armed forces and reduction in its size. In addition, a number of civil institutions were to be created, including a new civilian police force (the PNC), a human-rights institution and a "Truth Commission". The UN set in place a resident observer mission (ONUSAL) to verify compliance within a set time limit. A land transfer programme, expected to transfer ten percent of agricultural land to demobilized combatants and refugees, was inaugurated and a tripartite commission, including the government, workers and private sector, set up to formulate further social and economic policies. On December 15, 1992, the day the FMLN registered as a formal political party, the civil war was formally ended.

■ EL Salvador at peace

Recovery from the brutalization of civil war was slow. Many disaffected former combatants remained on the fringes of society, while unemployment soared and the circulation of firearms went unchecked. Delinquency, crime and violence ensued. The first postwar **elections**, held in March 1994, resulted in Armando Calderón Sol of the ARENA party assuming the presidency, beat-

ing the FMLN's Rubén Zamora. The new government pursued a neo-liberal, free-market economic policy and privatized large sectors of the economy, including the controversial sale of Antel, the state telecommunications company. IMF loans were used to stabilize the currency and encourage growth in GDP.

On the downside, the cost of living rose, poverty increased and unemployment reached unprecedented levels, while large-scale privatization further concentrated wealth in the hands of the elite. Public dissatisfaction increased with the government's perceived failure to comply with the Chapultepec Accords and with the amnesties granted to members of the military accused of committing human-rights atrocities. The profound divisions in society that had originally led to civil war grew wider than ever, and **civil violence** intensified.

Following its failure in the 1994 elections, the FMLN's fortunes were revived by impressive results across the country in the March 1997 **municipal elections**, including winning the capital's prized mayoral seat. However, failure to build on these results allowed ARENA's Francisco Flores to triumph in the **presidential elections** of March 1999, though only 40 percent of the electorate turned out to vote – highlighting widespread contempt for politicians of both major parties.

Much of the country concentrated on the hardships of daily life. **Hurricane Mitch** hit the country in October 1998, killing 374 and making 56,000 people homeless. The government's response was slow, and much of the international effort was focused on harder-hit Honduras and Nicaragua. Infrastructure was destroyed, agricultural output badly damaged and disease spread across the affected areas, primarily the low-lying flood plain of the Lempa and San Miguel Grande rivers.

A report by the Universidad de Centroamérica (UCA), in March 2000, listed El Salvador as one of the **most violent** countries in Latin America, with widespread gang warfare, narcotrafficking and civil violence. A spate of kidnappings of business people for ransom has gone largely unchecked, and the small-talk of the nation is littered with the term *delincuencia*. One attempt to combat civil disorder is the highly controversial US military training base which President Flores has allowed to be established in El Salvador – avowedly to fight drug trafficking, though Salvadoreans are still naturally suspicious of US military intervention in their domestic affairs.

■ Dollarization and after

On 30 November 2000, the Asamblea Legislativa approved the ARENA government's plan to **dollarize** the domestic economy – El Salvador thus became the third Latin American nation, along with Ecuador and Panamá, to elect to use the US dollar in all aspects of its domestic economy. The main thrust of dollarization was to create an attractive economic environment for the foreign investment El Salvador desperately wants to attract, and a massive publicity campaign was launched across the country using the motto "Good for you, good for the country". For many Salvadoreans, however, the prospect of welcoming the "Yanqui" dollar reopens still healing wounds, recalling the massive amount of US funding that flooded into the country during the 1980s to prop up the cruel right-wing government during the civil war. As veteran FMLN leader Schafik Hándal put it: "After this, I wouldn't be surprised if they passed a law so that every 'señor' must now be called 'mister' ". At about the same time, the government also announced its elaborately titled **Plan de Nación**, a public–private investment in public infrastructure totalling over 900 million dollars. Most of this money came from the sale of the state telecommunications company Antel, and will be devoted to building a new road network and developing Cutuco into the largest Pacific port in Central America.

El Salvador was again brought to the world's attention when a devastating **earthquake** ripped through the country on the morning of 13 January 2001. Measuring 7.6 on the Richter scale, the earthquake killed over 1000 people and left more than 5000 injured; some 145,000 homes were destroyed and a further 120,000 were badly damaged. Two further earthquakes in the weeks that followed killed another 250 people and left tens of thousands more homeless. Hardest hit were the coastal areas, although most of the country was affected in some way. For a country already struggling, these earthquakes represented a monumental disaster, while it's estimated that the cost of repairing the widespread damage and destruction will run into billions of dollars.

The next **presidential elections** are scheduled for 2004, by which time El Salvador will have a fully operating dollar economy. In the meantime, the issues of poverty, unemployment and civil violence will remain at the forefront of Salvadorean politics and society. National unity will be sorely tested over the coming years as El Salvador is forced to recalculate the economic cost of natural disaster.

CHAPTER 12

SAN SALVADOR AND AROUND

S prawling across the Valle de las Hamacas at the foot of the mighty Volcán San Salvador is the urban melee of **SAN SALVADOR**, El Salvador's chaotic, frenetic and polluted capital. It's a city which is unlikely to win many hearts – on first impressions at least – with its crumbling buildings, raucous traffic and surrounding fringe of shantytowns. Earthquakes have robbed the city of most of its colonial architecture and under-investment in public buildings is often painfully obvious, while the legacy of war has left large slices of society without employment or opportunity. The daily theatre that passes for street life in the city centre reflects all of these factors, showing the public face of a metropolis that goes about its business without recourse to many of the advantages of Western cities.

For all that, San Salvador is a modernizing city, and the authorities are making a determined effort to create a more attractive environment in the old **centro histórico**. The plazas and parks have all been renovated and many of the city's street traders moved into indoor markets in order to free up pavement space and aid traffic flow. Extra police have been deployed on the streets and, although much work remains to be done, the city is a more pleasant place to visit than just a few years ago. A stay, however short, in El Salvador's capital is probably inevitable, and many people find it easier to get used to the place than they imagined, appreciating the diversions and services it offers – restaurants, bars, shopping, cinemas – that are unavailable in the rest of the country.

San Salvador is also a surprisingly green city, with a canopy of lush vegetation shrouding even the most unlikely of neighbourhoods, and a ring of encircling mountains that seem at times close enough to touch. Dominating the skyline to the north is **Volcán San Salvador**, accessible via the town of **Santa Tecla**, 13km from the city, while in the hills to the south lies the lush, extensive **Parque Balboa**, from where there are vistas right across to the Pacific coast. Beneath the park to the east is the predominantly indigenous village of **Panchimalco**, with its splendid colonial church. Fifteen kilometres east from the city is the country's largest crater lake, **Lago de Ilopango**, stunningly beautiful and with views on a clear day across to the peaks of Volcán Chichontepec (see p.327), whilst to the west are the natural gorge, waterfalls and pools of **Los Chorros**, a favourite weekend retreat for harrassed city dwellers.

Some history

There has been a city in the vicinity of the present capital since around 1054, when the Pipils founded the city state of **Cuscatlán** in the Zalcuatitán valley, stretching between what are today the towns of San Jacinto and Santa Tecla. Although the Spanish first arrived in the area in June 1524, they did not succeed in establishing a settlement until

For an explanation of **accommodation price codes**, see p.287.

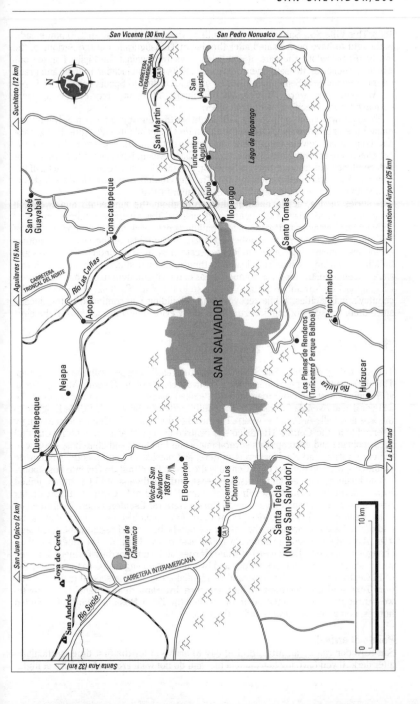

1528. This **Villa San Salvador**, to the south of where Suchitoto (see p.318) now stands, is thought to have been named after the day of Transfiguration of the Saviour of the World (El Salvador), the date of a conclusive victory against the Pipils. For reasons which are not clear, the settlement was moved to its present location in 1545, and granted the title of city in September 1546. By 1570, according to Spanish chronicler López de Velasco, there were 150 Spanish inhabitants, of whom sixty or seventy were *encomenderos*, a specific type of landholder.

Rapid growth came only in the **late eighteenth century**, after San Salvador was named the first *intendencia* within the Reino de Guatemala in 1785, stimulating trade and commercial development. Growing pressure within the country and across the isthmus to break away from Spain was particularly evident here; Delgado's first call for independence was issued from San Salvador, and the city became the first capital of the **Central American Federation** in 1824. The city continued to grow slowly and steadily, becoming capital of the Republic of El Salvador in 1840.

A series of destructive **earthquakes** throughout the nineteenth and twentieth centuries levelled most of the centre and ensured that virtually nothing remains of colonial San Salvador; today, the oldest buildings date back only to around the end of the nineteenth century. On October 10, 1986, in the midst of the civil war, another earthquake, measuring 5.4 on the Richter scale, destroyed around 60,000 houses and buildings, leaving six hundred dead and thousands injured and homeless. As if this were not enough, the air force bombed areas of the city thought to be hotbeds of guerrilla support in November 1989, in response to the FMLN's "final offensive" on the country's major cities. While recovery and rebuilding has continued in the decade since then, the scars of conflict are still painfully evident in some sections of the city.

Arrival and city transport

Though initially daunting, San Salvador's **layout** is easily grasped with the aid of a map. The city's central intersection is at the northwest corner of the Catedral Metropolitana, at the junction of the city's main **avenida** (called Avenida España to the north of the cathedral, and Avenida Cuscatlán to the south) and main **calle** (called Calle Delgado to the east and Calle Arce to the west). The heart of the capital, **El Centro** – increasingly referred to as the **Centro Histórico** – is centred on a point just north of the Catedral Metropolitana and encompasses several important buildings and churches, along with the city's major markets. Northwest of here, just outside El Centro, is the **Centro de Gobierno**, while to the east of El Centro is the major **Terminal de Oriente** bus station.

The business and residential districts **west and northwest** of El Centro are linked by the **Alameda F. D. Roosevelt**, which runs due west of El Centro to **Plaza de las Américas**, before changing its name to **Paseo General Escalón**, where it's fringed by quiet, wealthy residential districts. Many of the foreign embassies are located at the far end of the Paseo, as are a number of luxury hotels, banks and restaurants. The major **49a Avenida** crosses the Alameda 600m east of the Plaza de las Américas, then changes its name to **Boulevard de los Héroes** as it runs northeast, where it's lined with restaurants, bars and nightclubs and two major shopping malls. To the **southwest** of El Centro are further business and residential areas and the second major bus station, **Terminal de Occidente**. The **Carretera Interamericana** branches out southwest through the city; to the north of this lies the **Zona Rosa**, a suburb of secluded houses, upmarket restaurants and nightclubs.

Points of arrival

San Salvador can be an **intimidating** city to arrive in for the first time, particularly after dark. If you have luggage, take a taxi and do not walk around El Centro at night.

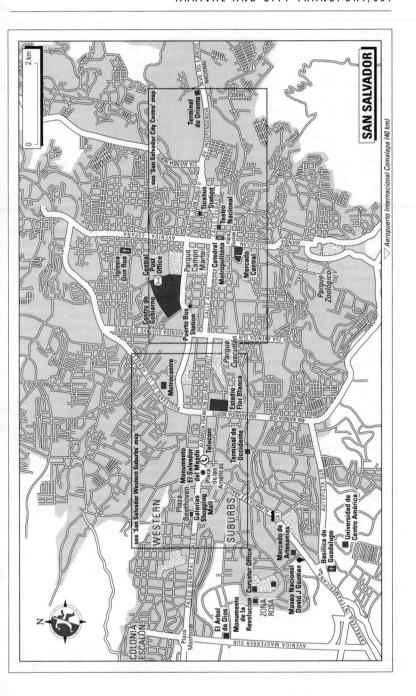

SAN SALVADOR

Aeropuerto Internacional Comalapa (40 km)

USEFUL BUS ROUTES

#29 – from Terminal de Oriente to Metrocentro via El Centro.

#30B – along Blvd de los Héroes, up Alameda Roosevelt and part of Paseo Escalón, then turning west to run past the Zona Rosa.

#34 – from Terminal de Oriente through El Centro to Terminal de Occidente and out along the Carretera Interamericana, past the Mercado de Artesanías.

#44 – along Blvd de los Héroes, onto 49a Av Sur close to the Terminal de Occidente, past the Universidad de Centroamérica and out past the US Embassy to Santa Elena.

#52 – along Alameda Juan Pablo II, past Metrosur and on to El Salvador del Mundo (opposite the Telecom office), then up Paseo Escalón past the Galerías shopping mall.

#101A/B/C/D – from El Centro up Alameda Roosevelt to Plaza de las Américas, then on to Santa Tecla.

The international airport, **Aeropuerto Internacional de El Salvador**, is located at **Comalapa** 44km from the city centre. The easiest option into the city is to take a **taxi** – well-run radio cabs wait outside (US$12–18 rising to US$20–30 after dark; about 1hr). Taxis Acacya run a **colectivo** service (9am, 1pm & 5.30pm; US$3) from the airport to their office close to El Centro at 19a Av Nte at 3a C Pte 1107. Alternatively, flag down any passing **bus** for the city at the stop in front of the terminal on the highway (5am–8pm; 45min–1hr; US$0.50).

Depending on the company, **international buses** arrive either at the Puertobus terminal by the Centro Gobierno (from Guatemala and Honduras), or at the Terminal de Occidente, Blvd Venezuela in the southwest of the city (from Guatemala). Ticabus buses from Costa Rica, Nicaragua and Guatemala have their own terminal at C Concepción 121 in El Centro.

For details of **buses from San Salvador**, see pp.313–314.

City transport

It's essential to get to know how the **bus system** works – the heat, pollution and danger of some neighbourhoods makes walking a bad idea, and crossing the road can be hazardous, to say the least. Bus services in San Salvador are comprehensive, frequent and fast. Newer city buses are red and white or green and white, though these are vastly outnumbered by the legions of older buses and minibuses that ply the same routes and come in all shapes, colours and sizes. There's a **flat fare** of about US$0.20 to anywhere in the city, which should be paid to the driver; minibuses are slightly more expensive (US$0.25–0.4). There are some marked **stops** (*parada de buses*), generally outside large public buildings, shopping centres and so on. Otherwise look for groups of people waiting by the road; drivers will usually let you board at red lights and the minibuses tend to hoot anywhere along a route to alert you to their presence. Services trail off after around 7pm, finishing altogether at around 9pm – at which time you should be thinking of taking taxis everywhere in any case.

City taxis ply the streets and wait around bus terminals, markets and major shopping areas. **Fares** should be settled before you get in – trips within the city should cost around US$3.50–5 depending on distance and time of day.

Accommodation

Although prices in San Salvador are substantially higher than in, say, Guatemala or Honduras, the city's budget accommodation – most of it in or east of El Centro – is not generally conducive to peace of mind or a pleasant stay. The area **east of Plaza**

Barrios and along C Concepción towards the Terminal de Oriente is distinctly unpleasant after dark, although we have listed the better hotels there. The **streets west of Plaza Barrios** are more sane, although dimly lit and virtually empty after nightfall. For peace of mind, it's worth investing a few dollars more to stay in the **western suburbs**, where you'll find some good-quality small hotels and guesthouses, as well as a selection of international-standard hotels where services – and prices – are everything you would expect in any capital city.

If you're arriving for the first time in the city, wherever your hotel, take a **taxi**.

El Centro

American Guest House, 17a Av Nte 119, between C Arce and 1a C Pte (☎271 0224, fax 271 3667). Gloomy rooms with a choice of private or shared bath, plus hot water and baggage storage. Management is helpful and the café in front serves all meals. ③–④.

Custodio, 10a Av Sur 109, across from Mercado Ex Cuartel (☎221 5810). A bit stark, but clean and friendly; rooms with bath cost more. ②.

El Castillo, 17a Ave Nte at C Pte Bis 227 (☎221 2435). Secure, clean and friendly hotel located slightly away from the heart of El Centro; one of the safest, cleanest and friendliest options in the area. Some rooms have private bath and TV, and a laundry service is available. ③–④.

Family Guest House, 1a C Pte Bis 925, between 15a and 17a Av Nte (☎222 9252, fax 221 2349). Clean, spacious rooms with hot water. The atmosphere is friendly, and it's a good place for solo women travellers. There's also a café serving all meals. ③–④.

Hospedaje Izalco, C Concepción 666 (☎222 2613). One of the best accommodation options in the area, with clean rooms, good beds and a luggage-storage service. The hotel itself is secure, though the surrounding streets are not nice after dark. ③.

León, C Delgado 621, between 10a and 12a Av Nte (☎222 0951). Basic, acceptable rooms with bath; those on the lower floors or with fan are slightly more expensive. ②.

Pasadena II, 3a C Pte 1075, between 17a and 19a Av Nte (☎221 4786). Clean, simple rooms, all with bath, in this safe hotel just behind the Puertobus terminal. ③.

San Carlos, C Concepción 121, between 10a and 12a Av Nte (☎222 8975). Clean and secure hotel, though given the area, which is a nightmare, the only reason to stay here is to catch an early Ticabus from the terminal next door. ③.

Western suburbs

Alameda, Alameda Roosevelt 2305, at 43a Av Sur (☎260 0299, fax 260 3011, *hotelalameda@salnet .net*). Affordable luxury hotel, with swimming pool, sauna, bars, restaurant, and a private beach on the Costa del Sol (see p.342) for guests' use. ⑦.

Amate Guest House, 25a C Pte 1302 at 23a Av Nte (☎ & fax 225 7616). Very quiet and friendly guesthouse, with three light, airy rooms, all with bath, in an old house set in a beautiful garden. Breakfast is included, and other meals are available on request. ④.

Camino Real Intercontinental, Blvd de los Héroes, opposite the Metrocentro (☎211 3333, fax 211 4444, *camino@salnet.net*). This landmark concrete monolith is the haunt of the rich and those travelling on expenses, with all the comfort and facilities you would expect of an international-standard hotel. ⑨.

Clementina's Casa de Huespedes, Av Morazán 34 at C Washington, Col Libertad (☎225 5962). Peaceful, friendly place; the owner is a good source of information on political and cultural affairs. ④.

Florida, Pasaje los Almendros 115, off Blvd de los Héroes, Urb La Florida (☎260 2540, fax 260 2654). Business hotel conveniently located for El Centro and the western suburbs, although the rooms are somewhat small. The roof terrace has nice city views. Breakfast included. ④.

Good Luck, Av Los Sisimiles 2943, Pasaje 5, Col Miramonte (☎260 1655, fax 260 1677). Large, bright and very clean rooms with private bathrooms and hot water. The restaurant next door serves all meals. ⑤.

Grecia Real, Av Los Sismiles 2922, Col Miramonte (☎ & fax 260 1820). Good-value, decent-sized rooms with bath, TV and phone; slightly more expensive with a/c. ⑤.

Hacienda, Alameda Roosevelt 2937, Urb Santa Monica (☎245 2463, fax 245 2464). Clean and spacious rooms, all with bath, though the front ones tend to get noisy. There's also a pool and a weekend disco. The café at the front serves breakfasts. ④.

Happy House, Av Los Sisimiles 2951, Col Miramonte (☎260 1568, fax 260 8633). Slightly dilapidated but friendly hotel, with clean rooms, courtyard and communal area. Breakfast is available on request. ④.

Lonigo, C El Mirador 4837, Col Escalón (☎264 4197, fax 263 2456, *hotellonigo@vianet.com.sv*). Beautifully renovated new hotel in a quiet neighbourhood. Rooms have private bathroom, a/c, TV and hot water, and there's also a swimming pool and secure parking. Bus #52 to El Centro runs from outside and there's a taxi office next door. Breakfast included. ⑥.

Miramonte, C Talamanca 2904, at Pasaje No 4, Col Miramonte (☎ & fax 260 1880). Friendly hotel in a quiet neighbourhood, and a good place for a spot of self-indulgence, with a wide range of rooms of varying size, comfort and price – all have bath; some also have balconies. Breakfast available on request. ⑤–⑧.

Occidental, 49a Av Nte 171, between Alameda Roosevelt and 1a C Pte, Col Flor Blanca (☎260 5724). Good-sized but dark rooms, with TV; some also have basic bathrooms. Rooms at the front get very noisy from the traffic. ③.

Ximena's Guest House, C San Salvador 202, Col Centro América (☎260 2481, fax 260 2427, *ximenas @navegante.com.sv*). Probably the only real "traveller's" hostel in the city, in a safe residential area close to bars and restaurants. There's a big dorm (②) and a variety of rooms (some with private bath), plus a communal TV area and courtyard. English is spoken, and staff can help arrange tours. ③–⑤.

The City

San Salvador is never going to win any prizes for elegance, and the rough edge to life here can come as a shock to those used to the more tranquil and colonial atmosphere of other Central American cities. There's a singular lack of museums and galleries, and little actually to do other than people-watching and soaking up the unique atmosphere. **El Centro** gives a vivid snapshot of Salvadorean daily life and character, as well as containing some churches and other buildings of interest. Towards the **west** things get easier, with a number of parks, including **Parque Cuscatlán**, providing acres of green relief from the traffic and noise, and the **Paseo General Escalón** and the **Zona Rosa**, offering modern cinemas, bars, clubs, shops and upmarket restaurants. The best museum in the city, commemorating those killed in the years of conflict, is based in the **Universidad de Centroamérica**, in the far southwest.

El Centro

San Salvador's authorities are making real efforts to rid **El Centro** of its traffic pollution, wall-to-wall street stalls and decaying buildings. Progress is slow, however, and although the parks, plazas and buildings in the **Centro Histórico** have received a generous makeover and some of the street sellers forcibly moved on, there is still a tangible sense of pollution, noise and decay, and it's unsafe to walk around after dark. Despite the dirt and crowds, however, there's a sense of real life here which isn't always apparent in the more upmarket suburbs to the west.

At the heart of the city is the newly rejuvenated **Plaza Barrios**, with its freshly planted trees giving some semblance of shade, and plaques commemorating the six Jesuit priests murdered at La UCA in 1989 (see p.295) and the revolutionary FMLN soldiers. The northern edge of the square is dominated by the **Catedral Metropolitana**, its new facade strikingly decorated with colourful contemporary murals by Salvadorean artist Fernando Llort. The building dates back to 1888, but was severely damaged on a number of occasions, most recently by fire in 1951. Subsequent repairs were suspended by Archbishop Oscar Romero, who argued that funds should be diverted to feeding the hungry – his murder in March 1980 is widely perceived as the event that sent the country spiralling into civil war. After the archbishop's assassination, mourners carrying his

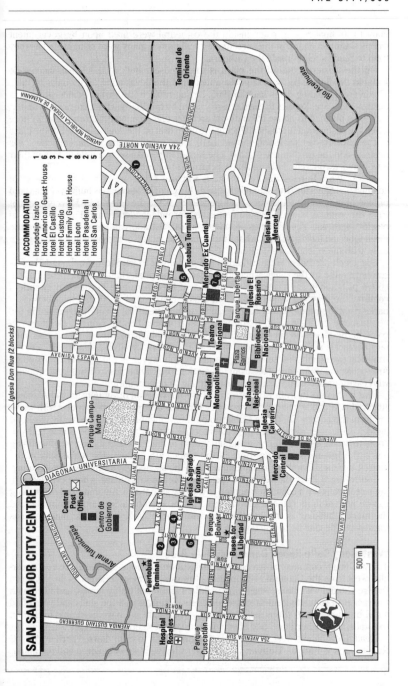

SAN SALVADOR CITY CENTRE

ACCOMMODATION

Hospedaje Izalco	1
Hotel American Guest House	6
Hotel El Castillo	3
Hotel Custodio	7
Hotel Family Guest House	4
Hotel Leon	8
Hotel Pasadena II	2
Hotel San Carlos	5

Iglesia Don Rua (2 blocks)

Terminal de Oriente

Río Acelhuate

AVENIDA REPÚBLICA FEDERAL DE ALEMANIA

24A AVENIDA NORTE

AVENIDA INDEPENDENCIA

Iglesia La Merced

Ticabus Terminal

Mercado Ex Cuartel

Parque Libertad

Iglesia El Rosario

1DA AVENIDA SUR

2A AVENIDA SUR

ALAMEDA JUAN PABLO II

10A AVENIDA NORTE

5A CALLE ORIENTE

1TTA CALLE ORIENTE

AVENIDA ESPAÑA

Teatro Nacional

Plaza Barrios

Biblioteca Nacional

Catedral Metropolitana

Palacio Nacional

Iglesia Calvario

AVENIDA CUSCATLÁN

Parque Campo Marte

Mercado Central

AVENIDA 29 DE AGOSTO

BOULEVARD VENEZUELA

DIAGONAL UNIVERSITARIA

Central Post Office

Centro de Gobierno

Arenal Tutunichapa

BOULEVARD TUTUNICHAPA

ALAMEDA JUAN PABLO II

Iglesia Sagrado Corazon

CALLE ARCE

Parque Bolívar

Buses for La Libertad

Puertobus Terminal

Hospital Rosales

Parque Cuscatlán

AVENIDA GUSTAVO GUERRERO

23A AVENIDA NORTE

25A AVENIDA SUR

N

0   500 m

body to its final resting place inside the cathedral were fired upon by government troops stationed on top of the surrounding buildings – many were slaughtered as they tried to reach shelter inside the cathedral.

On the western edge of the plaza is the imposing bulk of the Renaissance-style **Palacio Nacional**, the seat of government until the devastating earthquake of 1986. The current building dates back to 1905, having replaced an earlier edifice which was destroyed by fire. Repairs to the damage caused by the 1986 earthquake are still underway – it's planned to house the national archives and a national history museum here when the restoration is finished. Facing the cathedral on the southern edge of the plaza is the **Biblioteca Nacional**, moved here after a large part of the collection was destroyed in the earthquake of 1986. The remaining books seem a little forlorn in their new home, a concrete building that was formerly a bank.

East of Plaza Barrios along 4a C Ote is **Parque Libertad**, previously the heart of colonial San Salvador. The stained concrete church of **El Rosario** is built over the tomb of José Matías Delgado, father of independence, while the **Iglesia la Merced**, rebuilt from the original, where Delgado first called for independence in 1811, is a couple of blocks southeast. There's an impressive – in San Salvadorean terms – vista from the Plaza Libertad looking north, where the dome and facade of the cathedral rise majestically, with the volcano as a backdrop.

One block northeast of the cathedral is the compact **Plaza Morazán**, bounded on its southern edge by the renaissance-style **Teatro Nacional**. Built with the profits of the coffee plantations and reflecting the impact of French culture in the early twentieth century, the restored interior – all red plush, marble and decorative plasterwork – harks back to grander times. Regular musical and theatrical events (advertised in the newspapers) are held here. If you walk east from the theatre along C Delgado you come to the **Mercado Ex Cuartel**, a hangar-like building on the site of a former military barracks, selling a reasonable range of handicrafts from El Salvador and Central America; the quality and selection of local crafts, however, is wider at the Mercado de Artesanías (see opposite). East from the market, the city begins to disintegrate rapidly, with earthquake-damaged buildings struggling to remain upright.

Five blocks north from El Centro, near the intersection of Av España and Alameda Juan Pablo II, is the green expanse of the **Parque Campo Marte**, popular with workers from the nearby Centro de Gobierno on their lunchbreaks and for family weekend picnics. Continue north along the eastern edge of the Parque Campo Marte and you come to perhaps the most commanding church in the city – and its largest functioning one – the **Iglesia Don Rua**. Built in the nineteenth century, the white bulk of the church towers above the surrounding houses; the stained glass windows are stunning.

Southwest of Plaza Barrios is the sprawling **Mercado Central**, whose ever-expanding street stalls are a constant irritation to the city authorities. Anything and everything can be bought in its ruinous and cluttered alleys, even on a Sunday. Looming behind the market building is the **Iglesia Calvario**, whose dark, neo-Gothic bulk remains impressive, despite its dereliction.

West along Calle Rubén Darío and Calle Arce

The two major commercial streets of **Calle Rubén Darío** and **Calle Arce** run in parallel west from the Catedral Metropolitana towards the western suburbs. In El Centro they're choked with stalls, wandering peddlers and black traffic fumes, and filled with the racket of competing music-cassette sellers. Struggle past the stalls and you'll find small businesses and shops selling anything you might not have been able to find on the stalls, at a higher price, and cheap, fast-service restaurants and cafés.

Head a few blocks west, however, and things begin to calm down. Further along C Rubén Darío is **Parque Bolívar**, usually swarming with street children and the underemployed – more useful as a point for orientation (and the place to catch bus 102 to La Libertad) than for a respite from the city. One block west and three blocks south of Parque Bolívar on 17a Av Sur is the government printing press, with a small bookshop selling Spanish-language works on the history and culture of El Salvador. One block north of the Parque, on C Arce, is the nineteenth-century **Iglesia Sagrado Corazón**, under repair since earthquake damage. C Arce ends a few blocks west of here, in front of the nineteenth-century **Hospital Rosales**, constructed in Belgium, transported in pieces and put together in the city.

South of the hospital, **Parque Cuscatlán**, a large expanse of green and shady walkways and grass lawns, offers respite from the heat and noise for office workers on their lunch break, and weekend amateur football teams. At this point C Darío becomes the Alameda Roosevelt, heading out towards the richer western suburbs.

The western suburbs

From Parque Cuscatlán, **Alameda Roosevelt** runs west towards Blvd de los Héroes. This latter is lined with fast-food restaurant chains, more upmarket restaurants and what is reputedly the largest shopping mall in Central America, the **Metrocentro**, three storeys of expensive boutiques, sports-goods outlets selling mainly US brands at US prices and a couple of well-stocked, though pricey, souvenir shops. The bookshop on the second level has a decent selection of English-language fiction and general interest books, postcards and US magazines, and there's also an Internet café and food hall. The mall remains unpopular with local left-wingers, who argue that the country's problems will be solved by building new homes, schools and hospitals, rather than rushing to indulge a US-inspired consumerism.

Alameda Roosevelt continues west to the **Plaza de las Américas**, isolated amid eight lanes of traffic. Here, surrounded by small grassy lawns and benches, stands the national symbol, the **Monumento El Salvador del Mundo**, a large plinth showing Jesus standing on top of the globe. The main **Telecom** office (with international telephone and fax services, plus Internet facilities) is also located here, as are a number of banks and fast-food outlets. From here, the road changes its name again, to **Paseo General Escalón**, lined with ritzy restaurants, banks and upmarket businesses. The Paseo continues west, passing **Plaza Beethoven** (now officially renamed Plaza República de Argentina, though most people, including bus and taxi drivers, use the original name), the **Galerías** shopping mall (including a good bookshop, cinema and Internet café) and the **British Embassy**, before reaching **Plaza Masferrer**, home to an enormous national flag and some good *pupuserías*. The **El Árbol de Dios** art gallery (Mon–Sat 9am–6pm), south of Plaza Masferrer, on Av Masferrer Sur at C la Mascota, has a large collection of paintings and sculptures by Salvadorean artist Fernando Llort, renowned in particular for his naif style; there's also a pricey restaurant here. Beyond Plaza Masferrer are the rich suburbs of **Colonia Escalón** and **Lomas Verdes**, stretching high up onto the slopes of Volcán San Salvador.

Southwest along the Carretera Interamericana

Heading off from the Plaza de las Américas, the Interamericana runs through the southwest quarters of the city and out to western El Salvador. About 2km along this road is the **Mercado des Artesanías**, with a wide selection of handicrafts from all over the country. Good buys here include hammocks, painted wooden items from La Palma and bright hand-towels woven with Llort's naif-style paintings; prepare to bargain, although prices are around fifty percent higher than in the villages of origin. Turn into Av la Revolución, just past the market, and a couple of hundred metres up is the **Museo**

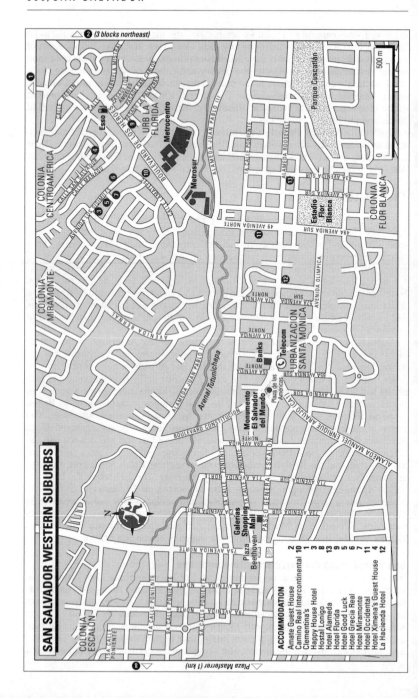

SAN SALVADOR WESTERN SUBURBS

Parque Cuscatlán

Estadio Flor Blanca

URB LA FLORIDA

Metrocentro

Metrosur

Esso

COLONIA CENTROAMERICA

COLONIA MIRAMONTE

COLONIA ESCALÓN

COLONIA FLOR BLANCA

URBANIZACION SANTA MONICA

Banks

Telecom

Monumento El Salvador del Mundo

Plaza de las Américas

Galerias Shopping Mall

Plaza Beethoven

Arenal Tutunichapa

BOULEVARD DE LOS HEROES

ALAMEDA JUAN PABLO III

BOULEVARD CONSTITUCIÓN

PASEO GENERAL ESCALÓN

AVENIDA OLIMPICA

ALAMEDA ROOSEVELT

ALAMEDA MANUEL ENRIQUE ARAUJO

ALAMEDA JUAN PABLO III

AVENIDA BERNAL

500 m

N

ACCOMMODATION

Amate Guest House	2
Camino Real Intercontinental	10
Clementina's	1
Happy House Hotel	3
Hostal Lonigo	8
Hotel Alameda	13
Hotel Florida	9
Hotel Good Luck	5
Hotel Grecia Real	6
Hotel Miramonte	7
Hotel Occidental	11
Hotel Ximena's Guest House	4
La Hacienda Hotel	12

(3 blocks northeast) — 2

Plaza Masferrer (1 km) — 8

Nacional de Antropología "Dr David J. Guzmán", a rather grand project, named after an eminent Salvadorean biologist, which when it opens in 2001 will contain the nation's largest collection of cultural artefacts and anthropological displays, plus exhibits of modern Salvadorean life and science. Opposite the museum, the **Feria Internacional** is the site of regular, and very popular, international trade fairs and also has an open-air music venue which hosts a range of Latin music stars.

Av la Revolución continues uphill for another kilometre or so, into the heart of the leafy Col San Benito, ending in front of the **Monumento de la Revolución**, a vast, curved slab of concrete bearing a mosaic of a naked Goliath with head thrown back and arms uplifted. Built to commemorate the revolutionary movement of 1948, the monument's location in one of the wealthiest areas of the city and overlooking one of its best hotels, the *Marriott*, is supremely ironic. East of the monument stretches the **Zona Rosa** entertainment district, with expensive restaurants, nightclubs and boutiques. The district's main drag, Blvd del Hipódromo curves uphill for 400m from the monument to the **Corsatur** (Corporación Salvadoreña de Turismo) office (see p.286).

Heading further out along the Carretera Interamericana, on the left, is the elegant white mansion and lush gardens housing the Foreign Ministry and, where the road meets the Autopista del Sur, what is possibly the most beautiful church in San Salvador, the **Basilica de Nuestra Señora de Guadalupe**. Built after World War II and consecrated in 1953, the basilica is dedicated to the Virgen Morena, or Black Virgin, patroness of the Americas. Inside are beautiful stained-glass windows and a 1950s mural of the Virgin and angels over the altar. Stretching behind the basilica is the campus of the **Universidad de Centro América** ("La UCA"; also known as the Jesuit University), pleasantly laid out amid shady grounds.

The extremely moving **Centro Monseñor Romero** (Mon–Fri 8am–noon & 2–5pm; free) at La UCA commemorates both the assassinated Archbishop Romero and the six Jesuit priests, their housekeeper and her daughter, who were murdered here by the security forces in November 1989. Volunteer students act as guides to the small museum, which houses clothing, photographs and personal effects of Romero and the priests, along with those of other human-rights workers killed during the years of conflict. There are diagrams and explanations of the campus massacre, as well as eyewitness descriptions of other low points during the war, such as the massacres at Río Sumpul (May 1980) and El Mozote (December 1981). Outside, a small rose garden has been planted in tribute; the circle of six bushes is for the six priests, the white rose the in the centre is for Monseñor Romero.

A short distance south of the university, the tranquil **Jardín Botanico la Laguna** (Tues–Sun 9am–5.30pm) sits incongruously at the edge of an industrial park and at the foot of old volcanic cliffs. The gardens contain plants from all over the world, set among shady trees and small streams, and are a good place to escape the city for an hour or two. Bus #101D or #44 will drop you off about five minutes' walk from the entrance.

Eating, drinking and entertainment

The best **restaurants**, **clubs** and **bars** are concentrated in the western suburbs, catering to those with the money and time to indulge. There are also small pockets of expat and tourist nightlife, particularly in and around *Ximena's Guesthouse* and *La Ventana* bar in Colónia América, behind Blvd de los Héroes. In El Centro and the less wealthy areas of the city, places tend to shut relatively early. There are lots of **cinemas** scattered around the city, mostly showing subtitled Hollywood releases. For **listings**, keep a look out for *Ke Pasa*, a free weekly entertainment guide available in bars, restaurants and cafés, which gives details of upcoming cultural, music and nightlife events. *The Revue*, Guatemala's English-language magazine, now includes an El Salvador section and is widely available throughout the city. As well as providing articles on new tourism projects in El Salvador it also advertises bars, restaurants and cafés popular with tourists and resident NGO workers.

Eating and drinking

The cheapest **places to eat** are the comedores in El Centro, although the richer suburbs occasionally throw up a few surprises; the **Plaza Masferrer** has a number of roadside eateries that stay open until quite late, while the unnamed comedor opposite *Ay Jalisco* restaurant, off the Blvd de los Héroes, caters to local workers with cheap, quick and good local food. Anywhere in the city, however, you're bound to stumble over a *pupusa* stall sooner or later, whilst the markets and bus stations are full of stands selling cheap meals and snacks. The **Blvd de los Héroes** area has a few good restaurants, while the **Paseo Escalón** and **Zona Rosa** are more cosmopolitan, with pricey international cuisine – book ahead at weekends. There are numerous international and local fast-food chains throughout the city, although they're mainly concentrated around the **Monumento El Salvador del Mundo** and along **Blvd de los Héroes**. The prices quoted below are for an average meal with a beer or juice.

El Centro

Café Don Pepe, 4a C Pte and 9a Av Sur. Sodas, juices, pastries and snacks in a lively atmosphere; daytime only.

Koradi, 9a Av Sur 225, at 4a C Pte. One of the few places catering to vegetarians (though it's open in the daytime only), with soy burgers, wholewheat pizzas and great juices (US$4–7). Closed Sun.

Mr Donut, C Arce and 21a Av Nte (and branches around the city). Nominally one of a chain of doughnut-and-coffee shops, though also serves excellent full breakfasts, lunches and light evening snacks. US$2–4.

Pan Latino, C Arce at 9a Av Sur. Welcome break from the maelstrom outside, serving coffees, cakes, *tamales* and sodas.

Pan Milenio, C Arce, opposite *Pan Latino* (plus other branches throughout El Centro). Excellent cakes and pastries, and plenty of seating to relax and enjoy a coffee. US$2–3.

Pupusería Irma No. 1, 1a C Pte 416 (opposite *Mr Donut*). Excellent and cheap rice *pupusas* and sodas. US$1–3.

Pupusería Nelly's, Av Bernal 210, north of Alameda Roosevelt between Blvd de los Héroes and Blvd Constitución. One of the city's best and friendliest places for a *pupusa* – try one made with cheese and *loroco* (a type of herb). US$2–3.

Around Blvd de los Héroes

Ay Jalisco, Pasaje los Almendros. Moderately priced Mexican and Central American food, although the portions are a little on the small side. US$5–9.

Dallas, Blvd de los Héroes by Pasaje las Palmeras. Seafood and steaks at moderate prices with very attentive service. Try the *ceviche*. US$7–12.

El Pueblo Viejo, Metrosur mall. Slightly above-average prices for generous portions of Salvadorean food, steaks and seafood, plus live music at weekends. A popular place for lunch. Closes at 8pm; US$9–14.

Hang Ly, C Lamatepec behind the *Camino Real* hotel. Large and almost authentic portions of Chinese food. US$4–8.

La Luna, C Berlin 228, Urb Buenos Aires. Arty restaurant, theatre and nightspot serving a good range of vegetarian and meat dishes. US$5–8.

Las Tinajas, Blvd de los Héroes 1140, in Edificio F.Q. Good, cheap breakfasts and set lunches; quick service. US$1–3.

La Ventana, C San Antonio Abad 2335, Col Centroamerica. European-run restaurant and bar with an interesting selection of dishes inspired by cuisines from around the world. Very popular at the weekends with expatriates, tourists and moneyed Salvadoreans. US$5–9.

Neskazarra, Av Maracaibo 612, Col Miramonte. Well-prepared Spanish and Mediterranean dishes and good sangría in a friendly atmosphere. US$4–8.

Panes Con Pavo, Av Pasco, at C Lampatepec (behind *Camino Real* hotel). Good *panes* and huge juices; more of a lunch than evening spot. US$4–6.

Señor Tortuga, C Sisimiles, at C Lamtepec. Mariscos and beer at reasonable prices. US$5–9.

Sol y Luna, Blvd Universitario 217. Popular among the local students, with good vegetarian food, pastries and fruit juices. US$3–5.

Paseo Escalón and the Zona Rosa

Chili's, Blvd Hipódromo 131, Col San Benito. Tex-Mex in a fun atmosphere. US$4–7.

Fruity Snacks, Av Olímpica 2930, at 57a Av Sur. Great little place for cheap breakfasts and lunch with superlative juices, if you happen to be in the area. US$1–3.

Kalpataru, C La Mascota, Urb Maquilushuat. Not easy to find but well worth the effort. Slightly pricey but innovative vegetarian fare, including *pupusas* with unusual fillings like stir-fried broccoli and curried vegetables. US$316.

Kreef, Paseo Escalón, at 77a Av Sur. German-style *bockwürst*, steaks and big sandwiches, though it's not cheap. The attached delicatessen is a favourite hangout for expats. US$7–13; closed Sun evening.

La Panatiére, Blvd del Hipodromo 211. The coolest afternoon café in the Zona Rosa, and a good place to enjoy a leisurely cappuccino and pastry and watch San Salvador's rich kids at play.

Pizzeria Vesuvio, 79a Av Sur 10, Col La Mascota. Although a little way from the Zona Rosa, it's well worth the effort of getting here for the superb wood-oven-baked pizza and wide range of pasta. Very popular in the evenings. US$7–12.

Punto Literario, Blvd del Hipódromo 326. Arty café serving coffees, drinks and light meals. US$3–6.

Ultima Alucinación, 7a C Pte 5153 at Av Masferrer Nte. Belgian-owned place serving good, pricey European cuisine. Or have a drink at the attached *Le Rendezvous des Artistes* bar. US$10–16; closed Sun evenings and Mon.

Nightlife

The entire population of the city appears to disappear at nightfall, and even in the Zona Rosa, the action takes place inside, rather than on the street. Many of the restaurants have **live salsa/merengue** music and dancing at the weekends; two of the best are *Villa Fiesta*, Blvd de los Héroes opposite the Hospital Bloom, and *Quinto Sol*, 15a Av Nte and 1a C Pte, Col Centroamerica. *La Luna*, C Berlin 228, Col Centroamerica, and *La Ventana*, C San Antonio Abad 2335, are relaxed **bars** with a more European feel, popular with local professionals and foreigners. *El Arpa*, Avenida "A" 137, Col San José, is San Salvador's obligatory Irish pub, while *Los Celtas*, C San Antonio Abad at C Principal 2339, keeps the Scottish flag flying.

In the **Zona Rosa**, *Mario's* and the *Reggae Bar* are both patronized by a lively crowd. Blvd del Hipódromo, around C la Reforma, has a number of loud, street-side bars which start getting full from around 10pm; many, including *Zky* and *Señor Frog's*, appeal to a younger, moneyed set. *Sr Cactus*, on C la Reforma, is more mellow, with a pleasant garden, attracting an older crowd. The *Lapsus* **nightclub** on the Paseo Escalón plays local music and Euro-bop until late.

There are a couple of **cinemas** in El Centro – including a huge Cinemark at Metrocentro and Galerías, and a multiscreen complex at Redondel Masferrer at the top of Paseo Escalón – and many others scattered around the city; the daily newspapers list programmes. *La Luna* (see above) shows a different film on video every weekday night, starting at around 7pm, while the Alianza Française (☎223 8084) on 51a Av Nte 152 runs French film seasons.

Listings

Airlines Many of the airlines are based around the Alameda Roosevelt/Paseo Escalón districts. Aerolineas Argentinas, Alameda Roosevelt 3006 (☎260 5464, fax 260 5450); Air France, Edificio Edim-Lama, Blvd del Hipódromo 645, Col San Benito (☎263 8192, fax 263 3416); Alitalia, Edificio Credomatic, 55a Av Sur at Alameda Roosevelt (☎298 1855, fax 224 3302); American Airlines, Edificio La Centroamericana, Alameda Roosevelt 3107 (☎298 0777, fax 298 0762); Avianca, Fountainblue Plaza, Modulo B, Apto 3, 87a Av Nte (☎263 2992, fax 263 2991); British Airways, 43a Av Nte 216 (☎260 9933, fax 260 6576); Continental, Torre Roble (Metrocentro), Blvd de los Héroes (☎260 2180, fax 260 3331); Copa, Alameda Roosevelt 2838 and 55a Av Nte (☎260 3399, fax 260 5481); Grupo Taca (incorporating Aviateca, Lacsa, Nica and Taca), Edificio Caribe, Nivel 2, Paseo Escalón (☎298 5055, fax 223 3757); Iberia, Centro Comercial Plaza Jardin, Local C, C Santa Tecla at Av Olímpica (☎223 2600, fax 223 8463); KLM, Centro Comercial Feria Rosa, Local 218-B (☎243 2513, fax 243 2514); Lan Chile, Edificio Imcolinas, Blvd del Hipódromo 253 (☎298 4067, fax 223 2525); Lufthansa, Fountainblue Plaza, Modulo B 1, 87a Av Nte (☎ & fax 263 2850); Mexicana, *Hotel Presidente Marriott*, Av la Revolución, Col San Benito (☎243 3633, fax 243 3634); United Airlines, Centro Comercial Galerías, Local 14, Paseo Escalón 3700 (☎279 3900, fax 298 5536).

American Express 55 Av Sur, Edificio Credomatic, between Alameda Roosevelt and Av Olímpica (☎245 3774); Centro Comercial la Mascota 1, Carretera Interamericana at C la Mascota (☎279 3844, fax 223 0035) – take bus #101B (to Santa Tecla), which passes the building.

Banks and exchange Most banks ask for the original receipt when cashing travellers' cheques; an exception is Banco Hipotecario, at Av Cuscatlán between 4a and 6a C Ote and other branches around the city. If you need colones, all banks will cash dollars, including Banco Cuscatlán, Banco Salvadoreño, Banco Agrícola and Banco de Comercio (Ban Co). You can get over-the-counter cash advances on Visa and Mastercard at most branches of Banco de Comercio and Banco Salvadoreño; a few also have ATMs.

Bookstores The bookshop in the Metrocentro mall has a selection of English-language books and some US magazines. Punto Literario, Blvd del Hipódromo 326, has English, French, German and Spanish literature. Centro Cultural La Mazorca, C Antonio Abad 1447, Col El Roble, has a small range of Central American literature and political texts (Spanish only) and a small craft shop, while *La Ventana* restaurant (see p.311) has a small selection of political and social texts (in English and Spanish) and US magazines and newspapers.

Car rental Renting a car is a good way to get to the more inaccessible parts of the country; expect to pay around US$45 a day for a small car and up to US$120 a day for a Space Wagon or Jeep. Check that the price includes insurance and that emergency assistance is available. Companies include: Avis, 43a Av Sur 147, Col Flor Blanca (☎260 7157, fax 260 7165), and at the airport (☎339 9268); Budget, Condominio Balam Quitze, Paseo Escalón (☎263 7174, fax 263 7166); Hertz, at C Los Andes, Block J-16, Col Miramonte (☎260 1728, fax 260 1101), and at the airport (☎339 9481); Tropic, Av Olímpica 3597, Col Escalón (☎279 3236, fax 279 3235, *tropic@es.com.sv*); Uno Rent-a-Car, Edificio Sunset Plaza, Av Jerusalen and C la Mascota, Col Maquilishuat (☎263 9366, fax 263 9371).

Embassies Most embassies are located in or around the Paseo Escalón and Zona Rosa districts – except for the US embassy which is on the road to Santa Elena (take bus #44). Argentina, 79a Av Nte and 11a C Pte 704, Col Escalón (☎263 3674, fax 263 3687; Mon–Fri 8am–noon); Belize, Condominio Medico B, Local 5, 2nd Floor, Blvd Tutunichapan, Urb La Esperanza (☎226 3682, fax 225 3540; Mon–Fri 8am–noon & 1–5pm, Sat 8am–2pm); Canada, C las Palmas 111, Col San Benito (☎279 4659, fax 279 0765; Mon–Fri 8am–noon); Costa Rica, Av Albert Einstein 11-A, Col Lomas de San Francisco (☎273 3111, fax 273 1455; Mon–Fri 9am–noon & 1–3pm); Guatemala, 15a Av Nte 135, Col Bloom (☎222 2903, fax 221 3019; Mon–Fri 8am–1.30pm); Honduras, 3a C Pte 3697, between 69a and 71a Av Nte, Col Escalón (☎223 4975, fax 223 2221; Mon–Fri 8am–1pm); Mexico, C Circunvalación at Pasaje No 12, Col San Benito (☎243 2037, fax 243 0437; Mon–Fri 8.30am–5pm); Nicaragua, 71a Av Nte 164 at 1a C Pte, Col Escalón (☎223 1223, fax 223 7201; Mon–Fri 8am–12.30pm & 2–4pm); Panamá, Edificio Copa, Alameda Roosevelt 2838 at 55a Av Nte (☎260 5453; Mon–Fri 8.45am–1pm); UK, Paseo Escalón 4828, Col Escalón (☎263 6527, fax 263 6516; Mon–Thurs 8am–1pm & 2–4.30pm, Fri 8am–1pm); US, Blvd Santa Elena, Antiguo Cuscatlán (☎278 1188, fax 278 6011; Mon–Fri 8.30am–4.30pm).

Immigration office Ministerio del Interior, Centro de Gobierno, Alameda Juan Pablo II (☎221 2111; Mon–Fri 8am–4pm) is the place to get stamps, tourist cards and visas extended.

Internet access New Internet outlets are opening all the time, though at present they are mainly located around student areas and in the large shopping malls. Access costs about US$4 per hour. Café Ciber Lógica, Centro Comercial Las Américas Local 15, Calle Arce between 19a and 21a Av Sur (there are a number of other Internet outlets in the same mini-mall); Cyber Café, level 2, Metrocentro shopping mall; Cyber Café Galerías, Paseo General Escalón (3 blocks north of Plaza Beethoven; take bus #52), level 3, Galerías mall; Galaxy Bowling, Plaza Beethoven; Cyber Café El Salvador, Av Rio Lempa 18, Jardines de Guadalupe; Café Internet Merliot, Centro Comercial Plaza Merliot; Telecom office, Plaza de las Américas; Café Internet Trazo, Av Don Bosco, C los Cedros 103 (by the west gate of the National University); Bar Café Internet, Av Pasco at C Aconcagua 11, Col Miramonte (behind the *Camino Real* hotel).

Laundry Try Lavandería Lavapronto, C los Sismiles 2944, near the *Camino Real* hotel (Mon–Sat 7am–7pm), or the nearby Lavapronto, C los Sismiles 2926. An average load should cost US$2–3. Most hotels either provide a laundry service – though at a slightly higher price than the local *lavanderías* – or let you wash clothes in the laundry sink.

Libraries and cultural institutes La UCA has a very good library, while the Centro Cultural Salvadoreño (Mon–Fri 8am–noon & 2–5pm), opposite the Metrocentro on C los Sisimiles, has an ageing collection of Salvadorean and English-language works. The Biblioteca Nacional is open to the public, but you have to show ID (Mon–Fri 8am–5pm).

Medical care There's a 24-hour pharmacy at Farmacia Internacional, Edificio Kent, Local 6, Av Juan Pablo II at Blvd de los Héroes. Embassies have lists of recommended doctors in various fields, and the Medicentro at 27a Av Nte and 21a C Pte has a number of doctors specializing in different fields. Hospital Rosales, 25a Av Nte at C Arce (☎222 5866) provides emergency medical care.

Police The main station is in the unmissable Scottish castle-like building which occupies an entire block on 10a Av Sur at 6a C Ote (☎271 4422).

Post office Behind the Centro de Gobierno on Blvd Centro de Gobierno; look for the large building with UPAE on the side. The *lista de correos* (Mon–Fri 8am–5pm, Sat 8am–noon) is at window 12 in the main section. There are smaller offices in the lower level of the Metrocentro mall and by the Europa supermarket on Plaza Beethoven.

Telephone office Telecom, the French-owned former state phone company, has an enormous glass office at La Campana, Plaza de las Américas (take any bus heading for El Salvador del Mundo and get off by the monument).

Travel agents Plenty along the Alameda Roosevelt/Paseo Escalón for booking or changing flights.

Moving on from San Salvador

To get to the **airport**, Taxis Acacya leave from their office in El Centro (see p.302) at 6am, 7am, 10am and 2pm (about 1hr; US$3). Remember that there is a departure tax (US$28) on international flights.

Scores of companies run **domestic buses** from a number of different terminals. Heading **west**, they leave from the **Terminal de Occidente** on Blvd Venezuela, west of El Centro; all of these also pick up and drop off on the Carretera Interamericana at the Basílica de Guadalupe. Buses **east** and **north** leave from the **Terminal de Oriente** on Blvd del Ejército Nacional, east of El Centro. Buses to **Usulután, Zacatecoluca, Costa del Sol** and **San Pedro Nonualco** leave from the **Terminal del Sur**, about 8km from El Centro on the airport highway (city bus #26 from Av España, by the Catedral Metropolitana, runs to the terminal). A number of faster *"directo"* buses, run by various companies, leave from the **Terminal de Oriente** for cities and towns further **east**. These are pullman-style, stop less often and are slightly more expensive. For **San Miguel** and **La Unión**, buses leave every hour on the hour between 6am and 4pm; for **Santa Rosa de Lima**, they run every hour on the half-hour. **Tickets**, however – as on standard buses – are not normally bought in advance; to be sure of getting a seat, turn up well before the bus leaves.

Tours

The agents listed below all arrange **set tours**, starting from around US$30 per person. Though these can save a lot of hassle, especially if you're short of time, they can be rather rushed, whisking you on and off the tourist bus at a rapid rate. All (apart from El Salvador Divers) offer similar tours to archeological sites (primarily Joya de Cerén and San Andrés) and areas of scenic beauty (such as Bosque Montecristo and Cerro Verde), along with some activity trips.

Amor Tours, 73a Av Sur at Av Olímpica (☎223 5131, fax 279 0363, *amortour@sal.gbm.net*).

El Salvador Divers, 3a C Pte 5020-A, at 99a Av Nte (☎264 0961, fax 264 1842, *www.elsalvadordivers .com*). Diving trips along the Los Cóbanos/Los Remedios stretch of the Pacific coast and crater diving at Lake Coatepeque, plus PADI courses and equipment rental.

Salvador Tours, Villas Españolas, local 3-b, Paseo General Escalón (☎264 3110, fax 263 6687, *saltours@es.com.sv*). Archeological and ecological tours across the country, plus surfing and beach trips.

Set Adventure Tours, Av Olímpica 3597 (☎279 3470, fax 279 3235, *set.adventures@salnet.net*). 4WD trips, rafting, bird-watching and volcano-climbing.

INTERNATIONAL BUS SERVICES FROM SAN SALVADOR				
DESTINATION	**DURATION**	**COMPANY**	**TERMINAL**	**FREQUENCY**
Guatemala City	5–6hr	Puertobus (☎222 2158)	Puertobus Terminal	12 daily
		El Condor (☎224 6548)	Terminal de Occidente	3 daily
		Comfort Lines (☎221 1000)	Puertobus Terminal	2 daily
		Mermex (☎279 3484)	Terminal de Occidente	2 daily
		King Quality (☎271 1858)	Puertobus Terminal	2 daily
		Ticabus (☎222 4808)	Ticabus Terminal	1 daily
		Pullmantur (☎243 1300)	Hotel Marriott	2–3 daily
Talisman (Mexican/ Guat border)	9hr	El Condor (☎224 6548)	Terminal de Occidente	3 daily
Tegucigalpa	7hr	King Quality (☎271 1858)	Puertobus Terminal	2 daily
		Cruceros del Golfo (☎222 2158)	Puertobus Terminal	1 daily
Managua (connections the following day for San José and Panamá)	11hr	Ticabus (☎222 4808)	Ticabus Terminal	1 daily

Around San Salvador

San Salvador is an excellent transport hub, and within easy reach of a number of destinations which offer immediate relief from the heat and crowds. Head in any direction and in well under an hour the harshness of the city gives way to lush, rolling countryside.

Santa Tecla, Los Chorros and Volcán San Salvador

Heading **west**, the Carretera Interamericana runs 14km through light industrial and residential districts to the small, busy town of **SANTA TECLA**, briefly the capital in 1854 and also known as Nueva San Salvador. Although considerably more relaxed than the capital, there is little reason to linger here. Six kilometres beyond, just off the highway is the *turicentro* of **Los Chorros** (daily 7am–5pm; US$0.90), beautifully situated in a natural gorge. Small waterfalls cascade through mossy volcanic slopes into a series of landscaped pools, suitable for bathing; there are public changing rooms and showers and a couple of comedores provide meals. Come on a weekday, unless you prefer your scenery with crowds. If you're in a group and feel brave enough to ignore the warnings about robbers, the surrounding hills provide pleasant walks. **Buses** for Los Chorros (#79) leave from 11a Av Sur and C Darío (every 15min; 40min); alternatively, take any Santa Ana bus from the Terminal de Occidente and ask to be dropped at the gate.

From Santa Tecla, a road heads north, up and around the heavily cultivated slopes of **Volcán San Salvador**, at 1960m the fifth-highest volcano in the country. Its summit is punctured by a 540m-deep crater, **El Boquerón**, which contains a smaller cone created in the last eruption in 1917. You can get to the top by public transport and then either walk around the crater (about 2hr) or down the wooded slopes inside it. **Bus** #103 (hourly) and pickups run from 4a Av Sur and C Hernández in Santa Tecla to the top, with the last bus back down leaving in mid-afternoon. Bear in mind that **taxi** and pickup drivers are reluctant to make the journey up to the crater in the afternoon, for fear of robbery – in any case, early morning is the **best time** to go, when the views from the summit are clearest. You can also walk up to the crater, though robberies are frequent; the police at the entrance may be willing to provide an escort for groups.

Joya de Cerén and San Andrés

Continuing west, the Carretera Interamericana runs through the flat and fertile Zapotitán Valley. Some 15km past Santa Tecla, a road branches off to the north and immediately splits; the left-hand fork here leads past the Maya site of **Joya de Cerén** (Tues–Sun 9am–4pm; US$3), designated a World Heritage Site by UNESCO in 1993. Known as the "Pompeii of the Americas", the site houses the remains of a village destroyed in a volcanic eruption around 600 AD. Lava from this and subsequent eruptions buried the site under up to six metres of ash until its accidental discovery in 1976.

The site itself will disappoint those accustomed to the imposing Mayan edifices of Guatemala and Honduras. Its importance, however, lies in the wealth of detail provided about the daily lives of the Maya. Eighteen structures have been discovered, although only ten have so far been excavated, including houses, storage rooms and one believed to be used for religious rituals or communal events; not all are open to the public, however. Artefacts found at the site, including jars containing petrified beans, utensils and ceramics, as well as the discovery of gardens for growing a wide range of plants including maize, beans, agave and chilli peppers, have helped to confirm a picture of a well-organized and stable society, relatively wealthy, and with trade links throughout the Central American isthmus. A small, informative museum at the site details the development of the Maya culture and outlines the course of excavations (Spanish-language only).

San Andrés

Five kilometres west along the Carretera Interamericana is another important Maya ceremonial centre, **San Andrés** (Tues–Sun 9am–4pm; US$3), set among rolling fertile agricultural land. San Andrés is one of the largest pre-Columbian sites in El Salvador, originally covering more than three square kilometres and supporting a population of about 12,000. The site reached its peak in the Late Classic era, around 650–900, establishing itself as the regional capital for the settlements in the Zapotitán Valley.

Only sections of the ceremonial centre have been excavated and the remains of seven major structures are visible – sadly, they've been preserved using rather too liberal amounts of concrete. The **Acropolis** (or south plaza) forms the major part of the centre, a raised platform supporting a number of pyramids and annexes. Structure 1 on the south edge was a temple; on its north face are the remains of an altar. Access to these pyramids was restricted to the governing elite, whose living quarters lay along the northern and western edges of the Acropolis; the bases of two of these have been reconstructed. The pyramids along the eastern edge of the Acropolis were possibly burial chambers. North of the Acropolis lay another plaza, used for markets and communal events. The largest pyramid (Structure 5) lies on the eastern edge of this plaza, but has not yet been excavated. Following the collapse of the Maya Empire from around 900 AD, San Andrés was not taken over by incoming Pipils, although the remains of a small farm dating from the Early Postclassic era (900–1200 AD) have been found close by. Ruins from what would have been the surrounding residential districts, still visible up to fifty years ago, have now also been lost to farming activity. You can wander freely around the site, which is also a popular spot for picnicking family groups at the weekends. The informative museum (Spanish-language only) has a small replica of what the site would have looked like in its prime.

Any Santa Ana-bound **bus** from San Salvador's Terminal de Occidente will drop you off on the highway at the access road to the site, from where it's about five minutes' **walk** to the site entrance. You can also walk between San Andrés and Joya de Cerén, but to be safe it's best only to do this in a decent-sized group. A path leads across the fields behind San Andrés, coming out about 4km northeast at an old railway track and abandoned station, just off the San Juan Opico road. From here it is another 3km or so to Joya de Cerén. From San Andrés you can also continue on to Santa Ana (see p.351) – buses can be flagged down on the highway – or return to San Salvador.

Lago de Ilopango

Heading **east** from San Salvador, the Carretera Interamericana runs through a succession of dismal slums and dreary suburbs, once independent towns, now incorporated into the city. A couple of kilometres past the domestic airport at Ilopango, a road branches south and winds down to **Lago de Ilopango**, offering stunning views across the water to the mountains on the other side. The country's largest and deepest crater lake, Ilopango is a contrast of blue waters and dramatic, thickly vegetated cliffs tumbling into the water, surmounted to the east by the peaks of San Vicente volcano.

At the weekends, the city crowds pour in, most of them heading for the **turicentro** (daily 8am–6pm; US$0.90) at the poor, dusty hamlet of **APULO**, on the northern shore of the lake, where there are small restaurants, a swimming pool, changing rooms and a section of beach, although the water is slightly grimy. A number of small boats tout for custom here (US$10 an hour), and drifting around the Isla de Amor, Isla de los Patos and the Cerros Quemados (created in an 1880 eruption) is a pleasant way to spend an hour or so. From Apulo a road heads round the shore, past the grounds of the private Club Salvadoreño to the hamlets of **CORINTO** and **SAN AGUSTÍN**; shortly before Corinto, where it drops closer to the water's edge, there's access to small rocky **beaches** and cleaner stretches of water. If you're tempted to **stay** the night, the *Hotel Vista del Lago* (④) sits about 2km above the lake, on the access road from the highway. The views are stunning, but the rooms – all with bath and a/c – are run-down.

South to Los Planes de Renderos

Heading **south**, a narrow, paved road clears the city surprisingly quickly and winds up to **Los Planes de Renderos**, a little-visited suburban area set in the hills around San Salvador. The air is much fresher here than in the city and the *mirador* lookout point affords superb views of San Salvador, the volcano and Lake Ilopango. Los Planes is also a famous for its numerous *pupuserías*, including the barn-like *Pupusería Paty* which serves some of the best *pupusas* in El Salvador. Also worth a visit is *Casa de Piedra*, an open-fronted bar and restaurant with spectacular night-time views of San Salvador – it's at km 8.5 on the Carretera Los Planes de Renderos. Twelve kilometres from San Salvador is the **Parque Balboa**, a somewhat run-down *turicentro* (daily 8am–6pm; US$0.90), but still a pleasant getaway. About forty minutes' walk inside the park is the **Puerta del Diablo**, a split rock formation at the summit of the Cerro Chulo, with spectacular views to the coast and across to Volcán San Vicente volcano.

Just before the entrance to Parque Balboa, a road branches off to wind down to the coast; a turning after about 2km leads to the small town of **PANCHIMALCO**, spectacularly set at the foot of the lush slopes of Cerro Chulo, with the Puerto del Diablo overlooking the town to the west. The area is inhabited by the Panchos, descendants of the Pipils, although traditional dress is rarely seen nowadays. The colonial church, built in 1725, is the oldest surviving church in the country, and there's a huge ceiba tree in the main square. Usually a sleepy, quiet place, things become livelier during the town's annual **festivals** (see p.288).

travel details

BUSES

San Salvador to: Costa del Sol (#495, Terminal del Sur; every 30min; 3hr); Joya de Cerén (#108, Terminal de Occidente; every 30min; 1hr); Lago de Ilopango (#15, 3a C Pte at 1a Av Nte; every 10min; 45min); La Union (#301, Terminal de Oriente; every 15min; 3–4hr); Panchimalco (#17, Av 29 de Agosoto; every 15min; 45min); Parque Balboa (#12, Av 29 de Agosto, south of the Mercado Central; every 15min; 30min); San Andrés (#201, Terminal de Occidente; every 10min; 1hr); San Miguel (#310, Terminal de Oriente; every 15min; 3–4hr); Santa Ana (#201, Terminal de Occidente; every 10min; 1hr 20min–2hr); San Vicente (#116, Terminal de Oriente; every 10min; 1hr 30min).

For details of **international services** from San Salvador, see p.314.

CHAPTER 13

THE NORTH

orth of San Salvador, hilly pastures and agricultural land give way to the remote, rugged and sparsely populated **Chalatenango** and **Cuscatlán provinces**, a region of poverty and pride, all but closed to outsiders. The Spanish found few natural riches to attract them this far north, and the wealth generated by the indigo and coffee plantations of the lowlands never reached here. Successive generations of campesinos have struggled to make a living in this harsh terrain, separated from the capital by distance and mindset. The sustained underdevelopment of the area created fertile ground for dissent and support for the **FMLN**, who controlled large parts of the department of Chalatenango for significant periods during the 1980s. Both army and guerrillas struggled to take control, leaving communities devastated in their wake and refugees fleeing across the border to Honduras. The scars of this are still evident, as – helped by various international aid agencies – villages struggle to repopulate and rebuild, against a background of continuing economic hardship, marginalization and growing civil violence.

Understandably, then, the welcome extended to foreigners can be initially rather cool; tourism is not a widely understood concept and travelling here is neither easy nor comfortable and – in rare instances – can be **dangerous**. Although so far no foreigners have been killed, the murder rate is high, particularly in Chalatenango, where many locals have been hijacked, held up with guns and shot. Though this usually happens to people in cars, you should also take great care if walking in the countryside around Chalatenango, and never carry anything of value. A little common sense, however, along with persistence, does bring results. Quite apart from the breathtaking mountain views and clear, fresh blue skies, there are a couple of genuinely appealing places to see: chiefly the tranquil and friendly **Suchitoto**, considered to be the finest colonial town in the country, set on the shores of **Lago de Suchitlán**; and the mountain village of **La Palma**, with its cottage handicraft industry. The Pipil ruins of **Cihuatán**, though somewhat specialist in appeal, are an easy trip from the capital. In addition, the glorious **Metapán Alotepeque** mountain range offers walking and hiking possibilities.

Suchitoto and Lago de Suchitlán

Set amid beautiful rolling countryside 18km east of Aguilares, near the site of a pre-Columbian Pipil town, **SUCHITOTO** lies on a small ridge above the southern edge of **Lago de Suchitlán**. The town's height of glory came when the original Villa San Salvador was located near here in 1528. In the many years since the capital was relocated, life has generally been quiet, except during the 1980s, when the area became the scene of bitter fighting as the army struggled to dislodge the FMLN guerrillas from their mountain strongholds in the area. The roads up and around Cerro Guazapo still bear the crumbling remains of the trenches and dugouts used by both sides, now quietly submerged beneath green vegetation.

For an explanation of **accommodation price codes**, see p.287.

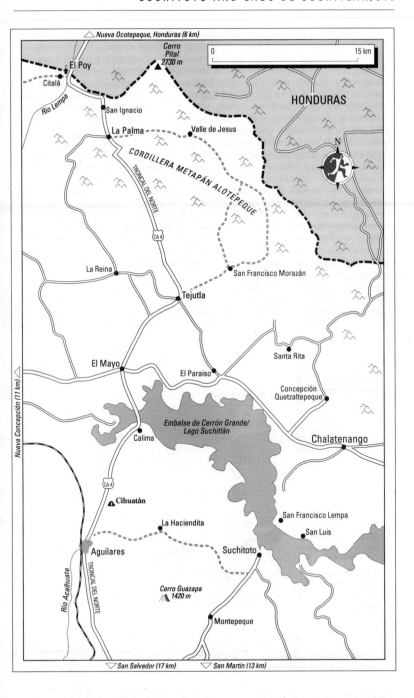

Today, Suchitoto (the Nahuatl name means "city of birds and flowers") is experiencing a renaissance, having been designated a national site of cultural heritage in 1997. It's a small and friendly place and makes for a relaxing getaway from San Salvador, as well as boasting some of the finest remaining examples of colonial architecture in the country, with low, red-tiled adobe houses stretching along the town's streets. In the centre, the whitewashed **Iglesia Santa Lucía** – now being slowly but extensively restored – is worth a look, with a particularly fine wooden altar. The **Teatro de las Ruinas** is currently under reconstruction but is planned to host music, dance and cultural events when it opens again shortly. The **Museo de Alejandro Cotto** (US$3.50) is a beautifully restored colonial house replete with a fine collection of local paintings, sculpture, indigenous artefacts and musical instruments. The friendly **Casa de Cultura** (Mon–Fri; free), opposite the church, has displays on local history and can give information on walks in the area. The shaded **Parque San Martín**, a couple of blocks east of the church, commands stunning and seemingly endless views across the blue waters of the lake; there's a small kiosk in the park and it makes a great spot to sit with a cold drink and enjoy the scenery. From the east and north ends of town, paths lead down to the lake shore, where you can swim, and where a couple of small bars make good spots for a relaxing lakeside beer. A small boat sometimes runs around the lake and to the small island in the middle, or local fishermen may be persuaded to take you out onto the water – the going rate is US$8–10, but be prepared to bargain.

Some 8km south of Suchitoto are the remains of **San Salvador Cuidad Vieja**, the original capital of El Salvador, founded in 1528, and now one of the most important archeological sites in the country – though there's not much to see as yet, and most of the remains are still buried under layers of earth. Ten minutes from Suchitoto by car,

SUCHITOTO

Ⓐ & Museo de Alejandro Cotto△

ACCOMMODATION
Casa de los Mestizos 1
Posada Suchitlán 2

RESTAURANTS
Comedor Trifinio E
El Obraje D
La Fonda A
Pupusería a la Vista C
Villa Balanza B

0   100m

at kilometre 34.8 on the Carretera San Martín, the renovated hacienda *Güancora La Bermuda* (☎226 1839; ⑤) offers a small range of excellent accommodation set amid magnificent gardens complete with swimming pool; there's also some fine walking in the area.

Practicalities

Of Suchitoto's limited **accommodation**, the *Posada Suchitlán* (☎335 1064; ⑥; reservations recommended at weekends) on 4a C Pte, a couple of blocks north of the lookout, is a very comfortable place to pass a few days. The large, well-furnished rooms are set around small patios, and the attached restaurant serves until 9pm. The Swedish owner is a mine of information on the area and its history. *Casa de los Mestizos* (③), on 3a Av Nte, has small, basic rooms with private bathroom and a bar which serves light meals and hosts various music and cultural events at weekends. The only other accommodation in town, *El Viajero* (①), 3a C Pte, two blocks up from the market building, has very basic, dark and dirty rooms. Some locals also rent out **rooms** – ask at *La Fonda* restaurant for Carmen, who has a double room (④), or at the Alcaldía for Gustavo Mixco, who also has rooms for rent (①).

For **eating**, *La Fonda*, at the northern end of town on Av 15 de Septiembre, serves well-prepared fresh fish, meat and chicken, and has great views over the lake. Near the church, *El Obraje* is simpler, but good. *Villa Balanza*, facing Parque San Martín, serves European and local dishes for US3–6. *Pupusería a la Vista*, near Parque San Martín, offers views of the lake and serves good *pupusas* each evening. The cheap and cheerful *Comedor Triunfinio*, at the entrance to town, serves good lunches for US$2–3. There are also a couple of small comedores on the main plaza.

The quickest way to get to Suchitoto from San Salvador is by **bus** via the small town of San Martín (every 15min; 90min); the last service back to the capital is at 5.30pm. For onward connections north to Chalatenango and La Palma you'll need to take the bus to Aguilares (hourly; 1hr 30min) along the extremely rough but serviceable dirt road that heads west from Suchitoto (you can also get to Suchitoto from San Salvador via Aguilares, but it's quicker and easier to go via San Martín).

Cihuatán

The main highway north, CA-4, or the **Troncal del Norte**, runs the 95km or so from San Salvador to the Honduran border at El Poy. A favourite target of guerrillas during the war, the road is still under repair, although most of the work is now complete. Some 35km from the capital, the workaday town of **AGUILARES** has little of interest for visitors but is conveniently close to the ruins of **Cihuatán**, 4km north. Though it's the most important Postclassic site in the country, a visit here is probably only for real archeology buffs; most of the buildings remain unexcavated and there is very little by way of information.

Although sporadic excavations have been carried out over the last hundred years, the true dimensions of the site did not become fully apparent until the felling of tree cover began in the 1950s. Sadly, the area is now acutely deforested, and nothing remains of the extensive woods amid which the site stood. Originally covering an area of around four square kilometres, Cihuatán (meaning "Place of Women" in Nahaut) was founded sometime after the first waves of Pipils (or Toltecs) began arriving in El Salvador in the tenth century. There is no evidence of occupation prior to this and the site was abandoned and destroyed around 1200, for reasons unknown. Residential areas surrounded two ceremonial centres, divided by a natural depression and covering an area of about half a square kilometre. Most of the excavations to date have been of the so-called West Ceremonial Centre, stretching west from the Río Acelhuate, where around twenty structures have been identified, including stepped pyramids and an I-shaped pelota court, bearing a clear Mexican influence, reflecting the origins of the Pipils. Artefacts found – including remains of ritual jars, some in the shape of human heads, ceramics and representations of the gods Tlaloc (rain) and Mictlanteuctli (underworld) – indicate trading and other links with settlements in Guatemala, the Gulf Coast and the high ground of Central Mexico.

The site is now administered by Concultura (Edificio A-5, Third Floor, Centro de Gobierno, San Salvador; ☎221 4364). There are no set **opening hours**; take a taxi from Aguilares and ask the resident guard for permission to look round. All **buses** running from the capital to Chalatenango or La Palma pass through Aguilares.

Twenty minutes north of Aguilares by car or bus, at kilometre 46.5 on the Troncal del Norte, is **La Hacienda de Colima** (☎ & fax 226 4144, *alfalit@netcomsa.com*; ②), a renovated hacienda with its own stunning forest reserve which encloses a variety of ecosystems and is home to numerous species of flora and fauna. The views of Lake Suchitlán and the nearby volcanoes are magnificent, and local guides are available to help you explore the area. The rooms have mosquito nets and there's a pool, café, numerous walking trails and a campsite. To get there, take any bus headed for La Palma or El Poy and ask the driver to let you off at the entrance. For more information visit the Alfalit office at Blvd Universitario 2034, Col San José, San Salvador.

Northeast to Chalatenango

From Aguilares, the highway continues north 19km to the major road junction at **El Mayo**, with its collection of scrubby comedores and bus shelters. From here, paved highways run west to the small town of Nueva Concepción, and east through agricultural and pasture lands along the fringes of the lake to **CHALATENANGO**. An important commercial centre, Chalatenango – established as a Spanish settlement in the seventeenth century – has the rough-and-ready feel of a frontier settlement, an atmosphere enhanced by the raised wooden walkways fronting the buildings of the centre. During the early 1980s this was a stronghold of the FMLN, who at one point claimed to have control of 26 out of 33 towns in the department. Today, much of the physical damage has been repaired, but the huge military garrison still looms over the central plaza, next to the church, and both the city and department have the reputation of being the most lawless areas of the country. Casual visitors are likely to be unaffected by this, but in recent years there has been a rising trend in car-jackings, armed **burglaries** and – very rare – bus hold-ups.

Incongruously, Chalatenango lies in a beautiful setting, southeast of the La Peña Mountains and overlooking the distant Cerron Grande to the west. **Walks** in the surrounding hills are possible, but seek local advice and don't go alone; in addition to dangers from humans, some of the surrounding areas were mined during the war and have yet to be cleared. Just outside town to the east is the **Agua Fria Turicentro** (daily 7am–5pm; US$0.90), with swimming pools filled by the nearby Río Armulasco. Twelve kilometres northwest of Chalatenango, the village of **CONCEPCIÓN QUEZALTE-PEQUE** is chiefly noted for its **hammock** industry. Workshops and homes around the village turn out colourful items in nylon and, less commonly, cotton and *mezcal* fibre. Prices are about half those in San Salvador; the hammocks are also sold in the market at Chalatenango at roughly the same prices as here.

There's no earthly reason to stay in Chalatenango: neither the atmosphere nor amenities are conducive to a pleasant stay. If you get stuck, **accommodation** is limited to the unmarked *Hospedaje La Inez* (opposite the Antel office on C San Martín, one block west of the central plaza; look for the pink door and the purple *Uva* sign; ①). The none-too-clean rooms and basic washing facilities are somewhat redeemed by the friendliness of the owners. There's a similar dearth of **places to eat**; try *Comedor*

Portalito opposite Banco Cuscatlán on 4a C Pte or *Comedor Carmary* on 3a Av Sur for *comida a la vista*. **Buses** arrive and depart from 3a Av Sur and 6a C Pte, a couple of blocks from the Parque Central.

La Palma

From the El Mayo junction, Highway CA-4 begins its climb up into the mountains of the Cordillera Metapán Alotepeque passing through the small, unexciting town of Tejutla, before making the slow, winding ascent to the Honduran border. The tortuous bus journey is compensated for by the views, with pine-clad mountains falling away to either side, and distant, hazy ranges and volcanoes seeming to stretch on forever (for the best views sit on the left-hand side of the bus on the way to La Palma from Tejutla).

LA PALMA, supposedly named after the indigenous custom of building houses out of palms, is a sleepy mountain village founded in 1915 under the name Dulce Nombre de la Palma. Its calm is really only broken during the annual **fiesta of Dulce Nombre de María**, in the third week of February. Today the village is chiefly famous for its **artesenías**, which are sold all over the country – naif-style wooden and ceramic handicrafts and toys, brightly painted with representations of people, villages and farming life. This cottage industry, instituted by Salvadorean artist Fernando Llort in the 1970s, is now the economic mainstay of the village, with workshops turning out hundreds of pieces a week. Most workshops sell their goods on the spot and are pretty relaxed about visitors turning up to watch the work; prices are somewhat cheaper than in San Salvador. On the main road through the village is the **gallery** of Salvadorean artist Alfredo Linares (Mon–Sat 9am–noon & 1–4pm), displaying his fine watercolours and pen-and-ink representations of the area and its peoples. Prices for the originals are not particularly low, but postcards and prints are also sold.

North of La Palma are several fine **hiking trails**, including, for the adventurous, El Salvador's highest mountain, **Cerro Pital** (2730m), 10km away on the border. A rough road branches east just before La Palma to run to Las Pilas on the lower slopes of the mountain; a dirt road also leads up from the village of **San Ignacio** (see below). Hiking to the summit is an adventure of two or three days, for which you will need to be fully equipped. If you don't mind not reaching the top, the trails provide day hikes of varying lengths – the owners of the *Hotel La Palma* are a good source of information on walks and guides.

Practicalities

Accommodation in La Palma includes *Hotel La Palma* (☎335 9012; ②), supposedly the oldest functioning hotel in El Salvador. Comfortable and rustic, it is probably the best option in town, and the owner is a useful source of local information. A rather overpriced restaurant serves all meals. *Hotel y Restaurante La Montaña* (☎335 9249; ⑦) has comfortable double rooms with a/c, TV and bathroom, a video room, swimming pool and bar terrace with magnificent mountain views; the price includes three meals a day. *Posada Real* (④) near the Parque Central, has basic cabin rooms with shared bathroom; a small restaurant-cum-*pupusería* serves lunches. Other **places to eat** include *La Estancia* restaurant, on the main road through the village near the hotel; and *La Terraza*, one block past the church – though both tend to shut early in the evening.

To the Honduran border

The highway continues past La Palma to the Honduran border at El Poy, 11km away, a thirty-minute journey by bus. The village of **SAN IGNACIO**, 6km from La Palma, also has a few craft **workshops** and two **places to stay**. The rather basic *La Posada* (②) on the square is run by the owner of *Hotel La Palma* in La Palma and has basic but clean rooms with shared bathroom; there's also a TV room, and the lobby sells artesanías from Ilobasco, La Palma and San Ignacio. The upmarket *Hotel Entre Pinos* (☎335 9370, fax 335 9382; ⑦) is on the highway, just before the village. The large, very comfortable rooms have bathrooms with hot water and great views, plus a restaurant, pool, bar, conference facilities, hiking trails and horseback-riding. Just short of El Poy, a road branching to the left crosses the Río Lempa and runs to the village of **CITALÁ**, 1km away. From here a daily bus leaves at 5am, running west along a rough but scenic mountain road to **Metapán**, for access to Bosque Montecristo (see p.357) and the Guatemalan border at Anguiatú, a journey of three to four hours. There's a basic *posada* (①) close to the centre of the village.

EL POY itself is a drab, dusty village with a collection of small comedores and general stores. Crossing the border here is straightforward and quick; there is a US$2 entrance charge for Honduras, but no entry or exit charges for El Salvador. A lot of trucks use this route, but private traffic is light; crossing early in the day is advisable. The last **bus** from the border for La Palma and San Salvador leaves at 4.30pm. On the Honduran side buses run the 10km to Nueva Ocotepeque (see p.402) every forty minutes or so until 5pm.

travel details

BUSES

San Salvador to: Chalatenango (#125, Terminal de Oriente; every 15min until 5pm; 2hr 30min); El Poy (#119, Terminal de Oriente; every 30min until 4pm; 4hr 30min); La Palma (#119, Terminal de Oriente; every 30min until 4pm; 4hr); Suchitoto (#129, Terminal de Oriente; every 15min; 1hr 30min).

CHAPTER 14

THE EAST

The rough and wild terrain of **eastern El Salvador** remained, in the main, unexplored territory for the pre-Columbian Pipils, who did not venture far beyond the natural frontier of the Río Lempa into this "land that smokes" of lofty volcanoes, hot plains and mountain ranges. Its Lenca inhabitants developed their society in isolation from the west, and it was only with some reluctance and difficulty that the Spanish conquered this frontier. Today, the region still remains separated from the capital by distance and experience, with the wealth of the coffee plantations around San Vicente and San Miguel contrasting cruelly with the rural poverty found elsewhere. Refugees from communities devastated by the civil war – eastern El Salvador saw the worst of the fighting – have in the last decade returned to try and pick up the pieces in this wild and beautiful area, but their struggle against poverty is painfully apparent. Travelling here, while difficult, is thought-provoking and moving; expect some reservation, even hostility, from locals and be prepared to understand and accept the difficulties – of continual poverty, unemployment, poor infrastructure and growing civil violence – that people still face.

The charming city of **San Vicente** makes a convenient base for hiking up the lofty peaks of **Chichontepec** and swimming in the **Laguna de Apastepeque**. Bustling **San Miguel**, the third-largest city in the country, is a transport hub, and a good place to recuperate from life on the road, with the largely unexcavated archeological site of **Quelepa** and the wetlands reserve of **Laguna el Jocotal** within easy reach. Buses head north from here to the tranquil mountain villages of the **Ruta de la Paz**, and the moving **Museo de la Revolución Salvadoreña** at **Perquín**.

For an explanation of **accommodation price codes**, see p.287.

East to San Vicente

From San Salvador, the Carretera Interamericana edges its way through industrial units, shanty towns and the grimy suburbs on the edge of the city, before arriving at **COJUTEPEQUE**, 32km from the capital. There's little to see here other than the shrine of the **Virgen de Fátima** of Portugal, a statue which was brought here in 1949. Housed at the top of the Cerro de las Pavas, about thirty minutes' walk from the centre of town, the shrine attracts worshippers and petitioners on Sundays particularly. The summit also gives wonderful views over Lago de Ilopango.

Some 6km beyond Cojutepeque, a road branches north through beautiful rolling countryside to the small town of **ILOBASCO**, noted for its brightly painted earthenware decorated with animals and everyday scenes. Look out for the town speciality known as *sorpresas* (surprises) – detailed scenes of village life contained in small, egg-shaped shells. From here, a road runs 35km east to **SENSUNTEPEQUE**, a pleasant, quiet town (with a couple of hospedajes) set amid marvellous mountain scenery, though there is little actually to do unless you're here during the November fiestas. East of Cojutepeque on the Interamericana, a paved road leads off to the small village of **SAN SEBASTIÁN**, famous for its hammocks and patterned cloth sheets and bedspreads. Although prices here are cheaper than in San Salvador expect to bargain, especially in the market. Regular direct **buses** run to Sensuntepeque, San Sebastian and Ilobasco from San Salvador's Terminal de Oriente (see p.313).

Further along the Carretera Interamericana, some 25km from Cojutepeque, a junction marked by ramshackle cane bus shelters gives onto the branch road for the attractive city of **San Vicente**, set in the Jiboa valley at the foot of **Volcán Chichontepec**. The approach is perhaps one of the most spectacular in the country; the road sharply descending to the valley floor on one side, while across on the other rises the conical bulk of the twin-peaked volcano, dwarfing everything in sight, including the white spires of the city nestling below.

San Vicente

SAN VICENTE was founded in 1635 by fifty local Spanish families in accordance with the 1600 Law of the Indies, which prohibited the Spanish from living among the indigenous people. Gathering under the shade of a tempisque tree near Río Alcahuapa on December 26, 1635, the families formally inaugurated San Vicente de Lorenzana, in honour of the Spanish martyr San Vicente Abad.

Until the 1980s, the biggest threat to the stability of San Vicente came on February 16, 1833, when the forces of Anastasio Aquino, leader of the Nonualco indigenous uprising, arrived in the city. "Inebriated with alcohol and success", they removed the crown from the statue of San José in the Iglesia El Pilar (see opposite) and crowned Aquino "Emperor of the Nonualcos". The rebels then returned to Santiago Nonualco, some 30km away; here, Aquino was captured by government forces on April 23 and later sent back to San Vicente and hanged.

Today, San Vicente is a calm, low-slung city, in a rich agricultural area producing sugar cane, cotton and coffee. It was attacked several times by guerrillas during the 1980s – an obvious military presence remains, with a huge barracks near the centre – and was also very badly hit by one of the earthquakes in 2001, during which the Iglesia El Pilar and the Torre Kiosko were badly damaged. The central **Parque Cañas** acts as a focus for the city, dominated by the **Torre Kiosko**, an eye-catching open-work clock-tower, which you can climb for great views of the cathedral and Parque. On the eastern edge of the Parque is the rather bare city cathedral; walk down its side, along C Daniel Díaz, and you come to the original tempisque tree, under which the city was founded, and which was declared a historic monument in 1984. Two blocks south of the Parque on Av Mirondo Sur is the **Iglesia El Pilar** (or Iglesia Nuestra Señora del Pilar, to give it its full name); the statue of San José – complete with crown – remains in the church. The church has a beautiful carved wooden altar, and a plaque by the entrance honours José Simeon Cañas, the man who abolished slavery in El Salvador.

The military barracks takes up an entire block between Iglesia El Pilar and the Parque; a walk west up the side of the barracks brings you to the extensive **market**, stretching over several streets. **Hammock** vendors can be found on most street corners – the hammocks are made in the surrounding villages and add a notable splash of colour to the town.

Practicalities

Buses coming from the highway run through the Parque and south to the bus station on Av Canónigo Lazo at C Indalecio Miranda; stand with the cathedral on your immediate left and Av Canónigo Lazo is straight ahead. Buses run from San Salvador every ten minutes, with the last leaving for the capital at 6.30pm. There are no direct buses to San Miguel; you'll need to catch any San Salvador-bound bus the short distance to the Interamericana (ask the conductor to tell you when to get off) and then catch any San Miguel-bound bus, which run every fifteen minutes from San Salvador. For phone calls the **Telecom** office is on the corner of the Parque next to the De Todo supermarket. The **post office** is on C 1 de Julio, one block down from the barracks. **Banks** include a Banco Hipotecario and Banco Agrícola on the Parque, and an Ahorromet Scotiabank on the corner of 1a Av Nte and C Quiñonez de O. **Internet** access is available at Computer Solutions, above a shop at C Quiñonez de O at 2a C Pte.

The town's best **accommodation** is the new and very clean *Villa Españolas* on Av José Maria Cornejo, a block north of the Parque (☎393 0322; ③); all rooms have private bath. On the Parque itself is the scruffy but amenable *Hotel Central* (☎393 0383; ②–③), which has rooms with TV and a/c, and an attached restaurant serving adequate meals. Friendliest of the bunch is the *Casa de Huéspedes el Turista* on C Indalecio Miranda and Av Maria de los Angeles, one block southwest of the Iglesia El Pilar (☎393 0323; ②), where all the rooms have bath, TV and hammocks.

Of the **places to eat**, first choice is *Casa Blanca* at C Alberto de Merino 13 (daily 11am–9pm), for its reasonably priced meat and fish dishes. *Restaurante Taiwan*, on the Parque next to *Hotel Central*, has average *comidas a la vista*, but, despite its name, no Chinese food. The restaurant at *Hotel Central* serves simple meals and is a good place for people-watching; both these close at around 8.30pm, depending on how many diners there are. *Comedor Rivoly*, on Av Maria de los Angeles, one block west of the Parque, has good breakfasts and *comidas a la vista*, whilst *El Cuco*, next to the bus station on Av Canónigo Lazo, serves tacos and sandwiches. *Restaurant Acapulco*, one block south and one block west of Iglesia El Pilar, serves good set lunches with salad and/or rice. For ice cream, try *Pops*, on the Parque next to the Alcaldía.

Around San Vicente

Everywhere in San Vicente is dominated by the towering bulk of **Volcán Chichontepec** (also known as Volcán San Vicente) to the southwest. Meaning "Hill of Two Breasts" in Nahuatl, the twin peaks rise to 2181m, making it the second-highest volcano in the country. It's considered to be dormant, with cultivated lower slopes and the steep summit left to scrub and soil. A number of **paths** lead up the slopes, from the village of **San Antonio** on the east side, or from **Guadelupe** on the northwest flank. From either, it's a stiff walk of at least two hours to the top; good walking shoes are essential, as is strong sun protection and lots of water. From the summit there are panoramic views north across the Jiboa valley, with San Vicente nestling distantly at the bottom, and west across to Lago de Ilopango. **Buses** to San Antonio and Guadelupe leave every hour or so until mid-afternoon from San Vicente's market.

Laguna de Apastepeque, 3km northeast of the city, is a small, well-maintained *turicentro* (daily 8am–6pm; US$0.90) set round a crater lake, with clear, clean blue waters and shady banks. The good swimming makes this an extremely popular spot among families at weekends. Nearby is the more secluded Laguna Ciega. Bus #156 to Apastepeque leaves from the bus station regularly until 6pm. Near Verapaz, 10km east of San Vicente, are the natural hot-springs **Los Infernillos**, used for years as a medicinal retreat because of their high sulphur content; buses (from the station) leave all day for the village.

Eight kilometres from San Vicente on the road to Tecoluca, the ruins of **Tehuacán** (Tues–Sun, irregular hours; US$2) lie on the eastern slopes of Chichontepec. A former Pipil settlement, the site covers an area of about three square kilometres, but unless you're a real archeology buff, there is very little to see. Excavations have uncovered the remains of a series of terraces oriented north–south, a central plaza, walls and roads and a pyramid. In the plaza are what are thought to be the foundations for the elite residences and a temple. Stone and earthenware artefacts taken from the site bear a clear resemblance to Mexican artefacts from the same era, indicating the common heritage of the Mexican Toltecs and migratory Pipils.

San Vicente to San Miguel

Beyond San Vicente, the Carretera Interamericana continues through low mountains and coffee plantations before crossing the **Río Lempa**, 30km past the city. This formidable natural boundary once afforded the Lenca inhabitants of the eastern territories some measure of protection, first against the Pipils and then against the Spanish. The Pipils called the area east of the river Popocatepetl, or "the land that smokes", presumably because of the number of active volcanoes.

The first section of the highway gives bus drivers ample opportunity to fine-tune their high-speed cornering technique before crossing the mighty Lempa on the brandnew **Puente Cuscatlán**, which replaced the old bridge bombed by the FMLN in January 1984. The remains of the original bridge lie slumped in the river, a sobering reminder of El Salvador's recent history. At the village of Mercedes Umaña, about 45km from San Vicente, a road heads south to the rough town of **Berlín**, the scene of much activity during the war and today the location of an important geo-thermal power plant. From here, hourly buses run along a road around the **Volcán Tecapa** to the more pleasant town of **SANTIAGO DE MARÍA**, which has a couple of simple hotels. Halfway between the two towns is Alegría, from where paths lead up the volcano to the sulphurous crater lake **Laguna de Alegría**, an energetic walk of about one hour. This area is predominantly coffee-growing country, with plantations lining the slopes of the rolling mountains. From Santiago, buses run up to **El Triunfo** on the Carretera Interamericana, then continue on to San Miguel; from both Berlín and Santiago there are also regular connections south to Usulután.

Beyond El Triunfo the scenery changes: coffee pastures give way to dry plains dotted with the cones of volcanoes; to the south the land falls away to pasture lands and coastal mangrove swamps. A major crop in this area is *henequén* (sisal); fields of serried ranks of the distinctive, spikey grey-green plants line the highway into the distance.

San Miguel

Some 136km from San Salvador is the bustling, hot and flat city of **SAN MIGUEL**. Sitting at the foot of the prodigious **Volcán Chaparrastique**, the city is the expanding commercial hub for the east of the country. More relaxed than San Salvador and with less claim to grandeur than Santa Ana (see p.351), the city doesn't offer much by way of tourist attractions. It is, however, a pleasant enough place to spend a couple of days resting up between bus journeys, and makes a good base for exploring the nearby Lenca archeological site of **Quelepa** and the wetland reserve of **Laguna el Jocotal**. San Miguel is also a regional transport hub, and the starting point for buses to **La Unión** and the port of **Cutuco** (bus #304), the stunning beaches of **El Cuco** (#320) and **El Tamarindo** (#385), and the bus to **Perquín** and the highland villages of the **Ruta de la Paz**. And no one should pass up the chance to eat at *La Pema*, El Salvador's most famous restaurant, just outside the city.

San Miguel really comes alive in November for the **Fiestas Novembrinas** (November Fiestas), particularly during **Carnival** on the 29th, whose music, fireworks and street dancing represent the climax to two months of celebrations for the festival of **Nuestra Señora de la Paz**, the city's patroness (see p.332). A relatively modern affair, the carnival was instituted only in 1958, but has quickly grown to be the largest carnival in Central America (or so they say). If you're around during the festival look out for people wandering around holding large plastic iguanas aloft – the locals are nicknamed *garroberos* (iguana eaters) due to their penchant for the lizards' meat.

Some history

Shortly after founding Villa San Salvador in 1528, the Spanish began to turn their minds to the territory east of Cuscatlán, motivated by the need to consolidate their gains against both the hostile indigenous population and against rival conquistador forces, based in Nicaragua under Pedrarias Davila. Exasperated by the capture of an expedition led by Diego de Rojas by these forces in 1530, Pedro de Alvarado dispatched **Luis de Moscosco** to finalize the conquest of the east. Around May 8, 1530, the day of San Miguel Arcángel, de Moscosco founded **San Miguel de Frontera**, on a site thought to have been in the vicinity of the Lenca city of Chaparrastique ("place of beautiful gardens"). Surviving a number of ferocious uprisings, the settlement thrived after **gold** was found in the area in 1537, being granted the title of city in 1574. A fire in March 1586 destroyed much of the town, however, and it was moved the few kilometres to its present location at the northern base of Volcán Chaparrastique.

Initially the least important of the Spanish cities, San Miguel soon began to grow wealthy, at first on the profits of gold and trade, and then on the coffee, cotton and *henequén* grown on the surrounding fertile land. A number of **religious order**s also brought a certain prestige to the city – by 1740, the city boasted two convents and two friaries – and in 1812 it was granted the title of "most noble and faithful city". Another nickname, sometimes still used, was "pearl of the east", because of its great wealth.

Guerrillas were active in the city and surrounding area during the 1980s and the city's barracks and electrical installations were attacked on several occasions. The city was also used as a wartime trading centre for arms and weaponry, which may explain why, even today, there remain an unusual number of gun shops across the city. Now, however, there is a less visible military presence than in other towns in the east and north, and the city's flat streets hum and rattle self-importantly with commerce and trade.

Arrival and information

All **buses** coming from San Salvador or points east and south of San Miguel arrive at the well-ordered main terminal on 6a C Ote and 8a–10a Av Nte, four blocks (or ten

SAN MIGUEL

ACCOMMODATION		RESTAURANTS	
Hotel A&Z	2	Bati Jugos Carlitos	C
Hotel del Centro	1	Oasis	D
Hotel Hispanamericano	5	Pupusería Chilita	A
Hotel San Rafael	4	Tacos Taurino	B
Hotel Terminal	3		

minutes' walk) east of the centre. The **Telecom** is on the corner of Parque Guzmán next to the Alcaldía, whilst the **post office** is on 4a Av Sur at 3a C Ote, south from the cathedral. **Banks**, including BanCo, Banco Cuscatlán and Banco Salvadoreño (which gives Visa cash advances), cluster around the west side of the Parque and along 4a C Oriente. For shopping, there's a new **Metrocentro** on the Interamericana (also called Av Roosevelt) at the edge of town, also with banks, supermarkets, restaurants and a cinema; any bus heading south down Av Roosevelt will drop you outside. There's a Super Selectos supermarket on Av Roosevelt at 11a C Pte, and a Dispensa Familiar supermarket in town on Av Gerrardo Barrios at C Chaparrastique. **Internet** access is available at the Euro Cyber Café, part of the Academía Europea at Av Roosevelt 300 Sur (US$2 per hour) and the Academia Interamericana de Tecnología on 2a Av Nte near the cathedral (US$2.50 per hour).

Accommodation

San Miguel's handful of upmarket **hotels** lie along Av Roosevelt (the Carretera Interamericana) to the west of town, about fifteen minutes' walk from the centre. Most of the other choices are around the bus terminal, inevitably a rather sleazy area. Given its daytime bustle, San Miguel is very quiet at night, with empty, ill-lit streets, and after dark it's best to take one of the abundant yellow taxis – most journeys around the city shouldn't cost more than US$2.

AROUND THE BUS TERMINAL

Hotel A & Z, 6a Av Nte between 6a and 8a C Ote. Well-located hotel with small rooms with TV, a/c and bath – OK, if a bit overpriced. ④.

Hotel del Centro, 8a C Ote 505 at 8a Av Nte (☎ & fax 661 5473). This very friendly, helpful and spotlessly clean hotel is a beacon of light in the surrounding sleaze; the comfortable rooms all have bath and TV. ③–④.

Hotel Hispanamericano, 6a Av Nte bis at 8a C Ote (☎661 1202). One of the better options around the bus terminal, although it has definitely seen better days, with large but dingy rooms, some with a/c. ②.

Hotel San Rafael, 6a C Ote 704 (☎661 4113). Friendly and secure place. The clean rooms all have bath and hammock, and there's also a communal TV area, attached café (6am–8pm) and a nice view from the roof. ②.

Hotel Terminal, 6a C Ote (☎661 1086). Opposite the bus terminal, with clean and pleasant rooms, all with bath, TV and a/c. The attached restaurant is open until late. ④.

IN TOWN AND ALONG AVENIDA ROOSEVELT

Hotel Caleta, 3a Av Sur 601 between 9a and 11a C Pte (☎661 3233). Clean and quiet hotel, popular with travelling businessmen during the week. There's a small courtyard with hammocks, and some rooms have private bath. Staff can also help arrange surf trips to secluded beaches. ②.

Hotel China House, Av Roosevelt Km 137, near the Esso garage at the entrance to town, (☎669 5029). Safe and secure hotel, set back from the main road, with its own parking. Rooms are arranged around a courtyard – all have TV and fan, and some have private bath. ③–④.

Hotel El Mandarín, Av Roosevelt Nte 407 (☎669 6969, fax 669 7912). Luxury, San Miguel style. All rooms have bath, a/c, phone and TV, and there's an attached restaurant (open until 9pm). Credit cards accepted. ⑤.

Hotel Milian, Av Roosevelt Nte at 10a C Pte (☎669 5052). Comfortable rooms with bath; the hotel also has a pool. ④.

Hotel Trópico Inn, Av Roosevelt Sur 303 (☎661 1800, fax 661 1288). Large new luxury hotel with top-quality service and comfort. All rooms have TV, a/c, bath and phone. ⑤.

The City

The heart of San Miguel is the shady **Parque David J. Guzmán**, named after the eminent nineteenth-century Migueleño biologist and member of the French Academy of Science. On the east of the Parque sits the **Cathedral**, built in the 1880s, and on the south is the Alcaldía. The city is laid out in the usual quasi-grid system, with the main avenida (Av Gerardo Barrios/Av José Simeón Cañas) and the main calle (C Chaparrastique/C Sirama) intersecting at **Parque Gerardo Barrios** two blocks southwest of Parque Guzmán. Parque Barrios itself is mostly overrun by an extensive market, a sprawling affair in whose narrow warrens upfront traders encourage you to buy all manner of food, clothes and other goods.

Just south of the cathedral is the **Antiguo Teatro Nacional**, a Renaissance-style building completed in 1909; performances occasionally take place here, particularly during fiesta time. Seven blocks west of the centre, the appealing **Iglesia Capilla Medalla Milagrosa**, set in pretty gardens, was built by the French nuns who used to work in the hospital that once stood next door.

Restaurants and cafés

There are plenty of **places to eat and drink** in San Miguel. By day, there are a number of reasonable lunch places in town, especially in the area around the bus terminal, where cheap comedores and pastry cafés offer quick and simple meals. By night the focus shifts to the comedores and fast-food chains (including *Wendy's* and *Pizza Hut*) along Av Roosevelt between 7a and 11a C Pte.

Bati Jugos Carlitos, 1a Av Nte and 4 C Pte. Small café serving excellent snacks, lunches and coffee, plus extremely good papaya *licuados*.

Comedor Esmeralda, 8a Av Nte between 4a and 6a C Ote. Good, basic breakfasts and *comidas a la vista*. Closed Sun.

El País, Av Roosevelt Sur opposite the *Hotel Trópico Inn*. Popular and reasonably priced Mexican food with outdoor tables.

Gran Tejano, 4a C Ote, just up from the Parque. Large and reasonably priced steaks and meat dishes.

La Barrita, 4a C Ote, two blocks up from the cathedral. Well-prepared and reasonably priced meat and chicken dishes in an informal setting. Closed Sun.

La Pema, 5km from town on the road to Usulután (☎667 6055). El Salvador's most renowned restaurant. It's not cheap, but the huge servings of *mariscada*, a creamy soup with every conceivable type of seafood, and the bowls of fruit salad served as an accompaniment will mean you won't feel like eating again for a while. Come here and treat yourself. Daily 11am–5pm.

Oasis, 4a C Ote, opposite *Pizza Hut*. Possibly the best juices and *licuados* in the country; huge glasses go for around US$1.50. Closed Sun.

Pupusería Chilita, 8a C Ote at 6a Av Nte. A barn of a neighbourhood *pupusería*, particularly popular at the weekends. Three or four *pupusas* and a fruit juice make an adequate meal. Open until around 9.30pm.

Pupusería El Paraiso, on Parque Guzmán. Well-prepared *pupusas* and *comida a la vista*.

Tacos Taurino, Av José Simeon Cañas at 4a C Pte. Lunch kiosk, with tables set out on the pavement, serving hot lunches and tacos. Very popular with local office workers.

Around San Miguel: Quelepa and Laguna El Jocotal

A short distance northwest of San Miguel, about 1.5km from the highway, is the pretty little village of **QUELEPA**, beyond which lie the **Ruinas de Quelepa**. Though not much of this predominantly Lenca site has so far been excavated, and there's little actually to see, the walk there and around makes for an enjoyable half day or so.

Quelepa was a flourishing city which reached its peak between 625 and 1000 AD, from which period date its I-shaped pelota court and small pyramids. A jaguar-head altar, fragments of ceramics and other artefacts – now in storage in San Salvador – indicate that the inhabitants had trade links with cultures to the west, since most of the finds are in the style of – or possibly even from – Maya sites in Honduras and Mexico. The absence of Toltec-influenced artefacts also suggests that Quelepa was exclusively Lenca, rather than Pipil. Around forty structures have been identified at the site, which was abandoned around 1000 AD, amongst them a series of tombs. A paved road – parts of which still exist – through the site would have led to the summit of the 300m Cerro Grande to the south. The friendly **Casa de Cultura** in Quelepa displays a collection of artefacts from the site – fragments of household utensils, ceramic figures and small ceremonial heads.

The **site** itself lies about 2km northeast of the village of Quelepa, between the Río San Estéban and a low range of hills. Follow 4a C Ote out of the centre of San Miguel and down to the river, cross over and ask for directions at the white house on the other side. At first glance there appears to be nothing but fields of *henequén* and the odd herd of cows, but the small mounds in the fields are the remains of the pyramids, and close searching may bring to light the remnants of some walls. A nice way to return, if you don't mind getting your feet wet, is by wading up the shallow river itself. **Bus** #90 leaves Parque Guzmán in San Miguel frequently, dropping you off on the highway, fifteen minutes' walk from the village. Bus #90G, which runs directly to the village, leaves from the same place, but less often.

Laguna El Jocotal, a small wetlands reserve supported by the World Wildlife Fund, lies around 18km southwest of San Miguel, just off Highway CA-2 on the road to Usulután. This peaceful, clear stretch of water, surrounded by reed beds with low hills in the distance, is the nesting and feeding ground for numerous species of birds, including snow herons and the blue-winged zarzeta, which can be seen year-round. The best time to visit is in the early morning, when a helpful warden is usually around the small dock to explain the conservation work, and you can rent a boat to explore the waterways. **Buses** running between San Miguel and Usulután pass the access road to the reserve, from where it's a walk of about ten minutes to the lake shore.

North along the Ruta de la Paz to Perquín

North of San Miguel, the beautiful and sparsely populated mountainous department of Morazán experienced some of the war's worst atrocities, with massacres and bombing raids a regular occurrence. Much of the region is now encompassed by the so-called **Ruta de la Paz**, part of a major project to rebuild much-needed housing, schools and infrastructure, as well as to develop tourism in the region – the "Ruta" encompasses the area as a whole, rather than referring to any specific route though it. Three **buses** leave San Miguel daily for Perquín (3hr), Corinto, San Francisco Gotera (generally referred to simply as Gotera) and the small towns and villages between. Alternatively, take one of the more frequent buses to Gotera, from where a well-organized cooperative runs regular covered pick-ups (5am–4.30pm) to and from the Parque Central in Perquín for the same price as the bus fare.

North of San Miguel, Highway CA-7 runs 25km to **SAN FRANCISCO GOTERA** (usually called simply "Gotera"), an edgy and unfriendly place, although set in a beautiful location. There's no real reason to stay here, but if you do get stuck, the *San Francisco* (①–③), on Av Morazán at 3a C Pte, just up from the market, is the nicest place in town. Two paved roads head north from Gotera. One takes you to the small village of **CACAOPERA**, home to a colonial church dating back to 1660, with walls up to 5m thick. The **Museo Guinakirika** ("community" in the local Ulúa language) has fine exhibits of indigenous tradition and culture, as well as photos and arts and crafts.

There's a friendly little comedor across the street, good for breakfasts and lunch. From Cacaopera, a road goes northeast to the town of **CORINTO**, an important commercial hub whose main claim to fame is the **Grutas del Espíritu Santo**, a series of caves bearing pre-Colombian wall art said to date back some 10,000 years. The caves are located about 15 minutes north of the village on foot through some pleasant scenery. Corinto can be reached on a day-trip from San Miguel (bus #327 from the main terminal).

The second road north from Gotera begins to climb into the mountains, with *henequén* fields and cattle pasture giving way to pine forests and superb mountain vistas, while the air turns pleasantly fresh. About 10km north of Gotera, the road passes the fringes of **CIUDAD SEGUNDO MONTES**, a collection of new villages housing repatriated refugees and named after one of the six Jesuit priests assassinated by the military in 1989. Sympathetic visitors are welcome to tour the communities and talk with the residents, and staff at the reception office (closed Sun) in the main village – **San Luis**, on the highway – can explain local community projects. **Accommodation** is available in dormitory rooms in San Luis (①).

From Arambala you can also hire a pick-up to take you to **EL MOZOTE**, scene of the country's most atrocious wartime massacre. In the week of 11–18 December, 1981, the elite, US-trained, Atlacatl army battalion attacked the village, killing some 1000 people, whose bodies were subsequently burnt or buried in mass graves. The few eye-witness testimonies to the events were ignored for years, and the bodies of the victims were exhumed in 1992. Today, what remains of El Mozote is virtually a ghost town, although families are slowly moving back. A moving monument to the victims features an iron sculpture of the silhouette of a family and boards carrying the names of those killed.

Perquín and the Museo de la Revolución Salvadoreña

After passing through Arambala, the road begins its final climb to **PERQUÍN**, a small and – given its history – surprisingly friendly mountain town, set in the middle of glorious walking countryside. During the war the town was the FMLN headquarters, from where they broadcast to the nation on the (literally) underground station Radio Venceremos ("We Will Triumph"). Attempts by the army to dislodge the guerrillas mostly failed, leaving the town badly damaged and deserted. Today, the "town that refused to die" has repaired most of its buildings, although the scars of war are evident everywhere, and nearly everyone has a horrendous tale to tell. Even so, there is today a sense of optimism and a determination to rebuild the community.

Perquín's main draw is the moving **Museo de la Revolución Salvadoreña** (Tues–Sun 9am–4pm; US$1.25), set up by ex-guerrillas in the wake of the 1992 peace accords. The curators travelled throughout the country collecting photographs and personal effects of those who died during the fighting, and notices request that visitors donate more in order to expand the collection. There is a succinct summary (in Spanish) of the process leading to the beginning of the armed struggle; displays of arms and weaponry confiscated from the army and weapons – including missile launchers, bombs, guns and grenades – disabled after the signing of the peace accords; and examples of international propaganda aimed at bringing the events in El Salvador to the world's attention. Outside is the **bomb crater** left by a 1981 explosion and a mock-up of a guerrilla camp – the crude bent-wood and palm-leaf constructions offered little shelter but could be erected and dismantled quickly. Behind the museum you can see the remains of the helicopter that was carrying Domingo Monterrosa (architect of the El Mozote massacre; see opposite) when it was shot down by the FMLN in 1984. The most moving exhibits are perhaps the anonymous transcripts of witnesses of the massacre, and drawings by refugee schoolchildren, depicting events as they saw them.

A separate room contains the transmitting equipment and studio used by **Radio Venceremos**. Using subterranean sound rooms to evade detection, the station broadcast every afternoon throughout the war on a number of frequencies, transmitting the guerrillas' view of events, as well as interviews and music. After the peace accords, the station received an FM licence in August 1992, and is now based in San Salvador – ironically, in offices rented from a member of the ARENA Party. Now a commercial, mainstream station playing a mixture of Latin American sounds and US rock, Venceremos has been heavily criticized by some of its former listeners for accepting all manner of commercials, as well as electoral advertisements from all political parties.

If you decide **to stay** in Perquín, the friendly *El Gigante* (①), five minutes' walk from town back down the road to Gotera, has clean, communal rooms with shared bath, and a small comedor. The more upmarket *Hotel Perquín Lenca* (☎680 4046, fax 680 4080, *perkin@netcomsa.com*; ④), 1.5km south of town, has solid wooden cabins with bath, hot water and hammocks, and an excellent restaurant and bar. Breakfast is included, and advance booking is recommended. Other **places to eat** in town are the small comedores, *Blanca* and *Las Palmeras*, both just off the main square, and the friendly *La Muralla* on the Parque.

East to the Honduran border

East of San Francisco Gotera, a road continues through hot, low hills to **SANTA ROSA DE LIMA**, a messy but thriving place, with a large daily market, cheese industry and a well-maintained church. There's not much to do here, but it makes a useful stopover if you're coming from Honduras. The best of the few **places to stay** is *Hotel El Recreo* (☎664 2126; ②) on 4a Av Nte between C Giron and 1a C Ote, which has clean rooms with bath. The basic but adequate *El Tejano* (☎664 2459; ①), on C Giron between 6a and 8a Av Nte, is slightly cheaper, but has a 7am checkout. For **eating**, the very clean *Comedor Chayito*, at the corner of C Giron and 1a C Ote, does a good cheap *comida a la vista* (7am–6pm), while for something with a bit more splash try *Taquería Tex Mex* on Av G Arias between 1a and 3a C Ote. **Banks**, including Banco Cuscatlán, are clustered around the plaza at the centre of town. The **Telecom** is on C Giron, just down from the church.

Beyond Santa Rosa, the road continues for a further 10km before connecting with the Carretera Interamericana to run to the border at **EL AMATILLO**. Formed by the Río Goascoran, the border crossing is easy but busy, used by international buses and teeming with moneychangers and opportunistic beggars. On the Honduran side, buses leave regularly until late afternoon for Tegucigalpa and Jícaro Galán, 42km from the border; there are also direct buses to Choluteca, for onward connection to the Nicaraguan border along the Carretera Interamericana. A bank on the Salvadorean side changes dollars, colones and lempiras, though the rates are slightly better with the moneychangers. There is a US$2 fee to enter Honduras.

travel details

BUSES

San Miguel to: El Amatillo (#330, every 10min until 5.30pm; 1hr 30min); La Unión (#324, every 10min until 6pm; 1hr); Perquín (#332A, 3 daily; 3hr); San Francisco Gotera (#328, every 10min until 5.30pm; 1hr); Santa Rosa de Lima (#330, every 10min until 5.30pm; 1hr 30min); San Salvador (ordinary service, #301, every 15min until 6pm; 4hr; "directo" service hourly; 3hr); Usulután (#373, every 10min until 5.30pm; 1hr).

San Salvador (Terminal de Oriente) to: San Miguel (ordinary service, #301, every 15min until 6pm; 4hr; "directo" service hourly; 3hr); Santa Rosa de Lima (ordinary service #306, every 30min until 2.30pm; 5hr; "directo" service 4 daily; 3hr); San Vicente (#116, every 10min until 6pm; 1hr 30min).

San Vicente to: San Salvador (#116, every 10min until 6pm; 1hr 30min); Usulután (#417, 5 daily until early afternoon; 2hr).

CHAPTER 15

THE PACIFIC COAST

l Salvador's **Pacific coast** stretching from the Río Paz in the west to the Río Goascorán in the east, is a 300-kilometre sweep of sandy tropical beaches, dramatic cliffs, mangrove swamps and romantic islands. The **Carretera Littoral**, which runs along the coast, links the towns and villages, and public transport runs regularly to many places, but it's worth renting a car for a few days to reach some of the more remote and beautiful beaches. While there are clusters of **tourist facilities** here and there, don't expect the amenities of international resorts. Instead, the beauty of this part of the country lies in relaxing on clean, wide beaches or spending time in the relatively untouched fishing villages of the coast. Unfortunately this region was very badly affected by the January 2001 **earthquake**, whose epicentre was located about 35km out to sea. The Carretera Littoral was badly damaged in places, as were many of the coastal towns, while many villages between La Libertad and Santa Tecla were obliterated. Though much rebuilding work should have been completed by the time this book is published, evidence of the quake will take a few years to clear away.

The most accessible stretch of coast near San Salvador – and thus very crowded at weekends – is the small fishing town of **La Libertad**, set among some of Central America's best surfing beaches. Head west up the coast, towards Guatemala, and there are more untouched beaches, including **Los Cóbanos** and **Barra de Santiago**, and the tranquil forest reserve at **Bosque El Imposible**. To the east, the small city of **Zacatecoluca** is the main jumping-off point for the Salvadorean playground of the **Costa del Sol**, home to the coast's most upmarket resort hotels. A little further down the coast are the green waterways and islands of the mangrove swamps of the **Bahía de Jiquilísco** and what many consider to be the finest beach in the country, **Playa El Espino**. Further east are the fine beaches of **El Cuco** and **El Tamarindo**, both busy at weekends but delightfully deserted during the week. In the extreme east of the country is the faded port town of **La Unión**, from where you can catch irregular lanchas to the tranquil **islands** of the Golfo de Fonseca.

La Libertad

Just 34km south of San Salvador, **LA LIBERTAD** (in full, Puerto La Libertad, but often reduced by bus conductors to simply "El Puerto"), once a major port and still an important fishing town, has – more by luck than judgement – re-invented itself as a tourist spot, neatly set between the beaches of the Costa del Bálsamo in the west and the Costa del Sol in the east. It's a popular place, particularly crowded at the weekends, when the hordes from the capital pour in to eat, drink and relax by the sea. La Libertad also has El Salvador's highest concentration of gringos, including a year-round community of international surfing bums who spend their time hanging out and waiting for the right break.

For an explanation of **accommodation price codes**, see p.287.

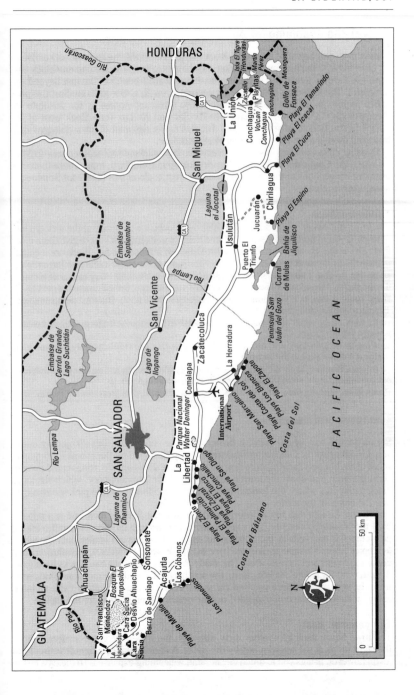

Arrival and accommodation

Buses from San Salvador (bus #201 from Parque Bolívar is the most direct) arrive in La Libertad at C Barrios, by the market, two blocks in from the sea and one block east from the Parque. Returning to the capital, buses leave from 2a C Ote just beyond the *turicentro*. The **Telecom** (with Internet access) is on 2a C Ote at 2a Av Sur; the **post office** is just round the corner. There's also **Internet** access at the Instituto de Computación, C El Calvario between 1a Av Sur and Av Luz (one block west of the Parque). The Banco Salvadoreño on C Barrios at the east end of town **changes dollars**, and there's a De Todo **supermarket** next door.

Heading east, town bus #540 runs every two hours inland to **Zacatecoluca** (p.342). To reach the **Costa del Sol**, take a bus or pick-up to Comalapa, from where there are frequent connections to the beaches. Heading west, a direct bus (#287) for **Sonsonate** leaves daily at 6am.

Accommodation

The more upmarket hotels, some with their own pools, are generally at the western end of town. If you're hoping to get a room on a holiday weekend, it's best to give them a call first. The better cheap alternatives are listed below; if these are full, there are a couple of basic hotels around 2a C Ote and 1a Av Nte. Some of the restaurants also have rooms.

Hacienda de Don Lito, 5a Av Sur at the end of 4a C Pte (☎335 3166). Very comfortable rooms, though slightly over-priced. All have bath, and there's a restaurant, bar and swimming pool. ⑤.

Hotel Amor y Paz, 4a C Pte between 1a and 3a Av Sur (☎335 3187). Basic but adequate rooms, although none has bath. ③.

Hotel Rick, 5a Av Sur 30, at the end of 4a C Pte (☎335 3033). Friendly, if a bit grubby, and popular amongst visiting surfers. ②.

La Posada de Don Lito, next door to the *Hacienda de Don Lito* (☎335 3166). Same owners and similar accommodation to the hacienda. ⑤.

La Posada Familiar, 3a Av Sur at 4a C Pte (☎335 3252). Very friendly and popular place with basic but good-value rooms, some with bath. A small comedor serves meals. ②.

Punta Roca, opposite *Hotel Rick*. Spacious a/c rooms with bath, plus great views of the bay. ⑥.

The town and beaches

Set on a small bay, whose curve is bisected by the main wharf (*muelle*) jutting out to sea, **La Libertad** is a shabby coastal town, badly damaged by the recent earthquake. Most of the old port buildings are now no more than shells and the roads could do with serious repair. Just about the town's only "sight" is the "car cemetery" which stretches along 1a Av Sur, where the twisted caracasses of accident-damaged pick-ups and cars line the edges of the street.

Even so, La Libertad has an energy and atmosphere all of its own, and is a popular base for the nearby beaches. The main action occurs around the wharf when the fishing fleet comes in and sells its catch; when not in use, the boats are hauled onto the wharf for repair. There's a small **turicentro** here (daily 7am–5pm; US$0.90), with showers and changing rooms and a picnic area. The shady Parque Central sits two blocks back from the seafront; **2a C Ote**, running along the southern edge of the Parque, one block back from the seafront, is where you find the police station, Casa de Cultura (with an interesting, if limited, collection of pickled marine creatures) and **buses** for the capital.

The beaches: east

The town beach itself gets rather dirty, although the waves are good; surfers wait for the right break at the western end by the rocks. A short distance either direction from town, however, brings you to much cleaner and welcoming expanses. To the east lie the small and crowded beaches of Flores and Obispo and, 5km from La Libertad, the beautiful **Playa San Diego**, with its clean, white and seemingly endless stretch of sand, deserted during the week except for a few fisherman. A turtle-nestling reserve is also being set up here to help protect this endangered species. Bus #80 runs from 4a Av Sur in La Libertad to Playa San Diego every 30min, following a dirt road which turns off the Carretera Littoral a couple of kilometres from town to run parallel along the length of the beach. Views to the sea are blocked by the ranks of private homes behind locked gates, but if you get off the bus outside the *Paradiso* restaurant, there's a path just to the left of the new *Hotel Villa del Pacífico* that leads down to the sand. This is also the place to look for **accommodation**: the *Paradiso* restaurant has small, basic rooms (②), while the *Hotel Villa del Pacífico* (⑤) has a/c rooms with bath, plus restaurant and pool set in manicured gardens right by the beach.

A little further along the Carretera Littoral, past the turn-off for the beach, is the entrance to **Parque Nacional Walter Deninger**, an extensive stretch of dry forest, supporting a range of flora and fauna. Over half the park was destroyed by fire in 1986, since when ISTU have been working on reforesting the area and encouraging the return of wildlife – check with their office in San Salvador (see p.286) about the park's opening hours.

The beaches: west

West of La Libertad, the Carretera Littoral winds up and around the thickly wooded hills to palm-fringed and generally uncrowded **Playa Conchalío**, though it gets popular at weekends (there have also been reports of robberies here, especially after dark, so be careful). *Hotel Los Arcos* (☎335 3490; ④) sits on the highway by the road leading down to the beach, with a restaurant that serves all meals. Further along the main road is the intriguing *Hotel Santa Fe* (☎335 3672; ③–④), whose owner designed and named the hotel in honour of the architecture of his favourite US city – look out for the guitar-shaped swimming pool. All rooms have private bath, and some also have air-conditioning.

Continuing west, at kilometre 42, is **Playa El Tunco**, named after the rock formation in the sea that, before it was eroded, resembled a pig. El Tunco's crowning glory is the *Restaurante La Bocana*, which serves huge seafood platters and ice-cold beer and is extremely popular at weekends. Just behind the beach are a couple of basic **places to stay**: *Tortuga Surf Lodge*, offering simple rooms in a pleasant setting (③), and *El Tubo Surf Lodge*, with small and very basic rooms around a courtyard (②).

Playa El Tunco merges with **Playa El Zunzal** (or Sunzal), a very popular surfing beach somewhat spoiled by the carelessly cemented frontage of the Club Salvadoreña. At the west end of the beach is the new *Café El Sunzal*, built into the rocks overlooking the beach, which serves excellent but pricey seafood and Salvadorean cuisine and is frequented by San Salvador's smart set. A few kilometres further on, **Playa El Palmarcito** is overlooked by the relaxing and comfortable *Atami Beach Club Resort* (you'll need to reserve ahead in San Salvador at 69a Av Sur 164, Col Escalón, ☎223 9000; ⑤). At kilometre 53, the small and uncrowded **Playa El Zonte** is a favourite among surfers; the new *Horizonte Surf Camp* just back from the beach has clean cabins (②), a kitchen, hammock and camping facilities; there's also a small pool and nice gardens.

From La Libertad, local **buses** #80A and #80B run past Playa Conchalío to El Tunco and Zunzal (every 30min until 5.30pm); while bus #192 leaves every two hours for Playa El Palmarcito.

Eating and drinking

Eating in La Libertad is not a problem, unless you don't like fish (although there are a couple of decent *pupuserías*). The Salvadorean speciality **mariscada**, a creamy seafood soup, is available everywhere and should be tried at least once. The more expensive **restaurants** are gathered at the western end of town. *El Viejo Alta Mar*, *Sandra* and *Karla*, all on 4a C Pte between 1a and 3a Av Sur, are all reasonably priced and serve the catch of the day along with meat and chicken standards, as well as offering glimpses of the beach from the dining tables. The slightly more expensive US-owned *Punta Roca*, towards the far end of 4a C Pte, has a great sea view and a range of well-prepared fish and meat dishes; the restaurant at *Posada de Don Lito* attracts a slightly more formal crowd. The **beach comedores** all serve fish, but at much lower prices. For huge juices and basic meals try *Comedor Paty* in town on 2a Av Sur just down from the Parque.

West to Guatemala

The section of coast west of Playa El Zonte on the way to Guatemala contains a number of good beaches, best reached by car. The hub of the region is the small, hot city of **SONSONATE**, another place severely hit by the 2001 earthquake. Set in tobacco and cattle-ranching country, Sonsonate is a bustling, commercial place, and though it's not on the coast itself, you'll invariably pass through it at some point. There's little of tourist interest here, except during festival time – chiefly the annual **Verbena de Sonsonate**, held at the end of January, when there's a host of music and drama performances, and the more colourful **Semana Santa**, when crowds flock to join the street processions and intricate pictures are drawn in coloured sawdust on the pavements. Sonsonate is also the transport hub for connections to the western beaches and the mountain towns of Juayúa and Apeneca.

Buses arrive at the main terminal on C 15 de Septiembre, seven blocks east of the centre and fifteen minutes' walk from the Parque Central. Of the limited **accommodation** in the centre, the *Hotel Orbe* (☎451 1416; ②) on Av Fray Mucci Sur and 4a C Ote, two blocks east of the Parque, has reasonably clean rooms with private bath. *Hotel Modelo* (☎451 1679; ③), on the corner of C Obispo Marroquín and 10a Av Sur (on the main street between the bus terminal and Parque), has nice clean rooms with TV, a/c and bath – it's noisy by day but quiet at night. The best option is the comfortable *Hotel Agape* (☎451 1456; ④), set in beautiful gardens on the outskirts of town, 2km along the road to San Salvador – take bus #53A or #53J from the crossroads by the bus terminal. There are a number of **restaurants** along this road, while in the centre a row of comedores overlooks the river by the attractive white bridge, on 4a Av Nte.

Los Cóbanos and Los Remedios

Los Cóbanos, 25km due south of Sonsonate, is a favourite beach for Salvadorean holiday-makers, and somewhat crowded at the weekends. Although rather rocky, this pretty, gently curved beach makes a nice contrast to the palm-fringed expanses further down the coast. Walk round the headland at the west end of the small bay and you come to the quieter beach of **Los Remedios**. A couple of places have **cabañas** for rent: *Solimar* (②) is the nicest (although closed during the week), while the *Mar y Plata* (②), set slightly back from the seafront, is slightly run-down. A number of small shacks serve fresh fish and other meals. **Bus** #257 leaves Sonsonate every hour for Los Cóbanos until early evening, and there are also occasional direct buses from San Salvador; the last bus leaves the beach at 5pm.

Acajutla to Cara Sucia

Beyond Sonsonate, the major town on the coast is the port of **ACAJUTLA**, the site of Pedro de Alvarado's first encounter with the Pipils in 1524, but today a hot, decaying and distinctly edgy place; it's better to stay at Sonsonate. Acajutla lies 4km from the Carretera Littoral, which from here runs the flat 46km or so to the Guatemalan border at La Hachadura, a beautiful journey with the slopes of the Cordillera Apaneca rising to the north and rolling pasturelands to the south. After 10km, the highway passes the access road to **Playa de Metalío**, a quiet, palm-fringed beach, whose beauty is somewhat marred by the refuse washed up from Acajutla. More remote, **Playa Barra de Santiago** lies 15km further up the coast, across a small estuary by the fishing village of Barra de Santiago. A rough road leads the 7km from the highway to the estuary; one bus a day in the morning runs along it from Sonsonate. At the estuary, bargain with a fishing boat to take you across to the village and the beach.

A further 10km west, the dusty village of **Cara Sucia** lines the highway just east of the Río Cara Sucia. The nearby archeological site of Cara Sucia was a Maya settlement made wealthy by trade in salt. Initial excavations uncovered a number of structures including two pelota courts, and though there's not much to see today, it's a peaceful place for a picnic. There is no public transport to the site; from the crossroads 50m past the bridge at the end of the village take the road leading left, opposite *Comedor Nohemy*, for about twenty minutes until you reach the Cooperativa Cara Sucia buildings on the right; ask the guard to let you through and follow the track round the buildings, taking the right-hand fork to the ruins.

From Cara Sucia the highway continues the last few kilometres to **La Hachadura**, a busy border crossing used by the international buses heading for Mexico. There's a small hospedaje on the Guatemalan side, and buses to Esquintla and Guatemala City.

Bosque El Imposible

The road leading right at the crossroads in Cara Sucia provides access to one of El Salvador's greatest hidden glories, the forest reserve of **Bosque El Imposible**, so called because of the difficulty of traversing the mountain tracks to get into it. Covering over 31 square kilometres and rising through three climatic zones across the Cordillera de Apaneca, the reserve contains more than 400 species of trees and 1600 species of plants, some of which are unique to the area. Bird-watchers may glimpse some of the more than 300 species, including the emerald toucan, trogons, hummingbirds and eagles, while the park provides a secure habitat for a diverse range of animals, including anteaters, the white-tailed deer, ocelots and the tigrillo, plus over 500 different species of butterfly.

Getting to El Imposible without a private vehicle is time-consuming; the operators listed on p.314 all run tours here. It costs US$6 to enter the reserve, which is managed by a non-governmental organization, SalvaNatura (77a Av Nte 304, Col Escalón, San Salvador; ☎263 1111, fax 263 3516, *salvanatura@saltel.net*) – you'll need to apply for written permission to visit at least one week in advance, and pay at the same time. When you reach the park the only money you need to pay is if you wish to hire a guide (they hang around the entrance; be prepared to bargain). SalvaNatura also have a small office in the nearby village of **San Francisco Menéndez**, the main point of access for the reserve, reached by a turning off the main highway 4km past Cara Sucia. Some pick-ups run from Cara Sucia to the entrance, but be prepared to leave early and also to haggle. There's another entrance to the park at the Desvio Ahuachapío turn-off from the Carretera Littoral, halfway between the Sonsonate–Acajutla road and Cara Sucia, and about 13.5km from the park itself. This sector of the reserve is called **San Benito**, and there's a small community, **Caserío San Miguelito**, actually inside the park, with shops selling handicrafts and a comedor. As yet, there is no formal provision for staying in the reserve – though SalvaNatura are planning to build a hotel in a nearby village; contact them for details.

Zacatecoluca and the Costa del Sol

Heading east from La Libertad, the Carretera Littoral swings inland, running north of the international airport to the small city of **ZACATECOLUCA**, with its impressive whitewashed Catedral Santa Lucía, in front of which stands a monument to the city's most famous son, José Simeon Cañas – if a priest is around he may let you climb the tower to see the marvellous views over the town and its volcano. Zacatecoluca was a pre-Columbian Nonualco city with about two thousand inhabitants when the Spanish first arrived. No records of conflict exist and in 1594, Don Juan de Pineda reported to the Spanish court that "there are three pueblos next to each other that are good, called San Juan and Santiago Nonualco and Zacatecoluca. In Zacatecoluca there is a corregidor who administers in the name of your majesty." In 1833, however, the indigenous revolt led by Anastasio Aquino from the nearby village of Santiago Nonualco posed a serious threat to the newly independent country. Supported both by local tribes and poor mestizos, and meeting with little effective resistance, Aquino at one point looked capable of marching on and taking the capital. Instead, his army contented itself with sacking Zacatecoluca before moving on to San Vicente, giving government forces time to regroup.

Apart from its big daily market, there's little of interest in Zacatecoluca except its proximity to the nearby beaches, but it's a pleasant enough place, with a couple of acceptable **hotels**. Just across the street from the bus terminal, *Hotel Primavera* (☎334 1346; ②), at Av Juan Viacortez 23, has tidy rooms with bath and hammock, while round the corner *Hotel Brolyn* (☎333 8410; ②), at 7a C Ote 25, is similar but slightly more expensive. **Buses** run every fifteen minutes from San Salvador's Terminal del Sur to Zacatecoluca, while bus #193 from Zacatecoluca runs all the way along the Costa del Sol.

The Costa del Sol

Due south of Zacatecoluca lies El Salvador's premier beach playground, the **Costa del Sol**, a fifteen-kilometre strip of palm-fringed beaches running between the ocean and the Jaltepeque Estuary. The clean expanses of sand here are good for swimming, and the place seethes at the weekends as the crowds pour in. From the highway, an access road runs the 20km south to the beginning of the beach strip and east along its length to La Puntilla at the end. Another road branches off 8km before the coast to the fishing town of **La Herradura**, from where boats can be rented to explore the estuary's mangrove swamps and small islands, some of them inhabited. **Buses** run down the Costa del Sol from Zacatecoluca, taking around an hour and a half to reach La Puntilla; there are also direct buses from the Terminal del Sur in San Salvador.

Behind the first beach along the strip, **Playa San Marcelino**, the rather plush *Costa del Sol Club* has swimming pools, sports facilities and a restaurant – try negotiating at the gate to be allowed in for the day. Some 3km east is **Playa Costa del Sol**, where a *turicentro* (daily 7am–6pm; US$0.90) rents cabañas and has a couple of small restaurants. There's also some upmarket accommodation here in the form of the *Izalco Cabaña Club* (☎223 6764; ⑥) and the *Tesoro Beach Hotel* (☎334 0600; ⑨) at the far end of the beach. A few kilometres further on, at kilometre 66, is **Playa Los Blancos** and the *Mini Hotel y Restaurante Mila* (③–④), the area's most reasonably priced hotel, with small but comfortable rooms and a swimming pool. At the far eastern tip of the Costa del Sol, **La Puntilla** has a number of comedores and cheap lodgings – you'll be approached by owners as soon as you step off the bus. Lancha owners run trips from here across to the Isla de Tasajera, around the mangrove swamps of the Estero de Jaltepeque and up the Río Lempa.

Bahía de Jiquilísco

East of Zacatecoluca, the Carretera Littoral crosses the Río Lempa at San Marcos Lempa before running through lush, green coffee country to the city of **USULUTÁN**, on the southern slopes of the volcano of the same name. Usulután is of little interest to tourists except as a transit point; *La Posada del Viajero* (☎662 0217; ②) close to the centre on 6a C Ote between 2a and 4a Av Nte, is a clean and friendly **place to stay**. The bus station is about six blocks east of the centre, on C Grimaldi, which leads down to the Parque Central. The **Telecom** and a number of banks are clustered around the square, and there's Internet access at Tipo's Cyber Café on 6a Av Nte and 4a C Pte.

About 20km southwest of Usulután, down a road lined with sugarcane fields, is **PUERTO EL TRIUNFO**, a small village and port set on the shore of Bahía de Jiquilísco, separated from the ocean by the San Juan del Gozo peninsula – this area was badly hit by Hurricane Mitch in 1998 and much rebuilding work continues. Formed by coastal mangrove swamps, the beautiful bay features 12km of waterways and a number of islands. Passenger boats cross to hamlets on the islands and to the village of Corral de Mulas on the peninsula; if you miss these – they tend to leave early in the day – boats can be rented for a return crossing or for a few hours exploring the waterways around the smaller islands of Tortuga, Madre Sal, Los Cedros and San Sebastian. A long, fine sandy beach forms the ocean-side of the peninsula; a road runs its length, branching off the highway at San Marcos Lempa. You can **camp** on the islands and the peninsula, and there is a small, basic and apparently nameless **hotel** (①) in Puerto El Triunfo, with a restaurant serving huge fish dishes.

At the far eastern end of the Bahía de Jiquilísco is one of El Salvador's remotest – and finest – beaches, **Playa El Espino**, whose wide expanse of soft sand backed by coconut palms is virtually deserted, even at weekends (though rumours persist that much of the land around the beach has been purchased by developers and will soon be covered in resort hotels). There's a slow and infrequent **bus** from Usulután (2–3 daily; 1hr 30min–2hr) to the beach, though, obviously, things are much easier with your own transport.

Eastern beaches

Thirty kilometres beyond Usulután the Carretera Littoral turns south; you can connect with buses north to San Miguel (see p.329) at the junction here. After passing the small, unexciting town of Chirilagua, 14km away, a side road winds over the low mountains to another popular and beautiful beach, **Playa El Cuco**, which, once you're past the dusty and rather unfriendly little village, stretches endlessly into the distance, empty of tourists during the week. For **accommodation**, *Hospedaje Vasquez*, *Hospedaje Palmeras* and the unfriendly *Hotel Colato* in the village all offer windowless, concrete boxes for which you should pay no more than US$4–5. A better option is to walk out of the village, parallel with the beach, where you will find *Piñar de Mar*, a friendly new hotel offering small but clean rooms with bath (③); there's no sign but look for the double blue gates and a notice saying "se alquilen cuartos". A little further along is the *Hotel Leones Marinos* (⑤–⑥), an old hotel, currently being renovated and extended, which offers a range of comfortable and good-value rooms, plus a café and restaurant. Further down the beach is the luxurious *Trópiclub* (☎661 1800, fax 661 1399; ⑤), with its own restaurant and pool. Playa El Cuco is accessible by direct bus (1hr 30min) from the terminal in San Miguel. The ride is one of the finest bus journeys in the country, winding up and over the mountains, with spectacular views of the valleys and the ineffable Volcán San Miguel (sit on the right side of the bus on the way to El Cuco).

Beyond Chirilagua, the highway runs parallel the coastline, passing through the tidy little town of Intipuca before turning north again, around the western slopes of Volcán Conchagua and up to La Unión. Some 5km past Intipuca, a side road gives access to **Playa El Icacal**, 7km south. An untouched expanse of wide soft sand fringed by coconut palms, the beach has good swimming and is perfect for a day doing nothing. There's no accommodation, although a few comedores serve meals. Buses from La Unión (#383) and San Miguel (#385) continue on to **Playa Negras**, **Playa Las Tunas** and **Playa El Tamarindo** – all of them stunning, with wide beaches and good swimming. The *Tropi Tamarindo* (☎649 5082; ⑦) at El Tamarindo and the *Torola Cabaña Club* (☎604 4516, fax 264 1170; ⑦) at *Las Tunas* are both expensive but have first-rate facilities. The *Hotel Playa Las Negras* (⑤) is slightly cheaper, and is fronted by a sublime expanse of sand – although currently closed, it's expected to re-open under new ownership during 2001.

La Unión and around

The port town of **LA UNIÓN** sits in a stunning location on a bay on the edge of the Golfo de Fonseca. Faded since its glory days as El Salvador's largest commercial port, La Unión's streets of low white houses crumble a little further every day in the ferocious heat. Though the atmosphere around the town is not pleasant, La Unión is the jumping-off point for the islands of the **Golfo de Fonseca**. The port of **Cutuco** is shortly to undergo a redevelopment plan that will turn it into the largest Pacific port in Central America. There are a few reasonable places to stay and eat in town, and the Honduran border crossing at El Amatillo (see p.390) is an easy journey away.

Practicalities

The **bus terminal** is on 3a C Pte, 4a–6a Av Nte, three blocks west from the Parque Central; most buses run through the Parque before terminating here. The **Telecom** is on 1a C Ote at 5a Av Nte, two blocks east of the Parque. If you want to **change money**, Banco Agrícola is at 1a C Pte and Av General Cabañas, and Ahorromet Scotiabank is at 1a Av Nte on the Parque. **Internet** access is available at the Centro de Computación, just off the Parque on C San Carlos.

The town's best **accommodation** is at the *Hotel Portobello* (③–④) on 4a Av Nte at 1a C Pte, which has clean a/c rooms with bath. *Hotel San Francisco* (☎604 4159; ②–③), on C Gral Menéndez 9a–11a Av Sur, five blocks east of the Parque, is also good, with clean rooms with bath; some also have a/c. *Hotel Centroamericana* on 4 C Pte, 1–3 Av Sur is secure and friendly; all rooms have a/c and bath, and some also have TV (☎604 4129; ③–④).

Places to eat include the airy *Restaurante El Sinai* on C San Carlos, one block down from the *Portobello* (daily until 8pm), which has good and moderately priced seafood, while *Restaurante El Marinero*, on 3a C Pte at Av Gral Cabañas, is the closest you'll come to a pavement café, with a large covered veranda from which to watch the street activity. For good **breakfasts**, try the cavernous *Restaurante El Viajero* next to the De Todo supermarket just off the Parque; there's also a *pupusa* kiosk at the entrance to the restaurant.

Around La Unión

PLAYITAS, 8km southeast of La Unión, is a small fishing village, with a somewhat dirty beach, whose main attraction is its proximity to the **islands** in the Golfo de Fonseca and its stunning views, which on clear days stretch across the gulf to the mainland of Honduras and, in the far distance, the mountains of Nicaragua. The smallest of the islands, **Zactillo** and **Martín Pérez** (to the left looking out to sea) seem almost close enough to touch, while ahead and to the right are the larger **Conchagüita** and, beyond, the island of **Meanguera**, both of which have small villages – Meanguera, in particular, is becoming a popular getaway and there is a small hotel here, the pretty *Hotel Isla Meanguera* (☎648 0072; ①–②), with simple rooms with shared bath. Irregular **passenger launches** leave for the larger islands; with a little bargaining, you should be able to find a private boat to drop you off for a few hours to enjoy the secluded beaches and clean waters, before returning to pick you up.

The whole Gulf region has long been associated with fables of the European **corsairs**, who made regular incursions along this coastline in the seventeenth and eighteenth centuries. Conchagüita was sacked by English pirates in 1682, who used it as a strategic base from which to attack ships sailing to Europe; the original inhabitants moved to the mainland and the island remained deserted until the 1920s, when settlers began moving back. In the centre of the island, on the Cerro del Pueblo Viejo, are the remains of a tiny pre-Columbian settlement; a path to the north of the ruins leads up to a large rock bearing engravings, which some believe is a map of the gulf, used strategically to plan defence.

Behind Playitas looms **Volcán Conchagua** (1243m), with beautiful views across the gulf to Nicaragua and Honduras and out across the Pacific. The friendly village of **CONCHAGUA**, sitting on its northern slopes, was founded by the inhabitants of Conchagüita at the end of the seventeenth century. The climate is fresher here, a pleasant relief from the heat of La Unión, and walks around the village give views across the Gulf. From Conchagua to the summit of the volcano is a strenuous, hot walk of two or three hours. As in most remote parts of El Salvador, walking alone is not recommended.

Eight kilometres west of La Unión is the junction with the Carretera Interamericana, which here swings north to run 27km up to the Honduran border at **El Amatillo** (see p.390). There are no direct buses to the border from the town; instead, take any of the frequent buses to Santa Rosa de Lima and change there.

travel details

BUSES

La Unión to: Conchagua (#382, every 30min until 6pm; 30min); El Tamarindo (#383, every 30min until 4.30pm; 1hr 20min); Playitas (#418, hourly until 4pm; 30min); San Miguel (#324, every 10min until 6pm; 1hr 30min); San Salvador (#304, every 30min until 2.30pm; 4hr); Santa Rosa de Lima (#342, every 15min until 5.30pm; 1hr 30min).

San Salvador to: Costa del Sol (#495, from Terminal del Sur, every 30min until 4pm; 2hr); La Libertad (#102, from Parque Bolívar, every 15min; 1hr); La Unión (#304, from Terminal de Oriente, every 30min until 2.30pm; 4hr); Los Cóbanos (#207, from Terminal de Occidente, every hour until 3pm; 2hr 30min); Sonsonate (#205 or #207, from Terminal de Occidente, every 10 min until 6pm; 1hr 30min); Usulután (#302, from Terminal del Sur, every 10min until 4pm; 2hr 30min); Zacatecoluca (#133, from Terminal del Sur, every 15min until 6.30pm; 1hr 30min).

Sonsonate to: Barra de Santiago (#285, 1 daily; 1hr 30min); La Hachadura (#259, every 10min until 5.30pm, passing the access roads for Playa Metalío and Barra de Santiago; 2hr; or #286, via San Francisco Menéndez; 4 daily; 2hr 30min); Los Cóbanos (#257, hourly until 5pm; 45min); San Salvador (#205 or #207, every 10 min until 6pm; 1hr 30min).

Usulután to: El Cuco (bus to San Miguel, then pick up the #320, every 30min; 1hr 30min); El Icacal (#373, every 10min; 30min to junction and pick up #385, 2 daily at 6am & 8am; 1hr); Puerto El Triunfo (#363, every 10min until 5.30pm; 1hr); San Miguel (#373, every 10min; 45min); San Salvador (#302, every 10min until 4pm; 2hr 30min); Zacatecoluca (#171, every 90min until 5pm; 1hr 30min).

Zacatecoluca to: Costa del Sol (#193 every 30min until 5.30pm; 1hr 30min); San Salvador (#133, every 15min until 6.30pm; 1hr 30min); Usulután (#171, every 90min until 5pm; 1hr 30min).

CHAPTER 16

THE WEST

M ore tranquil than in the north, the rich landscapes of western El Salvador in many ways offer a perfect introduction to the country. Soft mountain chains edge back from the valleys, dominated by the vibrant green expanses of coffee plantations from which the area gains its wealth. Spared from the most violent hardships of the conflict of the 1980s, the friendly towns and cities here are more amenable to visitors than in many places, and a relatively well developed tourist infrastructure makes travelling easier than in other regions.

The joy of this part of the country consists largely of soaking up the atmosphere. The mountain towns of **Apaneca** and **Juayúa**, in the south of the region, and the nearby city of **Ahuachapán** are perfect for a few days' relaxation, and are conveniently situated near the border with Guatemala – Ahuachapán in particular is a great little place to acclimatize yourself to El Salvador. The larger city of **Santa Ana** is a mellow contrast to the capital, while the peaks of **Cerro Verde**, **Volcán Santa Ana** and **Volcán Izalco**, the sublime crater lake of **Lago de Coatepeque**, and the pre-Columbian site of **Tazumal** are all close by. In the north of the region, near the Guatemalan border, the accommodating little town of **Metapán** gives access to the **Bosque Montecristo**, where hiking trails weave through unspoilt cloudforest amid some of the most remote and perfectly preserved mountain scenery in this part of the world.

The Cordillera Apaneca to Ahuachapán

Stretching east for more than 70km from the Guatemalan border, the glorious mountains of the **Cordillera Apaneca** are covered in a patchwork of coffee plantations and acres of pine forest, and are traversed by the so-called **"Ruta de las Flores"**, which stretches between the villages of Concepción de Ataco and Nahuizalco, named after the abundant white coffee flowers which are visible during May and the wild flowers that colour the hills and valleys from October to February. The population of the village of **NAHUIZALCO**, set on the southern edge of the range about 10km north of Sonsonate (see p.340), is mostly descended from the region's indigenous peoples, although few wear traditional dress any longer. The town thrives on the manufacture of wicker, with workshops lining the main street. Some of the pieces, such as baskets, are small enough to take home; gentle bargaining is acceptable. There's also an intriguing **evening market** where fruit and vegetables are sold by candlelight.

Beyond Nahuizalco, the air cools and freshens as the road winds its way up into the mountains proper; there are superb vistas down to Sonsonate and across the plains to the coast. Fifteen kilometres from Sonsonate is **JUAYÚA** (pronounced "hwai-oo-a"), whose magnificent **Templo del Señor de Juayúa**, built in colonial style in 1955, houses the **Black Christ of Juayúa**, carved by Quiro Cataño, sculptor of the Black Christ of Esquipulas in Guatemala (see p.237). Consequently the town is something of a pilgrimage site, particularly during the January festival. **Accomodation** is available at the

For an explanation of **accommodation price codes**, see p.287.

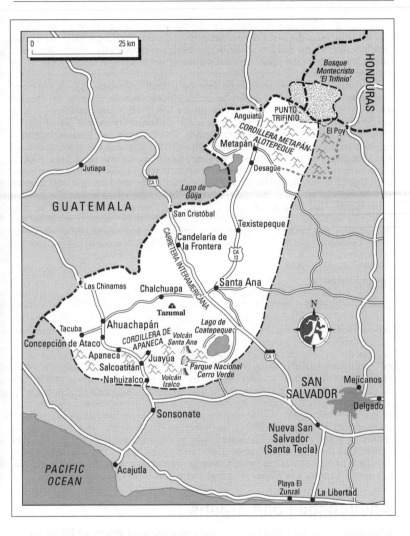

Casa de Huéspedes de Doña Mercedes (☎452 2287; ④), 2a Av Sur at 6a C Ote 3–6, a cheerful place with comfortable rooms, hot water and cable TV – it gets busy at weekends and holidays. The *Alojamiento Las Azaleas* (☎452 2383; ③), C Merceditas Cáceres Ote at 2a Av Sur, is more basic but clean, and also has a decent restaurant. Of the **places to eat**, *La Calera* on the Parque serves good coffee, cakes and light meals.

Apaneca and the Laguna Verde

A short leg further along the road from Juayúa is another quiet and charming mountain town, **APANECA**, founded by Pedro de Alvarado in the mid-sixteenth century. The town retains an air of friendly tranquillity, despite being popular with weekend visitors and home to one of the best-known restaurants in the country, *La Cocina de mi Abuela*, which draws wealthy San Salvadoreans and foreign residents alike. During the week, you're likely to have the place – and the wonderful surrounding mountain scenery – to yourself.

The town is easily accessible by **bus** from both Sonsonate (1hr 30min) and Ahuachapán (1hr). The best-quality **accommodation** is at the *Cabañas de Apaneca* (☎450 5106, fax 450 5137; ⑥), which has twelve comfortable wood cabins set in lush gardens overlooking the mountain slopes, and a good on-site restaurant (for which you should book ahead at weekends and holidays). There are two new **hostels**, located at opposite ends of the town (both are well signposted from the Parque): the *Hostal Rural Las Orquídeas* (☎433 0061; ③) has four clean, simple rooms with hot water – book in advance at weekends; the *Hostal Rural Las Ninfas* is very similar. The best place to **eat** is *La Cocina de mi Abuela* (11.30am–5pm Sat & Sun only; ☎450 5203 ext 301), housed in a beautifully decorated colonial-era house. The nicest tables are on the covered veranda at the back, with scenic views. Alternatively, the *Restaurante Fonda Lamatepec*, near the *Cabañas de Apaneca*, also serves excellent, if pricey, Salvadorean cuisine in a fine setting – fish fresh from Laguna Verde will set you back about US$8. Otherwise, eating options in town are limited to the row of friendly little **comedores** opposite the church.

Laguna Verde

There's little to do in Apaneca itself, but it's an enjoyable and not too strenuous walk through woods and fincas to the **Laguna Verde**, a small crater lake 4km to the north-east of town. Fringed by reeds and surrounded by mist-clad pine slopes, the lake is a popular destination, and at the weekends you're likely to share the path with numerous families and groups of walkers.

From the highway on the edge of town, follow the dirt road to the right of the Jardín de Flores garden centre, which winds up and round the mountain, passing several fincas and a couple of small hamlets, overlooked by the weekend retreats of wealthy San Salvadoreans. An enjoyable shortcut is to walk up the dried-up stream bed through the woods, which links the bends of the road; this is more of a scramble and it's quite easy to get lost – ask directions from anyone you meet. The hamlet just above the lake, reached after about ninety minutes, has sweeping views on clear days; the white city sheltering in the valley below is Ahuachapán, while to the north is the peak of Cerro Artillería on the Guatemalan border. The grassy slopes around the lake make a good spot for a picnic and you can swim. Closer to town to the north, the smaller and less impressive **Laguna Las Ninfas** is an easy forest walk of about 45 minutes.

Ahuachapán and around

From Apaneca the road winds its way down to the city of **AHUACHAPÁN**. This area, and the lands further north, are some of the oldest inhabited regions of what is today El Salvador, due in large part to the extremely fertile soil. Artefacts found in the region date back to 1200 BC and the first early Maya. Ahuachapán is also one of the oldest Spanish settlements in the country, made a city in 1862, and has generally been a place of quiet bourgeois comfort; two attacks by Guatemalan troops – in 1863 and 1864 – were both firmly rebutted. The early twentieth-century British visitor Percy Martin noted: "The people as a whole seemed to me to be very well-to-do, and evidences of refinement and solid comfort were to be met with on all sides . . . I was also impressed with the absence of the usual number of drinking shops, of which I counted scarcely more than six in the whole town. The town is a quiet, sleepy and eminently peaceful place of residence where one might dream away one's life contentedly enough."

Today the city's main industry is geothermal electricity generation, at one time supplying seventy percent of the country's power; consequently there are usually a number of European and Japanese technicians stationed here.

Arrival and accommodation

Buses arrive at the terminal on Av Commercial, 10a–12a C Pte, eight blocks from the Parque Central. Two main streets, 2a Av Nte and Av Francisco Menéndez, run parallel from the bus terminal to the cathedral on the Parque. The **Telecom** is at 3a C Pte and 2a Av Sur by the Parque, while the **post office** is at 4a C Ote and 1a Av Nte. To **change money**, Banco Cuscatlán and Ahorromet Scotiabank are on Av Francisco Menéndez and C Gerardo Barrios, and Banco de Comercio is on the corner of 4a C Pte and Av Francisco Menéndez. **Internet** access is available at the Cybercafé Cupac, Av Francisco Menéndez and 1a C Pte (US\$2.20 per hour). There are two supermarkets, De Todo and Despensa Familiar, by the bus terminal.

Of the city's **accommodation**, *La Casa Blanca* (☎443 1505, fax 443 1503; ④), on 2a Av Nte at C Barrios a couple of blocks from the Parque, is housed in a well-decorated colonial building and has large, clean rooms, all with bath and TV. The restaurant, set around a small courtyard is slightly overpriced, but good for sitting with a coffee or a beer. For those on a budget, *Hotel San José* (☎443 1820; ③), on 6a C Pte between Av Commercial and 2a Av Nte, close to the market, has clean, dark rooms. The nicest place to stay, however, is *Hotel el Parador* (☎443 0331; ⑤), 2km out of town on the road to the Guatemalan border post. All rooms have bath, hot water and TV, and there's a restaurant and a small pool open to the public.

The City and around

Apart from its quiet, gently fading streets, and the lively daily **market** around the bus station, the only things to see in Ahuachapán are its **churches**. The imposing white edifice of the **Iglesia Parroquia de Nuestra Señora de la Asuncíon**, on the Parque Central, dominates the centre of the city and acts as the focus for the annual fiesta in the first week of February. Dating from the 1950s, the spare **El Calvario**, on 6a C Pte at 2a Av Nte, is home to a fine sculpture of a crucified Christ.

Immediately south of the city, the hump of **Cerro Ataco** is a safe and not too difficult climb of about two hours – follow 2a Av Sur out of town and pick any one of the small paths which go up to the summit. The body of water visible to the northwest, off the road to Las Chinamas, is the **Lago de Llano**, a small, lily-fringed lake extensively fished by locals. It's a thirty-minute stroll along the main road from the centre of town to the lake, or you can catch bus #60 (regular departures from the market) to the rather depressing village of Las Brisas, 500m from the lake.

Some 5km east of town, near the hamlet of El Barro, are the **ausoles** (geysers) which form the basis of the local geothermal industry. The plumes of steam forced up from the earth hang impressively over the lush green vegetation and red soil – particularly impressive in the early-morning light.

Eating and drinking

Like most Salvadorean provincial cities, Ahuachapán is not overly blessed with **places to eat**. All restaurants tend to close relatively early, around 9pm, except for the *El Parador*, *El Paso* and *La Posada* restaurants – in a row on the Las Chinamas road in the northern outskirts of town – all of which serve meat and seafood standards, and occasionally have live music at the weekends. In the centre, *Tacos El Zocalo* and *Jardín de China*, next door to each other on 1a Av Sur at 1a C Ote, offer Ahuachapán's version of Mexican and Chinese cuisine respectively; both are good places for a relaxed drink as well as a meal. *La Estancia*, housed in a rather run-down white building on 1a Av Sur at C Barrios, has well-prepared standards at average prices. *Pollo Campero*, at 3a C Pte and Av Francisco Menéndez, has fast-food chicken and chips, plus some Salvadorean dishes, while *Mixta "S"*, 2a Av Sur by the Parque, is more of a fast-food place, with a range of simple meals, snacks and juices. For sitting and people-watching, try the stands in the Parque serving coffee and snacks.

Around Ahuachapán

Fifteen kilometres west of Ahuachapán is the quiet mountain village of **TACUBA**, reached via a winding and scenic road with grand views of coffee plantations and the mountains and national park of Bosque El Imposible. An important settlement existed here long before the Spaniards arrived, and the village retains strong folkloric traditions, although you'll only really notice these at fiesta time. There's not much to do in Tacuba itself, though it makes a fine base for exploring the nearby mountains and valleys. There are few **places to stay** other than private lodgings and the excellent new *La Cabaña de Tacuba* (☎417 4332; ⑥), set amid beautifully cultivated gardens and offering a fine range of accommodation, including large double rooms and suites. The price includes three meals a day and the owner can supply information on nature trails and hiking in the area.

To Las Chinamas and Guatemala

From Ahuachapán, a reasonably good and very scenic road runs the 20km or so to the **Guatemalan border** just past **Las Chinamas**. Local buses leave for the border every fifteen minutes, taking about an hour. International buses from Santa Ana also pass through at about 5.30am. There is no ticket office – stand on 6a C Pte more or less opposite the *Hotel San José* and flag them down. Buses run to Guatemala City from Valle Nuevo on the Guatemalan side.

Chalchuapa and Tazumal

Heading northeast from Ahuachapán, the road winds down through the last spurs of the cordillera onto a broad and scenic plain, running to **CHALCHUAPA**, which in addition to its faded but beautiful colonial church produces jade artesanías, including replicas of Maya artefacts. Chalchuapa's main draw is the archeological site of **Tazumal** (Tues–Sun 9am–5pm; US$3), located on the edge of town. The most important site in El Salvador, the ruins are – by comparision with sites in Honduras and Guatemala – rather small, although they do have their own, impressive beauty. Tazumal is an easy trip from Ahuachapán or Santa Ana. **Buses** from Ahuachapán (1hr) and Santa Ana (30min) drop passengers off at a small plaza a few blocks from the centre of town; from here, walk uphill for about four blocks and turn left at the sign.

What is now the town of Chalchuapa was the seat of power for a strong and thriving Maya population from 900 BC onwards. The inhabitants produced "Usulután" ceramics, key items of commerce in the Maya zone, and also controlled the trade in obsidian from Guatemala. This early society was literate – evidence suggests that they had both calendar and writing systems – and highly stratified, while artefacts indicate strong links with Olmec civilizations in Mexico. The catastrophic eruption of Volcán Ilopango in around 250 AD, covering an area of ten thousand square kilometres in ash, did not affect Chalchuapa as badly as the central zone of the country; the area quickly repopulated and **Tazumal** gradually became the main settlement.

The site as a whole was constructed in thirteen different stages over a period of 750 years, mostly during the Late Classic period (600–900 AD). Of the nine structures identified, only two remain in reasonable condition, with a third partially excavated; the rest have been destroyed by the expansion of the town. The central and largest structure – a stepped ceremonial platform, influenced by the style of Teotihuacán in Mexico – dates back to the Classic period (300–900 AD); traces of a platform dating back to between 100–200 AD have been found beneath it. A number of smaller temples were originally attached to the main structure. At the base of its northern edge, a number of tombs (Late Classic period) have yielded artefacts such as Tiquisate ware from Guatemala, jade jewellery, items for religious rites and a flask containing powdered iron-oxide. The last was used for decorating a ceremonial stone *hacha* or head, used during games of pelota. The pelota court itself lay on the southern edge of the structure.

Tazumal as a Maya city was abandoned around the end of the ninth century, during the collapse of the Classic Maya culture; unusually, Pipils moved in and occupied the site. Structure 2, to the west of the main platform, is a Pipil pyramid dating back to the Early Postclassic period (900–1200 AD). The new residents also constructed another pelota court, to the northwest corner of the site. Tazumal was finally abandoned around 1200 AD, with the focus of settlement in the area moving towards the centre of the current town.

An informative (Spanish only) **museum** displays artefacts discovered during excavations. The nearby ruins of **El Trapiche** and **Casa Blanca** are currently being excavated and aren't yet open to the public.

Santa Ana

Self-possessed **SANTA ANA**, the second most important city in El Salvador, lies in a superb location in the Cihautehuacán valley. Surrounded by green peaks, with the slope of Volcán Santa Ana rising to southwest, the gently decaying colonial streets exude a certain bourgeois complacency. Cooler and far mellower than San Salvador, and regarding itself as being above the unseemly commercial bustle of San Miguel, it's a good place to relax, admiring the handful of grandiose buildings or simply walking the streets soaking up the atmosphere. The natural attractions of **Lago de Coatepeque**, the forest reserve of **Cerro Verde** and the **Santa Ana** and **Izalco** volcanoes are all easy day-trips away.

Some history

The conquistadors passed through the valley soon after their arrival in El Salvador, discovering a Pipil town of about three thousand inhabitants where Santa Ana now stands. A Spanish settlement, however, was not founded until July 1569, when the disgraced Bishop Bernardino de Villapando arrived in the valley en route from Guatemala. Commenting on the beauty and fertility of the area, he ordered work to begin on a church dedicated to **Nuestra Señora de Santa Ana**, the saint of the day of his arrival. Completed in 1576, this occupied the site of the present cathedral until it was destroyed in the early twentieth century to make way for the new building.

The settlement grew relatively quickly: by 1770 the population was almost as large as that of San Salvador, with 589 Spanish and ladino families, and 138 indigenous families. Agriculture – particularly sugar cane, and latterly coffee – and ranching contributed to the city's wealth, and by the end of the nineteenth century Santa Ana was secure in its position as El Salvador's second most important city, with around 30,000 inhabitants, and buildings commensurate with the city's status, such as the theatre and cathedral, sprang up. Today, with a population of over 225,000, Santa Ana retains an air of restrained, provincial calm which is generally only ruptured during the **July fiesta**, when a host of events bring the streets to life.

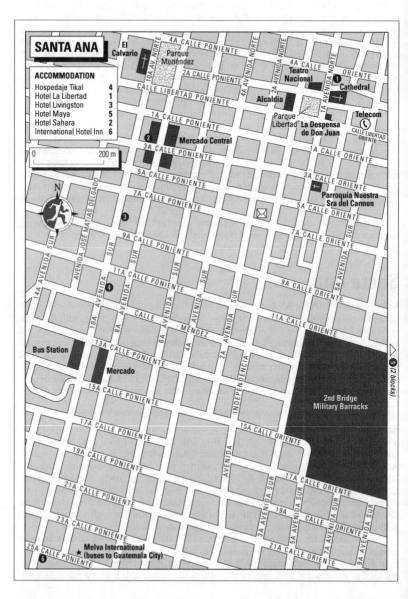

SANTA ANA

ACCOMMODATION
Hospedaje Tikal	4
Hotel La Libertad	1
Hotel Livingston	3
Hotel Maya	5
Hotel Sahara	2
International Hotel Inn	6

0   200 m

El Calvario

Parque Menéndez

4A CALLE PONIENTE
2A CALLE PONIENTE
CALLE LIBERTAD PONIENTE
1A CALLE PONIENTE
3A CALLE PONIENTE
5A CALLE PONIENTE
7A CALLE PONIENTE
9A CALLE PONIENTE
11A CALLE PONIENTE
CALLE MÉNDEZ
13A CALLE PONIENTE
15A CALLE PONIENTE
17A CALLE PONIENTE
19A CALLE PONIENTE
21A CALLE PONIENTE
23A CALLE PONIENTE
25A CALLE PONIENTE

10A AV NORTE
4A AVENIDA NORTE
2A AVENIDA NORTE
1A AVENIDA NORTE
4A CALLE ORIENTE

Teatro Nacional
Cathedral
Alcaldía
Parque Libertad
Telecom
La Despensa de Don Juan
CALLE LIBERTAD ORIENTE
1A CALLE ORIENTE
3A CALLE ORIENTE
Parroquia Nuestra Sra del Carmen
5A CALLE ORIENTE
7A CALLE ORIENTE
9A CALLE ORIENTE
11A CALLE ORIENTE
15A CALLE ORIENTE
17A CALLE ORIENTE
19A CALLE ORIENTE
21A CALLE ORIENTE

Mercado Central

AVENIDA JOSÉ MATÍAS DELGADO
14A AVENIDA SUR
10A AVENIDA SUR
8A AVENIDA SUR
6A AVENIDA SUR
4A AVENIDA SUR
2A AVENIDA SUR
INDEPENDENCIA
AVENIDA
3A AVENIDA SUR
5A AVENIDA SUR
7A AVENIDA SUR
9A AVENIDA SUR

Bus Station
Mercado

2nd Bridge Military Barracks

Melva International (buses to Guatemala City)

N

(2 blocks)

Arrival and information

Buses arrive at the main terminal on 10a Av Sur between 13a and 15a C Pte, nine or so blocks southwest of the central district; city bus #51 runs to the centre from the terminal, or you can walk it in about fifteen minutes. The **Telecom** is on C Libertad at 5a Av Sur, just down from the Parque Central, and the **post office** on 7a C Pte between Av Independencia and 2a Av Sur. **Banks** cluster around 2a Av Nte behind the Alcaldía, and include the Banco de Comercio, Banco Agrícola, Banco Salvadoreño and Banco Hipotecario; Banco Cuscatlán is on the corner of 3a C Pte and Av Independencia. The original **Mercado Central**, on 8a Av Sur, 1a–3a C Pte, burned down in October 2000, but a temporary replacement is now in operation on the same site – a good place to buy virtually anything. There's a smaller, mainly fruit and vegetable market, around the bus terminal, and a La Despensa de Don Juan **supermarket** on the Parque Menéndez.

Accommodation

Santa Ana's status as the country's second city is not reflected in its range of **accommodation**, although there are a couple of reasonably comfortable hotels, one convenient for the bus terminal, and the other closer to the Mercado Central. This area, around 8a and 10a Av Sur, also has a concentration of cheap and basic places to stay, though it's not recommended to wander around it alone at night.

Hospedaje Tikal, 10a Av Sur between C Méndez and 11a C Pte (☎440 4127). Clean and well-run hospedaje with small, basic rooms. ①–②.

Hotel La Libertad, 4a C Ote at 1a Av Nte (☎440 2358). Perhaps the nicest budget place in the city, in a great location right by the cathedral with clean, basic rooms (some with bath). Bring your own padlock for the doors. ②.

Hotel Livingston, 10a Av Sur between 7a and 9a C Pte (☎440 1801, fax 447 0435). Safe, but rooms are small and box-like, with shared baths. ②.

Hotel Maya, 11a C Ote at 11a Av Sur (☎441 3612). Good, secure place, with motel-style rooms, some with bath; a 20min walk from the centre. ⑤.

Hotel Sahara, 3a C Pte between 8a and 10a Av Sur (☎ & fax 447 8865, *hotel_sahara@yahoo.com*). The city's best, with large comfortable rooms, good service, bar and a restaurant open until 10pm. ⑥.

International Hotel Inn, 25a C Pte and 10a Av Sur (☎440 0810, fax 440 0804). Convenient for the bus terminal and international buses. The rooms are rather small but comfortable, all with TV and bath, but watch out for the cockroaches. ④.

The City

The heart of Santa Ana is the **Parque Libertad**, a neatly laid-out plaza with a small bandstand, where people gather to sit and chat in the early evening. The main intersection (Av Independencia Sur/Nte and C Libertad Pte/Ote) skirts its southwest corner. On the eastern edge of the Parque is the magnificent **cathedral**, an imposing neo-Gothic edifice completed in 1905. Inside, brick arches soar upwards and images – some dating back four hundred years – line the walls to the altar. Inset into the walls are plaques from local worshippers giving thanks to various saints for miracles performed. On the northern edge of the plaza, the **Teatro Nacional**, completed in Renaissance style in 1910, was funded by taxes on local dignitaries. Once the proud home of the country's leading theatre companies, the building became a movie theatre before falling into disuse. Facing the cathedral on the western edge of the plaza is the **Alcaldía**, another fine Renaissance-style piece of architecture – for Paul Theroux its facade possessed the "colonnaded opulence of a ducal palace".

Another important church, **El Calvario**, five blocks west of the Parque on 10a Av Nte by Parque Menéndez, is was reduced to ruins in the January 2001 earthquake. South of the Parque Central, on 1a Av Sur, sits the **Parroquía de Nuestra Señora del Carmen,** built in 1822; in 1871 it was briefly occupied by peasants from the area around Volcán Santa Ana who, spurred on by Guatemalan president Rafael Carrera's calls for the indigenous peoples to reclaim their land, ran riot through the city. After the uprising fizzled out, those who refused to give themselves up were hunted through the mountains and killed.

Eating and entertainment

Santa Ana has a reasonable number of moderately priced **places to eat; nightlife,** however, is not high on the city's list of priorities, and most restaurants tend to shut around 10pm, even at the weekends. The **cinema** on C Libertad at 3a Av Sur is virtually the only place to go after nightfall; it shows standard Hollywood films, subtitled.

Cafe Cappuchino, Av Independencia at C Libertad Pte. A relaxed, leafy café just off the plaza, serving coffees, good juices, beers and simple meals.

Café Fiesta, 1a C Pte and 1a Av Sur. Large restaurant with loud music, serving cheap-and-cheerful lunches.

Cafetería Central, 2a Av Sur between 1a and 3a C Pte. Good for large breakfasts and cheap lunches.

Cafetin El Ciclista, corner of 2a Av Sur between 3a and 5a C Pte. Popular with locals for its lunches and *comida a la vista*.

El Tucan Gourmet, Av Independencia Sur 33. Good but not cheap meat and seafood dishes.

Kiko's Pizza, Av Independencia between 7a and 9a C Pte. Huge pizzas: the regular size is more than enough for two.

K'y'Jau, C Libertad between 4a and 6a Av Sur. Popular restaurant, serving large portions of authentic Chinese food.

Los Horcones, next to the cathedral on Parque Libertad. The best views in the city, with seats on an open terrace facing the cathedral and plaza. Well-prepared standard dishes, and great juices.

Los Patios, 21a C Pte between Av Independencia and 2a Av Sur. One of the smartest places in Santa Ana, serving good meals in a nice courtyard at reasonable prices.

Around Santa Ana: the three peaks

South from Santa Ana, the three **volcanic peaks** of Cerro Verde, Santa Ana and Izalco together form a concise, living example of geological evolution. The oldest, **Cerro Verde,** is now a softened, densely vegetated mountain harbouring a national park. **Santa Ana,** nominally active, has cultivated lower slopes giving way to a bare, lava-covered summit, whilst juvenile **Izalco,** one of the youngest volcanoes in the world, is an almost perfect, bare lava cone of unsurpassed natural beauty.

Cerro Verde and Volcán Santa Ana

From the El Congo junction, 14km southeast of Santa Ana, a narrow road winds up through coffee plantations, maize fields and pine woods to the **Parque Nacional Cerro Verde** (daily 7am–5.30pm; US$1), occupying the crater of the long-extinct volcano. This is the most accessible reserve in the country, and consequently you're unlikely to be able to walk the short trails in solitude, particularly at the weekends. The dense forest shelters numerous species of **plants,** including pinabetes and more than fifty species of orchids. **Animal** life in the park includes armadillos, deer and cuzuco, though they tend, wisely, to stay out of sight; you're more likely to spot **birds,** including the native xara – with a shimmering blue body and black head – hummingbirds and toucans.

Cerro Verde is very well managed, with clear trails and lookouts over Volcán Santa Ana and, far below, Lago de Coatepeque. From the entrance gate a short track leads up to the car park, to the left of which is a small orchid garden. The main trail, the so-called **sendero natural**, leads from the top of the car park, looping clockwise through the reserve. Despite the weekend crowds this is an enjoyable walk of around forty-five minutes through the green calm of the forest. Smaller trails branch off through the trees.

Three **buses** a day run directly from Santa Ana to the car park, the last leaving the city in mid-afternoon (1hr 30min). The last bus from the car park leaves at 5pm and runs to El Congo only, from where you can pick up another service to Santa Ana or San Salvador. Alternatively, you could rent a taxi for a few hours or take the **tour bus** which runs every Sunday from outside the Catedral Metropolitana in San Salvador – it currently leaves at 6.30am, but it's worth double-checking. There are basic **cabañas** (①) by the car park, although you have to bring your own food and water; you can also **camp** – ask the wardens where you can pitch your tent.

Volcán Santa Ana

From a signed turn about ten minutes into Cerro Verde's sendero natural, a path branches down to the left, leading eventually to the summit of the **Volcán Santa Ana**, known also "Llamatepec" or "father hill". The highest volcanic peak in the country, at 2365m, Santa Ana is still considered active, although it hasn't erupted since the early twentieth century. The process of forestation is far less advanced here than in Cerro Verde, and the outlines of the volcano far starker.

The walk to and from the summit takes two or three hours each way. From the signed turn on the sendero natural, a downhill walk of about twenty minutes brings you to the Finca San Blas, beyond which the path begins to wind up though woodlands. After about 45 minutes, the gradient gets steeper, woodland cover gives way to rock and, towards the summit, lava. Three newer craters sit inside the larger older one – which takes about an hour to circumnavigate; there's a small, green sulphur lake at the bottom of the newest crater.

Volcán Izalco

Just below Cerro Verde on the road down is a stunning lookout west over the majestic **Volcán Izalco**, a bleak, black volcanic cone which is in startling contrast to the green slopes surrounding it. Beginning as a small hole in the ground in 1770, the volcano formed rapidly over the next two centuries as lava began to pour continously from the earth. Clearly visible from the ocean, the volcano – known to sailors as the "lighthouse of the Pacific" – was used to navigate until it finally stopped erupting in the 1960s.

It is possible to **walk up** Izalco, although locals advise against it, particularly alone, and robberies are not unknown. Local police can occasionally be persuaded to escort groups of five or more. A marked trail leads from the lookout down for about thirty minutes to a saddle between the two volcanoes. From here it takes at least an hour to climb the completely bare slopes of volcanic scree to the summit.

Lago de Coatepeque

East from the El Congo junction (14km from Santa Ana), a winding branch road descends 3km to the stunning crater lake of **Lago de Coatepeque**, shadowed by the three peaks. The bus ride descends the winding road towards the deep blue waters, fed by natural hot springs, passing a mirador (ask the driver to let you off here) from where there are panoramic vistas. Much of the shore is bounded by private houses, however, and access to the water is difficult.

Follow the road round to the left when it reaches the lake to reach the *Hotel Torremolinos* (☎446 9437; ⑤), which has large, clean rooms, rents out boats and has a small, private beach which you can use for a small fee. Much nicer, however, is the *Hotel de Lago* (☎446 9511; ⑤) just up the road, with large, shady gardens and a restaurant overlooking the lake. An excellent budget choice is *Amacuilco* (②), on the main road at the water's edge just before *Hotel Torremolinos*, a relaxed, lovingly maintained hostel with four-bed dorm rooms (US$10 per person), a purpose-built café on a pier over the lake, and free use of a canoe.

Buses leave Santa Ana every thirty minutes for the lake, running past the three hotels. If you're heading back to San Salvador, take the Santa Ana bus as far as El Congo then walk down the slip road to the main highway and catch any passing bus running from Santa Ana to the capital.

To San Cristóbal and the Guatemalan border

Beyond Santa Ana, the Carretera Interamericana heads northwest for 30km, through the small town of **Candalería de la Frontera** and on through gentle, green rolling countryside to the Guatemalan border at **San Cristóbal**. There are frequent buses from Santa Ana (1hr) to the crossing, which is efficient, not too busy, and has no exit or entry charges. There aren't any banks at the border, but numerous moneychangers offer reasonable rates for dollars, colones and quetzales. On the Guatemalan side, buses run to Asunción Mita, with connections to Guatemala City.

From Santa Ana to Metapán

Leaving Santa Ana, CA-12 heads north through agricultural plains and badly deforested hills, becoming wilder after it passes through the dusty town of **Texistepeque**. Sixteen kilometres further on, at the hamlet of Desagüe, a dirt road leads 2km or so to serene **Lago de Güija**, surrounded by low hills; Río Ostúa, flowing through the lake, forms the border with Guatemala. On the **Las Figuras** arm of land – accessible on foot during the dry season – stretching out on the left side of the lake shore are a number of faint pre-Columbian rock carvings; the area around the lakeshore was populated exclusively by indigenous groups until well into the seventeenth century. You can rent boats from here to the small island of **La Tipa** in the lake.

Ten kilometres beyond the lake the small, friendly town of **METAPÁN** is scenically situated on the edge of the mountains of the Cordillera Metapán-Alotepeque, which run east along the border with Honduras. Having survived a number of setbacks, including two devastating fires which nearly destroyed the town, Metapán was one of only four communities which supported Delgado's first call for independence in 1811, when rioting citizens opened the jail and attacked representatives of the Spanish crown. The **Iglesia de la Parroquia**, completed in 1743, is one of El Salvador's finest colonial churches, with a beautifully preserved facade. Inside, the main altar is flanked by small pieces worked in silver from a local mine while the ornately decorated cupola features paintings of San Gregorio, San Augustín, San Ambrosio and San Jéronimo.

Practicalities

Metapán is blessed with a few decent hotels and a number of good, cheap comedores. The comfortable *Hotel San José* (☎442 0556; ④) on the edge of town by the bus terminal, a few blocks from the centre, has comfortable **rooms**, all with bath and TV, plus a restaurant (open until 9pm). A few doors along is the new and well-managed *Hotel y Restaurante Centroamérica* (☎442 0066; ②–③), which has small, simple rooms and a small restaurant serving all meals. In the town, the friendly *Hotel Christina* (☎442 0044; ②–③), on 4a Av Sur and C 15 de Septiembre, has a range of good, clean rooms with and without bath – some also have hot water and TV. More basic is the *Hospedaje Central* (②) on 2a Av Nte at C 15 de Septiembre in the centre of town.

For **eating**, a number of good comedores line up along 2a C Pte, including *Panadería y Pupusería Elizabeth* and *Comedor La Esperanza*, which serves excellent breakfasts and lunches; for fast food, there's a *Chicken Bell* and a *Pollo Master* further down. There's a De Todo **supermarket** next door to the *Hotel San José*. If you need to **change money**, there's a Banco Salvadoreño on the park, a Banco de Comercio at Av Ignacio Gomez and C 15 de Septiembre, and a Banco Cuscatlán on the corner of 3a C Pte and Av Dr Isidro Menéndez.

Around Metapán: Bosque Montecristo

The main reason for staying in Metapán is for access to the international reserve of **Bosque Montecristo**, jointly administered by the governments of El Salvador, Honduras and Guatemala. The reserve rises through two climatic zones centred on the **Cerro Montecristo** (2418m), at whose summit the borders of the three countries converge. The higher reaches of Montecristo, beginning at around 2100m, are home to an expanse of virgin **cloudforest**, subject to an average annual rainfall of two metres and 100 percent humidity. Orchids and pinabetes thrive in these climatic conditions, while huge oaks, pines and cypresses, some towering to over 20m, swathed in creepers, lichens and mosses, form a dense canopy which prevents sunlight from reaching the forest floor. The numerous species of **wildlife** – which tend to be shy of humans – include mountain foxes, howler and spider monkeys and the occasional jaguar. The abundant birdlife includes quetzals, hummingbirds, striped owl and Elliot's colibri. The lower slopes of the reserve consist mainly of mixed pine and broadleaf forest cover, much of it secondary growth, replanted since the early 1970s – acute deforestation having provided the impetus for the creation of the reserve in the first place.

Getting to Montecristo

The untouched beauty of the upper heights of Montecristo is due in large part to its remoteness; the only road in is a dirt track running northeast from Metapán. All the **tour operators** listed on p.314 can organize trips here; the more people in a group the cheaper it will be. If coming **independently**, the road from Metapán branches right off the highway just before the *Hotel San José*. If you're not in a private vehicle (4WD necessary), occasional pick-ups make the journey; otherwise, you'll have to come to a private arrangement: ask around the market, though note that pick-up owners drive a hard bargain, regularly citing the poor state of the road as a reason for keeping their price high. Montecristo is managed by the National Parks and Wildlife Service (in Illopango ☎227 0622; in Metapán ☎442 0475), and you'll need to get permission to enter it in advance. You're not allowed to enter on foot. Note that the cloudforest is closed to visitors from May to October, and that there's an entrance fee of US$1.50.

The park **entrance** is 5km from Metapán; after another 2km you come to the Hacienda San José, also known as the Casco Colonial, where the wardens are based and where you have to register. From here the road continues for another 14km before reaching **Los Planes** (1890m), 16km inside the park, where there's a **tourist centre**, comprising a well-organized recreation area with a small restaurant, camping area and the wonderful **Jardín de Cien Años** orchid garden. If **camping**, bring food and water.

From Los Planes a marked trail leads to **Punto Trifinio**, the summit of Cerro Montecristo, where the three countries meet. Walking straight to the summit will take around three hours; the path leads through the cloudforest, however, and you can branch off in any direction (be careful not to get lost) – bring warm clothing and good footwear. Trails also lead from just below Los Planes to the peaks of Cerro el Brujo and Cerro Miramundo.

Crossing into Guatemala: north to Anguiatú

Regular buses (around 30min) make the 13km trip from Metapán along CA-12 to **Anguiatú** and the **Guatemalan border** – the most convenient crossing if you're heading for Esquipulas in Guatemala (see p.237). Formalities here are straightforward, though if you're coming in the other direction note that the last bus to Metapán leaves at 6.30pm. There are no banks, but lots of moneychangers.

travel details

BUSES

Ahuachapán to: Chalchuapa (#210, every 15min until 6pm; 1hr); Las Chinamas (#263, every 15min until 5.30pm; 1hr); San Salvador (#202 & #204, every 10min until 6pm; 3hr 30min); Santa Ana (#210, every 15min until 6pm; 1hr 30min); Sonsonate (#249, every 30min until 5.30pm; 2hr 30min).

Metapán to: Anguiatú (#211A, every 30min until 6.30pm; 30min); Santa Ana (#235, every 30min until 6.30pm; 1hr 30min).

San Salvador to: Ahuachapán (#202 & #204, from Terminal de Occidente every 10min until 6pm; 3hr 30min); Santa Ana (#201, from Terminal de Occidente, every 10min until 5.30pm; 2hr; *directo* service every 20min; 1hr 20min).

Santa Ana to: Ahuachapán (#210, every 15min until 6pm; 1hr 30min); Cerro Verde (#248 to Sonsonate runs via the car park; 3 daily; 1hr30min); Chalchuapa (#277, #218, every 10min;

40min); Lago de Coatepeque (#220 "El Lago", every 30min until 5.30pm; 1hr); Metapán (#235, every 30min until 6.30pm; 1hr 30min); San Cristóbal (every 15min until 5.30pm; 50min); San Salvador (#201, every 10min until 5.30pm; 2hr; *directo* service every 20min; 1hr 20min).

Sonsonate to: Ahuachapán (#249, every 30min until 5.30pm; 2hr 30min); Apaneca (#249, every 30min until 5.30pm; 1hr 45min); Juayúa (#249, every 30min until 5.30pm; 1hr30min); Nahuizalco (#249, every 30min until 5.30pm; 30min); Salcoatitán (#249, every 30min until 5.30pm; 1hr 15min); Santa Ana (#216, every 15min until 5.45pm; 2hr).

INTERNATIONAL BUSES

Santa Ana to: Guatemala City (hourly from 5.30am to 4pm; 4–6hr; buy ticket one day in advance from Melva International, 25a C Pte, 6a–8a Av Sur; ☎440 1608).

PART FIVE

HONDURAS

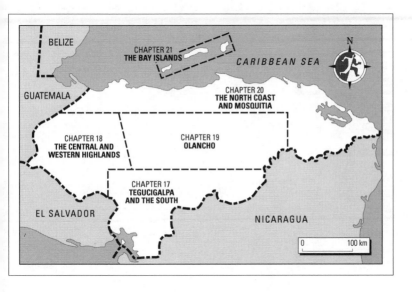

BELIZE

CHAPTER 21
THE BAY ISLANDS

CARIBBEAN SEA

N

GUATEMALA

CHAPTER 20
THE NORTH COAST
AND MOSQUITIA

CHAPTER 18
THE CENTRAL AND
WESTERN HIGHLANDS

CHAPTER 19
OLANCHO

CHAPTER 17
TEGUCIGALPA
AND THE SOUTH

EL SALVADOR

NICARAGUA

0   100 km

Introduction

The original Banana Republic, a byword for corruption and poverty, **Honduras** is all too often overlooked by foreign tourists. Many of those who do make it here head straight for the ruins of **Copán**, one of the finest Maya sites in the region. Some even miss that, in their rush to get to the palm-fringed beaches and clear Caribbean waters of the **Bay Islands**. Beyond these prime tourist sites, however, is a land of inspiring, often untouched natural beauty.

The second-largest country in Central America after Nicaragua, Honduras sprawls from the Atlantic to the Pacific coast, from Caribbean flatlands through the cooler mountainous interior, and south to the sun-baked shores of the Golfo de Fonseca. West to east, the forested highlands on the border with Guatemala give way to the vast, undeveloped savannas and wetlands of the Mosquitia. While eco-tourism is a relatively new concept here, more and more Hondurans are becoming aware of the role the country's extensive network of **national parks and reserves** plays in protecting irreplaceable natural resources. Almost a quarter of Honduran territory is protected, but a lack of funding and growing pressure on the land mean this status often exists more on paper than in reality. Nonetheless, the remoter reaches of the parks still host an astonishing array of flora and fauna, amid some of the finest stretches of virgin **cloudforest** and **tropical forest** in Central America.

Honduras's close alliance with the US, while preventing the bitter conflicts that beset its neighbours in the 1980s, has not alleviated the country's acute **social and economic problems**. After Nicaragua, this is Latin America's poorest nation, with levels of deprivation that can be disturbing to witness: some eighty percent of Hondurans live in poverty and forty percent are unable to read or write. Exacerbating the pressure on economic and environmental resources is a rapidly growing population, now approaching seven million, much of it absorbed by the ever-increasing shantytowns ringing the main cities.

It is in the cities that the pressures are most evident: life is fast and harsh and social intercourse is conducted at times with gratuitous abruptness. Move out into the rural areas, however, and the open generosity and genuine friendliness displayed by those who have little else are what leave an enduring impression. On the north coast, where the population is more ethnically diverse, the heat and sunshine combine to create a way of life that's more Caribbean than Latin.

■ Where to go

Most visitors pass through the capital, **Tegucigalpa**, at some stage, where a stay, however short, is enlivened by the generally relaxed ambience, and the presence of facilities and services you won't find elsewhere. Though small, the city has a reasonable range of places to eat, drink and make merry. A couple of hours on the bus from Tegucigalpa brings you to the peaceful mountain towns of **Santa Lucía** and **Valle de Ángeles**, with hiking close by in the cloudforest of **La Tigra**. Further away is the little-visited getaway of **Isla El Tigre**, becalmed in the warm waters of the Golfo de Fonseca and perfect for a few days spent doing nothing much at all.

Many travellers head straight for the western highlands and the Maya ruins of **Copán**, one of the finest archeological sites in Central America. Though it's an arduous trip from the capital, there are some worthwhile places to break the journey, notably **Comayagua**, a couple of hours from Tegucigalpa, the former colonial capital, which has a wealth of historic churches and a couple of good museums. The equally charming colonial city of **Santa Rosa de Copán** also makes a logical destination on the way to or from Copán.

In the east of the country, the rugged, sparsely populated region known as Olancho is home to the rarely visited national parks of **La Muralla** and **Sierra de Agalta**. The latter contains the most extensive stretch of virgin cloudforest remaining in Central America. Heading towards the Caribbean you're almost certain to pass through Honduras's energetic second city, **San Pedro Sula**, the commercial centre of the country and a useful transport hub. Just an hour or so south of town is one of Central America's premier spots for ornithologists, the placid, blue, fresh waters of **Lago de Yojoa**.

Frequent buses fan out from San Pedro to the **north coast**, with its pristine white beaches, clear warm waters and endless sun. **Tela**, **La Ceiba** and **Trujillo** are all lively towns with a thriving nightlife, while the fishing village of **Omoa** moves at a quieter pace. For a glimpse of a different way of life, make for the friendly **Garífuna** villages dotted along the coast. Also

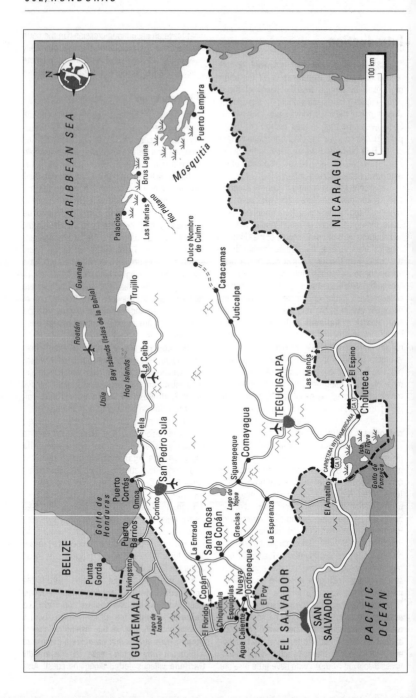

within easy reach is the coastal wetland reserve of **Punta Sal**, near Tela, sheltering a multiplicity of bird and marine life amid mangrove swamps and marshes. It requires a little more planning to get into the heart of **Pico Bonito**, a mountainous reserve near La Ceiba, but the effort is spectacularly rewarded.

The jewel in the crown of Honduras's natural resources, however, is the biosphere reserve of the **Río Plátano** in Mosquitia. Encompassing one of the finest remaining stretches of virgin tropical rainforest in Central America, the region is largely uninhabited – a trip here really does get you off the beaten track.

Finally, the **Bay Islands** are the ultimate base for a beach holiday, with world-class snorkelling and diving, and an extravagantly rich cultural mix.

When to go

As in much of Central America, the **climate** in Honduras is dictated more by altitude than by season. In the central highlands, the weather is temperate, pleasantly warm in the daytime and cool at night. It's hardly surprising that the Spanish focused their attention here, abandoning the flatlands and the northern coast, which can be unpleasantly hot at any time of year. While the Pacific and Caribbean coasts at least offer the relief of breezes and cooling rain showers, San Pedro Sula and other lowland towns can be positively scorching in summer.

Honduras's **rainy season**, known as "winter" (*invierno*), runs from May to November, though how much it will affect your trip depends on where you're travelling. In much of the country it rains for only a few hours in the late afternoon, though along the northern coast and in Mosquitia rain is a constant feature all year round. October and November are perhaps the only months you might want to avoid these parts: this is **hurricane season**, when heavy rains can cause serious flooding, washing away roads and cutting off all transport.

Getting around

There are a number of alternatives for **getting around** Honduras, depending on how fast you want to travel and where you want to get to. Buses are the cheapest way to go, but occasional flights cut down on the long, often tedious journeys through the country's mountainous terrain.

Driving allows you to take things at your own pace and to reach the more remote areas that are rarely served by buses, while boats are the most atmospheric way of reaching the Bay Islands. There's also an extremely slow, cheap and uncomfortable weekly train service between Puerto Cortés and Tela – for enthusiasts only.

Buses

Bus services in Honduras are some of the best in Central America, with frequent departures from the main transport hubs of Tegucigalpa, San Pedro Sula and La Ceiba, backed up by networks of local services. On the longer intercity routes there's usually a choice of bus, with an increasing number of luxurious a/c express buses (*ejecutivos* or *de lujos*) plus slower and less comfortable services (*directos*); local buses are typically much slower and more crowded. Timetables tend to be strictly observed, so plan ahead and double-check departure times if you want to avoid getting stuck. **Fares** are extremely low on most routes, at around US$0.8 an hour or less, though prices can triple on some of the really smart services – travelling between Tegucigalpa and La Ceiba can cost as much as US$18, depending on the service you choose. For intercity trips, it's worth buying a ticket well in advance, you'll usually be issued with a seat number. Virtually all direct buses stop to pick up passengers at certain points along the route – if there are no seats left, you stand.

Taxis

Taxis operate in all the main towns, tooting as they cruise by anyone who looks remotely like a tourist. Meters are nonexistent, so you should always agree a price before getting in. For safety reasons, it makes sense to use taxis to get around in the big cities at night – a cross-city fare will rarely exceed US$3.50, with US$2 a standard price for a short journey. For trips further afield it can be worth hiring a taxi for a few hours, or even the whole day. Fares are negotiable, but bargaining hard will get you a reasonable deal, particularly if you're in a group.

Driving and hitching

Renting a **car** is the simplest way to get to the more isolated national parks without having to rely on buses. Well-maintained highways connect the main cities, running between the north and south coasts and along the coasts themselves. There are also numerous dirt roads connecting the isolated villages of the highlands. Bear in mind, however, that these can be in quite appalling condition for large parts of the year, and at times completely impassable; check local advice on conditions before setting out. **Rental** starts at around US$45 a day for a small car, US$60 for larger models and 4WDs. Check the rental agreement carefully to ensure that insurance and emergency assistance are included.

Hitching is very common in rural areas, and generally safe. Keep an eye out for pick-up trucks with lots of people in the back, and stick out your thumb. You're expected to offer payment at the end of the ride, usually the same as the bus fare – though it may occasionally be refused.

■ Cycling

Cycling is a scenic way to travel around under your own steam, although negotiating the main highways can sometimes be a hair-raising experience. You'll need to bring your own bike, preferably a mountain bike to cope with the terrain. Since bicycles are a common form of transport in rural areas, there are repair shops in most places, although it's wise to anticipate potential problems and come equipped with your own tools and spares.

■ Boats

A fast scheduled **boat** service – the *MV Galaxy II* – operates between La Ceiba and Roatán/Utila, running in both directions daily. Tickets are slightly cheaper than the airfare and the journey takes an hour to Utila (US$12) and two hours to Roatán (US$13). The boat is comfortable, with an air-conditioned lounge, video service and snack bar. There are also unscheduled **cargo boat** departures for Mosquitia and Guanaja from La Ceiba and Trujillo – the only way to find out about these is to go to the dock and ask.

■ Planes

Internal **flights** are very affordable in Honduras, with all prices fixed by government, and faced with a six- or seven-hour bus journey from Tegucigalpa to the north coast, many people opt to fly. Flying is also the easiest way to reach the Bay Islands, and the only practicable way to get to the Mosquitia.

A small number of domestic airlines offer competitive fares, with frequent departures between Tegucigalpa and San Pedro Sula, La Ceiba and the Bay Islands. A one-way ticket between Tegucigalpa and San Pedro will cost around US$30, whilst La Ceiba to Utila or Roatán is US$18–20 and La Ceiba–Palacios around US$40. There's a **departure tax** of US$1.30 for internal flights and US$25 for international flights.

Costs, money and banks

Honduras's currency is the **lempira** (L), which consists of 100 centavos. Coins come as 1, 2, 5, 10, 20 and 50 centavos and notes as 1, 2, 5, 10, 20, 50 and 100 lempiras. For day-to-day living, Honduras works out extremely cheap for foreigners. At the current **exchange rate** of L15.4 to US$1, a cup of coffee typically costs around US$0.30, a soft drink around US$0.40 and fresh juice US$1. A meal in an ordinary café will be around US$2–3.

Honduras has a number of national **banks**, of which the biggest are Banco Atlántida, Bancahsa, Banco de Occidente and Ficensa. All of these change **travellers' cheques** – American Express is the most widely accepted brand, while Visa and Thomas Cook are also usually cashed without a fuss; other brands are frequently rejected, especially in more remote areas.

At present **Honduran ATMs don't accept foreign credit cards**. Visa card holders can get cash advances in several banks, including Banco Atlántida; Mastercard holders will have much more of a problem – currently only Credomatic (with branches in Tegucigalpa, San Pedro Sula and La Ceiba) accepts this card. All debit cards, including Cirrus and Plus, are currently useless in Honduras except for the Visa debit card. Banks in Tegucigalpa and San Pedro Sula are usually **open** Monday to Friday 9am to 4.30pm and Saturday 9am to noon; in smaller towns most shut for an hour at lunchtime and close up to an hour earlier in the afternoons. All banks are closed on public holidays and on the Monday following an election.

Information

The very helpful **Instituto Hondureño de Turismo**, in the Edificio Europa, Av Ramón Cruz and C República de México Tegucigalpa (☎238 3974, fax 222 6621, *touristinfo@iht.hn*), can provide general **information** about where to go and what to see in the country; they also have booths at Tegucigalpa and San Pedro Sula airports, and a free information service in the USA (☎800 410-9608). They also have good links with the main tour operators and the luxury hotels.

National parks and reserves are administered by the government forestry agency, **COHDEFOR** (Apdo Postal #1378; ☎223 7703, fax 223 2653). If you intend spending much time in any of the parks, it's worth visiting their headquarters in Tegucigalpa for detailed information on flora and fauna. The office is a little difficult to find, just off the Carretera al Norte in Comayagüela.

Accommodation

The choice of **accommodation** is widest in Tegucigalpa, San Pedro Sula, Copán and along the north coast, where there's a range of rooms to suit all pockets; outside these areas, the choice begins to narrow. Except in very remote regions, you'll always find a room, but don't count on it being particularly comfortable or spotlessly clean. Of the Bay Islands, Utila is the cheapest, with prices not much higher than on the mainland. Roatán has a few places catering to backpackers and a good selection of mid-range and luxury hotels, while Guanaja is geared heavily towards the luxury, all-inclusive scuba-diving package holiday market.

On the mainland, expect to **pay** around US$3 per person for a basic, acceptable room outside the capital and big cities, more if you want a private bath. Paying US$10 and above will secure you a reasonably well-furnished room, with extras such as TV, a/c and hot water. A twelve percent tax is sometimes, but not always, added to the bill; an additional five percent "tourist tax" is also added in some luxury places. Prices are higher in Tegucigalpa and San Pedro Sula: US$3 rooms do exist but are invariably located in the worst areas;

decent budget rooms begin at around US$7 and mid-range at US$20, while those in the top hotels start at around US$85. Normally the only time you need to reserve in advance is at Semana Santa or during a big local festival, such as the May Carnival in La Ceiba.

The only formal provision for **camping** is at Omoa, Copán Ruinas and in some of the national parks. Elsewhere, pitching a tent is very much an ad hoc affair. Tempting though they may seem, the north coast beaches are **not safe** to be on after dark and camping is highly inadvisable. Elsewhere, if you intend to camp, make sure you ask permission from the landowner first.

Eating and drinking

The range of **places to eat** in the big cities is wide and increasing all the time. Smart restaurants serving European, Latin American and Honduran cuisine abound in Tegucigalpa and San Pedro Sula, and the more touristy places, such as Copán and the Bay Islands, have a selection of excellent restaurants. Elsewhere, the choice narrows to comedores serving set lunches and dinners, consisting of the usual mix of beans, rice, tortilla and meat, and – very often – a Chinese restaurant, although the authenticity of these is variable.

■ What to eat

Honduran **specialities** worth trying include *anafre* and *tapado*. The former is a fondue-like dish of cheese, beans or meat, or a mixture of some or all of these. The latter is a rich vegetable stew, often with meat or fish added. North-coast cuisine has a strong Caribbean influence and fresh fish and seafoods feature heavily. *Guisado* (spicy chicken stew) and *sopa de caracol* (conch stew with coconut milk, spices, potatoes and vegetables) are dishes that should be tried at least once. *Pan de coco* (coconut bread) is often served with meals in the north and makes a delicious

---

ACCOMMODATION PRICE CODES

All accommodation reviewed in this guide has been graded according to the following price scales, which represent the cost of a **double room in high season**, excluding any taxes.

① up to US$5	④ US$15–25	⑦ US$60–80
② US$5–10	⑤ US$25–40	⑧ US$80–100
③ US$10–15	⑥ US$40–60	⑨ US$100 and over

snack in itself; Tela in particular is famed for its coconut rolls, sold on the beach by women and children. Probably the most common street snack, sold all over the country, is the *baleada*, a white-flour tortilla filled with beans, cheese and cream; two or three of these constitute a decent-sized meal.

■ **Drinking**

Though there are a few venerable European-style cafés in the big cities serving fine **coffee**, most places serve up a weak brew made from poor quality beans. **Fruit juices** are usually excellent, however, and available everywhere, most commonly in the form of *licuados* or *batidos* (blended with milk), or *frescos* (blended with water). Orange and other fruit juices are widely sold in cartons, but invariably have sugar added. Tap **water** is unsafe to drink; bottled, purified water is sold everywhere and many hotels supply it free to guests. The usual brands of **fizzy drink** are ubiquitous. Honduras produces five brands of **beer**, all of them made by the same company. Salvavida and Imperial are heavier lagers, Port Royal slightly lighter, and Nacional and Polar very light and quite tasteless. **Rum** (*ron*) is also distilled in the country, as is the Latin American gut-rot, *aguardiente*. Imported European and South American wines are available in more expensive restaurants, though at a price.

Opening hours, festivals and holidays

Business hours are generally Monday to Friday 9am to noon and 2 to 4.30 or 5pm, and sometimes from 9am to noon on Saturdays. Government offices work Monday to Friday 8.30am to 4.30pm, often with an hour's break for lunch. Government offices, post offices and many other businesses close on national holidays and the first Monday after an election. The major **public holidays** are listed in the box above.

All towns and villages have an annual **fiesta patronale** to commemorate the local saint. Some last only a day, some for a week or more, with a variety of events attracting people from far and wide. One of the largest is Carnaval in La Ceiba, more correctly known as **La Feria de San Isidro**. Held during the week leading up to the

PUBLIC HOLIDAYS
Jan 1 New Year's Day
March/April Semana Santa: Thursday, Friday and Saturday before Easter Sunday
April 14 Day of the Americas
May 1 Labour Day
Sept 15 Independence Day
Oct 3 Birth of Francisco Morazán
Oct 12 Discovery of America
Oct 21 Armed Forces Day
Dec 25 Christmas Day

third Saturday in May, the festivities culminate in a street parade through the centre of the city, followed by performances of live music on sound stages until the early morning. The celebrations in San Pedro Sula in the last week of June, culminating on June 29 (a holiday in the city), and in Punta Gorda (Roatán), from April 6 to 12, celebrating the arrival of the Garífuna, are both worth making an effort to get to. The biggest festival of all, however, is that of the **Virgen de Suyapa** – patron saint of the country – in the first week of February, when pilgrims from around the country flock to Tegucigalpa to worship and celebrate.

Mail and telecommunications

Letters posted from Honduras generally take around a week to get to the US and up to two weeks to reach Europe. Receiving letters via poste restante, however, is more hit and miss: mail may take weeks to work its way through the system, and there's always the chance it won't be given to you when it does arrive. The main **post offices** in Tegucigalpa and San Pedro Sula are open Monday to Friday 8am to 7pm and until 1pm on Saturdays; smaller offices open from Monday to Friday 8am to 5pm, with a lunch break, and on Saturdays until noon.

International phone calls are astronomically expensive from **Hondutel** offices (there's a branch in every town), the state-run company that President Flores has been unsuccessfully trying to privatize. A three-minute call to the US or Canada currently costs US$11.50, to Europe US$14.80 and to Australia or New Zealand US$18.20; it's also possible to make collect calls for a hefty fee. The branches in Tegucigalpa and San Pedro Sula are open 24 hours; elsewhere, offices are open daily from 7am to 9pm.

Unsurprisingly, given the rates, most travellers choose to avoid Hondutel if at all possible. In all the main tourist destinations and most cities there's now a cybercafé or communication centre offering discounted international call rates. While hardly a bargain, rates are typically set at around 70 per cent of Hondutel's tariffs. Many cybercafés also offer **Web phone calls**, which cut international call rates to the price of surfing the Net, though line connections are notoriously crackle- and delay-prone. Police have periodically raided cybercafés and confiscated Web phone equipment, however, as Hondutel have tried to make the practice illegal – but it's well worth asking if the facility is available.

Another alternative option is to purchase an **international calling card** from your home phone company before you travel. Once in Honduras, AT & T card holders should dial ☎8000 123 for an operator, while MCI card holders should dial ☎8000 121.

There are also **public phone** booths scattered around the major towns, which take 20 and 50 centavo coins; some also now accept Hondutel phone cards (L50 and L100). Local calls are very inexpensive, national calls cost L2 for a three-minute call. **Fax** services are available in most Hondutel branches (US$1.40 per page to send to North America, US$2.30 to the EU, US$2.45 to Australia or NZ), rates are cheaper in cybercafés. Note that there are **no area phone codes**; the international country code for Honduras is ☎504.

Internet use has mushroomed in Honduras in the last few years, and many hotels and businesses are now on-line. There are also cybercafés in all the big cities and in most places where travellers congregate. Rates vary considerably: from US$2.80 an hour in San Pedro Sula to a whopping

US$12 an hour in Utila and Roatán, where an annoying quirk of the phone system means that no calls can be classified local.

The media

There are six daily **newspapers** in Honduras, though all are owned by politicians, so don't expect dynamic investigative reporting – the Honduran papers overwhelmingly favour the opinions of their proprietors. *El Periódico, La Tribuna* (owned by President Flores) and *El Heraldo* are published in Tegucigalpa, *La Prensa, El Tiempo* and *El Nuevo Día* in San Pedro Sula. Of these, *El Tiempo* is the most liberal, and has been regularly critical in the past of the activities of government and the armed forces. *La Tribuna* is also fairly moderate in its political stance; *El Heraldo* and *La Prensa* – which has the highest circulation at around 42,000 – are both conservative but with good international coverage. Though all the print media impose a certain level of self-censorship, particularly when reporting the actions of the armed forces and government, reporting standards are steadily improving.

There are two excellent **English-language** publications. The weekly *Honduras This Week* newspaper has in-depth coverage of Honduran events, as well as tourist and business information and a superb Web site (*www.marrder .com/htw*). It's available from English-language bookshops in the capital and in the big hotels in Tegucigalpa, San Pedro Sula, Copán, La Ceiba and Roatán. *Honduras Tips* (*www.hondurastips .honduras.com*) is a very informative free **magazine**, geared to tourists, with useful hotel, restaurant, bar and nightlife listings, transport information (including pretty accurate nationwide bus timetables) and some features. You'll find it in many hotels and guesthouses.

Honduras's airwaves are filled with over 150 **radio stations**, most in private ownership, which broadcast to some 3.5 million listeners weekly; Radio Honduras is the government-owned station. All the six terrestrial **television** networks are in private hands, with around one-third of households owning sets; there are also numerous cable networks broadcasting films, news and light entertainment from Latin America and the US. Programmes on US channels are usually in English with Spanish subtitles.

USEFUL PHONE NUMBERS

191 National phone operator
192 Information
195 Cruz Roja (Red Cross)
197 International operator
198 Fire brigade
199 Police

Shopping

While the **artesenías** available in Honduras may not be as wide-ranging or as colourful as those in Guatemala, there are a number of crafts that are instantly recognizable as Honduran. The range of **carved wooden goods**, particularly those produced around Valle de Ángeles is extensive, from simple bowls and dishes to elaborate chests and doors, while in the highlands and around Copán **ceramics**, including replicas of Maya pottery and artefacts, are produced. On the north coast the speciality is cotton **hammocks**, along with **Garífuna** handicrafts, music and paintings. Good-quality **cigars** are sold in Tegucigalpa, Santa Rosa de Copán and Copán, and a number of companies in Tegucigapla and San Pedro Sula sell high-quality **leather goods** at around half European prices.

For everyday goods, the general **markets** in every town usually provide a bewildering range of cheap clothing, food and household goods. More expensive boutiques and supermarkets are limited to Tegucigalpa and San Pedro Sula.

Safety and the police

Large parts of Honduras remain relatively safe for tourists, and travel in rural areas is generally an informative exercise in mutual trust and respect. In the cities however, **street crime** is a serious and growing concern; pickpocketing and bag or jewellery snatches are predominantly opportunistic and can be prevented by exercising basic caution. While the centre of Tegucigalpa is reasonably safe at night, consider taking a taxi if it's late or you're on your own; Comayagüela, particularly around the market area, is not considered safe to walk around at all at night.

On the north coast **drugs** enter the equation: San Pedro Sula has a thriving gang culture and the highest crime rates in the country, while in the north coast towns, Tela particularly, muggings and physical attacks (including rape) on tourists have increased. Once again, the chances of anything occurring can be reduced by using some common sense: don't flash around money or valuables, and try to remain aware of where you are and how you are returning to your hotel. None of the beaches around the towns are considered safe at night.

The **police**, though now separate from the armed forces, are unlikely, overall, to be of much help if something does happen, but any incidents of theft should be reported for insurance purposes.

Work and study

Honduras is waking up to the demand for **language schools**, though it's by no means in the same league as neighbouring Guatemala, with just a few schools operating in Tegucigalpa, Copán and La Ceiba. Courses can be taken for any length of time you choose and always include the option of staying with a family. Schools generally also arrange cultural and social activities.

Opportunities for paid employment are few and far between in Honduras. Perhaps easiest to come by are jobs **teaching English** at one of the small language schools – try under listings for *Academias de Idiomas* in the yellow pages. On the other hand there are probably thousands of

---

LANGUAGE SCHOOLS

La Ceiba

Centro Internacional de Idiomas, Av San Isidro 12–13 (☎ & fax 440 1557, *www.worldwide.edu/honduras/cici*). Small and friendly school offering weekly courses of four hours a day one-to-one tuition for US$220 with homestay, US$145 without. Air-conditioned classrooms; transfer credit is available from US universities.

Copán

Escuela de Español Ixbalanque, a block and a half west of the Parque (☎ & fax 651 4432, *ixbalan@hn2.com*). Runs a one-week course for US$175 including homestay, twenty hours of tuition and afternoon activities.

Guacamaya, three blocks north of the Parque (☎ & fax 651 4360, *www.guacamaya.com*). Similar fees and courses to the Ixbalanque school.

Tegucigalpa

Conversa, Av República de Brasil 2419, Colonia Palmira (☎236 5170, fax 236 7420, *www.worldwide.edu/honduras/conversa*). Professionally run school with flexible study programmes – twenty hours of tuition plus homestay costs US$185 per week.

vacancies for **voluntary workers** (Honduras has more Peace Corp people than any other country in Latin America), as organizations have flooded into Honduras to rebuild the nation after Hurricane Mitch.

History

When the Spanish arrived in the sixteenth century, Honduras was populated by a number of different tribes. In the northeast – the Mosquitia, parts of the north coast and Olancho – were the **Pech** and **Sumu**, related to the South American Chibchans, while the north-central region was occupied by the **Tolupan**, migrants from possibly as far away as the present United States. Western Honduras was home to the **Maya**, while the **Lenca**, also believed to be descended from the Chibchans, inhabited the centre of the country. The **Pipils**, migrants from present-day Mexico, lived to the south, along the Golfo de Fonseca, with the Toltec-speaking **Chorotega**, also from Mexico, inhabiting the area around Choluteca.

Of these, it is the **Maya** about whom most is known. Archeologists believe that settlers began moving south into the Río Copán valley from around 1000 BC; construction of the city of **Copán** began around 100 AD. By the time of the founding of the royal dynasty in 426 AD, Copán exerted control as far north as the Valle de Sula, east to Lago Yojoa and west into what is now Guatemala. Home to the governing and religious elite, and supporting a total population of around 24,000, the city was the pre-eminent Maya centre for scientific and artistic development; today it is one of the world's foremost archeological sites. When, for reasons which are not entirely clear, Maya civilization began to collapse around 900 AD, Copán was abandoned, although the area it previously controlled remained inhabited.

Following the collapse of the Maya empire, the **Lenca** became the predominant group in Honduras, absorbing other indigenous cultures and settling in small, scattered communities, supported by subsistence agriculture and hunting and gathering. The Lenca established trade links as far north as Mexico and interacted peaceably with the Maya and Pipil.

■ Discovery and conquest

On July 30, 1502, on his fourth and final voyage, **Columbus** arrived off the island of Guanaja. Naming it the "Isla de Pinos" (Island of Pines), he then continued exploring the Central American coastline, accompanied by a Pech trader encountered coming from the direction of Guatemala. Sailing east along the coast, the fleet first stopped at Punta Caxinas, close to present-day Trujillo, where the first Catholic Mass in Latin America was held on August 14, 1502. Sailing on into harsh storms, the fleet rounded a cape where, encountering calmer waters, Columbus is reputed to have exclaimed "Gracias a Dios que hemos salido de estas honduras" (Thank God we have now left these depths), christening both the cape – Cabo Gracias a Dios – and eventually the country. Initially, however, the Spanish called these new lands Higueras, the name used by the indigenous groups they encountered.

Twenty years elapsed before the conquistadors returned to take possession of the new territory, the nominal conqueror being **Gil González Dávila**, who sailed up the Pacific coast from Panamá and partially explored the lands that now form Nicaragua and Honduras. In 1524, however, **Hernán Cortés** despatched his lieutenant **Cristóbal de Olid** to claim the whole of the isthmus on Cortés's behalf. Olid landed on the north coast in May 1524 and founded the first Spanish settlement, Triunfo de la Cruz on the Bahía de Tela; his own claims on the territory were abruptly ended by assassination later that year. Cortés himself, desperate to stamp his ownership on the new lands, left Mexico for Honduras in 1525, arriving on the north coast in the spring and ordering the founding of Puerto Caballos (now Puerto Cortés) and Trujillo. Aware that his absence from Mexico was undermining his position, however, Cortés returned there in April 1525. Five years later **Pedro de Alvarado**, despatched from Guatemala, arrived to govern the territory. Under Alvarado, the city of San Pedro Sula was founded in 1536, and control of the inland regions was secured.

■ Lempira's rebellion

There was sporadic but persistent **resistance** to the Spanish advance by the indigenous groups they encountered, although the power of these was lessened by their geographical dispersal and the lack of a single powerful group. No significant threat to the Spanish was posed until **Lempira's rebellion** in 1536. A Lenca *cacique* (chieftain) from what is today Erandique in southwest

Honduras, Lempira was a charismatic leader, popularly believed to be invincible. Persuading the tribes of the centre and western highlands to unite in rebellion, he amassed a force of up to 30,000 men, retreating with them to the natural mountain redoubt of Peñol de Cerquín. From here he signalled the outbreak of hostilities by killing three Spanish passers-by. The mass insurrection that followed was at first impossible for the Spanish to control; at one point Comayagua was burnt down and Gracias, San Pedro de Puerto Caballos and Trujillo besieged. Outright rebellion continued for three years, before the Spanish, having lured Lempira down to participate in peace talks, shot and killed him in 1539. With no leader at their head, Lempira's forces were easily overcome and the Spanish hold on the land assured.

■ The colonial period

With Honduras under control, the Spanish increasingly focused their attention on the interior of the country, in large part because of the inhospitable climate of the coastal settlements and their vulnerability to pirate attacks. Discovery of **gold** in the Valle de Comayagua in 1539, and of **silver** at Goascorán and around Tegucigalpa over the following forty years, seemed to promise untold riches. The designation of Comayagua as capital in 1573 reflected the displacement of economic activity away from the coast.

For the indigenous inhabitants, the consolidation of Spanish power was catastrophic. Contemporary population records are notoriously inaccurate, but from an estimated 400,000 in 1524, the population probably fell to as low as 15,000 by 1571. Those who survived the diseases of the Old World were initially enslaved and shipped either overseas or into the mines. Social structures collapsed and communities were forcibly dispersed, with the highland tribes being most affected, since they had the greatest contact with the colonists. Incredibly, considering their impact, the number of colonists numbered fewer than 300 throughout the seventeenth century.

For the Spanish the steep **decline in population** was above all else a severe hindrance to economic development. Though at their peak the mines provided a comfortable living for their owners, from the seventeenth century onwards the labour shortage made working deeper seams impracticable, and profits dropped sharply as a result. The depopulation of the countryside also hindered the development of a sustainable agricultural sector. *Encomienda*, the system of demanding labour and tribute from the indigenous population, theoretically ensured a supply of workers; in practice, labour scarcity meant that food production rarely rose above subsistence levels, capable only of supplying immediate local needs.

By the early 1800s, the Honduran economy was in crisis. Mining was virtually defunct and a series of severe droughts hit both agriculture and livestock. Society was sharply divided, with a thin layer of the relatively wealthy – state functionaries, merchants, a handful of mine and hacienda owners – above a poor mass of mestizos and indigenous peoples. A middle class was nonexistent and any kind of unifying national infrastructure absent; by independence in 1821, Honduras still had no national printing press, newspapers or university.

■ Independence

News of **independence** from Spain reached Honduras on September 28, 1821. While the Liberals of Tegucigalpa celebrated, the Conservatives of Comayagua declared their intention of joining the American monarchy under the Mexican Agustín Iturbide. Following Iturbide's deposition, the provinces of Central America declared themselves an independent republic on July 1, 1823. In the civil war that almost immediately followed, the Honduran **Francisco Morazán** – Liberal and sometime soldier – succeeded in defeating Conservative forces in Guatemala and, elected president of the republic in 1830, tried to institute a séries of far-sighted reforms in government, the Church, the judicial system and education. Opposed by Conservatives across Central America, his vision of the potential of a united republic was not enough to persuade even his own countrymen. There were sporadic uprisings and eventually civil war broke out again; Morazán failed to crush the Conservative-backed 1837 rebellion of Rafael Carrera in Guatemala, and – when Honduras and Nicaragua went to war against El Salvador – resigned in 1839. The Central American Republic was finished.

Rivalry in the newly independent **Republic of Honduras** between Liberals and Conservatives was as strong as ever. Rallying various bastions of local power to their respective flags, they plunged the country into an almost permanent state of political and military conflict,. The economy, too, was deeply unstable: subject to financial mismanagement by governments of both colours, lacking an export sector to secure foreign revenues and a national infrastructure to push growth, and undermined by flourishing corruption. The effects of this were clearly illustrated in the ill-fated venture to construct a national railway system. Sensing the opportunity to make a quick profit, British banks loaned a desperate government £6 million in 1867–70. Of this, only around £100,000 was ever received and barely 90km of track laid. The resulting debt – which over the next fifty years rose to £30m – was not fully paid off until 1953.

■ Marco Aurelio Soto and the Liberal reform

The man credited with beginning the modernization of Honduras was **Dr Marco Aurelio Soto**, a Liberal who was elected president in 1876. He and his successor Luis Bográn reformed the powers of judiciary and Church, professionalized the armed forces and put communications and education infrastructures into place. What was created, in short, were all the elements, above a common language and religion, necessary to make Honduras a unified state capable of taking its place in the world. Recognizing the need to participate in the international economy, Soto also instigated agricultural reforms in order to develop the coffee and sugar cane industries for export.

Believing that foreign capital was the key to economic development, he encouraged **foreign investment** by US, British and European companies on extremely favourable terms, conversely laying the basis for the country's enduring economic problems. In the mining industry, for example, investors had an obligation to do little more than employ workers, while the government undertook to build roads, ports and any infrastructure necessary to get equipment in and the finished product out. At the El Rosario mine near Tegucigalpa – at one point the most productive mine in the western hemisphere – which accounted for 45 percent of the country's export income at the turn of the century, ninety percent of shares were in foreign (mainly US) hands.

■ The banana republic

The same thinking lay behind the development of the **banana industry** in the late nineteenth century, the industry that was to become the dominating factor in Honduras's future. More than happy to accept government concessions, which included exemption from customs duties and ownership of mineral rights, US fruit companies began to move into the rich agricultural lands of the north coast. Three companies – United Fruit, Vacarro Bros (later Standard Fruit) and the Cuyamel Fruit Company (bought out by United Fruit in 1929) – soon became dominant, all but wiping out small-scale producers. Further concessions, granted in return for promises to build railways, allowed the companies to steadily increase their holdings, which by 1924 amounted to two thousand square kilometres on the north coast and control of seventy percent of Honduras's total exports. Through expansion of interests, the companies also gained control of the country's railways, principal factories and major energy and telegraph companies, set up banks and acted as intermediaries in negotiations over foreign loans.

Political power and influence followed economic might. Cuyamel cultivated strong links with the Liberal Party, while United Fruit – whose support extended to instigating armed uprisings – bankrolled the Conservatives, now known as the National Party. A succession of weak and short-lived governments struggled to keep control in the face of the dominant interests of the fruit companies and, behind them, the United States, as the virtually autonomous north coast spun away from the impoverished centre and south.

■ The development of modern Honduras: 1932–1963

With the 1932 election of National Party president **Tiburcio Carías Andino** were laid the foundations for the modern state of Honduras. A virtual dictator for sixteen years until he was forced to step down in 1948, Carías strengthened the armed forces and cracked down on political opposition, the press and trade unions. Conversely, his economic austerity programme succeeded in balancing the economy and his authoritarian leadership forged a new national cohesion. His successor, **Juan Manuel Gálvez**, set up a central bank, a public service sector, and expanded the nascent export industry of coffee, sugar and light manufacturing.

This strengthened government was thus better placed to deal with the worst excesses of the banana companies, reflected in the **Banana**

Strike of May 1954. Originating with Puerto Cortés dockers, the strike spread to 35,000 United and Standard Fruit workers, and then to workers in other industries. Ended by a settlement in early July, thrashed out between government, employers and unions, most demands went unrecognized. The two main achievements of the strikers, however – legitimization of labour unions and the drafting of an enduring framework of labour protection laws – made the strike a watershed in Honduran history.

A **coup** in October 1956 introduced the **military** as a new element into the hierarchy of power. Though civilian government resumed in 1957, with the election of Liberal Ramón Villeda Morales, a new constitution the same year gave the armed forces the right to disregard presidential orders they perceived to be unconstitutional, strengthening vastly the position of the military and affecting the development of the state over the next twenty years.

■ Military influence – and the Football War

In October 1963 a second coup installed **Colonel Oswaldo López Arellano** as provisional president. Though elected constitutionally in 1965, López remained a ranking officer – eventually rising to Brigadier General – forging an unhealthily close alliance between the military and the National Party, in effect his personal political vehicle. During twelve years in power he decimated the Liberal opposition and reversed most of his predecessor's social reforms. Free-market economic policies led to an increase in unemployment and landlessness, while the profits which were creamed off government development projects fuelled unprecedented corruption. In an attempt to counter growing unrest over land, López introduced limited agrarian reform in 1967, in the shape of rural co-operatives, though these were far more acceptable to the fruit companies than the trade unions. Above all, however, his first period of office is remembered for one of the more bizarre conflicts in modern Central American history, the so-called "**Football War**".

On July 14, 1969, war broke out on the Honduras–El Salvador border. Ostensibly caused by a disputed result in a soccer match between the two countries, the conflict stemmed from tensions generated by a steady rise in illegal migration of campesinos from El Salvador into

Honduras in search of land. In April 1969 the Honduran government gave settlers thirty days to return to El Salvador and began forced expulsions; sporadic violence broke out, with cynical manipulation of the situation in the press by right-wingers on both sides of the border.

In June, the two countries began a series of **qualifying matches** for the 1970 World Cup, the first of which, held in Tegucigalpa, was won 1–0 by Honduras. At the second game, won 3–0 by El Salvador, spectators at the San Salvador ground booed the Honduran national anthem and attacked visiting Honduran fans. The third and deciding match was pre-empted by the El Salvadorean army bombing targets within Honduras and advancing up to 40km into Honduran territory. After three days, around two thousand deaths and a complete rupture of diplomatic relations, the Organization of American States (OAS) negotiated a ceasefire, establishing a three-kilometre-wide demilitarized zone along the border. Tensions and minor skirmishes continued, however, until 1980, when a US-brokered peace treaty was signed. Only in 1992 did both sides accept an International Court of Justice ruling demarcating the border in its current location.

An experiment in democratic government, under Ramón Cruz in 1971–72, was marked by economic chaos and civil unrest, and ended abruptly with a second coup restoring Lopéz to power in December 1972. A new programme of industrialization, with the government responsible for investment and accumulation of capital, was – given the by now endemic corruption at senior levels of government, in the military and in business – a recipe for disaster. Millions of dollars of national and international loans and aid money were siphoned off to private bank accounts, and while limited agricultural reform succeeded to a degree in redistributing underutilized land, it was not enough to contain rural unrest.

The "**Bananagate**" scandal, the payment of US$1.25m to government officials by United Brands (previously United Fruit) in return for reducing the taxes on fruit exports, eventually forced López to leave office in April 1975. Under his successors, **Colonel Juan Melgar Castro** (1975–78) and **General Policarpo Paz García** (1978–81), agrarian reform slowed to a trickle, repression of civil rights and freedom of speech increased, and corruption among military and government personnel grew to almost laughable levels. In a society sharply divided between rich and poor, almost seventy percent of rural households were unable to meet essential consumption costs, while five percent of the population controlled over half the land.

■ The lost decade – "USS Honduras"

Following the Sandinista revolution in Nicaragua in July 1979 and the election of Reagan to the US presidency in November 1980, Honduras found itself at the centre of US geo-political strategy – the "fourth border of the US", a state of affairs with which the government was only too happy to comply. The **elections** of November 1981, held under US diplomatic pressure, brought **Roberto Suazo Córdova** to power. Though a Liberal, Suazo was closely allied to the rabidly anti-Communist **Colonel Alvarez Martinez**, head of the police force (the FSP), then under military control, and later Commander in Chief of the armed forces. These two men allowed Honduras to become the focus for the US-backed Contra war in Nicaragua, accepting in return over US$1.5bn of direct economic and military aid from the US during the 1980s. US-funded training camps along the border were used on occasion to launch Contra attacks into Nicaraguan territory, while the Honduran army provided logistical support and participated in manoeuvres with the steadily growing numbers of US troops based in the country.

Domestically, the relationship between the military and government grew ever closer. **Human rights** violations rose alarmingly, with the army implicated in at least 184 "disappearances" of activists from labour organizations and peace movements. Forced conscription was common, and lengthy jail sentences were introduced for activities deemed subversive, including street demonstrations. In 1984, army officers, increasingly anxious over Alvarez's actions, forced him into exile. Though repression eased somewhat, the relationship between the military and government continued to be close, with corruption at senior levels in both institutions positively encouraged by the endless flow of dollars from the US.

■ Neo-liberalism and Hurricane Mitch

Honduras's role as a geo-political lynchpin diminished after Reagan left office and both the Contra war and the civil war in El Salvador were resolved. As the military became less obvious in day-to-day life, forced conscription was ended and most of the US troops stationed in Honduras were recalled, the country's endemic economic and social problems were thrown into stark relief.

National Party president **Rafael Leonardo Callejas** came to power in 1989 and introduced a neo-Liberal austerity programme, floating exchange rates, privatizing the state sector and cultivating foreign and private investment. Successful in the short term, particularly in forging relations with international lenders, the programme led to a sharp rise in poverty levels and failed ultimately to secure significant investment. Jurisdiction over legal and government affairs was slowly wrested back from the military by a resurgent judiciary, but monitoring groups reported that human rights abuses were still common. Callejas also singularly failed to tackle the issue of corruption, and was himself formally indicted for misappropriation of public funds in 1994.

In 1993, the widely respected Liberal candidate, businessman-turned-politician **Carlos Roberto Reina**, was elected president. Faced with an economic recession and rapidly devaluing Lempira, Reina put his claims to be capable of engineering moral renewal to the test by taking action on most overt cases of high-level corruption. He was not able, however, to prevent the economy sliding further into recession, or to halt a steadily worsening spiral of social instability. This last, fuelled by growing poverty and greater involvement with drug-smuggling between South and North America, affected the north coast in particular.

Reina's successor, Liberal **Carlos Flores Facussé**, took office in January 1998, after elections marred by allegations of corruption and vote-rigging on both sides. **Facussé** immediately set about trying to reduce Honduras's massive international debt, organizing a series of meetings with the IMF and World Bank. Though Flores had been elected with a campaign pledge to reverse the cycle of deepening poverty and social despair through investment and a programme of national conciliation, he largely maintained the free-market economics of his predecessors. Corporation tax was slashed and sweeping privatization plans were proposed in an austerity package formulated to gain debt relief, while sales tax was hiked from 7 to 12 per cent.

But just as these policies were being implemented, and before debt relief had been granted,

Hurricane Mitch began brewing offshore in October 1998. The category-five hurricane first battered Guanaja, laying siege to the Bay Island for three days before ripping across mainland Honduras, unleashing colossal volumes of rainfall in an apocalyptic trail across the country. After causing landslides and storm surges that killed over a thousand people in the capital Tegucigalpa, Mitch pursued an erratic path back across Honduras, triggering devastating mud slides and floods in neighbouring Nicaragua and along the path of the Chamelecón and Ulúa rivers from the Western highlands to San Pedro Sula. Though the final death toll will never be known, it's estimated that Mitch killed over 7000 people in Honduras, 4000 in Nicaragua and around 400 in Guatemala and El Salvador. Thousands more remain unaccounted for.

President Carlos Flores declared that Mitch had set Honduras back fifty years, and the world's media reported a cataclysmic picture of damage and devastation. These initial assessments came to seem over-pessimistic, however, as the nation – aided by teams from all over the world – steadily pulled itself together again, quickly patching up much of the key infrastructure. A year after the hurricane, all the main highways were open and most of the hundred bridges damaged by Mitch had been or repaired or rebuilt, and tourists were returning.

Yet reconstruction aside, it quickly became clear that Mitch had seriously exacerbated the nation's fundamental weaknesses and inequalities. The **economy** remains critically weak and almost totally dependent on inward investment, which chiefly goes into the *maquila* garment-assembly factories of the north. This industry, dominated by Korean and US companies, enjoys tax-free status and pays notoriously poor wages, while prestige technology companies opt to settle in the stable pastures of Costa Rica, where they can draw on a well-educated workforce. **Crime rates** have soared since Mitch, as violent gangs settle turf wars in the streets of San Pedro Sula and cocaine trafficking has become a key industry. The discredited police force retain a reputation for systematic corruption and have been implicated in the widespread killing of street children in the large cities.

As the December 2001 elections approached, life for most Hondurans remained a struggle in a country gripped by poverty and lack of opportunity. The key campaign issues are likely to reflect this, with unemployment, the state of the economy and law and order being uppermost in people's minds. The new president faces other formidable challenges: renegotiating Honduras's massive external debt and co-ordinating the fundamental developmental reforms with the numerous international organizations that have settled in Honduras after Mitch.

CHAPTER 17

TEGUCIGALPA AND THE SOUTH

N estling in a mountain valley 1000m above sea level, **Tegucigalpa** is one of the more enjoyable Central American capitals, thanks to a combination of faded colonial charm and a refreshing climate. This is a city built on a human rather than a monumental scale: from the small colonial core, home to many museums and churches, wealthy residential and embassy districts spread out to the south and east, while across the Río Choluteca to the west lies **Comayagüela**, Tegucigalpa's shabbier, more industrial twin – together the two comprise the administrative **Distrito Central**. Although the nation's economic focus has long since shifted to San Pedro Sula, Tegucigalpa continues to function as the political and governmental centre of Honduras.

The city sights might keep you busy for a day or two, but it's worth planning a longer stay in the capital in order to venture out into the pine forests and mountain ranges that encircle the city. To the east, the colonial mining villages of **Santa Lucía** and **Valle de Ángeles**, both easily reached by local buses, evoke a time when this was a rough frontier, and rich seams of silver provided the wealth on which Tegucigalpa was built. Just a short distance further north is one of the country's most accessible cloudforest reserves, the **Parque Nacional La Tigra**; though commonly visited on a day-trip from the capital, an overnight stay allows time to see more of the forest.

South of Tegucigalpa stretches the stark, sun-baked coastal plain of the Pacific. Tourists are few and far between in this region, whose only real attraction is **Isla El Tigre**, a little-visited volcanic island set in the calm waters of the Golfo de Fonseca. The most likely reason for travelling here is to cross the border into Nicaragua or El Salvador; heading east into Nicaragua, you may well have to change buses in the regional capital, **Choluteca**, whose well-preserved colonial centre makes it an appealing stopover.

Tegucigalpa

Much of **TEGUCIGALPA**'s appeal is understated, with its main pleasure to be found in wandering the winding, narrow streets of the old centre, which meander haphazardly up the lower slopes of **Cerro Picacho**, the city's dramatic, mountainous backdrop. Along these streets, crumbling colonial buildings give way to gently decaying nineteenth-century mansions and modern, airy homes, each a watermark of the city's history. Even the constant cacophony, gridlock and pollution of the traffic-choked centre doesn't detract entirely from the charm, and the comings and goings of hordes of

For an explanation of **accommodation price codes**, see p.365.

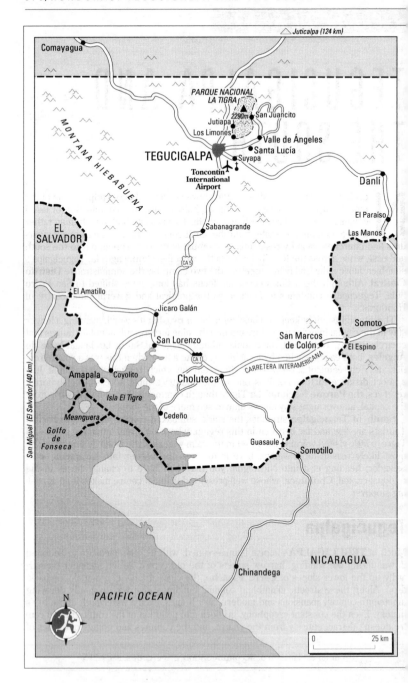

vendors, beggars, idlers and passers-by provide entertainment for free. More concrete attractions include several well-preserved colonial **churches**, in particular the eighteenth-century cathedral on the Plaza Morazán, a handful of national **museum and art collections**, and several small, well-patronized parks.

Yet just west of the old centre, the character of the city rapidly becomes more menacing as you approach the banks of the Río Choluteca. On October 29, 1998, ten-metre-high floods caused by **Hurricane Mitch** ripped through the river valley, tearing down buildings in a tide of devastation that killed around a thousand people. Today virtually nothing has changed since the floods – vast mud deposits and garbage clog the banks and hundreds of vultures circle overhead in some worst scenes of urban decay in Central America. Cross one of the bridges and you're in **Comayagüela**, always a poor barrio but now distinctly threatening after dark as poverty levels have increased following Mitch. Most visitors come here to visit sprawling **market**, or are simply passing through one of the city's **bus terminals**, which are dotted around Comayagüela's streets. Keep a very close eye on your possessions as you change buses.

Some history

Before the arrival of the Spanish, the Tegucigalpa valley was inhabited by small Lenca groups who gradually moved south and settled along the Río Choluteca, as far as what is today Comayagüela. Exactly when the conquistadors first arrived in the valley is unclear; records make no mention of the area until the 1560s, when silver deposits were found in the hills to the east, around Santa Lucía (see p.387). The discovery of further deposits in the surrounding hills attracted growing numbers of settlers, who pushed the indigenous inhabitants out to what are now the outlying barrios of Comayagüela. **Real de Minas de San Miguel de Tegucigalpa** was founded on September 29, 1578, and in 1608 granted the status of *alcaldía*, with authority over a rash of mining settlements in the valley and surrounding hills. Town status came in 1768 and that of city in 1807, with profits from the silver mines aiding the construction of fine colonial churches and houses.

Its mining wealth and location at the centre of cross-country trade routes made Tegucigalpa an increasingly clamorous rival to the then capital, Comayagua. Following **independence** – initially spurned by both cities through fear that the other might be named capital – it was decided to alternate the seat of government between the two, a plan that was riddled with shortcomings but nevertheless staggered on until 1830, when parliament was permanently restored to Comayagua. Fifty years later, however, the Liberal President Soto shifted power back to Tegucigalpa, enraged by the failure of Comayagua's innately conservative leaders to support him. In 1932, the city and its poor relation to the south, Comayagüela, were united under the title **Distrito Central**.

Since the late nineteenth century, when the economic focus of the country began to shift to the bountiful fruit plantations of the north coast, Tegucigalpa has become somewhat eclipsed by San Pedro Sula. In essence a chaotic small town grown large, the business of government remains the city's main industry. In the words of a local saying, "Tegucigalpa thinks, San Pedro works".

Arrival, information and city transport

Both international and domestic flights arrive at **Toncontín International Airport**, 7km south of the city. **Taxis** wait outside the terminal, but you can save a couple of dollars by walking 50m down to the highway and hailing one there; the journey to the centre should cost around US$4. City bus #24 ("Río Grande–Lomas") passes the airport frequently, running through Comayagüela and into the centre of Tegucigalpa in around forty minutes, depending on the traffic. At the airport there's a **bank**, a small **Hondutel** telephone office, a number of **car rental** agencies and the *Cyber City* **Internet café** outside the arrivals hall.

Tegucigalpa has no central **bus terminal**; each international or intercity bus line has its own terminal, most of them scattered around Comayagüela. The main exception is buses to and from Danlí and the Nicaraguan border at Las Manos, which run from the Mercado Jacaleapa, Col Kennedy – you can catch a collectivo taxi (US$0.30) there from Puente La Isla below the Congreso Nacional building.

The helpful **Instituto Hondureño de Turismo**, in the Edificio Europa, Av Ramon Cruz and C República de México (Mon–Fri 8.30am–4.30pm; ☎238 3974, fax 222 6621, or call toll-free in Honduras on ☎800/222 TOUR, *touristinfo@iht.hn*), provides maps of the country and major cities, as well as bilingual information on the main tourist attractions, such as Copán. There's always someone available who speaks English. Keep an eye out for *Honduras Tips*, a privately published, quarterly magazine, available in many of the better hotels and some gift shops, which gives a good overview of sights, hotels and restaurants across the country. For more detailed **maps**, try the Instituto Geográfico Nacional, 15a C off the Blvd de Comunidad Europea, Comayagüela (Mon–Fri 8.30am–noon & 2–4pm; ☎225 0752).

City transport

City buses are frequent and extremely noisy; they're generally old US school buses, though unfortunately not painted in the glorious colours seen elsewhere in Central America. Urban routes start running at around 6am and finish around 9pm. Route names and numbers are painted on the front and fares are extremely cheap (US$0.20 anywhere within the city), though none pass very close to the Parque Central. Any bus signed "San Miguel" (including the #21) runs past the US embassy and the tourist office along Av Juan Gutemberg.

Taxis come in a range of shapes and colours, but are easy to identify by the numbers painted on their sides. They announce their availability by incessant honking and are often shared, with passengers dropped off in turn. There are no meters but a trip in the city should be around US$2, a little more at night.

Accommodation

The central and eastern parts of **Tegucigalpa** contain a reasonable range of upmarket **hotels** and pleasant, less expensive accommodation, convenient for museums, restaurants and enjoying the bustling evening street life. A nice alternative, though not particularly cheap, is to stay in one of the **B&B guesthouses**, which are mostly located outside the centre in the district of Colonia Palmira. Though Comayagüela contains a number of **budget** places, few travellers now stay there because of security concerns. All accommodation is marked on the maps opposite or on p.381.

Tegucigalpa

Coxfort Inn B & B, 2 C Col Palmira (☎ & fax 239 1197, *coxfort@mayanet.hn*). Convivial American-owned guesthouse in a prestige location high above the city, with spacious, individually decorated rooms (all with TV and some with kitchen facilities), a small pool and secure parking. ⑥.

Hotel Granada, Av Juan Gutemberg at Av Cristóbal Colón (☎237 2381). Best budget deal in town, with basic but clean rooms, some with bath, plus hot water and a communal TV area. Very good value and consequently always popular. ①–②.

Hotels Granada 2 & 3, Subida Casa Martín, Barrio Guanacaste (☎237 4004, 237 0798 or 237 0812). Similar to – and just round the corner from – the original *Hotel Granada*. All rooms, including triples and quadruples, have private bath. You'll pay a little extra for a TV. ③.

Hotel Honduras Maya, Av República de Perú, Col Palmira (☎220 5000, fax 220 6000, *www.hondurasmaya.hn*). This luxury modern hotel is something of a city landmark, its bold outline bedecked in Maya glyphs. The upper rooms have great views over the city, and facilities include a restaurant, café, large pool, souvenir shops, car rental and a travel agency. ⑨.

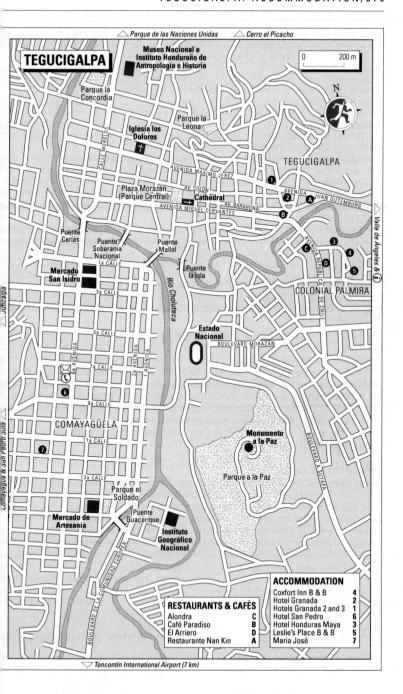

TEGUCIGALPA

△ Parque de las Naciones Unidas   △ Cerro el Picacho

Museo Nacional e
Instituto Hondureño de
Antropología e Historia

Parque la
Concordia

Parque la
Leona

Iglesia los
Dolores

CALLE MORELOS

AVENIDA MAXIMO JEREZ

TEGUCIGALPA

Plaza Morazán
(Parque Central)

AV. COLON

Cathedral

AVENIDA MIGUEL CERVANTES

AVENIDA JUAN GUTEMBURG

AV. BARAHONA

1
2 A
B

Puente
Carías

Puente
Soberania
Nacional

Puente
Mallol

Puente
la Isla

3
C
D
4
5

AVENIDA REPUBLICA DE CHILE

COLONIAL PALMIRA

Mercado
San Isidro

1a CALLE

3a CALLE

Río Choluteca

Valle de Ángeles & ℹ △

Estado
Nacional

5a CALLE

7a CALLE

2a AVENIDA

6a AVENIDA

BOULEVARD MORAZÁN

6

9a CALLE

COMAYAGÜELA

11a CALLE

7

Monumento
a la Paz

BOULEVARD A SUYAPA

13a CALLE

Parque a la Paz

Parque el
Soldado

Puente
Guacerique

Mercado de
Artesanía

Instituto
Geográfico
Nacional

BOULEVARD DE LA COMUNIDAD EUROPEA

0   200 m

N

Comayagüela a San Pedro Sula △   △ Júcacalpa

▽ Toncontín International Airport (7 km)

RESTAURANTS & CAFÉS

Alondra	C
Café Paradiso	B
El Arriero	D
Restaurante Nan Kin	A

ACCOMMODATION

Coxfort Inn B & B	4
Hotel Granada	2
Hotels Granada 2 and 3	1
Hotel San Pedro	6
Hotel Honduras Maya	3
Leslie's Place B & B	5
Maria José	7

Hotel La Ronda, Av Jeréz at C las Damas (☎237 8151, fax 237 1454). Now looking a little in need of a refurbishment, but still offering a central location and comfortable rooms, all with a/c and TV, and the price includes breakfast. There's a decent restaurant and a relaxed bar downstairs. ⑦.

Hotel MacArthur, Av Lempira 454, Barrio Abajo (☎237 9839, fax 238 0294, *homacart@datum.hn*). Convenient for the centre and popular with business travellers; all rooms have hot water, fan and TV – you pay more for a/c. The small café downstairs serves expensive breakfasts. ⑤.

Hotel Maya Colonial, C Palace, just north of the Parque Central (☎237 2643). An air of faded charm, a good central location and adequately furnished rooms, though there's no hot water. ②.

Leslie's Place B&B, Calzada San Martín 452, Paseo República de Perú, Col Palmira (☎239 0641, fax 239 5912, *www.dormir.com*). Comfortable and friendly hotel with a pleasant patio, but perhaps a shade pricey. The stylish rooms all have a/c, TV and phone. ⑦.

Nuevo Hotel Boston, Av Máximo Jeréz 321, between C el Telegrafo and C Morelos (☎237 9411). This well-run perennial favourite is a great place for meeting people. The friendly management keep everything spotlessly clean and very secure. There's free coffee, an elegant communal TV area and inexhaustible supplies of hot water. The large, old rooms at the front are nicer, despite the traffic noise. ③.

Comayagüela

Hotel Maria José, 12a C, 7–8 Av (☎237 7292). Good-value family-run establishment, offering clean and pleasant rooms with private bath, hot water, TV and fan. The café downstairs is open for breakfast through to dinner, closing mid-evening. ②.

Hotel San Pedro, 6 Av 8–9 Av (☎222 8987). You'd hardly want to spend too long in this hotel – the ninety rooms with or without private bath are very basic – but it remains a popular choice with travellers because of its location close to the bus terminals. ①–②.

The City

The heart of Tegucigalpa's **old city** is the pleasant Plaza Morazán, bordered on one side by the **cathedral**; a number of the more interesting churches and museums, plus many hotels, lie within easy walking distance of the square. East from the centre, two major roads, **Av Jeréz** (which becomes Av Juan Gutemberg and then Av la Paz) and **Av Miguel Cervantes** (changing its name to Av República de Chile), run out through the richer suburbs and embassy district. Tegucigalpa's main artery, **1a Avenida** (later called Blvd de la Comunidad Europea), splits the city in two from north to south, running parallel to the Río Choluteca then continuing out past the airport to destinations south. Across the river, west from central Tegucigalpa, lies **Comayagüela**, with its huge market and bus terminals.

Around the old centre

Plaza Morazán, Tegucigalpa's central square, functions as a meeting point, marketplace and site of general entertainment. Hawkers vend, beggars beg, people stop and chat, and on Sundays the place swarms with workers enjoying their day off. As busy after dark as during the day, the plaza makes a pleasant place to while away the time and people-watch. The statue at the centre commemorates the national hero **Francisco Morazán**, a soldier, Liberal and reformer who was elected president of the Central American Republic in 1830. The house where he was born, two blocks west on Av Cristóbal Colón, is now the **Biblioteca Nacional** (Mon–Fri 8.30am–4pm). On the east edge of the plaza, the blinding white facade of the **Catedral San Miguel**, completed in 1782, is one of the best preserved in Central America. Inside, look out for the magnificent hand-worked Baroque-style gilded altar, and the baptismal font, carved in 1643 by indigenous artesans from a single block of stone. Three blocks east from the plaza, on Av Paz Barahona, the **Iglesia San Franciso** is the oldest church in the city, first built by the Franciscans in 1592, although much of the present building dates from 1740.

Just to the south of the Parque Central, next to the Iglesia La Merced on C Bolívar, the **Galería Nacional de Arte** (Mon–Fri 9am–4pm; US$1) is home to an extensive collection of Central American art. Displays on the ground floor range from prehistoric petroglyphs and Maya stone carvings to colonial paintings and religious art, while upstairs rooms are devoted to the gallery's surprisingly ambitious twentieth-century

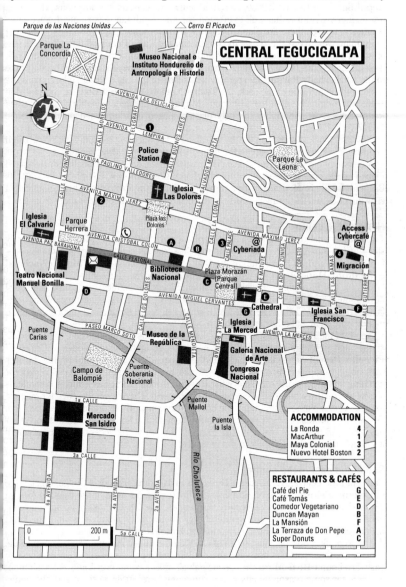

CENTRAL TEGUCIGALPA

Parque de las Naciones Unidas △   △ Cerro El Picacho

Parque La Concordia

Museo Nacional e Instituto Hondureño de Antropología e Historia

AVENIDA LAS DELICIAS

CALLE MORELOS
AVENIDA
CALLE EL TELÉGRAFO
CALLE BUENOS AIRES
CALLE SALVADOR MENDIETA

Police Station

AVENIDA PAULINO VALLEDORES
AVENIDA MÁXIMO JEREZ

Parque La Leona

Iglesia Las Dolores

Plaza las Dolores

Iglesia El Calvario

Parque Herrera

AVENIDA CRISTOBAL COLÓN

CALLE LA CONCORDIA

AVENIDA PAZ BARAHONA

CALLE LA LEONA

CALLE PALACE
AVENIDA MÁXIMO JEREZ

Access Cybercafé @

CALLE ADOLFO ZUNIGA

Cyberiada

CALLE MAUTE

Migración

CALLE LAS DAMAS

Teatro Nacional Manuel Bonilla

Biblioteca Nacional

CALLE PEATONAL

Plaza Morazán (Parque Central)

AVENIDA MIGUEL CERVANTES

CALLE SALVADOR CORLETO

CALLE GUTIÉRREZ

CALLE LOS DOLORES

Cathedral

Iglesia San Francisco

CALLE MENDIETA
CALLE BOLÍVAR

Iglesia La Merced

AVENIDA LA MERCED

Puente Carías

PASEO MARCO SOTO

Museo de la República

Galería Nacional de Arte

Campo de Balompié

Puente Soberanía Nacional

Congreso Nacional

Puente Mallol

1a CALLE

Mercado San Isidro

Puente la Isla

3a CALLE

6a AVENIDA
4a AVENIDA
2a AVENIDA

Río Choluteca

5a CALLE

0 — 200 m

ACCOMMODATION

La Ronda	4
MacArthur	1
Maya Colonial	3
Nuevo Hotel Boston	2

RESTAURANTS & CAFÉS

Café del Pie	G
Café Tomás	E
Comedor Vegetariano	D
Duncan Mayan	B
La Mansión	F
La Terraza de Don Pepe	A
Super Donuts	C

collection. Originally a convent and then the national university, the building's Neoclassical facade sits rather uncomfortably alongside the stained concrete hulk of the **Congreso Nacional**, the country's seat of government, next door.

One block west of the Galería Nacional de Arte, at Paseo Marco Soto and C Mendieta, the late nineteenth-century presidential palace housed the **Museo Histórico de la República** from 1992 until 2000, though it's currently closed for renovations. The museum formerly held a rather dull exhibition tracing Honduran development since independence, though there are plans install new exhibits sometime in 2002.

Running **west from the plaza**, the pedestrianized **Calle Peatonal** (literally "pedestrian street") is lined with shops and cafés and thick with innumerable street vendors. Walk west along here for twenty minutes or so, dodging the moneychangers, and you'll come to the small, shady **Parque Herrera**, where many of the city's street children pass the day. On the south side of the park, the **Teatro Nacional Manuel Bonilla**, completed in 1915, was originally intended to honour Miguel de Cervantes; within the grey-stone Renaissance-style shell is an ornately plaster-worked interior, based on the Athenée Comique in Paris. Check the local press or ask at the box office for details of current shows. Five blocks north from the theatre along C la Concordia is another welcome patch of green, the **Parque La Concordia**, dotted with replicas of Maya sculptures.

A couple of blocks northwest from the central plaza, set on the small pedestrianized Plaza Los Dolores is the white, domed **Iglesia Los Dolores**, completed in 1732. Its Baroque facade is decorated with a representation of the Passion of Christ, featuring a crowing cock and the rising sun; inside, the ornately worked gold altar dates from 1742.

North of the centre

Two blocks west of the Iglesia Los Dolores, a right turn onto C Morelos and a fairly steep fifteen-minute walk brings you to the Villa Roy, an eighteenth-century mansion – formerly the home of President Lozano Díaz – that's now home to the **Museo Nacional e Instituto Hondureño de Antropología e Historia** (Tues–Sun 8.30am–3.30pm; US$1.50). Inside, a comprehensive exhibition covers the political, economic and social development of the republic, alongside a display of less interesting presidential artefacts. The institute below the villa has a small reference library with books and information on Copán and other archeological sites.

North of the Plaza Morazán, older suburbs – previously home to the wealthy middle classes and rich immigrants, now long gone – edge up the lower slopes of **Cerro El Picacho**. Decent views can be had from the **Parque La Leona**, about twenty minutes walk uphill from the centre along C Las Damas, but if you can, it's worth continuing (or catching a bus) up to the top, where the **Parque de las Naciones Unidas** commands a view across the whole of the city and valley beyond. There's ample space for picnicking and strolling among the trees; the cramped zoo, near the entrance, is best avoided. On Sundays **buses** run here every half-hour from behind Los Dolores church; on other days, take an El Hatillo bus from the Parque Herrera to the access road, from where it's about fifteen minutes' walk to the entrance.

South and east of the centre

East from the centre, **Av Máximo Jeréz/Juan Gutemberg** skirts the northern edge of **Colonia Palmira**, an upmarket district which contains most of the capital's foreign embassies, luxury hotels and wealthy residences. The **US embassy**, a common reference point, lies along Av Juan Gutemberg, about thirty minutes' walk from Plaza Morazán. Another city landmark, the modern **Hotel Honduras Maya**, can be found on the Av República de Chile, just south of Col Palmira, fifteen minutes' walk east from the centre. Continue past the hotel for about a kilometre and an overpass gives access to eastward-bound **Blvd Morazán**, Tegucigalpa's major commercial and entertainment artery – for some reason no city buses run along here. At its western end, the boulevard terminates at the **Estadio Nacional**, home to both international and domestic soccer games. The vaguely Greek temple-like monument visible to the south of here on the low Cerro Juana Laínez is the **Monumento a la Paz**, built to commemorate the treaty ending the 1969 Football War (see p.372). A road up to the monument starts from the fire station behind the stadium.

Comayagüela

The surging brown waters of the polluted Río Choluteca form a suitable border to Tegucigalpa's twin, **COMAYAGÜELA**, which sprawls away through down-at-heel business districts into industrial areas and poor barrios. There's little to see here and the workaday streets, invariably choked with traffic, have a much less relaxed feel than those of Tegucigalpa. At night there's an undeniably rough edge to the place, and even the inhabitants of Tegucigalpa prefer not to venture here.

San Isidro, the capital's main **market**, sprawls around 6a Av and 1a C, just across the Puente Carías river bridge from C Morelos in Tegucigalpa. Stalls jostle for space along the narrow alleys and pavements, sometimes spilling over into the streets themselves, and buses crawl through the crowds, sometimes only inches from the vendors. The atmosphere is hot and frenetic, with the smell of raw meat rising in hot weather. Keep an eye on your possessions while walking around here. About ten minutes' walk past the market, at the intersection with 12a C, is the Banco Central de Honduras building; check in the newspapers for details of the occasional **exhibitions** hosted in the art gallery here.

In the heart of Comayagüela, at 3a Av and 15a C, is the small **Mercado de Artesanía**, housed in a rather gloomy building that never seems to get very busy. Stands sell handicrafts from around the country at prices lower than in Tegucigalpa's shops, although the selection is narrower.

Out from the city: the Basilica de Suyapa

Six or so kilometres east of the centre, the flat plains are broken by the monolithic white bulk of the **Basílica de Suyapa**. Built in colonial style in the 1950s, to provide a new home for the **Virgen de Suyapa**, the patron saint of Honduras, the church's lofty, bare interior serves to highlight the striking blue stained-glass windows. According to legend, however, the Virgin has resisted all attempts to place her permanently in the new edifice, each time mysteriously returning to her original home, a simple chapel behind the church. According to legend, the tiny 6cm-high statue of the Virgin was discovered in 1743 by two campesinos returning to Suyapa from working on Cerro del Pilingüín. Finding themselves still a distance from the village as dark fell, they decided to pass the night in the open air. One of them noticed he was lying on something that felt like a stone and threw it to one side, without looking at it. Within a few minutes, however, the object had returned to the same place. The next day, the two carried the little statue down to Suyapa where, placed on a simple table adorned with flowers, the Virgin began to attract increasing numbers of worshippers. A certain Captain José de Zelaya y Midence built the chapel to house the statue in thanks for recovery of his health.

You can see the statue behind the wooden altar in **La Pequeña Iglesia**, the much simpler, original eighteenth-century chapel, sheltered behind the Basilica. These days it is only moved to the new building temporarily, during the February festival of the Virgen de Suyapa, when thousands of pilgrims from across the country come to worship. City buses to Suyapa run regularly from the Mercado San Isidro in Comayagüela.

Eating, drinking and entertainment

Great culinary experiences and nightlife are not what Tegucigalpa is noted for, although a fairly wide selection of cuisines is available in a reasonable number of **places to eat**. The more expensive restaurants are generally found in the eastern colonias and along the Blvd Morazán, while the centre boasts a number of cheap and cheerful café-style eateries; quality varies but the portions are generally large. Unless otherwise stated, all the places listed below are open daily.

With a few exceptions, most **bars** in the centre are fiercely local hangouts, and as a visitor you may get an indifferent reception. The atmosphere is more relaxed in the upmarket spots on the Blvd Morazán and along **Blvd Suyapa** towards the university. While nothing like on the scale of most European capitals, this is also the place to come for **clubs**, especially at weekends.

For films, there are a few **cinemas** around the centre, with more modern complexes in the outer suburbs. All show first-run Hollywood movies, generally with subtitles. Closest to the centre are **Aires Tauro** on the Subida Casa Martín, off Av Juan Gutemberg, and **Cine Variadades**, C Mendieta at Av Cristóbal Colón.

Restaurants and cafés

Alondra Av República de Chile, Col Palmira. The most elegant restaurant in town, patronized by the nation's elite, with an expansive, European-inspired menu, decent wine list, and a gorgeous peaceful setting around a verdant garden. Relatively expensive (around US$18 a head), but worth a splurge.

Café del Pie inside a small mall just south of the cathedral. Despite the location, this little café is well worth seeking out for its delicious coffee (including espresso and cappuccino), tasty sandwiches and cheap lunches.

Café Paradiso, Av Paz Barahona at C la Plazuela. Quiet place with a tiny patio, serving good coffees and snacks. They also show foreign films, and there's a well-stocked Spanish-language bookshop attached. Closed Sun.

Café Tomás just behind the cathedral on C Matute. Popular with locals and foreigners, this venue combines a pleasant patio, an atmospheric bar (with a restaurant planned) and a short snack and breakfast menu – it's also home to Shakespeare's Books.

Comedor Vegetariano, Av Cervantes at C Morelos. Inexpensive vegetarian comedor. Though the eating area is slightly barren, the huge set meals, including soup, a daily special and dessert, are a bargain at around US$3. Closed evenings and Sun.

Duncan Mayan, Av Cristóbal Colón, 2 blocks west of Parque Central. Busy barn of a place, popular amongst workers on their way home, with large helpings of local food, burgers and snacks from US$1.50.

El Arriero, Av República de Chile 516, just past *Hotel Honduras Maya*. Expensive but excellent steak and seafood restaurant – a substantial meal goes for around US$12.

La Mansión Av Miguel Paz Barahona. Great buffet-style restaurant, set around a quiet courtyard, serving very inexpensive and tasty breakfasts and lunches.

La Terraza de Don Pepe, Av Cristóbal Colón, opposite the Biblioteca Nacional. Family restaurant dishing up large portions of local and Chinese-style food, as well as snacks. The tables on the roadside terrace are nicer, if you can stand the fumes.

Restaurante Nan Kin, in the *Hotel Nan Kin*, Av Juan Gutemberg at Calzada San Miguel. Large, tasty and reasonably priced Chinese dishes, and good service.

Super Donuts, C Peatonal and other locations. Doughnut shop which also does good-value Honduran-style breakfasts, pancakes and fruit, from around US$1. Closed Sun.

Nightlife

In the centre, *Café Tomás* (see above) has a sociable **bar** and patio for relaxed alfresco drinking – with regular performances from Garífuna and Honduran folk bands – and it's also a good place to meet other travellers. Along Blvd Morazán, *Taco Taco* and *Confetti* bars are both popular with Honduran students and get very lively at weekends. *Piano Bar la Hacienda*, also on Blvd Morazán, goes for a little more sophistication, serving cocktails and hosting variable live music. For dancing, *Plaza Garibaldi*, also on Blvd Morazán, stays open all night, playing Latin American rhythms. Those intent on serious **clubbing** should head out to Blvd Suyapa and the happening venues of *Ozona, Arena's,*

Coconut Grove and *Planeta Sí Pango*. The capital's dance scene mainly revolves around merengue and salsa sounds plus a little Latin house and European and American pop.

Listings

Airlines Air France, Galería la Paz 116, Av la Paz (☎237 0216, fax 237 0189); Alitalia, 4 Av & 9C, Col Alameda (☎ & fax 239 4246); American Airlines, Ground Floor, Edificio Palmira, Col Palmira (☎232 1414, fax 232 1380); British Airways, Blvd Comunidad Europea (☎225 5102, fax 225 0341); Continental Airlines, Edificio Palic, Av República de Chile (☎220 0997, fax 220 0990); Copa, Floors 2–4, Edificio Europa, Col San Carlos (☎231 2469, fax 231 2479); Grupo Taca (Lacsa, Nica, Aviateca, Avianca), Edificio Interamericana, Blvd Morazán (☎239 0915, fax 231 1517); Iberia, Edificio Palmira, Col Palmira (☎232 7760, fax 239 1729); Isleña, Galería La Paz, Av La Paz (☎237 3410, fax 237 3390); Japan Airlines, Galerías La Paz 312, Av La Paz (☎238 0425, fax 237 9914); KLM, Edificio Cicsa (☎232 6414, fax 232 6320); Lacsa, see Grupo Taca; Lufthansa, 2nd floor, Centro Comercial Plaza del Sol, Av La Paz (☎236 7560, fax 236 7580); Rollins, airport (☎234 2766); Sosa, airport (☎233 7351, fax 234 0137); Varig, Edificio Sempe, Blvd Comunidad Europea (☎225 5102, fax 225 0341).

American Express The local agent is Mundirama Travel Service, Edificio Cicsa, Av República de Panamá, close to the *Hotel Honduras Maya* (Mon–Fri 8am–noon & 1–5pm, Sat 8am–noon).

Banks and exchange Virtually all banks will change dollars and travellers' cheques. The Coin SA Casa de Cambio on C Peatonal may offer better rates for cash than the banks, whilst the money-changers on the street invariably offer rates slightly better than the official one. Banco Atlántida, on the Parque Central and elsewhere, gives advances on Visa cards, whilst Credomatic, C Mendieta at Av Cervantes, gives advances on Visa and Mastercard.

Bookstores Metromedia, on C República de Colombia in Col Palmira, has a wide range of English-language fiction, non-fiction and travel, as well as secondhand books, US newspapers and magazines. Shakespeare's Books, inside *Café Tomás* (see opposite) has around 9000 secondhand books, mainly fiction. Librería Guaymuras, Av Cervantes at C Las Damas, is good for Spanish-language fiction and political, economic and social texts, whilst the bookshop inside *Café Paradiso* also has a reasonable range of contemporary Honduran politics, history and economic titles. The *Hotel Honduras Maya* and other luxury hotels have US newspapers and magazines and *Honduras This Week*.

Car rental Avis, Av República de Perú, in front of *Hotel Honduras Maya* (☎239 5711, fax 239 5710; airport ☎233 9548); Budget, *Hotel Honduras Maya* (☎232 6832, fax 233 5170; airport ☎233 5161); Hertz, Centro Comercial Villa Real, in front of *Hotel Honduras Maya* (☎239 0772, fax 232 0870); Molinari, 1a Av, 10a C 1002, Comayagüela (☎237 5335, fax 238 0585; airport ☎233 1307); National, airport (☎233 4962).

Embassies Belize, ground floor of *Hotel Honduras Maya* (☎ & fax 239 0134; Mon–Fri 9am-1pm); Canada, Edificio los Castaños, 6th floor, Blvd Morazán (☎231 4538, fax 231 5793); Costa Rica, Colonia El Triangulo (☎232 1768, fax 232 1876; Mon–Fri 8am–3pm); El Salvador, 2 Av 205, Col San Carlos (☎236 8045, fax 236 9403; Mon–Fri 8.30am–noon & 1–3pm); Guatemala, 4 C at Arturo López Rodezno 2421, Col Las Minitas (☎232 9704, fax 231 5655; Mon–Fri 8.30am–3pm); Mexico, Av República de México 2402, Col Palmira (☎232 6471, fax 231 4719; Mon–Fri 8–11am); Nicaragua, C11, Block M1, Col Lomas del Tepeyac (☎232 4290, fax 231 1412; Mon–Fri 8.30am–1pm); Panamá, Edificio Palmira 200, Col Palmira (☎231 5508, fax 232 8147; Mon–Fri 8am–1pm); UK, Edificio Palmira, 3rd Floor, Col Palmira (☎232 0612, fax 232 5480; Mon–Thurs 8am–noon & 1–4pm, Fri 8am–3pm); US, Av La Paz (☎236 9320, fax 236 9037; Mon–Fri 8am–5pm).

Immigration Dirección General de Migracíon, Av Máximo Jeréz, just east of *Hotel Ronda* (Mon–Fri 8.30am–4.30pm; ☎238 1957).

Internet access Cyberiada (daily, open 24hr) on Av Máximo Jeréz, two blocks north of the cathedral, is very well set up, while a little further down the same road Access Cybercafé, Centro Comerical, Av Máximo Jeréz (opposite the *migración*) is also reliable – both charge around US$2.25 an hour.

Laundry Mi Lavandería, 2 Av, 3–4 C, Comayagüela, has coin-operated machines and a laundry service (Mon–Sat 7am–6pm, Sun 8am–5pm); Super Jet, Av Juan Gutemberg, just past the *Hotel/Restaurante Nan kin*, offers a reliable laundry service and dry-cleaning (Mon–Sat 8am–6.30pm).

Library The Biblioteca Nacional is open to the public for reference use only, on production of a passport (Mon–Fri 8.30am–4pm); you'll need to be very specific about what you're after.

Medical care Contact your embassy for a list of recommended doctors. Emergency departments (24hr) at Hospital Escuela, Blvd Suyapa (☎232 6234), and Hospital General San Felipe, C La Paz by the Bolívar monument.

Photography Kodak on Av Cervantes by the central plaza and Konica on the C Peatonal have a rapid and reliable developing service and sell film.

Police Go to the FSP office on C Buenos Aires, behind Los Dolores church, with any problems.

Post office C Peatonal at C El Telegrafo, 3 blocks west of the main plaza (Mon–Fri 8am–7pm, Sat 8am–1pm). Window 1 on the ground floor deals with the *lista de correos*.

Supermarkets Más Por Menos on Av la Paz, just past the river bridge, has a wide selection of canned and packaged goods and household items.

Telephone office First try the cybercafés (see previous page) for discounted international phone rates; Cyberiada also offers Web phone calls. Hondutel is at Av Cristóbal Colón at C El Telegrafo. Phone services operate 24hr, and reverse-charge calls to Europe are available. The fax office is open Monday to Friday 7am to 5pm.

Travel agents Numerous agents around the central plaza and in Col Palmira can book or change flights. Alhambra Travel (☎220 1700) in the *Hotel Honduras Maya* is quick, friendly and efficient.

Moving on from Tegucigalpa

Tegucigalpa is the transport hub of the nation, with regular **bus departures** for all the major towns and numerous smaller ones. Departures **south** to the Golfo de Fonseca, **north** to San Pedro Sula and **east** to Olancho are frequent and the roads good; you'll need to buy tickets before boarding if you're taking an intercity bus. Getting to desti-

BUSES FROM TEGUCIGALPA		
Unless otherwise stated, all terminals are in Comayagüela.		
DESTINATION	**COMPANY**	**DEPARTS FROM**
All Central American capitals (except Belize City)	Ticabus	16 C, 5–6 Av (☎220 0579)
Choluteca	Mi Esperanza	6 Av, 24 C (☎225 1505)
Comayagua	El Rey	12 C, 7 Av (☎237 1462)
Danlí/El Paraíso	Discua Litena	Mercado Jacaleapa, Col Kennedy, Tegucigalpa (☎232 7379)
North coast	Empresa Cristina	8 Av, 12 C (☎220 0117)
	Empresa Etrusca	12 C, 8–9 Av (☎220 0137)
	Viana (luxury buses)	Blvd Fuerzas Armadas (☎235 8585)
Olancho	Discovery	7 Av, 12–13 C (☎222 4256)
	Empresa Aurora	8 C, 6–7 Av (☎237 3647)
San Pedro Sula	Cotraibal	8 Av, 12–13 C (☎237 1666)
	Hedman Alas (luxury buses)	11 Av, 13 C (☎237 7143)
	Transportes Norteños	12 C, 6–7 Av (☎237 0706)
	El Rey	12 C, 7 Av (☎237 1462)
San Salvador	King Quality	Barrio Guacerique, Blvd de la Comunidad Europea (☎233 7515)
	Cruceros del Golfo	Barrio Guacerique, Blvd de la Comunidad Europea (☎233 7415)

nations off the main highways – Copán, the west, and the north coast, for example – is not as straightforward; in most cases there's no alternative to a slow and tiring bus journey on bad roads, though **flying** to the north coast is one alternative. Leaving Tegucigalpa by bus can be bewildering initially; routes are generally operated by several companies, out of their own private terminals. The major companies are listed in the box opposite, with terminal addresses and phone numbers.

Tours

A number of companies run **organized tours** to destinations in Honduras including Copán and the Bay Islands, usually for a minimum of two people. This can be an easy – if not particularly cheap – way to see the main sights. Explore Honduras, based in Edificio Medcast 206, Blvd Morazán (☎236 7694, fax 236 9800, *www.explorehonduras.com*) and Trek de Honduras, Av Julio Lozano 1311, Col Alameda (☎239 9827, fax 239 0743, *trek@hondurasnet.com*), are both reliable operators. La Moskitia Ecoaventuras, Apdo Postal 3577, Col Walter 1635, Barrio La Leona (☎ & fax 237 9398, *www.honduras.com/moskitia*), is highly recommended for organized tours to Mosquitia.

Around Tegucigalpa

Tegucigalpa's excellent local transport links make for easy day-trips to a number of destinations in the surrounding countryside. Set in the pine-clad mountains to the east are the tranquil colonial former mining villages of **Santa Lucía** and **Valle de Ángeles**, while to the north, charming **San Juancito** is a point of access for the cloudforest of **Parque Nacional la Tigra**, one of the most accessible national parks in the country. It is possible to visit the park in a day, but it's worth planning to spend at least a night there to fully enjoy the forest and wildlife. Finally, overland travellers may well make use of the Las Manos **border crossing**, the closest entry point into **Nicaragua** from the capital.

Santa Lucía

Twelve kilometres east of the capital, set amid the pine-clad mountain slopes so characteristic of the central highlands, **SANTA LUCÍA** is a legacy of the days when the riches to be gained from silver mining brought settlers to the area in droves. Built by the Spanish in the late sixteenth century, the fortunes of this archetypal colonial village – all whitewashed houses and red-tiled roofs set on a steep hillside – rose and fell with those of the mines. Its citizens' finest hour came in 1572, when King Felipe II, in gratitude at the stream of riches being produced, presented them with a carved wooden Crucifix. Now residing in the church, this is honoured annually during the fiesta of the **Cristo Negro** in first two weeks of January. The scenic views from Santa Lucía, over the mountains and down to Tegucigalpa, make for a relaxed half-day or so spent ambling around the steep, cobbled streets and surrounding forest. **Buses** for Santa Lucía leave Tegucigalpa's Mercado San Pablo, Col Reparto, every thirty minutes until 6pm; the last bus back leaves around 5.30pm.

Valle de Ángeles

Beyond Santa Lucía, the road continues to rise gently amid magnificent scenery, winding through forests of pine whose slender trunks reach up towards clear blue skies. Eleven or so kilometres from Santa Lucía is **VALLE DE ÁNGELES**, another former mining town, now reincarnated as handicraft centre and scenic getaway for *capitalaños*.

Perched on the edge of a valley, surrounded by green, wooded mountains, the town slumbers during the week in preparation for the weekends of hard business when the tourists pour in. **Buses** from Tegucigalpa run through the centre of town, passing the Parque Central and terminating a couple of blocks away. Everything in the town is only a few minutes' walk from both the Parque Central and the bus terminal.

The town is chiefly noted for its high-quality, carved wooden goods – including bowls and household items, trunks and ornaments – but there is also a wide range of leather and ceramics. Numerous small shops around town sell crafts, and gentle bartering is possible if you're serious about buying. The covered **Mercado Municipal de Artesanías**, by the bus stop, offers an overview of the range and quality of handicrafts available, while Lessandra Leather, close to the bus stop, sells very high-quality leather goods – bags, belts, purses and so on – at decent prices.

Although many people visit Valle de Ángeles as a day-trip, combining shopping with a walk in the surrounding woods, there are a couple of **places to stay**. The *Posada de Ángel* (☎ & fax 766 2233; ⑤) in the centre of town boasts comfortable rooms, all with bath, set around a courtyard, where the pool is also open to day visitors. Ten minutes' walk north of town on the road to San Juancito, *Los Tres Pinos* (*rubio@david.intertel.hn*; ②) has three very comfortable rooms set in a garden; the American owner arranges horse-riding and tours of the area. Reservations for both places are usually necessary at weekends and are recommended even during the week. For **eating**, try *Restaurante Epocas* (closed Mon) on the Parque Central, which also functions as an antique shop: a range of excellently prepared Honduran dishes are served in the dark, candle-lit interior. *El Anafre*, next door (closed Mon & Tues), serves large portions of spaghetti.

Direct **buses** for Valle de Ángeles (1hr) leave Tegucigalpa every hour until 6pm from an open lot near the Hospital General San Felipe. To get there, follow Av Juan Gutemberg/La Paz past the Bolívar Monument and turn right at the Esso petrol station; the terminal is about 100m further along on the left. The last bus back to Tegucigalpa is at 5pm.

San Juancito

Heading north from Valle de Ángeles, a dirt road curves round the mountains, eventually linking up with the highway to Olancho – the tortuously slow progress of buses along this bumpy, winding route allows you plenty of time to gaze at the raw beauty of the mountain scenery. **SAN JUANCITO**, 10km from Valle de Ángeles and set about 1km below the road, down an unmetalled turn-off, is a charming, shabby village of wooden houses, set in the narrow Río Chiquito valley. Most visitors pass through quickly on their way to the cloudforest of Parque Nacional la Tigra (see below), but this friendly little place makes for a pleasant stopover before returning to Tegucigalpa. The only **accommodation** is the *Hotelito San Juan* (①), with an attached café, close to where Tegucigalpa buses stop; the affable owner also runs the nearby *pulpería*. There's good home cooking at the *Mesa del Minero* comedor, just above the village on the road to the park, and its veranda offers great views across the valley and village.

Direct **buses** to San Juancito (2hr) leave from the Mercado San Pablo, Col Reparto in Tegucigalpa every morning at 8am. It's also possible to reach the village from Valle de Ángeles: take any bus or pick-up heading for Cantarranas, all of which pass the turn-off road, from where it's a ten-minute walk. Returning to Tegucigalpa there's a bus daily at 8am, with a second supposedly departing at 1pm on Saturdays.

Parque Nacional La Tigra

The oldest reserve in Honduras, **Parque Nacional La Tigra** (daily 8am–3pm; US$10) was given protected status in 1952 and designated a national park in 1980. Only 14km from Tegucigalpa, its accessibility and good system of trails make it a popular destination; by the same token, however, the diversity of flora and fauna is not as great as that found elsewhere. Previously owned by the El Rosario mining company, the slopes above San Juancito were almost completely denuded through heavy logging earlier this century; the company also cut a road through the heart of the forest to provide easier access to Tegucigalpa, destroying much of the original cloudforest in the process. What can be seen in the central sections of the park open to visitors, therefore, is secondary growth. Nonetheless, parts of the park still shelter abundant oak trees, bromeliads, ferns, vines, orchids and other typical cloudforest flora, along with **wildlife** such as deer, white-faced monkeys, ocelots, quetzals and toucans – though your chance of seeing any animals is slight, since they tend to stick to parts of the park that are out of bounds to visitors. Early mornings are the best time for seeing some of the estimated 200 species of **bird**. The well-laid **trails** across La Tigra provide some easy hiking, either on a circular route from the visitor centre or across the park between the two entrances; it's worth staying a couple of nights if you want to see everything in the park.

THE TRAILS

All the park's **trails** branch off the old logging road, which heads up from El Rosario, climbing 600m over a 2200m pass before descending to the western entrance at Jutiapa. The most pristine patch of forest is around the two highest peaks, **Cerro la Peña de Andino** (2290m), on the southern side of the park, and **Cerro El Volcán** (2270m), though both of these are out of bounds to visitors.

One of the more interesting routes, **La Cascada**, branches left off the logging road about twenty minutes past El Rosario, and heads north, around the curve of the mountain, to a waterfall; about halfway the path passes the old mine workings of Peña Blanca. It takes around an hour to reach the waterfall along a mostly flat trail. From the waterfall follow the path signed for Jutiapa, which after a relatively strenuous half-hour rejoins the logging road. Turn left here and after a few minutes take another trail on the left, which curves downhill through the thick cloudforest canopy. Take your time to admire the gnarled tree limbs, hung with vines and bromeliads, above the carpet of spongy mosses. A gentle walk along here brings you out, around thirty minutes later, just above the Jutiapa entrance.

PRACTICALITIES

From San Juancito, a dirt track, accessible only by 4WD, winds up the mountainside to the abandoned mining village of **El Rosario**. Though only a couple of kilometres long, the track is very steep and exposed. On foot, it takes one hot hour to reach the **entrance** to the park, where an enterprising family with a fridge sells cold drinks; they also cook meals with prior notice. A further ten minutes' walk from the park entrance brings you to the wooden buildings of the mining company, perched above the road on a steep hillside. One of these houses the **visitor centre**, which has boards describing the geography and wildlife of park; the friendly warden is usually around to answer questions and can provide trail maps. **Guides** (US$8.50 per day) are also available, though they only speak Spanish. **AMITIGRA**, a private organization based in Tegucigalpa at Edificio Italia, Col Palmira (☎235 8494, fax 235 8493, *amitigra @sigmanet.hn*), run the park and can provide information. Theoretically you're supposed to contact them before you visit the park if you want to reserve space in the simple, clean **dormitory** behind the visitor centre, but in practice this doesn't seem to matter. Dorm beds cost a hefty US$10 per night, though you can **camp** for US$3.50 per person. Nights can get very chilly, so bring a sleeping bag.

There is a second **entrance** on the western side of the park, reached via the village of Jutiapa, 17km east of Tegucigalpa. Though slightly easier to get to from the capital, this is a less popular entry point with very few facilities. To get there, take a **bus** from Av Colón (near the *Hotel Granada*) in the city centre to the village of Los Limones

(4 daily; 1hr), from where it's a stiff five-kilometre uphill walk, passing through the village of Jutiapa (2km) on the way.

East to Nicaragua: Las Manos

The **Las Manos** border crossing, some 120km from Tegucigalpa, is the most convenient place to enter **Nicaragua** from the capital. Buses run regularly to the town of El Paraíso, 12km from the border, from where minibuses and pick–ups shuttle to the border every thirty minutes or so. With an early enough start, it's possible to reach Managua the same day.

Discua Litena runs six direct **buses** to El Paraíso (2hr 15min) daily, from its terminal at the Mercado Jacaleapa, Col Kennedy, in the southeast suburbs of Tegucigalpa, a fifteen-minute taxi ride from the centre. The same company also runs a more frequent service to the regional capital of **Danlí**, some two hours from Tegucigalpa, from where there are half-hourly buses to El Paraíso.

The border post itself is a collection of huts housing the *migración* and customs officials. Both sides are open daily until 5pm and crossing is generally straightforward. There are no banks, but eager moneychangers accept dollars, lempiras and Nicaraguan córdobas. There's a US$0.50 exit tax to leave Honduras. On the Nicaraguan side, trucks leave every hour for Ocotal, from where you can pick up buses to Estelí and Managua.

Southern Honduras

South of the capital, the pine-clad mountain ranges drop down through rolling green pasture lands to the arid heat of the Pacific coastal plains. A world away from the clear air and gentle climate of the highlands, this region nonetheless has its own particular, stark beauty, defined by dazzling light and ferocious temperatures. Traditionally this is a poor region, and in recent years many of the campesinos and cattle ranchers who struggled to eke a living here have moved north to swell the barrios of Tegucigalpa and San Pedro Sula.

Tourists are scarce hereabouts, since there are relatively few attractions to make the journey worthwhile. For a change of pace from the capital, however, the shrimping town of **San Lorenzo** and the colonial city of **Choluteca** both make convenient stopovers on the longer route to Nicaragua, and with time to spare, the island of **Isla El Tigre** in the Golfo de Fonseca is a perfect, deserted getaway.

The main transport junction in this part of the country is at the village of **Jícaro Galán**, at the intersection of Highway CA-5 and the Carretera Interamericana, some 100km south of Tegucigalpa. Buses heading in all directions stop here to exchange passengers before continuing **west** to the border with El Salvador at **El Amatillo**, 42km away, or **east** across the coastal plain to **Nicaragua**.

West to El Salvador

Seedy, steamy and hot **El Amatillo**, point of entry for **El Salvador**, teems with border traffic, extrovert moneychangers and opportunistic beggars. Crossing here is straightforward, however, with the border post open daily (6am–10pm). There's no fee to enter El Salvador. A bank on the El Salvadorean side changes dollars, lempiras and colones, but you'll get slightly better rates from the moneychangers.

The quickest way to El Amatillo by **bus** is to take an express service from Tegucigalpa to Choluteca, changing at Jícaro Galán onto the Choluteca–El Amatillo service. Over the border in El Salvador, buses leave for Santa Rosa de Lima – 18km away, and the closest place offering accommodation – and San Miguel (58km; see p.329) every ten minutes until around 6.30pm.

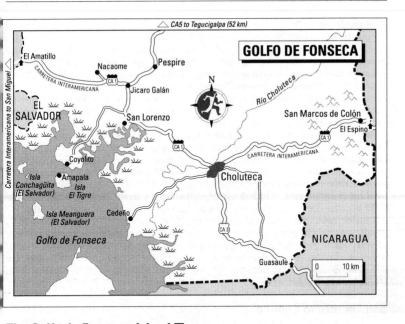

The Golfo de Fonseca: Isla el Tigre

Forty or so kilometres from Jícaro Galán, boats depart the fishing village of Coyolito for the volcanic **Isla El Tigre**, whose conical peak rises sharply against the sky across the sparkling Golfo de Fonseca. So far, tourist development on the island has been minimal, and its beaches, calm waters and constant sunshine make for a perfect getaway. A dirt road runs all the way around the island, giving access to some glorious deserted beaches and a couple of hotels. From the southern side of the island there are stunning views across the gulf to Volcán Cosiguina in Nicaragua, and in some places to Isla Meanguera and the mainland of El Salvador beyond. The island's peak can be climbed in a steep and very hot two- to three-hour walk; ask for directions to the start of the trail, about fifteen minutes' walk southwest of Amapala, the island's only town.

Previously the country's major Pacific port and now a cheerfully decaying, nineteenth-century relic, **AMAPALA** was founded by special decree in October 1833. A brief stint as capital of the country in 1876 preceded a long slide into obscurity, exacerbated when port activities were transferred to Puerto de Henecán, further east along the coast, in the early twentieth century. Today the town is a sleepy place where nothing much happens, even during the annual **fiesta de Santa Cruz** on May 5. Wooden houses, some still brightly painted, cluster up the hillside from the main dock, a picture that's completed by a large, plain wooden church, a small Parque Central and an even smaller market building. The economy of both the town and the island is now based on small-scale agriculture and a small shrimp plant.

It takes four or more hours to walk the 22-kilometre road round the island. Transport is limited to taxis; drivers hang around at the end of the dock and charge US$4–5 for a one-way trip around the island. Around twenty minutes west from Amapala is **Playa Negra**, a pretty, curving volcanic sand beach, with the secluded white-sand **Playa Gualora** fifteen minutes further on; both beaches have accommodation (see overleaf).

Practicalities

To **get to the island**, you need to reach **COYOLITO**; the turn-off is around 12km southeast of Jícaro Galán on the Carretera Interamericana, marked by a Dippsa fuel station; local buses wait on the highway to collect passengers for the slow but beautiful 30km journey through agricultural land and mangrove swamps to the village. There's a steady flow of **launches** between Amapala and Coyolito from 7am until late afternoon, although frequency tends to drop off after lunch; alternatively, fishermen can ferry you across to the island and – if you're willing to bargain hard – through the mangrove swamps east of Coyolito to **San Lorenzo** (see below).

Accommodation in Amapala is limited to two basic hospedajes. The unsigned *Hotel Internacional* (①), just to the left of the dock, has large, airy rooms above a family home and a balcony overlooking the water. A couple of streets back from the seafront, the *Hotel Ritz* (①) charges even less, but rooms are smaller and there's no view. For **eating**, the *El Faro Victoria* restaurant by the dock serves fish and chicken dishes and snacks; the family at the *Hotel Morazán* (which doesn't rent rooms, despite its name), two blocks to the right from the dock, cook meals on request; there are also comedores in the market.

Outside town, the renovated *Hotel Villa Playa Negra* (☎237 0632, fax 238 2457; ⑤–⑥), set on rocks above Playa Negra, has a pool, restaurant and comfortable rooms, all with private bath, but you pay extra for a/c; they also rent out motorbikes (US$16 per day). For a more atmospheric location head for the *Villas Karissa* (☎237 9281, fax 232 6288; ④–⑤) on Playa Gualora, where there's a selection of clean cabañas, each sleeping up to five people.

San Lorenzo to Choluteca

Just east of the Coyolito turn-off, dusty **SAN LORENZO** stretches for a couple of kilometres between the highway and the coastal mangrove swamps. This is a lively, friendly town, and a reasonable stopover en route to or from Choluteca and Nicaragua. For **accommodation**, you could try the basic but clean *Perla de Pacífico* (①–②), on the main street. Down by the waterfront, past the town's shrimp-packing plant, the *Hotel Miramar* (☎881 2039, fax 881 2106; ⑤) has somewhat overpriced rooms, although the view from the restaurant over the mangroves and beyond to Nicaragua is spectacular, particularly at sunset. The hotel also has a swimming pool which is open to non-residents. Beyond the *Miramar* there's a row of clean seafood **restaurants** open for lunch and dinner; in the centre of town, the unnamed restaurant just down from the *Perla de Pacífico* prepares excellent fish and chicken dishes.

San Lorenzo is served by hourly **buses** from Coyolito. These stop on the highway at the fuel station, where you can pick up intercity services heading either west or east to Choluteca, 55km away.

Choluteca

Honduras's fourth-largest city, with a population of slightly over 100,000, **CHOLUTECA**'s main attraction is its old colonial centre, one of the finest in the country. The municipal authorities spent years restoring the city's historic streets, and despite the ravages of Hurricane Mitch, the graceful buildings survived the mud and floods without too much damage. Most places of interest are grouped around the Parque Central, itself a pleasant place to enjoy the cooler evening air. Dominating the square, the imposing seventeenth-century **cathedral** is worth a look for its elaborately constructed wooden ceiling. On the southwest corner of the parque, the building now housing the Biblioteca Municipal was the birthplace of **José Cecilio del Valle**, one of the authors of the Central American Act of Independence in 1821 and elected

President of the Federation in 1834, though he died before taking office. There are plans to turn the biblioteca into a municipal museum.

Choluteca makes a convenient stopover en route to or from the Nicaraguan border, but once you've seen the centre, there's not much reason to hang about in the stifling heat. The main **bus terminal** is about ten blocks northeast of the Parque Central, a twenty-minute walk or US$1 taxi ride. Buses run regularly along the Carretera Interamericana in both directions: west to El Amatillo and east to San Marcos de Colón for El Espino and the Nicaraguan border. There are also direct buses to Tegucigalpa from the Mi Esperanza terminal.

Should you need **to stay**, the *Hotel Pierre* (☎882 0676; ③–④) on Av Valle, two blocks east of the Parque Central, is comfortable if not overwhelmingly friendly; rooms all have bath and TV, and some have a/c. Further down Av Valle, *Hotel Bonsai* (☎882 2648; ③) is one of the better cheap hotels, basic but very clean. There isn't much in the way of **places to eat**, though the *Café Colonial* on 4 C SO, a couple of blocks from the parque, and the *Comedor Central* on the Parque itself, both serve good-value meals.

Routes to Nicaragua

From Choluteca, the Carretera Interamericana runs northeast along the valley of the Río Choluteca before beginning to ascend gently into the mountains. **San Marcos de Colón**, 110km from Choluteca, is a friendly little town, with basic accommodation, including the clean *Hotelito Mi Esperanza* (②), two blocks from the central square, and banks, though they'll only change cash dollars. Buses terminate here, and to get to **El Espino** and the border, 10km away, you need to take one of the frequent colectivo taxis (US$0.75). The border post itself (open daily 8am–5pm only) is quiet and straightforward, with moneychangers on both sides. On the Nicaraguan side, regular buses run to Somoto, 20km from the border.

An **alternative route** to Nicaragua is to take Highway CA-3 from Choluteca, which swings south then east for the 38km to **Guasaule** on the Río Negro. Buses for Guasaule leave from the Mercado Nuevo in Choluteca, a few blocks east of the Parque Central, calling in at the bus terminal on the way; the journey takes about 45 minutes. There's regular transport from Guasaule on to Chinandega, León and Managua.

The main domestic and international bus routes from Tegucigalpa are covered in the box on p.386.

Tegucigalpa to: Choluteca (18 daily; 3hr); Danlí (12 daily; 2hr).

Choluteca to: El Amatillo (hourly; 1hr 30min); Guasule (hourly; 45min); San Lorenzo (hourly, 45min); San Marcos (every 45min; 1hr 15min).

CHAPTER 18

THE CENTRAL AND WESTERN HIGHLANDS

I n their haste to reach the archeological site at Copán, or the palm-fringed beaches on the north coast, all many travellers see of the **central and western highlands** is the view from a bus window. To hurry through from the capital to San Pedro Sula – Honduras's second city and the gateway to the coast – would be to miss much, though, as this is the heartland of the country, an expanse of rugged, pine-clad mountain ranges, split by fertile valleys and scattered with villages and a handful of colonial towns. The highlands are also home to the country's highest concentration of indigenous peoples, many of them descendants of those who fought with Lempira against the Spanish conquistadors. Perhaps because it is so little visited, this is one of the friendliest parts of the country, and you're likely to be received with genuine warmth wherever you go.

From the capital, the main **CA-5** highway offers the most direct route through the highlands to San Pedro Sula and the north coast. Along this road, the first place of interest is **Comayagua**, formerly the nation's capital and still boasting some beautiful churches and other remnants of colonial architecture. Not far to the north lies Honduras's biggest lake, the vast blue **Lago de Yojoa** – an ornithologist's paradise, though Hondurans are more likely to come here for a weekend of fishing and boating.

With a little patience, you can take a bus along the painfully slow route that branches west off the CA-5 at Siguatepeque. Huddled beneath the jungle-covered escarpment of the **Montaña de Celaque**, the cobbled town of **Gracias**, another colonial centre built on the wealth provided by local silver mines, is a relaxing base for hikes in the pristine cloudforest reserve of the **Parque Nacional Celaque**. Beyond here the road improves and it's an easy trip northwest to the region's main town, **Santa Rosa de Copán**. Long the centre of the highland tobacco-growing industry, Santa Rosa has no particular sights to speak of, but is a supremely relaxing place to stay, and still unspoilt despite its growing popularity with tourists.

One of the chief attractions of western Honduras – and indeed of the country – is the ancient site of **Copán**. Though a little smaller than the major Maya sites in Guatemala or Mexico, Copán is equally impressive, thanks to its wealth of fabulous carvings and its wonderful site museum, perhaps the best in the Maya region.

Comayagua

The conquistadors' first city and the capital of Honduras until independence, faded **COMAYAGUA** lies just 85km north of its rival, Tegucigalpa, at the northeast end of the fertile Comayagua valley. Today, the main reason to visit is the architectural legacy of

For an explanation of **accommodation price codes**, see p.365.

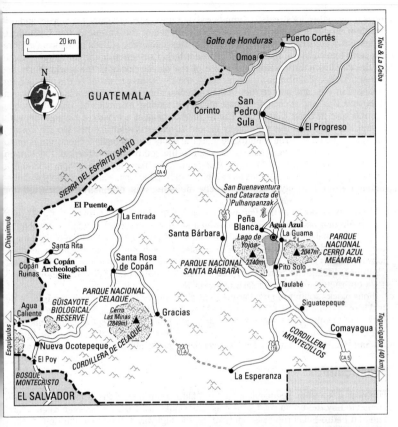

the colonial period, in particular the dramatic cathedral overlooking the Parque Central. The first Spanish settlement was established here on December 8, 1537, and destroyed soon afterwards during the Lempira rebellion (see p.369). Swiftly rebuilt in 1539, Santa María de Comayagua, as it was first known, rapidly became wealthy thanks to the discovery of **silver** in the vicinity. King Felipe II of Spain bestowed on Comayagua the title of city in December 1557, and in 1573 it became the administrative centre for the whole of Honduras. Following independence, however, the city's fortunes began to decline, particularly after Tegucigalpa was designated alternate capital of the new republic in 1824, an ignominy compounded by the city's sacking and burning at the hands of Guatemalan forces during the civil war in 1827. Backwater status was sealed conclusively in 1880, when President Soto permanently transferred the capital to Tegucigalpa, supposedly because Comayagua was too conservative for his liking. Although Comayagua is today a relatively rich and important provincial centre, its rivalry with Tegucigalpa has barely wavered over the centuries.

The Town

Most sights of interest are within a few blocks of the large **Parque Central**, which is graced by a pretty tiled bandstand, a fountain and a smattering of resident shoeshine boys. Few of the city streets are numbered, but the centre is relatively compact and orientation straightforward. On the southeast corner of the Parque is the **Cathedral**, whose intricate facade consists of tiers of niches containing statues of the saints. More properly known as the **Iglesia de la Inmaculada Concepción**, the cathedral is home to the twelfth-century Reloj Arabe, one of the oldest clocks in the world. Formerly housed in the Alhambra in Granada, Spain, the clock was presented to the city by King Felipe II in 1582 and now resides in the cathedral's bell tower, which was built between 1580 and 1708 and is considered one of the outstanding examples of colonial Baroque architecture in Central America. The highlight amongst a wealth of Baroque artwork inside the church is the elaborately carved seventeenth-century Retablo del Rosario altarpiece; go early if you want to see it, as the doors are normally locked from noon to 2pm and in the evenings. Across the road to the south of the cathedral, the **Museo Colonial** (Mon–Sat 9.30–11.30am & 2–5pm, Sun 10am–noon & 2–5pm; US$0.75), housed in the Casa Cural, holds an exhibition of religious art, statues, chalices and documents from the city's churches. The building was originally constructed for Comayagua's **university**, the first to be established in Central America, in 1678.

Two blocks north of the Parque Central, on the Plaza San Francisco, the **Museo Arqueológico** occupies a newly renovated single-storey building that used to be the government palace (Tues–Sun 8.30am–4pm; US$1.30). The small but interesting range of exhibits include a pre-Columbian Lenca stela, polychrome ceramics and some terrific jade jewellery; there's also a little café. On the same plaza is one of the city's oldest churches, **Iglesia de San Francisco**, originally established by Franciscan monks in 1574 but rebuilt following an earthquake in 1809.

Four blocks south from the Parque Central is another colonial church, the **Iglesia de la Merced**. Built between 1550 and 1558, though its facade dates back only to the early eighteenth century, this was the city's original cathedral, holding the Reloj Arabe until 1715, when the new cathedral was consecrated. Several blocks further south, the **Iglesia de San Sebastián**, completed in 1585, was built specifically for indigenous worshippers.

Practicalities

Highway CA-5 from Tegucigalpa passes 1.5km southwest of the centre, to which it's connected by the broad road known as "the Boulevard". **Buses** between Tegucigalpa and San Pedro Sula drop passengers off on the highway at the top of the Boulevard, a US$0.50 taxi ride or twenty-minute walk from the Parque Central. Transportes Catrachos also run hourly buses to and from Tegucigalpa from a terminal five blocks south of the Parque. There are several **banks** on or just off the Parque Central, including Banco Atlántida and Bancahsa. **Hondutel** and the **post office** are alongside each other on the street behind the cathedral. An extensive **general market** runs along 1 Av NO, 2–3 C NO, starting three blocks south of the cathedral.

Unfortunately for the visitor, the range of places to stay in Comayagua is quite narrow. Of the small number of **hotels** in and around the market area, the *Hotel America Inc*, 1 Av NO at 1 C NO (☎772 0360; ③), has rather spartan but clean rooms, all with bath and a/c. *Hotel Emperador*, on C Central at the Boulevard (☎772 0332; ②), is of a similar standard, while the *Hotel Norymax Colonial*, at the other end of C Central, in front of the school (☎772 1703; ③), is perhaps the nicest in this part of town, with clean comfortable rooms and flower-filled balconies. At the northern end of town, just off the Boulevard, *Hotel Quan* (☎772 0070, *hquan@hondutel.hn*) is a good alternative base, with a choice of either modern motel-style accommodation (④) or less pleasant but cheap budget rooms (②), some with private bath.

For **eating**, *Restaurante Palmeras*, at 4 C NO on the Parque Central, serves substantial breakfasts, daily lunches and low-priced snacks in a pleasant setting. One block down, *Fruit y Tacos* does excellent *licuados*, plus burgers and tacos, though the service can be a little downbeat. But by far the best place in town is the *Villa Real*, a block southeast of the plaza, a very stylish restaurant set in a beautifully restored colonial town house. There's an extensive menu, including pasta (US$4) and grilled meats and fish dishes (US$6–7), plus a gorgeous, well-stocked little bar.

Lago de Yojoa and around

North of Comayagua, the Carretera del Norte (CA-5) climbs across the pine-forested expanse of the Sierra de Montecillos before reaching **Siguatepeque**, about halfway between Tegucigalpa and San Pedro Sula, after 30km or so. Beyond Siguatepeque, the highway begins to descend from the mountains and the air becomes appreciably warmer. Some 35km north of Siguatepeque is the spectacular, sparkling blue **Lago de Yojoa**, a natural lake around 17km long and 9km wide. Its reed-fringed waters, sloping away to a gentle patchwork of woods, pastures and coffee plantations, are overlooked by the mountains of Cerro Azul Meámbar to the east and Santa Bárbara to the north and west. Both of these contain small but pristine stretches of **cloudforest** and are protected as national parks.

An ornithologist's dream, the waters and marshes of the lake attract over 350 species of **bird**, the highest concentration in the country. In a previous incarnation in the 1960s, the lake was a magnet for sports fishermen from all over Central America, who came here to fish for the predatory **black bass**, introduced into the lake in 1954. Stocks of these depleted rapidly, due to overfishing during the 1970s; recent judicious management has succeeded in encouraging regrowth and obtaining a fragile equilibrium between humans and nature.

The lake is a favourite with middle-class *Hondureños* at the weekends, when its peace and quiet is shattered by the buzz of jetskis; during the week, however, the waters – and surrounding hotels – are virtually empty, and Yojoa makes a supremely relaxing base for a couple of days rowing on the lake, observing the bird life and exploring the surrounding countryside. Ecolago, in Edificio Midence Soto, by the Parque Central in Tegucigalpa (☎237 9659), is an independent organization set up to monitor the health of Lago de Yojoa, and can provide **information** on the lake and its environs.

The eastern and northern shores

The CA-5 from Tegucigalpa runs along the lake's eastern shore, passing through the small village of **PITO SOLO**, at its southeast tip. The *Los Remos* hotel here (☎552 0618; ④), the only accommodation at this end of the lake, is somewhat shabby and overpriced, and it's better to head on to one of the hotels further on (see below). Fresh lake fish is served up at the row of comedores in the village, and at another cluster about 2km further along the highway. On the lakeshore 15km north of Pito Solo is the comfortable new *Honduyate* hotel (☎990 9386; ⑤), owned by an English-Honduran couple and with a fine restaurant attached. The highway north divides at the junction of **La Guama**, 7km further north, from where a dirt road runs east for 5km to the entrance to **Parque Nacional Cerro Azul Meámbar** (daily 8am–4pm). Named after its highest peak, the blue-hued Cerro Azul Meámbar (2047m), this is one of the smaller reserves in the national network, with a core of untouched cloudforest. Anyone planning to hike here should be prepared for precipitously steep gradients in the upper reaches of the reserve, with sheer rock-faces, dense vegetation and tumbling waterfalls. With luck, you might spot quetzals, and spider and white-faced monkeys. Cerro Azul is managed by a private organization, PAG, based at 3 C, 1–2 Av NO, Siguatepeque (☎773 2741), with another office in Tegucigalpa (☎232 8287); they can provide information on hiking and hiring guides. The park's **education centre** at the entrance occupies the old coffee finca of Los Pinos and has **accommodation** in the form of cabins with bunks (①), plus information on a number of short walking trails that are being opened up. There's no public transport to the park.

A paved road heads northwest from La Guama along the northern shore of the lake, passing the *Hotel Agua Azul* (☎991 7244; ④), one of the most agreeable hotels in the area. Though the rustic cabins are a little run-down, they enjoy a magical setting among wooded grounds sloping down to the waterside, and the restaurant's veranda has fabulous views across the lake; there's also a pool, and the hotel rents boats and organizes horse-riding on request. **AGUA AZUL** village, just past the hotel, has some basic stores and a couple of comedores – the only eating places around here outside the hotels. Continuing along the road:, it's 6km to the *Finca Las Glorias* (☎556 0461, fax 556 0553; ⑥) an equally characterful but more pricey hotel; fishing trips and tours of the surrounding coffee finca are available. Four kilometres further on, the shabby, overgrown village of **PEÑA BLANCA** is the commercial focus for the area. There are several cheap comedores here, including the *Comidas Rapidas* right on the main junction, and also simple, clean double and triple rooms at the *Hotel Maranata* (②). **Buses** running along the highway will stop at Pito Solo and La Guama if requested; there's an hourly service from the latter to Peña Blanca.

North to the Catarata de Pulhapanzak

North of Peña Blanca is one of the highlights of the lake region, the **Catarata de Pulhapanzak** (daily 8am–6pm; US$0.75; plus US$0.40 per person for camping), a stunning, 43-metre-high cascade of churning white waters on the Río Lindo. Claimed to be the prettiest waterfall in the country, the cascade is at its most dazzling in the early mornings, when rainbows form in the rising sun. A narrow trail on the right-hand side – very steep and wet – descends past several viewpoints to the riverbank at the bottom of the falls. The area immediately around the falls has been designated a public park, with comedores and a swimming spot. Right by the entrance, a grassy expanse is identified as the "ceremonial plaza" of a centre of Lenca culture believed to have been sited here, although no excavation has been carried out.

Pulhapanzak is an easy fifteen-minute walk from the village of **San Buenaventura**, 8km north of Peña Blanca; buses ply the dirt road between the two every hour.

The western shore

The towering peak of the **Cerro Santa Bárbara** (2740m) forms a superb backdrop to the waters of the western shore of the lake, which is far less developed and accessible than the eastern. The peak is encircled by the dense, green cover of the **Parque Nacional Santa Bárbara**, consisting of virgin cloudforest, plus thick stretches of pine and mixed broadleaf forest on the lower slopes. The reserve is as yet relatively undeveloped for tourism and there are no facilities, though guides can by found by asking in the lakeside hotels. Nestling at the base of the reserve, by the water's edge, is the archeological site of **Los Naranjos**, once an extensive Maya settlement, though at present there's little to see other than earth-covered mounds.

Taking the junction to the left at Pito Solo brings you onto Highway CA-20, heading west along the lower fringes of the park. Fifty-three kilometres along this road is **Santa Bárbara**, a friendly town situated amid coffee plantations. Buses run to the central plaza and there are a couple of decent hotels in the surrounding blocks.

La Esperanza to Gracias

West of the Tegucigalpa–San Pedro Sula highway lie Lempira and Intibucá, the departments that make up the **western highlands** of Honduras, a stunningly beautiful landscape of pine forests, sparsely inhabited mountains and remote villages. These two departments contain the highest concentration of indigenous peoples in the country and the small, lively town of **La Esperanza**, 68km southwest of the highway, is –

despite increasingly rapid absorption into mainstream culture – the place where you're most likely to see traditional dress being worn.

The drawback to travelling around here is the state of the roads: most are unsurfaced and can become impassable during the wet season. Private vehicles are infrequent, and public transport frustratingly slow and uncomfortable. If you're prepared to put up with the delays, however, you can take a cross-country route through La Esperanza to the colonial town of **Gracias** and the stunning cloudforest of the **Parque Nacional la Celaque**. At this point the infrastructure begins to improve, and it's an easy journey on to Santa Rosa de Copán (see p.401).

La Esperanza

Three kilometres north of Siguatepeque a good paved road leaves the main CA-5 high-way and heads west to **LA ESPERANZA**; the route is served by buses every couple of hours until mid-afternoon. Centre of commerce and trade in the region and capital of the department of Intibucá, the town livens up during the **weekend market**, a colour-ful and noisy affair, when Lenca farmers from surrounding villages pour into town. While there's nothing of much interest to buy, it's worth hanging around to observe the intensive bartering and socializing that goes on. Should you need to stay, *Hotel Solis* (☎898 2080; ②), one block east of the market, has clean rooms, some with private bath.

Gracias

Up to five hours from La Esperanza on the one daily bus, **GRACIAS** lies in the shadow of the **Montaña de Celaque**, the peak that forms the centrepiece of the nearby **Parque Nacional Celaque**. This is one of the oldest towns in Honduras, and served briefly as the seat of the Audiencia de los Confines, the centre of government under the Spanish, until this was transferred to Antigua, Guatemala, in 1548. Life since then has been a spiral of gentle decline with little happening to disturb the town's sleepy rural charm. Today, a handful of run-down buildings around the Parque Central hint faintly at former glories; the building that once housed the Audiencia is a block south of the square – it's now used by the Church.

Castillo San Cristóbal (daily 8am–5pm; free), a restored fort on a small hill, five minutes' walk above the western edge of town, provides wonderful views over the town and west across to Celaque, particularly in the late afternoon. The fort was built, but never ultimately used, to defend the area against Guatemalan troops during the nine-teenth-century civil wars; the walls contain the tomb of Juan Lindo, president of Honduras from 1847 to 1852. About an hour's walk south of Gracias are a set of natur-al **hot springs** (daily 8am–8pm; US$1.20), with small purpose-built pools for bathing in the 36–39°C waters; a comedor at the site serves basic meals, snacks and drinks. The path to the springs starts on the right just after the first river bridge on the road to La Esperanza, at the southeast edge of town.

PRACTICALITIES

The **bus terminal** is an empty lot three blocks west of the Parque Central; buses head-ing west arrive and depart from here, while local buses from La Esperanza stop at the southeast edge of town. There's a fairly regular service to Santa Rosa de Copán, sup-plemented by private pick-ups. Banco de Occidente, one block west of the Parque, changes dollars cash and travellers' cheques. **Hondutel** and the **post office** are next to each other, one block south of the Parque. The local **COHDEFOR** office, which sells photocopied maps showing the trail through Celaque, is five blocks north of the Parque. Provisions for hiking in the park can be bought at the small general **market**, on the same street, south of the Banco de Occidente.

Three blocks west of the plaza, *Guancascos* (☎656 1219, fax 651 1273; ④), owned by a dynamic Dutch woman, offers the best **accommodation** in town, with spotless and very attractive rooms, some with fine views; its restaurant also offers the best cooking in town and is the favoured hangout for most Western travellers plotting hikes in the hills. *Hotel Colonial*, just off the Parque Central (☎656 1258; ②–③), is a good budget place: it's clean and some of the rooms have bath and TV. *Hotel Erick*, one block north of the Parque (☎656 1066; ①/②), is also basic but very tidy. Just to the north on the same street is *Hotel Fernando* (☎656 1231; ②/③), another good option with quiet rooms set around a pretty courtyard.

For **eating**, *Guancascos* draws most diners but *Café Colonial* in the *Colonial* hotel, does good local breakfasts and daily set lunches, as well as snacks, while *La Galera*, a block from the plaza, does Mexican-style food at rock-bottom prices.

Parque Nacional Celaque

Parque Nacional Celaque (US$2, plus US$1 per night), best approached from Gracias, contains one of the largest and most impressive expanses of virgin cloudforest in Honduras. The focus of the park is the **Montaña de Celaque**, a volcanic escarpment and the source of eleven rivers – "Celaque" means "box of water" in the Lenca language – which boasts the highest peak in Honduras, the **Cerro Las Minas** (2849m), at its centre. Thick forests coat the slopes of the escarpment, rising from pine through to the cloudforest covering the escarpment plateau.

The park entrance is 6km west of Gracias; take the unmetalled road that runs through the village of Mejicapa, 2km away, from where a marked track leads uphill to the entrance. Few private vehicles run along here, and the walk can get very hot. From the entrance, a track leads for another 2km or so through the pine forest to the **visitor centre**, where there are bunk rooms, showers and cooking facilities; you'll need to bring plenty of food and water with you, though the friendly warden's family can provide meals on request. It gets cold at night and the trails are invariably wet and muddy, so sleeping bags, decent boots and a change of warm clothing are essential. *Restaurant Guancascos* in Gracias (see above) functions as an unofficial **information centre** for the park. As well as selling booklets and maps and renting some camping gear, they can also arrange lifts up to the visitor centre.

Gentle rambles are possible through the woods surrounding the visitor centre. A more adventurous option is the six-kilometre marked trail through the forest up to the peak of Cerro Las Minas. It's not really necessary to hire a guide for the trail, though you'll definitely need one if you're planning to undertake one of the more difficult treks on the southern slopes: ask at the COHDEFOR office in Gracias. In the upper reaches of the park much of the main trail consists of forty-degree slopes, so this is not a hike for the unfit. Plan on spending at least one night camping, if the summit is your aim; there are two designated camping spots along the way.

THE TRAIL TO CERRO LAS MINAS

Starting behind the visitor centre, **the trail up Cerro Las Minas** follows the river for about five minutes, then crosses over and heads steeply uphill before running southwest along and up the slope of the mountain, through pine forest. It's at least an hour's walk from the visitor centre to the core area of the park, at 1800m, and the first of the camping sites, **Campamento Don Tomás**, is another hour and a half away. Here there's a shack to sleep in (check with the warden at the centre that it will be unlocked), a stream (not suitable for drinking from), and space for tents.

From the campsite, the path, marked with tags, continues very steeply upwards for around two hours before levelling out on the plateau (2560m); **Campamento Naranjo** is at the edge of the plateau by a stream (drinkable), and has room for a few tents. Here the cloudforest proper begins, wrapped in a hushed, cathedral-like calm, and dripping wet at any time of year. Oaks and liquidambars loom overhead, draped in vines and bromeliads and banked by mosses and ferns. Thousands of years of geographical isolation has resulted in several endemic species of flora, including the abundant *oreopanax limpiriana* and globus yew. Sit quietly for a while and you may be lucky enough to catch a rare glimpse of the shimmering green and red quetzal, though hearing the characteristic rattle of a woodpecker echoing from somewhere nearby is more likely. Sightings of animals are even rarer, but you might want to keep an eye out for spider monkeys, pumas, tapirs, coyotes and white-tailed deer.

From Campamento Naranjo to the peak is another two hours, much of it an easier climb, except for the last half-hour or so. The ancient tree cover is more stunted at the summit, a result of almost continual cloud cover and temperatures that frequently drop below freezing. Generally the clouds and vegetation combine to limit the views, but when it's clear there are breathtaking vistas southwest, down the densely covered dark green slopes of the escarpment.

Santa Rosa de Copán and southwest to the border

It's an easy ninety-minute bus ride 45km northwest from Gracias to **SANTA ROSA DE COPÁN**, a wonderfully preserved, cobbled colonial relic built on the proceeds of the tobacco industry. Tourists are relatively few, mainly because the view across the Río Chamelicón valley is about all there is to see here. Nevertheless, Santa Rosa's location, along the main north–south transport route, usually makes a stop here inevitable.

Santa Rosa was once home to the Crown Tobacco Office, which regulated the cultivation of the crop, set official prices and handled sales, and today the golden weed is still central to the local economy. These days the old Tobacco Office in the centre of town houses offices belonging to the **Flor de Copán Cigar Company**. The building also used to house a cigar factory until a few years ago when it moved to new premises (open Mon–Fri 7am–noon & 1–5pm, Sat 7am–noon) 2km northwest of the town centre, next to the bus station. Around 30,000 hand-rolled cigars are produced daily, mostly for export. You can observe the process on a free tour (Spanish only) or simply by glancing through the windows of the rolling room, which face the street. Boxes of cigars can be bought at the small on-site shop at bargain prices.

At the centre of town is the delightful, shady **Parque Contreras**, with the cathedral on its eastern side. **Calle Centenario**, lined with shops and restaurants, runs along the southern edge of the Parque, past the old cigar factory a couple of blocks to the west and the **market** a couple of blocks east.

Practicalities

All **buses** arrive at a terminal just off the highway, about 2km northwest of the centre, at the bottom of the hill. There are six services a day to Ocotepeque for El Salvador and Guatemala (overleaf), and a constant stream north to San Pedro Sula (see p.421) via La Entrada, and the Copán turn-off. From the terminal it's a stiff twenty-minute walk into town, or US$0.50 per person in a colectivo taxi. **Hondutel** and the **post office** are on the western edge of the Parque, with Banco Atlántida to the south. You can surf the **Internet** at either *Pizza Pizza* (see overleaf) or Computec, 2 Av, two blocks southeast of the Parque – both charge about US$4 per hour.

The **Casa de Cultura**, two blocks south of the Parque, has some fairly limited **information** about the area, but you're better off talking to Warren Post, the helpful owner of *Pizza Pizza*, who knows the region well. If you want to really explore the western highlands, Lenca Land Trails, based in the *Hotel Elvir* (see overleaf), offer a number of excellent trips to national parks including Celaque, indigenous villages and hot springs. There's also a good community **Web site** (*http://sites.netscape.net/srcopan*) devoted to the town.

Santa Rosa has a moderate range of **places to stay**. By far the nicest place in town is the *Hotel Elvir* on C Centenario at 2 Av SO (☎662 0103, *lenca@hondutel.hn*; ⑤), which has large, colonial-style rooms, all with bath and TV, and a good restaurant and café. The *Hotel Continental*, at 2 C NO, 2–3 Av NO (☎662 0801; ③), is slightly cheaper, while the *Hotel Copán* at 1 C NE, 3 Av NE (☎662 0265; ②) and *Hotel Rosario* at 3 Av NE (☎662 0211; ②) are two good budget bets. The *Hotel Grand Mayaland* (☎662 0233; ④), opposite the bus terminal, offers modern, impersonal rooms, but is convenient for transport.

Santa Rosa's small number of **eating and drinking** places is increasing with the growing number of tourists. One of the newer outfits is the French-owned *Paris Restaurant and Bar* on C Centenario, two blocks west of the Parque, whose excellent – but fairly pricey – menu changes daily. Both the courtyard dining area and wooden bar are also good for a quiet drink. One block south is *Chiky's Antijitos Mexicanos*, 1 C SO at 1 Av SO, serving inexpensive burgers, tacos and Honduran food in a relaxed atmosphere. Three blocks away, to the east of the Parque Central, *Restaurant Well*, 2 C SE, 2–3 Av SE, is a friendly place serving large portions of authentic Chinese food at reasonable prices; a couple of blocks further on, the US-owned *Pizza Pizza*, C Centenario, 5–6 Av NE, cooks up good pizza and pasta. Finally, there's always something tasty available in the pleasant café and restaurant inside the *Hotel Elvir*.

The route to Nueva Ocotepeque and the border

From Santa Rosa de Copán, highway CA-4 heads southwest through low valleys before climbing through the eastern flanks of the Cordillera de Merendón. **El Portillo**, a small, shabby roadside hamlet, marks the highest stretch of paved road in the country, at 2010m. Fifteen kilometres beyond the pass is **NUEVA OCOTEPEQUE**, the last town in Honduras before the border with both El Salvador and Guatemala and served by several buses a day from Santa Rosa. Modern and unremarkable – it was founded after a flood destroyed the colonial village of Ocotepeque in 1934 – the town is redeemed by its setting at the base of the towering Cerro el Sillón (2310m). Most visitors pass straight through en route to El Salvador or Guatemala, but if you need **to stay** the best budget option is *Mini Hotel Turista* (①–②), next to the main square, while the *Hotel Maya Chortí* (☎653 3377; ④), two blocks from the bus station, has very pleasant and good-value rooms, all with TV and a/c. The Banco de Occidente, just up from the hotel, changes dollars cash and travellers' cheques, but you'll get better rates for Guatemalan quetzales and Salvadorean colones at the borders.

Southeast of town lies the **Reserve Biológica la Fraternidad**, or the **Bosque Montecristo**. Cerro Montecristo, at the centre of the reserve, is where the borders of El Salvador, Guatemala and Honduras meet. Access from the Honduran side is extremely difficult; the visitor centre and few tourist facilities that exist are reached through **Metapán** in El Salvador (see p.355)

The border: El Salvador and Guatemala

Buses run 10km south to the El Salvadorean border at **El Poy** regularly until late afternoon. El Poy itself is a drab, dusty little place but the crossing is straightforward; it is as well to cross as early in the day as possible, since public transport onwards within El Salvador is infrequent, and stops altogether mid-afternoon. There are no banks, but a profusion of moneychangers – change enough to keep you going until you reach San Salvador. There's no fee to enter El Salvador.

El Poy has no **accommodation**, but there are basic hotel facilities in El Salvador at the village of Citalá, 1km away, and more upmarket places at San Ignacio, 5km from the border, and La Palma, the nearest town, 11km south of the border (see p.323). Buses to La Palma and on to San Salvador leave every thirty minutes until 4.30pm.

Some 18km west of town is the **Guatemalan** border crossing of **Agua Caliente** (open 6am–6pm). Buses make the thirty-minute trip to the border every half hour or so until 4pm. There are six daily buses from the border, running every two hours between 7.30am and 3.30pm direct to San Pedro Sula (6hr); alternatively, take the first bus to Nuevo Ocotepeque and change buses there. There are no banking or accommodation facilities on the Honduran side. Over in Guatemala, minibuses leave every twenty minutes for Esquipulas (see p.237) until 6pm.

Copán and around

Set in serene, rolling hills 45km from Santa Rosa, **COPÁN** is one of the most impressive of all Maya sites. Copán's pre-eminence is not due to size – in scale it's far less impressive than sites such as Tikal or Chichén Itzá – but to the overwhelming legacy of artistic craftsmanship that has survived over hundreds of years. Not surprisingly, the site is heavily promoted by the Honduran government and tour operators and now ranks as the second most visited spot in the country after the Bay Islands.

Copán Ruinas Town

The archeological site of Copán lies one kilometre south of the small town of **COPÁN RUINAS**, generally simply referred to as Copán, a charming place of steep cobbled streets and red-tiled roofs set among green hills. Despite the weekly influx of hundreds of visitors, which now contributes a large part of the town's income, it has managed to remain largely unspoilt and genuinely friendly. Many travellers are seduced by Copán's delightfully relaxed atmosphere, clean air and rural setting, and end up spending longer here than planned, studying Spanish, eating and drinking well, or exploring the region's other minor sites, hot springs and beautiful countryside.

Arrival and information

Most **buses** enter town from the east, by a small football field, with some continuing up the low hill to circle the Parque Central; buses from Guatemala enter town from the west. The **post office** is just behind the museum; **Hondutel** is just south of the plaza. There's an excellent community **Web site** (*www.copanruinas.com*) where you'll find useful hotel and restaurant listings, local news and links; you can choose between several **Internet** cafés in town, including two branches of Maya Connections, one is just south of the plaza and the other is inside the *Hotel Los Gémelos* – rates hover around US$5 an hour.

Direct luxury air-conditioned Hedman Atlas **buses** (☎651 4106) leave Copán for San Pedro Sula daily at 2pm (2hr 45min). Two other bus companies, Gama and Casarola, also run less expensive direct and non-direct services to San Pedro Sula; while slower local buses run every two hours to La Entrada, from where there are plenty of connections to San Pedro Sula.

Accommodation

Many of the town's older **hotels** have undergone refits to attract the ever-expanding organized tour market, while a swathe of new mid-range places help keep prices competitive. There's not too much choice at the budget end of the market, however, where places fill up quickly at busy times of the year.

Casa de Café B&B, at the southwest edge of town, overlooking the Río Copán valley (☎651 4620, fax 651 4623, *www.todomundo.com/casadecafe*). A charming place, with ten comfortable and airy rooms, all with wood panelling and nice individual touches, private bathrooms and steaming hot water, plus a fabulous garden where you could lie in a hammock and enjoy the views all day. A huge ranch-style breakfast is included, and there's free coffee all day, plus a library and TV. ⑥.

Hacienda San Lucas, 1.8 km south of the plaza (☎651 4106, *sanlucas@copanruinas.com*). Wonderful converted farmhouse accommodation and camping set in the hills south of Copán, with startling views over the valley. There's an attached restaurant with excellent home-cooked food, plus horse-riding and hiking trails to the Los Sapos site. Breakfast included. ⑤.

Hotel Los Brisas de Copán, one block north of the Parque Central (☎651 4118). Twenty-two very clean and good-sized, though slightly soulless, rooms, all with bath, hot water and TV. There's also parking, and a terrace bar is planned. ④.

Hotel Los Gémelos, close to the bus stop (☎651 4077). Very friendly backpackers' stronghold, still going strong, with basic but spotless rooms, all with shared bath. The family provide hot water if enough people ask, and also run the adjacent Maya Communications Internet café. ②.

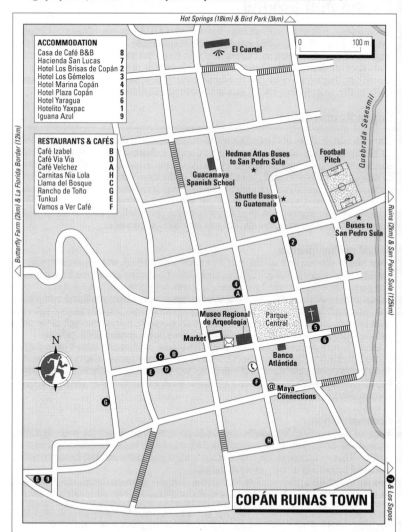

Hotel Marina Copán, just northwest of the plaza (☎651 4070, fax 651 4477, *hmarina@netsys.hn*). The most luxurious place in town by a long shot. The stylish rooms all have a/c and TV, and there's a small pool, a sauna, a gym and a bar on site. ⑧.

Hotel Plaza Copán on the east side of the plaza (☎651 4508, fax 651 4039, *placopan@netsys.hn*). Twenty-one good-value rooms, some overlooking the square and all with a/c and cable TV; also has a small kidney-shaped pool. ⑥.

Hotel Yaragua, half a block east of the plaza (☎651 4050). Smallish but comfortable and excellent-value rooms, set around a verdant little courtyard, all with good-quality double beds and cable TV. ④.

Hotelito Yaxpac, a block north of the plaza (☎651 4025). Run by a friendly family, with four good-value, simple, clean rooms – all have private bath, and some also have little balconies. ②.

Iguana Azul, next to the *Casa de Café B&B* and under the same ownership (☎651 4620, fax 651 4623, *www.todomundo.com/iguanaazul/index.html*). The definitive budget choice, with three private double rooms and two very pleasant dormitories, all with shared bath and decent mattresses. Pretty garden, communal area and laundry facilities, plus great travel information. Dorms US$4.50 per person, doubles ②–③.

The Town

Half a day is enough to take in virtually all the town's attractions. The **Parque Central** – lined with banks, municipal structures and an attractive, whitewashed Baroque-style church – was originally designed by visiting archeologists Tatiana Proskouriakoff and Gustav Stromsvik, though its original elegance has been somewhat spoilt by grandiose remodelling initiatives, including a series of sweeping pillars and arches, unleashed by a local mayor in the last few years. It does remain a popular place to kill time however, its benches filled with cowboy-booted farmhands and camera-touting visitors in the late afternoon. A number of **souvenir shops** on or close to the Parque Central sell Honduran ceramics, wood and leather crafts; all are broadly similar in terms of price and range. Tabacos y Recuerdos, next to *La Posada* hotel, has a wide selection of Honduran cigars.

On the west side of the plaza, and somewhat eclipsed by the new sculpture museum at the site itself, though still worth a visit, is the **Museo Regional de Arqueología** (Mon–Sat 8am–4pm; US$2). Inside are some impressive Maya carvings from the Copán region, including the glyph-covered Altars T and U and **Stela B**, depicting the ruler Waxaklajuun Ub'aah K'awiil (Eighteen Rabbit), along with some remarkable intricately detailed eccentric flints – ornamental oddities with seven interlocking heads carved from obsidian. There are also two remarkable **tombs**, one containing the remains of a female shaman, complete with jade jewellery and the skulls of a puma, deer, and two human sacrificial victims. The other (10J-45) was constructed for an early Classic period ruler of Copán and only discovered in 1999 during road-building work. Archeologists found a vaulted burial chamber, dating from the sixth century, where the as yet unknown leader was buried with numerous ceramics and two large carved jade pectoral pieces.

Just behind the museum (turn right beyond the post office), the tiny municipal **market** is worth a browse, while there's a wonderful view over the town and surrounding countryside from **El Cuartel**, the old military barracks up the hill five blocks north of the Parque Central.

On the outskirts of town, a twenty-minute walk from the plaza along the road to Guatemala, is a small **butterfly park**, Enchanted Wings (daily 8.30am–5pm; US$5), owned by an English enthusiast and his Honduran wife. Unfortunately, Copán's cool winter nights periodically wipe out some of the forty or so specimens – many of which are collected from the steamier tropical environs of the north coast – so you may not find an abundance of butterflies, though look out for the speckled brown "giant owl" and the scarlet-and-yellow "helicopter", two of the hardier species. Butterflies hatch in the morning hours, so if you plan to go to the centre, it's best to time your visit accordingly if you can. On the other side of town, 3km north of the plaza, a new **bird park** with macaws and toucans is set to open in late 2001.

Eating and drinking

Copán has a wide range of places to **eat** and **drink**, many of them catering specifically to the tourist market, and standards are usually very high, with generous portions and good service. Virtually all restaurants stop serving at 10pm.

Café Izabel, one block west of the plaza. Unpretentious comedor serving a range of well-prepared local dishes; the vegetable soup is particularly good.

Café Via Via, two blocks west of the plaza. Belgian-owned establishment with a nice little streetside terrace and magazines to browse through. Good sandwiches, breakfasts, pancakes and omelettes.

Café Velchez, northwest corner of the Parque. Pleasant European-style café, serving good but fairly pricey coffees, juices and *licuados*, alcoholic drinks (including wine by the glass), cakes and light meals. There's a cigar bar upstairs – good for people-watching.

Carnitas Nia Lola, two blocks south of the Parque. The most atmospheric place in town, this highly popular restaurant-bar serves large portions of delicious grilled and barbecued meats, plus vegetarian dishes, at reasonable prices. It's equally popular as a drinking venue, with an early-evening happy hour and a good mix of locals and visitors.

Llama del Bosque, two blocks west of the Parque. Slightly old-fashioned restaurant with a big menu including local breakfasts, meat and chicken dishes, baleadas and snacks.

Rancho de Toño, three blocks west of the plaza. Vast new *palapa*-style restaurant specializing in fresh fish, with huge, reasonably priced portions and friendly service.

Tunkul Bar and Restaurant, across from *Llama del Bosque*. Busy garden restaurant-bar with good food, including burritos, vegetarian dishes and the near-legendary garlic chicken, plus lively music and a happy hour (8–9pm).

Vamos a Ver Café, one block south of the Parque. Busy Dutch-owned garden café, popular with travellers, with delicious homemade soups, sandwiches and snacks.

Listings

Banks Banco Atlántida on the Parque will change travellers' cheques, cash dollars and quetzales (at poor rates) and give advances on Visa cards.

Book exchange Justo a Tiempo, two blocks southwest of the plaza (Mon–Sat 7.30am–5.30pm); the friendly American owner also serves great cakes and coffee.

Immigration The *migración* is on the west side of the Parque next to the museum (Mon–Fri 7am–4pm).

Language schools Copán is an excellent place to study, with two Spanish schools to choose between, though it's a more expensive learning centre than Guatemala – four hours of classes plus full family-based accommodation and meals costs US$175 a week. Guacamaya (☎ & fax 651 4360, *www.guacamaya.com*), three blocks north of the plaza, has the better reputation of the two schools, though Ixbalanque (☎ & fax 651 4432, *ixbalan@hn2.com*), a block and a half west of the plaza, is also worth considering.

Laundry Justo a Tiempo, two blocks southwest of the plaza (Mon–Sat 7.30am–5.30pm).

Shuttle buses Contact Monarcas (☎651 4361), two blocks north of the plaza, for direct shuttles to Guatemala City and Antigua (US$25 per person).

Tour operators Go Native Tours (☎651 4432, *ixbalanqu@hn2.com*), a block and a half west of the plaza, and Yaragua Tours (☎ & fax 651 4050, *yaraguatours@hotmail.com*), half a block east of the plaza, both offer similarly priced tours. Trips include visits to the hot springs (see p.412; US$10 per person), horse-riding (from US$15 for 3hr), the Finca El Cisne coffee farm (US$30), El Rubi waterfall (US$15), and a spectacular local cave, the Cueva el Boquerón (US$70). Xukpi Tours (☎651 4435) is an excellent specialist bird-watching outfit run by the very knowledgeable guide Jorge Barraza.

Copán ruins

COPÁN RUINS lie 1.5km east of town, a pleasant fifteen-minute walk along a raised footpath that runs parallel to the highway. Entrance to the site (daily 8am–4pm; US$10 including the Las Sepultras ruins, though access to the archeological tunnels is an extra US$12) is through the **visitor centre** on the left-hand side of the car park, where a small exhibition explains Copán's place in the Maya World. Inside the visitor centre

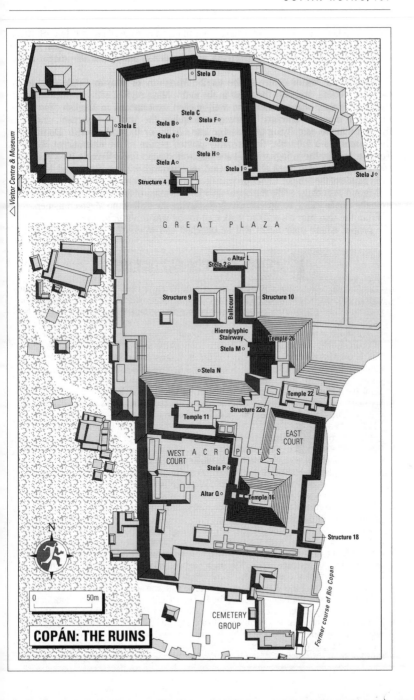

there's a ticket office and a desk where you can hire a registered site **guide** (US$10 for 2hr) – an excellent investment if you really want to get the most out of Copán. On the other side of the car park is a **cafeteria**, serving drinks and reasonable meals, and a small souvenir shop.

Opposite the visitor centre is the terrific **Museum of Mayan Sculpture** (daily 8am–4pm; US$5), arguably the finest in the entire Maya region, with a tremendous collection of stelae, altars, panels and well-labelled explanations in English. You enter through a dramatic entrance doorway, resembling the jaws of a serpent, and pass through a tunnel (signifying the passage into *xibalba*, or the underworld). Dominating the museum is a full-scale, flamboyantly painted replica of the magnificent **Rosalila Temple**, built by Moon Jaguar in 571 and discovered intact under Temple 16. A vast crimson and jade coloured mask of the Sun God, depicted with wings outstretched, forms the main facade of the temple. Other ground-floor exhibits concentrate upon aspects of Maya beliefs and cosmology, while the upper floor houses many of the finest original sculptures from the Copán valley, comprehensively displaying the skill of the Maya craftsmen.

From the museum it's a 200m walk east to the **warden's gate**, the entrance to the site proper, where your ticket will be checked and where there are usually several

A BRIEF HISTORY OF THE RUINS

Once the most important **city state** on the southern fringes of the Maya world, Copán was largely cut off from all other Maya cities except **Quiriguá**, 64km to the north in Guatemala (see p.226). Archeologists now believe that settlers began moving into the Río Copán valley from around 1400 BC, taking advantage of the area's rich agricultural potential, although construction of the city is not thought to have begun until around 100 AD.

Copán remained a small, isolated settlement until the arrival in 426 AD of an outsider, **Yak K'uk Mo'** (Great Sun First Quetzal Macaw), the warrior–shaman who established the basic layout of the city and founded a royal dynasty which lasted for 400 years. It's unclear whether he was from either Teotihuacan, the Mesoamerican superpower, or Tikal (which was under strong Teotihuacan influence at the time), but Yak K'uk Mo' became the object of an intense cult of veneration, first established by his son **Popol Hol** and continued by subsequent members of the dynasty over fifteen generations.

Little is known about the next seven kings that followed Popol Hol, but in 553 AD the **golden era** of Copán began with the accession to the throne of **Moon Jaguar**, who constructed the magnificent Rosalila temple, now buried beneath Temple 16. The city thrived through the reigns of **Smoke Serpent** (578–628 AD), **Smoke Jaguar** (628–695 AD) and **Eighteen Rabbit** (695–738 AD), as the great fertility of the Copán region was exploited and wealth amassed from control of the jade trade along the Río Motagua. These resources and periods of stable government allowed for unprecedented political and social growth, as the population boomed to around 28,000 by 760 AD, the highest urban density in the entire Maya region.

Ambitious reconstruction of the city continued throughout this era, using local andesite, a fine-grained, even-textured volcanic rock that was easily quarried and particularly suited to detailed carving, as well as the substantial local limestone beds, which were ideal for stucco production. The highly artistic carved relief style for which Copán is famous reached a pinnacle during the reign of Eighteen Rabbit – whose image is depicted on many of the site's magnificent stelae and who also oversaw the construction of the Great Plaza, the final version of the ball court and Temple 22 in the East Court.

Following the audacious capture and decapitation of Eighteen Rabbit by Quiriguá's Cauac Sky, construction at Copán came to a complete halt for seventeen years, possibly indicating a period of subjugation by its former vassal state. The royal dynasty subsequently managed to regroup, however, flourishing gloriously, albeit briefly, once more. **Smoke Shell** (749–763 AD) completed the construction of the **Hieroglyphic Stairway**,

squabbling macaws to greet your arrival – these are tame and sleep in cages by the gate at night.

The Great Plaza

Straight through the avenue of trees lies the **Great Plaza**, a large, rectangular arena strewn with the magnificently carved and exceptionally well-preserved stelae that are Copán's outstanding features. Initially, the visual impact of this grassy expanse may seem a little underwhelming: the first structure you see is **Stucture 4**, a modestly sized pyramid-temple, while the stepped buildings bordering the northern end of the plaza are low and unremarkable. This part of the Great Plaza was once a public place, the stepped sides bordered by a densely populated residential area. The grandest buildings are confined to the monumental temples that border the southern section of the plaza, rising to form the Acropolis, the domain of the ruling and religious elite.

Dotted all around are Copán's famed **stelae** and altars, made from the local andesite. Most of the stelae represent **Eighteen Rabbit**, Copán's "King of the Arts" (Stelae A, B, C, D, F, H and 4). **Stela A**, dating from 731 AD, has incredibly deep carving, although the faces are now eroded; its sides include a total of 52 glyphs, translating into a famous

one of the most impressive of all Maya constructions, in an effort designed to symbolize the revival. Optimism continued during the early years of the reign of **Yax Pasah** (763–820 AD), Smoke Shell's son, who commissioned **Altar Q**, which illustrates the entire dynasty from its beginning, and completed the final version of **Temple 16**, which towers over the site, around 776 AD. Towards the end of his rule, however, the rot set in: skeletal remains indicate that the decline was provoked by inadequate food resources created by population pressure, resulting in subsequent environmental collapse. The seventeenth and final ruler, **Ukit Took'**, assumed the throne in 822 AD, but his reign proved miserably inauspicious. Poignantly, the only monument to his reign, Altar L, was never completed, as if the sculptor had downed his tools and walked out on the job.

The site was known to the Spanish, although they took little interest in it. A court official, Don Diego de Palacios, in a letter written in March 1576, mentions the ruins of a magnificent city "constructed with such skill that it seems that they could never have been made by people as coarse as the inhabitants of this province". Not until the nineteenth century and the publication of *Incidents of Travel in Central America, Chiapas and Yucatán* by **John Lloyd Stephens** and **Frederick Catherwood** did Copán become known to the wider world. Stephens, the then acting US ambassador, had succeeded in buying the ruins in 1839 and, accompanied by Catherwood, a British architect and artist, spent several weeks clearing the site and mapping the buildings. The instant success of the book on publication and the interest it sparked in Mesoamerican culture ensured that Copán became a magnet for archeologists.

British archeologist **Alfred Maudsley** began a full-scale mapping, excavation and reconstruction of the site in 1891 under the sponsorship of the Peabody Museum, Harvard. A second major investigation was begun in 1935 by the Washington Carnegie Institute, which involved diverting the Río Copán to prevent it carving into the site. A breakthrough in the understanding not only of Copán but of the whole Maya world came in 1959 and 1960, when archeologists Heinrich Berlin and Tatiana Proskouriakoff first began to decipher **hieroglyphs**, leading to the realization that they record the history of the cities and the dynasties.

Since 1977, the Instituto Hondureño de Antropología e Historia has been running a series of projects with the help of archeologists from around the world. Copán is now perhaps the best understood of all Maya cities, and a series of **tunnelling projects** beneath the Acropolis have unearthed remarkable discoveries including the Rosalila Temple, buried beneath Temple 16, in 1989, which is now open to the public. In 1993, the Papagayo Temple, built by Popol Hol and dedicated his father Yax K'uk Mo', was uncovered, and in 1998 further burrowing unveiled the tomb of the founder himself.

inscription that includes the emblem glyphs of the four great cities of Copán, Palenque, Tikal and Calakmul – a text designed to show that Eighteen Rabbit saw his city as a pivotal power in the Maya world. **Stela B** depicts a slightly oriental-looking Eighteen Rabbit, bearing a turban-like headdress that's intertwined with twin macaws, while his hands support a bar motif, a symbol designed to show the ruler holding up the sky. **Stela C** (730 AD) is one of the earliest stones to have faces on both sides and, like many of the central stelae, it has an altar at its base, carved in the shape of a turtle. Two rulers are represented here: facing the turtle (a symbol of longevity) is Eighteen Rabbit's father, Smoke Jaguar, who lived well into his eighties, while on the other side is Eighteen Rabbit himself. **Stela H**, perhaps the most impressively executed of all the sculptures, shows Eighteen Rabbit wearing the latticed skirt of the Maize God, his wrists weighed down with jewellery, while his face is crowned with a stunning headdress.

THE BALL COURT AND HIEROGLYPHIC STAIRWAY

South of Structure 4, towards the Acropolis, is the I-shaped **ball court**, one of largest and most elaborate of the Classic period, and one the few Maya courts still to have a paved floor. It was completed in 738 AD, just four months before Eighteen Rabbit's demise at the hands of Quiriguá; two previous versions lie beneath it. Like its predecessors, the court was dedicated to the great macaw deity, and both sloping sides of the court are lined with three sculptured macaw heads. The rooms that line the sides of the court, overlooking the playing area, were probably used by priests and members of the elite as they watched the game.

Pressed up against the ball court, protected by a vast canvas cover, is the famed **Hieroglyphic Stairway**, perhaps Copán's most astonishing monument. The stairway, which takes up the entire western face of the Temple 26 pyramid, is made up of some 72 stone steps; every block is carved to form part of the glyphic sequence – around 2200 glyph blocks in all. It forms the longest-known Maya hieroglyphic text, but, unfortunately, attempted reconstruction by early archeologists left the sequence so jumbled that a complete interpretation is still some way off. What is known is that the stairway was initiated to record the dynastic history of the city: some of the lower steps were first put in place by Eighteen Rabbit in 710 AD, while Smoke Shell rearranged and completed most of the sequences in an effort to reassert the city's dignity and strength in 755 AD. At the base of the stairway the badly weathered **Stela M** depicts Smoke Shell and records a solar eclipse in 756 AD.

Adjacent to the Hierogylphic Stairway, and towering over the extreme southern end of the plaza, are the vertiginous steps of **Temple 11** (also known as the Temple of the Inscriptions). The temple was constructed by Smoke Shell, who is thought to have been buried beneath it, though no tomb has yet been found. At its base is another classic piece of Copán carving, **Stela N** (761 AD), representing Smoke Shell, with portraits on the two main faces of the stela and glyphs down the sides. The depth of the relief has protected the nooks and crannies, and in some of these you can still see flakes of paint – originally the carvings and buildings would have been painted in a whole range of bright colours, but for some reason only the red has survived.

The Acropolis

From the southwestern corner of the plaza, a trail runs past some original drainage ducts, beyond which stone steps climb steeply up the side of Temple 11 to a soaring cluster of temples, dubbed the **Acropolis**. This lofty inner sanctum was the reserve of royalty, nobles and priests; the political and ceremonial core where religious rituals were enacted, sacrifices performed and rulers entombed. The whole structure increased in size over four hundred years, the temples growing higher and higher as new structures were built over the remains of earlier buildings. A warren of excavated tunnels, some open to the public, bore through the vast bulk of the Acropolis to the Rosalila Temple and several tombs. From the summit of Temple 11, beside a giant ceiba tree (a tree held sacred to the Maya), there's a panoramic view of the site below, over the ball court and Great Plaza to the green hills beyond.

A few metres east of Temple 11 are the **Mat House** (Structure 22A), a governmental building distinguished by its interlocking weave-like patterns, and **Temple 22**, which boasts some superbly intricate stonework around the door frames. Constructed by Eighteen Rabbit, Temple 22 functioned as a "sacred mountain" where the elite performed religious blood-letting ceremonies. Above the door is the body of a double-headed snake, its heads resting on two figures, which in turn are supported by skulls. The decoration here is unique in the southern Maya region, with only the Yucatán sites such as Kabáh and Chicanna having carvings of comparable quality.

THE EAST COURT

Below Temple 22 are the stepped sides of the **East Court**, a graceful plaza which also bears elaborate carvings, including life-sized jaguar heads with hollow eyes which would have once held pieces of jade or polished obsidian. In the middle of the western staircase, flanked by the jaguars, is a rectangular Venus mask, carved in superb deep relief. Rising over the court and dominating the Acropolis, **Temple 16** is the tallest structure in Copán, a thirty-metre pyramid completed by the city's sixteenth ruler, Yax Pasaj, in 776 AD. In order to build Temple 16 Yax Pasaj had to build on top of the **Rosalila Temple**, though the temple was built with extraordinary – and atypical – care so as not to destroy the earlier temple; generally, it was Maya custom to ritually deface or destroy obsolete temples or stelae. The temple served as a centre for worship during the reign of Butz'Chan (578–628 AD), or Smoke Serpent, Copán's eleventh ruler, a period that marked the apogee of the city's political, social and artistic growth, so the discovery of the Rosalila has been one of the most exciting finds of recent years. You can now view the brilliant original facade of the buried temple by entering through a short **tunnel** – an unforgettable, if costly (US$12), experience, as it may be sealed again in future years. The admission price does at least include access to two further tunnels, which extend below the East Plaza past some early cosmological stucco carvings – including a huge macaw mask – more buried temple facades and crypts including the Galindo tomb.

At the southern end of the East Court is **Structure 18**, a small square building with four carved panels, and the burial place of Yax Pasaj, in AD 821. The diminutive scale of the structure reveals how quickly decline set in, with the militaristic nature of the panels symptomatic of the troubled times. The tomb was empty when excavated by archeologists and is thought to have been looted on a number of occasions. From Structure 18 there's a terrific perspective of the valley, over the Río Copán, which eroded the eastern buildings of the Acropolis over the centuries until its path was diverted by early archeologists. South of Structure 18, the **Cemetery Group** was once thought to have been a burial site, though it's now known to have been a residential complex, and home to the ruling elite. To date, however, little work has been done on this part of the ruins.

THE WEST COURT

The second plaza of the Acropolis, the **West Court**, is confined by the south side of Temple 11, which has eight small doorways, and Temple 16. **Altar Q**, at the base of Temple 16, is the court's most famous feature and an astonishing monument of ancestral symbolism. Carved in 776 AD, it celebrates Yax Pasaj's accession to the throne on July 2, 763. The top of the altar is carved with six hieroglyphic blocks, while the sides are decorated with sixteen cross-legged figures, all seated on cushions, who represent previous rulers of Copán. All are pointing towards a portrait of Yax Pasaj which shows him receiving a ceremonial staff from the city's first ruler, Yax K'uk Mo', thereby endorsing

Yax Pasaj's right to rule. Behind the altar is a small crypt, discovered to contain the remains of a macaw and fifteen big cats, sacrificed in honour of his ancestors when the altar was inaugurated.

Las Sepultras

Two kilometres east of Copán along the highway is the smaller site of **Las Sepultras** (daily 8am–4pm; entrance with the same ticket as for Copán), the focus of much archeological interest in recent years because of the information it provides on daily domestic life in Maya times. Eighteen of the forty-odd residential compounds at the site have been excavated, yielding one hundred buildings that would have been inhabited by the elite. Smaller compounds on the edge of the site are thought to have housed young princes, as well as concubines and servants. It was customary to bury the nobility close to their residences, and more than 250 tombs have been excavated around the compounds – given the number of women found in the tombs it seems likely that the local Maya practised polygamy. One of the most interesting finds – the tomb of a priest or shaman, dating from around 450 AD – is on display in the museum in Copán Ruinas town.

Around Copán

There are a couple of places within easy reach of Copán that make an extra day or two's stay here worthwhile. Closest is the small Maya site of **Los Sapos**, a delightful walk south from town. Ten kilometres or so in the opposite direction, the picturesque waterfall of **El Rubí** is the perfect spot for a picnic, while the **hot springs** fifteen kilometres north of town are a pleasant place to soak away your cares. Copán is also a convenient spot to cross over into Guatemala, with the **El Florido** border crossing just 12km to the west.

Los Sapos, dating from the same era as Copán, is set in the hills to the south of town, less than an hour's gentle walk away. The site, whose name derives from a rock carved in the shape of a frog, is thought to have been a place where Maya women came to bear children, though unfortunately time and weather have eroded much of the carving. To get there, follow the main road south out of town, turn left onto a dirt track just past the river bridge and follow this as it begins to climb gently into the hills, past the *Hacienda San Lucas* farmhouse hotel (see p.404). The views across the tobacco fields of the river valley are beautiful, and there are plenty of spots for swimming along the way.

Pick-ups leave Copán regularly throughout the day for the peaceful town of **Santa Rita**, 9km northeast. At the river bridge, just before entering the town, a path leads up to **El Rubí**, a pretty double waterfall on the Río Copán, about 2km away. Surrounded by shady woods, this is the perfect spot for a swim in the clear, cold water, followed by a picnic. Follow the path as it climbs along and above the right-hand bank of the river for about twenty minutes; just past a steep stretch and small bend to the right, a narrow path runs down through the pasture on the left to a pool and high rock, on the other side of which is El Rubí.

Around 15km north of Copán are some **hot springs** (*aguas termales*; US$0.75), set in lush highland scenery dotted with coffee fincas and patches of pine forests. Once there you can either wallow around in man-made pools or head to the source via a short trail where cool river water and near boiling-hot spring waters combine. One way to get to the *aguas termales* is to hitch a ride on a passing pick-up, which are reasonably frequent from outside the *Hotel Paty* in Copán and also pass the bird park; expect to pay around a US$1 for the ride, which takes about 50 minutes – but don't leave it any later than 3.30pm if you're planning to hitch back to Copán. Alternatively, speak to one of Copán's tour operators (see the listings on p.406); Yaragua Tours can arrange a half-day pick-up trip at 2pm for US$10 per person for a minimum of four people.

Into Guatemala: El Florido

The Guatemalan border is just twelve kilometres west of Copán, and crossing here at the **El Florido** border post – usually busy with travellers coming to and from the ruins – is pretty straightforward, though it can be slow. There's no bank, but the ever-present moneychangers handle dollars, lempiras and quetzales at fairly good rates. Minibuses and pick-ups leave from the Parque in Copán Ruinas about every thirty minutes until around 4pm; there's also a fast shuttle bus to Guatemala City and Antigua (see listings on p.175 for details of tour operators). There's no fee to enter or leave either country, though both sets of officials will almost certainly try to prise a dollar or two from you. From the border, buses leave every thirty minutes (the last is at 4pm) for Chiquimula (1hr 15min), 57km away down a smooth, newly paved road.

North to La Entrada and El Puente

Northeast from Copán the CA-11 winds its scenic way through lightly wooded mountains and fertile pasture to **LA ENTRADA**, a distinctly unlikeable junction town 55km northeast of Copán. La Entrada's only redeeming feature is its proximity to the small site of El Puente (see below); if you get stuck here, *Hotel San Carlos* (☎898 5228; ④), at the junction of CA-11 and CA-4, is the best of the available **accommodation**.

El Puente

Breaking the journey in La Entrada does give you a chance to visit the archeological site of **El Puente** (daily 8am–4pm; US$5); a signed turn on the CA-11 4km before La Entrada gives access to the site, 6km away. Opened in 1994, El Puente gets few visitors, which makes its location – amid the grassy fields flanking the Río Chinamito – all the more enjoyable, although after the glories of Copán, the scale of the site is inevitably disappointing.

Once a sizeable **Maya** settlement, dating back to the Late Classic period and under the authority of Copán, El Puente contains more than two hundred structures. To date, only a small number have been excavated, including religious buildings and structures for the use of the elite, built around what was the main plaza. The most important of these (Structure 1) is an eleven-metre-high, six-stepped pyramid, oriented east–west and thought to be a funerary temple; the long pyramid along its lower edge contains burial chambers. The small **museum** at the entrance to the park, about 1km from the restorations, has an informative exhibition on the site itself and on Maya culture in general.

There's no public transport to the site, but hitching is considered safe; traffic is more frequent in the mornings. A round-trip taxi fare from La Entrada will cost around US$10, including an hour at the ruins.

travel details

BUSES

Comayagua to: Tegucigalpa (18 daily; 1hr 30min); Siguatepeque (18 daily; 1hr).

Copán to: La Entrada (10 daily; 1hr 30min); San Pedro Sula (5 daily; 3hr).

Gracias to: Santa Rosa de Copán (hourly until 6pm; 1hr 30min).

La Entrada to: San Pedro Sula (every 30 mins; 1hr 30mins)

La Esperanza to: Gracias (1 daily; 4–5hr).

Nueva Ocotepeque to: Agua Caliente (every 30min until 4pm; 1hr); El Poy (every 40min; 30min).

Santa Rosa de Copán to: Copán (2 daily; 3hr); La Entrada (8 daily; 1hr 30min); Nueva Ocotepeque (6 daily; 2hr); San Pedro Sula (every 30 min; 3hr; 3 direct services daily; 2hr 30min).

Siguatepeque to: La Esperanza (every 2hr until mid-afternoon; 2hr).

CHAPTER 19

OLANCHO

S tretching east to the Nicaraguan border and north into the emptiness of Mosquitia, the sparsely populated uplands of **Olancho** are widely regarded as Honduras's "wild east", an untamed frontier region with a not totally undeserved reputation for lawlessness and violence. Traditionally the *Olanchanos* hold little respect for authority, and it's true that rebellion has played a major role in their history. The first Spanish settlers arrived in 1524, enticed to this mountainous region by Aztec tales of vast gold deposits, and immediately encountered resistance from the region's indigenous tribes. There was little peace for the next two hundred years as Pech, Lenca and other tribes periodically revolted against the Spaniards, who had set up slave camps to mine the rich gold deposits. The marauding presence of British pirates, who controlled the Caribbean coast to the north for most of the eighteenth century, further isolated Olancho, breeding an independent spirit and a distaste for governmental influence. Throughout the first forty years of the new Honduran republic there were bitter rebellions against Tegucigalpa, revolts which were only finally quelled in 1863 after a campaign of terror by President José Medina.

Since then Olancho has become one of the richer regions of Honduras, its wealth largely generated from exploitation of the huge forest reserves (much of it illegally logged) and cattle ranching (which has encroached into many of the national parks and reserves). A powerful local oligarchy, drawn from these industries and supported by military and police connivance, has led to environmental issues being given very peripheral priority, while activists opposing these interests have been threatened and killed. Olancho remains something of a law unto itself, and though communications have improved vastly in recent years, there is still the sense travelling here that you have entered a very different country. Nevertheless, the relatively few visitors who do pass through will receive a brusque yet genuine welcome.

Although Olancho makes up almost a fifth of Honduran territory, tourist attractions are few, and the high, forested mountain ranges interspersed with broad valleys often make travelling difficult and slow. However, these same ranges harbour some of the country's last untouched expanses of tropical and cloudforest: the national parks of **La Muralla** and **Sierra de Agalta** are awe-inspiring, while the smaller, more accessible reserve of **El Boquerón** offers ample opportunity for gentler hikes. Along the valleys, now given over to pastureland for cattle, are scattered villages and towns. Both **Juticalpa**, the department capital, and **Catacamas**, at the eastern end of the paved road, are good bases for exploring the region, while the friendly mountain settlement of **La Unión** acts as both gateway to La Muralla and a convenient stopover en route to the north coast.

Olancho's **climate** is generally pleasant, with the towns at lower altitudes hot during the day and comfortably cool at night; up in the mountains it can get extremely cold after dark. Once off the main highway, **travelling** becomes arduous, with the dirt roads connecting the remoter villages served by infrequent and invariably slow public transport.

For an explanation of **accommodation price codes**, see p.365.

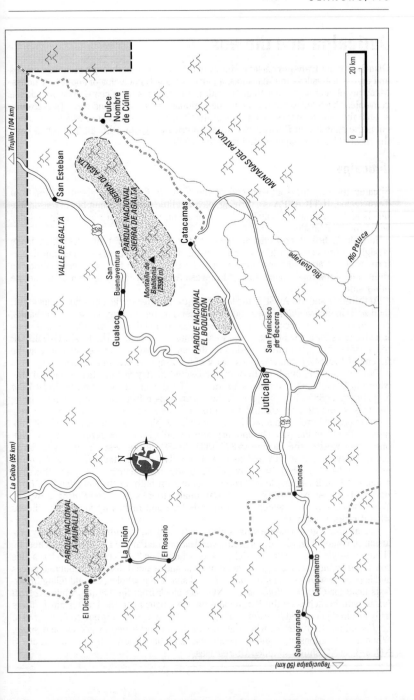

Juticalpa and the east

Olancho's main **transport** artery, Highway CA-15, runs east through mountain passes and across flat valleys to Catacamas, a journey from Tegucigalpa of about four hours. Many people get no further than **Juticalpa**, the region's main centre, which makes a convenient base for expeditions into the national parks. North and east of Catacamas stretch the remote, impassable peaks of the Sierra de Agalta, part of which is protected as the magnificent **Parque Nacional Sierra de Agalta**. Difficult to reach at best, the reserve is easiest approached from the north.

Juticalpa

Situated towards the southern end of the Valle de Catacamas, about 170km from Tegucigalpa, **JUTICALPA** is a thriving, pleasant little city with a number of reasonable hotels and restaurants. Capital of the department, its streets are busy night and day with provincial bustle and commerce.

Juticalpa's **bus terminals** are just off the highway on 1 Av SE, which leads straight to the centre, a fifteen-minute walk north. Local buses – including departures east to Catacamas and northwest to La Unión – run from the terminal on the right side of the road (facing town); Empresa Aurora's Tegucigalpa services use the other side.

At the other end of 1 Av SE is the leafy **Parque Banderas**, the city's heart, busy with food stalls in the evenings. The majority of hotels and restaurants, along with the banks, post office and other facilities, are on the streets around the Parque. The general **market** stretches for a few blocks to the west, along C Perulapan. The local COHDEFOR office (☎885 2253), with **information** on the national parks, is in a green house at the far end of 1 Av SO, about two blocks west of the Empresa Aurora terminal.

Don't expect too much in the way of cosseted luxury in Juticalpa, or indeed anywhere in Olancho. Of the **places to stay**, by far the smartest is the new *Hotel Villa San Andrés* (☎885 2405; ⑤), just off the highway 2km from the centre, whose large spotless rooms all have a/c and TV. In town there are a couple of comfortable, reasonably priced hotels and a handful of more basic places, all within a couple of minutes' walk of the Parque. The modern and friendly *Hotel Honduras*, 1 Av, 1 C NO, one street west of the Parque (☎885 1331; ②–③), is the best on offer, with large rooms, all with bath and TV and some with a/c. The similar *Apart Hotel La Muralla*, nearby at 1 C, 2 Av NO (☎ & fax 885 1270; ②), has smaller rooms, and there's a range of clean if rather gloomy rooms, some with bath, at the longstanding *Hotel Atuñez*, 1 C, 1 Av NO (☎885 2250; ②–③); finally, there's the *Hotel Rivera,* 2 Av, 1–2 C SO (☎885 1154; ①), which is cheap and clean and makes up for in friendliness what it lacks in comfort.

Juticalpa's range of **restaurants** is also pretty modest, though there's a healthy profusion of comedores, plus the *Restaurante Asia* on the Parque for cheap and cheerful Honduran-style Chinese dishes. Behind the cathedral on 2 Av NE, *El Rancho* has a nice courtyard setting, serves a good range of meat and seafood dishes at moderate prices and is popular with locals for a quiet beer and snack. For wholesome and filling breakfasts head for *Cafeteria Regis* on 1 C NO, one block from the Parque, while *Tropical Juices*, with branches on the Parque and on 1 Av, halfway to the bus terminal, offers truly inspired juices and *licuados*. For a genuine Olancho-style cowboy cook-up head to *La Fonda*, on the highway, where giant steaks and barbecued meats spit and sizzle. When the attractions of eating and people-watching have worn thin, the **cinema** at 1 C NO, 2–3 Av NO shows subtitled US releases.

El Boquerón

Twenty kilometres east of Juticalpa, **El Boquerón** is one of the last remnants of dry tropical forest in Honduras, and home to a wide variety of wildlife including over 180 species of bird – quetzals, toucans and taragones have all been spotted here. It's easily accessible as a day-trip from the city, though there are facilities should you want to camp. To see the forest properly, you need to follow the moderately strenuous track through the reserve, which cuts through a small patch of cloudforest.

Any of the buses running along the highway between Juticalpa and Catacamas will drop you at the marked **entrance** to the reserve, a journey of about twenty minutes. From here, the reserve stretches back along the **Canyon de Boquerón**, a kilometre-deep natural rift. The path takes you through forest and into the canyon along the left-hand bank of the **Río Olancho**, where there are plentiful opportunities for swimming. After around an hour, the path crosses the river and heads uphill away from the canyon through open pastureland to the hamlet of **LA AVISPA**; getting here takes about three hours in total. Beyond the village, the path loops steeply uphill around Cerro Agua Buena (1433m) and through the **cloudforest** section; here you've the greatest chance of seeing elusive bird and animal life, since the trees are stunted and the vegetation less dense than in other reserves. From this point on it's all downhill, the path emerging after a couple of hours on the highway at Tempisque, a few kilometres west of the main entrance. An early start would allow you to complete the walk in one day; alternatively, use the designated camping spots at the main entrance and at La Avispa – bring food and water. It's an easy matter to flag down **buses** to Juticalpa or Catacamas along the highway.

Catacamas

CATACAMAS, situated midway along the Valle de Catacamas beneath the southern flanks of the Sierra de Agalta, is a much smaller version of Juticalpa, 41km away. Very few tourists come here – Catacamas marks the end of the paved road – which no doubt contributes to the affable, small-town charm of the place. It has a more spectacular setting than its larger neighbour: a short walk up to the **Mirador de la Cruz**, fifteen minutes from the centre on the northern side of town, gives superb views over the town and valley, and across to the Montañas del Patuca.

Buses terminate on the Parque Central, from where it's pretty easy to find your way around. The banks, post office and other essentials lie on the couple of streets north of the Parque, while most hotels are to the west. Of the very limited **accommodation** available, *Hotel Colina*, 1 Av SW, just down from the Parque (☎899 4488; ②), is by far the best, with reasonably comfortable rooms, all with bath, TV and fan, set round a courtyard. Almost next door, the *Hotel Oriental* (①–②) has a selction of basic but clean rooms, some with private bath, while the *Hotel Rapallo* (①), one block away, is spartan and dingy, but would do in an emergency. For **eating**, *Restaurante Pollo Rico* and *El Riconcito Típico*, both a block north of the Parque Central, serve unexceptional meat and chicken dishes, while the *Buffet Ejectivo* in the Parque scores for cheap buffet food.

Parque Nacional Sierra de Agalta

Draped across the sweeping ranges of the Sierra de Agalta, the vast **Parque Nacional Sierra de Agalta** shelters the most extensive stretch of **virgin cloudforest** remaining in Central America. Since the establishment of the reserve in 1987, pressure on the land has remained acute, and large swathes of the lower forest of pine and oak have been cleared to provide pasture for ranching. Though there are signs that the environmental message is getting through – not least because the reserve is the watershed for the region and the source of the rivers Sico and Patuca, among others – the reserve still receives little real protection. It's a different story in the higher reaches of the mountains, where the core of the reserve is so remote that both vegetation and wildlife have remained virtually untouched. Here a typical cloudforest of oaks, liquidambar and cedar, draped in epiphytes, vines and ferns, cover the higher slopes in a dense cloak, giving way, above 2000m, to an almost primeval dwarf forest, where the trees grow only to a height of around five metres.

This isolation ensures a protected, secure environment for a biologically diverse range of **animals and birds**, many of them extremely rare. Tapirs, jaguars, ocelots, opossums and three species of monkey are among the 61 recorded species of mammal, although you'll need a great deal of luck to spot them. More evident are the birds, of which over four hundred species have been recorded, including 33 species of hummingbird. There are also numerous butterflies and reptiles.

The reserve's remoteness makes **independent access** difficult. There's no accommodation other than official camping spots, for which you'll need to bring all equipment and supplies. The easiest points of entry are along the northern edge of the Sierra, via the small towns of **Gualaco** and **San Esteban**, which you can reach off Highway C39 between Juticalpa and Trujillo. Hiring a **guide** is pretty much essential for hiking on the often difficult trails: ask at the COHDEFOR offices in Gualaco, San Esteban or Juticalpa. A daily bus to Trujillo, passing through both towns, leaves Juticalpa at 4am, and there are plenty of additonal pick-ups from the marketplace in Juticalpa.

La Unión and La Muralla

Some 110km from Juticalpa in the west of the department of Olancho, **LA UNIÓN** is a pleasant mountain town and the most convenient point of departure for **Parque Nacional La Muralla**, 15km north. Its location, around halfway along a backdoor bus route between Tegucigalpa and La Ceiba, also makes it a handy stopover between the capital and the north coast. However, if you're considering travelling along this remote road it's essential you determine the current **security** situation first, as there have been regular hold-ups and robberies (of buses and private cars) in the last few years. Check in the COHDEFOR office in Juticalpa (see p.416) before you set out.

Accommodation in La Unión is limited to the very basic *Hotel La Muralla* and *Hotel Karol* (both ①). There are a couple of **comedores** around the Parque Central for meals. If you intend to visit La Muralla, you need to register at the **COHDEFOR** office (Mon–Fri 8am–5pm), three blocks from the Parque Central; the office can also help organize transport into the park.

Parque Nacional La Muralla

La Muralla (daily 8am–4pm; free) takes its name from the appearance of the reserve when viewed from a distance – "the wall" of a high massif densely covered with leafy forest, forming an island of incredible biological diversity amid the surrounding low-level mountain ranges. Cocooned in the centre of the reserve is an extensive stretch of virgin cloudforest which, despite its remoteness, is more accessible to visitors than the Sierra de Agalta. The park's dazzling array of **bird life** and its well-planned visitor facilities make a visit here very rewarding.

Forest cover in La Muralla ranges from pine woods at the level of the entrance (1400m) through to cloudforest from around 1800m. The mountains slope steeply, rising to the peak of **Las Parras**, at 2064m the highest point. For bird-watchers, quetzals, hummingbirds, kites and toucanets are among the species likely to be spotted; the aguacatillo tree in front of the visitor centre is a major food source for quetzals and, if you're lucky, they can be seen feeding there in the early mornings. More evasive are the white-tailed deer, jaguars, pumas, grey foxes and howler monkeys that inhabit the park.

It's possible to visit La Muralla as a day-trip from La Unión, although since bird-spotting is best done in the very early morning, it's wise to plan on spending the night here. The shortest **trail**, El Pizote, swings from the visitor centre in a two-hour loop up through the damp hush of the cloudforest and back down again. Though steep, wet and slippy, this can be done unguided and benches are provided at the best points for bird-watching; guides are recommended, however, for greater understanding of what you're seeing. Longer trails run across the reserve to the **Cascada de Mucupina** (8hr return) and to **Monte Escondido**, a two-day hike.

Access to La Muralla is via the **visitor centre** at the southwest end of the reserve, about 15km north of La Unión on the road to El Díctamo village. Here you can pick up trail maps and information on wildlife; there are also dorm **beds** (reservations through COHDEFOR in Tegucigalpa: ☎223 7703) and **camping space**, with two more camping spots further into the reserve. Bring plenty of food and water and some warm clothes.

travel details

BUSES

Catacamas to: Juticalpa (hourly; 1hr).

Gualaco to: Trujillo (1 daily; 6hr).

Juticalpa to: Catacamas (hourly; 1hr); Gualaco (1 daily; 2hr 30min); La Unión (1 daily; 4hr); San Esteban (1 daily; 4hr); Tegucigalpa (Empresa Aurora, 12 daily; 3hr).

La Unión to: La Ceiba (1 daily; 7–8hr); Tegucigalpa (Cotraibal, 3 daily; 5hr).

San Esteban to: Trujillo (1 daily; 4hr).

CHAPTER 20

THE NORTH COAST AND MOSQUITIA

A world away from the forested mountain ranges of the interior, Honduras's **north coast** stretches for 300km along the azure fringes of the Caribbean. A magnet for Hondurans and foreign tourists alike, most are drawn solely by the prospect of sun, sea and entertainment, which is provided in abundance by the coastal towns of **Tela**, **La Ceiba** and **Trujillo**, with their broad expanses of isolated beach, clean warm waters, dozens of restaurants and buzzing nightlife. Dotted in between the main towns are a number of laid-back **Garífuna** villages blessed with unspoilt beaches, where a stay is likely to be more peaceful. **San Pedro Sula**, the region's major city and transport hub, provides amenities of a strictly urban kind.

When beach life loses its appeal, there are several natural reserves in the region to visit. The national parks of **Cusuco**, **Pico Bonito** and **Capiro y Calentura**, whose virgin cloudforest shelters rare wildlife, offer hiking for all levels of fitness; the wetland and mangrove swamps at **Punta Sal** and **Cuero y Salado** require less exertion to explore.

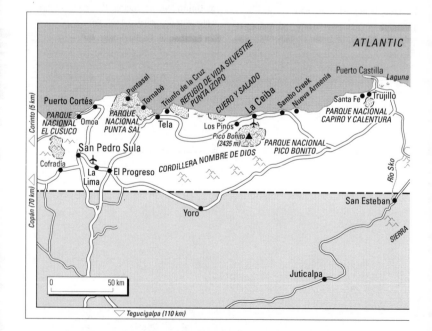

For an explanation of **accommodation price codes**, see p.365.

Occupying the eastern corner of Honduras is the remote and undeveloped expanse of the **Mosquitia**, at whose heart lies the **Río Plátano Biosphere Reserve**, an extensive swathe of virtually pristine tropical rainforest. Travelling here requires a spirit of adventure and the ability to lose track of time, but the effort it takes is well rewarded.

The two **dry** seasons – December through to April, and August to September – are the best times to visit the north coast. Temperatures rarely drop below 25–28°C, but the heat is usually tempered by ocean breezes. Outside the Mosquitia, **transport** is reasonably good, with frequent buses along the fast, paved highway that links the main coastal towns; as usual, reaching the remoter villages and national parks requires some forward planning. There's abundant **accommodation** to suit all price levels – the only time it's necessary to book is around Semana Santa, when hordes of Hondurans head for the beach and prices often rise.

San Pedro Sula

Honduras's second city, and the country's driving economic force, **SAN PEDRO SULA** sprawls across the fertile Valle de Sula at the foot of the Merendón mountain chain, just an hour from the coast. Flat and uninspiring to look at, and for most of the year uncomfortably hot and humid, this is a city for getting business done in rather than sightseeing. It's also the transport hub for northern and western Honduras, meaning that a visit here is usually unavoidable, even if only to pass through. On a more positive note, in terms of **facilities** San Pedro rates alongside Tegucigalpa, with its own international

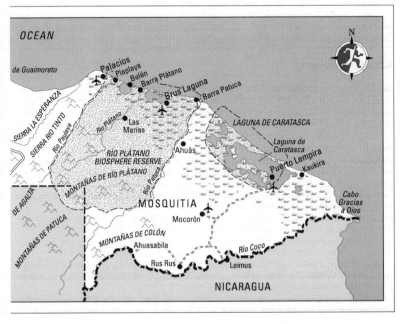

airport, foreign consulates, and a wide range of hotels, restaurants and shopping outlets – travellers coming from the north rarely need to visit the capital. If you do choose to stick around for a day or two, it's not difficult to organize a trip out to one of the country's finest **cloudforest reserves**, the Parque Nacional El Cusuco (see p.426).

One of the first Spanish settlements in the country, founded by Pedro de Alvarado in 1536, today's San Pedro bears almost no trace of its pre-twentieth-century incarnation. Burnt out by French corsairs in 1660 and virtually abandoned during a yellow-fever epidemic in 1892, the city struggled to maintain a population of more than five thousand, and today only a few wooden buildings remain as proof of its long past. Fortunes began to rise with the growth of the **banana** industry in the late nineteenth century, when the city rapidly cemented its role as Honduras's commercial centre. With its outer reaches continuing to sprout factories, many of them foreign-owned, and a population now in the region of 600,000, San Pedro ranks as one of the fastest-growing cities in Central America.

Arrival and information

The **Aeropuerto Internacional Villeda Morales**, the point of arrival for both domestic and international flights, lies 12km southeast of the city. As yet, there is no public transport between the airport and the city centre; **taxis** charge around US$8. **Buses** arrive at their own separate terminals, most within a few blocks of each other in central San Pedro (see p.427 for addresses).

San Pedro's regular grid layout makes navigation easy: avenidas run north–south and calles east–west, numbered in ascending order from the central 1 Avenida and 1 Calle, which intersect two blocks east of the cathedral. The city is further divided into quadrants, whose labels – southwest (SO), southeast (SE), northwest (NO) and northeast (NE) – are always used in directions. The bus terminals, many hotels and the main commercial area are in the southwest sector, close to the centre. Running west from the Parque Central, 1 Calle is also known as the Blvd Morazán for the twelve blocks before it meets the **Av Circunvalación** ring road, which separates the city centre from San Pedro's wealthiest residential districts; this is where many of the more upmarket restaurants are located. Beyond the Circunvalación, 1 Calle becomes Blvd los Próceres.

Accommodation

San Pedro's **accommodation** ranges from a spate of new four- and five-star luxury hotels, including a *Holiday Inn* and *Camino Real*, to sleazy, dollar-a-night dives. Expect to pay at least US$12 for an acceptable double room with bath in a secure hotel; double that, and TV and air conditioning become standard. The area south of the market can get rough at night, and although foreigners are unlikely to be targeted, it's not really a place to be wandering around after dark.

Ambassador, 7 C & 5 Av SO (☎557 6825, fax 557 5860). Reasonably comfortable rooms, all with bath and a/c. Not a particularly pleasant area at night, but convenient for many of the bus terminals. ④.

Bolívar, 2 C & 2 Av NO (☎553 3224, fax 553 4823). Good-value hotel in a central location with an upmarket feel. The large rooms all have bath, a/c and TV, and there's a small pool and terrace downstairs, plus a rather characterless bar and restaurant. ⑤.

Ejecutive Real del Valle, Edificio Maria Emilia, 6 Av, 4–5 C SO (☎553 0366). A comfortable place with a welcoming atmosphere. All rooms have a/c, bath, hot water and TV. ④.

Gran Hotel Conquistador, 2 C SO, 7–8 Av (☎552 7605). Small and very friendly place, four blocks west of the Parque Central. Rooms are small but clean and all have bath, a/c and TV. ⑤.

Gran Hotel San Pedro, 3 C, 1–2 Av SO (☎553 1513, fax 553 1655). Large, rambling place that's popular with travellers. The choice of rooms ranges from basic ones with shared bath to reasonably spacious options with large beds, private bath, a/c and TV. ②–④.

Gran Hotel Sula, 1 C 0, at the Parque Central (☎552 9999, fax 552 7000, *www.intertel.hn /tourism/gransula*). Venerable city landmark set in an excellent location in the main square. The

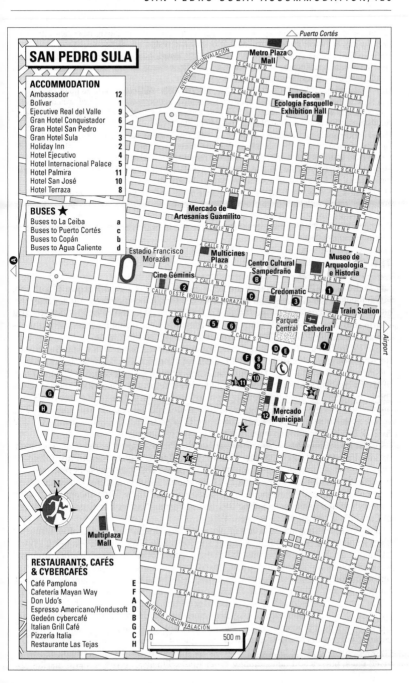

△ *Puerto Cortés*

SAN PEDRO SULA

ACCOMMODATION

Ambassador	12
Bolívar	1
Ejecutive Real del Valle	9
Gran Hotel Conquistador	6
Gran Hotel San Pedro	7
Gran Hotel Sula	3
Holiday Inn	2
Hotel Ejecutivo	4
Hotel Internacional Palace	5
Hotel Palmira	11
Hotel San José	10
Hotel Terraza	8

BUSES ★

Buses to La Ceiba	a
Buses to Puerto Cortés	c
Buses to Copán	b
Buses to Agua Caliente	d

Metro Plaza Mall

Fundación
Ecología Fasquelle
Exhibition Hall

Mercado de
Artesanías Guamilito

Estadio Francisco
Morazán

Multicines
Plaza

Cine Géminis

Centro Cultural
Sampedraño

Museo de
Arqueología
e Historia

CALLE OESTE (BOULEVARD MORAZÁN)

Credomatic

Parque
Central

Train Station

Cathedral

△ *Airport*

Mercado
Municipal

Multiplaza
Mall

N

RESTAURANTS, CAFÉS & CYBERCAFÉS

Café Pamplona	E
Cafetería Mayan Way	F
Don Udo's	A
Espresso Americano/Hondusoft	D
Gedeón cybercafé	B
Italian Grill Café	G
Pizzería Italia	C
Restaurante Las Tejas	H

0   500 m

business-class rooms have everything you'd expect for the price, including balconies with views over the city, and there's also a small pool, 24hr café and restaurant. ⑧.

Holiday Inn, 1 C, 10–11 Av (☎550 8080, fax 550 5353, *www.holiday-inn-sps.com*). New luxury block set in a pleasant residential area, with classy, commodious rooms, all with huge beds and many with wonderful views. Special weekend rates available. ⑧.

Hotel Ejecutivo, 10 Av & 2 C SO (☎552 4289, fax 552 5868). Well-run mid-range hotel, located in a quiet residential area a ten-minute walk from the centre. The large rooms all have two double beds, a/c, bathroom with power showers, and TV; the price includes a simple breakfast. Slightly cheaper rooms are available in a second block directly opposite. ⑤–⑥.

Hotel Internacional Palace, 8 Av, 3 C SO (☎550 3838, fax 550 0969, *www.intertel.hn /tourism/palace*). Refurbished hotel offering upmarket accommodation at reasonable prices. All rooms have bath, hot water, a/c and TV, and the rooftop pool and bar are a good place to cool off. ⑥.

Hotel Palmira, 6 C, 6–7 Av SO. Basic but cleanish place conveniently located beside the Casarola bus terminal for Copán; all the rooms have private bathrooms, and some also have a/c. ②–③.

Hotel San José, 6 Av, 5–6 C SO (☎557 1208). One of the city's better budget hotels, offering clean, good-sized rooms with bath and a choice of fan or a/c. ②.

Hotel Terraza, 6 Av, 4–5 C SO (☎550 3108). Safe, good value and convenient for the centre and bus terminals. Rooms all have bath and hot water (some also have a/c), and the café downstairs serves decent breakfasts. ③–④.

The City

San Pedro Sula's Parque Central, the large and recently re-paved **Parque Barahona**, is the focus of the city centre, teeming with vendors, shoeshine boys, moneychangers and general malcontents taking the air. On its eastern edge, the colonial-style **Catedral Municipal** was actually only completed in the mid-1950s; facing it across the Parque is the unremarkable Palacio Muncipal, home to the city adminstration.

San Pedro has few tourist attractions, but one place that is worth a visit is the **Museo de Arqueología e Historia** (Wed–Mon 9am–4.15pm; US$0.65), a few blocks north of the Parque at 3 Av, 4 C NO. The museum's collection (mostly labelled in Spanish only) of pre-Columbian sculptures, ceramics and other artefacts, the majority recovered from the Sula valley, outlines the development of civilization in the region from 1500 BC onwards; weaponry and paintings from the colonial period continue the theme. While you're in the area, check out what's on at the **Centro Cultural Sampedrano**, 3 C, 3–4 Av NO (☎553 3911), which regularly hosts concerts and plays.

A block southeast at 1 C and 7 Av (above the *Pizzería Italia*) is the ecological foundation **Fundación Ecologista Hector Rodrigo Pastor Fasquelle** (Mon–Fri 8am–noon & 1–5pm, Sat 8am–noon; ☎552 1014 or 557 6598), an excellent resource centre with information about the ecology of Honduras. Displays feature pictorial and written explanations of the development of cloudforests and the wildlife encountered in the country's varied habitats, including the nearby Parque Nacional de Cusuco (for details of Cusuco's information office, see p.427).

San Pedro has a good selection of places to buy Honduran **handicrafts**. Ten or so blocks northwest of the Parque Central, the **Mercado Guamilito**, 9 Av, 6–7 C NO, is an indoor market with numerous stalls selling hammocks, ceramics, leatherwork and wooden goods. If you can carry them, the cotton hammocks are a good buy; gentle bartering should get you better prices. A couple of shops on the Calle Peatonal, just off the Parque Central, sell similar stuff, though prices are higher and the range not as wide.

For the more eclectically minded, **Le Merendon**, a taxi ride out of the centre at 18 Av, 6 C SO, is a thatch-roofed display-area-cum-beer-garden with an offbeat selection of works by artisans from around the country; look out for the huge straw animals and the ceramic garden decorations. **Danilo's**, a couple of streets away at 18 Av B, 9 C SO, is an outlet for one of the best leather-goods producers in the country, selling excellent-value bags, purses and belts, among other items. Finally, the vast general market, the

Mercado Municipal, is between 4–5 Av SO and 5–6 C SO, though stalls spill onto the streets around for several blocks.

Eating, drinking and entertainment

As you'd expect in such a business-oriented city, there's a good selection of **places to eat** and a diverse range of evening entertainment. The more down-to-earth places can be found in the centre, while the stretch of Av Circunvalación south of 1 C – the so-called "**Zona Viva**" – is the place to go for upmarket restaurants, bars and clubs. There's a number of modern multi-screen **cinemas** – including the Multicines Plaza de Sula at 10 Av and 4 C NO; Cine Tropicana, at 2 C, 7 Av SO; and the Cine Géminis, 1 C, 12 Av NO – all are within easy walking distance of the centre and show new US films and the occasional Latin American offering.

Cafés and restaurants

Café Pamplona, Parque Central. Always crowded with locals, this place has kitsch 1970s decor, an extensive menu, decent coffee and reasonable prices – but don't expect too much in the way of service. Closes 8pm.

Café Skandia, in the *Gran Hotel Sula*. Air-conditioned and open 24hr, the *Skandia* is something of a San Pedro institution, offering reasonably priced sandwiches, light meals and snacks.

Cafetería Mayan Way, 6 Av, 4–5 C SO, next to the *Hotel Terraza*. Slightly sleazy, but popular with travellers for the good breakfasts, set lunches and daily specials at down-to-earth prices. Open until 2am Fri and Sat.

Don Udo's, 1 C, 20 Av SO (☎552 5225). Dutch-owned restaurant that's held to be one of city's finest, offering a broad range of European and local dishes and a decent wine list. Prices are not cheap, but worth it for a splurge; expect to pay from US$15 a head for a full meal with wine. Sunday brunches are less formal. Mon–Sat evenings, Sun 10am–2pm.

Espresso Americano, just west of the Parque Central on 3 C SO. Modern *Starbucks*–style coffee house with good mochas, cappuccinos, and even frappaccinos.

Italian Grill Café, 8 C, 16 Av SO (☎552 1770). Authentic Italian place offering generously sized pasta dishes which include a side salad and focaccia bread. Suprisingly moderate prices, though wines are expensive. Closed Sun.

Pizzería Italia, 1 C, 7 Av NO. Cosy little place with wonderful time-warp furnishings, serving good pizza (around US$4) and a small selection of pasta dishes (around US$5).

Restaurante Las Tejas, Av Circunvalación, 9 C SO. Popular place for Honduran-style lunch and dinner, with a wide selection of well-prepared seafood, as well as meat and chicken dishes.

Shauky's Place, 18 Av, 8 C SO. Easy-going bar and restaurant with tables set around an open-air gravelled garden. Delicious steak and meat dishes costing around US$7, and there are a few vegetarian choices too. Mon–Sat from 4pm.

Bars and clubs

After dark, the best bet for a cheap **drink** in the central zone is to start out at the *Cafetería Mayan Way* (see above) or *Johnny's*, by the market, an idiosyncratic spirits-only bar where locals go to shoot the breeze to the accompaniment of 1950s bebop. Out in the suburbs, *Frog's Sports Bar*, Blvd Los Próceres, 19–20 C SO, has pool tables and giant TV screens. **Clubbers** should head for either *Henry's* or *Confetti's* in the Zona Viva for Latino pop and Euro dance, while *El Quijote* at 11 C, 3–4 SO, is probably the most exclusive place in town, attracting a flash, label-conscious crowd.

Listings

Airlines American Airlines, Centro Comercial Firenze, 16 Av, 2 C (☎558 0518 or 558 0521, fax 558 0527); British Airways, Edificio Sempe, Carretera a Chamelecon (☎556 6952 or 552 3942, fax 556

8764); Continental, Plaza Versalles, Av Circunvalación (☎557 4141, airport ☎668 3208); COPA, *Gran Hotel Sula* (☎550 5586); Iberia, Edificio Quiroz 2 C, 1–2 Av (☎557 5311, fax 553 4297; airport ☎668 3218); Isleña, Edifico Trejo Merlo, 7 Av, 1–2 C (☎ & fax 552 8322); Sosa, 8 Av, 1 C SO (☎550 6545, airport ☎668 3223); Taca, Av Cirunvalación & 13 Av NO (☎550 5262, airport ☎668 3333).

American Express Agencia de Viajes Mundirama, Edificio Martinez Valenzuela, 2 C, 2–3 Av SO (☎553 1193, fax 557 9022).

Banks and exchange Banco Atlántida has a number of branches in the downtown area, including one on the Parque Central, for exchange and Visa advances; Banco de Occidente, 6 Av, 2–3 C SO, changes cash and travellers' cheques; Credomatic, 5 Av, 1–2 C NO, advances cash on Visa and Mastercard.

Bookshops The cigar shop in the *Gran Hotel Sula* has a small assortment of English-language fiction, books on Honduras and US magazines and newspapers.

Car rental Avis, Blvd Morazán 58 (☎552 2872); Budget, Aeropuerto Villeda Morales (☎566 2267, fax 553 3411); Dollar, 3 Av, 3–4 C NO (☎552 7626); Molinari, *Gran Hotel Sula* (☎553 2639, fax 552 2704; airport ☎566 2580).

Consulates Belize, Km 5, road to Puerto Cortés (☎551 0124, fax 551 1740); El Salvador, 6th floor, Edificio Rivera, 3 C, 5–6 Av SO (☎553 3604; Mon–Fri 9am–noon & 2–3.30pm); Guatemala, 8 C, 5–6 Av NO (☎553 3560; Mon–Fri 8.30am–2pm); Mexico, 2 C, 20 Av SO, 205 (☎553 2604; Mon–Fri 8.30–11.30am); UK, 13 Av, 11–12 C SO, No 62 (☎557 2046; Mon–Fri 9am–noon).

Immigration Direcion General de Migración, Calle Peatonal, above the Moreira Honduras souvenir shop (☎553 3728; Mon–Fri 8am–4pm).

Internet access The number of cybercafés in town is growing rapidly. Hondusoft is the most central, on the first floor of the Edificio Gran Via, just south of the Parque Central on C Peatonal; rates are just $2 an hour. On the west side of town, Gedeón, Local 1A, Plaza GMC, 6 Av Norte, 2–3 C NO, is very well set up, with rows of gleaming iMac machines; rates are US$2.65 an hour.

Laundry Lavandería Express 9 Av, 3 C NO (Mon–Sat 8am–5pm).

Medical care There's an emergency department at the Clínica Bendaña, Av Circunvalación, 9–10 C SO (☎553 1618).

Police ☎552 3128.

Post office 9 C, 3 Av SO (Mon–Fri 7.30am–8pm, Sat 7.30am–12.30pm).

Telephone office Hondutel, at 4 C, 4 Av SO, is open 24hr; fax service is available 8am–5pm. Gedeón (see "Internet" listing above) have Web phone-call facilities.

Travel agents and tours Agencia de Viajes Mundirama, Edificio Martinez Valenzuela, 2 C, 2–3 Av SO (☎553 0192, fax 557 9092), is an efficient place to book or change international air tickets, or try the reputable Transmundo de Sula, 5 Av, 4 C NO (☎550 1140). Mesoamérica Travel, Edificio Picadelli, 11C, 2–3 Av (☎557 0332, fax 557 6886, *www.mesoamerica-travel.com*), is an excellent tour agency with trips to reserves including Punta Sal near Tela and Cusuco, the Bay Islands and Mosquitia. Maya Tropic Tours, based in the *Gran Hotel Sula* (☎557 8830, *mayatt@netsy.*hn), also offer trips to Copán and Cusuco.

Moving on

San Pedro Sula is the main transport hub for this part of Honduras, with frequent **bus departures** for Tegucigalpa, Santa Rosa de Copán and all destinations along the north coast. Bus companies operate out of their own terminals, most of which are conveniently located within a few blocks of each other in the centre of the city (see opposite for addresses). An (L) after the company names denotes a luxury service. There is also an intermittent **train** service between Puerto Cortés and Tela – check in the station at 1 C E, 1 Av N.

Around San Pedro: Parque Nacional El Cusuco

Some 20km west of San Pedro in the Sierra del Merendón, the stunning **Parque Nacional El Cusuco** (daily 6am–5pm; US$10) supports an abundant range of animal and plant life, much of it rare and threatened. Though inevitably affected by the prox-

BUSES FROM SAN PEDRO SULA			
DESTINATION	**COMPANY**	**ADDRESS**	**FREQUENCY AND DURATION**
Copán	Hedman Atlas (L)	3 C, 8–9 Av NO (☎553 1361)	1 daily; 2hr 45min
	Casasola/GAMA	6 C, 6–7 Av SO (☎558 2861)	5 daily; 3hr
Gracias	Gracianos	6 C, 6–7 Av SO	2 daily; 5hr
La Ceiba (via Tela)	Viana (L)	Av Circunvalación (☎556 9261)	2 daily; 2hr 45min.
	Cotraibal	1 Av, 7–8 C SO (☎552 8740)	5 daily; 3hr
	Catisa Tupsa	2 Av, 5–6 C SO (☎552 1042)	12 daily; 3hr
Nuevo Ocotepeque	Toritos	6 Av 8–9 C (☎553 1174)	7 daily; 5hr
Puerto Cortés	Impala	2 Av, 4–5 C SO (☎553 3111)	12 daily; 1hr–1hr 15min
	Citul	6 Av 7–8C (☎553 0700)	11 daily; 1hr–1hr 15min
San Salvador	King Quality	6 C, 7–8 Av SO (☎558 1659)	1 daily; 7hr 30min
Santa Rosa de Copán	Toritos	11 C, 6–7 Av SO (☎553 4930)	6 daily; 2hr 45min
Tegucigalpa	Hedman Alas,	3 C, 8–9 Av NO (☎553 1361)	10 daily; 3hr 45min
	Saenz	8 Av, 5–6 C SO (☎553 4969)	6 daily; 3hr 45min
	El Rey	7 Av, 5–6 C SO (☎553 4969)	10 daily; 4hr
	Norteños	6C, 6–7 Av (☎552 2145)	11 daily; 4hr 15min
	Viana	Av Circunvalación (☎556 9261)	4 daily; 3hr 45min
Trujillo	Cotraibal	1 Av, 7–8 C SO (☎552 8740)	5 daily; 6hr

imity of human settlement, Cusuco is still a joy to visit and not too difficult to reach from San Pedro. To see as much as possible, the best plan is to arrive in the afternoon, camp overnight and walk the trails early in the morning.

The lower reaches of the park have long been settled by humans and were heavily logged during the 1950s, contributing to disastrous floods during the 1970s. Here the mixed pine and broadleaf forest is secondary regrowth. At around 1800m the **cloud-forest** begins, its dense oaks and liquidambars reaching 40m in some places, stacked over avocados and palms, all supporting mosses, vines, orchids and numerous species of heliconias, recognizable by the red or orange brackets holding the blossoms. Studies carried out in the park in 1992–95 revealed the existence of at least seventeen species of plant hitherto unknown in Honduras.

Four **trails**, ranging between 1km and 2.5km, have been laid out among the lower sections of cloudforest (there is no access to the highest, steepest sections of the reserve), taking you through a hushed world of dense, dripping, multi-layered vegetation. If you're incredibly lucky, you might spot the reserve's namesake, the *cusuco* (armadillo), as well as salamanders, monkeys and even a jaguar, though you're more likely to spot some of the reserve's dazzling range of birdlife: quetzals can be spotted from April to June, and trogons, kites and woodpeckers are among the more numerous of the 100-plus species of bird living here.

Practicalities

Cusuco is managed by the Fundación Ecologista Hector Rodrigo Pastor Fasquelle, whose office is above the *Pizzería Italia*, 1 C, 7 Av NO, in San Pedro Sula (☎552 1014). Information leaflets are usually available, and they can also advise on getting to the reserve. The main point of **access** is via the small town of **COFRADÍA**, 18km southwest of San Pedro off highway CA-4. From here, a dirt road continues for another 26km to the village of **BUENOS AIRES**, 5km beyond which you'll find the park **visitor centre**. Getting there independently is time-consuming: you need to take a westbound bus to Cofradía (buses to and from La Entrada or Santa Rosa pass through) and then wait for onward transport. Other options include renting a car – a 4WD can make the whole journey in about two hours, depending on the state of the road – or taking a tour from San Pedro (see listings on p.426). The visitor centre has displays on the park's wildlife, trail maps, a dormitory (①) and a camping site.

The northwest coast: Puerto Cortés and Omoa

North of San Pedro Sula, Highway CA-5 runs through the flat agricultural lands of the Sula valley, amidst lush, tropical scenery. After 60km the four-lane highway reaches the coast at **PUERTO CORTÉS**, Honduras's main port, where the unstinting heat and dilapidated wooden buildings merely add to the rough and ready feel of the place. There's nothing here to entice you to stop, but if you do, *Hotel El Centro* (☎665 1160; ②/④), at 3 Av, just west of the Parque Central, has basic but serviceable singles and doubles, some with cable TV and private bathrooms, while *Hotel Villa Capri* (☎665 6136, fax 665 6139, *villa-capri@lemaco.hn*; ⑦), close to the docks at 1 C and 2 Av, has the best rooms in town, all with a/c.

Three companies run **buses** between San Pedro Sula and Puerto Cortés, including the reliable Citul, whose offices are at 6 Av, 7–8 C SO in San Pedro; they have services every thirty minutes between 6am and 6pm, and the journey time is one hour. The Citul terminal in Puerto Cortés is a block north of the main plaza at 4 Av and 4C – if you're heading on to Belize or Guatemala, the **migración** (Mon–Fri 8am–noon and 1–5pm; ☎665 0582) is conveniently close by at 5 Av and 4 C, one block to the north. To **change money**, head for Banco Atlántida on the south side of the plaza, or to the market just to the west, where the largest shoe-stall owner cashes dollars at fair rates. There's **Internet** access at Plaza Marinakys, 2 Av and 6 C (Mon–Sat 8am–6.30pm), two blocks east of the Parque.

Moving on from Puerto Cortés, there are buses to Corinto, for **Guatemala**, every ninety minutes (8am–3.30pm; 4hr) and hourly connections to Omoa (1hr); buses leave from the Transportes Citral terminal on 3 C a block west of the Parque. It's also possible to travel from Puerto Cortés by fast skiff, the *Gulf Cruza*, to **Belize**, with weekly departures on Mondays at 10am from the old bridge at La Laguna, 3km south of the town centre. The journey to Belize City (US$75) takes around seven hours, with stops at Belizean immigration at Big Creek and at Placencia (4hr; US$50). For more information and the latest schedules and prices call ☎665 1200 or 665 5556.

Omoa

Spreading inland from a deep bay at the point where the mountains of the Sierra de Omoa meet the Caribbean, the fishing village of **OMOA** has become increasingly popular in recent years, with travellers coming here for total rest and relaxation. Once a strategically important location in the defence of the Spanish colonies against marauding British pirates, today the village dozes lethargically under the heat of the Caribbean sun, with its one outstanding sight, the restored **Fortaleza de San Fernando de Omoa** (Mon–Fri 8am–4pm, Sat & Sun 9am–5pm; US$1.30), standing in mute witness to this colourful history. Now isolated amidst tropical greenery a kilometre from the coast, having been beached as the sea has receded over the centuries, the triangular fort was originally intended to protect the port of Puerto Barrios in Guatemala. Work began in 1759 but was never fully completed, due to a combination of bureaucratic inefficiency, problems with materials and labour shortage. The steadily weakening Spanish authorities then suffered the ignominy of witnessing the fortress being temporarily occupied by British and Miskito military forces in October 1779.

The rather narrow village **beach**, lined with colourful fishing boats, offers stunning views west across the curve of the bay and the mountain backdrop. At weekends hordes of day-trippers turn up and it's often too crowded for comfort. Better **swimming** can be had by walking five minutes or so out of the village in either direction, while fifteen minutes around the headland to the east is a much wider and usually emptier expanse of beach.

Practicalities

Buses between Puerto Cortés to Corinto pass the southern end of the village, close to the *migración* (daily 8am–5pm in theory, though it's often unmanned), which is right on the highway. The coast and hotels are 2km away to the north, past the fortress and the **Hondutel** office.

Rising numbers of foreign tourists have led to the opening of a handful of reasonably comfortable **places to stay**. Heading towards the beach from the highway, you'll come to the Swiss-run *Roli's Place* (☎ & fax 658 9082, *RG@yaxpactours.com*; ②), an excellent budget base with camping (US$2 per person) and mosquito-screened dormitories (US$3.50 per person); they also have **Internet** access for US$5.80 per hour. Close to the seafront, the new *Pia's Place* (☎658 9076; ②) is run by a friendly long-term *gringa* resident and offers basic clean rooms and dormitory accommodation (US$3 per person). Next door, by the waterfront, the comfortable *Bahía de Omoa* (☎658 9076; ④), also run by Pia, has large, modern rooms, all with private bath and a/c. Pia also organizes snorkelling trips to the spectacular Sapadillo cayes, in Belizean waters northwest of Omoa, when there's sufficient demand. For a good **meal** head to the *Botín del Suizo* restaurant for European and local dishes or one of the *champas* on the beachfront – small, palm-thatched restaurants serving well-cooked seafood and other dishes. Try the clean and friendly *Fisherman's Hut*, or *Champa Virginia*, where a substantial meal costs just US$3–4.

Moving on from Omoa to **Guatemala** it's an excruciatingly slow and bumpy bus ride southwest to the town of **Corinto**, 2km from the border. Buses run every ninety minutes along this route, which is steadily being patched up after Hurricane Mitch wiped out all the bridges in 1998. It currently takes up to three hours to cover the (flat) 50km to Corinto, though the journey time will fall as the road improves and bridges are rebuilt. Corinto currently has its own **migración** (daily 8am–5.30pm), though a new joint Guatemalan–Honduran customs and immigration point is due to open at the border itself (2km north of town) in 2003. At present, frequent pick-ups shuttle to and from the border, from where you catch a minibus (every thirty minutes) over the recently built Arizona bridge, along a new paved road which crosses the Río Motagua. Minibuses pass though the village of Entre Ríos, for Guatemalan migración, to Puerto Barrios, an hour from the Honduras border.

If you're pressed for time, adventurous souls can charter a lancha from Omoa to make the two-hour – and invariably very wet – boat journey over to Lívingston in **Guatemala**. Ask around in the guesthouses or the *Botín del Suizo* for a captain; the price is around US$260 for the trip, which can be divided between up to ten people.

Tela and around

East of San Pedro, highway CA-13 runs through fertile lowlands, past serried ranks of banana trees which stretch for mile after endless mile. **La Lima**, 15km from San Pedro, is the definitive company town, headquarters for United Fruit ("Chiquita" brand) operations in Honduras. At **El Progreso**, a dusty town a further 15km east, the highway swings north to enter the stunning scenery of the **coast**.

With its magnificent natural setting midway round the Bahía de Tela, surrounded by sweeping beaches, **TELA** should be a dream getaway. The town is a magnet for Hondurans and young European travellers alike, and though the police have reined in some of the gangs of would-be lotharios, there remains something of a seedy undercurrent about the place that can either add to its charm or bring a sense of unease, depending on your point of view. However you feel about Tela itself, the wealth of fantastic natural reserves within just a few kilometres of the town make it well worth a visit.

Arrival and information

There are no direct buses between San Pedro and central Tela; buses to La Ceiba and Trujillo stop along the highway outside town, from where taxis (US$0.50) ferry passengers into the centre, five minutes away. Most local services, including the half-hourly buses to and from La Ceiba, use the terminal at 9 Av, 9 C NE, near the market; buses to the surrounding villages use the terminal close by at 8 Av, 10 C NE.

Hondutel and the **post office** are next to each other at 4 Av, 7–8 C NE, two blocks south of the Parque Central. For **changing money**, both BanParqueco Atlántida and Bancahsa are just west of the Parque on 9 Calle, the main drag. For excellent **information** about the town and region visit the useful community Web site (*www.tela-honduras .com*) or visit Garífuna Tours, at 9 C and 5 Av NE (☎448 1069, fax 448 2904, *www .garifuna.hn*), who run superb tours including trips to Punta Sal and Punta Izopo (US$18 per person) and also offer **Internet** access for US$3.20 per hour. You can also check your email at the *Mango Café* (see opposite). **Prolansate**, the organization that manages Punta Sal and other reserves in the area, can help with information and advise on access; they're based at 9 C, 3 Av NE (☎ & fax 448 2042).

Accommodation

Given Tela's somewhat faded status, it's not surprising that many of the hotels are run-down and uninviting. There are also a couple of prime examples of the Honduran beach-front genre of architecture, where all the rooms face inland or onto internal corridors. Many of the new places tend to get busy at weekends, when it pays to book ahead.

Bahía Azul, 2 Av, 11 C NE (☎448 2381). On the beach just west of the centre; you pay for the location but not the sea views (there aren't any). Rooms, some with TV, are comfortable, but lacking in character and rather overpriced. ④.

Grand Central, opposite the train station, 400m south of the Parque (☎ & fax 448 1099, *grancentral @hotmail.com*) Smart new French-owned apartment-hotel: the stylish apartments all have kitchens and very comfortable beds. ⑤.

Hotel Marazul, 11 C, 4 Av (☎448 2343). A long-term travellers' stronghold, with clean, cheap rooms and a small café. ②.

Hotel Marsol 2 Av, 9 C NE (☎448 1781). New place with a selection of clean, spacious and very good-value rooms, all with a/c, TV and bath. ③–④.

Maya Vista, 9 C, 10 Av (☎448 1497, *www.mayavista.com*). Canadian-owned hilltop hotel, overlooking the ocean, with a selection of comfortable rooms and attractive new apartments, some with full kitchen facilities and a/c, plus a great restaurant. Rooms ④, apartments ⑤.

Puerto Rico, 5 Av, 11 C NE (☎448 2413). Another seafront special, where only six or so of the small, clean rooms, all with private bath, face the beach. ③–④.

Tela, 9 C, 4 Av NE (☎448 2150). Rambling, wooden building in the town centre, with large, clean rooms all with bath and fan. ②–③.

Villas Telamar, Tela Nueva (☎448 2196, fax 448 2984). Occupying what used to be executive housing for Tela Railway Company employees, this idiosyncratic piece of luxury has wooden houses spread across shady grounds, a stretch of beautiful beachfront and facilities including a pool, tennis courts and nine-hole golf course. Accommodation is either in individual rooms or in villas sleeping up to fourteen people. ⑦–⑨.

The Town

Today's Tela is a product of the banana industry. In the late nineteenth century United Fruit nominated what was then a backwater as its headquarters, and set about building a company town – **Tela Nueva** – on the west bank of the Río Tela; the old village became known as **Tela Vieja**. When the company removed its headquarters to La Lima in 1965, the town began to slip back into its former somnolence, although fortunes today have been somewhat restored by the growth in tourism.

The centre of Tela, encompassing the **Parque Central** and main shopping area, lies about 2km north of the highway and two blocks from the beach. To the west the seafront is lined with hotels, to the east with discos. Five blocks west from the Parque Central, the **Río Tela** divides the old town from Tela Nueva. A ten-minute stroll covers practically all the delights of downtown. One target to make for is the small **Museo Garífuna**, by the river on 8 C NE (Mon–Sat 7.30am–noon, 2–5pm; US$0.40), where lively exhibits cover all aspects of the Garífuna way of life, music and traditions, supplemented by a gift shop and the *Mango Café* restaurant (see below). However, it's the **beaches** that most people come for; those in Tela Vieja, though wide, are more crowded and consequently less clean than the stretch of pale sand in front of the *Villas Telamar*. Much better beaches can be found along the bay outside town.

Eating, drinking and nightlife

Tela has an interesting mix of **places to eat**, with foreign-run restaurants, catering to the steady flow of European and North American visitors, competing with locally owned seafood places. Most of the hotels along the beach also have terrace restaurants, facing out across the water. One staple that shouldn't be missed is the delicious and addictive *pan de coco* (coconut bread) sold by Garífuna women and children on the beach and around town.

Tela has a thriving weekend **nightlife**, when the cluster of discos by the beach at the east end of the town boom out salsa, reggae and Euro dance until the small hours. Be aware, though, that things get rough at times, and take extra care when walking around – attacks are common. Out on the beachfront road, east from the Parque, you can grab a cocktail or beer at the atmospheric *Casa Azul*, from where it's a short stroll to all the main dance halls – *La Gaviota* and *El Submarino* are both popular, while the *Happy Port* puts on regular live music. For a more tranquil drink with a view, try the *Delfín Telamar* at the *Villas Telamar* on the beach or the *Mango Café* (see below), which organizes regular evenings of Garífuna music and dancing.

Cesar Marisco's, on the beach at 3 Av NE. Renowned for the quality of its seafood, in particular the *sopa de caracol* (conch soup), of which a more than adequate serving costs US$5. The outdoor eating area makes a nice place to relax in the evenings.

Jardín Corona, on the Parque Central. Cheap and straightforward Honduran fare; breakfasts are particularly good value. Closes at 7pm Mon–Sat, 3pm on Sun.

Luces del Norte, 11 C, 5 Av NE. Popular with foreign tourists, serving up a good range of seafood dishes, though food can be slow in coming – you might want to while away the time reading a title from the book exchange.

Mango Café 8 C NE, below Museo Garífuna. The most popular place in town amongst international travellers, with a great riverside site and friendly service. Dishes include delicious Italian food, or try the Garífuna style *tapado*, a wonderful seafood and coconut soup.

Maya Vista inside the *Maya Vista* hotel. Classy and fairly expensive menu of well-executed meat and fish dishes, plus huge breakfasts. There's an engaging atmosphere most nights, and tables overlook the ocean.

Restaurante Casa Azul, 11 C, 6 Av NE. Snug place tucked into the ground floor of an old house. The Italian menu features pasta and meat dishes, and there's also a small bar. A substantial meal and drinks will set you back about US$9.

Restaurante Puerto Rico, in the *Hotel Puerto Rico*. Large covered terrace with views across the beach and a well-prepared range of the usual Honduran standards and seafood dishes.

Tuty, 9 C NE, just off the Parque Central. Huge breakfasts and excellent juices; worth the inevitably long wait. Closes 7pm.

Around Tela

Even if you don't like Tela, the town redeems itself with an abundance of places to visit in its vicinity. These include **Garífuna villages** on either side of town, sited along the bay on pristine beaches, the **Punta Sal** and **Punta Izopo** wildlife reserves, and **Lancetilla**, 5km south of town, probably the finest botanical reserve in Latin America. For getting to all of these places you can take taxis or rely on local buses, but renting a bike is probably the most enjoyable way to get around.

The Garífuna villages

Heading **west** from Tela, a dirt road edges the bay between the seafront and the Laguna de los Micos, which forms the eastern edge of Punta Sal (see below). Seven kilometres along this road is the sleepy Garífuna village of **TORNABÉ** and, beyond that, **MIAMI**, set on a fabulous stretch of beach at the mouth of the lagoon. Though Tornabé has a few brick-built houses, Miami is unique, consisting of nothing but traditional palm-thatched huts. Accommodation in Tornabé is limited to *Chola's* (①), which has very simple huts owned by a friendly couple, and *The Last Resort* (☎230 0491 or 996 3318; ⑨), an idyllic getaway with small, comfortable, air-conditioned cabins and a decent restaurant; they also rent boats for exploring the lagoon. There's nowhere formal to stay in Miami, though if you ask around someone will probably find a place where you can hang a hammock. **Buses** run from Tela's marketplace to Tornabé several times a day until late afternoon; from here, three pick-ups continue on to Miami from Monday to Saturday. Weekends are the best time to visit, when you'll get to witness performances of Garífuna music – haunting and melodic drum-driven rhythms in which the influence of Africa can be clearly heard.

Some 7km **east** along the bay from Tela, the village of **TRIUNFO DE LA CRUZ** occupies the site of the first **Spanish settlement** on the mainland. Cristóbal de Olid landed here on May 3, 1524, but the colony was abandoned within a few months and the area not resettled until the Garífuna began arriving at the end of the eighteenth century. Basic accommodation is available, and a couple of small restaurants serve good seafood – try *Jorge's*. The scenic walk along the beach from Tela takes around two hours, passing the smaller village of **LA ENSENADA** on the way, though it's not advisable – especially for women – to walk alone or to take anything valuable with you. Intensive tourist development is mooted for the area around the village, but as yet the expanses of palm-fringed beach remain untouched.

Punta Sal and Punta Izopo

The **Parque Nacional Janet Kawas** (daily 6am–4pm; US$1), commonly known as **Punta Sal**, is a wonderfully diverse reserve encompassing mangrove swamps, coastal lagoons, wetlands, coral reef and tropical forest, which together provide habitats for an extraordinary range of animal, bird and plant life. Lying to the west of Tela, curving along the bay to the headland of Punta Sal, the reserve covers three lagoons: Laguna de los Micos, Laguna Tisnachí in the centre and the ocean-front Laguna El Diamante, on the western side of the headland. Over one hundred species of bird are present here, including herons and storks, with seasonal migratory visitors bumping up the numbers; animals found in the reserve include howler and white-faced monkeys, wild pigs, jaguars and, in the marine sections, manatees and marine turtles. **Boat trips** along the Río Ulúa and the canals running through the reserve offer a superb opportunity to view the wildlife at close quarters. Where the headland curves up to the north, the land rises slightly to Punta Sal (176m); a trail over the point leads to small, pristine **beaches** at either side.

It's possible to visit parts of Punta Sal independently by renting a boat in Miami to explore the Laguna de los Micos and surrounding area, though most people opt to join the trips organized by Garífuna Tours (see p.430). You could also hike the scenic eight kilometres from the village to the headland along the beach. For information on the reserve contact **Prolansate**, 9 C, 3 Av NE in Tela (☎ & fax 448 2042), the non-governmental organization that manages Punta Sal and other reserves in the area. Janet Kawas, after whom the reserve is named, was a former president of Prolansate and instrumental in obtaining protected status against intense local opposition. Her murder, in April 1995, has never been solved.

Jardín Botánico de Lancetilla

The extensive grounds of the **Jardín Botánico de Lancetilla** (Mon–Fri 7.30am–3pm, Sat & Sun 8am–3pm; US$5), 5km south of Tela, started life in 1925 as a United Fruit species research and testing station. Now managed by COHDEFOR, the reserve has grown into one of the largest collections of fruit and flowering trees, palms, hardwoods and tropical plants in Latin America. Within Lancetilla's boundaries are an arboretum, a still-functioning research station and a biological reserve – the last covers two-thirds of the total grounds and contains one of the only remaining stretches of virgin tropical wet forest on the Atlantic coast. The stability of the environment has also encouraged numerous species of birds to make their home here.

To **get to** Lancetilla, take the San Pedro highway for a couple of kilometres to the signposted turn-off south, from where it's a further 3km. Guided tours of the arboretum are available, and visitors are also free to wander at will along the marked trails; maps are available at the visitor centre. You need a whole day to visit the arboretum and then cross the reserves, through bamboo groves, to some small **swimming holes** on the Río Lancetilla. There's a **comedor** and a small **hostel** (US$4 per bunk) at the visitor centre; beds should be reserved through Prolansate in Tela (see above).

La Ceiba

Some 190km east along the coast from San Pedro Sula, steamy **LA CEIBA**, the lively capital of the department of Atlántida, is one of the more approachable Honduran cities. Though the town is completely bereft of architectural interest and its sandy beaches are strewn with garbage, it does at least enjoy a stunning setting beneath the steep, green slopes of the Cordillera Nombre de Dios. The city is bustling and self-assured by day, with a cosmopolitan mix of inhabitants including the large Garífuna community, but it's the night that's really celebrated in La Ceiba, when visitors and locals gather to sample the city's vibrant dance scene. Things really come to a head during La Ceiba's **Carnaval** in May, when 200,000 revellers descend on the town.

Ceiba, as it's generally known, owes its existence to the **banana** industry: the Vaccaro Bros (later Standard Fruit and now Dole) first laid plantations in the area in 1899 and set up their company headquarters in town in 1905. Although fruit is no longer shipped out through La Ceiba, the plantations are still important to the local economy, with crops of pineapple and African palm now as significant as bananas.

Though for many travellers Ceiba is no more than a stop-off en route to the Bay Islands, there are some good beaches just 10km or so outside town. Alternatively, with more time and a little planning – or the services of a tour operator – you can explore the cloudforest of the nearby **Parque Nacional Pico Bonito** or the mangrove swamps of the **Refugio Vida Silvestre**.

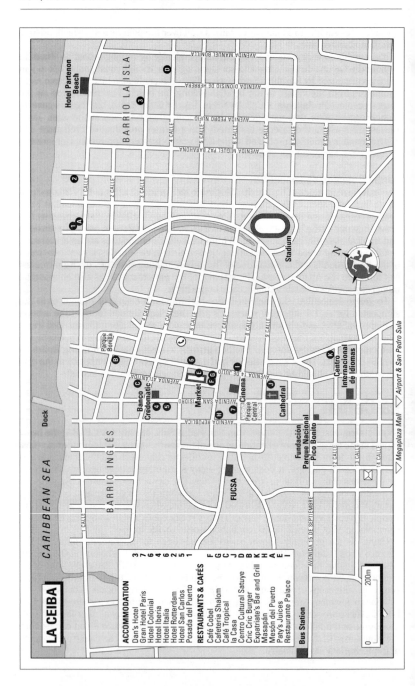

LA CEIBA

CARIBBEAN SEA

Dock

BARRIO INGLÉS

BARRIO LA ISLA

Hotel Partenon Beach

AVENIDA MANUEL BONILLA

AVENIDA DIONISIO DE HERRERA

AVENIDA PEDRO NUFIO

AVENIDA MIGUEL PAZ BARAHONA

1 CALLE
2 CALLE
3 CALLE
4 CALLE
5 CALLE
6 CALLE
7 CALLE
8 CALLE
9 CALLE
10 CALLE

Stadium

Parque Bonilla

Banco Credomatic

AVENIDA ATLÁNTIDA

AVENIDA SAN ISIDRO

AVENIDA REPÚBLICA

AVENIDA 14 DE JULIO

Market

Cinema

Parque Central

Cathedral

FUCSA

Fundación Parque Nacional Pico Bonito

Centro Internacional de Idiomas

Megaplaza Mall ▷ ▽ Airport & San Pedro Sula

AVENIDA 15 DE SEPTIEMBRE

Bus Station

N

ACCOMMODATION
Dan's Hotel   3
Gran Hotel Paris   7
Hotel Colonial   6
Hotel Iberia   4
Hotel Italia   6
Hotel Rotterdam   2
Hotel San Carlos   5
Posada del Puerto   1

RESTAURANTS & CAFÉS
Café Cobel   F
Cafetería Shalom   G
Café Tropical   C
la Casa   J
Centro Cultural Satuye   D
Cric Cric Burger   B
Expatriate's Bar and Grill K
Masapán   H
Mesón del Puerto   A
Paty's Juices   E
Restaurante Palace   I

0   200m

Arrival and information

Long-distance and local **buses** arrive at the main terminal, 2km west of the centre; taxis downtown, usually shared, charge US$0.50 per person. Those arriving by **air** will find themselves at the **Aeropuerto Internacional Golosón**, 9km from the centre, off the main highway west to San Pedro Sula. From the terminal, the taxi fare into the centre is US$4.50, or around US$3 if you flag one down on the highway, where you can also pick up buses heading into the city. The **ferry** to and from **Roatán** and **Utila** in the Bay Islands uses the Muralla de Cabotaje municipal dock, about 5km to the east of the city. There's no bus to the dock; taxis charge US$4–5 from the city centre and around US$8 from the airport.

FUCSA, which manages the Refugio de Vida Silvestre Cuero y Salado (see p.439), has an office in the Edificio Ferrocarril Nacional, two blocks west of the Parque Central (Mon–Fri 8–11.30am & 1.30–4.30pm, Sat 8–11.30am; ☎ & fax 443 0329, *fucsa@laceiba.com*).

Accommodation

Given La Ceiba's status, both as a provincial and party centre, there's a wide range of **places to stay**. The only problem will be in deciding whether you want to be near the centre, or closer to the nightlife along 1 C. Prices inevitably tend to rise around Carnaval time in May, when reserving ahead becomes essential.

Dan's Hotel, C 3, Barrio La Isla (☎ & fax 443 4219). Very friendly and quiet family-run place in the Garífuna barrio of La Isla. Spotless rooms, all with bath, cable TV and a/c. The owners will cook breakfasts and other meals on request. ④.

Gran Hotel Paris, Parque Central (☎443 2391, fax 443 1614, *www.granhotelparis.com*). Recently refurbished landmark hotel in an excellent location on the main plaza. The large, comfortable rooms all come with a/c, phone and TV, and there's a pool, a quiet bar, restaurant and cybercafé. Excellent value for money. ⑥.

Hotel Colonial, Av 14 de Julio, 6–7 C (☎443 1953, fax 443 1955). One of the more upmarket downtown places: all the rooms have bath, TV and phone, and facilities include a decent restaurant, a bar and, bizarrely enough, a sauna. ⑤.

Hotel Iberia, Av San Isidro, 5–6 C (☎443 0401). Noisy location, though the spacious rooms are fairly good value: all have two double beds, bath, a/c and TV. ⑤.

Hotel Italia, Av 14 de Julio, next to the *Colonial* (☎443 0150). Rooms are large and clean, but somewhat sparsely furnished; all have baths, however, and the place is secure. ②.

Hotel Rotterdam, 1 C, Av Barahona, Barrio La Isla (☎443 0321). Reasonable-value, Dutch-run hotel, just up from the beach, with adequate rooms, all with bath. ②.

Hotel San Carlos, Av San Isidro, 5–6 C (☎443 0330). Well-run and very popular travellers' stronghold set in the heart of town above a bakery, with a selection of clean, safe rooms, all with fans. ②.

Posada del Puerto, beachfront, off 1C (☎440 0030). Very homely, friendly beachside guesthouse. All rooms have excellent quality beds and pleasant decor, plus a/c and TV; there's also a guests' living room and kitchen, and a large restaurant, under the same management, next door. ⑤.

The City

Most things of interest to visitors lie within a relatively small area of the city around the shady and pleasant **Parque Central**, with its pools of terrapins and a slumberous-looking caiman or two. The unremarkable whitewashed and powder-blue **Cathedral** sits on the southeast corner, diagonally opposite the *Gran Hotel Paris*. Running north from the Parque almost to the seafront, Av San Isidro, Av Atlántida and Av 14 de Julio form the main commercial district, lined with shops, banks and a couple of supermarkets. It's worth a look around the bustling main general **market** which sprawls along the streets around the decrepit old wooden market building on Av Atlántida. For a more sanitized shopping experience, check out the vast new Megaplaza **mall** on the southern outskirts of town, where there's also a cinema, supermarket and restaurants.

Night action takes place along **1 C**, which runs parallel to the seafront. Nicknamed the "Zona Viva" due to its preponderance of bars and clubs, 1 C extends west from the old dock and over the river estuary into **Barrio La Isla**, a quieter residential district, mainly home to Garífuna, once it leaves the seafront. All the **beaches** within the city limits are, sadly, too polluted and dirty for even the most desperate to want to brave the rough water. Better by far is to head east to the much cleaner beaches a few kilometres out of town (see p.438).

Eating, drinking and entertainment

Not for nothing does La Ceiba have a reputation as the place to party. The **Zona Viva** hums most nights of the week, though weekends are really explosive, with a profusion of places to drink and get down. A hedonistic local crowd, plus a steady trickle of tourists and a growing number of resident expats, both in front of and behind the bar, have helped to create a buoyant atmosphere. While the range of **places to eat** is not that extensive, it's not impossible to find good Honduran and international food, though restaurants generally stop serving at around 10pm. There's a **cinema** just east of the Parque Central on 8 C, and two screens at the Cines Milenium in the Megaplaza south of town (you'll need a taxi) for the usual subtitled Hollywood fare.

If you can make it, the most exciting time to be in La Ceiba is during **Carnaval**, a week-long bash held every May to celebrate the city's patron saint, San Isidro. Dances and street events in various barrios around town culminate in an afternoon parade on the third Saturday of the month. Led by a float carrying the Carnaval Queen, the parade moves slowly down the gaudily bedecked Av San Isidro. Bands on stages placed along the avenida then compete to outplay each other throughout the evening and into the early hours. The 200,000 or so partygoers who attend Carnaval every year flock between the stages and the clubs on 1 C, where the dancing continues until dawn.

RESTAURANTS AND CAFÉS

Café Cobel, 7 C, Av San Isidro. A fast-turnaround place serving breakfasts and lunch, mainly to office workers. The food is good, as are the juices, and the portions large.

Cafeteria Shalom, inside a small mall on 7 C, between Av Atlántida and Av 14 de Julio. Perhaps the most unexpected find in La Ceiba, this superb Israeli-owned canteen serves delicious Middle Eastern food including falafel, kebabs and stuffed peppers. Excellent lunch buffet special for US$2.25. Open daily 7am–8pm.

Café Tropical, Av Atlántida, 4–5 C. Cheerful café serving from early morning to around 10pm. Good *pollo frito* features heavily in the daily set menus.

Centro Cultural Satuye, 4 C, Av Herrera, Barrio La Isla. Light-hearted and informal Garífuna restaurant. Loud live music in the evenings.

Cric Cric Burger, Av 14 de Julio, 3 C. Good burgers, steak sandwiches and other snacks served to the accompaniment of very loud music. The side tables are a good place to watch comings and goings in the street.

Expatriate's Bar and Grill, 12 C, two blocks east of Av San Isidro. Airy, North-American-owned thatched bar with a good range of excellent vegetarian dishes, grilled chicken and fish and barbecued ribs. Welcoming atmosphere and popular with resident foreigners, so it's also a good source of local information. Closed Tues & Wed.

La Casa, 9 C, Av San Isidro–Av 14 de Julio. Centrally located comedor, with tables set around an open patio, serving a wide range of Honduran food for around US$1.50 a head.

Masapán, 7 C, between Av La República and Av San Isidro. Consistently popular self-service cafeteria, open 24-hours, with a cheap buffet of Honduran and American-style food.

Mesón del Puerto, on the seafront, just off 1 C, Barrio La Isla. Excellent but pricey beachside restaurant with good service and a delicious menu of grilled meats.

Paty's Juices, 14 de Julio, 6–7 C. Friendly family-owned place ideal for rich, delicious and inexpensive fresh juices, *licuados* and fruit salads.

Restaurante Palace, Av 14 de Julio, 8 C. Big barn of a place serving pretty good and fairly authentic Chinese dishes.

BARS AND CLUBS

African Dance, 1 C, two blocks east of the river, Barrio La Isla. A Garífuna dance hall, with live punta, plus some Latin and reggae, with dancing most nights of the week.

Cherry's, on the beach at the end of Av 14 de Julio. Popular club, open all week and packed at the weekend. Plays a mixture of Latin American rhythms, reggae and country music.

El Mussol, 1 C, 7 blocks from the bridge in Barrio La Isla. Probably the smartest club in the Zona Viva, with drink prices a little higher than in other venues.

Safari, just over the river in Barrio La Isla. Another popular club, attracting a predominantly local crowd.

Scape's, just over the river in Barrio La Isla. Lively beachfront bar, with food, pool tables and a dancefloor.

Listings

Airlines Isleña (☎443 0179), Sosa (☎443 1399) and Taca (☎443 1912) are all on the Parque Central; all three also have ticket desks at the airport, as do Rollins Air (☎443 ☎2177) and Cayman Airways (☎440 0863).

Banks Banco Ficahsa, just west of the Parque Central on 8 C, will change travellers' cheques, while Credomatic, Av San Isidro, 5–6 C, is the place for Visa and Mastercard cash advances.

Book exchange The Rain Forest Store, C La Julia, off 9 C (☎443 2917), has a reasonable stock.

Car rental Molinari, *Gran Hotel Paris* (☎443 2391, fax 443 0055).

Hospital Hospital Euro Honduras, 1 C, Av Atlántida, Barrio el Centro (☎443 0244), is a modern and well-equipped private hospital, with a 24hr emergency clinic and English- and German-speaking staff.

Immigration Av 14 Julio, 1–2 C (Mon–Fri 8am–noon & 2–4pm; ☎442 0638).

Internet access There are several cybercafés in La Ceiba, including the efficient Hondusoft (Mon–Fri 8am–8pm, Sat 8am–6pm) on the upper floor of the Centro Comercial Panyotti shopping mall at 7 C between Av Atlántida and Av 14 de Julio, with fast connection rates for US$3.50 an hour, plus Web phone facilities. Intercon, at Av San Isidro, 6–7 C (Mon–Sat 8am–8pm, Sun 9am–7pm), is another reliable place; rates are US$3 an hour.

Language school Centro Internacional de Idiomas, Av San Isidro, 12–13 (☎ & fax 440 1557, *www.worldwide.edu/honduras/cici*) is a good Spanish school with a/c classrooms. Rates are US$220 weekly for four hours of one-to-one tuition and homestay, including all meals.

Laundry Lavandería Super Clean, 16 C, Av San Isidro.

Police ☎441 0795 or 199.

Post office Av Morazán and 13 C, south of the Parque.

Telephones Hondutel, at Av Ramón Rosa, 5–6 C, is open 24hr; or use the Internet cafés (see above) for Internet phone dial-ups.

Travel agent Paso Travel Service, Av San Isidro, 11–12 C (☎443 3186).

Tour operators Several excellent companies arrange trekking trips to Pico Bonito (see overleaf) and whitewater rafting on the Río Cangrejal: try La Moskitia Ecoaventuras, Parque Bonilla, Av 14 de Julio at 1 C (☎442 0104, *www.honduras.com/moskita*); Euro Honduras Tours, Av Atlántida at 1 C (☎443 3874, *eurohonduras@caribe.net*); Jungle River Rafting, Av Miguel Paz Barahona, Barrio La Isla (☎440 1268, *jungle@laceiba.com*): or Ríos Honduras (☎995 6925, *www.paddlehonduras*.com).

Around La Ceiba

The broad sandy **beaches** and clean water at Playa de Perú and the village of Sambo Creek, both a short distance east along the coast, are easily reached as day-trips from the city. A trip to explore the **cloudforest** within the Parque Nacional Pico Bonito requires more planning, although the eastern edge of the reserve, formed by the Río Cangrejal, is more easily accessible, offering opportunities for swimming and whitewater rafting.

The beaches: Playa de Perú and Sambo Creek

Ten kilometres east of the city, **Playa de Perú** is a wide sweep of clean sand that's pop-ular at weekends. Any bus running east up the coast will drop you at the turn-off on the highway, from where it's a fifteen-minute walk to the beach. About 2km past the turn-ing for Playa de Perú, on the Río María, there's a series of **waterfalls** and **natural pools** set in lush, shady forest. A path leads from Río Maria village on the highway, winding through the hills along the left bank of the river: it takes around thirty minutes to walk to the first cascade and pool, with some muddy sections and a bit of scrambling during the wet season.

There are further deserted expanses of white sand at the friendly Garífuna village of **SAMBO CREEK**, 8km beyond Río Maria. You can eat excellent fresh fish at a couple of good restaurants in the village, and there are cheap beds at the basic *Hotel Hermanos Avila* (①) or more comfortable *Hotel La Canadien* (☎440 2099, fax 440 2097; ④), a new hotel with pleasant rooms, a great beachside plot and a pool. Olanchito or Jutiapa buses from La Ceiba will drop you at the turn-off to Sambo Creek on the highway, a couple of kilometres from the village; slower buses run all the way to the village centre from La Ceiba's terminal every 45 minutes.

Parque Nacional Pico Bonito

Directly south of La Ceiba, the Cordillera Nombre de Dios shelters the **Parque Nacional Pico Bonito** (daily 6am–4pm; US$6), a remote expanse of tropical broadleaf forest, cloudforest and – in its southern reaches, above the Río Aguan valley – pine for-est. Taking its name from the awe-inspiring bulk of Pico Bonito (2435m) itself, the park is the source of twenty rivers, including the Zacate, Bonito and Cangrejal, which cas-cade majestically down the steep, thickly covered slopes. The park also provides sanc-tuary for an abundance of wildlife including armadillos, howler and spider monkeys, pumas and tigrillos – an abundance which is largely due to the park's inaccessibility. The lower fringes are the most easily penetrable, with a small number of trails laid out through the dense greenery.

The easiest place to get into the park is via the *Lodge at Pico Bonito* (☎440 0388, *www.picobonito.com*; ⑧–⑨), a world–class **jungle lodge** with amazing bungalow accom-modation, gourmet cuisine, a pool and a sublime setting in the foothills of the forest reserve. To get there head for the village of **Los Pinos**, 12km from La Ceiba on the Tela highway, from where the hotel is signposted, 3km away up a dirt side road. Trails from the lodge snake up through the tree cover to a lookout from where Utila is visi-ble, and down to beautiful river bathing pools. Tour companies in La Ceiba operate day- and overnight trips to Pico Bonito from around US$40 per person (see previous page).

Just below *Lodge at Pico Bonito* are two further attractions. The Finca Mariposa **but-terfly park** (US$5), a signposted 600m from the hotel, is home to more than forty species in a large, screened garden house. A further 2km from the butterfly park, but better reached from a one-kilometre-long dirt road from Los Pinos, the small AMARAS **wildlife refuge centre** (☎443 3824, *fupnapib@kaceiba*.com; US$2) takes in monkeys, big cats (including jaguars), macaws and parrots confiscated from traffickers and pre-viously kept as pets, and where possible prepares them for release back into the wild – volunteers are needed and visitors welcome.

The **Río Cangrejal**, forming the eastern boundary of the park, boasts some of the best class III and IV rapids in Central America; **whitewater rafting** and **kayaking** trips are organized by some of the tour companies listed on the previous page. There are also some magnificent swimming spots, backed by gorgeous mountain scenery, along the river val-ley. It's tricky to get to the river under your own steam, but you could contact the German-owned Omega Rafting (☎440 0334, *omegatours@laceiba.com*), who run a small **hotel** (②) geared for eco-travellers on the banks of the Cangrejal – transport from La Ceiba, full board and a day spent either trekking, horse-riding or rafting costs US$50 per person.

Refugio de Vida Silvestre Cuero y Salado

Thirty kilometres west from La Ceiba, the **Refugio de Vida Silvestre Cuero y Salado** (daily 7am–4pm; US$10) is one of the last substantial remnants of wetlands and mangrove swamps along the north coast. The reserve is home to a large number of animal and bird species, many endangered, including manatees, jaguars, howler and white-faced monkeys, sea turtles, hawks, along with seasonal influxes of migratory birds. Though nominally protected since 1987, the edges of the reserve are under constant pressure from local farmers wishing to drain land for new pastures.

The best way to see the reserve is to take a **guided tour**, not least because the guides know the spots where you're likely to see some wildlife. **FUCSA**, the body that manages the reserve, has an office in La Ceiba (see p.435) and runs regular tours (US$18 per boat), which you'll need to book in advance. They also have a small **campsite** at the reserve, with tents for hire (US$7) which can sleep four.

To get to the reserve **independently**, catch an hourly bus from La Ceiba's terminal to the village of La Unión, 20km or so west. From here, you can either make your way on foot through the fruit plantations – it takes around an hour and a half to walk the 8km – or travel by *burra*, a flat, poled railcar (locals charge between US$6–10, depending on numbers, to shunt you along the tracks). The last bus back to La Ceiba leaves La Unión mid-afternoon.

Trujillo

Perched above the sparkling waters of the palm-fringed Bahía de Trujillo, with the green backdrop of Cordillera Nombre de Dios rearing up behind, **TRUJILLO** immediately seduces the small number of tourists who make the 90km trip here from La Ceiba. Though you'd never guess it from the town's sleepy demeanour, this is an important city, capital of the department of Colón. All the elements for a relaxing stay are in place – warm, sheltered waters, clean beaches, and a good range of hotels and restaurants – and having endured the three- to four-hour journey from La Ceiba, few are in a hurry to leave.

The area around Trujillo was settled by a mixture of Pech and Tolupan groups when Columbus first disembarked on the American mainland here, on August 14, 1502. Trujillo itself was founded by Cortés's lieutenant, Juan de Medina, in May 1525, though it was regularly abandoned due to attacks by European pirates. Not until the late eighteenth century did repopulation begin in earnest, aided by the arrival, via Roatán, of several hundred Garífuna from the island of St Vincent. In 1860, a new threat appeared in the shape of the US filibuster William Walker, who in June of that year briefly took control of the town; executed in September 1860 by the Honduran authorities, he is buried in Trujillo's cemetery. The twentieth century has been distinctly less eventful, except for a severe battering at the hands of Hurricane Mitch, though few buildings in town were destroyed. There's often far more activity these days at **Puerto Castilla**, at the eastern end of the bay, the busy port through which passes the produce of the region's plantations.

Arrival and information

Buses enter Trujillo from the east, passing an airstrip, crossing over the Río Negro at the bottom of the hill and terminating at the top in the Parque Central. The town proper stretches south up the hill from here; north, a sloping path leads down to the seafront, which is lined with palm-thatched *champas*. Very few of the streets are signposted. Bancahsa and Banco de Occidente (for Visa and Mastercard cash advances) have branches one block west of the Parque, with the small general market just to the south. **Hondutel** and the **post office** are next to each other three blocks south from the southeast corner of the Parque, and there's a small **migración** (Mon–Sat 8am–noon, 1–5pm; ☎434 4451) 1km southwest of the Parque in Barrio Cristales.

One kilometre south of town, up the hillside in the *Villas Brinkley* (see below), **Turtle Tours** (☎434 4444, fax 434 4431, *ttours@hondutel.hn*) offers a range of very tempting but moderately priced tours, including snorkelling excursions, canoe trips and city walks, plus five-day expeditions into the Mosquitia for US$375 per person. A new **language** school, the Escuela de Idiomas Trujillo, is located close to the *migración* on the road to the Museo Rufino Galán (☎434 4135; *www.spanishschool.hn*); it costs US$180 per week for five hours of study daily and full family-based board and accommodation.

Accommodation

There's plenty of **accommodation** to choose from in the town centre, close to the restaurants and bars, though since Trujillo has never really featured on the tourist trail there are fewer rock-bottom cheapies than in La Ceiba or Tela. There are also a couple of excellent places in glorious settings just outside town, and you can **camp** at the *Campamento Hotel* (see below).

Campamento Hotel & Restaurant, on the beach 4km west of town (☎434 4244, fax 434 4200). Comfortable, a/c wooden cabañas in an idyllic setting, scattered around extensive grounds reaching down to a private beach. There's also an open-air restaurant serving well-prepared seafood and other dishes, and safe camping (US$3 per tent) with access to a bathroom. ④–⑤.

Cristopher Colombus Hotel, on the beach by the airstrip (☎434 4966, fax 434 4971). A large, green architectural curiosity, redeemed by its location and patronized by wealthy Hondurans, with facilities including a pool and tennis courts. Rooms ⑥, suites ⑨.

Hotel Cocopando, 1km west of centre in Barrio Cristales (no phone). The town's best-value budget hotel, in a beachside setting with simple, clean and pretty rooms and a great comedor downstairs. Gets noisy at weekends when the neighbouring dance hall fires up. ②.

Hotel Colonial, just south of the Parque (☎434 4011). Well-situated hotel, with big beds and bath, a/c and TV in all rooms, though the downstairs ones are rather dark. The management could do with a little customer-service training. ④.

Hotel Emperador, by the market (☎434 4446). One of the town's nicest cheaper places, with clean rooms, all have bath and fan, set round a courtyard. ②–③.

O'Glynn, three blocks south and one block east of the Parque (☎434 4592). Friendly place with simple, clean accommodation in the original hotel plus large modern rooms with a/c and TV in a new annexe. ③–④.

Villas Brinkley, on the hillside, 1km south of town (☎434 4444 or 434 4545). One of the most pleasing hotels in Honduras, with a really relaxed, welcoming ambience and superb views from the terrace over the whole stretch of the bay and its glistening waters. There's a range of tastefully furnished and recently renovated rooms, all with bath and some with a/c and kitchen. The hotel also has a pool, and the restaurant is a good place to come for a meal even if you're not staying here. ③–⑤.

The Town

The town proper stretches back five or so blocks south of the **Parque Central**, which is just fifty metres from the sea cliffs. On the northeast edge of the Parque is the sixteenth-century **Fortaleza de Santa Bárbara** (daily 8am–noon & 1–4pm; US$0.10), the site of Walker's execution. Low-lying and built of dark stone, it hangs gloomily on the edge of the bluffs, overlooking the coastline it was singularly unsuccessful in defending against pirate attack.

Much of Trujillo's charm lies in meandering through its rather scruffy streets, where the heat of the sun is alleviated by a constant breeze. Southwest from the centre, a couple of blocks past the market, is the **Cementerio Viejo**. where Walker's grave lies amid the at times floridly decorated memorials to the town's dead. Turn right past the cemetery and a ten-minute stroll brings you to the privately run **Museo Rufino Galán** (daily 7am–5pm; US$1), a somewhat eccentric collection of junk, amongst which are buried a few interesting pre-Columbian ceramics. Behind the building are a couple of small, moss-surrounded river pools in which to bathe. Back at the Parque Central, walk west for ten minutes and you'll reach the **Barrio Cristales**, the site of the country's first mainland Garífuna settlement, founded in 1797. The Gari Arte shop here stocks Garífuna handicrafts and music tapes.

Trujillo's outstanding feature by far is its **beaches**, long stretches of almost pristine sand. The glorious sweep of the Bahía de Trujillo is as yet unaffected by excessive tourist development, and its calm, blue waters are perfect for effortless swimming. The beaches below town, lined with *champas,* are clean enough, but the stretches to the east, beyond the airstrip, are emptier. It's also possible to walk east along the beach to the reserve of **Laguna de Guaimoreto** or west to the Garífuna village of **Santa Fe** – see below.

Eating, drinking and entertainment

The best **places to eat** are the informal *champa* bar-restaurants on the beach, where you can dine in the warm evening air, listening to the waves. The main cluster is on the beach below town – *Rogue's Gallery*, owned by Jerry from California, is one of the most popular. There's another group to the east by the airstrip, about twenty minutes' walk away – note that it's not advisable to walk back along the beach after dark.

Later on in the evening, *Disco Horfez* and *Disco Truxillo* in the centre of town both heave at the weekends to Latin American rhythms, while *Black and White*, on the beach in Barrio Cristales, attracts a mainly Garífuna crowd. All the venues are generally pretty relaxed compared to many places on the north coast, although trouble is occasionally reported.

Bahía Bar, on the beach by the airstrip. Long-established, foreign-owned beach *champa* with a wide menu of seafood, good juices and sandwiches.

Café Oasis, southwest off the Parque. The leafy courtyard setting and the welcome relief of a vegetarian menu, as well as good juices, don't quite excuse the occasionally slack service. There's an excellent book exchange, however, and the café is a good place for information.

Gringo's Bar, next to the *Bahía*. Everything a tropical beachside bar should be, with well-cooked food, good breakfasts and an easy-going atmosphere.

Papa Jack Café and Salon, two blocks southwest of the Parque. A place to have a quick drink more than anything, but the sandwiches and other snacks are reasonably priced.

Pizza Pantry, two blocks southwest of the Parque. As well as reasonable pizza, the broad menu includes seafood, steaks and breakfasts.

Restaurante Lempira, at the *Villas Brinkley* (see opposite). Feast on well-cooked European and Honduran dishes whilst admiring the fabulous views, then walk it all off on the stroll back to town.

Rincón de los Amigos, on the beach below town. Friendly *champa* serving excellent seafood (including paella) in a relaxed atmosphere. Live Garífuna music at weekends.

Rogue's Gallery, on the beach below town. Engaging American-owned bar-restaurant with superb seafood and plenty of hammocks for day-time chilling. Also has a book exchange.

Around Trujillo

Expanses of white-sand **beach** stretch for miles around the bay from Trujillo, all clean, wide and perfect for gentle swimming; don't take anything valuable with you, though, and don't venture onto them after dark. Walking east from town along the beach, for 5km or so, you come to the **Laguna de Guaimoreto**, a small reserve of mangrove swamps that is home to thousands of migratory birds, monkeys and other wildlife. Visits to a **crocodile farm**, the Hacienda Tumbador, on the south side of the laguna are also included in tours of the laguna organized by Turtle Tours (see opposite).

Ten kilometres **west** from Trujillo, the Garífuna village of **SANTA FE** is even more relaxed than Trujillo, though the beach isn't as attractive. Even so, it's worth a visit if only to sample the exquisite local seafood dished up by the *Comedor Caballero*, and there are also a couple of basic hotels (both ②) in the village if you want to stay. A dirt road connects Santa Fe with Trujillo, travelled by three **buses** daily in either direction, or you could walk it in about two hours.

On the other side of the mountain peaks directly above Trujillo lies the dark green swathe of **Parque Nacional Capiro y Calentura** (daily 6am–5pm; US$3.75). Protecting stretches of tropical and subtropical rainforest, the reserve's huge cedars and pines tower amid the thick canopy of ferns and flowering plants and vines, many of them used for medicinal purposes. Following the devastation wrought by Hurricane Fifi in 1974, much of the cover is secondary growth, but it still provides a secure habitat for howler monkeys, reptiles and a colourful range of birdlife and butterflies. You can walk into the reserve by following the dirt road past the *Villas Brinkley*, which winds, increasingly steeply, up Cerro Calentura to the radio towers just below the summit, a ten-kilometre walk, best done in the relative cool of early morning; alternatively, you could negotiate with a taxi driver to take you to the top and then walk down.

Taking a hot bath in the heat of the Caribbean may not strike everyone as an appealing thought, but a soak in the clean and very hot mineral waters of the **Aguas Calientes** springs (daily 7am–9pm; US$2), 7km inland from Trujillo, feels delightfully decadent. The experience can be topped off with a drink at the bar of the rather slick *Agua Caliente* hotel in the grounds (☎434 4249; ⑤). Any bus heading to Tocoa will drop you off at the entrance to the springs; buses stop running at around 6.30pm.

La Mosquitia

Honduras's northeast corner is made up of the remote and sparsely populated expanse of **La Mosquitia**. Bounded to the west by the mountain ranges of the Río Plátano and Colón, with the Río Coco forming the border with Nicaragua to the south, this vast region comprises almost a fifth of Honduras's territory. With just two peripheral roads and a tiny population divided among a few far-flung towns and villages, entering the Mosquitia really does mean leaving the beaten track.

To the surprise of many who come here expecting to have to hack their way through jungle, much of the Mosquitia is composed of marshy coastal wetlands and flat savanna – likened by some to the landscape of South Carolina. The small communities of **Palacios** and **Brus Laguna** are access points for the **Río Plátano Biosphere Reserve**, set up to protect one of the finest remaining stretches of virgin tropical rainforest in Central America. **Puerto Lempira**, to the east, is the regional capital.

The largest ethnic group inhabiting the Mosquitia are the **Miskitos**, numbering around 30,000, who spoke a unique form of English until as recently as a few generations ago. There are much smaller indigenous communities of **Pech**, who number around 2500, and **Tawahka** (Sumu), of whom there are under a thousand, living around the Río Patuca.

Some history

Before the Spanish arrived, the Mosquitia belonged to the Pech and Sumu. Initial contact with Europeans was comparatively benign, the Spanish showing slight interest in the area, preferring to concentrate on the mineral-rich lands of the interior. Contact with Europeans intensified when the **British** began seeking a foothold on the mainland in the seventeenth century, establishing settlements on the coast at Black River (now Palacios) and Brewer's Lagoon (Brus Laguna), whose inhabitants – the so-called "shoremen" – engaged in logging, trading, smuggling and fighting the Spanish.

Britain's claim to Mosquitia, nominally to protect the shoremen, though their real reason was to ensure a transit route from the Atlantic to the Pacific, supposedly ended in 1786, when all Central American territories except Belize were ceded to the Spanish. In the 1820s, however, taking advantage of post-independence chaos, Britain again encouraged settlement on the Mosquito Coast and by 1844 had all but formally announced a protectorate in the area. Not until 1859 and the British-American Treaty of Cruz Wyke did Britain formally end all claims to Mosquitia.

   The initial impact of mestizo Honduran culture on Mosquitia was slight. Since the creation of the administrative department of Gracias a Dios in 1959, however, indigenous cultures have become gradually diluted: Spanish is now the main language and the government encourages mestizo settlers to migrate here in search of land. Pech, Miskito and Garífuna communities have become more vocal in recent years in demanding respect for their cultural differences and in calling for an expansion of health, education and transport infrastructures.

Palacios, Brus Laguna and Ahuas

Sited on what was the British settlement of Black River, **PALACIOS** lies just west of one of the Río Plátano Biosphere Reserve's three coastal lagoons, Laguna Ibans. Served by regular flights to and from La Ceiba, this is frequently the starting point for organized trips to the Río Plátano Biosphere Reserve and a logical place for independent travellers to set out from. Adequate **rooms** (both ②) can be had in the hotel run by local whizzkid Don Felix Marmol, who is also the Isleña agent, or the *Jungle Lodge* by the airstrip, where the rooms are a little better.

   Dotted along the Caribbean shoreline around Palacios is a cluster of interesting Garífuna villages, including **Batalla**, just to the west of town across the Palacios lagoon, and **Plaplaya**, about 8km to the east, where a **turtle project** has been established. Highly endangered giant leatherbacks, the largest species in the world (reaching up to 3m in length and 900kg in weight), nest in the beaches around the village between April and June. There's a resident peace corp worker stationed here to oversee the project, and volunteers are welcome. **Raistá**, the next coastal settlement, three hours' walk from Plaplaya, is a friendly Miskito village and also the base for a new **butterfly farm** (daily 8am–5pm; US$2.50, including tour), which exports exotic specimens to other parks in Honduras and North America. There's simple accommodation here (①) and the manager's wife cooks tasty, inexpensive meals. There are more rooms for rent in **Belén**, right next door to Raistá on the outer edge of Laguna Ibans, and in **Barra Plátano**, a two-hour walk east from Belén along the beach. Boats to the Río Plátano reserve and Las Marías can be hired in any of these villages, or from Palacios.

Thirty kilometres east along the coast from Palacios, on the southeastern edge of the Laguna de Brus, is the friendly Miskito town of **BRUS LAGUNA**. A basic hospedaje here serves for the relatively few visitors who make it this far. Regular **flights** connect the town with La Ceiba, and guides and boats can be hired for multi-day trips, travelling up the Río Sigre (or Sikre) into the southern reaches of the Río Plátano reserve.

A little under 40km inland from Brus Laguna as the crow flies is the Miskito village of **AHUAS**, scattered across the savanna. The village is only a kilometre from the Río Patuca, which forms the border of the Río Plátano reserve, and narrow cargo boats take passengers on the four-hour trip upriver to **Barra Patuca** on the coast. Rooms can be found by asking around near the airstrip.

The Río Plátano Biosphere Reserve

The **Río Plátano Biosphere Reserve** is the most significant reserve in Honduras, sheltering an estimated eighty percent of all the country's animal species. Visitors usually come here to experience the tropical rainforest; yet within its boundaries – from the Caribbean in the north to the Montañas de Punta Piedra in the west and the Río Patuca in the south – the reserve also covers huge expanses of coastal wetlands and flat savanna grasslands. Sadly, even international recognition of the importance of this diverse ecosystem, signalled by its World Heritage status, hasn't prevented extensive destruction at the hands of settlers: up to sixty percent of forest cover on the outer edges of the reserve has disappeared in the last three decades.

Getting to the heart of the Río Plátano reserve requires travelling up the Río Plátano, through savanna and secondary forest growth, to the small village of **LAS MARÍAS**, a Pech and Miskito settlement about seven hours upstream from the coast. There are two basic hospedajes in the village (both US$4 per person), each serving meals, and plenty of prospective **guides** are available to help you explore the river and surrounding jungle for US$8–10 a day. The local guides have organized themselves a rotation system, co-ordinated by the leader Martin Herrera, so that everyone gets some work once in a while. Unfortunately this means that individuals cannot be recommended and it's pot luck whether you get a good or poor guide.

Upstream from the village begins the primary forest cover, pressing in against both banks of the river. Few experiences can match the initial impression of entering the **rainforest**, as towering trees – mahogany, tamarind, oak – reaching up to 50m or more, break through the dense canopy to the sunlight. Smaller in size are the forest's palms, ceiba and avocados, hung with vines and epiphytic ferns, whilst still closer to ground level are sprays of brilliantly coloured magnolias and lush ferns. Periodically shattering the cathedral-like calm are the raucous screams of troops of howler and spider **monkeys**, while tapirs, white-faced coatis, pacas, anteaters and squirrels are also hidden among the trees – sightings of most animals, however, are frustratingly rare. Flashes of the brilliant plumage of **macaws**, **parrots** and **toucans**, a bright contrast against the dim light, are easier to come by.

Puerto Lempira

Capital of the department of Gracias a Dios, **PUERTO LEMPIRA** is the largest town in Mosquitia, with a population of 11,000. Set on the southeastern edge of the biggest of the coastal lagoons, Laguna de Caratasca, some 110km east of Brus Laguna, the town survives on government administration and small-scale fishing and shrimping. The best of the available **accommodation** is at the *Hotel Flores* (④–⑤) in the centre of town, where the small rooms all have a/c and bath; the *Hospedaje Modelo* (②) opposite is basic but clean. There are several small **restaurants** close by. Banco Atlántida, next to Hotel Flores will change travellers' cheques and gives Visa cash advances. **Mopawi** (☎898 8659), the Mosquitia development organization, has its headquarters in the town, three blocks south of the main dock.

Puerto Lempira is hardly a transport hub, but the only traffic-frequented roads in Mosquitia lead west from here across the savanna to the village of Ahuasbila, an eight-hour drive, passing through Morocón and Rus Rus on the way. A side road shears off to Leimus on the Nicaraguan border; a truck leaves Puerto Lempira early each morning for Leimus, taking around five hours. There's a new Honduran **migración** post (daily 6am–8pm), but nothing on the Nicaraguan side, so you'll have to get your entry stamp in Puerto Cabezas.

travel details

BUSES

La Ceiba to: Tegucigalpa (12 daily until 3pm; 7hr); Trujillo (12 daily until 4pm; 4hr).

Puerto Cortés to: Corinto (5 daily; 4hr); Omoa (hourly; 1hr).

San Pedro Sula See box on p.427.

Tela to: El Progreso (every 30min; 1hr 30min); La Ceiba (every 30min; 2hr).

Trujillo to: La Ceiba (12 daily until 4pm; 4hr); San Pedro Sula (5 daily until 2pm; 6hr); Tegucigalpa via San Esteban and Juticalpa (1 daily at 4am; 10hr).

FLIGHTS

Brus Laguna to: La Ceiba (Rollins & Sosa; 3 weekly).

La Ceiba to: Ahuas (Sami; 5 weekly); Brus Laguna (Rollins & Sosa; 5 weekly); Palacios (Isleña; 1 daily Mon–Sat); Puerto Lempira (Isleña & Sosa; 7 weekly); Tegucigalpa (Taca, Sosa, Rollins & Isleña; 7 daily); Trujillo (Isleña & Rollins; 1–2 daily).

Palacios to: La Ceiba (Isleña & Rollins; 1–2 daily); Trujillo (Isleña; 1 daily Mon–Sat)

Puerto Lempira to: La Ceiba (Isleña & Sosa; 7 weekly).

San Pedro Sula to: Belize City (Taca, 1 daily); Cancún (Aerocaribe 1 daily); La Ceiba (Isleña, 2 daily, Rollins 3 daily, Sosa 1 daily); Miami (Iberia, 2 weekly; American Airlines, 1 daily, Taca 1 daily); Tegucigalpa (Taca, 2 daily; Isleña, 1 daily).

CHAPTER 21

THE BAY ISLANDS

Strung in a gentle curve less than 60km off the north coast of Honduras, the **Bay Islands (Islas de la Bahía)**, with their clear, calm waters and abundant marine life, are Honduras's main tourist attraction. Resting on a coral reef, the islands are a perfect destination for cheap diving, sailing and fishing, while less active visitors can sling a hammock and relax in the shade on the many palm-fringed sand beaches. Composed of three main islands and some 65 smaller cayes, this sweeping 125km island chain lies on the **Bonacca Ridge**, an underwater extension of the Sierra de Omoa mountain range that disappears into the sea near Puerto Cortés. **Roatán** is the largest and most developed of the islands, while **Guanaja**, to the east, is an upmarket resort destination with some wonderful dive sites. **Utila**, the closest to the mainland, is a target for budget travellers from all over the world.

Even old hands get excited about **diving** the waters around the Bay Islands, where lizard fish and toadfish dart by, scarcely distinguishable from the coral; eagle rays glide through the water like huge birds flying through the air; parrotfish chomp steadily away on the coral; and barracuda and harmless nurse sharks circle the waters, checking you out from a distance. In addition, the world's largest fish, the **whale shark** (which can reach up to 16m in length) is a resident of the Cayman Trench, which plummets to profound depths just north of the islands. It's most frequently spotted in October and November, when dive boats run trips to look for it, but can be encountered close to Utilan waters year round.

The **best time to visit** the islands is from March to September, when the water visibility is good and the weather is clear and sunny; the rains start in October, while November and December are usually very wet, with squally showers continuing until late February. Daytime temperatures range between 25 and 29°C year round, though the heat is rarely oppressive, thanks to almost constant east–southeast trade winds. **Mosquitoes** and **sandflies** are endemic on all the islands, and at their worst when the wind dies down; lavish coatings of baby oil help to keep the latter away.

Some history

The Bay Islands' history of conquest, pirate raids and constant immigration has resulted in a society that's unique in Honduras. The islands' original inhabitants are thought to have been the **Pech**, recorded by Columbus on his fourth voyage in 1502 as being a "robust people who adore idols and live mostly from a certain white grain from which they make fine bread and the most perfect beer". Post-Conquest, the indigenous population declined rapidly as a result of enslavement and forced labour. The islands' strategic location as a provisioning point for the Europe-bound Spanish fleets ensured that they soon became the targets for **pirates**, initially Dutch and French, and subsequently English. The Spanish decision to evacuate the islands, eventually achieved in 1650, left the way open for the pirates to move in. Port Royal, Roatán, became their base until the mid-eighteenth century, from where they launched sporadic attacks on ships and against the mainland settlements.

For an explanation of **accommodation price codes**, see p.365.

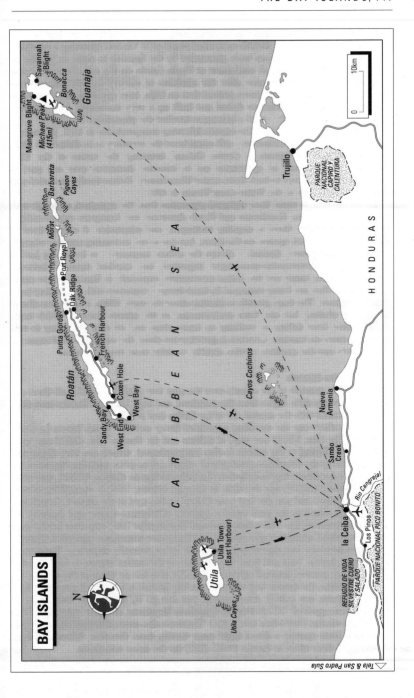

BAY ISLANDS

N

Guanaja

Mangrove Bight
Savannah Bight
Bonacca
Michael Peak (415m)

Barbareta
Pigeon Cayes
Môrat

Port Royal
Oak Ridge
Punta Gorda
French Harbour
Coxen Hole
West Bay
West End
Sandy Bay

Roatán

C A R I B B E A N   S E A

Cayos Cochinos

Trujillo

PARQUE NACIONAL CAPIRO Y CALENTURA

H O N D U R A S

Nueva Armenia

Sambo Creek

Río Cangrejal
La Ceiba
Los Pinos

REFUGIO DE VIDA SILVESTRE CUERO Y SALADO
PARQUE NACIONAL PICO BONITO

Utila Town (East Harbour)
Utila
Utila Cayes

10km
0

◁ Tela & San Pedro Sula

After the pirates left, Roatán was deserted until the arrival of the **Garífuna** in 1797. Forcibly expelled from the British-controlled island of St Vincent following a rebellion, most of the 3000-strong group were persuaded by the Spanish to settle in Trujillo on the mainland, leaving a small settlement at Punta Gorda on the island's north coast. Further waves of settlers came after the abolition of slavery in 1830, when white Cayman Islanders and freed slaves arrived first on Utila, later spreading to Roatán and Guanaja. These new inhabitants fished and built up a very successful fruit industry, which exported to the US – until a hurricane levelled the plantations in 1877.

Honduras acquired rights to the islands following independence in 1821, yet many – not least the islanders themselves – still considered the territory to be British. In 1852, Britain declared the islands a Crown Colony, breaking the terms of the 1850 Clayton–Bulwer Treaty, an agreement not to exercise dominion over any part of Central America. Forced to back down under US pressure, Britain finally conceded sovereignty to Honduras in the Wyke–Cruz Treaty of 1859.

Today, the islands retain their **cultural** separation from the mainland, although with both Spanish-speaking Hondurans and North American and European expats settling in growing numbers, there is ongoing re-shaping and adaptation. A unique form of **Creole English** is still spoken on the street, but due to the increasing number of mainlanders migrating here, Spanish – always the official language – is becoming just as common. This government-encouraged migration has sparked tensions between English–speaking locals and the Latino newcomers, especially in Roatán, where many islanders feel they are being swamped by land–hungry outsiders with whom they have little in common. The huge growth in tourism since the early 1990s, a trend that shows no signs of abating, has also been controversial, as the islands' income, which traditionally came from fishing or working on cargo ships and oil rigs, is coming to rely more and more on tourism. Concern is growing too about the environmental impact of the industry and the question of who, exactly, benefits most from the boom.

Getting to the islands

The growth in tourism to the islands over the past few years means that all three are served by several daily flights from the mainland, and both Utila and Roatán have daily boat connections with the coastal city of **La Ceiba** (see p.433).

Most travellers use the excellent scheduled **ferry service** which leaves La Ceiba daily for Utila (1hr; US$12 one way) at 9.30am and for Roatán (2hr; US$13 one way) daily at 3pm. **Flying** to the islands is also uncomplicated; tickets are very cheap and standardized by the Honduran government – there are no price variations between airlines. There are fifteen flights daily from La Ceiba to Roatán (30min; US$20), four daily to Utila (20min; US$17), and five daily to Guanaja (40min; US$33). Availability is very rarely a problem, and you can buy your tickets on the spot at the airport, though you should book ahead in the peak holiday seasons (Christmas–Easter and August). All internal flights from San Pedro Sula (1hr) and Tegucigalpa (1hr) stop over briefly in La Ceiba. Schedules change at short notice and flights are sometimes cancelled altogether; bear in mind that you may be late arriving or, more crucially, departing. The domestic **airlines,** Isleña, Taca and Sosa, have offices on the central square in La Ceiba and at the airport; another internal carrier, Rollins Air, also has an office at the airport.

From Belize, the easiest way to get to the Bay Islands is **to fly** to Roatán with Taca (US$274 return; see p.385). Alternatively, you can go by **boat** from Belize City or Placencia (see pp.60 & 115) to **Puerto Cortés** in Honduras, and then continue by bus to La Ceiba via San Pedro Sula (see p.421). There are also several **international flights** to Roatán: Taca operate a direct flight once weekly from Houston, Miami and New Orleans; call their office in Roatán (☎445 1387) for the latest schedules.

Utila

Smallest of the three main Bay Islands, **UTILA** is a key destination for budget travellers, and one of the cheapest places in the world to learn to **learn to dive** – and even if you don't want to don tanks, the superb waters around the island offer great swimming and snorkelling possibilities. Utila is still the cheapest of the Bay Islands, with a cost of living only slightly higher than that on the mainland, although prices are gradually rising. Life is laid-back and people are generally friendly; crimes against tourists are very rare, though watch out for the periodic dancehall brawl. As elsewhere, respect local customs in dress and don't walk around in your bathing suit. Note also that drinking from glass bottles on the street is prohibited.

Arrival and information

All boats **dock** in the centre of **Utila Town** (also known as East Harbour), a large, curved harbour that's the island's only settlement and home to the vast majority of its 2000-strong population. The island's principal main road, a twenty-minute walk end to end, runs along the seafront from The Point in the east to Sandy Bay in the west. A new airport is currently being hacked out of the jungle 3km north of Utila Town, at the end of the island's other main road, **Cola de Mico Road**, which heads inland from the dock; until it opens (which will be sometime in 2002, if the necessary finances materialize), all planes land at a dirt **airstrip** in The Point.

Wherever you arrive, you'll be met by representatives from the dive schools laden with **maps** and information on special offers. Many schools offer free accommodation during their courses, but it's worth checking out the various options before signing up. For more objective **information**, the Utila branch of BICA (Bay Islands' Conservation Association) has a visitor and information office on the main street east of the dock, though its opening hours are erratic (usually Mon–Fri 9am–noon and a couple of hours in the afternoon).

It takes just twenty minutes to stroll from the airstrip to the far western end of town. **Bikes** can be rented from Delco, next to Henderson's grocery store, just west of the dock, the *Mango Café* (see p.452) and other places around town – rates start at US$2 a day for an old bike, and around US$5 for a decent mountain bike (not that you'll need it). Some locals use four-wheeled motorbikes to get around and occasionally pick up hitchers.

Accommodation

Utila has more than 25 affordable guesthouses and hotels, and a profusion of rooms for rent; there's always somewhere available, even at Christmas and Easter. Most of the dive schools have links with a hostel, so that enrolling on a scuba course gets you a few free or discounted nights' accommodation. Everywhere is within walking distance of the dock and airstrip, and the accommodation listed below is in the order that you come to it, walking west along the road from the airstrip. There are no designated places to **camp** except on the cayes.

FROM THE AIRSTRIP TO THE MAIN DOCK

Sharkey's Reef Hotel, behind *Sharkey's Reef Restaurant*, near the airstrip (☎425 3212, *hjackson @hondutel.hn*). Set in a peaceful garden, the rooms here all have a/c, private bathrooms and cable TV, and some have kitchens. There's also a terrace with great views over the lagoon. ⑤–⑥.

Trudy's (☎425 3103). A popular place with large, clean rooms, and you can swim from the dock at the back. ①.

Cooper's Inn (☎425 3184). One of the best budget places on the island, with clean, basic rooms and friendly management. ①.

Rubi's Inn, two minutes' walk from the dock (☎425 3240). Very clean, with airy rooms and views over the water; kitchen facilities are available. ①.

COLA DE MICO ROAD

Blueberry Hill, just beyond Thompson's bakery, on the opposite side of the road (☎425 3141). Characterful cabins with basic cooking facilities, run by friendly owners, but ear plugs are essential at weekends when the *Bucket 'o' Blood* bar opposite fires up. ①.

Mango Inn, five minutes' walk up the road from *Blueberry Hill* (☎425 3335, *www.mango-inn.com*). A beautiful, well-run place, timber-built in Caribbean style, set in shady gardens and offering a range of rooms, from thatched, a/c bungalows to pleasant dorms. Also has a book exchange and laundry service, and the attached *Mango Café* is a lively spot serving good food. Dorms ①, rooms ③, bungalows ④; rates drop by at least fifty percent if you dive with the associated Utila Dive Centre.

SANDY BAY

Tropical Hotel, opposite Hondutel telephone office (no phone). Very popular backpackers' stronghold, the small functional rooms all have fans and there's a communal kitchen. ①.

Utila Lodge, behind Hondutel (☎425 3143, *ulodge@hondutel.hn*). Comfortable a/c rooms, though they're almost exclusively occupied by divers signed up on weekly packages ($735 per person including all meals). It also has its own dock, and the owners can arrange fishing trips. ⑨.

Seaside Inn, opposite Gunter's Dive Shop (☎425 3150). A reasonable place, with plain but clean rooms (some with private bath), plus small apartments. ①–②.

Margaritaville Beach Hotel, ten minutes' walk west of the dock (☎425 3266). Tranquil seafront location well away from the main dock, with large, airy rooms, all with private bath. ②.

Diving

Most visitors come to Utila specifically for the **diving**, attracted by the low prices, clear water and abundant marine life. Even in winter, the water is generally calm and common sightings include nurse and hammerhead sharks, turtles, parrot fish, stingrays, porcupine fish and an increasing number of dolphins. On the north coast of the island, Blackish Point and Duppy Waters are both good sites; on the south coast the best spots are Black Coral Wall and Pretty Bush. The good schools will be happy to spend time talking to you about the merits of the various sites.

Rather than signing up with the first dive school representative who approaches you, it's worth spending a morning walking around checking out all the schools. **Price** is not really a consideration, with the dozen or so dive shops all charging around US$140 for a three- to five-day PADI course; advanced and divemaster courses are also on offer, as are fun dives, from US$12. **Safety** is a more pertinent issue: for peace of mind, you should make sure that you understand – and get along with – the instructors, many of whom speak a number of languages. Also, before signing up, check that classes have no more than six people, that the equipment is well maintained and that all boats have working oxygen and a first-aid kit. Anyone with asthma or ear problems should not be allowed to dive. A worthwhile investment is the diving **insurance** sold by BICA for US$3 a day, which covers you for medical treatment in an emergency.

Recommended schools include the Utila Dive Centre (*www.utiladivecentre.com*) on the road between the dock and the dirt airstrip; Gunter's Dive Shop (*ecomar @hondutel.hn*), two minutes' walk west of the dock, which also rents out sea kayaks; Alton's (*altons@hondutel.hn*), two minutes' walk west of the airstrip; and Underwater Vision (*tamara@psi.net.hn*), opposite *Trudy's*. Salty Dog's, a minute's walk west of the dock, has **underwater photography** equipment for rent, and many of the dive shops also rent out **snorkelling** equipment for around $10 a day.

It's important to bear in mind that the coral reef dies every time it is touched. BICA has been installing buoys at each of the sites to prevent boats anchoring on the reef and all the reputable schools will use these.

Swimming, snorkelling and walking

The best swimming near town is at the **Blue Bayou,** a twenty-minute walk west of the centre, where you can bathe in chest-deep water and snorkel further out; there's a US$1 charge to use the area, which also boasts a small sandy beach and rickety wooden pier where you can sunbathe in peace away from the sandflies, and a food stand selling snacks and beers. Hammocks are slung in the shade of coconut trees and there's snorkelling gear available for rent (US$1.50 per hour). Blue Bayou is also the site of the **Utila Sea Turtle Conservation Project,** a privately run scheme set up with support from BICA, where hawksbill and loggerhead turtle eggs are incubated, and the hatchlings fed and then released; visitors are welcome. East of town, **Airport Beach,** at the end of the dirt airstrip, offers good snorkelling just offshore (though access is more difficult), as does the little reef beyond the **lighthouse**. The path from the end of the airstrip up the east coast of the island leads to a couple of small coves – the second is good for swimming and sunbathing. Five minutes beyond the coves, you'll come to the **Ironshores,** a mile-long stretch of low volcanic cliffs with lava tunnels cutting down to the water.

Another pleasant five-kilometre walk or cycle ride is along the Cola de Mico Road across the northern tip of the island to **Pumpkin Hill** and beach, passing the site of the new airport. The 82-metre hill, the eroded crest of an extinct volcano, gives good views over the island and across to the mainland and the dark bulk of Pico Bonito (see p.438). Down on the beach, lava rocks cascade into the sea, forming underwater caves – there's good snorkelling here when the water is calm, though it's not safe to free dive down into the caves.

The Cayes

Utila Cayes – eleven tiny outcrops strung along the southwestern edge of the island – were designated a wildlife refuge in 1992. **Suc Suc** (or Jewel) **Caye** and **Pigeon Caye**, connected by a narrow causeway, are both inhabited, and the pace of life here is even slower than that on Utila. Small launches regularly shuttle between Suc Suc and Utila (US$1), or can be rented to take you across for a day's snorkelling, if you have your own equipment. *Vicky's Rooms* on Suc Suc (①) offers basic **accommodation**, and there are a couple of reasonable restaurants and a good fish market.

Water Caye, a blissful stretch of white sand, coconut palms, pellucid water and a small coral reef, is even more idyllic given its absence of sandflies. Camping is allowed (bring all your food, equipment for a campfire and water), and a caretaker turns up every day to collect the US$1 fee for use of the island (hammocks can be rented for an extra US$1). Water Caye is also the ultimate desert-island venue for occasional full-moon parties and a spectacular annual two-day July rave, with European house and techno DJs, organized by Sunjam and the *Mango Inn* (see *www.sunjam.com* for information). **Transport** to the caye is organized during such events; at other times, dive boats will often drop you off on their way to the north coast for a small fee, or you can ask the owner of the *Bundu Café* (see overleaf).

Eating

Lobster and **fish** are obviously staples on the islands, along with the usual rice, beans and chicken. With the tourists, however, have also come **European and American foods** – pasta, pizza, burgers, pancakes and granola. Since most things have to be brought in by boat, **prices** are higher than on the mainland: main courses start at around US$4, and beers cost at least US$1. For eating on the cheap, head for the evening stalls on the road by the dock, which do a thriving trade in *baleadas*. Note that many restaurants stop serving at around 10pm.

Bundu Café, on the main street, east of the dock. Serves European-style breakfasts and lunches and lassi-style milkshakes. Also has a book exchange.

Captain Jack's, five minutes' walk west of the dock. Dutch–Utilan owned café-restaurant serving excellent-value lunches, including burritos and sandwiches, freshly squeezed orange juice, and delicious dinners such as fish cakes and grilled kingfish steaks.

Cross Creek, at the Point. Superb Caribbean cooking from one of Utila's best chefs, served in a quiet spot beside the lagoon and majoring in flavoursome pan-fried fish and seafood. It's fairly expensive though: expect to pay around $10 a head for a meal plus drink.

Delaney's Island Kitchen, three minutes east of the dock. Simple, well-executed island cooking, plus a few Western dishes like pasta.

Golden Rose, two minutes west of the dock. Good-value Caribbean and Honduran dishes, popular with dive instructors and locals.

Jade Seahorse, on Cola de Mico Road. Serves great breakfasts and *licuados*, and good seafood.

Mango Café, in the *Mango Inn*. A popular place with an interesting selection of tasty and well-presented European food, espresso and cappuccino, and a lively bar. Closed Mon.

Mermaid's Corner, at *Rubi's Inn*. Popular pasta and pizza restaurant with a great atmosphere, though service can be very slow.

RJs, at The Point, beside the bridge. Popular with dive crews and students, with a gregarious atmosphere and famously excellent meat and fish barbecues.

Thompson's Bakery, Cola de Mico Road. A near-legendary place to hang out, read, drink coffee and meet other travellers while sampling the good-value breakfasts or the range of daily baked goods – try the johnny cakes.

Nightlife

Despite its tiny population, Utila is a fearsomely hedonistic party island. The hottest place in town for travellers is the *Coco Loco Bar,* just west of the dock, which draws a lively bunch of party heads with its extended happy hour and regular house, techno and reggae parties. *Casino*, by the dock, attracts a more local crowd with thundering reggae and a dash of salsa and merengue. During the rest of the week, the *Mango Café* is a popular spot for cheap beer and a quiet drink, while the *Bucket 'o' Blood*, very close by on Cola de Mico Road, boasts a bombastic sound system but fewer drinkers. Further along the Cola de Mico Road towards the new airport, the huge open-air *Bar in da Bush* can get very lively at weekends.

Listings

Airlines Tickets for Sosa and Rollins, covering domestic routes in Honduras, can be purchased in the captain's office by the dock.

Banks Banco Atlántida and Bancahsa, both close to the dock, change money and offer cash advances on Visa cards (Mon–Fri 8–11.30am & 1.30–4pm, Sat 8–11.30am); at other times try Henderson's store, just to the west.

Bicycles can be rented for around $5 a day from Delco, just west of the dock, or from the *Mango Café*.

Books The *Bundu Café,* on the main street, east of the dock, has a book exchange.

Doctor The Community Medical Center is two minutes west of the dock (Mon–Fri 8am–noon).

Immigration office Next to Hondutel in Sandy Bay (Mon–Fri 9am–noon & 2–4.30pm).

Internet access Two minutes west of the dock, Bay Island Computer Services offers Internet access for $12 an hour, plus discounted international calls.

Port office In the large building at the main dock (Mon–Fri 8.30am–noon & 2–5pm, Sat 8.30am–noon).

Post office In the large building at the main dock (Mon–Fri 9am–noon & 2–4.30pm, Sat 9–11.30am).

Telephones The best rates for international calls are at Bay Island Computer Services (see "Internet access", opposite) and the Reef Cinema. Avoid the Hondutel office, next to the *migración*, where the rates are extortionate.

Travel agents Tropical Travel and Utila Tour Travel Center, both east of the dock on the airstrip road, can confirm and book flights to La Ceiba and elsewhere in Central America.

Roatán

Some 50km from La Ceiba, **ROATÁN** is the largest of the Bay Islands, a curving ridged hump almost 50km long and 5km across at its widest point. Geared towards upmarket tourists, the island's accommodation mostly comes in the form of all-in luxury resort packages, although there are some good deals to be found. Like Utila, Roatán is a suberb **diving** destination, but also offers some great hiking, as well as the chance to do nothing except laze on a beach. **Coxen Hole** is the island's commercial centre, while **West End** is the place to head for absolute relaxation.

Arrival and getting around

Regular flights from La Ceiba and occasionally further afield land at the **airport**, on the road to French Harbour, 3km from Coxen Hole – the main town on the south side of the island. A taxi to West End from here costs $10, or you could walk to the road and wait for one of the public minibuses which head to Coxen Hole every 20 minutes or so (US$0.70) and change there. There are an information desk, a hotel reservation desk, car rental agencies and a bank at the airport. The **ferry dock** is in the centre of Coxen Hole.

A paved road runs west–east along the island, connecting the major communities. **Minibuses** leave regularly from Main Street in Coxen Hole, heading west to Sandy Bay and West End (every 20min until late afternoon) and east to Brick Bay, French Harbour, Oak Ridge and Punta Gorda (every 30min or so until late afternoon); fares are US$0.70–1. However, if you really want to explore, you'll need to **rent a car** or **motorbike**: in addition to the agencies at the airport, Sandy Bay Rent-a-Car (☎445 1710, fax 445 1711) has offices at Sandy Bay and West End and rents out Jeeps for $45 per day, and motorbikes for $25 a day.

Coxen Hole

COXEN HOLE (also known as Roatán Town) is dusty and run-down, and most visitors come here only to change money or shop. All of the town's practical facilities and most shops are on a hundred-metre stretch of **Main Street**, near where the buses stop. For tourist **information** about the island and its events, pick up a copy of the *Coconut Telegraph* magazine from the Cooper Building; you'll find the headquarters of BICA (Mon–Fri 9am–noon & 2–5pm) here as well, if you want to brush up on Roatán's flora and fauna.

To change **travellers' cheques** or dollars or get a Visa cash advance, try Bancahsa, or Credomatic. The **migración** and the **post office** are both near the small square on Main Street, while **Hondutel** is behind Bancahsa. HB Warren is the largest **supermarket** on the island, and there's a small and not too impressive general **market** just behind Main Street. The island's best-set-up **Internet** café, Paradise Computers (Mon–Fri 9am–5pm, Sat 9am–1pm), is a five-minute walk from the centre of town on the road to West End, and though rates are very high (around $12 an hour), the epic cappuccinos and delicious carrot cake help compensate a little. Librería Casi Todo, in the same building as the *Qué Tal Cafe* (see overleaf), sells secondhand **books**.

It's unlikely you'll want **to stay** here unless you have a very early flight. If you do, the *Hotel Cayview*, on Main Street (☎445 1222; ⑤), has comfortable rooms with a/c and private bath, while the *Hotel El Paso* (☎445 1367; ④), nearby on the same street, has clean rooms, but communal bathrooms only. There are a number of cheap comedores, serving standard Honduran **food**, while *Qué Tal Cafe*, on Thicket Street, just past Paradise Computers, serves European-style breakfasts and snacks.

Sandy Bay

Midway between Coxen Hole and West End, **SANDY BAY** is an unassuming community with a number of interesting attractions. The **Institute for Marine Sciences** (Sun–Tues & Thurs–Sat 9am–5pm; US$3), based at *Antony's Key Resort* (see below), has exhibitions on the marine life and geology of the islands and a museum with useful information on local history and archeology. There are also bottle-nosed **dolphin shows** (Mon, Tues, Thurs & Fri 10am & 4pm, Sat & Sun 10am, 1pm & 4pm; US$4), and you can dive or snorkel with the dolphins (US$100 and US$75 respectively; must be booked in advance on ☎445 1327). Across the road from the institute, several short nature trails weave through the jungle at the **Carambola Botanical Gardens** (daily 8am–5pm; US$3), a riot of beautiful flowers, lush ferns and tropical trees. Twenty minutes' walk from the gardens up Monte Carambola, the **Iguana Wall** is a section of cliff that's a breeding ground for iguanas and parrots. From the top of the mountain you can see across to Utila on clear days. Bordering the gardens, Sandy Bay's newest attraction is the **Tropical Treasures Bird Park** (Mon–Sat 10am–5pm; US$5, including guided tour), with toucans, parrots and scarlet macaws.

There are several places **to stay** in the Sandy Bay area, all of which are clearly signposted, including the attractive *Beth's Hostel* (☎445 1266; ④); the *Oceanside Inn* (☎445 1552; ⑥), with large rooms and a good restaurant; and three dive resorts, the best of which is *Antony's Key Resort* (☎445 1003, fax 445 1140, *www.anthonys-key.com*; weekly packages from $600), one of the smartest places on the island, with cabins set among the trees and on a small caye. Popular places **to eat** include *Rick's American Café*, set on the hillside above the road and serving giant US-style burgers, and *Monkey Lala*, next door, offering superb seafood.

West End

With its calm waters and incredible white beaches, **WEST END**, 14km from Coxen Hole, makes the most of its ideal setting, gearing itself mainly towards independent travellers on all budgets, with a good selection of attractive accommodation. Set in the southwest corner of the island, round a shallow bay, the village has retained a laid-back charm, and the gathering pace of tourist development has done little to dent the locals' friendliness.

The paved road from Coxen Hole finishes at the northern end of the community, not far from **Half Moon Bay**, a beautifully sheltered sandy beach ringed with hotels. Turning to the south at the end of the paved road from Coxen Hole, a sandy track runs alongside the water's edge through the heart of West End, passing a merry bunch of guesthouses, bars and restaurants, set between patches of coconut palms. You can **rent cars** from Roatán Rentals, at the north of West End, or Sandy Bay Rent-a-Car close by; Captain Van's rents out bicycles, mopeds and motorbikes (though their rates are pricey). The sole **Internet** café, *Chit Chat Flat*, located towards the southern end of West End, charges $12 an hour for pretty lethargic connections.

ACCOMMODATION

Most of the accommodation in West End and Half Moon Bay is charmingly individualistic, and heavy discounts are available during low season (April–July & Sept to mid-December), particularly for longer stays.

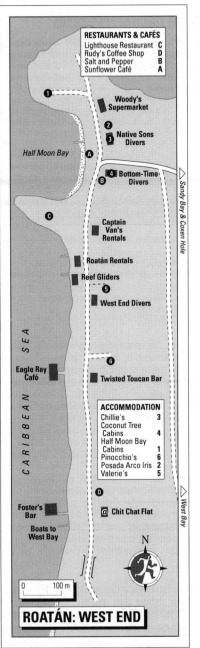

RESTAURANTS & CAFÉS
Lighthouse Restaurant C
Rudy's Coffee Shop D
Salt and Pepper B
Sunflower Café A

Woody's Supermarket

Native Sons Divers

Half Moon Bay

Bottom-Time Divers

Captain Van's Rentals

Roatán Rentals

Reef Gliders

West End Divers

Eagle Ray Café

Twisted Toucan Bar

ACCOMMODATION
Chillie's 3
Coconut Tree Cabins 4
Half Moon Bay Cabins 1
Pinocchio's 6
Posada Arco Iris 2
Valerie's 5

Foster's Bar

Boats to West Bay

Chit Chat Flat

CARIBBEAN SEA

Sandy Bay & Coxen Hole

West Bay

N

0   100 m

ROATÁN: WEST END

Chillie's, Half Moon Bay (☎445 1214, *mermaid @globalnet.hn*). Very well-set-up, English–Honduran-owned backpackers' stronghold, with dorm beds and private rooms, a kitchen and camping available. Also home to Native Sons Divers. ③.

Coconut Tree Cabins, at the entrance to the village (☎445 1648, *www.coconuttree.com*). Comfortable, spacious cabins all with covered porches, fridges and hot water. ⑤–⑥.

Half Moon Bay Cabins, Half Moon Bay (☎445 1075). Upmarket place with secluded cabins scattered around wooded grounds close to the water's edge; all have fan or a/c. There's also a lively restaurant and bar. ⑤.

Pinocchio's (☎445 1481, fax 445 1008, *pinocchio69@bigfoot.com*). Occupies a wooden building set on a small hill above the village, with clean, airy rooms with bath. The owners are very friendly and there's a good restaurant downstairs (see below). ⑤.

Posada Arco Iris, Half Moon Bay (☎445 1264, *http://roatanet.com/scuba/posada.htm*). Set in attractive gardens just off the beach, with excellent, imaginatively furnished and spacious rooms, studios and apartments, all with fridge and hammocks, and some with a/c. ④–⑥.

Valerie's, about 100m along West End, then up a signposted dirt track (no phone). Venerable love-it-or-hate-it West End chaotic bohemian set up with a profusion of quirky accommodation, including two trailer-style rooms and a large dorm (US$5 per person); guests can also use the kitchen. ②–③.

EATING AND DRINKING

There's a more than adequate range of **places to eat** in West End, with fish, seafood and pasta featuring heavily on many menus. **Drinking** can drain your pocket fast, and it's best to seek out the half-price **happy hours** at many of the restaurants and bars; starting at around 4.30pm, many of them last until 10pm. The *Twisted Toucan*, halfway along the seafront is usually the happening place in town most nights, except Fridays, when everyone heads to *Foster's* for the weekly reggae jump up.

Lighthouse Restaurant, close to the seafront between West End and Half Moon Bay. Big portions of reasonably priced Caribbean food served up in friendly, diner-like surrounds.

Pinocchio's, in the hotel of the same name. One of the finest restaurants in West End, with an eclectic range of creative, but fairly pricey, European meat and fish dishes. Closed Wed.

WATERSPORTS IN AND AROUND WEST END

Diving courses for all levels are available in West End. Prices are officially standardized, with a four-day PADI open-water course costing around US$250, but it's worth asking around as some schools include basic accommodation, and sporadic price wars break out between the schools. Fun dives are set at US$30 a dive, though again substantial discounts are often on offer, with ten-dive packages set at US$200 or below. Recommended West End-based **schools** include Ocean Divers (*oceandivers@global.hn*), West End Divers (*www.roatan.com/wed*), Reef Gliders (*paradise@global.hn*) and Bottom-Time Divers (*www.coconuttree.com*), while Native Sons (*mermaid@global.hn*), another good school, is located at *Chillie's* hotel in Half Moon Bay. There are also two decent dive schools in West Bay (see below).

The reef lying just offshore provides some superb **snorkelling**, with the best spots being at the mouth of Half Moon Bay and at the Blue Channel, which can be accessed from the beach 100m south of *Foster's* bar. You can also rent **sea kayaks** from the *Sea Breeze Inn*, close to the entrance road; expect to pay around US$12 for a half day or US$20 for a full day. Underwater Paradise, based in the Half Moon Bay Resort, runs popular, hour-long **glass-bottomed boat** tours for US$18 per person.

Rudy's Coffee Stop Legendary breakfasts of banana pancakes, omelettes, fresh coffee and juices. Closed Sun.

Salt and Pepper, at the entrance to the village. Wide-ranging gourmet menu including French, Japanese and Thai dishes. Expect to pay upwards of US$10 a head with wine, but the relaxed atmosphere and excellent cooking make it worth the money.

Sunflower Café, close to the centre of Half Moon Bay. Cheerful North American-owned café serving delicious omelettes, bagels and muffins. Open 7am–3pm only.

West Bay

Two kilometres southwest of West End, towards the extreme western tip of Roatán, is the stunning white-sand beach of **WEST BAY**, fringed by coconut palms and washed by crystal-clear waters. The beach's tranquillity has been mildly disrupted by a rash of cabaña and hotel construction, but provided you avoid the sandflies by sunbathing on the jetties, it's still a sublime place to relax and enjoy the Caribbean. There's decent snorkelling at the southern end of the beach too, though the once pristine reef has suffered in recent years from increasing river run-off and the close attentions of unsupervised day-trippers.

From West End, it's a pleasant 45-minute stroll south along the beach and over a few rock outcrops; alternatively you can take one of the small launches that leave *Foster's Restaurant* regularly – the last one returns around 7pm (9pm in high season). A dirt road also runs here: from West End, head up the road to Coxen Hole and take the first turning on the right. If you want **to stay**, the Swiss-owned *Bananarama* (☎992 9679, *www.roatanet.com/bananarama*; ⑤) has comfortable little wood cabins with mosquito nets and 24-hour hot water, while for something really luxurious, head for the Canadian-owned *Island Pearl Resort* (☎991 1858, *www.roatanpearl.com*; ⑨), which boasts stunning two-storey houses equipped with kitchens and hot tubs plus a gourmet restaurant set in a spacious beachside plot. Both hotels have good in-house dive schools.

Northern Roatán

Leaving Coxen Hole, the paved road runs northeast past the small secluded cove of **Brick Bay** to **FRENCH HARBOUR**, a busy fishing port and the island's second largest town. Less run-down than Coxen Hole, it's a lively place **to stay** for a couple of days, and all the accommodation is right in the centre. *Harbour View Hotel* (☎455 5390;

④) has reasonable rooms with bath and hot water, while the more upmarket *Buccaneer Hotel* (☎455 5032; ⑥) has a pool and a large wooden deck overlooking the water. The best place **to eat** is *Gio's*, by the Credomatic building on the waterfront, where you can dine on excellent but pricey seafood; for more local fare, try *Pat's Place*, 50m further on.

From French Harbour the road cuts inland along a central ridge to give superb views of both the north and south coasts of the island. After about 14km it reaches **OAK RIDGE**, an attractive fishing port with wooden houses strung along its harbour. There are some nice unspoiled **beaches** to the east of town, accessible by launches from the main dock. The best place **to stay** is the clean and pleasant *Hotel San José* (☎435 2328; ③–④), on a small caye a short distance across the water from the dock. Launches run from the main dock to the caye on demand (US$0.50).

About 5km from Oak Ridge on the northern coast of the island is the village of **PUNTA GORDA**, the oldest Garífuna community in Honduras. The best time to visit is for the anniversary of the founding of the settlement (April 6–12), when Garífuna from all over the country attend the celebrations. At other times it's a quiet and slightly dilapidated little port with no historical buildings. The very basic *Los Cincos Hermanos* (②) offers fairly clean **rooms** and has an attached comedor.

From the end of the paved road at Punta Gorda you can continue driving along the dirt track which runs east along the island, passing the turn-off for the secluded **Paya Beach** after around 1.5km, where there's a new dive hotel, the pleasant little *Paya Beach Resort* (☎924 2220, *www.payabay.com*; ⑦ including all meals). A further 5km or so along is **Camp Bay Beach**, an idyllic, undeveloped stretch of white sand and coconut palms, though there are plots of land for sale here so things may change soon. The road ends at the village of **PORT ROYAL**, on the southern edge of the island, where the faint remains of a fort built by the English can be seen on a caye offshore. The village lies in the **Port Royal Park and Wildlife Reserve**, the largest refuge on the island, set up in 1978 in an attempt to protect endangered species such as the yellow-naped parrot, as well as the watershed for eastern Roatán.

The eastern tip of Roatán is made up of mangrove swamps, with a small island, **Morat**, just offshore. Beyond is **Barbareta** caye, which has retained much of its virgin forest cover. The *Barbareta Beach Resort* runs inclusive packages (in the US ☎888/450 3483; from US$220 for three nights), with diving, windsurfing, hiking, mountain biking and fishing tours available. The reef around Barbareta and the nearby **Pigeon Cayes** offers good snorkelling; launches can be hired to reach these islands from Oak Ridge for around US$35 for a return trip.

Guanaja

The easternmost Bay Island, **GUANAJA** was the most beautiful, densely forested and undeveloped of them all until Hurricane Mitch laid siege to it for over two days during October 1998, lashing the land with winds of up to 300kph. Though buildings have been patched up and reforestation projects have been implemented, the landscape will take decades to recover. Guanaja is some 25km long and up to four kilometres wide, and is divided into two unequal parts by a narrow canal – the only way to get between the two sections of the island is by water-taxi, which adds both to the atmosphere and to the cost of living. The island is very thinly populated – most of Guanaja's 12,000 inhabitants live in **Bonacca** (also know as **Guanaja Town**), a crowded settlement that sits on a small caye a few hundred metres offshore. It's here that you'll find the island's shops, as well as the bulk of the reasonably priced accommodation. The only other settlements of any substance are **Savannah Bight** (on the east coast) and **Mangrove Bight** (on the north coast).

Arrival and information

Guanaja **airstrip** is on the larger section of the island, next to the canal. Aside from a couple of dirt tracks there are no roads, and the main form of transport is small launches. **Boats** from the main dock in Bonacca meet all flights and rides can be hitched on private boats to Mangrove Bight for a nominal fee. There are no scheduled **boat** services to Guanaja from the mainland, but regular cargo ships sail to the island from La Ceiba and other ports in Honduras.

Virtually all the houses in Bonacca are built on stilts – vestiges of early settlement by the Cayman islanders – the buildings clinging to wooden causeways over the canals, many of which have now been filled in. The main causeway, running for about 500m east–west along the caye, with a maze of small passages branching off it, is where you'll find all the shops, banks and businesses. You can change dollars, travellers' cheques and get cash advances at Bancahsa, to the right of the dock (Mon–Fri 8–11.30am & 1.30–4pm, Sat 8–11.30am).

Accommodation

Most of the hotels on Guanaja are luxury all-inclusive dive resorts offering weekly packages. You'll also find a small number of mid-range hotels in Bonacca – though none are particularly good value for money.

BONACCA

Hotel Miller, halfway along the main causeway (☎453 4327). In a slightly run-down building, though the rooms are in reasonable condition; most have hot water and, for a little extra, a/c and cable TV. ④.

Hotel Nights Inn, at the extreme western end of the causeway (☎453 4465). New family-run place with very clean and comfortable, fairly spacious rooms, all with cable TV and a/c. ⑤.

Hotel Rosario, opposite the *Hotel Miller* (☎453 4240). Modern building with comfortable rooms, all with private bath, a/c and TV. ④.

THE REST OF THE ISLAND

Bayman Bay Club, on the north side of the island (☎991 0281, *bayman@caribe.hn*). Large and pleasantly furnished cabins set in plenty of space on a wooded hillside above a small beach. Packages including dives and all meals cost US$700–750 per person per week.

Island House Resort, on the north side of the island (☎ & fax 453 4146). Pleasant accommodation in a large house run by a friendly local dive instructor, close to several expanses of beautiful beach. Rooms with full board ⑥, with full board and diving ⑦.

Posada del Sol, on the south side of the island (☎ & fax 453 4186, *posadadelsol@aol.com*). Stylish cabins scattered around sixty acres of ground, with amenities including a pool, tennis courts, sea kayaks and snorkelling equipment. All-inclusive dive packages from US$775 per person.

Around the island

Though Guanaja's Caribbean pine forests were flattened by Mitch, there's still some decent **hiking** across the island. A wonderful trail leads from Mangrove Bight up to **Michael's Peak**, the highest point of the entire Bay Islands (412m) and down to Sandy Bay on the south coast, affording stunning views of Guanaja, Bonacca and the surrounding reef. Fit walkers can do the trail in a day, or you can camp on the summit, provided you bring your own provisions.

Some of the island's finest white-sand **beaches** lie around the rocky headland of **Michael's Rock**, near the *Island House Resort* on the north coast, with good snorkelling close to the shore. **Diving** is excellent all around the main island, but particularly off the small cayes to the east, and at Black Rocks, off the northern tip of the main island, where there's an underwater coral canyon. To get to these sites you'll have to contact one of the hotel-based dive schools: the *Island House Resort* usually has the best rates at around US$70 for two dives including equipment. **Fishing** and **snorkelling** can be arranged with local boatmen, who charge US$10–15. In many areas, however, the reef is close enough to swim to if you have your own snorkel gear.

Eating and drinking

There are several **restaurants** in Bonacca, though most close on Sundays. None is particularly cheap, however, as most of the supplies have to be shipped in from the mainland. In Bonacca itself, try *Bonacca's Garden*, halfway along the main causeway, or the *Best Stop*, next to the basketball court, for snacks, cakes and yummy sticky buns. The funkiest **bar** in town is *Nit's Bar*, just east of the main dock, where the clapboard walls shake to classic reggae sounds, while you'll find Guanaja's best margaritas at the air-conditioned *The End of the World* bar on the main causeway.

Cayos Cochinos

Lying 17km offshore from the mainland, the **CAYOS COCHINOS (Hog Islands)** comprise two, thickly wooded main islands – **Cochino Grande** and **Cochino Pequeño** – and thirteen cayes, all of them privately owned. The small amount of effort it takes to get there is well worth it for a few days' utter tranquillity. Fringed by a reef, the whole area has been designated a **marine reserve**, with anchoring on the reef and commercial fishing both strictly prohibited. The US Smithsonian Institute, which manages the reserve, has a research station on Cochino Pequeño. On land, the island's hills are studded with hardwood forests, palms and cactus, while Cochino Grande has a number of trails across its interior, and a small peak rising to 145m.

Organized **accommodation** on the islands is limited to the *Plantation Beach Resort* on Cochino Grande (☎442 0974, *www.plantationbeachresort.com*), which does weekly dive packages for around US$800, including all meals and three dives a day; they collect guests by launch from the Muralla de Cabotaje dock in La Ceiba on Saturdays (US$75 return). It can be more rewarding, however, to stay in the traditional Garífuna fishing village of **CHACHAUATE** on Lower Monitor Caye, south of Cochino Grande. Here, the villagers have allocated a hut for visitors to sling their hammocks for a minimal charge, and will cook meals for you. Basic groceries are available in the village, though you should bring water and your main food supplies with you from the mainland.

Unless you're staying at the *Plantation Beach*, the only way to the Cayos is to charter a boat from the Muralla de Cabotaje dock at La Ceiba (US$60–80 return for up to six people, but be sure to bargain hard), or from the Garífuna village of **Nueva Armenia**, (around US$40 return for a charter), 40km east of La Ceiba. One bus a day runs to Nueva Armenia (2hr) from La Ceiba; more frequent buses to Trujillo, Tocoa and Olanchito all pass through Jutiapa, 8km inland from Nueva Armenia, from where you can hitch or walk. There is a basic hotel (①) in Nueva Armenia and a few simple eating places.

travel details

FLIGHTS

La Ceiba to: Roatán (Isleña, 7 daily; Sosa, 4 daily; Rollins Air, 4 daily); Utila (Rollins, Mon–Sat 2 daily; Sosa, Mon–Sat 2 daily); Guanaja (Isleña, Mon–Sat 2 daily, Sun 1 daily; Sosa, Mon–Sat 2 daily).

BOATS

MV Galaxy runs daily between La Ceiba and Roatán (2hr; US$13) and Utila (1hr; US$12).

PART SIX

NICARAGUA

Introduction

Wedge-shaped **Nicaragua** may be the largest country in Central America, but it is also one of the least visited. Even after more than a decade of peace, Nicaragua is synonymous in the minds of many with civil war; this reputation, when coupled with the dilapidated infrastructure of a country that has fought its way not only through a bloody conflict but also an American economic blockade, scares many off. Still, many travellers who spend any time there find – much to their surprise – that Nicaragua is their favourite country in the isthmus. Perhaps because it doesn't yet fully cater for the tourist experience, Nicaragua is an incorrigibly vibrant and individualistic country, with plenty to offer travellers prepared to brave Nicaragua's superficial obstacles of economic chaos, cracked pavements and crammed public transport.

Cuba aside, Nicaragua is unique in Latin America in having pulled off a bona fide revolution of the people. The **revolution** of 1978–79 and the civil war that followed in the 1980s, while ravaging the country, has also given it one of the most dramatic of recent histories. At times it seems that every Nicaraguan has both horrifying and uplifting personal stories to tell. And even though Nicaragua's long-suffering people would rather forget many aspects of the war, the country's political past continues to inform every minute of its present.

During the 1980s Nicaragua was the destination of choice in Central America for young, socialist-minded *internacionalistas* – foreign volunteer workers who came to the country to aid the Revolution by working in the education and health sectors. From 1996 onwards, the Alemán government discontinued many of the programmes that brought the *internacionalistas* to Nicaragua and tourism slumped, which was bad news for the country's hotel owners and tour operators. Recent years, however, have seen tourist numbers increase as part of the general upturn in interest in Central America.

In comparison with the Maya ruins of Guatemala or the national parks of Costa Rica, Nicaragua offers few traditional tourist attractions – almost no monuments or ancient temples remain, and earthquakes, revolution and war have laid waste to museums, galleries and theatres. For years the country has suffered from a chronic lack of funding, and high inflation and unemployment have also impoverished Nicaragua's infrastructure. However, no one visits Nicaragua and remains immune to the country's extraordinary **landscape** of **volcanoes** (17 in all), **lakes, mountains** and vast plains of **rainforest**. A smattering of **beaches** – the majority of them on the Pacific Coast – continues to attract the budget **surfing** and backpacking crowd, while culture and **the arts** are very much alive in Nicaragua, and it is here you can buy some of the best-value high-quality crafts in the isthmus.

More than anything, though, the pleasures and rewards of travelling in Nicaragua come from interacting with the inhabitants of the country's complex society. Its **people** are well-spoken, passionate, engaged and engaging – Nicaraguans tend to be witty and exceptionally hospitable. The best thing you can do to enjoy Nicaragua is to arrive with an open mind, some patience and a willingness to practise your Spanish.

■ Where to go

Most of Nicaragua's population lives in the hot, relatively dry and **fertile Pacific lowlands**, where much of the country's agriculture is centred. This region is also the political and cultural centre of the country – nearly everything thought of as being inherently Nicaraguan, whether food, music, dress or dance – comes from this area. Virtually every traveller passes through the capital, **Managua**, if only to catch a bus; but there's little to detain the tourist in the capital and many quickly make tracks for **Granada**, with its splendid lakeside setting and wonderfully atmospheric colonial architecture. The town of **Masaya**, 26km southeast of the capital, is the arts-and-crafts centre of the country, and both Nicaraguans and foreign tourists descend upon its Mercado Nacional de Artesanía for some of the best crafts in Central America.

Ecotourism is beginning to have some impact In the **Lago de Nicaragua** area, with more and more travellers visiting Isla de Ometepe and the Solentiname Islands. Volcano-viewing and hiking are the attractions of Ometepe, with its thrilling twin volcanoes rising out of the freshwater lake. Further south in the lake, near the Costa Rican border, the Solentiname archipelago and the Río San Juan are some of the most pristine areas in Central America, where flora, fauna and a unique tradition of primitive naif painting prevail.

Nicaragua's mountainous **central region** is distinctly different, with a cooler climate and strikingly independent peoples. Much of the country's rich mellow export-grade **coffee** is grown here, and farms dominate the scented landscape of blue-green pine-covered mountains. Hiking and bird-watching near the mountain town of **Matagalpa** are the main tourist attractions.

Physically cut off from the rest of the country, the Caribbean lowlands – called the **Atlantic Coast** in Nicaragua – actually make up nearly fifty percent of the country's landmass. Hot, humid and perpetually rainy, this area is sparsely populated and little-visited. Most of its inhabitants gain a living from fishing and subsistence agriculture. Politically and culturally distinct from the rest of Nicaragua, the region governs itself autonomously, regularly fighting tooth and nail with the central government. Descended from

escaped African slaves and from the indigenous peoples, the Miskito, Rama and the Suma (who account for the majority of Atlantic Coast inhabitants) speak English – a legacy from the days when the area was a British protectorate. Food, dance, music and religion on the Atlantic Coast are West Indian rather than Spanish: rice-and-beans is cooked with coconut milk and the radio play is strictly reggae in the hot and ramshackle jungle towns of **Bluefields** and **Puerto Cabezas**. The beautiful – and as yet unspoilt – **Corn Islands**, just off the coast of Bluefields, offer a welcome respite from the stresses of mainland life.

■ When to go

Nicaragua has two distinct seasons, the dry and the wet. The **rainy season** is called *invierno* – winter – and corresponds roughly with the

Northern Hemisphere summer, from May to November. *Verano* – **summer** (December–April) – is hot and often uncomfortably dry; dust covers everything, and the heat seems to rise to a kiln-like intensity. Fewer travellers come in the rainy season – which alone could be a reason for choosing to put up with the daily downpour. The seasons are most pronounced on the **Pacific coast**, where rain often falls in the afternoons from May to November, although the mornings are dry. Influenced by the Caribbean trade winds, the **central mountain region** has sporadic rainfall all year, although it is drier in the "summer". Its climate is cooler year-round, with misty clouds covering its blue-green mountain summits. The **Atlantic Coast** is wet – *very* wet – year-round, and almost unbelievably hot and humid. As in the rest of the Caribbean region, September and October are the height of the tropical storm season.

Getting around

Finding your way around Nicaragua, whether on crowded school buses, sturdy old lake-boats, or in little single- and double-engined planes, is at least half the fun of travelling in the country. Most journeys, with the exception of the trip to or from the Atlantic Coast, are relatively short and manageable. Public transport, especially buses, is geared toward the domestic population, and is very cheap.

■ Buses

Everywhere you go in Nicaragua you see packed **buses** careering down the highway, dodging the occasional pothole, roof racks full of luggage and insides packed to the hilt. For the vast majority of Nicaraguans the bus is the only affordable way to travel, and despite the crush the service is good; people are friendly and will help you with your bags and with directions. The standard bus in Nicaragua is an old American or Canadian Blue Bird school bus – not uncomfortable, unless you have long legs. An increasing number of express minivans also service the more popular routes – they stop less frequently, have better suspension and are often driven by frustrated Formula One racers.

Managua is the **transport hub** of the country, and from here you can get virtually anywhere by bus. The most popular routes are Managua–

Masaya–Granada; Managua–Rivas–San Juan del Sur; and, in the north, Managua–Leon and Managua–Matagalpa/Estelí. With some Spanish and a little fancy footwork you can get from almost any Nicaraguan town to another. Local services tend to be far less frequent and stop more often than "express" services between towns.

Most **intercity buses** begin running between 5am and 7am and the last buses leave about 5 or 6pm. Fares are very cheap – it used to be said you could cross Nicaragua by bus for less than US$1. That's not the case any more, but most trips cost no more than US$1–2. If you are carrying luggage you may be charged half-fare – sometimes even full fare – for it. This is standard practice and there's no point arguing. Luggage is either put on the roof rack or at the back of the bus; the latter is a bit safer. You can tip the bus conductor a córdoba or two to keep an eye on it. Luggage is unloaded from the back door – try to watch proceedings to make sure your pack isn't stolen. Pickpocketing is also common – best to carry valuables in a money belt or inside pocket, and to keep any small backpacks on your front.

Departure times are frequent, usually every thirty minutes, or when the bus is full. Bus **stops** are never marked, but are usually located at the local market. You can flag down buses on the highway, but this means they'll probably be full and you'll have to stand. The conductor will collect your fare shortly after the bus departs, though he may not have change for big notes, in which case he'll take your money and return when he has collected enough fares to give you your change.

Camionetas

Though they're less common than just a few years ago, adventurous travellers can still try Nicaragua's cut-rate transport of choice, the **camioneta**. During your time in Nicaragua you'll doubtless see pick-up trucks loaded with people hurtling down the highway. A kind of collective transport, cheaper even than the bus, camionetas run on almost all routes, but you have to ask around to find the departure point.

■ Taxis

Although you'll mostly see **taxis** in cities – either battered Ladas or smart new imported models – they also make long-distance journeys. Although a taxi from, say, Granada to Rivas, will cost several times the bus fare, it's still a good deal, especially if you're in a group, since drivers charge by the distance travelled rather than by the number of passengers. Another option is to hire a taxi to take you around for the day; this tends to be more expensive – at least double the price of a town-to-town journey, costing US$45 per carload or more. In all cases, negotiate the fare before getting into the cab.

■ Driving and hitching

Renting a car in Nicaragua is most reliable in Managua (for a list of companies, see p.496), although some of the more upmarket hotels in Granada and León may also be able to arrange car hire for you.. You need a valid licence, passport and a credit card. Make sure you take out full-cover **insurance**, as road accidents in Nicaragua are on the increase. Throughout the country road signage is quite poor, and you'll need to ask directions frequently. Most roads are now paved, at least, although fuel remains expensive by Central American standards. As with other Central American countries, don't drive at night – it's less a question of crime than the lack of streetlighting disguising potholes, sudden deviations in the road, or even the road disappearing altogether, as well as cattle straying onto the highway.

Nicaraguans are a little surprised to see foreigners **hitching**, although it's very common for locals to do so. You'll only see women hitching when accompanied by men, however, and it's wise to follow this rule as a traveller. You will be expected to pay for your lift, but usually no more than US$1–1.50, even for trips of a couple of hours. Competition for lifts out of Managua and other large towns is fierce: most hopefuls stand under a patch of shade on the highway just outside the city – if the competition is tough or drivers unresponsive they give in and take the bus.

■ Boats

For the many people who live around Nicaragua's numerous waterways and two large lakes, **boats** provide a vital link. Travellers, however, tend not to use boats much, since in most cases good bus or plane connections are also available. The longest boat journey in the country, from Granada on the west side of Lago de Nicaragua to San Carlos on the southeast corner of the lake, is a

cheap, although slow (up to 14hr) way to cross this enormous inland sea. The Nicaraguan boat trip you're most likely to experience is the hour-long ride in a lancha – a medium-sized, motorized wooden craft – between San Jorge, near Rivas, and Moyogalpa on Ometepe island.

The trip from Managua and the Pacific lowlands to the Atlantic Coast can be made partly by boat, using either the slow public ferry or the high-speed *panga* (a large, motorized canoe carrying up to 20 people) that run from the hamlet of El Rama at the head of the Río Escondido to the coastal town of Bluefields. On the eastern side of the country nearly all travel is by boat along the complex network of rivers and lagoons of Mosquitia. All these services are private, and geared towards locals. Journeys are unscheduled, long and unpredictable, and you'll have to ask around in Bluefields and Puerto Cabezas for connections.

A ferry makes a twice-weekly journey between Bluefields and the **Corn Islands**, though this 6–8 hour journey can be notoriously rough on occasions and many travellers opt to take a flight on the return leg. A twice-daily *panga* runs between **Corn Island** and **Little Corn Island** – the journey is great fun and takes about an hour, although you'll probably get wet.

■ Planes

Faced with a ten-hour bus trip followed by six hours on a slow river jungle-cruise, many people heading to Nicaragua's Atlantic Coast from Managua choose to **fly** at least one way. The private domestic airlines La Costeña and Atlantic Airlines operate reliable (and very scenic) flights between Managua, Bluefields and the Corn Islands for about US$60 one way. Both operators offer similar prices, fly with equal frequency and also go to Puerto Cabezas in the northeast corner of the country, which is inaccessible by road for at least half the year, and to San Carlos, near the border with Costa Rica, another relatively inaccessible location.

Costs, money and banks

Nicaragua's **currency** is the **córdoba**, written as C$. The córdoba is divided into 100 centavos. Notes come in denominations of 100, 50, 20, 10, 5 and 1 córdobas, and 25, 10 and 5 centavos.

Coins come in denominations of 5 and 1 córdobas, and 50, 25, 10 and 5 centavos. The centavos and the one-córdoba notes come in very handy; you'll learn quickly to get rid of the 100 and 50 notes, as in most places they're about as welcome as a stack of Russian roubles and no one – except maybe bus conductors – ever seems to have change.

Nicaragua is no longer as cheap as it used to be. The IMF and World Bank policies have had their effect, and **prices** have risen accordingly. In general bus transport, food bought at markets and some accommodation are still bargains; restaurant meals, petrol, car rental and more upscale hotel accommodation, especially in Managua, are surprisingly expensive. As a rule, the budget traveller in Nicaragua, staying in hospedajes, taking buses instead of taxis, and eating in markets or at food stalls, can get by on as little as US$10 a day, although US$15–18 is a more comfortable aim.

■ Banks and exchange

The banking system in Nicaragua is improving, though one of the main hassles of travelling around the country is the refusal of many banks to acknowledge the existence of **travellers' cheques**; which means that you'll always be carrying a huge wad of grubby córdobas with you. The situation is, however, better than before, and **Bancentro** – with branches in all major towns and cities – will change travellers' cheques, although at much poorer rates than cash.

The most ubiquitous banks are Bancentro, Banco de América Central, Banpro and Banic, which are found in almost every Nicaraguan town. In larger places like Managua, León and Granada, many new private banks are cropping up: these offer more or less the same service as other banks – and they won't cash travellers' cheques either – but in slightly less totalitarian surroundings. Banks are usually open from 8.30am to 4.30pm and may close for an hour or more over lunch (12.30–1.30pm); many are also open on Saturday mornings. All will change US dollars, but no other currency.

To change travellers' cheques you can go to private currency exchange houses, called **casas de cambio**, though at present these are only found in Managua. You'll need both your passport and, as a rule, the purchase receipts with the serial numbers. Changing cheques into dollars rather than

córdobas incurs a fee of around US$3. The rate for changing dollar travellers' cheques at casas de cambio is slightly worse than the bank rate.

Credit cards such as Visa and Mastercard are accepted in some of the more expensive hotels and restaurants and you can often use them to pay for car rental, flights and tours. All branches of Credomatic bank advance cash on major cards. ATMs that accept foreign-issued cards can be found at the Plaza Inter shopping mall in Managua and in some banks in León and Granada.

Moneychangers (*coyotes*) operate in the street, usually at the town market, but avoid changing dollars in the street – it's easy to get ripped off. If you must, avoid dealing with more than one person at a time, and watch out for sleights of hand (like replacing a US$100 bill with a US$1). Take a taxi after changing money.

The **exchange rate** at the time of writing was 13.05 córdobas to the dollar, and is now relatively stable. Dollars are a useful standby across Nicaragua, and this will increase with the widespread acceptance of the dollar across Central America.

Information

Managua's **Inturismo** office (see p.484) is the country's only real tourist information centre. Though the staff are friendly, they can't offer much practical help and you're unlikely to come away with much more than a bunch of colourful leaflets. Ask for a copy of the bimonthly *Guía Fácil Nicaragua* (US$1), a useful publication packed with countrywide events listings and features. If Inturismo don't have it, you should be able to pick it up in the bigger hotels.

Useful English-language **Web sites** include *www.guideofnicaragua.com*, which has up-to-date information, maps and features on travelling in Nicaragua, and *www.intur.gob.ni*, the official government tourist site. For more general information about the country visit *www.centralamerica.com/nicaragua*.

Accommodation

Most travellers to Nicaragua find themselves at some point in a Nicaraguan **hospedaje** – a small, pension-type hotel, most often family-owned and run. Most hospedajes are basic but characterful, though some, especially those in old Spanish colonial-style houses, are truly characterful places, with big rocking chairs ringing plant-filled patios and a lively family life going on around. As a rule, basic hospedajes still charge under US$5, although with inflation prices are moving into the US$5–10 range; most require payment in cash, usually in córdobas, although many accept dollars. Breakfast is not normally included in the price, and in most places you'll have to share a bathroom, though in only the most basic of hospedajes will you have to provide your own toilet paper and towel. More upmarket hospedajes occasionally offer the option of air conditioning; since electricity is so expensive this can double the price of the room. Nicaraguan units tend to be old and noisy and in most places a/c is not really necessary – you can get by with a ceiling fan.

Hotels tend to be fancier, with air conditioning, possibly cable television, and other services like tours and car rental. Outside Managua they're very thin on the ground, although a few, like the *Europa* and *Colonial* in León and Granada's *Alhambra* and *Colonial*, may merit the US$25 or so they charge for a room. You can pay by credit card – and occasionally with travellers' cheques – and an air-conditioned "international" restaurant is usually attached.

In Nicaragua, as in the rest of Central America, "**Motels**" and "**Auto Hotels**" are not used for sleeping. Better described as "love" motels, they advertise an amazing array of comforts, including a/c, hot water, cable television, security and – most importantly – "privacy".

Throughout the country **camping** is problematic, although not impossible; unlike in Costa Rica, say, there is little tradition of camping in Nicaragua, and sand flies, mosquitoes, rain and theft are only a few of the deterrents to setting up a tent. If you're determined, the most promising areas in which to camp are beach towns like San Juan del Sur, Isla Ometepe and the Corn Islands.

Eating and drinking

Nicaraguan **food**, like that in many Central American countries, is based around the ubiquitous **beans, rice and meat** – and plenty of it. Everything is cooked with oil; even the rice is fried, often with a little onion and some finely sliced red chiles or small capsicums. If this sounds like gastronomic hell, take heart – *comida nica* grows on you and you may find yourself craving a plate of **gallo pinto** (beans and rice) once you've left the country. Homegrown Nicaraguan beef is also very tasty. The downside is that **vegetarians** will usually have to stick to a diet of rice-and-beans and fried plantains, although vegetarian restaurants are cropping up in the major towns, and the foreign-owned hospedajes in Granada serve a good variety of meat-free dishes.

■ What to eat

Nicaraguan meals are very much centred on meat, usually **chicken**, **beef** or **pork**, most deliciously cooked *a la plancha*, on a grill or griddle, and served spitting on a hot plate. **Seafood** is equally good: on the coast you'll be offered ocean fish such as snapper and bass, with freshwater fish on the menu around Lago de Nicaragua. Fish are usually served whole, deep fried and served with a rich tomato or garlic sauce. Weekends are traditionally the time to eat **nacatamales**, parcels of corn dough filled with either vegetables, pork, beef or chicken, which are wrapped in a banana leaf and boiled for a couple of hours.

On the Atlantic Coast the cuisine becomes markedly more **Caribbean**, and sweeter, spicier tastes invade the recipes. Although rice and beans is still a staple dish, you'll often find that the rice has been cooked in delicious mild coconut milk, and the fresh **coconut bread** is delicious. **Ron don** – "run down"; in local parlance "to cook" – is a stew of local yucca, chayote and other vegetables, usually with meat added, which is simmered for at least a day and traditionally eaten at weekends.

Nicaragua's secret national treasure is the Eskimo **ice cream** company, which produces an extraordinary range of home-grown flavours, embracing many local fruits and nuts, including chocolate with almonds, coconut, pistachio, star fruit, rock melon and mango. For the more exotic flavours you may have to go to an Eskimo shop or a supermarket.

■ Where to eat

Throughout Nicaragua **streetside kiosks** sell hot meals, usually at lunchtime. You'll soon become familiar with the ubiquitous plastic tablecloths, paper plates and huge bowls of cabbage salad set beside small barbecue grills. The food is generally well prepared and safe to eat: most Nicaraguans have their lunch this way, or in small **comedores** or **cafetines**, restaurants with ten or so seats that do a lunchtime *comida corriente*, a good-value set plate of meat, rice and salad. **Street vendors** sell a variety of snacks including nuts, popcorn and banana chips, along with succulent bags of chopped mango, pineapple, papaya and melon. In the early evening, small stalls open up in most towns on or around the central plaza selling cheap and filling fried foods with rice and salad.

■ Drinking

Nicaragua has two local brands of **beer**, Victoria and Toña, both lagers. Each has its aficionados, who refuse to drink the other, but they really taste quite similar, although Toña is a little darker and nuttier. You can buy them in cans, but to get them from your local shop you will need to exchange some "empties" – Nicaragua operates a strict recycling program for beer bottles and with no empties to exchange you'll pay double the price.

Local Flor de Caña **rum** comes in both dark and white, gold, old, dry and light, and is an excellent buy at just US$4–7. It's usually brought to the table with a large bucket of ice and some lemons, but you can mix it with soft drinks for something a little less potent.

Given Nicaragua's heat, it's just as well that there's a fascinating range of cold drinks, or **refrescos** (usually shortened to *frescos*), to choose from. These are made from a large range of grains, seeds and fruits, which are liquidized with milk, water and ice. *Cebada en grano* is a combination of ground barley and barley grains mixed together with milk and coloured pink – like most drinks it is flavoured with cinnamon and lots of sugar. *Pinolillo* is a maize drink with spices, served in large, carved, oval containers made from the seed of the jickory tree; the *semilla de Jicaroa* itself is made into a delicious drink that looks and tastes rather like chocolate. *Cacao* is also widely available, and often sold in small sealed plastic bags at traffic lights. You can now buy these drinks in powdered form in the supermarket, ready to mix with milk and a little ice in the blender. Just about every fruit imaginable is made into a *fresco*, including watermelon, star fruit, papaya, rock melon (a small, local variety of melon) and oranges. During the rainy months, keep your eye out for *pitahaya* juice. Made from the fruit of a cactus, it's a virulent purple in colour and incredibly tasty. You can also eat the fruit raw, but be warned that you'll stain your hands and mouth a deep purple. Some drink stands and street vendors specialize in **raspados**, a cup full of ice scraped off a large block and topped with flavouring, anything from milk and chocolate to currants (*grosellas*).

Opening hours, festivals and holidays

Shops and **services** in Nicaragua still observe Sunday closing: otherwise you'll find most things open from 8am to 4pm, with the exception of **banks**, which normally close at 3pm. Some **museums** and **sites** close for lunch, normally shutting their doors between noon and 2, before reopening again until 4pm. Supermarkets, smaller grocery shops and the small neighbourhood shops called *ventas* generally stay open until 8pm. **Bars** and **restaurants** tend to close around 11pm, except for nightclubs and dance clubs – most of which are in Managua – which stay open until 2am or later.

Christmas and Easter are still the biggest **holidays**. At **Easter** especially the whole country packs up and goes to the beach: buses are packed, hotel rooms on the coast are at a premium, and flights to the Corn Islands are fully

PUBLIC HOLIDAYS

January 1 New Year's Day
Easter week Semana Santa
May 1 Labour Day
July 19 Anniversary of the Revolution
September 14 Battle of San Jacinto
September 15 Independence Day
November 2 All Soul's Day (Día de los Muertos)
December 7 & 8 Inmaculada Concepción
December 25 Christmas Day

booked. **Christmas** and **New Year** are mainly celebrated in the home, but you'll find most things closed between December 23 and 25 and on January 1. The holiday marking the **Revolution**, on July 19, is still celebrated ardently by Sandinistas and is usually accompanied by parades and marches. In addition, each town in Nicaragua has its own **patron saint** and will observe the saint's day with processions and celebrations called Toro Guaco, when you might catch a glimpse of old customs inherited from the Aztecs mixed with mestizo figures like the masked *viejitos* (old ones – masks of old men and women worn by young and old alike). In all cases Nicaraguans love to dance, and you will probably see folkloric dances in the streets, usually performed by children.

Mail and telecommunications

The **mail** service in Nicaragua is fairly fast: though letters to Europe can take up to two weeks, they reach North America in about eight days. Theft from letters is an increasing problem, especially with mail sent into Nicaragua, so it's wise not to trust cash or anything valuable to the postal service. You can send **international mail** from any Nicaraguan town, although Managua, León and Granada have the best service. Mail sent from the Atlantic Coast will probably take the longest to reach the rest of the world.

Every Nicaraguan town of any size has an **Enitel** office, the recently privatized state telecommunications and postal service (most people still refer to it by the old joint name of Enitel/Telcor). Except in Managua, all Enitel offices have separate sections for phone and mail services (the phone sections are generally open

much later, usually until around 10pm). While the phone service is more reliable than it used to be, calling out of the country can still be a hassle.

There are virtually no coin-operated phones in Nicaragua. Major towns like Managua, León and Granada have new Publitel **cardphones**. Cards are available from Enitel offices and supermarkets and work by code, not magnetic strip (don't insert them into the telephone). They can be useful for making **domestic** calls (and calls to neighbouring countries), although it's often easier, cheaper and more reliable to make calls from an Enitel office. Outside major towns, all telephone calls have to be placed at an Enitel office.

Calling abroad, you'll have to pay a visit to an Enitel office and wait in line with huge numbers of Nicaraguans. You can ask to reverse the charges or pay for your call afterwards in córdobas – tell the operator how long you wish to talk and they'll calculate the approximate cost for you. You'll then be sent to a numbered booth, where you wait for your call to be patched through – a sometimes frustrating process. Most Enitel offices are open long hours, from 7am until 10pm Monday to Friday, with reduced hours at weekends. Alternatively, many countries have **direct-dial numbers** that get you through to either a member-card operator (AT&T, Sprint or MCI) or your home country operator for a reverse-charge call. Calling Nicaragua from abroad, the **country code** is ☎505.

Fax machines are common in Nicaragua, although except in Managua Enitel does not provide a public fax service. If you stay at a mid-range or upmarket hotel you'll probably be able to send a fax abroad for a fee; otherwise – and especially outside Managua – you're out of luck.

Internet services are becoming more widespread, with better and cheaper connections across the country. There are plenty of places with reasonably priced Internet access in Managua, León, Granada and Estelí, usually costing between US$2.50 and US$4 per hour, although in smaller or more remote towns the lack of competition can mean that, where available, the cost of Internet access is much higher.

The media

The Sandinistas were widely criticized for **censoring** Nicaragua's media during the 1980s, and though Nicaragua's press is now technically free, in 2000 the Alemán government introduced stringent new standards for journalists requiring them all to be university educated, professionally qualified and – the crux of the argument – government approved. Opponents say that these new conditions restrict the right to free speech.

Of the national **newspapers**, the most authoritative is *La Prensa*, founded in 1926. During the Chamorro years it was criticized for being too supportive of that government (Violeta Chamorro was on the editorial board, and her daughter was the paper's editor), though it now takes a slightly more independent line and attacks corrupt politicians irrespective of party allegiance – in the run-up to the 2001 presidential elections it was equally critical of all the candidates. The other widely available daily is the black-and-white *El Nuevo Diario*, which is leftist but more sensationalist and populist in tone. *El Mercurio* is less widely available and yet more sensationalist.

The only **English-language newspaper** is the monthly *Nica News*, which often prints features on tourist destinations and reproduces flight schedules and the like. The problem is getting hold of it; try the *Casa del Cafe* in Managua, which also sells the Spanish-language Latin American edition of *Newsweek*. Foreign newspapers, even those readily available in other Central American countries, such as the *Miami Herald* or the *New York Times*, are virtually impossible to buy in Nicaragua.

Cable television is becoming increasingly widespread across Nicaragua, providing access to a range of international news, sports and movie channels. Many poorer Nicaraguans still get their news from the **radio**, while a number of FM stations pump out pop music, generally a mix of English and Spanish.

Safety and the police

Poverty and unemployment in Nicaragua have contributed to a rising crime rate. **Petty theft** is the most common form, especially on buses. Nicaraguans suffer from this as well as tourists, and locals take the usual precautions of not carrying anything valuable in an outside pocket, and spreading valuables and money over several pockets or purses; travellers should do the same. Opportunistic forms of theft aside, the only place where you need to worry about assault is in Managua. Here it's best not to walk around at night or to go out alone to bars or nightclubs, and be alert when leaving banks or casas de cambio,

where thieves have recently targeted both foreigners and Nicaraguans. Never leave anything of value on the beach, even for a few minutes, as it is almost guaranteed to be stolen. Larger hotels will have safes where you can leave your passport and other valuables. **Women** should be wary of going out alone or even in a group at night – the chief threat is being harassed by drunken men spilling out of bars in groups.

The **police** in Nicaragua are generally reliable, except perhaps the traffic police *(policia de tránsito)*, who are infamous for their opportunistic targeting of foreigners and who will take any chance to give you a fine (*multa*). To **report a crime** you must go to the nearest police station. If you need a police report for an insurance claim, the police will ask you to fill out a *denuncia* – a full report of the incident. If the police station does not have the *denuncia* forms, ask for a *constancia*, a simpler form, signed and stamped by the police. This should be sufficient for an insurance claim. Visitors to Nicaragua must carry their passport on them at all times. A photocopy is acceptable; police checks are not as common as they used to be. Keep passports secure in an inside pocket all the time, and keep a photocopy separately when travelling.

In an **emergency**, dial ☎128 for the Red Cross (Cruz Roja); ☎115 for fire (*bomberos*); ☎118 for police; or ☎119 in the case of a traffic accident.

Work and study

Gone are the heady days of the 1980s, when **internacionalistas** (foreign voluntary workers) came from Europe, North America and other Latin American countries to help the Revolution. By all accounts this was a rewarding experience for the mostly young people who found voluntary work placements in Nicaragua, doing anything from road-building to picking organic coffee.

Now, with the political shift to the right, *internacionalistas* still come to Nicaragua, but in much reduced numbers compared to those of ten or fifteen years ago. As overseas NGOs and aid agencies take over, it is becoming increasingly difficult to find good voluntary positions in Nicaragua. One place you can try is the Casa Ben Linder in Managua (three blocks south and one and a half blocks east of the Monseñor Lezcano statue; ☎266-4373), the Nicaraguan base for a number of primarily US voluntary groups and agencies. Most towns have a local IXCHEN **women's centre** (*casa de la mujer*), whose work is largely based on health, family welfare and community issues. Women are always welcome to visit and if your Spanish is good and you have some qualifications, they may be able to advise you regarding voluntary work with women.

Unless you are sponsored by an overseas government, agency or voluntary organization, however, opportunities for work are few, and what does exist is likely to be unpaid. In a country where unofficial unemployment figures hover around seventy percent, foreigners will only find casual work as **teachers** of English. Even so, the Nicaraguan government is strict in its immigration policy and to undertake any paid work you need a long-stay working visa; if you are sponsored by an overseas company they will probably take care of this for you. The address of Managua's migración office is given on p.496.

History

In comparison with its neighbours to the north, in Nicaragua you often get the impression that history didn't begin until the arrival of the Spanish. Few traces of Nicaragua's pre-Conquest history remain; certainly there are **no major monuments** of the likes of Tikal or Copán, and historians and archeologists are doubtful whether cities of equivalent size and complexity ever existed here, though modern Nicaragua retains aspects of its ancient history in its language, food and customs.

Events far to the north in Mexico determined the future of the country that would come to be called Nicaragua. After the fall of the Aztec city of Teotihuacán in 1000 AD, displaced **Mexica** (Aztec) migrated southward through the isthmus on the strength of a prophecy that they were to settle where they saw a lake with two volcanoes rising from the water – which they found in the striking form of Isla de Ometepe in Lago de Nicaragua.

Two groups of pre-Columbian peoples settled on the shores of the lake. Roughly divided into the **Chorotegas** and the **Nahuas**, it is still possible to tell who settled where by place names – Momotombo, Masaya, Niquinohomo and Nandaime come from the Chorotegan language, while Managua, Masatepe, Tipitapa and Chinandega are Nahuatl words. The food – maize, beans, chillies and chocolate – and culture of these people continued to closely resemble that of the Aztecs, even after centuries of living far away from metropolitan Aztec culture.

These people called themselves the **Niquirano** and were governed by chief **Nicarao**, a rich *cacique* (chief) from near present-day Rivas who came to be called Nicaragua by the Spanish, giving the modern country its name. In 1522 Nicarao welcomed **Gil González de Avila**, an intrepid explorer who had made his way to Nicaragua on foot and by boat from Panamá and Costa Rica, becoming the first Spaniard to arrive in the area. Nicarao allowed his people to be baptized and to mix interracially with the Spanish conquerors.

The inhabitants of central Nicaragua, the **Chontales**, **Matagalpas** and **Populucas**, were a different ethnic group, related to the Maya of Honduras, and offered far more resistance to the Spanish, though their language and peoples did not survive the Conquest. On the Atlantic coast the pre-Miskito **Sumus** and **Ramas** (of whom little is known) made up the indigenous population. Nearly all the coastal peoples, except the Rama, mixed racially with the Afro-Caribbean population who came to its shores as freed or escaped slaves from British West Indian colonies.

■ The colonial era

Although the very first Spanish conquistadors glimpsed the eastern coast of Nicaragua as early as 1508, it was not until 1522, three years after Hernán Cortez landed on the coast of Mexico, that a Spanish expedition sailed up the Río San Juan into the Lago de Nicaragua. Two years later an expedition led by **Francisco Fernandez de Córdoba** founded the first cities, Granada and León, after suppressing local indigenous groups.

The story of colonial Nicaragua is a familiar one of rapacious looting of resources, exploitation of indigenous peoples as slave labour, and genocide – in part caused by new diseases to which the pre-Columbian peoples had no immunity. On the Atlantic Coast, where the Europeans did not settle, diseases did not decimate the indigenous population to the same extent. Throughout the colonial period the Spanish Crown did not concern itself much with its new hot, volcanic wedge of territory – the gold of Mexico and Peru was far more absorbing. Instead, Nicaragua was used as a source of **slave labour** and many indigenous Nicaraguans were sent to work in the Peruvian mines. The Spanish did not make much of an effort to penetrate remote parts of the country or to establish other towns, and by the end of the 1500s León and Granada were still the only settlements. The country remained poor, the central mountains unexplored through fear of the fierce indigenous peoples who still lived there, while the Atlantic coast was plagued by pirates. Not much would change in Nicaragua for nearly three hundred years.

■ Independence

By the beginning of the nineteenth century Spain had begun to lose its grip on power in Nicaragua. As in other New World colonies, in Nicaragua only *peninsulares* – those born in Spain – could hold positions of influence. Fuelled by the frustrations of the local-born elite, a revolt staged in 1811 in El Salvador ignited aspirations of independence throughout the region. Along with the other Central American countries, in 1821 Nicaragua gained independence from the Spanish Crown as part of the **Central American Federation**, before becoming a fully independent nation in 1838.

Following independence, the new republic of Nicaragua attracted the interest of the US, who believed that the Río San Juan and Lago de Nicaragua represented a possible route for transporting goods and passengers between the Atlantic and Pacific sides of the isthmus. In 1849, the American **Cornelius Vanderbilt**, in partnership with the Nicaraguan government, formed the **Accessory Transit Company**. The company was granted exclusive rights to build a canal across the isthmus, and was also allowed to establish a transit route across Nicaragua along which passengers and mining equipment were moved during the Californian Gold Rush (the journey from the east to the west coast of the US by sea via Nicaragua was actually quicker than that across the US by land). This was a period of relative prosperity for Nicaragua – and for Vanderbilt, who made a fortune – with giant steamboats plying the choppy waters of Lago de Nicaragua, filled with overdressed east-coast ladies in crinolines sweating under the fierce sun alongside rough gold-rush hopefuls.

■ William Walker

William Walker was an ambitious and megalomaniacal – or just plain mad, depending on your interpretation – American adventurer. A native of Tennessee, schooled in law and journalism, Walker had vast political ambitions. The Liberals of León foolhardily handed him the chance to fulfil them by inviting him to Nicaragua to help them gain power over their arch-rivals, the Conservatives of Granada.

In 1855 Walker set foot on Nicaraguan soil and soon afterwards, with just sixty mercenaries, gained control of Granada – and, by default, the entire country. Walker installed a puppet government, though real power remained in his own hands. In 1856, alarmed by the situation, Costa Rica declared war on Walker, but an epidemic of cholera forced the Costa Ricans to withdraw. The same year Walker held a rigged election and declared himself President of the Republic. By making English the country's official language and **legalizing slavery**, Walker managed to alienate all Nicaraguans; Cornelius Vanderbilt, still a force in Nicaragua, was determined to have him out, and the other Central American countries, fearing Walker's activities might spark rebellions in their own territories, began plans to topple him.

Nicaragua paid dearly for the eventual overthrow of Walker, which came only with help from Guatemala and Costa Rica: many Nicaraguans lost their lives in the fighting, and as he retreated Walker ordered the beautiful colonial city of Granada burned. The final battle of 1856–57, in Rivas, near the Costa Rican border, would come to be known as the **"National War"**. Intervention by the US forced the issue and on May 1, 1857, Walker and his remaining followers were escorted by marines out of Rivas and onto a ship back to the US.

Three years later, during a further bout of adventuring in Central America, Walker was captured by the British and handed over to Hondurans, who executed him in Trujillo.

■ The US invasion

For the next three decades, power see-sawed, not always peacefully, between Liberals and Conservatives. Even so, the period from 1857 to 1893 was one of such unusual stability and prosperity that Nicaraguan historians often refer to it, somewhat nostalgically, as **"The Thirty Years"**. This period coincided with the growth of what was to become Nicaragua's most important export: **coffee**, fuelled by Europe and America's seemingly insatiable desire for the drink.

Despite the prosperity afforded the country by the coffee trade, at the beginning of the twentieth century Nicaragua's economy was dominated by the overwhelming presence of US companies, usually in alliance with Nicaraguan landowners – a pattern which was to characterize economic relations for most of the coming century. Angered when, in 1904, the US chose Panamá for the site of the **Transisthmian Canal**, ·president José Santos Zelaya countered by inviting Germany and Japan to construct a rival canal across Nicaragua. Though this canal never left the drawing board, the subsequent worsening of relations with the US prompted a **civil war** in October 1909, with the nationalist Liberals and the US-friendly Conservatives again at each other's throats. In response, the US inaugurated a precedent in Nicaragua – and in the region as a whole – by landing four hundred US marines on the Caribbean coast. Zelaya resigned soon after.

From 1912 until 1933 the US kept a token number of troops in Nicaragua, more as a reminder of US influence than as any real military threat. Pro-US Conservatives held onto power until a further outbreak of unrest in 1926 prompted the US to send more marines, ostensibly to protect US citizens.

One of the opponents of the US presence in Nicaragua was **Augusto César Sandino**, a socialist who waged independent guerrilla activity, manned by his own personal army of peasants and workers. He eventually joined the Liberals' fight against the Conservatives and their US allies. In response to Sandino's activities – their excuse was the maintenance of "internal security" – in the first years of the 1930s the US took over the country's military and developed the Nicaraguan National Guard, which was to become such a significant force under the next political figure looming on Nicaragua's horizon – Somoza.

■ The Somoza years

The long era of **Somocismo**, or Somoza-family rule, began in 1934. In his role as head of the country's National Guard, **General Anastasio "Tacho" Somoza García** ordered the **assassination of Sandino**, by then the liberal candidate for the upcoming election. With Sandino dead, rigged elections were held and Somoza was sworn in as president of Nicaragua in 1937.

Well-educated in the US, where he attended a school run by the US marines, fluent in English and Americanized, Somoza was also well-connected in Nicaragua through the kind of network of family influence that has always been so significant in Central American political life. Perhaps his privileged lifestyle and reliance upon his family's influence were responsible for Somoza's exceptionally cynical character; in any case, it was clear he had little sympathy for the majority of his compatriots. Indeed he ruled in typical Latin American strongman fashion as a *caudillo*, or dictator, as he ruthlessly pursued the enrichment of himself, his family and his coterie of associates. He cultivated the National Guard as his own personal army and gave it power far beyond the usual sphere of a military force, until it virtually controlled the radio stations, the postal services and even the health system.

For the Somoza family, at least, the **1940s** were prosperous. Somoza supported the Allies, at least in name (intimates of Somoza during this time recall Somoza replacing his office portrait of Hitler with one of Churchill), but for most of the decade he busied himself with accumulating a personal fortune, buying up land, the national airline, even the national dairy.

Somoza remained in power through continuously rigged elections and re-elections, or appointments of puppet governments. In 1955 the Nicaraguan Congress amended the constitution to allow Somoza to be re-elected again. But by then political opposition was growing. Somoza's end came unexpectedly, both for him and the country, brought about by the independent action of **Rigoberto López Pérez**, a 27-year-old poet, who shot the dictator dead in the streets of León in 1956. The National Guard responded by shooting Pérez some fifty times.

As it turned out, little changed, despite Perez's dramatic and passionate action. Somoza's son, **Luis Somoza Debayle**, also US-educated, took the position of interim president. At the same time his younger brother **Anastasio "Tachito" Somoza Debayle** assumed command of the National Guard. Following in their father's footsteps, they stayed in power through manipulation of the constitution and electoral process. A long period of repression followed, during which dissidents were regularly tortured and imprisoned.

Opposition grew, however, and in the 1967 elections the Conservatives and Christian Social Party banded together to create the **National Opposition Union** (Unión Nacional Opositora, or UNO). Nonetheless, vote rigging and harassment of voters ensured Somoza's election as president. Luis Somoza died of a heart attack soon after and power was left concentrated in the hands of Anastasio Somoza – now both president and head of the National Guard.

■ Growing opposition

At a few minutes past midnight on December 23, 1972, Managua was rocked by an incredible seismic disturbance, causing the near total collapse of the city. By the time the ground stopped rumbling – just thirty seconds later – some 10,000 people were dead and about 50,000 families homeless.

Every Nicaraguan recognizes the **earthquake of 1972** as a national turning point. The earthquake was followed by the looting of the shattered shops of Managua's former commercial core, in which poor Managuans were joined by soldiers of the National Guard. Much of the emergency earthquake relief supplies sent from abroad were also intercepted by the Guard, acting on Somoza's orders, and then sold off to victims in the street. Businesses and homeowners were unable to claim compensation on damaged property because the Somoza-owned insurance companies refused to recognize their claims. All classes of Nicaraguans were appalled by the epic cynicism and greed behind Somoza's actions; by 1974 his personal wealth was estimated at some US$400 million. Even businessmen and the elite, both traditionally loyal to Somoza, deserted camp.

Although the downtown core of Managua was never reconstructed, an effective opposition to the dictator was built out of the rubble of the 1972 earthquake. The **Frente Sandinista de Liberación Nacional** (FSLN), named after Sandino, became a rallying point for dissidents. Founded in the late 1950s by law students at the National University in León as a Marxist-Leninist response to the dictatorship, by the early 1970s the FSLN had gained widespread support, especially in the countryside and among students.

The FSLN's first major success took place on December 27, 1974, when guerrillas raided the home of a government official and held several relatives of Somoza to ransom, gaining a US$1 million payout. The guerrillas fled abroad, and though the opposition was buoyed by the success of the rebels' audacity, in response Somoza stepped up the repression, surveillance, torture and murder of suspected dissidents.

Opposition to the Somoza regime accelerated in 1977, both within Nicaragua and in the US, whose new president, Democrat Jimmy Carter, made continuing military assistance to the Somoza regime contingent on the improvement of human rights. In October of that year a group of Nicaraguan intellectuals met secretly in Costa Rica to form the first coherent anti-Somoza alliance, and to work out a plan of action. The catalyst that began the Revolution was engineered by the dictator himself when, on January 10, 1978, **Pedro Joaquín Chamorro**, opposition leader and editor of *La Prensa*, was assassinated by the National Guard, acting on Somoza's orders. Mass demonstrations and a general strike followed, crippling the country and galvanizing the opposition. Meanwhile, in response to attacks on civilians and increasing reports of torture and murder, the US cut off the Somoza regime by suspending military aid. Unrest had its effect on the national economy and inflation, and unemployment reached new heights.

The most dramatic event staged by the FSLN took place on August 22, 1978, when guerrillas stormed the National Palace while Congress was in session. After 2000 government members had been held hostage for two days, President Somoza was forced to meet the demands of the FSLN. A humiliation for Somoza, the audacity of the guerrillas once again inspired the population. By the end of 1978, demonstrations and outbreaks of fighting had spread around the country.

■ Revolution

As 1979 opened, Somoza's declaration that he would stay in power until 1981, two years past his mandate, sparked a national crisis. As guerrilla attacks by the opposition increased, the Nicaraguan economy nosedived. By now, though, the FSLN was in a stronger position, having acquired arms from sympathetic countries like Cuba. In May the FSLN launched its main offensive in Estelí and Jinotega. No longer merely a group of guerrilla insurrectionists bent on staging dramatic stunts, the **Sandinistas** were now a formidable fighting force: their influence had spread to the provinces, and their military strategy was centrally organized.

In June, a Nicaraguan **government-in-exile** was established in Costa Rica. Among the five-member governorship of the country were two people who would play key roles in the political future of Nicaragua – **Daniel José Ortega Saavedra** of the FSLN and **Violeta Barrios de Chamorro**, the widow of the assassinated *La Prensa* editor. By June the country was largely in the hands of the Sandinistas, although Managua remained under the control of Somoza and his National Guard. Isolated, Somoza was forced to resign and soon after boarded a plane to Miami. He eventually moved to Paraguay, where he was assassinated by South American leftist guerrillas in 1980.

Triumphant, the government-in-exile ceremoniously entered the city of León the day after Somoza's departure. A day later the FSLN forces entered Managua, and the Revolution was won, officially, on July 19, 1979. With the Revolution ended a long – perhaps even 500-year-long – era of feudalism in Nicaragua. However, the price had been high: around 50,000 were dead and over 120,000 had fled the country into exile.

■ The Sandinista years and the Contra War

As the 1970s became the 1980s, the challenge facing the **new Sandinista government** was enormous. The country's infrastructure was in ruins: food was scarce, health care nonexistent and diseases like cholera and malaria rampant. But the mood of the country – among the leadership as well as the general population – was buoyant, even ecstatic. By all accounts, the Sandinistas' energy for reconstruction was enormous. Within days new ministers took over buildings formerly owned by Somoza companies, set up government offices, and got down to the business at hand.

First on the agenda for the Sandinistas was the resuscitation of the **economy**, severely damaged by Somoza's appropriation and by war. Foreign debts had to be renegotiated, loans secured, and economic aid directed. Somoza's properties were nationalized – some two thousand farms, accounting for twenty percent of Nicaragua's agricultural land.

Operating under emergency measures, the governing junta suspended all the mechanisms of Somocismo, including the constitution, presidency, Congress, and all courts. A new army, the Sandinista People's Army (**Ejército Popular Sandinista** or EPS), was formed along with a Sandinista-controlled police force. With the help of training by Cuban and Soviet armed forces, the

EPS soon developed into the most powerful standing army in Central America.

Another task facing the Sandinistas was the construction of a civil society, which had never really existed in Nicaragua. They set about forming various unions and interest groups, of which the largest still exist in some form: the Sandinista Workers' Federation (Central Sandinista de Trabajadores–CST) and the Luisa Amanda Espinoza Nicaraguan Women's Association (Asociación de Mujeres Nicaragüenses Luisa Amanda Espinoza or AMNLAE). In transforming the civil, military and judicial arms of Nicaragua, the Sandinistas made themselves ubiquitous, and within only a year of taking over the country they were in control of most aspects of Nicaraguan society.

The first democratic elections held under the Sandinistas, in 1984, were won by Daniel Ortega with a 67 percent majority. This was the first time most Nicaraguans had ever voted, and the first time since 1928 that the US did not have a hand in the electoral process. The Sandinistas were not universally popular, however, particularly in the **Atlantic Coast** region. Independent, traditionally suspicious of anyone of Spanish descent and not of a leftist bent, the Miskito, Rama and Creole peoples of the Atlantic Coast never really got behind the Revolution, especially after the Sandinistas made attempts to forcibly relocate indigenous groups and to impose leftist ideology upon them. Many coastal dwellers – the Miskito especially – were so disenchanted by the Sandinistas that they would make easy recruits in the civil war that was to come.

The main blow for the Sandinistas came in the form of **Ronald Reagan's** election to the presidency of the US in November 1980. Convinced that Nicaragua's leftist policies and its friendship with Cuba and the Soviet Union meant the spread of Communism in US' backyard, the Reagan administration **suspended aid** to Nicaragua in 1981 and thereafter waged an open campaign against the Sandinistas. The **Contra War** – "contra" being short for *contrarevolucionarios* – was launched with nearly $20 million of US military assistance. The troops, based in training camps in Honduras, were mostly made up of former National Guard soldiers who had fled the country on Somoza's departure, though they were soon joined by other groups, including Miskitos. Although it's true that sectors of the population were disgruntled with the Sandinistas, the presence of the universally hated ex-National Guard in the Contra forces caused most Nicaraguans to distrust the Contra movement.

By the mid-1980s the Contra War was causing widespread disruption in the country. What with open US support for the movement, as well as the ambivalent positions of Honduras and Costa Rica – both used as launching pads by the Contras – the Sandinistas felt increasingly isolated, and began to clamp down on political opposition. Revoking their promises for an open political society, they banned opposition in the media – including *La Prensa*, ironically an organ of dissent during the Somoza years – and prevented rival political parties.

Arguably it was the five-year-long **US trade embargo** that succeeded in strangling the Nicaraguan economy and undermining the Sandinistas. Within a few years, though, US support for the Contras was shaken by the **Irangate** scandal, during which it emerged that Oliver North was a lynchpin in a CIA scheme to sell weapons to Iran illegally, using the proceeds to fund the Contra activities.

The first serious initiative for peace in Nicaragua was taken by neighbouring Costa Rica's president, **Oscar Arias Sánchez**. The Arias Plan for peace in Central America, launched in February 1987, had the backing of the US and was signed by the presidents of five Central American republics. An initiative to stop conflict within Nicaragua and El Salvador, and to repair relations between Nicaragua and Honduras, the Plan was welcomed as the first serious attempt to solve by diplomatic means the political problems between nations in the region. In March 1988 the FSLN and the Contras signed a ceasefire agreement.

■ 1990–1996: The Chamorro goverment

The **elections** scheduled for February 1990 were to be a test for the Sandinistas' staying power as a political force: opposition was gathering strength and in 1989 no fewer than fourteen political parties, with nothing in common except their opposition to the leftists, formed a coalition, the **National Opposition Union** (Unión Nacional Opositora, UNO), and appointed Violeta Barrios de Chamorro, then-publisher of *La Prensa*, as their presidential candidate. Head of a coalition of opposition forces that had the support of the US government and Nicaraguans living in Miami,

Doña Violeta, as she is known in Nicaragua, had all the ingredients of a leader. Her status as the widow of a murdered hero of the Revolution also gave her a moral authority that few, other than Daniel Ortega himself, could match.

Ortega ran again for the Sandinistas, who adopted an anti-US stance, condemning the UNO as a puppet of US foreign policy. The UNO was fractured and disorganized, fighting what seemed to be, at least on the surface, a less charismatic campaign, which concentrated on promises of peace and reviving the national economy.

The international community and neighbouring Central American countries watched the elections carefully, expecting the Sandinista organizational know-how and showmanship to win through. Perhaps no one was more deeply shocked than Daniel Ortega when on February 25, 1990, Violeta Barrios de Chamorro emerged victorious with 55 percent of the vote against Ortega's 41 percent. Both international observers and Nicaraguan commentators could only conclude that the Nicaraguan people had voted for peace, fearing that another Sandinista government would bring continuing war and poverty. By the end of the 1980s the more well-to-do echelons of society (at least, the ones who had not fled to Costa Rica or Miami) had the distinct impression they had been better off under Somoza. Death had hit at nearly every family, and many people felt the Sandinistas had brought further hardship on the country by inviting the scrutiny of the US and the subsequent blockade. One way or another, Nicaraguans had decided it was time for a change.

Although there were extreme right-wing forces in her coalition, Violeta was seen as an acceptable moderate and with Chamorro's election victory came peace: the US lifted their embargo and cut off supplies to the Contras. After some delay, both sides were disarmed and plans were drawn up to re-integrate soldiers into society, a process that later came to grief as small bands of Contras and Sandinistas re-armed to fight for better conditions for veterans.

However you feel about their politics, the **achievements** of the Sandinistas were enormous. When they took over after Somoza's departure, about sixty percent of Nicaragua's population was illiterate. Literacy workers were dispatched to every corner in the country, armed only with a chalkboard and a gas lamp, and by the end of the Sandinista years the figure had been reduced to thirteen percent. They also transformed the role of women: several women led battalions into combat during the Revolution, and women made up about twenty percent of soldiers in the Sandinista army. Because the war effort ate up around half the national budget for many years, basic programmes in health education and culture were heavily reliant on foreign funding and international volunteers. These *internacionalistas*, as they were called, for many years made up an important part of Nicaraguan society. As a result of this contact, Nicaraguans are generally more aware of what is going on in the rest of the world than other Central Americans of similar background, and display a remarkable cosmopolitanism, even in very remote areas. In many ways, the Sandinistas effected a near-total transformation of Nicaraguan society.

With Chamorro's victory, the World Bank and the International Monetary Fund began negotiations to relieve Nicaragua's debt burden in exchange for a programme of **economic restructuring**. The government initiated a plan to rein in the inflation rate in the first 100 days – during the first few years of the decade inflation was running at about 410 percent. The honeymoon didn't last long; the country was in a shocking state, the result of a drawn-out war, a crippling US embargo and falling production. Nicaraguans were tired of the constant state of crisis and the steady deterioration of the standard of living. For them, things only got worse.

The new government's plan to halt inflation failed and the economic restructuring, without any of the cushioning in place under the Sandinistas, resulted in two paralyzing **general strikes**, which forced the government to alter much of its programme. Violeta Chamorro's inner circle, the members of the cabinet who effectively decided policy, managed to resolve the crisis by working with the Sandinista leadership during the months of the strikes; in doing so, they alienated the extreme right-wing element in the coalition, which wanted to crush Sandinismo once and for all.

To her credit, Violeta Chamorro managed to hold the government together during the six-year term, but during the **1996 election campaign** right-wing forces gathered around the former Mayor of Managua, **Arnoldo Alemán**. His party, the Partido Liberal Constitucionalista (PLC), was a splinter group of the larger National Liberal Party (PLN), the political vehicle of Anastasio Somoza.

The Sandinistas' chances of defeating the Liberals suffered a blow a year before the election when there was a damaging split in the party. A moderate faction led by ex-Vice President Sergio Ramirez broke away, leaving Sandinista leader Daniel Ortega in charge of the remnants. The result was that Alemán and the PLC won the election – narrowly and controversially – and formed another coalition government, this time more openly committed to the destruction of Sandinismo and more closely aligned with the Catholic Church and the US policy of global integration.

■ The Alemán government

Many Nicaraguans saw the **Alemán victory** as proof that the counter-revolutionary movement had not only won, but had welcomed Somocismo back into Nicaragua. For many Sandinistas, this was a dispiriting, even heartbreaking, conclusion. In addition, many political neutrals were concerned that the Alemán administration would lead to **political cronyism** and **corruption** – failings of which his mayoral administration of Managua was frequently accused.

The Sandinistas and the governing PLC clashed repeatedly in the early years of the Alemán presidency, although both parties also suffered internal conflicts caused primarily by the authoritarian styles of the party leaders. In 1998, the reputation of FSLN leader Daniel Ortega was severely tested by accusations of rape and sexual abuse made by his stepdaughter Zoilamérica Narvaez. Ortega disappeared from public office to fight the charges – which were never proven, although his stepdaughter continued to accuse him – but later returned to the political fray and began to exercise an even tighter grip over the FSLN. Meanwhile, President Alemán also strengthened his control over the governing PLC party, as allegations of fraud and corruption, along with doubts over his mental stability, began increasingly to be heard.

The PLC approached the problem of reviving Nicaragua's economy with the standard neoliberal cure-alls of globalization, privatization and free-market economics. But although Nicaragua achieved rapid economic growth, the **distribution of wealth** remained concentrated in the hands of a privileged few, while the initial economic successes were followed by a period of severe recession. Inevitably, widespread financial hardship was accompanied by growing accusations of illicit enrichment within government circles – one report suggested that Alemán had amassed a personal fortune of between US$26 and US$40 million during 1990–97.

As if the life of most Nicaraguans was not already hard enough, in October 1998, **Hurricane Mitch** hit the region, causing massive flooding and landslides in central and northern Nicaragua. Many bridges, roads and villages were washed away, 500,000 homes were damaged and some 2500 people were killed. The hurricane also had a devastating impact on agriculture across the country, with widespread crop damage, while many towns were cut off for weeks by the intense flooding and burst rivers. The financial damage, though hard to calculate, ran into billions of dollars.

■ The new millennium

By the beginning of the new millennium, most statistics rated Nicaragua the second poorest country in the Americas, after Haiti, with two million Nicaraguans living on an income of less than a dollar a day, and the first year of the new century saw no signs of improvement. Foreign donor countries threatened to suspend aid for **post-Hurricane Mitch reconstruction** because of the government's lack of transparency and the uncertain distribution of foreign donations. And although the tourist and manufacturing industries showed signs of growth, the economy remained depressed, while two banks, Interbank and Bancafé, collapsed amid scandal and allegations of fraud that tainted both the FSLN and the PLC. As if this were not enough, an **earthquake**, with its epicentre in Laguna de Apoyo, killed six

people in Masaya and damaged over 4000 homes; this was followed in October 2000 by persistent rains provoked by **Hurricane Keith** which caused further widespread damage and made many people homeless in the west and north of Chinandega.

Politically, 2000 also saw some dubious horse-trading between the two leading parties, as the FSLN and the PLC worked together to create a new electoral law which now excludes many small political parties from participating in the political process. The new law was put to test in the **municipal elections** in November 2000 when violence flared in parts of the north, as election results were severely delayed, despite it being clear that the Sandinistas had won in many areas, including the prized mayoral seat of Managua. Discontent was also strongly felt in the Northern Atlantic region, where the indigenous YATAMA party was excluded from the election process.

Support for the Sandinistas was still growing at the beginning of 2001, though this was due more to the Alemán government's unpopularity rather than any clearly stated political manifesto of its own. It remains to be seen, however, whether an FSLN government – should it win the forthcoming election – will be able to convince the world of its ability to manage the economy, while the election of Republican George W. Bush to the US presidency could contribute to a further hardening of the FSLN's anti-US stance. Politics aside, most Nicaraguans are tired of conflict, and more than anything want peace, justice and democracy, although faced with poverty, unemployment, ongoing recession, uncertainty over land ownership and political instability, these dreams seem more remote than ever.

CHAPTER 22

MANAGUA AND AROUND

H otter than an oven and crisscrossed by anonymous highways, there can't be a more tourist-unfriendly capital than **MANAGUA**. Less a city in the European sense than a conglomeration of neighbourhoods and commercial districts, Managua offers few sights or cultural experiences of the type you can have in other Central American cities – in fact, most visitors are so disturbed by the lack of street names or any real centre to the city that they get out as fast as they can. Being a tourist in Managua does require some tenacity, but there *are* things to enjoy, and as Nicaragua's largest city and home to a quarter of its population, the city occupies a key position in the nation's economy and psyche. Unfortunately, it's difficult as a tourist in Managua to enter into "real" Nicaraguan life unless you have a local contact, due both to the lack of public spaces and meeting places like cafés or galleries and the fact that Managuans' social life is based in their own neighbourhoods, in churches, discos and playgrounds.

Set on the southern shore of **Lago de Managua**, the city is hot, low-lying and swampy, the flatness of its setting relieved only by the few eroded volcanoes and volcanic craters a few kilometres inland. The city is home to Nicaragua's few national museums and cultural organizations, most of them in the old **ruined centre**, whose historic cathedral is worth visiting, along with the Palacio Nacional, a museum of Nicaragua's culture and the home of its national library. Still, the reality is that there are few sights of interest, though the good news is that most of the city's modest attractions can be found within a few blocks of each other – an advantage in the draining heat.

Meanwhile, attempts are being made to establish a new commercial centre in the south along the **Carretera a Masaya**, just over the hill of Laguna de Tiscapa. A new Metrocentro shopping centre has opened here, along with hotels, restaurants, bars and cinemas, while the nearby district of **Altamira** boasts a number of elegant restaurants and cafés serving tourists and the city's smart set. Another feature of post-earthquake Managua is the proliferation of *centros comerciales*, mostly low-slung North American-style **shopping malls**, with banks, supermarkets and secure parking.

Even if the city's tourist sights have been given a lick of paint (for the most part paid for by the Dutch, Austrian or Chinese governments), the majority of Managuans are still very poor. This begs a mention only because **street crime** is on the rise, and Managua has developed a reputation as a dangerous city – not so much for foreigners as for Managuans, since gang warfare is an increasing problem. Even so, it's best to travel by taxi, even in the daytime; not to walk around at night; and generally to be on your guard.

For an explanation of **accommodation price codes**, see p.468.

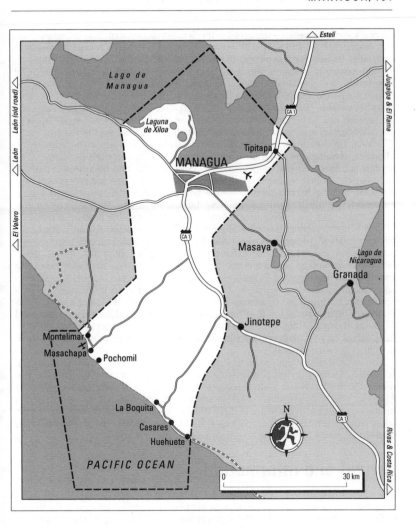

Some history

Founded as a new capital city by the Spanish in 1858 as a foil to the warring political factions of León and Granada, from the beginning Managua was intended to represent the political middle ground. But the ground itself proved the problem: Managua sits smack on top of no fewer than eleven **seismic faults**, and the ground by the lakeshore is sandy and unstable. The earthquake of March 1931 destroyed most of the city, and what Managuans managed to rebuild was largely razed by a fire just five years later. Again the city was rebuilt, with modern commercial buildings of four or five storeys, wide streets, traffic lights and shops, only to be completely devastated by another **earthquake** on December 23, 1972. This one claimed over ten thousand lives and left many more homeless.

For a variety of reasons – the greed of the Somoza dictatorship, who intercepted foreign emergency aid and sold it to victims at inflated prices; the refusal of insurance companies (mostly Somoza-owned) to pay out disaster damages; and the Revolution – the **old centre** of Managua was never rebuilt, while fighting during the **1978–79 Revolution** caused further damage to buildings. The Sandinista government wanted to rebuild the centre, using donated foreign funds, but this never happened and for many years "downtown" Managua remained a ruined shell of scruffy fields, skeletal ruins and old parking lots turned into graffiti-sprayed basketball courts, while squatters colonized the derelict spaces and constructed makeshift homes among the ruins.

During the Contra war many people fled violence in rural areas and migrated to Managua, creating new **neighbourhoods** and expanding the city's perimeter. (The wealthy still tend to live in neighbourhoods called *repartos* and *residenciales*; *colonias* were largely created by the Sandinistas in order to house specific professions, like teachers, and the barrios tend to be the poorer areas, where squatters and rural migrants try to eke out a living.) Following the war, during the 1990s, the city's mayor – and Nicaragua's future president – Arnoldo Alemán began the process of restoring the old centre, erecting expensive fountains and, unfortunately, having many of the famous murals of the Sandinista era painted over, thereby losing forever some of Latin America's best examples of political street art. Elected president in 1996, Alemán determined to resurrect the long-neglected central district, centred on an opulent new **Casa Presidencial** (Presidential Palace). Built against seismologists' advice, this salmon-and-mustard-coloured carbuncle is widely detested, and seen by Managuans as a reminder of the greed and mismanagement that has plagued them under Alemán's government. Other parts of the area have also been re-landscaped with new plazas and fountains, though the old centre still lacks focus and few local people spend any time here, except on weekend evenings when they come to watch the music-and-light show in front of the old cathedral.

The 1990s also saw the return of some of the **"Miami boys"** – businessmen and influential families who had fled revolutionary Nicaragua to settle in Miami. The current political climate has enticed some to return, and with them have come their American values, air-conditioned 4WDs and alarm-studded mansions. New bars and restaurants catering to the tastes of these *nicas ricas* have sprung up, and – even if the cover charges are high, the drinks expensive and the clientele more South Floridan than Nicaraguan – they have at least improved the nightlife scene.

Arrival and information

The majority of travellers arrive in central Managua on the **international** Ticabus services from either Honduras or El Salvador in the north or from San José in Costa Rica to the south. Buses from within Nicaragua arrive at one of several crowded, noisy and generally chaotic **urban marketplaces** that also serve as bus terminals. For **drivers** Managua is a disconcerting city in which to arrive; the lack of a definable centre and landmarks – not to mention road signs or directions – makes driving into the city a stressful experience, especially coupled with zealous traffic cops and aggressive Managuan drivers.

The good news about arriving by air or bus is the abundance of **taxis**. If you know where you are going to stay, it's helpful to have the address given to you in terms of neighbourhood and distance from a well-known **landmark**; no one uses street addresses in Managua, and taxi drivers will find places by its relation to a well-known city fixture. Distances are measured in metres as much as in blocks – in local parlance 100m is a city block or *cuadra*. Sometimes an archaic measure, the *vara*, is also used: one *vara* (a yard) is interpreted as roughly equivalent to a metre. To confuse the issue still further, many Managuans do not use the **cardinal points** in their usual form: in Managua north becomes *al lago* – towards the lake; *al sur* is south; *arriba* – literally, "up", is to the east; and *abajo*, "down", is to the west. So, "del Hotel Inter-Continental una cuadra [cien metros] arriba y dos cuadras [doscientos metros] al lago" means one block east and two blocks north of the *Hotel Inter-Continental*. For clarity, we've used blocks and the usual cardinal points in addresses throughout.

By air

All international flights and the vast majority of domestic ones arrive at Managua's **Augusto César Sandino International Airport**, 12km east of Managua. The one bank there, Banpro, changes US dollars and gives cash advances at a reasonable rate but won't change travellers' cheques. You can pay for everything (including a taxi to the centre) in dollars, but if you really want **córdobas**, outside banking hours you'll have to hike across the Carretera Norte outside the airport and try the *Hotel Las Mercedes*. Local and international **telephone** calls (including Sprint and USA Direct services) can be made at the airport's Enitel office (daily 7am–6.45pm). You'll find **car rental** agencies in the arrivals hall at the northern end of the airport.

The **buses** that ply the Carretera Norte into town are always crowded; should you manage to squeeze onto one, you'll be a tempting target for the many practised thieves operating on Managua's buses – taxis are definitely the way to go. A **taxi** from the arrivals gate into town costs US$7, although this figure can double after dark; walking out to the Carretera Norte can save you at least two dollars on the fare.

When you come to leave, note that all international departures are subject to a US$25 **departure tax** which must be paid (in dollars or córdobas) at check-in.

By international bus

The majority of travellers arrive in Nicaragua on the international Ticabus or King Quality services from San Salvador, Tegucigalpa or San José. All Ticabuses arrive at the **Ticabus terminal** (two blocks east and one block south of the old Cine Dorado) in barrio Martha Quezada, a neighbourhood just west of the Plaza Inter shopping centre and about as central as you get in Managua. The **King Quality** (222-6094) **terminal** is directly opposite Ticabus. If you come in on the **Sirca** services from San José, you arrive in the south of the city, near the Universidad Centroamericana, four blocks north of the Shell station.

Taxi drivers wait for the Ticabus to arrive; they may try to charge innocents a **gringo fare** (currently anything above US$1.20 for a journey within Managua), so be ready to argue for a reasonable fare and agree on a price before you get in. It's worth remembering that most of the affordable accommodation is only a very short walk away from the Ticabus terminal itself.

By domestic bus

Buses from elsewhere in Nicaragua arrive at one of three city markets. Coming from Masaya, Granada, Rivas or other destinations in the **south**, you'll arrive at the **Mercado Roberto Huembes** near the Carretera a Masaya on the southeastern edge of the city. A **taxi** from here to the centre should cost around US$1–1.50. Regular **express minivans** also run to and from Masaya and Granada from a small unmarked terminal on the highway opposite La UCA – all city taxi drivers will know how to find this terminal. Buses from the **north** and **east** – Estelí, Matagalpa, Jinotega, Ocotal, Somoto, Boaco, Chontales, San Carlos and El Rama – arrive at the terminal in the **Mercado Mayoreo** in barrio Concepción, near the airport. The Mayoreo is somewhat more organized and safer than other terminals. Buses from the **northwest** towns of León and Chinandega use the busy **Mercado Israel Lewites** in the southwest of the capital. No matter which market you arrive at, keep an eye on your belongings, especially at night. **Taxis** from Mayoreo to the centre will cost about (US$2–3). As always, agree on a fare before you get in.

Information

The only place in Managua equipped to provide information is Managua's **Inturismo** office, one block west of the old *Hotel Inter-Continental* (Mon–Fri 8.30am–12.30pm & 1.30–5pm; ☎222-2962). Taxis will know it as the Ministerio de Turismo or, more simply,

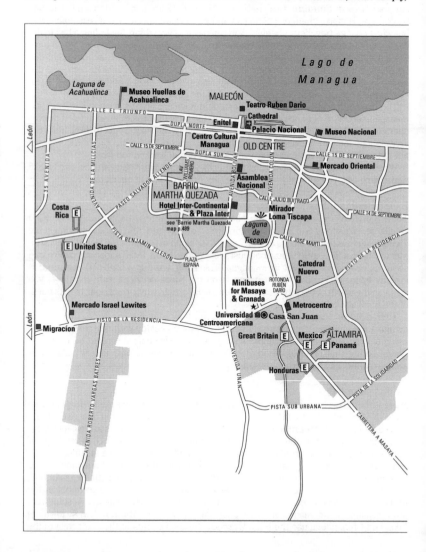

as the Turismo. If there's no one there, ask the security guard at the corner entrance to phone for you and someone will come and open the door. The staff are well-intentioned and some speak English, although they don't have much in the way of handouts. It's worth buying the excellent city map of Managua (US$2.50) from them, if available. You may also be able to pick up a copy here of the useful bimonthly *Guía Fácil Nicaragua* (US$1), which lists cultural events and entertainment throughout the country, with features on regions and tourist activities. Transport schedules are also sometimes included and there's usually a helpful map of Managua on the inside back cover. If Inturismo don't have any copies, try the *Casa del Café* (see p.493) and at the larger hotels.

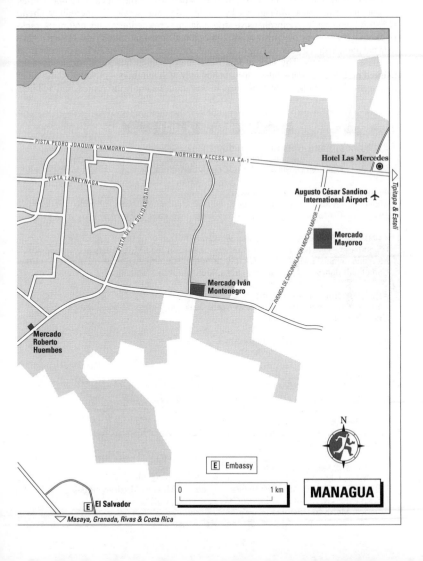

City transport

Managua's heat and incoherent layout make it a disconcerting city for travellers to negotiate, and some form of transport is essential. Buses are the cheapest way to get around, but the abundant taxis are more straightforward to use and safer, particularly at night.

Buses

If your confidence and Spanish are up to it, it's worth taking the **bus** at least once, for an insight into how most Managuans live. While the bus service is incredibly **cheap** (US$0.20) and fairly comprehensive, the amazing crowdedness and notorious **pick-pockets** – the two are obviously related – are a real deterrent. The crush makes it hard to avoid theft; keeping your money in an inside pocket or clutching your bag on your front are wise precautions. The lack of bus route maps, signed bus stops, or destinations marked on the bus itself – buses are labelled only with numbers – make anything other than a simple trip hopelessly confusing. However, locals know the routes, and will help

---

USEFUL BUS ROUTES

#108 Santa Clara – Socrates Sandino
Carretera Norte, Migración, Mercado Oriental, Nueva Rotunda Santo Domingo, Pista de la Resistencia, Máximo Jeréz, Centro Comercial Managua, Mercado Huembes.

#109 Socrates Sandino – Malecón
Malecón, Teatro Nacional Ruben Dario, Centro Cultural, Palacio Nacional, *Hotel Inter-Continental*, Largaespada, El Dorado, Mercado Huembes.

#110 Las Piedrecitas – Mercado Mayor
US embassy, Siete Sur, Pista de la Resistencia (or San Juan 11, as it has been renamed), Mercado Israel Lewites, the UCA (University of Central America), Altamira, Centro Comercial Managua, Mercado Huembes, Mercado Ivan Montenegro.

#112 Miraflor – Vía Libertad
Carretera Sur, Linda Vista, Carretera Norte, Malecón, Teatro Nacional Ruben Dario, Mercado Ivan Montenegro.

#113 Las Piedrecitas – Buenos Aires
Batahola Sur, El Carmen, Martha Quezada.

#117 Villa Jose Benito Escobar – San Juan
Carretera Norte, Villa Revolución, Rubenia, Mercado Huembes, Colonia Centroamérica, Centro Comercial Camino de Oriente, Av UNAN.

#118 Siete Sur – Manuel Fernández
Siete Sur, Pista de la Resistencia, El Recreo, Plaza España, Martha Quezada, Ciudad Jardín.

#119 Las Brisas – 19 Junio
Las Brisas, Linda Vista, Monseñor Lezcano, Plaza España, Pista de la Resistencia, Metro Centro, Los Robles, Carretera a Masaya, Mexican embassy, British embassy, Altamira, *Casa del Café*, La Colonia, Colonia Centro América, Mercado Huembes.

you find the right stop. Services start at 5am and continue until 10pm, becoming less frequent from about 6pm onwards. For a rundown of the main city bus routes, see opposite.

Certain parts of the city are **dangerous** and should be avoided by foreigners. If a bus breaks down or you get off in the wrong place and find yourself in an unfamiliar neighbourhood, don't walk around looking lost; approach a friendly-looking local and ask them to stay with you until you are safely in a taxi.

Taxis

Managua **taxis** are a plentiful mixture of spanking new imported models and heroic old Ladas that struggle around the city's streets. Taxis with red licence plates are officially registered and locals will tell you that these are safer and more reliable. Generally **cheap**, and with friendly, talkative drivers, they are always in good supply – listen out for honking drivers in search of custom. **Sharing** may sometimes save you a bit of money, and you could try flagging down an already occupied taxi if it seems to be going your way (equally, don't be surprised if a taxi you're already in takes other customers on board during your journey), though drivers will accept an additional passenger only if everyone is headed in vaguely the same direction. Fares are about US\$1–1.50 per person, depending on distance. Drivers may be open to negotiation if you are in a group going to the same destination.

Driving

Driving in Managua itself is not recommended. The city can seem like one endless freeway, with no street signs – confidence and a good city map are both essential. Should you get lost and find yourself in one of the various rough parts of the city, roll up your windows and lock doors, especially at traffic lights. It's not safe to leave your car on the street, but most upscale hotels have secure **car parks**. For exploring outside of Managua, however, a car is a definite bonus; see p.496 for a list of **rental** agencies.

Accommodation

Site of the Ticabus terminal, the **barrio Martha Quezada**, a neighbourhood twelve blocks south of the old ruined city centre and just west of the *Hotel Inter-Continental*, is the place for cheap, hospedaje-type accommodation, and also has some of the best hotels and guesthouses in Managua. Directions and **addresses** in the barrio use the local landmarks of the *Hotel Inter-Continental*, the Ticabus terminal, and the Cine Dorado (now closed), west of the Ticabus terminal.

During the Revolution years most foreigners stayed within this eight-by-five block area and it became something of an international community, filled with cafés and restaurants where politics and literature were debated over beers by visitors from all over the world. These days the barrio is definitely not the buzzing place it used to be. A mixture of middle-class homes and very poor dwellings, some with only corrugated iron for doors, the barrio's hot, eventless streets have a forlorn look. There's nothing much to do here except sleep, though there are still a number of good local **cafetines** and **restaurants**.

Accommodation in Martha Quezada is scattered in a two-block radius on either side of the Ticabus terminal. Arriving at the terminal, you will be met by touts, usually children, offering to take you to a hospedaje. They receive a percentage from the hotel owner for bringing people off the Ticabus and there's no harm in going with them, since you're under no obligation to stay if you don't like the hospedaje they take you to. Most hospedajes in Martha Quezada are family-run and – it must be said – not overwhelmingly friendly; new ones are opening all the time and there's a plentiful supply of reasonably priced rooms throughout the year.

There's no real concentration of hotels **elsewhere in the city**: several upscale airport-type hotels are located on the Carretera Norte near the international airport and near Metrocentro, and there are a few hotels in the residential neighbourhood of Bolonia, immediately south of barrio Martha Quezada. One or two other places can be found near the Universidad Centroamericana (UCA), towards the south of the city.

As elsewhere in Nicaragua, Managua accommodation tends to be spartan, with water and electricity prone to cuts. Because of the city's amazing heat and humidity, Managua is one place in the country where you might want to shell out for a noisy old **air-conditioning** unit, though this can cost up to double the price of a room with a fan. Many hospedajes in barrio Martha Quezada are open to discounts of a couple of dollars for groups or for long stays – it's worth asking.

Barrio Martha Quezada

Hospedaje El Bambú, one block east of the Ticabus terminal (look for the bamboo door). Friendly Marie-Elena and family run a hospedaje with six rather dark rooms with fan and shared bath, set around a pleasant covered patio area. Meals on request. For reservations, call Marie-Elena's sister Nubia on ☎222-3180. ②.

Hospedaje El Dorado, two blocks west of the Ticabus terminal. Very cheap and quiet family-run hospedaje set back from the street. Friendly and secure, but rooms are stuffy, grouped around a small interior patio. All rooms have ceiling fan; some also have private bath. ①.

Hospedaje El Molinito, half a block from the Ticabus terminal. Basic but reasonable-value budget hotel with small rooms and shared bath, popular with backpackers. Breakfast available.①.

Hospedaje Quintana, one block north and one block west of the Ticabus terminal. For many years a popular place among *internacionalistas*, this spotlessly clean, family-run hospedaje has big rooms with fans and sturdy beds. Some are quite dark, so look before choosing. Laundry service available. ②.

Hospedaje Santos, one block north and two blocks west of the Ticabus terminal (☎222-3713). Sprawling and ramshackle, this hospedaje is very popular among travellers, with tons of atmosphere, revolutionary art on the walls and an indoor patio with cable TV. Rooms, however, are dark and none too clean – try to get one upstairs, where ventilation is better. All have ceiling fan, and some come with private bath. ①.

Jardín de Italia, one block east and one block north of the Ticabus terminal (☎222-7967). Five comfortable, very clean and well-ventilated rooms with private bath; a/c rooms cost twice the price of those with fans. ③, ④ with a/c.

Los Felipe, opposite the *Hospedaje Santos*, one and a half blocks west of the Ticabus terminal (☎ & fax 222–6501). Clean and friendly new hotel with bright décor and helpful staff. The small but comfortable rooms have bath, TV and fan, and Internet and laundry services are available. A swimming pool and café are under construction. ③–④.

Margaritas (☎222-4106, fax 222-4240), one block north and one block west of the Ticabus terminal. Medium-sized hotel with 24-hour service, bar, restaurant and Internet access. A variety of rooms are available, some with TV, a/c and private bath – ask to see a selection before choosing. ②–④.

Morgut, in Bolonia, two blocks north and five blocks east of the Ticabus terminal (☎222-2166, fax 222-3543). Small and comfortable hotel in a relatively well-to-do area. All seven rooms have TV and the helpful staff can arrange tours and car rental. Advance reservations needed. ⑤.

Elsewhere in the city

Casa de Huéspedes Sáenz, Planes de Altamira #3, Carretera a Masaya, Altamira, one block from the *Hotel Princess* next to *La Piazzetta* restaurant (☎277-3733, *iva@datatex.com.ni*). Family-run guesthouse with spacious, impeccably clean rooms with TV, a/c and private bath in a residential neighbourhood between Metrocentro and Altamira. Breakfast included. ⑤–⑥.

Casa de Huéspedes San Juan, C Esperanza 560, behind the Universidad Centroamericana – known locally as "La UCA" (☎278-3220, fax 278-0419). Welcoming guesthouse in a quiet neighbourhood. The spacious rooms are arranged around a flower-filled patio; some have private bath, and all have fans. Meals are available with advance notice. The hotel is popular, so reserve in advance. ④.

RESTAURANTS & BARS

Antojitos	D
Antojitos Chinos	A
Bar Shannon	F
Las Cazuelas	B
Mirna's	E
Rincón Marino	C

ACCOMMODATION

Hospedaje El Bambú	9
Hospedaje El Dorado	7
Hospedaje Quintana	5
Hospedaje Santos	2
Hospedaje El Molinito	8
Hotel Los Felipe	3
Hotel Jardín de Italia	6
Hotel Margaritas	4
Hotel Morgut	1

Casa Fiedler, near Plaza España, two blocks south and two blocks west from the CST building (☎266-6622). Rooms are dark and unappealing, but the management is friendly and knowledgeable – the guesthouse has long been popular with visiting *internacionalistas*. Prices vary according to room – ask to see several. Travellers' cheques are accepted, and good breakfasts are available on request. ③.

Colon, (☎278-2490, fax 267-0191, *hcolon@ibw.com.ni*), two blocks east of *Domino's Pizza* on Carretera a Masaya, Altamira. Comfortable, small hotel located amid new restaurants and cafés in the smart Altamira district and offering a variety of rooms, some with a/c, TV and private bath with hot water. The restaurant serves all meals and credit cards are accepted. Reservations recommended. ⑤–⑥.

King's Palace Hotel, Carretera a Masaya Km 5, Altamira (☎277-4548, fax 278-2456, *hotelkingspalace@munditel.com.ni*). Unpretentious hotel located on a busy road between Metro Centro and Altamira, with sixteen comfortable rooms, some with a/c. The attached cafeteria has an outside terrace and bar and does good breakfasts. ⑤–⑥.

Las Mercedes, Km 11, Carretera Norte, very close to airport (☎263-1011, fax 263-1083, *lm@munditel.com.ni*). Best Western hotel catering for business travellers – the airport location makes it a useful stop if you're arriving late or leaving early. The comfortable rooms have TV, a/c and bath, and there's a reasonable on-site restaurant, plus bar and swimming pool. ⑧.

The City

For the visitor, sprawling Managua can be thankfully divided into a few distinct areas. The **old ruined centre** on the lakeshore is the site of the city's tourist attractions, such as they are, including the few impressive colonial-style buildings that survived the 1931 and 1972 earthquakes, like the slowly decaying old municipal **cathedral** and the magnificently restored **Palacio Nacional**. **Lago de Managua**, which forms such a pretty backdrop to the old centre, is severely **polluted** from raw sewage and regular dumpings of garbage, chemical waste, and mercury. The air doesn't seem any cleaner; winds from the lake blow dust around the city and old buses, schoolbuses and Ladas belch fumes into an increasingly crowded city.

Twelve blocks south from the old centre, most of Managua's hospedajes and restaurants are clustered in the **barrio Martha Quezada**, a district that was home to the international community during the Revolution. Just to the east, but visible from everywhere, is the city's main landmark, the **Hotel Inter-Continental** (not to be confused with the new *Inter-Continental Metro Centro* hotel at the Metrocentro shopping mall in the south of the city), whose white form, reminiscent of a Maya pyramid, sails above the city – it's about 1km south of the ruined old city centre, and not worth a visit in its own right, though you'll probably end up passing by it anyway as it stands at the junction of Av Bolívar, which runs north–south from the lake to Plaza España, and C Julio Buitrago, a major east–west thoroughfare. Many of the city's banks, airline offices and the well-stocked La Colonia supermarket can be found a further 2km south, around **Plaza España**. To the southeast of the city, a new commercial district has grown up along the **Carretera a Masaya** between the **Metrocentro** shopping centre and the upmarket suburb of **Altamira**.

The old centre

Most of Managua's "sights" are concentrated in the **old city centre**, completely trashed in the 1972 earthquake and until recently a haunting maze of fields, the concrete skeletons of buildings, burnt-out cars and impromptu basketball courts. Much of the old centre is now under redevelopment, with new plazas and monuments being constructed, and fairground rides and places to eat and drink springing up along the lake's edge. If you don't mind the heat, you can walk the twelve blocks from barrio Martha Quezada to the old centre, or take bus #109 north from the corner of Av Bolívar and C Julio Buitrago.

Plaza de la Republica

The centrepiece of the old centre is the recently renovated **Plaza de la Republica**. On the eastern side of the square stands the wrecked ash-grey Catedral Santiago de los Caballeros, known as the **Catedral Viejo**, an eerie monument to a destroyed city, decaying a little more with each passing day. Funds donated from foreign governments have enabled the cathedral to be re-roofed with a transparent fibreglass cap, and for cut stone to be laid on the formerly grass floor. The old clock, which used to front the right-hand tower and which still bore the time that the big earthquake struck (12.32am on December 23, 1972), has been taken down for cleaning. Inside, birds fly through the ruined interior, where semi-exposed murals still line the walls, as do leaning stone angels and saints, some of them with their wings cracked. Though the cathedral is officially closed to visitors, the guard will usually allow you in for a few córdobas (a small extra payment is required to take photos). There's a colourful **music and choreographed fountain** display in front of the cathedral daily at 6pm – it's particularly popular at weekends when families, young couples and a large portion of Managua's street traders descend on the normally empty plaza.

Since its blue marble and yellow stucco renovation it's hard to believe that the **Palacio Nacional** (daily 8am–4pm; US$1), next to the cathedral, was the scene of a cinematic **coup d'état**. On August 22, 1978, Sandinista commandos disguised as National Guard soldiers ran through these cool corridors and, in an audacious operation, captured the deputies of the National Assembly, effectively bringing to an end the rule of the dictator Somoza. This columned building was the seat of power during the long years of Somoza rule: the Colombian writer Gabriel García Márquez called it *el partenón bananero* – the banana parthenon. The Palacio is still a functioning government building but has had much of its interior turned into a **museum and art gallery**. Many of its walls are covered with colourful murals by foreign artists that run the gamut from Mexican Arnold Belkin's socialist-realist depiction of the Mexican and Nicaraguan revolutions to Russian surrealism. As well as rooms showing dark and derivative religious paintings, there are **modern Nicaraguan art** exhibits, and a rather good display of Nicaraguan handicrafts, plus a few pre-Columbian artefacts. Upstairs is the new home of the **Biblioteca Nacional**, which has been beautifully furnished and decorated with funds donated by the government of China.

To the southwest of the Palacio National is the distinctive green building which now houses the **Centro Cultural Managua** (☎228-4045, fax 228-4046). The former home of the Gran Hotel, the low-slung, tasteful wooden structure gives you a bit of an idea of how pre-earthquake Managua looked. The downstairs area hosts sporadic exhibitions and seminars, including the **Sábado de Artesanía**, a craft fair held on the first Saturday of each month. Prices are higher than in the Mercado Roberto Huembes (see p.495), the outdoor Managua market which has the largest selection of crafts, but lower than in the *galerías* and art shops. The centre's upper floors house many of the country's arts organizations and it's worth going upstairs just to see the **historic photographs** lining the corridor. Some show Managua before the 1972 earthquake – an attractive city of palm trees and some colonial architecture; others, taken immediately following the quake, show crumpled buildings, crushed cars and gaping holes in the road – a sobering juxtaposition.

Sadly, the plaza's north side is now home to the upstart salmon-and-mustard eyesore of the **Casa Presidencial**, finished in 2000. Constructed against the advice of eminent seismologists, the building is an unflattering monument to the style and substance of Arnoldo Alemán's vainglorious presidency, and a pale imitation of the far more arresting Palacio Nacional opposite, whose style it apes, but singularly fails to match.

The lakefront

Perched like a huge white futurist bird 200m north of the Plaza de la Republica, near the swampy shores of Lago de Managua, is the **Teatro Nacional Rubén Darío**, Managua's main cultural venue. Foreign orchestras and dance troupes on tour perform here, along with Nicaraguan theatre groups. Check the *Guía Fácil* or *La Prensa* for details of events – though bear in mind that theatre performances are in Spanish only. If the building is open, it's worth going inside to see the massive chandeliers, marble floors and the stirring view out to the lake from the enormous second-floor windows. Outside the theatre, a determined attempt has been made to transform the lakeshore boardwalk, or **Malecón**, with bars and food kiosks, plus a Ferris wheel and a couple of fairground rides. It gets quite lively at weekends, though it's fairly deserted during the week except for stray kissing teenage couples. Just south of the *Malecón* is the vast **Plaza de la Fe Juan Pablo II**, a recently constructed square whose central obelisk commemorates Pope John Paul II's two visits to Nicaragua. Like the *Malecón*, the plaza is rarely busy, and is also one of the fiercest sun traps in the city, though it looks better at night when floodlighting adds some definition to its vast expanse.

There are pleasant views across the lake to the north from the Malecón, where **Volcán Mombotombo** and little **Mombotombito** sit side by side against the horizon on the far shore of the lake, 50km away. Mombotombo's capacity for destruction is evoked in the **Museo Huellas de Acahualinca** (theoretically Mon–Fri 8am–noon & 1pm–3pm; US$2), just west of the Malecón in barrio Acahualinca (take a taxi or bus #112), a shabby little monument to a sort of Managuan Pompeii. On display are animal and human footprints from prehistoric unfortunates fleeing one of the volcano's frequent eruptions – preserved in volcanic ash, the footprints date back between 10,000 and 6000 years. In any other context this little display wouldn't merit a visit, but given that it's Managua, you might want to take a look if you have some time on your hands.

South of the old centre

Behind the *Hotel Inter-Continental*, a path winds upwards to the **Laguna de Tiscapa**, a small and unremarkable lake in the centre of the city. The views of the city are excellent, however, stretching north to Lago de Nicaragua and the distant volcanoes and south beyond the new cathedral towards Masaya. The area around Laguna de Tiscapa is loaded with historical importance: the presidential palace used to be situed here and the large, silhouetted statue of Sandino marks the spot of the revolutionary leader's assassination. The Somoza regime also built torture chambers near the lake.

About 1km south of the laguna is Managua's biggest concentration of residential and commercial neighbourhoods. The main thoroughfare through this southern part of the city is the **Carretera a Masaya**, bordered to the west by the university area and to the east by residential and shopping districts; this is also where you'll find the **Metrocentro** shopping centre, which boasts shops, a food court, banks, a modern cinema and the *Inter-Continental Metro Centro* hotel (not to be confused with the original *Hotel Inter-Continental* on the edge of the barrio Martha Quezada). A short walk from Metrocentro, in the middle of a field, is the unmissable Catedral Metropolitana de la Purísima Concepción, known simply as the **Catedral Nueva**, a remarkably unorthodox piece of architecture whose roof resembles a collection of large concrete hand-grenades. The interior is rather stark, with a bleeding figure of Christ encased in glass being the only interesting feature.

A further 1km south from the Metrocentro along Carretera a Masaya is the embassy neighbourhood of **Altamira**, the focus for new commercial and hotel construction in the city, which has a number of hotels, cafés, Internet offices and a good selection of international restaurants popular with the district's expat residents. A few kilometres further south on the Carretera a Masaya is the campus of the Universidad Centroamericana, or **La UCA**, as it's generally known, a tranquil place by Managuan standards, just off the major road to León and points north.

Eating and drinking

Wherever you walk in Managua – on the street, at the bus stop or even under a shady tree – you will find someone selling a drink or a *comida corriente*. Good, cheap food on the hoof is also easy to get in any of Managua's major **markets** – look out for *pupusas*, a Salvadorean concoction of cheese, tortillas, sauce and meat. Hygienically speaking, the food is safe to eat, and you can get a decent meal for as little as a dollar. Managua also has a surprisingly cosmopolitan selection of **restaurants**: Chinese, German, French, Italian, Peruvian, North American – even vegetarian. **Cafés** are thin on the ground, though, and the ones that do exist tend to be frequented by expats and wealthier Managuans.

Barrio Maria Quezada and around

Alemana, one block west of the *Antojitos* restaurant (see below). Good spot for a quick sandwich or piece of cake – there's also a large choice of rye and dark bread to take away. Closed Sun.

Ananda, next to the Montoya statue: from the Cine Dorado walk two blocks towards the lake then eight blocks west. Excellent vegetarian restaurant, set around a covered patio and garden, with a varied menu including a good-value *plato del día* and reasonably priced fresh juices. A meal plus drink will cost you around US$3–4. Closed Mon.

Antojitos, Av Bolívar, in front of the *Hotel Inter-Continental* (☎222-4866). Reasonable but expensive Mexican-Nicaraguan food and famous photographs of neon-lit downtown Managua before the 1972 earthquake.

Antojitos Chinos, C Julio Buitrago, one block west of *Hotel Morgut*. Acceptable Chinese cuisine served up in a huge thatched barn. Very popular at weekends. US$3–5 for a main course plus drink.

Las Cazuelas, opposite *Hospedaje Santos*. Small restaurant with a nice atmosphere serving local and international cuisine in the heart of barrio Martha Quezada. A meal will set you back around US$3–5.

Mirna's, one block west and south of the Ticabus terminal. Popular with locals and travellers staying in barrio Martha Quezada, this small, family-run place serves freshly prepared breakfasts and lunches – US$2–3 will buy you a good feed and drink.

Nacatamales el Dorado, in the *Residencial El Dorado*, over the Pista Radial, three and a half blocks south from the traffic lights (☎244-2755). Small place famous for its authentic Nicaraguan *nacatamales*, which is pretty much all they serve – one of the banana-leaf parcels washed down with a *refresco* will fill you up for US$0.75.

Rincón Catalan, one block west of the *Hotel Inter-Continental*. A favourite with well-to-do guests of the *Inter-Continental*, offering Spanish food with the emphasis on seafood and paella. A big meal with drinks costs around US$10.

Rincón Marino, one block west and half a block north of the Ticabus terminal. Rather upmarket for Martha Quezada, and a popular lunchtime choice for nearby office workers. The *arroz marinero* with shellfish and squid is good value at US$2.50, or try the *filete a la plancha* at US$4.

Altamira

Bongó, Km 5, Carretera a Masaya, just beyond the *King's Palace Hotel*. Upmarket restaurant serving a good range of Cuban food and drink. Regular music and promotional evenings. US$6–10.

Casa del Café, one block west of *Domino's Pizza* on the Carretera a Masaya. A favourite of wealthy Managuans and travellers, this open-air café serves good sandwiches, wonderful cakes and pies – try the *torta de limón* – and the best coffee in town. A two-course lunch costs US$10–20. They also sell English-language magazines and books downstairs, plus Nicaraguan export-grade coffee.

Cocina de Doña Haydée, Km 4, Carretera a Masaya, near the British embassy (☎278-7336). Well-established restaurant offering good Nica food in nice surroundings. It's also the only place in Managua to go for breakfast on a Sunday morning when everything else is closed.

La Casa de los Jugos, opposite *Pizzeria Valenti's*. In the heart of Altamira's restaurant zone, this is primarily a food store but also serves excellent fresh juices and *licuados* for a dollar a throw.

Los Ranchos, Km 3.5, Carretera Sur (☎266-0526). Popular steak joint serving huge portions – try the excellent brochettes or the filet mignon of tasty Nicaraguan beef. Count on US$10 for a full meal with dessert and a beer.

Panadería La Baguette, half a block west of the *Sorbet Inn* on the Carretera a Masaya. The makers of Managua's only genuine French-style baguettes (they're also sold in Colonia supermarkets) and a range of other delicacies.

Pizzeria Valenti's, one block east of *Domino's Pizza*, house no. 6 (☎277-5744). The outside patio, an ice-cold mug of draught beer and one of Valenti's excellent thin-crust pizzas make this unpretentious place one of the best in Managua. It's also good value considering the area: a pizza and a beer will cost about US$5.

Pollo La Radial, Col Maximo Jeréz, 20m south of the main entrance to Radial Santo Domingo on C Principal de Altamira (☎278-1114). Managuans say this budget family restaurant does the best chicken in town – it's roasted over a grill and served with rice, beans, plantains and salad. The atmosphere is relaxed, with swings and pets to keep children entertained.

Tacos Charros, Col Centroamerica, on the road to Mercado Huembes, in front of the Farmacia Vida. Tasty and cheap Mexican food in a busy, noisy atmosphere; good for a quick meaty taco if you're on your way to the Huembes market.

Nightlife and entertainment

There are plenty of places to **drink** and **dance** in Managua. Some of them are crowded with the young and reckless teenagers of the Nica rich. Others have grandmothers and adolescents dancing to the same music. The venues are often large ranchos, or palm-covered shelters, open to the warm Managua night air and whatever cooling breeze there happens to be. Most Nicas are fans of either rancho music (not unlike "country" – fairly unsophisticated and raucous) or merengue, but you can also hear plenty of salsa, disco and occasionally reggae.

Women generally don't go out dancing without a male escort as it can be dangerous on the street at night. Beware of overcharging in the shadier places – keep the bottles on the table and keep track of the bill if in doubt. While there have been reports of travellers being stung with outrageous bills and ending up in jail for non-payment, all the venues listed here should be OK. A beer that costs US$0.50 at a shop will cost you US$0.70–1.50 in a bar.

Bars and clubs

Bar Shannon, 50m from *Hospedaje El Bambú*. New Irish-owned bar in the heart of barrio Martha Quezada, though the design of the bar is more Nicaraguan than mock-Irish and the clientele is a good mix of locals and travellers. The owner can direct you to the popular late-night drinking and dancing spots on the fast-changing Managuan scene.

Cafe Amatl, one block south of the *Hotel Inter-Continental* (☎266-2486). The student crowd tends to hang out here because the outdoor ambience is nice, the food is pretty cheap (US$1.50) and the music good. Cover charge of US$1.50 if there's a live band.

Cats Club, one block north and two blocks east of the *Hotel Inter-Continental* (☎222-3232). Stylish club with a small but attractive dance floor and traditional salsa and merengue playlist, with a few US tunes thrown in. Expensive.

El Quetzal, in Col Centroamerica, in front of Registros Públicos. A barn-like dance joint where everybody gets up and dances into the small hours. Firmly off the tourist trail, with a neighbourhood atmosphere, cheap and filling Nicaraguan food and hot live salsa bands. Fri & Sat only.

La Bodeguita del Centro, in the Centro Cultural Managua. Small venue with concerts at weekends – by day it doubles as a lunch bar (try the healthy brown-bread sandwiches and *refrescos*, all for about US$2.50). There's a rare clean public washroom just outside the bar.

La Buena Nota, Km 3, Carretera Sur (☎266-9797). Famous throughout Nicaragua as the home base of Luis Enrique and Carlos Mejía Godoy, two popular guitar-playing and song-writing brothers who dominate the Nicaraguan music scene. Entrance US$6.

La Cavanga, on the northeast corner of the Centro Cultural Managua. A microcosm of Nicaraguan culture, this little bar plays traditional Nicaraguan music and is decorated with black and white photos of Old Managua and a few paintings by Ernesto Cardenal. It's one of the best bars in Managua, packed in the early evening with government workers and students having a beer or two.

Reggae City, Km 6, Carretera Norte (☎289-3803). The best Afro-Caribbean music venue and one of the best nights out in Managua, *Reggae City* has a family ambience, with kids and grandparents getting up for a dance. The fried chicken and cheap beer are a bonus. US$4 cover.

Ruta Maya, 150m east towards the fire station from the Montoya statue (☎222-5038). Famous music venue, hosting the band of the same name. Closed Sun.

Arts and entertainment

Cinema is a popular diversion for rich Nicas and the large foreign population in Managua – at US$3 and up, most other Managuans can't afford the price of a ticket. There's a four-screen Cinemark complex in the Metrocentro shopping mall showing the latest Hollywood movies, usually in English with Spanish subtitles, but it's best to check. Food in the cinemas is overpriced but there are plenty of restaurants nearby where you can get a good meal and a few beers. Similar films and similar prices can be found at the modern cinema complex in the Plaza Inter.

The **theatre** scene in Nicaragua is small but active, and is particularly strong in children's theatre, puppetry and folk dancing – good news for non-Spanish speakers – while adult theatre tends toward the Brechtian style that has been such a dynamic part of the theatre tradition throughout Latin America. The nation's main venue is the **Teatro Nacional Rubén Darío**. One of the few buildings in Managua to survive the 1972 earthquake, it is today recognized as one of the best theatres in Central America, with a main auditorium seating 1200 people, an exhibition space on the second floor, and an experimental theatre in the basement. Events are scheduled there most weekends and it's easy to get to, with bus #109 stopping right in front. Check the *Guía Fácil* or the listings in *La Prensa* for details of performances.

Shopping and markets

Managua's best shopping is to found in its characterful and varied **markets**. The **Mercado de Mayoreo** in barrio La Concepción, near the airport, is divided into separate areas or buildings for different types of produce: onions, lettuces, seafood, eggs, chickens, plantains and so on, and you can get a cheap meal at the market café while waiting to board buses heading north. In contrast, the famous **Mercado Oriental**, a few blocks southeast of the old centre, is a small, lawless city-within-a-city where you can buy just about anything, but need to keep a close eye on your pockets – take someone with you to watch your back and help carry your stuff. In the streets around the entrance to the market are several shops selling furniture and electrical goods. If you can carry it, it's worth buying a rocking chair here: beautifully made, they cost around US$25, and can be bought disassembled for carrying onto the plane.

Near the Carretera a Masaya in the south of the city, the **Mercado Roberto Huembes** is somewhat safer to wander around than the Oriental and has an excellent crafts section. You can find rocking chairs here, too, and some of the best hammocks in the world – everything from a simple net hammock, lightweight and perfect for the beach (US$3), to a luxury, two-person, woven cotton hammock with wooden separators and beautiful tassels (US$30). Products made of leather and skins are in abundance, but choose carefully as many of the species used are endangered. Traditional clothing is cheap, finely embroidered and perfect for the tropics. **Paintings** in the style of the artists' colony on the Solentiname Islands are available here, along with many fine pen-and-ink drawings and abstract works. You can buy Nicaraguan cigars (*puros*) as well as wicker products (*mimbre*) such as baskets, mats, chairs and wall hangings. Many of these crafts are produced using methods dating back to pre-Columbian times.

Markets apart, in these post-revolutionary days you can buy anything you want in Managua, and there are now plenty of large **supermarkets** along the Carretera Norte, as well as the well-stocked La Colonia supermarket just off Plaza España. You can also buy a lot of the basics at local *pulperías*, small shops set up in people's houses, which are never more than a couple of blocks away. **Fruit** and **vegetables** are cheapest at the weekend markets, when the growers come into town to sell their produce. Fresh produce tends to be more expensive elsewhere, unless you go to some of the bigger markets like the Oriental and the Mayoreo.

Listings

Airlines Air France, two and half blocks south of Rotonda Guegüense (☎266-2612 or 266-6615); Alitalia, one and a half blocks west of Los Pipitos (☎266-7030); American Airlines, Plaza España (☎266-3900); British Airways, in front of the old Hospital El Retiro (☎266-8268); Continental, Edif. Detirosa, Km 4.5, Carretera a Masaya (☎278-2834); Copa, Planes de Altamira, No. #9 (☎267-5438 or 267-0045); Iberia, Plaza España, Edificio Málaga (☎266-4296 or 266-4756); GrupoTaca, Edif. Barcelona, Plaza España (☎266-3136); JAL, north side of Plaza España (☎266-3588); KLM, in front of the west side of the Plaza España (☎266-8052/3); Lan Chile, Plaza España (☎266-7011 or 266-1381); United, Costado Este, Plaza España (☎266-6663).

Banks and exchange Central branches that exchange foreign currency include Banpro and Bancentro, both on the Carretera a Masaya near the *Hotel Princess*, and Banco de América Central, Plaza España. ATMs can be found on the basement and third floors of the Plaza Inter.

Car rental Auto Express, from the Plaza Inter traffic lights, one block to the lake and two blocks west (☎222-3816); Budget, one block west and one block south of the Montoya statue (☎266-6266); Hertz, Edificio Lang (☎266-8300 or Carretera a Masaya (☎266-8400); Hyundai, Km 5, Carretera a Masaya (☎278-1249 or 278-1382); Toyota, Casa Pellas, two blocks west of Gadala Maria (☎266-3620).

Embassies and consulates Canada, north side of Telcor, Zacarias Guerra (Mon–Thurs 9am–noon; ☎228-7574, fax 228-4821); Costa Rica, two blocks north and one block east of the Montoya statue (daily 9am–3pm; ☎266-2404); El Salvador, in Las Colinas, Pasaje Los Cerros, Av del Campo, Casa #142 (Mon–Fri 8am–2pm; ☎276-0160, fax 276-0712); Guatemala, Km 11.5, Carretera a Masaya (Mon–Fri 9am–1pm; ☎279-9834, fax 279-9610); Honduras, Km 12.5, Carretera a Masaya (Mon–Fri 9am–2pm; ☎278-3043, fax 279-8228); Panamá, one block north and half a block east of the *Hotel Colón* (Mon–Fri 8.30am–1pm; ☎266-8633); UK, Reparto Los Robles (Mon–Fri 9am–noon; ☎278-0014 or 278-0887, fax 278-4085); USA, Cancilleria, Km 4.5, Carretera Sur (Mon–Fri 7.30–9am; ☎266-6010 or 266-6012, fax 266-3865).

Immigration office Departamento de Inmigración Extranjería, Km 7, Carretera Sur (Mon–Fri 8am–noon & 2–4pm; ☎265-0014 or 265-0020; *www.migracion.gob.ni*).

Internet access *Kiosk*, Level 3, Plaza Inter (US$4/hr); *Kafé Internet*, Av Willams Romero, one block north of the Cine Dorado (US$3/hr); *Cyber Café*, Av Williams Romero, one block south of the Cine Dorado (US$3/hr); *Kafé Internet*, Km 5, Carretera a Masaya, adjacent to the *King's Palace Hotel* (US$3/hr). *Enitel*, main telephone office, three blocks west of the Catedral Viejo (US$3.50/hr).

Libraries and cultural institutes The Casa Ben Linder, three blocks south and one and a half blocks east of the Monseñor Lezcano statue (☎266-4373), is the Nicaraguan base for a number of primarily US voluntary groups and agencies. They maintain a small library.

Medical care The Hospital Bautista (Baptist Hospital) in barrio Largaespada, two blocks south and one and a half east of the Casa Ricardo Morales Aviles (☎249-7070 or 249-7277), is a good private hospital with an emergency department. Dr Enrique Sánchez Delgado, in Bosques de Altamira, Casa #417, two blocks east and half a block north of the Cine Altamira, speaks English and charges around US$30 for a consultation. Natural medicines are available from the Fundación Julie Marciacq in barrio José Isaías Gómez, two blocks east and two blocks north of the SINSA hardware store on C Principal de Altamira, Casa M-153 (☎278-6681).

Post office In the Enitel office (Mon–Fri 8am–4pm, Sat 8am–noon), three blocks west of the Catedral Viejo.

Supermarkets The two main chains are La Unión and La Colonia, which both sell everything you might possibly need, though at higher prices than in the markets. La Unión has branches in the Centro Comercial Ciudad Jardín and the Centro Comercial Belo Horizonte; La Colonia is in the Centro Comercial Plaza España and the Colonia Centroamerica Plaza de Compras.

Telephone office Enitel office three blocks west of the Catedral Viejo (daily 7am–10.30pm).

Travel agents Flights can be bought and reconfirmed at the following places; several also run organized tours (see p.499). Aeroamerica Tours, alongside the Banco Mercantil (☎266-3487); Aventurismo, half a block north of *Restaurante Wok*, Los Robles, Casa 143 (☎265-2063); Careli Tours, three blocks south of Plaza el Sol (☎278-2572); Tours Nicaragua, half a block east of San Francisco Church, Bolónia (☎266-8689); Senderos Tours, one block south and two blocks east of Gimnasio Hercules (☎278-3238); Tropical Tours, one block south and one west of La Casa de Obrero (☎266-1387); Tropical Travel, one block west and half a block north of Ciudad Jardín ITR (☎249-7548).

Out from the city

Beaches around Managua don't have the white sand and clear water of places like the Corn Islands or the beaches of San Juan del Sur and La Flor further south, but the water is warmer and they're easy to reach. Managuans visit on day-trips, particularly on national holidays, when the beaches – and public transport – get amazingly crowded, especially at Easter and Christmas: watch your belongings wherever you go.

The closest beaches to the city are **Pochomíl** and the nearby town of **Masachapa**, 3km beyond, around an hour and a half by hourly **bus** from the Mercado Israel Lewites. There's a small fee to enter Pochomíl, but once here you can settle in for the day, as there are restaurants all along the sand, and motorbikes and horses for rent. At the northern end of the beach, the *Villa del Mar* charges an extra entry fee of US$5 but has a freshwater swimming pool, toilets, showers, and large, comfortable ranchos where you can hang a hammock. The fee is redeemable in food and drink – a whole grilled fish costs US$7. You can rent rooms here, or at the hotel *Ticomar* (☎265-0210; ④) at the other end of the beach, which also has a/c rooms for four people (⑤). There are several very basic hospedajes (①) in nearby Masachapa, or you may be able to string a hammock up in one of the locals' houses along the beach. Masachapa is more of a fishing village and its beach is not as clean as Pochomíl. The **bus** from Managua goes to both places.

Southwest along the coast from Masachapa is the town of **Casares**, which has its own stretch of fairly rough, unshaded beach, and **Hueheute**, which is a bit rougher again. Near Casares is **La Boquita**, another area developed for tourism which charges a small entry fee and offers plenty of places to relax and eat. The beach here can be dangerous with large rocks hidden in the shallows, but the river mouth which opens onto the beach provides a safe place to swim. The only place to stay is at *Las Palmas del Mar* (☎412-3351; ④–⑤). There is a direct **bus** service from the Mercado Israel Lewites to La Boquita, but it's infrequent except on weekends and holidays; during the week, catch the bus to Diriamba and change there for La Boquita.

Montelimar resort

A short distance north of Pochomíl is the number-one – possibly the only – resort in Nicaragua, **Montelimar** (☎269-6752 or 269-6769, *www.barcelo.co.cr*). Once the beach house of the dictator Somoza, it was turned into a resort by the Sandinistas and is now run by a Spanish company, though like many other properties nationalized during the Revolution, it's currently subject to an involved property dispute with Somoza's relations. Nicaragua's only five-star hotel, *Montelimar* has a relaxed atmosphere with a lovely private beach, four restaurants, four swimming pools, a small zoo and casino, and planned activities such as dance classes, horse-riding, tennis, windsurfing and volleyball. Most people come on a package, but you can book once you've arrived in Nicaragua. A so-called "all-inclusive" resort, prices are between US$110 and US$150 for a double room, including all meals, drinks and snacks; day rates of US$45 are also available.

El Velero

The hilly coast around **El Velero**, some 40km north of Managua towards León, is wilder than the beaches further south, punctuated by cliffs and peninsulas. A holiday village of sorts, El Velero is less frequented by day-trippers than Pochomíl or La Boquita, and consequently far more relaxed. Shady huts line the beachfront, along with showers, changing rooms and a number of food stands. The beach itself is excellent for swimming, and children can play safely in a rock pool at low tide. You can **stay** here at the holiday centre, originally set up for goverment workers, and still run by the Instituto Nicaragüense de Seguridad Social. Rooms (③) have a/c and private bath and there's a restaurant and bar in the grounds. Call the INSS to make a reservation (Managua ☎222-6994, El Velero ☎311-5413).

To get to El Velero, take a bus to León, alight at Puerto Sandino and take a camioneta. All in all, it's a three-hour journey from Managua.

Moving on from Managua

Even if you don't particularly want to go to Managua, it's virtually impossible to avoid, since almost all buses go to and from the capital. The main routes of interest to travellers are the **international** routes from Guatemala City, Tegucigalpa in Honduras, and San Salvador in El Salvador, operated by Ticabus (☎222-6094) and King Quality (☎228-1454) – all these services pass through Managua and you may well have to overnight here if you're travelling south to Costa Rica or Panamá. In addition to Ticabus, Sirca leaves daily for San José from four blocks north of the Shell Station in the south of the city, on the Carretera a Masaya (near the university). A new luxury service between Managua and San José, run by Transnica (☎278-2090), departs from in front of the Ramac building daily at 7am and 1pm.

The busiest **domestic** bus routes are those between the capital and the provincial cities, particularly León in the northwest and Granada in the south. Other main routes run to Matagalpa, Estelí, Masaya and Rivas, the last for connections to the Costa Rican border and the beach town of San Juan del Sur. Express buses also run on most routes from the Mercado Mayoreo – quicker but more expensive than normal buses. You can get most of the way to the Atlantic Coast by bus, a bone-jarring ten-hour trip from Managua to the port of El Rama, from where boats go upriver to Bluefields on the Caribbean. An alternate route is with a private bus company called Empresa Vargas Peña (☎280-1812 in Managua; ☎822-1410 in Bluefields), who provide bus transport to Rama and then a connection by launch to Bluefields: the company has three departures daily from the Mercado Iván Montenegro (5am, arriving in Bluefields at 3pm; 2.45pm, with an overnight stay in El Rama; and 9.30pm, arriving in Bluefields at 7.30am).

Barring international bus services, tickets for which usually need to be bought between one and three days in advance, you can't reserve tickets on any buses within Nicaragua. Buses leave when they become full, which is usually pretty quickly – every fifteen or thirty minutes, with less frequent services leaving every hour or ninety minutes. For a rundown of the main bus routes from Managua, see the box below.

Grupo Taca has daily **international flights** between Managua and San José, while Copa handles flights to and from Panamá. The main **domestic airlines** are La Costeña (☎263-2142/3/4; *www.flylacostena.com*) and Atlantic Airlines (☎222-5787), which both

BUS ROUTES FROM MANAGUA

DESTINATION	DEPARTS FROM	FREQUENCY	DURATION
Chinandega	Mercado Israel Lewites	every 30min	2hr
Estelí	Mercado de Mayoreo	every 30min	3hr 30min
Granada*	Mercado Roberto Huembes	every 15min	1hr 30min
Jinotepe	Mercado Israel Lewites	every 30min	2hr 30min
León	Mercado Israel Lewites	every 15–30min	1hr 30min
Masaya*	Mercado Roberto Huembes	every 30min	45min
Matagalpa	Mercado de Mayoreo	every 30min	3hr
El Rama	Mercado de Mayoreo	5 daily	10hr
Rivas	Mercado Roberto Huembes	every 30min	3hr
San Carlos	Mercado de Mayoreo	3 daily	10hr
San José	Ticabus terminal	daily at 5.45am	7–10hr
San Salvador	Ticabus terminal	daily at 4.45am	8hr
Tegucigalpa	Ticabus terminal	daily at 5am	7hr
Tipitapa	Mercado de Mayoreo	every 15min	45min

*Regular express minibuses run to Masaya and Granada from an unmarked terminal on the highway opposite La UCA.

run frequent and reliable scheduled services, mainly to and from the Atlantic Coast. There are daily services to Puerto Cabezas and three flights weekly (Tues, Thurs & Sat) to Waspám on the northern Atlantic Coast; flights run to Bluefields several times a day, with two services daily to Corn Island. Advance reservations are essential. Both airlines have offices at the airport and agencies across the city.

Tours

Given the often erratic schedules of Nicaraguan transport, if you're short of time it's worth considering an organized tour, particularly to remote or difficult to reach areas like the Solentiname archipelago or the Río San Juan. There's not much choice of tour operators, but the ones that do exist are established and reputable.

Careli Tours, Calle Principal, Los Robles (☎278-2572, *info@carelitours.com*).

Nicarao Lake Tours, 120m east of the Bancentro in Bolónia (☎266-1694, *nir@nicaraolake.com.ni*).

Tours Nicaragua, Av Bolívar, one block south of the *Hotel Inter-Continental* (☎228-7063, *nicatour @nic.gbm.net*).

Solentiname Tours, Km 8, Carretera a Masaya (☎265-2716, *zerger@ibw.com.ni*).

CHAPTER 23

THE NORTH

N
icaragua's **north** is really two regions, divided by geography and climate as well as – to an extent – the character of their inhabitants. The **northwest** is largely an agricultural area, its hot, dry grassy plains given over to cattle farming, peanuts and cotton, and its horizons punctuated by dramatic volcanoes. Heading northwest from Managua, two roads lead to the colonial city of León and agricultural Chinandega, the only towns of any size in northwest Nicaragua. The only stop of any interest for visitors on the way to León is at the ruins of **León Viejo**, one of the very first Spanish settlements in Central America. Once the capital of Nicaragua, the city of **León** itself is of interest mainly for its cathedral, the largest in Central America, though students of Nicaraguan politics and history will also find the city interesting for its role as the birthplace of the FSLN. Further northwest is the hot rural town of **Chinandega** and the **Cosigüina Peninsula**, along with a chain of volcanoes including **Volcán San Cristóbal**, at 1745m the highest in the country, and the smaller **Volcán Cosigüina**, perched on the end of the peninsula. Good beaches are scarce on this stretch of the Pacific coast. **Poneloya**, a weekend and holiday destination for inhabitants of León, is wild and wave-raked and not really safe for swimming.

North of Managua the landscape is altogether different, with mountainous hillsides covered in bright-green coffee plants and cows grazing in cool alpine pastures. Set within a circle of mountains, the north has a more temperate climate and very productive soil, with plenty of tobacco plantations and an economy based on coffee, grains, vegetables, fruit and dairy farming. The journey north from Managua to Estelí, some 150km from the capital, is one of the most inspiring in the country, as the Carretera Interamericana winds through the grassy Pacific plains, skirting the southern edge of Lago de Managua before climbing slowly into a ribbon of blue mountains.

Many travellers coming from the south notice a distinct difference in the people as well as the geography: northerners are poorer and more battle-hardened, and can sometimes seem less forthcoming than Nicaraguans in other areas. In both the Sandinista Revolution years and during the Contra–Sandinista struggles of the 1980s, this region, and particularly **Estelí**, its largest town, saw heavy fighting and serious bloodshed. Because of their staunchly leftist character and legendary tenacity, Somoza bore a particular grudge against the inhabitants of Estelí and waged brutal offensives on the city. Scars have not really healed, either on the bombed-out buildings that still dot the streets of Estelí or in people's minds, and the region remains a centre of unflappable Sandinista support, as demonstrated by the party's sweeping victories in municipal elections in northern Nicaragua in November 2000.

León and around

The capital of Nicaragua until 1857, **LEÓN**, 90km north of Managua, is these days a quiet provincial city – though it would be even quieter were it not for the presence of

For an explanation of **accommodation price codes**, see p.468.

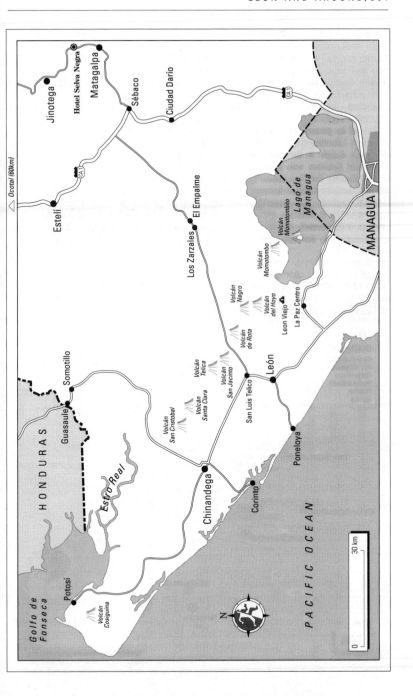

the **National University**, the country's premier academic institution. The original León was founded by Hernández de Córdoba in 1524 at the foot of Volcán Mombotombo, where its ruins – now known as León Viejo (see p.505) – still lie. The city was subsequently moved northwest to its present-day location soon after León Viejo's destruction by an earthquake and volcanic eruption in 1609. Today, the city's main attraction is its **Cathedral**, the largest in Central America, while an array of other churches – eighteen in all, displaying a fine spectrum of architectural styles and photographic opportunities – seem to spring up on practically every corner.

For all its present-day peace, León has a violent history. In 1824, tensions between the city's Liberals and the Conservatives of Granada erupted – a total of seventeen battles were fought in the city over the course of the next twenty years. In 1956 the first President Somoza was gunned down in León by the martyr-poet Rigoberto López Pérez. During the Revolution in the 1970s the town's streets were again the scenes of several decisive **battles** between the Sandinistas and Somoza's forces, and much of the damage caused – bullet-scarred buildings, cracked sidewalks – is still visible. Many key figures in the Revolution either came from León or had their political start here. The **National University** and the National Law School were (and perhaps still are) hotbeds of revolutionary ferment, and the presence of these institutions has contributed enor-

mously to León's Liberal bent. While the student population livens things up considerably, the town generally seems very quiet, baking gently under the ferocious sun, although the atmosphere quickens in the evenings, when Mass-goers tumble from the churches and food and drink vendors set up on the central plaza.

Arrival and information

Buses from Managua pull in at the market on C 6 Norte, in the east of town, from where you can hop in a taxi (US$0.60) or walk the eight blocks or so west into the centre of town. There's a small **tourist office** on the Parque Central next to the *Café El Sesteo* restaurant, which has a few maps and leaflets but not much else. The Viajes Mundiales office (Mon–Fri 8am–12.30pm & 2–5.30pm; ☎311-5920 or 311-6920) is the place to reconfirm outbound **flights** or book air tickets – they represent all Central American and international airlines.The **Enitel** telephone office (Mon–Sat 7am–10pm) is located on the west side of the Parque and has USA Direct and Sprint phone boxes from which you can connect to a US operator.

The **post office** is three blocks north of the Parque Central opposite the Recolección church. **Internet access** with good connections can be found at the UNAN office, two blocks north of the Parque. **Banks** are plentiful, and will relieve you of your dollars for córdobas at the official rate. Three of the main banks face each other on the intersection one block northeast of the cathedral: all keep the same hours (8am–noon & 1–4pm) and offer the same rates; Bancentro is the best of the three for changing travellers' cheques. Just to the east, Credomatic advances cash on credit cards – it's next to the well-stocked La Unión **supermarket** one block northeast of the Parque.

Accommodation

Although still poor for a city of its importance, the range of decent **places to stay** in León has increased in the last couple of years as new family-run guesthouses have opened up.

América, two blocks east of the Parque, near the market. Nice budget hotel in a good location: the rooms (with private bath) are rather dark and gloomy, but there's a pleasant courtyard with rocking chairs and plants and good breakfasts (but bad coffee). ②.

Austria, one block south from the Parque (☎311-1206, fax 311-1368, *haustria@ibw.com.ni*). Smart new hotel with good facilities including a bar, restaurant, Internet access, car rental and parking. All rooms have TV, a/c and bath with hot water. ⑥.

Casona Colonial Guesthouse, four blocks north of the Parque (☎311-3178). Clean and very friendly family-run guesthouse a few blocks from the city centre with good-sized double rooms with bath, comfortable beds and an excellent breakfast (not included in rate). ②–③.

Colonial, two blocks north of the Parque (☎311-2279, fax 311-3125). Very friendly hotel with bags of character and rocking chairs ranged around a huge inner courtyard, though it could do with a lick of paint and is rather overpriced for what you get. Some rooms have a/c and bath. ④.

Europa, 3 C NE, 4 Av (☎311-6040, fax 311-2577). Modern hotel with small, well-maintained rooms with comfy beds, TV and bath – some also have a/c. Note that quoted room prices don't include tax. ④–⑤.

La Posada del Doctor, four blocks north of the Parque, opposite the *Casona Colonial Guesthouse* (☎311-3178). New, clean and well-kept rooms, some with bunk beds, all with shared bath. ②.

The City

"León: ciudad heroica – primera capital de la revolución" say the street signs, and León certainly wears its FSLN heart on its sleeve. Although many of the old **Sandinista murals and graffiti** have been covered over there are still some fine examples around town, particularly near the university. (The best example is half a block north of the western edge of the Parque Central, where the ruins of the **Penelas y Sirera** department store, wrecked during fighting in 1979, feature a mural of a big-hatted Sandino, casting his shadow over the sidewalk, plus a reproduction of the letter Rigoberto López Pérez – see below – wrote to his mother before shooting Somoza.)

The city's most obvious attraction, however, is the colossal **Cathedral**, a cream-coloured structure of epic proportions towering over León from the Parque Central. Begun in 1747, it took anything from seventy to a hundred years to build, depending on who you talk to. Inside the only things of interest are the large statues of the Twelve Apostles and the tomb of local hero **Rubén Darío**, Nicaragua's most famous writer and poet, guarded by a statue of a weeping lion. Masses are held daily at about 5pm and are worth attending, if only to people-watch. Two blocks northeast of the Parque is one of Nicaragua's finest colonial churches, **La Recolección**, with a beautiful Mexican-Baroque facade dating from 1786 and some fine mahogany woodwork inside.

The **Parque Central** is the heart of the city, centred on a statue of **General Máximo Jerez** guarded by four lions and visited by a constant stream of locals, street vendors and tourists, who stop here to eat ice cream, bagged fruit or simply sit on a park bench. On the west side is one of the city's Sandinista strongholds, the decaying **Asociación de Combatientes y Colaboradores Históricos** building, while next door is the **Enitel** office, whose giant satellite tower unfortunately competes with the cathedral as the Parque's dominant structure. Enlivening the north side of the Parque is the grand **Casa de Gobierno** and the **Centro de Convenciones**, while on the northeast corner is the **Mausoleo Héroes y Mártires**, a star-shaped monument dedicated to those who died fighting for freedom during the civil war, surrounded by a large mural colourfully detailing Nicaragua's history from pre-Colombian times to the ending of the civil war.

A block west of the Parque Central, the **Parque Rubén Darío** features a statue of the rather bored-looking poet dressed in suit and bow tie. A few blocks further west is the **Museo Rubén Darío** (Mon–Sat 9am–noon & 2–5pm, Sun 9am–noon; free, but donations appreciated), housed in a substantial León residence which was actually the house of Darío's aunt, Bernarda. Inside, the lovingly kept rooms and courtyard garden are home to wonderfully frank plaques narrating the story of Darío's tempestuous personal life and diplomatic and poetic career, along with many of his personal possessions and commemorative items, such as Rubén Darío lottery tickets.

Two blocks north of the Parque Rubén Darío is the **Casa Rigoberto López Pérez**. Now a rather dowdy FSLN office, a plaque marks the spot where the young revolutionary Rigoberto López Pérez assassinated the dictator General Somoza on September 21, 1956, before himself being shot some fifty times by the National Guard. FSLN workers will allow you in to see the courtyard and the plaque dedicated to Pérez, and read the moving note which he wrote to his mother detailing his reasons for murdering Somoza. Many other monuments around the city evoke stirring memories of the hardship León endured during the Somoza dictatorship and civil war. Three blocks south of the cathedral lie the ruins of **El Veinte Uno**, the National Guard's 21st garrison and scene of heavy fighting in April 1979. One block further south stand the macabre remnants of **Somoza's jail** in which political prisoners were tortured and murdered.

Four kilometres west of the city centre is the barrio of **Subtiava**, which long pre-dates León and is still home to many of the city's indigenous population. It is also the site of one of the oldest churches in the country, the small adobe **parish church** of Subtiava. Recently renovated, the church is not always open, but worth a visit if you're catching a bus to or from the beach at Poneloya (see opposite).

Eating and drinking

León now boasts a large quantity of **places to eat**, although the standard of food varies and many restaurants remain alarmingly empty most of the time; as across most of northern Nicaragua, **pizza** seems to predominate. There are also a number of **comedores** on the edges of town and around the market. For good **cakes**, bread and pastries try the *Panadería y Repostería Morella,* opposite La Recolección church.

On Friday and Saturday nights, snappily dressed university students head to the only site of nocturnal life in town, the **disco/bar** *El Túnel del Tiempo* – an unthreatening venue playing mostly salsa and merengue. Look for the whitewashed building near the exit to Chinandega on the highway just outside the city – best to come and go in a taxi (around US$1).

Café El Sesteo, northeast corner of the Parque. The main café in town, the tastefully renovated, open-fronted *El Sesteo* is a popular – if slightly expensive – place to eat, drink and people-watch.

Flor de Sacuanjoche, one block north and two blocks west of La Merced church. Fine ambience, good music and well-prepared fresh meat, fish and chicken dishes, as well as some good vegetarian plates – expect to pay US$5–7 for a good meal.

Italian Pizza behind *El Sesteo*. Decent pizza restaurant decked out with flags of the world.

Los Pescaditos, barrio Subtiava, 4km west of the city. Popular and upmarket outdoor restaurant – try the buttery *camarones con ajillo*, washed down with a cold Victoria beer underneath the night sky.

Payitas, opposite La Merced church. Popular throughout the day with students, serving decent snacks, drinks and cakes.

Pizzeria Roma, 350m north of the Parque. While the pizza and pasta is nothing to write home about, portions are huge, the atmosphere is pleasant and you can pay with a credit card. Closed Mon.

Tip Top, one block northeast of the market. Good place for fried chicken and fast food.

Around León: Poneloya and León Viejo

Day-trip destinations from León include the Pacific beach of **Poneloya**, due west of the city and easily reached by bus. The mildly interesting historic monument of **León Viejo** is best reached in a car or taxi – a trip on public transport entails some fancy footwork to make the connections, and even then leaves you with a long walk.

Poneloya

For killer Pacific waves, **Poneloya**, 20km west of León, is the most impressive beach in the country. The water here is notoriously dangerous, due to a combination of powerful waves and rip tides, but it's the only beach within convenient reach of León, and many of the city's well-to-do residents have weekend homes here. Outside of peak times like Christmas and Easter, though, Poneloya seems rather run-down and forlorn, with restaurants closed and homes boarded up, and a rather bleak vista out to a sere Pacific. You really must take care if you **swim** here: waves come ashore with a supernatural force. Ask locals about rip tides (*corrientes peligrosos*) before venturing into the water, and never swim alone. The smaller beach at **Las Peñitas**, at the south end of Poneloya, is much safer.

Most travellers come to Poneloya for the day and sleep in León – a good option, since accommodation in Poneloya is limited. Options include the *Hotel La Posada de Poneloya* (☎311-4612 or 311-4812; ③), which is a bit run-down but serves good meals for about US$2; the good-value *Suyapa Beach* (☎311-6257; ②), includes a hearty breakfast); and the new *Barco del Oro* (no phone; ①–③) at Las Peñitas (the bus stops right outside), which has a variety of rooms, some with private bath, plus an on-site restaurant and bar, Internet access and cable TV, and **camping** facilities. **Buses to Poneloya** (40min) leave León every hour from the Terminal Poneloya on C Darío, near the Subtiava church in barrio Subtiava (see opposite). A taxi will cost about US$8 each way – good value if you're in a group.

León Viejo

Founded in 1524, the same year as Granada, **León Viejo**, 32km east of the modern city, was destroyed by an earthquake and volcanic eruption on December 31, 1609. The ruins themselves are interesting only for the cathedral (whose walls stand about thigh-high) and the broken stones of the former plaza. Otherwise there's little to see but a pile of rubble and grassy fields. The site is more or less unattended and there are no explanatory plaques. Still, the location is impressive, in view of the lake and under the looming shadow of Mombotombo. The only way to get to León Viejo comfortably is by car; there is a local bus from **La Paz Centro**, a hamlet about 60km north of Managua, but the service is irregular – best get to La Paz Centro very early in the day and ask around.

Chinandega to the Honduran border

The first thing you notice about **CHINANDEGA**, 35km northwest of León, is its extra-ordinary heat. Set on a plain behind the looming form of Volcán San Cristóbal, the area's dry, kiln-like climate is ideal for cotton-growing, the main economic activity, along with some groundnut cultivation and cattle farming. In Nicaraguan terms Chinandega is a fairly prosperous agricultural town. It's also home to the Flor de Caña rum distillery, Nicaragua's export-grade tipple, which sits on the outskirts of town.

Buses arrive at the market southwest of the centre, known as the **Mercado Bisne** – *bisne* being short for "business", as during the years of the Reagan-sponsored embargo much contraband came through here from **Corinto**, Nicaragua's main port, 21km west of the city on a sandy island reached by a bridge. (Corinto is still the only deep-water port in Nicaragua, and almost every molecule of shipping commerce passes through the town.)

Chinandega's incredible heat makes it one of the few places in the country where you may seriously want to consider air conditioning. The only comfortable **place to stay** is the *Hotel Cosigüina*, half a block south of the Banco Nacional de Desarrollo (☎341-3636; ④), which has ten rooms with private bath, cable TV, a/c or fan. If you really don't want to shell out, the friendly *Hotel Chinandega*, four blocks east and one and a half blocks south of the Parque Central (no phone; ②), isn't a bad option, though the bathrooms could use a scrub.

If you're heading to Guasaule and the Honduran border (see below) under your own steam, express **buses** from Chinandega run about every thirty minutes.

Guasaule and the border with Honduras

Most travellers experience **GUASAULE** from the safe capsule of the Ticabus, which whizzes you painlessly through this cumbersome **border post**. If you're travelling by local transport, note that the border tends to close before noon for lunch and open whenever the officials have had their fill, usually at 2pm. Take a few dollars: the exit tax is currently US$2, and it must be paid in US currency. It's about 1km between the Nicaraguan border post and the Honduran side, and you'll have to walk it unless some kind truck driver takes pity on you, as there are no colectivos.

If you're **entering Nicaragua** from Honduras the entry fee is US$5, plus a US$2 "processing fee" – the combined fee is **only payable** in US dollars. From the border a service departs for Chinandega – the nearest Nicaraguan town with acceptable accommodation – every thirty minutes or so. At Chinandega you can pick up an express bus on to Managua about every 30 minutes, or continue by bus to León.

Estelí and around

At first sight **ESTELÍ**, the largest town in the north, can seem downtrodden and poor. It does have its poor *barrios*, but is an engaging place and a hotbed of political activity.

Of all the towns in Nicaragua, in Estelí you can best get a sense of what the country must have been like during the Revolution and glimpse something of the vision that inspired so many people during the 1980s. The town continues to provide fierce support for the Sandinistas, and witnessed violent disturbances following the controversial delay in announcing the results of municipal elections in November 2000, when President Alemán stalled for time in the hope of provoking disturbances which would undermine the FSLN's credibility.

Although the war ended with the failure of the Sandinistas in the election of 1990, Estelí has been the scene of fighting as recently as 1994. In what has become known as the "**one-day war**", former Sandinista and Contra soldiers took up arms together to demand better conditions for veterans. At the same time they robbed a bank and their leader, "Pedrito El Hondureño" reportedly disappeared with the loot. The government responded by encircling the veterans in the centre of town with national police, soldiers and helicopter gun ships. About a dozen veterans were killed along with two civilians. A further uprising in 1997 came to nothing.

More recently the town's government has been particularly successful in attracting **overseas aid** and Estelí is filled with the offices of international organizations working on projects as diverse as cooperative and organic farming, women's rights and the environment. Estelí is also the site of a US$25 million reforestation project designed to clean up the water supply. In the early 1990s the town provided the location for the Ken Loach movie *Carla's Song*, the making of which no doubt funnelled a few córdobas into the local economy.

Arrival and information

Confusingly, Estelí now has **two bus terminals**, located five minutes' walk from one another to the south of town. Regular buses from Managua and Matagalpa stop at the bus station in the **old market**, about twelve blocks south of the Parque Central. The **new bus terminal** is located on the Interamericana, three blocks to the east, and in theory deals with all destinations north of Estelí, including Ocotal, Somoto, Jinotega and the Honduran border, plus express buses to Managua, Masaya and León. In practice, you can currently find buses leaving for all destinations from both terminals, although it's expected that all services will use the new bus terminal in the near future. In the meantime, it's worth checking both terminals for departure times and destinations.

The town is arranged on a narrow north–south grid, with most services clustered together in the small centre along C Transversal. The new **tourist information office** is at the back of the old hospital, eight blocks south and one block east of the Parque (there's a brand new artesanía market in the same building) – they're planning to start arranging **tours** into the surrounding countryside in the future. The **post office** (Mon–Fri 8am–7pm) is 25m west of Av Central; the **Enitel** office (daily 7.30am–9pm, Sat closed noon–1.30pm) is on C Transversal between Av 1 and 2 SE. **Internet access** can be found at Cyber Place on Av Central, two blocks north of the Parque, and at Computer Soluciones on the northwest corner of the Parque – both charge US$3.30 per hour. There are four **banks** on the corner of Av 1 NE a block west of the Parque: Bancentro changes travellers' cheques, while Credomatic/Banco de América Central advances money on credit cards. You can transfer money, make international phone calls and send faxes at the **Western Union office**, C 11 SE and Av 1 SE (Mon–Fri 9am–5pm, Sat 9am–noon & 1.30–4.30pm; ☎713-3566).

To some extent a leftover from the Sandinista years, when *internacionalistas* flocked here, there are a few **language schools** in Estelí. Los Pepitos, one block south from Teatro Nancy (☎713-2154), does weekly courses including accommodation for around US$130. Horizonte, between C 8 and C 9 SE (☎713-3424 or 713-4117), is a cheaper option – run by the Unemployed Women's Movement, it also offers courses in local cooking and crafts. CENAC (no phone; *cenac@tmx.com.ni*) offers language courses and homestays for US$140. The Galería de los Héroes y Mártires, one block south of the Parque, runs language courses based on learning about the area and the effects of the civil war.

Accommodation

Because Estelí sees quite a bit of gringo traffic in the form of aid workers, Estelí's **hotels** tend to be a little more expensive than in other parts of the country.

Hospedaje Chepito Av Central. Small, simple family-run hospedaje catering for the budget traveller. ①.

Hospedaje Mariela, one block north of old bus terminal on the way into town (☎713-2166). Small, simple rooms with shared bath. ②.

Hospedaje San Francisco Av Central. Small hospedaje with basic rooms and shared bath. ①.

Mesón, one block north of the cathedral (☎713-2655, fax 713 4029). Estelí's dowager hotel, the *Mesón* has something of the feeling of a faded country inn, with a wood-panelled restaurant and friendly management – the scrappy courtyard inside is a disappointment, but the rooms are comfortable and all have private bath. ③.

Nicarao, Av Central, just south of C 1 SE (☎713-2490). Small hotel, perennially popular with gringos, possibly thanks to its covered patio where you can relax, dine on the excellent lunch specials (US$2.50) and write your postcards. ②.

Panorama #1, C Transversal between Av Central and 1 SE (☎713-3147, fax 713-2386), and **Panorama #2**, at the other end of C Transversal (☎713-5023). Two largely indistinguishable hotels of the same name, and owned by the same management, have between them 25 clean new rooms, all with private bath. ③.

The Town

Although Estelí lacks the stunning mountain views of Matagalpa to the south, the centre of town is well-kept and pleasant to wander around, and the climate refreshingly cool. Much of the pleasure lies in soaking up the atmosphere, particularly along Av Central, where shops' wares spill out onto the street and the windows display cowboy boots and the local farmers' favourite Western-style hats.

The **cathedral** on the Parque has a rather austere façade and is one of the least interesting in the country. The south side of the Parque is dominated by the **Centro Recreativo Las Segovias**, which puts on regular music and sporting events, particularly basketball. There's another cultural venue around the corner, a block to the south, the **Centro Cultural**, which hosts art exhibitions, dancing and music events. Across the street, the **Artesanía Nicaragüense** has a reasonable selection of handicrafts, pottery, T-shirts and cigars. On the same block is the tiny **Galería de Héroes y Mártires** (daily 9am–5pm; donations), a moving and simple museum devoted to the Revolution and to the many residents of Estelí who died fighting in it (the women who work at the Galería are, for the most part, mothers and widows of soldiers who were killed), containing a collection of photographs, maps, newspaper clippings and some personal possessions of those killed.

Eating and drinking

Estelí's **eating** scene is rather disappointing unless you like pizza, or the Nicaraguan interpretation of it. In the early evening a couple of small kiosks open up on the Parque serving grilled meat, rice and salad for around US$2. *Café Palermo*, half a block south of the banks, concocts inspired pizzas for a price (large ones cost US$8), plus pasta and garlic bread, and lunch and dinner specials that you can wash down with wine by the glass. *White House Pizza* behind the cathedral is a popular pizza chain serving large pizzas for US$4–6, while *El Mesero*, opposite, is a reasonable choice for lunch or an early-evening meal. The spartan and easily missed *Comedor Popular La Soya* on Av Central, two blocks south of *Hotel Nicarao*, serves plentiful soya and rice dishes with soya milk-shakes for US$2. *Sorbetería Iris*, on the north side of the Parque, will quell any ice-cream cravings.

Around Estelí: Miraflor

The **Miraflor nature reserve**, 28km northeast of Estelí, covers 150 square kilometres of forest along with some small farms, one of the project's main aims being to find sustainable ways in which farming and environmental protection can co-exist – over five thousand locals currently produce coffee, potatoes and exotic flowers in and around the reserve.

Guides lead visitors along a **nature trail** around the shore of the Laguna Miraflor, explaining the area's fauna, flora and natural environment. Home to a mix of wet and dry tropical conifers and deciduous species, Miraflor is a great spot to view quetzals, woodpeckers, *guardabarrancos* (the national bird of Nicaragua) and *urracas*, a local type of magpie. It's also home to howler monkeys – which you are likely to hear, if not see, at least at dusk – and reclusive mountain lions.

Basic **accommodation** (②) in cabins is available. Visits can be arranged free of charge as part of the management authority's public education program: contact the Union de Cooperativas Agropecuarias Héroes y Mártires de Miraflor at C 9 NE and Av 5 NE in Estelí (☎713-2971, *miraflor@ibw.com.ni*), a few days ahead. Horse-riding trips can also be organized to the **caves** (*las cuevas*), once inhabited by the ancient Yeluca and Cebollal mountain people.

Ocotal and the Honduran border

A dusty highway leads north from Estelí to the Honduran border post at **Las Manos**. A few kilometres short of the border is **OCOTAL**, a pleasant town in its own right, and a useful stopover on the way to or from Honduras. **Buses** run between Las Manos, Estelí and Managua roughly every hour until around 3pm; the bus terminal is on the highway 1km from the town centre, which is a dusty twenty-minute walk or a short taxi ride.

The best **place to stay** in Ocotal is the new *Hotel Frontera* (☎732-2668, fax 732-2669, *hofrosa@ibw.com.ni*; ④–⑤), 1km north of town by the Shell station. All rooms have TV, a/c and bath with hot water, and there's also a bar, restaurant and swimming pool. If you're on a budget, the *Hospedaje Segovia* (②) on the main street is a good, cheap option. For **eating**, the town boasts a number of decent **comedores**, or you could try the *Pizzaría Doña Pizza* on the main street one block south of the **Enitel** office.

Matagalpa and around

Known as "La Perla del Septentrión" – pearl of the north – **MATAGALPA** is spoken well of by virtually everyone in Nicaragua, principally, you suspect, because of its relatively cool **climate**: at about 21–25°C, it's considered *tierra fría* in this land of 30°C-plus temperatures. Located 130km northeast of the capital on the Carretera Interamericana, Matagalpa is a small, quiet town set among blue-green mountains covered in coffee plantations. Most visitors come here to visit the **Hotel Selva Negra**, famous all over Nicaragua and one of the country's premier tourism attractions.

Thanks to its climate and coffee-growing potential, there's a significant European **immigrant** presence in the area – mostly Germans, Italians and Americans, whose ancestors moved here in the late nineteenth century. The town has strong **Sandinista** credentials, too: Tomás Borge, the former Minister of the Interior under the Sandinista government, was born and raised here, as was Carlos Fonseca, a key Sandinista gunned down by Somoza's National Guard in 1976.

Matagalpa's services, hotels and restaurants are spread out between the seven or eight blocks that divide the town's two principal **parques**, and you'll find yourself constantly trekking between the two. At the northern end of town, the **Parque Morazán** fronts the **Catedral de San Pedro**, dating from 1874. Unusually, the cathedral was constructed side on, with its bell towers and entrance facing away from the Parque. A large **Sandinista monument** showing three men firing guns stands on the east side of the Parque. Tiny **Parque Darío** in the south is the site of several hospedajes and restaurants. Two main thoroughfares, Av José Benito Escobar and Av Central, link the two squares.

The town's only museum, the **Casa Museo Comandante Carlos Fonseca**, 100m southeast of the Parque Darío, documents the life of Carlos Fonseca but is currently closed due to lack of funds, though it may reopen by the time you get here. At the Tienda de Cerámica Negra, two blocks north of Parque Rubén Darío, you can buy examples of Matagalpa's typical artesanía, including the distinctive **black pottery** (*cerámica negra*) whose style indicates a link between the indigenous people of the Matagalpa area and the Maya – this type of pottery is otherwise found only in southern Mexico.

Practicalities

Buses arrive at Matagalpa's **bus terminal** and market, southwest of the city centre; it's about a ten-minute walk from the terminal to Parque Darío. There's no tourist office in Matagalpa. A number of **banks** sit on Av Central just south of Parque Morazán: Bancentro will change dollars and travellers' cheques. For post and phone calls head for **Enitel**, a block northeast of Parque Morazán (phones: daily 8am–10pm; post: Mon–Fri 8am–5pm).

If you have to spend the night in Matagalpa, the choice of **accommodation** isn't great, and most tourists head out of town to stay at the *Hotel Selva Negra* (see opposite). The *Hotel Colonial* (①–②) and *Hotel Plaza* (①–②), located on opposite sides of Parque Darío, are both bargain-basement options with uncomfortable beds, thin walls and shared bath with occasional running water. One block north on Av José Benito Escobar is the small *Hotel Arauz* (②), with tiny but clean rooms with bath. Across the street is the *Hotel del Centro* (②), whose colonial courtyard leads to clean but gloomy rooms, all with bath.

The quickest and cheapest **eats** in Matagalpa are to be had at the comedores scattered around the Parque Darío. The most popular of these is the *Comedor San Martín*, 25m north of the corner of Parque Darío and Av José Benito Escobar, where a plate of chicken, rice, chillies and cabbage salad will set you back about US$2.50. The *Restaurante Jin-Shan*, one block south of Parque Morazán, serves good Chinese food (US$3–6 for a meal with drinks) at lunchtimes and early evening, while *White House Pizza*, one block north of Parque Morazán, dishes up acceptable pizza for US$4–6. The large, bamboo *Comedor El Bambú*, Av José Benito Escobar, offers good-value breakfasts and lunches for US$2–3. For ice cream, head to *Sorbetería Chupis* on Av Central.

The Selva Negra

North of Matagalpa, the **Selva Negra** is an area of dark-blue, pine-clad mountains named by the area's German immigrants in the nineteenth century in emulation of their home country's Black Forest, which it strangely resembles. An amazing variety of wildlife flourishes in these pristine and sparsely populated tropical forests, including over eighty varieties of orchids, many birds (including the elusive resplendent quetzal), and sloths, ocelots, margay, puma, deer and howler monkeys – all of which are more likely to be spotted here than anywhere else in the country. Due to its high altitude (around 1300m), the area has a spring-like climate and a mean temperature of 18°C, which is very refreshing by Nicaraguan standards. As well as the climate, travellers are attracted by the region's walking and wildlife-spotting opportunities. That said, you can't just head off into the mountains: much of the terrain is farmed or under coffee cultivation, and trails are virtually nonexistent.

Because it offers an accessible route to the forest and mountains, nearly everyone who comes here stays in the **Hotel de la Montaña Selva Negra**, 10km from Matagalpa on the road to Jinotega (☎612-3883; doubles ⑥, dorm beds from $15 per person). An establishment of national repute, prices are high by Nicaraguan standards, but worth it, with accommodation in individually designed cabañas set in beautifully landscaped grounds; there's also a good restaurant on site, and you can go horse-riding or hike one of the fourteen trails which wind through the cloudforest in the hotel grounds (take plenty of food and water). The hotel's owners, Eddy and Mausi Kuhl, come from a German family who arrived in Matagalpa in 1891 to grow coffee, and Eddy's finca still produces some of the best export-grade coffee in the country.

Jinotega

Set amid cool, lush mountains 34km north from Matagalpa, is the nondescript but pleasant town of **JINOTEGA**, famous for the coffee grown nearby. Many *internacionalistas* have been posted to Jinotega over the years, and the town has a friendly attitude toward strangers, though most travellers only stop here on day-trips from Matagalpa. It's worth coming to Jinotega simply for the ride, however, since the journey between here and Matagalpa is one of the most magnificent in the country, winding slowly up through misty green mountains, though the road is badly maintained.

If you get caught in between buses and have **to stay**, try Jinotega's friendly hostel, the *Sollentuna Hem* (①–②), five blocks north and two blocks east of the cathedral – it's popular with international travellers and has simple but homely rooms with private or shared bath. Another cheap and simple option is the *Hotel Primavera* (①), five blocks from the Parque on the main street, while closer to the centre the *Hospedaje Tito* (①–②), one and a half blocks north of the cathedral, has simple, spotlessly clean rooms. The cafeteria next door serves tasty *gallo pinto* breakfasts.

travel details

BUSES

Chinandega to: Guasaule (every 30min; 30min); León (every 30min; 1hr 30min); Managua (every 30min; 3hr).

Estelí to: León (2 daily; 2hr 30min); Managua (every 30min; 3hr); Matagalpa (every 30min; 2hr); Ocotal (hourly; 2hr).

Jinotega to: Matagalpa (hourly; 1hr 30min); Managua (5 daily; 3hr 30min).

León to: Chinandega (every 30min; 1hr 30min); Estelí (2 daily; 2hr 30min); Managua (every 30min; buses 1hr 30min, minibuses 1hr 10min); Matagalpa (2 daily; 3hr).

Matagalpa to: Estelí (every 30min; 2hr); Jinotega (hourly; 1hr 30min); Managua (every 30min; 3hr); León (2 daily; 3hr); Masaya (2 daily; 2hr).

CHAPTER 24

THE SOUTHWEST

he vast majority of Nicaragua's population lives in the fertile plain that makes up the **southwest** of the country. Bordered by Lago de Nicaragua to the east and the Pacific to the west, the area has been prized since pre-Columbian times for its agricultural potential. Studded by volcanoes – Volcán Masaya, Volcán Mombacho just south of Granada, and the twin cones of Ometepe's Concepción and Maderas – the southwest is otherwise a flat, low, grassy plain, ideally suited to cattle,

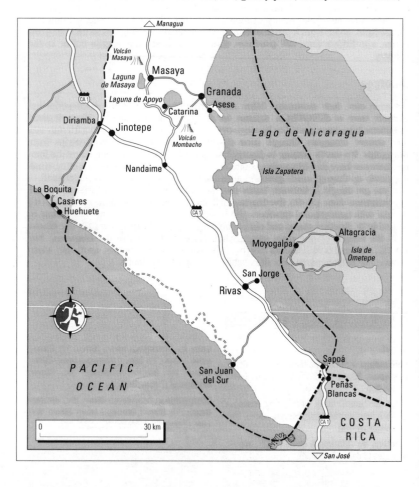

and most of what is left of Nicaragua's beef industry is concentrated here, while coffee plantations can be found at higher altitudes. The area has always been at the hub of the economy and politics of the country, and many of Nicaragua's most prominent political families, including the Chamorros, come from here.

The region's only two cities of any size are Masaya, 29km south of Managua, and Granada, 26km further south. **Masaya**'s enormous craft market attracts virtually everyone who comes to Nicaragua, while the nearby **Parque Nacional Volcán Masaya** offers the most accessible volcano-viewing in the country. With its fading classical-colonial architecture and lakeside setting, **Granada** is undeniably Nicaragua's most beautiful and popular city, and also makes a good base for exploring many nearby attractions including the **Isletas de Granada** and **Volcán Mombacho**. The road connecting Managua, Masaya and Granada passes through the picturesque **"Pueblos Blancos"**, or White Towns – Nindirí, Niquinohomo, Masatepe, Catarina, Diria and Diriomo – small sleepy settlements considered by Nicaraguans to embody everything that is authentically *nica*: typical indigenous-influenced food, crafts, and traditions and fiestas inherited from the Chorotgeta and the Mangue groups of native Nicaraguans. Some 75km south of Granada, **Rivas**, the gateway to Costa Rica, is of little interest in itself, though many travellers pass through on their way south or en route to **San Juan del Sur**, the most pleasant beach town in Nicaragua, where surfing, swimming and seafood are the main attractions.

Masaya and around

Set between the Managua–Granada Highway and the hulking form of Volcán Masaya, **MASAYA**'s stirring geography would make it an attractive town to visit even if it weren't also the centre of Nicaragua's artesanía production and home to two colourful **crafts markets**. These are of quite recent provenance – only during the Sandinista years did Masaya and the Pueblos Blancos develop their crafts tradition into a marketable commodity – but Masaya is now by far the best place in the country to buy hammocks, rocking chairs, traditional clothing, shoes and other souvenirs. Many of the crafts on sale came originally from the indigenous barrio of **Monimbó**, and the district continues to churn out a sizeable proportion of the region's handicrafts. Monimbó still has its own chief (*cacique*), whose authority was recognized in law in 1991, though other signs of true indigenous culture are scarce, and Masaya's cultural affinities are expressed mainly in its crafts and at fiesta time.

The most exciting time to visit Masaya is on Sundays between mid-September and mid-December, when the town indulges in a ninety-day period of revelry known as the **Fiesta de San Jeronimo**. The beginning of the fiesta sees one of the most fascinating processions in Nicaragua, the **Torovenado**, when Monimbó's large gay population comes out in style, indulging in a spot of cross-dressing and ridiculing those in power, including the politicians of the moment. A more recent invention is the popular **Jueves de Verbena** festival, held every Thursday evening throughout the year, when a spirited celebration of indigenous culture, music, dance and gastronomy is held in the renovated Mercado Nacional de Artesanía, and locals, tourists and musicians dance, sing, eat and drink the night away.

Most visitors come here on day-trips from Managua or Granada – a sensible plan, since Masaya doesn't have a large range of hotels and the bus services are fast and efficient.

For an explanation of **accommodation price codes**, see p.468.

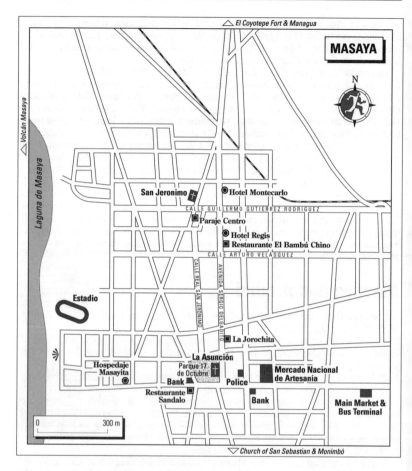

Arrival, information and accommodation

Buses from Managua's Mercado Roberto Huembes and from Granada arrive at the huge, dusty terminal next to Masaya's **main market**, to the east of town; it's a longish walk to the centre from here, so ask to be let off earlier, at the Iglesia San Jeronimo. Buses between Managua and Granada (plus those heading for Rivas and the Costa Rican border) also stop in town, at the **Mercado Nacional de Artesanía** (also known as the Mercado Viejo), one and a half blocks east of the Parque 17 de Octubre.

There's a very friendly and useful **tourist office**, staffed by local volunteers, in the Mercado Nacional de Artesanía, plus an official, but far less helpful, Mintur tourist office on the highway to Managua about 1km north of town (Mon–Fri 8am–4pm, Saturday 8am–noon; ☎522-2936). The **Enitel** office on the north side of the Parque 17 de Octubre (daily 7am–9.30pm) has public phones, including Sprint services to the US. Several **banks** offer an efficient dollar exchange service: Bancentro, next to the Enitel office will change travellers' cheques.

Masaya isn't really the place to bed down for the night; pickings are slim and **hotels** are not used to catering for tourists. Probably the best choices are the friendly and spotlessly clean *Hotel Regis* (②), half a block north of Cine González (☎522-2300; ②), which has ten clean rooms, separated by thin partition walls; and the *Hotel Montecarlo* (②), two blocks north of *Hotel Regis* (☎522-2166; ②), which has a nice plant-filled courtyard and pokey but good-value rooms. *Hospedaje Masayita* (no phone; ①–②), three blocks west of Banco de América Central, is basic and cheap, though not overwhelmingly friendly.

The Town

Masaya was hit by a severe earthquake in July 2000, but although many homes were damaged in the surrounding areas, the town has managed to repair the damage very quickly. It's still an attractive place to explore on foot: there's fairly little traffic in the streets and the heat is bearable. What little action there is in downtown Masaya takes place in the main square, the **Parque 17 de Octubre**. Bordering the square is the **Catedral de la Ascunción**, with images of various Central American saints inside, swathed in coloured satin and wilting gold lamé. More plain in its decor is the **Iglesia de San Jeronimo**, 600m north, the best example of colonial architecture in Masaya, despite its run-down condition. The statue of San Jeronimo on the altar depicts an old man wearing a loin cloth and a straw hat, with a rock in his hand and blood on his chest, evidence of self-mortification. For US$0.50 you can climb up to the bell tower for a sweeping view of the town.

Masaya's main attractions are its two crafts markets. The larger is located in the **main market** (open daily) next to the bus terminal, which is the best place in Masaya – and in Nicaragua as a whole – to buy craft items, many of them produced in Masaya and nearby towns. Goods on sale include paintings, many in the naif-art tradition of the Solentiname archipelago, large, excellent-quality hammocks, carved wooden bowls and utensils, simple wood-and-bead jewellery, cotton shirts, straw hats, and leather footwear, bags and purses. Bargaining is accepted, and although prices are generally quoted in córdobas, traders will accept US dollars (small bills are best), though you may get change in córdobas. The mercado is an easy walk from the centre, but if the heat is getting you down, grab one of the many taxis or horse-drawn carriages, which will take you anywhere in town for about US$0.75.

The Mercado Viejo, or Old Market, has been converted into the grandly named **Centro Cultural Antiguo – Mercado Nacional de Artesanía**, a pleasant mini-mall selling colourful pottery, carvings, bags, books and wall hangings. The prices are slightly higher than in the main market, but it has a nice atmosphere, a few cafés and restaurants and is the site of the weekly **Jueves de Verbena** party night. Check out the giant wall map of the country, which shows the places in Nicaragua where crafts are produced. If your Spanish is up to it, you could ask about visiting artisans at work in their homes and workshops. Just a block to the east are a couple of artisan shops, Los Tapices de Luís and Rincón de las Artesanías – worth visiting, but again pricier than the market.

The **Laguna de Masaya** beckons on the western side of town, seven blocks from the Parque 17 de Octubre. Despite its crystalline and inviting appearance, the laguna is actually highly polluted with sewage effluent from the town. The lakeside boardwalk, the Malecón, gives a stunning view of the smoking cone of Volcán Masaya (see p.516).

Eating and drinking

What it lacks in places to stay, Masaya makes up for in its tasty and cheap **eating** establishments. In the centre of town the best choice is the *Nuevo Bar Chegris* (closed Sun),

just around the corner to the south of the *Hotel Regis*, which is renowned for its bro-
chettas (meat on skewers), prawns in garlic sauce and chicken soup. Next door to the
Hotel Regis is the *Restaurante El Bamboo Chino*, which serves decent Chinese food
including "Chinese" tacos. At the southwest corner of Parque 17 de Octubre the
Restaurante Sandalo serves decent if greasy Chinese meals for about US$4. Best of all,
however, is the fabulous Mexican cuisine at *La Jorochita*, on Av Sergio Delgadillo, north
of La Asunción, where you can dine off tacos and fajitas for about US$2. The recently
opened *Paraje Centro*, opposite the former *Hotel Rex*, has an extensive menu including
sandwiches and fruit juices.

Coyotepe

Three kilometres out of town on the road to Managua is the old fort of **Coyotepe**. Built
on a hilltop by the Somoza regime to house political prisoners, the abandoned and
decaying structure commands stunning views of Masaya, Laguna de Apoyo and the volcanoes of Masaya and Mombacho, and also offers an eerie reminder of the atrocities
carried out here by Somoza's National Guard – bring a torch and you can poke around
in the darkened and eerie dungeons. The Sandinistas stormed the fort during the
Revolution – the National Guard responded by slaughtering all those inside. From
Masaya, take any Managua-bound bus and ask to be let off at the entrance, from where
a winding path leads up to the untended fort.

Parque Nacional Volcán Masaya

Just outside Masaya, the **Parque Nacional Volcán Masaya** (Tues–Sun 8am–3pm;
US$3.30) offers a glimpse into the smoking cone of the volcano and stunning views of
the area around Managua. Trails across the park take you through a lunar landscape
with its own unique flora and fauna, but be warned that walking unguided is not recommended, as it's very easy to get lost.

The **park entrance** lies between Km 22 and Km 23 on the Managua–Granada highway, about 4km from Masaya. You can get off any bus between Managua and Masaya
or Granada (except the express) at the entrance, from where you'll either have to hike
the tiring two-kilometre road up to the crater and back again or hitch a lift.
Alternatively, you could hire a taxi from Masaya. About 50m before the entrance to the
park, the *Dina #2* restaurant has tables set under little ranchitos and is a great place to
watch the sunset.

About 4.5km before the crater, along the approach road, is the **Centro de
Interpretación Ambiental** (Tues–Sun 8am–5pm), which houses an exhibition outlining the area's geology, agriculture and pre-Columbian history, along with an interesting three-dimensional display of the country's chain of volcanoes. The centre runs
infrequent **tours** (about US$1.50) on the trails around the area, to spot bird and plant
life (look out for the stunted bromeliads common to high-altitude volcanic areas).
There's a shady picnic area beside the centre and a viewing point on a rickety boardwalk out the back.

There are two **walking trails**, both about 5km long (at least a 2hr round-trip; take
water and food), starting at the Centro de Interpretación Ambiental and winding up the
side of the volcano. Volcán Masaya last erupted in 1772, but it was a powerful eruption,
as the depth of the crater testifies. The fumes coming from the crater are sulphurous
and you might find it difficult to breathe as you get near. Look out for the famous
chocoyos del cráter, small green parrots that have thrived in an atmosphere that should
be poisonous. They live on berries and leaves and seem to have built nests in the walls
of the crater. You're most likely to see them perching on the fence along the perimeter
of the parking lot at the Centro de Interpretación Ambiental.

The Pueblos Blancos

Scattered within a fifteen-kilometre radius of Masaya are the "Pueblos Blancos" or White Towns – **Nindiri, Niquinohomo, Masatepe, Catarina, Diria** and **Diriomo** – small pueblos held dear all over the country as the embodiment of all things Nicaraguan (or, more precisely, all things from the country's Pacific zone). They get their name from the traditional whitewash used on the houses, *carburo*, which is made from water, lime and salt. The white buildings are pretty, but that said, there's not much more actually to see, few places to sample any cuisine and no handicrafts obviously on sale. Although each town has its own specific artisan traditions and fiestas, and local identity is fiercely asserted, to the visitor they seem remarkably similar, sleepy towns with a few hangers-out around nearly identical central squares. Niquinohomo was the **birthplace** of Augusto César Sandino, and the house in which he grew up is marked by a plaque opposite the Parque Central.

If you want to visit just one, **CATARINA** is the prettiest. The main draw is **El Mirador**, a magical lookout point at the top of the village that stares right down into the blue waters of the collapsed crater lake of **Laguna de Apoyo**, with Volcán Masaya looming behind it. Restaurants, cafés and artesanía stalls have sprung up around the viewpoint. A regular local **bus** runs roughly every thirty minutes from Masaya's main bus terminal to Catarina. From Granada, take any Masaya or Managua bus and ask to get off at the Catarina turning, from where you'll need to take another short bus ride to the edge of the village.

Granada

Set on the western shore of Lago de Nicaragua some 45km southeast of Managua, **GRANADA** was once the jewel of Central America. The oldest Spanish-built city in the isthmus, it was founded in 1524 by Francisco Hernández de Córdoba, who named it after his home town in Spain. During the colonial period Granada became fabulously rich, its wealth built upon exploitation: sited only 20km from the Pacific, the city was a transit point for shipments of **gold** and other minerals that were mined throughout the Spanish empire, with the help of indigenous slave labour. Laden Spanish galleons would sail from Granada across the lake, down the Río San Juan, out to the Caribbean and then to Europe. The wealth of the city also attracted traffic in the other direction: Granada's gold stores proved tempting to buccaneers and it was sacked several times by English and French **pirates**, until the Spanish built their **Castillo**, a fort on the banks of the Río San Juan (see p.535).

Granada's wealth and the generations of *criollos* – people of Spanish descent born in the New World – who made it their home contributed to its conservative character. The split between liberal León, the only other city of any size in the country, and conservative Granada developed as early as the eighteenth century, and persists to this day. At the beginning of the nineteenth century, feelings of rivalry between the two cities were ignited by Nicaraguan independence. With the departure of the Spanish, a power vacuum developed and the elite of León decided to fill it by inviting the troublesome American, **William Walker** (see p.473) to fight their cause. Walker attacked and captured Granada, from where he ruled the country for two years until being finally driven out. On his retreat from Granada Walker ordered the city burned, and most of it subsequently fell into ruin (you can still see the black marks on the facade of the cathedral).

Granada never recovered its original splendour, though it's still the most architecturally arresting town in Nicaragua, while the city's recent tourist boom has led to a large-scale restoration of the old colonial buildings, many of them newly re-painted in

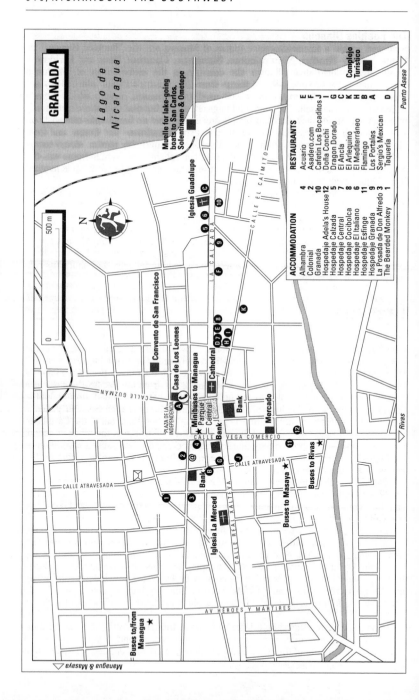

GRANADA

Lago de Nicaragua

Puerto Asese

Rivas

Managua & Masaya

ACCOMMODATION

Alhambra	4
Colonial	2
Granada	10
Hospedaje Adela's House	12
Hospedaje Calzada	5
Hospedaje Central	7
Hospedaje Cocibolca	8
Hospedaje El Italiano	6
Hospedaje Esfinge	11
Hospedaje Granada	9
La Posada de Don Alfredo	3
The Bearded Monkey	1

RESTAURANTS

Acuario	E
Asadero.com	F
Cafetín Los Bocaditos	J
Doña Conchi	I
Dragon Dorado	G
El Ancla	C
El Arlequino	K
El Mediterráneo	H
Flamingo	B
Los Portales	A
Sergio's Mexican	
Taquería	D

Complejo Turístico

Muelle for lake-going boats to San Carlos, Solentiname & Ometepe

Iglesia Guadalupe

Convento de San Francisco

Casa de Los Leones

CALLE GUZMÁN

PLAZA DE LA INDEPENDENCIA

Parque Central

Minibuses to Managua

Cathedral

Bank

Mercado

CALLE EL CAIMITO

LA CALZADA

CALLE VEGA COMERCIO

CALLE ATRAVESADA

Buses to Masaya

Buses to Rivas

Iglesia La Merced

CALLE ATRAVESADA

CALLE REAL XALTEVA

AV HÉROES Y MÁRTIRES

Buses to/from Managua

500 m

N

pastel shades. Today Granada is central to the Nicaraguan government's **tourism** ambitions, and a burgeoning network of foreign-owned bars, restaurants and hostels has already sprung up to service the increasing number of visitors. The city also makes a good base from which to explore the lake, volcanoes, the Zapatera archipelago and Isla de Ometepe, while more adventurous travellers might head on to the Solentiname Islands and San Carlos (see p.533).

Arrival, information and accommodation

Regular buses from Managua come into the **terminal** west of town, 700m from the Parque Central, from where you can walk or grab a taxi into the centre. Arriving from Rivas, Masaya and points south, buses pull up at the **mercado**, a short walk southwest of the centre. Express **minivans** from Managua and Masaya pull up outside the *Hotel Alhambra* on the Parque Central. If you're travelling from Costa Rica, the **Ticabus** for Managua will stop and let you off at its Granada office. The most exciting way to arrive, however, is by **boat** from San Carlos on the other side of Lago de Nicaragua (arrives Tues & Fri; 12–14hr), as half of Granada comes out to watch the old chug-tub boat dock.

Although spread out, Granada can be explored comfortably on **foot**, though in the midday heat you'll want to follow the example of Granadinos and walk on whichever side of the pavement is in shade. **Horse-drawn taxis** are a picturesque feature of the city, although the horses look thin and thirsty – they line up in front of the bandstand on the south side of the Parque Central. **Taxis** queue just across the street, in front of the *Hotel Alhambra*; if you take them from here it's slightly more expensive than hailing them on the street.

Information

Granada's small **tourist office** is on the Parque Central, just across from the cathedral. The green and white **Enitel** office is just along from the cathedral. All the **banks** in town change dollars; Bancentro, one block west of the Parque on C Atravesada, will change travellers' cheques., while Banco de América Central, on the south side of the Parque Central, has an ATM machine. The **post office** (Mon–Fri 8am–5pm), on C Atrevesada, has a reliable overseas mail service. The **cinema** on C Atravesada, opposite the post office, shows US films in the evenings.

There are **Internet** offices dotted around town – most charge around US$3 per hour – while many hospedajes and hotels also offer Internet access at slightly higher prices. The most popular office is at the *Café Converso* next to the Casa de los Leones; other offices include Computadoras de Granada, next to the Cathedral, and Compunet, on C La Libertad opposite *Hotel Colonial*.

Accommodation

The range of places **to stay** in Granada has improved immeasurably in just a couple of short years, and the city now boasts a complete range of accommodation options from budget hostels to upmarket hotels.

Alhambra, on the Parque Central (☎552-4486, fax 552-2035, *hotalam@tmx.com.ni*). Considered one of Nicaragua's finest hotels, this smartly designed, colonial-style establishment has rooms with a/c, TV, and bath with hot water, plus a bar and restaurant. Prices differ depending on which level you take a room – those higher up have better views over the Parque. ④–⑤.

Colonial, C La Libertad, just off the Parque (☎552-7581, fax 552-7299, *hotelcolonialgra@tmx.com.ni*). Smart new mock-colonial hotel. All rooms have a/c, TV, phone and bath with hot water, and there's also a bar and restaurant. Credit cards accepted. ④.

Granada, C La Calzada opposite the Iglesia Guadelupe (☎552-2974, fax 552-4128). Modern and unatmospheric hacienda-style hotel offering nice rooms with a/c, TV and bath (some have hot water), plus a bar and restaurant. Credit cards accepted. ⑤.

Hospedaje Adela's House, C Palmira, 25m from the market opposite terminal for buses to Rivas (☎552-7556). Simple, good-value hospedaje. All rooms have soft beds, fan and shared bath, and breakfast is served in an attractive tiled restaurant. ②.

Hospedaje Calzada, C La Calzada. Simple but popular family-run hospedaje with clean, simple rooms with fan and shared bath. A good-value breakfast is available – and the ping-pong table is also a big draw. ②–③.

Hospedaje Central, C La Calzada. The most colourful hospedaje in town, with murals, paintings and graffiti on all interior walls – accommodation is either in dorm beds (US$5–10 per person) or in rather basic rooms with shared bath. There's also a popular bar and restaurant serving "gringo" food. ③.

Hospedaje Cocibolca, C La Calzada (☎552-7227). Small but very popular hospedaje with homely and good-value rooms (some with private bath), plus cooking facilities, Internet access and cable TV. ②.

Hospedaje El Italiano, C La Calzada (☎ & fax 552-7047). Bright and airy purpose-built new hotel with a pleasant courtyard, bar and restaurant. The spacious double rooms all come with bath, TV and a/c. Reservations recommended. ⑤

Hospedaje Esfinge, C Palmira opposite market (☎552-4826). Good budget option with dorm beds (US$4–8 per person) and private rooms (some with bath) in large colonial house with bags of character – though rooms in the new extension are very small and airless. Also has laundry facilities, garden and a TV room. ②.

Hospedaje Granada, C La Calzada (☎552-3716). Pleasant, family-run hospedaje with its own swimming pool and simple, clean rooms, some with private bath, all with fan. ②–③.

La Posada de Don Alfredo, C 14 de Septiembre, one block from La Merced (☎ & fax 552-4455). Old colonial house restored in classic style, with a nice courtyard, romantic atmosphere and huge rooms (some with private bath) with high ceilings and good beds. ⑤

The Bearded Monkey, C 14 de Septiembre (☎552-4028, *thebeardedmonkey@yahoo.com*). Backpacker hangout in a renovated colonial house set around a large courtyard with hammocks, pool table, Internet access and TV. Accommodation is in large, impersonal dorms (US$10 per person) and three private rooms (all with shared bath). There's also a good restaurant and bar, and a daily happy hour. ②.

The Town

Though Granada's stately air has been punctured somewhat of late by the influx of tourists, it remains one of Nicaragua's most relaxing cities, and a pleasant place to spend a few days. There are few "must see" attractions in the city itself, and most of the pleasure is simply in strolling the streets and absorbing the colonial atmosphere – be sure to take a peak through the opened front doors along Calle La Calzada to see the magnificent interior courtyards which adorn some of the houses.

The centre of town is the attractive, palm-lined **Parque Central**, where locals and visitors spend hours sitting under shaded trees watching the world go by. A few small kiosks sell snacks and soft drinks, while an ice-cream seller wanders around ringing his hand bell in search of trade. On the east side of the Parque is the large but disappointing **Cathedral**, built in 1712 and damaged when William Walker ordered the city burned (you can still see the scorch marks); it has a peeling off-white facade and a rusting tin roof, and is often closed to the public.

Many of the city's most captivating **historic houses** are ranged around the Parque Central and the **Plaza de la Independencia**, immediately to the north. The palatial red house with white trim on the corner of Calle La Calzada, across from the cathedral, is the **Bishop's Residence**, with a columned upstairs veranda which is typical of the former homes of wealthy Granadino burghers. About 50m north of the cathedral on the Plaza de la Independencia is another stately old home, the **Casa de los Leones** (now renamed the Casa de los Tres Mundos). Built in 1724, it has been restored and turned into a culture and music centre, and visitors can wander among its covered and open courtyards and maze-like corridors – the wooden panelling and staircases found within are rare in this concrete-and-adobe country.

Originally dating from the sixteenth century but rebuilt in 1867 after Walker's attack, the historic **Convento de San Francisco** (daily 9.30am–5.30pm; US$3), 200m north and 150m east of the cathedral, has been converted into one of Nicaragua's best pre-Colombian museums, housing many of the **petroglyphs** recovered from Isla Zapatera. Hewn from black volcanic basalt in about 1000 AD, these petroglyphs depict anthropomorphic creatures – half man, half lizard, turtle or jaguar – which probably had ritual significance for the indigenous peoples who inhabited the islands. It was also from the confines of this convent that in 1535 **Frey Bartolomé de las Casas**, apostle of the indigenous peoples of Central America, wrote his historic letter to the Spanish Court, condemning the Indians' mistreatment at the hands of the Spanish. The Convento also houses the city **library**: many of Walker's filibusters are buried in the catacombs in its basement.

A few blocks southwest of the Parque Central, activity picks up (at least to a shuffle) at the **market**, a few blocks of indoor and outdoor stalls surrounding the old green market building. You can grab a quick and cheap bite here – the hot *tamales* and *gallo pinto* make a good breakfast.

The lakefront

Everywhere in Granada you can feel the welcome breeze off **Lago de Nicaragua**. The shoreline is about 1km east of the Parque Central; head down the wide boulevard of Calle La Calzada and the wind picks up as the huge vista of the lake stretches across the horizon. In the evenings Granadinos open the doors of their houses to let in the lake breeze, pull up the rocking chairs, and have a chat on inside patios.

The lakefront itself is pretty quiet, unless you happen to arrive as the boat from the other side comes in, when you can watch Granadinos meeting friends and family and see queasy passengers disembark as bananas, chickens and livestock are unloaded along the narrow dock. To the south a small park lines the lake, a few hundred metres beyond which is the entrance to the town's **Complejo Turístico**, a group of lakeside restaurants and bars, a narrow little beach and grassy areas – look for the strange little castle that marks the entrance. It's popular at weekends, but take care here after dark.

Eating and drinking

Granada offers a variety of **places to eat**. Budget travellers can grab a quick but basic bite at the town market, and street vendors sell nuts, popcorn and bagged fruit. In the early evening a couple of small food stands open up on the Parque Central, selling cheap and filling meat and rice dishes.

The city is peculiarly dead **at night**, and most travellers in search of alcohol and company tend to head to the bars at the *Hospedaje Central* or the *The Bearded Monkey*. Down by the lake, the places in the Complejo Turístico are much of a muchness and are usually fairly empty, except on Friday or Saturday nights, when locals go out to party. The *Colomar* bar-restaurant is slightly classier than other bars in the *complejo* – look for the gates and bamboo shoots outside. Many of these drinking dens advertise happy hours and special "disco" nights, but it's best to get there and back in taxi at night – local *machos borrachos* (drunk males) might make the walk back a bit of a hassle, especially for women.

Acuario, C La Calzada, opposite *Hospedaje Cocibolca*. Cheap and popular option serving good value Nicaraguan cuisine in the evening.

Asadero.com, C La Calzada, opposite Farmacia Loyola. Imaginative and varied meat and vegetarian platters for around US$5.

Cafetin Los Bocaditos, C Atrevesada. Good place for cheap breakfasts and lunches.

Doña Conchi, one block along C El Caimito from *El Mediterráneo*. Very good Spanish food, and slightly cheaper than *El Mediterráneo*.

Dragon Dorado, corner of C Real Xalteva and C Atrevesada. Reasonable – though slightly expensive – Chinese food.

El Ancla, Calle La Calzada, near Guadalupe Church. Succulent hamburgers or lake fish for about US$2.50; it has long opening hours and also takes credit cards.

El Arlequino, opposite *Doña Conchi*. Granada's best Italian eatery, seving good-quality seafood and pasta dishes for US$6–9.

El Mediterráneo, C El Caimito, two blocks from the cathedral. Elegant Spanish restaurant set around a romantic colonial courtyard dripping with atmosphere and serving good Spanish meat and seafood dishes for US$10–12.

Flamingo, C Atrevesada, next to the cinema. Popular canteen serving good lunches and cheap beer.

Hospedaje Central, C La Calzada. Similar range of dishes to *The Bearded Monkey*, though at slightly higher prices.

Los Portales, opposite the Casa de los Leones. Open-fronted restaurant serving acceptable Mexican and meat dishes for US$3–6.

Sergio's Mexican Taquería, next to *Hospedaje Central*. Popular burrito bar – a good feed will cost around US$5.

The Bearded Monkey, C 14 de Septiembre. Good selection of meat and vegetarian dishes.

Around Granada

Although Granada is a convenient jumping-off point for trips to Ometepe and Solentiname (see p.533), there are a couple of worthwhile day-trips closer by.

Isla Zapatera and the Isletas de Granada

About 20km south of Granada, in Lago de Nicaragua, **Isla Zapatera** is one of over three hundred islands scattered about the lake, believed to have been formed from the exploded top of Volcán Mombacho. Many of the pre-Columbian artefacts and treasures you find in museums in Nicaragua came from this group of islands, which must have once been of religious significance for the Chorotega-descended people who flourished here before the Conquest. At 52 square kilometres, Zapatera is the largest of the islands, skirted by attractive bays and topped by the much-eroded form of an extinct

---

LAKE TRANSPORT FROM GRANADA

The sturdy **tug-boat** that plies the choppy waters of Lago de Nicaragua between San Carlos and Granada has a changing schedule – check at the docks office (end of La Calzada) or pick up a copy of *Turistas: Revista Guía Granada*, a quarterly English-language magazine available from hotels and bars across Granada that publishes ferry schedules to and from Isla Ometepe and San Carlos. The trip from Granada to **Altagracia**, at the northeast tip of Ometepe, takes four to six hours, while the full journey across the lake from Granada to **San Carlos** takes anywhere from twelve to fourteen hours. According to the dock staff, demand for tickets is high at some times of year and people queue from 7am on the day of departure to be assured of a place. At other times you can just show up an hour before the boat is due to leave. Again, the best advice is to ask in Granada. Fares are very low: US$1.60 to Altagracia and US$3 to San Carlos. A speedier alternative if you're heading for Isla Ometepe is to take a bus to Rivas then a bus or taxi to San Jorge, from where eight lanchas a day (between 9.30am and 5.30pm) run to Moyogalpa on Isla Ometepe.

volcano. The island has recently been granted national park status, but that doesn't mean it's easy to get there. Unless you've got some nifty local connections, the only way to go is with a recognized travel agency, such as Servitur in Granada, or one of those in Managua that regularly offer archeological excursions to the island (see p.499). Guides should be able to show you **El Muerto** (The Dead), a site chock-full of the remains of tombs, several **petroglyphs**, and the scant remains – a few grassy mounds and stones – of **Sozafe**, a site sacred to the Chorotegas. These remains apart, there's really very little to see, bar lovely views of the lake. Most of the 300 islands are completely uninhabited, and food, drink and lodging are unavailable – hence the necessity for guided tours.

The alternative to a tour is to buzz round the 350 **Isletas de Granada** in a hired lancha. Boatmen in **ASESE**, a fifteen-minute drive or one-hour walk south of Granada, beyond the Complejo Turistico, charge around US$15 per hour for a boat for up to four people, (but be prepared to negotiate). You don't see much on the standard hour-long trip, so you may want to negotiate a two- or three-hour ride. Make sure the boat is covered, or take a hat and plenty of sunscreen – the sun out on the water is punishing.

Volcán Mombacho

Created in 1983, the **Reserva Nacional Volcán Mombacho** (Wed–Sun 8am–5pm; US$3) was set up to protect and study the unique ecology of **Volcán Mombacho**, whose slopes are home to one of only two **cloudforests** (the other is at Volcán Maderas on Isla Ometepe) in Nicaragua's Pacific region. The cloudforest is able to grow here due to the volcano's height – its peak is frequently covered in cloud – and the strong, cooling winds from Lago de Nicaragua. The reserve is run by the Fundación Cocibolca, whose interesting **research station** and **visitor centre** at the volcano's summit acts as the centre for the study and protection of the reserve's flora and fauna – which includes three species of monkey, 22 species of reptile, 87 species of orchid, 171 species of bird and some 50,000 species of insect. There's a well-marked **trail** around the four craters at the top of the volcano with signs explaining some of the reserve's unique flora and fauna. At the furthest point of the trail the views open out to provide a magnificent panoramic vista of Lago de Nicaragua, Granada, Las Isletas, Masaya and Laguna de Apoyo.

To get to the volcano take any **bus** from Granada bound for Rivas or Nandaime and ask to be let off at the turn-off for the park, from where it's another one-kilometre walk to the entrance, from where it takes two hours to walk to the top. Alternatively, for an extra US$1.75, you can take the "Eco-truck" to the summit – it leaves from the reserve entrance at 8.30pm, 10am, 1pm and 3pm.

Rivas

Most travellers experience **RIVAS** as a dusty bus stop on the way to or from Costa Rica, San Juan del Sur, or Ometepe, unaware of the important role this scruffy town has played in Nicaraguan history. Founded in 1736, it became an important stop on the route of Cornelius Vanderbilt's Accessory Transit Company, which ferried goods and passengers between the Caribbean and the Pacific via Lago de Nicaragua – Rivas's heyday came during the California Gold Rush, when its languid streets were full of prospectors travelling with the Transit Company on their way to the goldfields of the western US.

Rivas's ragged **market** and **bus terminal**, three blocks south and two blocks west of the Parque Central, is the transport hub of southern Nicaragua. From here you can catch buses north to Granada, Masaya and Managua; west to San Juan del Sur; and south to Sapoá and the Costa Rican border. Bus stops in the market are not marked but everyone knows where buses depart – ask around. If you're headed to San Jorge (for Ometepe), it's best to get a taxi (US$1.50) as buses are infrequent and leave from the highway, a good 1km hike from the market. **Moneychangers** frequent Rivas' bus stops, looking for Costa Rican-bound or departing gringos and offering Costa Rican colónes, Nicaraguan córdobas and US dollars at rates more or less the same as at the border. In town, Banpro, two and a half blocks west of the Parque Central, will change dollars.

Despite its history, Rivas is not a place you want to get stuck in for the night; several of the **hotels** rent beds by the hour. That said, the experience is survivable (earplugs help) and there are far worse dives in Nicaragua. The *Hotel Nicarao*, two blocks west of the Parque Central (☎463-3234; ②), is better than most, and its rooms are equipped with private bath and either a/c or fan. For rock-bottom budget travellers, the best bet is the *Hospedaje Internacional* next to the *Hotel Coco* (①), where you'll at least get a clean bed and a fan.

A quick, cheap **meal** can be picked up at any of the comedores on the Parque Central, where you'll find good chicken, pork or beef and rice dishes, and *tamales*. Surprisingly, Rivas has a vegetarian joint, *La Soya*, 50m north of the Parque Central, offering workaday salads and vegetable dishes.

San Juan del Sur

You would never suspect it today, but the sleepy fishing village-cum-beach town of **SAN JUAN DEL SUR** was once a lively place. In the mid-1800s this was a crucial **transit point** on Cornelius Vanderbilt's trans-isthmian steamboat line, on which people and goods were transported to goldrush-era California. Boats would sail up the Río San Juan, disembark at Granada, and then continue by rail or carriage to San Juan del Sur, from where Pacific-going vessels would head north.

San Juan del Sur's second age of glory was as a popular **holiday spot** for hordes of *internacionalistas* during the 1980s. Today it's the most popular beach town in Nicaragua, at least with foreign travellers – European backpackers and American surfers together make up the biggest contingent. San Juan del Sur's setting, in a lush valley with a river running down to the beach, is beautiful; the beach itself is a long wide stretch of fine dark sand running between two cliffs, with generally calm and shallow waters, suitable for swimming, and magnificent sunsets over the harbour. With excellent seafood restaurants and a number of reasonable places to stay, San Juan is the kind of town you could easily spend a few days in. To the south are some beautiful and remote beaches, good for surfing or relaxing (although not necessarily swimming – the surf is rough).

Arrival and information
Buses leave Rivas every hour, and take an hour to reach San Juan del Sur, pulling up outside the *Hospedaje Elizabeth* near the market. There's no tourist office in town, but you can get **information** from *Casa Joxi* or *Maria's Bar* – the latter also rents out **bicycles**. The **Enitel** office, two blocks south of *Hotel Estrella*, has an international phone service (daily 7am–10pm) and mail service (Mon–Fri 8am–6pm). There's no bank in town, but many establishments take credit cards, travellers' cheques and dollars.

Accommodation
San Juan del Sur has a good mix of accommodation, from well-appointed hotels to surfer's dens; the budget places are mainly located on the road to the beach from the bus terminal.

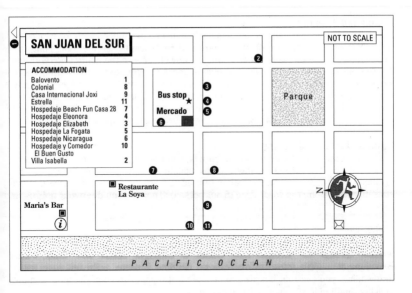

Balovento, behind the health centre (☎458-2298 or 458-2374). One of the town's larger hotels, with nineteen rooms, an a/c bar and a fairly good restaurant attached. ⑤.

Casa Internacional Joxi, 50m from the beach (☎468-2348). Nice but overpriced rooms and spotless dorms with bunkbeds (US$11). There's also pricey Internet access (US$9/hr), a restaurant and shop, and the owners rent out boogie boards and organize sailing trips. ④–⑤.

Colonial, just behind the beach (☎ & fax 458-2539, *hotel.colonial@ifxnw.com.ni*). Clean and well-maintained hotel – all rooms have a/c, TV and private bath. Breakfast included. ⑥.

Estrella, on the beach (☎458-2270). The second-storey rooms with balconies facing the beach have plenty of breeze and character and are ideal for sunset-watching. Minus points include the charm-less owners, mosquitoes, and the fact that rooms are divided only by partitions. There's also a restaurant serving all meals. ②.

Hospedaje Beach Fun Casa 28, a block back from the beach (☎458-2441). If you can stand the bargain-basement surfer clientele, *Casa 28* is a good budget option. Friendly management but poor beds. ①—②.

Hospedaje Eleonora, next to *Hospedaje Elizabeth* (☎458-2191). Small, safe and well-located family guesthouse, offering spartan concrete rooms with fan, shared bath and rather brusque service. ②.

Hospedaje Elizabeth, 75m east of the market, opposite bus stop (☎458-2270). A small, simple but friendly guesthouse with twelve rooms with private bath. You can pick up local maps here and rent bicycles. ①–②.

Hospedaje La Fogata next to *Hospedaje Eleonora*. Well-worn but friendly and characterful guesthouse. Most rooms have shared bath and fan, and you can get breakfast in the barn-like restaurant. ②.

Hospedaje Nicaragua, two blocks back from beach. Small and easily missed hospedaje with four spotless and impeccably maintained double rooms, all with a/c and private bath. The rocking chairs on the veranda are a nice touch. Good value. ②.

Hospedaje y Comedor El Buen Gusto, opposite the *Estrella* on the beachfront. Small rooms, but a nice upstairs balcony to relax on, plus a spotless restaurant. Breakfast included. ②.

Villa Isabella, northwest corner of the Parque (☎458-2568). Smart new hotel with good facilities and spacious rooms, all with TV, a/c and private bath. There's a bar and restaurant attached, and credit cards are accepted. ⑥.

Eating and drinking

Seafood is king in San Juan del Sur, and a whole baked fish, big enough for two, costs only US$7 or so. There are plenty of **bars** and **restaurants** serving food along the beachfront, though the same food is considerably cheaper in the market. *Restaurante La Soya* serves good vegetarian food plus fish and chicken dishes for around US$2, while the unmarked comedor opposite serves cheap and filling meals in the early evening. *Maria's Bar* has a good menu catering to Western tastes with dishes for around US$4–7. The seafront restaurants are also good places to have a beer and shoot the breeze at sunset. *Ricardo's Bar* is the town's liveliest **nightspot**.

Sailing, fishing and surfing

Fast developing a reputation for **water sports**, San Juan del Sur is already well-known as a good spot for **sailing**. All-day cruises, sailing south to Brasilito Beach, can be arranged – ask at *Maria's Bar* or look out for posters around town – and there are also sunset cruises along the coast (US$15 per person). There's good **deep-sea fishing** in this area and a number of companies organize trips. On a more modest scale, you can rent **fishing gear** from *Maria's Bar,* who also arrange fishing trips for groups of up to twelve people.

Diving trips in San Juan del Sur and other locations in Nicaragua can be arranged in advance through the Oceania Dive School in Managua (Bahía Dive Shop, Plaza Barcelona; ☎277-2104, *latincam@tmx.com.ni*). **Surfing**, however, is the real water sport in town, and you can rent boards and arrange transport to some of the more remote beaches south of town – again, ask at *Maria's Bar*.

The **Refugio de Vida Silvestre La Flor**, 19km south of San Juan del Sur, is an excellent spot to string up a hammock and spend a night. It has good surf, a beautiful white sandy beach and a stand of shady trees, and there are more great empty **beaches** within walking distance. It's also a guarded reserve dedicated to protecting the **sea turtles** that nest there in large numbers between October and December. Mosquitoes and voracious sandflies are abundant – take repellent. To reach La Flor you'll either need to arrange private transport or catch the once-daily bus that leaves San Juan del Sur in the mid-afternoon. There are a couple of tents at La Flor which are rented out on a first-come-first-served basis; otherwise, be prepared to string up a hammock.

South to Costa Rica

Crossing the border at the Sapoá–Peñas Blancas post is a time-consuming process, though leaving Nicaragua is at least faster than entering. Local **buses from Rivas** go as far as the border post at the shantytown of **Sapoá** (if you're leaving from San Juan del Sur, take the Rivas bus only as far as the highway and then catch a connecting bus – there's no need to go all the way back to Rivas). The bus pulls up directly in front of the barrier, which you cross (show your passport to soldiers in the little doghouses on either side), and enter the white Nicaraguan *migración*. Inside you must pay an exit tax (US$2) in dollars, and get your exit stamp from Nicaraguan *migración*. **Taxis** are available for the 3–4km trip to the Costa Rican border post (show passport again), from where it's about an 800m walk along the highway to the blue Costa Rican *migración*. Once inside, head for the "Entrada" window, where the *migración* official may ask to see an onward ticket. You'll be given a ninety-day entrance stamp and have to pay a fee of US$1, after which you pick up your passport from another window when you hear your name called out.

Local buses from **Peñas Blancas**, the name of the Costa Rican border post, run every hour to San José and points between. You can buy your ticket from one of the makeshift tables at the *migración*, after which you line up for the baggage check, a rudimentary fumble in your bag by Costa Rican customs officials. Once on the bus be prepared for many passport checks in the first few kilometres.

Inside the Costa Rican *migración* is a small Costa Rican **tourist office**, the ICT (Mon–Sat 8am–8pm, Sun 8am–noon). They're helpful, but don't have any hand-outs apart from glossy tourist brochures in Spanish only.

travel details

BUSES

Granada to: Managua (every 30min; 1hr 30min); Masaya (every 30min; 30min); Rivas (every 30min; 1hr 30min).

Masaya to: Diriamba (every 30min; 1hr); Granada (every 30min; 30min); Managua (every 30min; 45min); Rivas (every 30min; 2hr).

Rivas to: Diriamba (every 30min; 2hr); Granada (every 30min; 1hr 30min); Masaya (every 30min; 2hr); Managua (every 30min; 2hr 30min); San Juan del Sur (hourly; 1hr); Sapoá (for Costa Rica; hourly; 1hr).

San Juan del Sur to: Rivas (hourly; 1hr).

BOATS

For a rundown of the services from Granada to San Carlos, Ometepe and the Solentiname islands, see p.522 & 536.

CHAPTER 25

LAGO DE NICARAGUA

S tanding on the shore and looking out into its expanse, you can imagine the surprise of the Spanish navigators in 1522 when, nearly certain they were heading towards the long dreamed of route to the Pacific, they instead came upon **Lago de Nicaragua**. The lake – also known by its indigenous name, Cocibolca ("sweet sea") – is the largest **freshwater sea** in the Americas after the Great Lakes, and the tenth largest body of fresh water in the world. Over 177km long, about 58km wide and fed by forty rivers, the lake is not very deep (about 60m at its deepest point), though its waters can be rough.

Both Lago de Nicaragua and Lago de Managua were probably once part of the Pacific, until **volcanic eruptions** and earthquakes created the Pacific plain which separates the lakes from the ocean today. Fed by freshwater rivers over millennia, the lake water gradually lost its salinity, while the saltwater fish trapped in it evolved into some of the most unusual types of fish found anywhere on earth, including freshwater tarpon and swordfish. The lake is also visited by the **bull shark**, a voracious predator capable of moving between the ocean waters of the Caribbean and the fresh waters of the lake.

Crossing the lake can be quite an undertaking: Lago de Nicaragua is affected by what locals call a "short-wave phenomenon" – short, high, choppy waves – caused by the meeting of the Papagayo wind from the west and the Caribbean-generated trade winds from the east. Lakegoing craft are notoriously thick-set and slow; the waves

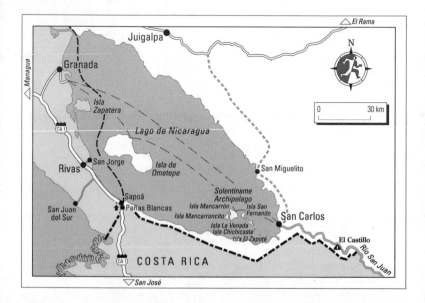

For an explanation of **accommodation price codes**, see p.468.

require them to advance slowly and in a zigzag pattern – one reason why lake crossings take so long. The lake's choppiness makes crossing it hell for those prone to seasickness, and there are occasional dangerous squalls, especially in November.

Travellers who have the patience to cope with erratic boat schedules (and preferably some Spanish, as settlements around the lake are few and isolated) are drawn by the area's unique **culture**. Many are captivated by the natural beauty of the **islands** that dot the southwest sector of the lake: twin-volcanoed **Isla de Ometepe** and the scattering of small islands known as the **Archipiélago de Solentiname**. Ernesto Cardenal, one of Nicaragua's best-known writers, lived for many years in Solentiname and the islands are also famous for their *pintores primitivos* – naif-style painters who depict lush landscapes in which jewel-coloured parrots and red jaguars poke their noses out of verdant jungles. In all, over 400 islands dot the lake, most of them inhabited, while others are used by well-to-do mainlanders as a place for holiday homes.

On its eastern edge the lake is fed by the 170-kilometre Río San Juan, which forms Nicaragua's southern border and runs out into the Caribbean. You can take a boat trip down the river to the remote **El Castillo**, an old Spanish fort on the banks of the Río San Juan, surrounded on all sides by pristine jungle and offering excellent opportunities for wildlife spotting. The Río San Juan and El Castillo are reached via the largest town on the east side of the lake, **San Carlos**, a muddy, bug-ridden town of little interest, used by travellers mainly as a transit point for exploring the river or travelling south to Costa Rica via Los Chiles.

Isla de Ometepe

"Va para la isla?" mainlanders ask you as you head to the San Jorge docks near Rivas to catch the boat to **ISLA DE OMETEPE**. And from the reverential way they say its name, you can tell Ometepe is considered a place apart from the rest of Nicaragua. The dramatic views from the mainland of its two magical **volcanoes** rising steeply from the waters of Lago de Nicaragua are not the least of its attractions, and on a clear day the view from the boat as you approach is truly spectacular. The island's name comes from the Nahuatl language of the Chorotegans, the original inhabitants of Nicaragua, who called it Ome Tepetl – "the place of two hills". Even on clear days wispy clouds cap the summit of the higher and more symmetrical of the two cones, **Volcán Concepción**, which at 1610m is Nicaragua's second-highest volcano. The dull mauve of Concepción's upper slopes, stripped of vegetation by altitude and lava flow, contrasts sharply with the almost shining green of the farms, secondary forest and tilled fields on its fertile lower slopes. To the south is extinct **Volcán Maderas**, smaller (1394m) and less perfectly conical in shape, but clothed with precious cloudforest. Until the last century Ometepe was technically two islands, separated only by a narrow canal, until an eruption of Concepción in 1804 filled the gap and sealed the narrow isthmus – Ometepe is now referred to as one island.

The island has probably been inhabited since the first migration of indigenous groups from Mexico arrived in this area, and a few stone sculptures and petroglyphs attest to their presence on the island – some can be easily seen if you go on a guided walk. It's not clear if there was any significant population on the island when Spanish farmers and cattle ranchers colonized Ometepe during the early 1600s. For hundreds of years Volcán Concepción was dormant, but one morning in 1804 the island's inhabitants woke up to find they had settled on an active volcano. Since then Concepción has erupted seven times, most recently in 1957: there has been no significant activity since.

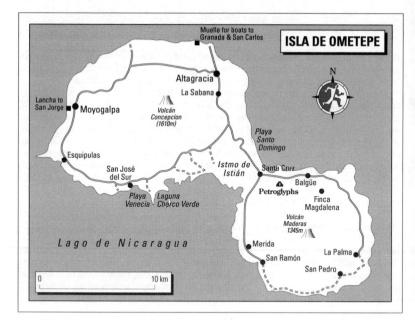

Still, the shadow of the volcano and its lava-scarred slopes looms everywhere on the island.

Ometepe has remained isolated from the outside world; until recently even contact with Granada was sporadic, while the Sandinista revolution and subsequent civil war had only a negligible effect. The island has an amazing **agricultural output**, owing to its unusually fertile volcanic soil, and is more prosperous than much of mainland Nicaragua. Most farms are smallholdings on the skirts of the volcano, growing citrus, bananas, coffee, cacao, watermelon and sesame, as well as dry-country products like tobacco and cotton. Towns on the island are well-kept and schoolchildren and the occasional cow share the dusty graded roads with island traffic.

Almost everyone who travels through Nicaragua comes to Ometepe, if only to sample the island's amazingly lush scenery and tranquil atmosphere. **Walking, hiking, volcano-viewing** and **horse-riding** are really the only activities on the island, and many visitors come specifically to scale the smaller of the two volcanoes, Maderas. The temperature on the island is slightly cooler than the mainland, as the heat is mitigated by lake winds.

Ometepe supports a population of 30,000 – quite large for an island of its size. Most people live around the foot of Volcán Concepción, which is where the two main towns, **Moyogalpa** and **Altagracia**, are found. A dirt and gravel **road** circles Concepción, though in the rainy season one stretch between Moyogalpa and Altagracia can become impassible, while another, very rough road (4WD only), goes about three-quarters of the way around Volcán Maderas.

Despite their relatively small size, the two volcanoes of **Concepción** and **Maderas** comprise quite different ecosystems. Concepción forms the easternmost extent of what is known as **Pacific tropical dry forest** – a dry and grassy type of vegetation. Most of Maderas, by contrast, is home to an ecosystem very similar to the **rainforest** areas of southeast Nicaragua. You can actually see the change taking place on Maderas as you move from the northwest part of the island to the south – the actual border zone, according to biologists, is around the hamlet of San Ramón. On Maderas you're likely to spot rainforest **animals** such as the white-faced monkey (*carablanca*) and howler monkey (*mono congo*), while bird-watchers will want to keep their eyes out for green parrots (*loro verde*) and the commonly sighted blue-tailed birds called *urracas*.

Island transport

The majority of travellers arrive in Moyogalpa on the **lancha from San Jorge** on the mainland; there are nine daily departures Monday to Saturday, and three on Sunday (see p.536 for detailed schedules); itineraries sometimes change between the rainy and dry seasons. There are also two boats a week **from Granada** (currently Mon & Thurs) to Altagracia, from where most travellers head straight for Moyogalpa, which offers a much better choice of hotels and services. A local bus service leaves Altagracia for Moyogalpa (last departure at 5.30pm). **Returning** to the mainland, you'll need to take an early-morning crossing if you want to travel on to Peñas Blancas on the Costa Rican border, though the 1.30pm crossing will still get you to Granada or Managua before buses stop running. Best to double-check the schedule the day before you plan to leave.

   Getting around the island isn't too arduous. A **bus** runs eight times daily, shuttling between Moyogalpa docks and Altagracia, a journey of about an hour. A far less frequent bus leaves Altagracia for Balgüe, on the northern side of Maderas, and the jumping off point for the *Finca Magdalena* and Volcán Maderas. Sunday services for all buses are less frequent.

   You can rent tough Suzuki Samurai **jeeps** from the *Hotel Ometepetl* for about US$56 for 24 hours, and most hotels rent **bicycles** by the hour (US$2) or by the day (US$8). An alternative to getting around under your own steam is to hire one of the several local **taxi** drivers-cum-guides to take you around the island. Fares depend on how far you are going, and it's far more economical if you can get a group together. A day's jaunt around Maderas as far as Merida or Balgüe will cost US$50 per carload.

Moyogalpa

The largest town on the island, **MOYOGALPA** is set on the northwest side of Volcán Concepción. The dock, where lanchas from San Jorge arrive, is at the bottom of the main street, a steep and narrow avenue lined by high pavements backed by hardware stores and agricultural supply shops. Occasional Land Rovers battle up and down the town's streets, their front axles hanging loose after too many potholes. Most transport in the town, though, is by tractor, or on rubber-wheeled, horse-drawn carts. Moyogalpa is home to many of Ometepe's services, lodgings and restaurants. There's no bank, but most shops, hotels and restaurants will **change dollars**. You can make calls and send mail from **Enitel** (Mon–Sat 8am–6pm) on the east side of the village.

   Most of Moyogalpa's **accommodation** is pretty basic. Probably the most popular budget option is the *Hotelito Aly*, 100m uphill from the dock, on the left (☎459-4196; ①–②), a large hospedaje with 25 basic rooms with narrow and uncomfortable beds plus a plant-filled courtyard with hammocks and a restaurant. Across the street, *Hotel Bahía* (①–②) has basic rooms with worn beds (some also have scruffy bathrooms) – those upstairs are better, with narrow balconies and volcano views. A restaurant serves all meals and there's a bar and "disco room" for weekend parties. For something a little more civilized, try the tranquil *El Pirata* hostel (☎459-4262; ④), two blocks north and one east of the tourist office, which has spacious doubles with a/c and bath, and a relaxing courtyard. Moyogalpa's most upmarket place is the *Hotel Ometepetl*, opposite the docks on the right (☎459-4276; ④), which has large, very clean if soulless rooms with fans. The management is friendly, and there's a good bar, restaurant and car-rental service.

There are only a few decent places in town **to eat**. *El Chele*, 50m uphill from the docks, and *Restaurante Ranchitos* on the main street both serve good Nica food and are popular at weekends, while the family-run *Comedor Familia* and *Soda El Chaguite*, just around the corner from the *Hotelito Aly*, serve good-value and freshly prepared *comida corriente* throughout the day. Both the *Hotel Bahía* and *Hotelito Aly* have cheap and cheerful restaurants attached serving standard Nicaraguan breakfasts, lunches and dinners.

Altagracia and Volcán Concepción

There's very little to detain the traveller in **ALTAGRACIA**, a sleepy town set slightly inland from the lake on Ometepe's northeastern side. Its **Parque Central** is nicely ringed by several pre-Columbian statues found on the island and, should you decide to stop here, there are two good **places to stay**. The *Hospedaje y Restaurante Castillo* (☎552-8744; ①–②), 100m south and 50m west of the church, has basic but spotlessly clean rooms, some with private bath. There's also a good restaurant, and horseback trips and guides for hiking up the volcano can be organized by the helpful owner. *Hotel Central*, two blocks south of the Parque Central (☎552-8770; ②), is a little more upscale and very comfortable. As well as regular rooms, some with private bath, there are good-value little cabañas that sleep up to four people; breakfasts, *comidas corrientes* and sandwiches are served in the little restaurant of the same name. *Hospedaje Don Kencho* (①–②), just along from *Hotel Central*, has box-like rooms with shared bath; the comedor at the front serves good-value meals. There's another decent **comedor** on the plaza opposite the bus station.

The hike up **Volcán Concepción** starts from just outside Altagracia and takes around eight hours for the round-trip. Much of the climb is extremely steep and it's a good idea to hire a guide – ask at the *Hospedaje Castillo*.

Playa Santo Domingo

Stretching for more than a kilometre on the east side of the isthmus separating Concepción and Maderas is the narrow, grey-sand **Playa Santo Domingo**. This is the only really swimmable beach on Ometepe (though the lake can be surprisingly rough at times), and many volcano-climbers and hikers spend a day soaking up some sun here. The beach is accessed from the main road circling Concepción, although the first kilometre or so of the road that forks off to Santo Domingo is in exceptionally bad condition (4WD essential). Beyond the beach there's not much to see, other than farmers riding out in the pre-dawn darkness and shy kids playing on the beach.

Of the two overpriced **places to stay**, the cheaper choice is the *Finca Santo Domingo* (③), a lovely rustic building offering simple dark rooms with fans, hammocks strung around the terrace, and good food – even if you don't stay here they will cook you large breakfasts and lunch for US$3–4. More upmarket is the adjacent *Hotel Villa Paraíso* (☎453-4675, in Managua ☎244-0181; ④): rooms are large, with fans and either shared or private bath, screened windows and rocking chairs on small patios. The covered restaurant, overlooking the lake and bordered by hammocks, is a great place to stop for lunch or for a beer.

Volcán Maderas

The hike up the verdant forested slopes of dormant **Volcán Maderas** is less arduous than the steep climb up and down Concepción, though it can be a wet, muddy and slippery walk, and you should exercise caution, especially on the descent. It takes about seven hours to get to the top and back down, so you need to set off early. Birds and howler monkeys can be heard (if not seen) all the way up, and the summit gives stunning views of Concepción and the lake. The crater itself is eerily silent and still, its lip covered by a mixture of dense, rainforest-like vegetation and a few bromeliad-encrusted conifers. Guides – a good idea – can be hired from the *Finca Magdalena* for around US$15. Make sure you take plenty of water (and don't forget sunscreen). The clear water in the crater lagoon is good for a (chilly) swim.

A nice place to stay whilst having a crack at climbing the volcano is the *Finca Magdalena*, an old hacienda with bags of character and stunning views across the lake, especially at sunset. Constructed in 1888, the finca was taken over by the Sandinistas and converted into a cooperative for the production of organic coffee, which is still grown here. Accommodation is in large dorm rooms (US$3–5 per person) with shared bath, or in a few small private rooms (②); the large restaurant serves good breakfasts, lunches and evening meals at reasonable prices. To reach the finca, you'll need to take the slow and bumpy bus ride through the banana plantations from Altagracia to **Balgüe**, on the northern slopes of Maderas, from where it's a twenty-minute walk up a signposted path. The finca always sends someone to meet buses arriving in Balgüe after dark, since the path isn't lit and is very difficult to find at night.

If you have time, it's worth exploring the towns dotted around the lower slopes of Maderas. **Petroglyphs** are scattered over this part of the island: a group of them is located between the hamlets of Santa Cruz and La Palma – you'll need someone to show you where they are; ask at the *Finca Magdalena* for a guide. Another easy one - our hike from the finca will take you to some very pleasant, but extremely cold, **waterfalls**.

The Solentiname archipelago

Lying in the southeast corner of Lago de Nicaragua, the **Solentiname archipelago** is made up of 36 islands of varying size which are becoming increasingly well known for their unspoilt natural beauty and remarkable **bird and animal life**. For a long time, though, it was the islands' colony of naif-art **painters** that brought fame to Solentiname. Priest and poet Ernesto Cardenal lived here for many years, writing and preaching liberation philosophy before becoming the Sandinistas' Minister of the Interior in the 1980s. His poetry and his promotion of the archipelago's primitive art and artisan skills brought Solentiname culture to the attention of the outside world, and it was Cardenal's work that led to the government declaring Solentiname a national monument in 1990.

The archipelago's largest islands are also the most densely inhabited: **Mancarrón**, **La Venada**, **San Fernando** and **Mancarroncito**. Most people stay on Mancarrón, where the islands' main hotel is located, and make trips to San Fernando and other nearby islands. Much of the **wildlife** in the area corresponds to that of northern Costa Rica, just over the border, and the dense jungles stretching from the eastern shore of Lago de Nicaragua to the Caribbean. The opulent birdlife includes parrots, macaws, egrets, storks and many kingfishers, while much of the islands' vegetation is pristine tropical forest.

Solentiname's **isolation** keeps all but the most determined independent travellers away, although tourist traffic in the form of organized tours is increasing. Travellers who give up trying to figure out the confusing and changeable boat schedules often come on a tour organized from Managua or Granada. There's absolutely nothing to do in Solentiname, except hunt out some of the *pintores primitivos*, if your Spanish is up to it. Make sure you bring plenty of córdobas with you – there's nowhere to change money on the islands.

Practicalities: Mancarrón

Boats make the two-hour trip to Mancarrón from San Carlos twice a week, on Mondays and Wednesdays at around 7am – although the departure time changes frequently.

Unless you come on a tour, this is currently the only way to get here by scheduled transport, although unscheduled private craft make the same trip, leaving constantly – ask around at the San Carlos docks.

Nearly everyone who comes to Solentiname **stays** in the *Hotel Mancarrón* (in Solentiname ☎552-2059, in Managua ☎260-3345; ⑤, including three meals a day), an old tiled-roof building set in grassland on the island of the same name. The hotel can fix you up with **boat tours** to nearby islands. A cheaper and potentially more interesting option is to bed down with a local family – even though it runs the hotel, the non-profit-making Solentiname Development Association (☎260-3345) on Mancarrón can put you in touch with locals; they can also hook you up with local **painters** and craftspeople and advise you on the boat schedule or anything else you need to know about Solentiname.

Río San Juan

At 170km long, the mighty **Río San Juan** is one of the most important rivers in Central America, and played a key role in the discovery and subsequent history of Nicaragua. In colonial times it was the route by which the nascent cities of Granada and León were supplied by Spain and emptied of their treasure by pirates, though nowadays the river area has staked its economic hopes on the more genteel pursuit of **ecotourism**. The river is relatively pristine, and no settlement of any size exists along the riverbank other than remote and sleepy villages whose inhabitants make their living by fishing and farming. If you want to experience the tropical flora and fauna and don't mind being hundreds of miles from civilization of any kind, then a boat ride on the Río San Juan is worth the hassle of getting there. **Wildlife** is abundant along the river, and travellers who venture up or downstream will certainly spot sloths, howler monkeys, parrots and macaws, bats, storks, caimans and perhaps even a tapir.

Most travellers see the Río San Juan from a boat en route between **San Carlos** on the eastern shore of Lago de Nicaragua and the old Spanish fort of the **El Castillo**, the only real tourist attraction in the area. The southern bank of the river forms the border with Costa Rica (although Costa Ricans have right of transit along it, the entire river is in Nicaraguan territory). See p.674 for trips on the Costa Rican side.

The Río San Juan area is alarmingly **remote** and you have to be prepared to do battle with the elements. Little food and drink is available, not to mention consumer goods, whether it be batteries or toothpaste. There are good hospitals on the Costa Rican side, in Los Chiles and in Ciudad Quesada, but you should be prepared for any emergency. Apart from that, the **basics** you will need are a light raincoat, plastic bags for cameras and other mechanical equipment, sunglasses, repellent, sunscreen, a torch, good boots, a spare (dry) pair of shoes, matches, candles, bottled water, towels and a first aid kid, including, if possible, a snakebite kit.

San Carlos

Sleepy and slatternly, **SAN CARLOS** has to be one of the most unprepossessing towns in the whole country. An air of lassitude, if not downright stasis, pervades its ramshackle buildings and muddy streets. This could, of course be the fault of the fire which destroyed most of the town in 1984, or the climate of heat and torrential rain, but there appears to be a general lack of civic pride or willingness to treat the place to a splash of paint. Travellers come through San Carlos from Los Chiles in Costa Rica in order to make the lake trip to Granada, or to go to Solentiname. Increasingly, more determined **ecotourists** are coming through to pick up a boat to the El Castillo and points further along the Río San Juan.

Getting to San Carlos

San Carlos can be reached by road, boat or air. The long, crowded and bumpy **bus** journey, which is erratic in the rainy season (always check that it's running), currently leaves Managua's Mercado Mayoreo bus terminal three times a day, taking nine or ten hours to reach San Carlos. If you plan on doing the heroic 300-kilometre **drive**, get your hands on a sturdy 4WD with high clearance.

Boats leave for San Carlos from Granada on Mondays and Thursdays at 2pm, arriving in San Carlos at 3 or 4am the next day (check return times from San Carlos to Granada before travelling). La Costeña and Atlantic Airlines **fly** from Managua to San Carlos three times weekly (check times in Managua), landing at the airstrip just north of town.

Practicalities

San Carlos's new Banco de Finanzas will **change dollars**; there's also an **Enitel** office (Mon–Sat 8am–5pm), but don't expect mail sent from here to get anywhere quickly. San Carlos has a lot of transient traffic, which is reflected in the spartan decor and indifferent management style of its **hotels**. There's little to choose between the four vaguely acceptable and not overly bug-ridden, sinister or noisy places in town. In front of the Plaza Malecón, by the lake, the *Hotel Azul* (☎283-0282; ②) is very basic; all rooms have fan and shared bath. The *Hotel San Carlos* in front of the market (②) is the place of choice for the local itinerant crowd, and pretty noisy. Rooms at the *Hospedaje Peña* (①) are cramped and run-down, while the shared bathroom is an experience. *Cabinas Leyka* (②–③), two blocks west of the Parque, is slightly more comfortable; all cabins have a/c and bath.

The best place **to eat** in town is the popular *Restaurante Kaoma*: it looks like a seedy underground drinking den but dishes up good, filling meat, fish and vegetarian (on request) plates for US$2–3.

Crossing into Costa Rica

To get to **Los Chiles in Costa Rica**, ask at the *muelle* (dock) for boatmen. There's currently no scheduled service, but you can always join one of the boats which ferry groups of Nicaraguans illegally over the river. The actual border post is 3km before you reach Los Chiles. Nicaraguan officials will give you an exit stamp; you get an entry stamp to Costa Rica at the Los Chiles **muelle**. Be aware that Costa Rican officials are rigorous in their checks on Nicaraguans in this area and there's always a chance that your boat will be sent back if you're travelling with Nicaraguans whose paperwork isn't satisfactory.

El Castillo

The full name of the Río San Juan's historic fort is La Fortaleza de la Limpia y Inmaculada Concepción, though everyone refers to it as **El Castillo**. Lying on a hillock perched beside a narrow stretch of the Río San Juan, the Castillo was built by the Spanish as a bulwark against the pirates who continually sacked Granada in the seventeenth century. The fort was more or less effective for over a hundred years, until the British finally took it in 1780, after which it was abandoned for nearly two centuries. The Nicaraguan Ministry of Tourism, with the help of funds from various overseas governments, has renovated and restored the low stone structure with an iron door and an access ramp, and has had several floors re-tiled. There's a library inside the walls with over a thousand books on the history of the castle and the Río San Juan area, plus a small **museum** (9am–5.30pm; US$1) with dusty armaments of the period and a few random artefacts found during the restoration of the castle.

Four **boats** a day leave San Carlos for El Castillo, a journey of about two and a half hours; the last returns at 2.30pm. You can rent a *panga* (motorized dugout boat) in San Carlos for about US$160 and holding up to eight people. Ask around at the docks and compare prices. The trip to and from the Castillo can be completed in a day, but if you want to hang around, the small village offers a few **places to stay**. The smart *Albergue El Castillo* (④) offers simple but comfortable rooms with fans in a well constructed cabin-style hotel with good river views. Of the budget options, the best is the *Hotel Richardson* (②), signposted from the dock, which has nice clean singles and doubles with private bath. *Alojamiento Aurora* (①) and *Alojamiento Manantial* (①), both on the left side of the dock, are both very basic, family-run concerns with small rooms and shared bath. **Places to eat** are restricted to the acceptable *Bar y Restaurante Cafetín*, built over the river next to the dock, and a small unmarked soda on the opposite side of the street.

Beyond El Castillo: Reserva Biológica Indio Maíz

Downstream from El Castillo, heading out towards the Caribbean, the northern bank of the Río San Juan forms part of the 3000-square-kilometre **Reserva Biológica Indio Maíz**, the largest nature reserve in Nicaragua – possibly in Central America. The climate here is very wet and hot, with the vast expanses of dense rainforest sheltering many species, including the elusive manatee, or sea cow, jaguars, tapirs, scarlet macaws, parrots and toucans. There is no real tourist infrastructure in the area; the usual way to see the Indio Maíz is from a boat on the Río San Juan – travelling toward the Caribbean, much of the left-hand bank of the river is the reserve. The pristine Indio Maíz vegetation stands in sharp contrast with the Costa Rican side, where agriculture and logging have eroded the forest.

travel details

BOATS

All boat services are subject to seasonal changes and cancellations at short-notice due to weather conditions.

San Jorge to: Moyogalpa (Mon–Sat 9 daily, Sun 3 daily; 1hr).

Granada to: Altagracia (Mon & Thurs at 2pm; 4hr); San Carlos (Mon & Thurs 2pm; 12–14hr).

Moyogalpa to: San Jorge (Mon–Sat 9 daily, Sun 3 daily; 1hr).

San Carlos to: El Castillo (4 daily; 2–3hr); Granada (Tues & Fri; 12–14hr); Mancarrón (Mon & Wed at 7am; 2hr).

BUSES

Managua (Mercado Mayoreo) to: San Carlos (3 daily; 9–10hr).

FLIGHTS

Managua to: San Carlos (Mon, Wed & Fri at 7am).

San Carlos to: Managua (Mon, Wed & Fri at 9am).

CHAPTER 26

THE ATLANTIC COAST

Nicaragua's **Atlantic coast** is low-lying, soaked with mangrove swamps behind which loom near-impenetrable jungles – a vast region comprising about half of Nicaragua's total landmass. This area was never destined to appeal to the Spanish conquistadors' desire for fertile agricultural land and gold. Further repelled by disease, inaccessible and endless jungle, dangerous snakes and persistent biting insects, the Spanish quickly made tracks for the more hospitable Pacific zone.

As a result, Spanish influence has never been great along Central America's Atlantic seaboard, and it was left to other nations to fill that gap. English, French and Dutch buccaneers had been plying the coast since the late 1500s, and it was they who first made contact with the **Miskito**, **Sumu** and **Rama** peoples who populated the area, trading goods for fish and turtle meat. In return, the indigenous peoples gave the pirates safe harbour and welcomed them into their settlements. Nicaragua's fierce Miskito tribe (now thought to number about 70,000) came particularly under the influence of the English, and from 1687 to 1894 the Atlantic coast of Nicaragua and Mosquitia as a whole was a British Protectorate known as the **Miskito Kingdom**. The declaration of this state in the midst of Spanish territory was the result of a strategic alliance between the English and the Miskito, who had a common interest in keeping the Spanish from gaining influence in the area. Armed by the British, the Miskito became the terror of the Sumu and Rama, who were finally subjugated by the larger group. In turn, from the late 1500s until 1894, when Britain unceremoniously ceded Mosquitia to Managua, the British navy, merchants and privateers gained unlimited rights to fishing and other local products, and enjoyed safe conduct along the coast and through the waterways of Mosquitia.

The **ethnicity** of the region today is complex. The Miskito, Sumu and Rama mixed with the slaves brought from Africa and Jamaica to work in the region's fruit plantations, and while many inhabitants are Afro-American in appearance, others have Amerindian features, and some combine both with European traits. For the most part black people from the Atlantic coast call themselves Creoles; if they acknowledge having Spanish blood, or Spanish is their first language, they may call themselves mestizos. **English** is widely spoken on the Atlantic coast, and English travellers may be surprised to be on the receiving end of a very warm welcome and some time-warp nostalgia for Britain.

During the years of the **Revolution** and the Sandinista government, the FSLN were met with suspicion on the Atlantic coast. In part this was due to the area's traditional mistrust of the government in Managua, and also to a lack of sympathy with the Sandinista's revolutionary values. A number of their socialist-revolutionary programmes conflicted with the region's traditional values, and Daniel Ortega's administration succeeded in driving many of the region's inhabitants – particularly Miskitos – over to the Contras. Nearly half the Miskito population went into exile in Honduras,

For an explanation of **accommodation price codes**, see p.468.

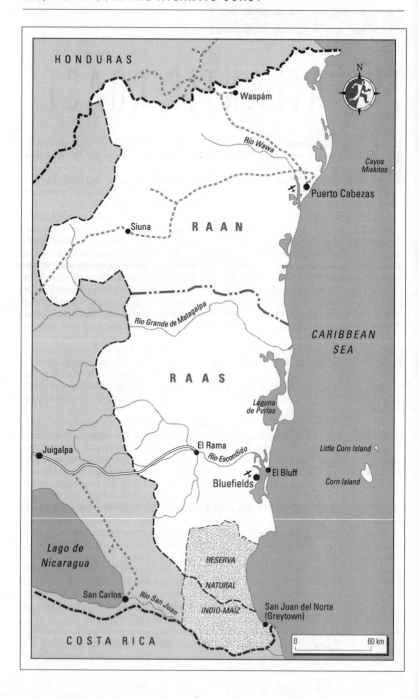

while in the south a much smaller number made their way to Costa Rica. In 1985 the Sandinistas tried to repair relations by granting the region political and administrative autonomy, creating the self-governing territories **RAAN** (Region Autonomista Atlántico Norte) and **RAAS** (Region Autonomista Atlántico Sur). In fact this controversial move served only to stir up further discontent in the region, being widely seen as an attempt to split the Atlantic Coast as a political force and make the north of the region compete with the south.

The only places in the area that attract visitors in any numbers are **Bluefields**, a raffish and charming Caribbean port town, and the **Corn Islands**, two small islands off Nicaragua's coast with sandy beaches, swaying palm trees, and a distinctly Caribbean cuisine and atmosphere. As for the rest of the coast, it remains a largely unknown and impenetrable tangle of waterways and rainforests, to be approached with caution and negotiated only by experienced locals. In the northern half of the region, **Puerto Cabezas** is the only town of any size. The region's main industries are mining and logging in the vast, dense forests of the RAAN. Although you can fly to Puerto Cabezas, few travellers make this long trip on a whim, since there's nothing really to interest tourists in or around the town itself. The possibilities for eco-tourism in this vast region are obvious, though a scarcity of resources and a lack of cooperation between central and local government have so far stymied all progress, while the long-discussed road linking Managua and Bluefields have similarly failed to leave the drawing board.

The Atlantic coast's extreme isolation and distance from the market economy mean that you can't count on getting **food, water and consumer goods** in most places outside of Puerto Cabezas and Bluefields. If you're intending to travel outside these areas, or to spend any length of time in the region, it's a good idea to stock up on consumer goods – both for yourself and for trade – in one of Managua's markets.

El Rama and the route to the coast

EL RAMA is a major transit point to the Atlantic coast, though most travellers only stop long enough to change from the Managua bus to a boat for Bluefields, or vice versa. With a largely transient population, the town's truck-stop atmosphere is not endearing, and the dilapidation, heat and bugginess doesn't help. If you don't manage to make the connection on the same day, you'll have to stay over. Least frightening of the cheaper options is *Hospedaje El Viajero* (①), an old colonial house one block north of the dock, with dark and stuffy rooms, but fairly friendly management; the nearby *Hotel Johanna* (①) is even more basic but OK. The *Hotel y Restaurante El Manantial* (①), a couple of blocks beyond *El Viajero*, is slightly more expensive but quiet and safe.

Five daily **buses** for El Rama leave from the Mercado Mayoreo bus terminal in Managua; the bumpy journey takes about eight hours. The public **ferry** (US$4) service between El Rama and Bluefields goes out of service from time to time. When it is running, it leaves in the mid-morning on Tuesday, Thursday, Saturday and Sunday. The trip can take five or six hours, so make sure you bring food and drink. A better bet is the high-speed **panga** which runs daily from 5.30am, although the schedule is a little confused – it appears to leave when full, but check at the dock. The *panga* takes two hours and costs US$9. An easier alternative is provided by the private bus company Empresa Vargas Peña (in Managua ☎280-1812, in Bluefields ☎822-1410), which offers a combined bus-and-*panga* service from Managua (Mercado Iván Montenegro) to Bluefields, leaving daily at 5am, 2.45pm and 9.30pm. All buses, except the 2.45pm which requires an overnight stop in El Rama, connect with a departing *panga* to Bluefields.

Bluefields

Despite its romantic name, there are no fields, blue or otherwise, near the steamy little lagoon town of **BLUEFIELDS**. The only town of any size on the Atlantic coast south of Puerto Cabezas, Bluefields gets its name from a Dutch pirate, Abraham Blaauwveld, who holed up here regularly in the seventeenth century, and it has retained the fugitive charm of a pirate town, perched on the side of a lagoon at the mouth of the Río Escondido. For most of the year it **rains** torrentially, except in May, when there's a short dry season, although it often rains then too. During these downpours the town – already ramshackle – can look somewhat forlorn.

Blufileños, as the town's inhabitants are called in Spanish, are mainly Creole, descended from Jamaicans. A fiercely proud and independent bunch, they are united in their mistrust of Managua and their delight in anything from the outside world, *de out* – meaning anywhere but the capital. A nostalgia for all things British, harking back to the days when the town imported steel from Sheffield, fabrics from France and dry goods from New Orleans, persists among the older generation. Both English and Spanish are spoken, although the English is heavily accented patois and takes some getting used to.

There's a lot of activity in town, and most of it takes place on the street, where card-table stalls sell batteries, tape players and other contraband goods from Costa Rica. Some examples of English colonial tropical architecture have survived the years: low-slung wooden buildings, bounded by grilled verandas, sitting alongside Caribbean-style cabañas – small wooden shacks painted in faded reds, greens and blues. You can't see the Caribbean from the town as houses block the view, and to get a sense of being at the ocean's edge you'll have to get a motorboat (*panga*) from the muelle over to the harbour and administrative hamlet of **El Bluff**, a collection of motley government buildings strung diagonally across the lagoon with the breezy open Caribbean at the end of a finger of land.

Hurricane Joan flattened Bluefields and the surrounding area in 1988, and there are still a few signs of the tremendous devastation. The town is occasionally plagued by electricity and water **shortages** – a good reason to bring a torch and batteries, as well as a few candles, and to stock up on bottled water when you can. You have to be on your guard a bit in Bluefields: the atmosphere can be tense, especially at night, when the several beer halls empty and the local machete-carrying machos tumble drunkenly onto the streets. Petty theft is on the rise, and tourists stick out painfully in this environment. Watch your belongings and be careful walking around at night.

Since 1995 Bluefields has received a shot in the arm in the form of the **URRACAN**, or Universidad de las Regiones Autónomos de la Costa Caribe Nicaragüense. The Bluefields campus is the largest of three on the coast – the others are in Puerto Cabezas and Siuna – and although most of the faculty are from the Atlantic coast region, volunteer professors also come from abroad, mainly Canada and the United States. The small campus is located about 1km from the centre of Bluefields, up the hill that backs the town to the northwest. During the last week in May, the streets of Bluefields are taken over by ¡**Mayo Ya!**, one of the most exciting fiestas in the country. Derived from the traditional May Day maypole celebrations of the British, ¡Mayo Ya! now features a mixture of reggae, folklore and indigenous dance that young Blufileños pair ingeniously with the latest moves from Jamaica.

Arrival and information

La Costeña and Atlantic Airlines **flights** from Managua land at the **airstrip**, 3km south of the town centre. Taxis will take you into town for about US$1. The public **ferry** from

---

MOSQUITOES AND NO SEE 'UMS

Bluefields can feel like the mosquito capital of the world, at least at dawn or dusk, when clouds of the creatures descend on any inch of exposed flesh. You need to take precautions: use plenty of repellent and wear long sleeves and trousers (along with socks). **Malaria** is present in the region, and you should fix yourself up with a regime of Chloroquine before you come and take the pills a week before you set foot in the area – see p.19. Coils, a mosquito net and a sleeping bag offer useful protection as well.

As if that weren't enough, the **sandflies** that populate the coast are even more virulent than the mosquitoes. Known throughout English-speaking Central America as "no see 'ums", sandflies are immune to every repellent known to man except, bizarrely, Avon's Skin-So-Soft body oil. This is not normally available in Nicaragua, but locals in the know may have procured a supply.

El Rama arrives at the dock about 150m north of the town's red-brick Moravian Church. From the dock you can walk to all accommodation in Bluefields' "centre" – a three-block by three-block area where all the hotels, restaurants and services are concentrated.

The few streets in Bluefields are named – and even have signs. Calle Central is the main drag and runs north–south alongside the bay. The three streets running east–west are Avenida Reyes, Avenida Cabezas and Avenida Aberdeen. However, no one really uses these names, resorting to the usual method of directing from **landmarks**: the Moravian Church, the Mercado at the end of Av Aberdeen and the Parque to the west of town are the most popular ones.

Banpro, almost opposite the Moravian church on C Central, will change dollars into córdobas, but won't handle travellers' cheques. In general, Bluefields is a dollar-friendly town – restaurants and hotels are only too happy to accept them. You can send letters from Enitel (Mon–Fri 8am–5pm), 50m east of the Parque, but don't expect them to arrive swiftly. Telephone calls, both domestic and international, can be made from the same building (Mon–Sat 8am–9pm).

Accommodation, eating and drinking

Cheap **lodging** in Bluefields is basic and some establishments attract a raffish local clientele – one reason why many places have a curfew of 10 or 11pm. Nearly destroyed by Hurricane Joan, Bluefields' most dependable budget option is the rebuilt *Hotel Hollywood*, 50m south of the Mercado (②). The place looks prepossessing, with lovely balconies and friendly proprietors, the shared bathrooms are clean, and the rooms quite large, but the thin partition walls don't reach the ceiling and it can be very noisy. Some rooms get a breeze off the water – ask to see several. A block and a half inland, the *Hotel Dorado* (①) is a little cheaper than the *Hollywood*; while it doesn't have the architecture and the lagoon-side setting, the second-storey balcony is a good place to sip a beer and it's quieter. Even more peaceful is the *Hotel Caribbean* (☎822-0107; ②), on Calle Naysi Ríos near the town centre, which has clean rooms with private bath and a/c. The *Hotel Marda Maus* (☎822-2429; ②–③), behind the market, is a bit more expensive and has the nicest rooms in town, with fan and a pleasant balcony.

At some point everyone in town ends up at the *Salon Siù*, a **café and restaurant** 50m south of the Moravian church and then 100m west and 75m north, whose time-warped 1950s ice-cream-parlour decor is peculiarly paired with tropicana. The sandwiches are tasty, the ice cream is excellent – for a real 1950s touch, try the *leche malteada*, or milkshake – and you might even catch a slight breeze if you sit next to one of the windows. It's open from 8am for tasty eggs-and-beans breakfasts (US$3). *Los*

Antojitos, 50m east of Enitel, is a friendly bar-restaurant with a bizarre Central American-cum-Asian menu (most dishes come with some form of soy sauce or chop suey) and enormous, good-value servings – try the *comida corriente* (US$3.50). Across from the market, *Pesca Frita*, true to its name, does some good if expensive fried fish and lobster in season, while the *Café Central*, about 150m up from the dock, serves reliable food until early evening.

The Corn Islands

Lying 70km off the Atlantic coast of Nicaragua, the **CORN ISLANDS** offer white beaches, warm, clear water, and even a bit of dreadlocked Rastafarian culture. Although there's not a lot to do, the islands are the epitome of relaxation, especially if travelling in Nicaragua is grinding you down – the kind of place you come to for a couple of days and end up staying a week.

Like many parts of the Caribbean coast, during the last century both the larger **Corn Island** and tiny **Little Corn** (or La Islita) were a haven for **buccaneers**, who used them as a base for raiding other ships in the area or attacking the inland towns on Lago de Nicaragua. These days it's drug-runners who use the islands as part of the transportation route for US- and Europe-bound cocaine. The islands' other notable trade is in turtle flesh – officially legal, though conducted in a rather clandestine manner; a short walk along the bay in either direction from the main settlement will lead you past houses that are used to store large numbers of turtles on their backs awaiting slaughter. Despite these somewhat shady aspects to the islands' life, they're safe to visit and the beaches are lovely.

Most visitors stay on **Corn Island**, home to all the services and with a decent selection of hotels and restaurants. Easily reached by *panga* from the bigger island, **Little Corn** is extremely quiet, with no real tourist infrastructure – most people come on a day-trip, or stay only one night. Bring sunscreen, mosquito repellent, a flashlight, snorkelling equipment and an emergency roll of toilet paper. Both English and Spanish are spoken on the islands.

Corn Island

Corn Island is fairly heavily populated for an island of its size, with over six thousand inhabitants living on its ten square kilometres. The island is still recovering from the onslaught of **Hurricane Joan** in 1988 that destroyed much of the housing and flattened trees. Many of the hardest-hit buildings have been summarily patched up, but even now signs of the destruction remain.

It's possible to walk round the entire island in about three hours. **Brig Bay** (just south of the fish-processing plant) is very tranquil and has a small wreck just off the shore in front of the *Hotel Paraíso Club*. **Long Bay**, across the air strip heading east, is quieter and less populated and there are plenty of places to swim in either direction. The southwest bay, the curiously named **Picnic Center**, is a fine stretch of sand near a loading dock – it's the site of a huge party during Semana Santa, when crowds of people come over from Bluefields and the locals set up stalls to sell food and drink. Further around the island is the **South End**, where there's some coral reef – good for snorkelling, though you'll need to bring your own equipment.

About 1.5km offshore to the southeast is the wreck of a **Spanish galleon** which lies in around 20m of clear water (given the islands' buccaneering past, it's likely that there are other wrecks in the area too). As yet there are no dive facilities on the island for exploring the wreck or the beautiful coral reefs. You can arrange **snorkelling** trips through the *Hotel Paraíso Club* (see overleaf), though you'll need to provide your own equipment.

Arrival, information and transport

An old Sandinista gunboat has been converted into a **passenger ferry** to Corn Island from Bluefields. It departs from the Bluefields dock at 8.30am on Wednesdays and Saturdays, returning on Thursdays and Sundays; the crossing can get very rough and takes five to eight hours (US$4; buy your ticket before boarding). **Freight ferries** leave most days for Corn Island and will take a small number of passengers; ask around at the docks.

A better option, at least for those prone to seasickness, is to take the **plane**, not least because the hour-long flight from Managua gives you an astounding perspective on the country as you fly over the volcanoes of Ometepe and across the perpetual green of the Atlantic coast jungle, before the plane flies over Bluefields and its surrounding waterways and heads out over the Caribbean. La Costeña (☎263-2142) and Atlantic Airlines (☎222-5787) both fly twice daily to Bluefields and Corn Island from Managua (US$100 return – flights leave Managua domestic terminal at 8am and 2pm). Both airlines have offices at Managua airport and on Corn Island, and also have booking agents across Managua. Flights land at the airstrip in the centre of the island. It's important to **confirm** your return flight once you arrive, particularly around Easter, when things get very busy.

From the airstrip it's five or ten minutes' walk to the beach front at Brig Bay, where you'll find some hospedajes. If you have a heavy pack it's sensible to take a **taxi** (US$1 per person anywhere on the island, US$2 after 8pm). You can also **rent a car** for US$13 an hour (enquire at the *Paraíso Club* – see overleaf) or a taxi for US$8 an hour. Otherwise, transport is provided by two local **buses**, which circle the island in opposite directions every forty minutes or so, commencing at 7am – a cheap way to have a look round. They pass the airport before heading into town or out to the southwest bay where the ferry comes in.

There's no tourist office, but the *Hotel Paraíso Club* has a notice board in their restaurant with some information on things to do. The Caley Dagnall **bank** will change travellers' cheques but doesn't give cash advances on credit cards. It's best to come armed with plenty of dollars or córdobas. You can make **phone calls** (but not send mail) at the Enitel office next to the Alcaldía, at the northern end of the island. For accidents and emergencies, go to the **hospital** in the centre near the baseball field.

Accommodation

Corn Island has some decent **hospedajes** and **hotels**, a number of which now have telephones, making it possible to reserve rooms; if you can't book in advance, come early if you want accommodation during the Easter period and expect to pay more. Another busy time is August 27, **Freedom Day**, which celebrates the abolition of slavery, an occasion for excess in a variety of forms and a large amount of crab eating – Picnic Center is the place to be for the party. Most of the hospedajes are scattered around the village and along **Brig Bay**, the beach area of the island.

Bayside Hotel, North End (☎285-5170). Comfortable, if expensive, double rooms with a/c and bath; the restaurant is built on stilts over the ocean. ⑥.

Casa Blanca, Brig Bay, three doors down from *Hospedaje Linda Vista*. Good, clean rooms with fans, mosquito nets and pleasant verandas with hammocks. ②–③.

Guest House Ruppie, Brig Bay. Small but clean rooms with fan and shared bath. ②.

Hospedaje Angela, behind the La Costeña office near the airport. Double rooms with fan in a delightful wooden family home with a pleasant balcony. ②.

Hospedaje Linda Vista, Brig Bay (look for the run-down two-storey house). Three very basic but acceptable rooms, with fan but no running water (washing water is supplied from a well), in a family house right on the beach front. ②.

La Princesa de la Isla, Woula Point, between Brig Bay and Picnic Center (☎285-5170). Charming, Italian-owned hotel offering large new rooms with huge bathrooms; the atmospheric restaurant serves fine Italian cuisine. ⑤.

Panorama, north of the dock. Decent rooms with fan. ④.

Paraíso Club (☎285-5111), at the southern end of Brig Bay. Attractive cabins and a pleasant restaurant under a large rancho – nice, but overpriced. ⑤–⑥.

Sun Rise Hotel, Sally Peachie (☎285-5187). Small and friendly hospedaje that seems a world away from anywhere. Rooms are quite adequate, if rather basic, and you can use the kitchen. There's a handicraft centre here too. ③.

Eating and drinking

More than anywhere else in Nicaragua, seafood lovers are in for a treat on the islands. It is easy to get a good feed of **fish, prawns or lobster** for a reasonable price (US$5–10). Although caught, killed and processed on the island, turtle meat is a rarity, but you may be able to find it on occasion. Excellent fresh coconut bread is sold in the grocery stalls from late afternoon.

The *Park Café*, a small red-and-white building next to the minuscule municipal park, cooks up good plates of fish, chicken and vegetables for US$3 from late afternoon to early evening, while the small but popular *El Cesteo*, near the airport, serves good breakfasts and lunches. *Fishers Cave*, next to the dock, is one of the few other options for breakfast. though the food's mediocre and the service is slow.

Little Corn Island

Only three square kilometres in size, **Little Corn Island** (La Islita) lies about 7km northeast of its larger sister. Largely undeveloped, the island boasts some beautiful **white sand beachs**, good swimming and snorkelling (bring your own gear) and plenty of peace and quiet – you can walk round and round the island and meet almost nobody else. The regular *panga* leaves the small jetty at the northern end of Brig Bay on Corn Island at 9.30am and 4pm daily, returning from Little Corn at 6.30am and 2pm (US$5). The trip takes an hour and you should expect to get wet.

Accommodation is currently limited to three options, although a new cabin-style hotel is currently being built on the south side of the island. *Bridgette's Hospedaje*, in the island's "village" opposite where the *panga* lands, has eight rather dingy rooms (①) and serves drinks and good meals. On the northeastern side of the island is the basic but very popular *Derrick's* (①–②), with small shared cabins, hammocks and camping space, plus its own beach. To get there, follow the path behind *Bridgette's* and walk for about thirty minutes (keep left when the path splits). On the eastern side of the island, on a bluff of land with great sea views, is the friendly US-owned *Hotel Casa Iguana* (*www.casaiguana.net*), which has four large, comfortable cabins with bath and potable water (⑤), two small and airless cabins (③), plus a restaurant and plenty of free tourist information. To get there, walk across the island from the village and turn right, a walk of about 15 minutes.

The RAAN: northern Mosquitia

The **northern coast** of Nicaraguan Mosquitia is one of the most impenetrable and underdeveloped areas of the Americas. No roads connect the area with the rest of the country, and the many snaking, difficult-to-navigate rivers and lagoons, separated by thick slabs of jungle, prevent the casual traveller – or any non-local, for that matter – from visiting the area.

Bordered at its northern extent by the **Río Coco**, Nicaragua's frontier with Honduras, Mosquitia is dotted by small settlements of the indigenous Miskito peoples. Few of these hamlets show up on any map, but the region is far from empty. The area was highly sensitive during the war years of the 1980s, when Contra bases in Honduras continually sent guerrilla parties over the long river border to attack Sandinista army posts and civilian communities in Mosquitia and beyond. The Sandinistas forcibly evacuated many Miskitos from their homes, ostensibly to protect them from Contra attacks, but also to prevent them from going over to the other side.

Few travellers come to **Puerto Cabezas**, the only town of any size and importance in the area: apart from the fact that there's nothing to do, getting around in these parts is difficult, if not dangerous – the RAAN still experiences isolated menacings by groups of re-armed former Contras. Although the situation is generally quiet, it's a region where people have very little money but a lot of guns, and it's important to know what you are doing if you venture outside the port town. More than anywhere else in Nicaragua, services are poor, consumer goods nearly nonexistent, and food hard to come by. Make sure you bring plenty of córdobas and perhaps a few dollars too. A detailed map of the area, a compass, and emergency provisions as well as the usual mosquito repellent, sunscreen and first aid kit, are all essential.

Puerto Cabezas

Small and scruffy **PUERTO CABEZAS** is the most important town north of Bluefields and south of La Ceiba in Honduras. Everyone seems to have come to this town of 30,000 people in order to do some kind of business, whether it be a Miskito fisherman walking the streets with a day's catch of fish dangling from his hand, a lumber merchant selling planks to foreign mills, or the government surveyors working on the all-season paved road through the jungle that may one day link the town with Managua. The town also serves as the base for YATAMA (Yapti Tasba Masraka Nanih Aslatakanka – which translates roughly as Children of the Mother Earth), a political party which fights for the rights of the indigenous Atlantic coast peoples, and which is fiercely opposed to central government, whether conservative, liberal or Sandinista.

Most travellers arrive by **plane**. The daily La Costeña or Atlantic Airlines flight from Managua touches down at the airstrip 2km north of town, from where taxis will take you into the centre for about US$1. The town's few amenities are all scattered within a few blocks of the Parque Central, a few hundred metres west of the seafront. An **Enitel** office and a solitary **bank** are the only services in town – the latter will change dollars if they have enough córdobas.

There's not much **accommodation**, unless you are into sleeping with rows of drunken men. The best choice at the moment is *Cayos Miskitos*, 100m east and 100m north of the Parque Central; although a little pricey, it's safe and clean, and you can watch Mexican cable TV (③–④). **Eating** in Puerto Cabezas is very expensive, and a seafood dish will cost you up to US$5, even though fishing is one of the area's main activities. For fish, try the *Restaurante Costa Brava*, 200m from the Parque Central. For something more upmarket, *Pizzeria Mercedita* has passable pizzas, and the *Cayos Miskitos* hotel has a fairly good restaurant attached. **Nightlife** is downright scary; although the town's nightspots play good Caribeña music, they cater exclusively to men and the overall aim is to get aggressively drunk – some establishments have weapons checks at the door. If you're up for the macho atmosphere, try the salsa at *Disco Scorpio* or the reggae and soca rhythms at the *Blue Beach*.

travel details

BUSES

Managua (Mercado Mayoreo) to: El Rama (5 daily; 8hr).

BOATS

All boat services are subject to change at short notice – check the latest schedules on the spot.

El Rama to: Bluefields (by ferry: Tues, Thurs, Sat & Sun mid-morning; 5–6hr; by *panga*: regular departures from 5am; 2hr).

Bluefields to: Corn Island (Wed & Sat 8.30am; 5–8hr).

Corn Island to: Bluefields (Thurs & Sun 8.30am 5–8hr); Little Corn (*panga*) (daily at 9.30am & 4pm, returns at 6.30am and 2pm; 45min–1hr).

FLIGHTS

La Costeña (☎263-2142) and Atlantic Airlines (☎222-5787) both fly from Managua to Bluefields several times a day, twice daily to Corn Island and once daily to Puerto Cabezas. Advance reservations are essential.

PART SEVEN

COSTA RICA

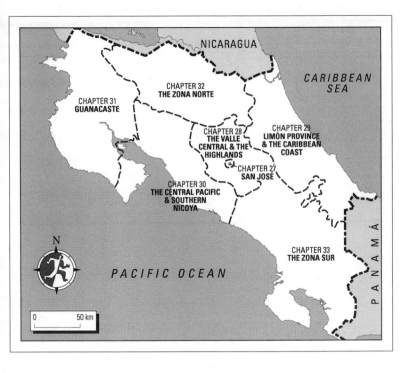

NICARAGUA

CARIBBEAN
SEA

CHAPTER 32
THE ZONA NORTE

CHAPTER 31
GUANACASTE

CHAPTER 28
THE VALLE
CENTRAL & THE
HIGHLANDS

CHAPTER 29
LIMÓN PROVINCE
& THE CARIBBEAN
COAST

CHAPTER 27
SAN JOSÉ

CHAPTER 30
THE CENTRAL PACIFIC
& SOUTHERN
NICOYA

CHAPTER 33
THE ZONA SUR

P A N A M Á

N

PACIFIC OCEAN

0   50 km

Introduction

In sharp contrast to the brutal internal conflicts in Guatemala or the grinding poverty of Nicaragua, **Costa Rica** has become synonymous with stability and prosperity – Costa Ricans enjoy the highest rate of literacy, health care, education and life expectancy in the isthmus. Unlike so many of its neighbours, the country has a long democratic tradition of free and open elections, no standing army (it was abolished in 1948) and even a Nobel Peace Prize to its name, won by former president, Oscar Arias, a key architect in the Peace Plan that helped bring an end to the conflicts in the region during the 1980s.

In recent years Costa Rica has also become the prime **eco-tourism** destination in Central America, if not in all the Americas, due in no small part to an efficient promotion machine that trumpets the country's complex system of national parks and wildlife refuges. Every year hundreds of thousands of visitors – mainly from the United States and Canada – come to walk trails through million-year-old **rainforests**, raft foaming whitewater rapids, surf on the **Pacific beaches** and climb the **volcanoes** that punctuate the country's mountainous spine. More than anything it is the enduring **natural beauty** that impresses. Milk-thick twilight and dawn mists gather in the clefts and ridges divided by high mountain passes; on the Pacific coast, carmine and mauve sunsets splash down into the sea like meteors; vaulting canopy trees and thick deciduous understoreys carpet large areas of undisturbed rainforest, and vestiges of high-altitude cloudforest offer glimpses into a misty, primeval universe, home to the jaguar, the lumbering Jurassic tapir and the truly resplendent quetzal.

One glib accusation you're almost certain to hear lobbed at the tiny nation is that it has **no culture or history**. It's certainly true that there are no ancient Mesoamerican monuments on the scale of Guatemala or Honduras, and just one percent of the population is of indigenous extraction, so you will see little native culture. However, anyone who spends some time in the country will find that Costa Rica's character is rooted in distinct **local cultures**, from the Afro-Caribbean province of Limón, with its Creole cuisine, games and patois, to the traditional *ladino* values embodied by the *sabanero* (cowboy) of Guanacaste. Above all, you're sure to be left with

mental snapshots of *la vida campesina*, or **rural life** – whether it be aloof horsemen trotting by on dirt roads, coffee-plantation day-labourers setting off to work in the dawn mists of the Highlands, or avocado-pickers cycling home at sunset.

■ Where to go

Though everyone passes through it, hardly anyone falls in love with **San José**, Costa Rica's underrated capital. Often dismissed as an ugly urban sprawl, the city enjoys a dramatic setting amid jagged mountain peaks, plus some excellent cafés and restaurants, leafy parks, a lively university district and a good arts scene. The surrounding **Valle Central** is the country's agricultural heartland, and also home to several of its finest volcanoes, including the huge crater of Volcán Poás and the largely dormant Volcán Irazú, a strange lunar landscape high above the regional capital of Cartago.

Though nowhere in the country is further than nine hours' drive from San José, the far north and the far south are less visited than other regions. The broad alluvial plains of the **Zona Norte** are often overlooked, despite featuring active Volcán Arenal, which spouts and spews within sight of the friendly tourist hangout of Fortuna, affording arresting night-time scenes of blood-red lava illuminating the sky. Off-the-beaten-path travellers and serious hikers will be happiest in the rugged **Zona Sur**, home to Mount Chirripó, the highest point in the country. Further south, on the outstretched feeler of the Osa Peninsula, Parque Nacional Corcovado protects the last significant area of tropical wet forest on the Pacific coast of the isthmus and is probably the best destination in the country for walkers – and also one of the few places where you have a fighting chance of seeing some of the wildlife for which Costa Rica is famed.

In the northwest, the cattle-ranching province of **Guanacaste** is often called "the home of Costa Rican folklore", and *sabanero* (cowboy) culture dominates here, with exuberant rag-tag rodeos and large cattle haciendas. **Limón** province, on the Caribbean coast, is the polar opposite to traditional *ladino* Guanacaste, home to the descendants of the Afro-Caribbeans who came to Costa Rica at the end of the nineteenth century to work on the San José–Limón railroad – their language (Creole English), Protestantism and the West Indian traditions remain relatively intact to this day.

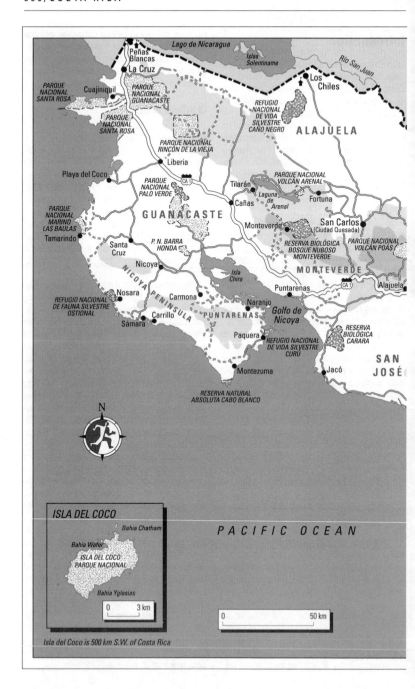

PARQUE NACIONAL SANTA ROSA

PARQUE NACIONAL GUANACASTE

Lago de Nicaragua

Peñas Blancas

La Cruz

Cuajiniquil

Islas Solentiname

Río San Juan

Los Chiles

REFUGIO NACIONAL DE VIDA SILVESTRE CAÑO NEGRO

ALAJUELA

PARQUE NACIONAL SANTA ROSA

PARQUE NACIONAL RINCÓN DE LA VIEJA

Liberia

CA 1

Playa del Coco

PARQUE NACIONAL PALO VERDE

Tilarán

PARQUE NACIONAL VOLCÁN ARENAL

Laguna de Arenal

Fortuna

Cañas

GUANACASTE

Monteverde

San Carlos (Ciudad Quesada)

PARQUE NACIONAL VOLCÁN POÁS

PARQUE NACIONAL MARINO LAS BAULAS

Tamarindo

Santa Cruz

P. N. BARRA HONDA

RESERVA BIOLÓGICA BOSQUE NUBOSO MONTEVERDE

Nicoya

Isla Chira

MONTEVERDE

REFUGIO NACIONAL DE FAUNA SILVESTRE OSTIONAL

Nosara

Carmona

Puntarenas

CA 1

Alajuela

Naranjo

Golfo de Nicoya

Carrillo

PUNTARENAS

Sámara

Paquera

RESERVA BIOLÓGICA CARARA

REFUGIO NACIONAL DE VIDA SILVESTRE CURÚ

NICOYA PENINSULA

SAN JOSÉ

Montezuma

Jacó

RESERVA NATURAL ABSOLUTA CABO BLANCO

N

ISLA DEL COCO

Bahía Chatham

Bahía Wafer

ISLA DEL COCO PARQUE NACIONAL

PACIFIC OCEAN

Bahía Yglesias

0   3 km

0   50 km

Isla del Coco is 500 km S.W. of Costa Rica

Close to the **Pacific coast**, Monteverde has become the country's number-one tourist attraction, pulling in the visitors who flock here to walk trails through some of the last remaining cloudforest in the Americas. Further down the coast is the popular beach of Manuel Antonio, with its picture-postcard ocean setting, plus the equally pretty but far less touristed beaches of Sámara and Nosara on the Nicoya Peninsula.

■ When to go

Although Costa Rica lies between 8° and 11° north of the equator, **local micro-climates** predominate and make temperatures and weather unpredictable, though to an extent you can depend upon the **two-season** rule. From roughly May to mid-November you will have afternoon rains and sunny mornings. The **rains** are heaviest in September and October and while they can be fierce, will only impede you from travelling in the more remote areas of the country – the Nicoya Peninsula especially – where dirt roads become impassable to all but the sturdiest 4WDs. In the **dry season** most areas are just that: dry all day, with occasional blustery northern winds blowing in during January or February and cooling things off. Otherwise you can depend upon sunshine and warm temperatures.

In recent years Costa Rica has been booked solid during the **peak season** – the North American winter months – when bargains are few and far between. The crowds peter out after Easter, but return again to an extent in June and July. During peak times you have to plan well in advance, faxing the hotels of your choice, usually pre-paying or at least putting down a deposit by credit card, and arriving armed with faxed confirmations and a set itinerary. Travellers who prefer to play it by ear can do much better off coming during the rainy or **low season** (euphemistically called the "green season"), when many hotels offer discounts. The months of November, April (after Easter) and May are the best times to visit, when the rains have either just started or just died off, and the country is refreshed, green, and relatively untouristed.

Getting around

Costa Rica's **public bus system** is excellent, cheap and quite frequent, even in remote areas. Getting anywhere by bus with a lot of baggage

can be a problem, however – many people travel light, leaving the bulk of their baggage somewhere secure (a San José hotel, for example) while on the road. **Taxis** regularly do long- as well as short-distance trips and are a fairly inexpensive alternative to the bus, at least if you're travelling in a group. **Car rental** is more common here than in the rest of Central America, but is very expensive.

■ Buses

Buses are by far the cheapest way to get around. The most expensive journey in the country (from Puerto Jiménez on the Osa Peninsula, to San José) costs US$7, while **fares** in the mid- to long-distance range vary from US$2.50 to US$5. **Tickets** on most mid- to long-distance and popular routes are issued with a date and a seat number; you are expected to sit in the seat indicated. Make sure the date is correct; even if the mistake is not yours, you cannot normally change your ticket or get a refund. Neither can you buy **return bus tickets** on Costa Rican buses, which can be quite inconvenient if heading to very popular destinations like Monteverde, Jacó and Manuel Antonio at busy times – you'll need to jump off the bus as soon as you arrive and buy your return ticket immediately to assure yourself a seat.

San José is the hub for virutally all bus services in the country; indeed, it's often impossible to travel from one place to another without backtracking to the capital. Different companies have semi-monopolies on various regions; for a run-down of **destinations and routes**, including international services, see pp.582–585.

On the most popular buses, like the service to Golfito, it's advisable to **book in advance**, though you may be lucky and get on without a reservation. Services to popular tourist areas in high season – especially Monteverde – get booked up very fast, so again you should buy your ticket several days ahead of travel. For information on bus **timetables** check *www.yellowweb.co.cr/crbuses.html*.

Though most Costa Rican buses are pretty good, the best of the bunch – arguably the best in Central America – is **Ticabus**, which runs the border routes from San José to Panamá or to Managua. Old converted US Greyhound buses, they have comfortable seats, adequate baggage space, air conditioning and very courteous drivers.

■ Driving

You have to exercise caution when **renting a car** in Costa Rica – companies have been known to claim for "damage" they insist you inflicted on their vehicle. By far the best policy is to rent a car through a Costa Rican travel agent or tour operator, which will cost you considerably less than doing it yourself. If you are travelling on a package, your agent will sort this out. Otherwise, go into an ICT-accredited travel agent in San José.

Car rental in Costa Rica is also **expensive**. Expect to pay about US$400 per week for a regular (non-4WD) vehicle, including insurance, and up to US$500 for 4WD. You will need a credit card, either Mastercard or Visa, which has sufficient credit for the entire cost of the rental, both at the beginning and end of the rental period. The majority of companies are based in San José, and you'll have to return the car there. The exception is Elegante, which has offices throughout the country. For a list of rental companies in San José, see p.581.

If you intend to drive in the rainy season (May–Nov), especially on the Nicoya Peninsula, or want to get to off-the-beaten-track places, or to Santa Elena and Monteverde, you'll need to rent a **4WD**. (Indeed, due to the condition of the roads some car-rental companies refuse to allow their regular cars to be driven to Monteverde between May and November.)

In recent years a system of **fines** (*multas*) for infractions like speeding has been introduced in Costa Rica. The **speed limit** on the highways is either 75km/hr or 90km/hr; it's marked on the sidewalk or on signs. If you're caught speeding you could find yourself paying up to US$65. **Fuel** is positively cheap by European standards: about

US$15 a tank on a medium-sized vehicle or about US$30 for a big 4WD.

■ Cycling

Costa Rica's terrain makes **cycling** a pleasure – indeed, it's easier to dodge the potholes and wandering cattle on a bike than in a car – and the range of places to stay and eat means you don't need to carry a tent. There is very little traffic outside the Valle Central, and Costa Rican drivers tend to be courteous to cyclists. Be warned, however, that if you cycle up to Monteverde, one of the most popular routes in the country, you're in for a slow trip: besides being steep, there's not much traction on the loose gravel roads.

San José's best **cycle shop** is Bicimania, at the corner of Paseo Colón and C 26. They have all the parts you might need, can fix your bike, and may even be able to give you a bicycle carton for the plane.

■ Planes

Costa Rica's two **domestic air carriers** offer a quite economical scheduled service between San José and many beach destinations and provincial towns. Sansa is the state-owned domestic airline; Travelair is its commercial competitor. Both fly small twin-propeller aircraft, servicing the same destinations. Of the two, **Travelair** (which flies from Tobias Bolaños airport in Pavas, 7km west of San José) is more reliable, and more frequent on some runs. **Sansa** (which flies from Juan Santamaría airport, 17km northwest of San José) is cheaper but less reliable – make your reservations as far as possible in advance and even then be advised that a booking means almost nothing until the seat is actually paid for. Reconfirm your flight in advance of the day of departure and once

<table><tr><td colspan="2">**GETTING AROUND COSTA RICAN TOWNS**</td></tr></table>

All Costa Rican towns of any size are intersected by an **Avenida Central**, which runs east–west, and a **Calle Central**, which runs north–south. From Avenida Central, parallel *avenidas* run odd numbers to the north and even numbers to the south. From Calle Central, even-numbered *calles* run to the west and odd numbers to the east. Avenidas 8 and 9, therefore, are actually quite far apart from one another, while Calles 23 and 24 would be at opposite ends of the city. "0" in

addresses is shorthand for "Central": thus Av 0, C 11 is the same as Av Central, C 11.

If you use street numbers as addresses, locals – and especially taxi drivers – won't have a clue where you are talking about. When possible use directions given in relation to local **landmarks**, buildings, businesses, parks or institutions, or according to the nearest intersection. People use **metres** to signify distance: in local parlance 100 metres equals one city block.

more on the day of departure, if possible, as schedules are likely to change at short notice. Sansa also offers good-value packages, usually two or three nights in more popular areas like Manuel Antonio. For a rundown of **schedules**, see p.583.

Costs, money and banks

Though prices have dropped from their peak of a few years ago, Costa Rica remains one of the most expensive countries in Central America. Some prices, especially for upper-range accommodation, are similar to those in the US, which never fails to astonish American travellers and those coming from the cheaper neighbouring countries. That said, with a little foresight you can still travel relatively cheaply.

■ Currency exchange and banks

The official currency of Costa Rica is the **colón** (plural colones). There are two types of **coin** in circulation: the old silver ones, which come in denominations of 1, 2, 5, 10 and 20, and newer gold coins, which come in denominations of 1, 5, 10 and 25. Public payphones do not yet take the new coins, and you will need the silver ones to make a call; otherwise, they're interchangeable. **Notes** start at 50, proceeding to 100, 500, 1000 and 5000. You'll often hear colones colloquially referred to as "pesos"; in addition, the 1000 is sometimes called the rojo (red). The colón floats freely against the American dollar, which means the **exchange rate** varies frequently; at the time of writing it hovers at around 300 colones to the US$1. Obtaining colones outside Costa Rica is virtually impossible: wait until you arrive and change some at the airport or border posts. If you miss banking hours then US dollar bills in small denominations will do.

When changing US dollars into colones, try to avoid Costa Rica's **state banks**: the Banco Nacional and Banco de Costa Rica (both with branches throughout the country; in many towns they are the only banks). Slow and bureaucratic, they will consume about an hour of your time. It's best to carry sufficient colones with you, especially in small denominations – going around with stacks of mouldy-smelling notes may not seem safe, but you should be all right if you keep them in a money belt, and it will save hours of time waiting in line. That said, however, if you are

doing a lot of travelling, it's comforting to know that many of even the smallest end-of-the-world towns now have a branch of at least one bank. In sharp contrast to the state banks are the efficient and air-conditioned **private banks**, the majority of which are in downtown San José (for addresses, see p.580). Private banks can legally charge what commission they like; the norm is about US$3 per transaction.

Banking hours vary slightly from branch to branch but tend to be Monday to Friday 8.30am to 3.30pm for state banks and slightly longer for private ones (which are also sometimes open on Saturday mornings). Most Costa Rican banks now have **ATMs**, though despite the fact that they carry VISA and Plus signs, foreign-issued cards at present only work in the ATMs of private banks such as Banco Popular, not in those of state banks such as Banco de Costa Rica and Banco Nacional.

You'll find **credit cards** especially useful in Costa Rica for making deposits for hotels via fax and for renting a car. In general, Visa and Mastercard are widely accepted, although retailers tend to accept only one or the other. In outlying areas, however, like the Talamanca coast, Quepos and Manuel Antonio and Golfito, some businesses may levy a six percent charge for credit card transactions; you may be better off taking plenty of cash.

Undeniably the safest way to carry money is to use **travellers' cheques**. These should be bought in US dollars only – Costa Rican bank staff will stare blankly at other currencies. However, do not expect to use travellers' cheques as cash except in mid- or upmarket hotels and guesthouses which regularly cater to foreigners.

■ Costs

The high cost of living is due in part to the **taxes** (18–25 percent) which are levied in restaurants and hotels, and also, more recently, to the International Monetary Fund, whose policies, aimed at restructuring the balance of payments deficit, have raised prices. Even on a rock-bottom **budget**, you're looking at spending US$25 a day for lodging, three meals and the odd bus ticket. Campers and hardy cyclists have been known to do it on US$15 a day, but this entails sleeping either in a tent or in somewhere pretty dire. You'll be far more comfortable if you count on spending at least US$20 a day for accommodation and US$12 for meals.

That said, **bus travel**, geared toward locals, is always cheap – about US$0.25 to US$1 for local buses, around US$4 or US$5 for long-distance buses (3hr or more). **Eating**, too, needn't be that pricey, while fruit, beer and cinema tickets will all seem very reasonable to visitors from most other countries. **Students** with ISIC cards may be entitled to some discounts at museums in Costa Rica. More useful is local student ID, available to visitors on language courses and other education programmes, which may get you discounts at museums and theatres.

Information

The best source of information about Costa Rica is the **Instituto Costarricense de Turismo** (ICT), Apartado 777, San José 1000, Costa Rica (☎506/223-1733, fax 223-5452) – you can write to them from abroad, though it may take a while to receive a reply, and you'll probably just be given the same glossy brochures that are handed out at embassies. You're better off visiting them in person at their office (see p.568) in the unprepossessing bunker underneath the Plaza de la Cultura in central San José, where the friendly bilingual staff will do their best to answer any queries you may have. On request, they'll also give you a free city map, plus a very useful and comprehensive bus timetable with recent additions and changes corrected on the spot. The office also has a full (though not necessarily up-to-date) list of practically all the hotels in the country, with prices, addresses and telephone numbers, a list of museums and their opening hours, and details of many San José restaurants and nightclubs. The small ICT booth at the **Santamaría International Airport** doesn't offer free timetables but may have the hotel lists. Apart from this, there are no tourist offices outside the capital, and you'll generally have to rely on locally run initiatives, often set up by a small business association or the chamber of commerce, or hotels and tourist agencies. A number of San José-based **tour operators** can offer guidance when planning a trip around the country; see p.586 for details.

On the **Internet**, *www.centralamerica.com* and *www.incostarica.net* both have links to thousands of Costa Rican Web sites; other sites with good links include *www.latinguia.com* and *www.terra.co.cr*. Weekly news on the country in English can be found at *www.ticotimes.co.cr*, and

Costa Rica's leading daily newspaper is online at *www.nacion.co.cr*.

Accommodation

Most towns in Costa Rica have a good range of places to stay, and even the smallest settlements have a basic pensión or hospedaje. The best **budget** accommodation tends to be in less touristed areas and caters more for nationals than foreigners. In the **middle and upper price ranges,** though facilities and services are generally of a very good standard, some hoteliers have decided they can pretty much charge what they please. If you don't mind spending US$45–70 a night for a room (especially in San José, and especially in the high season) then you can find somewhere quite comfortable. On a tighter budget, it's going to be more of a struggle.

Accommodation in Costa Rica is often in **cabinas**, usually either a string of motel-style rooms in an annexe away from a main building or hotel, or more often separate, self-contained units. They're usually – although not always – pretty basic, and most often frequented by budget travellers.

Few hotels, except those at the upper end of the range, have **double beds**; it's more common to find two or three single beds. Single travellers will generally be charged the single rate even if they are occupying a "double room", though this may not be the case in popular beach towns and at peak seasons.

In the high season (Nov–April), and especially at Christmas, New Year and Easter, you should **reserve** well ahead, especially for good-value hotels in popular spots, and for youth hostels. Although we often give *Apartado* (post box) numbers, it's far easier to reserve a room with a credit card by **fax** or **email**. If you want to get in touch but don't know the exact email address, it's worth trying the name of the hotel, all in lower case and without any spaces, followed by *@racsa.co.cr* – the email suffix for the vast majority of Costa Rican businesses. Failing that, most hotels in Costa Rica, even some very low-priced budget ones, now have fax numbers.

■ Camping

Though **camping** is fairly widespread in Costa Rica, gone are the days when people could pitch their tents on just about any beach or field. You'll have a far better relationship with locals if you ask politely whether it is OK to camp nearby; if they direct you to a campsite, they are doing so not because they don't like the look of you, but in an attempt to keep their environment clean.

In the beach towns especially you will usually find at least one well-equipped private campsite, with good facilities. Staff may also offer to guard your clothes and tent while you're at the beach. Alternatively, you might be able to find a hotelier (usually in an establishment at the lower end of the price scale) willing to let you pitch your tent in the grounds and let you use their showers and washrooms for a charge. Though not all national parks have campsites, the ones that do are generally good, with at least some basic facilities, and cost around US$2 per person per day. In some national parks, you may be able to bunk down at the ranger station.

When camping in Costa Rica never leave your tent or anything of value inside it unattended, or it may not be there when you get back. Never leave your tent open except to get in and out, unless you fancy sharing your sleeping quarters with snakes, insects, coati or toads. Finally, take your refuse with you when you leave.

■ Youth hostels

Costa Rica has a small network of twelve good and reasonably priced **youth hostels**, many of them in prime locations. They usually cost around $12–20 per night, and can be conveniently booked from the *Toruma* hostel in San José (see p.572). As with all accommodation in Costa Rica, bookings should ideally be made three months in advance if you're coming in high season – reserve by fax or phone directly with the hostel or through *Toruma*.

All twelve hostels can be reached by public transport and follow conservation regulations based on the sustainable development principle. Most of them have a range of double, triple and family rooms, and bed linen, towels and soap are included in the price.

Eating and drinking

Eating out in Costa Rica can be pricey. Main dishes can easily cost US$7–9, not including the service charge (10 percent) and the sales tax (15 percent). Tipping, however, is not necessary.

■ Where to eat

The cheapest places to eat in Costa Rica, and where most workers eat lunch, their main meal, are the ubiquitous **sodas**, halfway between the North American diner and the British greasy cafe. Sodas offer filling set *platos del día* (daily specials) and *casados*, combinations of rice, beans, salad and meat or fish, for about US$3. Many – at least in San José – are **vegetarian**, and in general vegetarians do quite well in Costa Rica. Most menus will have a vegetable option, and asking for dishes to be served without meat is perfectly acceptable.

Because Costa Ricans start the day early, they are less likely to hang about late in restaurants in the **evening**, and establishments are usually empty or closed by 10 or 10.30pm. Waiters tend to leave you alone unless they are called for. Non-smoking sections are uncommon, to say the least, except in the most expensive establishments; if you're looking for a smoke-free environment, try the vegetarian sodas.

■ What to eat

Ticos call their cuisine **comida típica** ("native" or "local" food). Simple it may be, but tasty nonetheless, especially when it comes to interesting **regional variations** on the Caribbean coast (Creole cooking) and in Guanacaste (where there are vestiges of the ancient indigenous peoples' love of maize, or corn).

Dishes you'll find all over Costa Rica usually include rice and some kind of meat or fish, often served as part of a special plate with coleslaw salad, in which case it is called a *casado* (literally, "married person"). The ubiquitous **gallo pinto** ("painted rooster") is a breakfast combination of red and white beans with rice, sometimes served with *huevos revueltos* (scrambled eggs). You should also try **ceviche** (raw fish "cooked" in lime juice with coriander and peppers), **pargo** (red snapper), **corvina** (sea bass), and fresh **fruit**, either by itself or drunk in *refrescos* (see below). Papayas, pineapple and bananas are all cheap and plentiful, along with some less familiar fruits like *mamones chinos* (a kind of lychee), *anona* (which tastes like custard) and *marañón*, whose seed is the cashew nut.

■ Drinking

Mellow-tasting Costa Rican **coffee** is among the best in the world, and it's usual to end a meal with a small cup – the coffee is traditionally served in a pitcher with a separate pitcher of heated milk. The best blends are export, which you can buy in stores and are served at some cafés. Also good are **refrescos**, cool drinks made with milk (*leche*) or water (*agua*), fruit and ice, all whipped up in a blender. You can buy them at stalls or in cartons, though the latter tend to be sugary. You'll find **herb teas** throughout the country; those served in Limón are especially good. In Guanacaste you can get the distinctive corn-based drinks **horchata** and **pinolillo**, made with milk and sugar and with a grainy consistency.

In addition to the many imported American **beers**, Costa Rica has a few local brands, which are not bad at all. Most popular is Imperial (light draught, American-style), followed by Bavaria (sweeter, more substantial and slightly nutty). Of the local low-alcohol beers, Bavaria Light is a good option; Tropical is a bit more watery.

There is an indigenous hard-liquor drink, **guaro**, of which Cacique is the most popular brand. It's a bit rough, but good with lime sodas. For an after-dinner drink, try Café Rica, a creamy **liqueur** made with the local coffee.

Costa Rica has a variety of **places to drink**, from shady macho domains to pretty beachside bars, with some particularly cosmopolitan establishments in San José. The capital is also the place to find the country's last remaining **boca bars**, atmospheric places which serve bocas (tasty little snacks) with drinks. **Gringo grottos** abound, especially in the beach towns, while in many places, especially port cities like Limón, Puntarenas and Golfito, there are the usual contingent of rough, rowdy bars, their seediness advertised by the giant

Imperial placards parked right in front of the doors to block views of the inside.

In general, Sunday night is dead: many bars don't open at all, while those that do, tend to close at around 10pm or so. Though Friday and Saturday nights are, as usual, the busiest, the **best nights** to go are often during the week, when you can enjoy live music, happy hours and other specials. The **drinking age** in Costa Rica is 18, and many bars will only admit those with ID. A photocopy of your passport page is acceptable.

Opening hours, holidays and festivals

Though you shouldn't expect the kind of colour and verve that you'll find at fiestas in Guatemala, Costa Rica has its fair share of holidays and

---

PUBLIC HOLIDAYS

Jan 1 New Year's Day. Celebrated with a big dance in San José's Parque Central.

Feb–March (date varies) Ash Wednesday. Countrywide processions; in Guanacaste horse, cow and bull parades, with bullfights (in which the bull is not harmed) in Liberia.

March–April (date varies) Semana Santa (Holy Week)

March 19 El día de San José (St Joseph's Day). Patron saint of San José and San José province.

April 11 Juan Santamaría Day. Commemorating the national hero who fought at the Battle of Rivas against the American adventurer William Walker in 1856.

May 1 Labour Day.

June 20 St Peter's and St Paul's Day.

July 25 Independence of Guanacaste Day (Guanacaste province only). Marking the annexation of Guanacaste from Nicaragua in 1824.

Aug 2 Virgin of Los Angeles Day. Patron saint of Costa Rica.

Aug 15 Assumption Day and Mother's Day.

Sept 15 Independence Day. Big patriotic parades celebrating Costa Rica's independence from Spain in 1821.

Oct 12 El día de la Raza (Columbus Day). Limón province only, marked by Carnaval, which takes place in the week prior to October 12.

Nov 2 All Soul's Day.

Dec 25 Christmas Day.

festivals, or **feriados**, when all banks, post offices, museums and government offices close. In particular, don't try to travel anywhere during **Semana Santa**, Holy (Easter) Week: the whole country shuts down from Holy Thursday until after Easter Monday, and buses don't run. Likewise, the week from Christmas to New Year invariably causes traffic nightmares, overcrowded beaches and a suspension of services.

Provincial holidays, like Independence Day in Guanacaste (July 25) and the Limón Carnaval (the week preceding October 12), affect local services only, but nonetheless the shutdown is drastic: don't bet on cashing travellers' cheques or mailing letters if you're in these areas at party time.

Mail and telecommunications

Costa Rica's recently privatized **postal system** is reasonably efficient, though you may have problems sending and receiving letters from remote areas. The most reliable place to send mail overseas from is San José's **Correo Central**, or main post office (see p.581), which is also the best place to collect post. In most cases – especially in Limón province, where mail is very slow – it's probably quicker to wait until you return to San José and post mail from there. **Opening hours** for nearly all Costa Rica's post offices are Monday to Friday from 7.30am to 5 or 5.30pm. Those in San José and Liberia also have limited Saturday hours.

■ Telecommunications

The Costa Rican state electronics company, **ICE** (Instituto Costarricense de Electricidad) provides international telephone, fax and Internet services via **RACSA**, the telecommunications subsidiary.

To make **international calls**, you can **call collect** from any phone or payphone in Costa Rica; simply dial ☎09 or ☎116 to get an English-speaking operator, followed by the country code, area code and number. AT&T, MCI, Sprint, Canada Direct or UK Direct calling-card holders can make credit-card calls from payphones. It's not a good idea to use a payphone to make international calls with colones – it's better to call from a hotel (though this can be expensive), a local *pulpería* (general store) or from the San José Radiográfica office (see p.582), where you can also send and

receive faxes, and use directories. Microchip telephone cards allow you to use special "Chip" payphones to make **local calls**; you can make international calls with the larger denomination cards but they won't give you much more than three or four minutes' speaking time.

The **country code** for the whole of Costa Rica is ☎506. There are no area codes and all phone numbers have seven digits.

Email

Most towns of any size in Costa Rica now have at least one **Internet café**, while places popular with tourists will usually have many more; charges are low, usually $0.75–$1 for 30 minutes. In addition, all Costa Rican post offices – even the most rural – now offer Internet access with prepaid cards which you can buy in the post office (300 colones for 30min, 500 for 1hr).

Many Costa Rican hotels and businesses now have **email**. If you don't know an address, it's worth trying the hotel or establishment name, followed by *@racsa.co.cr* – the usual suffix for email addresses in Costa Rica.

The media

Though the Costa Rican **press** is free, it does indulge in a certain follow-the-leader style of journalism. Leader of the pack is the daily *La Nación*, voice of the (right-of-centre) establishment and owned by the country's biggest media consortium. It also comes with a useful daily pull-out arts section, *Viva*, with **listings** of what's on in San José – the classifieds are handy for almost anything, including long-term accommodation.

La República is no less serious, but slightly more downmarket. *Al Día* is the populist "body count" paper. Alternative voices include *La Prensa Libre*, the very good left-leaning evening paper, and the thoughtful weekly *Esta Semana*, which offers longer, in-depth articles and opinion pieces. The *Semanario Universidad*, the voice of the University of Costa Rica, published weekly, certainly goes out on more of a limb than the big dailies, with particularly good coverage of the arts and the current political scene. You can find it on campus or in San Pedro.

Local **English-language papers** include the venerable and serious *Tico Times* and the full-colour *Costa Rica Today*, intended for tourists, with articles on activities and holidays. Both can be a good source of information for travellers, and the ads regularly feature hotel and restaurant discounts. You can pick up recent copies of the *New York Times*, *International Herald Tribune*, *USA Today*, *Miami Herald*, *Newsweek*, *Time* and sometimes the *Financial Times* in the souvenir shop beside the *Gran Hotel Costa Rica* in downtown San José and La Casa de Revistas on the southwest corner of Parque Morazan. Elsewhere, they're difficult to find.

There are many **commercial radio stations** in Costa Rica, all pumping out the techno and house tunes-of-the-moment alongside salsa, commercials, and the odd bout of government-led pseudo-propaganda. Most Costa Rican households have a **television**, which shows wonderfully awful Mexican/Venezuelan *telenovelas* (soap operas) and some not bad domestic news programmes.

Safety and the police

Costa Rica is generally considered a very safe country, and what crime does exist tends to be **opportunistic** rather than violent. The main thing travellers have to worry about is pickpocketing, and if you take a few common-sense precautions you should get by unscathed.

In downtown **San José** you need to be wary at all times. Wear a money belt, and never carry anything of value – money, tickets or passport – in an outside pocket. It has also been known for **luggage** to be stolen while you are distracted or while it is being kept supposedly secure in a left-luggage facility. Never hand your baggage to strangers, except the airport porters, who have official identification. If storing your bags in a hotel or guesthouse while you are travelling around the country, make sure it's locked, has your name prominently written on it, and that you have left instructions for it not to be removed by anyone but yourself, under any circumstances. **Car theft** – both of cars and things inside them – also occurs. You should not leave anything of value in a parked car – even locked in the trunk – anywhere in Costa Rica, day or night.

In addition, keep copies of your passport, your air ticket and your travellers' cheques, plus your insurance policy at home; and, if possible, keep extra copies in your hotel. In Costa Rica you have to carry **ID** on you at all times – for foreigners this means carrying your **passport**. A photocopy of your passport – of the information-bearing pages

> **EMERGENCY NUMBERS**
> **All emergencies** ☎911
> **Police** ☎117
> **Fire** ☎118
> **Traffic police** ☎222-9330 or 222-9245

and the page with your Costa Rican entry stamp – will do (the police understand tourists' reluctance to go about with their passports all the time), but if you are stopped and asked for ID, make sure you can produce the real thing – by going to your hotel, for example – in case the police demand to see it.

■ Reporting a crime

In the past year or so the **police** (*guardia*) presence in San José has increased dramatically. If you have anything stolen you will need to report it immediately to the nearest police post. In San José, the most convenient method is to head for the Organismo de Investigación Judicial (☎221-5337 or 221-1365) between Av 6 and 8 and C 15 and 19. In rural areas, go to the nearest *guardia rural* who will give you a report (you'll do better if you speak Spanish, or are with someone who does).

Any **tourist-related crime**, such as overcharging, can be addressed to the ICT in San José (see p.568).

National parks and reserves

Costa Rica protects 25 percent of its total territory under the aegis of a carefully structured system of **national parks**, **wildlife refuges** and **biological reserves** whose role in protecting the country's rich fauna and flora against the expansion of resource-extracting activities and human settlement has been generally lauded. In all there are currently some 75 protected areas, established gradually over the past thirty years.

In total the parks and reserves protect approximately four percent of the world's total wildlife species and life zones, among them rainforests, cloudforests, *páramo* (high-altitude moorlands), swamps, lagoons, marshes and mangroves, and the last remaining patches of tropical dry forest in the isthmus. Also protected are areas of historical significance, including a very few pre-Columbian settlements, and places considered to be of immense scenic beauty. Measures have also been taken to protect beaches where marine turtles lay their eggs, as well as a number of active volcanoes.

The **national parks**, which cover 12 percent of Costa Rica's protected land, provide more services and activities than the refuges and reserves, and tend to be more heavily touristed. That said, it's important to remember that none of the protected areas has been set up with tourists in mind – biologists, scientists and researchers make up a large portion of visitors. While we give information as to which **animals** inhabit the specific parks, bear in mind that you are in no way guaranteed to see them – although you'll probably see some of the more common or less shy ones, you'll be very lucky indeed to spot the larger mammals such as the jaguar, ocelot or tapir.

■ Visiting Costa Rica's parks

All national parks have entrance **puestos**, or stations, where you pay your fee and pick up a map. Typically, the **main ranger stations**, from where the internal administration of the park is carried out, and where the rangers live, are some way from the entrance *puesto*. It can be a good idea to drop by the main station, where you can talk to rangers (if your Spanish is good enough) about local terrain and conditions, enquire about drinking water, and use the bathroom. In some parks, such as Corcovado, you can sleep in or camp near the main stations. All parks now charge an **entrance fee** of $6 per day. If you want to camp overnight in any park, you'll have to pay for both days – $12 in total.

Outside the most visited parks – Volcán Poás, Volcán Irazú, Santa Rosa and Manuel Antonio – **opening hours** are somewhat theoretical. Many places are open daily, from around 8am to 3.45pm, though there are exceptions – Manuel Antonio is closed on Monday and may be closed on Tuesdays in the future, while other parks may open a little earlier in the morning. Unless you're planning on camping or staying overnight, there's almost no point in arriving at a national park in the afternoon. In all cases, especially at the volcanoes, you should aim to arrive as early in the morning as possible to make the most of the day and, in particular, the weather (especially in the wet season).

The only central office where you can make reservations and get detailed, up-to-date **information** or buy **permits**, where required, is the Fundación de Parques Nacionales (Av 15, C 23/25,

San José, ☎257-2239, *www.minae.go.cr/accvc*), who will contact those parks for which you need reservations, chiefly Santa Rosa, Corcovado and Chirripó (see the individual accounts in the Guide for more details). Other parks can be visited on spec.

Work and study

There are many **volunteer work and research projects** in Costa Rica, some of which include food and lodging. A good resource in the US for language study and volunteer work programmes is **Transitions Abroad**, a bi-monthly magazine focusing on living and working overseas (visit *www.transabroad.com* or write to Dept TRA, Box 3000, Denville, NJ 07834, USA). In Australasia, current details of student exchanges and study programmes are available from the AFS, PO Box 5, Strawberry Hills, Sydney 2012 (☎02/9281-0066, *www.afsaus.org.au*), or PO Box 11046, Wellington, New Zealand (☎04/384-8066 or 0800/600300. *www.afs.org/partners/nzlhome*). UK residents should contact the Costa Rican Embassy (see p.15).

■ Study programmes and learning Spanish

There are so many **language schools** in San José that choosing one can be a problem: though you can arrange a place through organizations based in the US (see box opposite), the best way to choose is to visit a few, perhaps sitting in on a class or two, and judge the school according to your own personality and needs. This is not always possible in high season (Dec–April) when many classes will have been booked in advance, but at other times it should be no problem at the majority of the schools we've listed.

As with most things, you will pay more for a Spanish course in Costa Rica than in other Central American countries. Some of the language schools in Costa Rica are Tico-run; others are arms of international (usually North American) education networks. Whatever the ownership, instructors are almost invariably Costa Ricans who speak some English. In addition, school noticeboards are an excellent source of information and contacts for travel opportunities, apartment shares and social activities. Most schools have a number of Costa Rican families on their books with whom they regularly place students for homestays.

VOLUNTEER PROGRAMMES IN COSTA RICA

Amigos de las Aves, 32-4001 Rio Segundo de Alajuela (☎441-2658). Works to establish breeding pairs of scarlet and great green macaws. Volunteers help care for the birds; no food or lodging offered.

ANAI, Aptdo 170–2070, Sabanillo (☎224-6090 or 224-3570, fax 253-7524, *anaicr@correo.co.cr*). Based in southern Talamanca, ANAI trains people to farm organically and manage forests sustainably. There are also volunteer programmes to help protect the Gandoca-Manzanillo Refuge and the turtles that come to the Caribbean coast each year (May–July), and working on ANAI's experimental farm (officially for a minimum of six months, but three-month stays can be arranged). Lodging and food included.

ASVO (Association of Volunteers for Service in Protected Areas), contact the director of International Voluntary Programmes (☎223-4533 ext. 135-182). Government-run scheme enabling volunteers to work in the national parks, helping guard protected areas, write reports and give environmental classes. Minimum two months.

DINADECO (Office of National Community Development; ☎235-0896, fax 253-1745, *l.fallas @gobnert.go.cr*). Costa Rican government institution which promotes citizen participation, family development, human-rights awareness and sexual equality. Foreigners are invited by the institution's International Cooperation Programme to get involved with individual development in small towns.

Humanitarian Foundation (☎282-9862, *gnystrom@racsa.co.cr*). Volunteers are placed in various programmes helping orphans, battered women, indigenous people and street children. $200 initial fee plus $225 per month for room and board.

Monteverde Institute, Aptdo 69–5655, Monteverde (☎645-5053, fax 645-5219, *mvipac @racsa.co.cr*). Volunteer projects in the Monteverde cloudforest including teaching, fieldwork on trails and other conservation efforts. Volunteers must know Spanish and commit for six weeks.

VOLUNTEER PROGRAMMES IN THE US

Caribbean Conservation Corp, PO Box 2866, Gainesville, FL 32602 (☎1-800/678-7853, in Costa Rica ☎225-7516, *www.ccturtle.org*). Volunteer research work on marine turtles at Tortuguero.

Global Service Corps, 300 Broadway, Suite 28, San Francisco, CA 94133-3312 (☎415/788-3666 ext 128, *www.globalservicecorps.org*). Service programmes in Costa Rica.

University Research Expeditions, University of California, Berkeley, CA 94720-705 (☎510/642-6586, *www.berkeley.edu*). Environmental and animal behaviour studies.

Volunteers for Peace, 43 Tiffany Rd, Belmont, VT 05730 (☎802/259-2759, *www.vfp.org*). Volunteer projects in Costa Rica and other Central American countries.

History

Archeologists know almost nothing about the various people who inhabited Costa Rica until about 1000 BC, though it is known that the area was a corridor for merchants and trading expeditions between the Mesoamerican empires to the north and the Andean empires to the south. Excavations of pottery, jade and trade goods and accounts of cultural traditions have shown that the **pre-Columbian** peoples of Costa Rica adopted liberally from both areas.

When the **Spaniards** arrived in Costa Rica in the early sixteenth century it was inhabited by as many as 27 different groups or clans. Most clans were assigned names by the invaders, which they took from the *cacique* (chief) with whom they

dealt. Many of these groups had affinities with their neighbours in Nicaragua to the north and Panamá to the south.

■ The arrival of the Spanish

On September 18, 1502, on his fourth and last voyage to the Americas, **Columbus** sighted Costa Rica, and four years later King Ferdinand of Spain despatched **Diego de Nicuesa** to govern what would become Costa Rica. From the start his mission was beset by hardship, beginning when their ship ran aground on the coast of Panamá. Forced as a result to walk up the Caribbean shore, the expedition met native people who, unlike those who had welcomed Columbus tentatively but politely with their shows of gold, instead burned their crops rather than submit to the authority of the Spanish. This, together with the impenetrable jungles – and the creatures who lived in them – and tropical diseases, forced the expedition to turn back.

Next came **Gil González** in 1521–22, who sailed from Panamá, where Spanish settlements had already been established, up the Pacific coast, which offered safer anchorages. The indigenous peoples, meanwhile, began a campaign of **resistance** that was to last nearly thirty years, employing guerrilla tactics, full-scale flight, infanticide, attacks on colonist settlements and burning their own villages. There were massacres, defeats and submissions on both sides, but by 1540 Costa Rica was officially a Royal Province of Spain, and a decade later the Conquest was more or less complete.

■ Early settlers

It seems more appropriate to discuss Costa Rica's *lack* of colonial experience, rather than a bona fide colonization. In 1562, **Juan Vásquez de Coronado** became the second governor of Costa Rica. Coronado has always been portrayed as the good guy, reputed for his favourable, if not benevolent, treatment of the indigenous peoples he encountered in his migration from the Pacific coast to the Valle Central. It was under his administration that the first settlement of any size or importance was established, and **Cartago**, in the heart of the Valle Central, became capital. During the next century settlers confined themselves more or less to the centre of the country. The Caribbean coast was the haunt of buccaneers – mainly English – who put ashore and wintered here after plundering the lucrative Spanish Main; the Pacific coast saw its share of pirate activity too, most famously when Sir Francis Drake put ashore briefly in the modern-day Bahía Drake in 1579.

This first epoch of the colony is remembered as one of unremitting **poverty**. Within a decade of its invasion Costa Rica was notorious and widely disparaged throughout the Spanish Empire for its lack of gold. The land of the Valle Central was fertile, but there was uncertainty as to which crops to grow. Coffee had not yet been imported to Costa Rica, nor had tobacco, so it was to subsistence agriculture that most settlers turned, growing just enough to live on. In 1719, the governor of Costa Rica famously complained that he had to till

his own land. To make matters worse, Volcán Irazú blew its top in 1723, nearly destroying the capital.

■ Independence

The **nineteenth century** was the most significant era in the development of the modern nation state of Costa Rica. Initially, after 1821, when Central America declared **independence** from Spain, freedom made little difference to Costa Ricans. Although status as a republic was granted in the summer of 1823, the news did not reach Costa Rica until well into the autumn, when a mule messenger arrived from Nicaragua to tell the astonished citizens of Cartago the good news. A **civil war** promptly broke out among the inhabitants of the Valle Central, dividing the citizens of Alajuela and San José from those of Heredia and Cartago. This struggle for power was won by the Alajuela-San José faction, and **San José** became the capital city in 1823.

Costa Rica made remarkable progress in the latter half of the nineteenth century, building roads, bridges, and railways and filling San José with neo-Baroque, Europeanate edifices. Virtually all this activity was fuelled by the **coffee** trade, bringing wealth that the settlers just a century earlier could hardly have dreamed of. Today high-grade export coffee is still popularly known as *grano d'oro*. The **coffee bourgeoisie** played a vital role in the cultural and political development of the country, and in 1848 the newly influential *cafetaleros* elected to the presidency their chosen candidate, Juan Rafael Mora. Extremely conservative and pro-trade, Mora came to distinguish himself in the battle against the American-backed filibusterer William Walker in 1856 (see p.473).

■ The twentieth century

The first years of the **twentieth century** witnessed a difficult transition towards democracy in Costa Rica. Universal male suffrage had been in effect since the last years of the nineteenth century, but class and power conflicts still dogged the country, with several *caudillo* (authoritarian) leaders, familiar figures in other Latin American countries, hijacking power. But in general these figures ended up in exile, and neither the army nor the Church gained much of a foothold in politics.

With the election in 1940 of the Republican (PRN) candidate **Rafael Calderón Guardia**, a doctor educated in part in Belgium and a devout Catholic, came the social reforms and state support for which Costa Rica is still almost unique in the region. In 1941 Calderón established a new **Labour Code**, which reinstated the right of workers to organize and strike, and a social security system providing free schooling for all. Calderón also paved the way for the establishment of the University of Costa Rica, health insurance, income security and assistance schemes, and thus won the support of the impoverished and the lower classes and the suspicion of the governing élites. One of those less than convinced by Calderón's policies was the man who would come to be known as "Don Pepe", the coffee farmer **José Figueres Ferrer**, who denounced Calderón and his expensive reforms. Figueres soon formed an opposition party, ideologically opposed to the PRN, calling them "communists". In March, **fighting** around Cartago began, culminating in an attack by the Figueres rebels on San José. Figueres wanted above all to engineer a complete break with the country's past and especially the policies and legacies of the Calderónistas. Seeing himself as fighting both communism and corruption, he not only outlawed the PVP, the Popular Vanguard Party – formerly known as the Communist Party – but also nationalized the banks and devised a tax to hit the rich particularly hard, thus alienating the establishment. A new **constitution** drawn up in 1949 gave full citizenship to Afro-Caribbeans, full suffrage to women and **abolished Costa Rica's army** in an attempt to save resources and limit political uncertainty in the country.

The **1960s** and **1970s** were a period of prosperity and stability in Costa Rica, during which the welfare state was developed to reach nearly all sectors of society. In 1977 the **indigenous bill** established the right of aboriginal peoples to their own land reserves – a progressive measure at the time, although indigenous peoples today are not convinced the system has served them well.

■ Storm in the isthmus: the 1980s

Against all odds, Costa Rica in the 1980s and 1990s not only saw its way through the serious political conflicts of its neighbours, but also successfully managed predatory US interventionism, economic crisis and staggering debt.

Like many Latin American countries, Costa Rica had taken out bank and government **loans** in the 1960s and 1970s to finance vital development. But in the early 1980s, the slump of prices for coffee and bananas put the country's current account in the red to the tune of millions. In September 1981, Costa Rica defaulted on its interest payment on these loans, becoming the first Third-World country to do so, and sparking off a chain of similar defaults in Latin America that resonated throughout the 1980s and threw the international banking community into crisis. Despite its defaults, Costa Rica's debt continued to accumulate, and by 1989 had reached a staggering US$5 billion, one of the highest per capita debt loads in the world.

To compound the economic crisis came the simultaneous political escalation of the **Nicaraguan Civil War**. During the entire decade, Costa Rica's foreign policy and to an extent its domestic agenda would be overshadowed by tensions with Nicaragua on the one hand and with the US on the other. Initially, the Monge PLN administration (1982–86) more or less capitulated to US demands that Costa Rica be used as a supply line for the Contras, and Costa Rica also accepted military training for its police force from the US. Simultaneously, the country's first agreement for a structural adjustment loan with the International Monetary Fund (IMF) was signed. It seemed increasingly clear that Costa Rica was on the path both to violating its declared neutrality in the conflicts of its neighbours and to condemning its population to wage freezes, price increases and other side-effects associated with IMF intervention.

In 1986 PLN candidate **Oscar Arias Sánchez** was elected to the presidency, and Costa Rica's relations with the US – and, by association, with Nicaragua – took a different tack. The former political scientist began to play the role of peace broker in the conflicts of Nicaragua, El Salvador, and, to a lesser extent, Honduras and Guatemala, mediating between these countries and also between domestic factions within them. In October 1987, just eighteen months after taking office, Arias was awarded the **Nobel Prize for Peace**, bringing worldwide attention to this tiny country.

Though Arias had gained the admiration of political leaders around the world, he proved to be less than popular at home. Many Costa Ricans saw him as diverting valuable resources and time to foreign affairs when he should have been paying attention to the domestic agenda, while increasing prices caused by the IMF's economic demands meant that conditions in Costa Rica were not much improved.

■ The 1990s

Until 1994, elections in Costa Rica had been relatively genteel affairs, involving lots of flag-waving and displays of national pride in democratic traditions. The elections of that year, however, were probably the dirtiest to date. The campaign opened and closed with an unprecedented bout of mudslinging and attempts to smear the reputations of both candidates, tactics which shocked many Costa Ricans. The PLN candidate – the choice of the left, for his promises to maintain the role of the state in the economy – was none other than **José María Figueres**, the son of Don Pepe, who had died four years previously. During the campaign Figueres was accused of shady investment rackets and influence-peddling. His free-market PUSC opposition candidate, Miguel Angel Rodriguez, fared no better, having admitted to being involved in a tainted-beef scandal in the 1980s. Figueres won, narrowly, though his term in office was plagued by a series of scandals. On a more positive note, in January 1995, a Free Trade agreement was signed with Mexico in order to try to redress the lack of preference given to Costa Rican goods in the US market by the signing of NAFTA. Costa Rica's economy received a further shot in the arm in 1996 when the communications giant INTEL chose the country for the site of their new factory in Latin America, creating thousands of jobs.

In February 1998 PUSC candidate **Dr Miguel Angel Rodriguez** was elected president, thus reinforcing the trend in Costa Rican politics for the past half-century, wherein power has been traded more or less evenly between the PLN and the PUSC. The new government committed itself to solving Costa Rica's most pressing problems, making improvements to the country's dreadful road system top priority, but financing this and other major public works by private investment. Increasingly, courting private money and catering to foreign interests are the order of the day. Still,

problems dog the economy in the shape of increasing balance of payments difficulties, as well as pressures on the banana market from Ecuador's growing competition – banana plantation labour in Ecuador costs US$3 a day, compared to US$18 in Costa Rica.

■ The future

Costa Rica's economic future rides on a wave created in the past, a constant see-sawing between the price of the country's bananas and coffee on world markets and the amount it pays for imports. Still, the economy continues to grow, in large part fuelled by **tourism**, and the government is beginning to claw back the massive public sector deficit through increased taxation, both on basic services like electricity and water and on restaurant meals and hotel bills.

As the Costa Rican economy grows, however, so do other indicators: inflation runs around 17 percent, while the annual **population growth** is as high as 3.2 percent per annum – Costa Rica has the highest rural population density in Latin America, and there is tremendous pressure on land. The prognosis for the campesino, that now nearly forgotten former backbone of the country, is not good, as peasant agriculture becomes increasingly anachronistic in the face of the big banana, coffee, palmito and pineapple plantations. Furthermore, the burden of the welfare state in Costa Rica has become increasingly difficult for the state to carry. High external debts to service the country's respected system of social welfare mean that a staggering 30 percent of the government budget goes on keeping up interest payments to foreign banks.

Meanwhile, the prognosis for the **environment** could be bleak if the authorities continue their strategy of attracting large hotel and development groups. Even bleaker is the fact that in recent years the country has gained a reputation as a **sex tourism** destination, with increasing evidence that minors are involved in the business. Even so, the country's legal and judicial institutions are doing their best to combat the country's most pressing social problems, such as drug trafficking, domestic violence and increasing crime and disorder.

CHAPTER 27

SAN JOSÉ

S prawling smack in the middle of the fertile Valle Central, **SAN JOSÉ** has a spectacular setting, ringed by the jagged silhouettes of soaring mountains – some of them volcanoes – on all sides. That's where the compliments end, however, and you'll be hard pressed to find anyone who has much good to say about the city's potholed streets and car-dealership architecture – not to mention the choking diesel fumes, kamikaze drivers and chaotically unplanned expansion. In the gridlocked centre things are wearingly hectic, with vendors of fruit, lottery tickets and cigarettes jostling on street corners, and thousands of shoestores tumbling out onto the sidewalks.

In general travellers talk about the city as they do about bank line-ups and immigration offices: a pain, but unavoidable. That said, if you've been travelling through the region, you'll find that compared to, say, San Salvador or Managua, San José is not only a reassuringly **safe** place (though street crime is rising) but also vibrant and cosmopolitan, with a sprinkling of excellent **museums**, some elegant buildings and landscaped parks, good cafés and the odd intriguing art gallery. Which is all to the good: most people find themselves spending some time here – the city is a major transportation hub, and many journeys across the country involve backtracking through the capital – learning to enjoy it, and even becoming perversely fond of the place.

Arrival

Arriving in San José is relatively stress-free: all the machinery to get you into town is well oiled and there is less opportunistic theft than at other Central American arrival points. San José's compact, frenzied city centre is contained within about fifteen blocks running east–west, and four blocks north–south. To the west, the main approach is the four-lane **Paseo Colón**, lined with car-rental agencies, upscale hotels, and office buildings. The centre of town is bisected by the largely pedestrianized **Avenida Central**, a very pleasant place to stroll, while most commercial activity is concentrated in the streets between Avenida Central and Avenida 7. The nondescript **Plaza de la Cultura** is considered to be the centre of town.

Near the post office, in the streets immediately west of Calle 2 is the frantic and sometimes insalubrious **Mercado Central** area, four blocks west of which is the **Coca Cola bus station**. The centre is subdivided into little neighbourhoods (barrios) that flow seamlessly in and out of one another: **Barrios Amón** and **Otoya**, in the north, are the prettiest, lined with the genteel mansions of former coffee barons, while further out toward San Pedro, **La California**, **Escalante** and **Los Yoses** are home to comfortable houses, the odd embassy and the *Toruma* youth hostel.

Further east, Avenida Central widens, heading out to the student suburb of San Pedro, home of the cool, leafy campus of the **University of Costa Rica** (UCR), one of

For an explanation of **accommodation price codes**, see p.556.

the finest in Central America. The three or four square blocks surrounding the university are lined with some of the liveliest bars and restaurants in San José, though in most of them you'll feel more comfortable if you're under thirty.

Many of San José's residents live in the **suburbs** surrounding the city – many shopping malls and embassies are located in the eastern suburb of **Curridabat** and nearby **Escazú**, a mountain town to the north and west of San José.

By air

Most international flights arrive at the modern new terminal at **Juan Santamaría International Airport** (☎441-0744), 17km northwest of San José and 3km southeast of Alajuela (see p.589). The **ICT office** here (daily 8am–4pm; ☎442-1820 or 442-8542) can supply maps and give advice on accommodation. There's also a **correo** (Mon–Fri 8am–5pm), next to the departure tax window, and a **bank** (Mon–Fri 6.30am–6pm; Sat & Sun 7am–1pm), downstairs on the departure level; colones are not necessary for taxis, but you'll need them for the bus.

The best way to get into San José from the airport is by **taxi**, which takes about twenty minutes in light traffic and costs US$12–14. Official airport taxis are orange and line

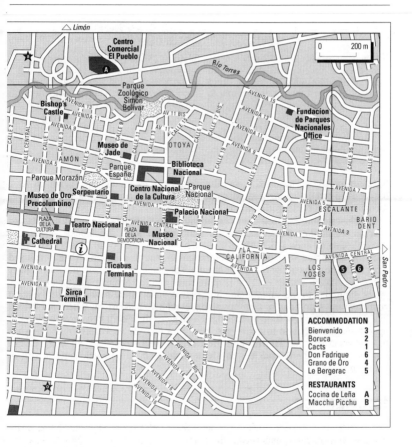

△ Limón

0   200 m

Centro
Comercial
El Pueblo
A

Río Torres

Parque
Zoológico
Simón
Bolívar

Bishop's
Castle

AVENIDA 13

AVENIDA 13

AV 11 BIS

CALLE 2

CALLE CENTRAL

AVENIDA 5

CALLE 3

AVENIDA 9

CALLE 9

AVENIDA 11

CALLE 13

CALLE 17 BIS

CALLE 17

AVENIDA 15

AVENIDA 13

AVENIDA 11

AVENIDA 9

Fundación
de Parques
Nacionales
Office

CALLE 31

CALLE 35

CALLE 37

Museo de
Jade

OTOYA

AMÓN

Parque
España

Biblioteca
Nacional

CALLE 9

AVENIDA 9

Parque Morazán

Museo de Oro
Precolumbino

Serpentario

Centro Nacional
de la Cultura

Parque
Nacional

AVENIDA 7

AVENIDA 5

CALLE 29

ESCALANTE

BARIO
DENT

CALLE 33

AVENIDA 3

△ San Pedro

AVENIDA 1

Palacio Nacional

CALLE 15

PLAZA
DE LA
CULTURA

Teatro Nacional

AVENIDA CENTRAL

PLAZA
DE LA
DEMOCRACIA

Museo
Nacional

CALLE 17

CALLE 19

CALLE 21

CALLE 25

CALLE 27

AVENIDA 1

AVENIDA CENTRAL

CALLE 35

Cathedral   i

LA
CALIFORNIA

CALLE 23

LOS
YOSES

5   6

CALLE 39

Ticabus
Terminal

AVENIDA 6

AVENIDA 8

Sirca
Terminal

CALLE CENTRAL

CALLE 3

CALLE 5

CALLE 7

AVENIDA 2

CALLE 29

CALLE 31

CALLE 33

AV 10 BIS

CALLE 23

AVENIDA 12 BIS

CALLE 13

CALLE 21

AVENIDA 14

AVENIDA 16

AVENIDA 18

ACCOMMODATION
Bienvenido	3
Boruca	2
Cacts	1
Don Fadrique	6
Grano de Oro	4
Le Bergerac	5

RESTAURANTS
Cocina de Leña	A
Macchu Picchu	B

up outside the terminal. You'll have no problems getting a cab, as the drivers will stampede for your business when you're practically still in customs. Taxi drivers accept dollars as well as colones.

Alternatively, the Alajuela–San José **bus** (every 3min between 5am & 10pm; every 15min at other times) stops right outside the airport's undercover carpark. Though it's much cheaper than a taxi there are no proper luggage racks inside and the buses are nearly always full – you can just about get away with it if you're carrying only a light backpack or small bag. Drivers will indicate which buses are on their way to San José (a 30min journey) and which to Alajuela. The fare is about 200 colones (US$0.75 – payable in local currency); pay the driver. The bus drops passengers in town at Av 2, C 12/14, where there are plenty of taxis around.

By bus

International buses from Nicaragua, Honduras, Guatemala and Panamá pull into the Ticabus station, Av 4, C 9/11 (☎221-8954), next to the yellow Soledad church. Since buses can arrive at odd hours, you may want to take refuge at one of the 24-hour eating spots nearby on Av 2 before looking for a room. One of the cheapest is the *Casa del*

SAFETY IN SAN JOSÉ

Although San José is a relatively safe city, there are dangers: mainly **mugging**, purse-snatching or jewellery-snatching. It's worth keeping a tight grip on your belongings around the Coca-Cola bus terminal – roughly from C 12 to 16 and between Av 1 and 3 – as well as around the Parque Central, Av 2, and the Plaza de la Cultura. Other dodgy areas, day and night, include C 12 around Av 8 and 10, and Av 4 to 6 and C 4 to 12, just southwest of the centre. If **driving** in the centre of the city, keep windows rolled up so no one can reach in and snatch your bag.

Also, watch out when **crossing the street**, anywhere in the city: drivers can be aggressive and accidents involving pedestrians are common.

Sandwich on the corner of C 9, and there's a taxi rank around the corner on Av 2 between C 5 and 9. Coming from Managua on Sirca, you'll arrive at the terminal at C 7, Av 6/8: taxis can be flagged down on C 7.

The closest thing San José has to a **domestic bus station** is **La Coca-Cola** (named after an old bottling plant that used to stand on the site), five blocks west of the Mercado Central at Av 1/3, C 16/18 (the main entrance is on C 16). Buses arrive here from the north and west (including Monteverde), and from Liberia, Puntarenas and most of the beaches of the Nicoya Peninsula. The name La Coca-Cola not only applies to the bus station proper – which is quite small and the arrival point for only a few buses – but also to the surrounding area, where many more buses pull in. Lugging your bags and searching for your bus stop around here makes it very hard not to look like a confused gringo, thus increasing the chances that you'll become the target of opportunistic theft: best to arrive and leave in a taxi. Be especially careful of your belongings around the **Tilarán and Monteverde bus stop** (C 14, Av 9/11): people waiting here for the 6.30am bus to Monteverde seem to be particularly at risk of attempted theft.

Information

San José's **ICT office** (Mon–Fri 9am–5pm; ☎223-1733, fax 223-5452, *www.tourism-costarica.com*), underneath the Plaza de la Cultura at C 5, Av 0/2, has free maps, leaflets and folders in which you can check out photos of hotels before you book, and free leaflets detailing the national bus schedule. They also hand out the free monthly *Culture Calendar*, which details concerts and festivals throughout the country.

In addition, the Sistema Nacional de Areas de Conservación (National System of Conservation Areas), or **SINAC**, runs a free phone line giving information in English and Spanish about Costa Rica's **national parks**: call ☎192 (Mon–Fri 8am–5.30pm). They can provide information on individual parks, particularly about transport and camping facilities. Basic information about opening hours, entrance tariffs and an explanation of the national parks system can be found at *www.minae.go.cr/areas/sinac.htm*. In San José you can get information, buy entrance tickets and make reservations for park shelters at the **Fundación de Parques Nacionales** office, Av 15, C 23/25, Barrio Escalante (☎257-2239, fax 222-4732, *azucena@ns.minae.go.cr*).

City transport

Central San José is easily negotiated on foot, though buses are useful in the suburbs. The mountain town of **Escazú** is about twenty minutes' ride to the west, and the university suburb of **San Pedro** about ten minutes to the east. After 10pm the buses stop running and **taxis** become the best way to get around.

Buses

Fast, cheap and frequent buses connect the centre of the city with virtually all of San José's neighbourhoods and suburbs; they generally run from 5am until 10pm. **Bus stops** in the city centre area seem to change every year. Currently, most buses to San Pedro, Tres Ríos and other points east leave from the stretch of Avenida Central between C 5 and C 15. You can pick up buses for Paseo Colón and Parque Sabana (labelled "Sabana-Cementerio") at the bus shelters on Av 2, C 5/7. At some point, the city authorities are hoping to move the bus stops out of the centre proper in order to cut traffic and pollution.

All buses have their routes clearly marked on their windshields, and usually the **fare** too. These are payable either to the driver or conductor when you board and are usually 60 colones (US$0.25), though the faster, more comfortable *busetas de lujo* (luxury buses) to the suburbs cost upwards of 80 colones (US$0.4). Bus drivers or conductors always have lots of change.

Taxis

Taxis are cheap and plentiful, even at odd hours of the night and early morning. Licensed vehicles are red with a yellow triangle on the side, and have "SJP" ("San José Publico") licence plates. A ride anywhere within the city will cost US$1–1.50, and about double that to get out to the suburbs. The starter fare – about US$0.50 – is shown on the red digital display; make sure the meter is on before you start (ask the driver to *toca la maría, por favor*). Tipping is not expected.

Driving

Though it's a bad idea to **rent a car** for getting around San José, you may need one for driving out of the city. Cars should never be left on the street anywhere near the city centre, since they are guaranteed to be broken into or stolen. Secure **parqueos** (guarded parking lots) dot the city; some are 24-hour, but most close at 8 or 8.30pm. If you have to leave your car on the street, look for the local security guard (they carry truncheons); and pay him 300 colones to guard it. For a list of car **rental companies** see p.581.

Accommodation

After a period of rapid growth – and high prices – in the hotel business during the tourism boom of the early 1990s, San José is at last getting more quality hotel rooms, with fairer prices in all categories, although characterful, friendly and good-value budget-to-moderate options are still elusive. Rock-bottom hotels tend, with a few exceptions, to be depressing cells that make the city seem infinitely more ugly than it is. The other recent major accommodation event in San José has been the arrival of international **hotel chains**, many of whose names – *Radisson*, *Holiday Inn* and *Best Western* – will be familiar to North Americans and Europeans.

If you're coming in **high season** (Dec–May), and especially over busy periods like Christmas and Easter, be prepared to reserve (and, in some cases, even pay) in advance – places that require payment in advance may give you a bank account number in Costa Rica for you to wire money to. Room **rates** vary dramatically between high and low seasons – the prices we quote are for a double room in peak season; expect to get substantial discounts at less busy times.

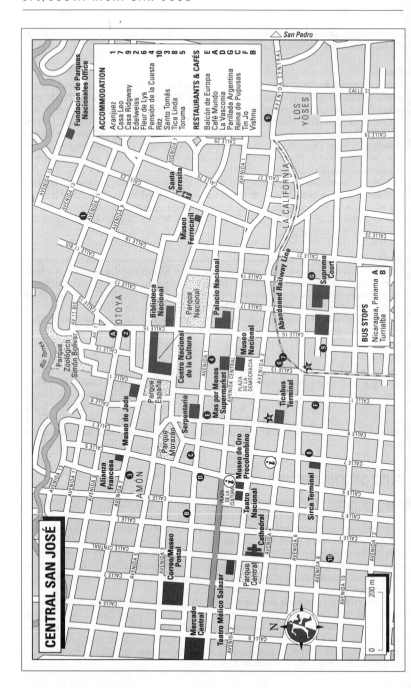

CENTRAL SAN JOSÉ

ACCOMMODATION

Aranjuez	1
Casa Leo	7
Casa Ridgway	9
Edelweiss	2
Fleur de Lys	6
Pensión de la Cuesta	4
Ritz	3
Santo Tomás	8
Tica Linda	10
Toruma	5

RESTAURANTS & CAFÉS

Balcón de Europa	E
Café Mundo	A
La Vasconia	D
Parrillada Argentina	G
Reina de Pupusas	C
Tin Jo	F
Vishnu	B

BUS STOPS

Nicaragua, Panama	A
Turrialba	B

Though staying in one of the budget hotels in the **city centre** is convenient, the downside is noise and pollution – Avenida 2 and parts of Avenidas 1, 3 and 5 can be noisy, but this is not a hard-and-fast rule, as the city authorities seem to like changing bus routes (the source of most street noise) every few years. The very cheapest rooms are in the insalubrious area immediately around La Coca-Cola, and while there are a couple of clean and well-run budget places here, the area is generally best avoided unless you've got an early bus to catch or are an aficionado of seedy hotels.

Not too far from downtown, in quieter areas such as **Paseo Colón**, **Los Yoses** and **Barrios Amón** and **Otoya**, are a group of more expensive hotels, many in old colonial homes.

Central San José

Aranjuez, C 19, Av 11/13 (☎256-1825, from the US & Canada call toll-free 1-877/898-8663, fax 223-3528, *www.hotelaranjuez.com*). Superb-value hotel in Barrio Aranjuez, a quiet area, but close to the centre. Rooms are arranged in converted houses that have been joined with communal sitting areas throughout, and there's a pretty garden around the back. The 23 rooms either have shared bath (③) or private bath and TV (④), and a good buffet breakfast and free local phone calls and email are included. It's often full, so reserve ahead.

Bienvenido, C 10, Av 1/3 (☎233-2161, fax 221-1872). One of the best downtown budget options, this family-run establishment has small clean rooms with private bath, and friendly staff who are particularly helpful with bus timetables and can arrange tours, but do not try to hard-sell them to you. Near La Coca-Cola, it's great if you want to catch an early bus, though the area is a bit dodgy. Credit cards accepted – unusual in this category. ②.

Boruca, C 14, Av 1/3 (☎223-0016, fax 232-0107). Central, basic and rather charmless hotel in the Coca-Cola district with small, musty and dark rooms – it's very cheap and clean, though, and has a secure atmosphere and friendly family management. ①.

Cacts, C 28–30, Av 3 bis (☎221-2928, fax 221-8616, *www.tourism.co.cr/hotels/cacts/cacts.htm*). Small, quiet and spotless hotel with sunny roof terrace, swimming pool and Jacuzzi. All rooms have ceiling fans, hot shower and TV, and the friendly owners also run a travel agency and can help with tours and reservations. ④.

Casa Leo, Av 6 bis, C 13/15 (☎222-9725). A good alternative if the *Casa Ridgway* (see below) is full, this small guesthouse has dorms (US$9 per person in a mixed-sex dorm) and basic private rooms (③) with shared bath and kitchen – all spotlessly clean and good value. The house can be hard to find; look for it next to the train tracks and tell your taxi driver it's a *calle sin salida*.

Casa Ridgway, C 15, Av 6/8 (☎233-6168 or 221-8299, fax 224-8910). Near the Ticabus stop, this homely Quaker guesthouse is San José's best budget option and a great place to meet other travellers. Accommodation includes clean single-sex dorms (US$10 per person), plus private singles (US$12) and triples (US$20) with communal bathrooms (there are no doubles), and there's also a shared kitchen, laundry and luggage storage – note that alcohol is banned and there's a "quiet time" after 10pm. Reserve ahead in high season, and try not to arrive after 8pm except by prior arrangement.

Don Fadrique, C 37, Av 8, Los Yoses (☎225-8166, fax 224-9746, *fadrique@centralamerica.com*). Upmarket but good-value hotel with restaurant and bar, located in the former home of Don Fadrique Gutierrez, early twentieth-century architect, general and philosopher. The hotel's halls are hung with Costa Rican art, and each of the twenty nicely furnished rooms comes with TV and private bath with hot water. Good low-season discounts. Breakfast included. ⑥.

Edelweiss, Av 9, C 13/15 (☎221-9702, fax 222-1241, *www.edelweisshotel.com*). Small, quiet hotel, situated in pretty Barrio Amón, with clean rooms (all with cable TV), wooden floors and piping hot showers, plus the use of a computer and safe. The excellent *Café Mundo* restaurant is just across the street. Breakfast included. ④.

Fleur de Lys, C 13, Av 2/6 (☎223-1206, fax 257-3637). Friendly hotel in an old San José house: each floor has a sunny, plant-filled atrium, and there's a nice restaurant/bar attached. Convenient downtown location near Ticabus and Av 2, but still quiet, and good discounts in low season. ⑤–⑥.

Grano de Oro, C 30, Av 2/4 (☎255-3322, fax 221-2782, *www.hotelgranodeoro.com*). Elegant converted mansion in a quiet area west of the centre, with 35 comfortable rooms and suites furnished in faux-Victorian style, with wrought-iron beds and polished wooden floors – they're popular with honeymooners and older Americans. All rooms have cable TV, mini-bar, phone and fax, and an excellent breakfast is served in the highly recommended restaurant. ⑤–⑦.

Le Bergerac, C 35, Av 0 (☎234-7850, fax 225-9103). For luxury without the price-tag, this elegant and relaxing top-end hotel is a good bet. The eighteen spacious rooms all have cable TV and phone, and some also have their own private gardens. A superb French restaurant, *L'Ile de France*, is prettily set in an interior courtyard. Continental breakfast included. ⑤–⑥.

Pensión de la Cuesta, Av 1, C 11/15 (☎ & fax 255-2896, *ggmnber@racsa.co.cr*). Tranquil and good-value rooms – though some are a bit gloomy – in a pink, colonial-style wooden house with a plant-filled lounge area, gold masks on the walls and decorated bedsteads. All rooms have shared bath, plus there's a communal kitchen, laundry service and luggage storage, and staff can also help with tours and car rental. ③.

Ritz, C 0, Av 8/10 (☎222-4103, fax 222-8849). Very clean and fairly large (25 rooms) central hotel with its own tour service – it's popular with European travellers, and is a good place to meet other backpackers. Management is friendly and the communal areas are pleasant, though rooms are rather dark – those with private bath (③) are twice the price of those without (②).

Santo Tomás, Av 7, C 3/5 (☎255-0448, fax 222-3950, *www.hotelsantotomas.com*). One of San José's best boutique hotels, located in quiet and elegant Barrio Amón, conveniently close to downtown. The hotel occupies an old mansion house decorated with burnished wood, Persian rugs and soft lighting. Rooms vary widely in size, character and price, though all have TV and telephone, and there's also a gift shop and free Internet and email access. ⑤.

Tica Linda, C 7, Av 6/8 (☎ & fax 222-4402). Venerable budget hotel, newly refurbished, with fairly spacious single, double or dormitory rooms, all with shared hot showers, kitchen, and TV. Despite the upgrade, manager José Luis has kept the lowest prices in San José, and the place continues to draw friendly backpackers from around the world. ①.

Toruma, Av 0, C 29/31 (☎ & fax 224-4085). Costa Rica's main HI hostel (see p.556), this beautiful establishment with Neoclassical exterior and high ceilings is a good place both to meet people and to make onward hostel, tour and travel reservations. Accommodation is in single-sex dorms (US$10 per person for HI members, US$13 for non-members – membership is available at the front desk) and a few singles, and there's also luggage storage, a safe and laundry. Book well in advance in high season. Non-smoking.

San Pedro

La Granja, off Av 0 in Barrio La Granja, San Pedro, 50m south of the *antiguo higuerón* – the site of a now disappeared tree which still serves as a local landmark (☎ & fax 225-1073). Great budget hotel in a family house with a pretty garden, near the university, bars and restaurants. Most rooms have shared showers. Also has some cheap singles (US$12), a TV lounge, communal kitchen and laundry service. ②.

Maripaz, 350m southeast of the *antiguo higuerón* (☎ & fax 253-8456, *maripaz@racsa .co.cr*). Small (5 rooms) B&B in the home of a welcoming Costa Rican family, located in a quiet and pleasant area close to the university and several language schools. Rooms come either with private or shared bath. ③–④.

Escazú

Casa de las Tias, San Rafael de Escazú (☎289-5517, fax 289-7353). Quiet, friendly and atmospheric place, with individually decorated rooms complete with private bath and hot water. No under-12s allowed. ⑤–⑥.

Posada del Bosque, Belo Horizonte de Escazú (☎228-1164, fax 228-2006). Very quiet, homely place, in large landscaped

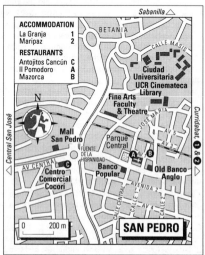

grounds, with comfortable no-smoking rooms with shared bath. The friendly owners can arrange tennis, swimming and horse-riding in the area. ⑨.

Posada El Quijote, Bello Horizonte de Escazú (☎289-8401, fax 289-8729, *quijote@racsa.co.cr*). Eight spacious rooms, all renovated in the style of a Spanish colonial manor and comfortably furnished with bath, hot water and cable TV. Breakfast is served in the lovely garden. ⑨.

The City

Few travellers come to San José for the sights. A city of nondescript buildings, energized by an aggressive street life – umbrella-wielding pedestrians pushing through narrow streets, noisy food stalls, homicidal drivers – San José is certainly not a place that exudes immediate appeal. It has its diversions, however, with plenty of places to walk, sit, eat, meet people, go dancing and enjoy museums and galleries. It's also a manageable city: all the attractions are close together, and everything of interest can be covered in a couple of days. Of the museums, the exemplary **Museo de Oro Precolombino** and **Museo de Jade** are the major draws. The less-visited **Museo Nacional** offers some interesting archeological finds, while the **Museo de Arte y Deseño Contemporáneo** displays some of the most striking work in Central America. San José is also a surprisingly green and open city, with small, carefully landscaped parks and plazas punctuating the centre of town.

Around the Plaza de la Cultura

The **Plaza de la Cultura** cleverly conceals one of San José's treasures, the **Museo de Oro Precolombino**, or Pre-Columbian Gold Museum (Tues–Sat 10am–4pm; US$4). The bunker-like underground space is unprepossessing, but the gold on display is truly impressive – all the more extraordinary if you take into account the relative paucity of pre-Columbian artefacts in Costa Rica. The exquisitely delicate work on show is almost entirely the work of the **Diquis**, the ancient inhabitants of southwestern Costa Rica. Most of the pieces are small and unbelievably detailed, with a preponderance of disturbing-looking **animals**. Information panels (Spanish only) suggest that the chief function of these portents of evil – frogs, snakes and insects – was shamanic. The *ave de rapiña*, or bird of prey, seems to have had particular religious relevance for the Diquis: there are tons of them here – hawks, owls and eagles, differing only incrementally in shape and size. Look out, too, for angry-looking arachnids; jaguars and alligators carrying the pathetic dangling legs of human victims in their mouths; grinning bats with wings spread; turtles, crabs, frogs, iguanas and armadillos, and a few spiny, unmistakeable lobsters.

San José's heavily columned, grey-brown **Teatro Nacional** sits on the corner of C 5 and Av 2, tucked in behind the Plaza de la Cultura. The theatre's marbled stairways, gilt cherubs and red velvet carpets would look more at home in old Europe than in Central America, and remain in remarkably good condition, despite the dual onslaught of the climate and a succession of earthquakes. Even if you're not coming to see a performance, you can wander around the post-Baroque splendour, although you'll be charged US$3 in colones for the privilege – another reason to come here for a show. The elegant attached café serves good coffee and European-style cakes.

Around the Parque España

On the north side of the **Parque España**, three blocks northeast of the Plaza de la Cultura, rises one of the few office towers in San José: the INS, or Institute of Social Security, building. This uninspired edifice is home to one of the city's finest museums, the **Marco Fidel Tristan Museo de Jade** (Mon–Fri 8am–4pm; US$3), home to the world's largest collection of American jade, ingeniously displayed with subtle backlighting to show off the multi-coloured and multi-textured pieces to full effect. You'll see a lot of **axe-gods**: anthropomorphic bird/human forms shaped like an axe and worn as a pendant. One entire room is devoted to male fertility symbols, and you'll also see X-shaped objects used to support the breasts of women of standing – a kind of proto-bra. Incidentally, the **view** from the museum windows is one of the best in the city, taking in the sweep of San José from the centre to the south and then west to the mountains.

Sprawling across the entire eastern border of the Parque España, the former National Liquor Factory (FANAL), dating from 1887, today houses the Centro Nacional de Cultura, home to the cutting-edge **Museo de Arte y Diseño Contemporáneo** (Tues–Sun 10am–5pm; US$2). The museum's cosmopolitan, multi-media approach features works by artists from across Latin America, alongside the work of Costa Ricans, and it's definitely worth a visit to see what's going on in the arts in the Americas. There's also a theatre in the complex – a wander around during the day may offer interesting glimpses of dancers and musicians rehearsing.

Lurking on the second floor of a nondescript building on the corner of Av 1 and C 9, the **Serpentario** (Mon–Fri 9am–6pm; Sat & Sun 10am–5pm; US$4) is one of Costa Rica's most useful attractions, where aghast tourists and fascinated schoolboys wander amid glass cases of snakes, poison-dart frogs and the odd lizard. Species on display include the fer-de-lance, bushmaster and jumping and eyelash vipers, while a rather forlorn-looking Burmese python lies curled up in the biggest case.

Heading one block south then one block east from the Sepentario brings you to the concrete **Plaza de la Democracía**, yet another of the city's soulless squares. Constructed in 1989 to mark President Oscar Arias' key involvement in the Central American Peace Plan, this expanse of terraced concrete slopes gently up towards a fountain and the impressive, fortress-like edifice of the **Museo Nacional** (Tues–Sat 8.30am–4.30pm, Sun 9am–4.30pm; US$2), home to the country's most important archeological exhibition. Highlights include petroglyphs, pre-Columbian stonework – the grinding tables and funerary offerings, in particular, show precise geometric patterns – and, in the **Sala Arqueológica**, wonderful anthropomorphic gold figures.

Centro Costarricense de la Ciencia y la Cultura

Near El Pueblo, at the north end of Calle 4, is the **Centro Costarricense de la Ciencia y la Cultura** (Tues–Fri 8am–4pm, Sat & Sun 10am–4pm; US$5). Located in a former prison, this complex devotes most of its space to the mildly interesting **Museo de los Niños** (Childrens' Museum), where Costa Rican kids can come to see interactive displays and learn about their country's history, culture and science. The complex also houses the **Museo Historico Penitenciario** (Penitentiary History Museum), which consists of a number of the original prison cells restored to their nineteenth-century condition, and some rather anodyne accounts of the country's penal history.

Around the Mercado Central

Northwest of the Parque Central and the commercial centre between Av 0/1 and C 6/8 is San José's **Mercado Central** (Mon–Sat 5am–5pm). Entering its labyrinthine interior you're confronted by colourful arrangements of strange fruits and vegetables, dangling sides of beef and elaborate, silvery ranks of fish. Shopping for fruit, vegetables and coffee here is cheaper than in a supermarket, and it's also the best place in town to get a cheap bite – not only that, but the view from a counter stool is fascinating, as traders and their customers jostle for *chayotes, mamones, piñas* and *cas.*

The surrounding streets, which even in the daytime can look quite seedy, are full of noisy traders and determined shoppers. All this activity encourages **pickpockets**, and in this environment *turistas* stick out like sore thumbs. Take only what you need and be on your guard.

Two blocks east and one block north of the Mercado Central, in the Correo Central, C 2, Av 1/3, the **Museo Postal, Telegráfico y Filatelico** (Mon–Fri 8am–4pm; free) exhibits old relics of telegraphic equipment – of interest to buffs only. Far more appealing is the pretty **flower market** in the square opposite, where carnations, orchids, begonias and scores of lush blooms create a blaze of colour and fragrance.

Paseo Colón and Parque la Sabana

Clustered around the main entrance to La Coca-Cola, off C 16, shops selling women's underwear, cosmetics and luggage compete for space with a variety of cheap snack bars and drinks stalls. Two blocks south, however, the atmosphere changes, as Av Central turns into **Paseo Colón**, a wide boulevard of upmarket shops, restaurants and car dealerships. At the very end of the *paseo*, the solid expanse of green today known as **Parque La Sabana** was until the 1940s San José's airport, and is now home to the country's key art museum.

The bright orange neocolonial edifice of the old air terminal in **Parque la Sabana** has been converted into the attractive **Museo de Arte Costarricense** (Tues–Sun 10am–4pm; $2), with a good collection of mainly twentieth-century Costa Rican paintings. The **Salon Dorado** upstairs is remarkable: four full walls of bas-relief wooden carvings overlaid with sumptuous gold, portraying somewhat idealized scenes of Costa Rica's history since pre-Columbian times.

On the southwest corner of Parque La Sabana, across the road in the Ministry of Agriculture and Livestock complex, is the quirky natural science museum, the **Museo de Ciencias Naturales La Salle** (Mon–Fri 8am–3pm; US$1). Walk right in, and after about 400m you'll see the painted wall proclaiming the museum; the entrance is at the back. Displays range from pickled fish and snakes coiled in formaldehyde to some rather forlorn taxidermy exhibits – age and humidity have taken their toll.

Sabana is also the best place in San José to **jog**. The cement track is usually full of serious runners in training, but you can run fairly safely all around the park. There's a small, dank changing hut, shower and lavatory beside the track, and you can leave your bag securely with the *señora* who takes the money (10am–4pm only).

San Pedro

First impressions of the student district of **San Pedro**, west of the city centre, can be offputting, with Avenida Central (also known here as Paseo de los Estudiantes) lined by gas stations, broken-up sidewalks, and dull malls as it passes through the area. Walk just a block away from the Paseo, however, and you'll find a lively combination of university student ghettos and elegant old residential houses, home to some of the city's best bars, restaurants and nightlife, catering to students, professors, residents and professionals.

Buses to San Pedro from the middle of town stop opposite the small **Parque Central**, centred on a monument to John F. Kennedy. Walking north from the square, through three blocks of solid sodas, bars, restaurants and abandoned railway tracks, you come to the cool, leafy campus of the **University of Costa Rica** (UCR), founded in 1940 and now one of the finest universities in Central America, with a busy, egalitarian and stimulating atmosphere.

Eating

For a Central American city of its size, San José has a surprising variety of **restaurants**. Many of the best places are in the relatively high-income and cosmopolitan neighbourhoods of **San Pedro**, along **Paseo Colón**, and in **Escazú**, but wherever you choose, eating out in San José can set your budget back on its haunches. The 23 percent tax on restaurant food can deliver a real death-blow, so it's cheapest to eat in the centre, at the sodas and snack bars, where the tax doesn't apply. A sit-down lunch of the *plato del día* at a **soda** will rarely set you back more than US$5, or for a quick sugar fix you could feast on *churros* dispensed over the counter. Healthier choices include *empanadas* and sandwiches to take out – combine this with a stop at one of the fruit stalls on any street corner and you've got a quick, cheap lunch. **Cafés** also abound: some, like *Giacomín*, have old-world European aspirations; others, like *Spoon*, are resolutely Costa Rican, with *Josefinos* piling in to order birthday cakes or grab a **coffee**. Of the major **ice-cream** chains *Pops* is the best, with particularly good fruit flavours.

Working *Josefinos* eat their main meal between noon and 2pm, when sodas especially can get very busy. Many restaurants close at 3pm and open again for the evening. In the listings below we have given a phone number only for places where you might need to **reserve** a table.

Restaurants

Antojitos Cancún, in the Centro Comercial Cocorí, 50m west of the Fuente de la Hispanidad roundabout, Los Yoses. Cheap, filling, Mexican food, not wholly authentic, but good for late-night snacks and cheap all-you-can-eat buffets. There's also draught beer and an outside terrace where you can sit and watch the 4WDs whizz round the fountain, plus live Mariachi on Fri and Sat from 10pm. Daily 11am–midnight.

Balcón de Europa, C 9, Av 0/1 (☎221-4841). City landmark: the food, largely pasta and Italian staples, is nothing special, but the atmosphere is great. Sepia photos of the early days line the wood-panelled wall, along with annoying snippets of "wisdom". Monster cheeses dominate the dining room, as does the game strummer who serenades each table. Closed Sat.

Café Mundo, Av 9, C 15, Barrio Otoya. The best food in San José, served amidst beautiful decor and a relaxed European atmosphere. The subtle and delicately cooked food is Italian influenced, and includes a variety of pasta dishes – the fetuccini with *camarones* (US$14) is good – as well as great puddings. The Caesar (US$4) and nicoise (US$8) salads are large but a bit overpriced – if you're on a budget, go for the pizza, or just come for a cappuccino (US$2). At night the bar attracts a largely gay clientele. Closed Sat & Sun.

Cocina de Leña, Centro Comercial El Pueblo (☎255-1360). Típico food, superbly prepared and served in rustic surroundings with big wooden tables, gingham tablecloths and menus on paper bags. Most meals are cooked in a wood oven – the succulent chicken dishes are recommended. Good for a quiet, upmarket night out. Dinner for two costs around US$35.

Grano d'Oro, Casa 251, C 3, Av 2/4 (☎253-3322). Upmarket restaurant with beautifully spare decor and a changing menu. Breakfast (from 6am) includes fresh fruit, eggs benedict and banana macadamia pancakes. Soups are excellent – try the classic black bean or corn chowder. Among the main courses, the beef is consistently delicious, as is white sea bass breaded with toasted macadamia nuts. Amazing desserts, including tiramisu and strawberry cream cheese. Book ahead and bring plenty of funds.

Il Pomodoro, San Pedro, 150m east of the entrance to UCR. One of the best pizza places in the city, with large pizzas – including a great vegetarian special – and cheap draught beer served in mugs and pitchers in a large and cheerful restaurant popular with the university crowd. Around US$18 for two.

Machu Picchu, C 32, Av 1 (☎222-7384). A consistent San José favourite, and the only truly South American place in town (the velvet llamas on the walls help) – though the appetizers, including *ceviche* and Peruvian *bocas*, tend to be more interesting than the main dishes. Count on around US$30 for two with beer or wine. Closed Sun.

Marisqueria La Princesa, north side of Parque la Sabana. One of San José's best restaurants, though it doesn't look much from the outside, with very cheap seafood – the shrimps with garlic (*camarones con ajillo*) are about half the price you'll find elsewhere.

Mazorca, 200m east and 100m north of San Pedro church. Macrobiotic restaurant just east of the entrance to UCR with homely, simple decor and menu (lunch is US$5; takeaways are also available). The tasty bread, soups, peanut-butter sandwiches and macrobiotic cakes make a welcome change from greasy *arroz con pollo*. Closed Sun.

Tin-Jo, C 11, Av 6/8 (☎221-7605). Quiet, popular and fairly formal Chinese-Thai place – the lemon-grass soup, bean-thread salad in lime juice and coconut milk curries are particularly good. Dinner with wine is around US$40 for two; skip the alcohol, or go for lunch, and you'll get away with half that.

Sodas

La Reina de Pupusas, Av 1, C 5/7, opposite Cine Omni on the corner of Parking Gigante. Salvadorean foodstall serving great snacks, including tortillas with *frijoles molidos* (refried beans), cabbage, mixed pickles and sausage or meat and cheese. The tortillas are large enough to be a meal in themselves, though very messy to eat.

La Vasconia, Av 1, C 3/5. Enormous menu featuring cheap breakfasts and lunch specials, including fairly cheap *ceviche*. The place to go to get off the tourist trail and mingle with stressed office workers.

Parillada Argentina, C 21, Av 6, 100m east of the Supreme Court. Watch the Argentine owners prepare exquisite chicken and beef or mozzarella, tomato and oregano *empanadas* (US0.75 each) to take away, or join the lawyers from the court next door and tuck into a massive lunch – the mini-parillada, with succulent beef, sausage, potato and salad (US$4) is quite enough for those with anything less than an Argentina-sized stomach. Open Mon–Fri lunch only.

Vishnu, Av 1, C 1/3. Obligatory pit stop for anybody visiting San José, this cheery vegetarian place serves delicious *platos del día* with brown rice, vegetables and soups, while the vegetarian club sandwich is a meal in itself at a bargain US$1.50. Fruit plates with yoghurt are a perennial favourite, and a *plato del día*, *refresco* and *café con leche* will set you back about US$4.

Cafés and bakeries

Café La Maga, inside the Centro Commercial Cocorí, just before the Fuente de la Hispanidad roundabout, Los Yoses. Currently one of the most popular places in town day or night, this café-bar doubles as an art gallery and stocks an enormous array of magazines dealing with Latin American and Spanish art, culture and literature.

Café Parisienne, *Gran Hotel Costa Rica*, Av 2, C 3/5. The closest thing in San José to a European street café, complete with wrought-iron chairs and trussed-up waiters, this is a wonderful place to sit and have coffee and cake on a sunny day. It's also one of the few establishments in the city that does continental breakfast.

Café Ruiseñor, Av 2, C 3/5. Coffee, fruit drinks, sandwiches and fantastic cakes served in a tranquil mint-green setting: the tables by the window are good for watching the goings-on in the Plaza de la Cultura.

La Esquina del Café, C 3 bis, Av 9. Small, quiet, aromatic café with excellent coffee, freshly roasted beans and friendly staff who will answer any questions about the entire coffee process, from bean to cup. Also serves good cappuccino with proper frothed milk, tasty desserts (you can try before you buy) and lunches of soups, salads and sandwiches. They also sell little bags of beans from Costa Rica's various coffee-producing regions.

Ruiseñor, 150m east of the Automercado in Los Yoses. Upmarket – and expensive – restaurant with a pleasant outdoor terrace and old-fashioned, European-style service and atmosphere.

Drinking and nightlife

San José's nightlife is gratifyingly varied, with scores of **bars** and **live music** venues. That said, a couple of the most popular venues of recent years, including the splendid Casa Matute, have had to close because of strict anti-noise regulations (curiously, these are only enforced for live music venues, as opposed to taped salsa blaring at 7am from your neighbour's room). Many bars change character drastically come Friday or Saturday, when they host jazz, blues, upcoming local bands, rock and roll, or South American folk music. Ticos aren't known for burning the candle at both ends – with the exception of the studenty bars in San Pedro, most places close by 2 or 3am; earlier on Sunday.

Most young *Josefinos*, students and foreigners in the know head to Los Yoses or San Pedro to drink. In **Los Yoses**, Av Central features a well-known "yuppie trail" of bars, starting roughly at the *El Cuartel de la Boca del Monte,* with its mobile phone-wielding contingent, and finishing at *Río,* a hugely popular American-style bar with an outdoor terrace. **San Pedro** is obviously geared toward the university population, with a couple of very studenty bars.

It's worth experiencing one of the city's **discos**: even if you don't dance, you can watch the Ticos burn up the floor. *Déjà Vu* is the place of the moment, while for traditional **salsa**, merengue, cumbia and soca try *La Plaza, Cocloco, Las Risas* or *Infinito*. **Cover charges** run to about US$4, though the big mainstream discos at El Pueblo (see below) charge slightly more than places downtown.

You need to be 18 to drink in Costa Rica. Even if you're well over age, if you look even remotely young, bring a photocopy of your passport as **ID**.

Bars and live music

Baleares, in San Pedro, 50m west of the Más y Menos supermarket. Live rock (Thurs–Sat) in a dark and cavernous bar popular with students and locals. There's usually a US$3 cover charge.

Bar Jazz Café, in San Pedro, next to the Banco Popular (☎253-8933). The best place in San José to hear jazz, with an intimate atmosphere and consistently good groups. The cover charge varies from US$5 to US$10, sometimes including a glass of wine, but is usually worth it.

Caccio's, 200m east and 25m north of San Pedro church. Insanely popular student hangout with guys wearing baseball caps and singing along to outdated songs – it's a great place to meet people, and the baskets of pizza and cheap cold beer are another bonus. Closed Sun.

Chelles, Av 0, C 9. Round the corner from its namesake (see below), this *Chelles* is a simple, brightly lit bar, with football on the television, cheap beers and *bocas*, and 24-hour service, drawing an eclectic crowd of weary businessmen and late-night revellers.

Chelles Taberna, C 9, Av 0/2 (☎221-1369). More like an English pub than a Latin American tavern, with smooching couples, serious guys in leather jackets and surly waitresses. It has a good range of drinks, though, as well as cheap, tasty *bocas*, and is open 24 hours.

El Cuartel de la Boca del Monte, Av 1, C 21/23. Probably the most popular bar in San José, at least with younger *Josefinos*, with a well-stocked bar, great food (lunch and dinner are served, as well as *bocas*), and some of the best live music in town from up-and-coming bands (Wed only). Dress hip and go early, preferably before 9pm, to get a seat. There's a door policy of sorts, but the bouncers never seem to turn foreigners away. Small cover (US$2.50) most nights. Open Wed–Sat evenings until 2am.

La Esmeralda, Av 2, C 5/7. Colourful, landmark institution, being the headquarters of the union of Mariachi bands, who whoosh by your table in a colourful swirl of sombreros and sequins before dashing off in a taxi to serenade or celebrate elsewhere in the city. Closed Sun.

La Maga, inside Centro Commercial Cocorí, just before the Fuente de la Hispanidad roundabout, Los Yoses. Currently one of the most popular places in town day or night, this café-bar doubles as an art gallery, and stocks an enormous array of magazines dealing with Latin American and Spanish art, culture and literature.

Las Risas, C 1, Av 0/1. One of the best downtown bars, on three floors. The disco at the top is good, with a small dance floor and lively young crowd. Bring ID – a copy of your passport will suffice — or the bouncers won't let you in. The cover charge of US$3 will usually get you two drinks or a tequila. Saturday is ladies' night.

La Villa, 150m north of the old Banco Anglo, San Pedro. Located in an atmospheric old house, frequented by students and "intellectuals" and plastered with political and theatrical posters, this is San José's best bar for beer and conversation, with Mercedes Sosa on the CD player, occasional live *peñas* and tasty *bocas*. Closed Sun.

Shakespeare, Av 2, C 28. Quiet, friendly place that's popular with people popping in for a drink before seeing a performance at the adjacent Sala Garbo cinema or Laurence Olivier theatre. Also has occasional live jazz.

Tapa Tapa, in the Multicentro Paco in Escazú (☎299-2320). Big, lively tapas bar, situated in a cavernous wooden room and boasting an utterly authentic menu, with manchego cheese, chorizo, anchovies, gazpacho and *calamares a la romana*. Some small tapas are served free with your beer (US$1.50); for larger *raciones* you have to order and pay separately.

Discos

Cocoloco, El Pueblo. Smart, well-dressed clientele, small dance floors, and the usual Latin techno-pop/reggae/merengue mix.

Déjà Vu, C 2, Av 14/16. A mixed crowd – gay, lesbian and straight – come for the hot and happening atmosphere, mostly house and techno with a few salsa tunes interspersed. There are two large dance floors plus a quiet bar and a café. The neighbourhood is pretty scary though – take a taxi. Cover charge varies from US$3 to US$5, though drinks are cheap. Closed Sun & Mon.

Dynasty, in Centro Comercial del Sur, Desamparados, south of central San José next to the old Pacific Railway station. Full of a young, hard-dancing crowd getting down to excellent *caribeña* tunes with reggae, plus the odd bit of garage, soca, merengue and calypso. Open Fri & Sat only.

Infinitos, El Pueblo. Similar to *Cocoloco*, with three dance floors playing salsa, US and European dance music, and 1970s romantic hits respectively. Attracts an older, smarter crowd, and excellent DJs. Closed Sun.

La Avispa, C 1, Av 8/10. Landmark San José lesbian disco-bar (men are also welcome) with a friendly atmosphere and mainly Latin music. There's a US$5 cover charge Thursday to Sunday. Closed Mon.

La Plaza, across from El Pueblo. Archetypical Latin American disco. Designed like a giant bull ring, the huge round dance floor is packed with couples dancing to merengue and superb waiters who twirl in their truncated tuxedos when business is slack. There's also a bar with a big TV screen flashing out a steady diet of music and sport.

The arts and entertainment

Bearing in mind the decreasing financial support it receives from the national government, the quality of the arts in San José is very high. *Josefinos* especially like **theatre**, and there's a healthy range of venues for a city this size, staging a variety of inventive productions at affordable prices. If you speak even a little Spanish it's worth checking to see what's on.

Costa Rica's **National Dance Company** has an impressive repertoire of classical and modern productions, some by Central American choreographers, arranged specifically for the company – again, ticket costs are low. The city's premier venues are the Teatro Nacional and the Teatro Melico Salazar, where you can see performances by the **National Symphony Orchestra** and **National Lyric Opera Company** (June–Aug), as well as visiting orchestras and singers – usually from Spain or other Spanish-speaking countries.

Going to the **cinema** in San José is a bargain, at around US$3 a ticket, though many venues have decamped to the suburbs – particularly to shopping malls, such as the Multiplaza Escazú, which you can only reach by car or taxi. There are still a few good downtown cinemas left, however, several of which retain some original features, along with plush, comfortable seats. Most cinemas show the latest American movies, which are almost always subtitled. The few that are dubbed will have the phrase "hablado en Español" in the newspaper listings or on the posters. For Spanish-language art movies, head to Sala Garbo.

Though obviously geared up for tourists, the **Fantasía Folklórica** held every Tuesday night in the Teatro Melico Salazar is the only forum in which traditional dances and songs of the Costa Rican countryside are performed. Shows vary between representations of, for instance, Guanacastecan dance and music and historic spectaculars such as the current long-running production *Limón, Limón*. Not nearly as cheesy as they sound, they're generally well staged and good fun if you like musicals.

For **details of all performances**, check the *Cartelera* section of the *Tiempo Libre* supplement in *La Nación* on Thursday and the listings in the *Tico Times*, which also distinguish between English- and Spanish-language films and productions.

Shopping and markets

San José's **souvenir and crafts shops** are well-stocked and in general fairly pricey; it's best to buy from larger ones, run by government-regulated crafts co-operatives, from

which more of the money filters down to the artisans. Items for sale include an abundance of pre-Columbian gold jewellery copies, Costa Rican liqueurs (Café Rica is best
known), T-shirts with jungle and animal scenes, weirdly realistic wooden snakes,
leather rockers from the village of Sarchí (see p.592), walking sticks, simple leather
bracelets, hammocks, and a vast array of wood carvings.

At the bottom of the Plaza de la Democracia, Av 0/2 and C 11/13, a long line of can-
vas-covered **artisans' stalls** sell hammocks, chunky Ecuadorean sweaters, leather
bracelets and jewellery, mostly of the leather-and-bead type. You'll also find some
Guatemalan textiles and decorative textile *molas* made by the Kuna peoples of Panamá
(see p.754), though all at steeper prices than elsewhere in the isthmus. Traders are low-
pressure and friendly, and gentle bargaining is allowed.

ANDA, Av 0, C 5/7. Indigenous crafts including wooden masks, colourful *molas,* and bags and
reproductions of Chorotega pottery.

La Casona, C 0, Av 0/1. Large marketplace with stalls selling the usual local stuff along with
Guatemalan knapsacks and bedspreads. Jewellery and Panamanian *molas* are the highlights.
Quality at some stalls is pretty poor, however, and there's not one good T-shirt in evidence. Great
for browsing, though.

Mercado Nacional de Artesanía, C 22, Av 2 bis. One of the largest stocks of souvenirs and crafts
in the country, featuring all the usuals: hats, T-shirts, Sarchí ox-carts, jewellery and woodwork,
including snakes and walking sticks.

Tienda de la Naturaleza, Curridabat, 1km past San Pedro on Av 0. The shop of the private
Fundación Neotropica, this is a good place to buy the posters, T-shirts and other paraphernalia
painted by English artist Deirdre Hyde that you see all over the country. She specializes in the landscapes of tropical America and the animals who live there – her jaguars are particularly good.

Listings

Airline offices Aeronica, C 11/13 (☎233-2483); Alitalia, C 38, Av 3 (☎222-6009); American, Paseo
Colón, C 26/28 (☎257-1266); Aviateca, at the airport (☎255-4949); Continental, C 19, Av 2 (☎296-
4911); Copa, C 1, Av 5 (☎222-6640); Iberia, C 40, Paseo Colón (☎257-8266); Lacsa, C 1, Av 5 (☎257-
9444); Ladeco, C 11, Av 1 (☎233-7290); Lufthansa, C 5, Av 7/9 (☎221-7444); Mexicana, C 1, Av 2/4
(☎257-6334); SAM, Av 5, C 1/3 (☎233-3066); Sansa, Av 5, C 1/3 (☎221-5774); TACA, C 1, Av 1/3
(☎222-1790); United Airlines, Sabana Sur (☎220-4844); Varig, Av 5, C 1/3 (☎290-5222).

Banks State-owned banks in San José include the Banco de Costa Rica, Av 2, C 4/6 (Mon–Fri
9am–3pm; Visa only) and Banco Nacional, Av 0/1, C 2/4 (Mon–Fri 9am–3pm; Visa only). Private
banks include Banco Mercantil, Av 3, C 0/2 (Mon–Fri 9am–3pm; Visa only); Banco Metropolitano,
C 0, Av 2 (Mon–Fri 8.15am–4pm; Visa only); BANEX, C 0, Av 1 (Mon–Fri 8am–5pm; Visa only);
Banco Popular, C 1 Av 2/4 (Mon–Fri 8.30am–3.30pm; Visa & Mastercard); and Banco de San José,
C 0, Av 3/5 (Visa & Mastercard).

Bookstores Mora Books, Av 1, C 3/5, in the Omni building (☎255-4136), has a good selection of
secondhand English-language books, CDs, guidebooks and magazines. Chispas, C 7, Av 0/1 (☎223-
2240), sells new and secondhand books, and has the best selection of English-language fiction in
town. It also sells a good array of guide books and books about Costa Rica (in English and Spanish),
plus the *New York Times*, *El País* and several English-language magazines. Lehmann, Av 0, C 1/3
(☎223-1212), has a good selection of mass-market Spanish-language fiction and non-fiction, as well
as lots of maps and children's books. The Librería Internacional, with branches 300m west of Taco
Bell in Barrio Dent (☎253-9553) and in the Multiplaza Escazú (☎298-1138), is the classiest of the lot,
and has the best selection of international fiction; they also stock travel books and Spanish-language
fiction, as well as books in English and German. Macondo, opposite the entrance to the library at
the university campus in San Pedro, is probably the best bookshop in town for literature in Spanish,
especially from Central America, as well as academic disciplines such as sociology and women's
studies. Universal, Av 0, C Central/1 (☎222-2222), is strong on Spanish books, fiction, titles on Costa
Rica (in Spanish), and maps of the country. Librería y Bazar Guillen at La Coca-Cola bus terminal is
a good place to browse for reading material before leaving on a long trip – if you're away from the
capital, you can order books from here by phone and the friendly owners will despatch them to you

by bus. 7th street books, C 7 Av 0/1 (☎256-8251) has both new and used books; it's good on English literature, and also has a wide selection of books and maps on Costa Rica in English and Spanish.

Car rental (where two numbers are given, the first is the company's downtown office, the second, the airport office): ADA, Av 18, C 11/13 (☎233-7733; ☎441-1260); Adobe, C 7, Av 8/10 (☎221-5425); Avis, C 42, Av Las Americas (☎293-2222); Budget, Paseo Colón, C 30 (☎223-3284); Elegante, C 10, Av 13/15, Barrio México (☎221-0066; ☎233-8605); Europcar/Prego, C 36/38 (☎257-1158, *www .pregorentacar.com*); Hertz, C 38, Paseo Colón (☎221-1818); Hola, in front of the *Best Western Irazú* on the airport highway (☎231-5666, *www.hola.net*); National, C 36, Av 7 (☎233-4044); Thrifty, C 3, Av 13 (☎257-3434); Tico, Paseo Colón, C 24/26 (☎222-8920; ☎443-2078).

Embassies and consulates Belize, 400m east of the Iglesia Santa Teresita, Rohrmoser (☎234-9969 or 234-9445); Canada, C 3, Av 1 (☎296-4149); Colombia, 175m west of Taco Bell, in Barrio Dent (☎283-6871); El Salvador, Av 10, C 33/35, Los Yoses (☎225-3861); Guatemala, 100m north and 50m east of *Pizza Hut* in Curridabat (☎224-5721); Honduras, 300m east and 200m north of ITAN, in Los Yoses (☎234-9502); Mexico, Av 7, C 13/15 (☎257-0633); Nicaragua, Av 0, C 25/27 (☎222-2373 or 233-8747); Panamá, C 38, Av 5/7 (☎257-3241); UK, 11th floor, Edificio Centro Colón, Paseo Colón, C 38/40 (☎258-2025); US, opposite the Centro Comercial in Pavas – take the bus to Pavas from Av 1, C 18 (☎220-3939).

Film processing San José is the only place in the country you should try to get film processed. That said, it's expensive and the quality is low: best wait until you get home if you can. Bearing in mind these caveats, try Universal, Av 0, C 0/1, which only processes Fuji; IFSA, Av 2, C 3/5, which only processes Kodak; or Dima, Av 0, C 3/5, which processes both Kodak and Fuji.

Hospitals The city's public (social security) hospital is San Juan de Díos, Paseo Colón, C 14/16 (☎257-6282). Of the private hospitals, foreigners are most often referred to Clínica Biblica, Av 14, C 0/1 (☎257-5252; emergency and after-hours number ☎257-0466), where basic consultation and treatment (such as a prescription for a course of antibiotics) starts at about US$100. San José has many excellent medical specialists – your embassy will have a list – and private health care isn't expensive.

Immigration The Costa Rican *migración* (Mon–Fri 8am–4pm) is on the airport highway opposite the Hospital México; take an Alajuela bus and get off at the stop underneath the overhead walkway. Get there early if you want visa extensions or exit visas. Larger travel agencies listed on p.586 can take care of the paperwork for you for a fee (roughly US$10–US$25).

Laundry Burbujas, 50m west and 25m south of the Mas x Menos supermarket in San Pedro, has coin-operated machines and sells soap; Lava y Seca, 100m north of Mas x Menos, next to Autos San Pedro, in San Pedro, will do your laundry for you, as well as dry-cleaning. Other places include Lava Más, C 45, Av 8/10, next to *Spoon* in Los Yoses; Lavamatic Doña Anna, C 13, Av 16; and Sixaola (one of a chain), Av 2, C 7/9.

Libraries and cultural centres The Alianza Francesa, C 5, Av 7 (Mon–Fri 9am–noon & 3–7pm; ☎222-2283), stocks some French publications; the Quaker-affiliated Friends' Peace Center, C 15, Av 6 bis (Mon–Fri 10am–3pm; ☎221-8299) has English-language newspapers, plus weekly meetings and discussion groups. Other libraries/cultural centres include the Biblioteca Nacional, C 15, Av 3 (Mon–Sat 9am–5pm) and the Centro Cultural Costarricense-Norteamericano, 100m north of the Am-Pm supermarket in Barrio Dent (Mon–Fri 7am–7pm, Sat 9am–noon).

Pharmacies Clinica Biblica, Av 14, C 0/1 (open 24hr); Farmacia del Este, on Av Central near Mas x Menos in San Pedro (open until 8pm); there are also many pharmacies in the blocks surrounding the Hospital Calderon Guardia, 100m northeast of the Biblioteca Nacional, in Barrio Otoya.

Post office The Correo Central (Mon–Fri 7am–5pm, Sat 7am–noon), C 2, Av 1/3, is two blocks east and one block north of the Mercado Central. They'll hold letters for up to four weeks (10 colones per letter; you'll need a passport in order to collect your post).

Sports The Sports Complex behind the Museo de Arte Costarricense on Parque La Sabana has a gym, running track and Olympic-size pool (US$3), though it's more often closed than open. Parque La Sabana has tennis courts, and is as good a place as any for jogging, with changing facilities and showers – there are lots of runners about in the morning, though there have been reports of assaults on lone joggers in the evening and it's wise to stay away from the heavily wooded northeastern corner of the park. Parque de la Paz in the south of the city is also recommended for running; in San Pedro you can jog at the UCR campus. The Club Deportivo Cipresses (☎253-0530), set in landscaped grounds 700m north of La Galera in Curridabat, offers day membership for US$7, which gives access to weights, machines, pools and aerobics classes. The nearest public pool to San José is at Ojo de Agua, 17km northwest of town; you can get a bus there from Av 2, C 20/22 (15min).

Supermarkets The cheapest is Mas x Menos (open daily until 9pm), which stocks mainly Costa Rican brands of just about everything. There are several branches in San José, including one on Av 0 between C 9 and 11, and one on Av 0, 300m north of the church in San Pedro. Branches of the Automercado and the Am-Pm supermarket are springing up all over the place. A more upmarket option is the Muñoz y Nanne complex (open daily until 9pm), on Av Central in San Pedro, where you can buy US brands at high prices.

Telephone offices Radiográfica, C 1, Av 5 (daily 7.30am–9pm; ☎287-0087), is the state-run office where you can use directories, make overseas calls, and send or receive faxes – unfortunately, it charges a flat fee of US$3 for the use of its phones on top of the price of the call.

Moving on from San José

San José is the **transport hub** of Costa Rica, and home to most bus companies, all express bus services, flights and car-rental agencies. Wherever you are in the country, technically you are never more than nine hours by road from the capital, with the majority of destinations being much closer than that. Eventually, like it or not, all roads lead to San José.

The tables on pp.584–585 deal with **express bus services** from San José. Regional bus information is covered in the relevant accounts in the Guide. As schedules are prone to change, exact departure times are not given here, though details are given where helpful in the accounts of the individual destinations; a full timetable is available free from the ICT office (see p.568).

BUS COMPANIES IN SAN JOSÉ

A bewildering number of **bus companies** use San José as their hub: the following is a rundown of their head office addresses and/or phone numbers, and the abbreviations that are used in the tables.

ALF	Transportes Alfaro, C 14, Av 3/5 (☎222-2750)
BA	Barquero (☎232-5660)
BL	Autotransportes Blanco, C 12, Av 9 (☎257-4121)
BM	Buses Metropoli (☎272-0651)
CA	CARSOL Transportes, C 14, Av 3/5 (☎224-1968)
CL	Coopelimón, Av 3, C 19/21 (☎223-7811)
CO	Coopecaribeños, Av 3, C 19/21 (☎223-7811)
CPT	Coopetraga, C 12, Av 7/9 (☎223-1276)
CQ	Autotransportes Ciudad Quesada, C 16, Av 1/3 (☎255-4318)
EM	Empresa Esquivel (☎666-1249)
ME	Transportes MEPE, Av 11, C 0/1 (☎221-0524)
MO	Transportes Morales, C 16, Av 1/3 (☎223-5567)
MRA	Microbuses Rapidos Heredianos, C1, Av 7/9 (☎223-8392)
MU	Transportes Musoc, C 16, Av 1/3 (☎222-2422)
PU	Pulmitan, C 14, Av 1/3 (☎222-1650)
S	SIRCA, C 7, Av 6/8 (☎222-5541 or 223-1464)
SA	SACSA, C 5, Av 18 (☎233-5350)
Tica	Ticabus, C 9, Av 4/6 (☎221-8954)
TIL	Autotransportes Tilarán, C 14, Av 9/11 (☎222-3854)
TRA	TRALAPA, C 20, Av 1/3 (☎221-7202)
TRC	TRACOPA, Av 18, C 2/4 (☎221-4214)
TRS	Transtusa, Av 6, C 13 (☎556-0073)
TU	Tuasa, C 12, Av 2 (☎222-5325)
Tuan	Tuan (☎494-2139)

INTERNATIONAL BUS SERVICES FROM SAN JOSÉ

Codes given under the "CO." column correspond to the relevant bus company (see box opposite). Advance purchase – at least a week in advance, particularly for Managua and Panamá City – is necessary for all routes.

TO	FREQUENCY	BUS STOP	DISTANCE	DURATION	CO.
David	1 daily	Av 3/5, C 14	400km	9hr	TRC
Guatemala City (overnight in Managua & El Salvador)	2 daily	C 9, Av 2/4	1200km	60hr	Tica
Managua	2 daily	C 9, Av 2/4	450km	11hr	Tica
Managua	Mon, Wed, Fri, Sun	Av 6, C 7/9	450km	13hr	S
Managua	1 daily	C22, Av 3/5	450km	11hr	Trasnica
Panamá City	2 daily	Av 4, C 9/11	903km	20hr	Tica
Paso Canoas (for Panamá)	7 daily	C 14, Av 5	349km	8hr	TRC
Peñas Blancas (for Nicaragua & Santa Rosa NP)	5 daily	C 16, Av 3/5	293km	6hr	CA
Sixaola (for Panamá)	2 daily	C 0, Av 9/11	250km	6hr	ME
Tegucigalpa (overnight in Managua)	2 daily	C 9, Av 2/4	909km	48hr	Tica

DOMESTIC FLIGHTS FROM SAN JOSÉ

Sansa, C 24, Paseo Colón/Av 1 (☎221-9414, reservations ☎257-9444, fax 255-2176, *www.gruptaca.com*)

TO	FREQUENCY	DURATION
Barra del Colorado	1 daily	30min
Fortuna	1 daily	30min
Golfito	2 daily	45min
Nosara	1 daily	1hr 25min
Palmar Sur	1 daily	1hr 30min
Puerto Jiménez	1 daily	1hr 15min
Quepos	4 daily	20min
Sámara	1 daily	1hr 45min
Tamarindo	3 daily	40min
Tambor	2 daily	20min
Tortuguero	1 daily	20min

Travelair, Tobías Bolaños airport, Pavas (☎220-3054 or 296-1102, fax 220-0413, *reservations@travelair-costarica.com*)

Golfito	1 daily	1hr 15min
Palmar Sur	1 daily	1hr 30min
Quepos	1 daily (low season)	20min
	3 daily (high season)	20min
Tamarindo	1 daily	40min
Tambor	1 daily	20min
Tortuguero	1 daily	30min

DOMESTIC BUS SERVICES FROM SAN JOSÉ

In the table below, the initials in the "CO." column correspond to the bus company that serves this route; see the box on p.582 for a list of companies and telephone numbers. Where advance purchase is mentioned, it is advised, and strongly recommended in the high season (HS) or at weekends (WE; i.e. from Friday to Sunday). You need buy your ticket no more than one day in advance unless otherwise indicated. NP = National Park; WR = Wildlife Refuge, NM = National Monument.

DESTINATION	FREQUENCY	BUS STOP	DISTANCE	DURATION	CO.	ADV. PURCHASE
Alajuela (and airport)	every 5min	Av 2, C 10/12	17km	35min	TU	no
Braulio Carrillo NP *see* Guápiles						
Cahuita	4 daily	C 0, Av 13	195km	4hr	ME	yes (HS)
Caño Negro WR *see* Los Chiles						
Cartago	every 10min	C 5, Av 18/20	22km	45min	SA	no
Chirripó NP *see* San Isidro						
Corcovado NP *see* Puerto Jiménez						
Fortuna	11 daily	C16, Av 1/3	130km	4hr 30min	BA	yes (HS)
Golfito	2 daily	C 14, Av 3/5	339km	8hr	TRC	yes (3 days)
Guápiles	every 45min	C 0, Av 13	30km	35min	CPT	no
Guayabo NM *see* Turrialba						
Heredia	every 10min	C 1, Av 7/9 & C 12, Av 2	11km	25min	MRA	no
La Selva/Selva Verde *see* Puerto Viejo de Sarapiquí						
Liberia	15 daily	C 24, Av 5	217km	4hr	PU	no
Limón	14 daily	C 0, Av13	162km	2hr 30min	CL/CO	no
Los Chiles	2 daily	C 12, Av 9/11	217km	5hr	CQ	no
Manuel Antonio NP *see* Quepos						

DESTINATION	FREQUENCY	BUS STOP	DISTANCE	DURATION	CO.	ADV. PURCHASE
Monteverde	2 daily	C 12, Av 7/9	167km	3hr 30min	TIL	yes (3–5 days)
Nicoya	6 daily	C 14, Av 3/5	296km	6hr	ALF	no
Nosara	1 daily	C 14, Av 3/5	361km	6hr	ALF	no
Playa Brasilito	2 daily	C 20, Av 3/5	320km	6hr	TRA	yes (WE)
Playa Coco	2 daily	C 14, Av 1/3	251km	5hr	PU	yes (WE)
Playa Flamingo	2 daily	C 20, Av 3/5	320km	6hr	TRA	yes (WE)
Playa Hermosa	1 daily	C 20, Av 1/3	265km	5hr	EM	no
Playa Jacó	3 daily	Av 3, C 18/20	102km	2hr 30min	MO	yes (WE)
Playa Junquillal	1 daily	C 20, Av 3/5	298km	5hr	TRA	no
Playa Panamá	1 daily	C 20, Av 1/3	265km	5hr	EM	no
Playa Potrero	2 daily	C 20, Av 3	320km	6hr	TRA	yes (WE)
Puerto Jiménez	1 daily	Av 9, C 14/16	378km	9hr	BL	yes
Puerto Viejo de Sarapiquí	8 daily	C 0, Av 13	97km	4hr	check with ICT	no
Puerto Viejo de Talamanca	4 daily	C 0, Av 13	210km	4hr 30min	ME	yes
Puntarenas	every 40min	C 16, Av 10/12	110km	2hr	PU	no
Quepos	3 daily	C 16, Av 1/3	145km	3hr 30min	MO	yes (3 days)
Sámara	1 daily	C 14, Av 3/5	331km	6hr	ALF	yes (WE)
San Carlos/Ciudad Quesada	14 daily	C 12, Av 7/9	110km	3hr	CQ	no
Sarchí	34 daily	C 8, Av 0/1	152km	1hr 30min	Tuan	no
Tamarindo	1 daily	C 14, Av 5	320km	6hr	TRA	yes (WE)
Turrialba	17 daily	C 13, Av 6/8	65km	1hr 30min	TRS	no
Volcán Arenal *see Fortuna*						
Volcán Irazú	1 Sat & Sun	Av 2, C 1/3	54km	1hr 30min	BM	no (but go early)
Volcán Poás	1 daily	Av 2, C12/14	55km	1hr 30min	TU	no (but go early)

Tours

The Costa Rican tourist boom of the last ten years has led to a proliferation of **tour operators**, and wandering around the city you face a barrage of tour agencies and advertisements: if you want to shop around it could take some time to sort yourself out. The following is not a comprehensive list of tour operators in San José, but all those that we've listed are experienced and recommendable, offering a good range of services and tours. They're all licensed (and regulated) by the ICT.

There are scores of others – be especially wary of fly-by-night operators, of which there are plenty. You often see, for instance, posters advertising cheap "packages" to Tortuguero or to Monteverde, both for about $80–100, less than half the price of a regular package. These cut-price tours are not packages at all, and never worth the price: in some cases you will be responsible for your own transport, accommodation will be the most basic, and no tours, orientation or guidance will be given – something you can easily arrange on your own, for the same price or less.

Camino Travel, C 1, Av 0/1 (☎257-0107, fax 257-0243, *caminotr@racsa.co.cr*). Young, enthusiastic staff with high standards and a mainly European clientele. Experienced in both upmarket and independent travel, selling individual tours and booking good-quality accommodation from their range of country-wide contacts. Can also help with bus and transport information and car rental. Convenient downtown office.

Costa Rica Expeditions, C Central, Av 3 (☎257-0766, fax 257-1665, *www.costaricaexpeditions.com*). Longest-established and most experienced of the major tour operators, with superior accommodation in Tortuguero, Monteverde and Corcovado, a superlative staff of guides and tremendous resources.

Costa Rican Trails, Av 15, C 23/25 (☎221-3011, fax 257-4655, *www.costaricantrails.com*). Small, friendly and very professional agency who will visit you in your hotel room to discuss their range of tailor-made and flexi-drive holidays in all price ranges. They're also experts in adventure sports, including rafting and motorbike tours.

Ecole Travel, C 7, Av 0/1 (☎223-2240, fax 223-4128, *www.travelcostarica.net*). Small agency, popular with backpackers, offering well-priced tours to Tortuguero and hiking trips to Chirripó (4 days) and the Osa Peninsula (3 days). They also run boats from Moín docks near Puerto Limón to Tortuguero.

Expediciones Tropicales, Av 11–13, C 3 Bis (☎257-4171, fax 257-4124, *www.costaricainfo.com*). Well-regarded agency with knowledgeable guides which runs the popular "Four-in-One" day-tour of Volcán Poás and nearby sights ($79; 11hr), as well as a host of other trips from San José at competitive prices.

Horizontes Nature Tours, C 28, Av 1/3 (☎222-2022, *www.horizontes.com*) Highly regarded agency concentrating on rainforest walking and hiking, volcanoes and bird-watching, all with an emphasis on natural and cultural history. Specialists in mountain biking and horse-riding too.

OTEC, C3, Av 1/3 (☎256-0633, fax 257-7671, *gotec@sol.racsa.co.cr*). Large agency specializing in adventure tours including fishing, trekking, surfing and mountain biking, plus hotel reservations and car rentals. One of the few tour operators to offer student discounts.

Serendipity Adventures, Turrialba (☎556-2592, fax 556-2593, *www.serendipityadventures.com*) Superior travel agency specializing in highly individual custom-made tours for self-formed groups with a sense of adventure. Serendipity make a point of searching out undiscovered parts of Costa Rica, are experts in canyoning and rappelling and the only company in Costa Rica to offer hot-air balloon trips. Tours are not cheap, starting at $2000 per person for eight days.

Simbiosis Tours, Aptdo 6939-1000 San José, (☎259-3605, fax 259-9430, *cooprena@sol.racsa.co.cr*). Runs packages to six co-operatives composed of low-income rural families sharing a common goal of exploring new and sustainable land uses. Projects managed by the co-ops include private reserves, nature trails, horse-riding trips and organic farms.

SpECOps (☎232-4028, *www.specops.com*). Adventure education group, comprising US Special Forces veterans and expert Costa Rican guides, specializing in white-knuckle thrills, jungle-survival courses and adventure film and photography.

CHAPTER 28

THE VALLE CENTRAL AND THE HIGHLANDS

osta Rica's **Valle Central** – literally "Central Valley", though it's actually an inter-mountain plateau poised at an elevation of between 3000 and 4000m – is a pre-dominantly agricultural region, with staggered green coffee terraces set amidst patchwork-quilt fields and loomed over by the blue-black summits of the sur-rounding mountains. Many of these are **volcanoes**, from smoking Poás in the north to precipitous Irazú in the east, and though there have been no real eruptions since Irazú blew its top in 1963, Poás and Irazú periodically spew light rains of fertile volcanic ash onto the surrounding farmland.

Although it occupies just six percent of the country's total landmass, the Valle Central supports roughly two-thirds of Costa Rica's population, containing the coun-try's most fertile land as well as its four most important cities – San José (covered in the previous chapter) and the provincial capitals of **Alajuela**, **Heredia** and **Cartago**. The chief attractions for visitors, of course, are the volcanoes, especially **Parque Nacional Irazú**, **Parque Nacional Poás** and **Volcán Barva**, and there's also good **whitewater rafting** on the Río Reventazón near Turrialba.

Most people use San José as a base for forays into the Valle Central; while the **provincial capitals** each have their own strong identity, with the exception of Alajuela they have little to entice you to linger. If you do want to get out of the city and stay in the Valle Central, the nicest places are the **lodges** and **inns** scattered throughout the countryside.

ALAJUELA AND AROUND

Alajuela province is vast, in Costa Rican terms at least, extending from **Alajuela** town, 20km northwest of San José, all the way north to the Nicaraguan border and west to the slopes of Volcán Arenal. The account below deals only with that part of the province on the south side of the Cordillera Central, spanning the area from Alajuela itself to the town of Zarcero, 59km to the northwest in the highlands. **Parque Nacional Volcán Poás** is the area's principal attraction, while the ride up to the crater gives good views over the whole densely populated and heavily cultivated province, passing flower-growing fincas, fruit farms and the occasional coffee field.

People also head out here to see the crafts factories at **Sarchí**, famous for its coloured wooden ox-carts; **Zoo-Ave**, the exceptional bird sanctuary and zoo just west of Alajuela on the way to La Garita; the **Butterfly Farm** at La Guácima; and the popu-lar **La Paz Waterfall Gardens**.

For an explanation of **accommodation price codes**, see p.556.

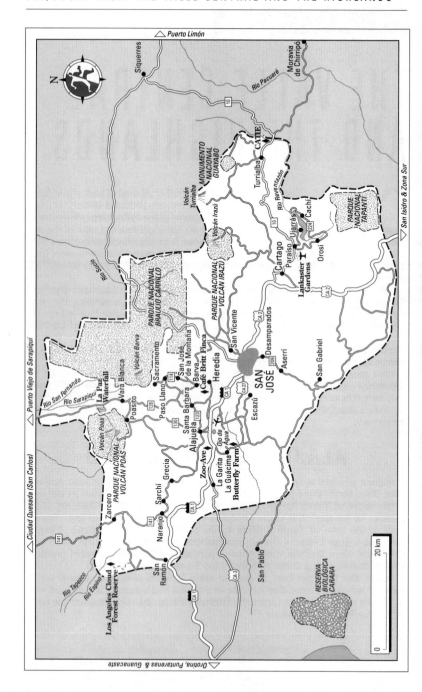

Alajuela

With a population of just 35,000, **ALAJUELA** is nonetheless Costa Rica's second city. Though it was founded back in 1657, at first sight there's little to distinguish it from San José, at least until the pleasant realization dawns that walking down the street you can smell bougainvillea rather than diesel. The city's few attractions, such as they are, are all less than a minute's walk from the Parque Central. Most impressive is the sturdy-looking whitewashed former jail that houses the **Juan Santamaría Cultural-Historical Museum**, Av 3, C 0/2 (Tues–Sun 10am–6pm; free), dedicated to Alajuela's most cherished historical figure, the drummer-boy-cum-martyr Juan Santamaría, who sacrificed his life to save the country from the American adventurer William Walker during the battle of 1856 (see p.473). The museum's curiously monastic atmosphere is almost more interesting than the small collection itself, which runs the gamut from mid-nineteenth-century maps of Costa Rica to crumbly portraits of figures involved in the battle of 1856.

Practicalities

Red-and-black Tuasa **buses from San José** arrive on C 8, four blocks west of the Parque Central, amongst an inhospitable confusion of bus stops, supermarkets and shoe stores. Alternatively, the beige-and-orange Station Wagon Alajuela bus from San José drops you off on Av 4, just west of Parque Juan Santamaría, two blocks south of the Parque Central. If you're **driving**, take the *pista* to the airport (General Cañas Highway) then the turn-off to Alajuela, 17km from San José – don't use the underpass or you'll end up at the airport. For getting around, **taxis** line up on the west side of the Parque Central

Alajuela is a quieter place to **stay** than San José, and just 3km from the **airport**, although there's not much choice, the hotels are of good standard. The small and cheerful *Mango Verde* hostel, Av 3, C 2/4 (☎ & fax 441-6330, *mangover@racsa.co.cr;* ③), is an excellent budget option, with simple en-suite rooms, a communal kitchen and an attractive blue-walled courtyard. The friendly *Hotel 1915*, C 2, Av 5/7 (☎441-0495; ⑤) is the town's best mid-range option: the comfortable and attractive rooms are arranged around an interior patio with rocking chairs and plants, and a delicious breakfast is included. *Charley's Albergue* on Av 5, 200m north and 25m east of the Parque Central (☎ & fax 441-0115, *www.isacam.com;* ⑥), has eleven large clean rooms with private bath and hot water, plus a TV lounge and kitchen. For details of accommodation around Alajuela, see overleaf.

When it comes to **eating**, *El Cencerro* on the south side of the Parque Central is the only restaurant in town with any pretensions, serving succulent beef dishes for US$10–15. For sticky cakes, an extensive selection of coffees and good-value lunchtime *casados*, head for *Ambrosia*, Av 5, C 2. *Lima de Antano*, Av 3, C 2, is a friendly family-run Peruvian café with excellent seafood, while *Bar La Troja*, a ten- to fifteen–minute walk south from the town centre along C 4, is the only vaguely lively place in town, with a rooftop bar, relaxed atmosphere and decent music.

Moving on, fast and frequent Tuasa **buses to San José** and **Heredia** leave from C 8 between Av 1 and Central (but note that some buses marked "Alajuela–San José" go via Heredia rather than direct to San José – check with the driver). All other buses depart from the loose collection of bus stops just south of Av 1 between C 8 and 10, including regular services for Sarchí and La Guácima Abajo (for the Butterfly Farm). It's a confusing area, and the departure points are not well marked, so ask around to make sure you're waiting at the right place.

Around Alajuela

Twelve kilometres southwest of Alajuela, **La Guácima Butterfly Farm** (daily 9.30am–5pm, last tour at 3pm; US$15; *www.butterflyfarm.co.cr*) breeds valuable pupae for export to zoos and botanical gardens all over the world. The farm also has beautiful views over the Valle Central, though in the wet season you should aim to get there early, as the rain forces the butterflies to hide themselves away, while the clouds obscure the view. On a sunny day, however, when the butterflies are active, it's a glorious sight. From Alajuela, **buses** (marked "La Guácima Abajo") leave from the area southwest of the main bus terminal; the Butterfly Farm is practically the last stop. Buses from San José (2hr) leave from Av 1, C 20/22 daily except Sunday at 11am and 2pm.

The largest aviary in Central America, **Zoo-Ave** (daily 9am–5pm; US$9), at Dulce Nombre, 5km northeast of La Garita, is just about the best place in the country to see the fabulous and many-coloured birds – especially macaws – which inhabit Costa Rica. The La Garita bus from Alajuela (15min) passes right by, leaving from the area southwest of the main terminal.

Accommodation around Alajuela

Around Alajuela, a few luxurious, country house-style **hotels** cater to a well-heeled clientele. *Orquideas Inn*, 5km outside Alajuela on the road to Poás (☎443-9346, fax 443-9740, *www.hotels.co.cr/orchideas.htm*; ⑥, no children) is a Spanish hacienda-style country inn with enormous rooms, landscaped gardens with pool, and attentive service. The luxurious *Xandari Plantation Inn*, 6.5km north of Alajuela (☎443-2020, in the US ☎805/684-7879, fax 442-4847, *www.xandari.com*; ⑨) is set in an old plantation house just north of town, with a swimming pool and walking trails on the premises; low-season rates are good value, and airport pick-up is included. The *Siempreverde Lodge*, 8km north of Alajuela (☎449-5134, fax 449-5003; ⑥), is a spotless new B&B with brightly coloured rooms and immaculate gardens.

Parque Nacional Volcán Poás

PARQUE NACIONAL VOLCÁN POÁS (daily 8am–3.45pm; US$6), just 55km from San José and 37km north of Alajuela, is one of the most easily accessible active volcanoes in the world, with a history of eruptions that goes back 11 million years. Poás's last gigantic blowout was on January 25, 1910, when it dumped 640,000 tonnes of ash on the surrounding area. At the moment it is comparatively quiet.

You need to get to the volcano before the clouds roll in, which they inevitably do, as early as 10am, even in the dry season (Dec–April). Poás has blasted out three craters in its lifetime, and due to more or less constant activity, the appearance of the **main crater** is subject to change – it's currently 1500m wide and filled with milky turquoise water from which sulphurous gases waft and broil. Although it's an impressive sight, you only need about fifteen minutes' viewing and picture-snapping.

The park features a few very well-maintained, short and unchallenging **trails**, which take you through a strange, otherworldly landscape, dotted with smoking fumaroles (steam vents) and tough ferns and trees valiantly holding up against regular sulphurous scaldings. Poás is also home to a rare version of cloudforest called **dwarf** or **stunted cloudforest**, a combination of pine-needle-like ferns, miniature bonsai-type trees, and bromeliad-encrusted cover, all of which has been stunted through an onslaught of cold (temperatures up here can drop to below freezing), continual cloud cover, and acid rain from the mouth of the volcano.

The **Crater Overlook trail**, which winds its way around the main crater, is only 750m long, along a paved road. A side trail (1km; 20–30min) heads off through the forest to the pretty, emerald Botos Lake, which fills an extinct crater and makes a good spot for a picnic. Named for the pagoda-like tree commonly seen along its way, the **Escalonia trail** (about 1km; 30min) starts at the picnic area (follow the signs), taking you through ground cover less stunted than that at the crater. Birds ply this temperate forest, among them the ostentatiously colourful quetzal, the robin, and several species of hummingbird. Although a number of large mammals live in the park, including coyotes and wildcats such as the margay, you're unlikely to spot them. One you probably will come across, however, is the small, green-yellow **Poás squirrel**, which is found nowhere else in the world.

Getting to Volcán Poás

Most visitors get to the volcano on a pre-arranged **tour** from San José (approximately US$35 per person for a 4–5 hour trip, including return transport and guide – see p.586 for details of tour operators). All kinds of combination packages with other Valle Central sites exist: the "Four-in-One" tour organized by Expediciones Tropicales (☎257-4171, *www.costaricainfo.com*) is reasonably priced and very popular, and also takes in the La Paz Waterfall Gardens, the Braulio Carrillo National Park and a boat ride on the Sarapiquí river (US$79 per person including breakfast, lunch and guide; 11hr). Alternatively, a Tuasa bus leaves daily at 8.30am from C 12/14, Av 2 in San José, travelling via Alajuela and returning from the volcano at 2.30pm (US$3 each way; 2hr). If you want to reach Poás before both tour buses and dense cloud cover arrive, you'll need either to drive or take a **taxi** from Alajuela (roughly US$30) or San José (US$45–50) – reasonably affordable if split between a group of people.

The park's **visitor centre** shows videos of the volcano and has a snack shop, which also serves hot coffee, though you're probably better off packing a picnic lunch. Make sure you bring a sweater and wet-weather gear with you in the rainy season. No **camping** is allowed in the park.

Accommodation near the park

If you want to get a really early start to guarantee a view of Poás' crater, there are plenty of places to stay in the vicinity, including a couple of comfortable **mountain lodges** on working dairy farms (though you'll need a car to get to them), and other, more simple and inexpensive places which can be reached on the daily bus to Poás. If you want **to camp**, the *Mountain View Campground* (☎482-2196; US$5 per tent per night), just before the *Chubascos* restaurant on the main road to Poás, has a pleasant garden site with hot showers.

La Providencia Ecological Reserve, 1km from the park entrance on the slopes of Poás (☎380-6315). Charming rustic *cabinas* on a working dairy farm, near the top of Poás, with spectacular views. The owners prepare excellent local food, rent out horses for trots up the volcano (US$20 for 3 hours) and organize trout-fishing trips. ⑤

Lo Que tu Quieras, 5km before the park entrance (☎482-2092). The least expensive option in the area, comprising three small *cabinas* with heated water and fireplaces, and a restaurant serving local dishes with huge picture windows and staggering views – stop for a drink on your way back from the volcano. Camping is permitted for a nominal fee. ③

Poás Volcano Lodge, 6km from the small village of Poásito – which is 10km before the entrance to Poás on the main mountain road from Alajuela and San José – take a right fork towards Varablanca (☎482-2194, fax 482-2513, *www.arweb.com/poas*). A working dairy farm, with patches of forest in the grounds and nine beautifully furnished rooms. Facilities include a basement games room and mountain bikes for hire. Meals (US$8–12) by arrangement. ⑥

La Paz Waterfall Gardens

A fifteen-kilometre drive east of Poás is one of Costa Rica's newest and most popular attractions, the **La Paz Waterfall Gardens** (daily 8.30am–4pm; US$24; *www .waterfallgardens.com*), an immaculate series of riverside trails linking five waterfalls on the Río La Paz, all set in a large colourful garden planted with native shrubs and flowers – there's also a large butterfly observatory and a hummingbird garden which is home to sixteen different species. From the reception centre, visitors take one of several self-guided tours which wind prettily through the site and along the river, where viewing platforms mean that at various points you're both above and underneath the waterfalls, the highest of which, **Magia Blanca**, crashes deafeningly down some 40m into swirling white water. The marked trails conclude at the top of the **La Paz Waterfall**, Costa Rica's most photographed cascade (it can also be seen from the public highway which runs over a large rickety bridge below).

There's currently no public transport to the gardens, and most people visit them as part of an organized tour from San José – Expediciones Tropicales (☎257-4171, fax 257-4124, *www.costaricainfo.com*) include La Paz as part of their "Four-in-One" highlights tour (US$79). If you're driving, take a right at the junction in Poasito towards Vara Blanca and, on reaching the village, take a left at the gas station and follow the well-marked signs for 5km.

Sarchí

Touted as the centre of Costa Rican arts and crafts, especially **furniture making**, the village of **SARCHÍ**, 30km northwest of Alajuela, is a commercialized place – firmly on the tourist trail but without much charm. Its setting is pretty enough, between precipitous verdant hills, but don't come expecting to see picturesque scenes of craftsmen sitting in small historic shops: the work is done in factories. The **Sarchí ox-cart** is a kaleidoscopically coloured, painted square cart meant to be hauled by a single ox or team of two oxen. Moorish in origin, the designs can be traced back to immigrants from the Spanish provinces of Andalucía and Granada. Though full-scale carts (US$1000) are, understandably, only rarely sold, smaller-scale versions (US$60–200) specially made for tourists are popular, as are Sarchí tables, bedsteads and leather rocking chairs (about US$70). Apart from the shops and factories, the only thing of interest is a bubblegum-coloured pink-and-turquoise **church** which looks out from atop the hill in Sarchí Norte (see below).

Practicalities

Sarchí is a spread-out place, divided into two halves. Large *fábricas* line the main road from **Sarchí Sur**, in effect a conglomeration of *mueblerías,* to the residential area of **Sarchí Norte**, which climbs the hill. There's just one small **hotel**, the *Hotel Daniel Zamora* (☎454-4596; ③), on a sidestreet opposite the soccer field in Sarchí Norte, which has clean rooms and hot water. For **lunch** or a snack, try *Soda Donald* beside the soccer field, which serves decent *refrescos* and ice cream, or *La Finca* restaurant, to the right of the Mercado de Artesanía souvenir shop as you drive north out of town, which serves very good maize soup and grilled steak.

Local **buses** from Alajuela run approximately every thirty minutes from 5am to 10pm. Buses back (via Grecia) can be hailed on the main road. From **San José** an express service (1hr–1hr 30min) runs from La Coca-Cola daily every thirty minutes from 5am to 10pm; the return schedule is the same. You could also take the bus to Naranjo from La Coca-Cola, every hour on the hour, and switch there for a local service to Sarchí – call the Tuan bus company for information.

The Banco Nacional on the main road beyond the church **changes dollars and cheques**, as does a smaller branch in the Mercado de Artesanía. If you need a **taxi** to ferry you back and forth between Sarchí Sur and Sarchí Norte, or to Alajeula or Zarcero, they can be called on ☎454-4028 or hailed on the street.

HEREDIA AND AROUND

Heredia province stretches northeast from San José all the way to the Nicaraguan border, skirted on the west by Hwy-9, the old road from San José to Puerto Viejo de Sarapiquí. To the east, the Guápiles Highway, Hwy-32, provides access to Braulio Carrillo and to Limón on the Atlantic coast. The moment you leave San José for **Heredia**, the provincial capital, the rubbery leaves of coffee plants spring up on all sides – the section of the province covered in this chapter is almost wholly given over to coffee production, and there are a number of popular "coffee tours", especially to the **Café Britt Finca** near Heredia town.

In the Valle Central, the province's chief attractions are dormant **Volcán Barva**, which offers a good day's climb, and the nearby **Rainforest Aerial Tram**, which allows you to see the canopy of primary rainforest from above, causing minimal disturbance to the animals and birds.

Heredia

Just 11km northeast of San José is the lively town of **HEREDIA**, boosted by the student population of the Universidad Nacional (UNA) at the eastern end of town. The town centre is prettier than most, with a few historical buildings, though a bit run-down. It's a natural jumping-off point for excursions to the nearby historical hamlet of **Barva** and to the town of San José de la Montaña, gateway to **Volcán Barva**. Many tourists also come for the **Café Britt Finca** tour, hosted by the nation's largest coffee exporter, about 3km north of the town centre.

Arrival and information

Tuasa **buses** leave San José for Heredia from C 1, Av 7/9 every 15–30 minutes and pull into Heredia at the corner of C Central and Av 4, a stone's throw south of the Parque Central. At night, **minibuses** leave San José hourly between midnight and 6am from Av 2, C 12/14. There's no tourist office in town. Banco Nacional at C 2, Av 2/4 and Scotiabank at Av 4, C 0/C 2 both have ATMs and change money and **travellers' cheques**. The **correo** (Mon–Fri 7.30am–5.30pm) is on the northwest corner of the Parque Central, while **taxis** line up on the east side of the Mercado Central, between Av 6 and 8, and on the southern side of the Parque Central.

Moving on from Heredia, **buses to San José** depart from C 0, Av 4 (about every 15min during the day). The town has no central bus terminal, but a variety of well-signed stops are scattered accross town, mainly around the Mercado Central, from where most local buses leave.

Accommodation

Decent **accommodation** in downtown Heredia is pretty sparse, though it's unlikely you'll need to stay in town, since San José is within easy reach and there are also several resort-type hotels in the country nearby, including one of the finest in Costa Rica. Although all are accessible by bus, you'll find it handy to have a car once you're there.

HEREDIA

Hotel America, C Central, opposite the San José bus stop (☎260-9292, fax 260-9293, *www .hotelamerica.net*). Clean if soulless rooms, some of them rather dark, though all have bathroom, fan, TV and hot water. ⑤

Hotel CEO, Av 1 (☎262-2628, fax 262-2639, *www.hotelamerica.net*). Quiet hotel with spotless but no-frills rooms with private bathrooms and hot water. ③

Hotel Verano, Av 6, C 4, at the western entrance to the Mercado Central (☎237-1616). Friendly budget option, though the beds and walls are very flimsy. ②

AROUND HEREDIA

Chalet Tirol, north of Heredia, well signposted on the road to Los Angeles via San Rafael (☎267-6222, fax 267-6228, *www.chalet-tirol.com*). Incredibly kitsch hotel in lovely pine forest on the edge of the Braulio Carrillo National Park, with ten alpine chalets in a grassy clearing plus a reproduction Tyrol village church and a square complete with fountain. There's also a renowned gourmet French restaurant, and guided walking tours are available. ⑦

Finca Rosa Blanca, on the road between San Pedro de Barva and Santa Barbara de Heredia (☎269-9392, fax 269-9555, *www.finca-rblanca.co.cr*). One of the best hotels in the country, like some giant white bird roosting above the coffee fields, with six themed suites and two villas, plus a gorgeous tiled pool which seemingly drips over the hillside. An excellent four-course dinner is served family-style round the large table in the fairy-tale hotel foyer. ⑨

The Town

Heredia's layout conforms to the usual grid system, centred on the quiet **Parque Central**, draped with huge mango trees and overlooked by the plain **Basílica de la Inmaculada Concepción**, whose unexcitingly squat design – "seismic Baroque" – has kept it standing through several earthquakes since 1797. North of the Parque, the old colonial tower of **El Fortín**, "The Fortress", features odd gun slats which fan out and widen from the inside to the exterior, giving it a medieval look: you cannot enter or climb it.

East of the tower on Avenida Central, the **Casa de la Cultura**, an old colonial house with a large breezy veranda, displays local art, including sculpture and painting by the schoolchildren of Heredia. The **Mercado Central**, Av 6/8, C 2/4 (daily 5am–6pm), is a clean, orderly place, its wide aisles lined with rows of fruit and veg, dangling sausages and plump prawns.

Eating and drinking

Perhaps because of its student population, Heredia is crawling with excellent cafés, patisseries, ice-cream joints and the best vegetarian and health-food **restaurants** outside San José. **Nightlife** is low-key, restricted to a few local salsa spots. If you're young or studently inclined, head for the four blocks immediately to the west of the university, which is where you'll find the best **bars** in Heredia.

Azzura Italiana, southwest corner of the Parque Central. Upmarket café with superior Italian ice cream, excellent *refrescos*, fresh sandwiches and real cappuccino and espresso.

El Bulevar, Av 4, C 5/7. Currently the in place for Heredia's student population, this lively bar is open to the street and does inexpensive beer-and-*boca* specials.

Le Petit Paris, C 5, Av 2/4 (☎262-2564). This French-owned oasis of calm has tables set out in a small garden and serves delicious French cuisine. The lunch menu changes daily, and there's live jazz on Wednesdays. Expect to pay around US$10–15 for a full meal. Closed Sun.

The Second Cup, foyer of the *Hotel America*, C 0, Av 2/4. Posh café with cappuccino, iced coffee and breakfast, as well as a good-value lunchtime menu (US$3). The tables outside on the main street are great spots for people-watching.

Around Heredia

North and east of Heredia the terrain climbs to higher altitudes, reaching its highest point at **Volcán Barva**, at the western entrance of the wild, rugged **Parque Nacional Braulio Carrillo**. Temperatures are notably cooler around here, and the landscape is dotted with dairy farms and conifers. The towns here – **Barva**, **Santa Barbara de Heredia** and **San Joaquín de Heredia** – are the favoured residences of expats, but there's little to detain the visitor.

Rainforest Aerial Tram

The invention of American naturalist Donald Perry, the **Rainforest Aerial Tram** lies just beyond the eastern boundary of Braulio Carrillo (5km east of Río Sucio; Mon 9am–4pm, Tues–Sun 6am–4pm; US$50 per person). The product of many years' research, most of it carried out at nearby Rara Avis in the Zona Norte (see p.676), the tram is the first of its kind in the world. Twenty **overhead cable cars**, each holding five passengers and one guide, run slowly along the 1.7km aerial track, skirting the tops of the forest and passing between trees, providing eye-level encounters along the way. The ride affords a rare glimpse of birds, animals and plants – including the epiphytes, orchids, insects and mosses that live inside the upper reaches of the forest – and, largely silent, it is less likely to frighten the animals. Don't come expecting to see particular animals, however, or you may be disappointed. Surrounding the tram track is a 3.5 square-kilometre **private reserve** used by researchers to study life in the rainforest canopy.

Practicalities

Less than an hour from San José, the aerial tram turn-off is on the northeast border of the Parque Nacional Braulio Carrillo, 5.3km beyond the (signed) bridge over the Río Sucio, on the right-hand side; from the turn-off it's another 1.5km. To get there **by bus**, catch the Guápiles service and ask the driver to drop you at the entrance. The return Guápiles–San José bus will stop when flagged down, unless full. Wear a hat, insect repellent, and bring binoculars, camera and rain gear.

Alternatively, and much more conveniently, you can organize a **tour** (US$65 per person) with the tram's San José office on C 7, Av 7 (☎257-5961, fax 257-6053, *www .rainforesttram.com*), which includes transport to and from your hotel, a guided aerial excursion and hiking on nature trails. Similar trips are offered (at a slightly higher price) by most San José travel agencies. There are also special early-morning birdwatching trips and torchlit night rides (until 9pm) – many canopy inhabitants only become active and visible in the dark – plus tours combining the tram with other regional attractions such as La Guácima Butterfly Farm or the Café Britt Finca.

North of Heredia to Volcán Barva

Set in a large verandaed house in landscaped coffee fields two kilometres north of Heredia, the **Museo de la Cultura Popular** (daily 8.30am–5pm; US$1.50) tries to give an authentic portrayal of nineteenth- and early twentieth-century campesino life. The kitchen has been preserved as it would have been on a coffee finca, and you can sample authentic food of the period, including *torta de arroz, pan casero*, and *gallos picadillos*, although apart from this there's little to do other than to wander around the house and the carefully kept gardens.

The colonial village of **BARVA**, about 1km further on, is really only worth a brief stop on the way to Volcán Barva to have a look at the huge cream **Baroque church**, flanked by tall brooding palms, and the surrounding adobe-and-tiled-roof houses – though Barva was founded in 1561, most of what you see today dates from the 1700s. The village also boasts an excellent Mexican restaurant, *El Charro de Fofo,* which serves all the usual Mexican staples like tortillas and refried beans in a cheerful corner spot 300m south of the village's main square on the road to Heredia. **Buses** to San José de la Montaña (for the volcano) stop opposite the soccer field.

On the way north from Heredia to Barva, look out for the signs to the **Café Britt Finca**, 1km south of Barva (daily tours at 9am & 11am, and at 3pm mid-Dec to April; US$15; *www.cafebritt.com*), the country's most important coffee exporter, and producer of one of its best-known brands. Costumed guides take you through the history of coffee growing in Costa Rica, showing how crucial the crop was to the country's development, with a rather slick multimedia presentation and a thorough description of the process involved in harvesting the beans. It all ends on a free tasting and, of course, the inevitable stop in the gift shop; they can pack and mail coffee to the US. The finca is signed from the road between Heredia and Barva and offers a pick-up from most San José hotels (US$25 including tour).

Parque Nacional Braulio Carrillo and Volcán Barva

The **PARQUE NACIONAL BRAULIO CARRILLO** (8am–3.45pm; US$6), 20km northeast of San José, covers 325 square kilometres acres of virgin rain- and cloudforest, though it's still little visited on account of its sheer size and lack of facilities, and most tourists experience the majestic views of cloud and foliage only from the window of a bus on their way to the Caribbean coast. Named after Costa Rica's third, rather dictatorial, chief of state, who held office in the mid-1800s, the park was established in 1978, mainly to protect the area from the possible effects of the Guápiles Highway that was then in construction between San José and Limón. Even when only seen from the highway, Braulio Carrillo's dense forested cover gives you a good idea of what much of Costa Rica used to look like about fifty years ago, when approximately three-quarters of the country's total terrain was virgin rainforest.

The park has two staffed ranger stations (*puestos*), one at Volcán Barva (see below) and the other at Quebrada Gonzalez, 2km east of the Sucio river bridge on the Guápiles Highway. There are picnic facilities and a well-marked trail leading from the *puesto* at Quebrada Gonzalez into the forest, but camping is not permited and there's no accommodation within this section of the park, though you can stay in very basic huts at the Volcán Barva *puesto*.

Slightly more accessible is the dormant **Volcán Barva** (daily 8am–3.45pm; US$6), a popular destination for walkers and climbers, though it's difficult to reach due to the lack of public transport and a bad stretch of road just before you reach the volcano – you'll need a 4WD, even in the dry season. The **main trail** (3km; about 1hr) up Barva's slopes begins at the park's *puesto*, 7km from the village of **Paso Llano** at the western edge of Braulio Carrillo, ascending through dense deciduous cover before reaching the cloudforest at the top. Along the way you'll get panoramic views over the Valle Central and southeast to Volcán Irazú; if you're lucky – bring binoculars – you might see the elusive, jewel-coloured quetzal (though these nest-bound birds are usually only seen at their preferred altitude of 3600m or more). It's easy to get lost on Barva. Take a compass, water and food, a sweater and raingear, leave early in the morning to enjoy the clearest views at the top, and be prepared for serious mud in the rainy season.

Practicalities

Buses from Heredia to Paso Llano leave daily at 6.30am, noon and 4pm. Buses back from Paso Llano to Heredia leave at 7.30am, 1pm and (most conveniently, but on weekends only) 5pm. Otherwise you'll have to get a taxi – ask in either of the restaurants mentioned opposite or try ringing local driver Lizandro Cascante (☎224-2400). From Paso Llano it's a four-kilometre walk (there's no bus) to the hamlet of Sacramento, followed by another 3km up a steep track to the Barva *puesto*,

If you want **to stay** near the volcano, there are basic **huts** (US$2 per night) and **camping** facilities (reserve in advance on ☎283-5906) at the Barva *puesto*. There are also a couple of surprisingly good places to stay in the hamlet of Guacalillo, 8km south of the volcano. *Hotel de Montaña El Portico* (☎237-6022, fax 260-6002) has enormous, simply furnished rooms with private bath (⑥) and attractive self-catering cabins (US$70 per night for up to 5 people), while the adjacent *Hotel Las Ardillas* (☎260-2172, *ardillas@racsa.co.cr*, ⑥) has very pretty *cabinas* with wall hangings and fireplaces, and a wonderfully cosy restaurant. There's also a tiled spa with mud treatments, massage and hypnotherapy (US$20–50/hr).

If you want to stock up on energy before climbing, several **restaurants** in the area serve típico food, including the *Campesino*, about 3.5km beyond Paso Llano en route to Volcán Barva, and the *Sacramento*, another 500m further on. *Soda El Bosque* in Sacramento, a picturesque little café stuffed full of junk-shop objects collected by its owner, serves up traditional *gallos* with various toppings, as well as breakfast and *casados*.

CARTAGO AND AROUND

Cartago province extends east of San José and south into the Cordillera de Talamanca, a region made fertile by deposits from Volcán Irazú. The section covered in this chapter is a heavily populated, farmed and industrialized region, centred on **Cartago** town, a major shopping and transportation hub for the southern Valle Central. The town itself is seldom used as a place to stay, however, and many of the area's attractions are usually visited on day-trips from San José.

It takes about forty minutes to reach Cartago on the good (toll) highway from San José. From Cartago there are road connections to Turrialba, on the eastern slopes of Irazú, and the Orosí valley, and south via the Interamericana over the hump of the Cordillera Central to San Isidro and the Valle de el General.

Cartago

CARTAGO, meaning "Carthage", was Costa Rica's capital for three hundred years before the centre of power was moved to San José in 1823. Founded in 1563 by Juan Vazquez de Coronado, like its ancient namesake the city has been razed a number of times, although in this case by **earthquakes** rather than Romans – two, in 1823 and 1910, conspired practically to demolish the place. Most of the fine nineteenth-century and fin-de-siècle buildings were destroyed, and what has grown up in their place – the usual assortment of shops and haphazard modern buildings – isn't particularly appealing. The highlight of the town is the pretty **Parque Central**, centred on the ruins of the **Iglesia de la Parroquía** (known as "Las Ruinas") – originally built in 1575, it was repeatedly destroyed by earthquakes but stubbornly rebuilt by the Cartagoans each time, until the giant earthquake of 1910 finally vanquished it for good. Only the elegantly tumbling walls remain, enclosing pretty subtropical gardens. From the ruins it's a walk of five minutes east to Cartago's only other attraction: the cathedral, properly called the **Basílica de Nuestra Señora de Los Angeles**, at C 16 and Av 2. rebuilt in a decorative Byzantine style after the original had been destroyed in an earthquake of 1926.

Practicalities

SACSA run frequent local **buses** to Cartago from their San José terminal on C 5, Av 18/20 (after 8.30pm, buses leave from in front of the *Grand Hotel Costa Rica*), running along Av 2 to C 19, then along Av Central and out through San Pedro – a journey of around 45 minutes. In Cartago, buses sometimes do a bit of a tour of town, stopping at virtually every block; wait to get off at the Parque Central. Like the other provincial capitals in the Valle Central, Cartago has no tourist office. The Banco de Costa Rica, Av 4, C 5/7, and Banco Nacional, C 1, Av 2, will change **travellers' cheques**, but it'll take a while. The **correo** (Mon–Fri 7.30am–6pm, Sat 7.30–12pm) is ten minutes from the town centre at Av 2, C 15/17. **Taxis** leave from the rank at Las Ruinas.

There's just one decent **hotel** in Cartago, the *Los Angeles Lodge* (☎551-0957; ④), on the square by the cathedral. Other accommodation in the town is frequented by commercial travellers and best avoided – in any case, getting stuck overnight in Cartago is an unlikely scenario, as there's a 24-hour bus service to San José. Of the town's few **restaurants**, the carvernous *La Puerta del Sol*, handily located by the cathedral, has a decent, reasonably priced menu and attentive staff. To get back to **San José**, hop on whichever bus happens to be loading up in the covered area on Av 4, C 2/4. Buses leave every ten minutes between 5am and midnight, and about every hour otherwise.

Around Cartago

Dominating the landscape around Cartago, mighty **Volcán Irazú** is the area's most popular excursion. On the eastern slopes of the Cordillera Central, the small town of **Turrialba** is something of a local hub for watersports, with Ríos Reventazón and Pacuaré, two of the best whitewater rafting rivers in the country, nearby. Turrialba has also become a small centre for river kayaking – whitewater kayaking, in effect – with one or two specialist tour operators. The town is also the gateway to the **Monumento Nacional Guayabo**, the most important archeological site in Costa Rica.

Parque Nacional Volcán Irazú

The blasted-out lunar landscape of **PARQUE NACIONAL VOLCÁN IRAZÚ** (daily 8am–3.45pm; US$6) is dramatic, reaching a highest point of 3432m and giving fantastic views on clear days to the Atlantic coast. The inactive **Diego de la Haya crater** is a creepily impressive sight, its deep depression filled with a strange algae-green lake. Some 32km north of Cartago, the volcano makes for a long but scenic trip, especially early in the morning before the inevitable clouds roll in. Disappointingly, there is little actually to do in the park after you've seen the crater from the mirador and there are no official trails, though it's possible to clamber along the scraggly slopes of a few outcroppings and dip into grey-ash sand dunes.

Practicalities

A visit to Irazú is strictly for day-trippers, since there's nowhere to stay in the park and camping is not allowed. Only one public **bus** runs to the park, leaving from San José's *Gran Hotel Costa Rica* at 8am on weekends and public holidays only – be there early in high season to make sure you get a seat. The bus stops to pick up passengers at Cartago (from Las Ruinas) at 8.30am. The return fare is about US$4.50 (US$2.25 from Cartago), which doesn't include the park entrance fee.

The bus pulls in at the crater parking area, where there are toilets, information and a **reception centre** containing a snack bar serving *tamales*, cakes and hot drinks, and a small gift shop which rents out waterproof ponchos (US$2) – it can get cold at the summit, so bring a sweater. The bus returns to San José at about 12.30pm. You can also get to Irazú on any number of half-day **tours** run by travel agencies in San José, which whisk you back and forth in a modern minibus for around US$35, not including the entrance fee.

Lankaster Gardens

Orchids are the main attraction at **Lankaster Gardens** (daily 8.30am–3.30pm; US$4), a tropical garden and research station 6km southeast of Cartago. While there are always some in bloom at any given time, the wet season (May–Nov) is less rewarding than the dry; March and April are the best months. To get to the gardens by **bus from San José**, take the Cartago service, get off at Las Ruinas, and change to a Paraíso bus. Get off when you see the *Casa Vieja* restaurant, about ten minutes out of town, and take the road off to your right, signposted to the gardens, then turn right again at the fork – a total walk of about 1km.

Turrialba and around

The pleasant agricultural town of **TURRIALBA**, 45km east of Cartago on the eastern slopes of the Cordillera Central, has sweeping views over the rugged eastern Talamancas, though there's little to keep you here long. Tourists are most likely to see it as part of a trip to the **Monumento Nacional Guayabo** or en route to a **whitewater rafting** or **kayaking** trip on the Ríos Reventazón or Pacuaré. Many of the mountain lodge-type hotels nearby have guided walks or horseback rides up dormant **Volcán Turrialba**, though the lack of trails means that the volcano is otherwise inaccessible to independent visitors.

Monumento Nacional Guayabo

The most important archeological site in Costa Rica, the **MONUMENTO NACIONAL GUAYABO** (daily 8am–3.45pm; US$6) lies 19km northeast of Turrialba and 84km from San José – it was discovered by explorer Anastasio Alfaro at the end of the nineteenth century, but not excavated until the late 1960s. Guayabo belongs to the archeological-cultural area known as **Intermedio**, which begins roughly in the province of Alajuela and extends to Venezuela, Colombia and parts of Ecuador. Archeologists believe that Guayabo was inhabited from about 1000 BC to 1400 AD; most of the heaps of stones and basic structures now exposed were erected between 300 and 700 AD. The central mound is the tallest circular base unearthed so far, with two staircases and pottery remains on the very top.

There are daily **buses** to Guayabo from Turrialba (Mon–Sat at 11am & 5.15pm, returning at 12.30 & 5.30; Sun at 9am, returning at 4pm), though the inconvenient timetable means you either have not enough or too much time at the site. Alternatively, you could walk back to the main road, a four-kilometre downhill hike, and then intercept the bus that goes from the hamlet of Santa Teresita to Turrialba. It currently passes by at about 1.30pm, but you should double-check the times with the *guardaparques* or you might be left standing at the crossroads for 24 hours. **Driving** from Turrialba takes about thirty minutes. The last 4km is on a bad gravel road – passable with a regular car, but watch your clearance. **Taxis** charge US$13 from Turrialba.

Accommodation

Turrialba isn't really a tourist town, but has some perfectly decent places to stay, from simple hotel rooms in town to picturesque mountain lodges in the surrounding countryside.

Albergue de Montaña Pochotel, 8km from Turrialba towards Limón (☎384-7292, fax 556-7615, *www.homestead.com/casalasorquideas*). Simple accommodation and traditional mountain fare in a stunning position with volcano views in all directions. Camping also allowed. ④

Interamericano, southeast corner of Turrialba, near the old train station (☎556-0142, fax 556-7790, *www.hotelinteramericana.com*). Basic, clean and very friendly, this is the best budget deal in town and an excellent place to meet other travellers. There's also a kitchen for guests' use, and the proprietor organizes kayaking and other tours. ③

Turrialtico Lodge, 7.5km from Turrialba on the road to Limón (☎ & fax 556-1111, *turrialt@racsa.co.cr*). A cosy lodge with 14 wood-panelled rooms, all with private bath and hot water; some have balconies overlooking the gorgeous surrounding countryside. The restaurant is renowned for its barbecued meat and other local specialities. Tours to Irazú and the Río Reventazón are available. ⑤

Volcán Turrialba Lodge (☎273-4335, fax 273-0703, *www.volcanturrialbalodge.com*). Quiet, modern and simply furnished farmhouse on the flanks of Volcán Turrialba, whose 14 rooms all have woodburning stoves and private bath; diversions include ox-cart rides and horseback tours to Turrialba crater. You can arrange for a pick-up from San José; otherwise you'll need a 4WD to get here over the badly rutted access road (call for directions). ⑥

Wagelia, Av 4, Turrialba, just beyond the gas station on the road from Cartago (☎556-1566, fax 556-1596). Small, clean and comfortable rooms with TV, fridge and phone, though it's popular and often full – ring in advance to reserve a room. ⑦

travel details

BUSES

Alajuela to: La Guácima Abajo (4 daily; 20min); San José (every 15min; 20min); Sarchí (hourly; 1hr); Volcán Poás (1 daily; 2hr); Zoo-Ave (every 30min; 15min).

Cartago to: Paraíso (every 30min Mon–Fri, hourly Sat & Sun; 30min); San José (every 20min; 40min).

Heredia to: Paso Llano (3 daily; 1hr); San José (every 15min; 15min).

San José to: Alajuela (every 15min; 20min); Braulio Carrillo (every 30min; 35min); Cartago (every 20min; 40min); La Guacima Abajo (Mon–Sat 2 daily; 40min); Heredia (every 15min; 15min); Sarchí (17 daily; 1hr 30min); Turrialba (16 daily; 1hr 30min); Volcán Irazú (1 Sat & Sun; 1hr 30min); Volcán Poás (1 daily; 2hr).

Sarchí to: Alajuela (hourly; 1hr); San José (17 daily; 1hr 30min).

Turrialba to: Guayabo (2 daily Mon–Fri; 1hr+); San José (16 daily; 1hr 30min).

CHAPTER 29

LIMÓN PROVINCE AND THE CARIBBEAN COAST

S parsely populated **Limón province** sweeps south in an arc from Nicaragua down to Panamá. Hemmed in to the north by dense jungles and swampy waterways, to the west by the mighty Cordillera Central and to the south by the even wider girth of the Cordillera Talamanca, Limón province can feel like a lost, end-of-the-world place. Here you can watch gentle giant sea **turtles** lay their eggs on the wave-raked beaches of **Tortuguero**; snorkel coral reefs at **Cahuita**; surf at **Puerto Viejo**; drift along the jungle canal from Tortuguero to **Barra del Colorado**, a major sports-fishing destination, or try animal- and bird-spotting in the many mangroves. The interior is criss-crossed by the powerful Río Reventazón and Río Pacuaré, two of the best rivers in the Americas for **whitewater rafting**.

Although Limón remains an unknown for the majority of visitors – especially those on package tours – it holds much appeal for eco-tourists, having the highest proportion of protected land in the country. In addition, more than anywhere else in Costa Rica, the Caribbean coast exudes a sense of **cultural diversity** and a unique and complex local history. The only town of any size, **Puerto Limón**, is a lively if jaded port town, with a large (mostly Jamaican-descended) Afro-Caribbean population, while in the south, near the Panamanian border, live several communities of indigenous peoples from the **Bribrí** and **Cabécar** groups.

There are few options when it comes to **getting around** Limón province. From San José to Puerto Limón you have a choice of just two roads, while from Puerto Limón south to the Panamá border at Sixaola there is but one narrow and badly maintained route (not counting the few small local roads leading to the banana fincas). North of Puerto Limón there is no public land transport at all: instead, private lanchas ply the coastal canals connecting the port of Moín, 8km north of Puerto Limón, to Río Colorado near the Nicaraguan border. There are also scheduled **flights** from San José to Barra del Colorado. A good, frequent and quite reliable **bus** network operates in the rest of the province, with the most efficient and modern services running from San José to Puerto Limón and on to Sixaola. **English** is spoken widely along the coast, not just in Limón but also in Tortuguero, due to the many Miskito-descended people from Nicaragua.

For an explanation of **accommodation price codes**, see p.556.

It's very **wet** all year round, with a smaller dry spell in January and February. South of Limón, September and October offer the best chance of rain-free days.

Puerto Limón

Once the Atlantic coast's principal port, today **PUERTO LIMÓN**, 165km east of San José, has a somewhat neglected air. There has been little activity at the harbour since the big-time banana boats started loading at **Moín**, 8km up the headland toward Tortuguero, and to make things worse, the city was ravaged by the 1991 earthquake, which left a trail of wrecked buildings in its wake. All in all, the place does have some rough edges, and while the scare stories Highland Ticos gleefully tell of the place are a bit exaggerated, it's worth watching your back. Generally speaking, tourists come to Limón for one of three reasons: to get a boat to **Tortuguero** from Moín, to get a bus south to the **beach towns** of Cahuita and Puerto Viejo, or to join the annual Carnaval-like celebration of **El Día de la Raza** (Columbus Day) during the week preceding October 12.

Arrival and information

Of the two roads from the capital to Puerto Limón, the **Guápiles Highway** (Hwy-32) is one of the best maintained in the country, and will get you to Puerto Limón in around three hours. The narrower and older Hwy-10, often called the **Turrialba Road**, runs through Turrialba on the eastern slopes of the Cordillera Central; it's considered dangerous and difficult to drive, and carries very little traffic.

Arriving in Limón can be unnerving at night – it's best to arrive in daylight, if only to orientate yourself. Coopelimón and Coopecaribeños **buses** do the **San José–Limón** trip, running more or less hourly from 5am to 7pm. You should buy your ticket in advance if travelling to Limón for Carnaval, although extra buses are laid on. Buses come into town from San José along Av 1, parallel to the docks and the old railroad tracks, pulling in at C 2, Av 1/2. Arrivals **from the south** – Cahuita, Puerto Viejo and Panamá (via Sixaola) – terminate at the Transportes MEPE stop at C 3, Av 4, 100m north of the mercado. Buses to **Moín** leave from beside *Soda La Estrella* at C 5, Av 3–4.

For **information**, you'll need to contact the San José ICT (☎223-1733), as there's no official tourist office in the entire province. The Banco de Costa Rica, on Av 2, C 1, will **change money**, as does Scotiabank, on Av 3, C2. The **correo** (Mon–Fri 7.30am–5pm, Sat 8am–12pm) is at Av 2, C 4, though the mail service from Limón is dreadful – you're better off posting items from San José. There's **Internet access** at the *Edutec Internet Café*, upstairs in the Centro Plaza Caribe on Av 3, C 4. **Taxis** line up on the corner of Av 2, C 1. Note that during the El Día de la Raza Carnival everything shuts for a week, including all the banks and the post office. Should you need **medical care**, head for Hospital Dr Tony Facio Castro (☎758-2222), at the north end of the *malecón*.

While Limón is not quite the mugger's paradise it's sometimes made out to be in the Highland media, standing on the sidewalk and looking lost is not recommended, nor is carrying valuables (most of the hotels in our list have safes). As opposed to other Costa Rican towns, Limón's *avenidas* run more or less east–west in numerical order, starting at the docks. *Calles* run north–south, beginning with C 1 on the western boundary of Parque Vargas, by the malecón.

Accommodation

It's worth shelling out a bit for a **room** in Limón, especially if you're travelling alone – this is a place where the comfort and safety of your hotel makes a big difference to your peace of mind. In midweek, the town's hotels fill up very quickly with commercial travellers; try to get to Limón as early as possible if you're arriving on a Wednesday or Thursday.

Staying **downtown** keeps you in the thick of things, and many hotels have communal balconies, perfect for relaxing with a cold beer above the lively street activity below. The downside of this is noise, especially at night. There's a group of quieter hotels outside town, about 4km up the road to Moín at **Portete** and **Playa Bonita**. A taxi up here costs less than US$1.50, and the bus to and from Moín runs along the road every twenty minutes or so. In all but the most upmarket places, avoid drinking the **tap water**.

Hotel prices rise by as much as fifty percent for **carnival** week, and to a lesser extent during Semana Santa, or Easter week. The least expensive times to stay are between July and October, and December to February, which (confusingly) are considered high season in the rest of the country. Limón has its share of dives, which tend to fill when there's a big ship in town. None of the places listed overleaf is rock-bottom cheap. If this is what you're after, you'll find it easily enough, but always ask to see the room first and inspect the bathroom, in particular.

In town

Acón, Av 3, C 2/3 (☎758-1010, fax 758-2924). Large central hotel with rather gloomy but well-equipped rooms with TV, a/c and hot water. Private parking. ④.

Caribe, Av 2, C 1, above the *Brisas del Caribe* restaurant (☎758-0138). Plain but spacious rooms with TV and fan, though they can be noisy at night. ③.

Miami, Av 2, C 4/5 (☎ & fax 758-0490). Friendly place whose clean rooms all have ceiling fans, cable TV and private bathrooms. ③.

Park, Av 3, C 1, by the *malecón* (☎798-0555 or 758-4364). The smartest option in town, popular with Ticos and travellers alike, so you'll have to book in advance. The most expensive rooms come with a sea view, slightly less expensive ones with a street view, and the cheapest, *plana turista*, rooms with no view at all. There's a good restaurant, too. ⑤.

Teté, Av 3, C4/5 (☎758-1122, fax 758-0707). Clean and well-cared-for hotel, with friendly staff – though nothing special, it's the best-value downtown option in this price range. Rooms on the street have balconies but can be noisy; those inside are a little darker, but quieter. ③.

Portete and Playa Bonita

Albergue Turistico Playa Bonita, Playa Bonita (☎793-3090, fax 798-3612). Good-value family pen-sión with seven simple but clean rooms set round a courtyard. ④.

CARNAVAL IN LIMÓN

Though in the rest of the Americas **Carnaval** is usually associated with the days before Lent, Limón takes Columbus' arrival in the New World – October 12 – as its point of celebration. The idea was first brought to Limón by a local man named Arthur King, who had been away working in Panamá's Canal Zone and was so impressed with that country's Columbus Day celebrations that he decided to bring the merriment home with him. Today **El Día de la Raza** (Day of the People) is basically an excuse to party.

The carnival features a variety of events, from Afro-Caribbean dance to Calypso music, bull-running, afternoon children's theatre, colourful *desfiles* (parades) and massive firework displays. Most spectacular is the **Grand Desfile**, usually held on the Saturday before October 12, when revellers in Afro-Caribbean costumes – sequins, spangles, fluorescent colours – parade through the streets to a cacophony of tambourines, whistles and blasting sound-systems.

Cabinas Maeva, Portete – look for the blue-and-white sign (☎758-2024). The best-value accommodation in Limón, with cute, yellow hexagonal *cabinas* nestling among palm trees, plus a beautiful pool and Neoclassical statues. ③.

The Town

Fifteen minutes' walk around Puerto Limón and you've seen the lot – you may even spot one of the vultures which occasionally hang out on street corners. **Avenida 2**, known locally as the "market street", is for all purposes the main drag, touching the north edge of Parque Vargas and the south side of the **Mercado Central**. The market is as good a place as any to start your explorations, and at times seems to be full of the entire town population, with dowager women minding their patch while thin men flutter their hands, clutching cigarettes and gesticulating jerkily. The sodas and snack bars here are good places to grab a bite.

Shops in Limón close over lunch, between noon and 2pm, when everyone drifts towards **Parque Vargas**, at the easternmost end of C 1 and Av 1/2, and the *malecón* (sea wall) to sit under the shady palms. A little shabby today, the park features a seafacing **mural** by artist Guadalupe Alvarea depicting colourful and evocative images of the province's tough history. From here the **malecón** winds its way north – avoid it at night, as muggings have been reported.

As for other activities in town, forget **swimming**. One look at the water at the tiny spit of sand next to the *Park Hotel* is enough discouragement. There are few **daytrips** worth making from Limón. The trip up the canals to Tortuguero (see p.607) takes three to five hours (with animal-spotting) one way, though it makes more sense to stay at least one night at Tortuguero if doing this trip. A better possibility for a short boat trip is up the **Río Matina** from Moín – with a guide, you might be able to spot sloths, monkeys, iguanas and caimans. You could try the friendly and knowledgeable Bernardo R. Vargas (☎798-4322, fax 758-2683), who also offers a packed one-day tour which takes in a walk in the rainforest at Aviarios de Caribe, the Parque Nacional Cahuita, a tour of local banana and coffee plantations and a city tour of Limón (US$35; 4–5hr).

Eating, drinking and entertainment

Limón has pretty good **food**, and variety too, but *Springfield* is the town's one authentic Creole restaurant, serving rice and beans cooked in coconut milk, jerk chicken and spicy meat stews. Inside the Mercado Central there's a host of decent sodas serving tasty *casados*. Outside Carnaval most people hang out with a beer in the evenings, but gringos in general and women especially should avoid most **bars** – especially those that have a large advertising placard blocking views of the interior. If you want to drink, stick to places like *Mares* or *Brisas del Caribe*. **Playa Bonita** is a great place for lunch or an afternoon beer if you're tired of town.

In town

Brisas del Caribe, C 1, Av 2, in the same building as the *Hotel Caribe*. Clean bar-restaurant with a good view of Parque Vargas. Except on nights when the sound-system is blasting, this is a quiet place to have a hassle-free coffee or beer. For food, there a Chinese menu, sandwiches, snacks and a good *medio casado* (half *casado*) for US$2.50.

Park Hotel, Av 3, C 1, by the *malecón*. The only restaurant in town where you feel you might actually be in the Caribbean – sea breezes float in through large slatted windows and all you can see is an expanse of blue sea and cloud. Excellent, though pricey, breakfast and standard Costa Rican fare.

Soda La Estrella, C 5, Av 3/4. The best lunch in town: top marks for *soda* staples, excellent *refrescos*, coffee, snacks, basic plates and daily specials, all accompanied by cordial service.

Springfield, north of the end of the *malecón*, across from the hospital. *The* place in Limón to get coconut-flavoured rice-and-beans with a choice of chicken, beef or fish (US$7). It's also one of the few places in Costa Rica to serve turtle, a local delicacy (though illegal). Try to arrive early, as the restaurant gets very full. Credit cards accepted.

Portete and Playa Bonita

Kimbambu, Playa Bonita. Beach-bar with excellent – though pricey – fresh fish cooked to order. Live music at weekends.

Maribú Caribe, Portete. Peaceful and friendly poolside bar-restaurant high above the sea, offering excellent food and *refrescos*.

MOVING ON FROM PUERTO LIMÓN

Heading north to **Tortuguero**, shallow-bottomed private lanchas make the trip up the canal from the docks at Moín (3hr). It's best to arrive at the docks early (7–9am) although you ought to be able to find boatmen willing to take you until 2pm. Expect to pay around US$50 each return for a group of four to six people; if you are travelling alone or in a couple, try to get a group together at the docks. The bus stop for **Moín** is at C 4, Av 5/6, 200m north of the Mercado Central, but the bus has no set schedule and only leaves when it's full (more or less every thirty minutes), so a taxi (US$3) may be a better option.

Buses to San José start running at 5am from the main bus terminal and continue hourly until 7pm. Direct buses to San José are run by Coopelimón and Coopecaribeños (see p.582), whose ticket windows are side by side; Coopetraga (☎758-0618) also has services from the main bus terminal to **Siquerres** and **Guápiles**, from where there are onward bus connections to the capital. Destinations **south of Limón** are served from the Transportes MEPE office (☎221-0524) at C 3, Av 4, 100m north of the Mercado Central, from where buses leave four times daily (from 7am until 6pm) to Cahuita (1hr) and eight times (also 7am until 6pm) to Puerto Viejo (1hr 30min–2hr). The **Sixaola** bus also stops in both places. Two buses (6am & 2.30pm; 2hr) go direct to **Manzanillo** village in the heart of the Gandoca-Manzanillo Wildlife Refuge, via Puerto Viejo.

Taxis line up on Av 2 around the corner from the San José bus stop: they'll do long-haul trips to Cahuita and Puerto Viejo (US$30–40), so if you're in a group, renting a taxi can be far more convenient than taking the bus.

Parque Nacional Tortuguero

Despite its isolation – 254km from San José by road and water, and 83km northwest of Limón – **PARQUE NACIONAL TORTUGUERO** (US$6) is extremely popular wtih visitors. The park is one of the most important nesting sights in the world for the **green sea turtle**, which, along with the hawksbill, lays its eggs here between July and October. First established in the 1960s, Tortuguero covers a large area – 189.5 square kilometres to be exact – protecting not only the turtle nesting beach, but also surrounding forests, canals and waterways. Except for a short dry season during February and March, Tortugero receives over 6000mm of rain a year, a soggy environment which hosts a wide abundance of species: fifty kinds of **fish**, numerous **birds**, including the endangered green parrot and the vulture, and some 160 **mammals**, some under the threat of extinction. It's the **turtles** that draw people here, however, and the sight of the gentle beasts tumbling ashore and shimmying their way up the beach to deposit their heavy load before limping back, spent, into the dark phosphorescent waves is truly moving.

The most popular way to see Tortuguero is on one of literally hundreds of **packages** that use the expensive "jungle lodges" across the canal from the village. These are usually two-night, three-day affairs, although you can certainly go for longer. Accommodation, meals and transport are taken care of, while guides point out wildlife along the river and canals on the way. The main difference between tours comes in the standard of hotels – check the reviews of the lodges on p.609 to help you choose. With a little planning, you can also get to Tortuguero **independently** and stay in cabinas in the **village**, which is a more interesting little place than initial impressions might suggest. Basing yourself here allows you to explore the beach at leisure – though you can't swim – and leaves you in easy reach of restaurants and bars.

Getting to Tortuguero

The journey up the canals from Limón to Tortuguero is at least half the experience. Expect a three- or four-hour trip (sometimes longer) by lancha, depending upon where you embark – if on a package tour, it will probably be **Hamburgo de Siquerres** on the Río Reventazón; if travelling independently, you'll find it easier to leave from **Moín**, near Puerto Limón (see p.602). Either way you'll pass palm and deciduous trees, mirror-calm waters, and small stilt-legged wooden houses, brightly painted and poised on the water's edge – along, of course, with acres and acres of cleared land. Quite apart from the wildlife, the canal is a hive of human activity, with lanchas, *botes* (large canoes) and *pangas* (flat-bottomed boats with outboard-motors) plying the glassy waters. Package tourists are disgorged at whichever of the lodges they are booked into.

If you're travelling **independently**, you ought to be able to find a boat at Moín willing to take you up the canal anytime from 6am until as late as 2pm. You can arrange with your boatman when you would like to be picked up to return (it's really not worth going for the day – if you do you'll have to make the return trip not later than 1.30pm to avoid getting stuck in the dark). Get a phone number from your boatman if possible, so you can call from Tortuguero village if you change plans. The lanchas drop you at Tortuguero dock, from where you can walk to the village accommodation or take another lancha across the canal to the more expensive tourist lodges. If you haven't booked a hotel, be aware that accommodation in the village can fill up quickly during the turtle-nesting seasons (March–May & July–Oct).

Alternatively, you can do what the locals do and take the 9am bus from San José to **Cariari**, then switch to a bus for the **Geest banana plantation**, from where a boat goes to Tortuguero, arriving in the village at 3.30pm. It's a long journey, but the boat ride costs only US$10 each way, and if you're travelling alone it makes sense. The return boat to San José leaves daily at 7am.

If you come **by air** on Sansa's daily flight (☎221-9414, fax 225-2176), which leaves San José at 6am and takes approximately 35 minutes, you'll arrive at the airstrip some 4km north of the village. There are no taxis from here to the village, though the more upmarket lodges will come and pick you up; otherwise, you'll have to walk.

The village

The peaceful village of **TORTUGUERO** lies at the northeastern corner of the national park, on a thin spit of land between the sea and the Tortuguero canal. With its exuberant foliage of wisteria, oleander and bougainvillea, the whole place has the look of a carefully tended tropical garden. Tall palm groves and clean expanses of mown grass are punctuated by zinc-roofed wooden houses, often elevated on stilts. This is classic Caribbean style: washed-out, slightly ramshackle and pastel-pretty, with very little to disturb the torpor until after dark.

A dirt path runs north–south through the village – the "main street" – from which narrow paths go off to the sea and the canal. Smack in the middle of the village stands one of the prettiest churches you'll see anywhere: pale yellow, with a small spire and an oval doorway. Just beyond the church is the colourful **La Crisalida Butterfly Garden** (daily 3–5.30pm; US$1), a community initiative manned by volunteers. The Jungle Souvenir Shop, at the northern end of the village across from the small jetty, is very well-stocked with T-shirts, wooden souvenirs and cards – if the sun is getting to you, this is the place to pick up a hat or sunscreen. The wares are less authentic at the purple Paraíso Tropical souvenir shop, which doubles as the village's Travelair agent, and sells tickets to San José.

Information

A display on the turtles' habits, habitat and history surrounds the **information kiosk** in the centre of the village. Officially you should buy tickets for turtle tours here; the park rangers open the kiosk at 5pm, and this is a good time to find a local guide (see below). In addition, Canadian naturalist and local resident Darryl Loth (☎392-3201, fax 710-0547, *www.safari.jumptravel.com*) runs a small information centre in the village and can arrange tours, such as boat trips and hikes up Cerro Tortuguero (see p.611). At the north end of the village, there's also a **Natural History Museum** (daily 10am–5.30pm; US$1), with a small but informative exhibition explaining the life-cycle of sea turtles and a short history of turtling in the area.

The *pulpería*, 50m south of the information kiosk, houses a public phone; there's another one at *Miss Junie's* restaurant which you can use for outgoing calls. There are no **bank** or moneychanging facilities in Tortuguero – bring all the cash you'll need with you – and though there's a **correo** in the middle of the village, mail may take three or four weeks just to make its way to Puerto Limón.

Village accommodation

Staying at Tortuguero on the cheap entails bedding down in one of the independent **cabinas** in the village. **Camping** on the beach is not allowed, though you can set up tent at the mown enclosure at the **ranger station** (about US$2 per day) at the southern end of the village, where you enter the park. It's in a sheltered situation, away from the sea breezes, with water and toilets, but bring a ground sheet and mosquito net, and make sure your tent is waterproof.

Cabinas Aracari, south of the information kiosk and soccer field (in Limón, ☎798-3059). New *cabinas*, all with private bath, cold water and fan, set in a beautiful tree-filled garden and run by a friendly local family. ②

TOUR OPERATORS TO TORTUGUERO

A number of operators in San José and Limón offer **packages to Tortuguero**, some with accommodation (in the lodges) and meals included. Though you could usually fix things up more cheaply yourself, these save a lot of hassle, and many of them are very good value.

Costa Rica Expeditions, C Central, Av 3, San José (☎257-0766, fax 257-1665, *www.costaricaexpeditions.com*). The most upmarket and efficient Tortuguero packages, with accommodation at the comfortable *Tortuga Lodge* (from US$300 for a three-day, two-night package, including flights from San José). They also do trips to Barra del Colorado.

Cotur, C 36, Paseo Colón and Av 1, San José (☎233-0155, fax 233-0778, *www .tortuguero.com*). Fairly good value three-day tours for about US$250 in high season, including transport by bus and boat, accommodation at the *Jungle Lodge*, meals and guides.

Ecole Travel, C 7, Av 0/1, San José (☎223-2240, fax 223-4128, *www.travelcostarica.net*). One of the longest-established companies going to Tortuguero and the best budget option, popular with students and backpackers – tours (from US$89 for two days and one night) start from Moín dock near Puerto Limón; Ecole also run boat trips from Moín to Tortuguero (US$55 return).

Grupo Mawamba, at the *Mawamba Lodge* in Tortuguero, or in San José at C 24, Av 5/7 (☎223-2421, fax 222-5463, *www.grupomawamba.com*). The best mid-range tour operator, providing superior but affordable packages staying at the *Mawamba Lodge*. The tours generally last three days and cost around US$219 per person, although longer stays can be arranged.

Cabinas Mary Scar, east of the *pulpería*, before the beach (in San Jose, ☎220-1478). Two new cabins with private bathrooms, plus some older *cabinas* with shared bathroom – they're slightly gloomy but very clean, and the bathroom is spick-and-span. Family atmosphere, with simple meals (about US$3) cooked on request. The least expensive option in Tortuguero. ②

Cabinas Sabina, east of the information kiosk, on the beach (no phone). Very simple, green *cabinas* whose main attraction is their setting on a nice strip of sand. The rooms are basic and dark (those upstairs have better ventilation), and the toilet and shower are in an outhouse, though they're perfectly clean. Bar on site. ②

Cabinas Tortuguero, south of the village, towards the entry to the national park (no phone). Tortuguero's best option, with five simple rooms (all en suite) in a lovely garden and Italian food available on request (breakfast US$3, lunch or supper US$5). ②

Miss Junie's, at the north end of the village, just before you reach the Natural History Museum (☎710-0523). Tortuguero's most popular cook (see overleaf) also has a few well-decorated and comfortable rooms with private bath (cold water only) and fan. ④

The lodges

Staying at Tortuguero's **lodges**, most of which are across the canal from the village, has its drawbacks. You're pretty much duty-bound to eat the set meals included in the package, and – unless you're at the *Laguna* or *Mawamba* – if you want to explore the village and the beach on your own you have to get a lancha across the canal (free, but inconvenient). The lodges only rent rooms to independent travellers if they have space, which they rarely do, owing to Tortuguero's perennial popularity, and no official prices are posted for non-package rooms.

El Manatí, 1.5km north of the village, across the canal (☎ & fax 383-0330). Tortuguero's best budget option, this peaceful family-run lodge has basic but clean rooms with private bath, hot water and fans, as well as several attractive two-bedroom *cabinas*. Breakfast included. ④

Jungle Lodge, 1km north of the village, across the canal (☎233-0155, fax 233-0778). Friendly, comfortable and unpretentious lodge, set in its own gardens, with en-suite rooms, a good restaurant, games room, a small disco, swimming pool, free canoes and a lagoon. Good value. ⑤

Laguna Lodge (☎225-3740, fax 283-8031, *www.lagunalodgetortuguero.com*). Attractive hotel with driftwood décor, riverside bar and rustic wooden cabins in a convenient village location, with easy access to the beach. Gorgeous pool and butterfly gardens, too, while the peaceful atmosphere is ideal for those who don't like large touristy lodges. Full tour services. ⑥

Mawamba Lodge, 1km north of the village (☎710-7282, fax 222-5463, *www.grupomawamba.com*). Large, ritzy and gregarious lodge. The well-organized facilities include a gift shop, daily slide-show, environmentally friendly boats and round-the-clock cold beers. The *cabina*-style rooms have ceiling fans and private bathrooms, and there's a large pool and jacuzzi, while the village and ocean are just a short walk away. ⑥

Pachira Lodge, opposite the village (☎256-7080, fax 223-1119, *paccira@racsa.co.cr*). Tortuguero's newest lodge, this luxurious establishment has spacious and attractive rooms in wood cabins, linked by covered walkways, with large en-suite, hot-water bathrooms, along with a pool, gift shop and imaginative tour options. ⑥

Tortuga Lodge, owned by Costa Rica Expeditions (☎257-0766, fax 257-1665, *www.costaricaexpeditions .com*). The plushest lodge in the area, though it's furthest from the village, with exemplary service, large, attractive en-suite rooms, a riverside swimming pool and elegantly landscaped grounds with walking trails. ⑦

Eating, drinking and nightlife

Tortuguero village offers good homely food, typically Caribbean, with wonderful fresh **fish**. The only disadvantage is that prices tend to be high: expect to pay up to twice as much for a meal as you'd pay in other parts of Costa Rica. For entertainment, the Centro Social La Culebra has a nightly **disco**, though the clientele can be a bit rough. *Bar Brisas del Mar* (known to the locals as *El Bochinche*) is better, with a large, semi open-air dance floor and a good sound-and-light system (when it's not visiting Limón). You can hear the sea from your table and the atmosphere is low-key except on Saturday nights, when the lively weekly disco attracts a large local crowd and goes on well into the small hours.

El Dollar, mid-village, on the waterfront. In a great position on the river, with decent local food cooked to order.

El Muellecito, next to the *pulpería*. Tortuguero's best breakfast option, with tasty pancakes and fruit salad.

Miss Junie's, north end of village path, 50m before the Natural History Museum. Solid Caribbean food – red beans, jerk chicken, rice, chayote and breadfruit, all on the same plate – by local cook Miss Junie, dished up with ice-cold beers in a large dining room with gingham tablecloths and cool white walls. Miss Junie also cooks for the park rangers, so you need to ask a day in advance or in the morning whether she can fit you in.

Miss Miriams, adjacent to village soccer pitch (and a good spot to watch the village teams in action). Cheerful and immaculate restaurant serving Caribbean food at very reasonable prices.

The Vine, opposite the Jungle Souvenir Shop. Café, run by the owners of the souvenir shop, with good coffee, cheesecake and brownies. Closed during the rainy season.

Tropical Lodge Bar, mid-village on the path to the national park entrance. Noisy and entertaining village bar with perfect sunset views over the river.

Visiting the park

Most people come to Tortuguero to see the turtles laying their eggs, the so-called **des-ove**. Few are disappointed, as the majority of tours during laying **seasons** (March–May & July–Oct) result in sightings of the moving, surreal procession of the reptiles from the sea to make their egg-nests in the sand. Most turtles come ashore during the relative safety of night. Often dozens of turtles emerge from the sea at the same time and march up the sands to their chosen spot. Each turtle lays eighty or more eggs – the collective whirring noise of sand being dug away is extraordinary.

Although Tortuguero is by no means the only place in Costa Rica to see marine turtles nesting (they use the Pacific beaches too), three of the largest kinds of endangered sea turtles regularly nest here in large numbers. Along with the **green** (*verde*) turtle, named for the colour of soup made from its flesh, you might see the **hawksbill** (*carey*), with its distinctive hooked beak, and the ridged **leatherback** (*baula*), the largest turtle in the world, which can easily weigh 300kg – some are as heavy as 500kg and reach 5m in length. The green turtles and hawksbills nest most concentratedly from July to October (August is the peak month), while the leatherbacks come ashore from March to May.

Turtle tours, led by certified guides, leave at 8pm and 10pm every night from the village. If you're not going with an organized group from one of the lodges, you'll need to buy park entrance tickets (US$6) from the kiosk in the village, which is manned by park rangers from 5pm to 6pm every afternoon. There are over a hundred certified guides in Tortuguero; they charge US$10 for the turtle tour (roughly half the price of a lodge tour) and tend to hang around the ticket kiosk at 5pm in search of custom. Guides are instructed to make as little noise as possible so as not to alarm the turtles, allowing them to get on with their business; everyone must be off the beach by midnight.

During the day, you can walk a single, generally well-maintained, self-guided trail (1km), the **Sendero Natural**, which starts at the entrance and skirts a small swamp. As for that long, wild **beach**, you can amble for up to 30km south and enjoy crab-spotting, bird-watching, and looking for turtle tracks, which resemble the two thick parallel lines a truck would leave in its wake. Swimming is not a good idea, due to heavy waves, turbulent currents and sharks. Remember that you need to **pay park fees** (US$6) to walk on the beach or along the trail.

Other activities around Tortuguero

Almost as popular as the turtle tours are Tortuguero's **boat tours** through the *caños*, or lagoons, to spot animals and birds, such as dignified-looking herons, cranes and kingfishers. Most lodges have **canoes** you can take out on the canal – a great way to get around if you're handy with a paddle, but do stick to the main canal as it's easy to get lost in the complex lagoon system northwest of the village. In the south of the village, Ruben Aragón, 50m north of the ranger station, right by the water, rents traditional Miskito-style boats and canoes for about US$8 an hour, or US$15 with a guide-paddler.

It's also possible to climb **Cerro Tortuguero**, an ancient volcanic deposit looming 119m above the flat coastal plain 6km north of the village. A climb up the gently sloping side (90min round trip) leads you to the "peak", from where there are good views of flat jungle and inland waterways. Ask at the village information kiosk or at the ranger station.

Cahuita village and Parque Nacional Cahuita

The tiny village of **CAHUITA**, 43km southeast of Limón, is reached on the paved Hwy-36 which runs from Limón to Sixaola on the Panamanian border. Like other villages on the Talamanca coast, especially Puerto Viejo de Talamanca (see p.615) and Manzanillo (see p.618), it has become increasingly popular with backpackers and surfers for its laidback atmosphere and walking opportunities, along with the added appeal of great Afro-Caribbean food. Near the village, the **Parque Nacional Cahuita** was formed mainly to protect one of the only living coral reefs in Costa Rica; many people come here to **snorkel** and take rides in glass-bottomed boats. Though it's mainly wet all year round, the local "dry" season is between March and April, and from September to October.

While tourism has undoubtedly brought prosperity to the village, it has also created problems in its wake – at one point Cahuita was known for its drugs scene and bouts of opportunistic theft, and it's worth being cautious: lock your door and windows, never leave anything on the beach and avoid walking alone in unlit places at night. Nude or topless bathing is definitely unacceptable, as is wandering though the village in just a bathing suit. With a bit of common sense, though, most travellers really enjoy the community and atmosphere here.

Arrival and information

The easiest way to get to Cahuita from San José is by **bus** on the direct Transportes MEPE service (4 daily; 4hr), which goes on to Puerto Viejo. Taking a bus from San José to Puerto Limón (3hr) and then changing for Cahuita (4 daily) is only marginally less expensive than taking the direct bus and increases travelling time by at least an hour. In Cahuita, buses stop at the central crossroads opposite the *Salon Sarafina* bar-disco, which has a colourful and detailed map of the village painted on its exterior. Current timetables are posted in front of the Cahuita Tours office, 200m north along the village's main street.

Information

If you're coming to Cahuita **from Puerto Viejo**, be sure to pick up a copy of the free *Costa Rican Caribbean Info Guide*, which unfolds into maps of the local area and a directory of accommodation and businesses in both villages. The only sources of visitor **information** in the village itself are the tour companies: Mr Big J's (☎755-0328), towards the Parque Nacional Cahuita *puesto* and beach, has a book exchange and laundry facilities. Cahuita Tours (☎755-0000) has public phones where you can make international calls, while Turistica Cahuita sells the *Tico Times*. There's **Internet** access at *Cabinas Palmar* (evenings only). There are no banks in town – the nearest are in Bribrí, 20km away, or Limón. Your best bet for **changing money**, travellers' cheques and obtaining cash advances on credit cards is the efficient cambio (7am–4pm) at *Cabinas Safari;* Supermarket Vaz changes cash only. The small police station (*guardia rural*) is on the last beach-bound road at the north end of the village; the **correo** next door (theoretically Mon–Fri 7.30am–5pm) keeps erratic hours, to say the least.

Accommodation

Though Cahuita is popular with budget travellers, it's not rock-bottom cheap. Groups get the best deal, as most **cabinas** charge per room and have space for at least three or four people. Though accommodation tends to be of the concrete-cell variety, standards are high, with fans, mosquito nets, clean sheets and bathrooms. Upstairs rooms are usually slightly more expensive, with sea breezes and maybe views.

The **centre of the village** has scores of options, the best of which are listed below – staying here is convenient for restaurants, bars and the national park. There's also accommodation in all price ranges along the long (3km or so) road that runs by the sea north along **Black-Sand Beach**. It's quieter here, and the beach is not bad, though women (even if travelling in groups) and those without their own car are better off staying in town, since a number of rapes and muggings have been committed along this road, though so far always at night and none recently. You should **book ahead** on weekends during the Highland dry season (Dec–April).

There are several **camping** options in the vicinity, the nicest being at the Puerto Vargas ranger station in the national park (see p.614).

In the village

Cabinas Jenny, on the beach (☎755-0256). Beautiful rooms, especially the more expensive ones upstairs, with high wooden ceilings, sturdy bunks, mosquito nets, fans and wonderful sea views. Deck chairs and hammocks are provided, and there are good stout locks on all doors. ③.

Cabinas Sol y Mar, towards Kelly Creek (☎755-0237). Small, basic rooms run by friendly locals; clean and safe. ③.

El Encanto B&B, past the police station in the north of the village (☎ & fax 755-0113, *encanto @racsa.co.cr*). Highly recommended B&B, with a gorgeous garden, three beautifully decorated doubles, and a delicious breakfast included in the room rate. There's a self-contained house available for rent too. ⑤.

Hotel Kelly Creek, beside the national park beach (☎755-0007, *kellycr@racsa.co.cr*). Four vast, wood-panelled rooms right by the park entrance, with mosquito nets and a good Spanish restaurant on site. ⑤.

Black-Sand Beach

Atlantida Lodge, next to the soccer field on the road to Black-Sand Beach, about 1km from the village (☎755-0115, fax 755-0213, *www.atlantida.co.cr*). The best of the village's pricier options: friendly, with patio, pretty grounds, good security and the nicest pool in town. The cool rooms are decorated in tropical yellows and pinks, with heated water, and there's free coffee and bananas all day. ⑤.

Bungalows Malu, beyond the soccer field (☎755-0006). Pretty individual *cabinas* in a large garden facing the sea, with an Italian restaurant on site. ③.

Cabinas Algebra, 2km or so up the road to Black-Sand Beach (☎ & fax 755-0057). Attractive *cabinas*, some distance from town but with the good *Bananas Restaurant* on site, run by friendly Austrian couple who offer haircuts, laundry service and free pick-up from the village. ③.

Cabinas Iguana, 200m south of *Soda Bambata* on a small side road (☎755-0005, fax 755-0054, *iguanas @racsa.co.cr*). Some of the best budget accommodation in town, with lovely wood-panelled *cabinas* set back from the beach and a big screened veranda, plus laundry service, book exchange and a small swimming pool. The friendly owners also rent out two apartments and a three-bedroom house with kitchen. ③.

The village

Cahuita proper comprises just two puddle-dotted, gravel-and-sand streets running parallel to the sea, intersected by a few cross-streets. Though it seems like anything nailed down has been turned into some kind of small business, you'll still see a couple of private homes among the haphazard conglomeration of signs advertising *cabinas* and restaurants. Few locals drive (bicycles are popular), so most of the vehicles you see kicking up the dust belong to tourists.

Cahuita's main street runs from the national park entrance at Kelly Creek to the northern end of the village, marked more or less by the soccer field. Beyond here it continues two or three kilometres north along Black-Sand Beach. The small park at the central crossroads downtown, with its three small busts of Cahuita's founding fathers, is the focal point of the village, where locals wait for buses to San José and catch up on recent gossip. Opposite, *Coco's* disco and bar is *the* place to hang out at night, while at weekends its breezy veranda is crammed full of partygoers from the city and gaggles of young backpackers soaking up the atmosphere.

You can swim on either of the village's two beaches, although neither is fantastic: the first 400m or so of the narrow white-sand beach is particularly dangerous on account of rip tides. **Black-Sand Beach** is littered with driftwood, although you can swim in some places. The beach south of Punta Cahuita in the park – sometimes called **Playa Vargas** – is better for swimming than those in the village, as it's protected from raking breakers by the coral reef, but is slightly awkward to get to. Backing the shores, a trail leads through the vast area of thick vegetation and mangrove swamps.

The principal daylight activity in Cahuita is taking a boat trip out to the Parque Nacional Cahuita's coral reef to **snorkel** – try one of the town's three tour companies – or you can snorkel off the beach at Playa Vargas. Though you can **surf** at Cahuita, Puerto Viejo (see p.615) has better waves – bring your own board, as there's nowhere yet in either village to rent equipment. Wherever you swim, either in the park itself or on Black-Sand Beach, don't leave possessions unattended, as even your grubby T-shirt and old shorts may be stolen. If you don't fancy snorkelling, Mr Big J's organizes **horse rides** along the beach and jungle hikes (US$20–30), and all three tour agencies in Cahuita offer combined Jeep trips to local villages and the beach (US$35).

Visiting the park

PARQUE NACIONAL CAHUITA (daily 8am–5pm; "pay what you want" if entering at Kelly Creek; US$6 at the Puerto Vargas entrance, 4km south of Cahuita along the Limón–Sixaola road) is one of the smallest in the country, covering the wedge-shaped piece of land from Punta Cahuita back to the main highway from Puerto Limón to Sixaola and, crucially, the **coral reef** about 500m offshore. On land, Cahuita protects the littoral, or coastal, rainforest, a lowland habitat of semi-mangroves and tall canopy cover which backs the gently curving white-sand beaches of Playa Vargas to the south of Punta Cahuita and Playa Cahuita to the north. **Birds**, including ibis and kingfishers, are in residence, along with white-faced (*carablanca*) monkeys, sloths and snakes, but the only animals you're likely to see are howler monkeys, and perhaps coati.

The park's one **trail** (7km), skirting the beach, is a very easy, level walk, with a path so wide it feels like a road, covered with leaves and other brush, and a few fallen trees and logs. The Río Perzoso, about 2km from the Kelly Creek entrance, or 5km from the Puerto Vargas trailhead, is not always fordable. Similiarly, at high tide the beach is impassable in places: ask the ranger at the Puerto Vargas *puesto* about the *marea*, or tide schedules. Walking this trail can also be unpleasantly humid and buggy: best to go in the morning.

Many **snorkellers** swim the 200 to 500m from Puerto Vargas out to the reef. Again, you should ask about currents, although the water here is calmer than at the beach next to Cahuita village.

Eating, drinking and nightlife

Cahuita has plenty of places **to eat** fresh local food, with a surprisingly cosmopolitan selection. As with accommodation, prices are not low – an evening meal starts at around US$5 – and service tends to be laid-back: leave yourself lots of time to eat. **Nightlife** in Cahuita revolves around having a beer and listening to music. At weekends the village's two discos get very sweaty, with customers spilling out onto the street and cranked-up sound systems playing on until the small hours.

Bar Hannia, in the centre of the village. Small friendly bar with good cold beer and a relaxed atmosphere.

ChaChaChas, next door to Cahuita Tours. Fantastic gourmet cuisine – exotic salads, grilled squid, seafood and Tex-Mex – at very reasonable prices and served in a pretty setting with fresh flowers on the tables and fairy lights at night.

Chao's Paradise, Black-Sand Beach. Groovy little joint serving up posh Creole cooking using the freshest ingredients.

El Parquecito, behind the village park. Best place in the village for breakfast, with fresh juices, pancakes and French toast.

Palenque Luisa, in the middle of the village opposite *Bar Hannia*. Good-value and popular restaurant with extensive menu including *casados*, fish and Creole dishes, plus live calypso music on Saturday nights.

Sobre Las Ollas, at the northern end of the village, right on the beach. Atmospheric and classy hangout with first-rate seafood – the lobster is particularly delicious – and the sound of lapping waves in the background, though it's not cheap. Closed Tues.

MOVING ON FROM CAHUITA

There are seven buses daily to **Limón**, where you can connect for **San José**, but if you're in a hurry to reach the capital it's faster and easier to take the direct non-stop service (4 daily; 4hr), run by Transportes MEPE. For **Puerto Viejo**, a local bus leaves Cahuita six times daily, taking forty minutes (first bus at 6am, last at 7pm), and continuing on from Puerto Viejo to **Bribri** and then **Sixaola**.

Vista de Mar (known by the locals as "El Chines"), by Kelly Creek. Barn-sized restaurant with a vast menu featuring inexpensive rice-and-bean combos, fish and Chinese food. It's popular with backpackers, and can get very crowded.

Puerto Viejo de Talamanca and around

The 12km of coast between the languorous hamlet of **PUERTO VIEJO DE TALA-MANCA**, 18km southeast of Cahuita, and Manzanillo village is one of the most beautiful stretches in the country. Though not spectacular for swimming, the **beaches** – Playa Chiquita, Punta Uva and Manzanillo – are the most picturesque on the entire coast; there's also plenty of accommodation, and it's livelier than Cahuita.

It's **surfing** that really pulls the crowds; the stretch south of *Stanford's* restaurant at the southern end of the village offers some of the most challenging waves in the country, and certainly the best on the Atlantic coast. Puerto Viejo's famous "**La Salsa Brava**" crashes ashore between December and March and from June to July. September and October, when La Salsa Brava goes away to wherever big waves go, are the quietest months of the year.

The **village** itself lies between the thick forested hills of the Talamanca mountains and the sea, where locals bathe and kids frolic with surfboards in the waves. It's a dusty little place in daylight hours but reasonably well cared for, with bright hand-painted signs pointing the way to *cabinas*, bars and restaurants. The main drag through the centre, potholed and rough, is criss-crossed by a few dirt streets and an offshoot road that

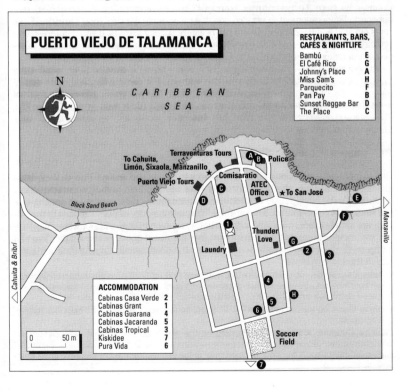

PUERTO VIEJO DE TALAMANCA

N

CARIBBEAN SEA

RESTAURANTS, BARS, CAFÉS & NIGHTLIFE
Bambú	E
El Café Rico	G
Johnny's Place	A
Miss Sam's	H
Parquecito	F
Pan Pay	B
Sunset Reggae Bar	D
The Place	C

To Cahuita, Limón, Sixaola, Manzanillo
Terraventuras Tours
Puerto Viejo Tours
Comisaratio
Police
ATEC Office
To San José
Black Sand Beach
Thunder Love
Laundry
Cahuita & Bribrí
Manzanillo

ACCOMMODATION
Cabinas Casa Verde	2
Cabinas Grant	1
Cabinas Guarana	4
Cabinas Jacaranda	5
Cabinas Tropical	3
Kiskidee	7
Pura Vida	6

0   50 m

Soccer Field

follows the shore. As in Cahuita, many Europeans have been drawn to Puerto Viejo and have set up their own businesses; also like Cahuita, most locals are of Afro-Caribbean descent. In recent years, Puerto Viejo's backpacker and surf-party culture has created a small **drugs scene**, though this is fairly low-key and shouldn't adversely affect your stay. Nevertheless, it's best to make sure your room is well secured at night, and to avoid wandering through the quiet fringes of the village alone in the small hours.

Arrival

All buses **from San José** to Puerto Viejo stop first in **Limón** and **Cahuita** (4 daily; 4hr 30min) and then go onto **Sixaola**, with the first one leaving San José at 6am and the last one at 3.30pm. The last bus back to San José goes at 4pm. Taking a bus from San José to Limón (5 daily) and changing there is only marginally less expensive, and will increase travelling time by an hour at least. Three buses daily go along the coast to **Manzanillo** (45min).

Information

Puerto Viejo has no tourist information office, but as with Cahuita, the village's tour operators can give you advice and maps. The most helpful operator is **Puerto Viejo Tours** (Tues–Sun 8am–12pm & 2pm–6pm; ☎ & fax 750-0411, *puertoviejotours@yahoo.com*) on the seafront, which has a wide range of tours, including rafting, snorkelling and birdwatching. They'll also change dollars and travellers' cheques, as will the nearby Comisaratio store. **Terraventuras Tours** (☎750-0426, *terraventuras@hotmail.com*) rent out snorkelling equipment at very reasonable rates, while the surf shop **Thunder Love** rents out surf and boogie boards and can organize surfing lessons. If you're interested in ecology, the proprietor of *Cabinas Tropical,* author and biologist Rolf Blancke, takes people out on excellent trips into the Gandoca rainforest (US$35 for a 12hr trip).

The **correo** (Mon–Fri 7.30am–6pm, Sat 7.30am–12pm) is situated in the small commercial centre three blocks back from the seafront. For camera film and other essentials, head for El Buen Precio **supermarket**, which has two public **phones** in front of it (as does ATEC). The **ATEC** office on the main road (daily 8am–9pm; ☎ & fax 750-0191, *www.greencoast.com/atec.htm*) has **Internet** access and an international telephone and fax service.

Accommodation

Due to its rapidly increasing popularity, places to stay in and around Puerto Viejo have mushroomed and you shouldn't normally have any problem finding accommodation, although it's still best to reserve a room in advance during high season and surfing-season weekends (Dec–March, June & July). The vast majority of places to stay in the **village** are simple *cabinas*, usually without hot water (sometimes without water altogether), while more upmarket establishments line the **coast** south of the village. You can **camp** on the beaches, but rock-bottom budget travellers usually forsake their tents and stay at the lovely *Kiskidee.*

Cabinas Casa Verde, one block south of the main drag (☎ & fax 750-0047, *cabinascasaverde@hotmail .com*). Fourteen fantastic-value *cabinas*, decorated with shell mobiles and pieces of washed-up coral, with very clean showers, ceiling fans, mosquito nets and space to sling hammocks. ④.

Cabinas Grant, on the main road (☎750-0292). Spotless, locally run hotel with basic but serviceable rooms. ②.

Cabinas Guarana, south of the main drag on the way to the soccer field (☎750-0244, *www .hotelguarana.com*). Excellent small hotel with attractive rooms, tiled bathrooms and a communal kitchen for guests' use. Check out the treehouse in the garden, from where there are great views over the village. ④.

ATEC AND TOURS TO THE KÉKÖLDI RESERVE

Skirted by the **KéköLdi** reserve, inhabited by about two hundred Bribrí and Cabécar peoples, Puerto Viejo retains strong links with **indigenous culture**. The Associación Talamanqueña de Ecoturismo y Conservación, or **ATEC** (☎ & fax 750-0191, *www .greencoast.com/atec.htm*) is a grassroots organization set up by members of the local community – Afro-Caribbeans, Bribri indigenous peoples and Spanish-descended inhabitants. As well as being able to tell you where to buy locally made products such as banana vinegar, guava jam, coconut oil, and jewellery made from coconut shells, seashells and bamboo, they arrange some of the most authentic and interesting **tours** in Costa Rica. If you're spending even just a couple of days in the Talamanca region, an ATEC-arranged trip is a must – contact their Puerto Viejo office at least one day in advance.

Cabinas Jacaranda, just north of the soccer field (☎750-0069). Basic but very clean budget option, with lively Guatemalan fabrics and a lush tropical garden. ③.

Cabinas Tropical, on the eastern edge of the village (☎ & fax 750-0283, *www.cabinastropical.com*). Small, quiet and scrupulously clean hotel with five large, comfortable rooms, and pet birds in the garden. ③.

Kiskidee, signposted along a path south of the soccer field (☎750-0075). Well worth the 15min trek up the hill – bring a torch at night – this is one of the most tranquil lodges in all Costa Rica, and at budget rates. The large veranda is good for bird- and animal-spotting, and there's spacious bunk accommodation and the use of a kitchen – stock up on food at the *pulpería* – but no fans and an outdoor toilet only. ②.

Pura Vida, near the soccer field (☎750-0002, fax 750-0296). Popular budget hotel which tends to fill quickly. The seven rooms all have private bath, ceiling fans and mosquito nets, and there's a pleasant veranda. ④.

Eating, drinking and nightlife

Puerto Viejo has a surprisingly cosmopolitan range of **places to eat**. Good, traditional **Creole food** is served at *Miss Sam's*, and the ATEC can put you in touch with village women who cook typical regional meals on request. Although quiet during the day, Puerto Viejo has a lively **nightlife**. If you're after a peaceful drink, one of the nicest spots in town is the spacious veranda in front of the Comisaratio store – buy your beer from the shop and drink it from the bottle as you watch the sun slide prettily into the sea.

Bambú, on the eastern edge of town. Beachfront reggae disco which gets absolutely packed on Mondays and Fridays; great fun.

El Café Rico, opposite *Cabinas Casa Verde*. Dutch-run café with the best coffee in town, tasty sandwiches, crepes and breakfast. Nice rooms (③) also available.

Johnny's Place, on the seafront near the police station. Large airy disco with bonfires on the beach. Very popular at weekends.

Miss Sam's, three blocks back from the seafront. Wonderful Caribbean home-cooking at very reasonable prices. Often full at lunchimes.

Parquecito, on the edge of town towards Manzanillo. Lively bar-restaurant with sea views, cold beer and good atmosphere – although the food's not up to much.

Pan Pay, behind *Johnny's Place*. Popular breakfast spot and bakery with croissants, cakes and delicious Spanish tortilla.

Sunset Reggae Bar, on the seafront near the bus stop. Groovy little bar with delicious pizza from the wood-fired oven, plus an entertaining Wednesday open-mike session with tables set out on the shore and passing musicians joining in.

The Place, one block back from the bus stop. Attractive café specializing in vegetarian dishes and seafood, popular with tourists who are sick of rice, beans and pizza – try the tasty coconut-flavoured curries.

South from Puerto Viejo to Manzanillo

The stretch south of Puerto Viejo, dotted by the tiny hamlets of **Playa Cocles**, **Playa Chiquita**, **Punta Uva** and **Manzanillo** (the main village), is one of the most appealing on the entire Atlantic coast. Palm trees lean vertiginously over small and little-visited beaches, while purples, mauves, oranges and reds fade into the sea at sunset, heralding the twilight mist that wafts in from the Talamancas. There's a low-hassle atmosphere, and excellent accommodation strung along the Puerto Viejo–Manzanillo road. Bus transport is infrequent, and you'll do best with a car.

The little-visited but fascinating **Refugio Nacional de Vida Silvestre Gandoca-Manzanillo**, bordering Río Sixaola and the international frontier with Panamá, incorporates the small hamlets of Gandoca and Manzanillo and covers fifty square kilometres of land and a similar area of sea. It was established to protect some of Costa Rica's last few **coral reefs**, of which **Punta Uva** is the most accessible. You can **snorkel** happily here. There's also a protected **turtle-nesting beach** south of the village of Manzanillo. **Playa Manzanillo** also has a large shelf of coral reef just offshore which teems with marine life and offers some of the best snorkelling in Costa Rica. The village itself is small and charming, with laid-back locals and a couple of great places to eat and hang out.

Accommodation

There are over 25 places to stay on the road from Puerto Viejo to Manzanillo – mostly mid-range options, plus a couple of elegant boutique hotels and several self-catering places.

Aguas Claras, Playa Chiquita (☎750-0180, fax 750-0386, *harbor@racsa.co.cr*). The best self-catering option in the area, set in luxuriant gardens just 200m from the beach. Each of the brightly painted wooden chalets has mosquito nets, a sitting area, balcony, clean bathroom, cold water, fully equipped kitchen and electricity. They sleep up to four people, but can only be rented by the week (US$240).

Cariblue, Playa Cocles (☎ & fax 750-0057, *www.cariblue.com*). Comfortable individual *cabinas* with an Italian restaurant, good souvenir shop and book exchange on site. ⑥

Casa Camarona, Playa Cocles (☎750-0151, *www.casacamarona.com*). Nineteen rooms, all with private bathroom and a/c, set in a first-class location right on the beach. There's also an attractive restaurant and good artesanía shop. ⑥

La Costa de Papito, Playa Cocles (☎ & fax 750-0080, *www.greencoast.com/papito.htm*). Six bungalows with large bamboo beds and balconies, set in pretty gardens and run by an effusive New Yorker. ⑤

Miraflores, Playa Chiquita (☎ & fax 750-0038, *www.mirafloreslodge.com*). Rustic, comfortable lodge opposite the beach, on an old cacao plantation with tropical flowers in the grounds. The decor is lovely, with Bribrí paintings, carvings and objets d'art. The upstairs rooms are brighter – with mosquito nets, mirrors and high bamboo ceilings – and there's an outside breakfast area. The owner has excellent contacts with local KéköLdi Bribrí communities and runs imaginative tours, including trips to Panamá in a motorized dugout. ④

Pangea, Manzanillo (☎224-2400, *pangea@puertoviejo.net*). Two beautifully decorated rooms, with private bath and breakfast included. ⑤

Shawandha, Playa Chiquita (☎750-0018, fax 750-0037, *www.shawandha-lodge.com*). Very chic French hotel comprising ten large bungalows with enormous beds and gorgeous tiled bathrooms. Rates include breakfast. ⑧

Villas del Caribe, Playa Chiquita (☎750-0202, fax 221-2801, *www.villascaribe.net*). Actually within the KéköLdi indigenous reserve, this hotel has very comfortable two-storey self-catering accommodation, with terrace, hot water, fan and organic garbage disposal. The grounds are right on the beach, with great sunset views. ⑥

Eating and drinking

Elena Brown's, just beyond *Miraflores* lodge, 5km south of Puerto Viejo. This long-established soda-cum-restaurant serves succulent local fish and chicken dishes, as well as inexpensive lunchtime specials and snacks.

El Rinconcito Alegre, Manzanillo. Small, cheerful café with *casados*, fresh fruit juices and seafood.

Maxis, Manzanillo. Large upstairs restaurant with great views over the beach and renowned seafood, including lobster. Gets packed at weekends.

Selvyn's Restaurant, about 8km south of Puerto Viejo. Long-established restaurant dishing up beautifully cooked local fish (served with coconut-flavoured rice-and-beans at weekends).

Bribrí and the Panamanian Border

From Puerto Viejo the paved road (Hwy-36) continues inland to **BRIBRÍ**, about 10km southwest, arching over the Talamancan foothills with views of the green valleys stretching ahead to Panamá. This is banana country, with little to see even in Bribrí itself, which is largely devoted to administering the affairs of indigenous reserves in the Talamanca mountains. Bribrí does, however, have one basic **place to stay**, *Cabinas El Mango* (no phone; ①), a couple of simple **restaurants** and a **bank**, the Banco Nacional, which changes money and travellers' cheques.

The border and on into Panamá

Sixaola–Guabito is a small crossing that doesn't see much foreign traffic, and for the most part formalities are simple, but you should get here as early in the morning as possible.

The Sixaola–Guabito border is open daily from 8am to 5pm Panamá time (one hour ahead of Costa Rica). Tourists leaving Costa Rica need to buy a **Red Cross exit stamp** (US$2 from the pharmacy in Sixaola); citizens of some nationalities may require a **tourist card** to enter Panamá (valid for 30 days); the Panamanian consulate in San José issues them, as does the San José office of Copa, the Panamanian airline (see p.580). Immigration requirements often change; check with the Panamanian consulate.

In Panamá, there's nowhere decent to stay before you get to Bocas del Toro (see p.780) – leave time to look for a hotel once you're there, and be aware that bus connections can be tricky.

travel details

BUSES

Cahuita to: Puerto Limón (4 daily; 1hr); Puerto Viejo de Talamanca (8 daily; 1hr 30min–2hr); San José (4 daily; 4hr); Sixaola (4 daily; 2hr).

Puerto Limón to: Cahuita (4 daily; 1hr); Manzanillo (2 daily; 2hr); Puerto Viejo de Talamanca (4 daily; 1hr 30min); San José (12 daily; 2hr 30min–3hr); Sixaola (1 daily; 3hr).

Puerto Viejo de Talamanca to: Cahuita (8 daily; 1hr 30min–2hr); Manzanillo (3 daily; 45min); Puerto Limón (4 daily; 1hr 30min); San José (4 daily; 4hr 30min); Sixaola (4 daily; 2hr).

San José to: Cahuita (4 daily; 4hr); Puerto Limón (12 daily; 2hr 30min–3hr); Puerto Viejo de Talamanca (4 daily; 4hr 30min); Sixaola (4 daily; 6hr).

Sixaola to: Cahuita (4 daily; 2hr); Puerto Limón (1 daily; 3hr); Puerto Viejo de Talamanca (4 daily; 2hr); San José (4 daily; 6hr).

FLIGHTS

Sansa and Travelair both fly the route below.

San José to: Tortuguero (1 daily; 35min).

Tortuguero to: San José (1 daily; 35min).

CHAPTER 30

THE CENTRAL PACIFIC AND SOUTHERN NICOYA

While Costa Rica's **Central Pacific** area is less of a geographical or cultural entity than other regions of the country, it does contain several of its most popular tourist spots, among them the number-one attraction, the **Reserva Biológica Bosque Nuboso Monteverde** (Monteverde Cloudforest Reserve), draped over the ridge of the Cordillera de Tilarán. Along with the nearby **Reserva Santa Elena**, Monteverde protects some of the last remaining pristine cloudforest in the Americas.

The Central Pacific and Southern Nicoya are also home to some of the best-known **beaches** in the country, including some which are easily accessible from San José. Each offers a distinctly different experience. A former tiny fishing village near the southwest tip of the Nicoya Peninsula, **Montezuma** is surrounded by a series of lovely coves, perfect for sunbathing and hanging out. On the mainland coast, the rough water and huge waves at **Jacó** make it one of the best places to surf in the country. Further south, **Parque Nacional Manuel Antonio** has several extraordinary beaches, with white sands and azure waters.

With the exception of the cool cloudforest of Monteverde, the **vegetation** is Pacific lowland. The **climate** is tropical, hot and rather drier than in the south – about 33°C is a dry-season average. It's not that much cooler in the wet months, when Quepos and Manuel Antonio, in particular, often receive torrential afternoon rains.

Of the two **routes from the capital** to Puntarenas and points south, the main one is the Interamericana, which climbs over the Cordillera Central before dropping precipitously to the Pacific lowlands, levelling out at the town of Esparza, a few kilometres beyond which is the turn-off for Puntarenas. Buses to Jacó and Manuel Antonio take the slightly shorter old road via Atenas and Orotina. Visiting Monteverde is always a bit of an expedition. Although it is just 170km from San José, the roads along the final 35km or so are unpaved and in poor condition. In the dry season you can do it with a regular car, but in the wet you need 4WD.

Most people cross over to the southern **Nicoya Peninsula** from Puntarenas on the ferries to Naranjo or Paquera. From Paquera there's public transport down to Tambor and Montezuma. From Naranjo you can continue south by car or north to Carmona and then up to Nicoya and Santa Cruz, but you'll need 4WD for either route.

For an explanation of **accommodation price codes**, see p.556.

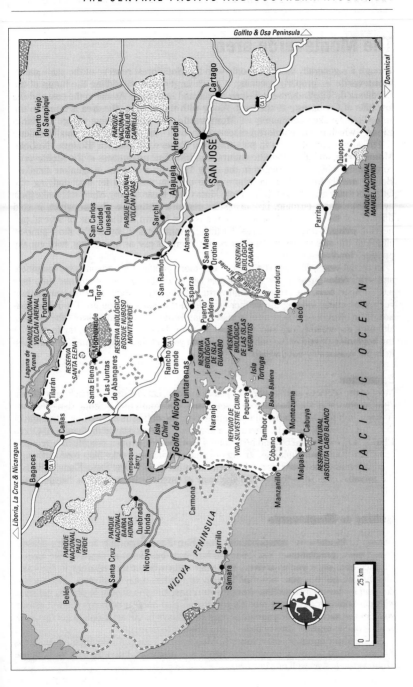

The Monteverde area

Though it's generally associated only with the cloudforest reserve of the same name, **Monteverde** is, properly speaking, a much larger area, straddling the hump of the Cordillera de Tilarán between Volcán Arenal and Laguna de Arenal to the east and the low hills of Guanacaste to the west. Along with the reserve, the area is home to the spread-out Quaker community of **Monteverde**, the neighbouring village of **Santa Elena** – which has a cloudforest reserve of its own – and several other small hamlets.

The area's appeal stems in part from the **Reserva Biológica Bosque Nuboso Monteverde**, and also from the cultural and historical uniqueness of the Monteverde community, which was created in the early 1950s by a number of **Quaker** families. Hailing mostly from Alabama, where some of them faced jail for draft-dodging, the Quakers today are completely integrated into Costa Rican society. Many still make their living from dairy farming, producing the region's distinctive **cheese** which is sold throughout the country. Abroad, the area is best known as the home of several pioneering **private nature reserves**. Of these, Monteverde is by far the most famous, although the less-touristed **Reserva Santa Elena** is just as interesting, with equally pristine cloudforest cover.

In recent years, Monteverde has become more popular than anyone ever imagined, and strict **rules** govern how many people can enter the reserve at any one time (see p.627). Apart from the crowds, Monteverde is quite **expensive**, although you can find very good cheap lodging the further away from the entrance you go. The **rainy season** (May–Nov) is the best time to visit Monteverde if you want to avoid the crowds, although the weather can stay rainy and grey for days on end. Ideally, try to come at the beginning or end of the rainy season, when you get the double benefit of fewer visitors but reasonably good weather.

Orientation

Most of the services and the cheaper places to sleep, eat and drink are in **Santa Elena**, 7km southwest of the Monteverde reserve and 5km south of the Santa Elena reserve. A major hub for the local farming communities, the village is centred on a triangle of three (often muddy) streets. There are a few more places to stay at the hamlet of **Cerro Plano**, 1km east, while beyond here comes **Monteverde** proper, essentially a group of dairy farms and smallholdings strung out along a winding, rocky 5km road. Although there are many hotels on this road, it's a much quieter place than Santa Elena, with only the metallic calls of bellbirds and the buzz of motorcycles and Jeeps breaking the silence.

Getting to Monteverde

Getting to Monteverde independently from **San José**, especially in the dry season, entails some pre-planning. You'll need to buy your bus ticket as much as five days in advance and, once you've arrived, buy your return ticket immediately. In the rainy months you can buy your ticket on the day or (better) a day in advance. There's less demand for bus seats travelling from **Puntarenas**, and you should be able to get away with not booking. In the dry months you should also **book a room**; in the wet season you can just turn up. Give yourself at least three days in the area; one to get up there, at least one to explore (two is better), and another to descend.

All the major operators offer **tours** to Monteverde from San José; their advantage is a better rate on the more comfortable hotels and transport, but otherwise you can see Monteverde just as well on your own.

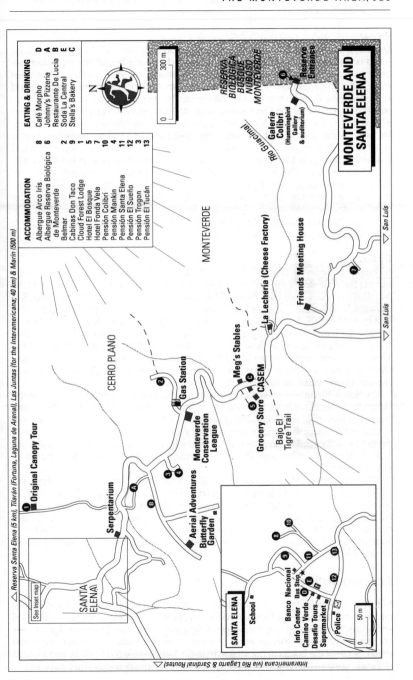

MONTEVERDE AND
SANTA ELENA

ACCOMMODATION

Albergue Arco Iris	8
Albergue Reserva Biológica	6
de Monteverde	
Belmar	2
Cabinas Don Taco	9
Cloud Forest Lodge	1
Hotel El Bosque	5
Hotel Fonda Vela	7
Pensión Colibrí	10
Pensión Mankin	4
Pensión Santa Elena	11
Pensión El Sueño	12
Pensión Trogon	3
Pensión El Tucán	13

EATING & DRINKING

Café Morpho	D
Johnny's Pizzeria	A
Restaurante De Lucia	B
Soda La Central	E
Stella's Bakery	C

RESERVA
BIOLÓGICA
BOSQUE
NUBOSO
MONTEVERDE

Reserve
Entrance

0   300 m

Galería Colibrí
(Hummingbird
Gallery
& auditorium)

Río Guacimal

CERRO PLANO

Original Canopy Tour

Serpentarium

Monteverde
Conservation
League

Aerial Adventures
Butterfly
Garden

Gas Station

Meg's Stables

Grocery Store   CASEM

Bajo El
Tigre Trail

MONTEVERDE

La Lechería (Cheese Factory)

Friends Meeting House

SANTA ELENA

SANTA ELENA

See Inset map

School

Banco Nacional
Info Center
Camino Verde   Bus Stop
Desafio Tours
Supermarket

Police

0   50 m

Interamericana (via Río Lagarto & Sardinal Routes)

▽ San Luis   ▽ San Luis

△ Reserva Santa Elena (5km), Tilarán (Fortuna, Laguna de Arenal), Las Juntas (for the Interamericana; 40 km) & Marin (500 m)

By car

Driving from San José to Monteverde takes about four hours via the Interamericana – two hours to the turn-off (there's a choice of three; see below), then another two hours to make the final mountainous ascent. One route, sometimes called the Sardinal route, takes the Interamericana north from Puntarenas towards Liberia, branching off at the **Rancho Grande** turning to Monteverde. Buses go a shorter route, continuing past Rancho Grande to the **Río Lagarto** turn-off – just before Río Lagarto itself – which is signed to Santa Elena and Monteverde. The least well-known route, which local *taxistas* swear is the best, is via **Las Juntas de Abangares**, a small town reached from a small road, labelled "145" on some maps, off the Interamericana. Once you've reached Las Juntas, drive past the main square, turn left and continue over a bridge; turn right, and follow the signs. The first 7km of this 37-kilometre road, via Candelaría, are paved, but have some spectacular hairpin bends – drive slowly. You can also reach Monteverde from **Tilarán**, near Laguna de Arenal. The road (40km) is often very rough, but provides spectacular views over the Laguna de Arenal and Volcán Arenal (see p.669).

Whichever route you take, you'll need **4WD** in the rainy season, when some agencies refuse to rent regular cars for the trip.

By bus

All **buses** arrive first in Santa Elena. Some then continue along the road to Monteverde, making their last stop at the Lechería (cheese factory). Most people arrive on one of the two direct services from **San José**'s Tilarán terminal (3hr 30min minimum, though it can often be more like 5hr, especially in the rainy season). Be particularly vigilant when waiting to board the bus – this service is a magnet for opportunistic thieves. When on the bus, keep everything with you if possible and valuables on your person. Note that taking the afternoon service from San José gets you to Monteverde after dark. From **Tilarán**, you can catch the 1pm bus (3hr), but in the rainy season, this may stop a few kilometres short of Santa Elena, leaving you with no option but to walk the remainder of the way. From **Puntarenas**, a daily bus leaves for Santa Elena at 2.15pm (3hr).

The **Santa Elena bus stop** is next to the church, at the top of the "triangle" near the Banco Nacional. From here, all amenities and many pensiones are no more than 100m away. The owners of pensiones and cabinas will come to the bus and try to entice you to their establishment; most are fine, so take your pick. If you are booked into one of the hotels on the road to the reserve, stay on the bus and ask the driver to drop you off, or, if you arrive on the bus from Puntarenas, arrange with your hotel to have a taxi meet you (US$5–6).

Moving on from Monteverde, buses to San José leave Santa Elena at 6.30am and 2.30pm daily. There's sometimes an extra service leaving at 2pm from Friday to Sunday; check the office beside the bus stop. For **Tilarán**, one bus leaves daily at 7am; for **Puntarenas**, the daily service departs at 6am. Two buses also leave daily at 5am and 6am for the two-hour journey to **Las Juntas**, from where you can get to Liberia and points north in Guanacaste. Check in the office beside the bus stop in Santa Elena; tickets are sold here too.

Accommodation

With the exception of a couple of pensiones on the road to Monteverde, the cheapest places to stay are in **Santa Elena**. All accommodation here is basic, but you'll get a bed and heated water at least, and almost certainly a warm welcome. Many small pensiones are run by locals and offer an array of services, from cooking to laundry and horse rental. Some of the hotels in the village triangle, like *Pensión Santa Elena* and *Pensión el Tucán*, are convivial places to meet up and swap information with other travellers.

Hotels in and around the **Monteverde** community tend to be pricey, and are mainly used by tour groups and older, better-heeled tourists. While you'll certainly be comfortable in these places – large rooms, running hot water, orthopedic mattresses, even saunas and Jacuzzis, are the norm – some travellers find the atmosphere a bit dour. You get little sense of a community, partly because Monteverde is not an obvious settlement, and many of the houses are set back in pasture, hidden from the main road.

Santa Elena

Albergue Ecológico Arco Iris, up a side street just behind the *Pensión Santa Elena* (☎645-5067, fax 645-5022, *arcoiris@racsa.co.cr*). The best-value mid-range accommodation in the area, with well-decorated and spacious cabins in quiet landscaped gardens in a central location; they also have cheaper rooms with bunkbeds (③) plus a family cabin (⑥). The delicious breakfast ($5) with German bread, granola, fresh fruit and eggs and toast is unequalled. ⑤.

Cabinas Don Taco, 300m north of the Banco Nacional (☎645-6023). Pleasantly furnished individual cabinas with private bath; some have good views over the area and, on a clear day, the Golfo de Nicoya. Breakfast included. ①–②.

Cloud Forest Lodge, 500m northeast of Santa Elena (☎256-0096 or 645-5058, fax 645-5168). Set in 70 acres of primary and secondary forest high above Santa Elena, on a steep road, this secluded hotel is now the classiest in the area. The eighteen well-appointed wood-panelled rooms all come with cable TV, a large private bathroom, and terraces with dizzying views over the Golfo de Nicoya. The hotel has its own 5km system of trails, plus a bar, restaurant, horse-riding tours and a 25 percent discount off the Original Canopy Tour, which is located here. It's best if you have your own transport, since it's a bit of a walk to Santa Elena or Monteverde. ⑥.

Pensión Colibrí (☎645-5682). Simple, family-run accommodation in small rooms with shared bath and heated water. Cooked breakfasts (not included in room rate) and lunchtime *casados* are available, and the owners also rent out horses. ①.

Pensión El Sueño, 25m east of the *correo* (☎645-5021). Fourteen cosy rustic wooden rooms right in the heart of Santa Elena; the cheaper ones, in the main building, have shared bath, while for around US$10 more there are nicer en-suite rooms out the back. There's also a small lounge with Sarchí leather rocking chairs for stargazing, a kitchen for guests' use and friendly *dueños* who cook a good breakfast (US$3) on request. Good low-season discounts. ②–③.

Pensión El Tucán, 100m south of the Banco Nacional (☎645-5017, fax 645-5462). The best rock-bottom budget rooms in town, with shared bath and heated water. Most rooms are located above the (good) restaurant of the same name: those with private bath cost a few dollars more, while the new cabins set away from the main builiding in quiet grounds come with private bath and balcony. ①–②.

Pensión Santa Elena, 50m south of the Banco Nacional (☎645-5051, fax 645-6060, *www .monteverdeinfo.com*). HI-affiliated place (members get ten-percent discount) right in the centre of things, with bargain rooms with shared bath for just US$5, though they're small, basic and sometimes dark, and the owner has been known to "forget" reservations. It's also a great place to meet other travellers, plus there's a kitchen, a pleasant candlelit dining area, email, international phone and fax, laundry service, and the owners can fix up horse-riding tours. ①–②.

Monteverde and around

Albergue Reserva Biológica de Monteverde, at the entrance to the Monteverde reserve (contact the Monteverde Conservation League on ☎645-5122, fax 645-5034). Accommodation right in the reserve, though it's often packed with researchers and students – tourists have second priority. Reservations are essential, and you'll need to pay half your room cost 45 days in advance. US$10 per person; US$23 with meals.

Belmar, Cerro Plano (☎645-5201, fax 645-5135, *belmar@racsa.co.cr*). The oldest of the area's many Swiss-style hotels, the perennially popular *Belmar* has 34 rooms, some of them enormous – those at the front benefit from astounding views out over the Golfo de Nicoya. Reception is well meaning but understaffed. ④–⑤.

Hotel El Bosque, in Monteverde, about 3km from the reserve entrance (☎645-5221, *elbosque@racsa.co.cr*). Twenty-eight rooms, rather pre-fab looking but affordably priced, with private bath, hot water and a good range of sizes from singles to triples. Some have views over the hills out towards the Golfo de Nicoya. ④.

Hotel Fonda Vela, Monteverde (☎645-5125, fax 645-5119, *fondavel@racsa.co.cr*). Set in quiet grounds fairly close to the reserve, the *Fonda Vela* is probably the best hotel in the area, expertly managed, with attentive staff, beautiful touches and a range of good-value rooms – plus a highly recommended restaurant. New rooms ("suites") aim for deluxe, with huge bathrooms and beautiful fixtures and furniture. Older rooms are more rustic but have greater charm, with wood-panelled walls and huge windows – most giving astonishing views, especially at sunset. The owner's father is an artist and classical musician, and sometimes gives concerts in the hotel. ⑤–⑥.

Pensión Manakín, Cerro Plano (☎645-5080). Friendly family pensión with some of the best budget rooms in the area, including basic dorm accommodation (US$10–15 per person), a couple of singles and a lovely double room which opens out onto the forest behind the house. There's a communal kitchen, and breakfast is included. ④.

Pensión Trogon, in Cerro Plano, next to *Pensión Manakín* (☎ & fax 645-5130). Good-value budget pensión with lots of animals, including monkeys, around. Cheaper rooms have shared bathroom; those with private bath cost an extra US$10. There's a collective cooking area, and breakfast (US$3) and dinner (US$4) are also available. Freddy Mejías, the friendly and energetic owner, offers a wide range of extra services including local transport and a laundry service. You can also camp in the grounds for US$3. ②–③.

The communities

In recent years **SANTA ELENA** has benefited – economically, anyway – from the influx of visitors to both the Monteverde reserve and, increasingly, to the Santa Elena reserve, 5km northeast. The **Info Center Camino Verde** in the centre of the village (☎645-5916, fax 645-6305) sells tickets to the Santa Elena reserve, the Sky Walk, Sky Trek, and the Monteverde Canopy Tour; they can also arrange guided tours to the Monteverde reserve and guides for the Sky Walk. Friendly and efficient **Desafío Tours** next door offer a similar range of services, plus **Internet access** (US$5/hr); they can also hook you up with whitewater rafting in the Fortuna area (see p.669) and run a speedy and enjoyable transfer from Monteverde to Fortuna and vice versa using horses, boat-taxi, and Jeep-taxi, which gets you to Fortuna in around 4–5 hours and costs about US$25. For a one-page handout with a map of the area and a helpful rundown of bus times and other transport details, head to the *Pensión Santa Elena*, 50m south of the Banco Nacional.

Gringos hang out at *Chunches* (Mon–Sat 8am–6pm; ☎645-5147), opposite the *Pensión Santa Elena*, which has a laundry, café serving espresso, US newspapers, and a useful noticeboard with details of tours, rooms and just about everything else. Its secondhand bookstore is especially good. Though it's better by far to bring plenty of colones, the Banco Nacional (Mon–Fri 8am–3pm) can change **travellers' cheques**, a service also offered to guests by many of the upscale Monteverde hotels.

MONTEVERDE proper is a seemingly timeless place, where milk cans are left out at the end of small dairy-farm driveways to be collected, modest houses sit perched above splendid forested views, and farmers trudge along the muddy roads in sturdy rubber boots. The focal points of the community are the **Lechería** (cheese factory), the **Friends Meeting House** and school, and the cluster of services around **CASEM**, the women's arts and crafts collective.

Reserva Biológica Bosque Nuboso Monteverde

The **RESERVA BIOLÓGICA BOSQUE NUBOSO MONTEVERDE** (Monteverde Cloudforest Reserve; daily 7am–4pm; US$10; *www.monteverdeinfo.com/monteverde _conservation_league*) is a large (105 square kilometres) private reserve which protects the last sizeable pockets of primary cloudforest in Mesoamerica. Administered by the Centro Científico Tropical (Tropical Science Centre) based in San José, it's hugely popular with foreigners and Ticos alike, who flock here in droves – especially during Easter week and school holidays – to walk the trails.

Few people fail to be impressed by the reserve's sheer diversity of **terrain**, from semi-dwarf stunted forest on the more wind-exposed areas to thick, bearded cloudforest vegetation, and some truly moving **views** of uninterrupted, dense green. The Monteverde reserve supports six different **life zones**, or eco-communities, hosting an estimated 2500 species of plants, more than 100 species of mammals, some 490 species of butterflies, including the rare blue morpho, and over 400 species of birds, among them the resplendent **quetzal** (best seen Jan–May). The cloudforest cover, however – dense, low-lit and heavy – makes it difficult to see animals.

Plant-spotting, however, is never unrewarding, especially if you take a **guided walk**, which will help you identify thick mosses, epiphytes, bromeliads, primitive ferns, leaf-cutter ants, poison dart frogs and other small fauna and flora. Serious rainforest walkers should plan on spending at least a day in the reserve; many people spend two or three days quite happily here.

Temperatures are cool: 15° or 16°C is not uncommon. Be sure to carry an umbrella and light rain gear. You should also bring binoculars, fast-speed film and insect repellent. It's just about possible to get away without **rubber boots** in the dry season, but you will most definitely need them in the wet. The reserve office and some hotels rent them out.

Practicalities

Except on Sundays, a **bus** leaves Santa Elena twice daily for Monteverde (Mon–Sat 6.15am & 1pm; US$0.80); alternatively, a **taxi** will set you back US$6 per carload – try to get a group together to share. If you decide **to walk**, be aware that the road is uncomfortably dusty in the dry season, and that there's a surprising amount of traffic, though nearer the reserve it becomes quieter and gives good views over the area. At the entrance, the **reserve office** is very well geared up to tourists, with a **visitor centre** where you can pick up maps and buy useful interpretive booklets for the trails. It also has a good souvenir shop and a small soda, which dishes out coffee, cold drinks and snacks, plus vegetarian *casados* at lunchtime. Also at the entrance, the **Galería Colibrí**, or Hummingbird Gallery (Mon–Sat 9.30am–4.30pm, Sun 10am–2pm) named after the birds that buzz in and out to feed at the sugared water fountains, sells nature slides, cards, jewellery and the like, as well as hosting slide shows on cloudforest topics.

In an attempt to limit human impact on the reserve, a number of **rules** govern entrance to Monteverde. The reserve imposes **a quota**, with a maximum of 120 people allowed in the reserve at any given time, but serious birders, wildlife spotters and those who would prefer to walk the trails in quiet, should avoid the **peak hours** of 8am till 10am, when the tour groups pour in. An alternative is to book a ticket a **day in advance** – your hotel can reserve you a place for the following day – and get here by 5.30am (not earlier – it's still too dark), when, even though the visitor centre is closed, you are able to go on the trails. Bookings cannot be made any more than 24 hours in advance.

For overnight and long-distance hikers, there are three simple **shelter facilities** along the trails – the closest is upwards of four hours' hike from the reserve entrance – which cost US$4 per person per night, plus the entrance fee for each day you're in the reserve (for example, if you stay in the reserve for one night, you'll pay two days' entrance fees plus accommodation, a total of US$24).

Tours and talks

Whatever sort of walk you go on in Monteverde – or anywhere else in the country, for that matter – it's worth realizing that you are more likely to be looking at plants, smaller animals and insects rather than staring into the eyes of pumas or tapirs. Bearing this in mind, the reserve itself runs excellent **guided walks**. Walks start at 8am sharp (or at 7.30am and 8pm if demand is high), last three to four hours and cost US$15 (plus the US$10 entrance fee). Ask in your hotel or call the reserve office a day in advance on ☎645-5112 or 645-5122 to secure a place, since there's a maximum of just nine people –

and make sure to arrive on time, too, or they'll set off without you. It might seem like a pricey tour, but the guides are informative and the experience supremely educational.

Another highly recommended way to experience another side of the rainforest – though not for those who are put off by the dark or by creepy crawlies – is the **night walk** (US$13), which leaves at 7.30pm each evening – you don't have to book for this tour, but turn up at the reserve office by 7.15pm to buy a ticket. Ask too, about the occasional **orchid walks**, available only at certain times of the year. All walks end with a **slide show**, during which you'll see some of the creatures you encountered in the reserve and many you did not, including the Monteverde golden toad.

If you can't or don't want to go on the official tours, there are a number of excellent local **guides** who can show you the reserve and the entire Monteverde area. Check at the visitor centre.

Reserva Santa Elena

Though it's less touristed than the Monteverde reserve, the **RESERVA SANTA ELENA** (daily 7am–4pm; US$7; *www.monteverdeinfo.com/reserve.htm*), 6km northeast of the village of Santa Elena, offers just as illuminating an experience of the cloudforest. Higher than the Monteverde reserve – poised at an elevation of 1650m – its three-square-kilometre area consists of mainly primary cover. Trails are steeper and more challenging, and there's a slightly higher chance of seeing quetzals in season. Established in 1992, it strives to be self-funding, assisted by donations and revenue from entrance fees, and gives a percentage of its profits to local schools. For maintenance and building projects it depends greatly on volunteers, usually foreign students.

Getting to the Santa Elena reserve from the village entails an arduous 5km walk over a boulder-strewn road, much of it uphill. **Jeep-taxis** (US$6) can be arranged by your hotel or can be picked up on Santa Elena's main street; the reserve can call a taxi to come and pick you up to take you back into town. More economically, a **collective taxi** (US$2) leaves for the reserve from in front of the Banco Nacional daily at 6.45am, 11am and 3pm, returning at 10.30am, noon and 3.30pm; make reservations a day in advance at the Info Center Camino Verde.

There's a **visitor centre** at the entrance, with washrooms and an information booth where staff hand out maps of the twelve-kilometre network of trails. Highly recommended **guided tours** can be arranged for between one and four hours (about US$20, including entrance fee); the reserve also rents out boots (US$6.50) and issues a succinct six-page leaflet discussing rainforests, cloudforests, epiphytes, seed-dispersal patterns and some of the mammals you might see in the reserve. **Guided nature walks** (US$15) are offered at 7.30am and 11.30am daily; **night tours** (US$15, inclusive of entrance fee) leave at 7pm daily. A line of **hummingbird** feeders have been strung along the entrance path, where you can watch these tiny, many-coloured birds zooming in and out of nectar-dishes.

Other Monteverde attractions

A number of attractions have sprung up around Monteverde in recent years, some of which have come to rival the reserves themselves in popularity. The **Original Monteverde Canopy Tour** (☎645-5243 or 257-5149, *www.canopytour.co.cr*, US$45), pioneered here by locals and now copied all over the country, is based at the *Cloud Forest Lodge* (see p.625) near Santa Elena. You can whizz from platform to platform via pulleys strung on horizontal traverse cables. It's not a particularly educational experience, nor do you normally see much plant, animal or bird life – you're moving too fast – but it's a nice little thrill. You have to reserve in advance for the tour, something a number of businesses in Santa Elena will do for you; the Info Center Camino Verde in Santa Elena also lays on free transportation, leaving daily at 7.15am, 10.15am and 2.15pm.

Three other places in the area offer canopy tours: the **Monteverde Canopy Tour** office on the road to the Reserva Santa Elena (☎645-5929, fax 645-5822, *www .canopytours.com*; US$35) is a well-equipped outfit whose tour comprises a 1600-metre ride through the canopy via fourteen platforms. They'll pick you up from your hotel; make reservations a day in advance, either directly with the office, through your hotel, or with the Info Center Camino Verde, who also lay on free transport if you book through them, leaving at 8am, 10.30am, 12.30pm and 2pm.

The **Sky Trek** (☎642-5238), located at the Sky Walk office on the road to the Santa Elena reserve, charges the same price (US$35) as the Monteverde Canopy Tour and has an extensive network of trails, platforms, suspension bridges and "ziplines" – the ropes you slide along from platform to platform. Tours leave at 7.30am, 9.30am, 11.30am, 1.30pm and 2pm; reserve at least a day in advance.

A more sedate ride through the forest is offered by **Aerial Adventures** (daily 6am–6pm; US$10; ☎645-5960), on the road to the Finca Ecológica in Cerro Plano. Rather like a rainforest ski-lift, the ninety-minute trip consists of a rather slow journey above the rainforest in hanging chairs. A different bird's-eye view of the forest can be had from the unique **Sky Walk** (daily 7am–4pm; US$12; *www.skywalk.co.cr*), an impressive series of bridges and paths built by Fernando Valverde, a biologist from Monteverde and world authority on the construction of rainforest suspension bridges. Located 3.5km along the road towards the Santa Elena reserve, the Sky Walk consists of a network of suspension-style footbridges, stretching from the ground to canopy level between acres of virgin rainforest. Bridges provide some really spectacular views – but take waterproofs.

Up the hill from Santa Elena on the way to Monteverde, the **Serpentario** (daily 9am–4pm) has a range of unnerving vipers in residence. The creatures are less menacing at the **Butterfly Garden**, in Cerro Plano (daily 9.30am–4pm; US$5), which, unlike most such places in Costa Rica, is geared to research rather than the export of pupae. For a smaller-scale rainforest walking experience, the **Reserva Sendero Tranquilo**, a private reserve in the grounds of a local farm behind the cheese factory in Monteverde, offers informative guided tours (book on ☎645-5010; around US$13 per person) through primary- and secondary-growth forest. The only part of the **Bosque Eterno de los Niños** (Children's Eternal Rainforest; part of the Reserva Santa Elena) that you are currently permitted to visit is the **Bajo El Tigre trail** (daily from 8am, last entrance at 4.30pm, though you can stay in the reserve until dusk; US$5), a short, unchallenging trek at lower elevations than in the cloudforest reserves, and with great views out to the Golfo de Nicoya – sunsets from here can be spectacular. The **Finca Ecológica** (daily 7am–5pm; US$6), south of Santa Elena, is, as the name suggests, an ecological farm where banana and coffee are grown. Animals in the area frequently come to snack at feeders the farm has set up; the most frequently sighted creatures are agoutis and coatis, as well as a resident sloth. A system of trails leads to a quiet waterfall, and you can also take a guided night walk here (US$13), leaving daily at 5.30pm and 7.30pm.

La Lechería (Cheese Factory; Mon–Sat 7.30am–noon & 1–4.30pm, Sun 7.30am–12.30pm) sells various types of Monteverde cheese and *cajeta*, a butterscotch fudge, as well as delicious ice cream. Guided tours (book on ☎645-2850; US$8) give you a behind-the-scenes glimpse into the world of cheese.

Other good options for a rainy afternoon are the **Orchid Gardens** in Cerro Plano (daily 9am–5pm; US$5), run by orchid enthusiast Gabriel Barboza, with over 400 different species of orchids on show, including the world's smallest. A **slide show** of Patricia and Michael Fogden's rainforest photos takes place year-round at the Monteverde reserve auditorium (daily 4.30pm; US$3).

You can't **ride horses** on the trails in the Monteverde or Santa Elena reserves, but a number of local outfitters hire them for trips through the surrounding countryside – as always in Costa Rica, the state of the horses varies wildly. In Santa Elena ask at the *Pensión Santa Elena* for Sabine Hein (☎645-5051, *www.horseback-riding-tour.com*), who has several healthy, well-cared-for horses and who knows the stunning countryside around Santa Elena well – you can stop at several look-out points with panoramic views out to the Pacific and the Nicoya Peninsula. On the road to Monteverde, Meg's Stables (☎645-5052), next to Stella's Bakery, hires out horses for around US$10/hr.

Eating, drinking and nightlife

In **Santa Elena**, most people eat in their **pensions**. The restaurant at the *Pensión el Tucán* (closed Sun), open to non-guests, serves good cheap food, especially *casados*, and is a good bet for breakfast. Doña Laura has a popular kiosk in front of the church serving *casados* – climb up on the wooden stools and chat with the regulars. For espresso, go to *Chunches*. *Teen's Bakery* has pastries and other snacks to take away. Cuisine in many of the top-end **Monteverde** hotels is very good indeed, and most of them open their restaurants to the public. Menus are usually fixed, and meals are served at set times. Drop round in person to book for dinner and see what's on the menu. Being a Quaker community, there is not much **drinking** to be done in the Monteverde area, even in gringo-filled Santa Elena. Most restaurants do have alcohol on the menu, but you'll notice a definite whiff of temperance in the air.

The **Monteverde Music Festival** (Jan–March) stages a blend of classical, jazz and modern music, from chamber orchestras to big bands. There are performances daily at 5pm, and a shuttle bus runs from Santa Elena to the venues – ask at your hotel.

Café Morpho, in the centre of Santa Elena, across from the church. The best bet in Santa Elena itself, offering healthy and well-prepared – if not particularly cheap – food, with a pleasant candlelit ambience in the evening.

Fonda Vela, in the *Hotel Fonda Vela*, Monteverde. Two restaurants at the hotel of the same name – a fairly formal and intimate fireside restaurant and a larger, slightly less staid one – with lovely views out over the property and a varied (though fairly expensive) menu including good, generous breakfasts and succulent dinner specialities – try the chicken in white wine and almonds (US$11).

Johnny's Pizzeria, Cerro Plano. One of the most popular restaurants in the area, both among tourists and locals, and it's not hard to see why, with superior cocktails, pizza (US$5) cooked in an open wood oven and superb service in a candlelit colonial décor. There's pasta, meat and fish on the menu too, but everybody seems to come for the pizza. During the day you can sometimes see hummingbirds in the quiet garden.

Pensión El Tucán, 100m south of the Banco Nacional. Open to non-guests, the restaurant at the *Pensión El Tucán* serves very tasty and cheap local food, especially *casados*. They're probably the best bet for breakfast in the village, with good gringo fare – the banana pancakes are recommended. Closed lunchtime and the whole of Sunday.

Restaurante de Lucia, between Santa Elena and Cerro Plano, 150m from the *Hotel Heliconia*. Excellent service, a not-bad wine selection and a varied menu, including perfect steak, chicken and pork done just as you like it.

Soda La Central, in the centre of Santa Elena. New soda, strategically placed in front of the bus stop to San José, Puntarenas and other points, with above-average *casados* (US$3) and tasty hamburgers with fries (US$2).

Stella's Bakery, opposite CASEM. Delicious chocolate-chip cookies, strudel, brownies and coffee in a pleasant café-like atmosphere, although the owner is surly. Daily 6.30am–4.30pm.

Around Monteverde: Tilarán

TILARÁN, 40km northeast of Monteverde, is a useful stop-off between Guanacaste to the west and the Zona Norte to the east. It's also about the best place in the country for **windsurfing** – the Tilawa Viento Surf & High Wind centre (☎695-5050, fax 695-5766) can arrange all kinds of rentals and advise on conditions on the Laguna de Arenal. There are a few **cabinas** in Tilarán: try *Cabinas El Sueno* (☎695-5347; ②), 150m from the northwest corner of the central Parque, with good rooms with private bath and a nice patio, or *Hotel Naralit* (☎695-5555; ②), for comfortable and spotless rooms. Tilarán has good **bus** connections with Cañas and the Interamericana, from where you can head on to Liberia and the Guanacaste beaches, or south to Puntarenas. The bus station is 100m north of the Parque Central.

Some 37km southwest of Santa Elena and 10km off the Interamericana, **LAS JUNTAS DE ABANGARES** was a small gold-mining centre in the late nineteenth and early twentieth centuries. Just off the road to Monteverde, 5km outside town on a rough (4WD only) little road is the **Ecomuseo Oro**, or "Gold-Mining 'Ecological' Museum" – one of the more bizarre uses of the "eco-" prefix in Costa Rica, since gold-mining is not known for respecting environmental integrity. Commemorating the activities of the Abangares Gold Fields Company, the small-scale exhibition features dusty photographs of the area's mini-gold boom, along with a ragbag collection of mining artefacts. The museum is meant to be open daily between 6am and 5pm, but is often closed; donations are gratefully accepted. Short trails pass through the pockets of tropical dryforest surrounding the building.

You can ask to be dropped off the bus from Santa Elena at the turn-off to the Ecomuseo, although it's a hot thirty-minute walk from here (follow the signs). If you're driving down the road from Monteverde, look for a fork on the left just before you hit the outskirts of Las Juntas, and the museum is signed from here. You'll need 4WD, or could drop your car in Las Juntas and hop in one of the 4WD **taxis** waiting at the rank around the corner from the church.

Puntarenas

Heat-stunned **PUNTARENAS**, 110km west of San José, has the look of raffish abandonment that haunts so many tropical port cities. What isn't rusting has long ago been bleached out to a generic pastel, and the town's cracked, potholed streets, shaded by mop-headed mango trees, are lined with old wooden buildings painted in faded tutti-frutti colours. Tourists come mainly to catch a lancha or ferry across to southern Nicoya – there's little to see or do in the town itself.

Arrival and information

Scores of **buses** arrive from San José every day. The bus stop is on the corner of C 2 and Paseo de los Turistas, near the old train tracks and the old dock that juts out into the gulf. **Local services** from Manuel Antonio and Quepos arrive just across the street from the San José bus stop, as do buses from Liberia and the daily service from Santa Elena, which currently arrives at about 9.30am.

The town centre is just a few blocks northwest of the San José bus stop. Here you'll find banks, the municipal market, and a slew of cheap hotels. The Banco de Costa Rica, Banco de San José and the Banco Nacional, virtually next to each other on the north shore near the docks area, offer **currency exchange**. If you get stuck, hotels like the *Gran Hotel Chorotega* can probably help you out, or you could try the more upscale ones like the *Tioga*, although these normally only change dollars for their own guests. Though it's easy enough to get around on foot, **taxis** scoot through the town, and can be flagged down. You can also wave down the **buses** that ply Avenida Central – the last stop is in front of the **Playa Naranjo ferry dock** at the western end of town.

Accommodation

The **cheap hotels** around the docks are useful if you want to catch an early lancha to Paquera. It's not a great area at night, however. More upmarket options – with the exception of the *Tioga* – congregate just east of the town centre, near the yacht club.

Wherever you stay, make sure your room has a fan that works.

Ayi-Con, 50m south of the mercado on C 2 (☎661-0164 or 661-1477). Venerable budget option near the Paquera lancha dock, catering mainly to Costa Ricans. Rooms are depressing cells with cold water, but it's cheap, clean, safe and central. ②.

Gran Hotel Chorotega, C 1, Av 3 (☎661-0998). Very basic downtown hotel near the docks. Rooms have a table fan, just about adequate for this climate, and private or shared bath. Well-run and very popular, it's often full of dockers and refinery workers at weekends. ①–②.

Tioga, Paseo de los Turistas, C 17/19 (☎661-0271, fax 661-0127). The nicest downtown hotel, with an elegant atmosphere, extra-friendly management and a/c rooms – those on the sea-facing side get the best views. There's also a soothing interior courtyard and a very pretty indoor pool. Rates include breakfast in the cafeteria-style restaurant. ④–⑤.

Eating, drinking and nightlife

Food, even fish, is pricey in Puntarenas: you'll be lucky to get *casados* or *platos del día* for less than US$6. As usual the **mercado** is a good place to pick up a cheap meal and a *refresco*, although you should avoid drinking anything made with the local water. The beachside sodas and kiosks near the **old dock** are more appealing places to linger for a quiet drink or a seafood lunch.

The best **restaurants** in town are on the Paseo de los Turistas. *Alohas* is most popular place in town for an evening drink, with an extensive and expensive menu, and nice breezy outdoor tables where you can sit looking out to sea. *Casa de los Mariscos*, between C 7 and C 9, has good seafood, though it's not cheap (US$6–10). *Restaurante La Terraza* at C 21/23 is the nicest place in town, with a reasonably priced menu concentrating on seafood, pizza and pasta. *Soda Macarena* at the bus stop has cheap and delicious food, including all kinds of fruit plates and toasted sandwiches; try their "Churchills" – similar to a crushed-ice *granizado*, but made with ice cream.

MOVING ON FROM PUNTARENAS

Puntarenas is a jumping-off point for the **southern Nicoya Peninsula**. The **Playa Naranjo and Paquera car ferries**, run by Coonatramar (☎661-1069, fax 661-2197), currently leave from the docks at the western end of town for Paquera (3 daily at 8.45am, 2pm & 8.15pm; 1hr 30min; US$10). Another company, Naviera Tambor, runs car ferries from here to Paquera at 5am, 12.30pm and 5pm. In summer (Dec–April), especially, arrive ninety minutes before sailing to be sure of a space. Bear in mind that, though it's possible to drive to Paquera from Naranjo in about an hour, the roads are not in great shape, and you'll need a 4WD. A much better option if you've got a car is to take one of the ferries to Paquera. Buses meet each Coontramar car ferry in Paquera (but not the Naviera Tambor ferry; best to get a taxi or try to hitch a lift) – it's a drive of about 45 minutes to Tambor and about an hour to Montezuma.

The **passenger ferry** (lancha) to Paquera currently leaves from behind the mercado, three times daily in the high season, twice in low season (1hr 30min; US$1.50). Schedules are posted outside the blue kiosk where you buy tickets. Buses for Tambor and Montezuma are timed to meet the Paquera lancha and leave once everyone is on board. Be quick to get off the ferry when it docks and you'll have a better chance of getting a seat on the bus. The only buses meeting the Playa Naranjo car ferry go north to Nicoya, a dusty and uncomfortable two-hour trip over horrible roads.

Buses leave at least every hour on the hour for **San José** from the San José bus terminal just off the Paseo de los Turistas on C 2. Services to **Liberia** (6 daily; 3hr) and **Santa Elena** (daily 2.15pm; 3hr 30min) depart from just across the road. For **Manuel Antonio**, take the Quepos service from the same place (3 daily; 2hr). This bus will also drop you off just 2km from **Jacó**.

The southern Nicoya Peninsula

The hour-long ferry trip across the Golfo de Nicoya from Puntarenas is soothing and slow-paced: the boat purrs through usually calm waters, passing island bird sanctuaries along the way. In the distance are the low brown hills of the Nicoya Peninsula, ringed by a rugged coastline and pockets of intense jungly green.

Much of the southern peninsula has been cleared for farming or cattle grazing or, in the case of **Tambor**, given over to tourism development. **Cóbano**, 6km inland from Montezuma, is the main town in the southwest of the peninsula, with a gas station, *correo*, *guardia rural* and a few bars. Most tourists pass right though on the way to **Montezuma**, one of the most popular beach hangouts in the country, reached by a reasonable dirt road lined with cattle pasture on both sides.

Montezuma and around

The popular beach resort of **MONTEZUMA** lies some 25km southwest of Paquera, near the southwestern tip of the Nicoya Peninsula. Some twenty-five years ago a handful of foreigners fell in love with the place and settled here. Then it was just a fishing village, largely cut off from the rest of the country; nowadays it's definitely been discovered: lights twinkle, and music pours out of restaurants and bars peopled by tatooed boys and batik-clad girls.

What brings everyone here is the astounding beauty of the setting. Montezuma and the coast south to Cabo Blanco feature some of the loveliest coastline in the country: white sand, dotted with jutting rocks and leaning palms, and backed by lush greenery, including rare Pacific lowland tropical forest.

Arrival and information

From where you get off the bus, at the bottom of the hill, you can see pretty much the entire centre of "town". *Chico's Bar* is straight ahead, as is the grocery store and the souvenir shop. To the right are two of the village's places for health-food and smoothies, the *Sano Banano* and the *Soda Monte Sol*.

Nearly everyone in town claims to be able to fix you up with tours. On the main drag, the helpful multilingual people at **Aventuras de Montezuma** (☎ & fax 642-0050, *avenzuma@racsa.co.cr*) have the largest range of tours, services and information in town, including trips to Isla Tortuga (US$40) and horse-riding on the beach and to local waterfalls (US$25). They also have an Internet café, international phone service, arrange car and motorbike rental, sell tickets for Travelair flights from Tambor to San José, and have information on current bus, ferry and flight times to and from Montezuma.

In the centre of the village, the **Montezuma Expeditions** kiosk rents out bicycles and motorbikes, and offers full-day trips to Isla Tortuga (US$40; including breakfast and time for snorkelling); diving trips (US$80, including equipment rental); four-hour horse-rides to waterfalls (US$25); and boat transfers to Jacó – though this can be a rough ride. They also arrange transfers to Cabo Blanco reserve and act as the local Sansa agent for flights to Tambor. The *Sano Banano*, adjacent to Aventuras de Montezuma, has an Internet café above its restaurant with satellite connection for about US$3 for thirty minutes.

Chico's shop, next to the bar and grocery store of the same name, sells sunscreen, film, clothing and telephone cards, which you can use in the **telephones** outside (if the lines are working). There's a **laundry** next to the *Sano Banano*, while for nice **souvenirs**, head to El Jardín gift shop (in the hotel of the same name). For **newspapers** and a lending library, try Librería Topsy, about 20m before the entrance to the beach. Some businesses in town close down between noon or 1pm and 4pm. Almost everyone

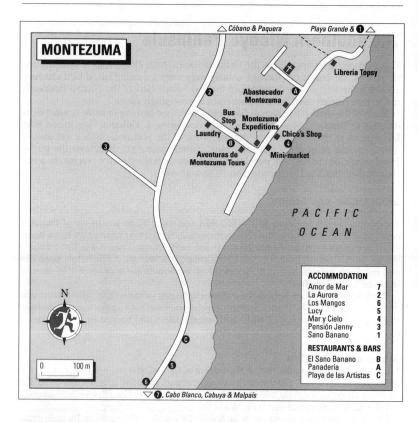

△ Cóbano & Paquera   Playa Grande & ❶ △

MONTEZUMA

Librería Topsy

Abastecedor
Montezuma   Ⓐ

❷

Bus
Stop   Montezuma
             Expeditions
Laundry   Chico's Shop
          Ⓑ   ❹
Aventuras de   Mini-market
Montezuma Tours

❸

PACIFIC

OCEAN

Ⓒ

Ⓢ

Ⓖ

N

0   100 m

▽ ❼, Cabo Blanco, Cabuya & Malpaís

ACCOMMODATION
Amor de Mar   7
La Aurora   2
Los Mangos   6
Lucy   5
Mar y Cielo   4
Pensión Jenny   3
Sano Banano   1

RESTAURANTS & BARS
El Sano Banano   B
Panadería   A
Playa de las Artistas C

seems to change dollars, or will accept **travellers' cheques** (but will give you a rate slightly below that of the banks). Still, it's best to bring some colones – you'll certainly need them for the bus and the ferry or lancha.

Accommodation

There's a good range of places to stay in Montezuma. **Prices** are moderate, as the village still caters to a young, studenty crowd who can't afford the rates of, say, Manuel Antonio, and even prices in some of the more upscale hotels drop in low season by about US$10–15. **Reservations** are useful in the dry season, especially at weekends, and are essential over Christmas and Easter. Most times, though, if you arrive on a late bus without a reservation, there is bound to be somewhere to stay, even if it's not your first choice.

Staying in the **village** is convenient, but can be noisy, due to the shenanigans at *Chico's Bar* and the odd car pulling in and out of the village. Elsewhere it's wonderfully peaceful, with choices out on the **beach**, on the road that heads southwest to the Reserva Absoluta Cabo Blanco, and on the sides of the steep hill about 1km above the village.

Camping is, according to various sources, either grudgingly permitted or vigorously frowned upon, so ask around – there have been problems with beach campers killing palm trees by building fires too close to their trunks, while the lack of sanitary facilities also raises hygiene questions. You would be better advised to stay at one of the organized camping sites between Montezuma and Cabuya, on the road to the Reserva Absoluta Cabo Blanco, where there are toilets, showers and barbecues.

Amor de Mar, 600m southwest of the village on the beach (☎ & fax 642-0262, *shoebox@racsa.co.cr*). Upmarket (for Montezuma) seafront hotel, well-managed by its German owners, set in pretty landscaped gardens on a rocky promontory, with hammocks swinging between giant mango trees. There's a good selection of rooms, with and without bathroom – those upstairs and facing the sea are best – and most come with veranda and ocean views. Good low-season discounts, and there's a small restaurant downstairs serving healthy breakfasts. ④–⑤.

La Aurora (☎642-0051, *aurorapacific@hotmail.com*). Pleasant, friendly and environmentally conscious pensión, with 16 varied rooms – the older budget rooms are good value, especially in low season, with fans, communal fridge, coffee- and tea-making facilities and shared bath. Upstairs rooms are a little more expensive but still very good value, while the new cabinas come with a/c and private bath with hot water; there's also an apartment with its own kitchen and terrace. ②–④.

Los Mangos, about 500m down the road to Cabo Blanco (☎642-0076, fax 642-0259). Expensive-looking but slightly dark bungalows, with large (hot water) showers and fan. The cheaper rooms – the best are upstairs – in the main building down by the road are good value, particularly for groups of four or six; some have their own verandas complete with rocking chairs. There's also a pool, Jacuzzi and a restaurant. ③–⑤.

Lucy (☎642-0273). A Montezuma stalwart (though the government once attempted to have it torn down as it violates the *zona marítima*, which prohibits building on the first 50m of beach) containing ten clean and basic rooms with cold-water showers and a nice seaside veranda upstairs. It's one of the village's best cheapie options, if a little quirky – weirdly, pictures of autumnal New England adorn the walls. The owner also offers a reasonable laundry service. ①–②.

Mar y Cielo (☎642-0261). Nice beachfront cabinas (sleeping 2–6 people), a cut above the basic category, with private bath, fan, cold water and sea breezes. As the name suggests, your view here is of sea and sky, though local sound effects might include nearby *Chico's Bar*, in addition to the crashing waves. ④–⑤.

Pensión Jenny, on the beach (☎642-0306). The cheapest place in town, with dorm beds (US$5) and basic clean singles (US$10) with shared bath in a house on the side of the road, overlooking the beach. ②.

Sano Banano, a 15min walk north of the village along the beach (☎ & fax 642-0638, fax 642-0068, *elbanano@racsa.co.cr*). A truly special place, one of the most characterful in country, with secluded circular cabinas, all featuring beachfront balconies and outside showers (some also have kitchenettes). The newer split-level apartments, also with beach views, are perfect for families, and there's a lovely freeform swimming pool with a waterfall, sun terrace and beautifully landscaped gardens. You have to not mind being close to nature – cabins are unscreened and there's lots of wildlife about. Bring a torch. ④–⑤.

The village and around

It's Montezuma's atmosphere, rather than its activities, which draw visitors, and other than hanging out and sipping smoothies, there's not much to do in the village itself, Despite the inviting palm-fringed white-sand beaches, **swimming** isn't very good on the beaches immediately to the north of Montezuma – there are lots of rocky outcroppings, some hidden at high tide, and the waves are rough and currents strong. It's better to head north along the lovely **nature trail** (1.5km; 30min) which dips in and out of several coves before ending at **Playa Grande**. There's reasonable swimming here, decent surfing, and a small waterfall at its eastern edge; some people also come here to sunbathe topless or nude, though this isn't particularly appreciated by local people.

Montezuma and its environs are laced with a number of **waterfalls**, the closest of which is about a one-kilometre walk down the road towards Cabo Blanco and then another 800m on a path through the dense growth (signed). Always take care with waterfalls, especially in the wet season, on account of **flash floods**, and under no circumstances try to climb them: many people have been injured – or even killed – in the attempt. Local tour operators lead **horse-rides** to falls that are otherwise difficult or impossible to reach on foot.

Isla Tortuga, off the coast of the peninsula near Curú, is a popular place to snorkel, swim safely in calm, warm and shallow waters, and sunbathe. Local boatmen can take you there and back for quite a bit less than you'd pay with one of the "cruise ship" companies doing the run from San José or Puntarenas, although tours from Montezuma are less posh – drinks, for instance, may be included, although lunch is usually not. It's best to stock up on supplies in the village and ask the boatmen if they have a cooler you can use.

The single most popular excursion in town, however, is probably to the **Cabo Blanco** reserve for a morning's walking. Although you can do this independently if you have your own (4WD) transport, most people take a tour. If you like **mountain biking** you could ride the 9km down to Cabo Blanco, walk the trails and bike back in a day. Mind the height of the two creeks en route, though, as you might not get through them on your bike at high tide.

Eating, drinking and nightlife

Just a few years ago all you could get to eat in Montezuma was fantastically fresh **fish**, practically straight off the hook, though nowadays this is complemented by tourist favourites like vegetarian pizza, granola, mango shakes and paella, not to mention more exotic dishes. Eating three meals a day will set you back a few colones, though: Montezuma's accommodation may still be moderately priced, but food is on the expensive side. If you're staying somewhere with a kitchen you can cut costs by grabbing food from Chico's store in the centre of the village.

Nightlife in Montezuma centres around *Chico's Bar*, an interesting mix of local kids, who arrive packed in the back of pick-ups, and tourists guzzling from a surprisingly wide bar stock and shouting above the music. More retiring types can take in the very popular nightly video shows (in English) at the *Sano Banano* at 7.30pm; you have to spend at least US$6 in the restaurant to get in.

Amor de Mar, at the hotel of the same name. Enjoy beautiful ocean-front views whilst sampling a range of light snacks, smoothies (made with homemade yoghurt) and superb, healthy breakfasts using delicious homebaked German bread.

El Sano Banano, in the village. Excellent North-American-style breakfasts and filling lunch and dinner specials – the fillet of fish (US$6) makes a good evening meal – plus crepes, vegetarian pizzas and vegetarian canelloni with spinach; organic produce is used where possible. If you have nothing else, try the incredible smoothies made with fresh fruit and yoghurt.

Panadería, in the village. Good coffee, ice cream and lovely cakes – if you want to take lunch to the beach, try the takeaway avocado, vegetable and hummous sandwiches. Closed Sun.

Playa de las Artistas, about 400m south of the village. Classy Italian-owned restaurant, with tables set romantically among the palm trees and nice touches like lampshades made out of coconut. The menu features exquisitely prepared Mediterranian cuisine with a local twist – the spaghetti with lobster and white wine sauce (US$11) is exquisite. Closed Sun.

Reserva Natural Absoluta Cabo Blanco

Nine kilometres southwest of Montezuma, the **RESERVA NATURAL ABSOLUTA CABO BLANCO** (Wed–Sun 8am–4pm; US$6), established in 1963, is Costa Rica's oldest protected piece of land. At almost twelve square kilometres, Cabo Blanco occupies the entire southwest tip of the peninsula. The natural beauty of the area is complemented by its unique biodiversity, with pockets of **Pacific lowland tropical forest** of a type and mix that are found nowhere else in the country. Animals that live here include howler monkeys, plus sloths and squirrels. Agoutis and coati are common, as are snakes – so watch your step. Sea birds nest down by the shore, using the islands off the very tip of the peninsula as their prime site, and you'll often see clouds of frigate birds hovering above.

You pay your entrance fee (US$6) at the ranger hut, where they'll supply you with a map of the trails, which also outlines the history of the reserve and species found in it. A **trail** (5km; 2hr) leads from here through tropical deciduous forest to **Playa Cabo Blanco** and **Playa Balsitas** – two very lovely, lonely spots, through they're not great for swimming. Be wary of the high tide (*marea*) – ask the ranger at the entrance when and where you're likely to get cut off if walking along the beach. It's very **hot**: 30°C is not uncommon, so bring a hat, sunblock and five litres of water per person. There's no real need to take a **guide** – ask at Aventuras de Montezuma in Montezuma if you do decide you want one. No camping is allowed in the reserve, but you can stay in simple **rooms** just outside the reserve in the house or campsite at *Lila's* (call the *Soda Fin de Luna* on ☎642-0327 and ask for Lila; ①); she'll also cook meals on request. From here it's less than a kilometre to the ranger station, convenient for keen early-morning animal spotters.

Practicalities

The **roads** down to Cabo Blanco are bad; you'll need 4WD to get there yourself, and watch the two creeks, which are deep at high tide. An old, road-hardened **bus** runs between Montezuma and Cabo Blanco, leaving from the side of Montezuma's *parqueo* at 8am, noon, 2pm and 7pm, returning to Montezuma at 7am, 9am, 1pm and 4pm daily except Sunday, although it may not run in the rainy season if it has been very wet. **Jeep-taxis** make the trip from Montezuma to Cabo Blanco for US$10 per person.

Playa Jacó

The best thing you can say about **PLAYA JACÓ** is that it's the closest beach to San José. Just three hours (102km) from the capital, it attracts a mix of surfers, weekenders and holidaying Ticos, from party-hearty students to working-class families. If you've been stuck in San José and are desperate to get to a beach, you might want to take advantage of the weekend specials at larger hotels like the *Best Western Jacó Beach*. But if you have dreams of swimming in the Pacific off pristine white sands, forget it – for one, the water is reported to be polluted near the estuaries; and elsewhere it can be dangerous.

Despite the caveats, it's impossible to overstate Jacó's popularity with surfers (May–Nov), Canadian package tourists (Dec–March) and Joséfinos (all year); be sure to make reservations during the high season (Dec–April), especially at weekends.

Arrival, information and getting around

Jacó straggles along a three-kilometre main road, little more than a strip of shops, restaurants and hotels. Turning off from this main drag are a few streets that head for the sea but never quite make it, petering out in attractive palm groves or the beach. This is the **centre** of town, although many accommodation options are found to the north or the south of this little nucleus.

From San José **buses** leave for Jacó daily at 7.30am, 10.30am and 3.30pm (2hr 30min–3hr). From Puntarenas, buses leave for Jacó at 5am, 11pm and 2.30pm (1hr). From Quepos, buses leave at 4.30am, 11.30pm and 3pm (1hr 15min). There may be extra services on holidays and holiday weekends, but if you intend to travel between Friday and Sunday, especially in the high season (Dec–April) or on public holidays, buy your ticket three days in advance. The bus stops at the extreme north end of the village at the Plaza Jacó mini shopping centre, where the ticket office is also found, behind the Banco de

Costa Rica. The *Best Western Irazú*, just outside San José on the way to Alajuela, has shuttle buses that go to its sister hotel, the *Best Western Jacó Beach*, daily.

The Banco de Costa Rica, in the Plaza Jacó at the north end of town, has an **ATM** that theoretically takes Visa, though as with all state banks, foreign-issued cards may not work. The bank itself will change **travellers' cheques**, as will the Banco Nacional in the centre of town and the larger hotels, like the *Best Western*. The Banco Popular at the south end of town on the main road also changes travellers' cheques but, more importantly, has an **ATM** that will accept foreign-issued Visa cards. The ICE office in the centre of town (Mon–Sat 8am–noon & 1–5pm) offers an international **phone** and fax service. Many places rent **mountain bikes** and **boogie boards** (about US$2/hr or US$10/day – though note that bikes aren't allowed on the beach) and **surfboards** (US$5/hr or US$20/day). You can also rent scooters, for which you'll need your licence and passport – try Señor Bill's (daily 7am–10pm) on the main road near the south end of town.

Locals advise against walking on the beach at night: hold-ups by knife-wielding characters have been reported. Otherwise, walking around town, even at night, should be safe, especially since a special contingent of bike-riding police have taken to patrolling the streets.

Accommodation

Jacó's cheapest **cabinas** generally cater to weekending *Josefinos* or surfers. Much of the mid-range accommodation is self-catering. In general, be prepared to pay more than either the town or, in some cases, the accommodation, merits. You'll need to **reserve** at holiday times, like Easter and Christmas, and weekends, for any of the places listed below.

Jacó is well endowed with **campsites** – all charge about US$3 a night to pitch a tent and have showers, toilets and beach access. Sites include *Camping and Cabinas Mariott* (nothing to do with its hotel-chain namesake), set in level, clear grounds at the north end of town; the shaded *Camping Madrigal*, at the southern end of the beach; and the newer *Camping El Hicaco*, in the centre of town, with nice grounds dotted with picnic tables.

Aparthotel Flamboyant, in the centre of town in front of the beach (☎643-3146, fax 643-1068). Good-value, well-kept apartments sleeping two people, with hot water, kitchen and ceiling fans. There's a pool and a good restaurant attached. ⑤.

Best Western Jacó Beach, north end of town (☎643-3246, fax 643-1000, *jacohotel@racsa.co.cr*). Well-established resort hotel, recently acquired by the Best Western chain and refurbished to a good standard. It's not the cheapest place in Jacó, but it has lots of facilities, including a big clean pool, restaurant, casino and weekend disco, plus kayaking, sports-fishing and sailing lessons. Rooms are decorated in anonymous chain-hotel style, but are perfectly comfortable, and come with private bath, a/c and cable TV. ⑦.

Cabinas Alice, on the beach towards the southern end of town (☎ & fax 643-3061). Twenty-two super-clean cabinas set in beautiful beachfront grounds with little to disturb the peace except the crashing of waves. All cabins come with fan and hot water, while some also have a small kitchen plus fridge and a small terrace; the older and more basic cabinas are slightly cheaper. Good restaurant attached. Visa accepted. ④.

Cabinas Antonio, at the north end of Jacó, near the San José bus stop (☎643-3043). Friendly establishment whose basic but well-priced cabinas come with fans and private bathrooms with hot water; there's also a restaurant. Low-season discounts. ③.

Cabinas Calú, in the centre (☎643-1107). Large, good-value rooms, if a bit dark, with hot water, although the central location can get noisy at weekends. The friendly owners also offer a laundry service. ③.

Cabinas Emily, on the main road on the north side of town (☎643-3513). Filled with surfers on a budget, these friendly, rock-bottom cabinas sport green cement walls and come with private bath (cold water only). A bit pricey for single travellers, but good value for two to four people sharing. There's a restaurant of the same name attached. ②.

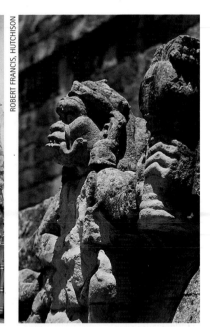

Traditional dance troupe, Honduras

Copán, Honduras

Men returning from work, Honduras

Church of La Recolección, Léon, Nicaragua

Masaya, Nicaragua

Playa Cocles, Costa Rica

Volcán Concepción, Ometepe, Nicaragua

Sandinista mural, Léon, Nicaragua

Marimba players, San José, Costa Rica

Central San José, Costa Rica

Guanaja, Bay Islands, Honduras

JULIO ETCHART

Kuna woman, San Blas Islands, Panama

DIEGO FERRARI

Santa Elena Cloudforest, Costa Rica

MOSER, HUTCHISON

Lockgates at the Panamá Canal

Club del Mar, southern end of town (☎ & fax 643-3194). Tastefully decorated, English-owned apartments on a quiet section of beach south of town, with a friendly family atmosphere and a range of amenities – there's also a pool, restaurant, a small library and a games room. ⑤.

Los Ranchos, in the centre (☎ & fax 643-3070). Arranged in attractive gardens around a pool, this welcoming hotel offers good value for single travellers and groups alike, with a variety of rooms and prices, from upstairs loft rooms (some with kitchenettes) to two-storey bungalows with kitchens sleeping two to four people. ④–⑤.

Mango Mar, in the centre, off the main drag towards the sea (☎643-3670). Small modern hotel set in beachside grounds, with a small pool and a Jacuzzi. The spotless en-suite rooms (those upstairs have good views) come with hot water and a/c; some also have kitchenettes. ⑤.

Mar de Luz, in the centre, on the landward side of the main drag (☎ & fax 643-3259). Well-kept hotel set in landscaped grounds away from the road, with thirty generous-sized rooms arranged around two large pools – plus a good security system in the form of the friendly Dutch owners' alert dachshunds. There's TV in the rooms, plus a communal TV, games area and a small library. Credit cards accepted. ④–⑤.

Villas Estrellamar (☎643-3102, fax 643-3453). Get-away-from-it-all place, with twenty bungalows (all with bath, hot water, fan, TV, kitchen and fridge) in quiet tropical gardens with a large pool. Good low-season prices. ⑤.

Activities and tours

Jacó is very much a beach town; other than sunbathing, surfing and a little cautious swimming, there's little to do. Experienced **surfers** can rent boards at a number of competing places in town; ask at *Los Ranchos* hotel for advice and recommendations. Renting a **mountain bike** (about US$10 a day) is useful for exploring the spread-out town. Some people rent **mopeds** (about US$35 a day) and head out onto the Costanera Sur highway to explore the 10km-long **Playa Hermosa**, 5km south of Jacó, another reputable surfing beach.

The biggest range of tours can be found at Jacó Adventures (☎643-1049, *jacoadventures @playajaco.com*), 100m south of the *Restaurante Colonial*. Their day-long tours to **Manuel Antonio** (US$35) are popular, and they also run rafting trips on the **Río Savegre** (US$89) and **kayaking** and **snorkelling** tours for US$55; day-trips to **Isla Tortuga** (US$70) are another perennial favourite.

Eating, drinking and nightlife

Considering how much local accommodation is geared toward self-catering, there's a good selection of **eating** establishments in Jacó. Many of the best hotels have very good restaurants, though as always in Costa Rica, if you're on a budget, make the lunchtime *casado* or *plato del día* your main meal.

Sedate during midweek in low season, Jacó can transform itself into a beer-drinking-contest hell during weekends and holidays. For **drinking**, bar *Zarpe* at the north end of town is recommended for cold beer and good, if slightly pricey, Mexican *bocas*. *Bar y Restaurante Bohio*, right on the beach, is a great place for a sunset drink – check out the church-pew benches and tables under a ranch roof. They sometimes lay on a very loud **disco**. Other discos include that at the *Best Western Jacó Beach*, the swankiest in town, though it's only open on weekends, and *Disco La Central*, on the beach right in the centre of town – popular with gringos, though again it only really gets going at weekends.

Alice, at the *Cabinas Alice*. Good family-run restaurant, serving fresh seafood and shellfish from a varied menu.

Bananas, in the centre. Popular for its reasonable breakfasts, including tasty pancakes, for US$3.

Barco de Mariscos, in the centre on the main drag. New venue specializing, as its name suggests, in well-prepared fresh shellfish.

MOVING ON FROM JACÓ

Buses for San José leave the bus stop at the north end of Jacó daily at 5am and 3pm (2hr 30min–3hr). It's also possible to continue to **Quepos** and the **Manuel Antonio** area by walking 2km out to the Costañera Sur and flagging down the Puntarenas–Quepos or San José–Manuel Antonio buses that pass on the highway. Buses from Puntarenas to Quepos (see p.647) pass by about ninety minutes after leaving Puntareanas – it's a good idea to check times with locals and to get out onto the highway a few minutes early, just to be sure.

Casita del Maíz, north end of town. One of Jacó's better sodas, popular with locals, with good *casados* made with fresh ingredients.

Chatty Kathy's, opposite the Max x Menos supermarket. One of the best places in town for breakfast, this Canadian-owned upstairs café serves pancakes, cooked breakfasts and delicious cinnamon rolls, as well as light lunches.

Colonial, on the main drag. Tastefully designed new bar-restaurant popular with travellers for drinks as well as main meals.

La Ostra, on the main drag. Long-established *marisquería* (seafood restaurant) set in a quiet rancho next to a creek, and good for both fish and shellfish. Credit cards accepted.

Quepos and Parque Nacional Manuel Antonio

The small corridor of land between the old banana-exporting town of **Quepos** and the little community of **Manuel Antonio**, outside the **Parque Nacional Manuel Antonio**, has experienced one of the most dramatic tourist booms in the country. The stunning, picture-postcard setting, with its spectacular white-grey sand beaches fringed by thickly forested green hills, is the main attraction, and there's also a huge variety of things to do – including walking the park's easy trails, whitewater rafting, ocean-cruising and horse-riding, to name but a few. The beauty of the area is due in part to the unique "*tómbolo*" formation of **Punta Catedral**, which juts out into the Pacific from the park. A rare geophysical phenomenon, a *tómbolo* results when an island becomes joined, slowly and over millennia, to the mainland through accumulated sand deposits. Other smaller islands, some of them no more than rocky outcroppings, straggle off from Punta Catedral and, from high up in the hills, watching a lavish sunset over the Pacific, it does seem as though Manuel Antonio is one of the more charmed places on earth.

That said, the huge tourist input has undeniably taken its toll on the whole area. In the last few years it has been perceived as **overpriced**, and budget travellers searching for cheap beaches have headed instead to Montezuma or to Sámara on the Nicoya Peninsula. Consequently, some hotels have had to drop their rates, and many places have gone from being overpriced to being merely expensive. You'll also need to take more precautions against **theft** than in the rest of Costa Rica. Never leave anything on the beach when you're swimming and, if you take the bus, don't let anyone handle your luggage. Wherever you stay, ensure your hotel room is locked at all times, and note that rental cars left on the street have become a favourite target.

Quepos

Arriving at the town of **QUEPOS** from San José, Puntarenas or Jacó, it's immediately apparent that you've crossed into the lush, wetter southern Pacific region. Vegetation is thicker and greener than up north, and you'll notice the proliferation of **sports-**

fishing imagery – of all the sports-fishing grounds in Costa Rica, the Quepos area has the most variety, and many small tour agencies cater more or less exclusively to sports-fishers. The town itself, backed against a hill and fronted by a muddy beach, can look pretty ramshackle, but it's a friendly place, with plenty of hotels, bars and restaurants. More important, however, is its proximity to Parque Nacional Manuel Antonio and its beaches, 7km south.

Arrival and orientation

Buses leave San José's La Coca-Cola for Quepos four times daily (at 7am, 10am, 2pm & 4pm; 4hr); there's a faster service, also leaving from La Coca-Cola, to Manuel Antonio (daily at 6am, noon & 6pm; 3hr 30min) which calls at Quepos en route to the national park entrance. At weekends, holidays and any time during the dry season, you'll need to buy your bus ticket for the Manuel Antonio service at least three days in advance, and your return ticket as soon as you arrive. All buses arrive in Quepos at the busy **terminal**, which doubles as the mercado, just one block east of the town centre. In addition to these two buses, Interbus's new **shuttle service** makes the trip between San José and Quepos daily using air-conditioned Mercedes minibuses (US$25 each way). They leave San José at 8am, returning from Manuel Antonio at 1.30pm, and will pick you up from your hotel at each end. For reservations, call ☎283-5573 in San José or contact Lynch Tours in Quepos (☎777-0161, *lyntur@racsa.co.cr*).

Due to the long drive and the condition of the roads, it's a good idea to **fly** from San José: this takes only fifteen minutes and, as Quepos residents like to point out, there are no potholes in the sky. Keep in mind that Sansa or Travelair flights are often booked weeks in advance, however, especially in the dry season. Alternatively, you could charter your own plane. The airstrip is about 5km north of town.

Information

To change **money and travellers' cheques**, head for the Banco Popular, just southwest of the bus terminal; the attached ATM accepts Visa and Mastercard. The Banco de Costa Rica and Banco Nacional also change travellers' cheques, but may be slower. The Banco de San José/Credomatic is the only place you can get cash advances on Mastercard, and is also open on Saturday mornings. Many businesses in town will change dollars, and there's a branch of Western Union (Mon–Fri 9am–noon & 1pm–6pm, Sat 9am-2pm) next to the *Café Milagro* just as you enter Quepos.

The **correo** (Mon–Fri 8am–5pm) is at the eastern end of town. There's a plethora of places with **Internet access**, including Los Amigos del Río, next to the church; *Internet Tropical*, in front of the *Hotel Malinche*, which also has an international phone service, plus good fruit *batidos* and toasted sandwiches; *Quepos Internet Café*, opposite the soccer field, which has a happy hour and student discounts. In the event of medical emergencies, Quepos has an excellent **hospital**, the Hospital Dr Max Teran (☎777-0200).

Accommodation

Budget travellers will have a hard time in the Manuel Antonio area, especially in the dry season, when hotels are full and charging their highest prices. The area's few budget options can be found in Quepos, which is more economical overall than Manuel Antonio both for accommodation and eating. Wherever you plan to stay, book well ahead in high season – as ever, things are cheaper and easier in the wet.

Cabinas Doña Alicia, on the northwest corner of the soccer field (☎777-0419). Good budget choice: the hot rooms (with comfortable double beds) all sleep up to four people, apart from a few good-value singles, a rarity in Quepos. All have private bath (cold water only), and the friendly owners keep everything spotlessly clean. ②.

Cabinas El Cisne, 200m north of the church (☎777-1570). Good-value rooms, with refrigerator, TV and standing fans, and friendly owners who keep everything clean. ③.

Cabinas Hellen, a block south of the mercado (☎777-0504). Clean cabinas in the back of a family home, with private bath, hot water, fridge, fans, small table and chairs, a small patio and a laundry service. Secure, and recommended for those travelling with children. Good single rates too. ③.

Cabinas Ramacé, opposite *Cabinas El Cisne* (☎777-0590). Similar to other cheap cabinas in Quepos, with clean – if bare – rooms with hot water and refrigerator in somewhat sterile surroundings. ④.

Hotel Malinche, just west of the mercado (☎ & fax 777-0093). Modern, "American"-style a/c rooms (③–④) with carpet, TV and balcony, and cheaper, older rooms (②) with ceiling fans and cold water – the latter are better value, especially for singles. Rooms vary, so if you don't like the first one they show you, ask to see another – those upstairs are better.

Hotel Mar y Luna, just northwest of the mercado (☎777-0394). Central, friendly budget hotel. Rooms are dark, but have private bath, heated water and fans, and there's a small plant-filled communal balcony, shared fridge and free coffee. ④.

Tours and activities

There's a good range of **tours** in the Quepos area, while many of the upmarket hotels in town or on the road to Manuel Antonio have their own tour-service desk. Most day-trips include equipment rental and guides where necessary, along with lunch and/or snacks. Note that though you can theoretically visit **Bahía Drake and the Osa Peninsula** – including Isla del Caño just off the coast of Osa – from Quepos, it's far cheaper to get there from Palmar or Golfito (see p.685) in the Zona Sur.

In the town centre, the friendly and reputable **Lynch Tours** (☎777-0161, fax 777-1571, *www.lynchtravel.com*) is a good source of unbiased information. They can get you to Dominical, Corcovado, and Bahía Drake either by bus or plane, and arrange transfers to nearly all parts of the country in air-conditioned Mercedes shuttle buses; they also arrange airport transfers (US$3) and handle plane-ticket sales and reservations. Their many local tours include horse-riding trips to a local waterfall (US$55), sports-fishing (US$500–1000 for full day's offshore fishing), sea kayaking (US$60), whitewater rafting (US$75–US$90), rainforest canopy tours (US$80), and ever-popular daytime or sunset cruises, some specifically to see dolphins (US$60).

Equus Stables (☎777-0001, *havefun@racsa.co.cr*), on the road to Manuel Antonio, can take you **horse-riding** on the beach – sunset is the time to go – and up into the mountains behind on a two-hour tour (US$35). As elsewhere in the country, it's worth having a look at how the horses are treated and stabled before you ride, since overwork and abuse of horses is fairly widespread and a thorny issue among travellers and riding outfitters. The area's best established **sports-fishing** outfitter is Costa Rica Dreams (☎ & fax 777-0593), while Isabel Guillen's Boutique El Pescador (☎ & fax 777-1596) is also recommended; a day's fishing will cost up to US$950. **Rafting** outfitters Los Amigos del Río (☎ & fax 777-1262) have offices in Quepos itself, next to the church, and between Quepos and Manuel Antonio (look for a large orange building on the left with inflatable rafts outside).

One of the most popular activities hereabouts are the **cruises** along the coast to Manuel Antonio. Sunset Sails (☎ & fax 777-1304; or book through Lynch Tours) offer dolphin-watching or sunset cruises (Dec–April only) in a classic wooden yacht, with stunning views of the coastline and offshore islands (US$60 for a 4hr cruise); they claim that whales and sea turtles are sometimes spotted. The cruise includes lunch and snorkelling, and there's time for a swim off the boat. Another popular excursion is the day-trip to **Hacienda Barú**, a private hacienda-cum-nature-reserve near Dominical (☎787-0003, fax 787-0004, *sstroud@racsa.co.cr*). They have a canopy observation platform from where you get a bird's-eye view of the upper rainforest canopy, and also offer horse-riding.

Eating and drinking

As in other tourist towns in Costa Rica, head to the sodas frequented by locals for the cheapest meals – *Soda El Costo de Oro*, next to the Banco Popular, is the cheapest place

MOVING ON FROM QUEPOS

Buses to Manuel Antonio leave from the terminal at the *mercado* (15 daily; 20min) between 5.30am and 9.30pm; there are slightly fewer in the rainy season. The service **to San José** (3hr 30min) departs at 5am, 8am, 2pm and 4pm. Buses **to Puntarenas** (3hr) leave at 4.30am, 10.30am and 3pm; the Puntarenas bus will also drop you at the entrance to Jacó (1hr 30min). **Taxis** line up at the rank at the south end of the *mercado*: the journey to Manuel Antonio costs US$3. If you're **driving**, you can get to San Isidro, Golfito and the Osa Peninsula, and other points in the Zona Sur via Dominical, 44km south of Quepos – although the road is usually in terrible condition and a sturdy 4WD is needed, it beats going all the way back to San José and taking the Interamericana south. For **plane** tickets and schedules to San José, visit Lynch Tours (see opposite).

in town, with fish *casados* for only US$2 and a busy lunchtime crowd of both locals and tourists. As a rule, **fish** is predictably good – order grilled *pargo* or *dorado* and you can't go far wrong. *Café Milagro*, on the sea wall has a real espresso machine and cakes – try the vanilla nut chill or iced raspberry mocha. The moderately priced *Restaurante Dos Locos*, just southwest of the mercado, is popular with travellers, with a cosmopolitan range of dishes – including large healthy sandwiches and Mexican cuisine – served up in a nice dining area open to the street. *D'Angolo*, across from *Dos Locos*, is a small Italian deli with a couple of tables and the place to come if you crave fettucini with real gorgonzola cheese (US$6) or if you're self-catering. *Isabel,* on the main street, has friendly, fast service and a menu of American and continental breakfasts, salads, pasta and rice dishes.

Quepos to Parque Nacional Manuel Antonio

Southeast of Quepos, a seven-kilometre stretch of road winds over the surrounding hills, pitching up at the entrance to the Parque Nacional Manuel Antonio. This road is now the site of a tremendous number of hotels: the most exclusive – and expensive – are hidden away in the surrounding hills, reached by side roads, and the very best overlook Punta Catedral, or Cathedral Point, which juts out picturesquely into the Pacific. Though there are some reasonably affordable places near the park entrance, and the occasional low-season discount, prices are high compared to the rest of the country.

La Buena Nota souvenir shop, on the road to Manuel Antonio between the *Hotel Karahé* and *Cabinas Piscis* (☎777-1002), functions as an information centre for the area, as well as selling camera film, foreign papers and magazines, and locally made handcrafted clothing, including some featuring *molas* (designs from the Panamanian Kuna peoples). There's **Internet access** in the unlikely setting of a restored railway car – brought all the way from northern Chile – in front of *La Cantina* restaurant across from the *Costa Verde* hotel.

The hotels below are listed **in the order you encounter them from Quepos**. All are well signed from the road. More than anywhere else, the choice is partial, each one representing the best value in its price range. Taking a **taxi** from Quepos to any of the hotels on the road to the park there's a set fare of around US$6. If you're going back to Quepos by taxi, it's cheapest to flag one down on the road. Fares are per person, and the driver may pick up a number of people along the way.

Accommodation

Cabinas Pedro Miguel (☎777-0035, fax 777-0279). One of the friendliest places in the area, Costa Rican-owned and managed and currently home to the Escuela del Pacífico language school. The family rent two little *casitas*, backed up against the rainforest, with mosquito nets, kitchenette and basic furnishings. There's also a small pool and a great cook-your-own restaurant. Low-season and midweek discounts are available, but book ahead. ⑤.

Hotel Plinios (☎777-0055, fax 777-0558, *www.hotelplinio.com*). Good selection of rooms (though some are a bit dark), all well-screened and nicely decorated with Guatemalan prints – the highest rooms give spectacular sunset views which you can watch from the raised platform beds. The land-scaped tropical gardens feature a pool and a four-kilometre nature trail, with stupendous views from the top. There's a very good restaurant too, and off-season discounts. ⑥.

El Mono Azul (☎ & fax 777-1954, *www.monoazul.com*). One of the best-value places in Manuel Antonio, with ten small but bright and clean rooms with fans (two have a/c), hot water and outside ter-race. A lovely pool and an excellent restaurant (see opposite) add further lustre. Book in advance. ④.

Hotel Las Tres Banderas (☎777-1284, fax 777-1478, *Banderas@centralamerica.com*). Situated in a quiet wooded area, this is one of the area's best hotels, though moderately priced. The large dou-ble rooms open onto a terrace or balcony, while the even more spacious suites are furnished with kitchenette and sofa bed. There's also a large swimming pool and a good restaurant. ⑤–⑥.

La Colina (☎777-0231, *lacolina@racsa.co.cr*). Located on the near-vertical incline locals call "car-diac hill", this lovely hotel offers rare, good-value mid-range rooms, all with private bath and ceiling fans or a/c; the suites with kitchenettes are good value for groups of three or more. There's a nice pool too, and breakfast is included. ⑤–⑥.

Tulemar (☎777-0580, fax 777-1325, *www.tulemar.com*). A great hideaway, and slightly cheaper than the area's other top-end hotels, with fourteen beautiful octagonal bungalows, many with panoramic views over Punta Catedral, built on stilts and set into the hillside. All are luxuriously furnished with a/c, VCR and TV, phones and well-equipped kitchenettes, and there's also a large swimming pool and nature trails in the grounds. Breakfast included. ⑥.

Makanda-by-the-Sea (☎777-0442, fax 777-1032, *makanda@racsa.co.cr*). Manuel Antonio's best top-range choice, with a friendlier atmosphere than at some other luxury establishments in the area. Accommodation is in elegant villas, all with kitchenettes and outside balconies or terraces, set in quiet gardens with ocean views. Breakfast included. ⑧.

Si Como No (☎777-0777, fax 777-1093, *sicomono@racsa.co.cr*). Architectural award-winning com-plex set on a hill overlooking the Pacific and Punta Catedral – there are beautiful views from near-ly every room. The hotel has solar-heated hot water, Jacuzzi, pool, swim-up bar and waterslide, as well as a small cinema with nightly screenings (free to guests). Rooms (and prices) vary from well-appointed doubles to fully equipped villas. The poolside *Rico Tico* grill serves excellent food, and breakfast is included. ⑧.

Hotel Villa Nina (☎777-1221 or 777-128, fax 777-1497, *www.hotelnina.com*). One of Manuel Antonio's best-value lower mid-range hotels. Most rooms have refrigerator, telephone, coffee-maker, a/c and a private balcony or terrace; those upstairs have ocean views. Breakfast is included, and there's a pool, a great rooftop bar, and sloths and monkeys in the trees. ④–⑤.

Costa Verde (☎777-0584, in the US ☎1-800/231-RICA, fax 777-0560). Friendly and professionally run hotel in a quiet area, with spacious rooms and studio apartments constructed from beautiful hardwood, rustic in feel but with all amenities and nice details such as decorative tiles and bal-conies with terrific ocean views. The best-value rooms are in D block, looking out directly onto Punta Catedral and offering the most stunning views in Manuel Antonio. There's a separate air-conditioned area for families, along with a restarant, bar, and a swimming pool with stunning views. ④–⑤.

Cabinas Espadilla (☎777-2135, ☎ & fax 777-0903, *www.espadilla.com*). The nicest place in Manuel Antonio village, although slightly overpriced – the cabinas with fan, sleeping three or four people, are the best value. Each room has private bath with hot water and kitchen, and the complex is set in attractive gardens with a nice pool. ⑥.

Hotel Vela Bar (☎777-0413, fax 777-1071, *velabar@maqbeach.com*). Small and reasonably priced hotel offering basic but pleasant rooms with private bath and fan or a/c – those with fan are better value. Close to the beach and park. ⑤.

Cabinas ANEP (☎777-0565). By far the most basic accommodation in the area, with dark and spartan – but clean – cabinas with fans and private bath set in quiet landscaped grounds close to the park and beach. Though technically reserved for members of the Costa Rican Public Employees Association, they'll take foreign tourists when there's space – usually midweek and in low season. ②.

Eating and drinking

Eating in Manuel Antonio is notoriously expensive and the area's few good-value restaurants, like *El Mono Azul* and *Mar y Sombra*, are understandably popular. The more upmarket hotels all have restaurants attached; some are very good, though most are expensive, or simply overpriced. Some restaurants in Manuel Antonio, including several of the best, close or have restricted hours in the rainy season – ask at La Buena Nota (see p.643) for information. For the more popular places – *Plinios, Karola's* and *Vela Bar* among them – you should call or stop by to make a reservation, especially at weekends and during high season.

Barba Roja, next to the *Divisimar Hotel*, on the road to Manuel Antonio, about 2.5km from the park entrance. Friendly and perennially popular place for high-quality American cuisine, including burgers and desserts.

Café Milagro, One of the best local places for breakfast (from 6.30am), with excellent locally roasted coffee and superlative cappuccino, pastries and cooked food served up in a pleasant environment.

El Mono Azul, in *El Mono Azul* hotel. Generous and reasonably priced plates of well-cooked chicken, fish, hamburgers and sandwiches. Check out the shop next to the restaurant – all proceeds go to a local project run by children to preserve the rainforest and the habitat of the squirrel monkey.

Karola's, near *Barba Roja*. Mexican cuisine, with burritos, seafood, vegetarian dishes and a macadamia nut pie that has entered local food legend. Closed Wed and in the low season.

Mar y Sombra, Manuel Antonio village, 500m from the park entrance, on the beach. In a shady palm grove, this sprawling, cheap place is the most popular in the village. You can have a drink on the beach, and eat típico food including good *casados*, and there's a disco at weekends. Try the fried fillet of fish of the day, simply done in garlic and butter, with fried plantains and salad.

Plinio's, opposite *Pedro Miguel* (☎777-0055, fax 777-0558). Quite simply one of the best restaurants in the country, open for breakfast, lunch and dinner. It's famous locally for its eggplant parmesan, though it's also worth trying the pot roast in red wine, the tiramisu, and the selection of reasonable Chilean wine. There's a nice relaxed bar, too, with good music.

Rico Tico Grill, at the *Si Como No*. Poolside dining with a view over the ocean and superbly cooked food – try the succulent fish brochettes – only slightly marred by excessively obsequious service. Try an exceptional cocktail or chilled fruit drink. Breakfast is also good, with the added entertainment – if you're lucky and up early – of watching the squirrel monkeys and coatimundi that live in the trees in front of the restaurant.

Vela Bar, Manuel Antonio village. The swankiest food in the village, with dishes (starting from around US$7) featuring good grilled fish, plus some vegetarian choices and paella.

Parque Nacional Manuel Antonio

By far the smallest Park in Costa Rica's system, **PARQUE NACIONAL MANUEL ANTONIO** (Tues–Sun 7am–4pm; US$6; *www.manuelantonio.com*), some 150km southwest of San José, fights it out with Parque Nacional Volcán Poás in the Valle Central for the title of the most popular national park in the country. It's hard not to appreciate the foresight that went into the establishment of the park in 1972: considering the number of hotels and restaurants sidling up to its borders, you can just imagine how developed the white sands would be today were they not protected. Even so, the park is suffering from the numbers it receives, and frequently reaches its quota of six hundred visitors a day.

Covering an area of just under seven square kilometres, Manuel Antonio preserves not only the lovely **beaches** and the unique *tómbolo* formation of Punta Catedral, but also **mangroves** and humid tropical **forest**. Visitors can walk only on the coastal section of the park. The eastern mountain section is off limits to the public, and is regularly patrolled by rangers to deter poaching, which is rife in the area, and incursions into the park from surrounding farmers and campesinos.

This forest is one of the few remaining natural habitats for **squirrel monkeys.** Other **mammals** in the park – you're likely to see many of the smaller ones – include

the racoon, coati, agouti, two-toed sloth and white-faced capuchin monkey. **Birdlife** is also abundant, including the shimmering green kingfisher, the brown pelican, which can often be seen fishing off the rocks, and the laughing falcon. Beware of the snakes that inhabit the park, draping themselves over the trails in imitation of jungle vines; you may not see them, but they're here.

The **climate** is hot, humid and wet, all year round. Though the rains ease off in the dry season (Dec–April), they never disappear entirely. The average temperature all year is 27°C, and it can easily go to 30°C and above.

Beaches in Manuel Antonio are known by a confusing number of different names, but because some are not safe for swimming, it's important to grasp which one is which. **Playa Espadilla**, also sometimes called Playa Primera, is actually outside the park, immediately north of the entrance. One of the most popular beaches in the country – it is very beautiful, with a wide stretch of smooth light-grey sand and stunning sunsets – it is also very dangerous, plagued by fast **rip tides**. However, lots of people do swim here – or, rather, paddle and wade – and live to tell the tale, and now that there are professional lifeguards around, it's considerably safer than it used to be, in the dry season, at least. Inside the park, swim only at **Playa Manuel Antonio** (also called Playa Tres or Playa Blanca), which is where everyone else will be, anyway. Immediately south of Punta Catedral, it is situated in a deeper and more protected bay than the park's other beaches. **Playa Espadilla Sur** (or Playa Dos) is very calm – like a swimming pool, say the rangers – but you can still get clobbered by the deceptively gentle-looking waves as they hit the shore.

Practicalities

Buses from Quepos and San José drop passengers off 200m before the park entrance. If you're staying at a hotel between the park and Quepos, and want to go to either by **taxi**, it's cheaper to flag one down on the road rather than ringing from the hotel – you'll be charged a per-person fare, and the taxi may pick up more people. If you're driving, note that there isn't much **parking** at the road loop at the end of Manuel Antonio village; arrive early in the morning for the best (shaded) spots, the going rate to have your car guarded is about US$1.50 per day. The entrance hut is on the other side of the bridge. Here you can pick up a colour map of the park which shows the beaches and trails and also gives information on the local climate and flora and fauna. There are toilets and showers at Playa Tres. There have been problems with **theft** in Manuel Antonio, usually as a result of people leaving valuables (like cameras) on the beach: the rangers, who often sit at the picnic tables, might be able to look after your stuff, but ask nicely, as it's not actually part of their job.

Guided **tours** are available with park-accredited guides for US$15 per person. The guides are informative and speak English. Ask at the park entrance, or ask your hotel to ring the park office to reserve a guide. Be aware that when you leave your car in the parking area in Manuel Antonio village you may be approached by "guides" offering their services at the same price as the official park guides. These "guides" have been known to rob their clients while in the park; though it's more likely that they simply won't be able to show you anything you couldn't see with your own eyes, as they're not trained. If in doubt, the park-accredited guides carry photo ID. Take care if walking alone in the park; a number of robberies have been reported. Although rangers are often on patrol and can nearly always be found near Playa Tres, by law they can't deny entrance to the park to anyone, even suspicious characters.

travel details

BUSES

Jacó to: Puntarenas (3 daily; 1hr); Quepos (3 daily; 1hr 15min); San José (3 daily; 2hr 30min–3hr).

Montezuma to: Paquera (3 daily; 1hr).

Paquera to: Montezuma (3 daily; 1hr); Tambor (3 daily; 40min).

Puntarenas to: Liberia (6 daily; 3hr); Quepos (3 daily; 3hr 30min); San José (14 daily; 2hr); Santa Elena (1 daily; 3hr 30min).

Quepos to: Jacó (3 daily; 1hr); Puntarenas (3 daily; 3hr); San Isidro (2 daily; 3hr 30min); San José (4 daily; 3hr 30min–5hr).

San José to: Jacó (3 daily; 2hr 30min–3hr); Manuel Antonio (3 daily; 3hr 30min); Santa Elena (2 daily; 4–5hr); Puntarenas (14 daily; 2hr); Quepos (4 daily; 30hr 30min–5hr).

Santa Elena to: Las Juntas (2 daily; 2hr); Puntarenas (1 daily; 3hr 30min); San José (2 daily; 4–5hr); Tilarán (1 daily; 3hr).

Tilarán to: Santa Elena (1 daily; 3hr).

FERRIES

Naranjo to: Puntarenas (4–5 daily; 1hr 30min).

Paquera to: Puntarenas (8–9 daily; 1hr 30min).

Puntarenas to: Paquera (8–9 daily; 1hr 30min).

FLIGHTS (Sansa)

Quepos to: San José (4 daily; 20min).

San José to: Quepos (4 daily; 20 min); Tambor (1 daily; 20min).

FLIGHTS (Travelair)

Quepos to: San José (4 daily high season, 1 daily low season; 20min).

San José to: Quepos (4 daily high season, 1 daily low season; 20min).

CHAPTER 31

GUANACASTE

Guanacaste **province**, hemmed in by mountains to the east and the Pacific to the west, and bordered to the north by Nicaragua, is distinctly different from the rest of Costa Rica. Though little tangible remains of the dance, music and folklore for which the region is famous, there is undeniably something special about the place. Granted that much of the **landscape** has come about essentially through the slaughter of tropical dry forest, it is still some of the prettiest you'll see in the country, especially in the wet season, when wide open spaces, stretching from the ocean across savanna grasses to the brooding humps of volcanoes, are washed in a beautifully muted range of earth tones, blues, yellows and mauves. Its **history**, too, is distinct: if not for a very close vote in 1824, it might have been part of Nicaragua, which would have made Costa Rica very small indeed.

Most tourists come for the **beaches**: specifically those where the **Nicoya Peninsula** joins the mainland (roughly two-thirds of the mountainous peninsula is in Guanacaste, with the lower third belonging to Puntarenas province). Several beaches are also nesting grounds for **marine turtles**. An enormous number of hotels, some all-inclusive resort types, are being built on both coasts, and with the opening of the Liberia airport to international traffic, winter charter tourism has well and truly arrived. Inland, however, mass tourism is less evident. Here the dry heat, relatively accessible terrain and panoramic views make Guanacaste the best place in the country for **walking** and **horse-riding**, especially around the mud pots and stewing sulphur waters of **Parque Nacional Rincón de la Vieja** and through the tropical dry forest cover of **Parque Nacional Santa Rosa**. The only **towns** of any significance for travellers are the provincial capital of **Liberia**, and **Nicoya**, the main town of the peninsula. If you are overnighting on the way to **Nicaragua**, La Cruz makes a useful base.

Much of Guanacaste has long been put under pasture for cattle ranching, and a huge part of the region's appeal is the **sabanero** (cowboy) culture, based around the hacienda (ranch) and *ganado* (cattle). This dependence on cattle culture has its downside, however, and much of Guanacaste is now degraded pastureland. Although impressive efforts to regenerate former tropical dry forest are under way – at Parque Nacional Santa Rosa and **Parque Nacional Guanacaste**, for example – it is unlikely that this rare type of life zone will ever recover its original extent.

The province is significantly greener, and prettier, in the "wet" season (May–Nov), generally agreed to be the **best time** to come, with the added benefit of fewer travellers and lighter rainfall than in the rest of the country.

Liberia and around

The spirited provincial capital of **LIBERIA** has a distinctively friendly and open feel, its wide clean streets and blinding white houses the legacy of the pioneering farmers and cattle ranchers who founded it. At present most travellers use the town simply as a

For an explanation of **accommodation price codes**, see p.556.

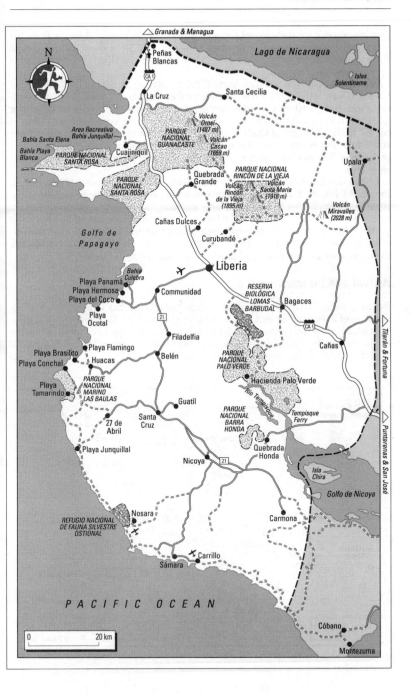

△ *Granada & Managua*

Lago de Nicaragua

Peñas
Blancas

CA 1

La Cruz

Santa Cecilia

◯ *Islas
Solentiname*

*Volcán
Orosí
(1487 m)*

*PARQUE
NACIONAL
GUANACASTE*

*Volcán
Cacao
(1659 m)*

*Area Recreativa
Bahía Junquillal*

Bahía Santa Elena

*Bahía Playa
Blanca*

*PARQUE NACIONAL
SANTA ROSA*

Cuajiniquil

*PARQUE NACIONAL
RINCÓN DE LA VIEJA*

Quebrada
Grande

Upala

*PARQUE
NACIONAL
SANTA ROSA*

*Volcán
Rincón
de la Vieja
(1895 m)*

*Volcán
Santa María
(1916 m)*

*Volcán
Miravalles
(2028 m)*

Cañas Dulces

*Golfo de
Papagayo*

Curubandé

Liberia

*Bahía
Culebra*

Playa Panamá
Playa Hermosa
Playa del Coco

Communidad

*RESERVA
BIOLÓGICA
LOMAS
BARBUDAL*

Bagaces

CA 1

Tilarán & Fortuna △

Playa
Ocotal

21

Cañas

Filadelfia

*PARQUE
NACIONAL
PALO VERDE*

Playa Brasilito
Playa Conchal

Playa Flamingo

Huacas

Belén

Playa
Tamarindo

*PARQUE
NACIONAL
MARINO
LAS BAULAS*

Guatíl

Hacienda Palo Verde

Río Tempisque

Puntarenas & San José △

Santa
Cruz

*PARQUE
NACIONAL
BARRA
HONDA*

*Tempisque
Ferry*

27 de
Abril

Playa Junquillal

Nicoya

21

Quebrada
Honda

*Isla
Chira*

Golfo de Nicoya

*REFUGIO NACIONAL
DE FAUNA SILVESTRE
OSTIONAL*

Nosara

Carmona

Carrillo

Sámara

PACIFIC   OCEAN

Cóbano

0   20 km

Montezuma

N

jumping-off point for the national parks of **Rincón de la Vieja** and **Santa Rosa**, an overnight stop to or from the **beaches** of Guanacaste, or a break on the way to Nicaragua. It's worth getting to know it better, however, for Liberia is actually one of the most appealing towns in Costa Rica.

Sometimes called the "**ciudad blanca**" (white city) on account of its whitewashed houses, Liberia is the only town in the country that seems truly "colonial". It has everything you might need for a relaxing stay of a day or two – well-priced accommodation (although not much choice), a very helpful tourist office and a couple of nice places to eat and drink. This may all change, of course, if the nearby international airport ever starts delivering passengers in large numbers, but for now Liberia is still the epitome of dignified (if somewhat static) provincialism, with a strong identity and atmosphere all its own.

Liberia also boasts several lively local **festivals**, the most elaborate of which is on July 25, **El Día de la Independencia**, celebrating Guanacaste's independence from Nicaragua with parades, horseshows, cattle auctions, rodeos, fiestas and roving marimba bands. If you want to attend, make bus and hotel reservations as far in advance as possible. The last week in September, the **Semana Cultural Liberia Ciudad Blanca**, offers similar goings-on but without the wild patriotic revelry of July's celebration; there's no need to book buses and hotels in advance during this period.

Arrival and information

Buses from San José pull in at Liberia's clean and efficient bus terminal on the western edge of town near the exit for the Interamericana – it's a ten-minute walk at most from here to the centre of town. **Addresses** in Liberia are most often given in relation to the church, the Parque Central, or the *gobernación*, a large white building accross from the church on the corner of C Central and Av Central.

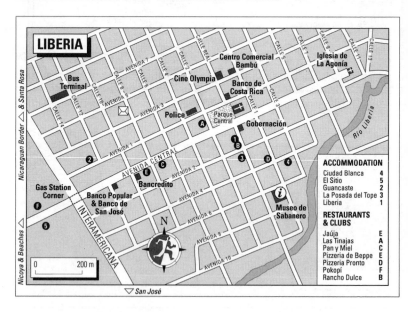

Information

Liberia's supremely helpful **tourist office** (Mon–Sat 9am–noon & 1–5pm, Sun 9am–1pm; ☎666-1606) is on C 1, five minutes' walk south of the Parque Central, in the same building as the Museo de Sabanero. Staff will book hotels, help with directions and place international phone calls at cost. In the high season, especially, they also function partially as a **tour service**, using local operators. Staff speak some English and give unbiased advice and information. The office is a non-profit-making service, and any donations are appreciated.

The efficient **correo**, Av 3, C 8 (Mon–Fri 7.30am–6pm, Sat 7.30am–noon), is a bit hard to find: it's between Av 3 and Av 5 in the low-slung white house across from an empty square field bordered by mango trees. Liberia's one **Internet café**, *Cybermania* (daily 8am–10pm), located in a small business centre on the north side of the Parque Central, is efficient, friendly, air-conditioned and cheap. There are plenty of **banks**, many of them on Av Central, leading into town. The Banco de San José deals with Mastercard and Cirrus, while the Banco Popular next door does VISA and Plus cards – both have ATMs. The next one along, Bancredito, seems to take both. The Banco de Costa Rica, across from the Parque Central, will change travellers' cheques, but its ATM only accepts Costa Rican-issued cards.

Accommodation

Liberia is a convenient place to spend the night if you're heading north to the border or the beaches. Because of tourist traffic to and from the beaches, the town is chock-full in the dry season, especially weekends, and it's imperative to have a **reservation** before you arrive. At other times, midweek especially, there's no problem with space.

Hostal Ciudad Blanca, 200m south and 150m east of the *gobernación* (☎666-2715). Spotless hotel with a small breakfast terrace/bar, and twelve modern, a/c rooms with TV, private bath and ceiling fans. Popular with American travellers bedding down before heading out to the beach. ⑤.

Hotel El Sitio, on the Nicoya road, 200m west of Gas Station Corner (☎666-1211, fax 666-2059, *htlsitio@racsa.co.cr*). Now part of the Best Western chain, this large motel-style hotel, shaded by huge Guanacaste trees, is a good option for families (despite a brash new casino on site), with an on-site pool and restaurant, and large rooms with a/c, TV and private bath. Buffet breakfast included. ⑤.

Hotel Guanacaste, Av 1, 300m south of the bus station (☎666-0085, fax 666-2287, *www .hostelling-costarica.com*). Popular, HI-affiliated hotel, with a traveller-friendly cafeteria-restaurant. The rooms are simple, clean and dark; all but two have private bath. The hotel fills up quickly, so book ahead. If you have a HI card you get 15 percent discount; you might wangle a further 10 percent with student ID. The management organizes a daily transfer (small charge) to Rincón de la Vieja, and sells bus tickets to Nicaragua. Visa and Mastercard accepted. ①–②.

Hotel Liberia, C 0, 75m south of the Parque Central, (☎ & fax 666-0161). Well-established, friendly youth-hostel-type hotel located in a historic house – look for the jolly papaya orange exterior. Rooms are set around a sunny but bare courtyard: the newer rooms in an annexe to the rear are better than the old ones, though they cost an extra US$5. Popular with vacationing foreigners and Costa Ricans alike – a reservation and deposit are required in the high season. The hotel staff also organize transport to Rincón de la Vieja. Visa accepted. ①–②.

La Posada del Tope, 150m south of the *gobernación*, on C 0 (☎666-3876, fax 385-2383, *hottope @racsa.co.cr*). Popular, cheap budget option in a beautiful historic house. The six basic rooms with fan and shared showers in the old part of the hotel are a bit stuffy, but clean; the more modern rooms across the street in a new annexe with cable TV cost about the same. There's a courtyard cafeteria-bar, plus free email, bike rental, and a rooftop telescope for star-gazing. The manager runs transport to Rincón de la Vieja for US$11 per person return. Visa and Mastercard accepted. ②.

The Town

Liberia's wide, clean streets are used more by cyclists and horsemen than motorists. It's pleasant to walk around in the shade provided by the mango trees, though in March and April watch out for the ripe fruit plopping down full-force at your feet. The town is arranged around its large **Parque Central**, properly called Parque Mario Cañas Ruiz. It's dedicated to *el mes del annexion*, the month of the annexation (July), celebrating the fact that Guanacaste is not in Nicaragua. Liberia's Parque is one of the loveliest central plazas in the whole country, ringed by benches and tall palms that shade gossiping locals. Its **church** is startlingly modern – somewhat out of place in this very tradition- al town. About 600m away at the very eastern end of town, the colonial **Iglesia de la Agonía** is more arresting, with a mottled yellow facade like a pock-marked, washed-out banana. On the verge of perpetual collapse – it has had a hard time from those earth- quakes – it's almost never open, but you could try shoving the heavy wooden door and hope the place doesn't collapse around you if it does give way. The town's most inter- esting street is **Calle Real** (marked as Calle Central on some maps). In the nineteenth century this street was the entrance to Liberia, and practically the entire thoroughfare has now been restored to its original colonial simplicity. The tourist office houses the **Museo de Sabanero**, or Cowboy Museum (Mon–Sat 9am–noon & 1–5pm, Sun 9am–1pm; donation appreciated), containing a small-scale display of objects from the big old ranch houses.

Eating, drinking and entertainment

Liberia has several **restaurants** that are particularly good for breakfast and lunch. Local treats include **natilla** (soured cream) eaten with eggs or *gallo pinto* and tortillas. For a real feast, try the various **desayunos guanacastecos** (Guanacastecan break- fasts): hearty food, made to be worked off with hard labour. For rock-bottom cheap **lunches**, head for the stalls in the bus terminal, *Las Tinajas* or the town's various fried chicken places.

For **drinking**, places like *Las Tinajas* and *Pizzería Pronto* are good for a quiet beer. The town's one **disco**, *Kurú*, next to the *Pokopí* restaurant, gets lively with salsa and merengue, especially on weekends and holidays. The main Saturday evening activity, however, involves the locals parading around the Parque Central in their finery, hang- ing out, having an ice cream, and maybe going to the movies at the **Cine Olympia**, 100m north of the church, which shows a variety of English-language movies, includ- ing the latest art-house releases, as well as the usual action-adventure blockbusters.

Restaurants and sodas

Jauja/Pizzeria de Beppe, Avenida Central. Good breakfasts and pizzas served in a pleasant out- door garden setting.

Las Tinajas, west side of Parque Central. The outdoor tables on the veranda of this old house make a good spot for watching the goings-on in the Parque while enjoying a *refresco* or beer. Basic *casa- dos* and excellent hamburgers (US$3) are also served. There's live music on Thursdays and Sundays.

Pan y Miel, next to the *Restaurante Jauja* on Avenida Central. More a cafeteria than a restaurant, with buffet breakfasts, good cakes and coffee.

Pizzería Pronto, C 1, 200m south of the church. Situated in an old adobe house, with wooden tables and décor and a covered garden patio, the friendly *Pronto* serves excellent – if smallish – piz- zas (US$4–5) cooked in a giant wood oven. The restaurant's bar is popular with gringos.

Pokopí, 100m west of Gas Station Corner, on the road to Nicoya opposite *Hotel el Sitio*. Fastidiously clean (they mop the floor every two seconds) and decorated with colourful toucans, this pleasant

---

MOVING ON FROM LIBERIA

As well as having good connections with **San José** (8 direct Pulmitan de Liberia buses daily, 4hr 30min), Liberia is also the main regional transport hub, giving easy access to Guanacaste's parks and beaches, and the Nicaraguan border.

For **Parque Nacional Santa Rosa**, take a La Cruz or Peñas Blancas (Nicaraguan border) bus (hourly) from the bus terminal. Take the earliest bus you can to give yourself time for walking, and ask the driver to let you off at Santa Rosa. You can also reach the park by colectivo taxi (US$15 per car) from the northwestern corner of the Parque Central. **Parque Nacional Guanacaste** isn't really reachable by bus; you could theoretically take the 3pm bus to Quebrada Grande village, from where it's a walk of at least two hours – but you'd still arrive after closing time. If you're heading for the border, take one of the hourly buses to **La Cruz** or **Peñas Blancas** (the border's official name) (1hr).

There are direct services to the more northerly of Guanacaste's **beaches**: for Playa Hermosa and Playa Panamá, two buses leave daily (11.30am & 7pm; 1hr). Playa del Coco is served by three or four services per day (5.30am, 12.30pm, 4.30pm and, high season only, 2pm; 1hr). You can also get to **Santa Cruz** (hourly 5.30am–7.30pm; 1hr), from where you can hook up with buses to Tamarindo, Junquillal and beaches further south. Buses for **Nicoya** leave on the hour from 5am to 7pm (2hr). Buses to **Puntarenas** leave at 5am, 8.30am, 10am, 11am and 3pm (3hr).

Colectivo taxis, shared between four or five people, can be good value if you're heading for **Parque Nacional Rincón de la Vieja** or the lodges near Las Espuelas ranger station. They line up at the northwestern corner of the Parque Central, and charge about US$25 for four people. Arguably the best way to get to Rincón de la Vieja is to travel with one of the various Liberia hotels – *Posada del Tope, Hotel Liberia* and *Hotel Guanacaste* – which arrange transport to the park. All services are open to non-residents, though hotel guests get first option.

---

restaurant serves huge, dripping burgers for US$3, and very tasty snapper in garlic butter (*pargo en ajillo*) for about US$7. Eat early on weekends, though: the *Kurú* disco starts up around 9.30pm, and might drown out your supper.

Rancho Dulce, 50m south of the *gobernación*. Tiny soda serving *casados*, sandwiches, *empanadas* and *refrescos*: great for a cheap lunch. You can sit at the tiny outdoor stools (if you have a small bottom) or tables.

Parque Nacional Rincón de la Vieja

The dramatically dry landscape of **PARQUE NACIONAL RINCÓN DE LA VIEJA** (daily 8am–4pm; US$6), northeast of Liberia, varies from rock-strewn savanna to patches of tropical dry forest and deciduous trees, culminating in the blasted-out vistas of the volcano crater itself. The land here is actually alive and breathing: Rincón de la Vieja last erupted in 1991, and rivers of lava still broil beneath the thin epidermis of ground, while **mud pots** (*pilas de barro*) bubble and puffs of steam rise out of lush foliage, signalling sulphurous subterranean springs. This is great terrain for **camping, riding** and **hiking**, with a comfortable, fairly dry heat – although it can get damp and cloudy at the higher elevations around the crater. **Birders**, too, will enjoy Rincón de la Vieja, as there are more than 200 species in residence.

Getting to the park

The local dry season (Dec–March especially) is the best time to visit Rincón de la Vieja, when the hiking trails and visibility as you ascend the volcano are at their best. To make management of the forest more efficient, the park has been split into two sectors:

Sector Pailas ("cauldrons") and **Sector Santa María**, each with its own **entrance** and ranger station. From Liberia most people travel through the hamlet of Curubandé, about 16km northeast, to the Las Pailas sector. The other ranger station, Santa María, lies about 25km northeast from Liberia. The **casona** that houses the ranger station here is a former retreat of US president Lyndon Baines Johnson, and, at more than 110 years old, is ancient in Costa Rican terms.

Both routes to the park are along stony roads, not at all suitable for walking. People do, but it's tough, uninteresting terrain, and it's really more advisable to save your energy for the trails within the park itself. Options for getting here from Liberia are covered in the box on p.653; **hitching** is also an option if you can find a truck driver making a delivery, possibly at one of the gas stations at Gas Station Corner on the Interamericana at Liberia. Alternatively, you could **rent a car** (you'll need a 4WD) and stay in one of the upmarket tourist lodges such as the *Hacienda Guachipelín* or *Rincón de la Vieja Lodge* (see below).

To get to the **Las Pailas sector** and the lodges, take the Interamericana north of Liberia for 6km, then turn right to the hamlet of Curubandé – you'll see signs for the *Guachipelín* and *Rincón de la Vieja* lodges. A couple of kilometres before the *Guachipelín* there's a barrier and toll booth, where you'll be charged US$2 to use the road. If you don't have your own transport, both lodges will pick you up from Liberia for an extra charge (US$10–25 return); they also offer **packages** from San José, with transport included. The **Santa María sector** and the *Rincóncito* lodge are reached by driving through Liberia's Barrio La Victoria in the northeast of the town (ask for the *estadio* – the soccer stadium – from where it's a signed 24-kilometre drive to the park).

Accommodation

There's a basic **campsite** near the Las Pailas *puesto*, and another slightly better equipped site at the Santa María *puesto* (US$3 per person), where there are lavatories and water for washing, though you should take your own cooking utensils, food and drinking water. If you have a sleeping bag, and ask in advance, you can also stay inside the musty bunk rooms in the Santa María ranger station (phone the ACG office at Santa Rosa for permission on ☎695-5598).

Albergue Buenavista, 31km northeast of Liberia (☎ & fax 661-8158 or 666-2069, *www .buenavistalodge.net*). A working cattle ranch – you can even ride with the cowhands if your horse-manship is up to it – with stupendous views over Guanacaste and some great trails through pockets of rainforest on the flanks of the volcano and up to the crater. There are some good-value dorm beds and singles (US$15–20), while double rooms are housed in individual bungalows, many set around a small lake in which you can swim. A restaurant serves up wholesome meals, and there are reasonably priced horseback and hiking tours available. If you're driving here, a 4WD is recommended; alternatively, you can arrange to be picked up from Cañas Dulces (accessible from Liberia by bus). ⑤.

Albergue Nueva Zealanda, in Quebrada Grande (marked as García Flamenco on many maps), about 35km northeast of Liberia (☎666-4300 or 666-3804, *www.tourism.co.cr/hotels/nzealandia*). Rustic and comfortable lodge, affiliated with the HI (ask at the *Hotel Guanacaste* for information on discounts), located on the northwest flank of Rincón de la Vieja park. Birds and animals abound, and horse-riding is offered. Rooms are in a wooden building on stilts. ⑤.

Hacienda Guachipelín, 5km beyond Curubandé on the edge of the park (☎284-2049, ☎ & fax 256-6995, *www.guachipelin.com*). A working ranch, the historic *Guachipelín* looks every inch the old cattle hacienda, with comfortable doubles in the main house and bargain dorm beds (US$10). Meals are extra – portions can be a bit mean, considering the cost. Attractions include a nearby waterfall, mud pots and some well-marked trails, while guides are available for a variety of tours, including riding and hiking to the volcano. Pick-ups from Liberia can be arranged, for a fee. ④.

Rincóncito, in San Jorge (☎666-2764, mobile 380-8193). The cheapest option close to the park, this farm is owned by a friendly family, and has plain but good-value *cabinas* with cold water and no electricity. The owners are a good source of advice on local transport, guides and directions, and can also arrange horse-riding, guided tours and pick-ups from Liberia (about US$35 return per car). Meals available (breakfast US$3, lunch and dinner US$5). ①–②.

Rincón de la Vieja Lodge, 5km northwest of the *Guachipelín* and 3.5km from the Las Pailas park entrance; follow the signs (☎ & fax 661-8198, *www.rincondelaviejalodge.com*). Popular lodge with simple, rustic accommodation, including doubles with private bath and hot water (⑨), and dorm beds with communal bathrooms and cold water (US$20 per person). There's a pool, reading area, and restaurant serving tasty and filling meals. Horse-riding, mountain-biking, a canopy tour and swimming in nearby waterfalls can all be arranged, and packages are available, with meals and some activities included. ⑨.

Visiting the park

You can walk Rincón de la Vieja's **main trail** to the crater from either the Santa María or Las Espuelas ranger stations. Whether on foot, horseback or a combination of the two, this is quite simply one of the best hikes in the country, if not *the* best. A variety of elevations and habitats reveals hot springs, sulphur pools, bubbling mud pots and fields of purple orchids, plus a great smoking volcano at the top to reward you for your efforts. **Animals** in the area include all the big cats, shy tapir, red deer, collared peccary, two-toed sloth, and howler, white-faced and spider monkeys. **Birders** will have a chance to spot the weird-looking three-wattled bellbird, the Montezuma oropendola, the trogon and the spectacled owl, among others.

From the Las Pailas *puesto* the summit is 7.7km away. Theoretically, if you start out early in the morning you could get to the top and back down before nightfall, but only if you don't mind rushing. The **summit** (1916m) of Rincón de la Vieja presents a barren lunar landscape, with a smoking hole surrounded by black ash and a pretty freshwater lake, Lago los Jilgueros, to the south. You can get hammered by wind at the top; bring a sweater and windbreaker. If you don't fancy the climb up the volcano, more gentle walks in the Las Pailas sector take you to fumaroles and mud pots, and you can also hike to two waterfalls, the *cataratas escondidas*.

Parque Nacional Santa Rosa

Established in 1971, **PARQUE NACIONAL SANTA ROSA** (daily 7.30am–4.30pm; US$6), 35km north of Liberia, is Costa Rica's oldest national park, having been established to protect an area of increasingly rare dry tropical forest. Today it's one of the most popular in the country, thanks to its good trails, great surfing (though poor swimming) and prolific turtle-spotting opportunities. It's also, given a few official restrictions, a great destination for **campers**, with a couple of sites on the beach.

Santa Rosa has an amazingly diverse topography for its size, ranging from mangrove swamp to deciduous forest and savanna. Home to 115 species of mammals – half of them bats – 250 species of birds and 100 types of amphibian and reptile (not to mention 3800 species of moth), Santa Rosa is of prime interest to biologists, attracting researchers from all over the world. Jaguars and pumas prowl the park, but you're unlikely to see them; what you may spot – at least in the dry season – are coati, coyotes and peccaries, often snuffling around watering holes.

The appearance of the park changes drastically between the **dry season**, when the many streams and small lakes dry up, trees lose their leaves, and thirsty animals can be seen at known waterholes, and the **wet months**, greener but affording fewer animal-viewing opportunities. From August to November, however, you may be able to enjoy the sight of hundreds of **Olive Ridley turtles** (*llora*) nesting on Playa Nancite by moonlight; September and October are best. Though too rough for swimming, the picturesque **beaches** of Naranjo and Nancite, about 12km down a bad road from the administration centre, are popular with serious **surfers**.

Santa Rosa's **La Casona** (Big House), one of Costa Rica's most famous historical sites, burned to the ground in May 2001, depriving the country of one of its oldest buildings, and also of the folkloric museum which the Casona had housed for many years. Plans for reconstruction are reportedly under way.

Practicalities

Santa Rosa's **entrance hut** is 35km north of Liberia, signed from the Interamericana. After paying the park fee, pick up a map and proceed some 6km or so, taking the right fork to the **administration centre** (☎666-5051, fax 666-5020), which also runs to Guanacaste and Rincón de la Vieja national parks. From here a rough road leads to the beaches; to drive these, even in the height of the dry season, you'll need a sturdy 4WD. The rangers discourage any driving at all beyond the main road; most people park their vehicle at the administration centre and walk.

If you're walking down to the beach, a ranger or fellow tourist will probably give you a ride, but on no account set out without **water** – a couple of litres per person, at least, even on a short jaunt. The easy-to-carry bottles of water with plastic handles sold at the gas stations on the road outside Liberia are particularly convenient – stock up before you come. You can also buy drinks at the administration centre.

Camping facilities at Santa Rosa are some of the best in the country. There are two sites, each costing US$2 per person, payable as you arrive at the administration centre. The shady **La Casona** campground has bathrooms and grill pits, while **Playa Naranjo**, on the beach (and only open outside the turtle-nesting season), has picnic tables and grill pits, and a ranger's hut with outhouses and showers plus, apparently, a boa constrictor in the roof. Wherever you camp, watch your fires (the area is a tinderbox in the dry season), take plastic bags for your food, do not leave anything edible in your tent (it will be stolen by scavenging coati) and, of course, carry plenty of water.

Parque Nacional Guanacaste

Some 36km north of Liberia on the Interamericana is the **PARQUE NACIONAL GUANACASTE** (daily 7.30am–4.30pm; US$6), much of which was until quite recently under pasture for cattle until influential biologist D.H. Janzenhelped create the park virtually from scratch in 1991. Raising over US$11 million, mainly from foreign sources, he envisioned creating a kind of biological corridor in which animals, mainly mammals, would have a large enough tract of undisturbed habitat in which to hunt and reproduce. The result of his work, the **Santa Rosa–Guanacaste** (and, to an extent, Rincón de la Vieja) **corridor**, represents one of the most important efforts to conserve and regenerate tropical **dry forest** in the Americas.

Covering the slopes of the dormant Orosí and Cacao volcanoes, with tropical wet and dry forests and a smattering of cloudforest, the Parque Nacional Guanacaste also protects the wellspring of the Río Tempisque, as well as the Ríos Ahogados and Colorado. More than 300 species of **birds** have been recorded, while mammals lurking behind the undergrowth include jaguar, puma, tapir, coati, armadillo, two-toed sloth and deer. It's also thought that there are about 5000 species of **butterflies** and moths.

Few people come to Parque Nacional Guanacaste. The only primary rainforest exists at the upper elevations and, of the three biological stations, you are currently allowed to visit only the one on Volcán Cacao. **Trails** are being cut, however, and there are pre-Columbian **petroglyphs** lying around at El Pedregal, near the Maritza field station at the bottom of Volcán Orosí. Ask the rangers at the entrance about the best way to see them; they are not on any currently existing trail, nor are they marked.

Practicalities

Facilities at Guanacaste are minimal. To get there, take the exit for Potrerillos on the right-hand side of the Interamericana, 10km south of the Santa Rosa turn-off. At

Potrerillos turn right for the hamlet of **Quebrada Grande** (on some maps called García Flamenco) and continue for about 8km – best to have a 4WD for this trip. You can **camp** at the main ranger station or there's a rustic, simple **lodge** at Cacao field station. Call in at Santa Rosa administration (☎666-5051, fax 666-5020) to check if it's open and how much they're charging for people to stay.

Crossing the border into Nicaragua: Peñas Blancas

Peñas Blancas (8am–noon & 1–4pm), the main crossing point into Nicaragua, is emphatically a border post and not a town, with just one or two basic sodas and no hotels. Aim to get here as **early** as possible, as procedures are ponderous and you'll be lucky to get through the whole deal in less than ninety minutes. In addition, buses on both side of the border are far more frequent in the morning, and fizzle out completely by 2 or 3pm. Things are smoothest if you come with Ticabus – all passengers are processed together and are given priority. Both Costa Rican and Nicaraguan border officials are quite strict, and there are many checks to see that your paperwork is in order. Canadians, Australians and New Zealanders need **visas**, which can be organized in San José (around US$25; or US$15 for a 72-hr transit visa).

Exit stamps and fee (75 colones) are paid on the Costa Rican side, where there's a restaurant and a helpful, organized Costa Rican **tourist office**. Moneychangers are always on hand and have colones, córdobas and dollars. After getting your Costa Rican exit stamp, it's a short walk north to the barrier. From here you can pick up a shuttle bus (US$2) 4km north to the Nicaraguan shantytown of **Sapoá**, where you go through *migración* (see p.526).

The Guanacaste beaches

Many of the **beaches of Guanacaste**, scattered along the rocky coastline from Bahía Culebra to Sámara on the west of the Nicoya Peninsula, are being aggressively developed for mass tourism. Most controversial is the fits-and-starts **Papagayo Project**, covering nearly the entire Bahía Culebra. Over the next fifteen years about 14,000 rooms are planned here, making it the largest tourist development in Central America (there are currently a total of just 13,000 hotel rooms in the whole of Costa Rica). That said, despite all the noise, the project seems to be permanently stalled. The **golf course** craze, however, shows no signs of abating. These pose a particular danger to the delicate environment, since golf courses require an enormous amount of water, which is often taken from wetlands, mangroves and other fragile habitats, never mind the fact that local people may have their water supply curtailed.

Despite the increasing development, the coast here has a lot to recommend it, not least **Parque Nacional Marino Las Baulas**, where droves of leatherback **turtles** come ashore to lay their eggs between October and February. If it's a good swim you want, however, best head down to **Tamarindo**, or better still to **Sámara** or **Nosara** on the Nicoya Peninsula.

It can take a long time to get to the Guanacaste coast from San José (5hr minimum, unless you fly) and in some places you feel very remote indeed. **Getting around** can take time, too, as the beaches tend to be separated by rocky headlands or otherwise impassable formations, entailing considerable backtracking inland to get from one to the other. Unless you're just going to one place, **bus** travel is tricky, although possible. By far the most popular option is to **rent a car**, which allows you to beach-hop with relative ease. Roads are not bad, if somewhat potholed – you'll do best with **4WD**, though this can prove expensive.

Playa Panamá and Playa Hermosa

Sheltered from the full force of the Pacific, the clear blue waters of **Bahía Culebra** on the **Gulfo de Papagayo** are some of the best for swimming and snorkelling in the country. The northernmost beach of the bay, **Playa Panamá**, with its grey volcanic sand, is still a nice quiet spot, although there is no shortage of upmarket hotels being built here, many of them by Italians. The resort-style hotel *Costa Smeralda* (☎672-0070, fax 670-0379, *smeralda@racsa.co.cr*, ⑧) has a nice pool, good restaurant and efficient management. Two **buses** daily do the hour-long trip from Liberia, on a good paved road, leaving Liberia at around 11am and 7pm. The turn-off for Playa Panamá is 3km beyond the Playa del Coco turn-off.

Playa Hermosa, on the southern edge of Bahía Culebra, 10km north of the nearest beach to the south, Playa del Coco, is calm, clean and good for swimming. Small islets dot the bay, and despite a recent building boom in the area, in the wet season Hermosa can be wonderfully quiet.

If you want to **stay** on the beach, the popular and friendly *Hotel el Velero* (☎670-0036, fax 670-0016, *elvelerocr@yahoo.com*; ⑥–⑦) has split-level rooms with balconies and sea views in lovely gardens filled with birds and lizards. There's also a good restaurant and a small pool, while a short path leads from the hotel down to the beach. Ask about often generous low-season discounts. *Rancho Vallejo* (☎672-0108; ②) is one of the few places left in Playa Hermosa that could conceivably be described as budget, offering simple, clean rooms with private (cold-water) bath, while *Villas del Sueño* (☎ & fax 670-0026, *www.villadelsueno.com*; ④) is a good-value small hotel with eight large and lovely rooms, all attractively furnished and with pretty tiled floors; there's also a small pool and a nice open-air restaurant.

Playa del Coco

Thirty-five kilometres west of Liberia, with good road connections, **Playa del Coco** was the first Pacific beach to hit the big time with weekending Costa Ricans from the Valle Central. Its accessibility, budget accommodation and good restaurants make it a useful place for a couple of days' jaunt or, if you have a car, as a base to explore the better beaches nearby.

Playa del Coco is a popular **snorkelling** and **diving** centre: try Mario Vargas Expeditions (☎ & fax 670-0351, *mvexped@racsa.co.cr*) in Coco itself, or Bill Beard's Diving Safaris (☎ & fax 672-0012, *diving@racsa.co.cr*) in nearby Playa Hermosa. The staff at Rich Coast Diving (☎670-0176, *dive@richcoastdiving.com*), on the main road about 300m from Playa del Coco, speak English, organize snorkelling and scuba trips (US$65–80 for a two-tank dive) and rent out mountain bikes.

Arrival and information

A direct **bus** (5hr) leaves San José for Coco daily at 10am, returning at 9.15am. You can also get to Coco on local services from Liberia (1hr), returning to Liberia at 7am, 9.15am (high season only), 2pm and 6pm. The town itself spreads out right in front of the beach, with a tiny **Parquecito** as the focal point. Minimal services include a minis-cule **correo** (Mon–Fri 7.30am–5pm) and public **telephones** on either side of the Parquecito. The Banco Nacional will change dollars and travellers' cheques; otherwise you can **change money** at *Flor de Itabo* (see opposite). **Taxis** gather in front of the *Restaurante Cocos* by the beach.

Accommodation

Coco has lots of fairly basic **cabinas**, catering to weekending nationals and tourists. In the high season, you should make sure to **reserve** for weekends, but can probably get away with turning up on spec mid-week, when rooms may also be a little cheaper. In the low season bargains abound. There's **camping** (US$4) at the Ojo Parqueo, 75m from the beach on the main road; they'll keep an eye on your belongings, and also sell water.

Cabinas Catarina, 100m before you reach the Parquecito (☎670-0156). The most basic budget cabinas in town, and a very good deal. Each *cabina* has a private bath with cold water only, and the friendly management will let you do laundry and cook meals in the small kitchen. ①.

Cabinas Chale, 500m up the road branching off to the right as you approach the beach (☎670-0036). Very plain a/c lodgings, but just 50m from the beach, with big rooms plus fridges (useful if you don't want to walk into town for a beer) and a pool. ④.

Cabinas El Coco, on the beach, 200m north of the Parquecito (☎670-0167). Comfortable, clean and friendly cabinas right on the beach. The rooms on the second floor are best, and come with shared or private bath, and fans. On Saturday nights, noise from the nearby disco can be troublesome. ③.

Flor de Itabo, on the main road coming into town, about 1km from the beach (☎670-0011, fax 670-0003). Tasteful, friendly and long-established hotel, decorated with lovely dangling shell mobiles and Guatemalan bedspreads. All rooms have private bath, a/c, hot water and TV. Non-residents can change money here, and use the pool for about US$3. There's also an excellent on-site Italian restaurant, *Da Beppe* (see below). ⑤.

Hotel/Cabinas Luna Tica, 100m south of where the road ends at the beach (☎670-0459). Rooms with private bath and cold water: those in the hotel are a bit airier than those in the cabinas, and some have fans or a/c. ③.

Villa Flores, on the road leading to the right before you reach the beach (☎670-0787, fax 670-0269). Quiet and comfortable, this hotel has rather dark rooms each with private bath and hot water – some have ceiling fans, others a/c (about US$10 more). The second-storey balcony is a great place to catch sea breezes. There's also a pool, Jacuzzi, small gym, and dives can be arranged. ⑤.

Vista Mar, signposted turn 1km north of the village (☎ & fax 670-0753, *www.arweb.com/vistamar*). A good-value and nicely maintained option, with eight spacious and pleasantly decorated rooms, either with shared or private bath with hot water, plus fan or a/c. There's a nice palm-fringed pool and a good restaurant serving Italian- and French-themed food. Breakfast included. ④–⑤.

Eating, drinking and nightlife

Coco has two very distinct types of **restaurants, sodas** and **bars**: those catering to nationals and those that make some sort of stab at cosmopolitanism to hook the gringos. Nightlife is generally quiet during the week, but things get livelier at the weekend, when the *Cocomar* **disco** starts up.

Bar Coco, opposite the Parquecito. A popular place in a prime position. Good for seafood lunches and dinners or just a beer in the evening.

Bar El Bohio, in the centre of the village. Extensive, gringo-friendly fare, running from Chinese to tacos, with menus in English.

CocoMar Bar and Disco, right on the beach, about 100m north of the Parquecito. Coco's only disco can be very loud at weekends, when it plays a mixture of salsa and reggae. On weekday evenings it's usually a bar unless someone decides to crank up the powerful sound system. Open until midnight; later at weekends.

Da Beppe in the *Flor de Itabo* hotel. The most ambitious food in town, with prices to match; the fillet of beef and fresh shrimp are recommended if you feel like splashing out. The popular *Havana Bar* is in the same building.

Pizzería Pronto, 500m before the beach on the right-hand side as you enter Coco. Green salads and large pizzas (the *jalapeña* is good) for about US$7, served beneath a pleasant canopy. Closed Tues.

San Francisco Treats, 200m from the beach. The San Francisco crowd who run this cheery melon-coloured restaurant offer treats such as home-made lasagne and roast beef sandwiches. Desserts – brownies and pies – are especially good.

Parque Nacional Marino Las Baulas

On the Río Matapalo estuary between Conchal and Tamarindo, **PARQUE NACIONAL MARINO LAS BAULAS** (8am–4pm, though open until late at night for guided tours in season; US$6, including tour) is less a national park than a reserve, created in 1995 to protect the nesting grounds of the critically endangered **leatherback turtles**, which come ashore here to nest from October to February. Leatherbacks have laid their eggs at **Playa Grande** for quite possibly millions of years, and it's now one of the few remaining such nesting sites in the world. The beach itself offers a beautiful sweep of light-coloured sand, and outside laying season you can surf and splash around in the waves, though swimming is rough, and plagued by crashing waves and rip tides. Despite its proximity to an officially protected area, someone seems to have given developers carte blanche to build at Playa Grande. What effect this will have on the millennia-old nesting ground of the turtles remains to be seen.

Around 200m from the park entrance, the impressive and educational **El Mundo de la Tortuga** exhibition (early Oct to mid-March daily 4pm to late; US$5) includes an audioguided tour in English and some stunning photographs of the turtles. You'll gain some insight into the leatherback's habitats and reproductive cycles, along with the threats they face and current conservation efforts. There's also a souvenir shop and a small café where groups on turtle tours are often asked to wait while a nesting turtle is located. It's open late at night – often past midnight – depending on demand and nesting times. There are two official entrances to Playa Grande, though **tickets** can only be bought at the southern entrance, where the road enters the park near the *Villa Baulas*. There are no bus services to the park. To **drive to Las Baulas**, take the road from Huacas to Matapalo, and turn left at the soccer field (a 4WD is recommended for this stretch during the wet season). Most people, however, visit the park by **boat** from Tamarindo, entering at the southern end rather than from the Matapalo road.

Playa Tamarindo

Stretching for a couple of kilometres over a series of rocky headlands, **Playa Tamarindo** is one of the most popular beaches in Guanacaste, attracting surfers and weekending Costa Ricans. **TAMARINDO** village, which has a sizeable foreign community, boasts a great selection of restaurants, a lively beach culture and some nightlife, at least during high-season.

Arrival and information

You can **fly** into Tamarindo on Travelair and Sansa (see p.583), and both have offices in town; **buses** arrive by the village loop at the end of the road. The loop effectively constitutes Tamarindo's small centre, with a Parquecito populated by New-Age jewellery-sellers – and even the odd pecking chicken – surrounded by restaurants. The small Banco Nacional, about 1km north of the loop, across from Supermercado Pelicano, will probably **change dollars**. There are **public telephones** on the Parquecito and several **Internet cafés** (costs are around US$2 per 30min), but most look so itinerant it's hardly worth listing their names. The Supermercado Tamarindo and Supermercado Pelicano sell basic foodstuffs. For **getting around** the area, and out to Playa Langosta, you could rent a scooter or a mountain bike from Tamarindo Rental Tours or from the surfboard/rental place next to *Cabinas Marielos*, or even rent a car for a day or two from Economy Rent a Car, next to the *Frutas Tropicales* soda on the main road.

Accommodation

Many of Tamarindo's **hotels** are very good, if expensive. You can **camp** at *Tito's* (US$5) at the south end of the beach; he also hires out horses for reasonable prices.

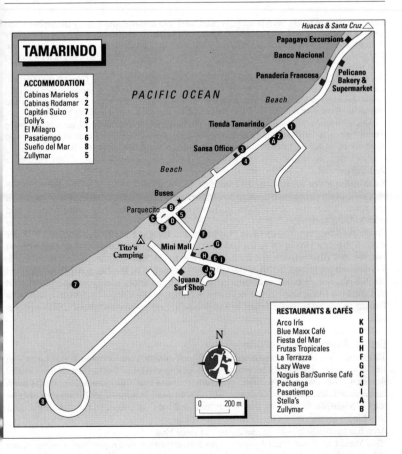

TAMARINDO

ACCOMMODATION

Cabinas Marielos	4
Cabinas Rodamar	2
Capitán Suizo	7
Dolly's	3
El Milagro	1
Pasatiempo	6
Sueño del Mar	8
Zullymar	5

RESTAURANTS & CAFÉS

Arco Iris	K
Blue Maxx Café	D
Fiesta del Mar	E
Frutas Tropicales	H
La Terrazza	F
Lazy Wave	G
Noguis Bar/Sunrise Café	C
Pachanga	J
Pasatiempo	I
Stella's	A
Zullymar	B

Cabinas Marielos (☎ & fax 653-0141). Basic rooms, light and clean, with fan, cold water and the use of a small kitchen, in pleasant and colourful grounds. The *dueña* is helpful and professional, though she insists on all rooms being booked and paid for in advance. ④.

Cabinas Rodamar (☎653-0109). Basic budget traveller's hangout, with dark and spartan cabinas set back from the main road. It's friendly, though, and you can use the shared kitchen. ②.

Capitán Suizo (☎653-0075, fax 653-0292, *www.hotelcapitansuizo.com*). Popular and upmarket Swiss-run hotel set in spacious landscaped grounds on the beach. The *cabina*-style rooms all have a balcony or terrace, fridge, ceiling fans or a/c, bathtub, hot water and an outside shower. The pool is bigger than most, and the atmosphere friendly and relaxed. There's also a cocktail bar, beautiful beach views and a buffet breakfast. Good low-season discounts. ⑦–⑧.

Dolly's (☎653-0017). Friendly place popular with surfers and budget travellers, but fills up fast. The rooms are basic verging on uncomfortable, with flimsy beds, fan and private bath – those upstairs are quieter and have sea views. There's a bar and restaurant attached. ③.

El Milagro (☎653-0042, fax 653-0050, *flokiro@racsa.co.cr*). A favourite with Europeans, featuring nicely decorated cabinas with private bath (cold water) and either fan (⑤) or a/c (⑥). Some rooms are generously proportioned, with French windows opening onto flowered terraces. The poolside restaurant serves great food. Breakfast included.

Pasatiempo (☎653-0096, fax 653-0275). Popular hotel with a relaxed and friendly atmosphere. The spotless rooms have ceiling fans and hot water – the larger rooms (sleeping 5) are a particularly good deal. The atmosphere is homely, with hammocks strung outside the rooms and around the nice pool, and there's also a lively restaurant and very popular bar (though it can get a bit loud in high season). ⑦.

Sueño del Mar, 1km from Tamarindo on the road heading south to Playa Langosta (☎653-0284, *www.tamarindo.com/sdmar*). Swing in a hammock on the ocean-facing veranda of this beautiful house, designed in Spanish-hacienda style with tiled roofs and adobe walls. The three rooms and one *casita* all come with pretty tiled showers, and rates include a tasty and filling breakfast. ⑦.

Zullymar (☎653-0140). Clean, spacious and – for Tamarindo – reasonably priced cabinas, set in pleasant grounds scattered with reproductions of pre-Columbian art. The rooms with fan and cold water are about half the price of than those with fridge, a/c and "hot" showers. ③.

Activities

Swimming is not great around Tamarindo, as the waves are fairly heavy and there are rip tides. Most people are content to paddle in the rocky coves and tide-pools south of the town. A number of outfitters in Tamarindo rent **surfboards**, **windsurfers** and **snorkelling equipment**; most charge US$15–20 a day for a surfboard and US$12 a day for snorkelling gear. You can also rent **bikes** and **boogie boards** (both about US$8 per day). Agua Rica Diving (☎ & fax 653-0094) have a good reputation and do certification courses and **dive trips** in the area – their trip to the Islas Catalinas is recommended. The Iguana Surf Shop, south of the village (☎ & fax 653-0148), has a larger selection of surfboards, boogie boards and snorkelling gear. In addition, numerous operators, such as Papagayo Excursions at the northern entrance to the village (☎653-0254, *papagayo @racsa.co.cr*), offer **turtle tours** to Las Baulas in nesting season (about US$15 per person).

Eating, drinking and nightlife

Tamarindo has an astounding number of good-quality, cosmopolitan restaurants – in fact, it's well on its way to becoming the gourmet capital of Costa Rica, if not Central America. The town's large Italian population means that this cuisine is perhaps over-represented, but French, Mexican, Costa Rican (and fusions of all these) can also be found. **Nightlife** focuses on the restaurants and bars – a couple of them with pleasant beachfront locations – in the centre of the village.

Arco Irís Impressively large vegeterian menu. Closed Mon.

Blue Maxx Cafe Good, filling American breakfasts, served with real cappuccino or espresso, and tasty fresh sandwiches and salads at lunch – a nice place to go for a coffee at any time of day.

Fiesta del Mar Recommended by locals for good quality "surf n' turf" (meat dishes served with seafood) at slightly above-average prices (US$10–12 for most main dishes). Good selection of non-alcoholic fruit drinks and fruit cocktails, too.

Frutas Tropicales One of the few genuinely cheap places in Tamarindo. As the name says, there's plenty of tropical fruit in this little snack bar – try the fruit *refrescos*. Otherwise, the menu is the usual soda fare, with *casados* (US$3.50) and hamburgers (US$3) both good bets. They also rent out a couple of cabinas (③).

La Terrazza Good, authentic Italian pizzas, with an impressive view of the village and beach from the upstairs dining room.

Lazy Wave This outdoor restaurant may look casual, but it dishes up some of the best cooking in the area, if not the country, with a very fairly priced menu (changes daily) distinguished by the delicacy and inventiveness of its ingredients and flavours. The bakery-patisserie is worth a visit too.

Noguis Bar/Sunrise Cafe Serves excellent breakfasts, with good breads, pastries and coffees, which you can either eat at the breezy seaside tables or take away.

Pachanga Intimate, candlelit restaurant, tastefully decorated, and with a dependable menu including *dorado* curry (US$8) and BBQ ribs (US$10). No credit cards.

MOVING ON FROM TAMARINDO

There's a direct bus to **San José** daily at 6am (6hr), and one to **Liberia** daily at 6am (1–2hr). Alternatively, you could take one of the daily buses to **Santa Cruz** at 10am and 3pm, from where you can connect with local services to Liberia or San José (call ☎221-7202 for schedule information). As always, bus timetables are likely to change. Buses currently stop at the town circle, in front of the Parquecito. Continuing down the west coast of the peninsula is only really possible if you have your own transport, preferably a 4WD, although you can pick up occasional services to Sámara or Nosara from Santa Cruz and Nicoya.

Travelair and Sansa both have daily **flights** to San José; Sansa also operate a daily flight to San José via Fortuna in the Arenal area (US$60). You can buy tickets from the Sansa office, on the road into town on the right-hand side, about 400m before you reach the village loop. The airstrip is located 2.5km north of town.

Panadería Francesa (although the sign still says "Johan's Bakery"). Small bakery serving delicious fresh croissants, *pan dulce*, *pain au chocolat*, banana cake, pizza, waffles and apple flan for breakfast.

Pasatiempo, in the hotel of the same name. Perennially good restaurant serving crowd-pleasers like Caesar salad (US$4) and a wonderfully succulent blackened fish with greens, or try the chicken breast with mango stuffing (US$8). Very reasonable prices, too, which isn't always the case in Tamarindo. If nothing else, try the superlative fruit cocktails and a few nibbles. Live music twice a week in high season.

Pelicano Bakery and Supermarket Tasty, high-quality sweets and sandwiches, with wholewheat sandwiches, coffee, desserts, bagels and takeout lunches.

Stella's One of Tamarindo's best restaurants, with good Italian pasta and fresh fish cooked in excellent, inventive sauces. A large menu encompasses wood-oven-baked pizzas and even – rare for Costa Rica – veal. Main courses US$8–12. Closed Sun.

Zullymar Unbeatable beachfront location – everybody seems to come here for a drink whilst watching the sun go down – and good food, with main dishes for US$5–7. Breakfasts are tasty and (for Tamarindo) good value, while the típico dishes – *pargo* and *dorado* fish *casados* in particular – are always well prepared.

Nicoya

Bus travellers making connections between, say, Tamarindo and Sámara sometimes end up having to spend a night in **NICOYA,** the main settlement of the peninsula. Set in a dip surrounded by low mountains, it's a hot place, but undeniably pretty, with a lovely **Parque Central**, centring on a preserved white adobe church (earthquake-battered, structurally unstable and currently closed).

Practicalities

Eight **buses** a day arrive in Nicoya from San José, a journey of around six hours. Some take the slightly longer route via the road to Liberia, but most use the Tempisque ferry (see box overleaf). Buses also arrive from a number of regional destinations, including Liberia (10 daily), Santa Cruz (16 daily), Sámara (3 daily) and Nosara (1 daily). Most buses arrive at Nicoya's spotless bus station on the southern edge of town, a short walk from the centre; the Liberia service pulls in across from the *Hotel Las Tinajas*. As usual, you'll find most **services** around the Parque Central, including the *correo* (Mon–Fri 7.30am–5.30pm) and the Banco de Costa Rica. The Banco Popular has an ATM that accepts foreign-issued cards – it's 100m east and 300m north of the Parque Central on the main road out of town. **Taxis** line up by the Parque, or call Coopetico (☎658-6226).

THE RÍO TEMPISQUE FERRY

The **Río Tempisque ferry** carries cars and passengers across the river between Puerto Moreno, 17km from the Nicoya–Carmona road, and a point 25km west of the Interamericana on the mainland. Crossing here will save you a 110-kilometre drive up and over the cleft of the peninsula, via Liberia, but leave yourself plenty of time on weekends (Fridays and Sundays especially) and holidays, when the line-up of traffic can mean waits of four to five hours. Whatever time you cross, and in whichever direction, be in line about an hour before departure. Unless curtailed by bad weather in the wet season, **eastbound** crossings take place on the half-hour between 6.30am and 8.30pm, **westbound** every hour on the hour from 6am to 8pm – it takes twenty minutes.

The friendly *Hotel Jenny* (☎685-5050; ②), 200m south of the Parque Central, is the cheapest **place to stay**, with old, basic rooms with air-conditioning, TV and phone. The similarly priced *Hotel Las Tinajas* (☎685-5081; ②), 100m northeast of the Parque Central, is nicer, with dark rooms inside the main building and lighter cabinas around the back. Good **restaurants** include the *Cafetería Daniela*, 100m east of the Parque, for breakfast and pastries; the sodas by the Parque for large *casados*; and, for Chinese food, the *Restaurant El Teyet*, across from the *Hotel Jenny*.

Playa Sámara

For sheer size, and for safety for swimming, **SÁMARA**, 30km southwest of Nicoya, is probably the best beach in Costa Rica, especially now that local residents and visitors have tackled the litter problem that once plagued its wide, flat sands. The waves break on a reef about a kilometre out, so the water near the shore is actually quite calm. It's also a great place to relax, and its distance from the capital means it's quieter than the more accessible Pacific beaches.

Arrival and information

Sansa and Travelair **planes** from San José arrive at the airstrip 6km south of town at Carrillo, from where 4WD taxis make the trip to Sámara for about US$6. The express **bus** from San José leaves daily at 12:15pm, 12:30pm and 6:15pm, and arrives at Sámara some six hours later, stopping about 50m in front of the beach right at the centre of the village. The express bus **back to San José** currently leaves at 4.30pm and 9am Monday to Friday, and at 7am and 1pm on Sunday. There are buses **to Nicoya** at 5am, 7am, 1.30pm and 4.30pm (2hr).

You can buy tickets for some bus services from the Transporte Alfaro office (daily 7am–5pm), next door to the *Pulpería Mileth* in the centre of the village, which also sells potato chips, suntan lotion and bottles of cold water, and is home to the village's public **telephone**. Sámara's **correo** (Mon–Fri 7.30am–6pm) – a small shack really – 50m before the entrance to the beach, offers minimal services, and there is nowhere to **change money** (other than at the large hotels), so bring plenty of colones, especially in low season.

There aren't as many **tours** or other activities at Sámara as around other places on the peninsula, due to the sheer distance and driving time it takes to get anywhere. Jorge Gonzalez does **taxi tours** (☎656-0081, mobile 390-4198) to the pottery-making village of Guatíl for US$40 per day, and to Rincón de la Vieja (US$70 per day, including park entrance). You could try Sámara Adventures (☎656-0655, *j_esqui@yahoo.com*), 100m south of the soccer field at the Super Samara, for tours to Ostional Wildlife Reserve, and for **whitewater rafting** and **sports-fishing** trips anywhere in the country.

Accommodation

Staying in Sámara is getting pricier, with few cheap cabinas. Though during the low season most hotels can offer better rates than the ones listed here, at high-season weekends you should have a **reservation** no matter what price range you're aiming for. *Camping Coco*, on the beach, is clean and well-run, with cooking grills, as is *Camping Playas Sámara*, at the north end of the beach, with toilets and showers (both US$3 a night).

Belvedere B&B, 100m down the road to Carillo (☎ & fax 656-0213, *belvedere@samarabeach.com*). Wonderfully pleasant and excellent-value hotel. The ten rooms and two apartments come with either a/c or fan (US$8 less), and all are brightly furnished in light wood, with mosquito nets and solar-heated water. There's also a Jacuzzi and whirlpool, and a good German breakfast is included. ④.

Casa Naranja, in the centre of the village (☎656-0220). Owned by Suzanne, an energetic ex-chef from Paris, this small, central hotel has three rooms (one with a/c) in a modern building. The very fair price includes a good French breakfast, and the attached bar-restaurant-creperie is highly recommended. Visa accepted. ④.

Giada, about 100m before you come to the beach, on the left (☎656-0132, fax 656-0131, *www.hotelgiada.net*). Small hotel set round a compact pool, with spotless banana-yellow rooms, good beds, overhead fans, private baths and tiled showers – the upstairs rooms are better for views and breeze. The friendly management also offer good-value dollar exchange (for guests only) and sell Sansa air tickets. ④.

Hotel Marbella, first left as you come into town from Nosara (☎ & fax 656-0122). Fairly cheap hotel, with a tiny pool – for plunging rather than swimming – and fourteen rather dark but brightly painted rooms. The helpful management can advise on transport in the area and also rent out bikes. ④.

Hotel Mirador de Sámara, 100m up the hill from the *Marbella* (☎656-0044, fax 656-0046, *www.miradordesamara.com*). Huge apartments (US$80) sleeping five to seven people, with large bathrooms, bedrooms, living rooms, kitchen and terrace, all with panoramic views over the town and beach. The bar is in an impressive tower with a 360° view for watching the spectacular sunsets, and there's a new pool with nice wooden sundecks. Good low-season and long-stay discounts, but the price means it's better value for four or more people, rather than couples.

Magica Cantarana, Playa Buena Vista, 1km north of Sámara on the road to Nosara (☎656-0071, fax 656-0260). In a quiet beachside setting, with plain but comfortable rooms in a modern two-storey building with swimming pool – the upstairs rooms with balconies are best. ④.

Eating, drinking and nightlife

There are a couple of very nice places to **eat** in Sámara, where you can enjoy a cold beer by the lapping waves. **Nightlife** is quiet, though things can get a bit loud on Friday and Saturday nights in high season, when the *Tutti Fruti* disco at the old *Hotel Playa Sámara* comes into its own.

Ananas, in front of the beach. Bar-restaurant, nicely set in a small rancho, serving incredibly tasty fruit salads, juices, breakfasts and coffee-and-cake combinations. Open for breakfast, lunch and afternoon coffee only.

Creperie Naranja, in *Casa Naranja* in the centre of the village. Authentic French cuisine (the owner is a former Paris chef) served in a small outdoor garden lit with candles in the evening. The wide menu offers, among other things, savoury crepes (US$3.50), French favourites like *duck à la orange* (US$5) and some incredible traditional cakes and desserts, flans, tartes and sweet crepes from US$3 to US$4 – pricey, but worth every penny.

Dorado, opposite the soccer field. German-run establishment with good fish dishes, particularly the filet of its namesake *dorado* (sea bass), although the *pargo* (snapper) is also very good – both are a real bargain at US$3 each with tasty vegetables.

El Ancla, next door to the *Delfín*. Relatively new restaurant on the beach, with a long menu of fish dishes and a pretty setting close to the water.

Isla Chora Inn, 400m down the Nosara road. Run by an Italian couple, with superb ice-cream and thin-crust pizza – the *pizza con mariscos* (US$7) is spectacular – as well as good pasta dishes and attentive service.

Nosara and around

The pretty drive from Sámara 25km north to the village of **NOSARA** runs along shady and secluded dirt and gravel roads punctuated by a few creeks – it's passable with a regular car in the dry season, but you'll need a 4WD in the wet. The village itself, properly called Bocas de Nosara, is set some 3km inland, between a low ridge of hills and the sea. Usually grouped together as **Playas Nosara**, the three beaches in the area – Nosara, Guiones and Pelada – are fine for **swimming**, although you can be buffetted by the crashing waves, and there are some rocky outcrops. Playa Guiones is the most impressive of the beaches: nearly 5km in length and with probably the best swimming, though there's precious little shade. The whole area is a great place to go beachcombing for shells and driftwood, and the vegetation, even in the dry season, is greener than further north. Some attempts have been made to limit development, and a good deal of the land around the Río Nosara has been designated a wildlife refuge.

In contrast to the busier Sámara, the vast majority of people who come to Nosara are North Americans and Europeans in search of quiet and natural surroundings. Much of the accommodation is slighly upmarket, and the owners and managers are more environmentally conscious than at many other places on the peninsula. A local civic association keeps a hawkish eye on development in the area, with the aim of keeping Nosara as it is, rather than having it become another Tamarindo or Sámara.

Arrival and information

Travelair and Sansa **fly** daily except Sunday to Nosara from San José, usually via Sámara, landing at the small airstrip. The San José **bus** comes in at the Abastecedor general store. There isn't much to the village itself apart from a soccer field, a couple of restaurants and a gas station (the latter is little more than a shack, with no pumps to show what it is – gas is siphoned out of a barrel). The Nosara Office Center (Mon–Fri 9am–noon & 1.30pm–5pm, Sat 9am–2pm), on the left as you enter the village, can send faxes and has the only **Internet access** south of Tamarindo (US$3 for 15min – pricey, but then there's no competition). They also reconfirm flights and sell tickets to San José on the private charter service Pitts Aviation. The **correo** (Mon–Fri 7.30am–6pm) is next to the airstrip, and public **phones** are in front of the police station, next to the Cruz Roja. You can rent **bikes** at Souvenirs Tuanis in the ramshackle old house on the corner of the village. If it's long-term accommodation or taxis to the Ostional refuge you're after, check out their notice board.

Accommodation

If you want to stay on the **beach** you've got two options: posh **gringo-run accommodation** or **camping**. There's a group of economical cabinas and hotels in the village – but you'll need to rent a bike or count on doing a lot of walking to get to the ocean.

Cabinas Chorotega, in the village (☎682-0105). Small, ten-room complex of pleasant cabinas with large rooms – those upstairs are best, though they're reached by an extremely steep staircase. There's a communal terrace with rocking chairs where you can sit with a beer and watch the scenery. ②–③.

Café de Paris, south end of Nosara, at the entrance to Playa Guiones (☎682-0087, fax 682-0089, *www.cafedeparis.net*). Well-appointed rooms set in bungalows arranged around the pool, all with private bath and hot water, and a choice of ceiling fans or a/c. Rooms range from standard doubles to suites with a/c, kitchen, fridge and a small rancho with hammocks. ④.

Casa Romantica, behind Playa Nosara (☎682-0019, *www.nosara.com/casaromantica*). Clean and well-kept family-run hotel, right on the beach, with bright rooms, all with hot water, fridge and terrace (along with a family room sleeping five people). There's also a pool and a fantastic on-site restaurant. If you fly or take the bus the owners will pick you up if you let them know in advance. ⑤.

Casa Tucan, 200m east from Playa Guiones (☎ & fax 682-0113, *casatucan@nosara.com*). Small, eight-room hotel, with brightly decorated rooms (four with kitchen, US$70), sleeping up to five people; all have private bath and hot water, and fan or a/c (US$10 extra). There's a good restaurant and bar, including a new juice bar, on the premises. Good low-season or long-stay discounts. The owner will pick you up if you fly in on Sansa or Pitts Aviation. ⑤.

Lagarta Lodge, signposted from the village (☎682-0035, fax 682-0135, *www.nosara.com/lagarta*). Set in a small private nature reserve, this lodge has excellent bird-watching and stunning coastal views – the rooms above the pool looking out onto the ocean have one of the best panoramas in the country. Rooms have private bath, hot water and fridges. A healthy buffet breakfast (not included) and evening meals are also available. ⑥.

Playas Nosara, on the hilltop, between Playas Guiones and Pelada; follow the signs (☎682-0121, fax 682-0123, *www.nosarabeachhotel.com*). Dramatically situated hotel on a headland overlooking the beach and pine-clad coastline. The large, clean, cool rooms with fans are priced according to the quality of the view (not all rooms overlook the beach). Unfortunately, ongoing building works can make the place look like a construction site. ④.

Eating and drinking

The Nosara area has experienced a mini-explosion of restaurants in the past few years. Many of them are very good, and prices are not as high as you might expect, given the area's relative isolation. There are a number of places in the **village**, most of them around the soccer field or on the road into town, though most of the better restaurants are huddled together near **Playa Guiones**, which is where the majority of tourists eat.

Bar-restaurant Tucan, next to the *Casa Tucan* hotel. The menu features seafood in adventurous fruit-based sauces, lobster, chicken, pasta and steaks (all US$7–12), served in a pleasant rancho strung with inviting hammocks and coloured lights. A new juice bar offers "create-your-own" drinks.

Café de Paris, at the southern entrance to Playa Guiones. The brioche and *pain au chocolat* confirm this bakery as a bona-fide overseas *département* of France, while the pleasant poolside restaurant serves sandwiches and pizzas for lunch (US$4–9).

Giardino Tropicale, south end of Nosara, on the road towards Sámara. Superior-quality pizza cooked in a wood oven and served in a pretty plant-strewn dining area.

Gilded Iguana, behind Playa Guiones. Upmarket bar with Mexican food that attracts the local expats, and well-priced lunch specials including filet of *dorado* (US$4) and fish and chips (US$3). Closed Mon, Tues & Sun.

Soda El Tico, across from the airstrip. Geared toward locals, though budget travellers might want to check out its comida típica, served in a small diner-type room.

Soda Vanessa, next to *Cabinas Agnell*, Nosara village. Recommended by locals for its cheap and well-prepared *casados*.

Refugio Nacional de Fauna Silvestre Ostional

Eight kilometres northeast of Nosara, Ostional and its chocolate-coloured sand beach make up the **Refugio Nacional De Fauna Silvestre Ostional**, one of the most important nesting grounds in the country for **Olive Ridley turtles** who come ashore to lay their eggs between May and November. You can't swim here, though, since the water's too rough, and is plagued by sharks.

If you're in town during the first few days of the *arribadas* you'll see local villagers with horses, carefully stuffing their big, thick bags full of eggs and slinging them over their shoulders. This is quite legal: villagers of Ostional and Nosara are allowed to harvest eggs, for sale or consumption, during the first three days of the season only. Don't be surprised to see them barefoot, rocking back and forth on their heels as if they were crushing grapes in a winery; this is the surest way to pick up the telltale signs of eggs beneath the sand. It takes about fifteen minutes to drive the gravel-and-stone road from Nosara to the refuge; alternately you can bike it or take a taxi.

travel details

BUSES

Liberia to: La Cruz (14 daily; 1hr); Nicoya (10 daily; 2hr); Parque Nacional Santa Rosa (5 daily; 1hr); Peñas Blancas (5 daily; 2hr); Playa del Coco (3–4 daily; 1hr); Playa Hermosa (2 daily; 1hr); Playa Panamá (2 daily; 1hr); Puntarenas (5 daily; 3hr); San José (8 daily; 4hr 30min); Santa Cruz (14 daily; 1hr); Tamarindo (1 daily; 1–2hr).

Nicoya to: Liberia (10 daily; 2hr); Nosara (1 daily; 2hr); Playa Sámara (3 daily; 2hr); San José (8 daily; 6hr); Santa Cruz (16 daily; 40min).

Nosara to: Nicoya (1 daily; 2hr); Playa Sámara (1 daily; 40min); San José (1 daily; 6hr).

Peñas Blancas to: Liberia (5 daily; 2hr); San José (3 daily; 6hr).

Playa del Coco to: Liberia (3–4 daily; 1hr); San José (1 daily; 5hr).

Playa Hermosa to: Liberia (2 daily; 1hr); San José (1 daily; 5hr).

Playa Panamá to: Liberia (2 daily; 1hr); San José (1 daily; 5hr).

Playa Sámara to: Nicoya (3 daily; 2hr); Nosara (1 daily; 40min); San José (2 daily; 6hr).

San José to: Cañas (6 daily; 3hr 30min); Junquillal (1 daily; 5hr); Liberia (8 daily; 4hr 30min); Nicoya (8 daily; 6hr); Nosara (1 daily; 6hr); Peñas Blancas (3 daily; 6hr); Playa del Coco (1 daily; 5hr); Playa Hermosa (1 daily; 5hr); Playa Panamá (1 daily; 5hr); Playa Sámara (3 daily; 6hr); Santa Cruz (5 daily; 5hr); Parque Nacional Santa Rosa (4 daily; 6hr); Tamarindo (1 daily; 6hr).

Santa Cruz to: Liberia (14 daily; 1hr); Nicoya (16 daily; 40min); San José (5 daily; 5hr); Tamarindo (2 direct daily; 1hr).

Tamarindo to: Liberia (1 daily; 1–2hr); San José (1 daily; 6hr); Santa Cruz (2 direct daily; 1hr).

FLIGHTS

Sansa

San José to: Liberia (1 daily); Nosara (Mon–Sat 1 daily); Playa Sámara (Mon–Sat 1 daily); Tamarindo (3 daily).

Travelair

San José to: Liberia (1 daily); Nosara (Mon–Sat 1 daily); Playa Sámara (1 daily); Tamarindo via Liberia (1 daily), Tamarindo via Fortuna (1 daily).

CHAPTER 32

THE ZONA NORTE

osta Rica's **Zona Norte** ("northern zone") spans the hundred-odd kilometres
from the base of the Cordillera Central to just short of the mauve-blue mountains of southern Nicaragua. Cut off from the rest of the country by a lack of
roads, the Zona Norte has developed a distinct character, with independent-
minded farmers and Nicaraguan refugees making up large segments of the population.
Neither group journeys to the Valle Central very often, and many people of the north
hold a special allegiance to and pride in their area.

Geographically, the Zona Norte separates neatly into two broad, river-drained plains
(*llanuras*), which stretch all the way to the Río San Juan on the Nicaraguan–Costa Rican
border. Less obviously picturesque than many parts of the country, the entire region
nonetheless has a distinctive appeal, with lazy rivers snaking across steaming plains
scarred by trails of blood-orange soil, and flop-eared cattle languishing beneath the
draped limbs of riverside trees.

Most travellers only venture up here to see the perpetually active **Volcán Arenal**,
using the nearby town of **Fortuna** as their base. To the east is the **Sarapiquí** area, with
its tropical forest **eco-lodges** and research stations of **La Selva** and **Rara Avis**.
Further north, the remote flatlands are home to the increasingly accessible **Refugio
Nacional de Vida Silvestre Caño Negro**, which harbours an extraordinary number
of migratory and indigenous birds.

The **climate** in the north is hot and wet, more so in the east than in the west near
Guanacaste, where there is a dry season. There's a serviceable **bus** network, though if
you're travelling outside the La Fortuna or Puerto Viejo areas, you'd probably do better with a car. As for other facilities, the area around Volcán Arenal is best geared up for
tourists, even boasting a couple of excellent five-star **hotels**. Between Boca de Arenal
and Los Chiles in the far north, on the other hand, there is a real shortage of accommodation, though fuel and food are in good supply.

Volcán Arenal and La Fortuna

That the Arenal region attracts such huge numbers of tourists is largely due to the
majestic **Volcán Arenal**, one of the most active volcanoes in the Western hemisphere.
Just 6km away, **LA FORTUNA DE SAN CARLOS**, or **Fortuna**, as it is more often
called, was until recently a simple agricultural town. Nowadays, true to its name, it's
booming, with visitors flocking to watch the lava ooze down the lip of the volcano like
juice from a squashed fruit.

Now very much geared to the tourist market, Fortuna is a curiously characterless
place, although people are friendly enough. There's nothing to do except book tours,
bed down and have a meal or a beer, and gaze at the volcano, looming 1633m above
town. One popular excursion is to Fortuna's two **cataratas** (waterfalls), just 6km from
the south side of the church in town and an easy day's hike (make sure to wear sturdy,

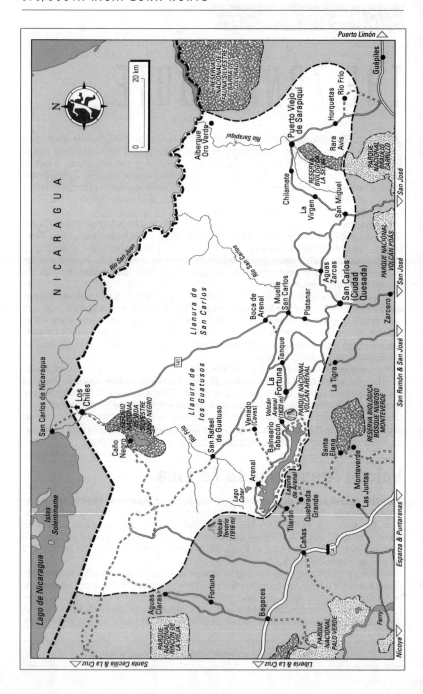

waterproof shoes) or half-day horse ride. Fortuna also has excellent **bus** connections, making it one of the main setting-off points for tours to the remote wildlife refuge of **Caño Negro** and something of a transportation hub for the region as a whole.

Note that as Fortuna becomes increasingly popular, opportunistic **theft** is rising; never leave anything unattended, especially in a car, and be careful about walking around alone late at night. Also be wary of "guides" who offer their services on the street.

Arrival and information

There are three **direct bus services from San José to Fortuna**, currently leaving La Coca-Cola at 6.15am, 8.40am and 11.30am. You could also take a direct bus from **San José to San Carlos**, where you can change for frequent buses to Fortuna (40km; 1hr). From Tilarán, take either the 8am or the 1.30pm bus (3hr). Buses from San José, San Carlos and Tilarán all stop by the soccer field in the middle of the village – it's never hard to orient yourself: the volcano is west.

Most hotels will **change money** for about the same rate as the Banco Nacional opposite the soccer field; apart from a few of the more expensive hotels, this is the only place to change travellers' cheques. There are **phones** scattered about town, most of which purport to take local and international phonecards, but only one or two of them actually work – they're the ones with the queues. There's **Internet access** at the Desafío Tours office, across from Rancho La Cascada, and the Aguas Bravas tour agency, on the main road opposite the soccer field, sells *La Nación*, the *Tico Times* and the *New York Times* – this is also the best place to **rent bikes** (around US$10/day for sturdy mountain bikes).

Taxis line up on the south side of the Parque Central – they rarely (if ever) use their meters, so agree a price before getting in and beware of overcharging. Try to negotiate a lower price than the first one you're quoted, or ask locals what they currently pay.

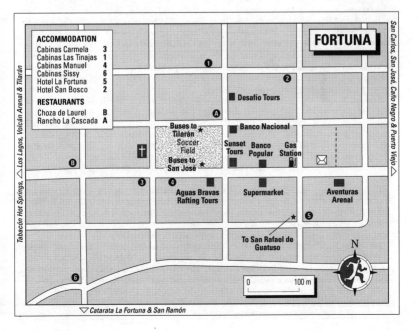

FORTUNA

ACCOMMODATION	
Cabinas Carmela	3
Cabinas Las Tinajas	1
Cabinas Manuel	4
Cabinas Sissy	6
Hotel La Fortuna	5
Hotel San Bosco	2
RESTAURANTS	
Choza de Laurel	B
Rancho La Cascada	A

Los Lagos, Volcán Arenal & Tilarán

Tabacón Hot Springs,

San Carlos, San José, Caño Negro & Puerto Viejo

❶
❷
■ Desafío Tours
Ⓐ
Buses to Tilarán
Soccer Field
Buses to San José
■ Banco Nacional
Sunset Tours
Banco Popular
Gas Station
✉
Ⓑ
❸
❹
■ Aguas Bravas Rafting Tours
■ Supermarket
■ Aventuras Arenal
❺
To San Rafael de Guatuso
❻

0   100 m

N

▽ *Catarata La Fortuna & San Ramón*

Accommodation

People with their own transport and a bit of money tend to stay in the **lodges** either on the road between Fortuna and La Tigra/San Ramón, on the road linking Fortuna and the Parque Nacional Volcán Arenal, or in one of the many pleasant hotels that border Laguna de Arenal. Budget travellers tend to stay in town – really the only option if you don't have your own transport. Most of the simple **cabinas** sprouting up all over town are pretty similar, with a few plain rooms and cold showers. Competition means that Fortuna is also one of the few places in the country where you might encounter **hotel touts** as you stumble off the bus. Note that single rooms are hard to find.

Alberge Ecotouristico La Catarata, 1.5km from of Fortuna on the road to Arenal, then 1.5km down a signed turn-off to the left (☎479-9522, fax 479-9168, *www.agroecoturismo.net*). This local initiative, part funded by the Canadian World Wildlife Fund, also includes a butterfly farm, an experi-

---

TOURS FROM FORTUNA

Price competition between tour agencies in Fortuna is fierce, but bear in mind that while you may save a few dollars by going with the cheapest agency, you could end up on a badly organized tour with under-qualified guides, or no lunch – get as many details as you can before you put down your cash. In general, it's worth going with a reputable tour operator, such as those listed below, and not with one of the freelance "guides" who may approach you; one was recently convicted of the rape of a female tourist whilst on a tour.

By far the most popular excursion is the late-afternoon hike around **Volcán Arenal**, followed by a night-time soak in the thermal pools at **Balneario Tabacón**, though few tours include the admission fee (US$15) in their prices. The volcano hike involves a walk through rainforest, much of it uphill, and a final scramble over lava rocks – take care, as they're particularly sharp, and few guides carry a medical kit. Bring a torch, too. The actual sight of the volcano – if you're lucky enough to be there on a clear night when there's activity – is amazing. Scarlet rivers of lava pour from the top, and you can hear the crunch of boulders landing as they are spewed from the mouth of the volcano. Also popular are horse-rides to the **Catarata de la Fortuna**, boat trips to **Caño Negro** (see p.675), and rafting down the **Río Sarapiquí**. A popular new trip is the transfer to **Monteverde** (4–5hr), using a combination of taxi, boat and horse – it's faster and much more interesting than taking the local bus.

Sunset Tours (☎479-9415, fax 479-9099, *www.sunset-tours.com*), on the main road, to the east of the soccer field, is pricier than other tour operators, but has professional, well-qualified guides. Their volcano tours (US$25) include the entrance fee to the national park, but not to Balneario Tabacón. They have a good day-trip to Caño Negro (US$45), as well as taxi transfers to Monteverde (US$30). Trips run by the professional **Aventuras Arenal**, 150m east of the soccer field (☎ & fax 479-9133), are almost identical and slightly cheaper, and they can also offer transport to just about anywhere in the country.

Desafío Tours (☎479-9464, fax 479-9178, *desafio@racsa.co.cr*) across from *Rancho La Cascada* are friendly, efficient and helpful rafting specialists and run half- and full-day tours (US$65–70) for all levels on the Ríos Toro, Peñas Blancas and Sarapiquí. They also offer the jeep-boat-horse-jeep transfer to Monteverde for an economical price, and can sort out flights, tours and accommodation anywhere in the country.

Jacamar (☎479-9767, fax 479-9456, *jacamar@racsa.co.cr*), next to the *Lava Rocks* restaurant, does an Arenal night tour (US$25), trips to Caño Negro (US$45) and gentle rafting excursions on the Río Peñas Blancas. Their boat-and-taxi (no horses) transfer to Monteverde costs US$25 and takes (they claim) just two hours. **Aguas Bravas** (☎479-9025, fax 229-4837), on the main road opposite the soccer field, offers whitewater-rafting trips on the Río Sarapiquí.

mental project to breed pacas and a medicinal herb farm. The eight rustic but comfortable cabinas all have private bath with hot water, and a hearty breakfast is included; the restaurant serves food made with organic produce from its garden. ③

Cabinas Carmela, opposite the church on the main road (☎479-9010). Good budget option, with ten spacious rooms (all with private bath and hot water) made slightly more homely by the wooden – as opposed to concrete – walls. ③

Cabinas Las Tinajas, 100m north and 25m west of the soccer field (☎479-9308, fax 479-9145). Small complex of four clean, well-furnished and airy cabinas, run by friendly owners; very good value. ③

Cabinas Manuel, opposite the church on the main road (☎479-9069). Simple, well-kept budget cabinas run by the helpful Señora Mercedes Castro. She'll also do your laundry for a reasonable price. ②

Cabinas Sissy, 100m south and 125m west of the soccer field (☎479-9256). Basic budget travellers' hangout, friendly and clean, with eight good-sized rooms with hot-water showers. You can also camp here for US$3. ①

Hotel Arenal Paraíso, 5km outside Fortuna en route to the volcano (☎460-5333, fax 460-5343, *www.arenalparaiso.decostarica.co.cr*). Attractive hotel with expensive-looking wooden cabinas, all with private bath with hot water (some also have fridges) and huge porches looking out directly onto the volcano. The adjacent restaurant serves good meals. ⑤

Hotel La Fortuna, 75m south and 100m east of the soccer field (☎479-9197). Basic but good-value hotel – the ten rooms come with shared or private bath. It's very popular with budget travellers, so book in advance. Breakfast included. ②

Hotel San Bosco, 100m northeast of the soccer field (☎479-9050, fax 479-9109). Rooms vary widely in price and size; some are large and a bargain, others are tiny – if you don't like the first room you're shown, ask for another. All have overhead fans and spacious baths with hot water. The hotel is managed by a friendly and informative local family, and there are excellent views of Arenal from the pool and Jacuzzi terrace on the upper level. Breakfast included. ④

Eating and drinking

Considering the number of tourists passing through, **restaurant** prices (US$5–7 per person for dinner) in La Fortuna are quite fair, catering for locals as much as visitors. The food is pretty much the same everywhere: the inevitable *casados, platos del día* and *arroz-con*-whatever. There's no evening activity to speak of; *Rancho la Cascada* and *Choza de Laurel* are where people head for a beer.

MOVING ON FROM LA FORTUNA

Despite its small size, Fortuna is something of a **transport hub**, and with a little planning you can get from here to Guanacaste, Puntarenas, Monteverde and Puerto Viejo de Sarapiquí without backtracking to San José. For **Puerto Viejo de Sarapiquí**, take a bus to **San Carlos** (6 daily; 1hr), where you can pick up a service east to Puerto Viejo. Buses currently leave San Carlos for Puerto Viejo at 6am, 10am and 3pm, but double-check these times, since if you miss your connection you'll need to stay the night. For **Monteverde**, there are two daily buses from Fortuna to **Tilarán**, at the head of Laguna de Arenal (3hr). The bus currently leaves at 8am and 5pm – if you take the later one you'll have to stay the night in Tilarán. You can connect in Tilarán with the Santa Elena service (for the Monteverde Cloudforest Reserve), which currently leaves at 1pm (3–4hr). There are also frequent local services from Tilarán to **Cañas** and the Interamericana, where you can pick up buses north to **Liberia** and the beaches of **Guanacaste**, or south to **Puntarenas**. To get back to **San José** from Fortuna, take the Garaje Barquero *directo* service (3 daily; 4hr 30min), which currently departs at 2.45pm, or head to San Carlos (see above) from where you can connect with hourly buses to the capital.

For those **driving**, the roads are good, with the exception of a perennially difficult patch between Fortuna and Arenal Town.

Parque Nacional Volcán Arenal

Though **Volcán Arenal** is one of the most active volcanoes in the Americas, whether you will see any lava flow depends very much on the weather. In the rainy season the spectacular night flows are very elusive, hidden by shrouds of mist and cloud. However, if nothing else you'll certainly hear unearthly rumbling and sporadically feel the ground shake – especially at night.

Volcán Arenal was afforded protected status in 1995, becoming part of the national parks system as the **PARQUE NACIONAL VOLCÁN ARENAL** (daily 8am–4pm; US$6). The park has some good **trails**, some of them across lava fields, while the four-kilometre "Tucanes" trail takes you to the part of the forest which was flattened by an eruption in 1968; you may also see some **wildlife** – birds (including oropéndolas and tanagers) and agoutis are particularly common. Although the park has a simple café, it's best to take a picnic lunch and plenty of water if you intend to spend some time walking. Hiking any distance up the volcano's sides has always been energetically discouraged, and fences now stop you doing so. If you arrive on a cloudy or rainy day (which is most of the year, unfortunately) and can't see the summit, the park's visitor's centre has video displays of the volcano's more spectacular activity.

You can't stay in or visit the park after dark except by taking one of the **night tours** which leave Fortuna every evening at about 3–4pm. Most operators run them even when it's cloudy, in the hope that the cloud will lift or the opposite side of the volcano will be clear. None offers you a refund if you don't see anything, however, so you might want to wait for a clear evening before signing up. In addition, Aventuras Arenal run a sunset **boat tour** on which you can watch the action from Laguna de Arenal.

The **park entrance** is 12km from Fortuna; look for the well-signed driveway off to the left. If you don't have your own vehicle, you can take a **taxi** from Fortuna to the west side of the volcano (around US$35 return per car, including waiting time of a few hours), but unless you're in a large group, it's cheaper – and less bother – to take a tour. The **bus** from Fortuna will drop you off at the entrance to the park and is much the cheapest option, though the return journey can be a bit tricky – unless you manage to connect with the bus coming from Tilarán or Arenal Town, your only option is to try to get a ride back with other park visitors.

The far north

The **far north** of the Zona Norte is an isolated region, in many ways culturally – as well as geographically – closer to Nicaragua than to the rest of the country. Most tourists come here to see **Refugio Nacional de Vida Silvestre Caño Negro**, a vast wetlands area and – at 192km from San José – one of the most remote wildlife refuges in Costa Rica. You can visit Caño Negro on a day-trip from the capital or on an excursion from Fortuna or any of the larger hotels in the Zona Norte; getting there independently, as with everywhere in Costa Rica, is more complicated.

Los Chiles

Few tourists make it to **LOS CHILES**, a border settlement just 3km from the Nicaraguan frontier, and other than soaking up the town's end-of-the-world atmosphere, there's little to do, except perhaps try to rent a boat or horse to go to **Caño Negro**, 25km downstream on the Río Frío (see opposite). The only other reason you might come to Los Chiles is to cross the Nicaraguan border, although the majority of travellers still cross at Peñas Blancas, further west on the Interamericana. Two **buses** per day run from La Coca-Cola in **San José** to Los Chiles (at least 5hr). The San José bus stops right outside the Mercado Central, while buses arriving from Ciudad Quesada often stop close to the docks.

Although Los Chiles has no official **tourist information**, the travel agency Servitur offers good advice, and everyone in town knows the current bus schedules and the times of the river-boat to the Nicaraguan border, though you'll need Spanish to ask around. **Migración** (officially Mon–Fri 8am–5pm; ☎471-1153) can answer more detailed enquiries, but it often closes before 5pm – get there by 3pm to be safe. You can supposedly **change dollars** and travellers' cheques at the Banco Nacional on the north side of the soccer field (Mon–Fri 8am–3.30pm).

Crossing into Nicaragua

The ferry service usually leaves the docks at 8am (Mon–Fri), but it's always worth checking first with officials in either Los Chiles or at the Nicaraguan consulate in San José (see p.581). The Los Chiles *migración* officials are relatively friendly, and you may be able to confirm current boat times with the groups of Nicas or Ticos who hang around the office.

Some nationalities need **tourist visas** to enter Nicaragua. Requirements are constantly in flux, so always check with the consulate in San José, which is the only place in the country that can issue the necessary documentation (allow at least 24hr for processing). Make sure that the **Nicaraguan border patrol**, 3km upriver from Los Chiles, stamps your passport, as you will need proof of entry when leaving Nicaragua.

From the border control point it's 14km up the Río Frío to the small town of **San Carlos de Nicaragua** (see p.534), on the southeast lip of the huge Lago de Nicaragua. You'll need some cash upon arrival; change a few colones for cordobas at the Los Chiles bank. From San Carlos de Nicaragua it's also possible to cross the lake to **Granada** and on to **Managua**, but again check with the consulate in San José; this is an infrequent boat service and without forward planning you could end up stuck in San Carlos for longer than you'd expected.

Refugio Nacional de Vida Silvestre Caño Negro

The largely pristine **REFUGIO NACIONAL DE VIDA SILVESTRE CAÑO NEGRO** (US$6), 25km west of Los Chiles, is one of the best places in the Americas to view huge concentrations of both migratory and indigenous birds, along with mammalian and reptilian river wildlife. Until recently its isolation kept it well off the beaten tourist track, though nowadays, more and more tours are visiting the area.

Getting to Caño Negro

Though most people come to the refuge on tours from Fortuna, you can also get to Caño Negro **independently**. Driving is easy enough in the dry season, while in the wet season a boat leaves from the Los Chiles docks (Tues & Thurs only at 7.30am; for information call ☎460-1301). On other days you can take your pick from several lanchas: get there early in the morning, compare prices and expect to pay at least US$65 per boat for the five-hour return trip – the people at Servitur in Los Chiles can also recommend someone reliable. Note that the first 25km of the trip down the Río Frío (taking an hour or more by lancha) does not take you through the wildlife refuge, which begins at the mouth of the large flooded area and is marked by a sign poking out of a small islet. Make sure your boatman takes you right into Caño Negro.

If you take a tour, the **entrance fee** is included. If not, you should pay at the **ranger station** on the north side of the lake, provided you can find someone to collect the money. You can also **stay** at the ranger station (☎460-1301; ①) – call from the public telephone at Caño Negro to reserve – though facilities are variable: you may be able to buy a meal, but bring your own supplies just in case. **Camping** is permitted in Caño Negro, but no formal facilities are provided and there's a charge of around US$4, payable to the ranger.

Unless you're an expert in identifying wildlife, the most rewarding way to enjoy the diverse flora and fauna of Caño Negro is to use the services of a **guide** who knows the area and can point out animals and other features of river life as you motor down to the refuge. If you come independently, asking at the docks or at Servitur in Los Chiles might turn up someone.

Sarapiquí

Steamy, tropical and carpeted with fruit plantations, the eastern part of the Zona Norte bears more resemblance to the hot and dense Caribbean lowlands than the plains of the north and, despite the toll of deforestation, still shelters some of the best-preserved **pre-montane rainforest** in the country. North by northwest from the Las Horquetas turn-off on the Guápiles Highway, the main road through the area makes a parabolic arc around the top of Parc Nacional Braulio Carrillo and stretches west to the village of San Miguel, from where Arenal and the western lowlands are easily accessible by road.

The region's chief tourist attractions are the biological research station **La Selva** and the eco-lodges of **Rara Avis** all of which offer access to some of the last primary rainforest in the country. The largest settlement, **Puerto Viejo de Sarapiquí**, is principally a river transport hub and a place for the fruit plantation workers to stock up on supplies and have a beer or two.

There are two options when it comes to getting **from San José** or the Valle Central to Puerto Viejo. The western route, which takes a little more than three hours, goes via Varablanca and the La Paz waterfall, passing the hump of Volcán Barva. This route offers great views of velvety green hills clad with coffee plantations, which turn, eventually, into rainforest. It's faster (1hr–1hr 30min) but less scenic to travel via the **Guápiles Highway**. The region receives a lot of **rain** – as much as 4500mm annually – and there is no real dry season (although less rain is recorded Jan–May), so wet-weather gear is essential.

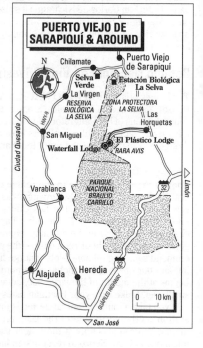

Rara Avis

RARA AVIS, 17km south of Puerto Viejo de Sarapiquí, and about 80km northeast of San José, offers one of the most thrilling and authentic eco-tourism experiences in Costa Rica, featuring both primary rainforest and some secondary cover dating from about thirty years ago. Established in 1983, Rara Avis is both a tourist lodge and a private rainforest preserve, dedicated to the conservation, study and farming of the area's biodiversity. Its ultimate objective is to show that the rainforest can be profitable for an indefinite period, giving local smallholders a viable alternative to clearcutting for their cattle. Rara Avis also functions as a **research station**, accommodating student groups and volunteers whose aim is to develop rainforest products – orchids, palms and so forth – as crops.

Rara Avis's **flora** is as diverse as you might expect from a premontane rainforest. The best way to learn to spot different flowers, plants, trees and their respective habitats is to go on a walk with one of the knowledgeable **guides**. Especially interesting plants include the **stained-glass palm tree**, a rare ornamental specimen, and the **walking palm**, whose fingertip or tentacle-like roots can propel it over more than a metre of ground in its lifetime, as it "walks" in search of water. **Orchids** are numerous, as are non-flowering bromeliads and heliconias. A mind-boggling number of **bird species** have been identified, and it's likely that more have yet to be discovered. Among the more common **mammals** are monkeys, tapirs, ocelots and jaguars, though the last three are rarely seen.

Getting to Rara Avis

Because of its isolation you'll have to spend at least one night in the reserve, though two or three would be preferable. If time is short, a **package** to Rara Avis including transport from San José may be worth considering (see p.586 for tour agents), but with a little planning it's perfectly possible – and more economical – to get there **independently**. To do this you need to take the bus from San José to near the small village of Las Horquetas, then a taxi to the village, from where a tractor-pulled cart makes the final 15km of the journey. You'll need to reserve accommodation at the reserve in advance, however you arrive.

As the tractor for Rara Avis leaves daily at 9am, you have to take the 7am bus to Río Frío/Puerto Viejo de Sarapiquí from San José. Make sure you get the express (*directo*) service via the Guápiles Highway (the bus via Heredia leaves thirty minutes earlier and takes the long western route to Puerto Viejo). It takes between an hour and ninety minutes from San José to reach the turn-off (*cruce*) for Las Horquetas – ask the driver to let you off. From here, a five-minute **taxi** ride will take you to the **Rara Avis office** in Las Horquetas (since all accommodation at the lodge must be pre-booked, they'll know you are coming, though it's worth calling ☎253-0844 to double-check that a taxi will be waiting for you). From the office, the tractor-cart will take you to Rara Avis. If you come with your own transport, there's a car park at the office, where you can leave your vehicle.

Getting to Rara Avis from Las Horquetas is at least half the fun, though not exactly comfortable. The uphill flatbed-tractor journey to the lodges takes two to four hours depending both on the condition of the "road" (actually a muddy rutted track) and on where you're staying. The pluses of this mode of transport include the sheer excitement – there's much multi-lingual cheering when the driver revs up the tractor and, squelching and spluttering, gets to the top of each slippery hill – and an exhilarating open-air view of the surrounding landscape, with plenty of time for toucan-spotting. Minuses include bumps and bruises, choking diesel fumes and a few worrying moments as the tractor slithers and slides up pitted hills.

If you miss the tractor, **horses** are available for hire from the villagers until noon (US$15) – any time after that is too late, as the trip takes several hours. Ask at the Rara Avis office when you arrive. The horses can get as far as the *El Plástico Lodge* (see overleaf), but if you're staying at the *Waterfall Lodge* or the *Riverside Cabin*, you'll have to walk the last 3km on a rainforest trail.

Leaving Rara Avis, the tractor departs at about 2pm from the *Waterfall Lodge*, passing the *Plástico* lodge at around 3pm. This means that it often arrives in Horquetas too late to rendezvous with the last bus for San José, which passes through at 5.15pm daily. If you miss this bus, the Rara Avis office in Horquetas can arrange for a taxi (about US$25 per carload) to the Guápiles Highway, from where you can flag down a Guápiles–San José bus, which pass by hourly until 7pm.

Accommodation

There are three **places to stay** at Rara Avis (all bookable on ☎253-0844 or 764-3131, fax 257-4876, *raraavis@racsa.co.cr*). Rates at all three include all meals, transport by tractor from and to Las Horquetas, and guided walks. The cheapest is the HI-affiliated *El Plástico Lodge* (US$45 per person in a dormitory; US$35 for students and HI members), in a cleared area 12km from Las Horquetas. *Plástico* is named after a convicts' colony that used to stand on the site, in which prisoners slept underneath plastic tarpaulins. It has dirt floors downstairs, bunk-style beds and hot water, a covered but open-view communal dining table and a sitting area. Despite its rusticity, it's all very comfortable, and the only way to see Rara Avis on the cheap.

The road from here to the more comfortable *Waterfall Lodge* (⑨) is only 3km, but it's uphill, through dense rainforest, and takes at least an hour by tractor from *Plástico*. If you are in good shape, the best way to get there is to hike the (fairly obvious) trail through the rainforest – you can pick up a map at the Rara Avis office in Las Horquetas. This should take about an hour: do not, under any circumstances, leave the trails, which are in good condition despite year-round mud. Set above a picture-perfect cascade, the *Waterfall Lodge* has rooms with running hot water, private baths, spacious balconies with hammocks, and fantastic views of utterly pristine rainforest and the hot, flat lowland plains stretching towards the Caribbean. It's an idyllic place to stay; the only sounds heard at five or six in the morning are the echoing shrieks of birds and *monos congos* (howler monkeys). Meals, cooked by local women and served three times a day, are delicious. There's no electricity (but plenty of kerosene lamps).

The third accommodation option is the still more isolated *Riverside Cabin* (⑨), about 500m from the *Waterfall Lodge* – if you stay here you'll have to be unfazed by walking through the forest at night with only a torch or a lamp. Even more isolated, in a vertical sense, is the **tree-top cabin** which has been built on a platform 30m up a rainforest tree – strictly for hardy outdoor types. Guides show you how to climb up using ropes and pulley-type gadgets. Once up, there are beds for two people and water (although this too has to be winched up the tree) and a chemical toilet. The prices are the same as the *Waterfall Lodge*, and the restrictions of staying here are obvious: once you're up the tree for the night, you're up.

Rara Avis activities

Rara Avis has a network of very good **trails**. From the *Waterfall Lodge*, nine or so trails weave through fairly dense jungle cover. All are well-marked, and give walks of thirty minutes to several hours depending upon the pace. While guided walks are fun and informative, guests are welcome to go it alone: you'll be given a map at the lodge receptions, but you should always let the staff know which trail you are following and about how long you intend to be. Rain gear is essential at all times.

Just below the *Waterfall Lodge*, a fifty-metre-high waterfall on the Río Atelopus plummets into a deep pool before continuing the river's slide down towards lower ground. **Swimming** in the icy-cold pool, shrouded in a fine mist, is a wonderful experience, but don't even consider it without a guide. Occasional *cabezas de agua* (flash floods) up in the highlands swell the river and cause sudden rushing torrents, with potentially fatal consequences – three people were swept to their deaths here some years ago.

Estación Biológica La Selva

A fully equipped research station, **ESTACIÓN BIOLÓGICA LA SELVA**, 93km northeast of San José and 4km southwest of Puerto Viejo de Sarapiquí (☎766-6565; in San José ☎240-6696, *laselva@ns.ots.ac.cr*; US$20) is probably the best place to visit in the Sarapiquí region if you are a botany student or have a special interest in the scientific life of a rainforest and, like Rara Avis, it is a superb birder's spot, with more than 400 species of indigenous and migratory birds.

Though tourists are secondary to research at La Selva, visitors are welcome, providing there is space – it's impossible to overstate La Selva's popularity, and in the high season it is sometimes booked months in advance, even for day-trips. Be sure to **reserve** way in advance by fax (710-1414) if you are coming between November and April. Visiting in the low season (roughly May–Oct) is a safer bet, but even then you should call first.

La Selva's ground cover extends from primary **forest** through abandoned plantations to pastureland and brush, crossed by an extensive network of about 25 **trails** varying in length from short to more than 5km long. Most are in very good condition, clearly and frequently marked, though some are pretty rough, and many can get very muddy indeed. Tourists tend to stick to the main trails within the part of La Selva designated as the **Ecological Reserve**, next to the Río Puerto Viejo. These **trails**, the Camino Circular Cercano, the Camino Cantarrana and the Sendero Oriental, radiate from the river research station and take you through dense primary growth, the close, tightly knotted kind of tropical forest for which the Sarapiquí area is famous.

Practicalities

The least expensive way of getting to La Selva **from San José** is to take the 7am Río Frío/Puerto Viejo de Sarapiquí bus (marked "Río Frío"), which, if you ask, will drop you off at the entrance to the road leading to the station. Note, however, that it's a two-kilometre walk down the road from the junction. The OTS (☎240-6696, fax 240-6783) also lays on a thrice-weekly bus (US$10) from its office in Curridabat, a suburb in the east of San José; though mainly reserved for researchers and students, it's worth asking if they can fit you in. Taxis make the four-kilometre trip **from Puerto Viejo de Sarapiquí** for about US$5.

If you want to **stay** at La Selva, you *must* book in advance, by calling the office number. The simple but comfortable **accommodation** (in San José ☎240-6696, fax 240-6783; in La Selva ☎740-1515, fax 740-1414; ⑥) at La Selva isn't cheap, but proceeds go towards the maintenance of the station. Researchers and students with scientific bona fides stay for less (④). Rates include three meals a day, served in the communal dining hall. A **day visit** costs about US$20 (including lunch); again, you have to reserve in advance, whatever time of the year you come.

Puerto Viejo de Sarapiquí

Just short of 100km northeast of San José, **PUERTO VIEJO DE SARAPIQUÍ** (known locally as Puerto Viejo, not to be confused with Puerto Viejo de Talamanca on the Atlantic coast) is an important hub for banana plantation workers and those who live in the isolated settlements between here and the Atlantic coast. Its only interest to independent travellers is as a jumping-off point from which to visit the nearby jungle lodges. Facilities are few, and inadequate even to cope with the demands of migrant workers, though there are plenty of *licorías* (liquor stores).

Numerous **buses** leave San José for Puerto Viejo; the **fast service**, via the Guápiles Highway and Las Horquetas, currently departs at 7am, 9am, 10am, 1pm, 3pm and

4pm, completing the 97-kilometre trip in just ninety minutes. Buses from San José to Puerto Viejo **via Heredia** (ask the driver if you're unsure which bus you're on – there's nothing on the front indicating which route it takes) take more like three hours and leave at 6.30am, noon and 3pm, returning from Puerto Viejo at 8am and 4pm – although the 4pm bus sometimes only goes as far as La Virgen, some 12km west of Puerto Viejo.

Though most people choose to stay in one of the lodges in the countryside outside the town (see below), if you're stuck, *Mi Lindo Sarapiquí* (☎766-6074; ②), on the main street, is the best-known spot in town, with a good restaurant that doubles as a bar at night – ask behind the counter in the restaurant for rooms, as there's no reception. Rooms are clean, fairly spacious and have private bath. Also on the main street is *El Bambú* (☎766-6005, fax 766-6132, *www.elbambu.com*; ⑤), the plushest accommodation in town, with nicely decorated rooms, all with fans, colour TV and hot water, pretty potted tropical plants and a restaurant, bar and full tour service.

Accommodation around Puerto Viejo de Sarapiquí

Although La Selva, and Rara Avis are the prime tourist destinations in this area, there are also a number of very attractive **hotels** and **lodges** dotted around Puerto Viejo that allow you to experience something of the rainforest. In general they're reasonably priced and accessible, and some offer **packages** from San José. If you're travelling by bus and the accommodation is west of Puerto Viejo, you should take the San José–Río Frío bus via Heredia (see above). Anything in Puerto Viejo itself or east is faster reached by the service to Río Frío/Puerto Viejo via the Guápiles Highway.

Ara Ambigua, 400m down a signed gravel road just to the right as you leave Puerto Viejo (☎ & fax 766-6971, mobile 393-5026). Lovely rustic cottages, nicely furnished and impeccably clean. Rooms come with private bath, hot water and fan, and prices are frankly a steal, with singles for just US$10. It's worth a visit just for the splendid food – try the chicken brochettes – dished up by owners Lisbeth and Delfin in the pseudo-Baroque restaurant, complete with giant gold-painted wooden chandelier. ③

La Quinta, 7km west of Puerto Viejo, and 5km east of La Virgen (☎ & fax 761-1052, *www .quintasarapiqui.com*). On the banks of the Río Sardinal, this comfortable lodge has 23 rooms, all with ceiling fans and hot water, set in bungalows scattered throughout the property. Activities include swimming in the pool or river, exploring the lodge's own cultivated lands, its butterfly garden and the new on-site exhibition, "Jewels of the Rainforest". There's a pleasant outdoor restaurant, and biking, horse-riding and bird-watching can all be arranged. ④

Posada Andrea Cristina, 1km west of Puerto Viejo (☎ & fax 766-6265). Simple rooms with fan and private bath – try the nice A-frame cabins, with high wooden ceilings – along with the best breakfasts, coffee and conversation in the area. Many people stay here for the family atmosphere and use

---

MOVING ON FROM PUERTO VIEJO DE SARAPIQUÍ

Puerto Viejo is a transport hub for the entire Zona Norte and eastern side of the country. From here it's possible to travel back to the **Valle Central**, either via the Guápiles Highway (1hr 30min or more) or via Varablanca and Heredia (3hr or more). You can also cut across country west to **San Carlos** (3hr) and on to **Fortuna** (3–4hr) and Volcán Arenal, from where it's easy to continue, via Tilarán, to **Monteverde** and **Guanacaste**.

By river it's possible to continue north from Puerto Viejo along the Río Sarapiquí to the Nicaraguan border then east along the Río San Juan to Barra and Tortuguero on the Caribbean coast. You'll have to rent a private lancha to do this pleasant journey, which can take anywhere between four and seven hours (you're going upstream). It's fairly pricey, unless you're in a group of eight or so – about US$300 (8–10 maximum capacity). Ask at Souvenirs Río Sarapiquí or at the docks.

it as a base to explore the area, including Tortuguero; the owners can advise on and arrange trips throughout the region. ⊙
Sarapiquí Ecolodge, 4km south of Puerto Viejo, across the river from Estación Biológica La Selva (☎766-6122; fax 253-8645). Based in the home and working farm of the Murillo family, offering many of the same facilities and activities as La Selva, including horse-riding, bird-watching excursions, boat trips and hiking (all cost extra). No luxury accommodation here, but the dormitory bunk-beds are comfortable enough, and prices include generous meals. US$15 per person.

travel details

BUSES

Fortuna to: San Carlos (6 daily; 1hr); San José (3 daily; 4hr 30min); Tilarán (2 daily; 3hr).

Los Chiles to: San Carlos (10 daily; 2hr 30min).

Puerto Viejo de Sarapiquí to: San Carlos (3 daily; 3hr); San José (via Guápiles Highway, 7 daily; 1hr 30min–3hr; via Heredia, 3 daily; 3–4hr).

San Carlos to: Fortuna (6 daily; 1hr); Los Chiles (10 daily; 2hr 30min); Puerto Viejo de Sarapiquí (3 daily; 3hr); San José (14 daily; 3hr); Tilarán (1 daily; 2hr).

San José to: Fortuna (3 daily; 4hr 30min); Los Chiles (2 daily; 5hr); Puerto Viejo de Sarapiquí (via Guápiles Highway, 7 daily; 1hr 30min–3hr; via Heredia, 3 daily; 3–4hr); San Carlos (14 daily; 3hr); Tilarán (4 daily; 4–5hr).

Tilarán to: Fortuna (2 daily; 2hr); San Carlos (1 daily; 2hr); San José (4 daily; 4–5hr); Santa Elena, for Monteverde (1 daily; 3–4hr).

CHAPTER 33

THE ZONA SUR

osta Rica's **Zona Sur** (southern zone) is the country's least-known region, both for Ticos and for travellers. Geographically it's a diverse area, ranging from the agricultural heartland of the Valle de el General to the high peaks of the Cordillera de Talamanca, most notably the mountain pass at Cerro de la Muerte ("Death Mountain"), and **Cerro el Chirripó** – at 3819m one of the highest peaks in Central America. South of Chirripó, the cordillera falls away steeply into the river-cut lowlands of the Valle de Diquis around Palmar, and the coffee-growing Valle de Coto Brus, near the border with Panamá.

The chief draw for travellers is the **Osa Peninsula** in the extreme southwest, home to the **Parque Nacional Corcovado**, one of the country's prime rainforest hiking destinations, and the remote and picturesque **Bahía Drake**. Less off the beaten track is the **Playa Dominical** area of the Pacific coast, a surfing destination whose tremendous tropical beauty is beginning to attract increasing numbers of visitors. **Golfito**, the region's only town of any size, suffered from an unsavoury reputation for years after the pull-out of the United Fruit Company's banana operations in 1985, though its fortunes have improved since being made a tax-free zone for manufactured goods from Panamá.

Despite the abundance of budget accommodation in the Zona Sur, you'll find yourself **spending** more than you bargained for simply because of the time, distance and planning involved in getting to many of the region's more beautiful spots. Many people prefer to take a package rather than travel independently, and travellers who stay at the more expensive rainforest lodges often choose to fly in.

Climatically the Zona Sur has two distinct regions. The first comprises the Pacific lowlands from south of Quepos roughly to the top of the Osa Peninsula, and the upland Valle de el General and the Talamancas, both of which experience a dry season from December to April. The second region – the Osa Peninsula, Golfito and Golfo Dulce – does not have so marked a dry season, while during the wettest part of the year, from around October to December, spectacular seasonal thunderstorms canter in from the Pacific. In the rainy season, some parts of Parque Nacional Corcovado become more or less unwalkable, local roads become impassable, and everything gets more difficult.

Dominical

The once quiet fishing village of **DOMINICAL**, 44km south of Quepos (see p.640), was until quite recently largely undiscovered, though since the paving of the road here it has seen increasing numbers of foreign visitors, lured by the beauty of the surroundings, the romantic sunsets and the get-away-from-it-all atmosphere. Wide and long, the palm-fringed, dark-sand **beach** is postcard-pretty, though often deserted except when **surfers** flock to chase the big waves. **Snorkelling** is good here, too, and there are a couple of pretty waterfalls nearby. Though it seems poised to become the country's next Manuel Antonio, development remains – for the time being at least – relatively low-key.

For an explanation of **accommodation price codes**, see p.556.

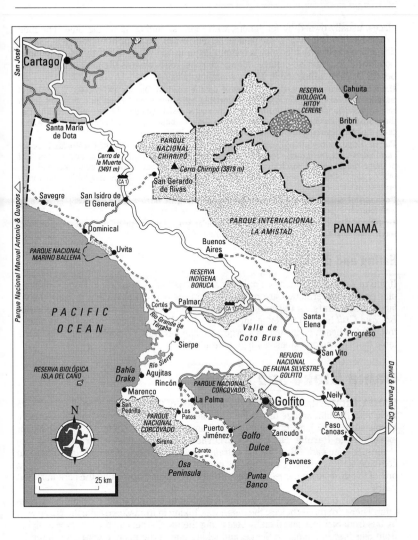

From San José the fastest route to Dominical is via the sleepy town of San Isidro de el General, on the Carretera Interamericana, from where there are reasonable bus connections; **from Guanacaste** and the Central Pacific, you'll do best to take the road south from Quepos. **Buses** from Quepos arrive at around 6.30am and 3pm daily, and continue to San Isidro (2hr).

Accommodation in the Dominical area

There's a surprising range of good **accommodation** in the Dominical area. Some is basic and caters mainly for surfers, but there are also a number of more upmarket places, usually owned by foreigners, with more springing up all the time. The most expensive hotels include some wonderful hideaways, good for honeymooners, romantics and escapists. Aside from accommodation in the village itself there's a string of hotels and self-catering cottages along the coast road towards the next hamlet and its beach, **Dominicalito**, and in the surrounding hills.

Hacienda Barú, 1km north of Dominical on the road to Quepos (☎787-0003, fax 787-0004, *www.haciendabaru.com*). Good-value, comfortable self-catering chalets set in a beautiful private reserve containing rainforest, mangrove and protected beach. Good for birders and orchid lovers – there are 250 varieties scattered around – plus there's a butterfly farm, turtle nursery and a fixed canopy platform on site; horse-riding tours are also available. ⑤.

Pacific Edge, 3km south of Dominical - follow the signed left-hand fork (☎381-4369, fax 771-8841, *pacificedge@pocketmail.com*). Secluded, simple and comfortable, on a ridge above the sea, with beautiful mountain and beach views. The four roomy chalets each have private shower and hammocks, and delicious meals, including bangers and mash (one of the owners is English) can be ordered in advance. ⑤.

Posada del Sol, on the main street opposite *San Clemente Bar* (☎ & fax 787-0085). Lovely hotel with four very good-value double rooms, all with private bath. ④.

Tortilla Flats, on the beach (☎787-0033). Popular small hotel with brightly decorated en-suite rooms overlooking the sea, plus on-site restaurant. ④.

Eating and drinking

If you're self-catering there's a *pulpería* and a small **supermarket** in Dominical itself, plus another supermarket just outside town in the pink Plaza Pacifica mall. Of the village's **restaurants**, *La Capannna* serves excellent Italian food, while the *San Clemente Bar and Grill* has a Tex-Mex menu with a little Italian and Cajun thrown in. *Thrusters*, towards the beach on the left, is a large barn-like **bar** with TV, pool tables, darts board, table football and an extensive range of drinks.

Bahía Drake and around

BAHÍA DRAKE (pronounced "Dra-kay") is one of the most stunning areas in Costa Rica, with the blue wedge of Isla del Caño floating just off the coast, and fiery-orange Pacific sunsets. Bahía Drake and the tiny hamlet of **AGUJITAS** make a good base for exploring the **Parque Nacional Corcovado** on the southwest corner of the Osa Peninsula – the park's San Pedrillo entrance is within walking distance, and hikers can combine serious trekking with serious comfort at either end of their trip by staying at one of the upscale rainforest eco-lodges that have sprung up around the park in recent years.

Like many other places in the Zona Sur, **getting to Bahía Drake** requires some planning. There are three choices: the tough way, hiking in from Corcovado; the cheap way, by bus from San José and then by boat along the Río Sierpe; and the luxury way, flying from San José to Palmar or Sierpe, and taking one of the many **packages** offered by hotels in the area, which include transport to your lodge.

Travelling **independently** you'll need to get a bus from San José to the banana processing town of Palmar Norte (6 daily; 5hr 30min), 120km southwest of San Isidro de el General; depending on what time you get in, you can then either bed down or get a local bus or taxi (about US$12) to **Sierpe**, where there are a few *cabinas*. In Sierpe, you must find a **boatman** to take you the 30km downriver to Bahía Drake (2hr). You need someone with experience, a motorized lancha, and lifejackets; Chichu Mora is recommended – ask Sonia Rojas at the Fenix *pulpería* to help you find him (and for any other general advice you may need). You can also hook up with a boatman in *Bar Las Vegas*, a rendezvous for tourists and boat captains – check out the ancient jukebox while you wait. The going rate for a one-way trip to Drake is currently about US$20 per person or around US$65–85 per boatload (usually a maximum of 8 people); ask around for the best rates.

Accommodation in and around Bahía Drake

Accommodation is clustered either in the tiny village of Agujitas itself, or on **Punta Agujitas**, the rocky point on the other side of the Río Agujitas. Virtually all the **eco-lodges** listed below do a range of **tours**, from accompanied excursions to Corcovado to boat-trips around Bahía Drake. The larger lodges are accustomed to bringing guests on packages from San José and can include transport from the capital, from Palmar, or from Sierpe. The packages (and the prices we give below) usually include three meals a day – there are few eating options in Bahía Drake otherwise. Although hoteliers will tell you you can't **camp** in the Drake area, people do – if you want to join them, pitch your tent considerately and be sure to leave no litter.

Cabinas Jade Mar, in the village (☎284-6681, fax 786-7366). One of the few village cheapies, and a good place to stay if you want to get a taste of local life, with extremely well-priced and pleasant, if basic, *cabinas*, kept very clean by the informative Doña Martha. All cabins have private bath, and hearty meals are included in the price. Inexpensive tours to Corcovado and Isla de Caño are also available. ⑤.

Cocalito Jungle Resort, Punta Agujitas (☎495-6821, fax 290-1280, *conexion@racsa.co.cr*). Small, family-run, Canadian-owned *cabinas* (with and without en suite) scattered around a main lodge, where delicious meals are served by candlelight in the restaurant. There's also safe swimming on the resort's small beach, mountain-bike rental and solar-heated water; all accommodation is well-screened. You can also camp here, and tents can be rented. ⑥.

Drake Bay Wilderness Resort, Punta Agujitas (☎ & fax 770-8012, in San José ☎256-7394, *www.drakebay.com*). The most established lodge in the area, providing a buffer zone between tourist and wilderness with rustic, comfortable *cabinas* or, if you want to rough it a bit, well-appointed tents – both options are well-screened. There's hearty local food, and the camp also has its own solar-heated water supply, night-time electricity, laundry service, plus excellent snorkelling and canoeing. It's popular, so best book and pay in advance. Packages include direct flights from San José to Bahía Drake. ⑨.

Jinetes de Osa, between Punta Agujitas and Agujitas (☎385-9541, *www.costaricadiving.com*). One of the less expensive options in Bahía Drake, right on the area's main beach – there's an on-site PADI dive school and most guests come here on good-value dive packages. Accommodation, some of it en suite, is simple but comfortable, and prices include three meals a day. ⑥.

La Paloma Lodge, Punta Agujitas (☎239-2801, *www.lapalomalodge.com*). Beautiful, rustic rooms in thatched hilltop bungalows, with private bath, balconies and hammocks – the airy, two-storey bungalows are best, being surrounded by forest and boasting spectacular views, particularly at sunset. *Pangas* (traditional canoes) are available for guests to paddle on the Río Agujitas behind the lodge, and there's also an attractively tiled swimming pool. Excellent service, with friendly and helpful staff. ⑨.

Rancho Corcovado, on the beach in front of Agujitas (☎384-1457, 240-4085 or 786-7059). Good-value, family-run hotel with beautiful views over the bay and simple, clean en-suite rooms. Rates all include full board, and camping and horse-riding tours are also available. ⑤.

Golfito

The former banana port of **GOLFITO**, 33km north of the Panamanian border, straggles for 2500m along the water of the same name (*golfito* means "little gulf"). The town's setting is spectacular, backed up against steep, thickly forested hills to the east, and with the glorious Golfo Dulce – one of the deepest gulfs of its size in the world – to the west. The low shadow of the Osa Peninsula shimmers in the distance, and everywhere the vegetation has the soft muted look of the undisturbed tropics.

Golfito's history is inextricably intertwined with the giant transnational **United Brands** company – locally known as "La Yunai" – which first set up in the area in 1938. United Brands built schools, recruited doctors and police, and brought prosperity to the area, but following fluctuating banana prices, a three-month strike and local social unrest, they eventually decided Golfito was too much trouble and pulled out in a hurry in 1985. The town died, and in the public eye became synonymous with rampant unemployment, alcoholism, abandoned children, prostitution and general unruliness.

Today, at the big old *muelle bananero*, container ships are still loaded up with bananas processed further up towards Palmar Norte. This residual traffic, along with tourism – Golfito is a good base for getting to the **Parque Nacional Corcovado** by lancha or plane – has combined to help revive the local economy. The real rescue, though, came from the Costa Rican government, who in the early 1990s established a **depósito libre** – or tax-free zone – in the town, where Costa Ricans can buy manufactured goods imported from Panamá without the 100-percent tax normally levied. Ticos who come to shop here have to buy their tickets for the *depósito* 24 hours in advance, obliging them to spend at least one night and, therefore colones, in the town.

Golfito straggles for ages without any clear centre. The town is effectively split in two – by a division in wealth as well as architecture. In the north is the **zona americana**, where the banana-company executives used to live and where better-off residents still reside in beautiful wooden houses shaded by dignified palms. Here you'll find the *depósito libre*, an unaesthetic outdoor mall ringed by a circular concrete wall. To the south, the **pueblo civil** (civilian town), is a very small, tight nest of streets; hotter, noisier and more crowded than the *zona*. It's here you'll find the good-value hotels and sodas, as well as the lancha across the Golfo Dulce to Puerto Jiménez and the Osa Peninsula.

Arrival and information

Buses from San José currently leave TRACOPA's terminal at 7am and 3pm (8hr). Buy your return ticket (see box opposite) as soon as you disembark. You can also **fly** here with Sansa; the airstrip is in the *zona americana*. The Banco Nacional, opposite the TRACOPA terminal, will change **travellers' cheques** and give cash advances on credit cards, but it's a tediously slow process. The **correo** is right in the centre of the *pueblo civil* and has **Internet** access. Land-Sea Tours (☎ & fax 775-1614, *landsea@racsa.co.cr*), on the waterfront at the southern end of the *pueblo*, organizes a wide range of tours, has a book exchange and is an excellent source of information.

Accommodation

Accommodation in Golfito comes in two varieties: swish places in the *zona americana*, catering to businesspeople and shoppers at the *depósito*; and decent, basic rooms in the *pueblo civil*.

Cabinas El Vivero, just south of the *depósito* (☎775-0217). Big, simply furnished rooms, shared kitchen and a friendly family atmosphere. *Dueño* Don Bob grows orchids and other plants in his nursery next door, and is a one-man history of the area. Very good value. ②.

Esquinas Rainforest Lodge, La Gamba, approx 7km from Km-37 on the Interamericana (☎ & fax 775-0901, *www.regenwald.at*). Friendly eco-lodge run by the Government of Austria as part of a model project combining development aid, nature conservation and rainforest research – all profits go to the local community. It's set in primary rainforest, with resident wildlife and on-site hiking

MOVING ON FROM GOLFITO

Buses to San José leave daily at 5am and 1pm – if you're getting the 5am bus you'll need to have bought your return ticket in advance. There are also flights to San José on Sansa. For **Corcovado** you'll need first to go to Puerto Jiménez, which can be reached either by lancha (daily at 11.30am; 1hr 30min; US$3), or small plane (about US$99 for up to 5 people) – contact the Alfa Romeo Aero Taxi office at the airstrip (☎755-1515).

trails. Wide range of packages available, plus a variety of tours, including ones to Corcovado and the Wilson Botanical Gardens. Fantastic meals are included in the room rate. ⑨.

Las Gaviotas, at the southern entrance to town (☎775-0062, fax 775-0544, *www.costaricasur.com /lasgaviotas*). Golfito's most upmarket accommodation, set in lovely gardens, and with the town's only pool. The good rooms all have private bath with hot water, a/c and cable TV, and the waterside rancho restaurant serves great local seafood. ⑥.

Samoa del Sur, on the main road between the *zona americana* and the *pueblo civil* (☎775-0233, fax 775-0573, *samoasur@racsa.co.cr*). Fourteen spacious though slightly gloomy rooms on the waterfront, with a large boat-shaped bar and on-site restaurant. ④.

The Osa Peninsula

In the extreme southwest of the country, and somewhat separate from the mainland, the **Osa Peninsula** is home to an area of immense biological diversity, much of it protected by the **Parque Nacional Corcovado**. Few people fail to be moved by the peninsula's beauty: whichever direction you approach it from, you see what looks to be a floating island, an intricate mesh of blue and green, with tall canopy trees sailing high and flat like elaborate floral hats. Most visitors base themselves in the tiny, friendly town of **Puerto Jiménez**. From here, you could feasibly "do" the whole peninsula in four days, but this would be rushing it, especially if you want to spend time walking the trails and wildlife-spotting at Corcovado – better to allot five to seven days; more if you want to explore Bahía Drake.

Puerto Jiménez and around

Relaxed and friendly **PUERTO JIMÉNEZ** – known locally simply as Jiménez – hasn't yet been overwhelmed by tourism, though it has plenty of places to stay and eat and good public transport connections. There's also the possibility of grabbing a lift with a truck to **Carate**, 43km southwest, from where you can enter Corcovado (see p.689). Drivers shouldn't try going further south – including to Carate – in anything less than a 4WD at any time of year. What looks like a good, firm dirt road can turn into a quagmire after a sudden downpour.

Arrival and information

There are two **buses** from San José via San Isidro to Jiménez (10hr), leaving the capital at 6am and noon and returning at 5am and 11am. A **lancha** for Jiménez leaves Golfito daily at 11.30am, returning at 6am, or you can **fly** in from San José or from Golfito.

The **Corcovado administration and information office** (Oficina de Area de Conservacion Osa; Mon–Fri 8am–noon & 1–4pm; ☎735-5036, fax 735-5276), which faces the airstrip, is staffed by friendly rangers who can answer questions, arrange accommodation and meals at the park's *puestos* (if you haven't already done so – in most cases it's better to arrange this before you arrive, see p.689). For other tourist information, try one of the town's various **tour companies**. The helpful Osa Tropical (☎735-5062, fax 735-5043, *osatropi@racsa.co.cr*) acts as the local Travelair and Sansa agent, has an international phone and fax service and can make accommodation reservations – it's on the main road 50m north of the gas station. Escondido Trex (☎ & fax 735-5210, *osatrex@racsa.co.cr*) offers a wide range of tours and has an office in the *Restaurante Carolina*. The tiny Banco Nacional changes **travellers' cheques** and dollars. The *correo*, opposite the soccer field, has public phones and **Internet** access, as does *Café Net El Sol* on the main drag.

The **town truck to Carate** goes daily except Sundays in the dry season at about 6am, but you'd do best to confirm this locally. You could ask staff at El Tigre supermarket, its departure point. In the wet season it goes less often, about three days a week. The price is about US$5 per person one way; you can arrange to be dropped off and picked up if you're staying at any of the places between Jiménez and Carate – ask the driver. If you don't get a place on the truck, a number of local taxi drivers have **4WDs**; try Orlando Mesen (☎735-5627; about US$60 return to Carate).

Accommodation

Jiménez's **hotels** are reasonably priced, clean and basic. Though it's best to reserve in the dry season, this may not always be possible, as phone lines sometimes go down. In the rainy season there are far fewer people about and you shouldn't need to book in advance. There are a few comfort-in-the-wilderness places **between Jiménez and Carate** around the lower hump of the peninsula, a couple of which make great retreats or honeymoon spots.

IN PUERTO JIMÉNEZ

Cabinas Agua Luna, on the waterfront near the lancha pier (☎ & fax 735-5393, *www.costaricasur .com/agualuna*). A range of comfortable waterfront accommodation, some of it quite smart, with cable TV, a/c and fridge. ③–⑤.

Cabinas Oro Verde, on the main street (☎735-5241). Nine very good-value and spotlessly clean rooms right in the middle of town, with restaurant, laundry service and friendly owners. ②.

Cabinas Puerto Jiménez, on the way into town from the Interamericana (☎735-5090). Quiet *cabinas* next to the water, with simple, clean and nicely furnished rooms. They're well-screened, with bath and fan, though some can be dark – ask to see a few before you choose. ②.

Doña Leta's Bungalows (☎ & fax 735-5180, *www.donaleta.com*). Nice group of eight bungalows, each with its own kitchenette and private bathroom with hot water, set in gardens facing the hotel's own small private beach. There's also a small restaurant, laundry service, kayaks for rent and (strangely enough) a volleyball court. ⑦.

Iguana Lodge, follow the signs for 5km out of Jiménez to Playa Platanares (☎735-5205, fax 735-5436, *www.iguanalodge.com*). Wonderful hotel run by very friendly US family with four two-storey *cabinas* in lovely gardens by the beach – all rooms face the sea and are attractively decorated. Rates include three delicious meals a day. ⑥.

BETWEEN PUERTO JIMÉNEZ AND CARATE

The following are listed **in order of their distance from Puerto Jiménez**. The first, *Bosque del Cabo*, is 25km south from Jiménez. The last, the *Corcovado Tent Camp*, is right next to the park entrance. All are signed from the road and include three meals a day in their room rates.

Bosque del Cabo, above Playa Matapalo, down a private road to the left off the Carate road (☎ & fax 735-5206, *www.bosquedelcabo.com*). Very secluded, beautifully decorated bungalows with stupendous views out to the Pacific and a good restaurant. There's also a waterfall and swimming hole nearby, along with lots of scarlet macaws. ⑨.

Lookout Inn, just north of Carate, and very convenient for its airstrip (no phone; *www.lookout-inn .com*). Three large rooms in a beach house set on rainforested hillside, with swimming pool and beautiful ocean views. Informal and fun atmosphere; tours available. ⑦.

Luna Lodge, set in the hills above Carate – call for a pick-up from the nearby Carate airstrip (☎380-5036, *www.lunalodge.com*). Remote, tranquil and beautiful lodge with welcoming owners and staggering views over the surrounding virgin rainforest. Healthy home-grown food and yoga classes available. ⑨.

Corcovado Tent Camp, about a 45min walk along the beach from Carate (book via Costa Rica Expeditions, see p.586). Twenty self-contained and fully screened "tent-camps" elevated on short stilts in an amazing beachside location, with bedrooms and screened verandas, communal baths and good local cooking. Very good value, with packages available (some including flights right to Carate) plus guided tours around Corcovado National Park (US$38–$68) and horse-riding. ⑥.

Eating and drinking

There's not much choice when it comes to **eating** in Jiménez, but you certainly won't starve. The most popular place in town (particularly with tourists and expats) is the funky little *Fish Store*, which does very good fish tacos, fish and chips and proper homemade burgers – it's a great place to hang out with a cool drink, even if you're not in the mood for food. Another good meeting place is *Restaurante Carolina*, on the main drag, which has a comida típica menu, while *Soda La Parada*, beside the Transportes Blanco bus stop, and *Soda El Ranchito*, next to the post office, are good places for a *casado* or *plato del día*.

Parque Nacional Corcovado

Created in 1975, **PARQUE NACIONAL CORCOVADO** ("hunchback"), 368km southwest of San José (daily 8am–4pm; US$6), protects a fascinating and biologically complex area of land, most of it on the peninsula itself. It also covers one mainland area just north of Golfito, which may soon be made into a national park in its own right. It's an undeniably beautiful park, with deserted beaches, some laced with waterfalls, high canopy trees and better-than-average wildlife-spotting opportunities. Many people come with the express purpose of spotting **margay, ocelot, tapir** and other rarely seen animals. Of course, it's all down to luck, but if you walk quietly and there aren't too many other humans around, you should have a better chance of seeing some of these creatures here than elsewhere.

Serious walking in Corcovado is not for the faint-hearted. The **terrain** varies from beaches of packed or soft sand, riverways, mangroves, *holillo* (palm) swamps to dense forest, although most of it is at lowland elevations. Hikers can expect to spend most of their time on the beach trails that ring the outer perimeters of the park. Inland, the broad alluvial Corcovado plain contains the **Corcovado lagoon**, and features the only sizeable chunk of tropical **premontane wet forest** (also called tropical humid forest) on the Pacific side of Central America. The Osa forest is as visually and biologically magnificent as any on the subcontinent: biologists often compare the tree heights and density here with that of the Amazon basin cover – practically the only place in the entire isthmus of which this can still be said.

The coastal areas of the park receive at least 3800mm of **rain** a year, with precipitation rising to about 5000mm in the higher elevations of the interior. This intense wetness, combined with a sunny respite, is ideal for the growth and development of the intricate, densely matted cover associated with tropical wet forests. There's a dry season (Dec–March), however, and the inland lowland areas, especially those around the lagoon, can be amazingly **hot**, even for those accustomed to tropical temperatures.

Practicalities

Unless you're coming to Corcovado with Costa Rica Expeditions and staying in their tent camp (see above), in the dry season, at least, you have to **reserve** in advance – this will include meals, camping space or lodging at the *puesto* of your choice (see below). The best way to do this is to fax the park's Puerto Jiménez office directly on 735-5276 or, if you're already in the country, visit the Fundación de Parques Nacionales in San José (see p.586), who will fax or telephone Corcovado on your behalf. You'll have to specify your dates and stick to them. It currently costs US$2 per night to camp at the *puestos*, or US$6 to sleep in the comfortable accommodation block at Sirena. You can either take **meals** with the rangers (US$3 for breakfast, US$6 for lunch and dinner – you pay in colones at the *puesto*) or bring your own food and utensils and use their stove. Food is basic – rice and beans or fish – but filling.

You should **bring** your own tent, mosquito net, sleeping bag, food and water, and plan to hike early – though not before dawn, due to snakes – and shelter during the hottest part of the day. Corcovado is set up so that the rangers at each *puesto* always know how many people are on a given trail, and how long they are expected to be. If you are late getting back, they'll go looking for you. This gives a measure of security, but, all the same, take precautions. Incidentally, it's especially important when coming to Corcovado to brush up on your **Spanish**. You'll be asking the rangers for a lot of crucial information, and few, if any, speak English. Bring a phrase book if you're not fluent.

Puestos and routes through the park

The *pulpería* in the village of **Carate**, about 43km from Jiménez, sells basic food-stuffs and you can camp for a nominal fee. From here it's a ninety-minute to two-hour walk along the beach to the park entrance at **La Leona** *puesto*. It's then a sixteen-kilometre hike – allow six hours, as you have to wind along the beach, where it's slow going – to **Sirena**, the biggest *puesto* in the park, where you can stay in the simple lodge, exploring the local trails around the Río Sirena. If you're walking from Bahía Drake, you'll enter the park at **San Pedrillo** *puesto* and walk to Sirena from there.

The small hamlet of La Palma, 24km north of Puerto Jiménez, is the starting point for the walk to the **Los Patos** *puesto*, a twelve-kilometre hike, much of it through hot lowland terrain. You need to arrive at Los Patos soon after dawn; if you want to stay in La Palma and get up early, *Cabinas Corcovado* (no phone; ①–②) is a good bet. The relatively new **El Tigre** *puesto*, at the eastern inland entrance to the park, is a good place to have breakfast or lunch with the ranger(s) before setting off on the local trails. To get there from Jiménez, drive 10km north and take the second left, a dirt track, signed to El Tigre and Dos Brazos.

All puestos have camping areas, drinking water, information, toilets and telephone or radio. Wherever you enter, jot down the details of the **marea** (tide tables), which are posted in prominent positions. You'll need to cross most of the rivers at low tide; to do otherwise is dangerous. Rangers can advise on conditions.

Walking the trails

The fifteen-kilometre trail from **La Leona to Sirena** runs almost entirely along the beach. You can only walk its full length at low tide, and if you do get stuck, the only thing to do is wait for the water to recede. If you can avoid problems with the tides, you should be able to do the walk in five to six hours, taking time to look out for birds. The walking can get a bit monotonous, but the beaches are uniformly lovely and deserted, and if you're lucky you may spot a flock of **scarlet macaws** in the coastal trees – a rare sight. You will probably see (or hear) monkeys, too. Take lots of sun-screen, a big hat and at least five litres of water per person – the trail gets very hot, despite sea breezes.

The really heroic walk in Corcovado, all 25km of it, is from **Sirena to San Pedrillo** – the stretch along which you'll see the most impressive trees. It's a two-day trek, so you need a tent, sleeping bag and mosquito net, and you mustn't be worried by having to set up camp in the jungle. Fording the **Río Sirena**, just 1km beyond the Sirena *puesto*, is the biggest obstacle: this is the deepest of all the rivers on the peninsula, with the strongest out-tow current, and has to be crossed with care, and at low tide only (sharks come in and out in search of food at high tide). Get the latest information from the Sirena rangers before you set out.

The trail across the peninsula from **Los Patos to Sirena** is 20km long. You may want to rest at the entrance, as this is an immediately demanding walk, continuing uphill for about 6–8km and taking you into high, wet and dense rainforest – and after that you've still got 14km or so of incredibly hot lowland walking to go. This is a trail for experienced rainforest hikers and hopeful **mammal**-spotters: taking you through the interior, it gives you a reasonable chance of coming across, for example, a margay, or the tracks of tapirs and jaguars. That said, some hikers come away very disappointed, having not seen a thing. It's a gruelling trek, especially with the hot inland temperatures (at least 26°C, with 100 percent humidity) and the lack of sea breezes.

The **El Tigre** area, at the eastern inland entrance to the park, is gradually becoming more developed, with short walking trails being laid out around the *puesto*. These provide an introduction to Corcovado without making you slog it out on the marathon trails, and can easily be covered in a morning or afternoon.

Paso Canoas and the Panamanian border

Duty-free shops and stalls lining the Interamericana announce the approach to **PASO CANOAS**. As you come into town, either driving or on the TRACOPA or international Ticabus service, you'll pass the Costa Rican customs checkpoint, where everybody gets a going-over. Foreigners don't attract much interest, however; customs officials are far more concerned with nabbing Ticos coming back over the border with unauthorized amounts of cheap consumer goods.

To cross from Costa Rica into Panamá, most nationalities need a **tourist card**: though UK citizens need only bring their passport. Tourist cards should be collected in advance from the **Panamanian consulate**, or from the office of Copa, Panama's national airline, in San José. Many people should also have a **visa** – Canadians, Australians and New Zealanders among them. You may also need a return ticket back to Costa Rica or an onward ticket out of Panamá to another country (though the cheapest TRACOPA fare will do), but bear in mind that immigration requirements frequently change, seemingly at whim, so always check with the Panamanian consulate before setting off.

The **migración** is on the Costa Rican side, next to the TRACOPA bus terminal. You'll have to wait in line, maybe for several hours, especially if a San José–David–Panamá City Ticabus comes through, as all international bus passengers are processed together. Arrive early to get through fastest. There's no problem **changing money**: there's a Banco Nacional on the Costa Rican side of the border and, beyond that, plenty of moneychangers. Note that you cannot take any fruit or vegetables across the border – even if they're for your lunch. They will be confiscated.

DAVID, the first city of any size in Panamá, is about ninety minutes beyond the border. Buses run from the Panamanian border bus terminal every hour or so until 5pm. From David it's easy to pick up local services, including the Ticabus to Panamá City, which you can't pick up at the border.

travel details

BUSES

Dominical to: Quepos (2 daily; 2hr); San Isidro (4 daily; 40min–1hr).

Golfito to: San José (2 daily; 8hr).

Palmar to: San José (7 daily; 5hr 30min); Sierpe (5 daily; 30min).

Paso Canoas to: San Isidro (2 daily; 6hr); San José (6 daily; 9hr).

Puerto Jiménez to: San Isidro (2 daily; 5hr); San José (2 daily; 10hr).

Quepos to: Dominical (2 daily; 2hr).

San Isidro to: Dominical (4 daily; 40min–1hr); Paso Canoas (2 daily; 6hr); Puerto Jiménez (2 daily; 5hr); San Gerardo de Rivas, for Chirripó (2 daily; 40min); San José (12 daily; 3hr).

San José to: Golfito (2 daily; 8hr); Palmar (7 daily; 5hr 30min); Paso Canoas (6 daily; 9hr); Puerto Jiménez (2 daily; 10hr); San Isidro (12 daily; 3hr).

Sierpe to: Palmar (5 daily; 30min).

FLIGHTS (Sansa and Travelair)

Golfito to: San José (4 daily).

Puerto Jiménez to: San José (2–5 daily).

San José to: Golfito (4 daily); Palmar Sur (1 daily); Puerto Jiménez (2–5 daily).

FERRIES

Golfito to: Puerto Jiménez (1 daily).

PART EIGHT

PANAMÁ

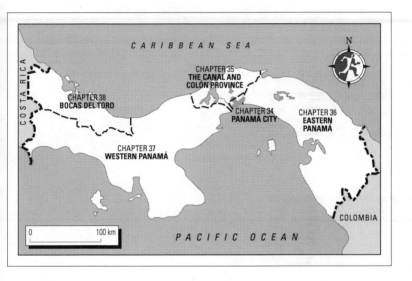

Introduction

Even before the construction of its famous canal, **Panamá**'s strategic location at the wasp waist of the Americas and at the meeting place of the Atlantic and Pacific oceans made it one of the great crossroads of the world. A narrow, S-shaped isthmus that stretches some 750km between Costa Rica and Colombia, Panamá remains a vital **thoroughfare** of international commerce, but is rarely visited by travellers. In part this is because the land bridge to South America, the Darién Gap, remains virtually impassable; in part because the use of the US dollar and the relatively high level of economic development make it a more expensive country to visit than other places in the region. But above all it seems that Panamá suffers from a serious image problem. Although the last US troops have now left Panamá and the canal is in Panamanian hands, to most outsiders the country remains a virtual colony of the US, artificially created in order to facilitate construction of the canal, while its culture is seen as a desperately compromised imitation of North America: urbanized, anglicized and Coca-colonized. Yet while it is true that no other country in Central America has been so dominated by the US – Panamá owes its very existence to US intervention – in fact the North American cultural influence, though strong, is but one among many. Spanish, African, West Indian, Chinese, Indian, European – all have contributed to a **compelling cultural mix**, creating perhaps the most cosmopolitan, open-minded and outward-looking society in Central America. At the same time, it is also home to some of the most unassimilated and culturally fascinating indigenous societies in Central America – within 30km of the high-rise banking district of Panamá City, for example, the indigenous **Emberá** still practise subsistence agriculture in the rainforest and hunt for their supper with blowpipes.

Most travellers who make it down to Panamá are surprised by its outstanding **natural beauty**. With 1600km of coastline on the Pacific and 1280km on the Caribbean side, Panamá boasts unspoiled beaches and coral reefs to match any in the region. And although it is Costa Rica that has achieved world renown as an **ecotourism** destination, in terms of pristine wilderness and ecological diversity Panamá has little reason to envy its neighbour. A biological bridge between conti-

nents, Panamá supports an astounding biodiversity, including over nine hundred species of bird, more than in the whole of North America. Over half the country is still covered by dense tropical rainforest, and large areas are protected by a system of national parks and nature reserves.

Although the government is keen to promote international tourism, for the moment Panamá remains one of the best-kept travellers' secrets in Central America. Of course, this means that in comparison to, say, Costa Rica, the **infrastructure** for visiting the protected wilderness areas is much more limited. But while this may put some people off, for others it simply adds to the sense of adventure – visitors to Panamá's national parks are unlikely to have to share them with more than a handful of other people. Moreover, wherever you travel in Panamá, the absence of a travellers' "scene" means you will be forced into much more direct contact with local people, an experience which, given the natural warmth and open-mindedness of most Panamanians and the fact that they have not yet become jaded with foreigners due to the impact of mass tourism, is undoubtedly one of the most rewarding aspects of any visit to this underrated and misunderstood country.

■ Where to go

Some two-thirds of Panamá's population live in the narrow corridor on either side of the canal, most of them in the capital, Panamá City, or in the well-developed Pacific coastal plain west of the canal. The rest of Panamá, east of the canal and north of the rugged mountain chain that runs like a spine down the length of the country, is heavily forested and sparsely inhabited, a virtual wilderness.

Cosmopolitan and contradictory, **Panamá City** is perhaps the most exciting capital city in Central America, combining the intrigue and frenetic energy of its international banking centre with the laid-back street-life of its old colonial quarter and the antiseptic order of the former US-controlled Canal Zone towns. Surrounded by some of the most accessible tropical rainforest in the Americas, it is also the best base from which to explore the rest of the country. Without doubt Panamá's best-known attraction for visitors, the monumental **Panamá Canal** can easily be visited from the city – you can watch mighty ships being raised and lowered through the locks or, even better, take a cruise yourself. Also within

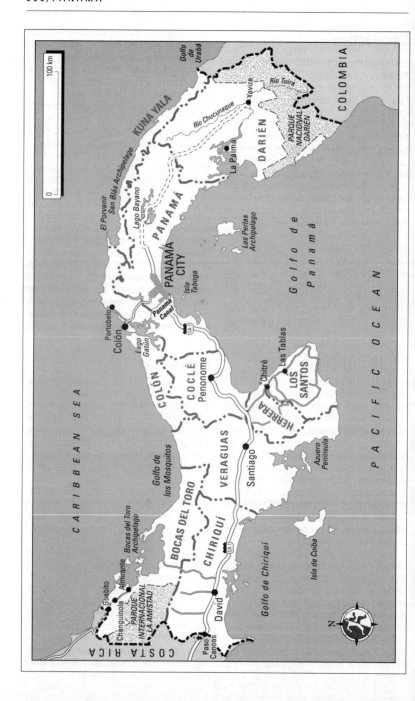

easy reach from the capital are the colonial ruins and pristine Caribbean coastline of the province of Colón. East of Panamá City stretches **Darién**, the wild, rainforest-covered frontier between Central and South America. Stretched out along its beautiful Caribbean coastline is **Kuna Yala**, the autonomous homeland of the Kuna, who live in isolation on the coral atolls of the San Blas Archipelago, accessible by light aircraft from the capital.

West of Panamá City and the canal, the Carretera Interamericana to Costa Rica runs through the Pacific coastal plain, Panamá's agricultural heartland. Densely populated in comparison with the rest of the interior, and with a decent road network, the attractions of this region include the folkloric traditions and coastal nature reserves of the **Azuero Peninsula** and the protected cloudforests of the **Chiriquí Highlands**, close to the Costa Rican border. The Caribbean coast west of the canal is virtually uninhabited except in the extreme northwest corner, in the isolated archipelago of **Bocas del Toro**, fast emerging as one of the most popular parts of the country amongst visitors thanks to its virtually unspoiled rainforests, beaches, coral reefs and unusual population of indigenous and West Indian-descended inhabitants.

■ When to go

Lying between 7 and 10 degrees north of the equator, Panamá is set well within the **tropics**, and consequently temperatures are constant year-round – around 25°–30°C – and vary only with **altitude**: the average temperature in the Chiriquí Highlands is about 19°C, but this is the only region in which you are ever likely to feel cold. **Humidity** is always very high. **Rainfall** varies markedly between the Pacific and Caribbean sides of the mountain chain that runs the length of the country: on the Pacific side, the annual average is about 1500mm, on the Caribbean, about 2500mm. The **best time** to visit Panamá is during the dry season between mid-December and April, known as *verano* (summer), though this seasonal variation is really only evident on the Pacific side of the mountains. On the Caribbean side, rainfall is spread more evenly throughout the year. Though heavy, the rainstorms during the May–December rainy season – *invierno* (winter) – rarely last long, and are no reason not to visit.

Panamá is in the **Eastern Standard Time Zone**, five hours behind GMT and an hour ahead of Costa Rica.

Getting around

Travel within Panamá varies as sharply as everything else in the country. While the **canal corridor** and the **western Pacific** region are covered by a comprehensive road network served by regular public transport, both **eastern Panamá** and **Bocas del Toro** are linked to the rest of the country by just a single road. Getting around these areas means relying on light aircraft and (generally unscheduled) boats.

■ Buses

Where there are roads, **buses** are the cheapest, easiest and most popular way to travel around Panamá. Panamá City is the hub of the network, with regular buses to Colón, Yaviza in Darién, Almirante (for Bocas del Toro) and all the cities and towns of western Panamá.

Buses vary in comfort and size, from modern, air-conditioned Pullmans to smaller minibuses and cramped, brightly painted old US school buses. Smaller towns and villages in rural areas are served by less frequent minibuses, pick-up trucks and flat-bed trucks known as *chivas* or *chivitas*, converted to carry passengers. Most buses are individually owned, and even when services are frequent, **schedules** change all the time. The cities and larger towns have bus terminals, otherwise buses leave from the main street or square. You can usually flag down through buses from the roadside, though they may not stop if they are full or going a long way.

Both Colón and David are also served by **express buses**, which are more expensive, more comfortable and faster than the normal service. The express bus to David and international buses to Costa Rica are the only ones worth **booking** in advance – in general, you can just turn up shortly before departure and you should get a seat. **Fares**, as elsewhere in Central America, are good value: the most you'll have to pay is US$11 for the seven-hour ride from David to Panamá City.

■ Driving and hitching

Driving in Panamá is pretty straightforward: roads (where they exist) are pretty good and distances relatively short. **4WD** is a good idea, particularly during the rainy season and if you want to drive to more remote rural areas, particularly Darién. Note that even the paved major roads in the canal corridor and the west can be badly maintained, and in Panamá City 4WD can be useful for negotiating potholes.

At around US$40 a day or US$200 a week (more for 4WD), **car rental** is reasonably cheap. It is also a good way of seeing the country, especially in the canal corridor and areas close to Panamá City. Most rental companies are based in Panamá City (see p.730) but some also have offices at the airport and in David. Always read the small print, make sure you are insured and check the car for damage before you accept it. **Filling stations** are easy to find on major roads and in most towns – many are open 24 hours – but there are fewer in rural areas, and in Darién you should carry an extra gas can in the car.

Traffic in Panamá City is fairly chaotic, and both there and in Colón **parking and security** are a problem. Car hijacking is growing, so keep your doors locked and (if you have air conditioning) your windows closed. Most hotels have their own parking lots, but otherwise when parking in the street someone is likely to offer to watch over your car for you in return for small change – though not exactly a demand for protection money, this is worth doing.

Hitching is possible, but private cars are unlikely to stop for you on main roads served by buses. In more remote areas, it is often the only motor transport available, and there is little distinction between private vehicles and public transport – drivers will pick you up, but you should expect to pay the same kind of fares as for the bus.

■ Cycling

Riding a bike in Panamá City is virtually unheard of, but in the west of the country, where roads are generally paved and traffic (away from the Carretera Interamericana) scarce, cycling is a popular way to get around, and most towns have somewhere offering parts and simple repairs. The stretch of road from the continental divide to Chiriquí Grande on the road from David to Bocas del Toro, in particular, is a cyclist's dream – some 40km downhill on a well-surfaced, little-driven road, through rainforest-covered mountains that march down to the Caribbean.

■ Boats and ferries

Scheduled **ferries** run from Panamá City to Isla Taboga and between Almirante and Bocas del Toro in the province of Bocas del Toro. **Smaller boats** – launches or dugout canoes with outboard motors – are an important means of transport in Bocas del Toro, Darién and Kuna Yala, and often the only way to reach islands or other remote areas. The only scheduled small boat services are the **water-taxis** in Bocas del Toro and between Puerto Quimba and La Palma in Darién. Otherwise you have to either wait for somebody who is going your way, or rent a boat and a boatman yourself. The latter is expensive, largely because outboard motors consume huge amounts of gas, but it becomes increasingly economical the more people there are to share the boat, and it can be the most exciting way to get around. Renting a canoe with an outboard motor and a boatman opens up unlimited possibilities for wilderness adventure – up jungle rivers to isolated villages or to uninhabited coastal islands.

Occasional **boats and ships** that take passengers run along the Pacific coast of Darién from Panamá City, sometimes continuing on to Colombia, though they have no fixed schedule. Similarly, tramp steamers run the length of Kuna Yala from Colón, and often continue to Colombia along the Caribbean coast, but both Kuna- and Colombian-owned ships are generally loath to take foreigners as passengers.

■ Planes

Cities and larger towns are served by regular flights by **Aeroperlas** (☎315 7500, *www.aeroperlas .com*), the principal domestic carrier, which also has regular flights to Darién. Other than Bocas del Toro and David, which are also served by **Mapiex Aero** (☎315 0888), most destinations are so close to Panamá City that it's scarcely worth flying, but flights are generally inexpensive (the longest flight, from Panamá City to David, costs around US$50), and on some routes (David to Bocas del Toro, for example) the views alone make it worthwhile. In eastern Panamá – Darién and Kuna Yala – on the other hand, light aircraft are the main and often the only way to get around. **ANSA** (☎315 0275 or 315 0299), **Aviatur** (☎315 0397 or 315 0314) and – the most reliable of the three – **Aerotaxi** (☎315 0275) have several flights a week to most of the major communities in Kuna Yala and towns in Darién.

■ Train

After being closed for me than a decade, the **transisthmian railway** (*www.kcsi.com/pcrc .html*), which runs alongside the canal between Panamá City and Colón, is due to reopen for passengers in 2001, offering an excellent way of seeing the canal and the surrounding rainforest. The only other train in Panamá is the banana railway from Changuinola in Bocas del Toro up to the Costa Rican border, though this is intended for banana workers and is much slower than making the same journey by road.

Costs, money and banks

Panamá is the most economically advanced country in Central America and has the highest GDP per head (although income distribution is so polarized that poverty remains widespread). This, together with the use of the US dollar as the national currency, makes **costs** higher than in other countries in the region.

■ Currency, exchange and banks

Panamá adopted the US dollar as its **currency** in 1904, and has not printed any paper currency since. Dollars are referred to interchangeably as **dólares** or **balboas**. Panamá does mint its own coinage: 1, 5, 10, 25 and 50 centavo pieces, which are the same shape and size as – and are used alongside – US coins. Fifty cents is also referred to as a "*peso*", and five cents as a "*real*", so 35 cents, for example, can also be described as "siete reales". US$100 and US$50 bills are often difficult to spend, for fear of forgeries or simply because change is difficult to come by, so it's best to make US$20 bills the largest you carry.

It is difficult to **change foreign currency** in Panamá, and you should change any cash into US dollars as soon as you can. In Panamá City there are Banco Nacional branches at the airport and on Via España in the El Cangrejo district, or you could try Panacambios, a *casa de cambio* also on Via España. Foreign banks will generally change their own currencies.

Travellers' cheques are the safest way to carry your money and are easy to change so long as they are issued by major companies (Visa, Mastercard) and are in US dollars. The three major **banks** in Panamá – Banco Nacional, Banco del Istmo and Banco General – will all change these, as will some of the international banks in Panamá City. Most banks are open from 8 or 8.30am to 3 or 4pm Monday to Friday, and some also open from 9am to noon on Saturday; almost all branches now have **ATMs.** Major **credit cards** are accepted in the more upmarket hotels and restaurants in Panamá City and the larger provincial towns. Visa is the most widely accepted, followed by Mastercard.

■ Costs

Though costs are low compared to Europe and North America, Panamá – along with Costa Rica and Belize – is one of the more **expensive** Central American countries. Sticking to a tight budget you can just about get by on around US$25 a day, though you should be prepared to spend more than that in Panamá City and in remote areas where basic goods have to be brought in by sea or air. A **basic double room** in a hotel or pensión will usually cost at least US$10, and you will often have to pay twice that to get somewhere comfortable. Fortunately, **bus transport** is inexpensive – more or less US$1–1.50 an hour – and if you stick to basic local **restaurants** you can eat well on a dollar or two for each meal. Because of low taxes and import duties, **imported consumer goods** – electronics, clothing and the like – are often cheaper than in Europe or North America (see "Shopping" on p.703 for more on Panamá's duty-free status).

Leaving Panamá, there's a US$20 **departure tax**, payable at the airport.

Information

The best source of information in Panamá is the Panamanian Tourist Institute, **IPAT** (*www .ipat.gob.pa*), which has its main office in Panamá City (see p.713) and several provincial branch offices. Though the government is keen to promote tourism, the idea that some foreign visitors prefer independent travel to package tours is still a novelty to most IPAT workers. You can get some useful information at the Panamá City office – advice, free maps, leaflets – but unless you go there with some fairly specific questions you may end up with little more than glossy brochures. The provincial offices are more variable, though even in the most rudimentary of them you should be able to find some useful information – a local map or brochures – and there is usually someone who speaks English. *The Visitor/El Visitante*, a free monthly **tourist promotion magazine** in English and Spanish available at IPAT offices, hotels and restaurants throughout Panamá, lists Panamá's attractions and upcoming events.

Panamá's **national parks** and other protected natural areas are administered by the National Environment Agency, **ANAM** (*www.anam .gob.pa*). The main office in Panamá City (see p.714) is in theory keen to promote ecotourism, though in practice they offer almost no information on visiting the parks. The ANAM regional offices, which administer the national parks directly, are generally more helpful and an essential stop before visiting parks where permission is needed or if you want to spend the night in a refuge (see opposite). Once again they are often unaccustomed to the idea of travellers visiting national parks independently, but are usually very helpful. Several **tour operators** based in Panamá City can also give you advice and information on visiting the rest of the country, though of course they will do so in the hope of selling you a tour.

The best **map** of Panamá (1:800,000; available in specialist map shops) is produced by International Travel Maps (345 West Broadway, Vancouver, BC, Canada V5Y 1P8). **In Panamá**, large-scale maps are available at the Instituto Geográfico Nacional Tommy Guardia (Mon–Fri 8.30am–4pm) on Via Simon Bolívar, opposite the entrance to the university in Panamá City.

Accommodation

In most areas of Panamá there is a wide choice of places to stay, though outside Panamá City and some resort areas few of the country's hotels are designed with foreign travellers in mind, particularly those on a budget. In general, **prices** are relatively high – the cheapest room may cost US$15–20 a night (the price for a single room varies little from that of a double) – but for this you'll usually get television, private bath, and air-conditioning. Cheaper rooms, with a fan instead of air-conditioning (you'll need one or the other), are often available, but staff will assume you are not interested in these unless you ask. **Hot water** is not considered a necessity and is usually only available in more expensive places, except in the Chiriquí highlands where it takes the place of a fan or a/c. In **Panamá City** most hotels are aimed at business travellers and prices tend to be even higher, while at the lower end of the market many hotels cater largely for Panamanian couples – some even have hourly rates – and are often full on the weekends, when prices go up.

You don't usually need to **book in advance**, except in the more upmarket hotels in Panamá City and at weekends or during public holidays. The ten percent **tourist tax** charged on hotel accommodation is usually included in the quoted price.

PANAMÁ ON THE WEB

An ever-increasing number of Panamanian businesses, government agencies and other organizations now have Web sites, and Internet addresses are given in the guide where relevant. The following are just a few of the more useful general sites.

www.ancon.org Web site of the National Conservation Association, Panamá's biggest and most influential environmental group, with excellent general information on Panamá's national parks, ecology and endangered species, as well as scientific papers and information on voluntary work.

www.ipat.gob.pa The site of the Panamanian Tourist Institute, IPAT, with plenty of basic information on Panamá's many attractions and good links to hotels, airlines, tour agencies and other related sites.

www.mundolatino.org/prensa/Panama Links to Panamanian newspapers and other media.

www.panamainfo.com Good general guide to tourism, business in Panamá, in English and Spanish, with excellent links to a wide range of Panamanian Web sites.

www.panamatours.com One-stop resource for travel to Panamá, with plenty of general information on Panamá as a tourist destination and links to all kinds of related sites.

www.pancanal.com Official site of the Panamá Canal Authority with plenty of information and news, a history of the canal in English and Spanish, plus pictures and a live Webcam.

www.thepanamanews.com Panamá's weekly English-language newspaper – a good place to keep up with the latest events.

■ Camping and places without hotels

There are no **official campsites** in Panamá, but it is possible to camp in remote rural areas and national parks, though you should always ask permission or at least let local people know that you are doing so. Other than on uninhabited islands in Kuna Yala or deep in the wilderness it is never really necessary – even in the smallest villages there's almost always somewhere you can sling a hammock or bed down for the night in return for a few dollars. If you do camp, a hammock and a plastic sheet or tarpaulin strung up against the rain are just as good as a tent. A **mosquito net** or mosquito coils (known as *mechitas* and widely available) are essential, as is a good insect repellent.

Almost all the national parks have ANAM (see p.714) **refuges** where you can spend the night for US$5–10, though this fee is not always charged. They are usually pretty basic, with bunk beds, cooking facilities and running water.

Eating and drinking

Known as *comida típica*, **traditional Panamanian cooking** is broadly similar to what you will find elsewhere in Central America. Basic, filling meals based on rice and beans or lentils served with a little chicken, meat or fish form the mainstay, though *yuca* (manioc) and plantains are also important staples.

■ Where to eat

The cheapest places to eat are canteen-like **self-service restaurants**, serving a narrow but filling range of Panamanian meals for a few dollars, which you will find almost everywhere. Larger towns usually have some more **upmarket restaurants** with waiter service where a main meat or fish dish may cost US$5–15, and in Panamá City there is no shortage of expensive and exotic restaurants. There is no **tax** to pay on

meals and **tipping**, though always welcome, is only expected in more expensive places or where service has been particularly good. All towns have US-style **fast-food** places, but **street vendors** are less common than elsewhere in Central America.

In **remote areas** with no real restaurant, there is usually someone in the village who will be prepared to cook you a meal, though it is always best to let them know in advance.

■ What to eat

Panamá's national dish is **sancocho**, a hearty chicken soup with *yuca*, plantains and other root vegetables flavoured with coriander, closely followed by the ubiquitous **arroz con pollo** (chicken with rice). **Seafood** is plentiful, excellent and generally cheap, particularly *corvina* (sea bass), *pargo rojo* (red snapper), lobster and prawns – the latter are one of Panamá's biggest exports. *Ceviche* – a cool, spicy dish of raw fish or seafood marinated in lime juice with onions and hot peppers – is a popular appetizer, though a disappointment to anyone who has eaten the more substantial South American version. Fresh **tropical fruit** is also abundant, but rarely on the menu at restaurants other than in juice form – you're better off buying it yourself in local markets.

Breakfast for most Panamanians is *fritura*, a combination of fried foods such as sausages, eggs, *patacones* (fried green plantains), *tortillas de maíz* (smaller and thicker than elsewhere in Central America) and *hojaldres* (fried dough – much tastier than it sounds). Popular **snacks** include *carimañolas* or *enyucados* (fried balls of manioc dough filled with meat), *empanadas*, *tamales* (a mix of maize porridge, vegetables and pork or chicken wrapped in a banana-leaf parcel and boiled) and *patacones*.

The diverse **cultural influences** that have passed through Panamá have also left their mark on its cuisine, especially in Panamá City, where there are hosts of reasonably priced French,

Greek, Italian, Chinese, Japanese and American restaurants. Elsewhere, almost every town has at least one **Chinese** restaurant – often the best option for **vegetarians,** as outside Panamá City there is little to choose from other than eggs, rice and beans – and dishes such as chow mein and fried rice often find their way onto the menus of even the most basic Panamanian restaurants. **US influence** is evident in the widespread availability of hamburgers and hot dogs. Perhaps the strongest outside influence on Panamanian food, though, is the distinctive **Caribbean cuisine** of the West Indian populations of Panamá City and the provinces of Colón and Bocas del Toro, which usually involves fish, seafood and rice cooked in hot spices, lime juice and coconut milk. Popular dishes include *saos* (pigs' trotters marinated in lime and chiles), and *fufu* (a stew of fish, plantains and manioc cooked in coconut milk). In Darién and other remote areas you may well be offered wild game – *conejo pintado* (agouti), a large rodent with sweet, greasy meat, is the most common bush meat.

■ **Drinking**

Coffee is generally good in Panamá, made espresso-style and served black. Weaker coffee is known as *café americano*. Otherwise, everyone drinks **cold drinks**, essential given the heat and humidity. The **drinking water** of Panamá City is so good that it is known as the "Champagne of the Chagres" after the river from which it is drawn, and iced water, served free in restaurants as a matter of course, along with the tap water in most towns and cities, is perfectly safe. Known as **sodas**, bottled fizzy drinks are available everywhere. Cheaper and more refreshing, though, are **chichas**, delicious blends of ice, water and the juice of any one of a dozen tropical fruits, served in restaurants or, in paper cones, by street vendors everywhere (except, that is, in Kuna Yala, where *chicha* is a ceremonial alcoholic drink made from fermented sugar-cane juice flavoured with coffee or cacao). *Batidos* are thick fruit milkshakes, often made with ice-cream. Also popular are **pipas**, green coconuts filled with coconut milk, often served ice cold from massive roadside fridges and drunk with a straw.

Beer is extremely popular in Panamá, and drunk as much for refreshment as for intoxication. Locally brewed brands include Panamá, Löwenbrau, Atlas, Soberana and Balboa.

Imported beers such as Budweiser and Guinness are only widely available in Panamá City. When it comes to getting drunk, most Panamanians turn to locally produced **rum** – Seco Herrerano (known as seco) and Carta Vieja are the most common brands – though imported whiskies and other spirits are widely available. Outside the more upmarket restaurants in Panamá City, wine is hard to come by.

Opening hours, holidays and festivals

Business hours vary from establishment to establishment, but generally **banks** are open from 8 or 8.30am to 3 or 4pm, Monday to Friday, while some also open on Saturday morning. **Businesses** and **government offices** are usually open Monday to Saturday from 8 or 9am to 4 or 5pm, while **museums** generally open the same hours from Tuesday to Saturday, with some also opening on Sunday morning. Some or all of these close for **lunch** from around 12.30pm or 1pm to 1.30 or 2pm. **Shops** are usually open from Monday to Saturday from 9am to 6pm.

Panamá has ten **national public holidays**, during which pretty much all government offices, businesses and shops close. Panamá City and Colón also each have their own public holiday, and there is one public holiday for government employees only. When the public holidays fall near a weekend many Panamanians take a long weekend (known as a *puente*) and head to the beach or the countryside, so it can be difficult to find hotel rooms.

Several of these public holidays coincide with **national fiestas** that continue for several days. **Carnaval**, in February or March, is the largest and wildest of these, celebrated with parades, drinking, water-fighting and dancing in Panamá City and across the country, most colourfully in Las Tablas. **Holy Week** (Easter) is celebrated with religious processions. In November, known as **"El Mes de la Patria"**, the anniversaries of the first declaration of independence and of both independence days (from Spain and Colombia) are celebrated by a succession of drum-band parades.

In addition, **local fiestas** are held by every small town to celebrate its own anniversary and saint's day. The most vibrant of these are the **Fiesta of the Black Christ of Portobelo** on October 21, when up to 50,000 purple-clad

PUBLIC HOLIDAYS

Jan 1 New Year's Day
Jan 9 Martyr's Day (in remembrance of those killed by US troops in the 1964 riots)
Feb–March (date varies) Carnaval
March–April (date varies) Good Friday
May 1 Labour Day
Aug 15 Foundation of Panamá City (Panamá City only)
Nov 3 Independence Day (from Colombia, 1903)
Nov 4 Flag Day (government holiday only)
Nov 5 National Day (Colón only)
Nov 10 First Cry of Independence
Nov 28 Emancipation Day (independence from Spain).
Dec 8 Mothers' Day
Dec 25 Christmas Day

pilgrims descend on that town (see p.743), and the numerous religious and folkloric fiestas of the towns of villages of the **Azuero Peninsula** (see p.765). In **Kuna Yala**, the Kuna celebrate their own independence day (the anniversary of the short-lived Dule Republic) in February, as well as several other dates throughout the year.

Mail and telecommunications

Other than in remote areas, **communications** in Panamá are good. Most small towns have a post office and telephone office, so keeping in touch with home is fairly easy.

Letters posted with the Correo Nacional (COTEL) cost US$0.35 to the US and US$0.45 to Europe. They should reach either destination within a week or two, though have been known to take far longer – it's best to post them in Panamá City. Most post offices have an *Entrega General* (Poste Restante, General Delivery) where you can **receive mail** – in Panamá City your correspondent must specify the post office zone: the most central is Zone 5, on Av Central/Via España. Post office **opening hours** are generally from 7am to 6pm Monday to Friday, 7am to 5pm on Saturday.

Panamá's recently privatized **telephone** company is owned by Cable and Wireless (C&W). **Local phone calls** are cheap, and there's a wide network of modern payphones that take phonecards sold in shops and street stalls. You can make **international collect calls** from these via the international operator (☎106), and both AT&T (☎109) and MCI (☎108) can place collect or credit-card calls to the US. Otherwise, C&W offices are the best place to make international calls or send **faxes**. Hotels tend to overcharge for phone calls. Panamá's **country code** is ☎507; there are no regional codes for internal calls. As elsewhere, there's a growing number of **Internet** cafés in the main towns.

The media

For a small country, Panamá has an impressive number of newspapers, and the **independent press** has flourished since the end of military rule. *La Prensa, La Estrella de Panamá, El Panamá America* and *El Universal* are all serious broadsheets, while *Critica Libre* and *El Siglo* are the most popular tabloids. **La Prensa** is probably the most effective critic of the present government, has a good international section and publishes entertainment listings. The **Panamá News**, a free fortnightly English-language newspaper covering local news and with an entertainment listings section, is widely available in Panamá City, as is the international edition of the *Miami Herald*. You can also find *Newsweek, Time, The Economist, The Financial Times* and several US papers on sale in the capital.

Most Panamanian households have a **television**, as so do most hotel rooms. There are four private television stations – channels 2, 4, 5 and 13 – offering a mix of Latin American soap opera, sport, US sitcoms, movies and news, as well as a government educational channel, Channel 11. Cable and satellite television is also widely available – particularly in more upmarket hotels – featuring CNN, BBC World, and a plethora of US sport and entertainment channels. There's a massive variety of FM **radio stations** in Panamá, and you'll seldom be out of earshot of a radio, blasting out anything from music and news to evangelical exhortations.

Shopping

For many visitors, **shopping** is the main reason to come to Panamá, and today people from all over Latin America and the Caribbean come here to buy **consumer goods** – electronics, designer fashion, jewellery – which are available here at a lower cost and in greater variety than elsewhere in the region. You can buy almost anything you might want in the bazaars and superstores of Panamá City, often at a lower price than in Europe or the US, and the country is also home to the second largest duty-free zone in the world: the **Colón Free Zone**. Goods from all over the world are traded here in vast quantities, and though most business is in bulk, you can find good bargains (though you may have to pay duty when you return home).

Panamá also produces some beautiful **handicrafts**. The most famous and exceptional are the **molas** – brightly coloured cotton cloths intricately decorated with abstract designs created by a system of reverse-appliqué – made by the Kuna people (see p.754). The *mola* has become something of a national symbol and are sold all over the country. The Emberá-Wounaan in Darién produce exquisite **carvings** in wood or *tagua* (a palm seed known as "vegetable ivory"), mostly of birds and rainforest animals, while the artisans of western Panamá, and in particular those of the Azuero Peninsula, produce a wide range of handicrafts including pottery, lurid fiesta masks, leatherwork, and straw sombreros. The brightly coloured dresses and fibre shoulder bags (*chacaras*) of the Ngobe-Buglé people also make beautiful and practical souvenirs. Sadly, authentic **Panama hats** come from Ecuador.

Almost all these handicrafts are available in Panamá City, in shops and in cooperative artesanía **markets** (listed in the Guide), but of course if you have the time it's much more rewarding (and cheaper) to buy them from the artisans themselves.

Safety and the police

Panamá has something of a reputation as a dangerous place to travel, but though **violent crime** is a problem – most shops, banks and hotels have private armed guards – outside certain areas Panamá is really no worse than anywhere else in Central America. You should take special care in **Colón** and in **Panamá City** (particularly in the San Felipe, El Chorillo and Calidonia districts), where **mugging** is a real threat, and always ask local advice about the relative safety of different areas. Other than your **passport**, which you are required to carry at all times, leave your valuables in your hotel when you can, keep them close to

your body when you can't, and carry a few dollars separately so that muggers do not search you for more (or become violent with disappointment). Late at night or when carrying luggage, it's a good idea to take a taxi – think of it as a cheap insurance policy. If you are **driving**, never leave your car unattended and, in Panamá City and Colón, keep your doors locked and windows closed to avoid being hijacked (see p.698).

Outside Colón and Panamá City, the only area where there is any particular danger is **Darién** and the easternmost part of **Kuna Yala**. This wilderness frontier with Colombia has long been frequented by Colombian Marxist guerrillas, bandits and cocaine traffickers, but since 1996 the situation has deteriorated dramatically, and several travellers attempting to cross overland to Colombia have been kidnapped, killed or have simply disappeared. It is still possible to visit Darién, including parts of the national park, and the situation may well get better, but at present **we do not recommend travel in this area**. Even when the situation has improved, you should check with the ANAM office in Darién by phone and in the press in Panamá City before going, and register with the police in every town. And if you are planning to travel to Colombia by sea, you should be aware that many of the boats that ply the coast are involved in smuggling.

If you are robbed or otherwise become the victim of a crime, you should report it immediately to the local **police** station, particularly if you will later be making an insurance claim. If treated respectfully, Panamanian police are generally honest and helpful. In Panamá City the **tourist police** (*policía de turismo*) are better prepared to deal with foreign travellers and more likely to speak English – they wear white armbands and are often mounted on bicycles.

Work

Although Panamá City teems with foreign workers, without a permit there are few opportunities for **work** in Panamá. There are some **English**

schools, but no shortage of teachers. With patience, luck or charm you may be able to find work crewing on a **yacht**, as a linehandler as it passes through the canal or even onwards into the Caribbean: for details see p.735. Finally, the environmental organization ANCON (☎314 0060, *www.ancon.org*) accepts volunteers to work on conservation programmes throughout Panamá.

History

Perhaps no country in the world has had its history so thoroughly determined by geography as Panamá. In prehistoric times this was a crucial land bridge in the migration routes by which the Americas were populated, and from the moment the conquistador **Vasco Nuñez de Balboa** emerged from the forests of Darién to become the first European to look out onto the Pacific Ocean on September 25, 1513, the history of Panamá has been the history of the route across the isthmus. Balboa claimed what he called the "Southern Ocean" in the name of the King of Spain, but received scant reward for his discovery – in 1519 his jealous superior **Pedro Arias Dávila** (known as Pedrarias the Cruel), the first governor of what was by then known as Castilla de Oro, had him beheaded for his troubles.

In the face of appalling losses from disease in the first Spanish settlements on the Caribbean, Pedrarias moved his base across the isthmus to the more salubrious Pacific coast, where he founded **Panamá City** in 1519. The new settlement became the jumping-off point for further Spanish conquests north and south along the coast, and after the conquest of Peru in 1533 began to flourish as the **transit point** for the fabulous wealth of the **Incas** on its way to fill the coffers of the Spanish Crown. From Panamá City, cargo was transported across the isthmus on mules along the paved Camino Real to the ports of Nombre de Dios and later Portobelo, on the Caribbean coast. A second route, the Camino de Cruces, was used to transport heavier cargo to the highest navigable point on the Río Chagres, where it was transferred to canoes that carried it downriver to the coast. Once a year huge trade fairs lasting several weeks were held at Portobelo, when the Spanish royal fleet arrived to collect the gold and silver that had accumulated in the treasure houses of Panamá and to trade European goods that were then redistributed across the Americas. The vast wealth that flowed across the isthmus was quick to attract the attention of Spain's enemies, and despite ever heavier fortification the Caribbean coast was constantly harassed by English and other European **pirates**. In the most daring attack, the English Henry Morgan sailed up the Río Chagres and crossed the isthmus to sack Panamá City in 1671.

Though the city was rebuilt behind defences so formidable that it was never taken again, the raiding of the Caribbean coast continued, until finally in 1746 Spain rerouted the treasure fleet around **Cape Horn**. With the route across the isthmus all but abandoned, Panamá slipped into decline, and settlement of the interior began to increase. Despite fierce resistance from indigenous groups the rest of the isthmus had been progressively conquered in the decades following the foundation of Panamá City. The forests of Darién and the Atlantic coast had been largely abandoned once the early colonial gold mines established there had been exhausted, and provided a refuge for unsubmissive tribes and bands of renegade slaves known as *cimarrones*, while the Pacific coastal plain west of Panamá City was gradually settled by farmers. **Trade** remained the dominant economic activity – whereas in most of the Spanish Empire political power lay in the hands of large landowners, in Panamá it was always held by the merchant class of Panamá City.

In 1821 Panamá declared its **independence from Spain**, but retained its name as a department of Gran Colombia, which, with the secession of Ecuador and Venezuela, quickly became simply **Colombia**. Almost immediately, though, conflicts emerged between the merchants of Panamá City, eager to trade freely with the world, and the distant, protectionist governments in Bogotá, leading to numerous half-hearted and unsuccessful attempts at independence.

Meanwhile, traffic across the isthmus was once again increasing, and exploded with the **discovery of gold in California** in 1849. Travel from the US east coast to California via Panamá – by boat, overland by foot, and then by boat again – was far less arduous than the overland trek across North America, and thousands of "Forty-niners" passed through on their way to the goldfields. In 1851 a US company began the construction of a **railway** across Panamá. Carving a route through the inhospitable swamps and forests of the isthmus proved immensely difficult, and thousands of the mostly Chinese and West Indian migrant workers died in the process, but when the railway was completed in 1855, the **Panamá Railroad Company** proved an instant financial success. Panamá's importance as an international thoroughfare increased further, but the railway also marked the beginning of foreign control over the means of transport across the isthmus. Within a year, the first **US military intervention** in Panamá – "to protect the railroad" – had taken place.

■ The French canal venture

In 1869 the opening of the first **transcontinental railway** in the US reduced traffic through Panamá, but the completion of the **Suez Canal** that same year at last made the longstanding dream of a canal across the isthmus a realistic possibility. Well aware of the strategic advantages such a waterway would offer – the journey of a ship travelling from, for example, Boston to San Francisco would be reduced from 21,000km to just 8000km if it could cross the continent by passing through Panamá rather than going all the way round Cape Horn – Britain, France and the US all sent expeditions to seek a suitable route. It was the French, though, who took the initiative, buying a concession to build a canal from the Colombian Government. In 1881, led by **Ferdinand de Lesseps**, the architect responsible for the Suez Canal, the Compagnie Universelle du Canal Interoceanique began excavations.

But despite De Lesseps' vision and determination, the "venture of the century" proved to be an unmitigated disaster. In the face of the impassable terrain – forests, swamps and the shifting shales of the continental divide – the proposed sea-level canal proved technically unfeasible, while yellow fever and malaria ravaged the workforce, killing as many as 20,000. In 1889 the Compagnie collapsed as a result of financial mismanagement and corruption, implicating the highest levels of French society in what the official described as "the greatest fraud of modern times".

But the dream of an interoceanic canal would not die. The US government, never keen on the idea of a canal controlled by a European power and convinced by its 1898 war with Spain of the military importance of a fast passage between the Atlantic and Pacific oceans, took up the challenge. President **Theodore Roosevelt** in particular was convinced that the construction of a canal across Central America was an essential step in pursuit of the control of all the Americas. At first the US favoured building a canal through Nicaragua, but the persuasive lobbying of Philipe Bunau-Varilla, a French engineer anxious to profit from the sale of the French rights and equipment, swung the crucial Senate vote in Panamá's favour. A treaty allowing the US to build the canal was negotiated with the Colombian government in 1903, but the Colombian Senate refused to ratify it. Outraged that "the Bogotá lot of jackrabbits should be allowed to bar one of the future highways of civilization", Roosevelt gave unofficial backing to Panamanian secessionists who had long been seeking independence. The small Colombian garrison in Panamá City was bribed to switch sides and a second force that had landed at Colón agreed to return to Colombia without a fight after its officers had been tricked into captivity by the rebels. On November 3, 1903 the **Republic of Panamá** was declared and immediately recognized by the US, whose gunships standing offshore prevented Colombian reinforcements from landing to crush the rebellion.

Though it is true that Panamá would never have come into existence as an independent republic without the involvement of the US, the independence movement was not wholly a US invention. The Panamanian merchant elite had good reason to seek independence – rule from remote Bogotá limited Panamá's ability to trade and involved it in Colombia's endless civil wars – and had attempted secession 33 times in the previous seventy years. The difference, in 1903, was the support of the US, and this, as the Panamanians were soon to discover, came at a high price.

■ The canal

A new **canal treaty** was quickly negotiated and signed on Panamá's behalf by Bunau-Varilla. It gave the US "all the rights, power and authority. . . which [it] would possess and exercise as if it were sovereign", in perpetuity over an area of territory – the **Canal Zone** – extending five miles either side of the canal. In return, the new Panamanian government received a one-off payment of US$10 million and a further US$250,000 a year. These conditions were so favourable that even American Secretary of State John Hay had to admit they were "very satisfactory, very advantageous for the US and we must confess . . . not so advantageous for Panamá." Panamá's newly formed national assembly found the terms outrageous, but when told by Bunau-Varilla that US support would be withdrawn were they to reject it, they ratified the treaty and work on the canal began.

It took ten years, the labour of some 75,000 workers and some US$387 million to complete the task – an unprecedented triumph of sanitation, organization and engineering during which chief medical officer Colonel William Gorgas established a programme that eliminated yellow fever from the isthmus and brought malaria under control. The US engineers abandoned the idea of a sea-level canal, and instead constructed a series of locks to raise ships up to a huge artificial lake formed by damming the mighty Río Chagres, an obstacle the French had never been able to overcome. Together the engineers solved the problems that had defeated the French, excavating over 160 million cubic metres of earth and rock, building the biggest concrete constructions (the locks), the biggest earth dam and creating the largest artificial lake the world had ever seen. On August 15, 1914, the SS *Ancon* became the first ship to transit the canal, which was completed six months ahead of schedule.

An enormous **migrant workforce**, which at times outnumbered the combined population of Panamá City and Colón, was imported to work on the canal's construction, and many – Indians, Europeans, Chinese and above all West Indians – stayed on after its completion, transforming the racial and cultural makeup of Panamá for ever. They worked under what was effectively an apartheid labour system, where white Americans were paid in gold and the rest – the vast majority of whom were black – in silver. Dormitories, mess halls and even toilets and drinking fountains were set aside for the exclusive use of one group or the other, and despite the success of the sanitary programme, mortality amongst black workers was four times higher than among whites.

Meanwhile, though their economy boomed during the construction, Panamanians soon came to realize that in many ways they had simply exchanged control by Bogotá for dominance by the United States. The de facto sovereignty and legal jurisdiction that the US enjoyed within the Canal Zone made it a strip of US territory in which Panamanians were treated as second-class citizens, denied the commercial and employment opportunities enjoyed by US "Zonians". And the US agreement to guarantee Panamanian independence came at the price of intervention – inside and outside the Canal Zone – whenever the US considered it necessary to "maintain order", a right they exercised eight times between 1903 and 1936. Though the Panamanian Government, largely controlled by a ruling elite known as the "twenty families", was ostensibly independent, in fact it was little more than a client of the US. "There has never been a successful change of government in Panamá," one US official admitted in 1944, "but that the American authorities have been consulted beforehand."

Despite a new treaty limiting the US right of intervention in 1936, resentment of US imperialist control became the dominant theme of Panamanian politics and the basis of an emerging sense of national identity. Maverick politician **Arnulfo Arias Madrid** – a racist and Nazi sympathizer who later became one of Panamá's most popular political figures – led demands for a further renegotiation of the canal treaty. But the US-backed Panamanian National Guard made sure that no president who challenged the status quo lasted long in office. Nevertheless, **anti-US riots** in 1959 and 1964 revealed the enduring popular resentment of US domination.

When Arnulfo Arias was deposed by the National Guard after winning the 1968 elections, it appeared to be business as usual in Panamá. But in fact the coup marked a turning point in Panamanian politics. After a brief power struggle Lieutenant Colonel **Omar Torrijos** established himself as leader of the new military government. Described by his friend Graham Greene as a "lone wolf", Torrijos broke the political dominance of the white merchant oligarchy – known as the *rabiblancos*, or "white arses" – in his pursuit of a pragmatic middle way between socialism and capitalism. Over twelve years he introduced a wide range of populist reforms – a new constitution and labour code, limited agricultural reform, nationalization of the electricity and communications sectors, expanded public health and education services – while simultaneously maintaining good relations with the business sector, establishing the Colón Free Zone and introducing the banking secrecy necessary for Panamá's emergence as an international financial centre. At the heart of Torrijos' popular appeal, though, was his insistence on the recovery of Panamanian control over the canal and his nationalistic opposition to US intervention in Panamanian affairs. After intensive negotiations a new canal treaty was signed by Torrijos and US president Jimmy Carter on September 7, 1977. Under its terms the US agreed to pass complete control of the canal to Panamá by the year 2000, and in the meantime it was to be administered by the **Panamá Canal Commission**, composed of five US and four Panamanian citizens. However, though a memorandum of understanding made it clear that the US had no right of intervention in Panamá's internal affairs, the US retained the right to intervene militarily if the canal's neutrality was threatened, even after the year 2000.

■ Noriega and the US invasion

With his main aim accomplished, Torrijos formed a political party, the **Partido Revolucionario Democratico** (PRD), and began moving towards a return to democracy in elections scheduled for 1984. In 1981, however, he died in a plane crash in the mountains of Coclé province. Though the crash was officially an accident, many Panamanians now believe that there was some involvement by the CIA or by Colonel **Manuel Noriega**, his former intelligence chief. Whatever the truth, Noriega soon took over as head of the National Guard, which he restructured as a personal power base and renamed the Panamá Defence Forces (PDF). Though fraudulent elections were held in 1984, by the following year Noriega had established himself as effective dictator of Panamá.

Noriega had been on the CIA payroll since the early 1970s and, whereas Torrijos had supported the Sandinistas in Nicaragua, Noriega quickly became an important figure in covert US military support for the Contras. Despite this, the undemocratic nature of his regime and revelations about his involvement in drugs trafficking began to prove embarrassing for his erstwhile employers, and in 1987 the US government began a campaign to drive him from power. Economic sanctions were followed by the indictment of Noriega for drug offences in February 1988, and after a US-backed coup attempt by dissident PDF

officers failed in March 1988 the confrontation between Noriega and the US began to slide out of control. On December 20, 1989 US president George Bush launched **"Operation Just Cause"**, and 27,000 US troops invaded Panamá. They quickly overcame the minimal organized resistance offered by the PDF. Bombers, helicopter gunships and even untested stealth aircraft were used against an enemy with no air defences, and over four hundred explosions were recorded in the first fourteen hours. The poor Panamá City barrio of El Chorillo was heavily bombed and burned to the ground, leaving some 15,000 homeless. Noriega himself evaded capture and took refuge in the papal nunciature before surrendering on January 5. He was taken to the US, convicted of drug trafficking and sentenced to forty years in a Miami jail, where he remains as the only prisoner of war in the United States. In 2000 he was up for parole, but this was turned down after George Bush said he would fear for his life if Noriega was released.

Estimates of the number of Panamanians killed during the invasion vary enormously – from several hundred to as many as 7000 – largely because little care was taken in counting the dead, and many were quickly buried in mass graves. That the invasion was illegal, however, was clear – it was condemned as a violation of international law by both the United Nations and the Organization of American States, both of which demanded the immediate withdrawal of US forces. President Bush gave four reasons for the invasion: "to safeguard the lives of Americans, to defend democracy in Panamá, to combat drug trafficking, and to protect the integrity of the Panamá Canal Treaty." But the defence of democracy in Panamá had scarcely been a US priority in the past, and Bush's concern with Noriega's extensive involvement in drug trafficking was also new. As director of the CIA in 1976 he had increased payments to Noriega, despite the CIA's detailed knowledge of Noriega's drug links. After the invasion the flow of drugs through Panamá actually increased. The invasion was also in direct violation of the canal treaty provision prohibiting US intervention in Panamanian politics, and though one US soldier had been killed in the build-up to the invasion, this alone was scarcely sufficient reason to invade an entire country.

The real reasons for the US invasion remain unclear. Certainly Bush's desire to appear tough in the domestic political arena played a part, and the invasion set an important precedent for further US military interventions in the post-Cold War world. To many Panamanians, though, the reasons were all too familiar: reassertion of US control over Panamá and its strategic waterway, and the destruction of the PDF. Not that most Panamanians opposed the invasion: unlike Torrijos, Noriega was deeply unpopular, and almost all were relieved to see the back of him. But most were angry at the excessive use of force and felt humiliated by the reassertion of US dominance that Noriega's removal involved. Some likened Operation Just Cause to a brilliant cancer operation by a surgeon who had been pushing cigarettes to the patient for forty years.

After the invasion, the US installed **Guillermo Endara**, winner of elections annulled by Noriega in 1989, as president. In 1994 he was defeated by Ernesto Perez Balladares, leader of the PRD – the party of both Torrijos and Noriega. After taking office, Perez Balladares implemented neo-liberal economic policies – privatization of state-owned companies, reduction of public expenditure – aimed at meeting payments on the vast external debt that was the legacy of the Torrijos years: Panamá still has one of the highest per capita **debt** levels in the world.

■ The handover of the canal

In an ironic twist, the presidential elections of 1999 to determine who would preside over the handover of the canal were contested between Martin Torrijos, son of the former military ruler, and **Mireya Moscoso**, widow of Arnulfo Arias, the man Torrijos ousted in 1968. As the deadline for the handover of the canal and the closure of the last US military bases drew near, politicians in the US began to express doubts about the withdrawal, arguing that it threatened US strategic interests. When the port facilities at either end of the canal were sold to a Chinese company, some even suggested this was part of a communist plot

to take over the canal. But negotiations to maintain a US military presence as part of a multilateral anti-drugs base broke down, and on 31 December 1999 Panamanians celebrated the final victory in their struggle to gain control of the canal and establish **full independence**.

The US withdrawal was a mixed blessing for the Panamanian economy. Many jobs were lost with the closure of the bases and the loss of the US personnel's spending power, but the hugely valuable real estate and infrastructure Panamá inherited created huge economic opportunities. Some of these opportunities are being realized, with major infrastructure and investment programmes under way in the reverted areas, though critics say they have been handed over too cheaply to private business and political cronies rather than being used to provide housing for the poor. And like the ruins of a once powerful empire, some of the US bases are now dilapidated and abandoned.

The handover of the canal itself was seamless, and so far the waterway seems to be working as well under Panamanian control as it did under the US – it's currently being widened to allow two-way traffic and there are plans to build a new set of locks to accommodate the growing number of ships which are currently too big to go through. There are also proposals to establish new dams to provide the extra water that will be needed if the number of ships going through the canal is to be increased, though these are bitterly opposed by thousands of peasants whose homes and land would be flooded. **Relations with the US** remain complex, with an ongoing dispute over the US failure to clean up toxic chemicals (including depleted uranium) and unexploded shells from the bases and firing ranges. And though Panamá has so far resisted pressure to join in US efforts to isolate left-wing rebels across the border in Colombia, it seems that the US military has not abandoned hope of someday returning to Panamá.

CHAPTER 34

PANAMÁ CITY

If the world had to choose a capital, the Isthmus of Panamá would be the obvious place for that high destiny.

Simon Bolívar, 1826

Few cities in Latin America can match the diversity, cosmopolitanism and sheer energy of **PANAMÁ CITY**: polyglot and post-modern before its time, in many ways it is closer in atmosphere to the mighty trading cities of Asia – Hong Kong or Singapore – than to anywhere else in the region. Situated on one of the great crossroads of the world, the city has always thrived on commerce, and its unique geographical position and the opportunities it presents have attracted immigrants from all over the globe. Though it is the undisputed political and social centre of Panamá and home to almost half its population, Panamá City's gaze is fixed firmly on the outside world, and its inhabitants pay scant attention to what they refer to rather vaguely as "the interior". Open-minded and outward looking, the population is among the sharpest and most sophisticated in Central America.

With a spectacular **setting** on the Pacific bay of the same name, with the canal on one side and lush, forested mountains rising behind, Panamá City encompasses some startling incongruities. On the southwest end of the bay stands the old city centre of **San Felipe**, a jumble of crumbling colonial churches and nineteenth-century mansions, while 4km or so to the northeast rise the shimmering skyscrapers of **El Cangrejo**, the modern banking and commercial district. Further east, amid the sprawling suburbs, stand the ruins of **Panamá Viejo**, the first European city to be founded on the Pacific coast of the Americas, while west of San Felipe the former US Canal Zone town of **Balboa** retains a distinctly North American character despite having been returned to Panamanian control in 1979.

Those who find the city's ceaseless commercial energy overwhelming, meanwhile, can easily escape: to **Isla Taboga**, the idyllic "island of flowers" some 20km off the coast; along the **Amador Causeway** that juts out into the Pacific beside the canal; or into the **Parque Nacional Metropolitano**, the only pristine tropical rainforest within the limits of a Latin American capital. Panamá City is also a good base from which to explore the rest of the country – the canal, Colón and the Caribbean coast as far as Portobelo can all be visited on day-trips.

Some history

The first European city on the Pacific coast when it was founded by the **conquistador** Pedrarias Davila on August 15, 1519, Panamá quickly flourished as the base for further conquest along the Pacific and as the point of transit for the vast booty so accrued on its way to the treasure houses of Spain. By the mid-seventeenth century it had a population of some 10,000 and boasted some of the grandest constructions in the New World. The opulence of "Panamá the golden" did not escape the notice of the **pirates** then ravaging the Spanish Main. In 1671 Henry Morgan captured the fort of San

For an explanation of **accommodation price codes**, see p.701.

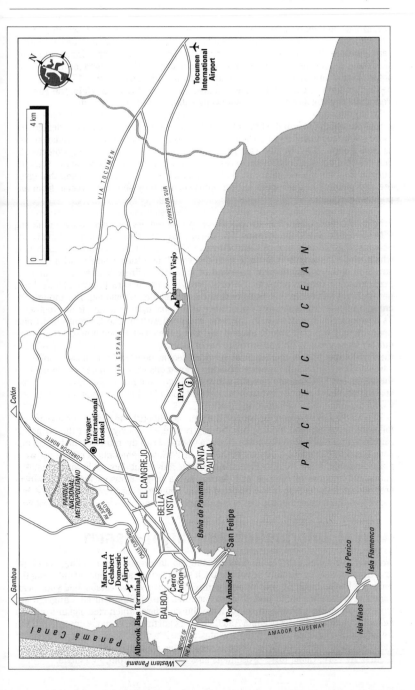

Lorenzo at the mouth of the Río Chagres, crossed the isthmus and descended on the city with a force of 1200 corsairs. After a bloody three-hour battle Morgan's desperate band defeated the much larger defending army and seized the city, already in flames after the defenders set light to its gunpowder magazines. They pillaged for three weeks before departing with 600 prisoners and a quantity of loot so vast that 175 mules were needed to carry it back across the isthmus. Known as **Panamá Viejo**, the ruins of Pedrarias' city still stand amid the sprawling suburbs of the modern city.

When the scattered survivors regrouped, they opted to rebuild the city on a rocky peninsula jutting out into the bay 10km to the west, a site deemed easier to defend and more salubrious than its swamp-bound predecessor. Founded in 1673 and today known as **San Felipe**, the new city was heavily fortified against pirate attack, protected by defences built at such enormous expense that the King of Spain was said to scan the horizon from his Madrid palace for a glimpse of the walls of Panamá, saying that given the vast quantity of gold spent in their construction they should be visible from any point on earth.

Though it never matched the glory of its predecessor (and was all but destroyed by fires in 1737 and 1756), the new city slowly prospered, its fortunes rising and falling with the traffic across the isthmus. The decline brought about by the rerouting of the Spanish treasure fleet around **Cape Horn** in 1746 was arrested after **independence**, which made Panamá free to trade with the world, and then reversed with the construction of the **transisthmian railroad** in 1855. The railroad, and subsequently the French and US canal construction efforts, brought immense prosperity and a wealth of new cultural influences that transformed the city and its population. But though the **canal** confirmed Panamá City's importance as a global trading centre, it also restricted its development. Hemmed in to the west and northwest by the US-controlled Canal Zone, the city was only able to expand east along the coast, which it began to do very quickly from about 1920. The introduction of banking secrecy laws in the 1970s led to the rapid expansion of the financial services sector, boosted by a massive influx of narco-dollars from South America. Banking regulations were tightened enormously in the 1990s, but **El Cangrejo** remains a hive of intrigue and many of its luxury high-rise apartments stand empty, the astronomical rents paid by their fictitious occupants providing a useful means of laundering money.

The **1989 US invasion** devastated the poor neighbourhood of El Chorillo and was followed by widespread looting, but the city recovered quickly, free of the economic sanctions imposed by the US on the Noriega regime. With the return of the last US military bases to Panamanian control at the end of 1999, vast amounts of real estate were made available. Many wealthy Panamanians have moved into homes in the former US-dominated suburbs of Albrook and Ancon, and a major infrastructure development programme is under way in the reverted areas, counteracting to some extent the economic slowdown caused by the loss of the spending power of US servicemen and women.

Arrival, information and city transport

Arriving in Panamá City can be disconcerting, so unless you are travelling very light or are within walking distance of your hotel, it's best to take a taxi. Spread out along the Bahía de Panamá, the city has no real centre, but once you've established your bearings it is relatively easy to find your way around. **San Felipe** and **El Cangrejo** are joined by **Avenida Central**, the city's main thoroughfare, which runs north from San Felipe through the district of Santa Ana then veers northwest, its name changing to **Vía España** as it continues through the downtown districts of Calidonia, La Exposición and the residential district of Bella Vista. Several other main avenues run parallel to Av Central: Av Perú, Cuba, Justo Arosemena and, along the seafront, Av Balboa.

Confusingly, most streets in Panamá City have at least **two names**: Av Cuba, for instance, is also Av 2 Sur, and the road known universally as Calle 50 is also Av 4 Sur or Av Nicanor de Obarrio. We have used the most common names in the following accounts.

By air

International flights arrive at Tocumen International Airport (☎238 4322), about 26km northeast of Panamá City. There are several **car-rental** offices here, a Cable and Wireless office with Internet access (6.30am–9pm) and an **IPAT** office (daily 8am–10pm) which has some basic tourist information, can book accommodation and will arrange a **taxi**, by far the best way to get into the city. These cost US$25 to hire individually or US$8 per person if you share with other passengers, though if you walk out of the airport and hail one on the street you should be able to negotiate a lower fare. You can also take one of the frequent **buses** from the airport that run into the city and along Av Balboa to Plaza Cinco de Mayo and Plaza Santa Ana. Take any bus marked Tocumen, Pacora or Chepo from the stop across the main road outside; a ticket costs only US$0.30, but there's not much room for luggage.

Domestic flights arrive at Marcos A. Gelabert airport (☎315 0400), also known as Albrook after the former US military airbase it occupies. All the domestic airlines have offices here, and there's also an IPAT information booth and several car-rental offices. A taxi into the city centre should cost about US$3, and occasional buses run to the SACA terminal on Plaza 5 de Mayo.

By bus

International buses from Costa Rica and beyond arrive at the Ticabus terminal on C 17, just off Av Central, next to the *Hotel Ideal*. This is a dodgy area, so unless you're staying there it's best to get a taxi to your hotel, particularly if you arrive at night. **Domestic buses** from almost everywhere in the interior of Panamá arrive and depart from the domestic bus terminal in Albrook, about 2km northwest of Calidonia, a massive, ultra-modern complex that's easy to use and has shops, restaurants and banks with ATMs. Buses heading into the city centre depart from well-marked stops outside; a taxi between the terminal and the city centre should cost about US$2. The only buses that do not arrive and depart from the Albrook terminal are those to Gamboa and elsewhere in the former Canal Zone, which leave from the SACA bus terminal just off Plaza Cinco de Mayo.

By sea

Irregular boats from Darién and Colombia dock at the **Muelle Fiscal** next to the Mercado Central on the seafront of Santa Ana. If you're heading for San Felipe, it's a short walk along the shore to the southeast. Otherwise, walk two blocks up the hill in front to Parque Santa Ana where you can catch a bus or hail a taxi to anywhere in the city.

Information

The main **IPAT** office (Mon–Fri 8.30am–4.30pm; ☎226 7000) is in the Atlapa Convention Centre on Av 6 Sur, out in the suburbs east of El Cangrejo, but it's not really worth hauling yourself all the way out there for the limited information available. Though they do their best to answer specific questions and some speak a little English, the staff are not really used to independent travellers asking for information and tend to limit themselves to dishing out glossy brochures. For simple queries, you're better off asking at the IPAT booth on the corner of Via España and C Ricardo Arias in El Cangrejo, or at the international and domestic airports. Generally, you'll find tour companies (see p.731) a better source of information on the interior of the country, though

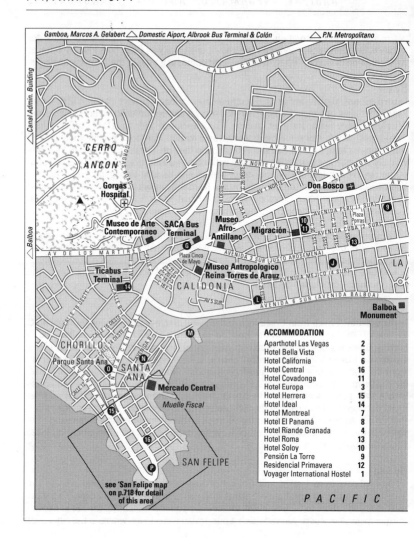

of course they'll want to sell you a tour. The *Voyager International Hostel* (see p.717) is
an excellent source of travel advice, though only for those staying there.

Panamá's National Parks and other protected natural areas are managed by the
National Environment Agency **ANAM** (☎315 0855), in Edificio 804 at the former US
military base of Albrook. Although promoting ecotourism is allegedly part of their policy, actually getting any information out of them is almost impossible – you're better off
going to the regional offices or heading straight to the parks. The **Kuna General
Congress** (☎225 5822) has an office on the first floor of the Azteca building on the corner of C27 and Av Mexico, where you can get general information on Kuna Yala and
permission to stay in the *Nusagandi Lodge* (see p.756).

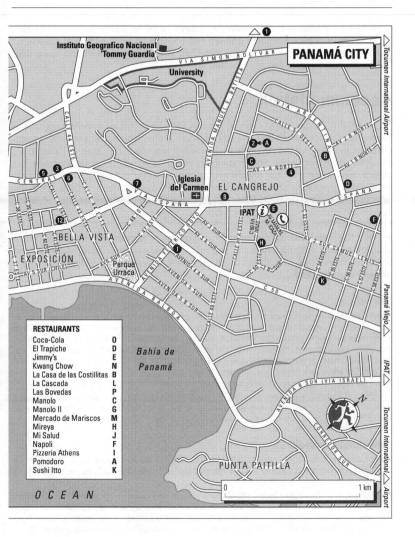

RESTAURANTS

Coca-Cola	O
El Trapiche	D
Jimmy's	E
Kwang Chow	N
La Casa de las Costillitas	B
La Cascada	L
Las Bovedas	P
Manolo	C
Manolo II	G
Mercado de Mariscos	M
Mireya	H
Mi Salud	J
Napoli	F
Pizzeria Athens	I
Pomodoro	A
Sushi Itto	K

City transport

Panamá City's public **buses** are the cheapest way to get around town and are an exciting experience in their own right. Known as *diablos rojos* – red devils – the brightly
painted former US school **buses** bounce along to loud reggae and salsa that blasts from
speakers more powerful than the engines themselves. They cost just US$0.2 per ride
and go to almost every corner of the city between 6am and midnight. However, most
are individually owned and there are no fixed **routes** or **schedules**: you just have to
look for the destination painted on the windscreen. Plaza Santa Ana is the main hub
where you can get buses to almost anywhere in the city.

Taxis are plentiful and inexpensive, with **fares** based on a zone system: US$1 plus US$0.25 for each zone boundary crossed and US$0.25 for each additional passenger. Most journeys within the city centre cost US$1–2, and none should cost more than US$3 – it's best to agree the fare in advance.

Accommodation

There are three main areas to stay in Panamá City. Most budget travellers opt for the faded splendour of **San Felipe**, the city's historic centre, which offers low-cost accommodation in run-down but atmospheric hotels that were once the finest in Panamá. It's a long way from most of the city's restaurants and nightlife, and is unsafe after dark, but an increased police presence and the gradual restoration of many of the area's historic buildings is gradually making it more appealing. The more upmarket hotels are in the safer neighbourhoods of **Bella Vista** and **El Cangrejo**, the centre of the city's nightlife, culture and commercial activity, which has some good mid-range options on its fringes. Between San Felipe and El Cangrejo, and with good access to both along the city's main arteries, the **Calidonia/La Exposición** area offers a compromise, with a wide choice of unexceptional modern hotels and pensions, including plenty of budget options and good mid-range deals. There's not much of interest in the area itself though, and here, too, you must be careful.

San Felipe

Hotel Central, C 5, Plaza Catedral (☎262 8044). The grandest hotel in Central America when it was built in 1884, the *Central* housed many of the key figures involved in the canal construction and was for decades the centre of the city's social life. Although rather run-down, it retains much of its former glory and enormous charm. Rooms are well-ventilated with high ceilings, and those at the front, though noisy at night, have balconies looking out across the square to the Cathedral. Good value, and worth a look even if you don't stay. ③–④.

Hotel Herrera, C 9, Parque Herrera (☎228 8994). Elegant though decaying nineteenth-century Neoclassical building with flower-covered balconies overlooking the park. Rooms are basic, and some of the furniture and mattresses seem almost as old as the building itself. Cheaper rates for shared bathroom, more expensive rooms available with a/c and fridge. ③.

Calidonia/La Exposición

Hotel Covadonga, C 29, Av Perú (☎225 3998 or 225 3989, fax 225 4011). Modern and clean, with a good 24hr restaurant and a small rooftop swimming pool. All rooms have a/c, phone, cable TV and hot water. ④.

Hotel Ideal, C 17 Oeste, Av Central (☎262 2400). Just off Av Central on the way out of San Felipe, halfway between Plaza Santa Ana and Plaza 5 de Mayo, next door to the Ticabus office. Surprisingly comfortable rooms with a/c and TV behind the grim exterior and chaotic reception area. Always busy and in a dodgy area. Restaurant, 24hr café, swimming pool, discounts for Ticabus passengers. ④.

Hotel Roma, Av Justo Arosemena, C 33 (☎227 3844, fax 227 3711, *www.pananet.com/hroma*). Friendly and helpful, with good tourist facilities. Large, comfortable rooms with hot water, a/c, cable TV, fridge. Swimming pool, gym, bar, 24hr cafe and a good Italian restaurant. A little overpriced, but cheaper rates may be negotiated. ⑤.

Hotel Soloy, Av Perú, C 30 (☎227 1133, fax 227 0884, *hgsoloy@pan.gmb.net*). Enormous Spanish chain hotel with 200 rooms, casino, 24hr restaurant, swimming pool, bar and a lively disco (Thurs–Sat). Comfortable, spacious rooms with uninspired decor, hot water, cable TV, a/c, fridge and mini-bar. Excellent value, but a bit too classy for the area. ⑤.

Pension La Torre, Av Perú, C 36 (☎225 0172). The upper floor of an incongruously elegant 1931 mansion – the Casa Patterson – on the corner above a cluster of restaurants. Entrance up the stairs behind a row of small trees on C 36. Basic, clean rooms with TV, a/c extra. ③.

Bellavista/El Cangrejo

ApartHotel Las Vegas, Av Eusebio A Morales, C 49B Oeste (☎269 0722, fax 223 0047, *www .lasvegaspanama.com*). Self-contained apartments with kitchen, bathroom, a/c, cable TV, phone and free coffee and ice, perfectly located two blocks from the centre of El Cangrejo. Smaller "mini-studios" with kitchenette also available. Good weekly and monthly rates. ⑥–⑦.

Hotel Bella Vista, Via España, Av Perú (☎264 4029). Unspectacular but reasonably priced rooms with a/c, cable TV, hot water and telephone. ③.

Hotel California, Via España, C 43 (☎263 7736, fax 264 6144). Large, modern and comfortable rooms with hot water, a/c, TV and telephone. ⑤.

Hotel El Panamá, C 49B Oeste, Via España (☎269 5000, fax 223 6080, *www.elpanama.com*). Formerly the *Hilton*, this five-star Art Deco hotel has plenty of character and is ideally located in the heart of El Cangrejo with luxurious decor, swimming pool, three bars, two restaurants, casino, gym, indoor tennis courts and all the other features of a top international hotel. ⑨.

Hotel Europa, Via España, Av Perú (☎263 6369 or 263 6911, fax 263 6749, *heuropa@sinfo.net*). Friendly, comfortable Art Deco hotel with 24hr restaurant, bar, pool and bizarre interior decor – the lobby looks like a 1970s disco. Rooms have a/c, TV, hot water and phone. ⑤–⑥.

Hotel Montreal, Via España, Justo Arosemena (☎263 4422, fax 263 7951). Excellent location – the closest in this price-range to the centre of El Cangrejo – but a lot of noise from Via España traffic. Small, poorly lit rooms with TV, hot water, phone and a/c. Those at the back are quieter. Bar, rooftop swimming pool and a modest restaurant. ④.

Hotel Riande Granada, Av Eusebio A Morales, Via España (☎269 1068 or 265 1962, fax 263 7197, *granada@sinfo.net*). Luxurious international hotel with excellent service and central location. 24hr café, bar, outdoor barbecue restaurant and pool surrounded by tropical plants. ⑦.

Residencial Primavera, Av Cuba, C 42 (☎225 1195). Rooms are poky and dark, but the friendly service and location in a quiet residential area on the edge of Bella Vista makes it excellent value. Small, and therefore often full. ②.

Voyager International Hostel, C Arcangel, C 62 Oeste, just off Tumba Muerto (☎260 5913 or 224 5389, *www.mipagina.com/pmahoste*). The only real backpackers' hostel in Panamá City. The shared dormitories with bunkbeds are cramped, but the atmosphere is friendly and it's a great place to meet other travellers and get information. Communal kitchen, washing-machine and living room; thirty minutes' Internet access and breakfast included. ④.

The City

The colonial city centre of **San Felipe** (also known as Casco Viejo – the old compound) is the most picturesque and historically interesting part of Panamá City and is home to many of its most important buildings, several **museums** (including the unmissable **Museo del Canal Interoceanico**). Crumbling **colonial churches** overlook quiet squares filled with monuments, and the narrow, cobbled streets are lined with ornate French and Spanish-influenced nineteenth-century mansions, some with cast-iron balconies draped with flowers, and painted white or in faded Caribbean pastels,.

Northwest of San Felipe the steep, forested hill of **Cerro Ancon** offers commanding views of the city and marks the boundary of the former Canal Zone, while the canalside area of **Balboa**, which retains the feel of a US provincial town, makes an interesting contrast to the chaotic vitality of the rest of the city. Balboa is also the jumping-off point for the peaceful **Isla Taboga**. North of the city, meanwhile, a stroll through the rain-forests of the extraordinary **Parque Nacional Metropolitano** offers an even more fundamental change of scenery.

San Felipe

For centuries the centre of the city's social and political life, and still home to the presidential palace, the colonial city centre of **San Felipe** was declared a UNESCO World

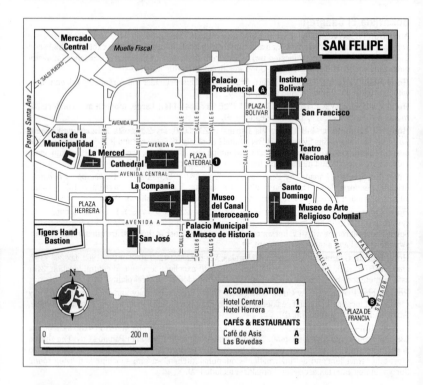

Heritage site in 1997 and is gradually being restored to its former glory after decades of neglect. Despite the upmarket restaurants and cafés which are beginning to open up, however, San Felipe is still a poor, run-down neighbourhood with a relaxed but slightly seedy streetlife – and though the ongoing restoration is making it a much more pleasant place to visit, the renovations are not popular with the district's poorer residents, many of whom face eviction. It is dangerous to walk the streets at night, and even during the day you should be careful when out of sight of the tourist police. The best way to see San Felipe is on foot, and **Plaza Catedral**, the main square, is a good place to start – you can reach it from the rest of the city by taxi or by walking down Av Central from Parque Santa Ana.

Plaza Catedral

Plaza Catedral, also known as Plaza de la Independencia – the proclamations of independence from both Spain and Colombia were made here – centres on a bandstand, ringed by benches shaded by trees and by busts of eminent Panamanians. Flanked by white towers inlaid with mother of pearl, the classical facade of the **cathedral** looks out on the square from the west. It was built between 1688 and 1796 using stones from the ruined cathedral of Panamá Viejo (see p.723). Three of its bells were also recovered from its ruined predecessor, and reputedly owe their distinctive tone to a ring thrown by Empress Isabella of Spain into the molten metal from which they were cast. Southeast of the cathedral is the Neoclassical **Municipal Palace**, whose small **Museo de**

Historia Panameña (Mon–Fri 8.30am–4.30pm; US$1) offers a cursory introduction to Panamanian history that pales in comparison beside its neighbour, the superlative **Museo del Canal Interoceanico** (Tues–Sun 9.30am–5pm; US$2; *www.sinfo.net /pcmuseum*). The museum expounds clearly and in great detail the history of the transisthmian route, from the first Spanish attempt to find a passage to Asia to the contemporary management of the canal, with many photographs and cinema footage and historic exhibits including the original canal treaties. All displays are labelled in Spanish, but if you call in advance they can arrange a free guided tour in English.

Across the square from the cathedral is the **Hotel Central**, built to replace the *Grand Hotel* and in its time the plushest hotel in Central America. The huge central patio was once a chandelier-lit palm garden where glittering balls were held, and it was here that jubilant crowds gathered in 1903 to celebrate Panamanian independence by pouring champagne over the head of General Huertas, the defecting garrison commander, for over an hour. Though run-down today, it retains much of its former splendour and is a characterful place to stay (see p.716).

Palacio Presidencial

On the seafront two blocks north of the square along C 6 the **Palacio Presidencial**, originally built in 1673, was home to successive colonial and Colombian governors before being rebuilt in grandiose neo-Moorish style in 1922 under the orders of President Belisario Porras. It is commonly known as the "Palacio de las Garzas" due to the white Darién herons that were introduced by Porras and have lived free around the patio fountain ever since. Rumour has it that when US president Jimmy Carter visited the palace before the signing the new canal treaty his security team sprayed the building with a disinfectant that proved fatal to herons, and replacements had to be rushed in under cover of darkness. The streets around the palace are busy with presidential guards, who may let you in for a glimpse of the interior, or at least close enough to photograph the exterior.

Plaza Bolívar and around

Walking a block back down C 6 and then two blocks east along Av B brings you out onto **Plaza Bolívar**, an elegant square dedicated in 1883 to Simon Bolívar, whose statue, crowned by a condor, stands in its centre. Bolívar came here in 1826 for the first Panamerican congress, held in the chapter-room of the old monastery building on the northeast corner of the square. Lined with carved wooden panelling and nineteenth-century portraits, the plush interior is currently being restored and may reopen to visitors. Next door stands the **church and monastery of San Francisco**, built in the seventeenth century but extensively modified since. The church is usually closed, but if you ask in the parish office on Av B someone there will open it up and show you around. Other than the carved wooden confessional dating to 1736, the interior is unspectacular, but the views across the city from the tower make it well worth visiting.

Just off the square to the south on Av B is the **Teatro Nacional**, designed by Genaro Ruggieri, the Italian architect responsible for La Scala in Milan. Extensively restored in the early 1970s and reopened with a performance by Margot Fonteyn, the British ballerina and long-term Panamá resident, in 1974, the theatre still stages performances in the evening and can be visited during the day (free, but ask the security guards' permission). Built to the most exacting acoustic standards, the splendid Neoclassical interior is richly furnished and decorated in red and gold, with French crystal chandeliers, busts of famous dramatists and a vaulted ceiling painted with scenes depicting the birth of the nation by Panamanian artist Roberto Lewis. Avenida B ends in a parking lot on the seafront. From here it is a 200m walk south along the seafront to the corner of Av A and C 1, past some immaculately restored nineteenth-century houses to the west and, overlooking the sea to the east, the ruined shell of the **Club de Clases y Tropas**, a recreation centre for Noriega's National Guard which was destroyed during the US invasion, with some Noriegista slogans still visible beneath the heavy graffiti on the walls.

Plaza de Francia and around

A 100m walk south along C 1 brings you out onto the **Plaza de Francia**, enclosed on three sides by the seaward defensive walls and site of a monument dedicated to the thousands of workers who died during the disastrous French attempt to build the canal (see p.706). The centrepiece of the monument is an obelisk topped by a proud Gallic cockerel which is ringed by busts of some of the key figures involved, including Ferdinand de Lesseps. There is also a plaque dedicated to Carlos Finlay, the Cuban doctor whose ground-breaking research on the causes of malaria and yellow fever was so important to the later success of the US canal. The Neoclassical **French Embassy** overlooks the square from the north, fronted by a statue of Mario Arosemena, a Panamanian politician who gave crucial support to the French venture. The elegant building to the east was formerly the Palace of Justice, badly damaged during the US invasion in 1989 and now home to the National Cultural Institute. In the colonial period the square was a military centre, and the vaults under the seaward walls served as the city's jails – built below sea-level, they would sometimes flood at high tide, drowning the unfortunate prisoners within. Known as Las Bovedas, some of the vaults have been restored: one houses a French restaurant (see p.728). From the square, steps lead up to the **Paseo Las Bovedas**, also known as the Esteban Huertas Promenade, which runs some 400m along the top of the defensive wall, all the way around the plaza and back to the corner of C 1 and Av A. Partially shaded by bougainvillea and with panoramic views, this is a popular place for courting couples.

Along Avenida A

Two blocks west along Av A from the corner with C 1 stands the ruined **Church and Convent of Santo Domingo**, completed in 1678 and famous for the **Arco Chato** (flat arch) over its main entrance. Only 10.6m high, the arch spans some 15m with no external support, and was reputedly cited as evidence of Panamá's seismic stability when the US Senate was debating where to build an interoceanic canal. In the chapel next door the absorbing **Museo de Arte Religioso Colonial** (Tues–Sat 9am–4.15pm; US$0.75) has a small collection of religious paintings, silverwork and sculpture from the colonial era. Four blocks west along Av A is the ruined shell of **La Compania**, a Jesuit church and university completed only eighteen years before the Society's expulsion from all Spanish America in 1767. Only the walls and ornate facade still stand.

A block further west on the corner with C 8 is the **Church of San José**, built in 1673 but since remodelled, exceptional only as home to the legendary baroque **Golden Altar**, one of the few treasures to survive Henry Morgan's sacking of Panamá Viejo in 1671 – it was apparently painted or covered in mud to disguise its true value. One block beyond San José, Av A emerges onto **Plaza Herrera**, a pleasant square lined with elegant nineteenth-century houses, some with cast-iron balconies imported during the French canal construction. This was originally the Plaza de Triunfo, where bullfights were held until the mid-nineteenth century, but was renamed in 1922 in honour of General Tomas Herrera, whose statue stands in its centre. Herrera was the military leader of a short-lived independence attempt in 1840; he went on to be elected president of Colombia but was assassinated before taking office in Bogotá in 1854. Just off Plaza Herrera to the west stands **The Tiger Hand Bastion**, a crumbling and indistinct pile of masonry that is the last remaining section of the city's defensive walls on the landward side. The walls came to symbolize the class divide between wealthy San Felipe residents and the poorer neighbourhood of Santa Ana, and were largely dismantled in the mid-nineteenth century.

Santa Ana

Shaded by trees, the small green **park** in the centre of **Santa Ana** – a busy transport hub – offers an island of tranquillity from the swirling traffic. A few blocks to the west, under the shadow of Cerro Ancon, is the poor barrio of **El Chorillo**, which was devastated during the US invasion, leaving hundreds dead and thousands homeless. It has since been rebuilt, but the concrete tenements that replaced the old wooden slum housing are already run-down and it remains a dangerous neighbourhood even during the day. Just beyond Parque Santa Ana on Av Central a right turn takes you down Calle **Sal si Puedes** ("get out if you can"), a steep, narrow street crammed with market stalls that runs two blocks down to the seafront and the covered **Mercado Central**, the lively food market. Beside the market to the southeast is the **Muelle Fiscal**, from where occasional boats to Darién and Colombia leave (see p.758).

The area between the market and Av B is known as the **barrio Chino** (Chinatown), the historic centre of Panamá City's large Chinese population, which began to arrive in the middle of the nineteenth century to work on the railway. The Chinese community is much more dispersed now, but the barrio retains a distinct oriental feel: there are Chinese supermarkets selling everything from dried shark fins to newspapers; restaurants where it is difficult to order unless you speak Cantonese; and, at the north end of C Juan Mendoza, an ornate gate that marks the official entrance to the barrio from Av Balboa.

The pedestrianized stretch of **Avenida Central** from Parque Santa Ana north as far as Plaza Cinco de Mayo is the liveliest and most popular shopping district in the city. Blasts of air conditioning and loud music pour from the huge superstores that line the avenue selling cheap clothing, electronics and household goods, as hawkers with megaphones attempt to entice shoppers inside. Nowhere is the sheer energy of the city and the enormous cultural diversity of its population more evident: stop for a while on one of the tree-shaded mosaic benches and you will see Hindus in saris, Kuna women in their traditional costumes, bearded Muslims in robes and skullcaps, *interioranos* in sombreros, Chinese, Afro-Antillanos and Latinos, all scrambling for bargains in the supercharged atmosphere of this post-modern bazaar.

Calidonia, La Exposición, Bella Vista and El Cangrejo

Ten blocks down, the pedestrianized section of Av Central ends as it emerges onto **Plaza Cinco de Mayo** and the maelstrom of traffic takes over again. In fact, this is two squares rolled into one: the first has a small monument to the volunteer firemen killed fighting an exploded gunpowder magazine in 1914 – the *bomberos* occupy a revered position in a city that has so often been devastated by fire. Opposite the monument a columned former railway station houses the disappointing **Museo Antropologico Reina Torres de Araúz** (Mon–Fri 9am–4pm; US$2), most of whose extensive collection of pre-Colombian artefacts is under wraps – just one room, featuring some finely carved stone statues from the ancient Barriles culture of Chiriquí, is currently open to the public, though a collection of pre-Colombian gold ornaments is due to go on show as soon as funding for adequate security measures can be found. Behind the museum is a large, open-air **handicrafts market**. The second square, Plaza Cinco de Mayo proper, is a little further down, with a black, monolithic monument emblazoned with

THE AFRO-ANTILLANOS

Some five percent of Panamá's population are **Afro-Antillanos** – descendants of the black workers from the English- and French-speaking West Indies who began migrating to Panamá in the mid-nineteenth century to help build the railroad and canal. West Indians, above all from Jamaica and Barbados, formed the vast majority of the labour force in both the French and the US canal construction efforts, living and working in appalling conditions – most of the 20,000 workers who died during the French attempt were West Indians and, despite the vast sanitary improvements, mortality among black workers was four times higher than among whites during the US construction. Despite the racial discrimination – lower wages, poorer conditions, strict segregation – they faced in the US Canal Zone, many West Indians stayed in Panamá City and Colón after the canal's completion, while others migrated to the banana plantations of Bocas del Toro. In Panamá as a whole they were widely considered second-class citizens or undesirable aliens. Populist politician Arnulfo Arias was an undisguised racist, and as president in 1940 pushed through a constitution that prohibited further immigration by blacks and denied the right to own property to those without an adequate knowledge of Panamanian history and the Spanish language. The inclusionary politics of the Torrijos regime eased discrimination: jobs in government and even business were made accessible to Afro-Antillanos and they became more widely accepted, but though today they are more socially integrated than the black communities of several other Central American republics, they remain among the most marginalized sectors of the population.

More than a century after their arrival in Panamá, the Afro-Antillanos maintain a vibrant and distinct **culture** whose influence is apparent in many aspects of contemporary Panamanian society. Many second- and third-generation Afro-Antillanos still speak English, or rather the melodic patois of the West Indies, and the street Spanish of Panamá City and Colón is peppered with Jamaican slang. The Protestant churches they brought with them from the West Indies continue to thrive; heavily spiced Caribbean dishes have permeated Panamanian cuisine; and their music, from jazz in the 1950s through to "reggaespañol" – the compelling combination of Spanish lyrics and hardcore Jamaican dancehall rhythms that took Latin America by storm in the 1990s – is popular across the country.

the nationalist slogan: "Ni limosnas, ni milliones, queremos justicia" ("neither alms, nor millions, we want justice").

Across the road, on the corner with Av Justo Arosemena, inside a small fenced garden stands a statue of **Mahatma Gandhi**, erected by the city's Hindu community and often garlanded in flowers. A block down Av Justo Arosemena on the corner with C 24 an unmarked wooden former church houses the **Museo Afro-Antillano** (Tues–Sat 8.30am–3.30pm; US$1), dedicated to preserving the history and culture of Panamá's large West Indian population. It is very small, but its exhibits – photographs, tools, furniture – give a good idea of the working and living conditions of black canal workers. There is also a small library and occasional events, including Afro-Antillano cookery courses and jazz festivals.

Beyond Plaza Cinco de Mayo, Av Central continues to the northeast, the city's main thoroughfare and still a busy shopping street as it runs through Calidonia and La Exposición. Two blocks away from Av Central on Av Cuba between C 29 and C 30, the **Museo de Ciencias Naturales** (Tues–Sat 9am–3.30pm, Sun 1pm–5pm; US$1) offers a basic introduction to Panamá's geology and ecology, with many stuffed animals – look out for the pickled fer-de-lance which killed the director of Panamá's old zoo in 1931. Four blocks further down Av Central, facing C 34, is the neo-Moorish **Church of Don Bosco**, built in the 1950s with open sides screened by iron grilles and a minaret-like tower. A short walk down C 34 brings you out onto Av Balboa on the seafront, and two blocks to the left, set in a small park shaded by palm trees, is the glorious **Balboa**

Monument. Erected in 1913 with Spanish help, Balboa stands atop a globe with a sword in one hand and a flag in the other, looking out in perpetual triumph on the southern ocean he "discovered".

As it continues northeast, Av Central changes its name to Via España and passes through the comfortable residential neighbourhood of **Bella Vista**. On the corner with Av Manuel E. Batista, the twentieth-century neo-Gothic wedding-cake **Del Carmen** church marks the beginning of **El Cangrejo**, the high-rise banking district and commercial heart of the city, centred on Via España between the church and Via Argentina, and on C 50. Most of the classier hotels and restaurants are here, as well as upmarket stores and shopping centres selling the latest designer fashions and state-of-the-art electronics. This is also where much of the city's nightlife is concentrated, and it's reasonably safe to walk around at night.

Panamá Viejo

On the coast about 6km east of El Cangrejo stand the ruins of **PANAMÁ VIEJO**, the original colonial city founded by Pedrarias Davila in 1519 and abandoned in 1671. Many of its buildings were dismantled to provide stones for the construction of San Felipe and in recent decades much of the site has been built over as the modern city has continued to spread eastward, but despite this a surprising number of the original buildings still stand, testimony to the skill of the Spanish masons who built them, and a walk among the ruins will give you a good impression of the former splendour of the first European city on the Pacific Ocean.

To **get to Panamá Viejo**, either take a taxi or catch any bus marked Panamá Viejo or Via Cincuentenario. If you're short on time and leaving Panamá by air, you can see quite a lot of the ruins by asking your taxi-driver to take the slow route to the airport via Panamá Viejo. The best place to start a visit is the **museum** (daily 9am–4pm; US$1.50), on Via Cincuentenario in the centre of the ruins, where a scale-model and audio-tape history in English or Spanish gives a good idea of what the city must have looked like. There is also a display of artefacts discovered during ongoing archeological excavations, including nails and rusty swords, pottery and astonishingly well-preserved Sevillan tiles, all well illustrated with reproductions of paintings by the Spanish artist Velasco showing these household items in use. The ruins are well marked with descriptions in English and Spanish and there are usually free maps available in the museum.

The site

The ruins are spread out either side of Via Cincuentenario, with many trees still scattered among them, remnants of the forest that engulfed the site after its abandonment (some buildings still have gnarled roots embedded in their walls). To the right as you come out of the museum is the former **Plaza Mayor**, overlooked by the three-storey square stone tower of the **cathedral**, built between 1619 and 1629 to replace an earlier wooden structure, and flanked by the square **cabildo** (town hall) to the right and the well-preserved bishop's house to the left. Behind the cathedral, through the grounds of the National Sport Institute, you can still see the foundations of the **casas reales** – the royal treasury, customs house, court and governor's residence that together formed the centre of royal power in Panamá Viejo, originally separated from the rest of the city by a moat and wooden palisade. Returning to the cathedral and turning right brings you to the **church and monastery of Santo Domingo**, the smallest religious structure but also the best preserved, with a tall buttressed tree growing inside. From here, Via Cincuentenario runs 400m north to the **Church of San José**, which survived the fire of 1571 and was the home of the famous golden altar which escaped Morgan's notice and is now in the church of the same name in San Felipe (see p.720). Another 200m brings you to the **King's Bridge**, the beginning of the Camino Real, the treasure route across the isthmus to Nombre de Dios (see p.746). Be careful if walking alone in this area: the ruins are surrounded by poor barrios and it's a long way from the tourist police who patrol the site.

The major ruins across the road from the cathedral are the **Church of La Compania de Jesus** (Jesuits) and the **Church of La Concepción**, both of which had their respective monasteries, of which little now remains. Close by, on Via Cincuentenario, only one wall of the **Hospital de San Juan de Dios** still stands. As you walk east along Via Cincuentenario, after 100m you pass the remains of the **Monastery of San Francisco**, where the Franciscan monks were said to have been massacred by Morgan's men while tending to the wounded. Some 200m beyond are the crumbling remains of the **church and monastery of La Merced**, where Francisco Pizarro took communion before embarking on the conquest of Perú. La Merced was considered the most beautiful church in the city and survived the fire in 1571 – Morgan used it as his headquarters – but its ornate facade was dismantled and moved to San Felipe, the cloisters are no more and the whole structure is sadly cut in two by the road.

The former Canal Zone

To the southwest of Calidonia and El Chorillo, Panamá City encompasses the former Canal Zone town of **BALBOA**, administered by the US as de facto sovereign territory from 1903 to 1979. Panamanians who lived or worked here were subject to US law and many of the residents, known as Zonians, still maintain a distinct and somewhat exclusive transnational identity. The English writer Graham Greene described the Zone as "an island of prosperity in a sea of poverty", and though the difference has faded after more than twenty years of Panamanian jurisdiction (and the same is now more true of the modern luxury suburbs to the east), Balboa retains many of the characteristics of a US provincial town; clean, well ordered and in stark contrast to the chaotic vitality of the rest of the city. To the east, the Canal Authority Building looks down on Balboa from the slopes of Cerro Ancon, a longstanding symbol of US power in the isthmus, now in Panamanian hands, while to the south is **Fort Amador**, a former US military base currently being transformed into a massive luxury tourism development. Beyond the fort a **causeway** stretches 6km out to sea between the bay and the canal approaches, linking the islands of Naos, Perico and Flamenco.

Cerro Ancon and Balboa

Along the border of the former Canal Zone runs Av de Los Martires, named in honour of the 21 Panamanians killed by the US military during the riots of 1964 (see p.707). Above it to the right rises the heavily forested **Cerro Ancon**, crowned by a huge Panamanian flag that is visible throughout the city. From the entrance on Av de Los Martires it's a steep twenty-minute walk to the summit, well worth it for the spectacular views of the city, the bay and the canal as far as Pedro Miguel locks, 10km away. There are toilets and a drinking fountain at the top, and often a contingent of tourist police – there have been muggings on the hill, so be wary, particularly if walking alone. The forest is surprisingly well preserved, and deer, agouti and iguanas are frequently seen, as well as plenty of birds. From the summit you have to return the way you came.

Just off the entrance on Av de Los Martires is **Los Pueblitos** (Tues–Sun 10am–10pm; US$1), a theme-park-style replica of the traditional villages of four of Panamá's different ethnic groups: an early twentieth-century *interiorano* village, complete with church, telegraph office and barber's shop; an Afro-Antillano village with cool wooden houses on stilts painted in faded Caribbean pastels; a circle of Kuna palm and cane huts, complete with an artificial beach; and a few of the open-sided, raised platform huts of the Emberá, set amid lush forest. Though aimed primarily at Panamanians, it's less tacky than it sounds, and worth visiting if you are not going to see the real thing. Folkloric dances are performed on Friday evenings, and restaurants in three of the four *pueblitos* serve appropriate traditional food.

Some 200m east of the entrance to Cerro Ancon on Av de Los Martires is a turn-off onto Gorgas Road, which winds round the side of Cerro Ancon to the Canal Authority Building in Balboa Heights, about twenty minutes away on foot. Just off Gorgas road to the right, the **Museum of Contemporary Art** (Mon–Sat 9am–4pm) has a small but unexceptional collection of modern art by obscure national and international artists, housed in a former Masonic temple of 1936. As you climb Gorgas Road you pass the **Gorgas Military Hospital**, named after the US military doctor William Gorgas who did so much to reduce the death toll from malaria and yellow fever among the canal construction workforce. A formidable stone construction, the hospital now houses the Palace of Justice. As it continues around Cerro Ancon, the road's name changes to Heights Road, lined with several luxury villas set amid well-manicured lawns, including, at **107 Heights Road**, the residence of the Panamá Canal Commission administrator.

Soon after, Gorgas road reappears to the right and winds down to the three-storey **Panamá Canal Authority Administration Building** (daily 7.15am–4.15pm; free), a classic example of US colonial architecture, built during the canal construction and still home to the principal administration offices. Inside, four dramatic murals by US artist William Van Ingen depict the story of the canal construction under a domed ceiling supported by marble pillars, and there are busts of De Lesseps, Roosevelt and Charles V of Spain. In front of the building, where a Panamanian flag now flutters proudly, a broad stairway runs down to the **Goethals monument**, a white megalith with stepped fountains that represent the canal's different locks, erected in honour of George Goethals, Chief Engineer from 1907 to 1914 and first governor of the Canal Zone. Beside the monument is **Balboa High School**, whose ordinary appearance belies the dramatic events it has witnessed. It was here in 1964 that Zonians attacked students attempting to raise the Panamanian flag, triggering the **flag riots** that left 21 Panamanians dead, and during the 1989 invasion the school was used as a detention camp for Panamanian prisoners, some of whom were allegedly executed by US soldiers. From here, the palm-lined El Prado boulevard runs a few hundred metres down to **Stevens' Circle**. This is Balboa proper, the main residential area of the former Canal Zone, and though the English-language road signs have now largely been replaced, its solid white buildings with red-tiled roofs and immaculate lawns still give it a distinctively North American feel.

Fort Amador and the causeway

From the Balboa YMCA, Calle Amador runs towards the causeway through **Fort Amador**, a former US military base returned to Panamá in 1996 that is being redeveloped as the centrepiece of Panamá's plans to promote tourism in the former Canal Zone. The complex will include luxury hotels, a marina, a cruise-ship terminal and a "biodiversity exhibition centre" designed by the internationally acclaimed architect Frank Gehry.

From Amador, a 6km **causeway** (Calzada de Amador) runs out into the bay, linking the tiny islands of **Naos, Perico and Flamenco**. Built during the canal construction with spoil from the excavation as a breakwater to prevent silting of the canal entrance, the causeway is a popular weekend escape for the city's residents who come here to jog, swim, stroll, rollerblade or cycle (you can rent bicycles at the entrance; US$2/hr), and to enjoy the sea air and the view of the city on one side and the entrance to the canal on the other. In the early years of Panamá City the islands served as deep-water moorings for ships, and after the causeway's construction they together formed Fort Grant, heavily fortified for canal defence. The causeway remained a restricted area until 1989, contributing to the conservation of the islands' varied ecology, and some of the military installations can still be seen, including rails that once carried fifteen-inch guns.

On **Naos**, 2km along the causeway, the **Smithsonian Marine Exhibition Centre** (Tues–Fri 1–5pm, Sat & Sun 10am–6pm; US$1) offers an excellent introduction to Panamá's marine ecology, including an aquarium where you can stroke octopus, starfish and sea cucumbers. The centre also organizes **guided tours** of the island's different ecological systems, which include mangrove, tropical dry forest and coral reefs (book by calling ☎227 4918, minimum ten people). There are a couple of small beaches on Naos which are popular for swimmers but, given the proximity of the city and the canal, they are not the cleanest. The second island, **Perico**, is so small as to be indistinguishable from the causeway, and the last, **Flamenco**, home to the National Maritime Service, is closed to the public.

Parque Natural Metropolitano

A couple of kilometres north from the city centre in an area of the former Canal Zone that reverted to Panamanian control in 1983, the 2.65-square-kilometre **Parque Natural Metropolitano** is an unspoilt tract of primary rainforest which is home to more than 200 species of birds, as well as mammals such as titi monkeys, white-tailed deer, sloths and agoutis. You don't need a permit from ANAM to visit the park, which is officially open from 6am to 5.30pm, though there is nothing to stop you coming earlier and, as elsewhere, the best time to see wildlife, particularly birds, is early in the morning. The **park office** (Mon–Sat 8am–4pm) and main entrance are on Av Juan Pablo II, just off C Curundu not far from the Curundu domestic bus terminal – occasional SACA buses from Plaza Cinco de Mayo pass close by. There is a small exhibition centre and library here, and three-hour **guided tours** can be arranged (US$2 per person; book in advance), though you can easily walk the park's three short trails without a guide. The best of these is the 2km **La Cienaguita trail**, which leads to a viewing point 150m above sea-level with fantastic views across the forest to the city.

Around Panamá City: Isla Taboga

Twenty kilometres off the coast and about an hour away by boat, the tiny island of **Taboga** is one of the most popular weekend retreats for Panamá City residents, who come here to enjoy its clear waters, peaceful atmosphere and verdant beauty. Known as the "Island of Flowers" for the innumerable fragrant blooms that decorate its village and forested slopes, Taboga gets very busy on the weekends, particularly during the summer, but is usually quiet during the week, and if you stay the night you will have the place largely to yourself.

The island was settled by the Spanish in 1524 and served as a deep-water port before such facilities were established on the mainland – it was from here that Francisco Pizarro set sail for the conquest of Perú. Frequent pirate raids led to the fortification of El Morro Island, opposite Taboga, which in the nineteenth century served as the headquarters of the Pacific Steam Navigation Company. In 1882 the French Canal Company built a sanatorium on Taboga for convalescing employees, among whom was the French post-Impressionist painter **Paul Gauguin**, who came to Panamá hoping to buy land on Taboga and "live on fish and fruit". However, the canal construction work was too hard and the price of land too high for his meagre wages, so on recovering he took his quest for paradise west across the Pacific to Tahiti.

The island

Taboga's one **fishing village** is very picturesque, with scrupulously clean narrow streets running between its whitewashed houses, and dozens of gardens filled with bougainvillea and hibiscus. Most visitors head straight for one of the sections of **beach**, either right in front of the village or in front of the *Hotel Taboga* (to the right of the pier as you disembark), where the water is calmer and the view of Panamá City magnificent. Despite what the hotel would have you believe, you don't have to pay to enter its part of the beach, though to use any of the *Taboga*'s facilities costs US$5, in return for which you'll be given tokens redeemable on food, drinks or other services in the hotel.

Behind the village, forested slopes rise to the 300m peak of **Cerro Vigía**, where a viewing platform on top of an old US military bunker offers spectacular 360-degree views. It's about an hour's steep climb through the forest to the mirador – follow the path some 100m up behind the church until you find a sign marked Sendero de los Tres Cruces, beyond which the trail is marked with posts numbered 1 to 8. The other side of the island is home to one of the biggest brown pelican breeding colonies in the world and together with the neighbouring island of Uraba forms a protected **wildlife refuge**.

Snorkelling and diving are also popular activities on Taboga as marine life is abundant, particularly around El Morro, the island opposite the village. The *Hotel Taboga* rents equipment, though for diving it is better to organize a trip with one of the dive companies in Panamá City.

Practicalities

A visit to Taboga is worth it for the **voyage** out alone. Launches leave from Muelle 18 in Balboa (4 daily between 8am and 10pm, returning between 3pm and 6pm, more frequently on weekends; regular boat 1hr, US$7 return; express boats 40min, US$8 return) and pass under the Bridge of the Americas and along the canal channel, passing several uninhabited islands before reaching Taboga.

There are two **places to stay** on the island: the family-oriented *Hotel Taboga* (☎250 2122 or 264 6096, fax 223 5739; ⑦) has comfortable rooms with a/c and TV, pool, tennis court, and snorkelling and scuba equipment for rent, but it's rather overpriced and has the feel of a 1950s holiday camp. In the village the cheaper and more atmospheric *Hotel Chu* (☎250 2035 or 263 6933; ④) has basic rooms and communal bathrooms in a brightly painted wooden structure on stilts on the seafront. There's a bar-disco, *El Galeon,* under the hotel, which is convenient if you want to stay up late drinking rum and dancing, but rather noisy if you don't.

Both hotels have **restaurants**; the *Chu* serves reasonable Chinese food and good seafood on a broad wooden balcony overlooking the sea, while the *Taboga* offers more varied and more expensive international and Panamanian cuisine, and a full buffet on the weekends. The cheapest food on the island is served by the two kiosks just outside the entrance to the *Hotel Taboga.*

Eating

Panamá City's cosmopolitan nature is reflected in its **restaurants**: pretty much every cuisine in the world can be found here, from US fast food to Greek, Italian, Chinese, Japanese and French. Most of the more upmarket options are concentrated in **Bella Vista** and **El Cangrejo** – Via Argentina has the widest range, many with outdoor tables that are good for people-watching – but you're never far from a range of good and inexpensive places to eat. Excellent **fish** and seafood are widely available, and there are a couple of specialist vegetarian restaurants – a welcome change from the rest of Panamá.

Bella Vista and El Cangrejo

El Trapiche, Via Argentina (☎269 2063). Upmarket traditional Panamanian cuisine in a cheerful atmosphere complete with waiters in *interiorano* sombreros. Very good three-course set lunch for US$6.50, good meat and fish, filling Panamanian breakfasts.

Jimmy's, corner of Via España and C Manuel M. Icaza. Busy 24-hour restaurant-cafeteria in the heart of El Cangrejo with a wide choice of Panamanian food from the self-service counter, grilled meat and fish from the outdoor barbecue, good sandwiches prepared to order and strong coffee. Good value and extremely popular.

La Casa de las Costillitas, Via Argentina, two blocks up from Via España. The same menu as *La Cascada* (below) with less outrageous decor and a more central location. Tues–Sun noon–11pm.

Manolo, C 49B Oeste, a block up from Via España. One of three restaurants so-named, this one offers a broad range of meats, fish and seafood as well as 12-inch pizzas for US$4.

Mireya, C 50 Este, a block away from the *Hotel Continental* on Via España. Inexpensive self-service vegetarian restaurant with a choice of about twelve different hot dishes and an excellent salad bar. Mon–Sat 6am–8pm.

Napoli, C 57, two blocks from Via España (☎263 8799). Large, usually busy upmarket Italian restaurant with reasonable pizza, excellent pasta and immaculate service. Closed Mon.

Pizzeria Athens, C 48E, C 50, behind the Delta garage. Very popular fast-food style restaurant with harsh fluorescent lighting and phones on the tables for ordering. Not the best pizza, but very good Greek dishes, including *sublaki*, *gyros*, roast aubergines (*berenjena*) and the inevitable Greek salad. About US$4–5 a head. Closed Wed. There's another branch on C 57, opposite the *Ristorante Napoli* (closed Tues).

Pomodoro, C 49B Oeste. Extremely popular upmarket Italian place with outdoor seating in an enclosed tropical garden serving good pizza and excellent pasta.

Sushi Itto, Av Samuel Lewis, Plaza Obarrio (☎265 1222). Fashionable Japanese restaurant with good sushi and sashimi from about US$9 a plate, a choice of set menus and some interesting Pacific fusion cuisine.

Santa Ana and Calidonia

Coca-Cola, C 12, Av Central, on Plaza Santa Ana. Self-proclaimed "oldest restaurant in Panamá" and something of an institution for the city's older residents, who gather to drink coffee, read the papers and discuss the news. Good, basic Panamanian meals for about US$3, and particularly good for breakfast.

Covadonga, C 29, Av Perú, next to hotel of same name. 24-hour restaurant with reasonably priced Panamanian and international food and some delicious Spanish specialities. Good for breakfast, especially the fruit salad at US$1.85.

Kwang Chow, Av B 13-80, just off Sal si Puedes. Excellent, moderately priced Chinese food and a largely Chinese clientele. Come here in the morning and ask for *desayuno chino* and you'll get the best dim sum this side of Shanghai.

La Cascada, Av Balboa, C 24. Enormous, surreal open-air restaurant "like an oasis, a dream, a mini-Disneyland in Panamá", according to its 16-page menu. Tables lit with multicoloured mushroom lights are set around a waterfall that tumbles over artificial rocks to feed a moat filled with goldfish and floating model ducks. Wide choice of meat and seafood, mostly grilled or fried in breadcrumbs, with the emphasis on quantity rather than quality. Starting at US$6, most meals are enough to feed a family of four for a week.

Manolo II, Plaza 5 de Mayo. A tranquil haven from the bustle of Avenida Central, this Spanish-run place specializes in meats and seafood, including a delicious *sopa de mariscos* for US$3.

Mercado de Mariscos, Av Balboa, C 23 Este. No-nonsense fish and seafood restaurant above the seafood market offering a wide choice of dishes at reasonable prices. Alternatively you can buy fresh seafood downstairs and they'll cook it for you for US$3 a pound. Closed Sun evenings.

Mi Salud, C 31, Av Mexico. Vegetarian health-food restaurant with tasty, filling meals for about US$2, very good fruit salads, juices and ice-cream. Also home-made bread and dietary supplements. Mon–Sat 6.45am–5.30pm.

Amador and San Felipe

Las Bovedas, Plaza Francia (☎228 8068). Exquisite French cuisine from about US$20 a head, under the arched brick ceilings of one of the old colonial dungeons. Excellent service, live jazz (Fri & Sat).

Mundo Aquatico, Calzador de Amador, just before Isla Flamenco. Reasonably priced seafood restaurant with excellent views of Panamá City across the bay. Particularly popular at the weekend, and it can be difficult to find a taxi back to the city at night.

Drinking, nightlife and entertainment

Panamá City is very much a **24-hour city**, whose residents like nothing better than to cut loose and eat, drink and dance into the early hours. Most of the upmarket places are around **El Cangrejo**, and it's easy and relatively safe to walk between them at night. Many restaurants double as **bars**, and there are several **discos** and **nightclubs**, playing a mixture of reggae, salsa, merengue and US and euro dance music. **Cover charges** tend to be high, but often include several (sometimes unlimited) free drinks. Be warned that many of the more upmarket nightclubs operate an unofficial racist policy whereby black Panamanians are effectively refused admission. The free bi-monthly English-language *Panamá News* has entertainment **listings** including live music and theatre (see overleaf).

At the other end of the market are the **cantinas** and bars around Av Central: hard-drinking dives where women are rarely seen. The wildest nightspots are out in the Afro-Antillan ghetto of Rio Abajo, but it is not a good idea to go there unless accompanied by locals.

Bella Vista and El Cangrejo

Bacchus, C 49A Este, Via España. Rather exclusive nightclub with impressive lightshow and massive sound system pumping out booming rave music. Women sometimes admitted free during the week; can be difficult to get into on Friday nights, despite the US$10 cover charge.

Beer House, Via España, Via Argentina. Appropriately named lively drinking dive with loud salsa and merengue and a young crowd.

Boy Bar, Av Ricardo Alfaro, Tumba Muerto. Panamá City's biggest and most popular gay nightclub, with a large dancefloor, impressive lightshow and pumping dance music. Out in the suburbs and difficult to find, so take a taxi. Fri–Sun 9pm–3am.

Café Dalí, C47, C Uruguay. Loud and popular bar/nightclub playing a mix of reggae, salsa and house music and occasional live performances. Free entry and drinks for women on Wednesday nights; US$5 cover at other times.

Coco Club bar, ground floor of the *Hotel el Panamá*. Classy and expensive even during the 5–8pm happy hour, but with excellent live salsa and merengue bands.

El Pavo Real, C 51E, C 50. "English" pub with darts, pool tables and live music every night from 11pm, popular with expatriates and wealthy Panamanians. Rather expensive food also available, including the inevitable fish and chips served in newspaper. Happy hour Mon–Thurs 3–7pm.

Las Tinajas, Av 2 Sur (C 51E), Av Federico Boyd (☎269 3840). Restaurant and bar serving traditional Panamanian food. Folkloric dance shows (Tues & Thurs–Sat from 9pm). Reservations recommended; US$5 cover charge. Closed Sun.

Mangos, C Uruguay, C 50. A currently very fashionable US-style bar and grill with good food and live rock music at the weekend.

Señor Frogs, Av 5A, C 48. Massive Mexican beach-party theme bar that attracts a young crowd with its raucous party atmosphere and the most enormous margaritas. Wed–Sun 9pm–late.

Amador, San Felipe and Santa Ana

Balboa Yacht Club, beside the Canal just off Av Amador. Currently in a temporary structure lacking the character and lively atmosphere of the original, which is being rebuilt for 2002, but still a good place for a drink while watching ships passing under the Bridge of the Americas. This is the place to ask about work as a linehandler on private yachts transiting the canal.

Café de Asis, Parque Bolívar. One of several upmarket bar-café's which have opened up in Casco Viejo as part of the regeneration of the colonial city centre.

El Barko, Calzador de Amador. Huge new open-air nightclub on Isla Flamenco at the end of the Amador causeway, currently the place to be seen for Panamá City's beautiful people. Food and drinks are good but expensive, and it can be difficult to get a taxi back to the city at night.

La Maravilla, C 18, Av B. One of several raucous drinking dives on C 18, with pool tables upstairs. Daily 10am–2am.

Entertainment

Panamá City isn't renowned for its love of high culture, but there are a couple of good **theatres** featuring national and international productions – check the *Panamá News* for listings. The Teatro Balboa, Stephens Circle, Balboa (☎262 5472) hosts jazz, folkloric dancing and theatre sponsored by the National Cultural Institute, while the splendid Neoclassical Teatro Nacional, Av B, Plaza Bolívar (☎262 3525), has theatre and ballet performances. **Cinema** is far more popular, and there are many places where you can see the latest Hollywood blockbusters, in English with subtitles – *La Prensa* lists current screenings. The Cine Universitario (☎264 2737) shows an eclectic range of films with the emphasis on the arty and obscure.

Panamanians of all social classes love to **gamble**, and as well as the ever-present lottery ticket sellers there are several tax-free **casinos**, all located in the major hotels: try the *El Panamá*, *Granada* or *Soloy*. **Cockfighting**, a bloody but immensely popular spectacle throughout the country, can be seen at the Club Gallistico (Mon, Sat & Sun; ☎221 5652; US$1) on the corner of Via España and Via Cincuentenario. **Horse-racing** meetings are held three times a week at the Hippodrome Presidente Ramon, out in the eastern suburbs.

Listings

Airlines Aeroflot, Unicentro Bellavista, Av Justo Arosemena, C 41 (☎225 0587 or 225 0497); AeroMexico, C 50, C 64, San Fransisco (☎263 3033); Aeroperlas, Aeropuerto Marcos A. Gelabert (☎315 7555 or 317 7500); AeroPerú, C Ricardo Arias (☎269 5777); Aerotaxi, Aeropuerto Marcos A. Gelabert (☎315 7520); Air France, C Abel Bravo, C 59 (☎223 0204); American, C 50, Plaza New York (☎269 6022); ANSA, Aeropuerto Marcos A. Gelabert (☎315 0275 or 315 0299); AVENSA, C Mario M. Icaza (☎264 9855); Avianca, Edificio Grobman, C Manuel M. Icaza (☎223 5225 or 264 3120); Aviatur, Aeropuerto Marcos A. Gelabert (☎315 0397 or 315 0314); British Airways, Av Ricardo J. Alfaro, Av Juan Pablo II (☎236 8335); Continental, Edificio Galerias Balboa, Av Balboa (☎263 9177); COPA, Av Justo Arosemena, C 39 (☎227 2522 or 227 5000); Cubana, C 29, Av Justo Arosemena (☎227 2122); Delta, C53E, Marbella (☎214 8118); Iberia, Av Balboa, C 43 (☎227 3966); KLM, Av Balboa, C Uruguay (☎264 6395); LanChile, Via Cincuentenario, Av 4 Sur (☎226 0133); Lloyd Aereo Boliviano, Edificio Bolivia, C 50 (☎264 1330); Lufthansa, C Abel Bravo, C 50 (☎223 9208); Mapiex Aero, Aeropuerto Marcos A. Gelabert (☎315 0888); TACA, Edificio World Trade Center (☎265 7814); United, C Abel Bravo, C 50 (☎213 9824 or 213 8362); Varig, Edificio Margarita, C 51 (☎264 2266).

American Express Torre Banco Exterior, Av Balboa (Mon–Fri 8.30am–4pm; ☎225 5858).

Banks and exchange Branches of the Banco Nacional de Panamá (BNP) (Mon–Fri 8am–3pm, Sat 9am–noon) and Banco del Istmo (Mon–Fri 8am–3.30pm, Sat 9am–noon) across the city change travellers' cheques and allow cash withdrawals on credit cards – most have ATMs. Both have branches on Via España in the heart of El Cangrejo. The closest to San Felipe is the BNP on the corner of Av Central and C 17 Este. Foreign currency is more difficult to change – foreign banks will generally change their own currency and there is one licensed exchange house, Panacambios (Mon–Fri 8am–4pm; ☎223 1800), Plaza Regency Building, Via España, opposite the *Hotel Continental*.

Bookstores Libreria Argosy, at the junction of Via Argentina with Via España, has a wide collection in Spanish and English.

Car rental Avis: C D, El Cangrejo (☎213 0555), Aeropuerto Marcos A. Gelabert (☎315 0434), Tocumen airport (☎238 4056); Budget: Via España, C 46 (☎263 9190), Tocumen airport (☎238 4069);

Hertz: C 55, El Cangrejo (☎263 6511), Tocumen airport (☎238 4081); National: C 50 (☎265 3333), Tocumen airport (☎238 4144); Thrifty: Via España, C 46 (☎264 2613), Tocumen airport (☎238 4955).

Email and Internet access There's a growing number of Internet cafés around the city. Try *Internet@café*, Via Venetta, C 49B Oeste, a block up from Via España behind the *Hotel El Panamá* (Mon–Fri 8.30am–6pm, Sat 9am–3pm); *Rut@57*, C 57, Obarrio (Mon–Sat 9am–9pm); above *Jimmy's* restaurant on the corner of Via España and C Manuel M. Icaza (Mon–Sat 9am–9pm).

Embassies and consulates Belize, C 5 Colonia del Prado (☎266 8939); Canada, World Trade center, C 58(☎264 9731); Colombia, Edificio Grobman, C Manuel M. Icaza (☎223 3535); Costa Rica, C G. Ortega, Via España (☎264 2937); Cuba, Av Cuba, Av Ecuador (☎227 0359); El Salvador, Edificio Citibank, Via España (☎223 3020); Guatemala, Via Argentina (☎269 3475 or 269 3406); Honduras, Edificio Tapia, Av Justo Arosemena, C 31 (☎225 0882); Mexico, Edificio Bancomer, C 50 (☎210 1523); Nicaragua, C 50, Av Manuel E Batista (☎269 6721); UK, Torre Swiss Bank, C 53E (☎269 0886); US, Av Balboa, C 40 (☎227 1777).

Immigration office The *migración* is on the corner of Av Cuba and C 29 (Mon–Fri 8am–3pm). Come here to extend your visa or to get permission to leave the country if you have been in Panamá for over three months – for the latter you will also have to visit the office of Paz y Salvo (Mon–Fri 8.30am–4pm) in the Ministerio de Hacienda y Tesoro on Av Cuba with C 35. At both offices it's best to arrive early and be prepared to queue.

Laundry Most upmarket hotels have a laundry service, and there are cheap, coin-operated *lavamaticos* all over the city, including Lavamatico America, Av Justo Arosemena, C27, and Lavamatic, C 3, Av Central.

Medical care There are doctors at the 24hr Centro Medico Bella Vista, Av Perú, C 35 (☎227 4022) and Centro Medico Paitilla, Av Balboa, C 53 (☎263 6060). Hospitals include the Hospital Santo Thomas, Av 5 Sur, C 34 E (☎227 4122).

Pharmacy Farmacia Arrocha, Via España, C 49E (open 24hr).

Photography Fujifilm, C Manuel M. Icaza, Via España, is one of many places that sells and develops print and slide film, and there are plenty of camera shops on Av 2 Norte, opposite the *Hotel El Panamá*.

Police Emergencies (☎104); tourist police (☎226 4021 or 270 2467).

Post office The most central post office is on Av Central at C 34, opposite the Don Bosco Church; there's another in El Cangrejo in the Plaza de la Concordia shopping centre on Via España (both open Mon–Fri 7am–6pm; Sat 7am–5pm).

Swimming pool Piscina Olimpica Adan Gordon, C31, Av Cuba, US$0.5.

Telephones Public phonebooths throughout the city take US$5, US$10 and US$20 phonecards, and some take coins. The main Cable and Wireless office (Mon–Fri 7.30am–5.00pm, Sat 7.30am–2.30pm) is in the Banco Nacional building on Via España.

Moving on from Panamá City

Panamá City is the **transportation hub** of the country – except for those to Gamboa, all domestic buses depart from the Albrook terminal (see p.713). Other than for the express bus service to David and the international bus to San José, there's no need to **book** bus tickets in advance.

Tours

A growing number of operators in Panamá City offer a range of guided **tours**, from city tours and canal cruises to trans-Darién treks and diving trips.

ANCON Expeditions, Edificio El Dorado, C Elvira Mendez (☎269 9414 or 269 9415, fax 264 3713, *www.ecopanama.com*). The highly rated commercial arm of the National Conservation Association offers tours with an ecological emphasis throughout the country, with expert bilingual guides. They also have their own exclusive lodges in Cana and Punta Patiño in Darién.

Argo Tours, 808 C Balboa (☎228 4328, fax 228 1234, *www.big-ditch.com*). Operate one of the ferries to Isla Taboga, and also run partial canal cruises every Saturday and full transits once a month, though they have been known to cut tours short.

Aventuras Panamá (☎260 0044, fax 236 5814, *avenpana@sinfo.net*). Whitewater rafting trips to Chagres National Park and fishing and diving excursions in the Pacific.

Panama Jones, C Ricardo Arias (☎265 4551, fax 265 4553, *www.panamacanal.com*). US-owned luxury tour operator offering a full range of trips throughout the country.

Scuba Panamá, Av 6 Norte, C 62A (☎261 3841, fax 261 9586, *www.scubapanama.com*). Countrywide diving trips, plus equipment sale and rental, and diving instruction.

MOVING ON FROM PANAMÁ CITY

Apart from buses to Gamboa (which leave from the SACA terminal, Plaza Cinco de Mayo) all buses depart from the modern Terminal de Buses in Albrook.

DESTINATION	FREQUENCY	DURATION	DISTANCE
Chitré	hourly	4hr	251km
Colón	every 20min	1hr 30min	76km
Colón (express)	every 20min	1hr	76km
David	hourly	7hr	438km
David (express)	2 daily	5hr	438km
Meteti	3–4 daily	7–8hr	225km
Paso Canoas	11 daily	9hr	494km
Paso Canoas (express)	3 daily	7hr	494km
Penonomé	every 20min	2hr 30min	150km
Santiago	every 30min	4hr	250km
Las Tablas	every 2hr	4hr 30min	283km
El Valle	every 35min	2hr 30min	134km
Gamboa	8 daily	45min	26km

INTERNATIONAL BUS SERVICE FROM PANAMÁ CITY

To **San José, Costa Rica** Ticabus, C 17, Av Central (☎262 6275). One bus daily, 14–15hr.

DOMESTIC FLIGHTS FROM PANAMÁ CITY

All flights leave from Marcos A. Gelabert domestic airport in Albrook.

DESTINATION	FREQUENCY	DURATION	OPERATOR
Bocas del Toro	3 daily	1hr 40min	Aeroperlas (☎315 7500)
			Mapiex Aero (☎315 0888)
Colón	14 daily	15min	Aeroperlas (☎315 7500)
David	4–6 daily	1hr	Aeroperlas (☎315 7500)
			Mapiex Aero (☎315 0888)
El Real	1 daily	50min	Aeroperlas (☎315 7500)
			Aviatur (☎315 0397 or 315 0314)
La Palma	1 daily	45min	Aeroperlas (☎315 7500)
			Aviatur (☎315 0397 or 315 0314)
Sambú	3 weekly	1hr 20min	Aeroperlas (☎315 7500)
			Aviatur (☎315 0397 or 315 0314)

To **Kuna Yala**: 2–3 flights daily Mon–Fri to (from northwest to southeast, 30min–1hr 15min): Porvenir (also Sat and Sun), Río Sidra, Río Azucar, Corazon de Jesus, Río Tigre, Playa Chico, Tupile, Ailigandi, Achutupo, Mamitupo, Ogobsucun, Mansucum, Mulatupu, Tubuala, Caledonia and Puerto Obaldia. Flights are operated by ANSA (☎315 0275 or 315 0299), Aviatur (☎315 0397 or 315 0314) and Aerotaxi (☎315 0275), and depart from Marcos A. Gelabert domestic airport in Albrook.

CHAPTER 35

THE CANAL AND COLÓN PROVINCE

R unning some 82km across the isthmus between the Atlantic and Pacific oceans, the **Panamá Canal**, one of the greatest engineering feats of all time, is the country's biggest visitor attraction, and an easy day-trip from Panamá City. Quite apart from its sheer magnitude, the canal also possesses an unexpected, rugged beauty. Though the corridor that surrounds this vital thoroughfare is home to almost two-thirds of Panamá's population, for much of its length the canal cleaves a narrow path through pristine **rainforest**, large tracts of which are protected within **Parque Nacional Soberania** and on **Isla Barro Colorado Isla**. These are among the most accessible tropical rainforest preserves in Latin America, and all of them support exceptional biodiversity. Soberania and Chagres also offer the opportunity to walk along the remnants of the **Camino de las Cruces** and the **Camino Real** – paved mule trains carved across the forested spine of the isthmus in colonial times, providing a convenient route by which the treasures that the Spanish accumulated could be transported from Panamá City to the Atlantic.

From 1903 to 1977 the strip of land that extends for five miles on either side of the canal was de facto US territory, known as the **Canal Zone**. The last US military bases closed at the end of 1999, when control of the canal was finally handed over to Panamá, but the well-ordered society the US established in the Canal Zone still remains, in delicious contrast to the tropical disorder and vibrant **Caribbean culture** of Colón and the surrounding coast, whose inhabitants are descended from the workers brought in to build the waterway. At the canal's Atlantic entrance, **Colón** is an infamously poor and dangerous – yet strangely compelling – city, steeped in history, while the Caribbean coast of Colón Province offers a perfect antidote to the city's sometimes depressing squalor. To the west, along the **Costa Abajo**, the formidable ruins of the colonial **Fort San Lorenzo** still stand guard over the mouth of the Río Chagres amid untouched tropical rainforest; while to the northeast stretches the **Costa Arriba**, an isolated region of pristine coral reefs and laid-back fishing villages, much of which is protected by the **Parque Nacional Portobelo**, set around the ruins of the colonial ports of **Portobelo** and **Nombre de Dios**.

The canal

Although Panamanians are keen to insist that their country is "much more than just a canal", the truth of the matter is that the **Panamá Canal** remains the country's defining feature, the basis of its economy and the key to its history. Were it not for the US

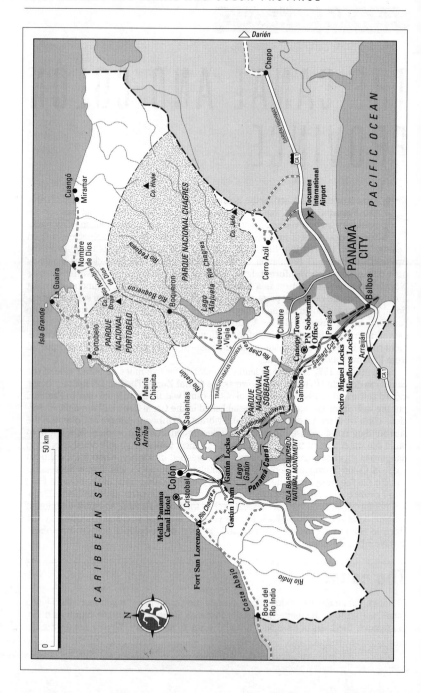

government's determination to build it, Panamá might never have come into existence as an independent republic, yet it is also the root cause of the US's deeply resented influence and interventions in national affairs. The struggle to establish control of the canal was central to the emergence of a Panamanian identity, and though after more than ninety years it was finally handed over to Panamanian jurisdiction at midnight on December 31, 1999, its future remains one of the most controversial issues in Panamanian politics.

The canal's **configuration** is such that the Pacific entrance is 43.2km east of the Atlantic entrance. From the Bahía de Panamá on the Pacific side, it passes under the broad sweep of the Bridge of the Americas and alongside the port of Balboa, running at sea-level some 6km inland to the **Miraflores Locks**, where ships are raised some 16.5m to Lago de Miraflores. About 2km further on, ships are raised another 10m to the canal's maximum elevation of 26.5m above sea level by the **Pedro Miguel Locks**, beyond which they enter the **Gaillard Cut** (formerly known as Culebra, but renamed in honour of Colonel William Gaillard, the US engineer who was responsible for its excavation). Described by the English Lord Bryce as "the greatest liberty ever taken with nature", Culebra was the deepest and most difficult section of the canal construction, a 13.6km cut through the rock and shifting shale of the continental divide. An enormous amount of excavation was required, and the work was plagued by devastating landslides. The cut is currently being widened to allow two-way traffic, part of an ambitious investment programme that may include the construction of a third set of locks to take the growing number of ships too big to use the existing locks.

After the confinement of the Gaillard Cut, the canal channel continues for 37.6km across the broad expanse of **Lago Gatún**, the largest artificial lake in the world when it was formed in 1913 by the damming of the Río Chagres. Covering 420 square kilometres, the lake is placid and stunningly beautiful; until you see an ocean-going ship appear from behind one of the densely forested headlands, it is difficult to believe that it forms part of one of the busiest waterways in the world. At the lake's far end ships are brought back down to sea-level in three stages by the **Gatún Locks**, easily visited from Colón, after which they run 3km through a narrow cut into the calm Atlantic waters of Bahía Limón.

Exploring the canal

By far the best way to experience the canal is by **boat or ship** – passing through the narrow confines of the Gaillard Cut or weaving between the forested islands of Lago Gatún is the only way to truly appreciate its awesome scale and beauty. The easiest way is to take an **organized tour** with Argo Tours in Panamá City (see p.731). A half-day, partial transit of the canal, through Miraflores and Pedro Miguel Locks and into the Gaillard Cut, costs around US$75, while a full-day complete transit, continuing into Lago Gatún and down through Gatún Locks, costs twice that – they usually run a partial transit every Saturday and a full transit once a month. Be warned, though, that they sometimes cut short tours if they feel there are not enough passengers: try to get a clear agreement on how long the tour will last and how far it will go before you hand over the money.

The other way is to get taken on as a **linehandler** on one of the private yachts that transit the canal – each yacht must take four linehandlers, who need no experience and are usually paid US$20–30 a day for the one- or two-day trip. The best way to find work is to visit the yacht clubs at Balboa or Cristobal and talk with yacht owners; there's a noticeboard at Balboa where you can offer your services, but direct contact is better. You may have to wait several days, though, and be aware that more yachts transit from the Atlantic to the Pacific than vice-versa.

Much of the canal can also be explored by **land**. A road served eight times daily by SACA buses from the Panamá City terminal on Plaza Cinco de Mayo runs 26km along the side of the canal, past the Miraflores and Pedro Miguel Locks, to the town of Gamboa on Lago Gatún, passing the entrance to Parque Nacional Soberania. This journey is described below; if time is short, you can easily find a taxi in Panamá City to take you to Miraflores, wait for an hour or so and take you back for about US$10. The Gatún Locks, on the Atlantic side, can also be visited via Colón. The **transisthmian railway** (*www.kcsi.com/pcrc.html*), which runs alongside the canal, is due to reopen for freight and passengers in 2001 after being closed for more than a decade. When it does, this will be an excellent way of seeing the canal and the surrounding rainforest, and is sure to be widely advertised in Panamá City.

Even experienced divers, jaded with the undersea wonders of the Caribbean and Pacific, should make an effort to **dive** in the Panamá Canal. Huge amounts of machinery and entire villages were submerged by the rising waters of Lago Gatún, and now make an unusual underwater attraction. Trips can be arranged through several of Panamá City's dive companies, including Scuba Panamá (see p.732).

The road to Gamboa

Gamboa is served by regular buses from the Plaza 5 de Mayo, though if you want to stop at points along the way you're better off hiring a taxi. The road to Gamboa leaves Panamá City to the north through a series of former US military bases, known as the "reverted areas", which were handed over to Panamá in the 1990s. One of these, Fort Clayton – once the nerve centre of US military operations throughout Latin America and the Caribbean – is being converted into an international university campus known as El Ciudad del Saber, (The City of Knowledge). Opposite Clayton, 9km from Panamá City, a side road leads a short distance to **Miraflores Locks**, which raise or lower ships the 16.5m between sea-level and the Lago Miraflores in two stages, each using fifty million gallons of fresh water which flows through tunnels 5m in diameter to fill each lock chamber in just ten minutes. Because of the extreme tidal variations in the Pacific, the first lock gates at Miraflores are the biggest in the whole system, each weighing a colossal 700 tons. The gates open in just two minutes, and ships are guided through by electric locomotives known as mules, taking thirty minutes. The **visitor centre** at Miraflores (daily 9am–5pm; free) has a scale model of the canal, a slide show and a viewing platform with a guided commentary in English and Spanish. The **best times** to see ships passing through are between 8 and 10am, when they come up from the Pacific side, and after 3pm, when they descend from the Atlantic side.

Some 1.5km further up the road, the **Pedro Miguel Locks** raise ships to the level of Lago Gatún. There are no special facilities, but you can watch ships here too. After Pedro Miguel Locks, ships enter the Gaillard Cut, which cannot be seen from land. Instead, the road continues 1km to the small canal town of Paraíso, a little way beyond which on the left is the **French Cemetery**, one of the few remaining traces of the doomed French attempts to build a canal in the 1880s. There's not much to see other than the graves in which a generation of France's finest engineers lie buried, but the place has the solemn atmosphere of a war cemetery. The road then climbs some 5km through dense rainforest to the **Parque Nacional Soberania office** (daily 8am–4pm; ☎229 7885). If you want to walk any of the trails in the park (see opposite) you'll need a permit from here; they charge US$3 for admission, and can provide guides for larger groups if arranged in advance.

A little further up on the crest of the continental divide are the **Summit Botanical Gardens and Zoo** (daily 8am–4pm; US$1), established by the US in 1923, with more than fifteen thousand different plant species spread out in its ample grounds. Handed over to Panamá in 1979 they are now a popular weekend destination for families from the capital, most of whom come for the zoo. Examples of most of Panamá's large mammals are imprisoned here in the name of environmental education, including pumas, jaguars, several species of monkey and an ocelot. Most have wild relatives in the surrounding forest, but your chances of seeing them are slim. There is also a captive breeding programme for the Harpy Eagle, Panamá's highly endangered national symbol.

From the summit, the road continues 9km to **GAMBOA**, where the canal channel emerges from the Gaillard Cut and follows the flooded bed of the Río Chagres into **Lago Gatún**. The headquarters of the Canal Dredging Division, Gamboa is something of a ghost town, as most canal workers now commute from Panamá City, and many of its functional, US imperial-style houses have been abandoned. There's a small marina where you can rent boats to take you out onto the lake, or back up the Chagres to the Las Cruces trail (see below).

Just outside the town overlooking the Chagres where it flows into the lake is the most ambitious of the new tourism developments to spring up around the canal in the wake of the US withdrawal, the **Gamboa Rainforest Resort** (☎314 9000, fax 206 5670, *www.gamboaresort.com*; ⑨). Set in the midst of the rainforest, the hotel itself is rather overpriced, but the resort is worth visiting as a day-trip from Panamá City for a ride on the **aerial tram** (Mon 1–4.30pm, Tues–Sun 8.30am–4.30pm; US$35). Rather like a ski-lift transferred to the tropics, the aerial tram climbs silently through the rainforest canopy for about 600 metres, offering a view of the forest ecosystem very different to what you see at ground level, plus a good chance of spotting wildlife, particularly monkeys and birds. At the summit, an observation tower offers a spectacular panorama over the canal, the lake and the Río Chagres winding lazily through dense vegetation. The ticket price also includes guided tours of a butterfly house, an orchid nursery, a serpentarium (where some of Panamá's most dangerous snakes are on display), and an aquarium with freshwater fish and reptiles.

Parque Nacional Soberania

Around Gamboa, the rainforest-covered watershed that is so vital for the canal's continued operation is protected by the 220-square-kilometre **Parque Nacional Soberania**. Just half an hour from Panamá City by road, Soberania is the most easily accessible national park in Panamá. There are three good **trails**, all of which pass over rugged terrain covered by pristine rainforest and offer reasonable chances of seeing wildlife such as monkeys and innumerable birds, or even (if you're very lucky) large mammals such as deer or tapir. You'll need a **permit** from the park office (see opposite).

The shortest and best-marked trail is the **Sendero El Charco**, which begins a few kilometres beyond the Summit Botanical Gardens on the road to Gamboa, stretches for about 4km, and takes about an hour to walk. The second is the old **Pipeline Road**, which begins a few hundred metres outside Gamboa and holds the world record as the place in which the highest number of bird species were identified in a 24-hour period, set by the Audubon Society in 1985. The trail stretches for 24km, ending on the shores of Lago Gatún, and so is too long to walk in a day.

The third trail is a remnant of the **Camino de las Cruces**, the colonial mule trail from Panamá City to the now abandoned village of Venta de las Cruces, where cargo was transferred to boats and taken down the Río Chagres to the Atlantic. The trailhead is marked by an old cannon near the park office along the Gaillard Highway, which forks right off the Gamboa Road and cuts across to the village of Chilibre on the Transisthmian Highway from Panamá City to Colón. The trail is still partially paved and runs about 10km through pristine rainforest to the banks of the Río Chagres, so you can either walk some distance down it and retrace your steps, or rent a boat in Gamboa to take you up the Chagres to Venta de las Cruces at the other end of the trail and walk back to the highway.

Just past the Summit Gardens on the road to Gamboa a right turn into the heart of Parque Nacional Soberanía takes you to the **Canopy Tower** (☎214 9724 or 264 5720, fax 263 2784, *www.canopytower.com*; ⑨, advance booking required), a former US radar station that has been converted into one of Latin America's most unusual eco-lodges. The tower is basically a fifteen-metre-high aluminium tube topped by a large geodesic dome that has been stripped of all military equipment and refitted with bright, comfortable rooms, with windows looking out onto the forest, a communal dining room with hammocks and a small ecological library. At the top of the tower, an open-air gallery offers a panoramic, canopy-level view of the surrounding rainforest, the canal and the skyscrapers of Panamá City and the Pacific Ocean in the distance. Though it's only been up and running for a few years, the *Canopy Tower* is already hugely popular with bird-watchers, particularly in October and March when migrating hawks and vultures pass over in their thousands. All meals and expertly guided tours of the forest in English or Spanish are included, and though it's relatively expensive, the tower offers an exceptionally good way of visiting the rainforest in comfort, and a unique example of how swords can be turned into ploughshares.

Isla Barro Colorado

As the waters of Lago Gatún began to rise after the damming of the Chagres, much of the wildlife in the surrounding forest was forced to take refuge on points of high ground that later became islands. One of these, **Barro Colorado**, administered by the Smithsonian Tropical Research Institute, is among the most intensively studied areas of tropical rainforest in the world. Though the primary aims of the reserve are conservation and research, you can visit it by contacting the Smithsonian in ANCON (☎212 8026, fax 212 8148, *www.stri.org*) – call well in advance, as visitor numbers are strictly limited and the waiting list is very long, though there are sometimes cancellations. The eight-hour trip costs US$70, which includes lunch and the boat trip across the placid waters of the lake. **Tours** of the island are conducted in English or Spanish by extremely knowledgeable guides, and provide an excellent introduction to tropical rainforest ecology. The island teems with wildlife – myriad species of bird, monkeys and tapirs – but as groups are a bit too large (up to fifteen people) and noisy, you're unlikely to see much.

The Transisthmian Highway and Parque Nacional Chagres

From Panamá City the **Transisthmian Highway** – the Transistmica – passes through the city's northern suburbs, over the continental divide and across the Río Chagres towards Colón. To the east of the Transistmica as it crosses the Chagres is **Lago Alajuela**, an artificial lake formed after the completion of the Madden Dam in 1934 which provides forty percent of the water needed for the operation of the canal, as well as all Panamá City's drinking water. The lake's watershed is protected by the **Parque Nacional Chagres**, 1290 square kilometres of mountainous rainforest comprising four different life zones that are home to over 300 species of bird, as well as several Emberá (see p.749) communities displaced by the flooding of Lago Bayano further east. It's relatively easy to visit the park as a day-trip from the capital: take any slow bus from Panamá City to Colón and ask the bus driver to let you off 29km from Panamá City at the turning for the lakeside village of **Nuevo Vigia**; then either walk the few kilometres to the village or wait for one of the irregular local buses. At Nuevo Vigia you can rent a canoe for about US$25 plus gas to take you across the lake and up either the Río Pequeni or Río Chagres into the park. The Emberá communities of **San Juan de Pequeni** and **Parrara Puru** (at the mouth of the Chagres) both accept visitors and are keen to sell handicrafts (wood carvings and the like) which they produce to supplement the subsistence hunting and agroforestry which are the only other economic activities they are allowed to practise in the park.

When water levels permit you can also visit the park by **whitewater rafting** down the Río Chagres to the lake, an exciting one-day trip from Panamá City, through level II and III rapids which are promoted as the "Chagres Challenge". The main operator is Aventuras Panamá (see p.732), though most Panamá City tour agencies are able to book the trip.

It is still possible to walk along the remains of the **Camino Real** through the park to Portobelo (4 days) or Nombre de Dios (2–3 days), though this is only recommended if you have plenty of tropical wilderness experience, and you should inform ANAM in Panamá City beforehand. The trailhead is at the village of **Boquerón**, 12km off the Transistmica from a turn-off just beyond the one to Nuevo Vigia; you may be able to find a guide in the village to take you, but don't count on it. You'll need a good map, a compass, a machete and food and equipment to survive for several days alone in the rainforest.

Colón and around

In all the world there is not, perhaps, now concentrated in a single spot so much swindling and villainy, so much foul disease, such a hideous dung-heap of moral and physical abomination as in the scene of this far-fetched undertaking of nineteenth-century engineering.

James Anthony Froude, British journalist, 1886

In fact, Froude never visited **COLÓN**, claiming that his curiosity was less strong than his disgust, but his opinion of the city during the French canal construction was widely shared by his contemporaries and were he to visit the city today he would find little to change his mind. Situated at the Atlantic entrance to the canal, with a population approaching 150,000, Panama's second city represents the dark side of the Caribbean that never makes it into the holiday brochures, and to most Panamanians its name is a byword for poverty, violence and urban decay. To a certain extent, this is fair enough – much of the city is a run-down slum, the streets strewn with rubbish and rife with violent crime. But despite decades of terminal decline, Colón retains the decadent charm of a steamy Caribbean port where pretty much anything goes, its former glory still evident in its many monuments and crumbling turn-of-the-century architecture. Moreover, if you can get past the initial hostility and suspicion, the people of Colón, mostly descendants of West Indians who came here to build the canal, are as warm and friendly as anywhere in the country, and enjoy a lively street culture that helps offset the desperate poverty that most of them face. Most visitors to Colón come here solely to shop at the **Colón Free Zone**, a walled enclave where goods from all over the world can be bought at very low prices – the starkest possible contrast to the rest of the city, which they avoid assiduously. Beside the Free Zone a similar enclave development known as Colón 2000 has been set up in a bid to persuade passengers on the many cruise ships that pass through the canal to disembark and spend some money, but it

WARNING

Though exaggerated, Colón's reputation throughout the rest of the country for **violent crime** is not undeserved, and if you come here you should exercise extreme caution – mugging, even on the main streets in broad daylight, is common. Don't carry anything you can't afford to lose, try and stay in sight of the police on the main streets, and consider renting a taxi to take you around, both as a guide and for protection. They charge about US$6 an hour.

has little to offer besides souvenir shops. Southwest of Colón, a road runs along the Costa Abajo to Gatún Locks, where ships are raised and lowered between sea level and Lago Gatún, and on to **San Lorenzo**, a formidable colonial fortress overlooking the mouth of the Río Chagres.

Some history

Founded in 1852 on filled-in mangrove swamps as the Caribbean terminal of the transisthmian railway, Colón was originally named Aspinwall after one of the railway's owners. The Colombian authorities' insistence that it be called Colón, after Christopher Columbus, led to a long-running dispute that only ended because letters from the US addressed to Aspinwall never reached their destination. The railway brought many immigrants and a degree of prosperity to the town, and though it slipped into decline in 1869 when the completion of the transcontinental railway in the US reduced traffic across the isthmus, its fortunes revived with the initiation of the French canal construction in 1879. The French founded the neighbouring port enclave of Cristobal, and vast quantities of men and material flowed through Colón, but it remained a poverty- and disease-ridden slum town famed for its depravity. Burned to the ground during an 1885 uprising led by **Pedro Prestan**, a Haitian later hanged in front of huge crowds on **Front Street**, the city was rebuilt by the French and prospered again during the US canal construction effort. Colón's heyday came in the 1950s, when it was among the most fashionable cruise destinations in the Caribbean, but despite its role as Panamá's main port and the success of the Free Zone (founded in 1949), the city slipped into gradual decline and the cruise ships stopped coming. Although the port and Free Zone continue to thrive, little of the money they generate stays in Colón, and many of the employees are bussed in from Panamá City. In the face of urban poverty as extreme as any in Latin America and unemployment levels approaching fifty percent, it is little surprise that many have turned to **crime**, particularly drug trafficking, as a way to survive. The most recent attempt to reverse the city's interminable decline is centred on reviving Colón as a destination for cruise ships, but even if successful the idea that this will transform the city's prospects seems a forlorn hope.

Arrival and information

The **bus terminal** is on the corner of Av Bolívar and C 13, two blocks away from Front Street. Buses arrive from and leave for Panamá City about three times an hour between 4am and 10pm; to and from Portobelo twice an hour from 5am to 8pm. If you arrive by **ship** from Kuna Yala you'll come in at Coco Solo port, a US$3 taxi ride from the city centre. **Yachts** coming through the canal dock outside the Yacht club in Cristobal. France's Field, Colón's **airport**, is a short taxi ride outside the city: Aeroperlas has fourteen **flights** a day between Panamá City and Colón, used mainly by business people visiting the Free Zone, but you'd have to be in a real hurry to want fly here, given the short distance between the two cities by land.

There is an **IPAT** office in Colón (Mon–Fri 8am–4pm; ☎441 9644), on Av Balboa with C 9 close to the entrance to Cristobal, but they don't have much information and will be very surprised to see you. The **post office** and a branch of the **Banco Nacional** are just around the corner on C 9; there are several more banks in the Free Zone.

Accommodation

There's a wide choice of **places to stay** in Colón, catering mostly to business people, and most of them would be seen as good value in any other city. If you are going to stay overnight, it's worth splashing out on a more expensive hotel with armed security and a restaurant so you won't have to go out at night.

Hotel Internacional, Av Bolívar, C 11 (☎445 2930 or 441 5457). Secure, with clean, spacious rooms with a/c, TV and hot water. Good restaurant and a rooftop bar. ⑤.

Hotel Sotelo, Av Guerrero, C 11 (☎441 7703). Small and dark, but with clean rooms with TV and a/c. There's also a bar, restaurant and casino. ⑤.

New Washington Hotel, Av Frente, C 2 (☎441 7133 or 441 8120, fax 441 7397, *nwh@sinfo.net*). The best place in town, in a recently refurbished historic building in elegant French style. The comfortable rooms have hot water, a/c and TV, while those at the front have balconies overlooking the sea. It's very secure, and has a bar, restaurant and casino. ⑦.

Pension Acropolis, Av Guerrero, C 11 (☎441 1456). Basic, with communal bathrooms; the best budget option in a moderately safe part of town. ②.

The City

From the bus terminal, a left turn takes you north up dilapidated **Front Street** (Av Frente), once the city's main commercial road, which runs along the waterfront of Bahía Limón. Most of the shops are closed and the elegant two- and three-storey buildings with pillared overhanging balconies are crumbling, their faded pastel paintwork covered in graffiti. Opposite the corner with C 8 is the abandoned **railway station**, built in 1909; beyond here the view of the bay is obscured by the shantytown settlement of La Playita, which is home to two hundred or so families of *precaristas*, as illegal urban squatters are known. How the plans to restore Front Street and turn it into a tourist centre will affect these families is uncertain.

Just off Front Street on C 6, the **Colón Boxing Arena** was built in the 1970s to nurture the mass of local talent. The city has produced numerous world champions, the most famous of whom was "Panama Al" Brown, the first Latin American world champion in the 1930s and one of the greatest boxers of all time. Four blocks down C 8 is the **cathedral**, built between 1929 and 1934 with high, neo-Gothic arches. Back on Front Street, it's six blocks north to **The New Washington Hotel**, built around 1850 to house railway engineers and rebuilt several times since. Famous guests have included Bob Hope, who entertained troops here during World War II, exiled Argentinian dictator Juan Perón, former British prime minister David Lloyd George and US president George Taft. Inside a palm-filled walled enclosure, its recently refurbished neo-colonial elegance, complete with chandeliers and ornate double staircase, is a reminder of Colón's former splendour as well as a gesture of confidence in the city's future. The seafront veranda is a good place to relax with a drink and watch the ships in the bay.

To the left of the hotel as you look towards the city is a small stone **Episcopal Church** that was the first Protestant church in Colombia when it was built, for West Indian railway workers, in 1865. Seven blocks east along the seafront, a statue of Christ the Redeemer, arms outstretched, faces down **Av Central**, which is lined with monuments, including, on the intersection with C 2, a statue of Columbus with an indigenous girl, donated to Panamá by Empress Eugenie of France in 1866.

Behind the bus terminal is the port enclave of **Cristobal**, formerly part of the Canal Zone and still one of Latin America's busiest ports, handling more than two million tons of cargo a year. Apart from the Yacht Club (see overleaf) there's not much of interest here and most of the port is off-limits to visitors anyway.

The Colón Free Zone

The southeast corner of Colón is occupied by the **Free Zone**, a walled city-within-a-city covering more than a square kilometre. This is the second biggest duty-free zone in the world after Hong Kong, with an annual turnover of more than US$10 billion. All manner of consumer goods are imported here and then re-exported across Latin America, and it is visited by thousands of businesspeople every week. The Free Zone is basically a forbidden city for Colón residents unless they work there, but you are allowed in if you present your passport at the gate. Inside, the contrast with the rest of Colón could not be greater – immaculate superstores line the Zone's clean, well-paved streets and the only smell is of money and expensive perfume. Most of the trade is in bulk orders, but you can buy individual items at low prices if you bargain hard or enlist one of the professional hagglers who tout their services at the entrance (they work for commission). Officially, what you buy must be held in bond and given to you at the airport as you leave the country.

Eating and drinking

Though there are several cheap **restaurants** in Colón serving the delicious local cuisine – usually seafood cooked to spicy Caribbean recipes – most are in dangerous parts of the city. In the evening, you are better off eating in or near your hotel.

Café Nacional, C 11 with Guerrero. Popular, with good, inexpensive food and a convenient location, which is fairly safe during the day. Closed Sun.

Cristobal Yacht Club, on the seafront inside the Cristobal port enclosure. The open-air restaurant, serving decent seafood, is expensive, but the atmospheric bar, shaped like a ship's prow, is a good place to hang out if you're looking for work as a linehandler on a yacht transiting the canal or heading out into the Caribbean.

Restaurante Hotel Internacional, on the ground floor of the hotel. Standard Panamanian and international food from about US$5, particularly good for breakfast. The rooftop bar (closed Sun), open to hotel guests only, is a good place to drink a sundowner and watch the ships lit up in the harbour at night while the city rages below.

Around Colón: Gatún Locks

From Colón, a road runs 10km southwest to **Gatún Locks**, where ships are raised or lowered from Lago Gatún to sea-level on the Atlantic side of the canal. Almost 2km long, Gatún Locks raise or lower ships the 26.5m between the lake and sea-level in three stages, and are among the canal's most monumental engineering features. The **visitors' centre** (daily 8am–4pm) has a scale-model of the canal, some photos of the locks during construction (their enormous size is most evident when viewed empty) and a viewing platform that offers the best vantage point to watch ships pass through (9–11am and after 3.30pm are the busiest times). There are also good views of the lake surrounded by dark, forest-covered mountains and of the vast **Gatún Dam**. More than 2km long and 800m wide at its base, this was the largest earthen dam in the world when it was built in 1906 to dam the Río Chagres and form the lake.

Occasional **buses** from the bus terminal in Colón can drop you at the locks; the road then goes on to cross the canal via a swing bridge which is only open when there are no ships passing through (each transit takes about an hour). It then forks, the left branch crossing the dam and following the west bank of the Chagres to the sea, then staggering along the **Costa Abajo** as far as the village of Boca del Río Indio. Costa Abajo is virtually undeveloped, with just a few fishing villages between the forest and the sea, and beyond Boca del Río Indio the coast is scarcely inhabited, stretching for 200km along the Golfo de Mosquitos to Bocas del Toro. Taking the right fork, not on the bus route, takes you to **Fort San Lorenzo**, at the mouth of the Río Chagres.

Fort San Lorenzo

With a spectacular setting on a promontory above the Caribbean overlooking the mouth of the Río Chagres, **Fort San Lorenzo** is the most impressive Spanish fortification still standing in Panamá. Until the construction of the railway, the Chagres was the main cargo route across the isthmus to Panamá City, and thus of enormous strategic importance to Spain. The first fortifications to protect the entrance to the river were built here in 1595, but the fort was taken by Francis Drake in 1596 and, though heavily reinforced, fell again to Henry Morgan's pirates in December 1670. Morgan then proceeded up the Chagres and across the isthmus to sack Panamá City. Further fortifications were insufficient to prevent English Admiral Edward Vernon from taking the fort again in 1740, but those that remain today, built during 1760–67, were never seriously tested, as by the time they were completed the era of the freebooters was coming to an end. The fort is well preserved, with a moat surrounding stout stone walls and great cannons looking out from the embrasures. It's an isolated place, surrounded by pristine rainforest, while the fort's view of the mouth of the Chagres and of the Costa Abajo can hardly have changed since the days of Drake and Morgan.

Fort San Lorenzo can only be reached by private car or **taxi** – you can rent one in Colón for about US$6 an hour. It's a drive of about forty minutes or so from Gatún Locks, passing through dense rainforest and the former US jungle training base of **Fort Sherman**, once home to the infamous School of the Americas, where military officers from all over Latin America received training before returning to their countries to commit appalling human rights abuses. Part of Fort Sherman has now been converted into the *Sol Melia Panamá Canal* (☎470 1100, fax 470 1200, *melia.panama.canal @solmelia.com*; ⑧), a luxury hotel aimed primarily at people doing business in the Colón Free Zone.

Portobelo and the Costa Arriba

The **Costa Arriba**, stretching northeast of Colón, features beautiful beaches fringed by dense tropical forest, the historic towns of **Portobelo** and **Nombre de Dios**, and excellent diving and snorkelling in the **Parque Nacional Portobelo**. If you're heading here from Panamá City you can avoid Colón by getting off the bus at Sabanitas and catching a bus from Colón to Portobelo.

Portobelo

Named by Christopher Columbus in 1502 after the magnificent bay on which it stands, **PORTOBELO** – "beautiful harbour" – was for centuries the most important Spanish port on the Atlantic coast of the New World, the northern terminus of the Camino Real. Today, it's a sleepy little town that sits amid the remains of the formidable fortifications built to defend the treasure fleets from pirate attack, and makes a good base from which to explore the rugged coastline and underwater treasures of **Parque Nacional Portobelo**. On October 21 each year Portobelo explodes into life as thousands of pilgrims descend on it from all over Panamá to pay homage to its patron saint, the miraculous **Black Christ**.

Some history
Portobelo was founded in 1597 to replace Nombre de Dios as the Atlantic terminus of the **Camino Real**, a year after the latter had been destroyed by Francis Drake. Set on a deepwater bay deemed easier to defend from the ravages of pirates, Portobelo was heavily fortified and for 150 years played host to the famous *ferias*, when the Spanish treasure fleet came to collect the riches that travelled across the isthmus on mule trains from Panamá City and to leave merchandise brought from Seville for distribution throughout the Americas. Unsurprisingly, the wealth concentrated in the royal

THE BLACK CHRIST OF PORTOBELO

There are several different stories as to how the **Black Christ** figure came to Portobelo. Some say that it was found floating in the sea during a cholera epidemic, which disappeared after the Christ was brought into the town, others that it was on a ship bound for Colombia that stopped at Portobelo for supplies and was repeatedly prevented from leaving the bay by bad weather, sailing successfully only when the statue was left ashore. Whatever its origin, though, the Black Christ is without doubt the most revered religious figure in Panamá. A small figure carved from black cocobolo wood with an agonized face and eyes raised to heaven, the Christ is reputed to possess miraculous powers. Every year on October 21 up to fifty thousand devotees, known as Nazarenos and dressed in purple robes, come to Portobelo for a huge procession that is followed by festivities that continue through the night – a wild and chaotic celebration of faith.

warehouses here was an irresistible target for the **pirates** who scoured the Spanish Main. Henry Morgan sacked the town for fifteen days in 1668 before moving on to San Lorenzo and thence to Panamá City, and subsequent refortification was not enough to prevent the English Admiral Edward Vernon from seizing Portobelo again in 1739. Vernon destroyed the fortifications and, though they were rebuilt at enormous expense, the Spanish treasure fleet was rerouted around Cape Horn and the Portobelo *ferias* came to an end. The Spanish garrison left after independence in 1821, and with the establishment of Colón as Panamá's principal Atlantic port, Portobelo slipped into the tropical indolence that characterizes it today.

The Town and ruins

Walking into Portobelo along the road from Colón brings you to the well-preserved **Santiago Battery**, constructed between 1753 and 1760 to the most exacting military standards of the day. From its stout battlements fourteen rusting cannons still look out to sea. Behind the battery the town itself begins, its ramshackle houses built on top of the ruins of the **Santiago de la Gloria Fort** and the many public buildings and merchants' houses destroyed by Vernon in 1739. The road leads onto the litter-strewn main square, flanked on one side by the colonial **Church of San Felipe**, built in 1776 and exceptional only as the home of the famous **Black Christ** (see above).

Just off the square stands the two-storey **Casa Real de la Aduana** (daily 8am–4pm; US$1), the royal customs house, which has recently been restored with Spanish help and now houses a small **museum**. A massive barn-like structure with solid walls of coral, the Aduana originally dates from the sixteenth century, but was rebuilt in its current form after being destroyed by Admiral Vernon. The Aduana was the biggest civil building in colonial Panamá and an important symbol of imperial power: this was where treasure was stored awaiting the arrival of the fleets from Spain, and the building also housed a barracks and offices for royal officials. As well as a brief exhibition outlining the history of Portobelo, including a relief map of the town at the peak of its glory, the museum also has a display of the purple robes donated each year to the Black Christ, accompanied by some fascinating testimonies from his devotees.

Looking out onto the bay behind the church, the **San Geronimo Battery** was built at the same time as the Santiago Battery and is equally well preserved, complete with cannons. There are more ruins, though they're largely covered by the forest that descends almost to the road from above the town, while across the bay the twin batteries of **San Fernando** are also in good condition – it's easy to find someone in the town to take you across in a boat for a few dollars, or ask at Diver's Haven (see opposite). Portobelo's most formidable defence, the **"Iron Castle"** of San Felipe, stood at the mouth of the bay on the opposite side, but was dismantled during the canal construction to uncover the basalt rock on which it was built, and most of its stones were used to build the breakwater in Colón.

Practicalities

Buses for Portobelo leave from Colón; if you are coming from Panamá City and want to avoid Colón, change at Sabanitas, 14km before Colón. The small **IPAT** office in Portobelo, tucked away behind the municipal offices on the main square, keeps irregular hours but is fairly helpful when open. The only **accommodation** in the village itself is above the *Bar-Disco La Aduana* (②), also on the main square, but the rooms are very basic and it gets very noisy at weekends. You're better staying at one of the places on the road towards Colón. The closest to town, about ten minutes away, are the cabañas formerly known as *Diver's Haven* (☎448 2914; ④), where you can rent basic concrete cabins with private bathrooms and pleasant patios overlooking the bay – there's no sign, but they're just behind the police station. Further along, *Cabañas El Mar* (☎448 2102 or 442 1647; ⑤) has more luxurious cabins with TV and a/c; while diving operators Scuba Portobelo (☎448 2147) have pleasant cabins that sleep up to four people for US$50. All are busy on weekends but charge less on weekdays. Several basic **restaurants** in the village serve inexpensive fish and seafood cooked to delicious local recipes with coconut rice – try the *Casa del Marisco*. There are also a couple of more upmarket restaurants on the road towards Colón: *Restaurante El Torre* and *Restaurante Los Canones*, both of which serve good seafood.

Parque Nacional Portobelo

The rugged coast around Portobelo is officially part of the Parque Nacional Portobelo, and although little is done for the area in terms of protection or administration (you don't even need permission from ANAM to enter) it does have good **beaches** and some of the best **diving** and **snorkelling** on the Caribbean coast, including coral reefs, shipwrecks and, somewhere in front of Isla de Drake, the as yet undiscovered grave of Francis Drake, buried at sea in a lead coffin after he died of dysentery in 1596. Most of this area can only be reached by sea; you can either hire a boatman in town or go on an excursion with Scuba Portobelo (see above), who rent snorkelling and diving equipment. They also offer full diving courses through Scuba Panamá in Panamá City (see p.732).

Isla Grande

Some 12km beyond Portobelo, a side road branches off the unpaved road to the tiny village of **La Guaira**, where launches can take you across to **Isla Grande**, a very popular weekend resort for residents of Colón and Panamá City. Though undeniably beautiful, friendly and relaxed, with some good beaches, Isla Grande is no more spectacular than other parts of Costa Arriba. It does, however, have better facilities – and higher prices. The best **swimming** beach is around the island to the right as you face the mainland; the beach round the other side is good for surfing. For **snorkellers**, there's plenty to see around the Christ statue in front of the village, though beware of the current beyond the reef and of passing boats.

There are plenty of **places to stay** on Isla Grande, spread out along the seafront path that passes for the main street. The least expensive is *Super Cabañas Jackson* (☎448 2483; ④), which has small, box-like rooms; *Posada Villa Ensueño* (☎320 6321; ⑤) and *Cabañas Cholita* (☎232 4561; ⑤) have spacious cabins with a/c set around gardens. During the summer and on weekends it's worth booking ahead, though on weekdays prices can be lower and you can turn up on spec. There are also several **restaurants** serving mostly fish and seafood (try octopus cooked in coconut milk or *fufu*, a filling fish soup): *La Cholita*, *Candy Rose* and *Villa Ensueño* are all very good. The **social centre** of Isla Grande is the seafront shack in front of *Super Cabañas Jackson*, where locals gather to drink beer, play dominoes and listen to loud reggae. There are three or four **buses** daily from Colón to La Guaira; the last one back to Colón leaves at 1pm (Mon–Sat) or 4pm (Sun).

Nombre de Dios

A further 23km beyond Portobelo along the unpaved road is the small village **NOMBRE DE DIOS**, founded in 1520 and Portobelo's predecessor as the Atlantic terminus of the Camino Real. Almost nothing remains of the Spanish settlement destroyed by Drake in 1596, and it is difficult today to believe that in 1550 half the trade between Spain and the Americas passed through this tiny port. It is a charming village, though, friendly and laid-back, with the calm waters of Bahía de San Cristobal in front and the lush forest descending like a curtain from the mountains behind. Of the beautiful deserted beaches close by, the best is **Playa las Damas**, which can be reached by walking an hour or so along the sands – you'll need to get one of the locals to show you how to wade across the sand bank in front of the Río Nombre de Dios. There are also plenty of good **snorkelling** spots (bring your own equipment). Several simple **restaurants** serve good fish and seafood, but unfortunately there's nowhere to **stay**.

Beyond Nombre de Dios, the road staggers about 20km along the coast as far as the hamlet of Cuangó, which has become a centre for illegal and highly destructive gold mining. The frontier of Kuna Yala is about 25km further along the coast, and you may be able to catch a lift from one of the boats that sometimes travel into the *comarca* from the village of **Miramar**, a few kilometres west of Cuangó, though this trip is best done in the opposite direction (see p.756). There are three to four **buses** daily between Colón, Portobelo and Nombre de Dios; the last bus back usually leaves Nombre de Dios at 1pm, though it's worth checking with the locals in case it leaves earlier.

travel details

BUSES

Colón to: La Guaira (3–4 daily; 2hr); Nombre de Dios (3–4 daily; 2hr); Panamá City (every 20min; express 1hr, local 1hr 30min); Portobelo (15 daily; 1hr).

Gamboa to: Panamá City (8 daily; 45min).

La Guaira to: Colón (3–4 daily; 2hr).

Nombre de Dios to: Colón (3–4 daily; 2hr).

Panamá City to: Colón (every 20min; express 1hr, local 1hr 30min); Gamboa (8 daily; 45min).

Portobelo to: Colón (15 daily; 1hr).

FLIGHTS

Panamá City to: Colón (14 daily Mon–Fri; 15min).

Colón to: Panamá City (14 daily Mon–Fri; 15min).

CHAPTER 36

EASTERN PANAMÁ: DARIÉN AND KUNA YALA

S parsely populated by isolated indigenous communities and the descendants of escaped African slaves, the eastern third of Panamá – some 19,000 square kilometres – is perhaps the last great untamed **wilderness** of Central America, the beginning of an immense forest that continues almost unbroken across the border into Colombia and down the Pacific coast to Ecuador. This was the first region on the American mainland to be settled by the Spanish, but though they extracted great wealth from gold-mines deep in the forest, they were never able to establish effective control, hampered by the almost impassable terrain and by the fierce resistance put up by its inhabitants, and harassed at every turn by European pirates and bands of renegade African slaves known as *cimarrones*.

Though historically the whole of eastern Panamá was referred to as Darién, today it is divided into two distinct regions, separated by a low chain of forested mountains that runs the length of the Atlantic coast. The Atlantic side of these mountains is **Kuna Yala**, the autonomous *comarca* (territory) of the Kuna people, one of the most wildly beautiful and culturally fascinating regions of Panamá. Here some forty thousand Kuna live in isolation on the idyllic offshore islands of the **San Blas Archipelago**, connected to the rest of the country only by boat or plane.

The rest of eastern Panamá is **Darién**, the almost impenetrable wilderness frontier between Central and South America and the largest and most isolated province in Panamá. Only one road penetrates Darién: known as the **Darién Highway**, it is an extension of the Carretera Interamericana, intended to connect the road systems of North and South America. But for the moment the 106km gap between the two – the **Darién Gap** – remains unbridged. Here the vast forests remain largely undisturbed, one of the most pristine and biologically diverse ecosystems in the world and home to the semi-nomadic Emberá-Wounaan. Along the border with Colombia huge areas of these forests are protected by **Parque Nacional Darién**, the largest and most important protected area in Panamá.

Eastern Panamá has always been a wild frontier, a haven for rebels and renegades that defies effective government control, and today the *cimarrones*, pirates and insubmissive indigenous tribes of the colonial era have been replaced by drug traffickers, bandits and guerrillas. In recent years the situation has got markedly worse, with the vicious, decades-long Colombian **civil war** spilling over into Panamá. The Marxist guerrillas of the Colombian Revolutionary Armed Forces (FARC) have long maintained bases in Darién, but now right-wing paramilitary groups backed by powerful landowners and drug traffickers have begun pursuing them, terrorizing isolated Panamanian communities they accuse of harbouring the guerrillas. The paramilitaries have also

For an explanation of **accommodation price codes**, see p.701.

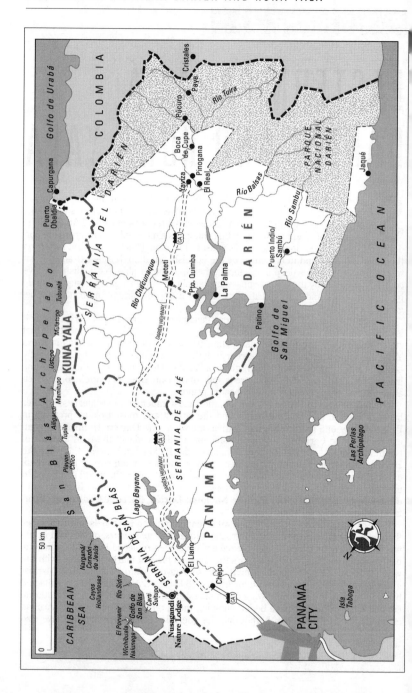

been waging a brutal campaign against poor peasants in Colombia, driving floods of refugees across the border, and unidentified armed groups have begun attacking Panamanian police outposts. Thus a climate of fear and suspicion reigns in Darién and the eastern extreme of Kuna Yala: remote villages have been abandoned, locals fear to travel by river, and thousands of extra police have been rushed in. While large areas of the region can still be visited safely, including almost all of Kuna Yala and parts of the Parque Nacional Darién, crossing the frontier by land, always a risky adventure, would now be crazy.

DARIÉN

With its mighty rivers, rugged mountain chains and vast, impenetrable rainforests, **Darién** is in many ways much closer to South than to Central America, its incredible biological diversity matched only by the cultural diversity of its population, which is made up of three main groups: black, indigenous and colonist. Other than a few Kuna communities, the indigenous population of Darién is composed of two closely related but distinct peoples, the **Wounaan** and the more numerous **Emberá**, classic semi-nomadic South American rainforest societies characterized by their traditional use of blowpipes for hunting and their encyclopedic knowledge of the rainforest. Easily recognizable by the black geometrical designs with which they decorate their bodies, the Emberá-Wounaan have been migrating across the border from Colombia for the last two centuries. Only since the 1960s have they begun to settle in permanent villages and establish official recognition of their territorial rights in the form of a *comarca*, divided into two districts: the **Comarca Emberá Cemaco**, in the north, and the **Comarca Emberá Sambú**, in the southwest. The black people of Darién, descended from the *cimarrones* and released slaves, are known as **Dariénitas** or **libres** (the free). Culturally distinct from the Afro-Antillano populations of Colón and Panamá City (see p.722), they live in the larger settlements, acting as intermediaries between the Emberá-Wounaan and mainstream Panamanian society. The **colonists**, meanwhile, are the most recent arrivals, poor peasants driven off their lands in western Panamá by expanding cattle ranches and encouraged to settle in Darién during the construction of the Darién Highway. Also known as **interioranos**, many colonists still wear their distinctive straw sombreros as a badge of identity and maintain the folk traditions of the regions they abandoned.

The **Darién Highway** was built in the 1970s and early 1980s to open up the region's supposedly empty lands to colonization and to complete the last link in the Carretera Interamericana from Alaska to Tierra del Fuego. At present it goes no further than Yaviza, 276km east of Panamá City, and the 106km **"Darién Gap"** between the road systems of Panamá and Colombia remains unbridged. Both governments are keen to complete the highway, but various factors have conspired to prevent this: the enormous expense; fears that a road link with Colombia would facilitate drug trafficking and the spread of foot-and-mouth disease from South America; and the opposition of environmentalists and indigenous groups. The environmental consequences of the progress that the highway was supposed to bring are sadly evident along its existing length: the lands on either side are heavily deforested, plundered by illegal logging companies and cleared and replaced by low-grade cattle pasture. For the moment the exceptionally rich rainforests that stand in the highway's path along the border are protected by the 5790-square-kilometre **Parque Nacional Darién**.

Given the **security concerns** currently affecting the border area, including parts of the national park and the Comarca Emberá Cemaco, a visit to **southwestern Darién** is a better option if you want to experience the ecology and culture of the region independently but without risking an encounter with armed groups. The provincial capital of **La Palma**, on the Pacific, is a good base from which to rent a boat to take you along the coast and up the Río Sambú into the Comarca Emberá Sambú.

Visiting Darién

Several tour companies in Panamá City (see p.731) run **tours** to Darién, ranging from short trips to two-week trans-Darién treks: ANCON Expeditions are the most experienced and have exclusive eco-lodges in the national park at Cana and on the Pacific coast at Punta Patiño. But it's easy enough to visit the region **independently**, though you'll need to bring your own equipment and supplies. The national park can be reached on foot from El Real, and you can rent guides and a canoe (gas is the biggest expense) in any of the region's towns to take you upriver into the forest and to visit indigenous communities.

The Darién Highway

East of Panamá City the **Darién Highway** is well paved as far as the busy cattle ranching centre of **Chepo**, 53km away. Beyond here it's unpaved, getting worse the further east you travel, and is often impassable in the wet season. Some 18km east of Chepo the highway passes through the quiet village of **El Llano**, where a side road leads up to the **Nusagandi Nature Reserve** in Kuna Yala (see p.756). Some 10km beyond El Llano the highway crosses the placid **Lago Bayano**, surrounded by well-preserved rainforest. Formed in 1972 by the construction of the hydro-electric dam that provides most of Panamá City's power, the lake is named after the king of the *cimarrones* who terrorized Panamá's colonial rulers in the 1500s. After defeating several armies sent against him, Bayano was captured in 1555 and taken to Seville, where he lived out the rest of his years as an honoured prisoner of the Spanish king. Though the provincial border is still some 90km further east, beyond the lake you are to all intents and purposes in Darién. From the lake, the highway rolls on for 196km through a desolate, deforested landscape, passing Emberá-Wounaan hamlets with their characteristic open-walled houses raised on stilts, and tin-roofed colonist settlements before ending on the banks of the Río Chucunaque at Yaviza.

Meteti

Fifty kilometres before Yaviza the highway passes through **METETI**, a small roadside *interiorano* settlement that has grown in importance as an administrative and commercial centre in recent years as a result of insecurity closer to the Colombian border. Plans to build an airstrip big enough to accommodate large military transport aircraft just outside Meteti have raised concerns that the town has been earmarked as a base for possible US intervention in Darién in the future. Meteti is the end of the road for buses from Panamá City, but there are usually a couple of buses a day that go on to Yaviza, and a side road leads some 20km down to **Puerto Quimba** on the Pacific coast, where **boats** can be taken across the Golfo de San Miguel to La Palma, the provincial capital (see p.752). Pick-up trucks leave Meteti for Puerto Quimba every 45 minutes or so between 5.30am and 6pm. You can find **accommodation** at the *Hotel Tres Hermanos Ortiz* (no phone; ②) by the roadside; the **restaurant** next door is simple but good. Meteti is also not a bad place to organize an expedition into the Comarca Emberá Cemaco to the north – you can probably find a guide and a canoe to take you down the Río Meteti to the Río Chucunaque, which forms the southern border of the *comarca* and runs parallel to the highway to Yaviza. Expect to pay US$10–20 a day for each guide, much more (for gas) if the canoe is motorized.

CROSSING THE DARIÉN GAP TO COLOMBIA

Though crossing the Darién Gap has always been a hazardous undertaking (and one of the most celebrated adventures in Latin America), given the present security situation we **do not recommend travel** in the region – several travellers have disappeared or been **killed** in the attempt in recent years, and at the very least you are likely to be robbed or kidnapped, even if you can find guides willing to take you (many of the villages in the region have been attacked or overrun by bandits and the inhabitants have fled). The route described below should only be used if the security situation in Darién improves, and even then you should remember that there is a **war** raging across the border in Colombia. *Always* check with the police in Yaviza before attempting to make this journey.

To cross the gap, you must first get permission from ANAM and the Colombian consulate in Panamá City (make sure you have your exit permission from *migración* if you have been in Panamá for more than three months). It takes seven or so days to get from **Yaviza** to **Turbo**, some 70km across the border, where you must register on arrival with DAS, the Colombian immigration agency. The route is by canoe or on foot to Palo de las Letras on the border, from where it is eight hours to Cristales, a park-guard station for the beautiful Parque Nacional Los Katios in Colombia where you can get a boat up the mighty Río Atrató to Turbo.

Yaviza

Founded by the Spanish in 1638 as a garrison town to establish colonial control over the gold mines further up river, **YAVIZA** is the terminus of the Darién Highway. Beyond here, the only transport is by water, and the river port is always busy with the plantain-laden Emberá canoes from the upriver communities of the *comarca* who come here to trade with the town's mostly black population. It is also a good base for trips into the Emberá Comarca Cemaco, and a short distance from the Parque Nacional Darién office in El Real. Sadly, though, with the recent upsurge in **bandit** and **paramilitary incursions** from Colombia, Yaviza is today once more beginning to resemble a garrison town, with nervous, heavily armed policemen and the thud of military helicopters. You should let the police know of your presence and your plans when you arrive and ask their advice before you continue.

Buses from Meteti arrive and depart from beside the dock at the entrance to town. From here the town's only real street runs down to a small square, just off which the friendly *Hotel Tres Americas* has simple **rooms** (③). There's a basic **restaurant** next door and a few others on the main street, as well as shops where you can buy supplies.

Parque Nacional Darién

Covering almost 5800 square kilometres of pristine rainforest along the border with Colombia, **Parque Nacional Darién** is possibly the most biologically diverse region on earth – over five hundred species of bird have been reported here. Inhabited by scattered indigenous communities, it is the only great forest in Central America that has not been affected by logging, and provides a home for countless rare and endangered species including jaguars, harpy eagles and several types of macaw. Given its isolation, the park is surprisingly accessible, especially from the village of El Real (see overleaf), where the park office is located. At time of writing parts of the park were safe to visit, but the security situation can change rapidly: phone the park office before you come down to check the current situation.

To visit the park you should first head to the park office in the small town of **EL REAL**, about half an hour by boat down the Chucunaque and up the Tuira from Yaviza. There's no scheduled boat service, but if you go to the dock in Yaviza in the morning you should find vessels which will take you for about US$4 per person. These boats go to meet the Aeroperlas (☎315 7500) and Aviatur (☎315 0397 or 315 0314) **planes** that arrive daily from Panamá City, returning the same day – the El Real airstrip, on the edge of town, serves Yaviza as well. There's basic **accommodation** at the *Hotel El Nazareno* (no phone; ②–③), a few stores, and a couple of simple restaurants (inform them in advance if you want an evening meal).

To the enter the park you need permission (US$3 per day) from the **Parque Nacional Darién office** (daily 8am–4pm; ☎299 6579) in El Real. Check here too about the relative safety and accessibility of the park's three **ranger stations**. Of these, only **Rancho Frío**, a three-hour walk through the forest from El Real, is currently safe to visit – the park office can provide a guide (US$10) to take you here. There are plenty of trails into the forest from Rancho Frío, including one to the peak of Cerro Pirre (1200m), considered one of the best bird-watching locations in the world. The other two ranger stations, **Cruce del Mono** and **Río Balsas**, are currently off limits to visitors, though they may reopen if the security situation improves. Cruce del Mono is considered the best station for seeing mammals. To reach it you must first go to Boca del Cupe, a small village about two hours up the Río Tuira from El Real (ANAM should be able to help organize a boat), from where it's a five-hour walk. Rió Balsas is about eight hours by boat down the Tuira and up the Balsas – renting a boat from Yaviza or El Real could cost anything up to US$200.

The ranger stations all have basic **lodges** where you can stay for US$10 a night. You should take food, bedding, mosquito repellent and nets or coils, a water bottle and purifiers, and a first aid kit. Gifts for the park guards (food, drink, batteries, newspapers) are much appreciated. ANCON Expeditions (see p.731) have a lodge deep in the park at the old **Cana Mine**, another excellent birding location which is accessible only by private light aircraft.

La Palma

With a spectacular setting south of the Darién Highway overlooking the Golfo de San Miguel – where the silt-laden waters of the Río Tuira flow into the Pacific Ocean with rugged, densely forested mountains rising on all sides – **LA PALMA** is the capital of Darién province, a lively commercial and administrative centre despite its isolation. There's not much to do here, but it's a friendly place largely unaffected by the fear gripping much of Darién (though you should still register with the police on arrival) and a good base from which to rent a boat to take you along the coast and up the Río Sambú into the **Comarca Emberá Sambú**.

Practicalities

La Palma clings to a steep slope that runs down to the seafront, along which runs its only real street, lined with houses on stilts projected over the water. **Planes** arrive and depart for Panamá City (and occasionally continue to Sambú) from the airstrip at the northwest end of the street – Aeroperlas and Aviatur both have small offices there. **Boats** from Puerto Quimba arrive on the beach below the main street. There are sometimes boats direct to Panamá City, but no scheduled service – this route has been largely superseded by the connection to the Darién Highway, though if you ask around in town you may turn up something.

There are two clean and pleasant **places to stay**: the elegant *Hotel Biaquirú Bagará* (☎299 6224; ④), with a beautiful patio overlooking the gulf, and the *Pensión Takela*

(☎299 6213; ④). The *Crismary*, opposite the *Takela*, is the town's most popular **restaurant**, and there are also a couple of unnamed places on the main street. For a small town, La Palma has some lively **nightlife** – check out the *Cantina Brisas del Tuira* on the seafront for booming all-night reggae. There's a **telephone office** on the main street, and a **Banco Nacional** (Mon–Fri 8am–3pm, Sat 9am–noon) where you can change travellers' cheques and make Visa card cash withdrawals.

Comarca Emberá Sambú

From La Palma it's a fantastic one-day boat journey to the **Comarca Emberá Sambú**, passing the forested islands in the mouth of the Golfo de San Miguel, along the wild coastline fringed with mangroves and deserted beaches and up the tidal estuary of the Río Sambú to the twin towns of **Sambú** and **Puerto Indio**. Sambú is a trading town with a mostly black population, while Puerto Indio is the capital of the Emberá Comarca. The two stand on opposite sides of the river, joined by a footbridge that is effectively a frontier between two different worlds: as you cross, the squat concrete homes of the *libres* are replaced by the open-walled thatched houses of the Emberá, raised high on stilts. The Emberá are keen to promote ecotourism, and Puerto Indio is a good place to find a guide and a canoe to take you upriver, deep into the Comarca. Away from Puerto Indio the Emberá live in dispersed communities along the river banks, hunting, fishing and cultivating small gardens that provide the only break in the otherwise pristine vegetation.

Practicalities

There are no scheduled **boat** services up the Río Sambú, but if you ask around in La Palma you should be able to find a cargo boat that will take you in return for a contribution to fuel costs, though you may have to wait for several days. Midway between La Palma and the mouth of the Río Sambú at **Patiño**, about 30km along the coast, there's a nature reserve with facilities for visitors run by ANCON Expeditions – you should contact them in Panamá City (see p.731) well in advance if you want to stay there. Sambú also has an airstrip served by Aeroperlas and Aviatur light **aircraft** from Panamá City (usually via La Palma) several days a week, though arriving this way you miss out on the spectacular boat trip.

There are no hotels in Sambú or Puerto Indio and only one basic restaurant, but you can find **accommodation** with local families, though you should ask the permission of the headman of Puerto Indio first. Travelling further upriver into the Comarca is a real adventure – there are no facilities and you will have to bring all your own supplies and either camp or stay with local families. Goods such as machetes, batteries and preserved food are often more useful than cash when it comes to paying for accommodation.

KUNA YALA

Stretching some 375km along the northeastern Caribbean coast of Panamá from the Golfo de San Blas to Puerto Obaldia, **Kuna Yala** is the autonomous *comarca* of the Kuna (or Dúle), the only region in the country populated and governed exclusively by indigenous people. Although their territory includes the narrow strip of land between the sea and the peaks of the Serrania de San Blas, almost all the Kuna live on the **San Blas Archipelago**, a chain of coral atolls that runs the length of the forested coastline like a string of pearls. They say there is an island for every day of the year (in fact there are slightly more), some forty of which are inhabited, with populations ranging from

---

KUNA CULTURE

Fishing is the mainstay of the traditional Kuna subsistence economy, but they also culti-vate food crops in clearings in the forest on the mainland and collect coconuts to sell to Colombian trading ships. Kuna society is regulated by a system of highly participative **democracy**: every community has a *casa de congreso* where the *onmakket*, or congress, meets regularly. Each community also elects a *sahila*, usually a respected elder, who attends the Kuna General Congress twice a year. The General Congress is the supreme political authority in Kuna Yala, and it in turn appoints three *caciques* and sends repre-sentatives to the Panamanian National Assembly. Colonial missionaries struggled in vain to Christianize the Kuna, and though some of the Christian sects that have made so much headway elsewhere in Latin America have now established a foothold in Kuna Yala, most Kuna cling to their own **religious beliefs**, based above all on the sanctity of Nan Dummad, the Great Mother, and on respect for the environment they inhabit. The Kuna also have a rich tradition of **oral history**, and the ritual interpretation of their past by poet-historians plays an important part in decision-making and in maintaining their collective identity. Though Kuna men wear standard Western clothes, **Kuna women** wear gold rings in their ears and noses and blue vertical lines painted on their foreheads; they don piratical headscarves and bright bolts of trade cloth round their waists, their forearms and calves are bound in coloured beads, and their blouses are sewn with beau-tiful reverse-appliqué designs known as **molas**. Depicting everything from fish and birds to complex abstract designs and even political slogans, *molas* are the most popular sou-venir for visitors to Kuna Yala and are on sale all over Panamá.

Although it is idiosyncratic, it would be wrong to consider Kuna culture as entirely tra-ditional and unchanging – its very strength comes from the Kunas' ability to absorb those aspects of the outside world that suit them and adapt them to their needs. The Kuna have travelled the world as sailors, many work in the US bases, and thousands work and study in Panamá City and Colón. Of course, this integration with the outside world poses some problems – egalitarian traditions are gradually being eroded and some resources, particularly lobster, are being overexploited to satisfy market demand. But if their history is anything to go by, the Kuna are likely to find ways of resolving these prob-lems without losing their culture and their identity.

---

several thousand to single families living on narrow sandbanks which are all but sub-merged at high tide.

The untamed beauty of its forested coastline, palm-fringed islands, coral reefs and bounteous marine life make Kuna Yala a good destination for a beach holiday, though transportation is difficult and there are few facilities. The real appeal, though, is the opportunity to observe the unique culture and lifestyle of the Kuna themselves.

Some history

Historians still argue over whether the **tribes** the Spanish first encountered on the coasts of Darién were Kuna, but it is clear that by the mid-sixteenth century the Kuna were migrating into Darién from the great Atrató swamp in present-day Colombia. Gradually driven onto the north coast by war with the Spanish and with the Emberá, their historic rivals, they began moving to the relative safety and isolation of the islands in the nineteenth century. A treaty signed with the Spanish in 1787 guaranteed a measure of independence, but in the early twentieth century the authorities of newly independent Panamá initiated efforts to "civilize" the Kuna, sending police and mis-sionaries to the islands. This twin assault on Kuna culture and autonomy and the despoilation of their natural resources by outsiders provoked an explosive reaction. In 1925 the Kuna rose up in what they still proudly refer to as **"the Revolution"**, killing or expelling the Panamanian police garrison and declaring an independent republic.

The government sent a punitive expedition but a US warship standing offshore prevented further bloodshed – the Kuna had sent representatives to Washington to request assistance before the uprising – and a settlement was made by which the Kuna recognized Panamanian sovereignty in return for a degree of autonomy. The support of the US has never been forgotten: to this day while outsiders in general are referred to as *uaga*, a derogatory term, North Americans are known as *merki*, a superior category, making Kuna Yala one of the few places in the region where it is advantageous to be (or to be mistaken for) a North American. Protracted negotiations in the decades after the revolution led to the final recognition of Kuna Yala as an independent self-governing *comarca* in 1952. No non-Kuna can own land or property in the *comarca* and the Kuna General Congress is responsible for all administration in accordance with the Kuna's own constitution – a degree of political autonomy far greater than that of any other indigenous people in Latin America.

Visiting Kuna Yala

Though the Kuna are generally keen to promote **tourism**, they are determined to control its development and limit its negative impacts. When in Kuna Yala, particularly in the more remote areas, it is important to remember that you are a guest of the Kuna and must abide by their laws. Always ask **permission** from the local *sahila* when you visit or wish to stay on an island, and ask before **photographing** anybody (expect to pay about US$0.25 per photo, more for group shots). The Kuna are particularly sensitive about the *casas de congreso* and the cemeteries on the mainland – never enter or photograph these without permission. Some islands charge a **fee** for visitors and most will assign a **guide** to take you around and make sure you respect the Kuna's sometimes strict social codes – full or partial nudity and public displays of affection, for example, are frowned upon.

Pretty much every **tour company** in Panamá City (see p.731) can organize trips to Kuna Yala, some to exclusive resort hotels, but it is easy to visit the *comarca* independently. The few islands with any organized tourist **facilities** are concentrated in the western end of the archipelago in the Golfo de San Blas. Here you can stay in basic guesthouses or small hotels where meals and boat-trips – to other islands, beaches and snorkelling spots, or into the forests of the mainland – are included in the price. Away from these islands the possibilities for adventure are endless – there's no reason why you shouldn't fly to any of the other islands or mainland communities where, once you have received permission from the *sahila*, you can find a family to stay with and rent a boat to take you around. You can also – with permission – get a boatman to drop you on one of the many uninhabited islands to camp, though you will need to bring all your own food and water. If you are planning any kind of **long stay** in Kuna Yala, you need permission from the Congreso General Kuna office in Panamá City (☎225 5822), on the first floor of the Azteca Building at the corner of C 27 and Av Mexico. They also sell books of Kuna history and poetry in Kuna and Spanish, and publish a useful pamphlet, "Tourism in Kuna Yala".

By air

The easiest way to reach Kuna Yala is by **plane**. Almost all the forty or so inhabited islands and the twelve mainland communities have airstrips close by, which are served regularly by ANSA (☎315 0275 or 315 0299), Aviatur (☎315 0397 or 315 0314) and Aerotaxi (☎315 0275) light aircraft from Marcos A. Gelabert domestic airport in Albrook. Flights cost between US$25 and US$45 one way. The airstrips are often bigger than the islands themselves and located on the mainland, and a small arrival and departure fee is usually charged. If you need to return to Panamá City on a specific day, you should book in advance, as there may not be space on the plane, or, if there are no guaranteed passengers, it may not come at all. The light aircraft are also not a bad way to travel between islands. If you wait at the airstrip you may be able to persuade the pilot to take you on to another island, though sometimes you will have to settle for going where he is going. The fare is flexible and goes direct to the pilot, so feel free to negotiate.

By sea

You can also reach the islands – and travel between them – by **boat**, renting one or asking around and getting a lift. In addition, several Kuna-owned trading ships travel between Coco Solo port in Colón and the islands, but they are generally unwilling to carry outsiders, as are the Colombian ships from Turbo or Cartagena that tramp up and down the archipelago trading basic goods for coconuts. You may be able to get them to take you between islands, but remember that this is a wild coast, and many of the ships that pass along it are involved in smuggling. If you can get on one, they are the least expensive way to travel throughout the archipelago – the three- to five-day trip from Coco Solo to Puerto Obaldia won't cost you more than US$30, meals included.

Smaller canoes from the village of **Miramar** on the Costa Arriba in Colón province (see p.746) occasionally travel to the islands around El Porvenir to deliver fresh fruit and vegetables. Though it's not really worth trying to come into Kuna Yala this way – you don't really want to hang around in Miramar waiting for a boat – it's an exciting way to return from the islands: the boats all pass by the *Hotel San Blas* in Nalunega (see opposite), and are usually happy to take passengers back to the Costa Arriba for about US$10. The archipelago is also popular with **private yachts**, and you may find one that's prepared to take you to Colombia via the islands – try asking around at the Balboa Yacht Club in Panamá City (for more on travelling to Colombia by yacht, see p.758).

On foot

You can **walk** into Kuna Yala across the Serranía de San Blas from the village of El Llano, 70km east of Panamá City on the Darién Highway, a two-day journey passing through the pristine Nusagandi Nature Reserve (see below). There are plenty of other adventurous walking routes across the Serranía from the coast of Kuna Yala to the tributaries of the Chucunaque, which you can then descend by canoe to reach the Darién Highway, but for these you will need guides.

Nusagandi Nature Reserve

The semi-abandoned road that runs some 47km from El Llano on the Darién Highway across the Serranía de San Blas to the coast is the **best land route** into Kuna Yala, and is easy to follow without a guide. Built in the 1970s as part of General Torrijos's planned "conquest of the Caribbean", the road originally extended to the coast opposite the island of Cartí, bringing a wave of colonists to the borders of Kuna Yala, clearing the forest for agriculture and cattle-ranching. The Kuna General Congress acted swiftly in response to this threat to the territorial and ecological integrity of the region, establishing a **nature reserve** covering some 1000 square kilometres – the first such reserve in Latin America to be set up and administered by an indigenous people. Today the road is usually passable by 4WD as far as the park guard station and **nature lodge** at **Nusagandi**, 27km from El Llano.

Visiting the reserve

To visit Nusagandi you need **permission** from the Congreso General Kuna in Panamá City (see p.714); they charge US$5 per day plus US$10 per night to stay in the Nusagandi lodge (see below). It's a short drive from El Llano to Nusagandi if you have your own vehicle, or about four to six hours on foot – you may be able to hitch, but don't count on it. As the road climbs the deforested southern slopes of the Serrania de San Blas, the desolate landscape of scrubby cattle pasture and recently planted timber plantations gradually gives way to lush vegetation as it approaches the border of Kuna Yala. Perched just over the continental divide, **Nusagandi** has excellent views of the jagged, forest-covered ridges that march down to the Caribbean, and on clear days you can see the islands laid out in the shimmering waters of the Golfo de San Blas. Set amid the pristine forests, the rather run-down **nature lodge** sleeps up to forty people in dorms, with a communal bathroom and a kitchen – you should bring all the food you need, plus a little extra for the park guards. The forest around the lodge is rich in wildlife, particularly toucans and various species of monkey. **Trails** pass waterfalls and *miradores*, and the knowledgeable park guards are usually happy to act as guides. Not that you need to go far to see wildlife here – you can simply lounge in the hammock on the patio and watch innumerable bird species flit by while the eerie dawn chorus of the howler monkeys echoes across the treetops.

Beyond Nusagandi, the 20km road down to the **coast** is impassable to vehicles but easy to follow on foot. It's a tough walk (6–8hr) through pristine forest, longer if you stop to observe the wildlife, so you should leave early in the morning. For the last two hours the road levels out as it reaches the narrow coastal plain where the Kuna farms are concentrated, but even here you are unlikely to see another soul. The only place where the road is difficult to follow is after it crosses a bridge over the Río Carti Grande – you should veer left here. An hour beyond the bridge you emerge at the coast beside the Carti airstrip, where you can find a boat to take you over to Carti (see overleaf) or one of the other islands.

The islands

Set just off the Punta de San Blas on the northern tip of the gulf, the island of **EL POR-VENIR** is the administrative capital of Kuna Yala and home to the airport for the nearby islands of **Wichubuala**, **Nalunega** and **Ukuptupu**, which are those best prepared to receive visitors. You can **stay** here at the *Hotel Porvenir* (no phone; ⑦), where all meals and various boat trips are included, but there's little reason to do so – apart from the airstrip, the Kuna-controlled *gobernación*, and a small beach, there's nothing much to the place. The hotels on Wichubuala and Nalunega send boats to meet arriving planes, and you are better off heading onto one of these straight away.

On **Nalunega**, the *Hotel San Blas* (☎290 6528; ⑥) is the biggest, longest established and best-value hotel on the islands. Fenced off from the village with its own stretch of beach, it offers a choice of basic rooms in a modern concrete building or cooler sand-floored cabins on the pleasant beach in front. Bathrooms are shared. The owner and several of the staff speak some English, and snorkelling equipment is available to rent. On **Wichubuala** the pleasant *Kuna Niskua* (☎225 5200 or 259 3610; *kunaniskua @hotmail.com*; ⑦) has pleasant rooms in the midst of the community. Between the two, *Cabañas Ukuptupu* (☎220 4781; ⑦) occupies the former Smithsonian marine research station, built on a tiny semi-submerged coral outcrop with cool, well-built rooms connected by walkways over the sea. Rates in these three hotels are good value when you consider they include three decent meals a day, usually with fish and sometimes with lobster, and numerous boat excursions to pristine beaches, busy Kuna communities or into the forests of the mainland. The most popular excursion is to **Achutupu** or Dog Island, where a wrecked Colombian cargo just off shore makes for excellent snorkelling.

CROSSING INTO COLOMBIA

As well as the hazardous land route through the Darién Gap (see p.751), you can also **cross into Colombia** along the coasts. Although there is no scheduled passenger boat service between Panamá and Colombia on the Caribbean side, several **private yachts** carry passengers between Colón and the Colombian city of Cartagena on an informal basis. This adventurous trip takes three or four days, passing through the San Blas Archipelago, and should cost about US$200 per person plus food – about the same as a flight to Cartagena. At time of writing three yachts were running this trip: the US-owned *Bonamanzi* (*cartagenasailing@hotmail.com*); the *Calamoro* (*calamoro@hotmail.com*); and a Belgian-owned boat (*mygreengo@hotmail.com*) – though these are not permanent operations and are bound to change. The *Voyager International Hostel* in Panamá City (see p.717) usually has up-to-date information on which yachts are carrying passengers on this route, and you can always ask around at the yacht clubs in Cristobal (Colón) or Balboa (Panamá City).

You can also enter Colombia on foot from **Puerto Obaldia**, a remote border outpost at the far southeastern extreme of Kuna Yala, served by light aircraft from Panamá City. It has a basic pensión and a couple of restaurants. After going through customs and *migración*, you can walk or take a motorboat down to Capurgana, a small fishing village and incipient holiday resort on the Colombian coast. From Capurgana boats head across the Gulf of Urabá to Turbo, where you must register with DAS, the Colombian agency that deals with immigration, and there are also regular light aircraft flights to Medellin and Cartagena.

On the **Pacific side**, occasional boats from the Muelle Fiscal in Panamá City run down the coast of Darién to **Jaqué**, 90km due south of La Palma (20hr), and sometimes continue to Juradó and Bahía Solano in Colombia (3 days), from where there are onward flights to Quibdó, Medellin and Turbo. You can get an exit stamp from the *migración* at the dock in Panamá City, but should check on entry requirements with the Colombian consulate there. Be warned, though, that the whole border area is busy with **guerrilla and paramilitary activity**: the police garrison at Obaldia has been attacked several times; the naval base at Juradó was destroyed by guerrillas in 1999, leading most of the town's population to flee to Panamá; and Turbo is at the centre of Urabá, the most violent region in Colombia.

Cartí Suitupo and the Cayos Holandeses

One of a cluster of densely populated islands close to the mainland about 10km south of El Porvenir, **Cartí Suitupo** (Cartí) is a busy community where about 1500 Kuna live crammed onto a tiny patch of land. There's a small, basic *dormitorio* (③), and a *cafeteria* serving basic **meals**, though these are not really oriented towards tourists, and if you stay here you'll be living in the midst of the community. There's no beach, but you can easily hire a boatman to take you out during the day, and there's even a small **museum** (US$2), which has a collection of Kuna arts and crafts including day-to-day objects and the miniature carved canoes used in funeral ceremonies. Cartí's **airstrip** is on the mainland, where the path down from Nusagandi emerges onto the coast. About 16km east of Cartí the airstrip at **Rio Sidra** serves the island of **Narasgandup**, where you can stay at the pleasant *Cabañas Narasgandup* (☎259 2746; ⑧) – the price here includes all meals, transport to and from the airstrip, excursions and the use of a private beach.

About 20km northeast of Río Sidra, the outlying chain of islands known as the **Cayos Holandeses** are amongst the most pristine and beautiful in the archipelago, and an excellent spot for snorkelling. To reach them, you'll have to arrange for a boat to come and fetch you at the end of your stay – it takes about two to three hours to and from El

Porvenir. Sea conditions can be rough, though, and you may have to pay up to US$50 to persuade someone to take you. One of the Cayos' few residents, Arnulfo Robinson, rents rustic cabañas (☎299 9058; ④) and prepares simple meals, though it's a good idea to bring drinking water and other supplies with you.

Narganá and Corazon de Jesús

For some Kuna the twin islands of **Narganá** and **Corazon de Jesús**, 40km east of El Porvenir, are a nightmare vision of what the future of Kuna Yala might be like if the *uaga burba* – the spirit of the outsiders – continues to spread. Few women here wear traditional dress; the buildings are mostly of concrete rather than cane and palm; there is a **Banco Nacional** but no *casa de congreso*; and whereas most communities do not allow missionaries onto their islands, here five different Christian sects compete for possession of the islanders' souls. In some ways this makes it an interesting place: the frontline in a long-standing cultural struggle. The fiercely traditional community of **Isla Tigre**, close by, offers a profound contrast and the surrounding coastline is very beautiful, with extensive coral reefs and many uninhabited islands with good beaches. You can **stay** at the very basic and dirty *Hotel Cadenita de Oro* (②), and there are several simple **restaurants**.

Ailigandi

Some 60km further along the coast towards Colombia, **Ailigandi** is an important regional centre with a population of some two thousand, many of whom are Baptists. You can **stay** at the *Hotel Ikasa* (☎224 8492; ④), a simple, clean concrete construction with a basic restaurant, or you may be invited to stay in someone's home. There's also a small communal **restaurant**. Once again, there is plenty of scope for excursions, and the island is also home to the **Hogar Cultural Kuna**, where wood carving, pottery, weaving and *mola* design are taught.

travel details

BUSES

Panamá City to: Meteti (3–4 daily; 7–8hr).

Meteti to: Panamá City (3–4 daily; 7–8hr); Puerto Quimba (every 45min; 30min); Yaviza (1–2 daily; 2–3hr).

Puerto Quimba to: Meteti (every 45min; 30min).

Yaviza to: Meteti (1–2 daily; 2–3hr).

BOATS

La Palma to: Puerto Quimba (10 daily; 45min).

Puerto Quimba to: La Palma (10 daily; 45min).

FLIGHTS

Panamá City to: El Real (1–2 daily; 50min); Kuna Yala* (2–3 daily Mon–Fri; 30min–1hr 15min); La Palma (1–2 daily; 45min); Sambú (4–5 weekly; 1hr 20min).

*flights to (from northwest to southeast): El Porvenir; Río Sidra, Río Azúcar, Corazón de Jesús, Río Tigre, Playa Chico, Tupile, Ailigandi, Achutupo, Mamitupo, Ogobsucun, Mansucum, Mulatupu, Tubuala, Caledonia and Puerto Obaldia.

CHAPTER 37

WESTERN PANAMÁ

W estern Panamá is divided into two by the rugged **Cordillera Central**, which begins not far west of the Panamá Canal and runs some 400km to Costa Rica. North of the mountains, the undeveloped Atlantic coast is covered in dense rainforest and inhabited by isolated indigenous groups. South of the mountains, the drier and more fertile coastal plain is largely deforested and heavily settled. This agricultural heartland is known as **el interior** (its inhabitants are known as *interioranos*), the homeland of *ladino* rural culture.

Before the arrival of the Spanish, this Pacific coastal region was home to the most sophisticated **indigenous societies** in the country, and it was here that the conquistadors met the fiercest resistance, especially that led by **Urraca**, a chieftain whose head now decorates the one cent coin. Gradually these societies were defeated and either assimilated or driven into the infertile highlands – where their descendants, the **Ngobe-Buglé**, still live – while the forests were cleared for agriculture and ranching.

The region's towns – **Penonomé**, **Chitré**, **Las Tablas**, **Santiago** and **David** – are dull, provincial market centres, and the surrounding agricultural lands scarcely match the untamed wildernesses found elsewhere in the country. Even so, there are several places worth checking out as you head west towards Costa Rica or Bocas del Toro. Close to Panamá City are some spectacular Pacific **beaches** and the cool mountain resort town of **El Valle**; while slightly further west near Penonomé the remnants of the pre-Columbian societies that dominated the region can be seen at **Parque Arqueológico el Caño**. South of the Interamericana is the **Peninsula de Azuero**, a fascinating agricultural region famed for its religious fiestas in which early Spanish folkloric traditions survive almost unchanged. In addition, although the peninsula is largely deforested, much of its coastal ecology remains well preserved. Surrounded by coral reefs, **Isla Iguana Wildlife Reserve** is one of the best places in Panamá for divers and snorkellers, while at **Isla Cañas Wildlife Reserve**, to the south, sea turtles arrive every year in their thousands. In the far west, near the Costa Rican border, the Cordillera Central rises to its highest peaks in the **Chiriquí Highlands**, a beautiful region of extinct volcanoes, dense cloudforests and idyllic mountain villages.

West from Panamá City

West of Panamá City the **Interamericana** runs along a narrow plain squeezed between the Pacific and the slopes of the Cordillera Central. The landscape becomes noticeably more **arid** as you travel west – deforestation and *El Niño* have made the crescent formed by the coastal plains of Coclé and Herrera provinces the driest region in Panamá, and the sugar-cane fields depend on irrigation water from the rivers that run down from the mountains to the north. At the border of Coclé province, 23km beyond Aguadulce and 213km from Panamá City, the road forks at Divisa: the Interamericana

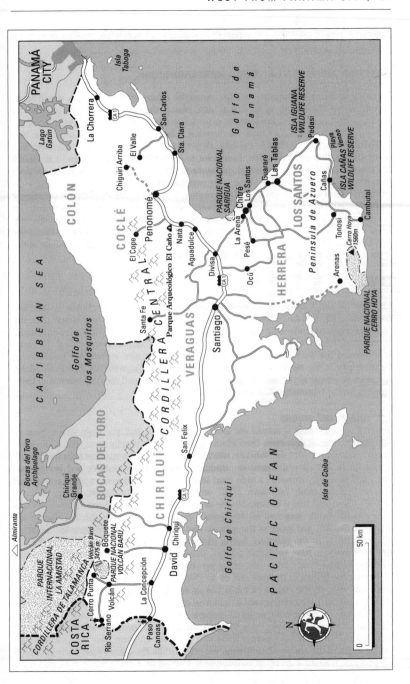

continues west to Santiago, the capital of Veraguas Province, while another road turns
south into the Peninsula de Azuero.

Beaches along the Carretera Interamericana

From Panamá City the Interamericana crosses the Bridge of the Americas, which soars
1600m across the mouth of the canal, and passes through the satellite town of La
Chorrera as it heads west towards the province of Coclé. For 50km beyond the village
of Bejuco, 29km west of La Chorrera, the coast is lined with some of the most beautiful
and popular Pacific **beaches** in Panamá, all just a few kilometres from the highway and
accessible by taxi or local buses. From east to west **Playas Gorgona** and **Coronado**
are the most fashionable weekend destinations for the wealthy residents of Panamá
City, while **Playa San Carlos** is the most popular with surfers.

Playa Santa Clara, 30km east of Penonomé, is probably the loveliest – a seemingly
endless stretch of white sand lapped by usually calm waters. There's a **restaurant**, *Las
Veraneras* (daily 10am–7.30pm), which serves decent fish and seafood, and locals rent
horses close by. They also have four delightful self-catering **cabañas** overlooking the
sea, *Cabañas Veraneras* (☎993 3313; ⑥), which sleep up to five, though if you eat at the
restaurant they won't mind if you camp on the beach.

El Valle

Just beyond San Carlos, 96km west of Panamá City, a side road climbs up into the
cordillera to **EL VALLE**, a small village set in an idyllic fertile valley that was once the
crater of a volcano, now long extinct. At 600m above sea-level, El Valle is comparatively cool, and the surrounding countryside is good for walking or horse-riding. The area
is renowned for its flowers and **orchids**, and is a popular retreat for residents of
Panamá City at the weekend, when it gets very busy. Otherwise it's a peaceful place,
where most people get around by bicycle or on horseback and the only noise is of lawn-
mowers and of hummingbirds buzzing among the flowers.

The village and around

Everything in El Valle is spread out along Avenida Principal, the main street. Next to
the church, a small **museum** (Sun 10am–2pm; US$0.25), run by nuns, has some good
exhibits on local history and folklore, while the nearby Sunday **market** sells fruit, handicrafts (including carved soapstone, traditional earthenware pottery and woven baskets) and flowers. Opposite, a side road leads up to **El Nispero**, a plant and orchid
nursery and zoo (daily 7am–5pm; US$2) where you can see monkeys, tapirs, the cele-
brated golden frog that is endemic to the area, and birds ranging from macaws and toucans to such exotic wonders as the *Gallina Inglés* – the English chicken. Cages are
cramped, though, and some of the animals look pretty miserable. Beside the church a
side road leads to the **thermal baths** (daily 8am–noon & 1–5pm; US$1) by the Río
Anton. Reputed to have medicinal powers, these make a great place to relax after a day
walking in the countryside – one of the joys of a visit to El Valle.

Across the bridge at the east end of Av Principal the road forks three ways. A thirty-minute walk up the right fork takes you up to **El Chorro Macho** (daily 8am–4pm;
US$2), a 35-metre waterfall set amid the forest of a private ecological reserve; for anoth-
er US$2 you can also use the delightful natural swimming pool in the river. The reserve
also operates exciting cable rides through the forest canopy, the so-called **"Canopy
Adventure"** (☎983 6547), costing US$40 for just over an hour. The left fork from the
bridge leads to the smaller **Las Mozas** waterfall, while the centre fork leads after a fifteen-minute walk to a group of **petroglyphs**. Carved on a huge white rock and high-

lighted with chalk and charcoal, the petroglyphs are pre-Columbian abstract designs, including spirals and anthropomorphic and zoomorphic figures; nobody knows when or by whom they were carved, let alone their significance. Further afield, innumerable trails climb up into the **cloudforests** of the surrounding mountains, which are excellent for bird-watching – try following the path up behind the petroglyphs to the peak of **La India Dormida**, the mountain ridge that looms over the valley to the west and whose silhouette resembles the sleeping form of a legendary Indian princess.

Practicalities

There's no bus terminal in El Valle, but all **buses** run down Av Principal. Buses from Panamá City (2hr 30min) arrive every 35 minutes or so between 7.30am and 6.30pm, and minibuses arrive every 45 minutes from San Carlos (20min). The small **IPAT** office (Wed–Sun 8.30am–4.30pm; ☎983 6474), in a kiosk next to the market, has lots of information, including good maps. The **Banco Nacional** has an ATM on Av Principal by the turn-off for El Nispero. The *Hotel Don Pepe* offers **Internet** access to clients (the *Residencial El Valle* is also planning to open an Internet café). You can rent **bicycles** (US$2/hr) from the *Residencial Don Pepe*, and **horses** (US$3.50/hr) from a little kiosk near the *Hotel Campestre*, about ten minutes' walk out of town to the northeast. In both cases you'll probably get a better price on weekdays, or for a whole day.

There's a good range of **accommodation** in El Valle, though it's relatively expensive and tends to fill up at weekends, when prices go up. The *Santa Librada* restaurant (☎983 6376; ②–③) on Av Principal is the best budget option, with several rooms of varying size, comfort and price; while the *Motel Niña Delia* (☎983 6110; ③), also on Av Principal, has small gloomy rooms and a pleasant patio and garden. Moving upmarket, the *Hotel Don Pepe* (☎983 6425, *www.pmaol.com/hotelpepe.htm*; ⑤) and the very similar *Residencial El Valle* (☎983 6536; ⑤), next to each other beside the market on Av Principal, both offer modern, comfortable rooms. The most luxurious place is the *Hotel Los Capitanes* (☎983 6080, fax 983 6505, *www.panamainfo.com/loscapitanes*; ⑦), which has spacious, well-furnished rooms set amid beautiful grounds. Locals sometimes rent out rooms – ask at IPAT.

There are several **restaurants** in town, though most only open at weekends. Of those that are open daily, the *Santa Librada*, on the main street, is by far the best, serving very good típica food; its sister restaurant, the *Santa Librada II*, is much the same. For basic, filling and inexpensive meals, try the restaurant inside the covered market. Opposite the market, *Pinocchio's* serves decent pizza and ice cream. The restaurant at *Los Capitanes* serves good but expensive international cuisine, with main courses from about US$10.

Moving on from El Valle you can either take a direct bus to Panamá City or a minibus to San Carlos, where you can flag down buses heading in either direction along the Interamericana.

Penonomé

Founded in 1581 as a *reducción de Indios* – a place where conquered indigenous groups were forcibly resettled so as to be available for labour service – and briefly the capital of the isthmus after the destruction of Panamá Viejo, the lively market town of **PENONOMÉ** was named after Nomé, a local chieftain cruelly betrayed and executed here by the Spaniards after years of successful resistance. Now the capital of the province of Coclé, apart from its small museum Penonomé doesn't have much to see, though it makes a good enough base for exploring the surrounding area.

From the bus terminal on the Interamericana Penonomé's busy commercial main street, called both Via Central or Avenida J. D. Arosemena, runs a few hundred metres down to the **Plaza 8 de Diciembre**, which features a statue of Simon Bolívar and the inevitable bandstand. It's flanked by several government buildings and the unspectacular **cathedral**. From the square, a short walk down C Damian Carles and a right turn opposite the covered market brings you to the run-down **Museo de Historia y Tradición Penonomeña** (Tues–Sat 9am–12.30pm & 1.30–4pm, Sun 9am–1pm; US$1), which has some good pre-Columbian ceramics decorated with abstract designs and colonial religious art. The streets around the market bustle with campesinos from local villages selling agricultural produce (and spending much of the proceeds in the town's many bars).

Practicalities

Buses from Panamá City arrive at the **terminal** at the intersection of Via Central and the Interamericana every twenty minutes or so, and it's easy to flag down any through bus going east or west along the Interamericana. There are two **places to stay**: the *Hotel Dos Continentes* (☎997 9325, fax 997 9390; ④) opposite the bus terminal is good value, with clean, spacious but unimaginative rooms with air-conditioning; rooms at the friendly *Residencial El Paisa* (☎997 9242; ③), just off the plaza on Av Manuel Amador Guerrero, are cramped and slightly stuffy.

Of the town's several **restaurants**, the best is at the *Hotel Dos Continentes*, which is popular and particularly good for breakfast. There are three restaurants called *Gallo Pinto*, each with menus as original as their name – the best is opposite *El Paisa*. On the Interamericana, *Las Tinajas* is a reasonably inexpensive self-service place, while *Parillada*, also on the Interamericana, offers reasonable pizza and barbecued meat. The **post office** is on Via Central, as is the **Banco del Istmo**, which has an ATM and changes travellers' cheques.

Around Penonomé: Chiguiri Arriba

From the market area in Penonomé, *chivas* (flatbed trucks converted to carry passengers) head off to villages scattered in the folds of the cool, forested mountains that rise to the north. One of these, **Chiguiri Arriba**, 29km away, makes an easy day-trip (1–2 *chivas* daily; leaving about 10am, returning in the afternoon; 1hr 20min; US$1.50). There are plenty of good hiking trails, spectacular views and a thirty-metre waterfall nearby – local children will happily guide you there for a small tip. Some 2km before the village is *La Posada del Cerro La Vieja* (☎263 7890 or 223 4553; ⑧), a luxurious **eco-resort** set amid beautiful gardens and a private forest reserve. Rates include all meals and guided excursions, on foot or horseback. They can also arrange longer trips across the mountains to El Valle or down through pristine rainforest to the Caribbean coast by trail and canoe along the Río Indio, though there's no reason – with a little Spanish, a local guide and the right supplies and equipment – why you can't do this independently.

El Caño Archeological Park and Natá

Some 25km west of Penonomé on the Interamericana, the **Parque Arqueológico El Caño** (Tues–Sat 9am–4pm, Sun 9am–1pm; US$1) is the most impressive pre-Columbian site in Panamá – though that's not saying very much, and compared to the Maya wonders elsewhere in Central America there's very little to see. An important ceremonial site from 500 to about 1200 AD, El Caño later became a cemetery that was still in use after the Conquest – horse remains have been found in some of the tombs – but the hundreds of stone statues that formed what was described as the "Temple of the Thousand Idols" were illegally decapitated by US archeologist Hyatt Verril in the early twentieth century, and the best of their zoomorphic and anthropomorphic heads are now in New York. Set amid cornfields and plagued by mosquitoes, the site consists of several funeral mounds, one of which is excavated and open to view, and lines of decapitated standing stones whose significance can only be speculated – some believe they were part of an astronomical observatory. A small **museum** displays ceramics and lesser stone statues, but otherwise there's nothing to delay you for more than half an hour. To reach the site from the marked turn-off on the Interamericana, walk ten minutes to the village of El Caño, beyond which it's another 25 minutes' walk.

A few kilometres beyond El Caño, **NATÁ DE CABALLEROS** was founded by Gaspar de Espinoza in 1522 and acted as the forward base for the Spanish conquest of what was then known as Veragua, facing continuous attack from the indigenous forces led by Urracá. Resistance was finally overcome in 1556, and Natá became an agricultural centre supplying the now long-abandoned gold mines on the Atlantic coast. Today Natá is a quiet backwater, notable only for the **Church of Santiago Apóstol**, built in 1522 and possibly the oldest church on the American mainland still in use. Set on the main square about five minutes' walk from the highway it boasts a fine Baroque facade and an intricately carved colonial altar.

The Peninsula de Azuero

Jutting out into the Pacific Ocean like the head of an axe (or adze, which is what *azuero* means), the largely deforested **Peninsula de Azuero** was one of the earliest regions of Panamá to be settled by Spanish colonists and is considered the cradle of Panamanian rural tradition and folklore. Predominantly agricultural, the landscape here is dry and scrubby, dotted with small villages little changed from colonial times, its narrow roads often blocked by herds of cattle being led to market by cowboys on horseback or the occasional ox-drawn cart. In many ways visiting the Azuero is like going back to seventeenth-century rural Spain – the peninsula's Spanish heritage is clearly evident in the traditional handicrafts and folkloric costumes, and above all in the vibrant religious **fiestas**.

Between fiestas, the principal towns of **Chitré** and **Las Tablas** are sleepy market centres where little happens, but the historic town of **Los Santos** and the eerie desert landscape of **Parque Nacional Sarigua**, both near Chitré, make interesting excursions. Further south, meanwhile, the peninsula's rich coastal ecology is well preserved. The small town of **Pedasi** is surrounded by deserted white-sand beaches, while the nearby **Isla Iguana Wildlife Reserve**, an offshore island surrounded by coral reefs, is one of the best places for snorkelling or scuba diving on the Pacific coast of Panamá. The rarely visited **Isla Cañas Wildlife Reserve**, further west, is an excellent place to observe nesting sea turtles. The mountainous western half of the peninsula, scarcely penetrated by roads, is home to the **Parque Nacional Cerro Hoya**, among the most beautiful and remote national parks in Panamá, accessible only by boat or by a long, unpaved road from Santiago.

Chitré

The capital of Herrera province and the largest town on the peninsula, **CHITRÉ** is a quiet market centre where life is conducted at a leisurely pace. Other than its small museum there's not much to see, but it's a good base for exploring the rest of the peninsula and its main transport hub. Chitré centres on the Parque Union, with the usual bandstand, benches and trees, flanked on one side by the **cathedral**, built at the turn of the century, with an impressive vaulted wooden roof. The cathedral faces down Av Herrera, the town's main street – walk down a block and turn left on C Manuel Correa to reach the **Museo de Herrera** (Tues–Sat 8am–noon & 1–4pm, Sun 8–11am; US$1), three blocks away. Set in an elegant colonial mansion, the museum has a collection of

---

FIESTAS IN THE PENINSULA DE AZUERO

The Peninsula de Azuero is famous throughout Panamá for its many **religious fiestas**, usually honouring a particular patron saint. Many date back almost unchanged to the days of the early settlers, and represent the most obvious expression of the region's Spanish heritage. Religious **processions** are accompanied by traditional music, fireworks and costumed folkloric dances which are as **pagan** as they are Catholic. Listed below are just a few of the major events; every village and hamlet has its own fiesta and there's almost always one going on somewhere – IPAT in Los Santos has good information on all these.

Jan 6 Fiesta de Reyes and Encuentro del Canajagua in Macarcas.
Jan 19–22 Fiesta de San Sebastian in Ocu.
Feb (date varies) Carnaval in Las Tablas (and everywhere else in the country).
March/April (date varies) Semana Santa, celebrated most colourfully in La Villa de Los Santos, Pesé and Guararé.
Late April Feria International del Azuero in La Villa de Los Santos.
June (date varies) Corpus Christi in La Villa de Los Santos.
June 24 Patronales de San Juan in Chitré.
June 29–30 Patronales de San Pedro y San Pablo in La Arena.
July 20–22 Patronales de La Santa Librada and Festival de la Pollera in Las Tablas.
Aug 15 Festival del Manito in Ocú.
Sept 24 Festival de la Mejorana in Guararé.
Oct 19 Foundation of the District of Chitré, in Chitré.
Nov 10 The "first cry of independence" in La Villa de Los Santos.

pre-Columbian pottery from the surrounding area and a good display on local folklore and customs, featuring traditional masks, costumes and musical instruments.

Practicalities

Buses from Panamá City pull in at the **terminal** on the outskirts of town, about ten minutes' walk from the centre. The **IPAT** office for the entire peninsula is in neighbouring Los Santos (see opposite). The best **hotel** is the *Rex* (☎996 4310, fax 996 4310; ④) on Parque Union, which has comfortable rooms with TV and a/c. The *Hotel El Prado* (☎996 4620 or 996 6859; ③), on Av Herrera near the cathedral, and the *Hotel Santa Rita* (☎996 4610, fax 996 2404; ③), just around the corner on C Manuel Correa, are both similar, with small, clean rooms and a choice of fan or a/c; the former has a balcony overlooking the street which makes it a good place for watching fiestas.

Of the town's many **restaurants** the best is the *Meson del Rex*, in the *Rex* hotel, its Spanish ownership evident in its red-checked tablecloths and excellent, reasonably priced cuisine. Also on the Parque, the open-air *Restaurante Aire Libre* has a limited menu but great breakfasts; while the self-service *Restaurante Estrella #2* offers cheap and filling típica meals. The *Panadería Chiquita* on Av Herrera is good for cakes, sandwiches and huge pizzas. The **Banco del Istmo** is on the corner of C M. Correa and Av Perez. The **post office** (Mon–Fri 7am–6pm) is a block down Av Perez, and there's **Internet access** at Econoútiles (Mon–Fri 8am–6pm, Sat 8am–4pm), a couple of blocks south of the Cathedral on Av Central.

Moving on from Chitré, buses to Las Tablas, Santiago and to villages in the interior of the peninsula leave from the **terminal**, while buses to Los Santos (every 10min; 10min) can be flagged down at any of the stops on the main streets in town.

Parque Nacional Sarigua

Ten minutes north of Chitré, the village of **La Arena** is famous for its pottery, sold on the roadside by the potters themselves. Further north, just before the village of Parita, a side road leads into **Parque Nacional Sarigua**, eighty square kilometres of salt flats ringed by dense mangroves, forming one of the strangest landscapes in Panamá – a harsh, arid desert entirely devoid of vegetation due to occasional flooding by high tides. The salt flats have existed for thousands of years, but deforestation and sea winds that carry salt further inland are causing them to expand, threatening the livelihoods of local farmers. Not that the flats support no life at all – the area provides an excellent breeding ground for shrimp, which are farmed commercially and attract numerous wading birds. Indeed, archeological remains suggest that these marine resources provided the basis for Panamá's oldest known human settlements – pottery, graves and arrowheads from between 5000 and 1500 BC have been found in the area, as well as mounds of discarded shells. There are several other small wildlife reserves on this stretch of the coast, including **Playa El Aguilito**, about 6km out of town, one of the best places in Panamá for observing migrating birds – for information, go to the ANAM office (Mon–Fri 8am–4pm; ☎996 2946) on the road to Los Santos.

To **reach Sarigua**, take any bus heading north from Chitré, get off before Parita and walk 4.5km along the marked dirt road or catch the irregular minibus (1 daily) to the village of Puerto Limón, 1.5km from the park. There's a rangers' station at the entrance to the park and a small **visitors' centre** (daily 8am–4pm), where you'll be charged the US$3 entrance fee.

La Villa de los Santos and Guararé

South of Chitré just across the Río La Villa, **LA VILLA DE LOS SANTOS** – often referred to simply as Los Santos – is where the first Panamanian declaration of independence from Spain was made on November 10, 1821. A small, quiet town, Los Santos comes alive twice a year: to commemorate the **"Cry of Independence"** on November 10, and during the eight-day rum-fuelled fiesta of **Corpus Christi** in late May or early June.

The **IPAT** office (Mon–Fri 8.30am–4.30pm; ☎966 8037 or 966 8013) on Parque Bolívar, the centre of the town, is fairly helpful, with plenty of information on the peninsula. Also on the parque, the **Museo de la Nacionalidad** (Tues–Sat 9am–4.30pm, Sun 9am–1pm; US$1) has a small collection of colonial religious art and documents relating to the independence declaration. The building – a crumbling eighteenth-century house where the declaration was signed – is actually more interesting than its contents, with a garden filled with traditional handicrafts and agricultural tools. Just off the parque, the **Church of San Anastacio**, begun in the eighteenth century, features several intricately carved Baroque colonial altars.

From Los Santos the road continues 20km south to Las Tablas, passing through the small town of **GUARARÉ**. It's worth stopping here for the **Museo Manuel F. Zarate** (Tues–Fri 8am–4pm, Sat 8am–noon; US$1), behind the church on the main square, which has a fascinating exhibition on the folklore and fiestas of the peninsula, featuring masks, costumes, old photographs and a collection of the finest *polleras* (see overleaf). Manuel Zarate was a local teacher and musician who was dedicated to conserving the rich folk traditions of the Azuero and in 1949 began the **"La Mejorana" National Folkloric Festival**, a competition of traditional music, dance and costumes from all over Panamá that is still celebrated in Guararé every September 24.

Las Tablas

LAS TABLAS was founded in the seventeenth century by refugees fleeing by sea from Panamá La Vieja after its destruction by Henry Morgan. The settlers dismantled their ships to build the first houses, hence the town's name: Las Tablas means "the planks". Turn up at any other time of year and it's almost impossible to believe that this quiet colonial market settlement hosts the wildest **Carnaval** celebrations in Panamá, but for five days in February the place is overwhelmed by visitors from all over the country who come here to join in the festivities. The town divides into two halves – **Calle Arriba** and **Calle Abajo** – that fight a pitched battle with water, paint and soot on streets awash with a seemingly endless supply of Seco Herrerano, the peninsula's vicious firewater. The fiesta of **Santa Librada** in July is less raucous but just as colourful, and incorporates the **pollera fiesta** – the *pollera* being the painstakingly embroidered colonial-style dresses characteristic of the peninsula that are something of a national symbol, and which are produced in the town.

Practicalities
Buses from Panamá City arrive at the Shell station a few blocks from the square, while those from Chitré pull in to the Parque Porras. For the moment the only **place to stay** is the *Hotel Zafiro* (☎994 8200; ④) on Parque Porras, which has modern rooms with a/c and TV plus a balcony overlooking the square that makes it good, though noisy, at fiesta time, when prices go up. If you want to come here for carnaval you're better off staying in Chitré, though even there accommodation is booked up well in advance.

There are several basic **restaurants** on and around the square: *Los Portales*, one block up Av B. Porras, is the most popular, while the *Jardín Praga* opposite is also good, and has a massive dance hall that is the centre of things on Friday and Saturday nights. For **Internet access** try the *Café Internet Las Tablas* (Mon–Sat 9am–6pm) on Av B. Porras. **Banks** include the Banco del Istmo on the square and the BBVA one block away on Av B. Porras. If you're heading into **Cerro Hoya** (see p.770) from this side of the peninsula you should get information and permission from ANAM (Mon–Fri 8am–4pm; ☎994 7313) on the outskirts of town on the road to Pedasi; you don't need permission to visit Isla Iguana and Isla Cañas. **Moving on** from Las Tablas, buses for Pedasi (hourly; 45min) and Tonosi (hourly; 2hr 30min) leave from the square or Av B. Porras.

Pedasi and around

From Las Tablas, a road runs 42km south through cattle country to **PEDASI**, a friendly, uneventful little village best known as the hometown of President Mireya Moscoso and as the jumping-off point for **Isla Iguana**. The are a couple of **places to stay**, both on the main street: the long-established *Residencial Moscoso* (☎995 2203; ③–④), has comfortable rooms with a/c and TV, and less expensive ones with shared bath and fans; while the newer *Hotel Dim* (☎995 2303; ④) has large, well-ventilated rooms and a charming garden with hammocks and a patio. Pedasi's two **restaurants**, the *Angela* and *Las Delicias*, on the same street, serve típica food; the latter is slightly more expensive. **Buses** from Las Tablas and along the coast to Cañas via Playa Venao pass along the main street. As well as Isla Iguana, there are several good **beaches** near Pedasi – Playas Destilladeros, Las Almendras, El Toro and Punta Mala – some of them within walking distance of town; there are a few taxis in town if you want to head for those further afield.

Isla Iguana

Some 7km off the coast of Pedasi lies **Isla Iguana**, an uninhabited wildlife reserve sur-rounded by the most extensive **coral reefs** in the Bahía de Panamá. The reefs are com-posed of twelve different types of coral and teem with more than 540 species of fish, making Isla Iguana one of the best sites for **snorkelling** or **diving** in the country (though unless you come here with an organized tour from Panamá City you'll need to bring your own equipment). Quite apart from this, the island has white sand beaches, crystalline waters and a colony of some five thousand magnificent frigate birds, though, despite its name, iguanas are scarce – their meat remains a local delicacy. Between May and November you may see **whales**, and even the most inexperienced angler has a good chance of catching big game fish.

You can **rent a boat** to the island from **Playa El Arenal**, a short taxi ride or thirty-minute walk from Pedasi down the dirt road to the right just past the gas station on the road out to Las Tablas – either hotel in Pedasi will happily arrange this for you. Fishermen charge US$40 per return trip (25min each way) in boats that carry up to eleven people – on the weekends, you may find other visitors to share the cost. You should take all the food and drink you need. You can **camp** on the island or sling a hammock under a makeshift shelter on the beach – take plenty of drinking water and arrange for a boat to collect you the next day.

Playa Venao

Thirty kilometres west of Pedasi, the beautiful black-sand **Playa Venao** is great for **surfing**. There's an international competition here every November – come any other time, though, and you'll not find it crowded. *Jardin Vista Hermosa* (☎995 8107) serves inexpensive **fish** and seafood and rents very basic concrete **cabañas** on the beach that sleep up to three people for US$16 a day, though if you eat at the restau-rant they don't mind if you camp. Unfortunately, they haven't got round to renting out surfboards yet.

Isla Cañas Wildlife Reserve

Separated from the mainland by dense mangrove swamp and with a 14km beach on its seaward side, **Isla Cañas** is the most important **sea-turtle nesting site** on Panamá's Pacific coast, being frequented by four of the world's eight species of sea turtle. Though archeological evidence suggests that people have been coming to the island to hunt tur-tles and harvest their eggs for many centuries, it was only settled in the 1960s. The set-tlers, who now number some 400, have cleared most of the land for crops, but the eggs have always been their principal source of income. Since 1988, the hunting of turtles has been prohibited and a cooperative has been established to control the harvest. Members watch over the beaches at night and collect the eggs as soon as they are laid, keeping 80 percent for sale and consumption and moving the rest to a nursery where the turtles can hatch and return to the sea in safety. The reserve was officially estab-lished in 1994, protecting the mangroves as well as the marine life, and the turtle pop-ulation has made a dramatic recovery since. Come here between May and January and you will almost certainly see green, hawksbill or Olive Ridley turtles laying their eggs at night – the latter sometimes arrive in massive **"arribadas"** of several thousand in one night between August and November, a truly magnificent sight. From December to March there's a good chance of seeing the leviathan-like leatherback turtle, which can weigh over 800 kilos.

Surprisingly, given the popularity of the similar Parque Nacional Tortuguero in Costa Rica (see p.607), there is as yet almost no tourist development at Isla Cañas, so if you make it down here you will almost certainly have the place to yourself. The island is also very beautiful by day – you can hire a horse and ride along the endless white sand or get one of the locals to take you through the mangroves in a canoe.

Practicalities

To **reach Isla Cañas** take a bus heading for the village of **Cañas** from Pedasi or Tonosi and tell the driver you want to go to the island – the port is down a side road a few kilometres from the village but buses go there on request. **Canoes** wait at the port to take people to the island (US$0.5 per person) through channels cut in the mangroves, though at low tide you may have to wade through mud to reach it. Once on the island you should head for the ANAM office (☎995 8002) to pay the US$3 **visitors' charge** and get information.

The cooperative that manages the turtles – the Cooperativa Isleños Unidos – has three rustic but clean **cabañas** (②) with outside bath and mosquito nets. The latter are absolutely essential, as is insect repellent. The cooperative also has a small **restaurant**, though you should let them know in advance if you want to eat, and for a small tip (a few dollars should suffice) they will assign a member to take you out on the beach at night to see the turtles – they may even let you eat an egg or two, freshly laid and still warm. **Buses** to Pedasi (1–2 daily; 2hr) and Tonosi (1 daily; 1hr) from Cañas usually come down to the port to collect passengers.

Tonosi and Parque Nacional Cerro Hoya

From Cañas the road continues 25km west to **TONOSI**, a small town set in a green valley ringed by mountains. There are several basic **restaurants** and a couple of pensiones, but there's no reason to stay here unless you get stuck on your way to Isla Cañas. **Buses** to Las Tablas cut through the mountainous interior rather than following the coast via Pedasi. West of Tonosi the southwestern tip of the peninsula is covered by **Parque Nacional Cerro Hoya**, pretty much the last remaining area of natural forest in the Azuero. Rainforest-swathed mountains rise from pristine beaches to heights of more than 1500m, encompassing five distinct life zones. The park's existence is challenged by settlers anxious to continue logging and clearing land for cattle-ranching on its eastern fringes, and partly as a result ANAM is keen to promote ecotourism so locals can enjoy some of the economic benefits of conservation.

To visit the park you must first visit ANAM in Las Tablas (see p.768) for permission and information; they may also be able to help with transport. There are two routes into the park. **From Tonosi** you can get into the park by renting a boat from the nearby coastal village of **Cambutal** to take you to **Cobachón**, a coastal settlement just outside the park boundaries where you can camp near the ranger station or arrange to stay with local families. The easier approach however is by bus **from Santiago**, 98km along the west coast of the peninsula to the village of **Arenas**, where the park rangers will charge you the US$3 entrance fee and should be able to arrange transport by boat further down the coast to **Restingue**, another ranger station set on a beautiful beach with a network of trails into the surrounding forest. There's a basic refuge where you can stay for US$5 and cooking facilities, but you need to bring bedclothes and all your own food supplies.

Santiago and the route west

The easiest way to continue west from the Azuero is to return to the Interamericana at **Divisa**, though it's possible to cut across the interior – via Pesé, Las Minas and Ocú – from Chitré. From Divisa, the Interamericana continues 36km west to **SANTIAGO**,

Panamá's fourth biggest city and a busy market centre, though it's an incorrigibly dull and provincial place, with little reason to stay except to break a journey.

Practicalities

Buses to Panamá City and Chitré arrive and leave from the terminal on C 10, which links the Interamericana with Av Central in the city centre, while through buses heading for David pull in at the service station close to the *Hotel Gran David* on the Interamericana. The *Gran David* (☎998 4510; ③) is the most convenient **place to stay**, with comfortable rooms set around a central garden with a swimming pool and a good **restaurant**. There are several other upmarket places to eat on this stretch of the Interamericana, and if you do go into the centre of town it's worth stopping at the 24-hour *Cafe El Aire Libre*, on Av Central, which is very popular for snacks, sandwiches and excellent coffee, as well as more substantial meals. The only real reason to go into town however is to visit one of the **banks** (with ATMs) on Av Central, which include a Banco Nacional and a Banco del Istmo. There's also a helpful **IPAT** office (Mon–Fri 8.30am–4.30pm; ☎998 3929) on Av Central, which has plenty of information on Veraguas's largely neglected tourist attractions, and a cyber-café, the *Internet Zone Café*.

West to David

From Santiago the Interamericana continues west into the rich agricultural province of Chiriquí. A large area of the forested slopes of the Cordillera Central to the north and the Caribbean coast beyond is recognized as the **Comarca Ngobe-Buglé**. Commonly but erroneously referred to as the Guaymí, the Ngobe and Buglé (or Bokata) are two closely related peoples who together form the largest indigenous group in Panamá. Recognizable by their women's brightly coloured dresses, the Ngobe-Buglé travel widely throughout the provinces of Chiriquí and Bocas del Toro to work on the farms, ranches and banana and coffee plantations – migrant wage labourers on the rich lands that once belonged to their ancestors.

David and around

The only one of three Spanish settlements founded in the area in 1602 to survive repeated attacks from indigenous groups, **DAVID** developed slowly as a marginal and remote outpost of the Spanish Empire – as late as 1732 it was overrun and destroyed by British-backed Miskito groups raiding from Nicaragua. Only as settlement of Chiriquí increased in the nineteenth century did David begin to thrive as a marketing and transportation centre. Today, despite being a busy commercial city – the third largest in Panamá – and the focus of Chiriquí's strong regional identity, it retains a sedate provincial atmosphere. Hot and dusty, with unexceptional modern architecture spread out on a well-planned grid (the only surviving feature of the original colonial settlement), David has few attractions but is a good place to break a journey between Panamá City and Costa Rica, Bocas del Toro or the Chiriquí highlands – the last can be visited as a day-trip, though it's much better to stay up in Boquete or Cerro Punta if you have the time.

Arrival and information

Aeroperlas **flights** from Panamá City, Bocas del Toro and San José arrive at the **airport**, about 5km out of town, a US$2 taxi ride away. Aeroperlas (☎721 1195 or 721 1230) have an office just off the Parque on C A Nte. **Buses** from Panamá City, Almirante,

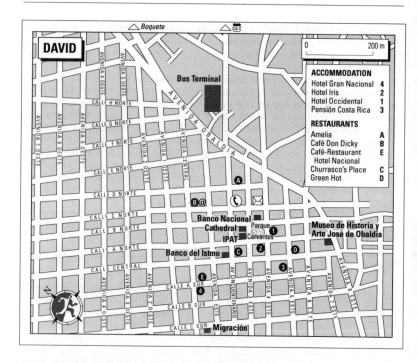

Boquete, Cerro Punta and Paso Canoas, and TRACOPA international buses from San José all leave from the terminal on Av Cincuentenario. If you're heading to San José or by express bus to Panamá City you should buy a ticket in advance. There's a self-service restaurant, *America* in the terminal and a left-luggage office that's open until 10pm. The not very helpful **IPAT** office (Mon–Fri 8.30am–4.30pm; ☎775 4120) is next to the cathedral on the Parque. If you're heading for Costa Rica and need a visa, the **Costa Rican consulate** (☎779 1923) is on the outskirts of town on Av 20 Este, while if you need a Panamanian visa extension or permission to leave the country, the **migración** (Mon–Fri 8am–3.30pm; ☎775 4515) is on Calle C Sur.

Accommodation

Accommodation in David is probably the best value in the country. There's a broad range, all in the city centre.

Hotel Gran Nacional, C A Sur, Av Central (☎775 2221 or 775 2222, fax 775 7729). Recently refurbished, this expensive but good-value establishment is by far the grandest place in town, with immaculate modern rooms featuring a/c, phone and TV. There's also a bar, pool, casino, and restaurant. ⑥.

Hotel Iris, Parque Cervantes (☎775 2251). Small, clean and comfortable rooms with a/c, TV and hot water, plus a café and communal balcony overlooking the Parque. ④.

Hotel Occidental, Parque Cervantes (☎775 4068 or 8340, fax 775 7424). Good value and spacious a/c rooms – those at the front of the building are brighter and share a balcony overlooking the Parque. ④.

Pensión Costa Rica, Av 5 Este, C A Sur (☎775 1241). Maze-like and ramshackle, with rooms of all shapes and sizes, each named after a different Panamanian town. A bit run-down and noisy, but friendly and full of character. ③.

The Town

David centres on **Parque Cervantes**, a good place to relax with a freshly squeezed sugar-cane juice and get your shoes shined in the shade of its immense trees. Three blocks southeast of the parque down C A Nte on the corner with Av 8 Este, the **Museo de Historia y Arte José de Obaldia** (Tues–Sat 8.30am–4.30pm; US$1) has a small but intriguing collection focusing on local history and culture, ranging from pre-Columbian artefacts and colonial religious art to relics from the Coto War with Costa Rica and photographs of David in the early twentieth century. The building is a beautiful colonial mansion that was home to successive generations of the distinguished Obaldia family – José was the founder of the province of Chiriquí, and later generations included presidents of both Colombia and Panamá.

Eating, drinking and entertainment

There are plenty of good-value **restaurants** in David, several of which double as nightspots at the weekends. Otherwise, entertainment generally revolves around the city's many nondescript bars and poolhalls, and a few discos – the *Brandywine*, a block away from *Pensión Costa Rica* on Av 5 Este, is a current favourite. You can catch the latest Hollywood blockbusters at the modern four-screen **cinema** next to the *Gran Nacional* hotel.

Cafés and restaurants

Amelia, C D Nte, Av Cincuentenario. One of several popular and inexpensive self-service restaurants on this block offering típica food. Daily 7am–3pm.

Café Don Dicky, C C Norte, Av Central. Very popular 24hr open-air café serving basic but good snacks and meals. Excellent sandwiches, fresh orange juice and the strongest coffee in town.

Café-Restaurante Hotel Nacional, Av Central, C A Sur. Decent pizza and meat and fish dishes for US$3–4 and a reasonable set lunch menu, but very slow service.

Churrascos Place, Av Cincuentenario, a block from the Parque. Bar and grill with good steaks and a set lunch menu for less than US$2. Open daily 24hr.

Green Hot, Av 5 Este, C Central. Small open-air restaurant serving good, inexpensive típica food. Particularly popular for breakfast.

Listings

Banks Banco Nacional (Mon–Fri 8am–3pm, Sat 9am–noon) is on Parque Cervantes; Banco del Istmo (Mon–Fri 8am–3pm) is a block away on the corner of Av Cincuentenario and C Central.

Car rental Budget (☎775 5597); Thrifty (☎721 2477).

Email and Internet access Internet Family, Av 1 Este, C C Norte (daily 8am–midnight).

Laundry Lavandería Panamá (Mon–Sat 7am–7pm), two blocks south of the Parque on Av 3 Este.

Post office The post office (Mon–Fri 7am–6pm, Sat 7am–5pm) is a block north of the Parque on C C Nte.

Shopping Deportes Hawaii, two blocks from the Parque on Av Cincuentenario, sells a wide range of snorkelling, camping and fishing equipment.

Telephone There's a Cable & Wireless office (daily 8am–4.30pm) on the corner of Av Cincuentenario and C C Norte.

On to Costa Rica

From David the Interamericana continues west 56km to the Costa Rican border at **PASO CANOAS**, passing through the saddle-making town of La Concepción, from where a side road heads up to Volcán and Cerro Punta (see overleaf). The **migración** at the border is open 24 hours, and there's an **IPAT** office (daily 6am–midnight) and a **Banco Nacional** where you can change travellers' cheques. Moneychangers will change Costa Rican currency. After passing through *migración* and customs (a formality unless you have anything to declare) you simply walk across the border, though queues for both can be long if international buses are passing through. If you're coming the other way, PADAFRONT **buses** for David (every 10min between 5am and 6pm; 1hr 20min) and Panamá City (11 daily; 7–9hr) depart from just beyond the border.

The Chiriquí Highlands

North of David rise the slopes of the **Cordillera Talamanca**, home to **Volcán Barú**, an extinct volcano that at 3475m is the country's tallest peak. These are **the Chiriquí Highlands**, a region of cloudforest-shrouded peaks, fertile valleys and mountain villages. The cool, temperate climate and stark scenery give the highlands a distinctly alpine feel, an illusion reinforced by the influence of the many European migrants who have settled here since the nineteenth century. Sadly, their agricultural success poses a grave threat to the survival of the region's spectacular **cloudforests**, which have been cleared at a devastating rate over the last fifteen years. Large areas are now protected by **Parque Nacional Volcán Barú** and **Parque Internacional La Amistad**, whose cloudforests are home to some of the country's most endangered **wildlife**, including jaguars, pumas, tapirs, harpy eagles and resplendent quetzals, and whose trails offer some of the best hiking in Panamá.

Two roads wind up into the highlands on either side of Volcán Barú. The first runs from La Concepción through the town of **Volcán** to **Cerro Punta**, the highest village in Panamá and the best base for visiting the cloudforests. The second climbs to **Boquete**, an idyllic coffee-growing town which has become a popular resort and is the best place from which to climb Volcán Barú. The trail that runs between the two, around the back of the volcano through the cloudforests, can be walked in a day.

The road to Cerro Punta

From La Concepción, the road to Cerro Punta winds up into the mountains through a lush valley with excellent views of the plain and the Golfo de Chiriquí before emerging at Hato de Volcán, usually known simply as **VOLCÁN**, a small town set on a broad plateau at the foot of Volcán Barú. Spread out along the road with no real centre, Volcán is a resort in its own right, and there are some good **trails** in the surrounding hills, including one to the protected Chiriquí lakes. You're actually better off staying in Cerro Punta if you want to visit the Parque Nacional Volcán Barú, but if you do choose **to stay** in Volcán, the comfortable *Motel California* (☎771 4272; ④), a US-style motel with hot water, close to the crossroads, is the least expensive option, and there are several **restaurants**, and a Banco del Istmo on the main road.

Cerro Punta

Set almost 2000m above sea level in a bowl-shaped valley surrounded by densely forested mountains, **CERRO PUNTA** is the highest village in Panamá, and often swathed in cloud. In the eighty or so years since it was settled, agriculture has expanded so rapidly that the town now produces some 80 percent of all the vegetables consumed in Panamá. This agricultural boom has been at the expense of the surrounding forests, however, and the local population is just beginning to face up to the consequences of deforestation, soil erosion and excessive pesticide use.

Despite these problems, the village and surrounding fields are still undeniably beautiful, filled with abundant flowers and buzzing with hummingbirds. The spectacular scenery, together with the cool, crisp mountain air (it even gets cold at night – a rare luxury in Panamá) makes Cerro Punta a perfect base for **hiking**, and the pristine cloudforests of La Amistad and Volcán Barú are both within easy reach. These parks are perhaps the best places in all Central America to catch a glimpse of the elusive quetzal, particularly in the dry season between January and April. Another worthwhile destination is the **Finca Dracula Orchid Farm** (daily 9am–3pm; US$7; ☎771 2070), about five minutes' walk beyond the *Los Quetzales Lodge and Spa* in Guadelupe (see below) and home to one of the most complete orchid collections in Latin America. Telephone in advance to arrange a visit.

Practicalities

Everything in Cerro Punta is spread out along the main road from David and a side road leading towards Parque Internacional La Amistad. **Buses** from David pull up on the one main street. There are a couple of **places to stay**: the *Hotel Cerro Punta* (☎771 2020; ⑤), on the main road, has clean, comfortable rooms with good views; while the friendly *Pensión Eterna Primavera* (no phone; ④), on the road towards La Amistad, has five overpriced and musty rooms. The newer *Los Quetzales Lodge and Spa* (☎771 2182, fax 771 2226, *www.losquetzales.com*; ⑥), in the hamlet of **Guadelupe**, 3km north of Cerro Punta, has pleasant rooms in a chalet-like building and a cramped but clean dormitory (US$12 per person). They can also organize tours with horses and guides into the parks and have three wonderful self-catering *cabañas* in the cloudforest, where you can watch quetzals and up to ten different species of hummingbird from your balcony while you eat breakfast – an amazing experience, if a bit steep at about US$100 a night. All the above have hot water. All buses to and from Cerro Punta collect and drop off passengers in Guadelupe – just let the driver know that's where you want to go.

The *Hotel Cerro Punta* has a reasonable **restaurant** with meals from about US$5, and there are several places in the village where you can get decent, inexpensive *típica* meals and excellent *batidos* – creamy milkshakes made with local strawberries and blackberries. In Guadelupe, the bakery and pizzeria at *Los Quetzales* is better than the rather overpriced restaurant upstairs; better still is the nearby *Refrescería La Canelita*, which is good for coffee, snacks, seafood and chicken.

Parque Internacional La Amistad

Covering 4000 square kilometres of rugged, forested mountains on either side of the border with Costa Rica, **Parque Internacional La Amistad** forms a crucial link in the "biological corridor" of protected areas running the length of Central America. Encompassing some nine life zones, the park supports an incredible biodiversity, including more than four hundred different bird species, making it the most important park in Panamá after Darién. Although almost all the Panamanian section of the park is in Bocas del Toro, it is only accessible from the Pacific side of the country.

To **get to the park** from Cerro Punta, walk or take a minibus to **Las Nubes**, a few kilometres away down the well-signposted side road. There's a permanently staffed **park office** here, where you must pay the US$3 admission charge; they also have an exhibition centre and a **refuge** (US$5 per night) – bring your own food and, ideally, a sleeping bag, as it gets cold at night. There are two well-marked **trails**, with *miradores* offering excellent views of the four highest mountains in Panamá (at least before the cloud descends) and a 55m waterfall, but though it teems with birds, the forest immediately around Las Nubes is secondary growth. The area was heavily deforested in the early 1980s when one of Noriega's cronies established an illegal cattle ranch here – the park office was his holiday home – and is only just beginning to recover. Longer trails lead into the virgin cloudforest further away, but you'll need to get one of the park guards to guide you, which they're usually happy to do.

The quetzal trail to Boquete

From Guadeloupe a partially paved road winds 6km up the western slope of Volcán Barú to **Respingo**, a park guard station at the entrance to **Parque Nacional Volcán Barú**, where the US$3 admission fee is rarely charged. There's no refuge, but you can camp. From Respingo **the quetzal trail** runs around the northern flank of the volcano to Boquete, a four- to six-hour hike, mostly downhill, through spectacular cloudforest. For the first hour or so the trail plunges down a steep valley and is difficult to follow, so you should get one of the park guards to guide you as far as a point known as La Victoria, beyond which the trail is easy to follow. It runs along the Río Caldera and eventually becomes a track before emerging at **Alto Chiquero**, another park guard station. From here it's another hour's walk to the tarmac road above Boquete, where you can hitch or walk the last few kilometres into town – take a left turn when you reach the tarmac. Walking the trail in the other direction, from Boquete to Cerro Punta, involves some very steep climbs. The Boquete-based tour agency Expediciones Tierras Altas (box opposite) can arrange guides and transport to hike this trail, starting at either end.

Boquete

Set in the tranquil Caldera Valley 37km north of David at just over 1000m above sea level, **BOQUETE** is the biggest town in the Chiriquí Highlands, the centre of coffee production and a popular weekend resort for the residents of David. The slopes surrounding the town are dotted with coffee plantations, flower gardens and orange groves, rising to rugged peaks that are usually obscured by thick cloud that descends on the town in a constant fine mist known as *bajareque*. Only when the cloud clears can you see the imperious peak of Volcán Barú, which dominates the town to the northwest.

Arrival and information

Buses from David arrive and depart from the Parque Central, and *transporte urbana* **minibuses** head up to the surrounding hamlets from the streets around the parque – taking one of these and then walking back to town is a good way to see the nearby countryside. IPAT has a massive **tourist information centre** (Mon–Fri 10am–7pm, Sat–Sun 11am–9pm) and café overlooking the town at **Alto Boquete** on the road towards David. The staff here are reasonably helpful, though few speak English, and you should be able to get a map and some basic information on walks in the countryside around Boquete. It's worth coming up here to enjoy the panoramic views, but otherwise you can get better advice from the hotels and tour companies in Boquete mentioned below.

There's a **Banco Nacional**, on the main road a block south of the Parque, which changes travellers' cheques and has an ATM. The **post office** and **telephone office** (Mon–Fri 7am–6pm, Sat 7am–5pm) are both on the main square, while **Internet access** is available at the *Internet Coffee Shop* (daily 8am–9pm) on the main road opposite *Restaurante La Conquista*. Bicycles and mopeds can be rented from Gringo's, on the main road opposite *Restaurante La Conquista*.

Accommodation

There are plenty of **places to stay** in Boquete, though prices are relatively high – all have hot water and tend to fill on the weekends, when prices go up.

ORGANIZED TOURS FROM BOQUETE

Rio Monte Ecological Tours (☎720 1327), at the *Panamonte* hotel, organize expensive tours and excursions by car to the volcano and to the owner's coffee finca, where you're almost guaranteed to see a resplendent quetzal between January and August. Expediciones Tierras Altas (☎720 1342 or 691 6152), across the bridge to the right as you head out on the road towards David, is run by enthusiastic young locals who offer similar tours at much lower prices, with the emphasis on hiking in the forests north of the volcano. Chiriquí River Rafting (☎720 1505, fax 720 1506, *www.panama-rafting.com*) runs year-round whitewater-rafting trips (US$75–100 per day) on the rivers that run down from the Chiriquí Highlands through grade II, III and IV rapids.

Hotel Rebequet, Av B. Porras, opposite the *Pensión Marilós* (☎720 1365). Clean and comfortable rooms, plus communal kitchens. ⑤.

Panamonte, on the way out of town to the north (☎720 1327 or 1324, fax 720 2055, *panamont@chiriqui.com*). The most luxurious accommodation in Boquete, in an elegant building with pool, restaurant and a beautiful garden. ⑦.

Pensión Marilós, Av B. Porras, opposite the *Hotel Rebequet* (☎720 1380, *http://marilos .freeyellow.com*). Similar to, but slight cheaper than the *Hotel Rebequet*. Rooms have shared bathrooms, and there's also a book exchange and cooking facilities. ④.

Pensión Topas, Av B. Porras (☎720 1005), Six rooms decorated with Tintin murals set around a nice garden and small pool with views of the volcano. The helpful and knowledgeable European owners can arrange guided excursions and horse hire. Excellent breakfast. ④.

Pensión Virginia, on the Parque Central (☎720 1260). Charming if slightly dilapidated accommodation with friendly owners. ④.

The Town and around

The town itself is a charming and – except during the annual Feria de las Flores y el Café (usually held in January) – peaceful place, spread out along the road that comes in from David and around two squares, the **Parque de las Madres**, decorated with flowers, fountains and a monument to motherhood, and the **Parque Central**, which bustles with activity during the weekend market. Sadly, recent developments have put Boquete's unique charm under threat. Foreign investment has flooded into the area in recent years, pushing land prices beyond the reach of most locals, and an all-inclusive luxury retirement condominium for up to five hundred people from the United States is currently under construction, prompting fears that the town is being turned into a kind of tropical theme park for wealthy foreigners.

The real attraction of Boquete, however, is walking or riding in the surrounding countryside. As well as the climb to the summit of the volcano – a strenuous day's walk or a couple of hours by car when the road is in good condition – there are plenty of less demanding walks you can make along narrow country lanes, with well-signposted attractions. One of these, heading out of town to the north towards the hamlet of **Alto Lino**, takes you past the **Café Ruiz** coffee processing plant, which offers free tours to visitors, demonstrating every stage of coffee production. If you take a right fork across a bridge shortly after this you'll reach the **Los Vernaderos Orchid Farm**, where visitors are also welcome.

Eating

There's a wide choice of **places to eat** in Boquete. *Restaurante La Conquista*, on the main road, has a hearty set lunch for US$2.25, excellent fresh trout and a glorious selection of thick fruit *batidos*, while *La Casona Mexicana*, as its name implies, offers good Mexican food. The pizza at *Pizzeria La Volcánica* (closed Sun), across the road, is good value and popular with the locals. The nameless café next door to the *Pensión Virginia* on the square offers burgers, sandwiches and típica meals amid classic 1950s US diner decor, and you can also get cheap típica food at *El Sabrosón*, on the main street a couple of blocks north of the Parque. Finally, the friendly *Café El Punto de Encuentro*, a left turn two blocks south of the Parque, serves good coffee and breakfasts.

Volcán Barú

Boquete's biggest attraction is undoubtedly the ascent of **Volcán Barú**. A 22km road winds up through spectacular scenery to the peak, from which on clear days (unfortunately few and far between) both oceans can be seen. The volcano receives 5m of rain a year, and is often enveloped in thick cloud, so outside the dry season, your best chance of experiencing the view is to be on the peak at dawn. This is only possible if you camp out, walk all night or drive up a couple of hours before, but even if the view is partially obscured it is still a worthwhile climb.

The first 6km of the road is paved, after which it becomes a rough track passable with 4WD only, and sometimes in the rainy season it becomes impossible even with 4WD – check conditions in town before you set off. To **walk** to the summit it's best to get a *transporte urbana* minibus or a taxi (US$4–5) to the end of the tarmac, beyond which it's a steep and strenuous four- to six-hour hike, and another six hours or so back to Boquete, unless you catch another minibus on the way down. If you're lucky you might be able to hitch a ride on a truck heading to one of the farms on the lower slopes, or even all the way to the summit with a telecommunications vehicle, but otherwise it's a long day's walk and you should take waterproof clothing and plenty of food and water.

The road up passes coffee plantations tended by Ngobe labourers, which soon give way to majestic cloudforest, whose tall trees are bearded with lichen and covered with orchids and bromeliads. As you climb, the views of the Caldera Valley, the plains around David and the islands of the Golfo de Chiriquí open up, the air becomes cooler, and the cloudforest gradually gives way to stunted, elfin forest and finally to bleak, high-altitude paramo. Surrounded by seven long-extinct craters and crowned by a cluster of telecommunications aerials, the **peak** is often shrouded in cloud, but don't let this dishearten you – even in the depths of the rainy season the cloud breaks every so often to reveal the sight of at least one of the oceans and of the forest-covered mountains marching west to Costa Rica. Trails lead down the other side to Volcán and Cerro Punta, but they are difficult to follow without a guide. You can **camp** on the grassy plateau just below the peak, but it gets very cold at night and there is rarely any water available.

travel details

BUSES

Boquete to: David (every 25min; 1hr).

Cañas to: Pedasi (1–2 daily; 2hr); Tonosi (1 daily; 1hr).

Cerro Punta to: David (every 20min; 2hr 30min).

Chiguiri Arriba to: Penonomé (1–2 daily; 1hr 20min).

Chitré to: Las Tablas (every 10–15min; 30min); Los Santos (every 10min; 10min); Panamá City (hourly; 4hr); Santiago (every 45min; 1hr 20min).

David to: Almirante (every 45mins; 3hr); Boquete (every 25min; 1hr); Cerro Punta (every 20min; 2hr 30min); Panamá City (12 daily; 7hr; 2 express buses daily; 5hr); Paso Canoas (every 10min; 1hr 20min); San José, Costa Rica (1 daily; 7hr 30min).

El Valle to: Panamá City (every 35min; 2hr 30min); San Carlos (every 45min; 20min).

Las Tablas to: Chitré (every 10–15min; 30min); Panamá City (every 2hr; 4hr 30min); Pedasi (hourly; 45min); Tonosí (hourly; 2hr 30min).

Los Santos to: Chitré (every 10min; 10min).

Panamá City to: Chitré (hourly; 4hr); David (12 daily; 7hr; 2 express buses daily; 5hr); El Valle (every 35min; 2hr 30min); Las Tablas (every 2hr; 4hr 30min); Paso Canoas (11 daily; 9hr; 3 express buses daily in evening; 7hr); Penonomé (every 20min; 2hr 30min); Santiago (every 30min; 4hr).

Paso Canoas to: David (every 10min; 1hr 20min); Panamá City (11 daily; 9hr; 3 express buses daily in evening; 7hr).

Pedasi to: Cañas (1–2 daily; 2hr); Las Tablas (hourly; 45min).

Penonomé to: Chiguiri Arriba (1–2 daily; 1hr 20min); Panamá City (every 20min; 2hr 30min).

San Carlos to: El Valle (every 45min; 20min).

Santiago to: Chitré (every 45min; 1hr 20min); Panamá City (every 30min; 4hr).

Tonosi to: Cañas (1 daily; 1hr); Las Tablas (hourly; 2hr 30min).

FLIGHTS

Aeroperlas (☎315 7500) and Mapiex Aero (☎315 0888)

David to: Bocas del Toro via Changuinola (2 daily Mon–Fri; 1hr 10min); Panamá City (4–6 daily; 1hr); San José, Costa Rica (4 weekly; 1hr).

Panamá City to: David (4–6 daily; 1hr).

CHAPTER 38

BOCAS DEL TORO

I solated on the Costa Rican border between the Caribbean and the forested slopes of the Cordillera Talamanca, **Bocas del Toro** (usually abbreviated simply to "Bocas") is one of the most remote and beautiful provinces in Panamá. Until the road across the cordillera from the province of Chiriquí was built in the early 1980s, Bocas del Toro was completely cut off from the rest of Panamá, and could be reached only by sea, air or via Costa Rica. From the volcanic slopes of the Cordillera Talamanca down to the Caribbean sea, most of the mainland is still covered by rainforest, apart from a narrow coastal strip where bananas are cultivated. Offshore, the **Bocas del Toro Archipelago** is home to an ecosystem so complex and well preserved that it has been described by biologists as "the Galapagos of the 21st century". This exceptional natural diversity is matched by the equally unusual make-up of the region's population. While the inland forests are still populated by indigenous groups – Ngobe-Buglé, Naso and Bribrí – the islands are dominated by the descendants of **West Indian** migrants, and English, or rather Guari-Guari – Jamaican patois embellished with some Spanish and Ngobere – remains the lingua franca.

Long one of the best-kept secrets in Central America, in recent years Bocas has begun to attract more and more visitors – thanks to its growing reputation and easy accessibility from Costa Rica, you're likely to see more travellers here in a day than in the rest of Panamá in a month. But though a tourism boom is well under way in the islands, it's yet to change the friendly, laid-back approach to life adopted by most of the inhabitants. And the pristine beauty of the archipelago's ecosystems – tropical forests, mangroves, deserted beaches, extensive coral reefs and crystalline waters teeming with rare marine life – is largely protected by the **Parque Nacional Marino Isla Bastimentos**. The only drawback is the unpredictable weather: the dry season is much less clearly defined than in the rest of the country and bright sunshine can give way to torrential tropical rain with alarming rapidity.

Most visitors head straight out to the islands and the provincial capital, **Bocas del Toro** – also referred to as Bocas Town, Bocas Isla or just plain Bocas – which is the best base from which to explore the archipelago. The coastal banana zone and its main town, Changuinola, are usually visited only by those heading to Costa Rica.

Some history

Christopher Columbus explored the coast of Bocas del Toro searching for a route to Asia during his fourth voyage in 1502, and many of the place names date from his visit – Islas Cristobal and Colón were named in his honour, Isla Bastimentos was where he took on supplies, Isla Carene where he careened his ships. But during the colonial era the Spanish had little success in taming the many warring indigenous tribes that populated the mountainous interior, and European pirates often sheltered in the calm waters between its many offshore islands. By the nineteenth century, English ships from Jamaica were becoming frequent visitors, arriving in search of hardwoods from the mainland forests and turtles, and in 1826 the town of Bocas del Toro was founded by

For an explanation of **accommodation price codes**, see p.701.

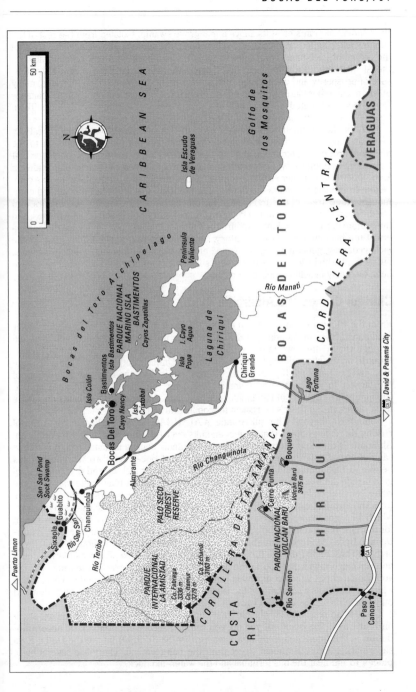

West Indian migrants on stilts above a mangrove swamp. Isolated from the rest of the country and plagued by malaria and yellow fever, the settlement developed slowly until the arrival of US banana companies towards the end of the century. Concentrated on the islands of the Bocas del Toro Archipelago, the banana plantations brought a measure of prosperity and encouraged further settlement by West Indian migrants, many of whom came here after working on the French canal construction. By 1895, bananas from Bocas accounted for over half of Panamá's export earnings, and Bocas Town boasted five foreign consulates and three English-language newspapers.

Early in the twentieth century, however, the banana plantations were repeatedly devastated by crop disease, leading the fruit companies to move production to the mainland around Changuinola, and the islands reverted to the tropical indolence that characterizes them today. The region's isolation from the rest of Panamá only ended in 1981, when the road across the isthmus from Chiriquí to Chiriquí Grande was completed. In the last few years the development of tourist facilities has accelerated enormously. Huge areas of the archipelago have been bought by foreign speculators who are dividing it up into lots for the construction of luxury hotels and holiday homes, and the regional economy is dominated by US interests in a way not seen since the banana era at the beginning of the last century. Certainly, the tourism boom has revived the local economy, generating much needed employment and income for local residents, but as the barbed wire enclosures go up, some are beginning to realize they may have been too hasty in selling their birthright.

Chiriquí Grande and Almirante

From the village of Chiriquí, 14km east of David on the Interamericana, a spectacular road runs across the continental divide, crossing the Fortuna hydroelectric dam and through the pristine forests that protect its watershed, to the small town of **Chiriquí Grande** on the shore of the Laguna de Chiriquí. Until recently this was the end of the road and the jumping-off point for the islands, but in 2000 the road along the shore of the lagoon to Almirante was completed, linking the coastal banana strip around Changuinola to the rest of Panamá for the first time. All boats to the islands now leave from Almirante, so there's no reason to stop in Chiriquí Grande.

Some 50km beyond Chiriquí Grande is **ALMIRANTE**, a ramshackle port town of rusting tin-roofed houses that project on stilts over the calm waters of the Caribbean, Almirante is the export terminal for the Changuinola banana industry and the place to catch a boat if you're heading out to the islands of Bocas del Toro. Through **buses** between Changuinola and David or Panamá City usually pick up and drop off passengers beside the road on the edge of town, a short taxi ride or ten-minute walk from the waterfront. Buses for Changuinola, where you can get connections for the border, leave from the terminal close to the port. Adjacent to the terminal is the train station, from which a banana workers' train runs to the border each morning – it's not really meant for tourists, but you might be able to persuade them to let you on for the ride. **Water-taxis** to Bocas del Toro (25min) leave every 45 minutes or so until about 6.30pm. If you arrive by bus, touts from the three water-taxi companies, Taxi 25, Bocas Marine Tours and Galapago's, will lead you to the port – the services are exactly the same, though you should check which company is leaving first before you buy a ticket. There's also a ferry – known as a *palanga* – to the islands four days a week, but this is very slow and only worth using if you have a car.

There is no reason to stay in Almirante unless you miss the last boat and get stuck on your way to the islands. If you do, you can find secure but pretty basic **accommodation** at the unmarked *Hotel San Francisco* (☎758 3779; ④), above the De La Rosa supermarket across the main street from the bus terminal. There are several basic **places to eat** near the bus terminal and the water-taxi dock.

Bocas del Toro

Connected to the rest of Isla Colón by a narrow causeway, the provincial capital of **BOCAS DEL TORO** is by far the best base from which to explore the islands, beaches and reefs of the archipelago, and also a charming place in its own right, with rickety wooden buildings painted in faded pastels, and a friendly and laid-back English-speaking population. There's nothing much to see, but that's hardly a problem – after a hard day in the sea and sun there's no better place to chill out with a cool drink, while the sun sets behind the forest-covered mountains of the mainland and the air fills with delicious cooking smells and the sound of calypso.

Arrival, orientation and information

Bocas is a small town and it's easy to find your way around. Most activity is concentrated on C 3, on the seafront. The **ferry** from Almirante docks at its eastern end, while Bocas Marine Tours **water-taxis** arrive beside *Le Pirate* restaurant on the same street, and Galapago's water-taxis tie up a couple of doors down; Taxi 25 water-taxis terminate just off C 3 on C 1. **Flights** with Aeroperlas (☎757 9341) and Mapiex Aero (☎757 9841) land at the small airstrip on the edge of town, just four blocks from C 3.

The **IPAT office** (Mon–Fri 8.30am–4.30pm, Sat & Sun 9am–4pm; ☎757 9642), housed in a grand new building on C 1, is one of the most helpful in Panamá and worth a visit if you're going to be spending a few days in the area. As well as providing tourist information, they also have **Internet access** and a well laid-out exhibition on the history and ecology of the archipelago. The environmental agency ANAM's office on C 3 can give permission to camp within the Isla Bastimentos Marine Park and may also be able to help organize a visit to see turtles laying their eggs between May and September. Information on many of the hotels and tour operators in Bocas can be found on the **Web site** *www.bocas.com*. The **Banco Nacional** behind the municipal building on Av E changes travellers' cheques and has an ATM. There's a Cable & Wireless telephone office (Mon–Fri 8am–noon & 1–4pm) on C 1, and you can rent **bicycles** from either Galapago's or Bocas Marine Tours, both on the seafront on C 3 (about US$1/hr or US$8/day).

Accommodation+

There's an ever-increasing range of accommodation in Bocas, with more and more foreign-owned places opening up. Things can fill up pretty quickly on weekends and during holidays, but you should always be able to find somewhere to stay: ask at the IPAT office if you get stuck.

Bahía, at the far end of C 3 by the ferry dock (☎757 9626, fax 757 9626). Spacious, recently refurbished rooms with a/c, TV and hot water in an imposing early twentieth-century wooden structure that was formerly the United Fruit Company HQ, with a communal balcony overlooking the sea. ⑤.

Bocas Inn, Av Norte, C 4 (☎757 9226). Airy wooden structure run by ANCON Expeditions as a field station for their tour groups, but independent travellers are also welcome. Clean comfortable rooms – those at the front share a large balcony with hammocks overlooking the bay – and there's a good environmental library for guests. Breakfast included. ⑥.

Casa Max, intersection of Av G and Av Norte (☎757 9120). Small, friendly place with clean, cheerfully painted rooms, comfortable beds and a homely feel. Free coffee and fruit. ④.

Cocomo-on-the-Sea, Av H, C7 (☎757 9259, *www.panamainfo.com/cocomo*). Spacious, comfortable a/c rooms, some with verandas looking out to sea. Breakfast included. ⑥.

Del Parque, C2 on the Parque (☎757 9008). Friendly family-run place with cool, clean rooms and a veranda overlooking the Parque. ⑤.

Las Brisas, on the corner of C 3 and Av Norte (☎757 9248). Rambling, ramshackle waterfront hotel with a great number and variety of rooms (③) – they're good value, and very popular with budget travellers. The modern annex nearby has more comfortable a/c rooms (⑤). Free coffee in the morning.

TOUR COMPANIES IN BOCAS DEL TORO

ANCON Expeditions (☎757 9226 or 757 9850, *www.anconexpeditions.com*). Excursions to the marine park and into the forests on the mainland – they're more expensive than other operators, but have powerful boats and good guides.

Bocas Water Sports, C 3 (☎757 9541, *www.bocaswatersports.com*). Professional, US-run diving and snorkelling excursions and equipment rental.

Starfleet Eco-Adventures, C 1 (☎757 9630, *www.starfleeteco.hypermart.net*). Canadian-owned company with a friendly, professional team offering diving and snorkelling excursions on a ten-metre catamaran and full PADI open-water diving courses (about US$250 plus equipment rental).

Transparente Tours, next door to *Le Pirate* restaurant on C 3 (☎757 9600). Run by experienced locals, this long-established company runs regular excursions into the marine park, along with other customized trips. They also rent out snorkelling equipment.

La Veranda, Av Norte, C6 (☎757 9211, *www.laverandahotel.com*). Welcoming guesthouse in a delightful traditional Caribbean house with spacious, well-decorated rooms around an open-air patio and a communal kitchen. ⑤.

Mangrove Inn Eco-Resort, a short boat trip around the west side of the peninsula – book in their office on C 3 (☎757 9594, *www.bocas.com/mangrove.html*). Purpose-built luxury eco-dive resort with comfortable wooden cabins on stilts over the water. Three meals a day included. ⑧.

Swans Key, C 3 just off the Parque (☎757 9090 or 757 9316, fax 757 9027, *swanscayisla@cwp.net.pa*). The most upmarket place in town, built in the local architectural style but with an incongruously opulent interior and elegant, well-furnished a/c rooms – it's popular with wealthy weekenders from Panamá City. Breakfast included. ⑧.

Eating

There's a wide choice of **restaurants** in Bocas, including an increasing number of foreign-owned pizza and pasta joints. Fish and seafood including lobster, conch and octopus are widely available and particularly delicious when prepared to local recipes with coconut milk and sharp Caribbean spices.

Blue Moon, C 3, opposite the *Hotel Bahía*. Waterfront Mexican restaurant serving reasonable food and good cocktails. Happy hour 5–7pm; closed Tues.

Buena Vista Deli and Bar, C 1, just off C 3. Set in a good waterfront location, with US sports on the satellite TV, this is the place to come for authentic US burgers, sandwiches and salads – as well as larger meals and excellent frozen margaritas – served up by cheerful, Hemmingway-esque owners. Closed Tues.

El Lorito de Don Chicho, C 3, opposite the square. Always busy, with a lively atmosphere and tasty, inexpensive, self-service Panamanian food; locals seldom eat anywhere else.

El Pecado da Sabor, above the Mangrove Roots shop on C 3, just off the Parque. Eclectic combination of delicious Thai, Lebanese and Mexican dishes made with the finest local and imported ingredients. If sin adds flavour, as the name suggests, the chef may be the devil himself. Tues–Sat evenings only.

Kun Ja, corner of C 3 and C 1. Inexpensive, no-nonsense Chinese food in a neon-lit room.

Parrillada Kuna, opposite the *Hotel Las Brisas* on the corner of C 3 and Av Norte. Popular Kuna-run place serving inexpensive seafood, good breakfasts and other filling meals.

Drinking and nightlife

Several restaurants double as **music** and **drinking venues** in the evening, and there are a few good **bars** where you can relax with a cold beer or a cocktail. On the weekends, many locals head to *Discoteca El Encanto* on the waterfront of C 3, or *Black and White* outside town on the road towards the isthmus to dance the night away to pounding reggae.

Blue Bull, inside Starfleet Eco-Adventures on C 1. Laid-back waterfront bar serving cold beer and excellent cocktails. Happy hour 5–7pm, and live calypso music at weekends.

El Barco Hundido, hidden down a narrow alley beside the Cable & Wireless office on C 1. Lively surfers hangout serving cold beer on a platform over the sea; many of the clientele arrive by paddling across the water on their boards.

Le Pirate, C 3, beside the Bocas Marine Tours water-taxi dock. Waterfront restaurant serving indifferent fish and seafood – it's more popular as a bar, especially for sundowners during the 4–6pm happy hour.

Loop, opposite the Mangrove Roots shop on C 3. Friendly local bar with pool tables; open 24hr.

Isla Colón

From Bocas Town, a dirt road runs across a narrow isthmus to Isla Colón and forks after about 1.5km – one branch heading across the centre of the island to Boca del Drago, about 14km away on the north coast, the other 8km up the east coast towards Bluff point. This road passes **Playa Bluff**, a beautiful long, white-sand beach which is visited by turtles between May and September. The surf here can be powerful and the currents strong, so be careful and don't swim alone.

BOCA DEL DRAGO is a small fishing community set on a broad horseshoe bay with calm waters perfect for swimming and a narrow beach fringed with palm trees and patches of mangrove and coral. You can stay here at *Cabañas Estefani* (✆626 7245, ③), which has two cosy self-catering cabins; the *Yarisnori* restaurant next door (closed Wed) serves simple, delicious fish and seafood. A **bus** runs to Boca del Drago from the Parque in Bocas Town on Monday, Wednesday, Friday and Sunday mornings, returning in the afternoon; alternatively you can hire a minibus-taxi in Bocas Town to take you to Boca del Drago (US$20–30) or Playa Bluff (US$10–15) and pick you up again later. Otherwise the best way to get around the island to rent a **bicycle** in Bocas Town (see p.783).

Bastimentos

Just across the water from Bocas Town on the western tip of **Isla Bastimentos** is the small fishing community of **BASTIMENTOS**, one of the parts of the island not included in the national marine park. Regular **boats** run between Bastimentos and Bocas Town (US$2 per person), and it's easy to hire a boatman in Bastimentos to take you on excursions into the park or elsewhere in the archipelago (see box overleaf). The community is not really set up for tourism, and so makes a good place to stay if you want a more authentic Caribbean experience than that provided by Bocas Town. A few places offer **rooms**, the best of which is the welcoming *Mr Wolf's Place* (✆757 9923; ③), which has two very comfortable rooms as well as rustic cabins in a flower-filled garden. The German Mr Wolf is very helpful, prepares breakfast and dinner, rents sea kayaks and snorkelling equipment, and can arrange excursions. *Pensión Bastimentos* (no phone; ③–④), on a floating wooden platform beside the dock, is also pleasant and friendly, with a good restaurant, while the *Sylvia Guest House* (✆757 9442; ②), a little further east, is more basic, but friendly and good value. In addition, a couple of upmarket beach cabaña complexes have opened near the eastern tip of the island, just outside the park boundaries. The secluded *Al Natural Resort* (✆757 9004, *www.bocas.com/alnatura.htm*; ⑦) has stylish rustic cabañas with solar-powered lighting and rainwater showers; transport to and from Bocas Town and three meals a day are included in the price. *El Limbo* (✆757 9888, *www.ellimbo.com*; ⑦) has comfortable cabañas, and rates include two meals a day and the use of snorkelling equipment.

EXCURSIONS FROM BOCAS TOWN AND BASTIMENTOS

The easiest way to visit the Isla Bastimentos marine park and surrounding areas is with one of the **tour companies** in Bocas Town (see p.784). A growing number of agencies offer day-trips to beaches and snorkelling spots in and around the park, typically costing US$10–20 per person and including a stop at a restaurant for lunch. You can also rent a boat from one of the many boatmen in Bocas Town or Bastimentos: with a group of four or more people this should work out the same price or cheaper than an agency tour, and also means you can decide exactly where you want to go. Prices vary according to the distance involved, the size of the boat, the power of the motor and your negotiating ability. Note that though a boat with a small motor may seem good value, you could end up spending most of the day chugging to and from your destination rather than in the water snorkelling or lying on the beach; in addition, check whether the boat has lifejackets. A typical day's excursion might include a visit to the Cayos Zapatillas in the morning, lunch and snorkelling at Crawl Key, and an afternoon on Red Frog Beach. Boatmen and agencies also sometimes take trips round the side of Isla Colón to Boca del Drago and on to **Swan Key** (Cayo Cisnet), a tiny island off the north coast that is an important nesting and resting site for migratory birds, including the rare red-billed tropic birds.

There are also endless possibilities for boat excursions **further afield**: west around the Peninsula Valiente to the Isla de Escudo de Verguas, which aficionados consider one of the best diving spots in the whole Caribbean, or up one of the rivers into the rainforests of the mainland to visit isolated Ngobe-Buglé communities. The Río Manati, which flows into Laguna de Chiriquí and the San San Pond Sock swamp, west of Changuinola, both support manatee, the extremely endangered and rarely seen Caribbean sea-cow, as well as turtles and a great variety of bird life. The price of gas makes excursions expensive, but the relative cost comes down if you can get a group of five or six people together. Most of the tour companies listed on p.784 (try Captain Cesar Smith at Transparente Tours) can organize such trips but don't promote them, as they don't think visitors are interested in much beyond sea and sand.

Parque Nacional Marina Isla Bastimentos

Most visitors to Bocas come to explore the pristine beauty of **Parque Nacional Marina Isla Bastimentos**, a 130-square-kilometre reserve that encompasses a range of virtually undisturbed ecosystems including rainforest, mangrove and coral reef. Deserted white-sand beaches and extensive reefs support an immense diversity of **marine life**, including dolphins, sea turtles and a kaleidoscopic variety of fish – a veritable paradise for snorkellers and divers. Foreign visitors to the park are supposed to pay a US$10 entrance fee, but this is only charged at Playa Larga and the Cayos Zapatillas (see opposite).

The best **beaches** are on the eastern side of Isla Bastimentos, which faces the open sea, though all have powerful surf which can make swimming dangerous. These can be reached on foot from Bastimentos village, or by boat when the sea is calm. The most popular and easiest to reach is **Red Frog Beach**, an idyllic stretch of sand which takes its name from the tiny but abundant bright-red frogs which inhabit the forest behind, and which are found nowhere else in the world. Red Frog Beach is accessible on foot from Bastimentos village, a fifteen-minute walk through the jungle – you must pay US$1 to the people who maintain the trail. A couple of beaches further east is Ola Chica, or **Polo Beach**, a longer and more secluded beach, partially protected from the surf by reefs – a spear-fishing hermit who has lived here alone for about thirty years sometimes cooks up his catch for visitors.

Further east – about a three-hour walk from Bastimentos village – the fourteen-kilometre stretch of **Playa Larga** is an important nesting site for **sea turtles** between

May and September. There's an ANAM ranger station here where you'll be charged the US$10 park entrance fee, and a basic refuge where you can **camp** for another US$10: you'll need to stay overnight if you want to see the turtles coming up to lay their eggs. You should get permission from the ANAM office in Bocas Town before coming here.

Southeast of Bastimentos island but still within the park are the **Cayos Zapatillas**, two idyllic coral-fringed islands where Henry Morgan is supposed to have buried his loot – though treasure-seekers have so far failed to find it and the pirate's curse is supposed to hang over anyone who does. The Zapatillas are excellent for snorkelling, but you must pay the park admission fee (US$10) at the ANAM station on one of the islands, where **camping** is also possible with permission from ANAM in Bocas Town.

Changuinola

Back on the mainland, the road to the border runs 29km west from Almirante through seemingly endless banana plantations to **CHANGUINOLA**, a typically hot and uninteresting banana town where almost everyone works for the Chiriquí Land Company ("The Company" – successor to United Fruit) which owns most of the surrounding land. **Buses** from Almirante and the border at Guabito arrive and leave from the terminal, which is usually busy with workers heading to the banana fincas, known by numbers rather than names. There's no reason to stop unless you get stuck between Costa Rica and Bocas, but if you do end up **staying** here, everything you might need can be found along the main road that runs alongside the terminal, including, the a/c *Hotel Carol* (☎758 8731; ③), a **Banco del Istmo** and several **restaurants** – the one in the bus station is good and inexpensive, while the *Chiquita Banana*, opposite, is more upmarket.

Crossing the border

From Changuinola the road runs 16km to the border with Costa Rica at **GUABITO**. There's little here except a few shops selling consumer goods to Costa Rican daytrippers and a **migración** (daily 8am–6pm), beyond which it's a short walk across a bridge to Costa Rica, where you can change currency.

travel details

BUSES

Almirante to: Changuinola (every 30min; 45min).

Changuinola to: Almirante (every 30min; 45min); David (8 daily; 5hr); Guabito (every 30min; 20min).

David to: Changuinola (8 daily; 5hr).

Guabito to: Changuinola (every 30min; 20min).

WATER-TAXIS

Almirante to: Bocas del Toro (every 45min; 25min).

Bocas del Toro to: Almirante (every 45min; 25min).

FLIGHTS

Aeroperlas (☎315 7500) and Mapiex Aero (☎315 0888)

Panamá City to: Bocas del Toro (3 daily; 1hr 40min).

Bocas del Toro to: David (Mon–Fri 1 daily; 55min); Panamá City (3 daily; 1hr 40min); San José, Costa Rica (5 weekly; 1hr 30min).

David to: Bocas del Toro (Mon–Fri 1 daily; 55min).

San José, **Costa Rica** to: Bocas del Toro (5 weekly; 1hr 30min).

CHRONOLOGY OF CENTRAL AMERICA

15,000 –12,000 BC
First waves of **nomadic hunters** from the north spread down through Mexico and the isthmus.

7500 BC
Settled agricultural communities develop throughout Mesoamerica – with maize cultivation and the domestication of animals – particularly in the northern regions.

1500 BC
Formative period of the **Maya culture** across Mesoamerica. Cultural and trade links established with, among others, the Olmecs of Mexico. Southern Central America – present-day Panamá and Costa Rica – develops links extending both north and south, with settled agricultural communities. Immigrants from South America migrate up the isthmus, reaching as far as Honduras by 1000 BC.

300 AD
Classic period of Maya culture in Mesoamerica begins. Emergence of the great city states at Tikal, Copán and elsewhere; scientific and artistic development reaches its peak. Trade contact made with the various groups living further south along the isthmus.

c. 900
Classic Maya culture begins to **decline**, with many of the great cities abandoned. The influence of Toltec and other **Mexican civilizations** travels down the isthmus; a Toltec–Maya civilization establishes itself in what is now Guatemala. The **Lenca**, descended from South American Chibchan groups, establish themselves in Honduras and El Salvador. Waves of **Nahua**-speaking groups migrate down the isthmus, reaching as far as northern Costa Rica.

1400–1475
Quiché overrun much of Guatemala, establishing a short-lived area of dominance.

1500
Central America inhabited by a number of different groups, none predominant and none ultimately capable of withstanding the subsequent Spanish Conquest. The Maya region is divided in a shifting pattern of alliances between rival city-states.

1502
Columbus lands on the island of Guanaja and first sights the Central American mainland. First Catholic Mass said at Punto Caxinas (Trujillo, Honduras); first exploration of the Atlantic coast.

1510
First Spanish settlement founded in Panamá by **Diego de Nicuesa**.

1513
Vasco Nuñez de Balboa crosses the isthmus of Panamá and becomes the first European to see the Pacific Ocean.

1519
Hernan Cortés lands in Mexico.

1522
Gil González Davila sails from Panamá up the Pacific coast, exploring as far north as Honduras.

1523
Pedro de Alvarado arrives in Guatemala and defeats the dominant Quiché tribe at Quetzaltenango. His army explores down into El Salvador.

1524
Cristóbal de Olid arrives in Honduras and founds the first Spanish settlement there. **Francisco Hernández de Córdoba** founds the cities of Granada and León in Nicaragua.

1524–40	**Spanish Conquest** of the isthmus proceeds, encountering and defeating resistance such as the Lempira rebellion in Honduras. The **Audiencia de los Cofines** – essentially the region's seat of government – is founded at **Gracias, Honduras**, in 1539.
1548	Seat of the Audiencia moved to **Antigua, Guatemala**; Guatemala becomes the predominant region during Spanish rule.
17th C	Development of **colonial rule** throughout Central America. Spain claims sovereignty over Belize but never effectively colonizes it. British and other pirates use the Atlantic coast of the isthmus and its islands as a refuge.
18th C	Colonial Central America remains a backwater, producing no great riches for the Spanish. **British claims** to Belize, Mosquitia and the Bay Islands are denied. Britain cedes all claims to land, except Belize, in 1786.
1773	A series of devastating **earthquakes** destroy Antigua, Guatemala; the capital is moved to **Guatemala City** in 1776.
1797	The **Garífuna** are forced to migrate to Roatán from the island of St Vincent. They quickly move on to settle along the north coast of **Honduras**.
1821	Mexico and Central America gain **independence** from Spain. Short-lived monarchy under the Mexican **Augustín Iturbide**. Panamá declares independence and becomes part of Gran Colombia, later simply **Colombia**.
1822	Iturbide is deposed.
1823	The Monroe Doctrine is announced, asserting US geo-political interests in Central America. Following Iturbide's deposition, the provinces of Central America (except Chiapas, now part of Mexico) declare themselves an independent republic – the **Central American Federation** – on July 1. Its first president is Salvadorean **Manuel José Arce**.
1824–39	**Civil war** almost immediately follows the creation of the republic, prompted by rivalry between Conservatives and Liberals. **Francisco Morazán** becomes president in 1830 and tries to institute reform of the Church and government. Fighting breaks out again with Morazán failing to crush the 1837 **rebellion** of Rafael Carrera in Guatemala. With Morazán's resignation in 1839 the Central American Federation is finished. The states become independent republics, except for Panamá, which remains part of Colombia.
1820s–1850s	**British** again assert claims to Belize, Mosquitia, the Bay Islands and north coast of Nicaragua. **Cruz Wyke treaty** cedes all territories except Belize.
1855	US filibuster **William Walker** is elected president of Nicaragua and announces intention of taking over the other republics before being driven out in 1857.
1860	Walker returns, capturing Trujillo in Honduras. Taken prisoner by British navy and executed by the Honduran army.
1862	Belize officially becomes part of the British Empire as the **Colony of British Honduras**.
1870s	Beginning of **coffee** boom in Guatemala, El Salvador and Costa Rica.

1890s	Beginning of **banana** boom in Guatemala, Honduras, Costa Rica and Panamá. Influence of US fruit companies begins to grow.
1903	**Panamá** declares **independence** from Colombia; new government recognized by US, which immediately presents a treaty for construction of the canal.
1904	Work on the **Panamá Canal** begins; completed in 1914.
1912	The US responds to a **rebellion in Nicaragua** by landing 2500 marines. The beginning of US domination of Nicaraguan politics.
1932	**La Matanza** (the Massacre): thirty thousand peasants and indigenous people, led by Augustín Farabundo Martí, murdered in El Salvador by security forces following an anti-government rebellion.
1934	Socialist **Augusto César Sandino** assassinated in Nicaragua on the orders of US-supported **Anastasio Somoza**. Somoza founds a dictatorship that will last 45 years.
1948	"**Revolution**" in **Costa Rica**; Figueres assumes presidency under the Junta of the Second Republic. The following year a new constitution introduces universal suffrage and abolishes the army.
1954	A CIA-backed military coup ends the Guatemalan presidency of socialist Jacob Arbenz. Start of **military rule** in **Guatemala** and a series of military-backed dictators.
late 1950s	Frente Sandinista de Liberación Nacional (**FSLN**) movement formed in **Nicaragua**.
1960	**Guerrilla war** begins in Guatemala's eastern highlands.
1963	Military coup installs **Colonel Oswaldo López Arellano** as president of **Honduras**. Beginning of overt military influence on government.
1964	Full internal self-government granted to **Belize**.
1968	**Panamá's** Guardia Nacional deposes the president, suspends the constitution and dissolves parliament. Lieutenant-Colonel (later General) **Omar Torrijos** assumes leadership of the country.
1969	Honduras and El Salvador engage in the five-day "**Football War**", essentially over a disputed border but triggered by a soccer match.
1972	**Earthquake** in **Managua** leaves over 10,000 dead and many more homeless. International aid money is appropriated by President Somoza. Opposition to the dictatorship grows.
1972	**El Salvador's President Duarte** exiled by the military, who assume government. Upsurge in guerrilla activity and creation of right-wing paramilitary "death squads". The kidnapping and extra-judicial killing of civilians increase.
1976	**Earthquake** in Guatemala leaves 23,000 dead and 77,000 homeless.
1977	**New Canal Treaty** allows for Panamá to assume control of most of canal zone, with total control to be handed over by the end of 1999, along with phasing out of US bases in the country.

1979	Somoza flees Nicaragua and **Sandinistas** march into Managua on July 19.
1980	In **El Salvador**, Archbishop Romero is murdered whilst saying mass. Armed uprising, led by the **FMLN**, begins and lasts throughout the decade.
1981	**Ronald Reagan** assumes presidency of US. During the "lost decade" of the 1980s, billions of dollars of military aid flows towards the right-wing government of El Salvador, while covert aid is used to fund the **Contras** and direct attacks on Nicaragua; a trade embargo is also imposed.
1981	**Belize** gains full **independence**.
1982	General **Ríos Montt** becomes president of **Guatemala**; ongoing repression in the countryside as the guerrilla war continues.
1983	**Manuel Noriega** assumes leadership of **Panamá** and remains in power, despite losing two elections, until forcibly removed in 1989.
1984	**"Irangate"** scandal blows up; US revealed to have funded Contra aid through arms sales to Iran.
1986	**Earthquake** in San Salvador leaves 600 dead and thousands homeless.
1986	Return to **civilian rule** in **Guatemala**, although military influence remains strong.
1988	US indicts Noriega of drug trafficking and involvement in organized crime. **Sanctions** imposed against **Panamá**, while internal repression increases.
1988–89	Costa Rican President Arias presents a **regional peace plan**, signed by Guatemala, El Salvador, Nicaragua and Honduras. Though it is never fully implemented, the departure of Reagan from office and the end of the Cold War ensures aid to the Contras slows to a trickle.
1989	El Salvadorean military murder six Jesuit priests and their housekeeper in **San Salvador**, while an estimated 4000 die in military offensives on cities.
1989	**US invade Panamá** in **"Operation Just Cause"**. Noriega seeks asylum in Vatican Embassy, eventually giving himself up in early 1990 (in 1992 he is extradited to the US and convicted of conspiracy to distribute cocaine). Estimates of the numbers killed during the invasion go as high as 7000.
1990	The FSLN lose the Nicaraguan election. **Violeta Chamorro** and her UNO government assume office. Contra fighting stops soon after and the US trade embargo is lifted.
1991	**President Serrano** of Guatemala recognizes Belize as an independent state, a decision not acceptable to Congress; the president attempts to govern independently – and is forced into resignation and exile.
1992	UN-negotiated **peace settlement** brings an end to twelve years of civil war in **El Salvador**, in which an estimated 75,000 people were killed. The FMLN becomes an opposition party, participating in elections in 1994, won by the right-wing ARENA party.

1996	**Alvaro Arzú** of the centre-right PAN party assumes the presidency of **Guatemala**. **Peace Accords** with guerrilla groups signed, ending over thirty years of civil war.
1998	Human rights leader Bishop Jean Geradi is murdered in **Guatemala City** following the publication of his investigation into abuses committed by the military during the civil war. Landslide victory for left-of-centre PUP in **Belize** elections. **Hurricane Mitch** devastates the region, killing thousands and causing billions of pounds worth of damage – **Nicaragua** and **Honduras** are especially badly hit.
1999	Self-confessed killer **Alfonso Portillo** becomes president of **Guatemala**.
1999	The US hands control of the **Panamá Canal** over to the Panamanian government.
2000	In **Nicaragua**, resurgent support for the FSLN sees them win the mayoral seat of Managua.
2001	**Guatemala** and **El Salvador** join Panamá in making the **US dollar** an official national currency.
2001	**Earthquakes** kill over 1000 people in **El Salvador**.

WILDLIFE

Be it the sinuous spotted jaguar, the technicolour macaw or the yellow-beaked toucan, tropical animals are more colourful and fabulous than their temperate-zone cousins, and nowhere is this more true than with the life forms of Central America.

The immense **geographical diversity** of the Central American isthmus accounts for the vast number of its resident animals, birds, insects and reptiles. And within each species you can observe an enormous variety, according to locality and **habitat**. For example, the freshwater turtles that inhabit mangrove streams are quite different from their larger sea-going cousins, and you won't see a jaguar on the dusty agricultural plains of northwest Nicaragua. Meanwhile, the crested harpy eagle seems to be locally extinct in Guatemala, but is thought to be alive and well in the matted density of the rainforests of Panamá's Darién Gap. You may encounter rare squirrel monkeys, delicate and savant-faced, which are endemic to a small wedge of the Pacific coast of Costa Rica. Similarly, Guatemala's bizarrely fluffy ocellated turkey can be seen only in the jungles of Petén.

The animals of the isthmus do have in common a general **genealogy** – many can be described as mixtures of temperate-zone (North American) and tropical (South American) fauna. Some of the animals you are more likely to see – because of their abundance and diurnal activity – look like outsize versions or variations of temperate-zone mammals: the agouti or paca (*tepezcuintle*), a large water-rodent, for exam-

ple, or the mink-like tayra (*tolumuco*), which may flash by you on its way up a tree. The Neotropical river otter (*nutria*) is a friendly creature, although extremely shy. The coati (often mistakenly called coatimundi; *pizote* in Spanish) looks like a confused combination of a raccoon, domestic cat and an anteater. There's also a tropical raccoon (*mapache*) that looks like its northern neighbour, complete with eye mask.

Despite its reputation as a wildlife haven, Costa Rica does not have Central America's most diverse vertebrate fauna – that honour goes to Guatemala. However, Costa Rican insects and birds are particularly numerous, with 850 species of birds (including migratory ones) – more than the US and Canada combined. Costa Rica is also home to a quarter of the world's known butterflies – more than in all Africa – about 3000 types of moth, and scores of bees and wasps. Despite all this abundance, you may spot a quetzal more easily in, say, the central mountains of Nicaragua, which are sparsely populated and undertouristed, and where there are still plenty of nesting sites remaining.

Nowhere in Central America – even in Costa Rica's or Belize's national parks – should you expect to see the larger (and shyer) mammals as a matter of course – the tapir, jaguar and ocelot are particularly elusive. Many of the more exotic mammals that inhabit the isthmus are either nocturnal, endangered, or made shy through years of hunting and human encroachment. Although encounters do occur, they are usually brief, with the animal in question fleeing in a haze of colour and fur or dipping quietly back into the shadows from which it first emerged. That said, however, it's quite likely that you'll come into (usually fleeting) contact with some of the smaller and more abundant mammals.

BIRDS

Bird life, both migratory and indigenous, is abundant in Central America and includes some of the most colourful birds in the Americas: the quetzal, the toucan and the scarlet macaw. The most famous bird of Central America is without doubt the brilliant green and red **quetzal**. With a range historically extending from southern Mexico to northern Panamá, the dazzling quetzal was highly prized by the Aztecs and the Maya. In the language of the Aztecs, *quetzali* means, roughly, "beautiful", and along with jade, the shimmering, jewel-coloured feathers were used as currency in Maya cities. The feathers were also worn by Maya nobles to signify religious qualities and social superiority, and formed the headdress of the plumed serpent Quetzalcoatl, the Aztec over-god. Hunting quetzals is particularly cruel, as it is well known that the bird cannot (or will not) live in captivity, a poignant attribute that has made it a symbol of freedom throughout Mesoamerica.

The male in particular, which possesses the distinctive feather train, up to 1.5m long, is still pursued by poachers. The quetzal is further endangered by the destruction of its favoured high-altitude cloudforest habitat. These days the remaining cloudforests – particularly Monteverde and the mountains of Cartago in Costa Rica; the Biotopo del Quetzal in Guatemala's Baja Verapaz; and the Volcán Baru and La Amistad national parks in Panamá – are among the best places to try to see the birds (March–May especially), although they are always difficult to spot, in part due to shyness and in part because the vibrant green of their feathers, seemingly so eyecatchingly bright, actually allows them to blend in well with the wet and shimmering vegetation in which they live.

The increasingly rare **scarlet macaw** (*lapa*), with its liberal splashes of red, yellow and blue, was once common on the Pacific coast of southern Mexico and Central America; they can also be found in the rainforests of Belize (where the Belize Zoo has started a conservation project aimed at protecting the remaining 300 birds), and in the Darien National Park in Panamá.

Parakeets are still fairly numerous and are most often seen in the lowland forested areas of the Pacific coast. You're also likely to see chestnut-mandibled and keel-billed **toucans** (*tucanes*), with their ridiculous – but beautiful – banana-shaped beaks. The chestnut-mandibled is the largest; their bills are two-tone brown and yellow. Keel-billed toucans have the more rainbow-coloured beaks and are smaller, which is sometimes taken advantage of by their larger cousins, who may drive them away from a cache of food or hound them out of a particular tree.

In the **waterways** and **wetlands** of the isthmus, most birds, at least in winter, are migratory species from the north, including herons, gulls, sandpipers and plovers.

The most common bird, and the one you're likely to come across hiking or riding in cattle country, is the unprepossessing grey-white **egret** (*garça*).Of the commonly found **raptors**, the laughing falcon (*guaco*) has the most distinct call, which sounds exactly like its Spanish name. The "laughing" bit comes from a much lower-pitched variation, which resembles muted human laughter. The shrunk-shouldered **vulture** (*zópilote*) is the one bird that almost everyone will see at some point, hanging out opportunistically on the side of major highways waiting for rabbits and iguanas to be thumped beneath the wheels of a passing vehicle.

MAMMALS

Central America's **mammals** range from the fairly unexotic (at least for North Americans and Europeans) white-tailed deer (*venado cola blanca*) and brocket deer (*cabra de monte*), to the lumbering, antediluvian Baird's tapir (*danta*) and the semi-sacred jaguar (*jaguar/tigre*). Now an endangered species, the **jaguar** is endemic to the New World tropics and has a range from southern Mexico to northern Argentina. Although it was once common throughout Central America, especially in the lowland forests and mangroves of coastal areas, the jaguar's main foe has long been man, who has hunted it for its valuable pelt and because of its reputation among farmers as a predator of calves and pigs. It is easily tracked, due to its distinctive footprint. Incredibly, the hunting of jaguars for sport was allowed to continue into the 1980s, although it was at least hampered by the fact that it is illegal to import jaguar pelts into most countries, including the United States.

Though you would be phenomenally lucky (or unlucky, depending on how you see it) to come across a jaguar in the wild, one of the sorriest sights you may come across is a jaguar caged in a hotel or private zoo, where it can do little but pace back and forth. Considered sacred by the Maya, the jaguar is a very beautiful mid-sized cat, nearly always golden with black spots, and very rarely a sleek, solid black. They feed on smaller mammals such as agoutis, monkeys and peccaries, and may also eat fish and birds.

Not to be confused with the jaguar, the **jaguarundi** is a small cat, also very rarely seen, that ranges in colour from reddish to black. Little-studied, the jaguarundi has short legs and a low-slung body, and is sometimes mistaken for the *tayra*, or tropical mink. All the cats have been made extremely shy through centuries of hunting. The one exception, which does not yield a big enough pelt, is the small, sinuous-necked **margay** (*tigrillo*), with its complex black-spotted markings and large, inquisitive eyes. It has been known to peek out of the shadows and even sun itself on the rocks in open view. The **ocelot** (*manigordo*) is similar, somewhere between the margay and jaguar in size, but is another animal you are very unlikely to see. Of all the cats, the sandstone-coloured **mountain lion** (*puma*) is said to be the most forthcoming. It's a big animal, and although not usually aggressive toward humans, it should be treated with respect.

Along with the jaguar, the **tapir** is perhaps the most fantastical beast inhabiting the Neotropical rainforest. Rather homely, with eyes set back on either side of its head, the tapir looks like something between a horse and an overgrown pig, with a stout grey-skinned body and a head that suggests an elephant with a short trunk. Their antediluvian look comes from their prehensile snout, small ears, and delicate cloven feet. Vegetarian creatures weighing as much as 300kg, they are extremely shy in the wild, largely nocturnal, and stick to densely forested or rugged land: consequently they are very rarely spotted by casual rainforest walkers. The tapir has proved to be very amiable in captivity, and is certain to be unaggressive should you be lucky enough to come upon one in the wild. Like the jaguar, its main foe is man, who hunts it for its succulent meat. Nowadays the tapir is protected to a degree, particularly in some of the national parks of Costa Rica and Panamá.

The **peccary** (*saíno*), usually described as a wild pig or boar, comes in two little-differentiated species in Central America: collared or white-lipped. They can be menacing when encountered in packs, when, if they get a whiff of you – their sight is poor so they'll smell you before they see you – they may clack their teeth and growl a bit. The usual advice, especially in Costa Rica's Corcovado National Park, where they travel in groups as large as thirty, is to climb a tree. However, peccaries are not on the whole dangerous and in captivity have proved to be very affectionate, rubbing themselves against you delightedly at the least opportunity.

One of the oddest animals is the tropical **anteater** (*hormiguero*), which you may well see vacuuming an anthill at some point. Top of the list for gregariousness – and sometimes noise – are the several species of **monkey** which inhabit the tropical lowland forests of the region. Most people can expect to at least hear, if not see, the **howler monkey** (*mono congo*), especially in the lowland forests: the male has a mechanism in its thick throat by which it can make sounds similar to those of a gorilla. Their whoops are most often heard at dawn or dusk. The **white-faced** or capuchin (*carablanca*) monkey is slighter than the howler, with a distinctly humanoid expression on its delicate face. This, combined with its intelligence, often consigns it to being a pet in a hotel or private zoo. The **spider monkey** (*araña*) takes its name from its spider-like ability to move through the trees employing its five limbs – the fifth one is its prehensile tail, which it uses to grip branches. The **squirrel monkey** (*mono tití*) is found mainly in and around Manuel Antonio National Park on Costa Rica's Pacific coast, and in parts of Panamá. Their delicate grey and white faces have long made them attractive to pet owners and zoos, and consequently they have been hunted to near-extinction in Costa Rica.

Two types of **sloths** (*perezosos*) live in the trees of the hotter regions of the isthmus: the three-toed sloth, active by day, and the nocturnal two-toed sloth. True to their name, sloths move very little during the day and have an extremely slow metabolism. They are excellently camouflaged from their main predators, eagles, by the algae that often covers their brown fur. In the first instance, at least, they are very difficult to spot, then, when you're used to the familiar hairy clump, you begin to notice them more often.

AMPHIBIANS AND REPTILES (ANFÍBIOS, REPTILES)

If you spot nothing else during your time in Central America, you'll almost certainly see a **frog** or a **toad**. Though they may look vulnerable, many tropical frogs and toads protect themselves by secreting poison through their skin. Using some of the most powerful natural toxins known, the frog can directly target the heart muscle of the predator, paralyzing it and causing immediate death. As these poisons are transmittable through skin contact, you should never touch a rainforest frog. Probably the best-known, and most toxic, of the frogs, is the colourful **poison dart frog**, usually quite small, and found in various combinations of bright red and blue or green and black.

The chief thing you'll notice about the more common frogs are their size: they're much stouter than temperate-zone frogs. Look out for the gaudy **leaf frog** (*rana calzonudo*), star of many a frog calendar. Relatively large, it is an alarming bright green, with orange hands and feet and dark-blue thighs. Its sides are purple, and its eyes are pure red to scare off potential predators.

Travelling along isthmus waterways, in most places you will see **caimans** sunning themselves on riverside logs, and massive **crocodiles** lolling on the mudflats. The crocs look truly fearsome, and usually confine themselves to fresh water – although the reefs off the Belize coast are home to some American saltwater crocodiles.

Pot-bellied **iguanas** are the most ubiquitous of the region's lizards. Despite their dragon-like appearance, they are very shy, and if you do spot them, it's likely that they'll be scurrying away in an ungainly fashion.

Central America is also home to a vast array of **snakes** (*serpientes, culebras*). Many of them are non-venomous, but it's worth knowing about a few of the ones that are in case you have a (statistically very unlikely) encounter. Bear in mind, though, that snakes are largely nocturnal, and for the most part at least as wary of you as you are of them. Of all the snakes it is the **bushmaster** (*cascabela, matabuey*) that inspires the most fear. A viper whose range extends from southern Mexico to Brazil, it is the largest venomous snake in the Americas – it can reach a size of nearly 2m. The most aggressive of snakes, it will actually chase people if it is so inclined. The good news is that you are extremely unlikely to encounter one, as it prefers the sort of dense, precipitous and mountainous territory tourists hardly ever venture into.

Once solely the inhabitant of rainforests, the **fer-de-lance** viper (*terciopelo*) has now adapted quite well to cleared areas, grassy uplands, and even some inhabited stretches, although you are far more likely to see them in places which have heavy rainfall (like the Caribbean coast) and near streams or rivers at night. Though it can reach more than 2m in length, the **terciopelo** (as it is most often called, in English

or Spanish) is well-camouflaged and very difficult to spot, its grey-black skin with a light crisscross pattern resembling a big pile of leaves. Along with the bushmaster, the terciopelo is one of the few snakes that may attack without provocation.

Considering the competition, it's not hard to see why the **boa constrictor** (*boa*) wins the title of most congenial snake. Often with beautiful semi-triangular markings, largely retiring and shy of people, the boa is one of the few snakes you may see in the daytime. Although they are largely torpid, it is not a good idea to bother them. They have big teeth and can bite (though they are not venomous) but are unlikely to stir unless startled. If you encounter one, either on the move or lying still, the best thing is to walk around it slowly, giving it a good 5m berth.

INSECTS (INSECTOS, BICHOS)

The many climates and microclimates of Central America support an enormous diversity of **insects**, of which **butterflies** (*mariposas*) are the most flamboyant and sought-after. Active during the day, they can be seen, especially from about 8am to noon, almost anywhere in the region. Most adult butterflies take their typical food of nectar – usually from red flowers – through a proboscis. Others feed on fungi, dung and rotting fruit. Best-known, and quite often spotted, especially along the forest trails, is the fast-flying **blue morpho**, whose titanium-bright wings seem to shimmer electrically.

The **lantern fly** (*machaca*) emits an amazingly strong mint-blue light, like a mini lightning streak – if you have one in your hotel room you'll know it as soon as you turn out the light. The **ant** kingdom is well-represented, especially in the humid forests. Chief among the rainforest salarymen are the **leaf-cutter ants**, who work in businesslike cadres, carrying away bits of leaf to build their distinctive nests. Endemic to the Neotropics, carnivorous **army ants** are often encountered in the forest, typically living in large colonies, some of more than a million individuals. They are most famous for their "dawn raids", when they pour out of a hideaway, typically a log, and divide into several columns to create a swarm. In this columnar formation then go off in search of prey – other ants and insects – which they carry back to the nest to consume.

MARINE LIFE

Of all the Central American marine areas, Belize's barrier reef and the Bay Islands of Honduras are probably the best places to spot sealife, whether while diving, snorkelling, or taking a boat trip. Belize, in particular, is home to a particularly rich concentration of marine life. The Caribbean **coral life** on the reef and in the Bay Islands is second to none in Central America, with oysters, the distinctive neon pink chalace sponge, the tentacled fire coral, and the apartment sponge – a tall thin tube with small holes stacked neatly through it.

Among the Caribbean coast's marine mammals, the friendliest has to be the sea-cow or **manatee**, elephantine in size, good-natured and well-intentioned, not to mention endangered. Manatees all over the Caribbean and Florida are declining in number, due to the disappearance and pollution of the fresh or saltwater riverways in which they live. You may come across them in the coastal areas of Belize. In Costa Rica your only reasonable chance of seeing one is in the Tortuguero canals in Limón province, where they sometimes break the surface. At first you might mistake it for a tarpon, but the manatee's overlapping snout and long whiskers are quite distinctive.

Five species of **marine turtle** nest on Central America's shores. Nesting takes place mostly at night and mostly in the context of *arribadas*: giant invasions of turtles who come ashore in their thousands on the same beach (or spot of beach) at a certain time of year, laying hundreds of thousands of eggs. Greens, hawksbills and leatherbacks come ashore on both coasts, while the Olive Ridley comes ashore only on the Pacific.

The strange blunt-nosed **loggerhead** can sometimes be seen in Belize, although they are still hunted for food there and so their numbers are in decline. The **green turtle**, long-prized for

the delicacy of its flesh, has become nearly synonymous with its favoured nesting grounds at Tortuguero in northeast Costa Rica. In the 1950s it was classified as endangered but, thanks in part to the protection offered by areas like Tortuguero, is making a comeback. Some greens make herculean journeys of as much as 2000km to their breeding beaches, returning to the same stretch year after year. *Arribadas* are most concentrated in June and October.

The **hawksbill** (*carey*), so-named for its distinctive down-curving "beak", is found all over the tropics, often preferring rocky shores and coral reefs. It used to be hunted extensively on the Caribbean coast for its meat and shell, but this is now banned. Poaching does still occur, however, and you should avoid buying any tortoiseshell that you see for sale. Capable of growing to a length of 5m, the **leatherback** (*baula*) is the largest reptile in the world. Its "shell" is actually a network of bones overlaid with a very tough leathery skin. Though it nests most concentratedly on the Pacific beaches, it also comes ashore on the Caribbean coast.

The **Olive Ridley** (*lora, carpintera* – also called the Pacific Ridley) turtle nests on Pacific beaches, particularly on its protected grounds at Playa Nancite in Santa Rosa National Park and Ostional near Nosara on Costa Rica's Nicoya Peninsula. They come ashore in massive *arribadas* and, unusually, often nest during the day.

The **black river turtle** and the **snapping turtle**, about which little is known (except that it snaps), also inhabit rivers and mangrove swamps, and may occasionally be spotted on the riverbanks.

Though **dolphins** (*delfínes*) and **whales** thread themselves through the waters of the Pacific coast, it's rare to see them, as they usually remain many miles offshore. **Sharks** (*tiburones*) can be found on both coasts, and though the vast majority of species are harmless, it's wise to ask around before going for a swim.

ECOTOURISM

Global **tourism** is a multi-billion dollar industry. With some 567m international tourists per year, the industry was worth, in 1995, around US$372bn – figures which are set to more than double by the year 2010. Though notoriously difficult to classify in any generally accepted form, **ecotourism** is estimated to account for as much as forty percent of the market. Through sheer numbers alone, such tourism is bound to have an impact even on societies which are sufficiently developed to be able to absorb it, and many of the relatively undisturbed areas that appeal to the ecotourist are located in precisely those societies that may be least able to absorb such an impact, and handle its possibly negative consequences.

Since the term was coined a decade or so ago, the **rationale** behind ecotourism has been that the relatively large sums of money dispensed by visitors from developed nations could be channelled successfully into protecting the natural resources they come to visit. By enabling local people to earn more by protecting their environment and encouraging visitors to come to it, both sides are able, theoretically, to benefit. In the words of the London-based Economics for Environment Consultancy, all natural resources have a "rent", or scarcity value. Local management of the resource and the capturing of this rent in the form of visitor fees, can be used to control the number of people visiting the resource, and allows for greater flexibility in determining and funding the best method of protection. This protection should be in line with local customs and traditions, and the evolution of the local society itself.

DEFINITIONS

Ecotourism is a tricky term to **define**. It is often seen in relation to what it is not: package tourism, wherein visitors have limited contact with nature and with the day-to-day lives of local people. But as more and more organizations and businesses hijack the eco prefix for dubious uses, the authentic ecotourism experience has become increasingly difficult to pin down. For some, ecotourism is a way of assuring themselves that they are a better tourist, and that they are giving something back. Others point to the fundamental **contradiction** between attempting to protect an area whilst encouraging large numbers of people to visit it – at heart, perhaps, the best way to be an ecotourist is not to be a tourist at all. Lying somewhere between these different views is the argument that if people are going to travel, they may as well do so in a low-impact manner that minimizes destruction of the visited environment and promotes cultural exchange.

One of the best attempts to put forward a workable definition has been made by **ATEC**, the Talamancan Ecotourism and Conservation Association in southwest Costa Rica, which seeks to promote "socially responsible tourism"

CODES OF CONDUCT

Though well-meaning, ecotourism **codes of conduct** can seem preachy and presumptuous. Still, in any attempt to define the term, or to go any way towards understanding its aims, it's useful to know what the locally accepted guidelines are. The Asociación Tsuli, the Costa Rican branch of the Audubon Society, has developed its own short code of conduct, called **Environmental Ethics for Nature Travel**:

1   Wildlife and natural habitats must not be needlessly disturbed.
2   Waste should be disposed of properly.
3   Tourism should be a positive influence on local communities.
4   Tourism should be managed and sustainable.
5   Tourism should be culturally sensitive.
6   There must be no commerce in wildlife, wildlife products, or native plants.
7   Tourists should leave with a greater understanding and appreciation of nature, conservation and the environment.
8   Tourism should strengthen the conservation effort and enhance the natural integrity of places visited.

by integrating local Bribrí and Afro-Caribbean culture into tourists' experience of the area, as well as giving residents pride in their unique cultural heritage and natural environment. They say: "Ecotourism means more than bird books and binoculars. Ecotourism means more than native art hanging on hotel walls or ethnic dishes on the restaurant menu. Ecotourism is not mass tourism behind a green mask. Ecotourism means a constant struggle to defend the earth and to protect and sustain traditional communities. Ecotourism is a cooperative relationship between the non-wealthy local community and those sincere, open-minded tourists who want to enjoy themselves in a Third World setting and, at the same time, enrich their consciousness by means of significant educational and cultural experience."

A CASE STUDY: COSTA RICA

Along with Belize, **Costa Rica** has become virtually synonymous with ecotourism in Central America and is widely regarded as being at the cutting edge of worldwide conservation strategy, an impressive feat for a small, cash-strapped Central American nation. At the centre of its internationally applauded conservation effort is a complex system of national parks and wildlife refuges which protect a full 25 percent of its territory. These statistics are used with great effect to attract tourists, the vast majority of whom still come to see the country's remarkably varied tropical flora and fauna.

However, for years the country has been in danger of being overwhelmed by its own popularity, attracting over 700,000 visitors annually – the population of the country itself is only 3.5 million. Not surprisingly, what most concerns biologists nowadays is how much damage is being caused by so many feet tramping through the rainforests.

In **Manuel Antonio National Park**, on Costa Rica's Pacific Coast, visitors can walk seaside trails, one of which circles the stunning Punta Cathedral, which juts out into the sea. As ecotourism experiences go, it's a soft option, easily reachable and sandwiched between beautiful beaches. Here the **squirrel monkeys**, an endangered species, have become too used to people. Ecotourists walking Manuel Antonio's trails complain about them behaving "as if they were in a zoo", begging for food and being cheeky, or alternately hiding from the

stress of having, on popular holidays like Easter, literally hundreds of people trudge through their habitat. Rangers at Manuel Antonio talk openly of the "psychological pressure" large numbers of visitors put on some animals. When the squirrel monkeys began to display symptoms of neurosis, officials took the decision to shut the park on Mondays, to give the animals a rest.

Monteverde and **Santa Elena**, two small farming communities high in the mountains of the Cordillera Central, are home to two reserves that together protect one of the last sizeable pristine pieces of **cloudforest** (high-altitude rainforest) in the Americas. In recent years increasing tourism has transformed the communities, and flotillas of tourist buses rattle up and down the muddy roads connecting the towns to the reserves. In the high season, the Monteverde administrators have had to set a 100-visitor-a-day ceiling in order to preserve the ecological integrity of the reserve. Both communities have resisted paving the 40-kilometre stretch of road which links them with the Carretera Interamericana, in an attempt to avoid a day-tripper culture where visitors would be bussed up to the reserve for the day and then back down to their beach hotels, spending little money but having the maximum impact on the local environment.

It could be argued that an underdeveloped country in need of foreign currency shouldn't complain about being too popular, especially when the type of tourism it has developed is so very "green". But Costa Rica highlights what some observers criticize about the concept of ecotourism – at least in Latin America – that it represents not so much an act of environmental altruism but is merely part of an imperialist, bourgeois agenda: wealthy first-world ecotourists can console themselves that they are saving the environment, but what about the 38 percent of Costa Rica's population who live in poverty and without access to land? Many tropical biologists have concluded that, in sum, if you love the rainforest, it would be better to stay at home and donate money to conservation organizations rather than travelling abroad to tramp through the forests and change local economies with the influx of your dollars. Ask any national park or private reserve administrator in Costa Rica about this and their response is nearly uniform – "People are going to come anyway. You can't stop them. Our job is to make sure the tourism is managed properly."

It's a delicate balance. Many powerful vested interests are lined up to log, mine and prospect for minerals in Costa Rica. As the country with the highest population density in Central America, there is also tremendous pressure on land, and parks are regularly invaded by squatters. There's no doubt that the financial success of ecotourism has guaranteed the survival of many natural places. All you have to do is look at the land *not* protected by the reserves – the lowlands around Monteverde, for example, which have now been almost completely cleared for pasture.

ECOTOURISM AROUND CENTRAL AMERICA

While there may be no lack of genuine enthusiasm for ecotourism across Central America, sadly in many cases a lack of money means that numerous wildlife, nature and marine reserves across the region have little real existence except on paper. Political turmoil during the 1980s and the grinding problems of poverty mean that – with the notable exception of Costa Rica – questions of environmental preservation and sustainability have until recently been largely neglected.

Honduras, for example, has an extensive national network of parks and reserves, many of which were designated protected areas only in 1987. Some, like Celaque in the central highlands and Cusuco near San Pedro Sula, are extremely well-managed and have ensured the protection of irreplaceable tracts of virgin forest and fragile ecosystems. Others exist as little more than lines on maps, and given the government's lack of resources, local people's need for land, and the at times illegal activities of large landowners, there's little realistic chance of changing this situation.

In **El Salvador**, a nascent network of national parks is now in existence. Perhaps the most advanced – in terms of a comprehensive project for both environmental protection and community development – is the Bosque Montecristo, part of the El Trifinio international biosphere, administered jointly by the governments of El Salvador, Honduras and Guatemala. The work carried out here places as much emphasis on the local indigenous communities as on environmental protection. Similar developments can

be seen in **Panamá**, whose Nusangandi Nature Reserve in Kuna Yala was the first reserve in Latin America to be set up and administed by an indigenous people.

Since the mid-1980s the number of foreign tourists visiting **Belize** each year has grown from fewer than 100,000 to well over 300,000 – the result of deliberate decisions taken by successive governments to promote tourism as the way to generate much needed foreign-exchange revenues. Moreover, given Belize's abundant natural resources – the second-largest barrier reef in the world, tropical forest, Maya ruins – this promotion has been founded on "greenness" and sustainability. Marine, wildlife and archeological reserves have been established, with local groups encouraged to take an active part in developing and maintaining ecotourist facilities. In Central America and the Caribbean, Belize is seen as having paved the way in creating a locally controlled industry that benefits both cultural traditions and the environment.

Certainly the country has benefited, with at least one quarter of its GNP now derived from tourist revenues. Underneath the surface, however, things are a less than rosy, with growing disquiet about the nature of so-called ecotourist development and fears that the industry is now spiralling beyond the control of Belizeans. Deliberate marketing of the country as a "green" destination has created a demand which it's thought can only be met by more and larger tourist developments, funded, if not managed, by foreign capital. The proposals to regenerate Belize City's waterfront were a case in point, having been drawn up initially under the sponsorship of US aid which aimed to create a "downtown" area studded with hotels, shops, restaurants and bars. Despite its appeal to tourists, such a development would be of little benefit to Belizean residents, who still have to put up with decaying infrastructure and increasing poverty and crime. Nor was it immediately apparent how much – if any – of the revenues generated by this project would flow directly to the local community. Similarly, plans for the redevelopment of Ambergris Caye sparked a long-running controversy when it emerged that the government proposed to transfer over one-third of the island to a US developer for the creation of an upmarket resort.

NEW INITIATIVES: THE WAY FORWARD

In recent years Mario Boza, prominent conservationist and a founder of Costa Rica's national parks system, has advocated a strategy of **macro-conservation**. Shifting the emphasis from individual country projects in favour of linking together chunks of protected land across national borders, he argues, will allow the creation of larger protected areas for animals that need room to hunt, like jaguars and pumas. Even more importantly, these initiatives will allow countries to make more effective joint conservation policies and decisions.

Macro-conservation **projects** include the Proyeto Paseo Pantera (all of Mesoamerica), El Mundo Maya (Belize, El Salvador, Guatemala, Honduras and Mexico), Si-a-Paz (Nicaragua and Costa Rica) and Parque Internacíonal La Amistad (Costa Rica and Panamá). The largest conservation project undertaken in the western hemisphere, the **Paseo Pantera** (Path of the Panther) is an interesting example of ecological co-operation between the Central American governments. When completed it is hoped this green corridor will allow unimpeded migration, north and south, of a wide range of animal, bird, and marine life. In some species this could be the answer to long-term survival (jaguars, for instance, need about 100 square kilometres in which to roam). Part of the strategy is to implement a tightly controlled ecotourism program, with tourist dollars helping to pay the green corridor's way.

Arguably, however, the most revolutionary change in conservation management, and the one likeliest to have the biggest pay-off in the long term, is the shift towards **local initiatives**. Some projects are truly local, such as the tiny grassroots organization TUVA on Costa Rica's Osa peninsula, which oversees the selective logging of naturally felled rainforest trees, or the ecotourism co-operative of Las Delicias on Costa Rica's Nicoya Peninsula, which provides professional guides to take tourists into Central America's largest underground caves. Another initiative, even more promising in terms of how it affects the lives of many rural-based Central Americans, is the creation of "buffer zones" around some national parks. In these zones campesinos and other smallholders can do part-time farming, are allowed restricted hunting rights and receive education as to the ecological and economic value of the forest. Locals may be trained as nature guides, and campesinos may be given incentives to practise non-traditional forms of agriculture and ways of making a living which are not so harmful to the environment.

In the Talamanca region of Costa Rica, ATEC (source of the "ecotourism definition" offered on p.802) takes tourists on tours of the local **indigenous** KeköLdi reserve. The Bribrí indigenous guides take outsiders into the local villages, on treks through the rainforest pointing out traditional medicinal uses of many plants, and demonstrate how many local products such as banana vinegar, guava jam and herbal teas are made. All tour fees go back into the local community. In the department of La Mosquitia, Honduras, the **Pech** indigenous people live in small villages near the headwaters of the Río Plátano, within the protected lands of the 5000-square-kilometre UNESCO Biosphere Reserve of the same name. Their income is supplemented by offering guide services and by selling miniature wooden carvings of *pipantes* (dugout canoes) and small bags of packaged cocoa. Some tour operators are taking tourists on multi-day jungle excursions in the area, and a fair portion of this revenue goes directly into the pockets of the indigenous Pech, Miskito and Garífuna communities visited.

Despite the problems outlined above, there's no question that ecotourism is the most effective way of preserving the natural environment while allowing it to pay its way. At present, though, the onus falls on eco-minded visitors to make sure their dollars are going to the right place. Probably the most positive sign for the future is the growth in community-based projects, a step forward in the development of an economically viable industry that's committed to protecting the stunning landscapes, wildlife and cultures of Central America.

BOOKS

The following is a list of the books that proved most useful – or enjoyable – in the preparation of this guide. General books are listed first, followed by individual sections on each country. Publishers are given in the format UK/US; where only one publisher is listed, this covers both the UK and US, unless specified.

CENTRAL AMERICA

HISTORY, POLITICS AND SOCIETY

James Dunkerley, *Power in the Isthmus* and *The Pacification of Central America* (Norton /Verso). Detailed accounts of Central American politics (excluding Belize) offering a good overview of events up to the early 1990s, particularly the region's civil wars. Well researched with plenty of statistics and charts, though the style is factual rather than flowing.

In Focus (LAB/Interlink Books). An excellent series of country guides giving concise, highly readable accounts of the people, politics and culture of each nation. Titles are currently available covering Costa Rica, Guatemala, Belize and Nicaragua.

Inside (LAB/Resource Center). A series of country guides covering the history, politics, economy and society of all the Central America nations. Though now rather out of date, each title is packed with accessible facts and analysis, and still makes useful background reading.

Peter Dale-Scott and Jonathan Marshall, *Cocaine Politics: Drugs, Armies and the CIA in Central America* (University of California Press). Polemical but well-researched exposé of CIA involvement in cocaine trafficking and political oppression in Cental America in the 1980s.

Reveals the truth behind the Iran–Contra scandal and gives the lie to the rhetoric of the war on drugs.

William Weinberg, *War on the Land: Ecology and Politics in Central America* (Zed Books/ Humanities Press). The author tells a story of intertwining conflicts and causes between conservation (and to a small extent ecotourism), land rights and politics in the individual Central American countries in a volume that deftly straddles the gap between academic studies of these subjects and the general-interest reader.

Ralph Lee Woodward Jr, *Central America: A Nation Divided* (Oxford University Press). More readable than Dunkerley, and probably the best general summary of the Central American situation, despite its daft title.

TRAVEL AND IMPRESSIONS

Simon Calder, *The Panamericana* (Vacation Work). Prolific writer, broadcaster and veteran backpackper Calder travels the entire Carretera Panamericana – the Pan-American Highway – from the Texas border to Yaviza in Panamá. An enormously funny and candid guide to the road and places just off it, the book is also packed with information and observations – the diagrams of border crossings are particularly useful.

Thomas Gage, *Travels in the New World* (University of Oklahoma Press). Unusual account of a Dominican friar's travels through Mexico and Central America between 1635 and 1637, including some fascinating insights into colonial life as well as some great attacks on the greed and pomposity of the Catholic Church abroad.

Aldous Huxley, *Beyond the Mexique Bay* (Flamingo, UK). Huxley's travels, in 1934, took him from Belize through Guatemala to Mexico, swept on by his fascination for history and religion, and sprouting bizarre theories on the basis of everything he sees. There are some great descriptions of Maya sites and indigenous culture, with superb one-liners summing up people and places.

Jeremy Paxman, *Through the Volcanoes* (Paladin). A political travel account investigating the turmoil of Central America and finding solace in the calm of Costa Rica. Paxman's travels take him through all seven of the republics, including Belize, and he offers a good overview of the politics and history of the region.

John Lloyd Stephens, *Incidents of Travel in Central America, Chiapas, and Yucatán* (Dover). Stephens was a classic nineteenth-century traveller. Acting as American ambassador to Central America, he indulged his own enthusiasm for archeology; while the republics fought it out among themselves he was wading through the jungle stumbling across ancient cities. His journals, told with superb Victorian pomposity punctuated with sudden waves of enthusiasm, make great reading. Some editions include fantastic illustrations by Catherwood of the ruins overgrown with tropical rainforest.

Ronald Wright, *Time Among the Maya* (Abacus/Henry Holt). A vivid and sympathetic account of travels from Belize through Guatemala, Chiapas and Yucatán, meeting the Maya and exploring their obsession with time. The book's twin points of interest are the ancient Maya and the violence of the 1970s and 80s, subjects which are covered with superb historical insight, whilst an encyclopedic bibliography offers ideas for further reading. Certainly one of the best travel books on the area.

ARCHEOLOGY AND MAYA CIVILIZATION

Michael Coe, *The Maya* (Thames & Hudson). Now in its sixth edition, this clear and comprehensive introduction to Maya archeology is the best on offer. Coe has also written several more weighty, academic volumes. His *Breaking the Maya Code* (Penguin/Thames & Hudson), a very personal history of the decipherment of the glyphs, owes much to the fact that Coe was present at many of the most important meetings leading to the breakthrough.

Joyce Kelly, *An Archaeological Guide to Northern Central America* (University of Oklahoma Press). Detailed and practical guide to 38 Maya sites and 25 museums in four countries; an essential companion for anyone travelling purposefully through the Maya region of Central America. Kelly's star ratings – based on a site's archeological importance, degree of restoration and accessibility – may affront purists but it does provide a valuable opinion on how worthwhile a particular visit might be.

Mary Ellen Miller and Karl Taube *The Gods and Symbols of Ancient Mexico and the Maya: An Illustrated Dictionary of Mesoamerican Religion* (Thames & Hudson). A superb modern reference on ancient Mesoamerica, written by two leading scholars. Taube's *Aztec and Maya Myths* (British Museum Press, UK) is perfect as a short, accessible introduction to Mesoamerican mythology.

Jeremy A. Sabloff, *The New Archaeology and the Ancient Maya* (Scientific American Library). Sabloff explains the "revolution" which has taken place in Maya archeology since the 1960s, overturning many firmly held beliefs and assumptions on the nature of Maya society, and explaining how the study of archeology relates to current environmental problems.

Linda Schele and David Freidel. These two authors, both in the forefront of the "new archeology", have been personally responsible for decoding many of the glyphs. While their writing style, which frequently includes "recreations" of scenes inspired by their discoveries, is controversial, it has nevertheless inspired a devoted following. *A Forest of Kings: The Untold Story of the Ancient Maya* (Quill, US), in conjunction with *The Blood of Kings*, by Linda Schele and Mary Miller, shows that far from being governed by peaceful astronomer-priests, the ancient Maya were ruled by hereditary kings, lived in populous and aggressive city-states, and engaged in a continuous entanglement of alliances and war. *The Maya Cosmos* (Quill, US), by Schele, Freidel and Joy Parker, is a more difficult read, but continues the examination of Maya ritual and religion in a unique and far-reaching way. *The Code of Kings* (Shribner, US), written in collaboration with Peter Matthews and illustrated with Justin Kerr's famous "rollout" photography of Maya ceramics, examines the significance of the monuments at selected Maya sites in detail. It's her last book – Linda Schele died in April 1998 – and now a classic of epigraphic interpretation.

Robert Sharer, *The Ancient Maya* (Stanford University Press). Classic, comprehensive and weighty account of Maya civilization, now in a completely revised and much more readable fifth edition, yet as authoritative as ever. Required reading for archeologists, and a fascinating reference for the non-expert.

FICTION

Rosario Santos (ed), *And We Sold the Rain: Contemporary Fiction from Central America*

(Ryan Publishing, UK). Put together in the late 1980s, this well-translated collection is still one of the best volumes of short stories from the isthmus, bringing together new contemporary writers of national stature from all the countries (many of them women). The introduction, by Jo Anne Englebert, gives an excellent overview of Central American literature in context.

WILDLIFE AND THE ENVIRONMENT

Catherine Caulfield, *In the Rainforest* (o/p). Still one of the best introductory volumes to the rainforest, dealing in an accessible, discursive fashion with many of the issues covered in the more academic or specialized titles. Much of the book is directed at the Amazon, but could easily be transposed to Panamá, Guatemala or Costa Rica – the author turns a wry eye on Costa Rica's cattle-ranching culture, as well as providing an interesting profile of the farming methods used by the Monteverde community.

Louise H. Emmons, *Neotropical Rainforest Mammals* (University of Chicago). Supported by François Feer's colour illustrations, this highly informative book is written by experts for non-scientists. Local and scientific names are given, along with plenty of interesting snippets.

Steve Howell and Sophie Webb, *The Birds of Mexico and Northern Central America* (Oxford University Press). The result of years of research, this tremendous work is the definitive book on the region's birds. Essential for all serious birders.

John C. Kricher, *A Neotropical Companion* (Princeton University Press). Subtitled "An Introduction to the Animals, Plants and Ecosystems of the New World Tropics" and containing an amazing amount of valuable information for nature lovers. Researched mainly in Central America, so there's plenty that's directly relevant.

BELIZE

HISTORY, POLITICS AND SOCIETY

Emory King, *The Great Story of Belize* (Tropical Books, Belize). Four slim, large-format volumes from a master raconteur. The meticulously researched narrative, full of events great and small and packed with larger-than-life characters, presents a vivid account of Belize's history from the first Spanish contact up to the 1990s.

Gerald S. Koop, *Pioneer Years in Belize* (Country Graphics, Belize). A history of the Mennonites in Belize, written in a style as stolid and practical as the lives of the pioneers themselves. A good read nonetheless.

Assad Shoman, *Thirteen Chapters of a History of Belize* (Angelus Press, Belize). A long-overdue treatment of the country's history written by a Belizean who's not afraid to examine colonial myths with a detailed and rational analysis. Primarily a school textbook, but the style will not alienate non-student readers. Shoman, active in politics both before and since independence, also wrote *Party Politics in Belize*, a short but highly detailed account of the development of party politics in the country.

Ann Sutherland, *The Making of Belize: Globalization in the Margins* (Bergin and Garvey, US). A recent study of cultural and economic changes in Belize, based on the author's experiences as a visitor and her observations as an anthropologist. The result is an enjoyable mixture of academic research, anecdotal insights and strong, even controversial, opinion; Sutherland reserves her strongest criticism for conservationists, whom she castigates as "eco-colonialists [who] totally disregard the interests of the Belizean people".

ARCHEOLOGY

Rosita Arvigo with Nadia Epstein, *Sastun: My Apprenticeship with a Maya Healer* (Harper). A rare glimpse into the life and work of a Maya *curandero*, the late Elijio Panti of San Antonio, Belize. Rosita Arvigo has ensured the survival of many generations of accumulated healing knowledge, and this book is a testimony both to her perseverance in becoming accepted by Elijio Panti and the cultural wisdom of the indigenous people. Arvigo has also written and co-authored several other books on traditional medicine in Belize, including *Rainforest Remedies*.

Byron Foster (ed), *Warlords and Maize Men – A Guide to the Maya Sites of Belize* (Cubola, Belize). An excellent handbook to fifteen of the most accessible sites in Belize, compiled by the Association for Belizean Archeology and the Belize Department of Archeology.

J. Eric S. Thompson, *The Maya of Belize – Historical Chapters Since Columbus* (Cubola, Belize). Interesting study of Belizean history in the first two centuries of Spanish colonial rule.

It's a little-researched area of Belizean history and casts some light on the groups that weren't immediately conquered by the Spanish.

FICTION, POETRY AND AUTOBIOGRAPHY

Zee Edgell, *Beka Lamb* (Heinemann). A young girl's account of growing up in Belize in the 1950s, in which the problems of adolescence are described alongside those of the Belizean independence movement. The book also explores everyday life in the colony, describing the powerful structure of matriarchal society and the influence of the Catholic Church. *In Times Like These* (Heinemann) is a semi-autobiographical account of personal and political intrigue set in the months leading up to Belize's independence.

Zoila Ellis, *On Heroes, Lizards and Passion* (Cubola Productions, Belize). Seven short stories written by a Belizean woman with a deep understanding of her country's people and their culture.

Felicia Hernandez, *Those Ridiculous Years* (Cubola Productions, Belize). A short autobiographical book about growing up in Dangriga in the 1960s.

Emory King, *Belize 1798* (Tropical Books, Belize). Rip-roaring historical novel peopled by the characters involved in the Battle of St George's Caye. King's enthusiasm for his country's history results in the nearest thing you'll get to a Belizean blockbuster, yet it's based on meticulous research in archives on both sides of the Atlantic. Wonderful holiday reading.

Carlos Ledson Miller *Belize – A Novel* (Xlibris, US). Fast-paced historical saga of a Central American father and his two sons – one American and one Belizean – who struggle against a forbidding land, and often with each other. The story opens in 1961, on the eve of Hurricane Hattie, then transports the reader across forty years from the unrest of colonial British Honduras to the turbulence of present-day Belize. A good read.

Various, *Shots From The Heart* (Cubola Productions, Belize). Slim anthology of the work of three young Belizean poets: Yasser Musa, Kiren Shoman and Simone Waight. Evocative imagery and perceptive comment relate experiences of a changing society. Musa's *Belize City Poem* (published separately) is a sharply observed, at times vitriolic, commentary on the

simultaneous arrival of independence and US dominated television on Belizean society.

WILDLIFE

Les Betelsky *Belize and Northern Guatemala – the Ecotraveller's Wildlife Guide* (Academic Press, UK). Although other, specialist wildlife guides may cover their subjects in more detail, this is the only reasonably comprehensive single-volume guide to the mammals, birds, reptiles, amphibians and marine life of the region. Helpfully, the illustration of each creature is given opposite its description, avoiding confusing page-flicking.

Alan Rabinowitz *Jaguar* (Arbor House, UK). Rabinowitz was instrumental in establishing Belize's Jaguar Reserve in 1984. This is an account of his experiences studying jaguars for the New York Zoological Society in the early 1980s and living with a Maya family in the Cockscomb Basin, Belize

SPECIFIC GUIDES

Kirk Barrett, *Belize by Kayak*. The most detailed book on this increasingly popular activity, though it's not widely available; contact Reef Link Kayaking, 3806 Cottage Grove, Des Moines, Iowa, USA.

GUATEMALA

HISTORY, POLITICS AND SOCIETY

Tom Barry, *Guatemala: A Country Guide* (Resource Center). A comprehensive and concise account of the political, social and economic situation in Guatemala, with a mild left-wing stance. Currently the best overview of the situation.

Anthony Daniels, *Sweet Waist of America* (o/p). This delightful book takes a refreshingly even-handed approach to Guatemala and comes up with a fascinating cocktail of people and politics, discarding the stereotypes that litter most books on Central America.

Jim Handy, *Gift of the Devil* (South End Press). The best modern history of Guatemala, concise and readable, with a sharp focus on the Maya population and the brief period of socialist government. Don't expect too much detail on the distant past, which is only explored in order to put the modern reality into some kind of context, but if you're interested in the history of

Guatemalan brutality then this is the book to read, as it sets out to expose the development of oppression and point the finger at those responsible.

Rigoberta Menchú, *Rigoberta Menchú – An Indian Woman in Guatemala* and *Crossing Borders* (Verso). Momentous story of one of Latin America's most remarkable women, Nobel Peace Prize winner, Rigoberta Menchú. The first volume is a horrific account of family life in the Maya highlands, recording how Menchú's famly were targeted, terrorized and murdered by the military. The book also reveals much concerning Quiché Maya cultural traditions and the enormous gulf between *ladino* and indigenous society in Guatemala. The second volume documents Menchú's life in exile in Mexico, her work at the United Nations fighting for indigenous people and her return to Guatemala. An astounding tale of a woman's spirit, courage and determination.

Víctor Perera, *Unfinished Conquest* (Califormia University Press). Written by a Guatemalan, this is a superb and extremely readable account of the civil war, and also has comprehensive coverage of the political, social and economic inequalities affecting the country. Immaculately researched, the book's strength comes from its extensive interviews with Guatemalans and its incisive analysis of recent history.

The Popol Vuh. The great poem of the Quiché, written shortly after the Conquest and intended to preserve the tribe's knowledge of its history. It's an amazing swirl of ancient mythological characters and their wanderings through the Quiché highlands, tracing their ancestry back to its beginning. The best version is translated by Dennis Tedlock and published by Touchstone in the US.

Jean-Marie Simon, *Eternal Spring – Eternal Tyranny* (W.W. Norton). Of all the books on human rights in Guatemala, this is the one that speaks with the greatest clarity, combining the highest standards in photography with crisp text. If you want to know what happened in Guatemala over the last twenty years or so there is no better book.

FICTION

Miguel Angel Asturias, *Hombres de Maíz* (Macmillan). Guatemala's most famous author,

Nobel Prize winner Asturias's fiction is deeply indebted to Guatemalan history and culture. *Men of Maize* is generally regarded as his masterpiece, classically Latin American in its magic realist style, and bound up in the complexity of indigenous culture. His other works include *El Señor Presidente*, a grotesque portrayal of social chaos and dictatorial rule, based on Asturias's own experience; *El Papa Verde*, which explores the murky world of the United Fruit Company; and *Weekend en Guatemala*, describing the downfall of the Arbenz government.

Francisco Goldman, *The Long Night of White Chickens* (Grove Press). The tale of a young Guatemalan orphan who flees to the US and works as a maid before finally returning home, where she is murdered. It's an interesting and ambitious story, flavoured with all the bitterness and beauty of Guatemala's natural and political landscape.

Gaspar Pedro Gonzales, *A Mayan Life* (Yax Te' Press, US). Absorbing story of the personal and cultural difficulties affecting a K'anjobal Maya from the Cuchumatanes mountains. The conflict between indigenous and *ladino* values becomes acutely evident as the central character seeks a higher education. Rich in ethnological detail and highly autobiographical, the book claims to be the first novel ever written by a Maya writer.

SPECIALIST GUIDES

William Coe, *Tikal: A Handbook to the Ancient Maya Ruins*. Superbly detailed account of the site, usually available at the ruins. The detailed map of the main area is essential for in-depth exploration.

EL SALVADOR

HISTORY, POLITICS AND SOCIETY

Robert Armstrong and Janet Shenk, *El Salvador: The Face of Revolution* (South End Press). Accessible history of the root causes and development of the civil war of the 1980s.

Tom Barry and Kent Norsworthy, *El Salvador: A Country Guide* (Resource Center). Concise study of contemporary political, economic and social affairs, with historical background, detailing the initiatives made in the years following the 1992 Peace Accords.

Charles Clements, *Witness to War* (Bantam Press). Fascinating account of a year spent by a volunteer US doctor working in the guerrilla zone of Guazapa in the early 1980s, offering a vivid portrayal of how the civil war affected a specific area – and by extension suggesting what conditions were like across the border in El Salvador.

Larry Dowell, **Mark Deinner**, *El Salvador* (Norton). Evocative and compelling collection of photographs taken during 1986, sharply delineating the progress of the civil war and its impact.

FICTION AND POETRY

Roque Dalton, *Taberna y Otras Lugares* and *Poemas Clandestinas*; *Pobrecito Poeta que era Yo*. Perhaps the most famous El Salvadorean poet, Dalton was also a journalist and revolutionary, and in constant open conflict with successive governments. Born in 1935, he was imprisoned and exiled on various occasions, but always returned to the land of his birth. He was a member of the People's Revolutionary Army (ERP) in the early 1970s, along with founder members of the FMLN. After differences of opinion led to his departing the movement he was assassinated on ERP orders in May 1975 near Guazapa; his death remains a landmark in Salvadorean literary history and still remains unsolved. *Taberna y Otras Lugares* and *Poemas Clandestinas* are both collections of poetry, while *Pobrecito Poeta que era Yo* is a novella.

Salarrué, *Eso y Más*, *Cuentos de Barro* and *La Espada y Otras Narraciones*. Born Salvador Salazar Arrué in 1899, Salarrué is one of the most widely known El Salvadorean writers. His short stories and novellas focus on the lives and realities of campesinos and non-metropolites.

Various, *Mirrors of War* (Zed Books). Wide-ranging collection of modern poetry and prose by Salvadorean writers, focusing on the causes and impact of the civil war.

HONDURAS

HISTORY, POLITICS AND SOCIETY

Tom Barry and Kent Norsworthy, *Honduras: A Country Guide* (Resource Center). Concise but comprehensive study of contemporary political, economic and social affairs, with some historical background.

William V. Davidson *Historical Geography of the Bay Islands, Honduras* (South University Press, US). A study of the physical and cultural development of the islands, including some interesting bits of background information.

TRAVEL AND IMPRESSIONS

Peter Ford, *Tekkin a Waalk along the Miskito Coast* (Flamingo Press). In the mid-1980s Ford gave himself the task of walking along the Caribbean coast from Belize to Nicaragua, resulting in this nice tale, with snippets of information on Garífuna history and contemporary development.

FICTION

Paul Theroux, *The Mosquito Coast* (Penguin). Well-known tale of the collapse of a man in the steaming heat of Mosquitia. Though entertaining, Theroux only touches on a remote corner of Honduras and the novel does little to enlighten the reader about the country as a whole. The movie, with Harrison Ford and Helen Mirren, was filmed in Belize.

Guillermo Yuscarán is the pen name of expatriate Willam Lewis, a long-time resident of Honduras. His novels and short stories, illustrating contemporary Honduran life, can be bought (Spanish and English-language; Nuevo Sol, Tegucigalpa) in bookshops in Tegucigalpa and San Pedro Sula.

SPECIALIST GUIDES

William L. Fash, *Scribes, Warriors and Kings* (Thames & Hudson). The definitive guide to the ruins of Copán, lavishly adorned with drawings, photographs and superb maps.

Cindy Garoute, *Diving the Bay Islands* (Aqua Quest, US). Glossy book with lots of great photos outlining the best places to dive off all the islands. Consider it essential if you're going to spend much time diving here.

NICARAGUA

HISTORY, POLITICS AND SOCIETY

John Brentlinger, *The Best of What We Are, Reflections on the Nicaraguan Revolution* (University of Massachusetts Press). An interesting journal of the period 1985–92 which attempts to explain that unity of thought and action, of real and unreal, of religion and magic, of life and death that is so present in Nicaragua even today.

Kent Norsworthy & Tom Barry, *Nicaragua: A Country Guide* (Resource Center). Good guide to the history, politics, economics, culture and society of modern Nicaragua, written in concise, lucid prose and including extensive reference notes and appendices.

Holly Sklar, *Washington's War on Nicaragua* (South End Press). A dissection of US policy on Nicaragua in all its ugly manifestations. Covers the Iran-Contra affair, the years of political double talk that undermined regional attempts to broker peace, the drug running, gun running and espionage that sought to destabilize the Sandinista regime, and the whole saga of the often clandestine US support for the Contras. A fascinating book.

Various, *Sandino's Daughters: Testimonies of Nicaragua Women in Struggle* (Rutgers University Press). Interviews with Sandinista women who participated at various levels in the struggle to liberate Nicaragua and later worked for the creation of a new and just society. First published in 1981, it's one of the most popular books written about that period.

TRAVEL AND IMPRESSIONS

Edward Marriott, *Wild Shore* (Picador). The author follows the Río San Juan from the Atlantic Coast to Lago de Nicaragua in search of the bull shark – the only shark able to live in both fresh and salt water – and the fisherman who make their living from hunting it. The result is an intriguing blend of natural and social history in which the bull shark emerges as one of the few constants in Nicaragua's turbulent history, and a symbol of survival in a country where exploitation has become a way of life.

Penny O'Donnell, *Death, Dreams and Dancing in Nicaragua*, (Australian Broadcasting Corporation). Written by an Australian radio journalist who, in her own words, avoided the "newsworthy" in favour of the "everyday stories of my neighbours and friends". It plods along at times, but also offers excellent insights into the challenges and pleasures of living and working alongside Nicaraguans.

Salman Rushdie, *The Jaguar Smile, A Nicaraguan Journey* (Picador). The result of a three-week trip to Nicaragua at the height of the Sandinista era in the mid-1980s, Rushdie was impressed – or seduced – by the Sandinista achievement. The only note of criticism he struck was with the lack of freedom of speech – ironically, the very subject that would come to be the defining theme in Rushdie's own life. The real charm of this slim narrative is Rushdie's witty portrait of cosy Managuan political society and its family affiliations.

FICTION AND POETRY

Gioconda Belli, *From Eve's Rib* and *The Inhabited Woman* (Curbstone Press). The only translated works – at once political and erotic – available by the well-known Nicaraguan poet and novelist, at first a political activist, an exile and then a member of the Sandinista government (although she has since disassociated herself from the party).

Ernesto Cardenal, *The Cosmic Canticle* (Curbstone Press). Thirty years of work went into the this narrative poem and mythic song – an epic work spanning the whole of Latin American history.

Ruben Dario, *Cuentos Completos* (Fondo De Cultura Enconimica); *Azul Cantos De Vida Y Esperanza* (Planeta); *Poesia* (Alianza). In Nicaragua, Dario is perceived more as a national hero than a writer, and as a kind of reference point in the national psyche. In his own work he was, like so many Latin American authors, a versatile writer, writing stories and essays as well as poetry, for which he remains best known.

Francisco Goldman, *The Ordinary Seaman* (Atlantic Monthly Press, US). Dark and depressing book about the fate of several Nicaraguan men contracted to work on a freighter. Their salvation from the wreck of post-Sandinista Nicaragua turns out to be a rotting hulk in Brooklyn harbour. Flight, exile, death and bittersweet memories form an enormous part of Nicaragua's culture since the revolution, and this book captures much of it.

COSTA RICA

HISTORY, POLITICS AND SOCIETY

Tjabel Daling, *Costa Rica In Focus: A Guide to the People, Politics and Culture* (Latin America Bureau, Interlink). The most authoritative and up-to-date country guide currently available, entertainingly illustrated with bits of Costa

Rican life, such as billboards and labels. The text offers an especially clear-eyed cultural and social analysis.

Marc Edelman and Joanne Kenen (eds), *The Costa Rica Reader* (Grove Atlantic, US, o/p). The best single title for the general reader, with chronologically arranged essays by respected historians – academic in tone but not inaccessible. See especially Chilean sociologist Diego Palma's essay on current Costa Rican politics and class conflict, which punctures the picture of Costa Rica as a haven of middle-class democracy.

Paula Palmer, *What Happen: A Folk History of the Talamanca Coast* (San José, Ecodesarrolos). The definitive – although now dated – folk history of the Afro-Caribbean community on Limón province's Talamancan coast. Palmer first went to Cahuita in the early 1970s as a Peace Corps volunteer, later returning as a sociologist to collect oral histories from older members of the local communities. Great stories and atmospheric testimonies of pirate treasure, ghosts and the like, complemented by photos and accounts of local agriculture, foods and traditional remedies. Available in English and Spanish (in Costa Rica only).

TRAVEL AND IMPRESSIONS

Allen M. Young, *Sarapiquí Chronicle: A Naturalist in Costa Rica* (Smithsonian Institute Press, o/p). Lavishly produced book based on entomologist Allen M. Young's twenty years' work in the Sarapiquí area and featuring a well-written combination of autobiography, travelogue and natural science, centring on the insect life he encounters.

ART AND ARCHEOLOGY

Between Continents, Between Seas: Precolumbian Art of Costa Rica (Harry Abrams, US, o/p). Produced as a catalogue to accompany the exhibit that toured the US in 1982, this is the best single volume on Costa Rica's pre-Conquest history and craftsmanship, with illuminating accounts of the lives, beliefs and customs of its pre-Columbian peoples as interpreted through artefacts and excavations. The photographs, whether of jade pendants, Chorotega pottery or the more diabolical of the Diquis' gold pieces, are uniformly wonderful.

FICTION AND POETRY

Fabián Dobles, *Ese Que Llaman Pueblo* (San José, Editorial Costa Rica). Born in 1918, Dobles is Costa Rica's elder statesman of letters. Set in the countryside among *campesinos*, this title is a typical "proletarian" novel.

Carmen Naranjo, *Los perros no ladraron* (1966), *Responso por el niño Juan Manuel* (1968), *Ondina* (1982) and *Sobrepunto* (1985). In keeping with a tradition in Latin American letters, but unusual for a woman, Naranjo has occupied several public positions, including Secretary of Culture, director of the publishing house EDUCA and ambassador to Israel. Her novel *There Never Was Once Upon a Time* (Latin American Literary Review Press, US) is available in English.

WILDLIFE AND THE ENVIRONMENT

Les Beletsky, *Costa Rica: Ecotraveller's Wildlife Guide* (Academic Press). This readable wildlife and natural history handbook, written by a professional wildlife biologist. is a good compromise between a guidebook and a heavy field guide. The text is accompanied by photos and drawings; the plates showing species with photos of their typical habitats are particularly useful. Includes detailed information on about 220 bird, 50 mammal and 80 amphibian and reptile species.

Daniel H. Janzen, *Costa Rican Natural History* (University of Chicago Press). The definitive reference source, with accessible and continuously fascinating species-by-species accounts. The introduction is especially worth reading, dealing in a cursory but lively fashion with tectonics, meteorology, history and archeology. Illustrated throughout with gripping photographs and available in paperback, but still doorstep-thick.

F. Gary Stiles and Alexander F. Skutch, *A Guide to the Birds of Costa Rica* (Black Press/Cornell University Press). You'll see guides all over Costa Rica clutching well-thumbed copies of this seminal tome, illustrated with colour plates to aid identification. Hefty, even in paperback, and too pricey for the amateur, but you may be able to pick up good secondhand copies in Costa Rica.

Philip J. De Vries, *The Butterflies of Costa Rica and their Natural History* (Princeton University Press). Much-admired volume, really for serious butterfly enthusiasts or scientists only, but illustrated with beautiful colour plates so you can marvel at the incremental differences between various butterflies.

PANAMÁ

HISTORY, POLITICS AND SOCIETY

David McCullough, *The Path Between the Seas: The Creation of the Panama Canal* (Touchstone, US). Compelling and authoritative account of the epic struggle to build the Panamá Canal. Detailed and well-resarched, it nonetheless reads like a novel.

John Weeks and Phil Gunson, *Panama: Made in the USA* (LAB). Detailed exploration of the unanswered questions behind the US invasion of Panamá in the context of the turbulent history of US–Panamanian relations and the struggle for control of the Canal.

TRAVEL AND IMPRESSIONS

Graham Greene, *Getting to Know the General* (Bodley Head, UK). Fascinating personal reminiscences regarding the author's unlikely friendship with General Omar Torrijos, dictator of Panamá from 1968 to 1981.

FICTION

Douglas Galbraith, *The Rising Sun* (Picador, UK). Tour de force of historical fiction set during the disastrous Scottish attempt to establish an independent colony in Darién during the late seventeenth century.

John Le Carré, *The Tailor of Panama* (Coronet/Ballantine Books). Fast-moving spy thriller by the great master of the genre, set in Panamá on the eve of US military withdrawal. Its satirical depiction of Panamá as a murky world of intrigue and corruption, populated by ambiguous characters, casued great controversy when it was first published.

SPECIALIST GUIDES

Michele Labrut, *Getting to Know Panama* (Focus Publications, Panamá). Enthusiastic introduction to the country's many attractions, detailed and up-to-date.

Robert S. Ridgely & John Gwynne, *A Guide to the Birds of Panama* (Princeton University Press). The definitive ornithological guide book for Central America – also covers Honduras, Nicaragua and Costa Rica – though it's bulky and expensive.

LANGUAGE

There's a bewildering collection of languages across the Central American isthmus, numbering well above thirty in all; fortunately for the traveller, there are two that dominate – English, primarily in Belize and the Bay Islands of Honduras, but spoken to some extent all along the Caribbean coast; and Spanish everywhere else.

ENGLISH

Belizean English may sound familiar from a distance and, if you listen to a few words, you may think that its meaning is clear. Listen a little further, however, and you'll realize that complete comprehension is just out of reach. What you're hearing is, in fact, **Creole**, a beautifully warm and relaxed language, typically Caribbean and loosely based on English, with elements of Spanish and indigenous languages. A similar dialect, Guari Guari, is spoken in the Panamanian province of Bocas del Toro. Written Creole, which you'll come across in Belizean newspapers, is a little easier to get to grips with. There's an active movement in Belize to formalize the language, and a dictionary is currently in production. Luckily, almost anyone who can speak Creole can also speak English.

To get a taste of the language on the streets in Belize, here are some simple phrases. For more, get hold of a copy of *Creole Proverbs of Belize*, usually available in Belize City.

• *Bad ting neda gat owner* – Bad things never have owners.

• *Better belly bus dan good bikkle waste* – It's better that the belly bursts than good victuals go to waste.

• *Cow no business eena haas gylop* – Cows have no business in a horse race.

In the **Bay Islands** of Honduras things are much simpler. English is English rather than Creole, and immediately understandable, albeit spoken with a unique, broad accent. Influenced by Caribbean, English and Scots migrants over the years, local inflexions turn even the most commonplace of remarks into an attractive statement. English, however, is slowly being supplanted by Spanish as the language heard on the street as growing numbers of mainlanders make the islands their home.

SPANISH

Those new to the region can take heart – **Spanish**, as spoken across Latin America, is one of the easier languages there is to learn and even the most faltering of attempts to speak it is greatly appreciated. Apart from the major tourist areas in Guatemala, Costa Rica, and in some parts of Panamá and Honduras, English is not widely spoken; taking the trouble to get to know at least the basics of Spanish will both make your travels considerably easier and reap countless rewards in terms of reception, appreciation and understanding of people and places.

Overall, Latin American Spanish is clearer and slower than that of Spain – gone are the lisps and bewilderingly rapid, slurred, soft consonants of the old country. There are, however, quite strong variations in accent across Central America: Guatemalan Spanish has the reputation of being clear, precise and eminently understandable even to the worst of linguists, whilst the language as spoken in Honduras – thick and fast – can initially bewilder even those who believed themselves to be reasonably fluent. Nicaraguans in particular take great pleasure in fooling around with language, creating new words, pronouncing certain letters differently and employing different grammar. There are enough Nicaragnismos – words and sayings particular to Nicaragua – to fill a 275-page dictionary. As far as pronunciation goes, the "s" is often dropped from word endings and the "v" and "b" sounds are fairly interchangeable.

For the most part, the rules of **pronunciation** are straightforward and strictly observed.

Unless there's an accent, words ending in d, l, r and z are **stressed** on the last syllable, all others on the second last. All **vowels** are pure and short.

A somewhere between the "A" sound of back and that of father.

E as in get

I as in police

O as in hot

U as in rule

C is soft before E and I, otherwise hard; *cerca* is pronounced "serka".

G works the same way – a guttural "H" sound (like the *ch* in loch) before E or I, a hard G elsewhere; *gigante* is pronounced "higante".

H is always silent.

J is the same sound as a guttural G; *jamón* is pronounced "hamoan".

LL sounds like an English Y; *tortilla* is pronounced torteeya.

N is as in English, unless there is a *tilde* (accent) over it, when it becomes NY; *mañana* is pronounced "manyana".

QU is pronounced like an English K.

R is rolled, **RR** doubly so.

V sounds like a cross with B, *vino* becoming beano.

X is slightly softer than in English, sometimes almost like SH, so that Xela becomes "sheyla"; between vowels in place names it has an H sound – México is pronounced "May-hee-ko".

Z is the same as as a soft C; *cerveza* is pronounced "servesa".

FORMAL AND INFORMAL ADDRESS

For English speakers one of the most difficult things to get to grips with is the distinction between formal and informal address – when to use it and to whom and how to avoid causing offence. Generally speaking, the third-person "**usted**" indicates respect and/or a non-familiar relationship and is used in business, for people you don't know and for those older than you. Second-person "**tú**" is for children, friends and contemporaries in less formal settings. (Remember also that in Latin America the second person **plural** – vosotros – is never used, so "you" plural will alway be ustedes). In day-to-day exchanges, genuine mistakes on the part of an obviously non-native speaker will be well received and corrected with good humour.

One idiosyncrasy is the widespread use of "**vos**" in Central America. Now archaic in Spain, it is frequently used in place of *tú*, as an intimate form of address between friends of the same age. In most tenses, conjugation is exactly the same as for *tú*. In the present indicative, however the last syllable is stressed with an accent (*tú comes/vos comés*); in "-ir" verbs in this tense, the final "i" is kept instead of changing to an "e" (*tú escribes/vos escribís*). In commands, the vos form drops the final "r" of the infinitive, replacing it with an accented vowel (*tú come/vos comé*). Take your lead from those around you – if you are addressed in the "*vos*" form it is a sign of friendship which should be reciprocated; on the other hand it is sometimes seen as patronizing to use it with someone you don't know well.

NICKNAMES AND TURNS OF SPEECH

Nicknames are very common in Central America, used in both speech and writing and for any situation from addressing a casual acquaintance to referring to political candidates. Often they centre on obvious physical characteristics – *flaco/a* (thin), *gordo/a* (fat), *rubio/a* (blond).

Often, these nicknames will be further softened by **diminution** – the addition of the suffix -*ito* or -*ita* at the end of nouns and adjectives, a trend used sometimes with a passion in everyday speech. You are quite likely to hear someone talk about their *hermanito* for example, which translates as "little brother" regardless of respective ages, whilst *mi hijita* ("my little daughter") can as easily mean a grown woman as a child.

Also very common are **casual street addresses**, used lightly in brief encounters and to soothe transactions. Heard in virtually every country are *(mi) amor* – used in much the same way as "love" in England and also between friends – as is *jóven* or *jovencito/a*, young one. More specific to each country (often but not always between men) are terms used to make casual questions or remarks less intrusive. *Papa* (literally "father") is used daily in Honduras, for example as in "*¿Qué hora tiene, papa?*" (What time is it?), whilst the Nicaraguans use *primo* (cousin). Panamanian men regularly address each other as *compadre*, often abbreviated to *compa*. In Nicaragua, the local term (a fond one) for foreigners is *chele/a*.

POLITESSE

Verbal courtesy is an integral part of speech in Spanish and one that – once you're accustomed to the pace and flow of life in Central America – should become instinctive. Saying *Buenos días/Buenas tardes* and waiting for the appropriate response is usual when asking for something at a shop or ticket office for example, as is adding *Señor* or *Señora* (in this instance similar to the US "sir" or "ma'am"). The response when thanking someone for a service is more likely to be *para servirle* (literally "here to serve you") rather than the casual *de nada* ("you're welcome"). The *tss tss* sound is commonly employed to attract attention, particularly in restaurants. In this very polite culture shouting is frowned upon.

On meeting, or being introduced to, someone, Central Americans will say *con mucho*

> **PHRASEBOOKS AND DICTIONARIES**
> It's worth investing in a good **phrasebook** and **dictionary** before you go. One of the best specifically Latin American dictionaries is the University of Chicago *Dictionary of Latin-American Spanish* (Pocket Books). Alternatively, HarperCollins produce the best general range of pocket dictionaries and grammars, which include many Latin American terms. The *Rough Guide to Mexican Spanish* can also prove extremely useful.

gusto, "it's a pleasure", and you should do the same. On departure you will more often than not be told *¡que le vaya bien!* ("may all go well") a simple phrase that nonetheless invariably sounds sincere and rounds off transactions nicely. In rural areas, especially, it is usual to greet even complete strangers met on the path with *!Adiós, que le vaya bien!* Don't be surprised if you're greeted with "*Adiós*", as this can mean both hello and goodbye.

A SPANISH LANGUAGE GUIDE

BASICS

yes, no	*sí, no*	open, closed	*abierto/a, cerrado/a*
please, thank you	*por favor, gracias*	with, without	*con, sin*
where, when	*dónde, cuando*	good, bad	*buen(o)/a, mal(o)/a*
what, how much	*qué, cuanto*	big, small	*gran(de), pequeño/a*
here, there	*aquí, allí*	more, less	*más, menos*
this, that	*este, eso*	today, tomorrow	*hoy, mañana*
now, later	*ahora, más tarde*	yesterday	*ayer*

GREETINGS AND RESPONSES

hello, goodbye	*¡hola!, adios*	I don't speak Spanish	*(No) Hablo español*
good morning	*buenos días*	What (did you say)?	*Mande?*
good afternoon/ night	*buenas tardes/noches*	My name is...	*Me llamo...*
How do you do?	*¿Qué tal?*	What's your name?	*¿Como se llama usted?*
See you later	*Hasta luego*	I'm English	*Soy inglés(a)*
sorry	*lo siento/disculpeme*	...American	*americano(a)*
Excuse me	*Con permiso/perdon*	...Australian	*australiano(a)*
How are you?	*¿Cómo está (usted)?*	...Canadian	*canadiense(a)*
Not at all/ You're welcome	*De nada*	...Irish	*irlandés(a)*
		...Scottish	*escosés(a)*
I (don't) understand	*(No) Entiendo*	...Welsh	*galés(a)*
Do you speak English?	*¿Habla (usted) inglés?*	...New Zealander	*neozelandés(a)*

NEEDS – HOTELS AND TRANSPORT

I want	*Quiero*	Is there a hotel nearby?	*¿Hay un hotel aquí cerca?*
Do you know...?	*¿Sabe...?*	How do I get to...?	*¿Por dónde se va a...?*
I'd like....	*Quisiera... por favor*	Left, right, straight on	*izquierda, derecha,*
I don't know	*No sé*		*derecho*
There is (is there)?	*Hay (?)*	Where is...?	*¿Dónde está...?*
Give me...	*Deme...*	...the bus station?	*....el terminal de bus?*
(one like that)	*(uno asi)*	...the train station?	*....la estación de*
Do you have...?	*¿Tiene...?*		*ferrocarriles?*
...the time	*...la hora*	...the nearest bank	*...el banco más cercano*
...a room	*...un cuarto*		(ATM is *cajero*
...with two beds/	*...con dos camas*		*automático)*
double bed	*/cama matrimonial*	...the (main)	*...el correo (central)?*
It's for one person	*Es para una persona*	post office?	
(two people)	*(dos personas)*	...the toilet	*...el baño/sanitario*
...for one night	*...para una noche*	Where does the bus	*¿De dónde sale el*
(one week)	*(una semana)*	to... leave from?	*camión para...?*
It's fine, how much is it?	*¿Esta bien, cuánto es?*	What time does it	*¿A qué hora sale*
It's too expensive	*Es demasiado caro*	leave (arrive in...)?	*(llega en...)?*
Don't you have	*¿No tiene algo más*	What is there to eat?	*¿Qué hay para comer?*
anything cheaper?	*barato?*	What's that?	*¿Qué es eso?*
Can one...?	*¿Se puede...?*	What's this called	*¿Cómo se llama este en*
...camp (near) here?	*¿...acampar aquí (cerca)?*	in Spanish?	*español?*

NUMBERS AND DAYS

1	*un/uno/una*	20	*veinte*	1999	*mil novecientos*
2	*dos*	21	*ventiuno*		*noventa y nueve*
3	*tres*	22	*veintidos*	2000	*dos mil*
4	*cuatro*	30	*treinta*	100,000	*cien mil*
5	*cinco*	40	*cuarenta*	1,000,000	*un millón*
6	*seis*	50	*cincuenta*	first	*primero/a*
7	*siete*	60	*sesenta*	second	*segundo/a*
8	*ocho*	70	*setenta*	third	*tercero/a*
9	*nueve*	80	*ochenta*	fifth	*quinto/a*
10	*diez*	90	*noventa*	tenth	*decimo/a*
11	*once*	100	*cien*		
12	*doce*	101	*ciento uno*	Monday	*lunes*
13	*trece*	200	*dos cientos*	Tuesday	*martes*
14	*catorce*	201	*dos cientos uno*	Wednesday	*miércoles*
15	*quince*	500	*quinientos*	Thursday	*jueves*
16	*dieciséis*	1000	*mil*	Friday	*viernes*
				Saturday	*sábado*
				Sunday	*domingo*

GLOSSARY

ABASTECEDOR A general store that keeps a stock of groceries and basic toiletries.

AGUACERO Downpour.

AGUARDIENTE Raw alcohol made from sugar cane.

AGUAS Bottled fizzy drinks; Coca-Cola, Sprite etc.

AHORITA Right now (any time within the coming hour).

ALCALDE Mayor.

ALDEA Small settlement.

AYUNTAMIENTO Town hall/government.

BARRANCA Steep-sided ravine.

BARRIO Neighbourhood, area within a town or city; suburb.

BIOTOPO Protected area of national ecological importance, usually with limited tourist access.

BOMBA Gas station.

CABAÑA Literally a cabin, but can mean anything from a palm-thatched beach hut to a US-style motel room. Usually applies to tourist accommodation.

CACIQUE Chief. Originally a colonial term, now used for elected leaders/figureheads of indigenous *comarcas* in Panamá.

CAMIONETA Small truck or van, or in Guatemala a second-class bus.

CAMPESINO Peasant farmer, smallholder, cowboy.

CANTINA Local, hard-drinking bar, usually men-only.

CARRETERA INTERAMERICANA Trans-national highway that runs 24,400km from Alaska to Tierra del Fuego, broken only by the Darién Gap between Panamá and Colombia.

CARRO Car, equivalent of *coche*.

CASA DE CAMBIO Currency exchange bureau.

CHAC Maya god of rain.

CHICLE Sapodilla tree sap from which chewing gum is made.

CHIQUILLOS Kids; also *chiquititos, chiquiticos.*

CHORREADOR Sack-and-metal coffee-filter contraption, still widely used.

CHURRIGUERESQUE Highly elaborate, decorative form of Baroque architecture (usually found in churches).

CLASSIC Period during which ancient Maya civilization was at its height, usually given as 300–900 AD.

COLECTIVO Shared taxi/minibus, usually following fixed route. Can also be applied to a boat – *lancho colectivo*.

COLONIA City suburb or neighbourhood, often seen in addresses as "Col".

COMEDOR Basic restaurant, usually with just one or two things on the menu, always the cheapest place to eat. Literally "dining room".

CONQUISTADOR "One who conquers": member of early Spanish expeditions to the Americas in the sixteenth century.

CONVENTO Convent or monastery.

CORDILLERA Mountain range.

CORRIENTE Second-class bus.

CREOLE Of mixed African/Caribbean and European descent; also refers to the English patois spoken in Belize and Caribbean towns throughout the region.

CUADRA Street block.

DESCOMPUESTO Out of order.

DON/DOÑA Courtesy titles (sir/madam), mostly used in letters or for professional people or the boss.

EFECTIVO Cash.

EJIDO Communal farmland.

EVANGÉLICO Christian evangelist or fundamentalist, often a missionary. Name given to members of numerous Protestant sects seeking converts in Central America.

FERIA Fair (market).

FINCA Ranch, farm or plantation.

FINQUERO Coffee grower.

GAMBAS Buttresses; the giant above-ground roots that some rainforest trees put out.

GARÍFUNA People of mixed African and Amerindian descent, with a unique language and strong African heritage, who live in on the Caribbean coast between southern Belize and Nicaragua.

GASEOSA Fizzy drink.

GASOLINERA Gas station.

GLYPH Element in Maya writing and carving; roughly the equivalent of a letter or numeral.

GRINGO/GRINGA Any white-skinned foreigner, particularly North Americans. Not necessarily a term of abuse.

GUACA Pre-Columbian burial ground or tomb.

HACIENDA Big farm, ranch or estate, or big house on it.

HENEQUÉN Fibre from *agave* (sisal) plant, used to make rope.

HOSPEDAJE Very basic pensión or small hotel.

HUIPIL Maya women's traditional dress or blouse, usually woven or embroidered.

I.V.A. Sales tax.

INDÍGENA An indigenous person; preferred term among indigenous groups, rather than the more racially offensive *índio:* indian.

INVIERNO Winter (May–Oct).

JORNALEROS Day labourers, usually landless peasants who are paid by the day, for instance to pick coffee in season.

JUEGO DE PELOTA Ball court.

LADINO A vague term – applied to people it means Spanish-influenced as opposed to indigenous, and at its most specific defines someone of mixed Spanish and indigenous blood. It's more commonly used simply to describe a person of "Western" culture, or one who dresses in "Western" style, be they of indigenous or mixed blood.

LICUADO Fresh blended fruit juice, made with water or milk.

MALECÓN Seafront promenade.

MAYA Indigenous people who inhabited Honduras, Guatemala, Belize and southeastern Mexico from the earliest times, and still do. Although they also lived in El Salvador, there are none left there today.

MESTIZO Person of mixed indigenous and Spanish blood, though like the term *ladino* it has more cultural than racial significance.

METATE Pre-Columbian stone table used for grinding corn.

MIGRACIÓN Immigration office.

MILPA Maize field, usually cleared by slash-and-burn farming.

MIRADOR Lookout point.

MISKITO Native American group living along the area of the Caribbean coast of Honduras and Nicaragua known as the Mosquitia.

MUELLE Jetty or dock.

NATURAL An indigenous person.

NEOTRÓPICOS Neotropics: tropics of the New World.

ORIENTE East; often seen in addresses as "Ote".

PALACIO Mansion, but not necessarily royal.

PALACIO DE GOBIERNO Headquarters of state/federal authorities.

PALACIO MUNICIPAL Headquarters of local government.

PALAPA Palm thatch. Used to describe any thatched/palm-roofed hut.

PASEO A broad avenue; also the traditional evening walk around the plaza.

PELOTA Ball, or ball court.

PENSIÓN Simple hotel.

PEÓN Farm labourer, usually landless.

PERSONAJE Someone of importance, a VIP, although usually used pejoratively to indicate someone who is putting on airs.

PLANTA BAJA Ground floor – abbreviated PB in elevators.

PLATERESQUE Elaborately decorative Renaissance architectural style.

PONIENTE West; often seen in addresses as "Pte".

POPUL VUH The Quiché Maya's epic story of the creation and history of their people.

POSTCLASSIC Period between the decline of Maya civilization and the arrival of the Spanish, 900–1530 AD.

PRECLASSIC Archeological era preceding the blooming of Maya civilization, usually given as 1500 BC–300 AD.

PULLMAN Fast and comfortable bus, usually an old Greyhound.

PULPERÍA General store or corner store. Also sometimes serves cooked food and drinks.

QUICHÉ Largest of the Guatemalan Maya groups, centred today on the town of Santa Cruz del Quiché.

RANCHO Palm-thatched roof; can also mean a smallholding.

REDONDEL DE TOROS Bull-ring, used for local rodeos.

REFRESCO Drink, usually made with fresh fruit or water, sometimes fizzy drink, although this can also be called a *gaseosa*.

SABANERO Cowboy.

SACBE Maya road, or ceremonial causeway.

SIERRA Mountain range.

SODA Costa Rican cafeteria or diner; in the rest of Central America it's usually called a comedor.

STELA Freestanding carved monument. Most are of Maya origin.

TECÚN UMÁN Last king of the Quiché Maya, defeated in battle by the conquistador Alvarado.

TEMPORADA Season: *la temporada de lluvia* is the rainy season.

TERRENO Land; small farm.

TIENDA Shop.

TÍPICO/TÍPICA Literally "typical". Used to describe food or, in Guatemala, the multi-coloured textiles geared to the Western customer.

TRAJE Traditional costume.

VERANO Summer (Dec–April).

INDEX

WHY ROUGH IT

Confirmed online reservations with Hostelworld.com

Will you have enough stories to tell your grandchildren?

©2000 Yahoo! Inc.

Yahoo! Travel

Do You
Yahoo!
?